CELEBRATING 20 HJT YEARS

Mastering Immigration Law Manual

© 2023 HJT Training

No part of this book may be reproduced or utilised in any form or by any electronic or mechanical means, including photocopying, recording or by any information storage and retrieval system without permission in writing.

HJT Training is a company limited by guarantee. Registered in England and Wales.
Reg no. 4891943

HJT Training Ltd
Level 17 Dashwood House
69 Old Broad Street
London
EC2M 1QS

enquiries@hjt-training.co.uk
hjt-training.co.uk

Although great care has been taken in the compilation and preparation of this book to ensure accuracy, the publishers cannot in any circumstances accept responsibility for any errors or omissions.

ISBN: 978-1-9164312-8-7

Version 2023

Contents

About 7
The Law Society's Immigration and Asylum Accreditation Scheme (IAAS) 8
The OISC Registration Scheme 9
Glossary of Abbreviations 10
CHAPTER 1: Immigration Control 11
    1.1 Key concepts 11
    1.2 Forms of control 13
    1.3 Permission to travel, enter and remain 15
    1.4 Sources of law 25
    1.5 Making applications to enter and remain in UK; and section 3C leave 32
CHAPTER 2: General Requirements of the Rules; Introduction to Guidance 57
    2.1 Navigating the Immigration Rules 57
    2.2 Common requirements of the Immigration Rules 60
    2.3 The general refusal grounds 74
    2.4 Policies, concessions and Operational Guidance 95
    2.5 Statutory duty to safeguard children 99
    2.6 Fairness 101
CHAPTER 3: Visitors 103
    3.1 Introduction to Visitors 103
    3.2 Appendix V: Visitor 103
    3.5 Refusals and appeals 115
CHAPTER 4: Non-business/family routesHome Office Concessions; Modern slavery and statelessness 118
    4.1 Routes outside the Points Based System (PBS) and Appendix FM 118
    4.2 Home Office concessions; &special categories under the Rules 123
    4.3 Victims of trafficking/modern slavery and their support 138
    4.4 Statelessness 149
CHAPTER 5: Long Residence and Private Life; Children; Proportionality in ECHR Art 8 cases 152
    5.1 Introduction 152
    5.2 Ten-year rule 153
    5.3 Private life under the rules 157
    5.4 Private life outside the rules 171
    5.5 Common considerations when assessing proportionality 182
    5.6 Unavailability of medical treatment abroad 188
    5.7 Making a private life application 193
CHAPTER 6: Family-Based Applications 196
    6.1 Family Life under Appendix FM 196
    6.2 Family life as a partner under Appendix FM 207
    6.3 Bereaved partners and domestic abuse 231
    6.4 Parent of a child in the UK (Appendix FM section EC-PT onwards) 236
    6.5 Children of partners and parents 240
    6.6 Adult dependent relatives 241
    6.7 Children of settled parent(s) 245
    6.8 Children born in the UK 250
    6.9 Refusals of leave to remain on family life grounds and appeals 251

CHAPTER 7: Immigration for Business, Work and Study **252**
    7.1 Introduction to the Business immigration routes 252
    7.2 The business, work and study routes 257
    7.3 Generic concepts within the work and study routes and family members of work and study migrants 284

CHAPTER 8: International Protection **291**
    8.1 The refugee definition 291
    8.2 Assessing risk: country evidence 303
    8.3 Being persecuted 310
    8.4 The Convention reasons 313
    8.5 Protection and relocation 317
    8.6 Non-refoulement 320
    8.7 Cessation Clauses 322
    8.8 Exclusion clauses 325
    8.9 Humanitarian Protection 329

CHAPTER 9: Asylum Process and Practice **334**
    9.1 Claiming asylum 334
    9.2 Asylum support & benefits for refugees 344
    9.3 Representing asylum seeking children 347
    9.4 Fast-track appeals 355
    9.5 Third country cases 358
    9.6 'Clearly unfounded' certificates, inadmissible claims from EU nationals, and fresh claims 365
    9.7 Benefits of recognition as a refugee 371
    9.8 Benefits of Humanitarian Protection 379

CHAPTER 10: Human Rights Law **381**
    10.1 Human Rights Act 1998 & ECHR 1950 381
    10.2 European Convention on Human Rights 383
    10.3 ECHR and immigration law – Articles 2, 3 and 8 385
    10.4 ECHR Articles 4, 5, 6, 8 and 14 392
    10.5 Discretionary leave 395

CHAPTER 11: European Union Law **400**
    11.1 Underlying legal principles, retained and saved free movement law and the EU Settlement Scheme .. 400
    11.2 Who benefited from EU rights? 412
    11.3 British citizens who benefitted from free movement rights 419
    11.4 Family members of qualified persons 423
    11.5 Generic concepts: dependency, prior lawful residence, sham marriages and comprehensive sickness insurance 431
    11.6 Rights of admission and residence (including Accession- and Association Agreements re the A8- and A2 states, Croatia, Turkey etc) 434
    11.7 Settled and pre-settled status ('ILR/LTR under Appendix EU') 449
    11.8 Excluding and removing EEA nationals from UK 493
    11.9 EEA rights of appeal 503
    11.10 Turkish cases: from the Ankara Agreement to the ECAA rules 509
    11.11 The Charter of Fundamental Rights 517
    11.12 Appendix S2 Healthcare visitors 520
    11.13 Appendix Service Providers from Switzerland 522

CHAPTER 12: British Nationality Law 526
12.1 A brief history of nationality law 526

12.2 Nationality Guidance 529

12.3 Birth or adoption in the UK on or after 1 January 1983 530

12.4 Birth outside the UK 538

12.5 Acquisition by naturalisation as an adult – ss6(1) & 6(2) 542

12.6 Challenging nationality decisions 548

12.7 Stopping being British 549

CHAPTER 13: Enforcement; Detention, Removal and Deportation 557
13.1 Detention 557

13.2 Immigration bail 576

13.3 Administrative removal 584

13.4 Deportation 586

13.5 Revocation of deportation order and appeal rights 599

13.6 The substantive law on deportation relevant to appeals 604

13.7 Extradition 607

13.8 Voluntary Returns 607

CHAPTER 14: Appeals, Administrative Review and Judicial Review 609
14.1 Appeals in the First-tier Tribunal 609

14.2 Rights and grounds of appeal 610

14.3 Certificates and out-of-country appeals 623

14.4 Appeals in the FTT 626

14.5 Onwards appeals to the Upper Tribunal 630

14.6 Onwards appeal to the Court of Appeal 633

14.7 Administrative review 633

14.8 A fully worked example of different remedies – Appeal, AR and JR 640

CHAPTER 15: Criminal Offences 642
15.1 Overview, Article 31 and Trafficking 642

15.2 Offences under the Immigration Act 1971 644

15.3 Offences under other legislation 647

CHAPTER 16: Professional Ethics 652
16.1 Ethical issues and professional practice 652

16.2 General duties 652

16.3 Basic principles 652

16.4 False representations 653

16.5 Appeals and duties to the court 654

16.6 Costs and client care 655

16.7 Supervision 655

16.8 Liens – retention of documents 656

16.9 Standard of work 656

16.10 Conflict of interest 657

16.11 Confidentiality 658

16.12 Money laundering 658

16.13 Terrorism, money laundering; confidentiality and GDPR 659

16.14 Complaints procedures 660

 16.15 Third party instructions 661
 16.16 Ethics questions in Accreditation exams 661
CHAPTER 17: Practical Skills **662**
 17.1 Introduction & best practice guides 662
 17.2 Immigration applications 662
 17.3 Asylum applications 663
 17.4 Skills guides – interviewing and drafting 666
Acknowledgements **669**

About

This manual, in conjunction with the Mastering Immigration Law online resource, explains even the most difficult concepts in an easy-to-understand way.

This edition has been comprehensively updated to include all major changes of the law as of October 2023 and is part of the Mastering Immigration Law online subscription.

With the ever-changing law, the Mastering Immigration Law online resource is extensively updated and amended every month to provide practitioners with the most up to date information; something not practically possible with a print resource, which is why this manual is only available with the online subscription rather than as a stand-alone publication.

The Mastering Immigration Law Manual has references to case law, policies and rules essential for any immigration practitioner. Throughout, we provide links to external sources to give you an opportunity to read further. These hyperlinks correspond to those in your online resource, accessed instantaneously through your computer or mobile device.

By bundling our Mastering Immigration Law manual and online resource, you'll never have to worry about the information being out of date; simply print off the relevant sections from the subscription to keep your knowledge as current as possible. Also perfect for sitting your assessments.

It is important to be well informed. Our work is tough enough without failing to keep up-to-date with all relevant developments. You can read about the challenges immigration lawyers face from a hostile public and media in YSA (Somalia) [2023] UKUT 74 (IAC).

Sources of information on immigration law are referenced and hyperlinked throughout Mastering Immigration Law subscription. Simply log in and you have an encyclopaedic resource at your fingertips.

We dedicate Mastering Immigration Law subscription and manual to our much missed friends and colleagues Gail Elliman, Navtej Ahluwalia & Jake Dutton

The Law Society's Immigration and Asylum Accreditation Scheme (IAAS)

The Legal Aid Agency (LAA), the government agency responsible for public legal funding, requires all advisers working under a legal aid contract in immigration law to be accredited under the IAAS. The IAAS is also open to solicitors and their staff who do not do publicly funded work, although the assessment process introduced in February 2016 focuses very much on the areas covered by legal aid (including the exceptional case funding scheme):

- Asylum law and practice
- Deportation and detention
- Trafficking and domestic violence
- Statelessness
- Pervasives: legal aid, appeals and other remedies, professional conduct

It is beyond the scope of this resource to describe the requirements of the accreditation scheme and the nature of the examinations at levels 1 and 2. HJT Training runs revision courses which address these issues:

- **The LAA** requires those providing advice and representation under an immigration legal aid contract to be accredited under the Law Society scheme. The LAA website (now incorporated into the Ministry of Justice's website) is notoriously difficult to navigate but does provide information about the requirement to be accredited (and reaccredited).
- **The Law Society**. The accreditation scheme is run by the Law Society. The Law Society website does provide information about the requirements of the scheme. See https://lawsociety.org.uk/support-services/accreditation/immigration-asylum/.
- **HJT training.** HJT provides the assessment and training materials for the IAAS re-accreditation process throughout the year.

Past examination papers are not publicly available. Those attending HJT Training courses will be given access to training materials, including sample questions.

The OISC Registration Scheme

The Office of the Immigration Services Commissioner (OISC) was created by the Immigration Act 1999 and regulates immigration advisers who are not solicitors and barristers or supervised by them. The OISC also regulates the provision of immigration advice in the not-for-profit sector.

The OISC has three levels of registration:

- level 1: basic immigration advice within the Immigration Rules
- level 2: more complex casework, including applications outside the Immigration Rules
- level 3: appeals

A recent addition to these levels is OISC Level 1 (EUSS), which accredits holders to deal with straightforward EUSS applications *only*. New, more comprehensive guidance as to the exact types of work one can do with this accreditation was published on 20 December 2019, and is entitled Guidance for EUSS advisers on authorised work at Level 1.

If an OISC Level 3 adviser wishes to conduct JR matters, they must be specifically authorised by OISC to do so, and the application for Judicial Review Case Management authorisation (JRCM) is here. HJT Training provides occasional courses on acquiring and making the most of the JRCM system.

For the main three levels, the OISC's Guidance on Competence (supplemented from time to time by OISC News) lays out the type of casework that can be undertaken by an adviser at each level of regulation. The 2012 version of the guidance is currently being updated. A person applying for regulation will also need to read and understand OISC Code of Standards (April 2016).

It is no longer possible to provide a comparison of the different levels of the two schemes, although the OISC's website continues to state that those who have passed the IAAS exams will not have to sit an OISC assessment at the comparable level.

Again, it is beyond the scope of this resource to describe the OISC scheme in detail. As with the Law Society scheme, there are knowledge and skills examinations and assessments that must be completed to register with the OISC (or to increase an adviser's level of registration). The assessments are administered and run directly by the OISC itself. HJT Training has a contract with the OISC to draft and mark the assessment papers.

Guidance on how to become an OISC regulated adviser maybe found on the OISC website

Detailed information on the assessment process, including some revision tips, sample papers, a mark scheme and detailed syllabuses are at: https://www.gov.uk/government/collections/competence-assessments-immigration-and-asylum-advisers .

The whole OISC collection Guidance and practice notes for authorised immigration advisers is available here.

As with the IAAS, those attending HJT Training courses will be given access to further preparatory and practice materials including further sample papers and mark schemes, and tips and techniques for those intending to take the OISC assessments.

The OISC has the responsibility to ensure that its regulated advisers understand the law and procedures of UK and EEA immigration control and how to apply it properly to their clients' cases. Consequently, the tests require examinees to clearly show their knowledge. If you are underprepared, they are not easy to pass. Many have underestimated their difficulty and the failure rate is high.

Neither HJT Training nor any other training provider can provide OISC accreditation or registration as this lies with the OISC alone. However, HJT Training does offer training that will assist a person seeking registration with the OISC and is an approved OISC training provider.

Please visit hjt-training.co.uk for all our public training courses.

Glossary of Abbreviations

MIL – Mastering immigration law

CoA - Court of Appeal (or occasionally, certificate of approval if used in the marriage context)

EUSSch – EU settled status scheme

EUSS – EU settled status

EUPSS – EU pre-settled status

FTT – First-tier Tribunal

FTTRs – First-tier Tribunal Procedure Rules

HO - Home Office

IRs – Immigration Rules (we tend to write IR when first referring to a set of rules but thereafter r1, r2 etc, for brevity)

JR – judicial review

Para – paragraph

Sch – Schedule

SSHD – Secretary of State for the Home Department

UKVI – UK Visas and Immigration

UT – Upper Tribunal

UTRs – Upper Tribunal Procedure Rules

Our full set of abbreviations for EUSSch is at MIL 11.7.1 – and don't forget the online MIL Index is itself a resource that may assist

©HJT

CHAPTER 1: Immigration Control

1.1 Key concepts
1.1.1 Exclusionary principles

The fundamental rule of immigration control is that it is exclusive in nature. That is, everyone is excluded from lawful entry or residence unless they are either exempted from control or have permission, typically called 'leave'. You can see an interesting history of legistative impacts on migration to the UK over time in the *timeline* published by the HO showing the effect of various policy changes from January 1983.

General rule
- Everyone is excluded

Unless
- Not subject to immigration control, or
- Permission ('leave') is granted

This basic rule, the founding principle of immigration law, is derived from s1 Immigration Act 1971. The 1971 Act still provides the framework for the UK's system of immigration control despite heavy amendments over the intervening years:

> (1) All those who are in this Act expressed to have the right of abode in the United Kingdom shall be free to live in and to come and go into and from, the United Kingdom without let or hindrance…
>
> (2) Those not having that right may live, work and settle in the United Kingdom by permission and subject to such regulation and control of their entry into, stay in and departure from the United Kingdom as is imposed by this Act…

Section 1(1) states that a person with 'the right of abode' will be free of immigration control, and section 1(2) that all others will need permission to come, stay, live, work, settle and depart. We will now look at the classes of migrant that that section creates: firstly, those exempt from control; secondly, those with the right of abode, thirdly, those subject to immigration control. Those subject to immigration control are likely to have to meet the criteria of the Immigration Rules (IRs) which are administered by the Home Office (HO).

1.1.2 Exemption from control

Sections 1(1) and 1(2) IA 1971 do not quite provide the full picture as to who is subject to or exempt from immigration control.

Those not subject to immigration control include those with the 'right of abode'. This group includes all British citizens, but a few others too, who may be British nationals (but not British citizens) or citizens of Commonwealth countries who were settled in the UK or married to men settled in the UK when the Immigration Act 1971 came into force. There is Guidance *Nationality – Right of Abode* on the right itself and on taking steps to deprive a person of the right.

Additionally, some foreign soldiers, members of international organisations and diplomats (and their family members) may also be exempt from immigration control. We address this class of migrant in more detail later (MIL 4.5).

Of course, the more famous exemption from immigration control was for EEA nationals. Section 1 of the 1971 Act, enacted prior to the UK joining the European Union (EU), makes no mention of any exception or carve out for EU or EEA citizens and their families. However, section 7 of the Immigration Act 1988 (repealed on 31 December 2020), exempted them from the requirement to hold leave to enter or remain. In fact, it was prohibited under European Union law that an Immigration Officer even endorse any form of immigration status in a passport of an EEA citizen. They do not require passports to travel elsewhere within the European Economic Area if they can otherwise prove that they are nationals of a member state. Post-Brexit, previously UK resident EEA nationals and others protected by EU law should be protected by the EU Settled Status regime, which has its own IRs. The UK Rules see these rights as domestic law, though they flow from the Withdrawal Agreement. The difference is likely to lead to litigation for years to come.

This subject is addressed in detail in Chapter 11: *European Union Law*. The terminology is also very different. Do not get confused between the two. As we have explained, from the UK's formal exit from the EU, which took place on 31 January 2020, and to the end of the transitional period/implementation period on 31 December 2020, EEA nationals and their families continued to enjoy free movement rights. They then enjoyed a grace period up to 30 June 2020 to regularise their immigration status under domestic law.

Since 1 January 2021, newly arriving European Economic Area (EEA) nationals and their family members are subject to UK immigration control. Most EEA nationals previously resident in the UK will retain enforceable EU rights. Until 11pm on 31 December 2019 EEA nationals enjoyed a right to admission and to reside in the UK under European Community law. Under EEA law there were some restrictions: eg economic activity, or criminality or abusing EEA rights. So, whilst EEA nationals and their family members did not have the right of abode, and were subject to some restrictions on their freedom of movement, they did not usually need to seek the permission of UK immigration officers to come or stay in the UK. Brexit brought this regime to an end, albeit that the changeover was cushioned by a transition period throughout 2020. For the provisions which now apply the rules to EEA/Swiss citizens generally, see section below.

The Guidance *Using your UK Visas and Immigration account* explains how those applying under the EUSS Scheme (EUSSch), or via the UK Immigration: ID Check app can sign in to view and prove their status when crossing the border and accessing certain services.

1.1.2.1 Provision for Irish citizens and the applicability of the rules to EEA/Swiss citizens following the end of Brexit transition

From 11pm on 31 December 2020 changes to IR5 (Introduction) and IR7 (Part 1) clarified the applicability of the IRs to Irish citizens. These changes also made it clear that in future the IRs would apply to EEA (other than Irish) and Swiss citizens. Section 3ZA of the Immigration Act 1971 provides that Irish nationals not need leave to enter or remain in the UK unless subject to a deportation order, exclusion decision or an international travel ban.

IR5 at rr5C-5E provides that

- Irish nationals who as a result of section 3ZA do not require leave to enter or remain are generally not covered by the IRs - but Irish nationals who are **not** exempt, **are** covered by them (r5C). The Explanatory Memorandum to the relevant rule changes (HC813) clarifies that applications from Irish nationals not covered by the rules will be invalid.
- The following parts of the rules **do** apply to Irish nationals: paragraph 11 in Part 1 (requirement for ID if travelling to the UK via the Channel Tunnel), Appendices: EU, S2 Healthcare Visitor, Service Providers from Switzerland, EU (Family Permit), AR (EU); and Part 11 (asylum) & Part 13 (deportation) (r5D). The explanatory memorandum adds that those Irish citizens who were resident continuously in the UK before the end of the transition period can, however, apply for settled or pre-settled status (EUSS/EUPSS) under the EU Settlement Scheme, but do not need to, even to sponsor family members under the scheme
- Irish nationals protected by s3ZA of the Immigration Act 1971 are considered settled for the purposes of the rules (r5E)

IR7 (Part 1, headed "leave to Enter"), which provides for which classes of persons require LTE, the words "the provisions of the 2006 EEA Regulations" [sic] are replaced by the words "section 3ZA of the Immigration Act 1971",

> 7. A person who is neither a British citizen nor a Commonwealth citizen with the right of abode nor a person who is entitled to enter or remain in the United Kingdom by virtue of section 3ZA of the Immigration Act 1971 requires leave to enter the United Kingdom.

1.1.2.2 Right of abode

The right of abode is an example of legacy terminology carried over from an earlier era of immigration control. As is discussed in Chapter 12: *British Nationality Law*, before 1948 anyone born in the UK or in any of its many colonies was a British Subject. From 1948, most British Subjects became Citizens of the United Kingdom and Colonies (CUKC). That status persisted until the great reform of citizenship laws in the British Nationality Act 1981.

For the two decades prior to the 1981 Act, however, politicians had sought to limit the right of residents of the colonies to live in the United Kingdom itself. The way in which this was achieved was to introduce the concept of the 'right of abode', which was independent from citizenship status. A person could therefore be a CUKC but not possess the right of abode, and therefore have no right to come to the UK itself unless they could meet certain requirements.

When the right of abode was initially introduced it was linked to another new concept, that of 'patriality'. Put simply, the right of abode was acquired through one's male ancestors having been born in the territory of the United Kingdom (rather than its colonies). The right of abode: guidance (periodically updated where countries depart and rejoin the Commonwealth) can be a helpful tool in assessing a potential application.

The original version of section 2 of the Immigration Act 1971 must be consulted if a query arises about the original meaning of the right of abode. The law has moved on considerably since those dark days, but the concept of the right of abode still persists.

There was a time when the refusal of the right of abode brought a full merits appeal before the FTT. However nowadays there would only be an appeal if the refusal of the right of abode also amounted to a human rights claim. That will be more difficult to show for people applying from abroad with limited UK ties. These days JR is usually the only remedy (MIL 14.8).

In Begum [2019] EWHC 2196 (Admin) the Administrative Court noted that the possession of the right of abode was a matter of precedent fact. This means that it needs to be assessed via a full review of all available evidence, including oral evidence if necessary. So whereas JR normally concentrates on public law errors rather than a merits review, challenges to decisions relating to the right of abode will be very similar to appeals in the FTT.

Today, British citizens hold the right of abode. Some individuals hold the right of abode but are not British citizens, but they are few in number and are addressed in Chapter 12: *British Nationality Law*.

The ongoing reform of the IRs is replacing the concept of leave to enter/remain with permission to enter/stay. Increasingly the new language is being added to the Rules though of course much of the vast corpus of immigration law continues to use the old terms.

1.2 Forms of control

In order to apply and enforce immigration laws, a number of forms of control have been introduced, operated by different officials. These officials work under the direction of the SSHD (SSHD). According to statute, it is the SSHD who makes immigration decisions, though they delegate the overwhelming majority of these to their civil servants.

As with everything that touches on UK immigration law and practice, understanding the organisations responsible for immigration control is difficult. The document *Our governance* identifes the Decision making, executive and managerial bodies in the Home Office.

From April 2013, at least on paper, immigration officials operate within a number of separate departments of the Home Office, UK Visas and Immigration (UKVI), the Immigration Enforcement Directorate (also called 'Home Office Immigration Enforcement'), and the UK Border Force. The first two previously operated as the UK Border Agency (UKBA). The UK Border Force was split off from the UKBA in March 2012.

The UK Border Force is responsible for controls at the border such as passport checks, juxtaposed controls operating from various ports abroad, and customs.

In earlier times, the functions of these three new entities were performed mainly by the Immigration and Nationality Directorate (IND) of the Home Office. This was then briefly re-constituted as the Border and Immigration Agency (BIA) before morphing into the UKBA.

Entry clearance work abroad (see below) was in previous years carried out by an organisation called UK Visas, a joint operation between the Home Office and the Foreign and Commonwealth Office. The separate identity for UK Visas has now been abandoned and the visa operation is carried out within the UKVI by Entry Clearance Officers (ECOs).

References to these predecessor organisations, particularly the UKBA, will still be encountered regularly (e.g. Home Office policies are often not updated with the appropriate terms). As the control of immigration is a direct function of the Home Office, we will usually refer in this manual to the body of immigration officials who make decisions on applications and enforce controls as 'the Home Office' (HO).

The main forms of immigration control (and the personnel responsible) are as follows:

Entry clearance
- Pre-entry control, more commonly referred to as a 'visa'

Leave to enter
- Permission to enter into the UK, either incorporated into the visa, or granted at port (to non-visa nationals visiting the UK)

Leave to remain
- Leave to remain in the UK, usually granted in-country

Limited leave
- Time limited leave (to enter or remain), granted for a certain period with a specified expiry date

Indefinite leave to enter or remain
- Unlimited leave that has no expiry date (but which can be lost, see below)

There are additional controls on employers and educational institutions. The UKVI must authorise them to recruit overseas workers and students through the system of sponsor licences and can penalise them if their recruits breach immigration laws. The Immigration Act 2014 introduced further controls, exercised by marriage registrars, private landlords, banks and the DVLA. Civil penalty schemes and criminal offences provide the incentive for these organisations to enforce immigration controls. There are appeals against civil penalties via conventional civil proceedings. You can see a useful summary of the correct approach in civil proceedings to the SSHD's Guidance explained in Link Spolka Z.O.O. [2021] EWCA Civ 1830. These measures, referred to collectively as "the *hostile environment* for illegal migrants" (MIL 1.3.6) were given more force, with significantly higher penalties for their breach, under the Immigration Act 2016.

Immigration Officers are endowed by legislation with wide powers to enforce immigration laws. Most of these powers originate in the 1971 Act (as amended) and include the power to search, seize, detain, question, arrest and enforce departure.

1.3 Permission to travel, enter and remain

Those with a right of abode can travel to and enter the UK with a British citizen passport, or another passport if stamped with 'right of abode' or a certificate of entitlement to the right of abode, without let or hindrance. Section 1 of the IA 1971 creates a regime by which anyone not exempt from UK immigration control will have their entry into, stay in and departure from the United Kingdom and their ability to live, work and settle here is determined by the Act. In short, they must have *permission* to do any of these things.

The term for 'permission' traditionally used in the Immigration Acts and Rules is that of 'leave', although we also need to mention the grant of permission to come to the UK before setting off, i.e. 'entry clearance'. People sometimes call their 'leave' a 'visa' (eg 'I want to extend my visa'): it is better for lawyers to use the correct legal term. However from December 2020 immigration routes have been restyled, and now it seems that it will be *permission* rather than *leave* will be the preferred language going forwards. MIL uses some abbreviations: LTE/LTR for leave to enter and remain, PTE/PTS for permission to enter/stay, EC for entry clearance and ETA for electronic travel authorisation.

Example

Elvis is Kosovan. He entered the UK illegally in the back of a lorry. He remained illegally for several years, never making any application to the Home Office. He decides to try to regularise his position by applying for leave.

He is an illegal entrant having entered the country clandestinely. Technically he is actually seeking leave to enter even though he has been here for many years. If his application were to succeed it might well be endorsed as leave to remain by the Home Office, simply because the decision will be made by officials of the UKVI working within the UK rather than at the border. There is no substantive difference between leave to enter and leave to remain once it is granted.

1.3.1 Entry clearance

Entry clearance is a form of pre-arrival control. Rather than allowing any person to arrive at a UK port and seek entry at that stage, requiring an Immigration Officer to make a snap decision on a potentially complex case, many of those seeking to enter the UK are required to possess entry clearance, a visa, before they physically arrive at an entry point to the UK. It is not required for Irish nationals (r24).

If a person is required to have entry clearance and does not they must be refused entry (r9.14.1 in Part 9).

The general position on who does and does not require entry clearance is this:

'Visa nationals'
- Always required: Nationals of countries listed in Appendix Visa: Visa National list to the Immigration Rules

Stay of more than 6 months
- Always required: immigration rule 24

If category-specific rule says so
- Always required: check individual rules (e.g. fiancé or marriage visitor)

CHAPTER 1: Immigration Control

> **Example**
>
> Alasdair is Canadian and wishes to enter the UK for two weeks, for a holiday. Canada is not listed in Appendix V of the IRs and Alasdair is not therefore a visa national. Entry as a visitor is granted for six months or less and the Rule does not require that entry clearance is obtained. Alasdair does not require entry clearance before he travels.
>
> Maria is Colombian and wishes to enter the UK for a one-year computing course. Colombia is listed in Appendix V and so Maria is a visa national. More relevant in this case is that she is seeking entry for a period exceeding six months, and the Student rule under which she needs to apply does specify that prior entry clearance is mandatory. Maria very definitely requires entry clearance before she travels.

This position is finessed by Appendix Visitor: Visa National List. The list can be amended at any time (eg Dominica, Honduras, Namibia, Timor-Leste and Vanuatu were added on 19 July 2023 by HC 1715). There is usually some transitional protection, eg permitting travellers who can evidence pre-bookings before the date in question to enter without a visa for a further month. Essentially one needs a visa pre-travel for any purpose unless one of the exceptions now found in the Visa National List applies (VN1.1):

- Transit visitors travelling on emergency travel documents issued by the authorities of countries not on the visa list
- Nationals of the countries at VN2.2 holding particular documents (issued by Hong Kong, Macao, China, the Holy See, etc) unless for marriage or for visits >6 months

Employees of some international organisations do not require a visa: see the Exemptions from Visa Applications list.

A non-visa national can, optionally, apply for entry clearance to travel to the UK for a visit; this would substantially reduce the risk of being refused entry on arrival. This would be very useful advice to give to a person who is at risk of refusal on arrival, for example because of a poor prior immigration history, a criminal record or having less than concrete ties to their country of nationality (i.e. being young, footloose and fancy free, or for an elderly person whose family are all settled here in the UK, see MIL 3.2).

Entry clearance is sought from an Entry Clearance Officer (ECO) at a British embassy, High Commission or consulate in the country where the applicant is '*living*' (r28) via an online application process. However applicants for visit visas, short-term study visas and under Temporary Work – Creative Worker lawfully resident overseas may apply to any visa application centre, British diplomatic mission or consular post overseas where entry clearance applications are accepted: see ECB05: where to apply, the policy.

- If granted, it takes the form of a sticker or vignette in the holder's passport, which is then presented to an Immigration Officer on arrival
- Those granted entry clearance/leave to enter for more than six months will be issued with a vignette in their passport (a short term biometric entry clearance visa valid for 90 days from the date they gave for their travel to the UK). The person will then need to collect their Biometric Residence Permit (BRP) within 10 days of arriving in the UK (in person from a nominated post-office or other location, e.g. a student would collect from their university). BRP letters are issued via email rather than in-person at VACs from 10 October 2022: if not received they may be chased at brpletterrequests@fcdo.gov.uk.
- BRPs for Skilled Workers and those granted international protection receive have their National Insurance Number (NINo) printed on their BRP: other groups do not.
- The HO plans to move to digitised immigration status by 31 December 2024 and so BRPs will no longer bear dates beyond that, notwithstanding that the underlying permission may be longer

> **Top Tip**
>
> British High Commissions exist in Commonwealth countries, British embassies are in non-Commonwealth countries, and consulates are just smaller posts away from the main High Commission or embassy. Much of the visa process, though, but not the decision making, is outsourced to 'commercial partners' of the diplomatic post.
>
> Although the UKVI still employs some ECOs outside the UK, much of the decision making now takes place in the UKVI's offices in Sheffield (UK).

Usually, by virtue of the Immigration (Leave to Enter and Remain) Order 2000, an entry clearance will also include the grant of leave to enter, which becomes effective on entry to the UK. However, on arrival an Immigration Officer may examine the leave to enter and has the power to cancel the entry clearance which contains the leave to enter under certain limited circumstances including (1971 Act, Schedule 2, paragraph 2A and immigration rule 321A):

- False representations made or false documents submitted, whether or not material to the application, with or without knowledge, in writing or orally; material facts not disclosed in relation either to the application or in obtaining supporting documents, either from HO or from elsewhere
- Sufficiently significant change in circumstances since entry clearance issued
- Medical grounds, criminal record or conduct, subject to a deportation order or exclusion; SSHD considers exclusion conducive to public good (see criminal record certificates MIL 7.7.5)

A person whose leave is cancelled at port may be able to lodge an administrative review ('AR') application if the decision falls within Appendix AR 4.2&3 to challenge the decision. In that event, they should be granted Immigration Bail (see Immigration Bail guidance) to enter the UK to make that application (MIL 14.7).

> **Example**
>
> Tasneem applies for entry clearance as a Student. The application is granted. While Tasneem makes arrangements to travel to the UK, though, her mother falls ill. Tasneem feels unable to leave her and does not travel.
>
> Her mother recovers and four months later Tasneem seeks entry to the UK. In the meantime, her course has started and her college has informed the Home Office that she has not enrolled.
>
> Even if the UKVI issues Tasneem a new 30-day vignette to travel to the UK, and they may not in these circumstances, when Tasneem arrives in the UK she can be stopped by an Immigration Officer and refused entry, even though she has a valid entry clearance. The basis of the refusal is para 321A(1), because there has been a change of circumstances since the entry clearance was granted.
>
> She will be able to challenge the decision by way of administrative review, and should be granted immigration bail to do so.

There are several other relevant provisions relating to entry clearance (see Part 1 of the Immigration Rules), including:

- Entry clearance applications for any purpose other than a visit or for short-term study must be made in the overseas post where the applicant resides or the nearest designated post if there is none: r28
- An application for entry clearance is to be decided in the light of the circumstances existing at the time of the decision, except that an applicant will not be refused an entry clearance, where entry is sought in one of the categories contained in paragraphs 296–316 in Part 8, or paragraph EC-C of Appendix FM (i.e. the rules relating to children coming to the UK with a view to settlement), solely on account of his attaining the age of 18 years between receipt of his application and the date of the decision on it: r27

CHAPTER 1: Immigration Control

- The obligation to determine an application based on present circumstances means that an ECO may refuse to grant a visa following a successful appeal: but only if there is a real change of circumstances or where genuinely new information has come to light: they should not search for further information with a view to undermining the result of the appeal –Rahman [2006] EWHC 1755 (Admin) (see MIL 14.4.3 on the binding force of appeal decisions)
- The entry clearance application will not be treated as having been made until the correct fee is paid: r30

Most entry clearance posts now employ an agent or courier firm to accept and process applications before forwarding them to the entry clearance post for decision. The visa application is made, usually online, to a Visa Application Centre (VAC) operated by these 'commercial partners'. The applicant is then given an appointment to attend the VAC in person, where they will submit any necessary documentation, pay the fee, have their biometrics enrolled, and be interviewed if necessary. It is not unknown for neat and tidy applications to be rearranged by the VAC staff, for better or worse. In some posts the practice now is for the person to attend the VAC for an appointment, but they then need to send their documents to the UKVI in Sheffield where the decision will be made. The online visa application process explains the specific procedures that apply in the country of application.

A Freedom of Information request led to the disclosure of a List of UKVI international application points and decision making centres. Following a meeting between ILPA and the Home Office, an email address was provided in February 2020 (SRSFESInt@homeoffice.gov.uk) to report ongoing issues with online systems for out of country applications.

1.3.1.1 Electronic travel authorisations

Electronic travel authorisations permitting travel to the UK are created by NBA 2022 s75 (adding s11A to IA 1971) from 28 June 2022. These are for travellers who are not British citizens or otherwise entitled to enter the UK (including the rest of the Common Travel Area) without leave. Appendix Electronic Authorisation provides the mechanics (for visitors and those on the Creative Worker visa concession) or transiting the UK: there is also brief generic Guidance and fuller casework Guidance Electronic Travel Authorisation, the latter for cases where the applicant's identity cannot be satisfactorily established automatically (eg via compliant digital photos) or where potentially adverse information regarding suitability for an ETA is identified.

The introduction is staged: from 15 November 2023 for nationals of Qatar, from 22 February 2024 for Bahrain, Jordan, Kuwait and Oman (ETA 1.2, rA24) (applications open on 1 February).

Key aspects of the system:

- ETAs are for those coming to the UK for up to 6 months for tourism, visiting family and friends, business or study, including under the Creative Worker visa concession, and for those transiting the UK, whether or not going through UK border control
- Those lawfully resident in Ireland are exempt from the ETA regime for journeys within the Common Travel Area (ETA1.4 & Guidance Electronic Travel Authorisation: Irish resident exemption) (if aged >16 they may be required to evidence such lawful residence ETA 1.6)
- There are Eligibility and Suitability (though not NHS debts) criteria: with mandatory refusal for custodial convictions in the last 12 months and a lifetime ban for receiving a sentence over 12 months (ETA2.2) or for overstaying, illegal entry, breaching conditions or using deception in an immigration application (ETA2.4) or making false representations or not disclosing material facts in a previous ETA application (ETA2.5) and litigation debt (ETA2.7). The Guidance states that convictions abroad for criminality not recognised in the UK require case specific consideration
- ETAs are valid for two years or until the passport used to support the ETA application expires (ETA4.1)
- ETAs may be cancelled due to deportation/exclusion decisions, criminal offences where the sentence was 12 months+ (there is a 1-year ban for lesser sentences), & for character/conduct/associations, overstaying/breaching conditions/illegal entry/deception, false representations,& NHS/litigation debts (ETA5)

- There are no appeals or administrative reviews available. Unsatisfactory grants (but not refusals/rejections) can be reviewed: recognising the right to human intervention to review a decision that has been made through a fully automated process

1.3.2 Leave/permission to enter or remain/stay

There is no real difference between leave (permission) to enter and to remain other than where it is granted, either at port (e.g. Dover, Heathrow) or in-country. Leave to enter can be automatically granted when passing through the automated gates at the UK borders – though only for visitors, transit visitors and parents of Tier 4 (child students) (Art 8A of Immigration (Leave to Enter and Remain) Order 2000) and nationals of EU Member States who are S2 Healthcare Visitors (Art 8B).

Leave/permission to enter will be granted on initial entry, and then if a further period of leave is sought and granted it will be called leave to remain. Where limited leave to enter or remain has been granted and remains current, the holder can depart from and re-enter the UK using that leave (unless it was granted for a single entry as a visitor).

Leave/permission can either be granted for a specific period, in which case it is referred to as limited leave, or can be granted for an indefinite period. Limited leave/permission will be subject to various standard conditions, typically controlling access to employment, study, recourse to public funds (specified within each route). Typically work is permitted save for as a sportsperson/coach. From 8 November 2022 'employment' will not include filling elected posts in local or devolved government (r6.2). Registration with the police for many migrants was required under Part 10 of the Rules for many years, until abolished on 4 August 2022 as per the www.gov page *UK visas and registering with the police*. Thus Part 10 was deleted on 9 November 2022.

Where leave/permission is endorsed on a passport that is lost, stolen, damaged or due to expire (or is endorsed on an immigration status document) can have their leave transferred to a biometric residence permit (BRP) by making an application under the *Transfer of Conditions Guidance*. Applications will be accepted only in the same name as their current valid passport. Any Home Office travel document must be produced at the same time, and will be cancelled. Name changes will be accepted where the new name is being used for all purposes, has been legally changed by deed poll or marriage, is reflected in their latest national passport from the relevant authorities, and where the real name has not previously been concealed. Justifiable reasons for previously giving different names or birthdates may be accepted so long as no material benefit was gained – if it was, cases will be referred to the curtailment team.

Top Tip

When immigration lawyers refer to **extensions of leave**, they are often referring to an extension of leave in the same immigration category. For example, a Student will be granted a limited period of leave to enter the UK to undertake the course for which they have been sponsored and will then have to apply for further periods of leave to remain if undertaking further studies.

Immigration lawyers often refer to an application for an extension of leave in a different immigration category as a variation application or as **switching**. For example, a Student might meet the love of their life, get married and want to apply for leave to remain as a spouse.

Whether in the same category, or a different one, both are extensions of leave (or **extensions of stay** as they are referred to in the IRs). Technically, even an application for asylum for a person with leave is an application to vary leave from student to refugee.

Note during 2020 it was possible to apply to switch categories where usually entry clearance would have been required, so you may see some unusual applications in clients' immigration history (MIL 4.2.19).

CHAPTER 1: Immigration Control

1.3.2.1 Indefinite leave to remain (ILR)

Indefinite leave is usually encountered as Indefinite Leave to Remain, or ILR. This may also be referred to as 'settlement', as that is what it amounts to. There are a few immigration categories in which Indefinite Leave to Enter is granted right at the outset (for children of settled parents and Adult Dependent Relatives), though most migrants will need one or more periods of limited leave before being able to apply for settlement (see MIL 5.7.1 for accelerated ILR).

Obtaining ILR is the ultimate objective of migrants wishing to remain long-term in the UK. Immigration categories which give access to ILR are called "settlement routes" (they are readily identifiable because there will be a sub-category of IRs governing access to ILR at the end of the relevant route). No conditions can be imposed on ILR and its duration is unlimited (see eg C1 [2022] EWCA Civ 30) – though it may be revoked (MIL 2.3.10). It may lapse if the holder leaves the UK for over 2 years (MIL 4.1.3)" There are specific criteria for English language and knowledge of life in the UK (MIL 2.2.6).

"No time limit" stamps are used to transfer proof of ILR from one's old passport to a new biometric residence permit, which should make travel easier and give a reliable proof of residence rights. NTLs went from being a relatively mundane piece of administration to one aspect of the Windrush scandal. On 1 January 1973 those ordinarily resident in the UK without time restrictions had their status converted to ILR. But the record keeping was haphazard. Hence now the Guidance *No time limit* explicitly warns decision makers to treat cases sensitively with every opportunity being given to prove one's case, bearing in mind the likelihood that those resident in the UK before 1 January 1973 did in fact obtain ILR. Indeed just having married or raised a family here before that date may suffice. From 6 April 2022 NTL applications are free of charge.

Modern immigration routes increasingly provide an opportunity to be granted limited leave if an ILR application fails (the ILR to PTS regime), so long as the application meets the relevant criteria and an opportunity to pay the IHS is taken up. If it is not paid the application will be invalidated. Though the ILR fee is not refunded. See *Settlement: guidance on when to vary a settlement application and grant permission to stay*, which notes that sometimes the IHS will not need to be paid, as for a child in local authority care. In September 2022 the HO noted in their *Tier 1 General review* that only 5% of ILR applications were refused.

Those Commonwealth citizens ordinarily resident and settled in the UK on 1 January 1973 received automatic ILR. A failure to respect the documentation difficulties that beneficiaries of this regime suffered was a major contribution to the Windrush scandal (4.2.14). Thompson [2023] EWHC 2037 (Admin) discusses the differences between ILR and ordinary residence alone.

1.3.3 Immigration categories or purposes

When entry clearance or a form of leave is sought, it must be sought for a specific purpose, such as to visit, study, work or live with a family member in the UK. The 'Immigration Rules', a document forming a key part of the UK's system of immigration control, sets out the different purposes for which entry to the UK can be sought.

The Immigration Rules are a unique form of legislation that the Secretary of State is authorised to amend by a relatively simple Parliamentary process called the negative resolution procedure. Essentially, any change to the Rules is simply laid before Parliament and then automatically becomes law (subject to the remote possibility of a "prayer" to reject the changes being brought by either House). These changes are published in documents called Statements of Changes. An objection to an amendment can be made by a Member of Parliament, but the objection only triggers a debate, and does not actually prevent the rule changes being implemented.

The current set of IRs ('the Rules') is officially called HC 395 (the reference number of the document in the House of Commons library). The current Rules were first introduced in 1994 and have been very heavily amended in subsequent years, growing from some 30 pages to well over 1000 as successive governments have sought to limit immigration into the UK. Amendments are made several times a year. The plethora of amendments and drafting techniques used by different draughtsmen over the years make the Rules difficult to navigate. The rules are commonly referenced by paragraph number. Sometimes we refer to 'para x" of the rules, though for concision we sometimes use "IR" for Rule: thus r 353 or IR353 = rule 353.

The following chapters examine the specific categories in more detail. The most popular categories (and their locations in the Rules) include:

- Visitors (Appendix V)
- Partners of British citizens or settled persons (Appendix FM)
- Parents of a child in the UK (Appendix FM)
- Children of settled parents (Part 8)
- Students (Appendix Student)
- Workers and their dependents (the Skilled Worker, Global Mobility and Temporary Worker appendices)
- Investment and business (Innovator, Global Mobility appendices)
- Asylum claims (Part 11)

However, there are many other categories under the Rules, some of which only exist for a relatively small number of immigrants.

1.3.4 Multiple entry; lapsing leave

The Immigration (Leave to Enter and Remain) Order 2000 (available in its original form online here) makes provision for recurring scenarios regarding the effect of entry clearances and also with respect to departure from the United Kingdom.

- Entry clearance takes effect as leave to enter if it specifies the purpose for which the holder wishes to enter the country and if it is endorsed with the conditions to which it is subject – this means that it can generally be said, of anyone who travels to the United Kingdom arriving on a particular date with entry clearance, that on that day they were granted leave to enter (Arts 2-5).
- Multi-entry visit visas operate as leave to enter on an unlimited number of occasions for so long as they are valid (for six months if six months or more remain of the visa's period of validity; or for the visa's remaining period of validity, if less than six months) (Article 4).
- Leave given for more than six months, or which was conferred by entry clearance (other than single-entry visit visas), does not normally lapse when a person leaves the Common Travel Area – but it does lapse where the holder has stayed outside the United Kingdom for a continuous period of more than two years (Article 13).

1.3.5 The different stages of immigration control

The following flowcharts provide examples of the different stages of immigration control a migrant will pass through in various categories of the Rules. The examples all assume that everything goes according to plan for the potential migrant – refusals, appeals and removals are not dealt with here.

CHAPTER 1: Immigration Control

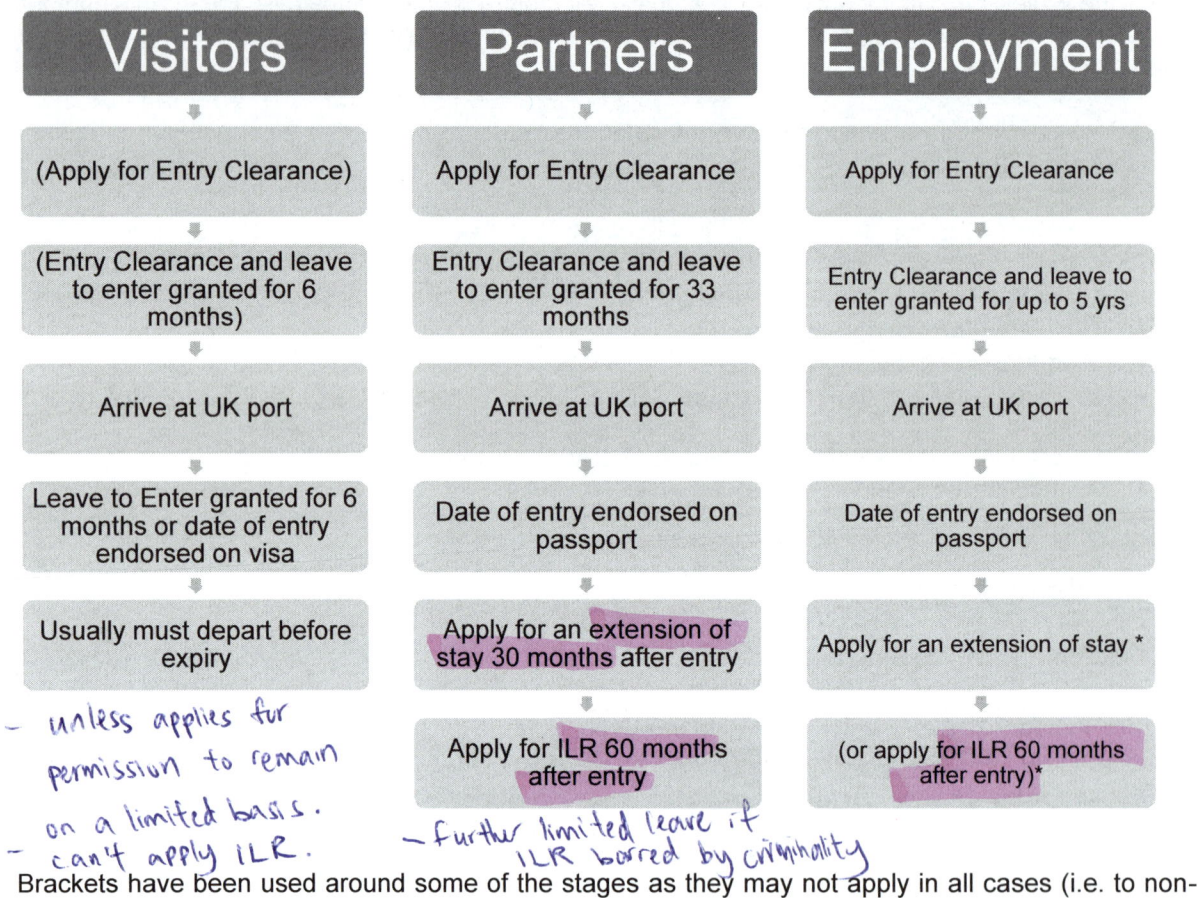

Visitors	Partners	Employment
(Apply for Entry Clearance)	Apply for Entry Clearance	Apply for Entry Clearance
(Entry Clearance and leave to enter granted for 6 months)	Entry Clearance and leave to enter granted for 33 months	Entry Clearance and leave to enter granted for up to 5 yrs
Arrive at UK port	Arrive at UK port	Arrive at UK port
Leave to Enter granted for 6 months or date of entry endorsed on visa	Date of entry endorsed on passport	Date of entry endorsed on passport
Usually must depart before expiry	Apply for an extension of stay 30 months after entry	Apply for an extension of stay *
	Apply for ILR 60 months after entry	(or apply for ILR 60 months after entry)*

Handwritten annotations:
- unless applies for permission to remain on a limited basis.
- can't apply ILR.
- further limited leave if ILR barred by criminality

Brackets have been used around some of the stages as they may not apply in all cases (i.e. to non-visa nationals arriving in the UK as visitors).

*The employment category above refers to Appendix Skilled Worker for convenience.

1.3.6 Overstayers and illegal entrants (and the hostile environment)

1.3.6.1 Illegal entrants

An illegal entrant (identified as liable to the mandatory ban in r9.8.7 by r9.8.1 Part 9 of the IRs) is statutorily defined at section 33 of the Immigration Act 1971:

> 'illegal entrant' means a person—
> (a) unlawfully entering or seeking to enter in breach of a deportation order or of the immigration laws, or
> (b) entering or seeking to enter by means which include deception by another person, and includes also a person who has entered as mentioned in paragraph (a) or (b) above;

So, the definition includes both a dishonest individual (e.g. who makes false representations in a visa application) and a clandestine entrant (who enters evading the immigration laws, say, in the back of a lorry).

1.3.6.2 Overstayers

An overstayer is someone who has remained beyond their leave to enter/remain, either the original grant, or beyond a statutory extension under s3C Immigration Act 1971 (see the definitions at para 6 under 'Interpretation' in the Introduction part of the IRs).

When advising these individuals, always consider whether they may be better off leaving the United Kingdom and applying to return from abroad, thereby remedying any flaws in applications that have so far failed. But beware any relevant *General refusal reasons* or *Suitability criteria* when doing so (see Chapter 2 at section 2.3: *the General Refusal grounds*). If they can avoid, for example, the mandatory one-year ban on return, by leaving the country before they have overstayed 90 days – or, where overstaying began on or after 6 April 2017, 30 days r9.8.5 Part 9), then they should seriously consider so doing. MIL 1.5.4 addresses applications by overstayers.

1.3.6.3 The Compliant/Hostile Environment

Some people fall foul of various aspects of immigration control, which can have serious adverse consequences for them. These days Home Office refusal letters list the various misfortunes that they will visit upon people who do not leave the country when they lack permission to remain here. These measures, collectively referred to by the government as 'the hostile environment for illegal migrants' (subsequently toned down to 'compliant'environment), introduced in the most part under the Immigration Act 2014, apply to employers, banks, landlords and the DVLA. The penalties for transgressors increase substantially under the Immigration Act 2016. There is an interesting House of Lords Library Briefing on the topic and a good summary in Balajigari [2019] EWCA Civ 673 §81.

The measures include:

- under the Immigration Act 2016 (s34), as from 12 July 2016, it has become a criminal offence to work (which is widely defined) in the UK without permission, and the illegal worker's wages can be seized as the proceeds of crime. Employing someone without permission to work can lead to civil penalties for employers of up to £20,000, and prosecution and imprisonment. The HO has produced a plethora of guidance documents for employers who want to avoid penalties: see eg *An employer's guide to right to work checks*. See MIL 7.9.4
- since February 2016 landlords have been required to carry out document checks to identify if a potential tenant has the right to rent in the UK, before they grant a tenancy, and to keep appropriate records during the tenancy and for at least 12 months after the tenancy has ended. The Immigration Act 2016 (s39) provides for prison sentences of up to five years for landlords who knowingly allow their property to be occupied by someone who is disqualified because of their immigration status. S40 of the new Act provides for the eviction of tenants who lose their permission to rent, without the need for the landlord to obtain a court order and with no right of appeal. JCWI has published a guide for tenants and those advising individuals in the private rented sector on the right to rent provisions in the 2014 Act (see also information from Shelter). The new measures on eviction came into effect on 1 December 2016.
- the immigration service may share people's details with financial services agencies to restrict access to credit
- the DVLA will not issue a driving licence and may be asked to cancel any existing licence. The Immigration Act 2016 creates a new offence of driving when unlawfully in the UK, with imprisonment of up to six months. Guidance on the current rules on revoking driving licences is in Offender management section of the Enforcement section of UKVI operational guidance
- undocumented migrants cannot open bank accounts. The 2016 Act goes further and requires bank accounts to be frozen and then closed. This has an extremely disruptive effect given that wages may be paid in and bills paid out. For how this is intended to be operated, see *Immigration status checks: guidance for banks and building societies*, *Guidance on money laundering reporting obligations* and guidance for those whose accounts are affected. See also Codes of Practice on freezing orders and the *Know your Customer* Guidance listing the various documents issued to migrants.
- The National Health Service (Charges to Overseas Visitors) Regulations 2015 were amended from 21 August 2017 to extend the secondary care settings in which charges can be raised, and from 23 October 2017 to provide for up-front payment, compulsory immigration status checks to be recorded on NHS records. For detailed information, refer to the ILPA Briefing and Department of Health guidance on overseas visitors charging regulations
- Lorry drivers are liable to civil penalties for carrying illegal entrants of up to £20,000 (by failing to secure their vehicle adequate, subject to defences such as checking for unauthorsied entry)– the regime is set out in the Carriers' Liability Regulations 2002 and summarised in the

CHAPTER 1: Immigration Control

Clandestine Entry Civil Penalty Guidance see the discussion of the approach in civil proceedings to the SSHD's Guidance - Link Spolka Z.O.O. [2021] EWCA Civ 1830

Employers and landlords may use the Home Office checking services to confirm the status of current and prospective employees and tenants/occupiers, though the information provided by the HO is not always accurate. In August 2021, a new, free online service entitled "Ask the Home Office to check your immigration status is correct" was introduced. It allows individuals to require the HO to correct its records, by filling an online form and emailing evidence in support. Disconcertingly the report of the Chief Inspector of Borders & Immigration cited in Open Rights Group & the3million [2021] EWCA Civ 800 noted that 10% of cases wrongly identified subjects as disqualified from holding a bank account.

By June 2020, the Enforcement Directorate was reported by the National Audit Office not to be in possession of an estimate of irregular migrant population or any figures to indicate whether the hostile environment did in fact have the desired effect of decreasing that population by deterrence or pressuring those present in the UK to leave.

Effect on the Windrush generation

In April 2018, media exposure of the impact on members of the Windrush generation and their descendants led to a public outcry, a change of Home Secretary and commencement of a review of the policy in general and the launch of the Windrush scheme on 30 May 2018 (see further MIL 4.2.14).

1.3.6.4 Right to rent

[handwritten: Jan 2024 = 1st breach: £5k per lodger, £10k per occupier. repeat: £10k, £20k]

In JCWI [2020] EWCA Civ 542 the Court of Appeal reversed the Administrative Court's decision that the "right to rent" scheme was unlawful. The Court of Appeal accepted that the evidence showed statistically significant discrimination against prospective tenants lacking a British passport. However, this was only indirect discrimination, as Article 8 does not give any general right to a home. Indirect discrimination is justified in matters of social policy unless the measures are found to be "*manifestly without reasonable foundation*". Here, as the ensuing discrimination was by private citizens (landlords) rather than government decision makers, the government had to be given wide leeway. Given there was no disproportionate interference with the right to be free from discrimination in matters touching on one's private life that affected all potential tenants, the scheme was lawful.

Certified digital identify service providers (IDSPs) can be used for identity checks using Identification Document Validation Technology (IDVT).

1.3.6.5 Right to work
Many migrants are encountered working in circumstances where a question arises as to their ability to do so (see MIL 13.3.1 for immigration raids).

For the conduct of right to work checks, see MIL 7.10.5. As noted above re right to rent, use of IDSPs is now encouraged, including for Disclosure and Barring Service (DBS – ie criminal record) checks. The pandemic adjustments to right to work and rent checks introduced on 30 March 2020 ended on 30 September 2022. From that date there must be a manual or HO online right to rent/work check or one using an IDSP.

1.3.6.6 No Recourse to Public Funds (NRPF)
Access to public funds is a politically controversial subject. So it is no surprise that many immigration routes contain a proviso that a grant is subject to a condition of no recourse to public funds, ruling out access to most benefits. But that restriction may well threaten the well-being of vulnerable migrants. The Rules permit the NRPF restriction to be lifted. 8% of limited leave grants under Appendix FM had the NRPF proviso lifted in 2014 (see ST [2021] EWHC 1085 (Admin)). Litigation has brought Rules changes recognising that the NRPF proviso should be lifted for those at imminent risk of destitution or contrary to a child's best interests or where there are exceptional circumstances affecting their income or expenditure (see eg the modern version of Appendix FM GEN1.11A, PL10.5(c), HK65.1). There is

always a discretion to lift NRPF, even for students and their dependents: PA [2023] EWHC 2476 (Admin).

There is Guidance *Access to public funds within family, private life and Hong Kong BN(O) routes*, which explains that
- The NRPF proviso applies to the Appendix FM, Appendix Private Life and Hong Kong BN(O) routes
- The test for destitution is not having adequate accommodation (ie being street homeless or relying on accommodation from a friend/charity, or if they have it, it is statutorily overcrowded or contravening public health Regs) or being unable to meet essential living needs (having regard to essential bills and expenses, the reasonableness of their accommodation costs, support from family and friends, savings/assets, and maintaining personal relationships and a reasonable level of social, cultural & religious life) (intentional disposal of funds or making loans may leed to refusal)
- Inspiration as to what is essential may be found in the regular *Reports on review of weekly allowances paid to asylum seekers and failed asylum seekers*.
- Proving "exceptional circumstances" requires compelling evidence
- Decision makers may need to make appropriate enquiries to clarify matters - they should look ahead at foreseeable events for three months (an assessment for s4/s95 support as asylum seekers will already have determined destitution, & generally local authority assessments should be respected)
- Benefits payments paid for specific essential needs for long-term mental health condition or disability re everyday tasks/mobility should not be regarded as relevant income absent evidence of non-essential spending

The NRPF Network provides a set of useful resources for anyone assisting those subject to NRPF conditions.

— child-compatible "best interests" test

1.3.7 The Common Travel Area

Many immigration provisions refer to the Common Travel Area ("CTA"). The CTA is a long-standing arrangement between the UK, the Crown Dependencies (Bailiwick of Jersey, Bailiwick of Guernsey and the Isle of Man) and Ireland. Essentially travel within the CTA is exempted from the requirements of immigration control by s1(3) of the IA 1971.

Under the CTA, British and Irish citizens (but not their third country family members) can move freely and reside in either jurisdiction and enjoy associated rights and privileges, including the right to work, study and vote in certain elections, as well as to access social welfare benefits, public housing, and health services. Indeed British residents in Ireland can even vote in the latter's elections, and vice versa.

However one cannot travel freely within the CTA where subject to a deportation or exclusion order. Article 3 of the Immigration (Control of Entry through Republic of Ireland) Order 1972 (sadly only the original version is online) lists various classes of individual who don't benefit from the deemed grant of leave for travellers from Ireland: including those who entered Ireland unlawfully from a place outside the common travel area and (from June 2021) those who last left the UK requiring, but not possessing, leave who have not since been granted further leave.

A person's leave potentially lapses when departing the CTA (IA 1971 s3(4)); but as discussed in section 1.3.4 there is statutory protection for most longer forms of leave which prevents such lapse.

The *CTA Guidance* explains access to work, education, healthcare and housing support within the CTA. The Guidance *Suitability: Admissibility to the Common Travel Area or other countries* explains the thinking on suitability refusals due to an applicant not being acceptable to the authorities in another part of the CTA or being unable to show their onwards inadmissibility to another country.

1.4 Sources of law

It is essential as an adviser to be able to navigate around the various pieces of law that govern UK and EU immigration control. This takes a lot of practice and will always remain a challenge. Immigration control is maintained through primary legislation, secondary legislation, the IRs, Home Office policy, and obligations under international conventions. On top of which the HO has a discretion to admit a person who does not satisfy any of the above.

All of these sources are amended from time to time and it will only be the most recently amended versions which will represent the current state of the law. The IRs are updated several times a year, the Immigration (EEA) Regulations which govern the free movement regime were amended many times (before Brexit brought their repeal), and statutes are regularly amended too. The parliamentary draftspeople prefer to amend existing legislation rather than starting from scratch.

The ongoing Immigration Rule reforms, plus the fall out of Brexit, will give rise to many further changes to the Rules and statutes, and will no doubt give rise to new and amended regulations. Reliance on old materials can produce serious problems for your clients, yet it is not always easy to find up to date versions.

Because the system of rules and regulations that makes up immigration law is so changeable, it is important to always check what you are doing against the law **as it is today** (or, where you are looking at refusal reasons, the law as it was at date of refusal): never presume the law is still the same as when you last looked. And it is a very good idea to know where a particular principle on which you rely has its source, so you can cite it in the event of a dispute down the line.

The senior judiciary often make this point: e .g. in DP (United States of America) [2012] EWCA Civ 365

> the frequent changes of the law in immigration field and the changes of Home Office policy guidance which are almost impossible for lawyers to keep up with, let alone ordinary people

We list, in the next unit, some of the most important legal sources and provisions. And of course the system is constantly changing: the government's *New Plan for Immigration* is taking effect via the Nationality and Borders Act 2022. It now seems that many of the NBA 2022's asylum appeal procedures will never see the light of day. Because the more radical approach of the the Illegal Migration Act 2023 is intended to prevent most asylum seekers from progressing their claims in the UK whatsoever.

1.4.1 Primary legislation

Available at http://www.legislation.gov.uk/ – usually, but not always, up to date if you hit the "Latest available" button! And it has a time travel feature accessible via the slide bar at the top of each section so you can access versions previously in force. It will be necessary to subscribe to an updating service such as Westlaw or Lexis.

We identify legislation as per the abbreviations at each heading below. The provisions within Acts are sections and sub-sections, within Regulations, individual regulations, within statutory instruments, Articles, and within Rules, individual rules.

You will see that there is a lot here. It is unrealistic to try and memorise it (in case you were thinking about doing so!). However, it **is** realistic to know which legislation deals with which major issue; then you can go to the contents page of the relevant legislation to see which part and which section deals with the issue that concerns you. You should practice (in your casework and/or exam revision) using your Phelan *Immigration Law Handbook* or the OISC level 1 and level 2/3 exam resource booklets, one or the other of which should be your core primary resource alongside HJT online courses and MIL, in order to link particular issues with particular legal provisions. HJT has made a great effort to include the most important legal materials for practitioners in the level 2/3 resources, and to update them several times a year.

Immigration Act 1971 (IA 1971)

- Continues to provide the framework of immigration control
- All persons without a right of abode are subject to immigration control (s1)

CHAPTER 1: Immigration Control

- The Secretary of State must lay down the rules to be followed (s1(4))
- Defines who has a right of abode (amended by other legislation) (s2)
- Provides that entry/stay is regulated by the grant of leave to enter or remain for either a limited or indefinite period (s3), and that leave continues whilst an application is awaiting decision (s3C)
- Provides for regulation and control of entry into and stay in the UK by the Secretary of State through powers (delegated to Entry Clearance Officers and Immigration Officers and under-secretaries at the Home Office) to grant (s4):
    - Entry clearance
    - Leave to enter
    - Leave to remain/further leave to remain
    - Make a decision to remove
    - Make a decision to deport
    - Make a decision to revoke a deportation order
- Provides for when a person may become liable for deportation (s3(5))
- Gives the power to remove only to certain countries or territories – specified in paragraph 8 of Schedule 2
- Defines various terms including illegal entrant (s33)
- Provides for the power to examine and detain passengers (Schedule 2)
- Provides for the grant of bail (Schedule 2)

British Nationality Act 1981 (BNA 1981)

- Redefined nationality and citizenship and limited 'right of abode' to newly created 'British citizens' (replacing Citizens of the United Kingdom and Commonwealth with six new categories of nationality and citizenship).:
    - s1 defines acquisition by birth or adoption
    - s2 defines acquisition by descent
    - s3 sets out the provisions for the registration of minors born outside the UK
    - s6 and Schedule 1 set out the criteria for acquisition by naturalisation
    - s4 to s4C sets out other registration provisions
    - s11 defines who acquired citizenship on commencement of the Act
    - s14 defines a 'British citizen by descent' and, in effect, also 'otherwise than by descent'. The distinction is important, as will be seen in Chapter 12: *British Nationality Law*.
    - s40 deprivation of citizenship

Special Immigration Appeals Commission Act 1997

- Created SIAC for security-sensitive appeals

Human Rights Act 1988 (HRA 1998)

- Incorporates the European Convention of Human Rights into UK law
- Provides for a domestic remedy (rather than having to go to the court in Strasbourg) for those asserting that a public official has breached their human rights protected under the ECHR

Immigration and Asylum Act 1999 (IAA 1999)

Largely superseded, but still relevant in certain important respects:

- amends IA 1971 to provide for entry clearance to have effect as leave to enter (s3)
- provides powers of administrative removal for persons (s10)
- provides for the registration of immigration advisors through the Office of the Immigration Services Commissioner (OISC), including the introduction of related criminal offences and enforcement powers
- provides for the support and dispersal of asylum seekers (though NBA 2022 will duly commence further provisions)
- provides for suspicious marriages to be reported by registrars

- creates new offences relating to facilitating/harbouring illegal entrants and increases powers of arrest and power to search premises and persons

Nationality, Immigration and Asylum Act 2002 (NIAA 2002)

- sets out rights of appeal to the immigration tribunal
- provides for certain asylum and human rights claims to be certified as clearly unfounded. An out-of-country (ie non-suspensive of removal) appeal was available until 28 June 2022: now there is no right of appeal whatsoever (s94)
- provides for establishment of accommodation centres and removal centres (ss16-42)
- allows for revocation of ILR (s76)
- grounds of appeal (s84)
- limitations on appeal rights (ss88-99)
- gives domestic life to Article 33(2) of the Refugee Convention (s72)
- provisions for juxtaposed controls with EEA countries
- a new Part 5, commencing on 28 July 2014, provides certain considerations as to the public interest that judges must have regard to when assessing an Article 8 claim
- The appeals provisions have been heavily amended, leaving only those who have made asylum or human rights claims with a right of appeal.

Asylum and Immigration (Treatment of Claimants etc) Act 2004 (AITCA 2004)

Current provisions include:

- immigration criminal offences aimed particularly at asylum seekers, including arriving without an immigration document (s2), not co-operating with removal (s35) and trafficking (s4)
- statutory negative presumptions about the assessment of credibility in asylum cases (s8)
- a regime for returning asylum seekers to safe third countries (now being amended by the NBA 2022 regime)
- various regulation-making powers, including to partially designate countries or groups for 'non-suspensive' appeals
- powers for electronic monitoring, or 'tagging', as a form of reporting restriction for those on immigration bail

Immigration, Asylum and Nationality Act 2006 (IAN 2006)

The major change introduced in this legislation was the abolition of appeal rights against entry clearance decisions for students and employment categories, which came into effect under the Points Based System (s4). Most other changes were relatively minor:

- introduces a new regime of civil penalty notices and fines for employers who employ immigrants without permission to work as well as a new criminal offence to replace s8 1996 Act (s15 to 26): s15 makes it an offence to employ a person subject to immigration control who lacks leave or whose leave does not permit them to work (or to pursue a particular kind of work)
- various provisions relating to information sharing and other enforcement powers (s27 to 42)
- removes registration as a British citizen as of right by introducing a good character requirement (s58)

UK Borders Act 2007 (UKBA 2007)

The changes instituted under the Act generally have little impact on day to day casework, save for the provisions on automatic deportations, subject to a human rights exemption and other exemptions. The Act also makes:

- provision for biometric immigration documents
- provision for imposing conditions on reporting and residence on those granted limited leave
- enhanced powers of detention for Immigration Officers

CHAPTER 1: Immigration Control

Tribunals, Courts and Enforcement Act 2007 (TCEA 2007)

- Creates a unified tribunal structure consisting of the First-tier Tribunal and the Upper Tribunal. Each is divided into different speciality 'chambers'.
- Immigration appeals were belatedly merged into the unified tribunal structure as of 2010 by the 2009 Act (below). An Immigration and Asylum Chamber was created in both the First-tier and Upper Tribunals.
- The right of appeal to the Court of Appeal is restricted by a second appeals test

Criminal Justice and Immigration Act 2008

- Sections 130-137 of this Act provide for a special immigration status for individuals who cannot be removed to their country of origin because of human rights concerns, but who have committed crimes falling under s72 NIAA 2002 or are excluded from refugee status by virtue of Article 1F of the Refugee Convention. Spouses, civil partners and children may also be subjected to the same status. The status can prohibit the person from working, subject them to heavy reporting and residence conditions and leaves them on a reduced welfare support package. It has not been introduced yet.

Borders, Citizenship and Immigration Act 2009 (BCIA 2009)

- New citizenship provisions were enacted: but, it would seem, never to be commenced, as announced by then coalition government
- Merged immigration adjudication into the unified tribunal structure (ie the FTTIAC and UTIAC).
- Power to transfer fresh claim JRs to the Upper Tribunal (a process which reached its culmination on 1 November 2013 from when almost all immigration JRs are heard in the Upper Tribunal)
- Powers to restrict what studies a person can undertake in the UK
- Most importantly, a new duty to safeguard and promote the welfare of children: section 55

Legal Aid, Sentencing and Punishment of Offenders Act 2012 (LASPO)

- Largely removes immigration matters from funding under legal aid
- Excludes migrants from the rehabilitation-of-offenders provisions

Crime and Courts Act 2013

- Allows for decisions to refuse an extension and to remove to be made at the same time
- Removes right of appeal for family visitors
- Restricts in-country appeal rights for those facing deportation on national security grounds

Immigration Act 2014 (IA 2014)

- Streamlines the decision-making process for removing migrants who do not have permission to be in the UK
- Restricts appeal rights to those who have made asylum or human rights claims
- Boosts the 'hostile environment' for irregular migrants. Provisions to prevent private landlords, banks and the DVLA providing their services to irregular migrants
- Restrictions on bail applications
- Rules for registering marriages

Immigration Act 2016 (IA 2016)

- new criminal offence of working illegally, with a power to seize the earnings of illegal workers
- further provisions relating to the 'hostile environment' – easier evictions, removal of driving licenses and the closing of bank accounts

CHAPTER 1: Immigration Control

- tagging of all foreign criminals awaiting deportation (where not detained)
- temporary admission becomes immigration bail
- human rights appeals potentially out of country absent risk of serious and irreversible harm
- restrictions on support for failed asylum-seeking families
- immigration skills charges for employers recruiting overseas
- restrictions on the detention of pregnant women

Nationality & Borders Act 2022 – NBA 2022

- Amendments to BNA 1981
  - giving access to citizenship for British Overseas Territories Citizens who lost out due to historic inability to transmit nationality
  - British citizenship for Chagos Islanders
  - a discretion to right historic wrongs in nationality laws and individual decisions
- New asylum law regime
  - introduction of differential treatment for refugees depending on their journey and or unlawful presence in UK and asylum claim's timing (subsequently paused in summer 2023)
  - refugee status qualification goes onto a statutory footing
  - a new inadmissibility regime for EU and "third country" asylum claims including a foundation for sending asylum seekers to Rwanda permanently
  - accelerated appeals procedures: priority removal and late evidence regimes penalising the late provision of evidence or making of claims and permitting abbreviated appeals direct to UT, and accelerated appeals for detainees (these provisions may never be implemented as IMA 2023 supercedes them)
- Extended definition of illegal entry as a criminal offence and new immigration offences
- New procedures for age assessment and modern slavery
- Visa penalties for citizens of countries which do not cooperate with removals from UK or which threaten international peace and security
- No right of appeal, out-of-country or otherwise, for refusals certified as clearly unfounded

Illegal Migration Act 2023 - IMA 2023

IMA 2023 is entering effect as usual in stages. Administrative provisions aside, as of Autumn 2023 some provisions had been introduced on commencement (s68) (lifetime bans on being granted LTR/ILR/British citizenship) and a general upgrade of FTT judges to potential UT status. And on 28 September 2023 the Illegal Migration Act 2023 (Commencement No. 1) Regulations 2023 introduced further sections (which MIL addresses where relevant): the new detention regime, a cap on the numbers of asylum seekers entering via safe and legal routes and a reporting regime thereon, the power to make Regs re seizing and searching electronic devices, and a new adverse credibility factor to consider for asylum seekers.

- Introduces radical measures to address small boat crossings – subject to government's success in Rwanda appeal in the Supreme Court & finding other willing third countries to host most of the UK's future asylum seeking arrivals
- Duty on SSHD to make arrangements for the removal of those arriving illegally in the UK via a third country – all asylum, human rights and trafficking claims to be inadmissible (save for UASCs under 18) & life bar on limited leave, ILR & British citizenship
- Automatic 28 days of detention
- Immigration detention powers challengeable only on conventional public law grounds
- Search and seizure powers re electronic devices
- Public order disqualification employed to bar these asylum seekers' access to trafficking protections
- Limited legal remedies against proposed third country removals

1.4.2 Secondary legislation

Some of this material is available on http://www.legislation.gov.uk/, but never in the amended form, so it is usually necessary to look separately at the original regulations and then any amendments to those regulations.

Immigration (Notices) Regulations 2003

- Governs the content of notices of immigration decisions
- Governs the service of the notice
- Requires a Notice of Appeal to be served with a Notice of Decision in certain circumstances
- Requires notices to be re-served where an asylum or human rights claim is made post-decision

Tribunal Procedure (First-tier Tribunal) Rules 2014

- Regulates appeal procedure in the Immigration and Asylum Chamber of the First-tier Tribunal, including time limits for lodging appeals. Still includes the Fast Track Rules (perhaps to be resurrected given the NBA 2022 promises new accelerated detained appeals). This is the place to start your search when looking for anything relating to appeals procedure.

Tribunal Procedure (Upper Tribunal) Rules 2008

- Governs appeals procedure in the entire Upper Tribunal, including the Immigration and Asylum Chamber

Immigration (European Economic Area) Regulations 2016 (EEA 2016)

- Transposes into domestic law the EU's freedom movement regime, and regulates residence, exclusion and appeal rights for EEA nationals and their family members.

Immigration Orders

- There are many Orders made under secondary legislation powers that can have an effect on immigration law. The most important is the Immigration (Leave to Enter and Remain) Order 2000 ('ILERO 2000'), which simplified immigration control for persons with visas & provides for the service and deemed service of immigration decisions not carrying the right of appeal.

- There are many other orders, the most useful of which are included in HJT's OISC level 2/3 exam resource.

Commencement Orders

- Bring into force the specific provisions of primary and sometimes secondary legislation – a recent example being The Immigration (European Economic Area) (Amendment) Regulations 2017.

1.4.3 Immigration Rules (HC395)

- Referred to in this manual as 'the Rules' or IRs
- https://www.gov.uk/government/collections/immigration-rules
- Unique legal status different to secondary legislation - made under section 3(2) of the 1971 Act
- Regulate who may and may not be granted entry clearance and/or leave to enter or remain
- HC395 is not actually law or secondary legislation as such and the SSHD retains discretion to allow entry outside the Rules(MIL 4.2.1)
- The HO cannot act more restrictively than is set out in the IRs and to do so would be unlawful

- Any substantive criteria for an immigration application must be located in the IRs. Not merely in the accompanying Guidance: see Alvi [2012] UKSC 33. This ruling initially led to a ballooning of the IRs' content, though with the reform of managed migration routes from 2020 there has been a relaxation as to the specified evidence for successful applications (MIL 2.2.2).

Statement of Changes

- Statements of Changes, each with their own 'HC' number, amend the IRs. They are available on the GOV.UK website from a link on the IRs page: Immigration Rules: statement of changes.

1.4.4 Operational Guidance

We deal with this at MIL 4.2.

For more on 'Operational Guidance' see the section on 'Policies, concessions and Operation Guidance' at 2.4.

1.5 Making applications to enter and remain in UK; and section 3C leave

Making an application for leave, whether from outside or within the UK, is always complex. The procedures for making the application are complex, and the substantive and evidential requirements of each application are complex too. None of this is helped by the constant changes to procedures, requirements, evidence and to the policies underpinning all of this.

The system now encourages most in-country applicants to apply online, with assisted digital support where necessary. A process also remains for receiving applications on paper for routes where there is no online application form, but paper forms can no longer be used for submission in person. The requirement for submission of passport photos was, also as part of those changes, dropped altogether. Documents can be uploaded: the Guidance Uploading evidence as part of your visa application explains how to do so.

The HO has an obligation to respect data protection rights and is only allowed to use, gather and share personal information where there is an appropriate legal basis to do so under the UK General Data Protection Regulations (UK GDPR) or the Data Protection Act 2018. Processing immigration applications and managing immigration control have an appropriate lawful basis. The Borders, immigration and citizenship: privacy information notice addresses compliance. Information is retained for 25 years (post-ILR/citizenship grant), 15 years otherwise, passenger name records at the border for 5 years, advance passenger information data for 10 years, arrest and detention records for 6 years.

1.5.1 Applications for a visa/entry clearance

Visa/entry clearance applications (terms which can be used interchangeably) must be made online (except in North Korea, where a paper application is still required though in June 2023 www.gov.uk reported these forms were no longer in use), and some other categories see the Guidance UK visa and immigration application forms), and since 1 November 2017 there has been a digital assist service available.

Information on entry clearance applications, processing times and local administrative arrangements for submitting an application can be found on the GOV.UK website at: Apply for a UK visa, which provides links as to the websites of the commercial partners and the local embassy or High Commission. Visa processing times can be found at: https://www.gov.uk/visa-processing-times. As at October 2022, visit, transit, and short-term study visas typically take 3 weeks, student visas 3 weeks, 3 weeks for working routes, returning residents, right of abode certificates of entitlement and biometric residence permit replacement, and family settlement applications (there are also customer service standards for family visas) have been promised turnarounds of 12 weeks at times in 2023, but more often, 24 weeks (though 9 months for international protection family reunion). For those who want quicker decisions, various priority services are available at an additional cost at some posts (MIL 1.5.7.3, 7.7.8).

An application for entry clearance should be made from the country in which the applicant is living (i.e. not merely passing through). Visit and short-term study visas are an exception – they can be made at any post where entry clearance applications are considered (r28), as can some Temporary Work categories (r28A).

The date of application may be important. An application is not legally made unless and until it is accompanied by the appropriate fee in local currency: r30. If the fee can be paid online, the application date will be the date the online application is submitted. Otherwise, the fee will be paid when the applicant attends the VAC in person for the biometric appointment. Where the IRs that apply to the application have been amended between the date of the online application and the date the fee is paid, it will be the amended rule that will be applied to the application.

Under r27, a child applicant who applies before their 18th birthday will not then be refused solely on the basis that they are over 18 at the date of decision. But leaving this too close to that date can be perilous: if the application is invalidated for one reason or another, the child may no longer be a minor at the date of decision.

Visa fees in local currency can be found at: https://www.gov.uk/visa-fees. A list of all fees is available on the fees and forms page. Where the application is being made for leave of more than six months (but not for indefinite leave to enter), there will usually be an immigration health surcharge (IHS) to pay on top of the fee (see below).

For more on the entry clearance process, see MIL 1.3.1 *Entry clearance*, above.

1.5.2 Applications for permission to stay /extension of stay

Applications for permission to stay (previously leave to remain) face various obstacles by which they may be refused, rejected and voided. Innocent mistakes by advisors can pitch a client headlong into the hostile environment. Until April 2022 it was possible to apply to vary one's leave whilst abroad. But the Rules' changes in HC1118 ended this possibility (deleting r33A). The explanatory note to these changes explains that those abroad should apply for entry clearance instead.

We consider below issues concerning the validity and timing of applications and further applications, including continuing leave under s3C of the Immigration Act 1971, and paragraphs 34 and 39E of the IRs. Understanding how these provisions operate together is difficult, but essential. To help you, there are some worked examples near the end of this chapter.

1.5.2.1 Timing of applications and decisions

The question of when to make the extension application is critical. For applications made on or after 24 November 2016, the Rules (but for some narrow exceptions: MIL 1.5.4);) require that the applicant must be lawfully in the UK at the date of application. That means they must not have overstayed their leave before making the application, even by one day. If they have, their application can be refused for that reason alone. There are some dispensations for applications under Appendix FM and Private Life applications (MIL 6.2.5).

The HO suggests a person applying for an extension/variation of stay makes the application no more than 28 days *before* their current leave expires. Although there is no prohibition on applying for an extension at any time during the person's leave, applying too early may not be a good idea as the person may lose out on the benefit of continuing leave under s3C should their application be refused very speedily before their leave expires (MIL 1.5.2.2 re s3C leave). For those on settlement routes, it is important that periods of leave granted are nearly completed before they are extended, to ensure the total settlement period will in fact accrue within the intended number of applications and extension periods. Otherwise an additional extension application may be necessary to reach the settlement period.

The Rules tell us when an application is treated as having been made (r34G):

- A postal application by paper form is treated as having been made on the date of posting (r34G(1)). The HO will take the date of posting as the date shown on the tracking information provided by Royal Mail or, if not tracked, by the postmark date on the envelope (so an application will not be made merely by putting it in a post box).
- Where a paper form is sent by courier or other postal services provider, the date on which it is delivered to the Home Office (r34G(2))
- Where the online process is used, the date on which the online application is submitted (r34G(3)) or, where the application includes a fee waiver application, the date the fee waiver was submitted online, so long as the completed application for leave to remain is submitted within 10 working days of the HO fee waiver decision being received by the applicant (r34G(4)) (see further MIL 1.5.8.4)

An extension of leave, if made by no later than the last day of a person's leave either online or sent by signed for delivery will be an 'in-time' application. See Ali [2021] EWCA Civ 1357 (MIL 1.5.4).

Applications take some time to be determined. There are premium services that may speed things along (MIL 1.5.7.3). The Guidance *Visa decision waiting times: applications inside the UK* gives some estimates: 8 weeks for student and partner, parent, child and adult dependant relative applications (and most business immigration routes), a more salutary 12 months for private life and 10-year route family cases. Start-up applicants and health and care workers should get decisions in a comparatively speedy 3 weeks. These timetables don't apply where something crops up to complicate things: the need for an interview, to verify documents or some special personal circumstances.

1.5.2.2 Automatic extension of leave ('continuing leave'/'3C leave')

The Home Office will take several weeks (at least) to decide an application for an extension of stay. For a person who has made an in-time application (i.e. before their leave ran out), this delay will usually result in their leave expiring after they have made the application, but before they receive the HO's decision on it. S3C of the Immigration Act 1971 deals with this problem. It provides that such a person will have 'continuing leave', which continues to run, automatically, when the person's leave that was granted to them has run out until that application is finally decided. The person's leave just continues, through the operation of the law, even though it will appear from a glance at their BRP to have expired.

S3C extends a person's leave throughout *three separate stages* of the application and appeals process:

1. where the person's leave runs out before the HO has decided the application, s3C automatically extends that leave until the application is either decided or withdrawn

2. if the application is refused, s3C further extends that leave by the period in which the person can lodge an application for administrative review or (in-country) appeal (the Guidance *Current Rights of appeal* addresses how the HO monitors this):

   - An application for administrative review must be lodged within 14 days of the person receiving the HO's decision to refuse the application (r34(1)(a)).

   - An appeal must be lodged within 14 days of the HO decision being sent to the applicant (Rule 19, The Tribunal Procedure (First-tier Tribunal) (Immigration and Asylum Chamber) Rules 2014)

3. where an appeal/AR has been lodged in-time, 3C leave continues for as long as the appeal or administrative review remains pending (i.e. until it has been withdrawn or is finally decided).

In the special case of EUSS appeals, where first an Administrative Review, then *also* an appeal (if AR is unsuccessful), can be brought, s3C leave is conferred:

- Under s3C(2)(ca) while an EUSS appeal can be brought (& under (2)(cb) whilst pending)
- Under s3C(2)(d)(i) while an EUSS AR could be brought (under (ii) while one is pending).

Note that

- An EUSS AR, under r34R(1A) must be lodged within 28 days, and if in detention within 7 days, of receipt of the decision notice
- An EUSS appeal must be lodged no later than 14 days after being sent the refusal decision notice or the dismissal of AR – Reg 19 (3B)(a)&(3D)(a) of the FTT Procedure Rules 2014.

Section 3C also extends the conditions attached to the previous grant of leave, so that a person who could previously work or study or claim benefits can continue to do so. Cancellation of s3C leave is possible under s3C(3A) for breaching conditions on leave or using deception (whether successfully or not).

Whilst a person is on the first kind of s3C leave before an application is determined, they may vary the application, by sending a new fee-paid application on the appropriate form (e.g. from an application as a partner under Appendix FM to an application under the 10 years' long lawful residence route, if they clock up the relevant residence pending the first application's determination). However, it is not possible to vary the application once it has been refused (s3C(4)): see JH (Zimbabwe) [2009] EWCA Civ 78.

For the interaction between s3C leave and the special extensions of leave granted under COVID concessions in mid-2020, please refer to section 4.2.19. See also MIL 5.2.1 for HO Guidance on withdrawn decisions and late appeals.

1.5.2.3 Situations where section 3C does not apply

It is important to understand how 3C works (and how it doesn't):

No s3C leave where refusal predates expiry of previous leave Section 3C does not kick in at any stage if the person's leave as granted to them expires *after* they have received a decision from the HO to refuse their application: that is, if they still have leave left at the date the decision is made. In that case, they will not benefit from 3C leave at any stage. They will become an overstayer as soon as the leave that was granted to them runs out, and will remain an overstayer unless and until they are granted further leave or depart from the UK. The fact that they have lodged an in-time appeal or Administrative review against the decision will not change the fact that they will become an overstayer when their leave runs out.

They will not benefit from section 3C because their leave ran out *after* rather than *before* they received the refusal decision. Their crime was to make the application too early. They could well be caught out even if making an application at a Premium Service Centre (PSC) on the last day of their leave, because if they are refused on the spot, they will still have leave until midnight of that day, and arguably will not then benefit from 3C leave whilst they challenge the decision. Consequently, the risk of refusal before the person's leave runs out will be a good reason not to apply in person at the PSC.

The HO suggests that if a person caught by this anomaly wants the protection of section 3C, they can make (yet) another application shortly before their leave expires, so that they will have 3C leave to cover them for the appeal or AR application that will already be pending.

To avoid this problem, a person who wants to extend or vary their stay should wait until their leave has almost expired before applying to extend or vary that leave to ensure that their leave has run out by the date of decision. If the application is then refused, they will benefit from continuing leave whilst they challenge the decision.

At one time, one could ensure one's leave had expired by the time a decision was made by applying by post (rather than at a 'same day' service). But since December 2018, most applications must be made online. IR34G(3) provides that the application is submitted when the online application is lodged. There will then be a time period, typically 10 days from that date, during which supporting documents must be sent, or a specified time period within which UKVCAS/SSC appointment be made for biometrics and document lodgement. Given the above danger of applying too early, the online application, and sending of documents/making of the appointment should be timed so as to ensure the decision cannot be made before leave expires.

No s3C leave where leave is curtailed As there is no longer a right of appeal against curtailment, a person whose leave is cancelled or curtailed by the HO does not benefit from continuing leave. They will become an overstayer immediately on their leave being cancelled or curtailed. Consequently, section 3D of the Immigration Act 1971, which worked in a similar way to s3C leave for those whose leave was curtailed, was deleted by the Immigration Act 2016.

No s3C leave where there is only a claim for JR Applications for JR are not one of the remedies which the statute includes as a basis for s3C leave. So, a client thinking about JR needs to understand that if it fails, any further application under the Rules may be ruled out because of the lengthy overstaying they have clocked up during the challenge.

However, if a JR application succeeds and strikes down the immigration decision which otherwise apparently ended the person's original or section 3C leave, s3C may be resurrected. In Saimon [2017] UKUT 371 (IAC) the UT found that where a UT decision refusing permission to appeal was set aside by a successful JR (i.e. what is often called a Cart JR after the case which first recognised this kind of challenge), the appeal becomes pending once again. It might be thought that this means that section 3C leave revives once more, given that a pending appeal is one of the bases for such leave. Though should an appeal be deemed abandoned due to a grant of leave to remain or voluntary departure from the UK *before* a Cart JR succeeds, s3C leave may not be resurrected in this way (MIL 14.6.1.5 and 14.5).

Akter [2021] EWCA Civ 704 confirms this possibility: there the question turned on the implication of references in correspondence to a JR claim which was being settled by a Consent Order as having "won". The Court accepts that this at least arguably implied that the underlying decision on the last application was being withdrawn: were that the case, any leave that would otherwise have expired would be revived.

Akinola [2021] EWCA Civ 1308 answered the long-vexed question as to the impact on s3C leave of the FTT extending time for a late appeal.
- When an extension of time is granted for an out-of-time appeal, section 3C(2)(c) is engaged by the resurrection of a pending appeal. This results in a revival of the section 3C leave
- But this protection of immigration status did not operate retrospectively - for to do so would have implications for the individual's legal relationship with third parties and the state
- When an extension of time is granted, the notice of appeal is effective from the date when it was filed, so that the appeal proceedings are instituted at that date rather than at the date when the decision to extend time is made or written notice of it is provided to the parties
- The Court of Appeal hoped that the SSHD would feel able to exercise her discretion to mitigate the disadvantages of the gap in relation to out-of-time appeals in the same way it understood she had done re withdrawn decisions. Indeed the 3C and 3D Guidance now states (from 15 October 2021, Version 11.0):
    "Where the Tribunal has extended time to appeal and the appeal is ultimately successful the person should not be disadvantaged by the break in their leave in any future application for immigration leave. For the purposes of deciding the application you should treat any gap in leave as if the person was lawfully in the UK where the appeal is allowed."

Akinola also finds that the withdrawal of an immigration decision by the SSHD reinstates s3C leave from the date the decision is withdrawn. But it does not reverse the previous legal position. A reconsideration of a migrant's case without an accompanying withdrawal of the previous decision had no impact on a person's past or present immigration status.

No s3C leave for extended family member applications: Ali [2022] UKUT 278 (IAC) explains that there was no legal requirement to treat persons with pending applications as extended family members (under the EEA Regs 2016) as if present with statutorily extended leave under s3C of IA 1971. The domestic law immigration regime and the EU regime had separate legal bases.

No s3C leave where leave has already expired at the time an application is made: obviously if one's leave has expired, there can be no extension of leave: because there is no leave to extend. Under r39E, the SSHD permits extension applications to be granted if made within a short period (these days, usually 14 days) of overstaying. Some advisors over time have had the impression that this overstaying tolerance somehow magics overstaying into an automatic extension of leave. It doesn't.

But s3C leave is extended where an outstanding application (made before the original leave expired) is varied by a new application (MIL 1.5.5). So an application in these circumstances might be used by way of a "sticking plaster" to cover a what would otherwise be a gap whilst a further application is under prepraration but not quite ready. Interestingly, where a varied application is treated as invalid by the HO, its predecessor remains extant for decision, which is another way in which s3C leave may be sustained: see Bajracharya [2019] UKUT 417 (IAC).

1.5.2.4 Confirming s3C leave

Those with s3C leave can easily fall victim to the hostile environment even though they remain lawfully resident in the UK. Some employers and landlords are now so nervous at the sanctions and penalties for wrong-doing, they may think twice about keeping someone on. Whilst they have access to HO guidance, which explains s3C leave to them and the circumstances in which they can rely on it to avoid HO sanctions, they may choose not to engage with it when dismissal or eviction appears the easier and safer option.

Top Tip

An adviser may need to help their client persuade an employer, landlord, bank or the DVLA that they are lawfully in the UK with continuing leave under s3C and, consequently, that their job, home, bank account, and car should not be taken away.

Remind the reluctant employer that the Home Office's 'An employer's guide to right to work checks' states, at page 25, that:

'If, on the date on which permission (as set out in the document checked) expires, you are reasonably satisfied that your employee has either:

- submitted an in-time application to us to extend or vary their permission to be in the UK; or
- made an appeal or an administrative review against a decision on that application;
- or is unable to provide acceptable documentation but presents other information indicating they are a non-EEA long-term lawful resident of the UK who arrived here before 1988

your statutory excuse will continue from the expiry date of your employee's permission for a further period of up to 28 days to enable you to obtain a positive verification from the Employer Checking Service.'

But problems can arise even where the employer does contact the HO checking service as the information available to HO staff can be out of date or inaccurate. Evidence that the application did reach the HO (recorded delivery tracking signature) will be useful in these circumstances, particularly as confirmation letters, if sent at all, often do not state the date of the application. Hopefully, in the face of a negative response from the HO, the employer can be persuaded to contact the HO again to clarify things with any new information you give them. One way of opening a channel of communication to the HO in these cases is for the person to contact their local MP's office, as the HO's MP Liaison Unit must respond within two weeks to the MP, whereas response times to the client are usually much slower.

CHAPTER 1: Immigration Control

1.5.3 Making a valid application

The validity requirements for applications were for some years found in IR34. But the reformed immigration routes from 1 December 2020 contain their own route-specific validity requirements. The validity requirements in these Appendices tend to include elements which were previously eligibility requirements, increasing the risk of rejections rather than refusals, and with it the loss of s3C leave. Always read each relevant Appendix for its own bespoke validity requirements. IR A34 now lists the routes to which the old generic regime still applies: including legacy routes, Appendices FM and Armed Forces, & the stateless. The _Guidance_ states that in general entry clearance applications will not be rejected as invalid as the technology is lacking, albeit that the IRs appear to apply validity criteria across the board.

Core validity criteria: The rest of this section deals with the core validity requirements which are common between the Appendices above and the cross-cutting Part 1 requirements. In short these are using the right form and paying the fee and IHS, providing any required biometrics, and providing a passport or other document which satisfactorily establishes identity and nationality.

Beyond these there may be other criteria: typically a control on switching into the route, a relationship to a Sponsor, presence in the UK at the application date, and in human rights routes, potential for waiving these criteria where claims are made alongside protection claims, or in an appeal with HO consent, during detention or at the point of removal.

Applications for leave to remain are made from within the UK. Since December 2018, they are generally made by completion of an online form. The options are to later send the signed form by post with supporting documents, or to attend an appointment with UKVCAS. As well as being made in-time, the application must be 'valid'. If the application is not valid, the HO will _reject_ it (rather than _refuse_ it). They will return it to the applicant with a 'Notice of Invalidity' and treat it as if it had never been made. A rejected application cannot be challenged by appeal or administrative review.

A decision that an application is invalid will bring the person's 3C leave to an end. The person may not then be able to make a further application. Consequently, if the decision on invalidity is incorrect, or the person has not been given an opportunity by the HO to correct the invalid application, the decision must be challenged (MIL 1.5.3.2).

A 'valid application' is defined in paragraph 6 of the Rules as an application made in accordance with the requirements of Part 1 of the Rules (rr34-34GB) (though aspects of the validity regime are disapplied by A34, in favour of the specific validity criteria within each route).

There are several elements to making a valid application:

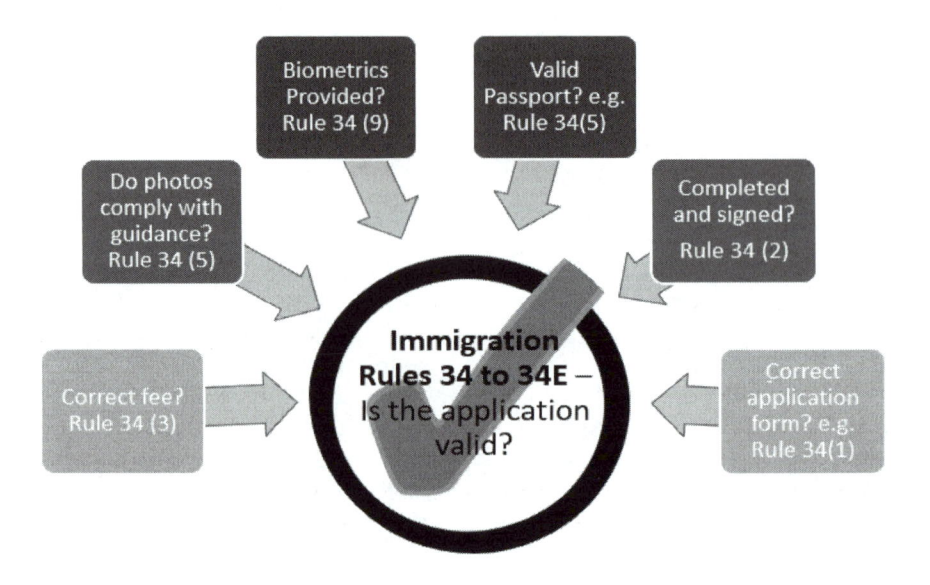

©HJT

CHAPTER 1: Immigration Control

The provisions as to validity can be found at IRs 34 to 34B (and in more modern immigration routes, within each route itself under the validity heading).

HO policy and guidance on these provisions is in the Applications section of the Immigration Staff Guidance, currently: <u>Applications for leave to remain: validation, variation and withdrawal</u> (hereafter referred to as the 'Applications Guidance').

The mandatory requirements are:

Use of the specified form, and the most up to date version of it (see list of forms below). The forms state on their front page the types of applications for which they can be used, and the date of issue.

If the relevant form remains a paper one it may bedownloaded directly from the UKVI <u>'fees and forms' page</u>.Ensure it is the correct form for the application in question. Before finalising and submitting the application, check again that it is still the most up to date version of the form available. Usefully IR34(1)(c) allows for an old version of a form to be used for up to 21 days after a new version goes online, although the current fee must always be paid (not that showing on the superseded form, if they are different). The paper forms are for the armed forces, domestic violence survivors, DLR for failed asylum seekers, refugees/stateless/HP holders extending leave, and various other forms of extension.

The Applications Guidance once stated applications made more than three months before possible invalidity was identified should still be treated as valid to avoid unfairly disadvantaging applicants: but no longer.

- **The payment of a specified fee**. Ensure, if the payment page is used, that the account remains in funds until the fee is collected. A full list of fees can be found at https://www.gov.uk/government/publications/visa-regulations-revised-table. There is Guidance on *Immigration and Nationality Refunds* listing the circumstances where a refund is available (eg where the application is void or withdrawn – not for administrative failings, addressed via ex gratia payments MIL 14.10)
- **The payment of the Immigration Health Surcharge (IHS)**, where applicable, in accordance with the process set out on the GOV.UK website (https://www.gov.uk/healthcare-immigration-application/pay) – see MIL 1.5.7.5
- **Parental consent:** where the main applicant is under the age of 18, their parent or legal guardian must provide written consent to the application
- **Two photographs** as described in the photo guidance. Note that this requirement does not apply in online applications as the photo used will be that taken at the biometrics appointment. However, where a paper form is still used, ensure you keep a photocopy of the photographs physically clipped to the form, so you will be able to prove they have been sent with the application.
- **Completion** of all the 'mandatory' sections of the form. Where an online form does not allow for certain answers, or does not allow the applicant to proceed to the next question unless an answer is provided where this is not available or applicable, another entry which fits the format should be made, and a careful note of this should be taken. The entry and the problems with the form or inapplicability of the question should then be clearly explained in the covering letter to avoid any allegation of misleading or inaccurate information having been provided.
- **Compliance with biometric requirements**, i.e. attending the Home Office or a post office for face and fingerprint scans within a specified timeframe. Biometric information must be provided in accordance with the process set out in the biometric enrolment letter and any subsequent warning letter issued in accordance with the Code of Practice about the sanctions for non-compliance with the biometric registration regulations.
  - There is Guidance such as the *Biometric Information: Introduction* (defining biometrics and explaining the difference between biometric residence documents for those subject to immigration control without leave under the EU Withdrawal Agreement, biometric residence cards for EEA nationals and e-visas, and explaining processes)
  - The Guidance Application *validation, variation, voiding and withdrawal of applications* ("Application Guidance") at the heading *Requirement: providing biometrics*

CHAPTER 1: Immigration Control

and proof of identity addresses sets out the various protections available: including various 14-day grace periods to rectify correctable mistakes, and if an application irredeemably invalid because a fundamental criteria cannot be satisfied, then an opportunity to vary the application to something more viable should be afforded

- Now the Guidance provides for waiver of biometric requirements on medical grounds (eg 'stretcher' cases) and for senior government officials on official visits, or in exceptional individual circumstances, eg compelling circumstances with no operational alternatives or where their status warrants excuse: see *Biometric information - enrolment*. In practice biometric waiver is sought from the Visa Application Landing Pages after the online visa application is made.
- The Guidance *Unable to travel to a Visa Application Centre to enrol biometrics (overseas applications)* explains that these applications must be a last resort after other attempts to resolve the problem have failed, eg waiting for the situation to improve or travelling to an alternative third country. By the time of KA & Ors [2022] EWHC 2473 (Admin) the HO readily acknowledged that biometric requirements could be waived.
- The Guidance *Biometric data-sharing process* explains that the Migration 5 ("M5") countries (the UK & USA, Australia, Canada, & New Zealand) agreed arrangements under the High Value Data-Sharing Protocol to check the fingerprints of up to 3,000 individuals between themselves annually, with a view to confirmed matches turning up previously unknown evidence of identity and immigration history.

- **Attendance at a UKVCAS centre (or Service and Support Centre (SSC)):** where the application is made online, and the person must attend a UKVCAS centre as part of the process, they are encouraged to go to an appointment and given a timescale to complete biometrics enrolmentas soon as possible. A reminder will be sent after 15 working days if no attendance has taken place.
- **An original, valid passport**, travel document or (unless the applicant is a Points Based System Migrant) national ID card issued to the applicant and to any dependant included in the application must be provided (rule 34(5)). The rule also allows the person to provide their most recent passport or national ID card if they do not have a current one (r34(5)(b)(ii))There are some exceptions, including (rule 34(5)(c)):
    o those whose document is with the Home Office
    o where it has been permanently lost or stolen and there is no functioning national government to issue a replacement
    o where the applicant is a victim of trafficking in receipt of a positive conclusive grounds decision, and it has been retained by an employer or other person
    o the applicant has made an application under the destitute domestic violence (DDV) concessionor DVILR rule
    o or as a stateless person or their family member or by a person in the UK with refugee leave or humanitarian protection
    o or the applicant provides a good reason beyond their control why they cannot provide proof of their identity.

As to proof of identity, the HO Application Guidance suggests:

IR34(5)(c) allows an applicant to provide a good reason beyond their control why they cannot provide any proof of identity. Reasons may include the following (this list is not exhaustive):
• there is no longer a functioning national authority to provide a new document
• there is no Embassy or consular service for their country in the UK
• there is a national authority to apply for a document, but they have run out of documents
• the applicant has made an application for a replacement document, but the issuing authority was not able to provide it before the application was made
• the applicant cannot obtain a document for reasons of national or personal security
• the national authority has unreasonably refused to provide a document, for example, if the national authority:
  o will only provide a passport if the applicant applies in person but there is no provision to apply in person in the UK
  o puts unreasonable barriers in place for the applicant
Paragraph 34(6) of the Rules states that you may ask the applicant to provide alternative satisfactory evidence of their identity and nationality. For example, this could be a combination of:

- birth certificate
- driving licence
- national health card
- national service document

There is a discretion for the HO to request alternative evidence (r34(6)).

1.5.3.1 Opportunity to correct an invalid application

Very importantly, where a person makes an invalid application, the HO *should* contact them before rejecting it as invalid, to give them an opportunity to correct the error or omission (IR34B). An applicant will have 10 business days (the Guidance now refers to 14 calendar days) to correct the application from the date on which the notification was sent. They will only get one chance to correct it, so if they miss that opportunity the applicant will receive a Notice of Invalidity. Discretion may only be exercised where fee & IHS have been paid and adequate proof of identity supplied.

Although the rule states only that the HO *may* contact the applicant to give them this opportunity, the Application Guidance states that caseworkers 'must' contact the applicant and give them at least 14 days to rectify the issue in relation to:

- Use of an incorrect form
- Payment of an incorrect fee
- Payment of only one fee although dependants are included
- Erroneous inclusion of a dependant where the form does not allow this
- Refusals of fee waivers
- Uploads of inadequate photos
- Any other validity requirements, whether in Part 1 or the routes themselves
- Multiple applications
- Variation application of an original application allowing dependants, where the variation does not
- Attempted variation application of an earlier application which has already been decided
- Applying under what looks like the wrong route

The guidance states that there is no obligation on the caseworker to contact the applicant where the missed requirement cannot be met (such as a minimum age requirement) and exercise of discretion (eg where an age requirement was missed by one day) is not considered appropriate. However where an applicant cannot perfect their application, 14 days' opportunity should be given to vary their application to another route.

If the HO decide that the application is invalid, and reject it *without having given the person the opportunity to correct it*, in accordance with r34B, that decision may itself be unlawful for failure to apply the Rules. Where the person has become an overstayer as a result, they must challenge the HO decision; firstly, because they will be subject to all the prohibitions of the hostile environment, including losing their employment (upon which they may have been relying for the application). And secondly, because they may not be able to make a further application in these circumstances!

Making an application as an overstayer is governed (in most categories of the Rules) by the requirements of r39E. Until 2022, where a person became an overstayer because the application they made was rejected as invalid, it was unlikely that fresh applications would meet the requirements of r39E. This was because that person is treated as having overstayed from the date their actual leave expired and not from the date the application was rejected as invalid (as noted in the Immigration Staff Guidance Applications from overstayers (non family routes) and the Supreme Court in Mirza [2016] UKSC 63). However now r39E protection applies from notification of invalidity as well as from refusals of applications (MIL 1.5.4).

Those who cannot make use of the r39E proviso must beware overstaying more than 30 days before leaving the UK as they may then face a re-entry ban when seeking to return (MIL 2.3.5.8).

Note that invalidity due to non-enrolment of biometrics is effective only from the date of notification of non-enrolment: until that date the application is conditionally valid (so s3C leave runs until said notice).

1.5.3.2 How to challenge decisions on invalidity

The HO sometimes wrongly treat applications as invalid, e.g. where the HO lose an applicant's photos or passport, and then allege the applicant did not include them with the application. Or the HO claim that they could not collect the fee from the applicant's bank, but the bank has no record of such an approach and the relevant account is in funds. These problems have been largely eliminated by the online procedures, which no longer require photographs and which require online payment by the applicant.

What of the situation where the HO alleges invalidity in circumstances where only the HO has records of what went wrong: eg where it is said that no payment authority was properly given so the card issuer refuses to pay the fee. Basnet [2012] UKUT 113 (IAC) explains that in these cases the HO bears the burden of proof. So the HO must produce its records of what allegedly went wrong. Subsequently Mitchell [2015] UKUT 562 (IAC) stressed the need to make a speedy challenge to such invalidity accusations, adding that the principle only applies where the migrant can show a prima facie case that their application was fully valid – eg proving they had sufficient funds to meet the payment in question at the relevant time. Ahmed [2018] UKUT 53 (IAC) emphasises the need to look at who was truly responsible: eg it was for the migrant to show that they had signed payment authority.

The current IRs aim to alleviate problems caused by invalidity, meaning that recourse to lengthy litigation will no longer be necessary. The discretion in IR 34B, by which the HO *may* give an opportunity to make good whatever led to the invalidity (MIL 1.5.3.1), read with the statement in the modern Guidance that an opportunity should *always* be given to rectify invalidity based on fees, should provide a fair and reasonable regime which avoids unduly harsh consequences due to innocent errors.

The question as to whether the application was invalid will be critical to the person's immigration situation. A wrongful allegation of invalidity, or a failure to give an opportunity to correct the application, should be challenged. Just making a new application may well store up future problems. Even if the applicant can make a new application, they may be significantly prejudiced by doing so as they will remain an overstayer unless and until they are granted more leave.

Because of the implications of the hostile environment, the HO need to be informed immediately of their mistake. That can be done by a letter of representations, or a letter submitted under the *pre-action protocol* for JRs. Send a copy to the decision maker, but also to the dedicated email address for PAP letters. Ultimately, as there is no right of appeal or administrative review against the rejection of an application, the remedy will be JR.

1.5.3.3 Void applications

There is a distinct regime from November 2022 for void applications. An application will be void where "it would not possible to grant" the permission for which they applied (r34KA). Such applications will be voided rather than considered (r34KB). Examples given are where someone exempt from immigration control applies for permission (except under Appendix EU), temporary permission applications where ILR has already been granted, new regular immigration applications made during the currency of a timely appeal, or where the applicant dies pre-decision (r34KC). Notice will be given under the regime in Appendix SN.

1.5.3.4 Mental capacity

It may be necessary for HO decision makers to bear in mind the mental capacity of migrants - ie being able to make decisions for themselves unless subject to impairment or disturbance in the functioning of their mind or brain (Mental Capacity Act 2005 s2(1), (2)). Where Guidance raises the issue (eg re asylum claim withdrawal MIL 9.7.1), it explains they should be assumed to possess capacity unless it is established otherwise on the balance of probabilities. Mental health conditions and disability due to mental impairment must also be considered. Reasonable adjustments may be necessary to avid a breach of Equality Act duties.

The Equality Act 2010 states that a disability is a physical or mental impairment that has a substantial and long-term adverse effect on a person's ability to carry out normal day-to-day activities. This could be due to a learning disability, cognitive disorder, or mental health condition. Reasonable steps must be taken to ensure an individual has capacity having regard to HO records and, if they lack representation, any available documentary evidence.

1.5.4 Applying as an overstayer – Rule 39E

Most immigration routes contain a Suitability rule barring a grant if in breach of immigration laws or on immigration bail. We will label this the standard immigration status proviso.

Whilst an applicant must normally apply for an extension of stay whilst their leave remains current, paragraph 39E of the Rules provides for two limited exceptions to this rule. Both give 14 days grace. The first exception requires "*good reason*" for the delay, and applies to any application, whether or not made following a refusal; the second exception applies where a timely application has been refused, and does *not* require "*good reason*".

The first exception – "good reason" (r39E(1))

Under the first exception (r39E(1)), an application made no later than 14 days after the person's leave has expired will be accepted and decided by the HO if the decision maker is satisfied that there was a good reason *beyond the control of the applicant or their representative*, provided in or with the application, why the application could not have been made in-time.

What is a *good reason beyond the control of the applicant or their representative*? Some examples are provided in the HO guidance, Applications from overstayers (non family routes) (in the Immigration Staff Guidance). These are:

- the applicant was admitted to hospital for emergency treatment (evidenced by an official letter verifying the dates of admission and discharge and the nature of the treatment)
- a close family bereavement
- an educational institution was not sufficiently prompt in issuing a Confirmation of Acceptance for Studies

When considering the reason given, the HO decision maker must give thought to:

- the plausibility of the reasons
- whether the reason was genuinely outside the applicant's control or whether the applicant is describing difficulties that could realistically have been surmounted
- the credibility of evidence provided

The second exception – application made within 14 days following refusal/invalidity

Under the second exception (r39E(2)), where an in-time application has been refused or rejected, a further extension application can be made within a 14-day period. It is not possible to benefit from the exceptions for overstayers twice in a row: so the refused application must itself have been an in-time application.

That 14-day period under para 39E(2) will begin on the day immediately following *one* of the events below:

- the refusal of a previous application, or
- the expiry of a period of 3C leave, or

- following the time limit for submitting an administrative review or appeal in relation to the previous application, or
- the conclusion of an administrative review or appeal

Essentially this means that one has 14 days from the refusal of an 'in-time' application, or from the ability or actual challenge to such a decision by AR/appeal, within which to make a further application which does not face automatic refusal for excess overstaying (see examples in the online MIL1.5.9).

If the application was made *more than* 14 days after the person's leave expired, the HO will not be able to accept it under the IRs ((absent very exceptional circumstances). Note though that for applications made before 24 November 2016, the IRs generally provided for late applications made up to 28 days after the person's leave had expired, without having to provide an explanation for the delay. The explanatory memorandum to HC667 explains:

> This 28 day period was originally brought in so that people who had made an innocent mistake were not penalised, but retaining it sends a message which is inconsistent with the need to ensure compliance with the United Kingdom's immigration laws

The third exception – overstaying between 24 January and 31 August 2020 (COVID exemption)

From 1 December 2020, para 39E can be applied retrospectively where an application was made following a period of overstaying between the above dates. Whilst this is clearly intended to address the consequences of the pandemic, nothing in the language of the Rule limits the overstaying protection to that cause.

The fourth exception – overstaying between 1 July 2020 and 31 January 2021 by current or former holders of Hong Kong BN(O) permission

Rule 39E(4) recognises the need to condone overstaying from the time that political unrest in Hong Kong created migration pressures and the route's opening on 31 January 2021. In fact leave outside the rules was available to those already in the UK before that date. To take advantage of this exemption, status must have been granted on the route, even if by the time r39E(4) is applied it is no longer current (see further MIL 4.2.20).

Where accepted by the HO, the application made within the 14-day period will be considered under the IRs in the normal way. But the applicant will continue to be an overstayer until further leave is granted. They will have committed a criminal offence by overstaying, albeit one that seems rarely to be prosecuted (IA 1971 s 24(1)(b)).

1.5.4.1 Adverse consequences of becoming an overstayer

Becoming an overstayer may have serious consequences, at least until further leave is granted. This may include all of the privations provided for by the 'hostile environment', including (but not limited to):

- Losing their right to work and to receive benefits as they do not have the benefit of a statutory extension of leave under s 3C of IA 1971
- They have potentially committed a criminal offence albeit one that seems rarely to be prosecuted, in that they have knowingly remained beyond their limited leave (IA 1971 s 24(1)(b)(i))
- They will commit a further offence if they continue to work or drive, and any benefits they may have previously been entitled to will stop
- They will be unable to rent property
- As a person without leave to remain they may be vulnerable to detention and removal and even if they would have a right of appeal, they may not get the chance to exercise it if they lack ready evidence of their links here. Under the 'relevant provisions' regime they will be a person who requires leave but does not have it, and so are liable to removal without notice under the 'single decision' procedure

- They will have broken their continuity of leave for future settlement purposes, and must re-start their settlement period all over again

The guidance to employers makes it clear that they cannot continue to employ a person who has overstayed, even if they have a current application awaiting consideration under the IRs. Every effort must therefore be made to make an in-time application, even if that means applying whilst the person awaits a new passport or before all the relevant documents are available. A person should be given time to correct an invalid application under IR34B, and missing documents can be submitted after the application is made if necessary (on the basis that the HO should consider all the documents they have at the date of decision). The 14-day period of overstaying under the Rules should only be relied on where there is absolutely no other option.

1.5.5 Varying an application

A person with an application pending at the Home Office can apply to vary that application if their circumstances change before a decision has been made. This is provided for in r34E of the Rules. For example, a person with an outstanding application for an extension of stay as a Student may clock up 10 years of lawful residence whilst awaiting a decision. They will want to vary that application so that they can instead be considered for ILR under the lawful long residence category. It is possible to vary an application up until the date that it is refused, but not after that date.

Any application to vary an application must be made in compliance with all the formalities as to fees and forms as required by r34. It must be made as a fully prepared fresh application and will be decided 'in accordance with the immigration rules in force at the date such variation is made' (r34F). For s3C purposes, the application will be treated as having been made at the date of the original application, so the person will keep their 3C leave in these circumstances.

R34E provides for a person to 'vary the purpose of an application'. The phrase 'vary the purpose' under r34E should not be given a narrow or technical reason. Such a variation could include a Student deciding to change their sponsor whilst an extension application is being considered by the Home Office. They will then need to make a wholly new Student application based on the new sponsorship, rather than simply submit their new CAS (Khan [2016] EWCA Civ 137).

Example

A person submits an application to extend their stay as a partner under Appendix FM. At the date of application, they have not been earning the required minimum specified gross annual income for the requisite period of six months. The application is likely to be refused. Some weeks later, however, before the application has been decided, they do now meet the financial requirement. They cannot simply send to the Home Office evidence of their new financial circumstances, because the Rules require that the requirement is met at the date of application.

Can they prepare and submit a whole new application to extend their stay as a partner, relying on their new financial circumstances, under para 34E? Whilst the law on this is hazy, HO practice seems to be to accept that they can do this and that the second application will be treated as a variation of the first.

1.5.6 Varying extant applications

From 6 April 2017, applicants can only have one outstanding application at a time.

Multiple applications are forbidden under Rule 34BB. Making a new application whilst there is an extant application will have the effect of **varying the existing application**. It may be sometimes necessary to to put in a "holding" application to protect one's position whilst another application is perfected (MIL 1.5.2.3).

- An applicant may only have one outstanding application extant

CHAPTER 1: Immigration Control

- A further application will be treated as a variation of the existing one (previously, a new application did not necessarily amount to a variation of the outstanding one, rather the two could proceed in tandem: Chaparadza [2017] EWHC 1209 (Admin))
- If simultaneous applications are made on the same day, both are treated as invalid: however the Home Office must give an opportunity to withdraw one or both within 14 days of the notification of potential invalidity being sent: absent a reply, all will be treated as invalid if the timings are unclear, otherwise only the most recent will proceed
- From 6 April 2022, where a protection or human rights claim is made as part of an application, and the application is subsequently varied, then the earlier claim will be treated as withdrawn if the application is granted: but if refused, will be treated as outstanding and will be considered at a time to be decided by the Home Office: r34BB(7)

The Home Office Guidance on *Applications for leave to remain* emphasises that a single form cannot be used for multiple applications.

Unless the application is made in respect of a human rights route (i.e. on the basis of family or private life), the HO policy is, unhelpfully, to ignore other issues raised in a covering letter or in a section 120 notice (see section 'Attempts to make multiple applications in a single form' in the Applications Guidance).

Varying extant applications

A person with an application pending at the Home Office can apply to vary that application to something else. For example, a person with an outstanding application for an extension of stay as a Student may clock up ten years of lawful residence whilst awaiting a decision. They will want to vary that application so that they can instead be considered for ILR under the lawful long residence category. It is possible to vary an application up until the date that it is refused. Any such further application must be made complying with all the formalities as to fees and forms (r34E), and will be decided 'in accordance with the IRs in force at the date such variation is made' (r34F). For section 3C purposes, however, the application will be treated as having been made at the date of the original application, so the person will keep their 3C leave in these circumstances (r34GB). The date of application for any dependant who was not part of the original application but is included in the varied one will be the varied application's date (r34GC).

Being able to 'vary the purpose' under r34E seems to allow one to make the same application again, as a variation of the first application, as a route to relying on better or more up-to-date evidence.

Eg a Student could decide to change their sponsor whilst a Student extension application is being considered by the Home Office. They will then need to make a wholly new application under Appendix Student based on the new sponsorship, rather than simply submit their new CAS (Khan [2016] EWCA Civ 137). Khan explained that the phrase '*vary the purpose*' under r34E should not be given a narrow or technical meaning.

Example

A person submits an application to extend their stay as a spouse under Appendix FM. At the date of application, they are not earning the required minimum specified gross annual income. The application is likely to be refused. Some weeks later, however, before they get a decision on the application, they now do meet the financial requirement.

They cannot simply send to the Home Office evidence of their new financial circumstances, because the Rules require that the requirement is met at the date of application. Can they send in a whole new application to extend their stay as a partner, relying on their new financial circumstances, such that the requirements of para 34E are met? Well, they can certainly try

1.5.7 Withdrawing an application

There are distinct procedures for withdrawing applications:

- An application can be withdrawn by written request or at www.gov.uk/cancel-visa (r34H)
- The date of withdrawal will be treated as the date the request was received (r34H)
- Decision makers may decline to accept the withdrawal and instead determine the application (r34I)
- Proof of identity will be returned to the applicant unless it is thought necessary to retain it (r34J)
- Travelling outside the common travel area pre-decision will be treated as the application's withdrawal (r34K)

1.5.8 Applications forms and fees

Applications for an extension of stay/leave (terms which can be used interchangeably) can be made by post or courier or, sometimes, in person or online (see more below on these different processes). Rather confusing some representatives refer to a person's immigration history via the application forms used to make an application rather the IRs underlying an application. This is bad practice as it is the route held under the IRs rather than the form used to achieve that status which is relevant to immigration history.

The specified forms, and a list of current fees can be found on the GOV.UK website at: https://www.gov.uk/immigration-operational-guidance/fees-forms

Dependants: Where explicitly stated on it, an application form can include dependants (r34C), including, where applicable, children over 18 . Otherwise, the dependant must use their own form.

Biometric residence permits: all applications for leave to remain automatically include an application for a BRP in that category.

In-country extension and regularisation applications

1.5.8.1 Forms

The main non-PBS, non-EEA application forms are as follows:

Form NTL (No Time Limit)

Use this online form to apply for a biometric residence permit confirming the person has indefinite leave. The same online form has also replaced previously paper Form TOC for limited leave. This will be necessary, for example, where the grant of leave was in a passport that has now expired.

Form FLR(M)

Use this online form to apply for an extension of stay as the partner (together with any dependent children) of a person present and settled in the UK, or of a person with limited leave in the UK with refugee leave or humanitarian protection. This will usually be for a partner application under Appendix FM on the five-year route.

Form FLR(O)

Note that this (once very famous) form is no longer in use. It was withdrawn for applications made on or after 1 December 2016. It has been replaced by forms FLR(HRO) and FLR(IR) – see below

CHAPTER 1: Immigration Control

Prior to it being withdrawn, this form was used to apply for an extension of stay for applications in any of the following categories:

- Academic visitor
- Domestic worker in a private household
- Academic visitor
- UK ancestry
- Visitor for private medical treatment
- Dependant of a person who has limited leave to enter or remain in the UK other than under the points based system
- General visitor
- Other purposes/reasons not covered by other application forms (including an extension of DL when the applicant had not previously been refused asylum)

Form FLR(FP)

Use this online form to apply for an extension of stay for applications in any of the following categories:

- Private life in the UK
- Family life as a partner (10-year route)
- Family life as a parent of a child in the UK (five-year and 10-year routes)
- Dependent child of a person who has, or is at the same time applying for, limited leave to enter or remain in the UK other than under the points-based system or UK Ancestry (10-year route)
- Leave outside the Rules on the basis of family or private life.

Form FLR(IR)

Use this online form for these types of application:

- visitors applying for visit visa extensions (except transit, Approved Destination Status and Permitted Paid Engagements visitors)
- UK ancestry
- domestic worker in a private household
- domestic worker who is a victim of slavery or human trafficking
- parent of a Child student
- dependant joiners (of a sponsoring family member) who are applying separately from the main applicant – dependants of a person who has limited leave to enter or remain in the UK, not including dependants of a person with leave under the Points Based System or dependants of a person in the UK with leave on the basis of family or private life
- relevant civilian employee
- member of an Armed Force who is subject to immigration control (course F)
- dependant of a member of Armed Forces which are not HM Forces (dependants of a member of HM Forces should complete FLR(AF))
- representative of an overseas business
- any other application for leave to remain that is within the IRs but is not covered by another form

Form FLR(HRO)

Use this online form for these types of application:

- leave outside the IRs based on compassionate and compelling circumstances
- leave outside the Immigration Rules
- human rights claim (excluding claims covered by forms FLR (M) or FLR (FP))

CHAPTER 1: Immigration Control

- medical grounds or ill health
- discretionary leave (DL) where you have previously been granted a period of DL but have not previously been refused asylum
- DL where you have been granted less than 4 years exceptional leave
- other claims not covered by another form

Form FLR(LR)

This online form is to apply for an extension of stay in the UK under the 10-year long residence rule (the form for ILR in this category is SET(LR), see below).

Form FLR(AF)

Use this online form to apply for an extension of stay for applications in any of the following categories:

- Limited leave as a HM Forces member on discharge
- Limited leave as the partner or child of a British or foreign or Commonwealth HM Forces sponsor under Appendix Armed Forces
- Limited leave as the partner or child whose sponsor was discharged from HM Forces
- Limited leave as the partner or child of a British HM forces sponsor applying under transitional arrangements under Part 8 of the IRs
- Limited leave as the partner or child of a foreign or Commonwealth HM forces sponsor applying under transitional arrangements under Part 7 of the IRs

For settlement the form is SET(AF), which is now also an online form.

Form FLR(P)

Use this form to apply for an extension of stay in the UK as a child under the age of 18 of a relative with limited leave to enter or remain in the UK as a refugee or beneficiary of humanitarian protection. Or as parents, grandparents or other dependent relatives aged over 18 of persons with limited leave to enter or remain in the UK as a refugee or beneficiary of humanitarian protection and for a biometric immigration document.

Form FLR(DL)

Form FLR(DL) is now an online form, and is intended for anyone who, following refusal of asylum, has been granted Discretionary Leave, and is now applying for a further period of Discretionary Leave or settlement, in accordance with the published Home Office Asylum Instruction on Discretionary Leave. Note that the refusal of asylum does not have to have been followed immediately by the initial grant of DL. There may have been many years between those decisions. This form must not be used by applicants applying for further leave on Article 3 medical grounds who must use form FLR(HRO).

Form FLR(S)

This online form is to apply for leave to remain in the UK, and a biometric residence permit, as a stateless person.

Form SET(M)

Use this online form to apply for ILR in the United Kingdom as the spouse (husband or wife), civil partner or unmarried partner of a person who is present and settled in the UK.

49

©HJT

CHAPTER 1: Immigration Control

Form SET(DV)

This online form is used specifically for applying for settlement under the IRs for victims of domestic violence whose relationships have broken down during the probationary period because of that domestic violence.

Form SET(F)

Use this online form to apply for ILR as the:

- Child under age of 18 of a parent, of parents or a relative present and settled in the UK
- Adopted child under the age of 18 of a parent or parents present and settled in the UK

Form SET(O)

Use this online form to apply for ILR in the United Kingdom when approaching five years of continuous leave to remain in the United Kingdom in one of the following categories:

- work permit holder
- dependant of work permit holder
- PBS dependant
- employment not requiring a work permit
- businessperson
- innovator
- investor
- self-employed lawyer
- writer, composer or artist
- Tier 1 (Entrepreneur) migrant
- Tier 1 (Entrepreneur) migrant – accelerated route
- Tier 1 (Investor) migrant
- Tier 1 (Investor) migrant – accelerated route
- Tier 2 migrant
- UK ancestry
- bereaved partner
- other purposes not covered by other application forms

Form SET(P)

Use this online form to apply for ILR in the United Kingdom when approaching five years of continuous leave to remain in the United Kingdom as a refugee or person granted humanitarian protection.

Form SET(LR)

Use this online form to apply for ILR (settlement) in the UK under the 10-year long residence rules. It is possible to extend leave for two years on this basis if not all requirements are met. The online version of former FLR(LR) is here.

1.5.8.2 Fees

These forms must be accompanied by the correct fee, which is payable on submission of the online form., and current fee levels can be checked here. Some of the most commonly encountered fees, which must be paid for each applicant, including dependants, after the October 2023 changes, are as follows:

CHAPTER 1: Immigration Control

Application	Fee
ILR	£2,885
LTR	£1,048
LTR for Skilled Worker (>3 year, 3 years+, standard & shortage occupations, healthcare)	£827/£1,500/£551/£1,084/£284/£551
Student and Child student	£490
Temporary Worker	£298

Different fees apply under Appendix Skilled Worker, dependent upon whether the job is in a shortage occupation, and the length of extension applied for.

There is a Exchange Rate Policy for calculating HO fees charged in foreign currencies.

1.5.8.3 Premium Service and online applications

The current online processes and procedures were introduced for the handling of in-country applications from November 2018. Before that date, most applications were made via paper forms and sent by post, with all original documents.

Fee payments are now generally completed online, and in most cases applicants must then book an appointment with a UKVCAS centre to enrol their biometrics and provide documents.

Documents can be uploaded before the appointment to save time and an extra scanning fee at the appointment. A great advantage of this is that this way applicants can retain their original documents.

The UKVCAS/Sopra Steria service centres differ according to whether free or charged appointments are available, whether enhanced services are offered (at an extra fee) or whether they provide services to those with extra support needs.

It is possible to pay extra for a faster decision to be made, if that service is available for the relevant category. The decision making service standard for the Priority Service is within 5 working days (£500) or, for the Super Priority Service, on the next working (£1000). Note the Super Priority Service is not available where the UK Immigration: ID Check App is used to confirm identity or for those lacking current leave applying on private and family life grounds. Since 30 November 2021, Skilled Worker (including Health and Care) and Student leave applicants using the app have access to some priority services.

The extra fee should show once the online form reaches the payment page, aspart of the total of the application fee and the relevant priority fee. If not, it is recommended to log in at another time when priority appointments have become available again. Once paid for, any type of biometrics appointment can be booked – the priority service is in relation to the decision making process after the biometrics appointment has occurred.

1.5.8.4 Fee exemptions and fee waivers

Current fees are specified in the Immigration and Nationality (Fees) Regulations 2018 (as amended). It is these regulations which are then transposed into the lists on the 'Fees and forms' page. Some categories are exempt under those regulations:

- Asylum and Article 3
- Leave outside the rules, under the Destitution Domestic Violence Concession
- Most applications for children under 18 who are looked after by a local authority (this does not include children supported under s17 of the Children Act 1989)
- Stateless persons and their family members, under Part 14

©HJT

CHAPTER 1: Immigration Control

- EC Association Agreement with Turkey (ILR for business persons is not included in this exemption)
- Discretionary leave as a victim of trafficking or modern-day slavery
- From 23 February 2022, Commonwealth veterans and Gurkhas with six years' will no longer have to pay a fee for ILR: *Visa fees scrapped for Non-UK Service Personnel*

When a person is not exempt from paying an application fee, but they cannot afford the fee, they can apply for a fee waiver (r6.2) if applying in one of the following categories as set out in the UKVI Fee Waiver Guidance:

- applications under the 5-year partner route where financial requirements are relaxed such that adequate maintenance rather than the target income must be shown
- applications under the 5-year parent/ private life routes
- applications for leave to remain under the 10-year partner, parent or private life routes based on ECHR Art 8
- applications for leave to remain on the basis of other ECHR rights
- extensions of DLR on ECHR grounds previously granted post-international protection refusal
- applications for further DL from victims of trafficking or slavery who have had a positive conclusive grounds decision from a competent authority of the national referral mechanism (NRM), have already accrued 30 months' DL and are seeking to extend it for reasons related to trafficking or slavery

Separate guidance on fee waivers for those applying under the Domestic Abuse (formerly Domestic Violence) provisions, is contained in the specific UKVI guidance for that category, and an Exceptional circumstances fee waiver policy for those prevented from leaving the UK due to COVID was introduced on 10 September 2020.

The Guidance on fee waivers located in Immigration Staff Guidance, Other cross-cutting guidance, now explains that a person may be granted a fee waiver if either:

- they are not able to pay the fee
- they are destitute
- they are at risk of imminent destitution
- their income is not sufficient to meet a child's particular and additional needs
- they are faced with exceptional financial circumstances

The standards of evidence applied in that guidance remain very high, so a close reading of this is recommended when preparing any fee waiver. Finances should be detailed via schedules of all income and expenditure, with receipts/bills verifying each item. Relevant considerations for decision makers are similar to those for nationality fee waivers (MIL 12.3.8.1).

Mahabir [2021] EWHC 1177 (Admin) gives a useful summary of the diverse provisions of the Immigration (Nationality and Fees) Regulations 2018 which provide for fee waivers in various kinds of case.

Fee waiver application procedure

Before 1 November 2018 a fee waiver application raised a real practical problem: by the time it was decided, the applicant's leave might have expired. So if the fee was *not* waived, the application would be deemed invalid. This was a major disincentive to making waiver applications unless finances were truly despereate. There was then an interim fix, the HO allowing unsuccessful applicants caught in this situation 10 days to pay the fee. But if they could not, they would then become an overstayer and enter the hostile environment.

Fee waiver applications are now online and are made and considered *before* the substantive application (MIL 1.5.2.1).The modern procedure protects the lawfulness of stay whilst the waiver is considered. .

CHAPTER 1: Immigration Control

If the fee waiver request is granted, the applicant will be able to submit an application for leave without an accompanying application fee.

If the fee waiver request is refused, the applicant may still submit an application accompanied by the relevant fee within 10 working days, for the initial application date (the date of the fee waiver application) to preserve continuing leave under these provisions.

Entry clearance fee waivers

Long-term advocacy from ILPA received its reward for entry clearance cases with the Guidance *Affordability fee waiver: overseas Human Rights-based applications (Article 8)*. A fee waiver must be granted if the applicant and sponsor are assessed and found either:

- to credibly demonstrate they cannot afford the fee
- that their income is not sufficient to meet their child's needs (bearing in mind the need to safeguard and promote the welfare of a child in the UK)

1.5.8.5 The Immigration Health Surcharge

The Immigration Health Surcharge (IHS) was introduced from 6 April 2015.

- For students, the youth mobility scheme & children, the charge is £470 per year applied for and
- For everyone else it is £624.

There is guidance available here and also here at Immigration Health Surcharge. This page lists who needs to pay, who does not, and who does not need to pay but requires an IHS reference number. The health surcharge will rise by 66% from around 16 January 2024. IHS fees will increase as follows per year of immigration permission at the point of application, to:

- £1,035 per year – for most applicants; and
- £776 per year – for students and their dependants, Youth Mobility Scheme applicants and children.

Payment is made as part of the online application process at the same time as the application fee is taken.

Liability for the charge is as follows:

- All applications for entry clearance *other than* those for indefinite leave to enter, fiances and visits of six months or less. Visitors will be expected to pay for NHS treatment at the point of use.
  NB: In some cases where the IHS should not apply, such as child settlement under Part 8, payment of the charge has been required at point of application, with a later refund if indefinite leave to enter (rather than a different, temporary form of leave) is granted.
- All applications from within the UK for any period of time other than ILR
- Health and care workers are exempt, and this exemption is backdated to 31 March 2020. Guidance on refunds is available here.

If an application is made for ILR but limited leave is granted, the surcharge will become payable and the Home Office will require payment before the BRP is issued. The Guidance sets out exceptions where an IHS reference number can be obtained without paying the IHS, for children in local authority care or relevant civilian employees with NATO or the Australian Defence Dept and their dependants.

1.5.9 Decisions – validity of notice; professional skills and conduct relevant to dealing with decisions

A well prepared and properly evidenced application which meets the requirements of the IRs *should* be granted by the Home Office. **In practice, applications may be refused for all kinds of reasons**, many of which may be unexpected and unwarranted. Decision makers may overlook documents that have been submitted, ignore representations and witness statements, and adopt interpretations of the law that may be inconsistent with their own guidance. There are *customer service standards* governing applications inside and outside the UK.

Advisors should **always warn clients** that they may receive a disappointing decision and that appeals, where available, are routinely allowed by immigration judges. Where there is no right of appeal, an administrative review may secure a favourable result.

Where an applicant may have the choice of **challenging a decision or applying again**, it will be necessary to **factor in** not only the relevant **costs and timescales**, but also a careful consideration of **s3C** of the Immigration Act 1971, the **consequences of overstaying** and, where **IR39E** applies, whether a further application can be made at all.

It will always **reduce the chance of a left-field decision if the application is well prepared, in form as well as in content**. The documentation should be easy to find and well ordered. Every application must be supported by a covering letter laying out the basic law relied upon, usually a category of the IRs or a provision of the Immigration (EEA) Regulations 2016, listing the enclosures, and explaining their purpose. Statements from the applicant (and other family members or others where relevant) are useful to explain the applicant's circumstances, put each document into context and show that each of the requirements of the rules is met.

On receipt of a negative decision advisers should look carefully at the **validity of the Notice of Decision**, and the **reasons of refusal**, and then consider the **availability of an appropriate remedy**, if any. The HO rarely reconsider decisions just due to a polite request unless there is a specific policy to do so (in rare and largely historic scenarios: e.g. the *Alvi* policy, the Reconsiderations policy in the Immigration Staff Guidance/other cross-cutting information which is of very narrow ambit, and Requests for reconsideration of old human rights claims that were refused before 6 April 2015 with no right of appeal). So a request for a review, outside the policy, is likely to be a waste of time unless it is accompanied by a formal complaint, or comes from an MP, or is put in the form of a pre-action protocol letter (MIL 14.8.3), or the Parliamentary and Health Service Ombudsman gets involved.

Acting in the **best interests of your client**, it will always be necessary to give them an **honest assessment of the merits of their case**. There is no point embarking on lengthy and costly applications and remedies, and it might be a breach of your professional duties to do so, if they are likely to fail (unless your client has given the project informed consent).

If a visa is issued with an incorrect endorsement, correction must be sought: at the visa application centre if the migrant is still abroad, via the online system if in a BRP or vignette endorsement. An application for variation of leave is necessary if three months have passed. See the Guidance *Correcting an incorrect endorsement: ECB19*.

Many migrants do not receive immigration decisions made with regard to their case. Of course, a decision can have huge consequences for the lawfulness of their stay in the UK. The government has an interest in ensuring that the consequences of decisions are not avoided by somebody claiming not to have received a decision, and accordingly the law enforce service in some scenarios.

Various principles can be identified regarding the need for **notice of decisions**:

- Generally speaking, a person must have notice of a decision before the decision can take legal effect against them: Anufrijeva [2003] UKHL 36
- Mere reference to an earlier decision in a later decision will not necessarily amount to adequate notice: see e.g Chaparadza [2017] EWHC 1209 (Admin)

- However, the various statutory instruments and Rules that govern service of decisions these days all contain a provision that a document that the Home Office can demonstrate was posted or emailed to the correct address for them or their representative (e.g. via records from their GCID computer case management system) is deemed served *unless the contrary is proved*. So a person needs to explain their arrangements for monitoring the post and keeping the Home Office up-to-date with their modern address in order to discharge the burden on them.
- For example decisions that do not carry a right of appeal are governed by the ILERO 2000. Article 8ZA-8ZB provides for various forms of service, including service to file where no other means of contacting an applicant is available. This was analysed in Alam [2020] EWCA Civ 1527. The Court explains that it can be presumed that service is effective where convincing evidence is put forward that an authorised method has been used. Cogent evidence would be needed to rebut this presumption. In Kalsi [2021] EWCA Civ 184 the CoA gives an example of a situation where notice might not have been established as given: where the evidence showed the decision had been signed for by a person with no organisational connection with the lawyers acting for the applicant.
- Mizanur Rahman [2019] EWHC 2952 (Admin) looks at how to prove a lack of service. This might include evidence that the SSHD had not actually sent the decision, but also covers the situation where cogent evidence is provided that the alleged recipient had not received the decision, for example because they had left that residence and could show they had consistently acted in good faith (by, for instance, taking steps to notify their change of address).

Top Tip

A true legal professional never assumes that the law remains the same since they last made a similar application. A policy can be withdrawn at any moment, and IRs can be altered without very much notice at all. Remember

☐ Always check the legal framework as it is *now* (and remember that the legal framework may include HO guidance/policy documents)
☐ Check whether any relevant Rules are about to be amended (and never let any client think the Rules are set in stone)
☐ Always check the legal framework as it *was at the date of decision* regarding cases where you are pursuing an appeal or JR

And they *always* know the foundation for any legal principle that they rely upon. For many years, for example, there was a policy that applied to children allowing them to remain in this country if they had resided here for seven years and their removal would be unreasonable; this was withdrawn several years ago, and was not resurrected until Appendix FM was introduced. Now it has an even firmer footing, as it is found in section 117 of the NIA 2002. Vague references to the 'seven year rule' risk failing to appreciate the differing legal foundations of the principle over time, moving as it did from policy, then disappearing, then being resurrected via the Rules before moving onto the statute book.

1.5.11 Safeguarding, information sharing and confidentiality

There is government *Information sharing Advice* for all frontline practitioners and senior managers working with children, young people, parents and carers who have to make decisions about sharing personal information on a case-by-case basis. It includes seven golden rules re information sharing, essentially emphasising there is no absolute bar to sharing information where safety and well-being may be at stake. Any information sharing should be necessary, proportionate, relevant, adequate, accurate, timely and secure.

Many HO policies now contain a section on safeguarding, where there is a concern that the applicant may be in danger, including child welfare and protection concerns. The right to confidentiality is not absolute. The law permits the disclosure of confidential information where there is an overriding public interest or lawful justification for doing so, for example, for child protection or the prevention of crime. FF [2021] EWHC 2566 (Admin) holds that HO is entitled to deal with a person's immigration affairs as being sensitive and confidential to them, and cannot be obliged to make them available to third parties (discussed also in *Exclusion Guidance*).

1.5.12 Assisted Returns

Not every migrant manages to secure permission to stay in the UK. The *Voluntary Returns Service* (VRS) is available for assisting departures (there is also Guidance *Practical Information for applicants*). The VRS will discuss whether voluntary return is appropriate and what level of practical support may be available, including financial assistance, the need for a travel document and travel plans. Interpretation services are available. Up to £3,000 of financial assistance is available.

1.5.13 Support for migrants

There are various schemes available for migrants. Welfare benefits law is a complex area in its own right. There is a useful House of Commons briefing *People from abroad: what benefits can they claim?* Generally speaking ILR is the gateway to mainstream benefits. Those with limited leave are usually granted on a "no recourse to public funds" basis. The IAA 1999 (s115) provides bars access to most social security benefits and tax credits for those subject to immigration control. There is a general move towards all benefits being paid via universal credit, though many people remain on legacy benefits. Most benefits require habitual residence in the UK to be established.

We deal with support for asylum seekers at 9.2.

CHAPTER 2: General Requirements of the Rules; Introduction to Guidance

2.1 Navigating the Immigration Rules

The IRs (HC 395) set out the rules for entry to and stay in the UK for people who are subject to immigration control. They form the centrepoint of UK immigration law. They must be consulted and strictly adhered to for all types of immigration applications for people subject to immigration control

The power to make the Rules comes from section 3(2) of the Immigration Act 1971:

> The Secretary of State shall from time to time (and as soon as may be) lay before Parliament statements of the rules, or of any changes in the rules, laid down by him as to the practice to be followed in the administration of this Act for regulating the entry into and stay in the United Kingdom of persons required by this Act to have leave to enter, including any rules as to the period for which leave is to be given and the conditions to be attached in different circumstances…

The Rules include a list of the purposes or categories under which people can enter and/or remain in the UK – e.g. for protection, to visit, to study, for employment, business and investment, and for family reasons. A few purposes though remain outside the Rules (see e.g. the concessions relating to carers and those involved in family proceedings in the section on policies and concessions in Chapter 4).

The landmark Supreme Court judgement in Alvi [2012] UKSC 33 held that all mandatory requirements, including evidential requirements, must be listed in the IRs. Before Alvi, many of these requirements could only be found in guidance documents. Together with the government's policy of increasingly micromanaging immigration, this means that the IRs have become extremely long and convoluted. This manual can only really provide an overview of the IRs, which now run to more than 1300 pages. Indeed, no textbook or training course can substitute for consistent reference to the constantly changing and hugely complex matrix of Rules.

There is no alternative but for advisers to work directly from the IRs themselves. The only up to date and comprehensive version of the IRs is on the GOV.UK website here, in the form of a drop-down index.

The IRs can be difficult to navigate. An ongoing simplification project aims to improve things: modern routes are found in a series of Appendices based on the same structure. Previously critical information was found in arbitrary places, scattered between the mainstream rules and an increasing number of appendices. Although one might expect substantive applications to be dealt with in the main body of the Rules, in fact mostly family migration cases are dealt with in Appendix FM. There is another Appendix that represents a sole code for visitor applications, even with its own sub-appendices. Even the paragraph numbering scheme often fails to follow any rational pattern. Nevertheless advisers must avoid the temptation to work solely from the guidance to applicants provided on the GOV.UK website as this is neither comprehensive nor always accurate.

Each category of the IRs (e.g. visitors in Appendix V, the Points Based System in Part 6A, family members in Appendix FM) has been drafted in different formats, but will generally contain;

- An outline of the purpose of the category
- A definition of criteria used in the category (though r6 of the Rules also contains important definitions of key words and phrases). It cannot be presumed that words in the IRs have their ordinary or common-sense meaning, so it is important to see how they are defined for the purpose of a particular rule.
    - The specific requirements that must be met for entry clearance or leave to enter, for an extension of stay, and for ILR where available. The requirements usually differ between these stages.

- In the older routes, specified (i.e. mandatory) documents – detailing both their form and content – that must be submitted with the application
- In modern routes, a standard scheme breaking down the criteria by reference to Validity, Suitability, and Eligibility (MIL 7.1.2 addresses this in the context of economic migration routes)
- The period of leave that will be granted
- The conditions that will be placed on the grant of leave (e.g. no recourse to public funds, prohibition on working – see more on conditions below)
- The circumstances in which the application will be refused

Many terms used by the Rules are defined by the Rules themselves, or within the definitions at Rule 6. Concepts within the Rules beyond these should be construed (see Mahad [2009] UKSC16):

> sensibly according to the natural and ordinary meaning of the word used, recognising that they are statements of the Secretary of State administrative policy.

Generally Guidance should not be used to construe the Rules. However exceptionally where the Rules' meaning is genuinely ambiguous, Guidance that is *in a migrant's favour* can be relied on: Afzal [2021] EWCA Civ 1909. Particularly where the consequences would be to otherwise make their status unlawful and thus subject to the "*compliant environment*". But Guidance *stricter than the Rules* cannot restrict their meaning: Pokhriyal [2013] EWCA Civ 1568.

Top Tip

It is important to read the IRs carefully and look for what is NOT in the IRs as much as what IS in them.

For example:

- ☐ Appendix Student contains no provision relating to a grant of ILR - so we can deduce a student cannot apply for ILR
- ☐ The Rules in Appendix Adult Dependent Relative are all expressed by reference to entry clearance applications, so there is no route under the Rules for an application to leave to remain in that capacity (i.e. there is no possibility, within the mainstream Rules, of switching into this category, or making an in-country application)
- ☐ The Temporary Worker categories make no reference to English language requirements (unusually for the PBS): so an applicant does not have to satisfy any such requirements.

2.1.1 Immigration history and subject access requests

When you first take on a case, it is imperative to obtain a proper immigration history of the individual. Some people may have a perfect record of their dealings with the Home Office, or, if they have received a refusal of an application, it may be that they can confirm that the Home Office has perfectly summarised their history. However, there may be cases where there is more to their history than is apparent from existing documents.

You can fill the gap via a 'subject access request', and for any case with a significant procedural history, it will be advisable for an appellant's representative to obtain this.

Subject access requests can be made as per the Guidance *Request personal information held in the borders, immigration and citizenship system*. Or by post (recorded delivery is essential), and the address is here: https://www.gov.uk/government/publications/requests-for-personal-data-uk-visas-and-immigration/request-personal-information-held-by-uk-visas-and-immigration. These will include entries from the HO's databases, the General Cases Information Database (GCID) and the immigration caseworking system Atlas (being rolled out from 2020). Another record keeping system is PRONTO (the police reporting and notebook organiser) which includes the digital pocket notebook, DPNB: enforcement activities should be recorded in these systems.

The system allows online applications for either *basic, specific* or *detailed* information requests. Each is free. The first two types should be answered within 30 days of identity being verified. Where multiple requests are made, only the first will be answered. Therefore the safest option would probably be to request detailed information.

A certified form of photo ID is required. However, such certification may now be done by OISC advisers or registered charities, as well as solicitors (refer carefully to the guidance in the forms to avoid delay).

There is a right of complaint to the Information Commissioner if the material is not provided in time, or is thought incomplete, and then onwards to the Information Tribunal. There is some guidance on disclosure on the HO website. However there are reports of serious failures by the HO to provide data within a reasonable timeframe in a *report by the Commissioner*. At user group meetings the HO have indicated they are short of resources and prioritising cases such as domestic violence, unaccompanied minors, and removals. Representatives should precisely identify any particularly important documents sought and bear in mind that basic requests may provide everything needed.

Sch 2, Pt 1, para 4 of the Data Protection Act 2018 contains the controversial immigration exemption under which the HO can refuse to provide information. In May 2021, the Court of Appeal held the exemption to be unlawful in Open Rights Group & the3million [2021] EWCA Civ 800. The revamped scheme was also found illegal in the 3million [2023] EWHC 713 (Admin) because key criteria appeared only in a policy document and there was no adequate assessment of risks to rights and freedoms.

Top Tip

Before starting to work out a client's future options, you should be able to produce a comprehensive immigration history in a form equivalent to this:

'Mr .... is a citizen of .... born. He obtained an entry clearance granted on .... and was granted leave to enter on .... as a .... His leave was subsequently extended in that capacity until .... [and subsequently in the same or other categories]. He made an application for further leave to remain as a ………….. on ………... and that was refused on ………..'

Without such details of a person's history, you are simply not in a position to comprehensively and accurately advise them of their present status and future options.

2.1.2 Transitional provisions

When changes are made to the IRs, transitional provisions often accompany them, dis-applying those changes to those who have already made applications or who entered the UK before the changes were made. So, depending on the particular transitional provisions, the 'old' Rules will continue to apply to some migrants, and the new Rules to others. In effect, there will be two or more sets of Rules running side by side, covering similar purposes, but applicable to different migrants. The default provision is that applications made before the new Rule enters force are considered by reference to the old one. But if the HO believes it is simply clarifying a Rule's meaning, rather than introducing new criteria, it is likely to enforce the change on everyone at once.

As an example, those who applied under the partner provisions as they were before 9 July 2012 (which are in Part 8 of the IRs), will have different requirements to meet from those who first applied after that date (under the Rules in Appendix FM). The Rules incorporate the transitional provisions (see Rules A277 to A280 (and weep!)), and it is necessary to carefully consider which particular rules and requirements apply to a particular case, depending on the migrant's date of first application in that category or date of entry. Happily there are very few people who have not escaped those routes into ILR.

Odelola [2009] 3 All ER 1061 establishes that where there are no transitional provisions, the Rules to be applied to an outstanding application will simply be those in force at the date of decision: whether or not they are the same Rules under which the applicant applied.

For those pursuing JRs where the Rule has been amended after they received their decision, the applicable rules will be those as they were at the date of decision. Usefully, there are archived versions of the IRs as they stood at various dates in the past on the GOV.UK website (see the Archive: Immigration Rules link on the IRs page).

> **Top Tip**
>
> Beware – the transitional provisions are seldom in the Rules. They may simply be in the Statement of Changes that introduced the particular Rule in question.
>
> Take, for example, HC 532 (which introduced a (then) new version of the private life rules– MIL 5.3.3): if you read the opening paragraphs, you will see that different provisions have different commencement dates, all set out under the heading Implementation; and that sometimes there is a more precise explanation of how a provision will apply, e.g. the IR276ADE change is found in para 6 of the statement of changes, and therefore dealt with by the commencement provision saying: *'The changes set out in paragraphs 4 to 12 and 49 to 64 of this statement take effect on 28 July 2014 … and apply to all applications to which paragraphs 276ADE ... apply and which are decided on or after that date.'*

2.1.3 Old rules and legitimate expectations

It is not unknown for a class of migrants to succeed in relying on an old rule. There have been a number of cases involving a claim of legitimate expectation by a migrant, typically where the rule (or even a policy outside the Rules) has changed between making the application and it being decided. Most typically this has happened where the UK authorities have made public representations indicating that people can settle here, as happened under the old Highly Skilled Migrant route.

To succeed on the grounds of legitimate expectation a clear promise has to be made that the Rules will remain the same (in general such expectation must be 'clear, unambiguous and devoid of relevant qualification': Bingham LJ in MFK [1990] 1 WLR 1545). The case of Bapio Action Ltd [2008] UKHL 27 provides a rare example of a case that succeeded on this basis. The action was brought by Bapio Action Ltd, a company formed by the British Association of Physicians of Indian Origin to represent the interests of junior overseas doctors who had been lured to the UK by promises of a career here but after arrival were being deprived of an opportunity to apply for jobs.

2.1.4 Closed immigration routes

From time to time routes within the Rules close to new applicants. These include, in recent times, Tier 1 (General) and Tier 1 (Post-study work). All of the Tier 1 (General) paras were deleted after ILR for Tier 1 (General) closed on 6 April 2018, including references in other routes for purposes of switching. The Tier 1 Entrepreneur route closed on 28 March 2019 and (more abruptly) Tier 1 Investor was shut down on 17 February 2022; but provisions remain in place for extensions and the grant of ILR for those already in the route.

Always bear in mind when advising clients that a particular immigration route, particularly the managed migration ones, may be terminated, albeit that one can anticipate 'sunset' clauses to soften the blow and allow for migrants on those routes to extend their leave pending being able to settle in the UK. A person who travels abroad when extending their immigration permission may find themselves unable to return if the application is refused. For no repeat application will be possible for a route that is now closed.

2.2 Common requirements of the Immigration Rules

Many different immigration categories include similar provisions, and rather than repeat the information it is more convenient to deal with them in one place.

2.2.1 Specified documents

Rule 39B lays out the general requirements as to 'specified' documents (i.e. specified in the IRs) that must be provided in support of an application. Where specified, supporting documentation must meet the requirements both in respect of form and content. A 'nearly' document just won't do! The heyday of specified documents is past and most routes provide for more flexibility (MIL 7.1.1).

A specified document must be verifiable, and so must include the contact details of the person or organisation creating the document. From 1 November 2018 original documents were (generally) no longer required. Copies or scanned copies can now be provided instead. If there are doubts about whether a document is genuine, verification rules will apply (MIL 7.7.9).

Where not in English or Welsh, a document must be accompanied by a full translation which includes the translator's credentials, the date and the translator's signature, and confirms that it is an accurate translation.

There were some document submission concessions available over the pandemic (MIL 4.2.19).

2.2.2 Evidential flexibility

Where a document is not available, a full explanation should be provided in a covering letter. The necessary document should be provided as soon as possible, and before a decision is made on the application.

Sending documents late is never ideal. One then runs the risk that an application is decided without regard to the late documents, because a decision is made unexpectedly speedily. Or the correspondence never reaches the file. Mudiyanselage [2018] EWCA Civ 6 holds there is no obligation on the HO to take account of late information – though it is best practice to do so. If the application expressly requests further time to send documents, a reasonable decision maker should give some leeway. Of course, where a critical document is not supplied by the time the decision is made, the application is likely to fail.

At one time there was no general requirement that the Home Office contact an applicant where documents were in the wrong format, or missing information (or missing altogether). However now the *Evidential Flexibility* Guidance explains

> 'if it appears that the applicant has made an error with, or omitted, supporting evidence, or further information or verification of evidence is needed to make a decision, you should normally provide an opportunity for the additional information to be provided ... from the applicant, the sponsor, or the awarding body or other organisation ... The rules do not now generally set out specific format requirements for most documents. This does not mean that format is irrelevant ... You must not refuse an application because the evidence is not in a particular format'

Though only where the missing evidence is material: not where the application would be refused either way. Applications should not be refused for want of a document that was not itself requested. 10 days should normally be given to rectify things. There is specific provision for UKVI's commercial partner Agents to invite applicants to return for a further appointment or upload missing documents.

2.2.3 Maintenance

Entry, leave to remain and settlement are usually contingent on a person being able to adequately maintain and accommodate themselves and any dependants without recourse to public funds. It is now enshrined in statute, at s117B(3) of NIAA 2002 which emphasises that the public interest, from an economic well-being perspective, is best served by admitting people who are financially independent.

This principle is put into effect across the Rules by a series of maintenance requirements, and by a condition placed on most grants of leave denying the holder recourse to public funds (which they would in any case be unable to claim due to welfare benefits law). Look, for example, at r245ZY which governs the conditions of a grant of Student permission: at 245ZY(c)(i) it states 'Leave to remain will be granted subject to ... no recourse to public funds'.

An equivalent rule is found in most categories, specifying the conditions of a grant including access to public funds.

There are also rules which permit a discretion to award access to public funds: see for example, within Appendix FM, GEN1.10, stating that where leave is granted under certain exemptions within the rules, that is 'subject to a condition of no recourse to public funds unless the decision-maker considers that the person should not be subject to such a condition'.

There are different regimes for meeting the financial requirement. Rules sometimes

- stipulate that a person must be able to maintain and accommodate themselves adequately without recourse to public funds;
- provide, as under the Points Based System, that an applicant must to demonstrate a fixed amount of savings in a prescribed form; or
- require, as for some applications under the family life categories of Appendix FM, a specified level of income and/or savings (unless the sponsor is in receipt of particular benefits).

This section looks at the requirements an applicant will need to meet in cases where the rule stipulates that they must be *able to maintain and accommodate themselves and any dependants adequately in the UK without recourse to public funds.*

This includes children applying to join or stay with their settled parent(s) in the UK (r287/298 in Part 8), and partners under Appendix FM where the settled partner is receiving one of the listed disability-related benefits (e.g. Rule rE-ECP.3.3).

Key principles on maintenance

- 'Public funds' are exhaustively defined
- There must be no additional recourse
- Income support provides an objective measure as to adequacy
- The adequacy requirement is not an excuse for inquiry into lifestyle
- Third party support is permitted in law, unless excluded by a specific rule (as it generally is now under the PBS and Appendix FM).

2.2.3.1 Meaning of public funds

Public funds are exhaustively listed in r6 of HC395 which contains a long list of forms of public funds. In a relevant case this list should be scrutinised with care. For now, we can summarise the relevant public funds as: housing supplied under the Housing Acts and housing benefit; attendance, disablement and carer's allowances; child benefit and social fund payments; jobseekers allowance; state pension credit, child and working tax credit; universal credit and personal independence payments; council tax reduction; certain discretionary payments or a payment from a Scottish welfare fund.

The list is exhaustive in the sense that any benefit not included in the Rule is not considered to be a public fund for the purposes of the IRs. As can be seen (by omission), there are some public funds, such as legal aid, education, contributory benefits such as contributory job seekers' allowance, and NHS care that are not included in the definition and are not therefore treated as public funds.

The UKVI Public Funds Guidance contains an extremely complex set of specific rules and exemptions which should always be checked when advising a client regarding their entitlements.

This is important because a person should not claim public funds or other services to which they are not legally entitled, to avoid problems with later immigration applications, e.g.

- the general grounds for refusal in Part 9 of the Rules include provisions for refusal for breach of conditions: r9.8.1-9.8.2 (the rules used to address this possibility more expressly see eg r322(4) a 'failure by the person concerned to maintain or accommodate himself and any dependants without recourse to public funds'; or
- cancellation of permission under r9.8.8 - once permission has been curtailed, a person would face removal under s10 IAA 1999 as a person who requires leave but does not have it.

The fact that a public fund or service is wrongly granted to them will not necessarily protect the applicant if they were not entitled to it.

The expression 'without recourse to public funds' is further defined in r6A to 6C . In short:

- entry is not prohibited where the sponsor is already claiming public funds but
- will be prohibited where the migrant relies on their sponsor's entitlement to increased or additional public funds as a result of their arrival in the UK.

The sponsor may use their pre-existing public funds to support the applicant

- as long as the level of support is still 'adequate' (see below).

This means that, for example, a sponsor already in receipt of disability living allowance can use those funds to support an applicant. This reflects the judgement in MK (Somalia) [2007] EWCA Civ 1521. This principle is recognised in Appendix FM where a partner or parent is in receipt of specified disability related benefits: thus, in an entry clearance case for a partner, as an alternative to meeting the strict financial requirements of holding certain levels of funds via admissible forms of evidence and savings, E-ECP.3.1 references an alternative route of showing adequate maintenance via E-ECP.3.3, which, if a relevant benefit is available, then poses the simple question as to whether adequate maintenance is available.

The definition of public funds in IR6 prevents reliance on any future additional entitlement to child benefit or tax credit to establish the relevant financial requirements in an entry clearance application but 6B permits reliance on those sources of funds in extension or settlement applications.

2.2.3.2 Required level of income

Outside reformed immigration routes and the income/savings-based requirements in most parts of Appendix FM, the maintenance requirement is whether the available funds are 'adequate', which is defined at r6:

> 'adequate' and 'adequately' in relation to a maintenance and accommodation requirement shall mean that, after income tax, national insurance contributions and housing costs have been deducted, there must be available to the family the level of income that would be available to them if the family was in receipt of income support

This definition (from 9 July 2012) largely reflected well established principles as to the meaning of 'adequate maintenance' outlined in cases including KA Pakistan [2006] UKAIT 00065. KA had held that the level of maintenance is adequate under the Rules if the funds available equate to that of a person or family receiving income support. In Yarce [2012] UKUT 425 the Upper Tribunal decided that the KA approach remained valid notwithstanding subsequent amendments to IR6. The case law has not yet confronted the change from old-style ("legacy") benefits to universal credit.

The latest and historic benefit levels can be checked on Rightsnet's website here.

Guidance on the Maintenance calculation is set out as follows in section 3 'Assessing Adequate Maintenance' in the IDIs Appendix FM 1.7A Adequate Maintenance & Accommodation August 2015

> How to assess adequate maintenance

The Upper Tribunal case of Ahmed [benefits; proof of receipt; evidence] Bangladesh [2013] UKUT 84 [IAC] directed the Home Office to evidence financial figures in all decision letters in which refusal was based on inadequate maintenance.

Therefore, decision makers considering an application for entry clearance, leave to remain, further leave to remain or indefinite leave to remain which has to meet a requirement for adequate maintenance must set out the financial position of the applicant/sponsor in all cases that fall for refusal using the following formula:

A – B ≥ C   A minus B is greater than or equal to C.

Where:
A is the net income (after deduction of income tax and National Insurance contributions);
B is housing costs (i.e. what needs to be spent on accommodation); and
C is the amount of Income Support an equivalent British family of that size can receive.

When preparing an Appendix FM application, the specified evidence requirements for those who are relying on 'adequate maintenance' by way of benefits and/or earnings/savings are set out in paragraphs 12 and 12A of Appendix FM-SE. The requirements are rather lighter as to the volume of documents: there is a specific calculation as to how savings are to be treated at paragraph 12B, by which total cash savings are divided into the number of weeks for which leave would be granted if the application succeeded and then added to the other available income. Further guidance as to this is found in the above linked Guidance 1.7A.

We deal with the exceptions where fixed criteria within the family migration and private life cases are not met below (MIL 6.2 & 5.4.8). Essentially leave may be granted exceptionally where there is a compelling case and/or where unjustifiably harsh consequences would otherwise arise.

Top Tip

Proving maintenance outside Appendix FM/Points Based System

In any immigration case where maintenance is in issue outside the strict requirements in Appendix A under the Points Based System or Appendix FM, make sure you make clear to the decision maker, be they the Home Office or an immigration judge, how it is that the level of income satisfies the income support level.

You can best do this by way of cross referencing from a witness statement, and/or via a table that shows the notional benefit entitlement.

Also explain

- any unusual patterns of income as shown by the bank statements provided
- discrepancies between earnings as suggested by pay slips and actual deposits into bank accounts
- any discrepancy between documents and the client's account of how they are paid and what their business activities actually are
- any other income from business interests or informal loans

2.2.3.3 Third party support

'Third party support' refers to support that is provided by an additional party, such as a parent, other relative or friend.

An applicant under Appendix FM cannot normally rely on third party support. Subject to para 1(b) of Appendix FM-SE. Third party support is there permitted by way of:

- Maintenance payments from a former partner
- Income from a dependent child now over 18 and remaining in the same household who is part of the Appendix FM financial requirements (i.e. because they were a minor when the application was originally granted, see E-ECP.3.2.(1)(a))
- A gift of cash savings, the source being declared, and now being held by the applicant, their partner, or an applicant child's parent, or in an adult dependent relative case, the sponsor or the applicant
- A maintenance grant or stipend associated with undergraduate or postgraduate study/research

It is only where 'exceptional circumstances' in GEN.3.1. of Appendix FM apply that the wider category of Third Party support in para 21A Appendix FM-SE becomes relevant (MIL 6.2.7).

The availability of third party support depends on the particular terms of the Rules. Under the visitor route, Appendix V now makes express provision for third party support, at V4.3, from a legally resident person 'with a genuine professional or personal relationship' with the proposed visitor, where they 'can and will provide support to the visitor for the intended duration of their stay'. The reformed immigration routes make individual provision for third party support (MIL 7.8.13).

And Appendix UK Ancestry permits such support. The language of UKA 5.1, *'can and will adequately maintain and accommodate themselves, and any dependants in the UK, or applying for entry clearance, without recourse to public funds'*, mirrors that of the old rule that was generously interpreted in *Mahad*.

Top Tip

Azim has been studying in the UK with the support of an uncle. He has now married a British citizen and wishes to remain as a partner. Neither he nor his spouse have jobs, but Azim's uncle is happy to support them until they can manage on their own.

In this case, where the uncle already has a history of providing support, there is good reason to think that the support will be adequate and that the offer is well considered and genuine. The uncle's support can only be relied upon for spouse applications either as a £62,500. If his uncle obliges, and Azim then holds this amount for 6 months before the application is made, it will be treated as his own savings rather than third party support (Appendix FM–SE 1(b)(iii)). Or it will need to meet the strictures of Appendix FM-SE 21A(8) as to its reliability in the context of 'unjustifiably harsh' consequences (MIL 6.1.4). Were Azim applying as a visitor, say, or under the ancestry category, he could still rely on his uncle's support; because in the former case there is specific provision for third party support, in para V4.3 of Appendix V. And the UK ancestry route uses similar wording for maintenance and accommodation as was found to include third party support in *Mahad*.

2.2.3.4 Sponsors and undertakings

A maintenance undertaking is mandatory under the adult dependent relative category of Appendix FM, which states:

> E-ECDR.3.2. If the applicant's sponsor is a British Citizen or settled in the UK, the applicant must provide an undertaking signed by the sponsor confirming that the applicant will have no recourse to public funds, and that the sponsor will be responsible for their maintenance, accommodation and care, for a period of 5 years from the date the applicant enters the UK if they are granted indefinite leave to enter.

The undertaking will be legally enforceable, so that the DWP or Home Office can recoup any public funds subsequently claimed by a disobedient migrant (r 35).

2.2.3.5 Joint sponsors

In AM (Ethiopia) & Ors [2008] EWCA Civ 1082, the Court of Appeal found that under Rule 317, the old version of the adult dependent relative category, it was possible for joint sponsors (e.g. two siblings) to give undertakings. This principle was upheld by the Supreme Court in Mahad [2009] UKSC 16

The equivalent category under Appendix FM, for adult dependent relatives, though, does not appear to allow for joint sponsors.

2.2.4 Adequate accommodation

Most categories of the IRs (but not the PBS) require that the applicant(s) and any family members they are joining in the UK have adequate accommodation available to them.

Key principles on accommodation:

- Third party provision is permitted
- Statutory overcrowding renders accommodation inadequate
- Adequacy can have a wider meaning than just available space

Unlike with maintenance, there has never been a problem with accommodation being provided by a third party: AB [2008] UKAIT 00018 and Mahad [2009] UKSC 16.

Accommodation must be adequate for the person coming to the UK and for those already occupying the accommodation. For people seeking entry on a long-term basis there are three considerations to the question of whether accommodation is adequate.

Firstly, in family cases, the sponsor/applicant must 'own or exclusively occupy' the proposed accommodation. This is not quite as onerous as it sounds as the guidance states that:

> Accommodation can be shared with other members of a family provided that at least part of the accommodation is for the exclusive use of the sponsor and his dependants. The unit of accommodation may be as small as a separate bedroom but must be owned or legally occupied by the sponsor and its occupation must not contravene public health regulations and must not cause overcrowding as defined in the Housing Act 1985

KJ [2008] UKAIT 00006 found this approach lawful.

Secondly, the proposed accommodation must not be overcrowded once the applicant arrives. Overcrowding is defined in paragraph 6 of the IRs by reference to the Housing Act 1985, the Housing (Scotland) Act 1987 or the Housing (Northern Ireland) Order 1988 (as appropriate). The test for whether a property will be overcrowded is based on the permitted number of persons in a room, and in the property as a whole.

The guidance states:

> A house is considered to be overcrowded if 2 persons aged 10 years or more of opposite sexes, who are not living together as husband and wife, must sleep in the same room. The Act also details the maximum number of people allowed for a given number of rooms or a given room floor area.

Account is taken only of rooms with a floor area larger than 50 square feet and rooms of a type used either as a living room or bedroom. Rooms such as kitchens or bathrooms are excluded.

Under the Housing Act, the number of people sleeping in accommodation must not exceed the following:

Rooms	Persons permitted
1	2
2	3
3	5
4	7.5
5	10
*	with an additional 2 persons for each room in excess of 5

For the purpose of the Act:

- a child under one does not count as a person.
- a child aged one to 10 years counts as only half a person.

> **Top Tip**
>
> In a case where the availability of adequate accommodation is in issue, make sure that you prove adequacy by reference to the statutory requirements: i.e.
>
> ☐ obtain a report from a professional or independent agent (some Councils' Residential Services departments now provide property inspections for immigration purposes); or
> ☐ refer to documented floor space, if there is a tenancy agreement or other documents showing the size and number of rooms

2.2.5 Conditions of Permission

There are various conditions that may be imposed on permission grants, relating to study, work, access to public funds etc. The IRs set these out within each of the relevant immigration routes, though the Home Office always has discretion to depart from them.

Where the IRs provide for them, conditions will be applied to a grant of limited leave which prevent or restrict the right to take employment, limit the place of study for students or the type of work permitted for sponsored workers, and prohibiting recourse to public funds. These conditions will be specified on the document granting leave (i.e. the visa or Biometric Residence Permit).

Access to healthcare is more restricted these days than in times past.

- The National Health Service (Charges to Overseas Visitors) Regulations 2015 ("Charging Regulations") are central to the legal regime
- There is a *useful toolkit from Doctors of the World* on how they work (not up-to-date but still useful)
- To avoid charges one must be ordinarily resident here, which essentially requires a permanent right to reside (eg British or Irish citizenship, ILR). Those lacking such status are termed **Overseas Visitors** for NHS purpose, whatever their immigration status (or lack of it). Additionally they must be living here lawfully having adopted their residence here voluntarily and for a degree of settled purpose for the time being, whether this is of short or long duration
- Attracting NHS debts can be one of the general refusal reasons (MIL 2.3.5.11)
- No charge may be made to anyone accessing accident and emergency services, family planning services, diagnosis and treatment of sexually transimitted illnesses and conditions listed in Sch 1 to the Regs (ranging from food poisoning to plague, including Covid); or for conditions due to torture, female genital mutilation, domestic abuse or sexual violence (provided the individual has not travelled to the UK simply to access such treatment) (Reg 9) – refugees and their UK-born babies (Reg 15) and modern slavery victims and their family members

(whether or not lawfully resident) (Reg 16) are also exempt and there is scope to recover past charges – also exempt are nationals of countries with whom the UK has reciprocal agreements (some of these provisos were introduced by the National Health Service (Charges to Overseas Visitors) (Amendment) (No. 4) Regulations 2022 from 28 December 2022)
- There is Guidance *Paying an NHS debt* explaining there are two months to pay the debt before it potentially goes on one's immigration record until it is paid

BRPs in family settlement entry clearance cases are issued with a National Insurance Number printed on the back.

At one time, where the grant of leave was silent in respect of a particular issue (i.e. the right to take employment), there would be no prohibition in that regard. The Home Office can also impose reporting, residence and other conditions on foreign nationals who are granted limited leave to enter or remain in the UK but this is not common.

A breach of conditions may and often does lead to removal from the UK. These days a decision would first be made to curtail leave under the relevant Rules; then s10 of the IAA 1999 would empower the person's removal as a person who requires leave and does not have it. A breach of conditions can also be the grounds upon which a subsequent application for an extension (rule 322(3)) or entry clearance (rules 320(7B) and 320(11)) is refused.

The HO is entitled to restrict access to work in general: there is unlikely to be a right to work in the UK outside of specific circumstances: Kulumbegov v Home Office [2023] EWHC 337 (KB) reviews the relevant authorities.

2.2.6 English language proficiency and knowledge of language and life in the UK

There are various sets of provisions addressing English language in the IRs. Some routes such as Appendix FM have their own bespoke provisions, the modernised managed migration routes refer to Appendix English Language, and some legacy routes still refer to Appendix B English Language. Essentially the criteria address the various means of proving language ability: having previously done so in another immigration application, coming from a majority English speaking country, having been taught at degree-level in English, or passing an English language test.

Where a test is taken (only with a HO-approved provider), the individual route usually identifies the relevant level required, via the Common European Framework of Reference for Languages (CEFR). Where the applicant relies on previous studies, Ecctis (formerly UK NARIC) must confirm whether awards from educational establishments outside the UK are deemed to meet the recognised standard of a Bachelor's or Master's degree or PhD in the UK, and that the degree was taught or researched in English to the relevant level.

Guidance over time has suggested that entry clearance can be cancelled where the migrant cannot converse without an interpreter and where there is no documentary evidence of their English language facility. Tazeem [2023] EWHC 1828 (Admin) holds that cancellation might be lawful at the border where a student migrant cannot converse in English: immigration officers needed no special training to assess this.

2.2.6.1 Appendix English Language

The introduction to this appendix lists the immigration routes for which this means of meeting the English language requirement applies. However the *level* at which proficiency is to be satisfied will be found in the *route* not in the *English language* Appendix itself.

Appendix English applies to a constantly updated list of immigration routes, ranging from most economic ruotes to Private life, Domestic Worker in a Private Household, the Hong Kong routes and Children staying with or joining a Non-Parent Relative (Protection).

CHAPTER 2: General Requirements of the Rules; Introduction to Guidance

This appendix is structured under the following headings and paragraph numbers:

- EL 1.1 Exemption
- EL 2.1-2.5 How the requirement is met
- EL 3.1 Met in a previous application
- EL 4.1 Majority English speaking country
- EL 5.1-Academic qualification
- EL 6.1 English language test
- EL 7.1-2 GCSE or A Level English
- EL 8.1-4 Additional ways Students can meet the English language requirement
- EL 9.1 Medical professional regulation for Skilled Workers

The caseworker guidance *Assessing the English Language requirement* summarises other available guidance on the English language requirement for routes not covered by this Appendix:

- for family partner or parent under Appendix FM and Armed Forces partners: the English language requirement guidance
- for Tier 1 Entrepreneur: see the English language Tier 1 guidance
- for settlement in other routes: Knowledge of language and life in the UK guidance

The scheme of the English language Appendix is to

- First to set out an exemption for those with a difficulty in meeting the requirement
- Second to summarise the five mainstream ways in which English proficiency can be evidenced
- Third to detail each of those methods: both the substantive requirement and the documents needed to evidence the requirement
- Fourth to provide some additional options for students

EL 1.1 Exemption

An applicant for settlement is exempt from the English requirement if on the application date they:

- are over 65 (a);
- are under 18 (b);
- have a physical or mental condition which presents them from satisfying the criteria (c); or
- There is a further exception for applicants aged over 18 who are applying for settlement as dependants and have spent more than 15 continuous years in the UK with permission, and have spent at least 75 hours in a guided learning English language class without being able to attain B1 level English. Such applicants must:
- provide confirmation from a qualified English language teacher that they have attended 75 guided learning hours of classes and, in the teacher's view, are unlikely to be able to attain B1 level English through further study; and
- show an English language speaking and listening qualification at A2 CEFR, ESOL entry level 2 or SCQF level 3.

EL 2.1-5 How the requirement is met

EL 2.1 provides that the English requirement is met if any of the requirements in EL3-6 are met.

For EC/PTS applications, the English requirement can also be met:

- by satisfying EL 7.1 to EL 8.4 (EL 2.2).
- by Skilled Workers satisfying EL 7.1 and EL 7.2 (EL 2.3(a)); or EL 9.1 (b).
- by Start-up or Innovator applicants, by meeting "EL" and EL 7.2 [NB: the omission of para numbers here appear to be an IRs drafting error]

CHAPTER 2: General Requirements of the Rules; Introduction to Guidance

Dependent partners and children applying for settlement can also meet the requirement by satisfying 3.2 of Appendix KOLL.

EL 3.1 Met in a previous application

Someone who has met the requirement at the same level in a previous application is treated as satisfying it again now.

EL 4.1 Majority English speaking country

Being a national of one of the following majority-English speaking countries suffices: Antigua and Barbuda, Australia, The Bahamas, Barbados, Belize, the British Overseas Territories, Canada, Dominica, Grenada, Guyana, Jamaica, Malta, New Zealand, St Kitts and Nevis, St Lucia, St Vincent and the Grenadines, Trinidad and Tobago, and the USA.

EL 5.1 Academic qualification

Proficiency can be established via an academic qualification listed in EL 5.2 which is evidenced as required under EL 5.3 or EL 5.4. The relevant qualifications in EL 5.2 are:

(a) a bachelor's- or master's degree or PhD awarded in the UK
(b) a degree or degree level qualification from a university or college in one of the majority-English speaking countries in EL 4.1 (except Canada), or in Ireland which meets or exceeds the UK standard for a bachelors- or master's degree or PhD
(c) a degree or degree level qualification which meets or exceeds the UK standard for a bachelors- or master's degree or PhD and which was taught or researched in English

The evidence required by EL 5.3 must be one of:

(a) a certificate from the awarding body
(b) a transcript issued by the university or college that awarded the qualification
(c) an official letter from the university or college containing information equivalent to a degree certificate

Qualifications awarded outside the UK must be further supported by confirmation from UK Naric (see MIL 7.4.3.17) that the qualification meets EL 3.2(b) or (c) (EL 5.4).

EL 6.1 English language test

The evidence for meeting the requirement via an English test is a valid digital reference number from an approved provider showing confirming passing an approved test to the required level within 2 years before the application (EL 6.1). Appendix O lists the approved tests and their providers.

EL 7.1-2 GCSE or A Level English

EL 7.1 provides that for EC/PTS applications as a Student, Skilled Worker, Start-up or Innovator or High Potential Individual migrant, and the Settlement Family Life and Private Life routes a GCSE, A level, Scottish National Qualification at level 4 or 5 or, Scottish Higher or Advanced Higher, in English (language or literature), can be used to meet the requirement if awarded:

(a) by an Ofqual, SQA, Qualifications Wales or CCEA regulated awarding body; and
(b) following education in a UK school whilst a minor.

The evidence required under EL 7.2 is a certificate or transcript issued by the awarding body. This class of qualifications is not available under the Appendix B English language.

EL 8.1-4 Additional ways Students can meet the English language requirement

These provisions only apply to applicants under Appendix Student (not Child Student).

Student applicants for at least degree level courses can meet the requirement if their sponsor has a track record of compliance and confirms on the CAS the facts and means by which they have assessed English proficiency (EL 8.1). This must be at least at level B2 CEFR in speaking, listening, reading and writing: or if the assessment has been made by a third party other than the student sponsor, the latter must confirm that they are satisfied that B2 will have been achieved by the end of the pre-sessional course (EL 8.2, ST 15.3).

Students can meet the requirement if they have taken an English language test and have been exempted from a component of that test by the test provider due to a disability. The sponsor must confirm their level of English suffices for the course (EL 8.3).

One can meet the requirement for a short-term study abroad programme of up to 6 months which is part of a course of study at degree level or above at a higher education institution in the US (EL 8.4(a)); so long as UK NARIC (see MIL 7.4.3.17) confirms the course leads to an academic qualification at UK bachelor's degree level or above (b).

EL 9.1 Professional regulation for Skilled Workers

Skilled Workers applying for EC/PTS meet the requirement if they are sponsored to work as a doctor, dentist, vet nurse or midwife and have passed an English Language assessment accepted by the relevant regulated professional body as a requirement for registration

2.2.6.2 Knowledge of English language and life in the UK for ILR

To obtain settlement (ILR) most applicants must demonstrate their knowledge of English language and life in the UK, or that they meet the narrow criteria for exemption.

Those applying for ILR in the refugee, humanitarian protection, bereaved spouses and domestic violence categories, and those with discretionary leave, do not have to meet this requirement (though they must do so if they are going on to seek British citizenship via naturalisation).

The life in the UK requirements are now found in two similarly named Appendices: Appendix KoLL and Appendix KOL (MIL 7.7.16).

- Many immigration routes are assessed via Appendix KoLL: applicants must pass the Life in the UK test, and separately evidence that they can speak and understand the English language at minimum B1 level of the Common European Framework of Reference for Languages (CEFR) (equivalent to an ESOL qualification at entry level 3). Individual rules generally refer to this Appendix thus: 'The applicant must have sufficient knowledge of the English language and sufficient knowledge about life in the United Kingdom, in accordance with Appendix KoLL'
- However most of the work-based routes are assessed via Appendix KOL UK (which conveniently summarises the routes to which it applies in its introduction)

From 1 December 2020, Appendix KOL UK applies to many routes. Presumably will eventually cover most if not all settlement applications.

Other routes are still covered by Appendix KOLL, and the policy around the Knowledge of Life in the UK test under either Appendix has not changed.

The Life in the UK Test requirement is met by sitting and passing an examination with multiple choice questions based on the book *Life in the United Kingdom: A Guide for New Residents*. The ESOL route (i.e. passing an ESOL qualification taught with citizenship materials) is no longer available.

Appendix KOLL

Under Appendix KoLL, applicants must pass the Life in the UK Test, and separately evidence their English language proficiency at minimum B1 level of the Common European Framework of Reference for Languages (CEFR) (equivalent to an ESOL qualification at entry level 3).

The language requirement can be met in several different ways:

- By being a national of a country listed in paragraph 2.2(a)(i) of Appendix KoLL (essentially the USA, and then Commonwealth countries in the Caribbean and Australia, New Zealand and Canada)
- By passing a secure English language test in speaking and listening at the minimum level with a provider approved by the HO A full list of tests and test centres is on the UK website together with frequently asked questions. Appendix O of the IRs which previously contained specifics regarding English Language tests has now been removed.
- Having an academic qualification at Bachelor's degree or higher level (excluding professional and vocational qualifications) from a college in a country listed in paragraph 2.2(a)(iii) of Appendix KoLL
- Having an academic qualification at Bachelor's degree or higher level (excluding professional and vocational qualifications) taught in English
- Having already met the B1 requirement in a previous grant of leave, and having had unbroken leave since that grant

Part 3 of Appendix KoLL lays out the exemptions:

- for those aged under 18 or over 65 at the date of their applications, and
- where the UKVI considers that, because of the applicant's mental or physical condition, it would be unreasonable to expect them to fulfil that requirement.

The official website for those booking and preparing to take the test is here and the terms and conditions for taking the test are on this separate page.

Some of those who are unable to pass either or both KoLL tests, despite their best efforts, may be able to rely on a reduced requirement after having spent 15 continuous years in the UK (as specified in paragraph 3.2 of Appendix KoLL of the IRs listing the routes for which this available). They will then need to pass an English language qualification at Level A2 of the CEFR. Nationals of the countries listed at paragraph 3.2(d) must take and pass the Life in the UK Test, however long that takes. The specified documents that must be submitted with the ILR application are in Part 4 of Appendix KoLL.

There is Guidance: *Knowledge of language and life in the UK*.

Rule 39C in Part 1 allows the UKVI to interview applicants for settlement to satisfy the Secretary of State that the KoLL requirements are met. If the decision-maker has reasonable cause to doubt (on examination or interview or on any other basis) that any document submitted by an applicant for the purposes of satisfying the requirements of Appendix KoLL was genuinely obtained, that document may be discounted for the purposes of the application. There is an evidential flexibility regime whereby missing documents can be sought (KOLL 4.3) (MIL 2.2.2 addresses similar regimes in detail).

A common problem for those sitting the HO's secure English Language Test is not having the appropriate ID, often because the HO holds it. There is guidance on the required ID in the 'immigration and borders' section of the UKVI website, here.

The rules require applicants to provide their unique reference number for the life in the UK test and the English Language test. (Appendix KOLL 4.15-4.16).

Requests for medical exemptions must be from the applicant's own GP or another GP at the same practice; or a GMC-registered consultant. The opinion should confirm that the condition will prevent one of the key KOLL elements being satisfied for the foreseeable future (KOLL 4.13ZA).

2.2.7 Tuberculosis tests

Appendix Tuberculolis provides that any person applying to enter the UK for more than six months (except under the Ukraine Scheme) or as a fiancé(e) or proposed civil partner or as a Returning Resident must provide a valid TB certificate, if they have resided in a country listed at TB6 for 6+ months, within the 6 months leading up to the application date (TB2).

- A TB certificate is only valid if it has not expired and is dated within 6 months of the application date issued by a medical practitioner approved by the SSHD for these purposes, as listed on this page, confirming that they have undergone screening for active pulmonary TB and are free from the condition
- The requirement to produce a certificate may be waived if the decision maker is satisfied the applicant is unable to produce one and it is reasonable to do so on the facts of the case (TB5)

2.2.8 Dependents of principal applicants

Most immigration routes specify whether dependents can apply under them. There is a generic requirement that addresses the Sponsor's immigration status at the date of the application: they must have permission in the route the dependant is applying under, or a valid pending application, or, if settled/a British citizen, have held permission in the route before becoming such (r34DA, though repeated in many individual immigration routes, eg ROB 20.2).

The same general scheme applies throughout the IRs to partners and children, with the usual criteria for validity and suitability. As to partners, leaving aside partner-specific routes such as Appendix FM and Appendix EU:

Partners must be

- 18+ years of age
- married or in a civil partnership, or be cohabiting in a similar relationship for 2 years pre-application
- in a genuine and subsisting relationship with an intention to cohabit during their UK residence
- be able to show that any previous relationship has permanently broken down and that they are not so closely related that marriage or civil partnership would be prohibited in the UK

Increasingly immigration routes at the ILR stage cross-refer to Appendix Relationship with Partner (MIL 6.2.10.1) and to Appendix Children for the criteria on age, independent life, care, relationship & parental consent (MIL 7.8.14.5).

Children must:

- establish the core validity criteria (MIL 1.5.3) and the suitability criteria (by reference to the general refusal reasons, with varying degrees of relaxation for human rights routes)
- show that both parents have permission to be in the UK (on the route or via ILR/British citizenship and is ordinarily resident here), unless one is the sole surviving parent, or has sole responsibility for the child (recognising the likelihood that other adults have some involvement with the child, as per the Guidance *Appendix Children*), or there are otherwise serious and compelling reasons for the grant (that Guidance lists possible scenarios, eg countries where single parentage is not tolerated, issues of safety)
- demonstrate suitable arrangements for their care and accommodation in the UK compliant with relevant UK law
- generally be unmarried and not be living independently, meaning they have no partner and lives with their parent subject to residing at boarding school, college or university (IR6.2)): there is a particularly full set of criteria at Part 8 r319H-SD: two separate forms of proof of residential address such as bank/credit card/driving licence/NHS registration/place of education, plus any payments for rent/board, and if living away from the family home, the reasons for so doing including proof of educational commitments and financial dependency on the parents). The Guidance *Appendix Children* states that living away from home with a boyfriend/girlfriend whilst studying would not necessarily render an applicant independent Decision makers will take account of separate addresses and may investigate the adequacy of accommodation proffered to meet the care requirements via open source checks; further information may be sought

CHAPTER 2: General Requirements of the Rules; Introduction to Guidance

2.3 The general refusal grounds

In this part of MIL we firstly address definitions and commonly used terms, and explain the architecture of Part 9 of the IRs. We then provide a diagram which summarises the many general refusal grounds, matches the old and new IRs and indicates broadly when decisions are discretionary or mandatory. Finally we go through each kind of general refusal reason in detail.

2.3.1 Introduction to the general refusal grounds

Immigration applications can be refused because they fail to meet the requirements of the route in question (for example eligibility or English language requirements). Or because the decision maker believes there to be a more fundamental problem with the application. The latter scenario is what Part 9 of the Rules deals with. Common problems arising in this context include clients being refused:

- Due to inconsistencies between the income claimed on their HMRC tax returns and in their immigration extension applications (leading to refusals on 'good character' grounds)
- Because past English language test results have been cancelled because a provider (usually ETS) has declared the results invalid (leading to refusals for dishonestly obtaining documents to support an immigration application)
- Due to omitting to disclose relevant information in an application form

For many years this has been known as the "*general grounds for refusal*". We will continue to so label it. From 1 December 2020 these grounds have been radically revised, with both a new structure and a completely new paragraph numbering system.

The new title for Part 9 is simply "*grounds for refusal*". Which has scope to confuse: because it does not differentiate between the grounds for refusal under individual immigration routes (eg on eligibility or suitability grounds) and Part 9's more generalised ones.

> **Top Tip**
>
> It will always be necessary to consider Part 9 (or the suitability criteria, if applicable) when taking a client's instructions, if necessary by asking direct questions to your client, in respect of criminal convictions (in the UK or abroad), their UK immigration history, and litigation/NHS debts.

Here are some terms frequently used in the context of the general refusal reasons:

- **"Conducive" refusals:** refusals which are on the grounds that exclusion/refusal is conducive to the public good. These refusals usually involve criminality.
- **"Good character" or "non-conducive" refusals**: refusals which are essentially due to character and conduct, but which falls short of the refusal for the "*conducive to the public good*" regime to kick in
- **Mandatory ban**: fixed periods for which time an application faces refusal.
    - **Mandatory ban for criminality**: for example any criminal offending covering a custodial sentence exceeding 12 months, or which is deemed to involve persistent offending or serious harm (eg r9.4.1). Convictions can be in the UK or abroad (r6).
    - **Mandatory ban for overstaying/dishonesty**: depending on the speed and manner of departure there are bans of various lengths (12 months for overstaying where one leaves voluntarily at one's own expense up to 10 years for deception in the present application (see the table at r9.8.7)
- **Breaches of immigration laws**: there are two separate definitions given in r6 (the Interpretation provision of the Rules). Note that present breaches include a *breach of conditions*, whereas past breaches *only* involve *overstaying, deception* and *illegal entry*. However once we reach the rules addressing previous breaches of conditions aside from overstaying, we see that it is only those breaches of conditions which were subsequently condoned by a subsequent grant of leave which are left out of account (r9.8.3).

CHAPTER 2: General Requirements of the Rules; Introduction to Guidance

- **Breach of immigration laws**: where the person is an overstayer, illegal entrant, is in breach of a condition of their permission (eg a prohibition on employment or study), or used deception in relation to their most recent application for entry clearance or permission (or committed historic deception in relation to a previous application, whether or not successfully r9.8.3A)
- **Previously breached immigration laws**: if the person overstayed or used deception in relation to a previous application for entry clearance or permission

- **Cancellation (including curtailment and adverse variations)**: Part 9 provides not only for the *refusal* of applications but also for their *cancellation* on suitability grounds. The reference to "*cancellation*" here covers also what was previously termed "*curtailment*": indeed the word "curtailment" does not appear in Part 9. The interpretation provisions of the Rules (r6) define cancellation to include curtailment and cancellation of entry clearance or permission. It also includes an "adverse" variation where a person's leave is shortened so that it ends sooner than it would otherwise have done. This is typically done where there has been some failure of sponsorship and the SSHD thinks it fair to give a short period in which the migrant may obtain an alternative sponsor. Powers to vary leave in the Rules may be interpreted as including a power to cancel: C1 [2022] EWCA Civ 30. See MIL 13.3.1 for administrative removal following cancellation.

2.3.2 Architecture of Part 9 Grounds for refusal.

Part 9 is split into five sections, as follows:

(1) Limitations on the application of Part 9
(2) Grounds for refusal, or cancellation of, entry clearance, permission to enter and permission to stay
(3) Additional grounds for refusal of entry, or cancellation of entry clearance or permission, on arrival in the UK (these often differentiate between mandatory refusal at the border for certain failures, and discretionary refusal where entry clearance has already been issued)
(4) Additional grounds for refusal, or cancellation, of permission to stay
(5) Additional grounds for cancellation of entry clearance, permission to enter and permission to stay which apply to specified routes

So to put that more simply, essentially the scheme is to

- Explain which bits of Part 9 apply to which species of immigration application, and
- Then to provide for a multitude of grounds that are generally applicable for most applications
- Add to that multitude some "Additional grounds" which bite only in particular circumstances: on arrival in the UK, for in-country cases only, and finally a few which apply only to particular routes.

Some initial points:

- The IA 1971 authorises the grant (and thus refusal) of leave, and s76 of the NIAA 2002 addresses revocation of ILR; the ILERO 2000 and Sch 2 of the 1971 Act empower cancelling entry clearance or permission. So the role of Part 9 is to set out how these general powers are to be exercised in the individual case
- Individual routes (usually) cross reference to Part 9 via the heading Suitability requirements: see for example for seasonal workers (SAW 2.1) "The applicant must not fall for refusal under Part 9".
- Some Rules have their own internal Suitability regime: see for example Appendix FM for partners, where we find Section S-EC: Suitability-entry clearance (and similar rules governing leave to remain too at Section S-LTR: Suitability leave to remain). There seems to be some inconsistency in the approach to cross-referencing: Appendix FM barely refers to Part 9. However r9.1.1(a) explains that many of its provisions do apply to Appendix FM applications
- Whilst Appendix FM does not impose a mandatory ban on return to the UK for breach of immigration conditions, r9.8.2 (contriving to frustrate the IRs) does apply to family applications

CHAPTER 2: General Requirements of the Rules; Introduction to Guidance

made under Appendix FM. It is often the basis upon which entry clearance applications, particularly those made under the partner category, are refused, where the applicant has what is considered by the HO to be a very poor immigration history (see below)

- Part 9 does not apply to an application for leave to remain on the grounds of private life under Appendix Private Life: except for the proviso that applications may be refused where the application is made for a purpose not covered by the Rules (9.1.1(b), 9.13.1)
- Part 9 does not apply to the post-Brexit EU routes: thus we can see that Appendix EU and Appendix EU (Family Permit), and Appendix S2 Healthcare Visitor and Appendix Service Providers from Switzerland are wholly excluded (9.1.1(d), (e), (j) and (k)): nor does it apply to Turkish businesspeople and workers under Appendix ECAA, except (in line with the general scheme of the Brexit era) where conduct post-dates the end of the transition period
- Typically the rules are paired, the first proviso addressing the circumstances in which an application might be refused, the second the circumstances in which it might be cancelled
- Refusals are sometimes mandatory ("must be refused" or "must be cancelled") or discretionary ("may be refused" or "may be cancelled"). As the introductory passages admit, decision making cannot solely be guided by the general refusal reasons: where fundamental rights are in play, it must also be compatible with the Refugee Convention or the ECHR (and it may well have to be proportionate to any interference with EU Treaty Rights acquired before Brexit)
- When new immigration routes are created, any exceptions to Part 9's general application is specified in the introductory "Section 1" of Part 9: eg when Appendix Temporary Permission to Stay for Victims of Human Trafficking or Slavery entered force in November 2022, it incorporated around half of the available refusal reasons

---

Top Tip

When taking instructions on a case where the general refusal reasons may be relevant:

(1) Check which immigration route is in play: Appendix FM, Appendix V Visitor, etc, and then check para 9.1.1 for the extent to which Part 9 applies to the route
(2) Work out where your client is in the immigration system: at the entry clearance stage, at the port of entry, applying for permission to stay, and then work out which of the refusal reasons at sections 2-4 apply (section 2 always applies, section 3 applies only on arrival, section 4 only applies to permission to stay cases)
(3) Work out whether your client needs face up to any route-specific refusal reasons under section 5: these essentially bite on dependents, and on sponsored and endorsed migrants, ie workers and students, and those in the global/exceptional talent route

---

Part 9 from 1 December 2020 is arranged by the issue motivating the refusal. It is helpful, particularly when looking at Section 1 r9.1.1(a)-(k) (which contains long lists of cross-references setting out which sections apply to which immigration categories) to gain an overview of how the numbering structure works. HJT does not normally cross-reference past and present IRs, taking the view that it is best to master the current provisions than refer to old ones. However, given the extensive case law relating to the old general refusal reasons, and the familiarity of many practitioners with the old numbering, the online MIL provides the previous versions for comparison.

2.3.3 Limitations on the application of Part 9

The limitations are quite dense reading, and sadly there is no substitute for staring carefully at each numbered paragraph to determine whether it may be applicable to your client's circumstances. However note:

- The limitations are usually expressed as a double negative: ie "Part 9 does not apply ... except ..." (so the numbered references *do* apply)

- Although at first sight it can be rather bewildering, on analysis we see that the general refusal reasons apply with full force to most regular immigration applications: for example the various Appendices governing study and work, and the surviving work/economic routes in Part 5 and Part 6 and Part 6A: the exclusions are essentially for private and family life (including the human rights oriented route r159I for domestic workers who are the victim of slavery or human trafficking), asylum and post-Brexit EU cases
- Appendix FM has rather a lot of *individual inclusions* notwithstanding its *general exclusion* from Part 9
- Permission for individuals under Appendix FM can be *cancelled* where an exclusion or deportation order is made (presumably following the grant of permission) (r9.1.1 referencing r9.2.2)
- Appendix FM's individual inclusions must be read alongside Appendix FM's own Suitability regime (so for example a partner seeking leave to remain under Appendix FM faces a mandatory refusal for imprisonment over 4 years under Appendix FM's own provisions (S-LTR.1.3) and for causing serious harm or persistently offending such as to show a particular disregard for the law (S-LTR.1.5), and a 10-year mandatory ban for sentences from 1-4 years under S-LTR.1.4: but also faces possible *discretionary cancellation* for offending (r9.4.5, brought into play by r9.1.1(a))
- There are four routes which are completely exempt from Part 9: Appendix E (dependents of Tier 1 Entrepreneurs), Appendix EU (Family Permit), Appendix S2 Healthcare Visitor and Appendix Service Providers from Switzerland - Appendix Electronic Travel Authorisation is also exempt

2.3.4 General principles regarding the general refusal reasons

The burden of proof lies on the SSHD to establish a general refusal reason: see eg <u>Shen</u> [2014] UKUT 236 (IAC) §25.

The Home Office provides detailed guidance to its caseworkers on the use of the general grounds. It can be found on the GOV.UK website:

- <u>General grounds for refusal</u> (immigration staff guidance)

2.3.5 The generally applicable grounds for refusal and cancellation

These grounds, found in Section 2 of Part 9, apply at *all stages* of the decision making process. From now on we will use the abbreviations EC (entry clearance), PTE (permission to enter) and PTS (permission to stay).

2.3.5.1 Exclusion or deportation order grounds (9.2.1-9.2.2)
An application for EC, PTE or PTS ***must*** be refused on SSHD's personal direction of exclusion (9.2.1(a)); or A is subject to an exclusion order (9.2.1(b)); or to a deportation order or decision to make one (9.2.1(c)). There is Guidance *Deportation and Exclusion – Suitability*.

EC or permission held ***must*** be cancelled on SSHD's personal direction for exclusion (9.2.2). This extends to individuals named in UN Security Council or EU Council instruments as recommended for refusal, unless so to do would contravene the ECHR or Refugee Convention, or the UK's Sanctions and Anti-Money Laundering Act 2018 (9.2.3-9.2.4).

An *exclusion decision* is a decision made personally by the SSHD directing an individual's exclusion. An *exclusion order* is the equivalent made under the EEA Regs 2016 <u>Campbell</u> [2013] UKUT 147 (IAC) examined the effect of the domestic variety, ie the *exclusion decision*:

- It involves the use of a non-statutory power exercised personally by the SSHD
- There is no right of appeal against the making of such an order (<u>Campbell</u> comes from the old era of immigration appeals where there were particular kinds of immigration decision

bearing a right of appeal, though the same thinking holds true given that the making of an exclusion order does not necessarily involve the refusal of a human rights claim): the FTT and UT would have power to consider the proportionality of the exercise of such a power in a statutory appeal brought on human rights grounds
- It would be wrong to impose any particular time period during which the decision's subject should not expect to be granted entry clearance to return: in general one might expect the public interest to diminish as time passed, at least when measured against strong family life
- Under the SSHD's policy there was effectively a two-stage process, by which the individual first applied for revocation of the exclusion decision and thereafter applied for entry clearance

2.3.5.2 Non-conducive grounds: character, conduct and associations (9.3.1-9.3.2)

Applications for EC, PTE or PTS *must* be refused where A's presence is not conducive to the public good on grounds of conduct, character, associations or other reasons (including convictions falling below the threshold to attract the criminality grounds) (9.3.1).

EC or PTE/PTS *must* be cancelled where presence in the UK is not conducive to the public good (9.3.2).

The Guidance on the *General grounds for refusal* explains the various factors that warrant consideration of potential refusal under the character, conduct and associations provisions. Single non-custodial convictions are unlikely to suffice; but many other forms of conduct, from deliberate or reckless building up of debts, corruption, assisting the evasion of immigration control, employing illegal workers, and deceitful dealings with HM Government, might do so. See MIL 2.3.5.3 for pending prosecutions.

Hussain [2021] EWCA Civ 2781 clarifies that the balance of probabilities applies to "*conducive to the public good*" decisions, with the qualification that the seriousness of the allegation is reflected in the quality of evidence which is to be subject to critical and anxious scrutiny.

There have been many 'good character' refusals under this Rules's predecessor (r322(5)) where the HO believes that the system has been 'played'. This most commonly arises where the applicant was previously in the Tier 1 General route (abolished some years ago). Migrants with a certain level of education and earning history could join Tier 1 General, applying from abroad (or switching into the route in the UK). The route closed to new applicants long ago, but it nevertheless features in many people's immigration history. There are a great many applicants still in the system because their cases were put on hold whilst they challenged refusals. Now their problems should have been recognised as amounting to a human rights claim and given a right of appeal.

- The SSHD observed a number of applicants under Tier 1 General who seem to have declared higher earnings to the HO on their immigration applications than they subsequently (or at the same time) declared to HMRC for tax purposes. Decision makers think this shows deliberate misuse of the immigration route – because these individuals have either downplayed their income for tax reasons or overstated their income for immigration purposes

- Many applicants now make corrections to their past tax returns with HMRC just before making settlement applications, to ensure their HMRC reporting tallies with the earnings claimed on immigration applications – but far from allaying Home Office concerns, tax corrections are treated as inherently suspicious.

- The *General grounds for refusal* guidance, when it comes to address *Deceitful or dishonest dealings with Her Majesty's Government* expressly says, addressing dishonesty, that it is 'not appropriate to refuse someone for a genuine mistake'. This suggests that 'good character' refusals require a finding of active dishonesty. Doubtless real tax dodging or earnings-exaggeration would qualify. However, the fact most of the examples given by the guidance involve criminality or outright serious dishonesty strongly suggests that the HO should not treat legitimate businesspeople as dishonest simply because of a difference in the figures reported, which can have plenty of innocent explanations. A small business may have ups and downs in its income, the tax year rarely equates perfectly to the immigration application year (the latter being the 12 months before the application date), and it is not unusual for businesspeople to have to correct their tax returns.

- JR is never a good remedy for this kind of refusal. JRs just review the HO decision. They are not determining an appeal on the merits. They are not determining the question of "Do I believe this unfortunate businessperson?" They are asking "Did the SSHD overlook material evidence or come to an utterly unreasonable conclusion when concluding she was not of good character?" And one cannot rely on post decision evidence, so one is limited to the material already put to the UKVI. Issues of UK connections are not relevant to applications under this route, and so don't help.

- The landmark decision of Balajigari [2019] EWCA Civ 673 changed the way these cases were dealt with, the CoA finding:

    - Active dishonesty is required for a good character refusal on tax discrepancy grounds, though misdemeanours did not necessarily have to be criminal in nature, nor have resulted in HMRC penalties
    - Procedural fairness demands that the dishonesty allegation is clearly made in the decision making process
    - The UT will have to determine dishonesty allegations for itself in JR proceedings where they are relevant to proportionality
    - In some cases, applicants might still be granted leave despite a finding of dishonesty, e.g. where this is in the best interests of a child
    - The question of whether unpublished dishonesty allegations (ie the possible damage to reputation caused by the SSHD terminating one's lawful status in the UK) can infringe private life is left open.

- The guidance General grounds for refusal: false representation has now been amended to include references to 'minded to refuse' letters, giving the applicant the chance to explain themselves. Akram [2020] EWCA Civ 1072 holds that where the applicant had been given an opportunity to answer the SSHD's concerns via a tax questionnaire sent to him in the course of the original immigration application, the procedure is likely to have been fair

Where the client has an appeal (eg because they have Tier 1 General as part of their immigration history but their latest application was a human rights claim), they can rely on fresh evidence of course, ranging from good character evidence to detailed corroboration from accountants.

> **Top Tip**
>
> People without the right of appeal might wish to consider where a human rights claim is the best way forward – they could argue that the allegation against their good character is part of their private life, and that this combined with their lengthy lawful residence in the UK means they have established private life here. The bad character allegation is essentially relevant to whether it is disproportionate to interfere with that private life. This is essentially the thinking in Ahsan [2017] EWCA Civ 2009. It might well be difficult for the Home Office to bar the right of appeal by certifying such claims as "clearly unfounded" – because they are supposed to assess whether a claim is "clearly unfounded" taking the case at its highest rather than resolving facts against an applicant.
>
> Many of these cases get into difficulties because applicants do not adequately explain the background to their case. Whatever stage of the process the person is at, they should consider addressing
>
> What is the precise allegation being made by the Home Office? The individual will need to work out precisely what earnings they did in fact declare to UKVI and HMRC, and explain their overall pattern of earnings and business activity
>
> Who was responsible for the tax liability reporting to HMRC? The client or an accountant offering a book-keeping service?

> Are UKVI attacking a single period or multiple periods (there will usually be two interactions with UKVI within the Tier 1 General route, the original application to enter the route and then the extension application)?
>
> Have UKVI correctly analysed the asserted discrepancy bearing in mind
>
> The difference between tax and "immigration application" years
>
> The various forms of earning: employed, self-employed, salary/dividends as a Director
>
> How significant is the difference between the earnings reported to UKVI and HMRC?
>
> How was it that the difference was not picked up by the client when signing off their annual tax returns (when their accountant is supposed to go through it with them) ?
>
> Has UKVI accepted the present earnings as genuine (if not, steps must be taken to prove that recent business activities are genuine, as well as addressing past earnings reporting)
>
> Are good character references available?
>
> In general the Home Office seems to raise these discrepancies by way of a questionnaire and sometimes an interview, before making their decision on the application, so clients need to put their best case at that point, otherwise the window of opportunity to submit further evidence may close.

Grant of FLR instead of ILR as a consequence of losing on good character but winning on family life grounds

2.3.5.3 Criminality grounds (9.4.1-9.4.5)

We use tables to minimise repetition below:

Mandatory grounds for refusal or cancellation	
9.4.1 An application for EC/PTE/PTS *must* be refused for	9.4.2 EC/permission held *must* be cancelled for
Identical for 9.4.1 and 9.4.2: (a) 12-month custodial (ie prison) sentence in the UK or elsewhere; or (b) persistent offender with a particular disregard for the law; or (c) having caused serious harm by offending.	
9.4.4 An application for EC or PTE for less than 6 months (including visitors) *must* be refused for (a) prison sentence under 12 months in the UK or elsewhere, which ended less than 1 year before application date; or (b) non-custodial sentence or out-of-court disposal recorded on criminal record in the UK or elsewhere where conviction was less than 1 year before application date	
Discretionary grounds for refusal or cancellation	
9.4.3 An application for EC/PTE/PTS *may* be refused (where 9.4.2. and 9.4.4. do not apply)	9.4.5 EC or permission held *may* be cancelled (where 9.4.2. does not apply)
Identical for 9.4.3 and 9.4.5: (a) prison sentence of under 12 months in the UK or elsewhere; or (b) non-custodial sentence or out-of-court disposal recorded on criminal record in the UK or elsewhere	

The Guidance *Grounds for refusal – Criminality* explains that there is:

- a single threshold for mandatory refusal on the basis of a custodial sentence of at least 12 months, replacing the previous three sentence-based thresholds
- a mandatory ground for refusal at the border for those entering as visitors or for less than 6 months

- a mandatory ground for refusal or cancellation on the grounds of serious harm, persistent offending or where it is conducive to the public good

- A definition is given for persistence, which is to be considered in the light of the number and frequency of offending, its pattern, seriousness, and any escalation, and whether any particular disregard of the law has been shown (ie whether the behaviour indicates "*a lack of willingness or capacity to adjust their conduct so that it remains within the law over a reasonable period of time*":

    'A persistent offender is considered to be a repeat offender who shows a pattern of offending over a period of time. This can mean a series of offences committed in a fairly short timeframe, or offences which escalate in seriousness over time, or a long history of minor offences for the same behaviour which demonstrate a clear disregard for the law'

- Serious harm may involve one or more violent, drugs-related, racially motivated or sexual offences will qualify, and sentencing remarks and offender management reports should be considered. The definition given is one that has:

    'caused serious physical or psychological harm to a victim or victims, or that has contributed to a widespread problem that causes serious harm to a community or to society in general.'

Mahmood [2020] EWCA Civ 717 addresses 'serious harm' for deportation purposes, and term 'persistent offender' is looked at in Chege [2016] UKUT 187 (IAC) (MIL 13.4.2.1).

Pending prosecutions

Sometimes there will be a pending prosecution. Where the prosecution is for an offence attracting a sentence that might materially impact on a decision, decision makers need to consider holding the case until the outcome of the court proceedings.

2.3.5.4 Exclusion from asylum or humanitarian protection grounds (9.5.1-9.5.2)

Discretionary ground	
9.5.1. An application for EC/PTE/PTS *may* be refused	9.5.2 EC or PTE/PTS *may* be cancelled
Identical for 9.5.1 and 9.5.2: (a) where SSHD has at any time decided that the individual should be excluded from refugee status or HP under 339AA/339D (ie for war crimes, crimes against humanity, and acts contrary to UN purposes, for refugee status; for past criminality, including committing international crimes, including offending in the UK which represents a danger to the community or the UK's security and the situation where their flight to the UK was to avoid punishment for a crime for HP); that HP should be revoked under 339GB (essentially the same reasons as under 339D); or that a person granted refugee status is in fact a danger to the UK under 339AC (being a danger to the community or the UK's security); or (b) where SSHD decides the above provisions would apply *were* the individual to claim protection, or where their protection claim was finally determined without reference to them	

It can be seen that r9.5.2(b) authorises exclusion where a protection claim was finally determined "*without reference*" to exclusion. Cases such as TB (Jamaica) [2008] EWCA Civ 977 hold that the SSHD cannot necessarily raise exclusion following judicial proceedings where the matter might have been raised but the point was not taken.

2.3.5.5 Involvement in a sham marriage or sham civil partnership grounds (9.6.1-9.6.2)

Discretionary ground	
9.6.1. An application for EC/PTE/PTS *may* be refused	9.6.2 EC or permission held *may* be cancelled
Identical for 9.6.1 and 9.6.2: where the decision maker is satisfied that it is more likely than not, that the person is or was involved in a sham marriage or civil partnership	

A sham marriage is defined (circuitously, the Rules' interpretation clause at r6 tells us we should refer to s62(3) of IA 2014, which then passes us onto s24(5) of IAA 1999, which says):

> "(a) either, or both, of the parties to the marriage is not a relevant national,
> (b) there is no genuine relationship between the parties to the marriage, and(c) either, or both, of the parties to the marriage enter into the marriage for one or more of these purposes—
> (i) avoiding the effect of one or more provisions of United Kingdom immigration law or the immigration rules;
> (ii) enabling a party to the marriage to obtain a right conferred by that law or those rules to reside in the United Kingdom."

The Guidance *Suitability: Sham marriage or civil partnership* explains when suspicions may arise: decision makers 'must be satisfied that there are reasonable grounds for suspecting' that a marriage is a sham. Action should be taken only where to do so is proportionate. The two parties may be treated differently if the evidence suggests one has been duped. The HO has stated that action may be taken beyond those who are party to the sham: this may include knowingly acting as a false witness or guest at the wedding, or introducing the parties. Giri [2015] EWCA Civ 784 (MIL 9.3.4) shows that the HO must be able to point to cogent evidence to establish her case on balance of probabilities (MIL 6.2.11 &, re EEA cases, 11.5.4). There is detailed Guidance *Marriage Investigations* which addresses how cases are considered, procedures and removal pathways; and the provision of notices for non-compliance under The Proposed Marriages and Civil Partnerships (Conduct of Investigations, etc.) Regulations 2015.

2.3.5.6 Providing false representations, documents, information, and material non-disclosure (9.7.1-9.7.4)

Discretionary grounds	
9.7.1 An application for EC/PTE/PTS *may* be refused	**9.7.3** EC or permission held *may* be cancelled
Identical for 9.7.1 and 9.7.3: if, in relation to the relevant application or in order to obtain supporting documents for this from SSHD or a third party (a) false representations were made or false information/documents submitted (whether or not to the person's knowledge, and whether or not relevant to the application); or (b) relevant facts were not disclosed	
9.7.4 Section 3C leave *may* be cancelled where the decision maker can prove it is more likely than not P used deception in the application for PTS	
Mandatory ground	
9.7.2 An application for EC/PTE/PTS *must* be refused where the decision maker can prove it is *more likely than not* that the individual used deception in the application	

These provisions have provoked much litigation, which has established:

- Deception requires active dishonesty – see for example AA (Nigeria) [2010] EWCA Civ 773. Or as it was put in Ozhogina [2011] UKUT 197 (IAC):

    it is necessary to show that a false statement was deliberately made for the purpose of securing an advantage in immigration terms

- The use of a false document itself justifies mandatory refusal on the *current* application, whether or not the applicant appreciated the falsity, AA (Nigeria); but where an application is being considered on the basis of whether *past* use of a false document should lead to a refusal of the *present* application, then active dishonesty must be shown: see eg Li [2018] EWCA Civ 2411
- A false document is one that is forged or has been altered to give false information: see e.g. Agha [2017] UKUT 121 (IAC):

there must have been an element of dishonesty in its creation and if this is not immediately obvious in a case of an inaccurate document then that element must be engaged with in any refusal.

- The burden of proof in establishing dishonesty is on the decision maker – JC China [2007] UKAIT 27 (unless of course the allegation is admitted, or has been judicially determined to have been made out in earlier judicial proceedings)
- The standard of proof is the balance of probabilities having regard to the severity of the allegation being made – Giri [2015] EWCA Civ 784). Giri also shows, however, that the more serious the allegation, the more cogent the evidence supplied in support of it must be in order to make good an allegation that can have serious consequences for a person's future. Evidence of 'sufficient strength and quality' is required, having appropriate regard to 'inherent probabilities'; see also Shen [2014] UKUT 236 (IAC).
- The SSHD must put applicants on notice of the precise terms of a dishonesty allegation being made against them to give them a proper opportunity to respond: this may require a "minded to refuse" letter before any final decision is notified: Balajigari [2019] EWCA Civ 673.
- It is difficult to see that the common law rule against self-incrimination could operate here: Walile [2022] UKUT 17 (IAC) makes the point that this relates to self-incrimination in the course of legal proceedings, not administrative applications
- Minor misrepresentations can be overlooked. As the guidance cited in Neshanthan [2017] UKUT 77 (IAC) puts it:

    Minor representations which have no bearing on the case can be ignored as long as the passenger is generally acceptable for their purpose of entry.

- The President explains in Muhandiramge [2015] UKUT 675 (IAC), that decisions in general refusal reason cases where dishonesty is alleged involve a "*moderately complex exercise*" in which "*the evidential pendulum swings three times and in three different directions*". To quote more of his evocative words directly:

    (a) First, where the Secretary of State alleges that an applicant has practised dishonesty or deception in an application for leave to remain, there is an evidential burden on the Secretary of State. This requires that sufficient evidence be adduced to raise an issue as to the existence or non-existence of a fact in issue: for example, by producing the completed application which is prima facie deceitful in some material fashion.
    (b) The spotlight thereby switches to the applicant. If he discharges the burden - again, an evidential one - of raising an innocent explanation, namely an account which satisfies the minimum level of plausibility, a further transfer of the burden of proof occurs.
    (c) Where (b) is satisfied, the burden rests on the Secretary of State to establish, on the balance of probabilities, that the Appellant's prima facie innocent explanation is to be rejected.
    A veritable burden of proof boomerang!

- DK and RK India [2022] UKUT 112 (IAC) rejects the notion that the burden of proof switches between the parties: the burden is assigned by law at the outset of proceedings. It might be judicially convenient to consider the matter in stages but that did not mean the burden moved between the parties. As of early 2022 most immigration practitioners were comfortable with the thinking in Muhandiramge and will have to digest the implications of DK and RK with care.

English language fraud refusals

One of the most common general refusal reasons involving dishonesty in recent years was in relation to proof of English language proficiency. A major provider of the TOEIC (Test of English for International Communication), Educational Testing Service Limited (ETS), reopened many of its test results following a television exposé of large-scale cheating. It consequently cancelled many thousands of results. When the SSHD learned of this in individual cases, decision makers invoked the ETS decision as evidence of dishonesty or deception, using the general refusal reasons where they were available, or relying on their equivalents within the Suitability criteria within Appendix FM. It has been said that there might have been 40,000 TOIEC fraud decisions made.

Very large numbers of these cases have proceeded to appeal or JR hearings. The available arguments have been set out in a series of cases:

- Gazi (IJR) [2015] UKUT 327 (IAC) points out were numerous inadequacies in the ETS fraud detection process
- SM and Qadir [2016] UKUT 229 (IAC): the ETS fraud detection process, whilst imperfect, is sufficiently reliable for the SSHD to treat it as raising a prima facie case of dishonesty. Once a migrant is cogently linked to a suspect test record, they must then answer that prima facie case with a reasonable amount of plausible detail including accurate recollection of the reasons for their choice of test centre and events on the day of the test, and other supporting evidence such as evidence of good character – if they fail to do so, then the SSHD will have discharged the overall burden of proof and the allegation of dishonesty will be upheld
- Iqbal [2017] EWHC 79 (Admin): the SSHD must disclose the "ETS look-up tool" linking the person whose honesty is challenged with a declaration of invalidity by ETS: if she fails to do so, then she will not have discharged the burden of proof of raising a prima facie case of dishonesty.
- MA Nigeria [2016] UKUT 450 (IAC): the evidence from ETS would probably suffice to win the day for the SSHD unless a good evidence-backed case was put in response. Any evidence of English language proficiency had to be relevant to the migrant's skills at the date of the test which was subsequently invalidated. Language skills might well have changed by the date of a hearing years later.
- Much of the criticism of the SSHD's and ETS's processes must now be read in the light of DK and RK India [2022] UKUT 112 (IAC). This decision makes challenges to TOEIC fraud allegations backed by ETS very difficult. The expert evidence indicated that there were two stages at which the procedures might malfunction: in determining whether a proxy had taken the test in question (ETS used software to identify suspiciously similar voice files, those cases then being analysed by its own staff), and then within the chain of custody linking the applicant to the impugned file. The UT found that either scenario was very unlikely. The HO evidence was amply sufficient to discharge the burden of proof and required a response from anyone who test result was attributed to a proxy. Akter & Ors [2022] EWCA Civ 741 confirms DK should be considered authoritative on these points.

Now there is Guidance *Educational Testing Service (ETS): casework instructions* which provides:

- It pursues 2 objectives identified in a *Written Ministerial Statement of 23 July 2019*:
  - it is necessary to balance 'a belief that deception was committed some years ago against other factors that would normally lead to leave being granted, especially where children are involved'
  - it is necessary to 'update operational guidance to ensure no further action is taken in cases where there is no evidence an ETS certificate was used in an immigration application'
- Where the ETS review showed a test result was "invalid", decision making should proceed on the basis of dishonesty being established
- But if the result was "questionable", an interview should have been conducted or an opportunity to retake the test given: if there was clear evidence that the latter opportunity was not taken up or answers at interview were not credible, dishonesty should be taken as established; if there was no interview around the time, or an English language test had been successfully retaken, the allegation should not be pursued
- ILR should not be refused if LTR/PTS had been granted since the issue arose
- Clearly unfounded certification was not appropriate unless there was strong evidence of deception (eg via a criminal conviction or finding in Tribunal proceedings) (absent other reasons justifying certification)
- There should be a minded to refuse stage if the dishonesty allegation was to be pursued in the face of an immigration application, unless there had been an independent judicial finding
- Successful appeals would normally proceed on the 5-year or 10-year settlement route

- Unsuccessful appellants failing on ECHR grounds but where the deception allegation was not established should receive six months LOTR to give an opportunity to make a further immigration application or leave the UK

Top Tips

NON-DISCLOSURE OF CONVICTIONS

Refusal for dishonesty often follows where a previous conviction has not been disclosed. Do bear in mind that in these cases there can be a double reason to refuse:

- the fact of the conviction
- dishonesty in withholding the fact of the conviction, which is itself a false representation

Application forms make it very clear indeed that any relevant convictions should be disclosed. Nevertheless, as we have seen above, a credible innocent mistake may be forgiven, as it will not exhibit the relevant dishonesty required by the case law.

It will be readily appreciated that the more sophisticated the migrant and their application, and the more glaring the omitted criminality, the more difficult it will be to maintain a case of innocent error: it is important to critically interrogate the instructions you are given regarding the surrounding circumstances and the state of mind of the applicant to ensure that the case is put in the best light.

ALLEGATIONS OF FORGERY

Where there is an allegation made that a document is false backed by an enquiry of the issuing institution, it is very difficult to rebut that allegation without making one's own enquiries of the institution. This should be done independently of the migrant client, whose credibility is in dispute: if they produce a further document themselves then a decision maker can simply say 'But you have already produced a document which the issuing institution says is forged'.

Further enquiries should go via the legal representative to the institution. Then it will not be open to the Respondent to discount the enquiries only because they are produced by the very person whose honesty is disputed.

2.3.5.8 Previous breach of immigration laws grounds (mandatory bans) (9.8.1-9.8.4)

Past breaches of immigration laws are dealt with by a refusal regime based on periods for which there will be a mandatory ban on returning to the UK. The refusal provisions (9.8.1-9.8.2) are linked to a series of exclusion periods set out in the table at 9.8.7.

At the entry clearance and permission to enter stage, an application for EC/PTE:

- ***must*** be refused for previous breach of immigration laws and the application was made within the relevant re-entry ban period in 9.8.7 (9.8.1(a)&(b))
- ***may*** be refused for previous breach of immigration laws, where the application was made outside the relevant re-entry ban period but the applicant has previously contrived, in a significant way, to frustrate the intention of the rules or there are aggravating circumstances like failure to cooperate with redocumentation or enforcement processes (such as absconding or failing to report), or using a false identity (9.8.2(a)-(c)).
- So we can see that there is mandatory refusal for applications made *within* the ban periods, and discretionary refusal for applications *after* the ban has expired, essentially based on the existence of an ***aggravated*** breach

At the permission to stay stage, an application for PTS:

- ***may*** be refused where P previously failed to comply with conditions of permission, unless permission has previously been granted in knowledge of the previous breach (9.8.3)

Breach of immigration laws and overstaying disregards

A "*breach of immigration laws*" for these purposes (9.8.4(a)-(d))

- Applies only to conduct committed whilst an adult
- Includes overstaying, a breach of conditions which was not condoned by a subsequent grant of leave, being an illegal entrant, or using deception in relation to an application (whether successfully or not)

- The Rules at r6 define overstaying as remaining beyond your last permission granted, including any statutory extension of leave under s3C/s3D IA 1971.
- Overstaying will be disregarded where the person left the UK voluntarily and not at the SSHD's expense (9.8.5(a)-(c)):
  - For up to 90 days where the overstaying began before 6 April 2017; or
  - For up to 30 days where the overstaying began on or after 6 April 2017; or
  - Where r39E applies
- Overstaying will be disregarded where this arose from a refusal or cancellation decision which was later withdrawn, quashed or reconsidered by direction of a court or tribunal, so long as that legal challenge was lodged within 3 months of the decision (9.8.6)

Re-entry bans

Re-entry bans apply as follows, depending on the conduct of the person concerned (9.8.7(a)-(f)):

a) 12 months if they left voluntarily at their own expense
b) 2 years if they left voluntarily at public expense, *within* 6 months of the later event: being given notice of liability to removal, *or* of no longer having a pending appeal/admin review, whichever is later
c) 5 years if they left voluntarily at public expense, *more than* 6 months after the later event of being given notice of liability to removal, or of no longer having a pending appeal or AR
d) 5 years if they left or were removed from the UK as a condition of a caution under s22 Criminal Justice Act 2003 (unless any prohibition to return remains extant)
e) 10 years if they were removed at public expense
f) 10 years if they used deception in an EC application (including a visit visa)

The "public expense" removal provisions at 9.8.7(b)-(c) are triggered by **notice of liability to removal**. This is defined in the interpretation clause to the Rules at r6:

> *a notice given that a person is or will be liable for removal under section 10 of the Immigration and Asylum Act 1999, and for notices that pre-date the Immigration Act 2014 coming into force, refers to a decision to remove in accordance with section 10 of the Immigration and Asylum Act 1999, a decision to remove an illegal entrant by way of directions under paragraphs 8 to 10 of Schedule 2 to the Immigration Act 1971, or a decision to remove in accordance with section 47 of the Immigration, Asylum and Nationality Act 2006*

Beyond the refusal provisions, permission (including s3C leave) *may* be cancelled where a person has failed to comply with conditions of their permission (9.8.8). The Cancellation Guidance explains that

> *the breach must be of sufficient gravity to warrant such action. You must not cancel leave when the breach is so minor that it would mean cancellation would be disproportionate.*

Previous HO guidance has pointed to other exceptions which it is not so easy to find in the current policies:

- Where the applicant has been accepted by UKVI as a victim of trafficking (RFL5.4)
- Where the applicant was in the UK illegally on or after 17 March 2008 and left the UK voluntarily (i.e. without being removed) before 1 October 2008 (RFL5.4)

Contriving to frustrate

The concept of contriving to frustrate the Rules (previously r320(11), now r9.8.2) was at one time explained in the Entry Clearance Guidance which listed the forms of 'service and support' which the Rules targets: various kinds of benefits, tax credits, gaining employment and accessing goods or services. Aggravating circumstances are specified: e.g. absconding, not complying with reporting conditions, recourse to NHS treatment to which one is not entitled, using false identities, involvement in sham marriages and vexatious attempts to avoid removal.

In Azerkane [2020] ECHR 380 the ECtHR reiterated its view that unlimited bans on re-entry were likely to be disproportionate than finite ones.

Many overstayers depart the UK rather than pursue lengthy legal proceedings here in order to try and return via the entry clearance route, so putting their immigration history into a better light. There is a danger that over-reliance on this Rule could undermine the public policy to encourage such departures. The UT made this point in PS India [2010] UKUT 440 (IAC), explaining that the HO should be careful when refusing applications from abroad from former overstayers to avoid discouraging compliance with the entry clearance route.

2.3.5.9 Failure to provide required information, etc (9.9.1-9.9.2)

An application for EC/PTE/PTS *may* be refused (9.9.1), and EC or permission held *may* be cancelled (9.9.2), where the applicant fails without reasonable excuse to comply with a reasonable requirement to be interviewed, provide information or biometrics, undergo a medical test or provide a medical report.

NB: the failure to provide biometrics, for application refusals, can be in relation to biometrics requested otherwise than in relation to the application (9.9.1(c)).

The Guidance *Suitability failure to provide required information, attend interview* reminds decision makers to determine whether a requirement was clearly reasonable based on the natural and ordinary meaning of the words, bearing in mind the likelihood that the applicant was aware of the requirement, how long they were given to comply and whether they requested an extension, their awareness of failing to comply (including any warning), their future ability to comply, and any reasonable excuse such as serious transport disruption, or medical issues. There are express limitations on medical examinations, which are not permitted for the purpose of establishing pregnancy or to elicit proof of relationships via DNA.

2.3.5.10 Admissibility to the Common Travel Area or other countries (9.10.1-9.10.2)

An application for EC/PTE/PTS *may* be refused if the applicant seeks to enter the UK with a view to travelling to another part of the CTA but does not satisfy the decision maker that they will be admitted there (9.10.1).

An applicant for EC/PTE/PTS *may* be refused if they fail to satisfy the decision maker that they are admissible to another country following their UK stay (9.10.2).

2.3.5.11 Debt to the NHS (9.11.1)

An application for EC/PTE/PTS *may* be refused where the HO has been notified of an outstanding NHS debt of at least £500.

There is bespoke Guidance: *Suitability: Debt to the NHS*.

- The level of cumulative NHS debt justifying refusal was £1,000 from 1 November 2011 to 6 April 2016. So where the applicant has accumulated debt of less than £1,000 before 6 April 2016, they should only be refused where further debts >£500 have accumulated since that date
- A person may have an NHS debt if they have received secondary healthcare (ie healthcare provided to the person by a hospital
- NHS bodies use their own internal processes to recover the debt and will only notify the HO once the debt has been outstanding for 2 months and there is no agreement to pay by instalments: the HO must have confirmation from a NHS body of the debt

CHAPTER 2: General Requirements of the Rules; Introduction to Guidance

- Decision makers should contact applicants to give them 10 days to confirm whether the debt has been paid (via receipts from the healthcare provider). "Recently discharged" debts are those paid within the last 6 months: in those cases the decision maker should consider whether paying off the debt may impact on the ability to meet the maintenance and accommodation requirements of the Rules
- If the application suggests that secondary healthcare may have been received but no charge was imposed, the case should be referred to the Interventions and Sanctions Directorate
- Decision makers must consider whether there are **compelling or compassionate circumstances** or **human rights considerations** that would make refusal disproportionate, and whether the applicant's true intention when previously applying for leave was to gain free access to chargeable healthcare. In general human rights arguments should be pursued via a human rights application
- Details of the actual medical treatment should not have been passed on to the SSHD by the NHS body and should not be retained on file
- Dependants' applications linked to the current application may be refused due to their own NHS debt, but that of the principal applicant should not be refused on NHS grounds

The UKVI Guidance *NHS debtors (version 6.0)* was found unlawful in MXK [2023] EWHC 1272 (Admin) because it failed to clarify that the only basis for cancelling leave in relation to NHS debts was in the light of false representations or material non-disclosure. The Guidance *NHS debtors* seems to be rather broader however than those misdemeanours. It also specifically addresses procedures for visitors on multiple entry visas.

> **Example**
>
> Fatima wants to come to the UK as a Skilled Worker. Some years ago, she spent time in the UK as a student and had a baby here. The NHS hospital charged her £7,000 for the cost of maternity services, but she left the UK without fully paying the debt. She came to an agreement with the NHS to pay off the debt at £100 per month and the debt is nearly cleared. She explains this in her covering letter when making her visa application. The ECO ignores her agreement with the NHS, and without giving any additional reasons refuses her application under r9.11.1.
>
> By failing to consider the agreement between Fatima and the NHS, the ECO has failed to exercise their discretion (i.e. has failed to consider all the relevant circumstances before deciding to refuse the application on a discretionary ground). Her remedy is an administrative review, followed by a JR if necessary: she can argue in these challenges that the ECO has applied the Rules incorrectly.

2.3.5.12 Unpaid litigation costs grounds (9.12.1)

An application for EC/PTE/PTS *may* be refused where there has been a failure to pay litigation costs awarded to the HO. Litigation costs are likely to arise in JR proceedings and civil claims (eg for false imprisonment following a person's release from detention): if unsuccessful in a JR the claimant is usually required to pay the SSHD's legal costs. If a claim succeeds, then usually they are not required to pay costs. Claims often settle with an agreement to reconsider a decision, which may or may not include an offer to pay the other side's legal costs. The Order concluding the JR proceedings, from the UT or Administrative Court, will include any costs order.

2.3.5.13 Purpose not covered by the Immigration Rules grounds (9.13.1)

An application for EC/PTE/PTS *may* be refused where PTE/PTR is sought for a purpose not covered by the IRs: see *Suitability: Purpose not covered by the Immigration Rules*

2.3.6 Additional grounds available at the UK border

These grounds comprise section 3 of Part 9, headed "Additional grounds for refusal of entry, or cancellation of entry clearance or permission, on arrival in the UK". There is distinct guidance on cancelling permission at the port of entry: *Suitability: refusal of entry on arrival in the United Kingdom and cancellation of extant entry clearance or permission*. If initial checks flag up any concerns then appropriate standard checks will follow: on the Police National Computer, Border Force/UKVI internal systems such as CID and CRS, referral to the Port Medical Inspector, and interviews.

2.3.6.1 Lack of prior entry clearance (9.14.1)

PTE *must* be refused where entry clearance is required but the passenger is required to hold entry clearance but does not have it.

2.3.6.2 Failure to produce recognised passport or travel document grounds (9.15.1-9.15.3)

PTE *must* be refused if the passenger does not produce a passport or other travel document which satisfies the decision maker of their nationality and identity. Stateless persons or refugees may provide a travel document issued by another country than that of their nationality (9.15.1). See MIL 1.5.3 for HO discretion re identity documents.

PTE *may* be refused if the passenger produces a passport which (9.15.2):

- Was issued by a territorial entity or authority not recognised as a state or dealt with as such by the UK government (9.15.2(a)) (the Guidance lists passports from the Republic of China (Nationalist China – Taiwan), Somalia, Iraq (S-, M- and N- series passports), and South African temporary passports, and documents from Yemen (Royalist authorities) and Turkish Republic of Northern Cyprus)
- The UK does recognise ordinary Taiwanese passports and Palestinian Authority travel documents
- Was issued by a territorial entity or authority which does not accept UK passports for immigration purposes (9.15.2(b)); or
- Does not comply with international passport practice (9.15.2(c)).

EC or permission held *may* be cancelled where they fail, on arrival, to produce a passport or travel document meeting 9.15.1 or 9.15.2.

"Passport" is defined in r6 of the Rules, as a document which:

> (a) is issued by or on behalf of the government of any country recognised by the UK, or dealt with as a government by the UK, and which complies with international passport practice; and
> (b) shows both the identity and nationality of the holder; and
> (c) gives the holder the right to enter the country of the government which issued the document; and
> (d) is authentic and not unofficially altered or tampered with; and
> (e) is not damaged in a way that compromises the integrity of the document; and
> (f) is used by the rightful holder; and
> (g) has not expired.

2.3.6.3 Medical inspector's advice (9.16.1-9.16.2)

PTE *must* be refused if granting entry would be against the advice of a medical inspector, unless strong compassionate grounds justify admission (9.16.1).

EC or permission held *may* be cancelled if granting entry would be against the advice of a medical inspector (9.16.2).

2.3.6.4 Consent for a child to travel (9.16.1-9.16.2)

PTE *may* be refused to a child if travelling without a parent or guardian where the relevant adult fails to provide written consent on request.

2.3.6.4 Returning residents (9.18.1)

A person seeking entry as a returning resident *may* be refused PTE if they do not meet the requirements of r18, or that they do not seek entry for settlement. We address this area in detail in MIL at 4.1.3.

CHAPTER 2: General Requirements of the Rules; Introduction to Guidance

2.3.6.5 Customs breaches grounds (9.19.1-9.19.2)
PTE *may* be refused (9.19.1), and EC or permission held *may* be cancelled (9.19.2), for a customs breach, irrespective of whether criminal prosecution is pursued. In cancellation cases the Guidance suggests having regard to the non-conducive (character and conduct refusal grounds too).

This is defined by r6 as a breach of any provision of the Customs and Excise Acts or any other breach relating to an assigned matter (ie any matter where the Customs Commissioners or HMRC have a power or duty which the SSHD may exercise at the border).

The Guidance *Grounds for Refusal – Customs breaches* (Version 1.0; 1 December 2020) explains that these breaches may involve prohibited or restricted goods, or goods which infringe intellectual property rights or may fail to declare goods which exceed their duty-free allowances. They can include, but are not limited to the following:

- possession of prohibited substances, including Class C drugs, even if for personal use
- possession of prohibited items such as offensive weapons, obscene material, certain products of animal origin (POAO)
- non-declaration of duty-payable goods
- possession of large quantities of goods such as alcohol and tobacco products beyond what could reasonably be classed as for personal use or gifts
- driving a vehicle which has been adapted to conceal goods

Decision makers should consider whether it is proportionate to refuse entry. Relevant considerations are past behaviour, the volume of goods detected and the harm they pose, the person's intentions, whether the conduct was incidental to the journey or its sole motivation, UK ties and mitigating evidence such as coercion.

2.3.6.6 Change of circumstances or purpose grounds (9.20.1-9.20.2)
EC or permission held *may* be cancelled if there has been a sufficiently significant change in circumstances since EC or permission was granted (9.20.1). The example given in the Guidance *General grounds for refusal – Considering entry at UK port* (section 3, v29.0; 11 January 2018) is a person coming to work in the UK but the job offer being withdrawn.

EC/PTE *may* be cancelled on P's arrival if their purpose in entering the UK is different from that specified in their EC (9.20.3). This may arise from answers at interview or inferences may be drawn from a baggage search.

2.3.7 General refusal grounds for permission to stay cases only

These are found in section 4 of Part 9, titled Additional grounds for refusal, or cancellation, of permission to stay.

2.3.7.1 Rough sleeping in the UK (9.21.1-9.21.2)
PTS or any other permission held by P *may* be refused or cancelled where the decision maker is satisfied that P has been sleeping rough in the UK. The interpretation clause in the Rules at r6 explains:

"Rough sleeping" means sleeping, or bedding down, in the open air (for example on the street or in doorways) or in buildings or other places not designed for habitation (for example sheds, car parks or stations).

2.3.8 Route specific cancellation powers

These are found in section 5 of Part 9, titled Additional grounds for cancellation of entry clearance, permission to enter and permission to stay which apply to specified routes. Scale-up workers are subject to the cancellations for sponsor-related failings only during their initial 6 months of sponsorship (9.33.1).

2.3.8.1 Ceasing to meet requirement of the rules (9.23.1)
EC or permission held *may* be cancelled if the migrant ceases to meet the requirements of the rule under which it was granted.

2.3.8.2 Dependent grounds (9.24.1)
EC or permission held as a dependent *may* be cancelled if the principal's permission is cancelled.

2.3.8.3 Withdrawal of sponsorship or endorsement grounds (9.25.1-9.25.3)
EC or permission held *may* be cancelled where sponsorship or endorsement is withdrawn. This possibility is relevant to those migrants who must have sponsors or endorsing bodies: Students; Child Student; Skilled Worker; Intra-Company Transfer; Intra-Company Graduate Trainee; Representative of an Overseas Business; T2 Minister of Religion; Sportsperson, Temporary Worker); Start-up; Innovator; or Global Talent, Global Mobility and Scale-up (9.25.1). Where a Global Talent migrant used a prestigious prize instead of endorsement to gain EC or PTS, and the prize is withdrawn, this *may* also be cancelled (9.25.3). Failing to undergo a Contact Point meeting is a general refusal/cancellation provision for Innovator Founders (r9.25.4).

Permission held by a Student *may* be cancelled where sponsorship is withdrawn due to a failure to attain Level B2 in speaking, listening, reading and writing English following a pre-sessional course (9.25.2).

The Skilled Worker guidance explains that if the applicant's sponsor loses its licence while the application is under consideration, the SSHD has a duty to inform the applicant promptly (as per Pathan [2020] UKSC 41 MIL 2.6).

2.3.8.4 Student does not start course or ceases to study (9.26.1)
EC or permission held by a Student or Child Student *may* be cancelled if

- they do not start, or cease, to study
- if the course start date is delayed by over 28 days or
- if they or their sponsor confirm that the course will cease before the CAS end date (9.26.1(a)-(d)).

The Guidance indicates that cancellation of permission for early course finishes should be to the new end of the course plus any additional period of wrap-up that was originally given.

2.3.8.5 Worker does not start work or ceases their employment (9.27.1)
EC or permission held by a Skilled Worker, person on the Intra-Company routes, Representative of an Overseas Business, T2 Minister of Religion, Sportsperson or Temporary Worker, Global Mobility and Scale-up (during their sponsorship period), *may* be cancelled if

- they do not start, or cease, to work for their sponsor
- the CoS start date for the job is delayed by over 28 days; or
- they or their sponsor confirm that the work has ceased or will cease before the CoS end date

The Guidance indicates that cancellation of permission to 60 days will be appropriate in these cases absent an aggravating factor.

2.3.8.6 Sponsor loses licence or transfers business (9.28.1)
EC or permission held by a Student, Child Student, Skilled Worker, person on the Intra-Company Routes, T2 Minister of Religion, International Sportsperson, Global Mobility, Scale-up (during their sponsorship period) or Temporary Worker *may* be cancelled if:

- Their sponsor has no licence; or
- The business is transferred to another business, institution or organisation which fails to apply for a sponsor license within 28 days of the transfer, or which is refused a licence, or the licence granted would not allow that business to issue a CoS/CAS to the migrant.

2.3.8.7 Change of employer (9.29.1)
Permission held in the routes Skilled Worker, person on the Intra-Company routes, T2 Minister of Religion, Sportspersons, Global Mobility, Scale-up worker (during their sponsorship period) or Temporary Worker *may* be cancelled for changing employer unless:

- They are a Government Authorised Exchange or Seasonal Worker and the change is authorised by the sponsor (9.29.1(a))
- The new employer sponsors them or the change is covered by TUPE Regulations (9.29.1(b))
- They are Sportspersons or a Temporary Workers: Creative or Sporting Worker and they are sponsored by a sports club and are being temporarily loaned to another club, to return to their sponsor; and such loans are specifically permitted by the relevant sports governing body; and the sponsor has made arrangements to continue to meet sponsor duties (9.21.1(c)(i)-(v))

2.3.8.8 Absence from employment (9.30.1)

Permission held in the routes Skilled Worker, Intra-Company, Representative of an Overseas Business, T2 Minister of Religion, T2 Sportsperson, Global Mobility, Scale-up worker (during their sponsorship period) or Temporary Worker *may* be cancelled if the individual is absent from work without pay or has their pay reduced for more than 4 weeks per calendar year, unless the absence is due to:

- Maternity, paternity or parental leave; statutory adoption leave;
- sick leave,
- assisting with a national or international humanitarian or environmental crisis if agreed by the sponsor; or
- taking part in lawful strike action
- performing jury service; or attending court as a witness (9.30.1(a)-(g)).

2.3.8.9 Change of job or lower salary rate (9.31.1-9.31.3)

Permission held in the routes Skilled Worker, Intra-Company, Representative of an Overseas Business, Minister of Religion, Global Mobility, Scale-up worker (during their sponsorship period) or T5 (Temporary Worker) *may* be cancelled in certain circumstances:

- Where the worker has changed jobs or receives a lower salary rate (so a salary rise is not caught, though the change must still be notified to the SSHD unless relating only to an annual increment or a temporary salary reduction permitted under the Sponsor guidance)
- Where a job loses its shortage occupation classification
- Where the job changes sufficiently that its SOC code changes (so a change in role within the same SOC code is fine) or
- A lower salary is received such that the going rate is no longer met, unless an exception applies. The exceptions are for:
  - A participant in a graduate training programme covering multiple roles who is changing SOC code within (or at the end of) that programme whose sponsor notifies the SSHD of the change of job and salary is protected from this (r9.31.2)
  - Salary drops due to permitted absences (r9.31.1)
  - For persons on the ICT route whose reduction is whilst they are abroad
  - For Skilled Workers who would nevertheless meet the 70 point requirement even after the change (r9.31.3). On 6 April 2021 r9.31.3(c) was amended to require the use of the same set of tradeable points (i.e. under the same option in the table at SW 4.2) to arrive at 70, to prevent sponsors reducing salaries below the level already assessed.
- A salary reduction coincides with a temporary reduction in the person's hours or a or phased return to work, for individual health reasons, so long as an occupational health assessment is provided and the reduction does not reduce the hourly rate in force for their last permission grant (9.31.3(d))

2.3.8.10 Endorsing body no longer approved (9.32.1)

EC or permission held as a Start-up, Innovator or Global Talent *may* be refused if their endorsing body ceases to be approved for endorsing migrants on the route on which P was endorsed.

Casework Tip

CONSIDERING A GENERAL REFUSAL CASE

When confronted by a possible general refusal scenario, bear in mind:

(1) Which general refusal reasons apply to the immigration route in question (r9.1.1)
(2) Are the refusals mandatory ("*must be refused*") or discretionary ("*may be refused*")?
(3) Are there any definitions in r6 or Part 9 that you should consider when determining whether the general refusal reason may bite in your particular case?

2.3.9 Cancellation of entry clearance/permission to enter or stay

Part 9 now includes cancellation within each of the paragraphs addressing particular scenarios. You can see whether a cancellation power is available by looking at the structure of each of the refusal grounds. Typically the 2nd paragraph of each ground addresses cancellation. Section 5 of Part 9 is wholly focussed on cancellation powers - all the scenarios covered there involve some material change of circumstances. As already noted, the term "cancellation" now generally replaces "curtailment", though the latter is still used in Appendix EU.

There is specific guidance *Cancellation and curtailment of permission*. It explains

- Typically permission will be cancelled such that 60 days remain. This is the case where cancellation is discretionary, where the matters are outside the migrant's control: as where a Sponsor loses their licence for reasons with which the migrant is not knowingly involved, or where a college does not run a course, or where a relationship breaks down without the settled spouse suffering domestic violence
- Immediate cancellation will be appropriate for
    - Knowing involvement in the matters underlying the decision: eg complicity with the actions leading to a Sponsor's loss of licence, or using fraud to obtain entry to the UK or involvement in a sham marriage
    - Serious non-compliance, such as being dismissed from one's job due to one's gross misconduct, or failing to find a new Sponsor within 60 days of the original employer stopping trading
    - Posing some risk of harm, as where a relationship has ended due to domestic violence committed by the migrant
- The cancellation process cannot be used to bestow further leave beyond that originally granted: so where there are less than 60 days' remaining, the period of leave left extant will also have to be less than 60 days
- Whilst decisions should be made on the available information "*in the majority of cases*", nevertheless "*it may be appropriate for you to ask an individual to provide additional information*" eg a letter from an appropriately qualified medical professional such as a NHS consultant
- "*You must establish the relevant facts and then carefully consider all an individual's relevant circumstances and the proven facts of the case before you make a final decision*": facts may be gleaned from the application or be stored on case files or on the electronic GCID records
- The existence of exceptional or compassionate circumstances is relevant: though it may be appropriate to expect the individual to make an application for an alternative form of leave to accurately reflect their circumstances
- Where there are exceptional compassionate circumstances due to pregnancy or a serious illness or medical condition (being in critical care or a coma are the examples given), or due to a child's welfare (eg completing exams) or because an individual would otherwise be left in a vulnerable position, decision makers should consider whether they should use discretion to grant more than 60 days extra PTS. Relevant considerations are whether the individual is fit to travel by any realistic means (bearing in mind the possibility of reasonable forward planning), how soon they can travel and whether they can reasonably be expected to make an application in a more appropriate immigration category
- Kumar [2023] EWHC 1741 (Admin) looks at cancellation powers for failing to comply with the examination and interview process. The arrivee was entitled to be fully aware of the issues concerning the decision maker and to the presence of a qualified lawyer at any substantive interview addressing cancellation. Permission could be cancelled only if the step with which

compliance was sought was objectively reasonable, and if the excuse for failing to comply was objectively evaluated.

2.3.10 Revocation of ILR

The NIAA 2002 at s76 makes specific provision for revoking ILR (including EUSS). In particular where

- They are liable to deportation but cannot be deported for legal reasons (typically where ECHR Art 3 or ECHR Art 8 prevent a person's removal)
- The leave was obtained by deception
- Where the Refugee Convention's cessation provisions kick in (MIL 8.7)

The Guidance Revocation of indefinite leave – section 76 explains that revocation decisions will

- Take account of any impact on a child particularly from "*official or independent*" sources
- Be preceded by a '*minded to revoke*' notification letter giving the person 20 working days to respond (at which point any allegation of dishonesty must be expressly notified) – the reply is not to be treated as a human rights claim as no removal action will necessarily ensue
- Where dishonesty is alleged, bear in mind that deception can include intentional misrepresentation or omission of the facts, making false representations, or submitting false documents – it must have been material to the grant of leave and decision makers will assess the evidence on balance of probabilities
- Await the outcome of criminal proceedings where a prosecution is pursued (though an unsuccessful prosecution, which will have involved the criminal "beyond reasonable doubt" standard of proof) does not prevent a deception finding on balance of probabilities)

Consider whether revocation should proceed having regard to the passage of time since ILR was granted (particularly where deception was previously overlooked through oversight), the possibility of the deception being an innocent error, and whether the deception was previously expressly condoned by an earlier decision maker or whether the surrounding facts were downplayed, and the vulnerability of the migrant: eg serious mental health issues, or being a victim of human trafficking or domestic violence

2.3.11 Remedies regarding the general refusal reasons

Of course, unless there is a refusal of a human rights or asylum claim, there will be no right of appeal: the only remedies will be administrative review or JR. A repeat application putting the full case at its highest is often the best option. A decision maker must properly consider any explanation for previous conduct deemed deceptive: Naidu [2016] EWCA Civ 156.

Appeals under the 'relevant provisions' of the NIAA 2002

The general refusal reasons often feature in appeals (MIL 14.4.6).

There is no direct avenue in these appeals to review the adverse exercise of discretion. In human rights appeals, general refusal issues will be relevant in assessing the public interest side of the balance when assessing proportionality. Presumably a mandatory refusal reason will carry more weight than a discretionary one.

Sometimes an appellant seeks to 'clear their name' of an allegation of impropriety to maintain a good immigration history for the future, even if they recognise that their appeal cannot succeed on its merits. Various points arise:

- If the decision letter raises issues that touch on the general refusal reasons without expressly citing them, the judge may consider them, subject to fairness (MO *Ghana* [2007] UKAIT 00014)

- Where factors were known to a decision maker which might have led to their use, but they do not take the point, the judge is entitled to presume that they are not relevant: RM India [2006] UKAIT 00039

Administrative review

The *Administrative Review* guidance explains that:

> *Administrative review is available both if the alleged error could have made a difference to the original decision or could have an unfair impact on the applicant's future applications, for example because they may now be refused on general grounds.*

So, a refused migrant may wish to use administrative review (MIL 14.7) to clear their name of allegations of misconduct relevant to the general refusal reasons even though they may recognise that their application is doomed to fail for other reasons. Although only some of the general refusal reasons are mentioned as case working errors at Appendix AR AR.2.11(a), any general refusal can be challenged given AR2.11(c):

> *Where the original decision maker otherwise applied the Immigration Rules incorrectly.*

Where there is no human rights or asylum refusal, and administrative review fails, then JR will be the only option (MIL 14.8).

2.4 Policies, concessions and Operational Guidance

Knowledge of policies and concessions is an important part of an immigration lawyer's arsenal. Many concessions from the past have now been withdrawn or incorporated into the rules (for example, there was once a 'seven years' child concession' which was, for non-British citizen children, rather similar to what is now found in section 117B(vi) of the NIAA 2002, and in Appendix Private Life and the Appendix FM exception at Ex.1).

There are different kinds of guidance.

- There are 'concessions' which effectively create alternative residence routes outside the IRs altogether (e.g. the carers policy) – we deal with these in Chapter 4.
- There is guidance that explains how particular IRs or the EEA Regulations will be operated and interpreted in practice: there is an ever-growing set of guidance of this kind. Indeed now virtually every part of the Rules has its own associated guidance. For example, the Immigration Staff Guidance Appendix FM Section 1.0b is where one would find definitions of concepts within the IRs such as 'insurmountable obstacles' (we deal with this guidance alongside the Rules in question in the following chapters). As was said in Sultana [2014] UKUT 540 (IAC), writing of the Immigration Directorate Instructions:

  > provided their terms are consistent with the provisions of the IRs to which they relate, they may, potentially, fulfil a further role, namely that of illuminating the rationale and policy underpinning the relevant Rules

- There is guidance that explains the procedures and processes by which an application will make its way through the system (for example, there is a detailed explanation of the way in which applications from the destitute will be deal with in the fee waiver guidance which is at time of writing located in Immigration Staff Guidance, Other cross-cutting guidance)
- There is guidance that has special force because it is *statutory guidance*: it is issued to explain the approach that will be taken to implementing a particular statutory duty. An example is Every Child Matters – Change for Children which contains very important material explaining how section 55 of the Borders, Citizenship and Immigration Act 2009 (which creates a duty to safeguard and promote the welfare of children in immigration cases) should be approached.

CHAPTER 2: General Requirements of the Rules; Introduction to Guidance

The special value borne by statutory guidance was noted in Medical Justice [2017] EWHC 2461 (Admin) §141
- There is guidance which summarises particular immigration routes and processes: this is essentially a guide for the use of unrepresented migrants (for example there is an overview of the Student visa requirements and process).

The majority of policies and concessions can be located in one or more of the collections below, which comprise sets of instructions to HO caseworkers, Immigration Officers and Entry Clearance Officers – now found on the GOV.UK website under the title Operational Guidance. These collections are broken down as follows:

- **Asylum guidance**: previously called the 'Asylum Policy Instructions' and the 'Asylum Process Guidance': guidance to HO staff dealing with asylum cases. Covers screening and routing, asylum support, children, detention and reporting, decision making, country information, appeals, and voluntary departures.
- **Immigration staff guidance**: guidance, mainly for HO caseworkers making decisions on non-asylum in-country applications, and for guidance which cuts across whole arenas of immigration law applications, e.g. the Other cross-cutting guidance which addresses topics such as administrative review, s3C leave, and various appeal-related policies. Includes many current policies and concessions, sometimes in the annexes, on a wide range of issues connected with immigration applications.
- **Entry Clearance Guidance (ECG)**: these comprise instructions to ECOs on how to interpret the IRs and assess applications. Much of the guidance to ECOs has now been put into the Immigration Staff Guidance collection, particularly where it overlaps with the HO policies on similar applications made from within the UK.
- **Enforcement** guidance – formerly Enforcement Guidance and Instructions (EIG): formerly known as the Operation Enforcement Manual – these are instructions to Immigration Officers carrying out removals and other enforcement action. The sections on bail and detention are useful. The chapters of the manual were renumbered, rendering references to specific chapters in case law obsolete.
- **European Casework Instructions (ECI)**: This guidance has now been moved to the Immigration Staff Guidance.
- **Nationality Guidance** – formerly Nationality Instructions (NIs): for nationality applications

These documents, voluminous and regularly updated, are vital tools in the armoury of the immigration adviser. These days they include a section "Changes from last version of this Guidance" which should itemise the important new elements. They outline most of the processes undertaken by the Home Office to control migration. They allow the adviser to step into the shoes of the Home Office decision maker to see, for example, how an application will be assessed against the IRs. Where the guidance is helpful to a case, it should be quoted in the covering letter or representations, and on appeal or JR.

These are very large documents and are frequently altered, so there is little point in keeping a hard copy: indeed it is positively dangerous to presume that the same policy matrix is in place when you next make an application as when you last acted for someone in that situation.

It is not easy to find exactly where the individual Guidance documents exist within the Operational Guidance section of the GOV.UK website, or even to know that they exist at all. Sometimes, they do not exist within a collection, so are impossible to locate from within the website itself. It may be easier to carry out an internet search on them – using the search term 'UKVI guidance + subject matter'.

You may want to create a library within your firm of particularly useful policies when you cite them in your casework (they can be saved onto a hard-drive as PDF files) – they may alter or sometimes disappear before your client's application is finally decided. You may be able to find a policy prevailing at a particular time. But you'll need to recall or ascertain its location within the structure of the historic Home Office website. The snapshots provided by the UK Government Web Archive show the contents of the Home Office website at particular times. Also the *Internet Wayback Machine* allows you to track old recurrences of a particular web address. You can subscribe (here) to a daily HO email service which informs you when guidance has been updated.

2.4.1 The relationship between rules and guidance

Always remember that guidance is neither law nor rule. Where it is inconsistent with the Rules, the Rules take priority. An advisor who relies on guidance paraphrasing the Rules *may* be cruising for a bruising encounter with the courts or Tribunals. This is particularly the case where the guidance simply summarises a particular part of the Rules for convenience. If guidance clearly and deliberately sets out a departure from the Rules then the HO may be bound by it. Nevertheless, the IRs are the complete legal code that applies to all applications, and for advisers it is the rules that need to be considered first and foremost. The guidance, though useful sometimes to help explain what the Rules mean, is not always accurate, up to date or comprehensive. If your client fits into a published interpretation of the Rules, it may suit you to rely on it, and if you obtain a favourable decision from the HO, all well and good. But you should always be aware of whether the source you are citing is consistent with the IRs or indicating a departure from them.

Alvi [2012] UKSC 33 explains the approach that must be taken by the Secretary of State in making changes to the regulation of immigration control, addressing the criteria that can be put into the Rules, as opposed to being located in informal guidance. It largely upholds the earlier decision of Pankina [2010] EWCA Civ 719. This is what people refer to as Pankina or Alvi principle. The judges say slightly different things, but Lord Dyson sums it up at [94]:

> a rule is any requirement which a migrant must satisfy as a condition of being given leave to enter or leave to remain, as well as any provision 'as to the period for which leave is to be given and the conditions to be attached in different circumstances' (there can be no doubt about the latter since it is expressly provided for in section 3(2)). I would exclude from the definition any procedural requirements which do not have to be satisfied as a condition of the grant of leave to enter or remain. But it seems to me that any requirement which, if not satisfied by the migrant, will lead to an application for leave to enter or remain being refused is a rule within the meaning of section 3(2).

And he added at [97]:

> all those criteria which are or may be determinative of an application for leave to enter or remain.

A series of cases were decided in the period between Pankina and Alvi which found that particular species of requirements were either properly dealt with in Guidance or should have been put into the Rules.

Further appendices have been added over time. This incorporation into the rules of what was previously guidance makes it all the more important that the rules are read and followed with extreme care. Happily modern routes increasingly feature more relaxed evidence requirements (MIL 7.1.1).

Top Tip

As we have seen above, when identifying an immigration route under the rules, there are always several places to look:

- The Immigration Rule in force at the time you are planning an application (or as at the date of decision when considering appeals and other remedies)
- Any definition of a word or concept within the Rules – this may be found in the general definitions in Rule 6, or in the introductory part of the relevant category
- Any Home Office policy – this may usefully explain or interpret the intended operation of the rule, and may additionally provide some leeway outside the Rule's strict confines – you may find these in the Operational Guidance, this Manual, or on the Refugee Legal Group, or on the ILPA website

2.4.2 Failing to follow a policy or promises

The Home Office cannot operate a policy that is stricter than the IRs. This is because it is the Rules that have the authority of parliamentary approval, as shown by the Pankina/Alvi litigation. However the HO may operate policies that cover situations not dealt with under the IRs, and thus may seem more generous than the Rules (so long as they do not directly conflict with them).

- In Pankina it was held that the policy guidance is, being guidance rather than rule, something that lacks the fixed status of law, and must therefore be interpreted sensibly and flexibly
- Munir [2012] UKSC 32 establishes that the HO was not required to consider a case under a policy which had been withdrawn by the decision date. Even where the migrant would have qualified under the policy as at the date it was withdrawn. Nor was the HO required to put such a change of policy before parliament. This is subject to any transitional provisions which expressly protect applicants (MIL 2.1.2)
- Where an ECO or the HO fails to act on a policy *outside the rules*, there may be remedies available, even though the policy or concession is not the law as such (being neither primary nor secondary legislation). Nadarajah [2005] EWCA Civ 1363 makes it clear that published policies should be followed unless there was a good justification for departing from them:

    > Where a public authority has issued a promise or adopted a practice which represents how it proposes to act in a given area, the law will require the promise or practice to be honoured unless there is good reason not to do so.

- We looked at legitimate expectations above (MIL 2.1.3). It will be hard to persuade a judge that a migrant has a legitimate expectation that the published law will be disapplied in their case. Thus in Emiantor [2020] EWCA Civ 1461 the appellant had been subject to deportation proceedings. These were discontinued whilst his appeal against a criminal conviction was pursued. He was released from detention. He had understood from the officials he dealt with that no deportation action would subsequently be initiated against him. The court found that it was inherently unlikely that the SSHD would have chosen to depart from the statutory duty to pursue automatic deportation procedures. A reasonable person would not think otherwise.

Challenging decisions involving policies

Arguments based on a failure to follow a relevant policy may be relied upon in various ways, depending on which remedies are available to a client. Whatever the route of challenge, the meaning of a policy is to be objectively established by the Tribunal or court that examines it – i.e. it should not simply be given the meaning that the HO attribute to it (though obviously on administrative review the HO is likely to adopt their favoured interpretation), see Lord Reed in Tesco Stores Limited v Dundee City Council [2012] UKSC 13

> policy statements should be interpreted objectively in accordance with the language used, read as always in its proper context

- If **administrative review** is available (MIL 14.7):
    - Failures to properly follow published policy can be challenged (AR2.11(d))
    - If the HO's administrative reviewer decides that there was a mistake made first time round, then they have options (AR.2.2):
        - They may withdraw the decision. A new decision will follow
        - Or they may maintain the decision, based on the same reasons, or they may withdraw one or more reasons, or they may add additional reasons: in the latter scenario there is a further right to administrative review
- If administrative review is not available, then **judicial review** is needed (MIL 14.8):
    - Failing to follow policy is a ground for JR as per Nadarajah cited above
    - Usually, this remedy will achieve no more than a reconsideration by the Secretary of State, properly applying the policy in question

- Very rarely, if a policy is expressed in absolute terms, the decision of the court may leave no real choice to the Home Office decision maker upon reconsideration
- If **an appeal is available** (because a human rights claim has been refused) (MIL 14.1):
  - In modern appeals there is no ground of appeal based on decisions being "*not in accordance with the law*". So it's human rights or nothing: Charles [2018] UKUT 89 (IAC)
  - Under this system, in determining a human rights ground of appeal, the Tribunal should take the policy into account in deciding whether or not an interference with private and family life is proportionate. As it was put in AG Kosovo [2007] UKAIT 00082:

    'a judicial decision-maker has to take into account any applicable policy, because if the policy itself 'tells in favour of the person concerned being allowed to stay in this country' it is a factor that has to be incorporated into an assessment of the argument going to the importance of immigration control'

Example

Under the IRs, a person with 10 years of continuous lawful residence who is of good character may be granted settlement: see Rule 276B. However continuous residence is strictly construed and there may not be any breaks (beyond 28 day periods of overstaying, 276B(v), except for permitted absences abroad, not to exceed six months, where the migrant leaves and returns with valid leave, 276A(a)). The Home Office policy document Long Residence sets out that there is a discretion to grant leave outside the Rules where there were 'compelling or compassionate circumstances, for example where the applicant was prevented from returning to the UK through unavoidable circumstances'. If this discretion was not recognised in a decision letter, then:

- A JR should succeed, with the decision being quashed, leaving the application outstanding before the decision maker to be reconsidered

- Modern appeals lack an 'in accordance with the law' ground to rely on, and all arguments have to be packaged into the human rights ground of appeal. The most likely relevant human right argument will be (usually) by way of Article 8 ECHR. There the first question is whether the long residence establishes private life which will face interference if the person is required to leave the country. If so, the second question should be answered in the appellant's favour. As the policy outside the Rules would be, so long as it is accepted thatshows that the public interest does not require a minor overstay abroad to be held against someone: see AG Kosovo
- You can actually see this kind of thinking in OS Hong Kong [2006] UKAIT 00031, though in the context of an old version of the long residence policy

---

2.5 Statutory duty to safeguard children

As well as the rules and policies set out in the previous units, there is one very important statutory duty which runs across the whole of immigration control, and which aims to ensure that the best interests of the child are always kept at the centre of decision making.

This has been introduced to bring the HO into line with the UK's commitments under the UN Convention on the Rights of the Child (MIL 5.3.2)).

Section 55 of the Borders, Citizenship and Immigration Act 2009 introduced an obligation to make arrangements to ensure that immigration functions are discharged having regard to the need to safeguard and promote the welfare of children who are in the United Kingdom. In so doing the Act aligns the section 55 duty with that imposed on public authorities under the Children Act 2004, s11(2).

The duty applies to the Home Office and also to those performing immigration functions, broadly defined. It only applies to children present in the UK. However, this is not to say that child welfare considerations are irrelevant to decision making in entry clearance cases: as stated in the headnote of T Jamaica [2011] UKUT 483 (IAC):

Where there are reasons to believe that a child's welfare may be jeopardised by exclusion from the United Kingdom, the considerations of Article 8 ECHR, the 'exclusion undesirable' provisions of the IRs and the extra statutory guidance to Entry Clearance Officers to apply the spirit of the statutory guidance in certain circumstances should all be taken into account by the ECO at first instance and the judge on appeal.

By section 55(3), a person exercising any of the specified functions must, in so exercising them, have regard to any guidance given to the person by the Secretary of State for the purpose specified in BCIA 2009, s55(1). The statutory guidance *Every Child Matters: Change for Children* was issued in November 2009. It explains that the s55 duty requires:

ensuring that children are growing up in circumstances consistent with the provision of safe and effective care; and undertaking that role so as to enable those children to have optimum life chances and to enter adulthood successfully;

having regard to their 'physical, intellectual, emotional, social and behavioural development' and their 'optimum life chances'; and their 'physical, emotional and educational needs' and 'the likely effect on [them] of any change in [their] circumstances'

Other important features of *Every Child Matters* as summarised in other UKVI documents are

- fair treatment which meets the same standard a British child would receive the child's interests being made a primary, although not the only, consideration
- no discrimination of any kind
- applications dealt with in a timely fashion
- identification of those that might be at risk from harm

The special value borne by statutory guidance was noted in Medical Justice [2017] EWHC 2461 (Admin) §141. There is an ongoing disagreement between the courts around the UK as to the importance of HO decision making having express regard to the statutory guidance. The Northern Ireland CoA is adamant that this is a failing that can seriously disadvantage children and that the Tribunal should do everything possible to rectify the problem in individual cases: CAO [2023] NICA 14.

None of this means that the rights of children are a trump card, however. Although the misdemeanours of parents should not be held against their children, the realities of the parents' immigration status must be given appropriate weight in decision making. If both parents are present unlawfully, the starting point is that the family should expect to return to their country of nationality: KO (Nigeria) [2018] UKSC 53.

Where children are affected by enforcement action (e.g. detention and removal), either directly or indirectly, the Office of the Children's Champion offers advice to UKVI decision-makers on the implications for the children's welfare, to enable an informed decision to be made giving due weight to their best interests. As far as the Home Office is concerned, neither the advice nor the best interests of the children need be determinative of the outcome of the case: but they must make a child's best interests a primary consideration.

The useful case of MK [2015] UKUT 223 (IAC) explains that:

- the duty does not have to be referenced in terms in decision letters, but it needs to have been given effect by the decision overall
- the Secretary of State should consider consulting children to ascertain their wishes and feelings in any given case
- whilst normally the Tribunal should consider s55 issues based on the material put before it, it may be necessary to seek further information from the migrant's side, such as expert medical (including mental health) reports, or from the Home Office side where they can be expected to have access to reports emanating from criminal proceedings or social services involvement, or where the views of children have not been sought
- Appeals and applications involving children should always be processed with the minimum of delay

The Safeguarding Advice and Children's Champion (SACC) offers specialist safeguarding and welfare advice on issues relating to children, including family court proceedings and complex child protection cases. Decision makers are advised to make a referral to the SACC whenever the facts of the case so demand, including where safeguarding issues arise within the family unit (see eg the *Revocation of protection status* guidance). Here is a typical *quarterly update on SACC processes*.

2.6 Fairness

Immigration law is an aspect of public law. So the Rules will always need to be interpreted in line with the common law's requirements of fairness. This includes issues such as receiving notice of a decision, having the opportunity to make representations before a decision is made on one's case by reference to an unexpected issue, and having a reasonable opportunity to discover facts relevant to one's application.

We set out most of the relevant authorities in one place at MIL 5.5.5 where we address generic proportionality issues in the context of private life. But these principles actually apply in all scenarios, not only where human rights are in play. To summarise the main points:

- One has to have notice of a decision for it be effective: Anufrijeva [2004] 1 AC 604 at §26-28
- Where the SSHD has made the wrong decision on someone's case (eg accusing them of dishonesty but where that allegation is subsequently withdrawn or judicially overturned), the SSHD should act creatively to put them back in the same position as they would have been in had the error never occurred: Ahsan [2017] EWCA Civ 2009 §120
- The SSHD should take account of any clearly established historic injustice in the way the individual or their community has been treated: Mousasaoui [2016] EWCA Civ 50
- If an individual is disadvantaged by a decision of the SSHD which misunderstands their application such as to put them on the wrong immigration route, arguably they should subsequently be treated no worse than if they had whatever relevant benefits that route offered: Musico [2020] EWCA Civ 1389
- Decision makers must interview applicants before refusing them on the basis of allegations of dishonesty, or due to serious concerns as to their character or conduct (see Balajigari MIL 2.3, 2.3.5.1), or due to matters which the applicant could not reasonably expect to be raised against them: see Tazeem [2023] EWHC 1828 (Admin) (& MIL example 3.5). Ambiguities in the interviewee's answers should be explored before an equivocal answer is treated as dishonest: Singh [2023] EWHC 2068 (KB)
- There is no absolute requirement for interviews to be recorded & transcribed. Absent a transcript, the best evidence of what transpired at interview is likely to be the manual note of interview plus any witness statement: Tazeem [2023] EWHC 1828 (Admin)
- It may be unfair not to offer access to the internet in order for an applicant to show their bank statements where the matter became relevant during their interview - De Aquino [2022] EWHC 2730 (Admin).
- The SSHD must notify an individual reasonably promptly of any matter that stands to defeat their application of which they could not reasonably be aware: Pathan [2020] UKSC 41 or over which the SSHD has exclusive control: Taj [2021] EWCA Civ 19, EK (Ivory Coast) [2014] EWCA Civ 1517. However this does not extend to notifying an applicant of an invitation to their sponsor to provide further information regarding the proposed role for which they are being sponsored: Topadar [2020] EWCA Civ 1525, nor to those who were overstayers when they applied: Ullah [2022] EWCA Civ 550
- Patel [2020] UKUT 351 (IAC) emphasises
  - **Historic** injustices (ie belated recognition by the UK authorities of wrongful immigration treatment in the past) are likely to have a profound or determinative effect in assessing a person's immigration position
  - **Historical** injustices which are clearly evidenced (case specific failings by the SSHD such as unreasonable delay in determining an application, failing to apply a relevant policy, or making a mistake as to the applicant's conduct) may be relevant to current decision making. Rahaman [2022] EWCA Civ 310 shows that perceived injustices arising from the natural workings of the historically inflexible PBS system don't make the grade.
- Ahmed [2023] UKUT 165 (IAC) looks at historical injustices in more detail. Some general observations were appropriate:

- It was likely that such injustice would start with a public law error by the HO
- Immigration functions would not have been unlawfully operated if case law had been properly applied even if subsequently overturned
- There must be evidence that the Appellant had suffered due to the wrongful operation of immigration functions: for example if a right of appeal had not been notified, it would need to be shown that there was an arguable prospect of the underlying appeal's success
- Taking steps to mitigate the injustice (such as seeking a new decision to generate a right of appeal) would be relevant to assessing the weight to be given the public interest: blaming the failures of legal advisors would not normally assist
- Beyond these scenarios there is very little scope to complain of unfairness. Increasingly the higher courts have emphasied that the common law requires *procedural* fairness but rarely protects *substantive* fairness in its own right: see eg Pathan [2020] UKSC 41 §154

CHAPTER 3: Visitors

3.1 Introduction to Visitors

The Visitors rules are now split up thus:

- Appendix V: Visitor
- Appendix Visitor: Permitted Activities
- Appendix Visitor: Visa national list
- Appendix Visitor: Permit Free Festival List
- Appendix Visitor: Transit Without Visa Scheme

The current rules are a little more relaxed than their predecessors with a view to compensating for the loss of EEA nationals' free movement rights. Now study for up to 6 months is permitted under the standard route, voluntary work of up to 30 days is permitted, students aged 16+ can receive research tuition, there is greater provision for academic visitors to conduct research on sabbatical, and international drivers can collect as well as deliver goods/passengers. Swiss nationals do not require entry clearance as marriage/civil partner (CP) visitors, and EEA and Swiss nationals may use their national ID cards as an alternative means to prove identity and nationality.

As at June 2023 applications take some 3 weeks to be decided.

3.2 Appendix V: Visitor

The introduction outlines the four types of visitor as being

1. Standard visitors who wish to undertake permitted activities
2. Marriage/civil partnership visitors, seeking to tie the knot or give notice to do so
3. Permitted Paid Engagement visitors, experts in their field coming for paid work for up to one month
4. Transit visitors, entering the UK for up to 48 hours en route to another country outside the CTA (unless the Transit Without Visa Scheme Appendix applies)

It reminds applicants that:

- They can only work if expressly allowed by Appendix Visitors: Permitted Activities.
- The maximum length of stay for each category is set out at V17.2.
- Multiple entry visit visas allow for staying in the UK for normally no more than 6 months at a time.

The Legal Framework

- Appendix V: Visitor
- Appendix Visitor: Permitted Activities
- Appendix Visitor: Visa national list
- Appendix Visitor: Permit Free Festival List
- Appendix Visitor: Transit Without Visa Scheme
- The Home Office guidance: Visit guidance, Considering human rights claims in visit applications, Transit guidance
- Guidance for applicants: marriage, permitted paid engagement, standard visitor visas, transit and ADS Agreement visits, Visiting the UK: guide to supporting documents

HO policy/guidance used to provide substantially more detail notice than now, and some of the older guidance may have useful things to say. Whilst it may no longer reflect HO policy, it will be hard for the HO to argue that older policy on substantially the same rules is no longer applicable.

3.2.1 General principles for visitors

Some general principles re the visit route:

- It is not possible to switch into a visit visa: exceptionally one can extend one's stay as a visitor
- Visa nationals require entry clearance. Included in the list of "visa nationals" (in Appendix Visitor: Visa national list) are nationals of countries listed in (a); stateless people (b); and those travelling on a document other than a passport (c). From 1 October 2021, there is a cross reference from (c) to rr11A&B in Part 1, to the effect that those covered by those paragraphs (EEA/Swiss nationals with certain types of status) can continue to enter the UK on their ID cards. Everyone else travelling on ID instead of a passport must apply for entry clearance.
- For nationals of Oman, Qatar, UAE and Kuwait, visa-free visits for up to six months are enabled via the Electronic Visa Waiver (EVW) scheme, which allows visa presentation at the border in electronic form (and a level of discretion regarding punctuation discrepancies with passports).
- A six-month visit visa costs £115
- Non-visa nationals may simply travel to the UK and then seek leave to enter as a visitor at the port of entry, unless seeking to visit for more than six months or visiting for the purposes of marriage of civil partnership, or of giving notice of such , but…
- Non-visa nationals *may* apply for a visa
- Each visitor in a group must fully satisfy the rules
- A visa will be valid, unless single or dual entry, for multiple uses during its lifetime (thus the term 'multiple entry' visa): it will usually be issued for six months. Where the person has built up a good immigration history, the HO may grant a long-term visit visa for two, five or 10 years, but which cannot be used for any single visit for more than six months. On each entry under a long-term visa, the person will be treated as having been granted leave to enter for six months (under the ILERO 2000).
- A different fee is payable according to the duration sought (2 years – £400, 5 years – £771, 10 years – £963). In a move to attract Chinese tourists to the UK, all standard visit visas issued in China will be valid for two years (but for no extra fee).

The route essentially works thus:

- There are provisions for entry, validity, eligibility and suitability, as typical of modern immigration routes
- There are a series of key requirements found in the **genuine visitor** provision V4.2: these are likely to be central to preparing an application and addressing refusals
- There are a series of additional eligibility requirements for various categories of visitor: for children, ADSA for Chinese tourists, private medical treatment, organ donation, short term study, academics coming for 6 months+, work related training, marriage/civil partnership, permitted paid engagements, transit, and also for visitor extensions
- There are then restrictions on what a visitor may do in the UK: found in the **prohibited activities and payment requirements** V4.4
- And there are numerous activities which are expressly permitted: found in Appendix Permitted Activities: V4.4 and this Appendix are likely to be the focus when advising individuals of their options when coming to the UK for a particular purpose

There is scope for the HO to take different approaches for applications from different countries, based on the perceived risk profile: this is done via the workflow routing process.

Non-visa nationals don't have to apply for a visit visa, of course. But it will be sensible for them do so if there is a risk they might be refused leave to enter on arriving in the UK without one. Thousands of individuals are refused entry to the UK each year. An up-front visa application can save the cost and frustration of travelling to the UK only to be held for several hours in the airport before being sent back home. However the ETA regime will eventually be rolled out for all nationalities (MIL 1.3.1.1).

Common refusal reasons at the port of entry include providing inadequate or inconsistent information; failing to convince the HO that they will leave the UK at the end of their visit, or not work here; or a lack of documentation addressing these issues. Where it can be predicted that a Border Force official may have such concerns, the visitor should be prepared to deal with them. A detailed letter from a representative explaining any issues of likely concern may help.

3.2.2 Entry, procedures and general refusal reasons

V 1.1-4 Entry requirements for visitors

Visitors require prior EC under V1.1. (and will otherwise be refused entry under V1.2) where the visitor is:

- A visa national as listed in Appendix Visitor: Visa national list, unless one of the exceptions in that Appendix applies or they are eligible under Appendix Visitor: Transit Without Visa Scheme
- Of any nationality (except Swiss) and applying in the marriage/CP visitor category
- Seeking to enter for over 6 months

V1.2 clarifies that visitors may enter the UK an unspecified number of times within the validity of EC granted, unless this was granted specifically as a singe or dual entry.

V1.3 provides that the following can apply for permission to enter at the border:

- Non-visa nationals (unless non-Swiss nationals coming to marry/enter into a CP or coming for more than 6 months)
- Visa nationals covered by an exception in the visa nationals appendix or entitled to transit without a visa.

Child visitors holding EC may be refused entry unless they travel with the person identified in their EC or hold EC stating they are unaccompanied. They may still be granted entry if adequate arrangements for travel reception and care have been made and their parent or legal guardian has provided consent (V1.4 read with V5.1&2)

V 2.1-6 Validity requirements for entry clearance or permission to stay as a visitor

V2.1-2 requires applications to be made:

- From outside the UK online on the specified form "Apply for a UK visit visa" (the old paper form is still here for reference) or,
- If applying in country to extend a visit visa Application to extend stay in the UK: FLR(IR)

Further validity requirements are that:

- The fee is paid and biometrics – as well as a passport or other document establishing nationality and identity - are provided (V2.3)
- EC applications are made to the relevant post abroad and PTS (permission to stay) applications are made by a person in the UK with a standard or marriage/CP visa (V2.4&5) (the Covid concessions permitted applications to be made from any visa application centre where the relevant one was closed due to coronavirus restrictions)

Where these requirements are not met, applications *may* be rejected and not considered (V2.6).

V 3.1-2 Suitability requirements for all visitors

These are not to

- fall for refusal under Part 9;
- be in breach of immigration laws unless r39E applies; or
- be on immigration bail (V3.1&2).

The Part 9 general refusal reasons (renamed Grounds for Refusal) which applying specifically to visitors (MIL 2.3 addresses the generic reasons):

- 9.4.4(a) EC applications *must* be refused where the applicant has been sentenced to 12 months of imprisonment anywhere, if they apply within 12 months of the end of the sentence.

- 9.4.4(b) EC applications *must* also be refused where the applicant was convicted of a criminal offence anywhere and received a non-custodial sentence or out-of-court disposal recorded on their criminal record, if the application is made within 12 months of that conviction

The 10-year re-entry ban for deception in previous applications in Part 9 r9.8.7(f) is now limited to entry clearance applications, expressly including visitor applications, as was previously the case in Appendix V's Suitability requirements at V 3.10(f)).

Other refusal or cancellation reasons under Part 9 also apply, and you should consult Module 2, section 2.3 Grounds for Refusal for further information.

V 4.1 (a)-(j) Eligibility requirements for visitors

All but transit visitors must meet the requirements in V4.2-6, plus other requirements for those applying: as a minor (V5.1&2); under the Approved Destination Status Agreement (V6.1); to receive private medical treatment (V7.1-3); as an organ donor (V8.1-4); to study as a visitor (V9.1&5); as an academic seeking EC for 12 months (V10.1); to receive work related training (V11.1-3); to marry/form a CP (V12.1&2); to undertake permitted paid engagements (V13.1-3) or if applying in-country for PTS (V15.1-4).

3.2.3 Genuine visitors

V 4.2.3 Genuine visitor requirement

The decision maker must be satisfied that the applicant will leave at the end of their visit and not live in the UK for extended periods or make the UK their main home through frequent or successive visits; that they will not undertake prohibited activities (V4.4-6); and that they have sufficient funds to cover all reasonable costs of their visit. "Reasonable costs" expressly include the cost of the return or onward journey, costs relating to dependants and planned activities (eg private medical treatment). Only funds held in financial institutions which meet FIN2.1 in Appendix Finance are taken into account (V4.2).

A third party who has a genuine professional or personal relationship with the visitor can provide sufficient funds for travel, maintenance and accommodation so long as this covers the duration of the visit and the third party is not in breach of immigration law at the time of decision or UK entry by the visitor (V4.3).

One of the most common reasons to come here is to visit family. The visit rules do not specify particular requirements for this class of visit. In Ahsrif 01/TH/3465, the Tribunal pointed out that:

> The whole point of a family visit is that the existence of family ties will normally furnish the reason for the visit, since it is hardly surprising that members of a family separated by many thousands of miles may from time to time wish to see each other.

Relevant factors in relation to intention include:

- The purpose or purposes of the visit (see Appendix Visitor: Permitted activities below)
- Immigration history: previous compliance with immigration laws is an excellent indicator of intention to leave – both regarding visits to the UK and elsewhere ('especially the USA, Canada, Australia, New Zealand, Ireland, Schengen countries or Switzerland' says the guidance). Where there have been previous breaches, evidence will need to be provided of a clear change in circumstances to allay the obvious concern.
- The immigration history and status of the sponsor, friend or relative that the person is visiting, or of such persons whom the HO may know to be in the UK, even where there is no stated intention to visit them
- Family links with own country, such as spouse, children, parents or relatives for whom the visitor is the usual carer
- Other links abroad, such as a job to return to or studies to complete

- Levels of income (it may be more difficult to suggest someone has a temptation to overstay if they earn an above average income in their own country, and where by doing so they would be exchanging that lifestyle for becoming an overstayer without the right to work). Watch out for the evidence supplied as to the availability of funds, because if bank statements do not dovetail with claimed earnings, the decision maker may be left doubtful as to whether they are being told the whole story
- Absence or otherwise of links in the UK – this could cut both ways, as having a sponsor is helpful, and having someone to visit provides a permitted purpose for the visit. On the other hand, if the family here has shown a 'pattern of immigration', some ECOs will suspect that, like them, the applicant will never leave. A failure to reveal the presence of a family member will be thought suspicious, and may give rise to an allegation of deception
- Whether a respectable applicant will seriously wish to exchange their life in the country of origin for what would effectively amount to being an outlaw in the United Kingdom, unable to work or study lawfully
- Whether documentary evidence can be verified
- Inconsistent information, e.g. discrepancies in the information provided by an applicant and statements made by their sponsor – the HO may contact sponsors to discuss the visit before the visit or upon the visitor arriving in the UK
- A search of the applicant's baggage

Also relevant as per the Visit guidance:

> the duration of previous visits and whether this was significantly longer than they originally stated on their visa application or on arrival – if this is the case, you should not automatically presume that the visitor is not genuine, but this may be a reason to question the applicant's overall intentions

The guidance does acknowledge that a person might 'extend their stay to do different permitted activities' from those they intended on entry. A person's intentions can change, but where they do, it will usually be sensible to explain to the HO why the visit was longer than expected.

Example

Don Juan applies for a visa to visit the UK, explaining that he is coming as a tourist to see the sights for a period of two weeks. He provides an outline and costed itinerary for his trip, evidence that he has the means to fund it, and a letter from his employer confirming that he is entitled to leave for two weeks. His application is successful and he is granted a visa for six months.

Shortly after arriving in the UK, he has a romance with a man he meets at a party, and cannot drag himself back home until six weeks have passed and the affair has run out of steam.

Having assessed his genuine intention to visit for a two-week holiday, the HO will be understandably miffed that he stayed for much longer. Next time he applies for a visit visa, they may suspect that that he lied to them about his intentions, his finances and his employment. He will need to explain why he stayed longer than intended, and how he was able to do so, given that the evidence he relied on in his earlier application all pointed towards a two-week holiday.

Another relevant factor is:

> whether, on the balance of probabilities, the information and the reasons for the visit or for extending their stay provided by the applicant are credible and correspond to their personal, family, social and economic background

This is self-explanatory. Where, on the facts of the case, this may be in issue, it may be sensible for the applicant to submit a detailed letter or statement explaining the purpose of the visit in detail, identifying any possible concerns, and rebutting them.

> **Example**
>
> Khadija, from Bangladesh, is in relatively low paid employment in her country, and her trip to the UK to see a friend is going to cost her six months of her normal salary. The HO may suspect that she has other intentions (e.g. to work in the UK and/or overstay).
>
> To improve her merits Khadija explains in a letter that she has been saving many years for this holiday, and provides evidence of a savings account into which she has deposited small sums over a long period of time. She also explains that she grew up with her friend, that they are particularly close, and her friend has family commitments in the UK which prevent her travelling to Bangladesh. She can also confirm that she fully understands the implications of breaching the immigration laws and does not want to prejudice any future visits by doing so. Her friend can also write a letter confirming the importance of their relationship and the difficulties she has in travelling to Bangladesh.

Frequent and successive visits

Para V4.2(b) states that the person 'will not live in the UK for extended periods through frequent or successive visits, or make the UK their main home'. This provision was initially added to the Rules following Sawmynaden [2012] UKUT 161 (IAC). She had spent 14½ out of the last 18 months here visiting her two daughters and six siblings and the refusal took the view that the long periods of time in she had spent here cast doubt on her true intentions. The Tribunal found:

(i) There is no restriction on the number of visits a person may make to the UK, nor any requirement that a specified time must elapse between successive visits.
(ii) The periods of time spent in the United Kingdom and the country of residence will always be important.
(iii) Both the expressed purpose of the visit and details of how time visiting in the past has been spent are material, together with the length of time that has elapsed since previous visits. There is nothing objectionable about a grandparent helping with childcare or an adult child helping with an elder's care needs.
(iv) The links that the appellant retains with her country of residence (including the presence of other family there) will be a material consideration.
(v) The Tribunal is required to ascertain what is the reality of the arrangement entered into between the appellant and the host in the United Kingdom. Is the reality that the appellant is resident in the United Kingdom and intends to be for the foreseeable future?
(vi) The issue may be approached by considering whether the reality is that the appellant is now no more than a visitor to her country of residence as the purpose of the return home is confined to using his or her presence there solely as the means of gaining re-admission to the United Kingdom.
(vii) This does not preclude the appellant from remaining in the country of residence for the least amount of time sufficient to maintain her status as a genuine visitor.
(viii) Family emergencies, whilst likely to result in a longer visit than the established pattern, should not be held against an applicant without adequate supporting evidence to that effect. Thus, the pregnancy of a daughter or daughter-in-law or the aftermath of the birth might explain a more-protracted stay (within the 6-month duration of a single permitted visit); so, too, a serious medical condition.
(ix) There may be comparisons with the person who owns homes in two different countries. Is he resident in both or a visitor to one of them?

Although the current rules might make it a little easier to refuse an application in Mrs Sawmynaden's circumstances, the Guidance is helpful. It highlights:

- the purpose of the visit and intended length of stay stated
- the number of visits made over the past 12 months, including the length of stay on each occasion, the time elapsed since the last visit, and if this amounts to the individual spending more time in the UK than in their home country
- the purpose of return trips to the visitor's home country or trips out of the CTA and if these are used only to seek re-entry to the UK

- the links they have with their home country or ordinary country of residence – consider especially any long term commitments and where the applicant is registered for tax purposes
- evidence the UK is their main place of residence, for example

    - if they have registered with a general practitioner (GP)
    - send their children to UK schools
    - the history of previous applications, for example if the visitor has previously been refused under the family rules and subsequently wants to enter as a visitor you must assess if they are using the visitor route to avoid the rules in place for family migrants joining British or settled persons in the UK

The Guidance emphasises that simply spending half one's time here would not justify refusal in itself. But given the existence of the "making the UK their home" proviso, applicants making frequent and lengthy visits here should be well prepared for a robust interview on entry and ready with evidence of their settled lives elsewhere.

Maintenance and accommodation

Sufficient resources to maintain and accommodate oneself adequately for the whole of the planned visit is necessary. The Guidance points out that there is no set level of funds required for an applicant to show this. The HO will expect enough information to be provided with the application to be able to assess the likely cost of the visit.

An applicant will need to provide very good and consistent evidence of their existing resources, including resources that they will continue to receive at home during their visit, and those available from any sponsor. The HO assessment will take account of any ongoing financial commitments the applicant has in their country of residence such as rent/mortgage payments and any dependants who they support financially, including those who are not travelling with them.

Where the majority of these funds have not been held in the relevant account for long, the HO will need evidence of the origin of the money. Any funds out of line with a person's stated income that are not explained and evidenced will be treated as suspect. Sometimes the only available evidence as to financial circumstances may be from friends or family, typically via statutory declaration: where that is provided, a visitor applicant is entitled to clear reasons as to why any such evidence is rejected: Sagra [2022] ScotCS CSOH_71.

Note also the additional requirements where the funds are being provided by a third party (V4.3).

3.2.4 Prohibited activities

V 4.4-6 Prohibited activities and payment requirements for visitors

The visitor must not intend to

- Work in the UK unless allowed under Appendices Permitted Activities, Permit Free Festivals or the Permitted Paid Engagements in V13.3. Working includes: taking employment or otherwise doing work for an organisation or business (or working as an au-pair, the Guidance adds); establishing or running a business as a self-employed person; work placements or internships; or direct selling to the public, or providing goods and services (V4.4(a)). Permitted activities must not amount to employment or filling/providing short-term cover for a role in a UK based organisation. Where the visitor is paid and employed outside the UK they must remain so (V4.5). Dias [2023] EWCA Civ 913 emphasises the difference between seeking to visit the UK whilst providing paid care to one's employer, as opposed to providing care for a friend or without charge.
- Receive payment from a UK source for activities in the UK apart from:
    - reasonable travel or subsistence expenses, including fees for board meeting attendance by a director

CHAPTER 3: Visitors

- international drivers undertaking activities permitted under PA 9.2
- prize money
- billing UK clients for time in the UK where the visitor's overseas employer has contracted to provide services to a UK company with the majority of such work being done overseas (payment must be less than the visitor's salary)
- salary payments by a multinational company made for administrative reasons from the UK
- for paid performances as an artist, entertainer or musician at a festival listed in the relevant Appendix
- for permitted paid engagements (V4.6).
- Study unless under Appendix Visitor: Permitted Activities (V4.4(b))
- Access medical treatment unless they meet the requirements to receive private medical treatment or donate an organ (V4.4(c))
- Marry/enter a CP unless they meet the marriage/CP visit requirements; or unless they are an EEA/Swiss citizen (V4.4(d))

It will be difficult to evidence that a person is not going to do something that is prohibited. The HO will suspect that those who are not well placed in their own country may think they can benefit from illegal employment in the UK. Such an applicant may want to address this potential concern directly in their statement. Similarly, a visitor coming to see a girlfriend or boyfriend may want to confirm they have no intention of marrying whilst they are here (unless of course they are applying for a marriage visit visa).

> **Top Tip**
>
> There are many applicants who will find it difficult to succeed in an application for a standard visit visa, particularly those who are from developing countries or who are not reasonably well-off individuals. The quality of the application will be fundamental to the prospects of success. Applicants should consider providing:
>
> ☐ detailed itinerary and costing for the trip
> ☐ a statement from the applicant explaining the purpose of the visit in detail, and any relevant background to the decision to come to the UK to visit. Why the UK? Why now?
> ☐ evidence how they will spend their time here (e.g. invitations from family members, or research into the sights they intend to visit)
> ☐ evidence of a settled life to return to at the end of the visit – work, employment, family responsibilities etc. Explain, with evidence, how the visit can happen, given those reasons to return – e.g. a letter from an employer confirming the person has been given leave for the relevant period, if necessary explaining how their absence will be dealt with, a letter from the college confirming the student will be on vacation at the relevant time, or evidence of alternative temporary arrangements for the care of dependants. Where there is no obvious incentive to return, the statement will need to be even more compelling. The object will be to persuade the HO that the person has a good life back home
> ☐ where the person has family here, this will often be seen as a negative factor. Explain their immigration history, and why, unlike them, the person has no wish to settle in the UK. Where the family have a poor immigration history, explain how the person is different
> ☐ evidence of funds
> ☐ if the cost of the visit may be considered to be disproportionate in light of the person's overall resources, the reasons for the visit will need to be clearly laid out. A person may well be willing to spend more on a visit to a close family member or friend than merely to see the sights
> ☐ their provenance (is the source of funds clear) and their accessibility. Unidentified deposits in bank accounts must be avoided. Approach evidencing the funds as you might do for an application under Appendix FM, ensuring that all the evidence is consistent (&providing an explanation if it is not)
> ☐ more evidence rather than less. If the applicant is working, payslips and bank statements, and letters from the employer (on headed notepaper) should be provided. If not, and in any case, other evidence of income from property or land, business accounts, tax returns etc. should be provided. If the applicant is studying, then plenty of evidence of that, and their progress in their studies, and an explanation as to how they can afford the time and funds for the trip
> ☐ evidence of accommodation
> ☐ evidence of previous compliance with immigration controls in the UK or elsewhere

CHAPTER 3: Visitors

> a clear statement addressing any facts which might be seen as potential weaknesses, previous reasons for refusal, and the applicant's intention to leave the UK at the end of their visit and not to work in the UK during it. HO decision makers are trained to identify potential weaknesses, so address them head on. A surfeit of honesty can be disarming
>
> Also:
>
> - make sure the application form is completed fully and accurately and the information on it is internally consistent and consistent with any other information the HO may hold on the applicant (eg from their own, or family members', previous applications
> - make sure documentary evidence is verifiable, and presume it will be verified
> - remember that friends and relatives here may be contacted by the HO to confirm their understanding of any relevant facts (e.g. the length and purpose of the visit) - check that relevant family members are alive to this possibility and familiar with the application details present the documentation in a way that is easy for the HO to access and understand. Provide good quality translations where necessary. Explain and cross refer to the documentation in a covering letter.

3.2.5 Additional eligibility requirements for classes of visitor

The online MIL deals with these criteria in detail.

The Guidance *Transit* explains the four forms of transit in detail and lists the criteria for assessing the genuineness of a purported transit and explains that permission may be given outside the Rules if there is a compelling case.

V 15.1-5 Additional eligibility requirements for permission to stay as a visitor [i.e. extension applications]

Those in the UK for private medical treatment must prove that they have met the cost of treatment so far and provide a letter from their doctor or consultant detailing the medical condition requiring further treatment; or an authorisation from their home country confirming that further NHS treatment, arranged under a reciprocal healthcare agreement, is required (V15.1).

Aademics seeking to extend their permission to stay must intend to do one or more of the activities in PA11.2 (Science and Academia); still be working in their field of expertise in which they are highly qualified and in which they worked at an academic or higher education institution prior to their visit (V15.2).

PLAB visitors seeking to resit their test must have confirmation of this in writing from the GMC (V15.3).

Those undertaking unpaid clinical attachment or dental observed posts must have passed the PLAB test (V15.1)

V 16.1 Decision

If all suitability and eligibility requirements are met, the application will be granted. If not it will be refused.

V 17.1-3 Period and conditions of grant for visitors

Visa holders must not access public funds, work (unless permitted by the PPEs in V13.3 or by appendices Permitted Activities, Permit Free Festivals) or study (unless permitted by PA2 and PA17). Under V17.1(d), permitted study or research may require an ATAS certificate.

The table at V17.2 sets out the maximum lengths of stay for each category , which is then elaborated upon at V17.3:

- Standard and marriage/CP visitors: 6 months
- Chinese tourists on the ADSA: 30 days
- PPE: 1 month

- Private medical treatment: 11 months (may extend for another 6 months after that for the same purpose)
- Academic visitors, their child or partner: 12 months (if undertaking one or more of the activities in PA11.2 (Science and Academia))
- Standard visitors may be granted PTS to make up no more than 12 months in total (including the period of EC); and may be granted PTS for up to 6 months to re-sit the PLAB test
- Standard visitors who have passed the PLAB test may be granted PTS to undertake an unpaid clinical attachment (as permitted by PA 10.1(a)) for up to a total period of 18 months (inc EC and first extension)
- Transit visitors: 48 hours
    - Transit without a visa: until 23.59 the day after arrival

3.3 Appendix Visitor: Permitted Activities (paragraphs PA1-PA18)

This separate Appendix sets out a summary table at PA 1 of permitted activities, and a roadmap of which provisions to refer to (further below) for each category:

a) Standard: all permitted activities in this appendix (only Chinese ADSA visitors are restricted to tourism)
b) Marriage/CP: marry or form a civil partnership, or give notice of this. They may also do all permitted activities in this appendix, other than study as set out in PA17.1-3.
c) PPE visitors may do the permitted paid engagements in Appendix V: Visitor at V13.3. and all permitted activities in this appendix other than study as described in PA 17.1-3.and transit as described in PA 18.
d) Transit visitor: transit the UK as described in PA 18.

The remaining appendix is ordered by headings according to subject matter. It is essential to put forward (and adequately evidence) one or more of the permitted activities. If the HO accepts the application is for a genuine purpose, that should help allay any concerns re overstaying or working illegally.

- **Tourism and Leisure**: includes visiting friends and family, going on holiday, taking part in educational exchanges or visits with a state or private school and attend recreational courses (not English courses) for up to 30 days (PA 2)
- **Volunteering**: up to 30 days for a charity registered with the Charity Commission for E&W or NI or the Office of the Scottish Charity Regulator (PA 3)
- **General Business Activities**: attending meetings, conferences, seminars and interviews; giving talks or speeches on a non-profit basis, negotiating and signing deals and contracts, attending trade fairs for promotion (not sales), visiting and inspecting sites, gathering information on behalf of overseas employers; briefings on UK based customers' requirements where the work is to be done outside the UK (PA 4) – the Guidance confirms jobseeking is permitted, so long as it goes no further than the interview stage, and so is remote working so long as they remain genuinely employed overseas and are not seeking to work here
- **Intra-corporate Activities**: employees of overseas businesses may advise, consult, troubleshoot, train and share skills and knowledge on a specific internal project with UK employees of the same corporate group, but not directly with clients. Regulatory or financial auditing may be carried out by an internal auditor visiting from an overseas branch of the same group of companies (PA 5&6)
- **Manufacture and supply of goods to the UK**: a visiting employee of an overseas company may install, dismantle, repair, service or advise on- machinery equipment or computer software or hardware or provide training in that regard, or train UK-based staff on these roles, in the context of a contract of purchase, supply or lease (including where the maintenance activities are supplied by a third party overseas firm so long as the contractual arrangements were set up at the time of the sale/lease). The company must be the manufacturer or supplier or be part of a contract for after sales services (PA 7). This little-known provision (described in the

CHAPTER 3: Visitors

Guidance as 'in place to provide for the commitments the UK has taken in trade agreements') seems to provide an avenue for unsponsored work in the uk, though the Guidance notes that decision makers may look askance at stays of more than 90 days

- **Clients of UK export companies**: a seconded employee of an overseas company which is a client of an UK export business can oversee the requirement for goods and services, so long as the two companies are not in the same group. (PA 8)
- Overseas roles requiring specific activities in the UK (PA 9)
  - **Translators, interpreters, PAs and bodyguards** employed overseas by an overseas businessperson may provide the relevant support to that person in the UK. PAs and bodyguards must not provide personal care or domestic work for that person in the UK
  - **Tour group couriers** contracted to an overseas company may enter and depart with a tour group organised by that company.
  - **Journalists, correspondents, producers or cameramen** may gather information for an overseas publication, programme or film
  - **Archaeologists** may participate in one-off excavations
  - **Market researchers and analysts** may conduct market research or analysis
  - **Overseas academic professors** may accompany students on study abroad programmes and provide a small amount of teaching that does not amount to filling a permanent teaching role at the host institution (PA 9.1)
  - **Drivers** may deliver or collect goods or passengers on a genuine international route and undertake cabotake operations. Drivers must be employed or contracted to an operator registered in a country outside the UK or be a self-employed operator and driver based outside the UK. The operator must hold an International Operators Licence or be operating on an own account basis" (PA 9.2&3.The definitions of cabotage operations, International Operator Licence, Own Account and Seafarers are at r6. Seafarers working on vessels on genuine international routes may deliver/collect passengers to UK ports from ports abroad, and within 60 days call at up to a further 10 UK ports to deliver/collect passengers to other UK ports, before travelling onwards abroad
- **Work-related training** (PA 10)
  - Medical, dental or nursing graduates may undertake unpaid clinical attachments or dental observer posts which involve no treatment of patients, or conduct independent research. They must provide the offer letter and confirmation they have not undertaken this activity before (PA 10.1 (a) read with V 11.1)
  - They may take the PLAB test with written confirmation from the GMC (PA 10.1(b) read with V 11.2); and the OSCE with written confirmation from the Nursing and Midwifery Council ((PA 10.1(b) read with V 11.3)
  - Overseas employees may receive training from an UK company (which is not available overseas), on work practices and techniques, which the recipients require for their overseas employment.
  - Corporate trainers contracted by the same international corporate group to which a UK company belongs can provide a short series of training to that company's employees
- **Science and academia** (PA 11)
  - **Scientists and researchers** may gather information and facts for a project relating to their overseas employment. They can also share knowledge or advise on an international UK-led project, so long as this does not amount to research in the UK (PA 11.1)
  - **Academics** may take part in formal exchanges with UK counterparts (including doctors) and undertake research for their own purposes while on sabbatical. Eminent senior doctors or dentists may participate in research, teaching or clinical practice but not thereby fill a permanent teaching post. (PA 11.2)
- **Legal: expert witnesses** can give evidence in court, and **other witnesses** may attend a hearing if summoned. **Overseas lawyers** may advise UK clients on international litigation or – transactions (PA 12.1&2)
- **Religion**: religious workers may preach or do pastoral work (PA 13)
- **Creative**

CHAPTER 3: Visitors

- **Artists, entertainers and musicians** may perform individually or as a group; participate in competitions and auditions; make personal appearances and participate in promotions, or in cultural events or festivals listed in Appendix Visitor: Permit Free Festival List (PA 14.1)
- **Personal, technical or production staff** of the above may support the activities in PA 14.1 or in V 13.3 (activities directly related to their profession if invited by a creative (arts or entertainment) organisation, agent or broadcaster) (PA 14.2 read with V13.3)
- **Actors, producers, directors or technicians** employed overseas as part of a film crew may participate in shooting a film programme or other media content financed and produced overseas (PA 14.3)

- **Sports**
  - **Sports persons** may participate in tournaments or events individually or as a team; make personal appearances and participate in promotion; participate in trials (not in front of paying audiences); and participate in unpaid short periods of training. Amateurs may join amateur teams or clubs to gain experience (PA 15.1).
  - **Personal or technical staff** of the above, or sports officials may attend the same event and support the above activities or those in V13.3(f) (activity directly related to profession if invited by a sports organisation agent or broadcaster). Personal or technical staff must be employed by the sports person overseas. (PA 15.2 read with V13.3(f)).
  - **Sports officials** may support tournaments/events where invited by a UK-based sports organisation, agent or broadcaster, or by a sportsperson themselves conducting permitted activities (PA 15.3)

- **Medical treatment and organ donation** (PA 16): this provision contains nothing but a cross reference to Appendix V: Visitor (Eligibility requirements for visitors coming to the UK to receive private medical treatment (V7.1-3) and to donate an organ (V8.1-4) (see above).
- **Study as a Visitor** (PA 17) – as per V 9.1-5 (see above): essentially with Accredited Institutions, <6 months, and with a UK Higher Education Provider if undertaking electives relevant to a course of study abroad, or coming for research. Kato [2012] ScotCS CSOH_146 holds that a generous approach should be taken to courses that visitors might pursue on the borderline, either via a broad construction of the Rules or via the SSHD's discretion.
- **Transit** (PA 18): this provision contains nothing but a cross reference to Appendix V: Visitor (Eligibility requirements for visitors coming to UK to transit V14.1&2)

3.4 Appendix Visitor; Transit Without Visa Scheme (paragraphs TWOV1-TWOV5)

This appendix sets out at TWOV 1 that, to be granted PTE (permission to ender, the new LTE), all TWOV 2 requirements must be met, plus one of the requirements in TWOV 3.

TWOV 2 requires that the person must

- Have arrived and will depart by air
- Be genuinely transiting via a reasonable route
- Not access public funds or medical treatment, work or study in the UK
- Genuinely intend to leave before midnight the day after arrival day
- Be assured entry to their destination country and all countries to be transited on the way there

TWOV 3 requires that the person must also be doing only one of the following:

- Be travelling to or from Australia, Canada, NZ or the USA and have a valid visa for the relevant country or entered that country with a valid visa within the last 6 months (TWOV3(a)&(b) – these do not apply to Syrian nationals holding a US B1 or B1 category visa)
- Hold one of the range of specific residence permits set out at TWOV 3 (c)-(k)

Any of the visas and residence permits in TWOV3 must not be in electronic format only (TWOV5).

The transit guidance under "DATV [Direct Airside Transit Visitor]: permission to enter" states that In exceptional circumstances, for example where a passenger's flight has been cancelled, it may be necessary to allow the passenger to enter the UK landside and in such cases you should consider granting leave outside the rules (LOTR) in line with the Border Force guidance on LOTR.

3.5 Refusals and appeals

Approximately 300,000 visit visa applications are refused each year (of a total of 2.2 million, so about 15%). Since 25 June 2013 there has been no right to appeal for visitors, nor a right to seek administrative review (except for cancellation on arrival, see above), so the remedies will be to apply again, or seek JR.

An appeal may be available if the visit visa is treated as a human rights claim, but this will be rare (see further below).

HO policy is that those refused a visit visa should apply again rather than bring a legal challenge. This may be true, if the HO's reasons for refusal can be fully addressed by providing relevant further information and better supporting evidence. However, where a person has been refused on the grounds of genuineness, it will be difficult to persuade the decision maker to take a different view. Tellingly, there have been no reported judgements from the Upper Tribunal (IAC) on JRs brought against the HO in such cases, which suggests the HO are conceding these claims at an early stage.

Pre Action Protocol letters threatening JR often bring reconsideration and indeed reversals of decisions. Especially when the orginal application was well evidenced and the PAP letter is well written and argued with precise reference to the relevant law and evidence. Belo [2023] NIKB 20 shows that an offer to reconsider a visitor refusal will not always mean the refusal is academic, as where the refusal would otherwise remain extant following the departure from the UK of a visitor refused at the border.

Top Tip

Generally speaking there are three possibilities when refused a visit visa - an appeal, an application for JR of the refusal or a fresh visitor application.

(1) Unless a good representative has already put the very best case forwards, usually a **fresh visitor application** is more likely to bear fruit. There is a big difference between a professionally presented application and one advanced by a private individual. If the ECO alleged dishonesty in the current or a previous application, it can be very difficult to persuade them to change their mind. But even so the best-evidenced case answering the ECO's criticisms should be put.

(2) If the visit involves **strong family life** which was well-evidenced in the application, then the refusal should, arguably, be recognised as **meriting a right of appeal** to the FTT.
   - Don't think you can't lodge an appeal just no right of appeal is recognised. The existence of a right of appeal is not just a question for the entry clearance post to decide – it is a question of law, based on whether a judge accepts that the decision appealed against amounted to the refusal of a "human rights claim" based on family life established between the family members in question (MIL 14.2.4).
   - The advantage of lodging an appeal is that the entry clearance manager will normally review the grounds of appeal and the evidence, and they may pragmatically reverse their decision (this can happen within weeks or months of the grounds of appeal being lodged);
   - If the FTT accepts there is an appeal, and then the appeal is listed and heard, then the Judge can look at up-to-date evidence and hear oral evidence from the UK-based family; and they can reverse the decision of the entry clearance post, rather than just require its reconsideration.
   - The disadvantages are that entry clearance appeals typically take a very long time to be listed, and the grounds for the appeal succeeding are rather narrow – basically you have to show that there is very strong enduring family life including emotional dependency between the various parties, not just that the visitor will be adequately maintained and accommodated and will leave the UK at the end of their visit. And appeals can derail, as the legal issues are relatively complicated, and the HO might successfully challenge the original FTT decision to recognise a right of appeal and put you back to square one. But even if the appeal failed on the strength of family life, the Judge might still overturn a dishonesty allegation, thereby improving the immigration history for future applications.

(3) There is also the **possibility of an application for JR** (MIL 14.8) made to the UT.

> - It is always available where the decision maker has acted unfairly or made an unreasonable decision
>   - most often it succeeds where the SSHD has overlooked relevant evidence.
>   - Or where the process has been unfair, eg as where the ECO refuses on the basis of extrinsic information of which he has become aware or doubts the applicant's veracity, or the authenticity of documents, or attributes other reprehensible conduct to him; or where the refusal reason is something which the petitioner could not reasonably have anticipated: GK [2020] ScotCS CSIH_69. See also Mushtaq (IJR) [2015] UKUT 224 (IAC).
>   JR is not an appeal on the merits and if all relevant evidence has been referred to in the refusal, the UT will be very unlikely to intervene, even if the refusal "feels" rather mean. And when granting a JR, judges cannot reverse the decision, they can only order that it be reconsidered.
> - Before issuing the JR it is necessary to write a Pre Action Protocol letter, which has to be considered by a senior decision maker, so operates like an entry clearance manager review. So sometimes one can get a quick reversal of a decision.
> - JRs have some financial risks, because if the claim fails you are liable for the government's legal costs as well as your own legal costs. Though the liability is modest in the initial stages: usually just for the cost of the government's written defence up to the stage where a judge grants permission or not. Then again, a strong JR has a good chance of recovering its legal costs.

Appeals on human rights grounds

Article 8 (Private and Family Life)

In an appeal on human rights grounds, arguments about intention to leave at the end of one's visit, or about ability to maintain and accommodate, will not be the main focus of the appeal. The Tribunal can only look at whether the interference with family life caused by the refusal is disproportionate. An ability to show that the Rules are met, though, will be important.

In the case of Mostafa [2015] UKUT 112 McCloskey J explained that refusals of entry clearance as a visitor *may* interfere with family life:

> this is likely to be limited to cases where the relationship is that of husband and wife or other close life partners or a parent and minor child and even then it will not necessarily be extended to cases where, for example, the proposed visit is based on a whim or will not add significantly to the time that the people involved spend together

Where it is accepted that a refusal of a visit visa interferes with family life, then:

> the underlying merits of an application and the ability to satisfy the IRs, although not the question before the Tribunal, may be capable of being a weighty factor in an appeal based on human rights but they will not be determinative.

This is accepted by the HO, whose guidance on visits and human rights (cited below) states:

> The applicant's ability to meet the requirements of the IRs is relevant to the proportionality of the decision to refuse a visit visa.

> **Top Tip**
>
> In an appeal on family life grounds, the case will have to be looked at through the five stage Razgar test. In a visitor appeal the most important stages are likely to be (1), (2) and (5).
>
> ☐ Is family life established – i.e. can it be said there is meaningful family life in existence notwithstanding that its participants live far apart? So, consider whether there is a regular pattern of visits over time which shows that this family's life has consistently existed across borders; or whether there is emotional/financial dependency going beyond the norm.

CHAPTER 3: Visitors

> - ☐ Will the immigration decision interfere with family life – the HO often argue that the immigration decision merely upholds the status quo, under which the Sponsor and Appellant are geographically separated. Consider whether there are real difficulties in maintaining family life via means other than a visit to this country (i.e. are visits from Sponsor to Appellant abroad realistic and affordable?).
> - ☐ Is the decision disproportionate – particularly if the Appellant actually satisfies every aspect of the IRs, in which case it may be thought that permitting the visit would be the least intrusive way of protecting the public interest: after all, the fact that the Rules are satisfied, including their requirements of maintenance, accommodation and intention to leave after the visit, does rather suggest that upholding the refusal is an excessive response to the issue.

The HO has produced guidance, <u>Considering human rights claims in visit applications</u>, that addresses these issues, posing a series of questions as to whether human rights are engaged:

1. Does the application say that it is a human rights claim?
2. Does the application amount to an implied human rights claim if it does not say that it is a human rights claim?
3. Are the matters raised capable of engaging human rights?
4. Does the human rights claim have any prospects of success?

The HO do not expect human rights issues to generally result from visitor refusals: they tell their decision makers that as

> visit visa applications do not generally engage human rights you should not imply a claim unless the information provided clearly indicates there is an implied claim.

They opine that family life will only be in play where the relationship is one of spouse/life partner, parent or minor child (though the case of <u>Advic v UK</u> [1995] ECHR 57 established the true test is whether in all the circumstances there is dependency or emotional ties exceeding the norm (MIL 6.2.6.1).

They add that Article 8 is not engaged in the following circumstances:

- an applicant applies to visit the UK temporarily but there are no reasons why the UK-based family members could not visit the applicant
- the applicant wishes to renew a private life established in UK

Relevant considerations will be whether:

- the person the applicant intends to visit has ever visited, or could visit, the applicant in their home country or a third country
- whether the circumstances of the person in the UK mean that travel is not possible for them
- whether a visit is necessary to maintain the current relationship (e.g. is the relationship actually based on personal contact?)
- family life exists for the applicant in their home country, with other family members who are residing there

For an up-to-date case law section, please refer to this section in our *Mastering Immigration Law* online resource. There you can read about various Court of Appeal cases that show the pitfalls in running visitor appeals on ECHR grounds and the approach to visits to the UK for the purpose of legal proceedings.

We address questions arising from Article 6 (right to a fair trial) for the purpose of visiting the UK to take part in legal proceedings elsewhere (MIL 4.2.10).

CHAPTER 4: Non-business/family routesHome Office Concessions; Modern slavery and statelessness

4.1 Routes outside the Points Based System (PBS) and Appendix FM

Most of the employment categories were, from 2009 to December 2020, located in Part 6A of the Immmigration Rules (& thus constituted "the PBS"). From 2020 they moved from Part 6A to the newly "simplified" distinct category Appendices (MIL 7) addressing Students, Skilled Workers, Innovator Founders, Global Talent, Global Mobility and Temporary Workers.

A few employment categories never made the journey into Part 6A in the first place (as they did not become points-based). Here are some other moves:

- Representatives of overseas businesses, formerly in r144-149 in Part 5, from 1 December 2020 in its own Appendix (now UK Expansion Worker within Appendix Global Mobility) (MIL 7.6)
- Domestic workers in private households, formerly in r159A–159H in Part 5, now with three Appendices for pre-2012 and post-2012 applicants and modern slavery victims) (MIL 4.1.1)
- Visit categories connected with work, formerly in Part 2, then in old Appendix V, now forming part of the current Visitor Appendices: Appendix V: Visitors; Appendix Visitor: Permitted Activities; - Visa national list; - Permit Free Festival List; - Transit without Visa Scheme (MIL 3)
- UK Ancestry – previously in Part 5, now in Appendix UK Ancestry (MIL 4.1.2)

4.1.1 Domestic workers in private households/overseas domestic workers

This route was seen originally as a purely economic one. However it developed a human rights twist as government came to appreciate the need to protect victims of modern slavery and other abuse. Changes introduced from 6 April 2012 limited this category to those accompanying their employer on a visit to the UK, with a maximum stay of six months. But there are some protections.

Those who entered under the rules in place before that date will continue to be able to apply for extensions for periods of 12 months at a time (previously under 159EA, and under 159G, now under Appendix Domestic Worker in a Private Household) for settlement after five years residence as a domestic worker. They must remain consistently within the route to qualify (DW 1.2A). The eligibility criteria are 30+ hours weekly employment (and no other employment) in their employer's household with terms and conditions as per Appendix Domestic Worker Statement showing adequate maintenance and accommodation. The usual suitability criteria apply re no overstaying save as per r39E.

Rules 159A–159H governed admission under the post-2012 category until 6 May 2021; . The from 6 May 2021, the requirements are now found in **Appendix Overseas Domestic Worker (paras ODW 1.1-8.2), which are almost identical.**

4.1.1.1 Domestic workers, trafficking and slavery

As extensively reported, the domestic worker route can encourage exploitation. The Guidance expressly warns caseworkers to look out for signs of trafficking. As explained in EK Tanzania [2013] UKUT 313, over time there have been various policies to protect domestic workers from exploitation via what amounts to forced labour, including the provision of leaflets to them concerning how to contact the United Kingdom immigration authorities, the employment rights which domestic workers would have in the UK, how to contact Trade Unions, the entitlement to the protection of the criminal law, the entitlement to free medical care, and information on the services provided by Kalayaan, an organisation providing independent advice and support on immigration and employment problems, along with contact details.

Following the coming into force of the Modern Slavery Act 2015 (MIL 15.1.4), the government implemented a minor concession for domestic workers. From 15 October 2015, this allowed domestic workers who had been determined by a conclusive grounds decision ("CGD") to be a victim of trafficking or slavery to extend their six-month visa by one further period of six months; 6 April 2016, there is a maximum of two years in the route.

From 6 May 2021, these applications are made under Appendix Domestic Worker who is a Victim of Modern Slavery. There are the usual modern IR provisions on validity and suitability. To be eligible one must previously have had permission as an Overseas Domestic Worker, or under Temporary Work – International Agreement (as a private servant in a diplomatic household), Domestic Worker in a Private Household, or, having received LOTR, having been referred into the National Referral Mechanism (NRM) and be in receipt of a positive Conclusive Grounds (CG) decision (DWMS3.1). And then a positive CG decision is required too (DWMS3.2).

The application must be made within 28 days of notification of that decision or within 28 days after a decision on another application pending while the conclusive grounds decision was made – or, where the applicant was last granted leave outside the rules, before this expires (DWMS 3.3)

There is no longer any requirement to maintain and accommodate themselves without recourse to public funds.

A grant will be subject to the conditions of no recourse to public funds (DWMS 5.2(a)) Employment is permitted as a domestic worker in a private household or a private servant in a diplomatic household, and supplementary employment is also permitted but only as a domestic worker in a private household. Study is permitted subject to the ATAs rules. (DWMS 5.2). Specific guidance 'Domestic Workers who are victims of slavery or human trafficking' is accessible here.

4.1.2 Appendix UK Ancestry (paragraphs UKA 1.1-36.1)

This route is for the grandchildren of British citizens who emigrated from thcitizensUK in times past. The children of such emigrants born outside the UK will usually have been born British, and will be free of immigration control, but *their* children born outside the UK will not have been born British. In some circumstances those second-generation children born outside the UK may register as British citizens (under ss3(3) or 3(5) of the BNA 1981), but if they cannot they may be able to come to the UK and settle under the relatively benign requirements of the UK ancestry route.

One of the main attractions of the ancestry visa is that it leads to settlement after five years. In addition, there are no restrictions on employment and the Immigration Staff Guidance on UK Ancestry suggests that examination of the applicant's ability to maintain themselves is relatively limited, providing they can do so by some means that include some sort of employment. It is not strictly necessary to show employment when applying for extensions, although it would certainly be helpful to be able to be able to do so. As no access to public funds is permitted before settlement, most individuals on this route will be in work or self-employment in any case.Commonwealth citizens are those identified as such in IR6: British Overseas Territories citizens, British Nationals (Overseas), British Overseas citizens and British subject, plus the countries identified in Sch 3 to the BNA 1981. There are two special cases identified in the Guidance whose citizens can participate: Zimbabwe (as to whom the UK government hopes will rejoin) and Cyprus and Malta, whose Commonwealth membership was for long obscured by their EU membership.

Appendix UK Ancestry

The introduction to Appendix UK Ancestry, in force since 1 December 2020, outlines the route as intended for Commonwealth citizens aged 17 of over, whose grandparent was born in the UK, the Channel Islands or the Isle of Man, seeking to live and work in the UK. Dependent partners and children can apply under this route, which also leads to settlement.

The appendix is structured as follows:

1. Validity requirements for UK Ancestry
2. Suitability requirements for UK Ancestry

3. Eligibility requirements for UK Ancestry
4. Decision on an application for UK Ancestry
5. Settlement on the UK Ancestry route
6. Decision on an application for settlement on the UK Ancestry route
7. Dependants of a person with UK Ancestry

Certain provisions are duplicated identically at the EC, PTS and ILR stages for main applicants and dependants, and thus are not listed below. They are that:

- For any application to be valid, the fe e and IHS must be paid and biometrics as well as a passport/acceptable travel document must be provided
- Prior EC is required in all cases before arrival in the UK
- To be valid, PTS applications by the main applicant require prior entry clearance in this category
- Applications not meeting all validity requirements *may* be rejected and not considered
- The Suitability requirement is not to fall for refusal under Part 9 and if applying for PTS not to be in breach of immigration laws. Where IR39E applies, that period of overstaying is disregarded.
- The Eligibility requirements include a TB test certificate where required under Appendix T
- Suitability and Eligibility requirements must be met or the application *will* be refused
- Upon EC/PTS grant, the following are permitted: work, including self-employment, voluntary work and study subject to the ATAS requirement in Appendix ATAS (MIL 7.4.3.11)
- Conditions on grants of EC/PTS include no access to public funds
- Administrative review is available on refusal

Set out below are only the remaining requirements

Validity requirements for UK Ancestry (main applicant)

- Use of the right online form – EC: UK Ancestry, Right of Abode or Returning Residents visa; PTS: Application to extend stay in the UK: FLR(IR) (UKA 1.1)
- A is a Commonwealth citizen who if applying for EC must be 17 or over at date of planned arrival (UKA 1.3 & UKA 1.4)
- The student work switching restrictions apply (MIL 7.4.4.6.4)

Eligibility requirements for UK Ancestry

- A must have a grandparent born in the UK or Islands (UKA 4.1)
- A must be able to maintain and accommodate A and dependants without recourse to public funds (UKA 5.1); funds are to be shown in accordance with Appendix Finance (UKA 5.2). Credible promises of third-party support from family or friends may be taken into account (UKA 5.3)
- A must be able to work and intend to seek and take employment in the UK (UK 6.1)
- Parental consent (MIL 7.8.14.5)

Decision on an application for UK Ancestry

Grants will be for 5 years (UKA 9.1)

Settlement on the UK Ancestry route (main applicant)

- Validity: this requirement mandates use of online form SET(O)(UKA 10.1) A must still be a Commonwealth citizen at the time of application (UKA 10.3).
- Eligibility: A must still meet the maintenance and ability to work requirements (UKA 12.1)
- Qualifying period: 5 years in the UK with permission on this route (UKA 13.1)
- Continuous residence: A must meet Appendix Continuous Residence (UKA 14.1)
- English: speaking and listening skills at B1 unless exempt (UKA 15.1) in accordance with Appendix English Language (UKA 15.2)

- KoLL: A must meet the requirements in Appendix KOL UK (UKA 16.1)

Dependants of a person with UK Ancestry

Dependants were previously covered under Part 5, but specific provisions now appear in this Appendix.

Validity: use of the correct online form "Join or accompany a family member" on the "Find and apply for other visas from outside the UK" form; for PTS Form FLR(IR) (UKA 18.1); Applicants for PTS must not have been a Visitor, Short-term Student, Parent of a Child Student, Seasonal Worker, Domestic Worker in a Private Household; or have hat LOTR (UKA 18.3).

Relationship requirements for partners

- A must either have permission on the UK Ancestry route; or be applying at the same time as their sponsor (S) who is being granted permission; or applying for PTS where their sponsor is settled (or British after becoming settled on the Ancestry route) (UKA 21.1).
- Unless married/in a civil partnership, 2 years' cohabitation is required, any previous relationship has permanently broken down and A and S are not so closely related that they would not be allowed to marry or form a civil partnership in the UK (UKA 21.2).
- The relationship must be genuine and subsisting (UKA 21.3) and A and S must intend to live together throughout A's stay in the UK.

Relationship requirements for children

- A must be the child of a person (P) who has permission on the UK Ancestry route; or who is applying at the same time (and is granted permission); or who is settled or British after settling on this route (UKA 22.1).
- A's parents must both be applying at the same time as A or be in the UK with non-visitor leave unless the parent with Ancestry leave is the sole surviving parent or has sole responsibility for A; or is British/settled and is or will be ordinarily resident in the UK; or there are serious and compelling reasons to grant A permission to come or stay with the parent with Ancestry permission – or the parent who is not the principal on the economic route is a British citizen or has ILR and is ordinarily resident here (UKA 22.2).
- Care requirement: suitable arrangements for care and accommodation which comply with UK law must be in place (UKA 23.1)
- Age requirement: A must be under 18 unless last granted permission as a dependent child (UKA 24.1); if aged 16 or over they must not be leading an independent life (UKA 24.2).

Financial requirement for partners and children: Adequate maintenance and accommodation for A, their sponsor and any other dependents without recourse to public funds (UKA 25.1). Funds must be shown as specified in Appendix Finance (UKA 25.2) and credible promises of third party support may be taken into account (UKA 25.3).

Conditions: A will be granted permission in line with S unless S has settled or become British, in which case A will be granted 30 months' permission to stay (UKA 27.1&2).

Settlement for dependants

- Validity: application on online form Set(O) (UKA 28.1); A must be present in the UK on application date (UKA 28.2). A's last grant of leave must not have been as a Visitor, Short-term Student, Parent of a Child Student, Seasonal Worker, Domestic Worker in a Private Household; or have hat LOTR (UKA 28.3).
- Eligibility for settlement – partners and children: A's sponsor must at the same time be granted Ancestry settlement or they must already have settled on this route or have naturalised after settling on this route (UKA 30.1). The relationship and financial requirements are identical to those at the EC/PTS stage.

- **English and KoLL:** A must show speaking and listening skills at B1 unless exempt (UKA 34.1) in accordance with Appendix English Language (UKA 34.2). A must meet the requirements in Appendix KOL UK (UKA 35.1).

There is no requirement for dependants to complete 5 years in the route before seeking ILR: they may apply for ILR alongside the principal applicant, as confirmed in an email from the UKVI policy department in November 2021.

Evidence

As there is no specified evidence under this category, evidence of ancestry must be provided that is compelling. That should include, when relying on blood relationships, the full birth certificates of the applicant, the relevant parent, and the grandparent, as well as marriage certificates where the applicant or direct ascendant relative has changed their names on marriage. An ability and intention to work can be proven by way of evidence of qualifications, current and previous work experience, CVs, job applications or offers in the UK, and, where there is a disability or illness, additional medical information confirming an ability to work.

4.1.3 Returning residents

These Rules moved to Appendix Returning Resident on 5 October 2023.

Leave lapses under ILERO 2000 (Art 13(4)(a))) where one has left the UK for more than 2 years. A person who *has* been away for more than two years but who can demonstrate that he has strong ties to the UK and intends to make it their permanent home may be granted indefinite leave to enter upon application for entry clearance. Note that ILR granted under Appendix EU ('settled status') lapses after five, not two years (MIL 11.7) (or four years for Swiss nationals: Art 13(4)(za)) – the Appendix now expressly covers these Brexit categories. No dependents are permitted; one can qualify only as a prinicpal.

There are the usual Validity (MIL 1.5.3 - the form is 'UKA/ROA/RR' or the 'Windrush Scheme application (Overseas) form) and Suitability (MIL 7.1.2) criteria – additionally applicants must have been granted ILR which has lapsed through operation of law. Windrush survivors may apply under this route; there is then no fee (RR1.2). Entry clearance is required and the TB proviso applies (MIL 2.2.7). Applicants must show an intention to settle in the UK (RR.4.1), that they did not receive publicly funded assistance to depart the country (RR.5.1), that they have maintained strong ties during their absence (RR.6.1). The usual parental consent criteria require (eg MIL 7.8.14.5). AR is available. Successful applications will be granted entry clearance for settlement (RR9.1).

The Guidance *Returning Residents* sets out relevant considerations:

- **Strength of UK ties**: family (particularly close family members, but extended family is relevant; regular contact will establish the strength of ties though it need not be in person), property & business (unlikely to suffice alone)
- **Length of original UK residence v time abroad and the reasons for going abroad** (travel and return with a particular employer, prolonged studies before returning to the UK, prolonged medical treatment and unintended abences eg due to pandemic)

Decision makers may revert to Applicant's for missing information.;

Previously the Rules and Guidance suggested a benign approach might be taken for absence due to service abroad with HM Armed Forces, for the UK Govt, as an employee of a quasi/government body, a British company or a United Nations organisation.

Where a person who has not applied for an entry clearance to return is refused leave to enter as a returning resident at the port, the Immigration Officer would at one time usually grant a period of six months leave to enter as a visitor. But the modern Guidance rules out visitor grants for rejected returning residents. In the past, many people may simply not appreciate the legal basis (or its full implications) for their admission, and may be surprised to later find they were being admitted as visitors rather than as a returning resident. From 12 April 2023 there was express protection of former ILR holders since granted leave as a visitor (IR19) though the Appendix does not carry this over. Those not seeking entry clearance under the Appendix will find there is no obvious appeal route (unless they made a human rights claim), and an application will have to be made outside the rules for the reinstatement of ILR. That being said though, a decision to grant leave to enter for six months may be unlawful if the Immigration Officer has failed to consider whether or not it is appropriate to grant entry as a returning resident (see Anderson FE (AP) [2013] ScotCS CSOH52).

4.2 Home Office concessions; &special categories under the Rules

The general strategy of the HO in recent years has been to try to minimise concessions outside the IRs. However there remain generic positions taken to cases outside the Rules, and old policies may remain relevant, at least for some older cases that are still in the system. The usual course of events now is that what are in fact concessions will be written quickly into the IRs as is clear from the listed categories below.

4.2.1 Applications outside the Immigration Rules

The HO always has a discretion to depart from the IRs. Sometimes it does so via a structured policy. But a reasonable decision maker must always recognise they have a discretion to depart from the Rules and policies if the facts of a particular case require this as part of their residual power and duty to make the right decision in any particular case – see for example Venables and Thompson [1998] AC 407.

However, there is no duty to depart from the Rules unless a coherent and exceptional case, backed by evidence, is put forward (for PBS see MIL 7.10).

From February 2018 the policy Leave Outside the Rules for non asylum, non human rights cases is more detailed than its predecessor (from 2006). That earlier version was discussed in Anderson [2013] ScotCS CSOH_52, which stressed that in the particular circumstances of the case always had to be considered and that a decision maker should not rule out the possibility of exercising discretion where appropriate. The current policy sets out:

- There will be cases where discretion should be exercised in the migrant's favour
- This might include cases where a person fits into one of the policies dealing with specific scenarios outside the Rules (e.g. the carers' policy mentioned below)
- The threshold for the grant of leave in such cases is that discretion will be exercised in 'rare' cases where are 'particularly compelling circumstances' (other than family and private life, medical, asylum or protection grounds)
- LOTR may be granted on a limited or unlimited (settlement) basis and may be applied for in the UK or from abroad
- The examples given are an unexpected event or a personal tragedy; medical grounds, so long as not the main reason, can be included but must be fully evidenced as with a health claim
- The process, according to the guidance, is to apply on the form for the route which most closely matches the applicant's circumstances. S & Anor [2022] EWHC 1402 (Admin) notes that the HO in fact considered LOTR applications whatever route was proposed by an applicant as the nearest available. Refusals may nevertheless be accompanied by an undertaking not to remove where factors raised in the application are sufficiently short lived. Afghan applicants under the ARAP scheme may not apply for LOTR via the ARAP form (MIL 4.2.15.1).

A policy to cover leave outside the rules is being drafted was promised to comply with the new ethical decision making model, created following the Windrush Lessons Learned review. For discretionary leave see MIL 10.5.2.

Other cases show

- Awa [2020] ScotCS CSOH_91: the SSHD should take account of all relevant considerations when assessing whether an application should be granted notwithstanding that it did not meet the Rules, which included the need to take account for a mishap in the immigration history (here, a letter going astray that had aimed to notify the applicant of a flaw with their application) that was not the fault of the applicant or the SSHD
- Decision making should show that "*the residual discretion here is not just false air and lives on in a meaningful and active way*": Sayaniya [2016] EWCA Civ 85
- Behary & Ullah [2016] EWCA Civ 702: there is an obligation to consider a grant when expressly asked to do so and briefly deal with any supporting material
- The PBS is a very prescriptive system and there is usually no meaningful discretion within it (as opposed to outside the Rules: see eg Kalsi [2019] EWCA Civ 2293)
- Whilst it was possible to vary a PBS application to an application outside the rules, this needed to be done expressly and clearly: Sarkar [2021] UKAITUR JR02246202

There is specific guidance *Suitability: Purpose not covered by the Immigration Rules*. Examples given as to where a grant of permission OTR might be appropriate are where there is a need for urgent medical treatment after becoming ill on a flight or where a Student discovers their college has closed after the summer vacation and wants to enter and seek a new Sponsor.

4.2.1.1 Grants of leave to remain outside the Rules on human rights grounds

The HO has a general position on cases that dont' fit its conception of human rights as found in the IRs. However over time the scope for matters to be considered outside the Rules has lessened: everything is under the Rules for family life applications made under Appendix FM (MIL 5.3, 6.1.4),.

Essentially the test the HO apply (see eg GEN3.2 in Appendix FM) is whether:

- there are exceptional circumstances present
- such that refusing the application would have unjustifiably harsh consequences
- for the applicant or for their family

4.2.2 The 'exceptional circumstances' review – rule 353B

All cases which are reviewed, having exhausted appeal rights or where further representations have been rejected as failing to meet the fresh claim threshold, will be considered by reference to r353B in Part 12. It is a residual consideration *under* the rules rather than being *outside* the rules, though it essentially amounts to a last-chance review of a case to see if there is any reason why the general presumption of removal should not be carried through.

> 353B. Where further submissions have been made and the decision maker has established whether or not they amount to a fresh claim under paragraph 353 of these Rules, or in cases with no outstanding further submissions whose appeal rights have been exhausted and which are subject to a review, the decision maker will also have regard to the migrant's:
>
> (i) character, conduct and associations including any criminal record and the nature of any offence of which the migrant concerned has been convicted;
> (ii) compliance with any conditions attached to any previous grant of leave to enter or remain and compliance with any conditions of temporary admission or immigration bail where applicable;
> (iii) length of time spent in the United Kingdom spent for reasons beyond the migrant's control after the human rights or asylum claim has been submitted or refused;
>
> in deciding whether there are exceptional circumstances which mean that removal from the United Kingdom is no longer appropriate. This paragraph does not apply to submissions made overseas. This paragraph does not apply where the person is liable to deportation.

At one time a person facing removal who had exhausted all rights of appeal received a residual consideration of all relevant circumstances under old r395C. Now under r353B the onus is on the person facing removal to raise any relevant matters to the HO's attention. Where those reasons engage Article 8 of the ECHR, the various private and family life provisions in the rules will be applied.

If an ECHR Art 8 claim gets nowhere, it is highly unlikely that the factors referred to in 353B will change the HO's mind. Chapter 53 of the EIG, 'Extenuating circumstances', now archived but still available via the same link (and not, as yet, replaced by a clear equivalent) laid out the considerations to be applied at this stage.

In Qongwane [2014] EWCA Civ 957 it was explained that r353B is essentially a 'safety-valve', and that factors in r353B such as character, conduct and associations, and compliance with conditions of leave, were listed *not* to indicate that a grant of leave was appropriate to people who did not fall foul of those criteria, but rather to emphasise that those factors alone in no way precluded the normal course of removal.

4.2.3 Legacy cases

On 25 July 2006, the then Home Secretary John Reid announced that his officials had found around 400,000 to 450,000 unclosed asylum files. These 'unresolved cases' soon came to be known as 'legacy' cases to most in the sector, and the HO committed itself to 'resolving' them by 2011. Some non-asylum files found themselves becoming legacy cases too. The exercise was officially referred to as the 'case resolution exercise' and a large team of HO caseworkers, the Casework Resolution Directorate (CRD) was established to deal with the backlog.

The HO announced in the summer of 2011 that the casework resolution exercise had been completed and that the CRD was to be wound up. The announcement said that all those who had not been granted leave under the exercise were either awaiting removal or were those with whom the HO had lost contact. However, there remained many thousands within the legacy who did not fit into either of those categories, and the announcement that the exercise was complete was clearly made many years prematurely. The remaining files, some 35,000 at the end of 2013, were being dealt with by the UKVI's Older Live Cases Unit in Liverpool.

Those granted leave under the case resolution exercise were granted ILR, until an unannounced change of policy on 20 July 2011, following which those granted leave were given only three years of discretionary leave. The many legal challenges to this change of policy have been unsuccessful. Many lawyers have tried to argue that the legacy appeared to operate different criteria than what could be found either in the IRs or outside them: what else could explain the experience of many practitioners that it amounted to a virtual amnesty?

Whatever justification lay behind the grants of leave to remain to all those lucky 'legacy' migrants whose cases were granted before 2011, the courts have not accepted that there was any free-standing legal regime in operation.

SH (Iran) [2014] EWCA Civ 1469 spelled the end of challenges to decisions to refuse LTR under the legacy. It is now accepted that, whatever impression may have been received by observers over the period of the legacy programme, the official HO position was only grant leave to remain where there was sufficient connection with this country as to make removal a disproportionate interference with private or family life.

We come back to the question of delay when we deal with the question of 'delay in asylum and human rights cases', in Chapter 5. But it's worth knowing that at one time the *Exceptional Circumstances* guidance made special mention of how decision makers should treat legacy delays. It was withdrawn on 19 October 2017, but it may be relevant for individuals who did suffer delays during a spell in the legacy queue.

Essentially it provided that :

- Lengthy residence in the UK including a significant period whilst a case was pending in the legacy queue may well contribute to strengthening a person's connections with this country (so long as they are independently strong enough to create family/private life) particularly where they exceed six years
- The mere fact that a person was in the legacy at some time, even for a lengthy period, is not otherwise relevant to their entitlement to remain here.

4.2.4 Immigration concession for Syrian nationals

The HO has a policy to let Syrians maintain their status if already present in the UK lawfully: this includes those here as visitors. This applies to:

- persons of Syrian nationality
- who are present within the UK
- whose country of habitual residence is Syria
- who have limited leave to enter or remain or whose leave has expired within the past 14 days

The policy operates by:

- relaxing various restrictions in the Rules that would otherwise bar extension applications, such as the various limitations on Students in relation to their type and duration of studies, and the six month limitation on visits
- lifting the switching controls that usually prevent the extension of certain forms of leave into the Points Based System and visitor categories
- letting dependents switch in line with the principal
- recognising that the unrest in Syria may prevent an applicant from providing all relevant documentation, and this may be condoned so long as the difficulties are adequately explained
- nevertheless requiring fees to be paid

Many Syrians benefited from the *Vulnerable Persons and Vulnerable Children's Resettlement Schemes* that operated from January 2014 until February 2021. Syrians arriving under this Scheme could (from July 2017) apply free to upgrade from HP to Refugee status (application form here).

4.2.5 Grenfell Tower survivors and relatives

UKVI policies for this small group of individuals are available for survivors and their relatives. Eligible individuals (living in the Tower or whose accommodation made uninhabitable by it, and not excluded for suitability reasons such as criminality or being subject to deportation proceedings – including partners and children at the time, any subsequent UK-born children, and other dependants ordinarily residing with them) were required to come forward by 31 January 2018 and were granted an initial 12 months' limited leave, extendable and on a 5-year ILR route (applications being possible from July 2022), subject to meeting security, criminality and fraud checks. The ILR form is here. Now the *Grenfell Tower Survivors' Settlement Policy* addresses ILR in this route. Late applications will be addressed via the usual LOTR regime (MIL 4.2.1).

4.2.6 Errors by a representative

It can often happen that a migrant is let down by a legal advisor: hopefully a former one. HO policy, now mentioned in one particular context in the Guidance *Further submissions*, considers whether an individual has been failed by their legal representatives – it is sometimes called the Kazmi discretion because it first arose in the case of Kazmi [1995] Imm AR 73, cited in LD (Algeria) [2004] EWCA Civ 804.

Cleary it is undesirable to permit representative error harm to migrants whose fundamental rights are at stake. See FP (Iran) [2007] EWCA Civ 13:

> Immigration judges will know of the great pressure that anyone working in the field of immigration and asylum is under with regard to case load and throughput ...
>
> there is no general principle of law which fixes a party with the procedural errors of his or her representative.

Where negligence is alleged, the Tribunal will generally expect the matter to be duly evidenced (BT Nepal [2004] UKIAT 00311):

> We wish to make it clear that, in general, we will not make a finding of fact based on an allegation against former representatives unless, first, it is clear that the former representatives have been given an opportunity to respond to the allegation which is being made expressly or implicitly against them, and secondly, we are either shown the response or shown correspondence which indicates that there has been no response.

In Mansur [2018] UKUT 274 (IAC) UT evaluated the impact of an immigration adviser's failings on the assessment of the subsequent proportionality of a HO decision on their Article 8 rights. On the facts of the case the inadequacy in the legal advice was effectively indisputable and it was clear the public interest would not be adversely affected by the grant of leave. Indeed the public would not expect someone to be prejudiced by clear-cut representative error.

4.2.7 The Active War Zone Policy

There was a time when the HO Operational Enforcement Manual included a passage at Chapter 12 para 12.3:

> enforcement action should not be taken against nationals who originate from countries which are currently active war zones. Country Information Policy Unit (CIPU) or Enforcement Policy Unit (EPU) will provide advice on this.

It is discussed in HH Iraq [2009] EWCA Civ 727. It ran for a good many years (quite how long was never identified) until 14 January 2008. Whilst it was then subsumed in the international protection given under Article 15(c) of the Qualification Directive to asylum seekers fleeing armed conflicts (MIL 8.9.3.2), and is unlikely to be beneficial in terms of securing leave to remain to anyone now, it may show that enforcement action should not have begun against someone, which would, for example, have the effect of stopping the clock in a person's accumulation of time under the old Fourteen Year Rule (which permitted settlement after 14 years so long as no enforcement action had begun).

It might also cast a lengthy period of non-removal in a different light, meaning that their basis of stay, whilst precarious, might nevertheless be viewed flexibly such that it, with other factors, makes a compelling claim for their departure being disproportionate.

4.2.8 Age and enforcement action

It was previously the case that enforcement action (i.e. removal or deportation) would not be pursued against the over-65s. That policy was withdrawn in late 2004. The latest policy was at chapter 53.7 of the EIG (archived on 19 October 2017, not replaced but still available), and states:

> Ministers have agreed that a person's age is not by itself, a realistic or reliable indicator of a person's health, mobility or ability to care for themselves. Many older people are able to enjoy active and independent lives. Cases must be assessed on their individual merits.

The onus is on the applicant to show that there are extenuating circumstances, such as particularly poor health, close dependency on family members in the UK coupled with a lack of family and care facilities in the country of origin, which might warrant a grant of leave.

Given the restrictive rules that now govern the admission of adult dependent relatives, which do not provide for 'in-country' applications and pose a very high threshold of dependency and lack of care arrangements or possibilities abroad, the benchmark for these cases would be set very high, outside the rules as well as within them.

4.2.9 Carers policy

There is no provision in the IRs for those seeking to enter the UK to care for a sick family member or friend. A person who wishes to enter the UK to provide short-term care or make alternative arrangements for the long term care of a friend/relative may do so under the Rules relating to general visitors.

Where an extension of stay is sought purely for the purpose of caring, the policy published at Chapter 17, section 2 of the IDIs will be applied. It states, that:

> Whilst each case must be looked at on its individual merits, when considering whether a period of leave to remain should be granted, the following points are amongst those that should be borne in mind by caseworkers:
>
> - the type of illness/condition (this should be supported by a Consultant's letter); and
> - the type of care required; and
> - care which is available (e.g. from the Social Services or other relatives/friends); and
> - the long-term prognosis.

The policy on carers suggests that three months leave to remain will be granted initially, with further periods of up to 12 months at a time to follow in exceptional cases subject to favourable medical and welfare reports. The grant of three months leave is granted 'on the strict understanding that during this period arrangements will be made for the future care of the patient by a person who is not subject to the IRs' (IDIs at 17.3.1). There is also a duty on the HO to make enquiries as to the provision of satisfactory care for the person receiving care in the event of removal of the carer.

4.2.10 Participating in legal proceedings generally

A person's right to fair trial may be adversely affected if they are removed from the United Kingdom in circumstances where that would damage their ability to effectively participate in a trial of their claim. This is likely to be the case where their removal would compromise their ability to instruct their lawyers and to give live evidence.

Historically the possibility has arisen most often where the litigation is actually being brought against the Secretary of State. There is a reference to the concept in the guidance Considering human rights claims in visit applications.

> Article 6 may be engaged when the applicant is:
>
> bringing legal proceedings against the SSHD (SSHD), for example seeking damages for unlawful conduct, and has been removed before the conclusion of those proceedings and there is an allegation of bad faith against the SSHD in respect of the removal (Quaquah (1999) EWHC (Admin) 100)

The location of this policy in the visitor route implies a particular line of thinking by the HO: i.e. that one should be expecting to leave the country and be permitted to return for the legal proceedings as a visitor, rather than remaining here throughout the whole run-up to the trial. The necessary length of residence will ultimately depend on the facts: proceedings where significant engagement with a legal team is essential before the trial which is not feasible via IT links may require a longer period of residence.

Without a court order for personal attendance, the policy says that it is only in 'exceptional circumstances' that the grant of entry clearance might be appropriate.

4.2.11 Family court proceedings

In the case of MS (Ivory Coast) [2007] EWCA Civ 133 it emerged that the HO had a policy whereby removal or deportation action will not be pursued where family proceedings are pending (MIL 6.2.6.2).

4.2.12 Children in the care of a local authority

Section 8 of Annex 3.2 FM of the IDIs sets out guidance to the following effect, which may be thought surprisingly generous compared to the stance the HO generally takes to children (e.g. in the case of unaccompanied asylum seeking children to grant leave until the age of 17.5 under rule 352ZC whereas the Annex 3.2 references to children shows that the policy applies whilst a person is a 'child' in the normal sense, i.e. remains under 18, and the one-year or four-year tranches of leave could clearly extend well past a person's 18th birthday):

- Decisions about the future of children in the care of the local authority should be left primarily in the hands of their social services department as they will be best placed to act in the child's best interests
- While the local authority may look into the possibility of arranging the repatriation of a child in their care, such action will only be taken if it is in the child's best interests
- Where they consider it may be in the child's best interests to be repatriated, they will normally make full enquiries to ensure that suitable arrangements are made for the child's care and to satisfy themselves that repatriation is indeed in the child's best interests.
- If the social services advise that it would be appropriate for the child to remain in the United Kingdom, consideration should be given to granting the child leave to remain
- If there is a realistic possibility of the child returning to his parent(s) and/or country of origin in the future, the child may be granted limited leave for periods of 12 months on Code 1
- Where there is no prospect of the child leaving, the child may be granted leave to remain for four years on Code 1
- In both cases, after four years of limited leave to remain, if there is no prospect of removal, indefinite leave to remain may be granted

So where a child is in social services care representatives should ensure that the views of the relevant social services department are clarified in good time before applying for further permission to stay. The policy gives the greatest weight to their views, and in relation to most children, it is hard to see what competing factors could outweigh them.

4.2.13 Gurkhas

Settlement for Gurkhas and their families is now catered for within the rules. But there remains a complex policy background which has been heavily interpreted in the case law . We give a summary here. To gain better understanding of where your particular client might fit in, you may wish to consult the following:

- Appendix Armed Forces
- Part 7 Armed Forces
- HM forces: partners and children: transitional arrangements Version 2.0 (December 2017)
- Annex K - Adult Children of Former Gurkhas
- Gurkhas discharged before 1 July 1997 and their family members

The latter two policies are rather similar. The rationale is to rectify the historic injustice whereby Gurkhas could not readily obtain ILR and, in turn, could not establish a launchpad to come to the UK themselves together with close family members to the UK; by the time that policies were introduced to rectify the injustice in 2009, for both the former soldiers and their spouse and minor children, many potential applicants had become adults. Ultimately the January 2015 policy change, first seen in Annex K, aims to identify those maintaining sufficiently clear ties with their parents to warrant entry clearance. The policy aims at adult children outside the UK, aged under 30, who are financially and emotionally dependant on the former Gurkha, were born after their parent's discharge in circumstances where they would have been brought to the UK sooner had the option existed, where they have not formed an independent family unit or lived apart from their Sponsor for more than two years. If any of these provisos are not satisfied, cases must still be considered by reference to ECHR Art 8.

4.2.14 The Windrush scheme

The devastating impact of the hostile environment (MIL 1.3.6) on a generation of long term residents who were unable to document citizenship or settlement entitlements to the standards expected by officialdom led to the 'Windrush scandal'. Ultimately the Home Secretary had to resign.

As it was put in Howard [2021] EWHC 1023 (Admin), the SSHD had recognised this group of people who had come to the United Kingdom from Commonwealth countries prior to 1973 as fully integrated into British society, and described them as "... *British in all but legal status*". They had been wrong-footed by a policy that equated lack of formal documentation with want of immigration status.

A UKVI information page and helpline was set up and The Immigration and Nationality (Requirements for Naturalisation and Fees) (Amendment) Regulations 2018 entered force on 30 May 2018 to give effect to the Windrush scheme (see casework guidance and an application form). The intention behind the scheme is for the HO to assist applicants in gathering evidence of long term residence held by various government departments. Citizenship and settlement fees are dropped as well as some requirements such as KoLL. Those assisting applicants may wish to refer to outlines of the complex legal situation prepared by organisations such as SLC, ILPA (see ILPA Monthly, May 2018), HJT's own blog post on nationality sources, and may still wish to advise their clients to make the following requests for documentation themselves:

- A full Medical records request from their GP - max charge £50, can stretch back decades even where changed GPs as file travels with patients
- UKVI Subject Access Request – detailed request but can cover decades
- HMRC Subject Access Request – records for any taxes or national insurance contributions that may have been made. NICs records go back to the 1970s.
- In addition, the National Archives will assist in trying to locate old, lost naturalisation certificates (which may be relevant to questions of nationality for family members). If located, certified copies are provided at a cost of £27.40.

The scheme essentially works by dividing up Windrush cases into several groups: the first group is Commonwealth citizens settled in the UK before 1 January 1973 or with the right of abode, those who were automatically British, those wishing to apply for British citizenship, those with the right of abode, those wishing to prove their settled status, and those whose ILR lapsed due to absence from the UK and wish to resume it. The second group is people of other nationalities with ILR before 1 January 1973; the third group is those of any nationality arriving between 1 January 1973 and 31 Deceber 1988 with settled status. Group 4 is children of Commonwealth citizens settled/holding the right of abode before 1 January 1973. On 24 January 2022 some corrections were made to the Guidance as the effect of s1(5) of the IA 1971 had not previously been properly stated (MIL 1.3.2.1).

The Windrush Compensation Scheme (WCS) for losses suffered has been established, the *Windrush Compensation Scheme Rules* state it is open to primary claimants, their family members and their estate, and there is detailed guidance on assessing the impact on an applicant's life (via a five-point table proposing damages of £10-100k) which emphasises that detailed documentary evidence of every aspect of a claim is not required; there are bespoke *application forms*. By December 2020 nearly £3m had been paid out; by September 2022 over £56.5m had been distributed. There is an *Equality Impact Assessment*. Individuals from a wide range of nationalities have been granted documentation after applying to the Windrush Scheme from within the UK, including a wide range of Commonwealth countries: 15,457 as per the *September 2022 Factsheet*. If applicants are unable to produce particular documents then the HO should give them every opportunity to obtain them (including supporting them in so doing) and put applications on hold for up to 6 months as per the *Windrush*

Compensation Scheme Guidance. The April 2023 Human Rights Watch report *"Hostile" Compensation Scheme Fails 'Windrush' Victims* critiques the scheme.

On 17 December 2018, a hardship fund was set up as an interim measure, promising amounts of up to £5,000 (see here: Windrush hardship fund Windrush scheme: support in urgent and exceptional circumstances, link added to page Windrush scheme and information).

The May 2020 ILPA monthly update reported that by 2020 the Windrush scheme had lost its initial 'humane' face - & 4000 cases remained outstanding, some for over one year. Meanwhile only 36 payouts had been made via the Windrush compensation scheme.

The courts have looked at some of the Windrush consequences:

- **Naturalisation:** Rose [2022] EWCA Civ 1068 holds there to be no direct connection between good character and long residence and integration (MIL 12.5.4)
- Noren [2022] EWHC 2942 (Admin) holds that simply being a descendant of a Windrush survivor does not constitute a historic injustice such as to justify conferring British citizenship on an adult child. There were too many variables as to what actions might have been taken by the parents had their own status been addressed sooner.
- Vanriel [2021] EWHC 3415 (Admin) holds that it is discriminatory for Windrush victims to have to meet the 5 years lawfully in the UK proviso where the obstacle to so doing was wrongful denial of entry to the UK
- Though Brown [2022] EWHC 534 (Admin) holds that the WCS was essentially lawful and there was no duty to pay any particular sum in compensation. It was not discriminatory to fail to provide statutory entitlement to British citizenship for all members of the Windrush generation
- **Fees:** Mahabir [2021] EWHC 1177 (Admin) finds that the SSHD's failure to afford family members of a Windrush victim seeking to join them in the UK preferential treatment in the charging of fees, given the Windrush context, was unlawful for being indirectly discriminatory against them. They were in a different position to other applicants because the outcome of their applications will bear directly on the family life of the Windrush victim already in the UK
- Thompson [2023] EWHC 2037 (Admin) notes that an alleged victim would need to establish that they held ILR and not simply show ordinary UK residence. The WCS is concerned with compensation for harm resulting from an inability to prove lawful status, that status being dependent on having either the right of abode or settled status. ILR would lapse after 2 years abroad and was thus not held as of right by a person asserting returning residence status.

4.2.15 Afghan citizens and their families

Some local staff in Afghanistan, such as interpreters, have worked in dangerous and challenging roles. In return for this service, a resettlement package was introduced, and a leave to remain category was added to the IRs in 2013 for certain 'relevant Afghan citizens'. As part of the resettlement package, entry clearance would be granted for five years with accommodation, benefits and employment support. HZ [2023] EWHC 660 (Admin) discusses the support arrangements including bridging accommodation noting that education needs and employment opportunities would have to be considered whether allocation accommodation. There is *Bridging accommodation* Guidance which address the inteirm measure pending moving to Settled Accommodation.

The policy context was set out in the conclusions and recommendations of a May 2018 defence select committee report Lost in Translation? Afghan Interpreters and Other Locally Employed Civilians. On 6 July 2018, this category at paras 276BA1 to 276BS1 in Part 7 was updated, and again on 1 April 2021.

Following the 2021 military withdrawal and subsequent takeover of power by the Taliban in Afghanistan, more Afghans have become eligible.

There are rather a lot of routes: you can read one account of them all in the *Afghanistan resettlement and immigration policy statement* and the House of Commons Briefing *UK immigration routes for*

Afghan nationals. There are four distinct schemes in place for certain Afghan nationals at the time of writing:

1. The Afghan Relocations and Assistance Policy "ARAP": at one time found in the IRs Part 7, under the heading "Entry clearance to come to the UK as a relevant Afghan citizen" rr 276BA1-276BA5, now in Appendix ARAP
2. The Afghan Citizens Resettlement Scheme "ACRS" – policy-based only and currently lacking a prescribed application process – in place since 6 January 2022
3. UKVI guidance document "Concessions to the Immigration Rules for Afghan nationals for work and study routes" published on 17 January 2022 – the HoC Briefing states that as at January 2023 there are no returns to Afghanistan (there being no commercial flights) and that whilst HO guidance does not suggest that all Afghans are at risk of serious harm, failed asylum seekers should make themselves known to the HO if they believe their situation has changed
4. The Afghanistan Locally Employed Staff Ex-Gratia Scheme, IRs Part 7 once again, r276BB1, BB6

Partners and minor children may accompany principal family members (R276BJ1- R276BS1). Routes 1 and 4, for "relevant Afghan citizens", give access to indefinite leave to enter (effectively ILR). Each of the routes give priority access to benefits by exempting Afghan citizens under each of these schemes from satisfying the past presence test: see eg HRA [2023] UKUT 109 (AAC).

Besides these schemes, applications have been pursued outside the Rules.

- S & Anor [2022] EWHC 1402 (Admin) holds that the selection of candidates for the original evacuation process ("Operation Pitting", which called forward a cohort adjudged particularly at risk) was inconsistent and arbitrary, often based on chance lobbying, leading to unjustified discrimination against other applicants. Individuals might have significantly contributed to the UK mission whether or not they worked in Kabul
- And on appeal S & Anor [2022] EWCA Civ 1092 confirmed that requiring applicants to give inaccurate information simply to access the online application process was irrational
- It is essential to ask the right questions during the application process to equip decision makers with the relevant information to assess these applications: ALO [2022] EWHC 2380 (Admin)
- It was lawful to treat Afghan applicants differently from Ukraine nationals in normally requiring biometric provision abroad before an application was accepted for consideration. The approach was justified because it was reasonable to conclude that Afghan nationals posed greater security risks given that terrorist organisations had recently operated from there, the pressure that would have been put on the UK's VAC network, the fact that the UK's diplomatic links and foreign policy objectives were different as between the two countries, and given that the Afghan scheme was a route to ILR whereas the Ukraine scheme envisaged return: AB [2023] EWHC 287 (Admin)
- CX1 & Ors [2023] EWHC 284 (Admin) finds it reasonable to require visitor online forms to be used to apply for LOTR – the free text boxes allow full information to be provided and Guidance warned that the available forms would not always be suitable in some respects
- GA [2023] EWHC 871 (Admin) holds that there was no clear, unambiguous and unqualified representation that potential applicants falling within the scheme's general description would have a right to make an application, simply that they may be included within a particular cohort

From 30 November 2022 ARAP received its own Appendix, rather than residing in Part 7 of the IRs. The Afghanistan Resettlement and Immigration Policy Statement of November 2022 introdcues that regime, setting out that the evacuation stage of the process is now over and that government is *"determined to ensure [evacuees] have the best possible start to life in the UK"*. "Operation Warm Welcome" should ensure that all those relocated to the UK can access the vital healthcare, housing, education and support into employment they need to fully integrate here. The Guidance *Managing vulnerable households* addresses how the HO will prioritise offers of settled accommodation, where it is available: the aim is to target offers firstly to those who have specific vulnerabilities such that they will struggle the most to find their own accommodation and integrate effectively into life in the UK.

The onlne MIL address the various routes in detail: ARAP, the Afghan Citizens Resettlement Scheme, concessions to the Rules, and the Locally Employed Staff Ex Gratia Scheme.

4.2.16 Section 67 leave – Dubs Amendment leave: unaccompanied minors

Paras 352ZG-352ZS in Part 11 were added on 6 July 2018 to provide for leave to remain and settlement for unaccompanied minors from mainland Europe, who have been transferred to the UK under s67 Immigration Act 2016. The commitment to transfer 480 children under this scheme was announced as fulfilled on 27 July 2020 (see Gov.uk Factsheet). Thus this route is now closed to new LTR applicants, but practitioners may come across ILR applications until 2025. The eligibility requirements for leave to remain on this route were as follows:

- where an applicant has made an asylum claim, any such claim has been refused
- not being excluded from refugee status under Reg 7 of the 2006 Protection Regs
- not being a danger to the security of the UK
- not being convicted of a particularly serious crime
- not falling within any of the (then) general grounds for refusal in para 322 of Part 9

For those applicants arriving in the UK after 1st October 2019 the grant of leave was automatic on their arrival. They were still entitled to claim asylum, but this was not required for the grant of leave (352ZHA).

Leave is granted for applicants and any minor dependants for five years with entitlement to work, study and have recourse to public funds.

SI2018/788 on 20 July 2018 amended legislation on Child Benefit, Tax Credits, Guardians' Allowance and Childcare Payments to provide for children on this type of leave.

ILR is available to those who

- have been granted s67 leave; or
- were transferred to the UK under s67, were granted leave as someone with refugee or HP status and have had that status ended or refused under paras 339A or 339G after a review

To qualify for ILR, a residence permit for s67 leave or under 339Q (refugee status/HP) must have been held for a continuous period of five years in the UK and all the conditions for s67 leave must still be met at that stage. In addition, the SSHD must not have the view that their character, conduct or association, or the fact the applicant poses a threat to national security makes their settlement undesirable. No fee is payable: SI 2018/999.

Travel document applications will be granted unless compelling reasons of national security or public order require otherwise, and if the applicant can prove their inability to obtain a national passport, or reasonable attempts were made and failed and there are compelling reasons to travel. This will not be a Refugee Convention document (as by definition those on s67 leave have been refused asylum), but the more expensive certificate of travel (£141 for children, £280 for adults).

4.2.17 Leave to remain for Calais children who joined family in the UK between 17 October 2016 and 13 July 2017

IRs 352I-X provided for a new form of leave for those children transferred to the UK between 17 October 2016 and 13 July 2017 as part of the Calais camp clearance to reunite with family, where they do not qualify for international protection (i.e. refugee status or humanitarian protection). 769 unaccompanied children were transferred to the UK, 549 of whom to reunite with family here. All of those children claimed asylum on arrival in the UK but a number would fall to be refused.

Those granted Calais leave, or dependants of those granted Calais leave, will receive a Residence Permit with a validity of five years. This is subject to exclusions based on the grounds of security and criminality, deception or omission of information relevant to acceptance under Calais leave. Residence permits can be revoked if Calais leave is revoked.

At the end of the five-year period, if the person's Calais leave has been renewed, they will be issued with another residence permit, valid for a further period of five years.

A person may apply for ILR after a period 10 years' continuous leave in the UK. ILPA's response to HC 1534 of 17 October 2018 criticizes this for being out of line with refugee leave, where settlement eligibility arises after five, not 10 years.

Travel documents are available via the Certificate of Travel (MIL 4.2.16)

Asylum Policy Instruction Calais leave, published on 3 December 2018, provides further detail.

4.2.18 Non-removable migrants and limbo

The theory of immigration control is that a person is either in the UK lawfully, because they have been granted permission or otherwise hold residence rights, or their stay is tolerated because they are pursuing an appeal or JR claim, or they are present unlawfully. The IMA 2023 introduces a new form of limbo for those falling under its s2 (MIL 9.1) - these individuals, mostly asylum seekers, will not be at the end of the line and the considerations arising in their cases may be rather different to the end-of-the-line community discussed below.

However, many people who have failed in their applications and appeals remain here. They are expected to make a voluntary departure if they have no pending application. There is no obligation on the HO to otherwise consider any arguments they have raised in a "one stop notice" updating the HO of their circumstances, unless they have made a formal application. Nor to generate an appealable immigration decision absent a proper application: Siddique [2016] EWCA Civ 570. If they cannot afford to make an application, then of course a fee waiver may be available.

What if they maintain that they cannot depart the UK because they cannot obtain travel documents, perhaps because their country of origin has no enthusiasm for accepting them back? Such individuals may well be liable to detention, though the HO has to be able to show that there is a real prospect of their removal for this to be lawful. They may be able to make an application under the Statelessness rules: but only if there is cogent evidence of lacking any country's nationality, they can prove they are not admissible to another country, and they pass the suitability thresholds (MIL 4.3). Often there isn't.

RA Iraq [2019] EWCA Civ 850 suggests that there would have be an exceptionally long period of limbo with no real chance of removal before leave need be granted . Where this situation potentially arises, then the impact on the individual's private life has to be balanced against the public interest in maintaining immigration control (bearing in mind that this is someone who has already been established as having no lawful entitlement to remain in the UK). Any culpability of the individual (for example, in failing to take every step open to them to persuade their national authorities to accept them back) would count strongly against the grant of leave. For this scenario to be relevant:

- first, it must be apparent that the appellant is not capable of being actually deported immediately, or in the foreseeable future;

- second, it must be apparent that there are no further or remaining steps that can currently be taken in the foreseeable future to facilitate his deportation; and

- third, there must be no reason for anticipating change in the situation and, thus, in practical terms, the prospects of removal are remote

The UT revisited the threshold at which the SSHD should be granting leave to persons who are not removable in AM [2021] UKUT 62 (IAC).

- The applicant must show serious and potentially long-lasting difficulties in the respondent's ability to have the individual removed – but they did not need to show that their removal was an outright impossibility
- Normally the individual would need to show that the difficulties with removal were beyond their own control: being found to have given misleading information to their own national authorities would usually prevent cases succeeding, even for a very long period (subject to mental health issues preventing them from ever putting the record straight)
- Where the chances of the applicant changing their mind were truly remote, and where the evidence was such that nobody could suggest immigration control would be threatened by setting a bad example (as where the individual had lived on the margin of society for their 20 years of limbo), there was no material public interest that would outweigh their private life

Antonio [2022] EWCA Civ 809 accepts that it might not be appropriate to grant leave to remain on limbo grounds where a person's refusal to disclose material information might change in the future.

The question of limbo may come alive in the context of the inadmissibility regime created by IMA 2023. The ECtHR has historically been unconcerned with the precise residence right a migrant receive, so long as "it allows the holder to reside within the territory of the host country and to exercise freely there the right to respect for his or her private and family life, the granting of such a permit represents in principle a sufficient measure to meet the requirements of that provision": Sisojeva v Latvia 60654/00 [2007] ECHR 325. However this leaves open whether failing to grant residence altogether to asylum seekers with unprocessed claims and who are not not facing imminent removal respects their private and family life.

4.2.19 Coronavirus policies, concessions and changes to procedure

From mid-March 2020, a great number of concessions and policies in response to the COVID-19 pandemic were announced. Not all were very clear; exceptional assurance in particular gave scope for confusion.

Whilst now historic (the exceptional assurance regime, permitting applicants unable to leave the UK and not intending to remain here on a basis that could be pursued under the Rules ended on 30 November 2022), these may remain relevant to understanding a client's immigration history. The general position is shown by this phrase from the *Student Coronavirus Guidance*: "The Home Office and its Ministers are very clear that no one will have a negative outcome through the immigration system due to a circumstance that was beyond their control."

In addition to the sources linked below, and to keep up with developments, readers may wish to consult

- UKVI's collection of COVID-19 policy documents and guidance (which covers some, but not all of the information)
- Refugee Council page Changes to Asylum & Resettlement policy and practice in response to Covid-19

The following policies and procedures appeared at various times on the pages Coronavirus (COVID-19): advice for UK visa applicants and temporary UK residents (which sets out a series of concessions) and Coronavirus (COVID-19): immigration and borders (which links to a series of policies, including ones for Students, Healthcare workers and Sponsors). The overriding thinking is as set out in the Coronavirus Student Guidance: '*The Home Office and its Ministers are very clear that no one will have a negative outcome through the immigration system due to a circumstance that was beyond their control.*'

Those in the UK

Those unable to leave the UK whose visa expired (or is due to expire):

- Between 24 January and 31 July 2020: could request a free, short "extension" by email

- Between 24 January and 31 August 2020: new applicants and those already on the above "extension" received an automatic extension to 31 August 2020, termed a "grace period": now IR 39E(4) condones overstaying over that period (MIL 5.2.4)
- Between 1 January 2021 and 30 November 2022 could request an extra period of leave termed an **"exceptional assurance"** to protect "against any adverse action or consequences" when leave expired, but which itself granted no leave (nevertheless, other leave could be applied for while the assurance is current) - evidence of inability to leave the UK was required. Applications were made to cihassuranceteam@homeoffice.gov.uk and the procedure is set out here. If circumstances changed preventing them leaving at the end of their exceptional assurance they could apply again for a further period of exceptional assurance. As time passed threshold became higher: eg where return was not possible because a country's borders remain closed or where quarantine arrangements are oversubscribed
- On 19 September 2020, the guidance was updated to confirm those with exceptional assurance could study, work or rent accommodation if their previous immigration status allowed this. However, to obtain leave, a full, paid application had to be made within the validity of the exceptional assurance
- If the leave held previously did not allow a further application or switching into the relevant category, an application could nevertheless be made if leave expired before 30 June 2021
- Those whose visa expired before or after 31 August 2020 could temporarily apply for leave, even in categories which would normally require entry clearance. However, those who did not apply for an "exceptional assurance" by 31 August 2020 could not use this discretion and the guidance required that they "make arrangements to leave the UK".
- The Exceptional circumstances fee waiver entered force on 10 September 2020: it allows UKVI to respond to the plight of migrants with a compelling and compassionate justification to waive fees due to exceptional circumstances significantly impacting on them for reasons beyond their control
- In June 2021, a new concession was added for those who travelled to the UK outside the validity of their entry clearance vignette due to COVID-19 impacts, and whose leave was therefore not activated. They could apply to activate their leave by emailing ECActivation@homeoffice.gov.uk, including the information and evidence as set out on this page. An updated BRP would then be sent out. This concession was removed on 28 January 2022

Application centre availability

- Those whose centres were closed at the time of their appointment should have been contacted to book a new appointment, their s3C leave being preserved

Tier 1 Entrepreneurs who suffered business disruption benefit from relaxed job creation criteria (MIL 7.2.3); disrupted start-up applicants also benefit (MIL 7.2.1.2.4); .
sstudents or Child Students benefit from some concessions (MIL 7.4.3.23).

Until 1 October 2020 frontline NHS workers received an automatic 1-year extension, free of charge, subject to making the application. NHS and other healthcare workers received various other dispensations, though tend to be of only historic relevance now. Non-EEA relatives of a healthcare worker deceased as a result of coronavirus should receive an automatic free grant of ILR, by way of the deceased's employer being contacted by UKVI. They can also contact UKVINHSTeam@homeoffice.gov.uk to enquire about the scheme. In June 2021, extended family members were added to those who may benefit from this settlement policy in compassionate and compelling circumstances.

For workers/renters generally:

- The Guidance Worker and temporary worker sponsors continues to state that that action will not be taken against employers whose employees are absent due to coronavirus
- Relaxed ("adjusted") checks were permitted until 30 September 2022 as per the Coronavirus (COVID-19): landlord right to rent checks and Coronavirus (COVID-19): right to work checks (thereafter see MIL 7.10.5)

Work visa applicants in most categories awaiting a decision:

- Could start work if they applied in-time and held a CoS for a job in the health and care category, or received a CoS before 19 January 2021
- But had to stop working if their application is rejected as invalid, or refused.

NHS workers could undertake supplementary work beyond 20 hours weekly in SoC codes beyond their primary visa until 4 October 2022.

Those outside the UK

- Should check any relevant travel bans, quarantine requirements and exemptions which will apply to them on their arrival, before making travel plans. Guidance on travel is here.
- May fit within the Covid Visa Concession Scheme (CVCS) to obtain permission to return to the UK where they left the UK before 17 March 2020 and who have, or are seeking to apply for, leave on an eligible route but were unable to return due to COVID travel restrictions meaning their leave expired whilst abroad

- Where 90-day travel vignettes expired replacements, valid for 90 days, can be requested by an online form
- Those who left the UK with valid leave before 17 March 2020 and who intended to apply for ILR or FLR, but were unable to return before leave expired had a window to apply until 21 June 2021
- ILR holders absent for 2 years or more due to coronavirus whose ILR therefore lapsed on or after 24 January 2020 should complete the Returning Resident application form. Holders of returning resident visas were able to request a refund via CIH@homeoffice.gov.uk but this concession closed on 21 December 2021.
- Holders of LTR under family or private life routes, who were unable to return to the UK before their leave expired because of Covid travel restrictions will have "*a short break of up to 6 months in continuous residence...overlooked*" if their leave expire between 1 March 2020 and 19 July 2021. They must apply for further leave as soon as possible.

Note that for ILR purposes absences from the UK in excess of 180 days, will only be overlooked where due to evidenced travel restrictions - not for Covid-related general or personal reasons.

Family life – applications for leave to enter or remain

- See MIL 6.2.3 for financial concessions
- See MIL 6.2.4 for immigration status concessions
- See MIL 6.2.2 for English test centre concessions
- As at 13 October 2020, the Guidance *Coronavirus (COVID-19): advice for UK visa applicants and temporary UK residents* stated for those deciding to stay in the UK due to the pandemic: "You'll also be able to submit an application form from within the UK where you would usually need to apply for a visa from your home country". At some time this concession was dropped.

4.2.19.2 HMCTS policies, concessions and changes to procedure
4.2.20 Hong Kong BN(O) Visa for BN(O) citizens and their close family members

The online version of MIL contains two useful sections on the routes for BN(O) citizens from Hong Kong and their family members, and the various Ukraine schemes. However, as these routes appear to have rather low refusal rates, and as we need to save space in the paper version, we do not put them into print.

4.2.21 Sudanese nationals

Although there is no published immigration concession available for nationals of Sudan, from 15 May 2023 the income-related benefits, universal credit, personal independence payment and disability and carers' Regs are amended by The Social Security (Habitual Residence and Past Presence)

(Amendment) Regulations 2023. It benefits persons lawfully resident in the UK previously residing in Sudan before 15 April 2023 who departed in connection with the violence which rapidly escalated on that date in Khartoum and across Sudan. They will be exempt from the residency tests and therefore be able to access benefits and services faster on arrival in the UK. Similarly housing legislation is amended so that housing and homelessness assistance can be provided by local authorities.

4.3 Victims of trafficking/modern slavery and their support

Victims of trafficking and of modern slavery are likely to have various needs. They may require international protection in which case they should apply for asylum - as where they fear retribution from their traffickers, or being re-trafficked (see e.g. PO (Nigeria) [2011] EWCA Civ 132). Once recognised as victims, they may benefit from various welfare services and may be granted short periods of discretionary leave. These rights arise under the Convention against Trafficking – formerly also under the EU Trafficking Directive 2011/36/EU though it is disapplied from 31 January 2023.

The Modern Slavery Act 2015 (ss1-2) creates offences for holding people in slavery or servitude (which may include the forced provision of any service, not just labour, under threat of penalty, which might include threats to report the victim to the HO), including for the purposes of exploitation (s3) so as to constitute trafficking: rather than define these terms itself it makes its reference point ECHR Art 4. The relevant HO guidance is available here, and further information relating to the NRM from this page.

Trafficking victims may need

- medical help, both physical and psychological,
- assistance re their current circumstances if they are detained or lack support and accommodation
- help with matters of criminal law

All of this may be new to many immigration advisers. Assisting trafficking victims is a specialist area and non-specialist advisors who have concerns that their clients may be victims of trafficking should seek expert advice. An extremely useful resource for those who are interested in this area is the *Human Trafficking Handbook: Recognising Trafficking and Modern-Day Slavery in the UK*. Guidance includes *Modern slavery: how to identify and support victims*. It explains the roles of public authorities and first responders, the decision making process, the vulnerability of child victims, and explains the support arrangements for adult victims including the Essential Living Rate for non-asylum cases.

Part 5 of NBA 2022 introduces significant reforms of the process from 31 January 2023:

- a statutory basis for the recovery period (ss61-62), providing assistance and support (s64), and for granting leave to remain (s65)
- disqualification on grounds of public order or acting in bad faith (s63)
- new legal aid provisions (ss66-67)
- disapplying the EU Trafficking Directive (s68)

There are further changes envisagd by IMA 2023 though not yet in force:

- a general disregard of slavery/trafficking claims for those falling under s2 (s5(1)(c)) (MIL 9.1)
- recovery periods and the duty to grant leave do not apply (s22(1)-(2)) unless the individual has received a positive reasonable grounds decision and is cooperating with a public authority re an investigation/prosecution into the conduct leading to that positive decision, where there are compelling reasons for thinking the migrant's presence is necessary for that cooperation and any threat they pose of significant harm to the public is outweighed by this necessity (s22(3), (5)) (this bar does not apply to the children of such a person for whom they have sole responsibility or for whom they have care: s22(7)). A person's leave under s65(2) NBA 2022 2022 may be revoked if granted after 7 March 2023

Annex F to the *Modern Slavery Statutory Guidance* sets out the details of support. Local housing authorities must secure accommodation for an individual if there is a reason to believe that they may otherwise be homeless, eligible for assistance and have a priority need (s188(1) Housing Act 1996)). They must not be considered 'intentionally homeless' if they have left accommodation because of violence or exploitation, or threats of the same. A referral should be made to the Modern Slavery Victim Care Contract (MSVCC) where there is a risk of destitution, though accommodation will only be provided prior to a reasonable grounds decision if other possibilities are unsuitable, or risk re-exploitation or destitution. The Guidance lists various kinds of accommodation considered suitable.

The support arrangements were conveniently summarised in JP [2019] EWHC 3346 (Admin):

> 'Basic trafficking support in the uk is provided by the Salvation Army under a contractual arrangement between the Salvation Army and the Secretary of State and includes specialist accommodation (where needed), a support worker to provide practical and emotional support, access to free healthcare in emergency or other limited circumstances, short-term counselling and financial support at a rate of £65 per week.
>
> Whereas under basic trafficking support a potential victim is entitled to access medical treatment only in emergency or other limited circumstances, under enhanced trafficking support, pursuant to Article 12(3) of ECAT, a potential or actual victim is entitled t" "necessary medical or other assistance to victims … who do not have adequate resources and need such he"p". Similarly, whereas under basic trafficking support a potential victim is not entitled to access the labour market, vocational training or education in thukUK, pursuant to Article 12(4) of ECAT, a potential or actual victim is entitled to that access.'

The SSHD via the MSVCC outsources the provision of accommodation and financial support to the Salvation Army. MD [2021] EWHC 1370 (Admin) found there was no legal requirement to provide support under the Contract to those receiving Asylum Support who had children. The judge noted the evidence of infrequent ad hoc payments to those with well-connected or persistent support workers was not reassuring – but the absence of alternative charitable arrangements did not create a funding obligation on the SSHD. PM [2023] EWHC 1551 (Admin) holds that trafficking victims in initial asylum accommodation should receive financial support of £65 per week and that the SSHD's failure to properly consult and investigate relevant considerations before cutting support in August 2020 was unlawful.

The *Allocation of Accommodation Policy* originally provided that possible victims referred to the NRM would not be suitable for being accommodated at Napier, the ex-MoD sites (in Wethersfield and Scampton), vessels, or for room sharing; however from 9 October 2023 cases will simply be considered on their individual facts.

ZV (Lithuania) [2021] EWCA Civ 1196 confirms that the obligation under Art 12(3)-(4) of the Anti-Trafficking Directive to provide necessary medical and other assistance and access to the labour market and vocational training did not apply to potential trafficking victims yet to receive a CGD. The requirement was to provide "necessary medical treatment", not only "emergency medical support/treatment". That implied psychological assistance, counselling and information responding to the welfare needs of the individual, objectively assessed in each case. No distinct formal assessment was required where the individual was in detention and thus under the care of professional staff.

The UK has duties to provide protection and services to victims of trafficking under the Council of Europe's Convention on Action against trafficking (CAT), under Article 4 of the ECHR and under EU law. Note also

- The provisions in the IRs relating to those granted leave under the domestic worker category who are then found to be victims of trafficking (MIL 4.1.1.1 on *Domestic workers, trafficking and slavery*, above)
- Trafficking victims should receive lifetime anonymity orders in any court/tribunal proceedings: R v BXR [2022] EWCA Crim 1483
- The specific Guidance *Adults at risk Detention of victims of modern slavery* (MIL 13.1.8)
- The modern slavery defences to criminal offending (MIL 15.1.4)

Here we provide an overview of trafficking. Those representing victims may wish to consult specialist organisations such as the Anti-Trafficking Legal Unit (ATLEU). There is also a guidance published by the Law Society. The government has suggested that trafficking claims may sometimes be an attempt to get roundt the immigration laws: the House of Commons Library briefing *Modern slavery cases in the immigration system* looks at the relationship between the UK's modern slavery laws and the asylum system, and recent debate about whether modern slavery laws are being exploited by people trying to avoid being removed from the UK.

4.3.1 The Convention against Trafficking

The Government ratified the Council of Europe Convention on Action against Trafficking in Human Beings (ECAT) on 17 December 2008 and implemented it from 1 April 2009.

Two HO guidance documents outline the policies and practices of the HO in regard to the UK's obligations under the Convention: Victims of modern slavery – frontline staff guidance and the Modern Slavery Act 2015: statutory guidance for England and Wales.

ECAT may be relied upon in public law proceedings, as explained in Minh [2015] EWHC1725 (Admin) at [53]:

> Since the UK Government has announced that its policy is to give effect to its obligations under the Trafficking Convention, that has consequences in domestic administrative law. Failure to apply the provisions of the Convention may give rise to a successful claim for JR: not because the treaty has any direct effect (because it does not), but because the Government has then failed to apply its own published policy … Thus, the Competent Authority should be taken to have intended to protect the victim's rights, combat trafficking and promote international co-operation (the objectives identified in the Convention) and to promote a human rights based approach.

This principle was in KTT [2021] EWHC 2722 (Admin) (followed in SV [2022] UKUT 39 (IAC)), in which the HO sought to argue that ECAT is not justiciable. The Court accepted that "*Article 14(1)(a) ECAT is potentially justiciable provided that the Defendant's stated policy was to make decisions in relation to discretionary leave in accordance with the requirements of that provision*". EOG [2022] EWCA Civ 307 confirms that whilst there may be no duty to incorporate every aspect of ECAT into domestic law, there was a public law duty to apply those particular aspects of ECAT which were incorporated into HO policy. From 31 January 2023 the NBA 2022 regime aims to reduce the impact of ECAT.

4.3.2 Definition of trafficking

Many victims will not understand themselves to have been trafficked or willing to disclose their true story. The two HO policy documents referred to above provide useful indicators of trafficking and should be consulted where there is concern that a client might be a victim of trafficking.

The Convention defines trafficking under Article 4. There are three crucial elements in the definition:

- the act of 'recruitment, transportation, transfer, harbouring or receipt of persons'
- by means of 'the threat or use of force or other forms of coercion, of abduction, of fraud, of deception, of the abuse of power or of a position of vulnerability or of the giving or receiving of payments or benefits to achieve the consent of a person having control over another person'
- for the purpose of exploitation, which includes 'at a minimum, the exploitation of the prostitution of others or other forms of sexual exploitation, force labour or services, slavery or practices similar to slavery, servitude or the removal of organs' (UN Convention No. 29 concerning forced or compulsory labour defines 'forced or compulsory labour' as 'all work or service which is exacted from any person under the menace of any penalty and for which the said person has not offered himself voluntarily')

Trafficking in human beings is a combination of these constituents: and the constitutents are likely to overlap. As summarised by in SP (Albania) [2019] EWCA Civ 951 the trafficking definition is to be read disjunctively rather than conjunctively and cannot otherwise be effective – slavery includes exploitation by the abuse of power which encompasses, among other practices, servitude, forced or compulsory labour and sexual exploitation.

Article 4 goes on to emphasise that a person's 'consent' to these practices is irrelevant to their status as a victim.

It is evident that a person may be brought to the UK in circumstances that have the flavour of trafficking but without one of the vital three ingredients being present, so it is important to always consider each dimension carefully. BWM, R. v [2022] EWCA Crim 924 warns that psychiatric experts should not pronounce on trafficking victim status.

4.3.3 Article 4 ECHR

The HO also has duties under Article 4 of the ECHR.

In Rantsev v Cyprus and Russia (2010) 51 EHRR 1, the European Court of Human Rights held that trafficking falls within the scope of Article 4 of the ECHR (see Chapter 10 for the text of Article 4), and that there is a procedural obligation under Article 4 to investigate alleged trafficking, and to put in place a legislative and administrative framework to prohibit and punish trafficking (sometimes called operational duties or measures).

The Supreme Court in MS (Pakistan) [2020] UKSC 9 found that any attempt to remove a trafficking victim from the United Kingdom before those procedural obligations have been discharged will normally be unlawful.

4.3.4 EU law

The protection available to trafficking victims was further strengthened by EU Directive 2011/36/EU on preventing and combating trafficking in human beings and protecting its victims. It was most useful vis-á-vis involvement in the criminal process and regarding support measures. However from 31 January 2023, s68 of the NBA 2022 disapplies its provisions from being EU retained law in so far as anything in the Directive is incompatible with the Act. We will see what effect this has on HO policy in due course.

4.3.5 Referral process

In order to ensure that trafficking obligations are met, the National Referral Mechanism (NRM) was created, to provide a framework for identifying victims of human trafficking and ensuring they receive the appropriate protection and support.

All agencies and organisations, who find themselves with grounds for concern that a person may be a victim of human trafficking, have a responsibility for ensuring the safeguarding needs of any potential child victim are assessed and addressed and for reporting their trafficking concerns to a first responder. There is a *Devolving child decision-making* pilot programme under way assessing whether the assessment is best done within existing safeguarding structures.

First responders are the agencies referringindividuals onto the National Referral Mechanism. A first responder may be (Victims of modern slavery – frontline staff guidance):

- a local authority
- UK Visas and Immigration (UKVI)
- Health and Social Care Trusts
- the police and National Crime Agency (NCA)
- Barnardo's
- the NSPCC's Child Trafficking Advice Centre (CTAC)

- an agency who deals with adults who have been trafficked (such as Gangmasters Licensing Authority, The Poppy Project, TARA, Migrant Help, the Medaille Trust, Kalayaan and the Salvation Army, Barnado's, NSPCC, Refugee Council and others)

Where a first responder finds themselves with grounds for concern that a person may be a victim of human trafficking, a formal referral is made into the National Referral Mechanism, a victim identification and support process which is designed to make it easier for all the different agencies that could be involved in a trafficking case – e.g. police, HO, local authorities and NGOs – to co-operate; to share information about potential victims and facilitate their access to advice, accommodation and support.

Given the likelihood that trafficking victims only get good quality legal advice some way along the process, initial decisions often have to be reconsiderd. In DS [2019] EWHC 3046 (Admin) the HO policy which limited the ability to request reconsiderations of negative trafficking decision was identified as unlawful. It was too restrictive in preventing legal representatives from applying for reconsideration. Now the policy states that a person acting on the applicant's behalf may request reconsideration. First Responders and Support Providers may be consulted by a competent authority; and if not putting a forward a reconsideration request themselves, should give written reasons. Reconsideration requests based on asserted breach of policy should be made within 3 months; if based on fresh evidence, there is no time limit.

BVN [2022] EWHC 1159 (Admin) holds that there is no obligation on the SSHD to advise a person as to the pros and cons of withdrawing from the NRM.

The National Referral Mechanism has been changed over time. The new digital system is live and can be found here. The old forms are still accessible here but will only be accepted under exceptional circumstances. First responders are under very serious pressures: the Kalayaan report *The National Referral Mechanism: Near Breaking Point* warns that front line staff in statutory services are often unaware of their legal responsibilities to identify and safeguard survivors, or being overstretched and underfunded for them to be able to respond sufficiently.

4.3.6 Competent Authorities, Reasonable and Conclusive Grounds decisions – and Disqualification from Protection

In line with the ongoing reform to trafficking processes the new Single Competent Authority (SCA) has replaced the Competent Authorities. Under the old system decisions about who is a victim of trafficking are made by one of the two *Competent Authorities* - the UK Human Trafficking Centre, where the person is a UK or EEA national, or where there is an immigration issue but the person is not yet known to HO, and the HO for situations where trafficking is raised as part of an asylum claim or in the context of another immigration process. Subsequently the HO created a new body, the Immigration Enforcement Competent Authority (IECA), for the stated purpose of identifying victims of modern slavery. Various NGOs warned against this measure as potentially weakening the protection afforded to victims.

The decision-making process remains the same and has two stages: the **reasonable grounds** decision (RGD) and then the **conclusive grounds** decision (CGD).

Part 1 The first part is the **reasonable grounds test**, which acts as an initial filter to identify potential victims.

Within 5 days of a referral, the SCA should apply a 'reasonable grounds' test to consider if the statement "I suspect but cannot prove" that the person is a victim of trafficking holds true. If the answer is positive, the person will be granted a minimum of 45 calendar days for recovery and reflection. No detention or removal action will be taken against the subject during this time.

Part 2 The second is a substantive **conclusive grounds decision** as to whether the person is in fact a victim.

Following a positive *reasonable grounds* decision, the SCA must make a second identification decision, on 'conclusive grounds', which is to conclusively decide, on the balance of probabilities, if the individual is a victim of trafficking. The expectation is that a CGD will be made at some time following the 45 day recovery and reflection period.

It has been argued that the balance of probabilities standard should not apply, given that trafficking decisions are akin to refugee status determination. MN [2020] EWCA Civ 1746 rejects this argument. Nevertheless the CoA accepts that many aspects of credibility assessment should bear in mind the principles developed over the years in asylum casework. Decision makers should analyse all the evidence in a rational order and not treat an account as lacking credibility simply because it was implausible: plausibility was just one aspect of the assessment. It was wrong for the guidance to label considerations like this as *"mitigating circumstances"*: because that term implied that there was a defect requiring explanation, contrary to the holistic assessment required.

Pasian [2022] ScotCS CSOH_21 holds that a CGD is unlawful for failing to take account of relevant considerations where it failed to give due consideration to information that the police had completed their enquiries into the Applicant's case.

As we discuss below, recognition to the conclusive grounds standard **may** bring a grant of leave to remain. It should usually bring serious consideration as to whether permission to work should be granted. LJ (Kosovo) [2020] EWHC 3487 (Admin) finds that the HO policy on work permission (Version 8.0) unlawfully discriminated against recognised trafficking victims whose asylum claims remained pending. In particular it failed to identify the discretion to depart from Immigration Rule 360 restricting asylum seekers' permission to work to jobs on the shortage occupation list. It was necessary to recognise a discretion to let people work where that might help their recovery from trafficking had to be recognised. Cardona [2021] EWHC 2656 (Admin) held that the *Application in respect of children* section of Version 8.0 of the Work Policy was unlawful for suggesting that generally their carers' ability to work was not relevant to childrens' best interests.

NBA 2022 s63(2) provides that potential victims disqualified from both the recovery period (MIL 4.3.7) and the grant of leave to remain (MIL 4.3.8). This applies where the individual

- is a threat to public order (s63(1)(a)) (essentially relating to terrorism or other national security matters, reaching the automatic deportation threshold (MIL 13.4.1.2), having been deprived of their British citizenship, or being excluded from the Refugee Convention, s63(3)) or
- has claimed to be a victim of slavery or human trafficking in bad faith (s63(1)(b))

4.3.7 Recovery period

Once a person is identified as a victim to the reasonable grounds standard, then he or she is owed assistance as identified by Article 12(1) of the CAT:

- appropriate and secure accommodation, psychological and material assistance;
- access to emergency medical treatment;
- translation and interpretation services;
- translated counselling and information as regards the person's legal rights and the services available to him or her;
- assistance to enable their rights and interests to be presented and considered at appropriate stages of criminal proceedings against offenders;
- access to education for children.

NBA 2022 s61 provides for a recovery period

- during which the person may not be removed from, or required to leave the UK (s61(2))
- running from the positive reasonable grounds decision (RGD) to the later of the ensuing CGD or 30 days after the RGD (s61(3))
- but where a further RGD is made by a competent authority, where the RGD is based on things done before the first RGD, then a second recovery period is available only as a matter of discretion (s62)

A preliminary needs assessment will be held following a positive RGD. Thereafter there must be a fuller one following a favourable CGD (see Atamewan [2013] EWHC 2727 (Admin). An agreed note between counsel in SSA (Ethiopia) [2023] UKAITUR JR2021LON001894 records:

> "a person who is accepted on conclusive grounds to be a victim of trafficking is given a Recovery Needs Assessment, the purpose of which is to allow support workers to work with victims in developing recommendations for support where they have ongoing recovery needs arising from their modern slavery experiences. An individual will continue to receive financial support under the Modern Slavery Victim Care Contract (MSVCC) for a minimum of 45 days after the Conclusive Grounds decision for as long as they are assessed to have a recovery need for it, in accordance with the Recovery Needs Assessment guidance. The provision of support is contingent upon there being a recommendation from the victim's support worker and an acceptance of that recommendation from the Single Competent Authority. Recommendations must include an exit date for the support to end, up to a maximum of six months, though further requests can be made for support thereafter."

EOG [2022] EWCA Civ 307 holds that "reasonable grounds" recognition as a trafficking victim does not require a short period of leave. Non-removability was all that ECAT required. This was notwithstanding that a prolonged period of uncertainty (averaging 462 days), living at subsistence level and unable to engage in gainful employment, was liable to be profoundly demoralising and inimical to the social and psychological recovery which ECAT aims to promote. Now NBA 2022 s64 adds s50A to the Modern Slavery Act 2015. This provides that "any necessary assistance and support" must be provided to identified potential victims – though those receiving further RGDs receive it only as a matter of discretion (s50A(3)-(4)).

> "assistance and support is "necessary" if the Secretary of State considers that it is necessary for the purpose of assisting the person receiving it in their recovery from any physical, psychological or social harm arising from the conduct which resulted in the positive reasonable grounds decision in question."

4.3.8 Legal Aid

A person who has had a positive reasonable grounds decision will be entitled to apply for legal aid from that point onwards to help them with the cost of legal representation to pursue their trafficking claim. The person will lose entitlement to legal aid if they then get a negative CGD. Legal aid may in any case be available for those who are pursuing an asylum claim, or JR, and at the application stage, whether or not a formal application is made for leave to remain. Public funding may also be available for compensation claims: see the ATLEU Guide to *Legal aid for victims of trafficking*.

4.3.9 Leave to remain/permission to stay for trafficking victims

Before the NBA 2022 regime entered effect, those found, in a CGD, to be victims of trafficking *may* have been granted a period of discretionary leave (DL) i.e. outside the Rules, under the DL policy (MIL 10.5.2): either due to their personal circumstances, to assist with police enquiries or to pursue compensation, unless they are entitled to a more generous form of leave (e.g. as a Refugee). Leave was normally granted for between 12 and 30 months, extended where necessary.

Now leave is granted under s65 NBA 2022. It essentially provides for grants of leave for recovery from physical or psychological harm, to seek compensation from exploitation, or to cooperate in investigations (s65(2)). But leave need not be granted where recovery is possible, or compensation pursued, from the victim's country of nationality or another territory where there is an agreement in place with the UK (s65(4), (5)).

Appendix Temporary Permission to Stay for Victims of Human Trafficking or Slavery (Appendix VTS) now deals with the criteria and grant of leave – it incorporates the key provisions of s65(2) as to eligibility and ineligibility. It is not a settlement route. It provides

- Applications for an extension of stay require that one is already on the route and has a positive CGD (VTS1) - no application is necessary to enter the route as consideration will automatically be given
- If refused PTS there may be no further applications under this route
- One can extend one's stay once in the route
- Applications can be refused for threatening public order or bad faith (VTS2.1) – or for the reasons set out in s65 NBA 2022 (VTS3.3, 3.4) – permission may be cancelled for the more serious general refusal reasons including for being a threat to public order which is defined as including committing terrorist offences or even any offence reaching the "foreign criminal" threshold as per UKBA 2007 s32 (ie receiving 12 months imprisonment) (VTS10)
- Reconsideration of a refusal may be sought once (VTS4) (the *Temporary Permission to Stay for Victims of Human Trafficking and Slavery Guidance* explains that reconsiderations will be via the DLR policy where decisions were made under it)
- Permission is granted for up to 30 months for recovery/investigation purposes, and up to 12 months for compensation purposes (VTS5.1) – work and study is permitted (subject to ATAS) as is access to public funds (VTS5.2)
- Dependent children in the UK may apply, subject to public order refusal, and will receive permission in line with the parent (VTS6-9)

The Eligibility criteria (VTS3.1 – sub-definitions in 3.2) are that the grant is necessary for

(a) assisting the person in their recovery (via NRM or other services, whether or not recovery is attained) from any physical or psychological harm (mental or emotional trauma, or causing behavioural change or physical symptoms that require psychological or psychiatric care, due to the "relevant exploitation", which must be the conduct leading to the CGD); or
(b) enabling the person to seek (ie having made a claim for) compensation in respect of the relevant exploitation, or
(c) enabling the person to co-operate with a public authority in connection with an investigation or criminal proceedings (confirmed by the CPS/relevant public authority) in respect of the relevant exploitation.

The Guidance *Temporary Permission to Stay considerations for Victims of Human Trafficking or Slavery* provides that

- Grants of permission are to be considered on balance of probabilities
- Grants of VTS may be appropriate for recovery in UK, though so too may be return to a place of familiarity where they can access wider support networks, such as their community, family or friends, or in another safe country (having regard to any dependent childrens' best interests)
- **Recovery** (up to 30 months): VTS's aim "*is not to assist in fulfilling recovery or to guarantee or achieve full recovery but to assist the victim with achieving recovery from psychological or physical needs that have arisen as a result of their exploitation*" – recovery from physical, psychological or social harm arising from the trafficking/slavery conduct is targeted, via evidence from medical professionals
- **Investigation:** All known details of the public authority or police officers investigating trafficking should be provided: the relevant Competent Authority will itself take reasonable steps to verify this
- **Compensation** (up to 12 months): the grounds must arise in relation to the relevant exploitation, and the claim's likelihood of success and whether it is necessary for the claimant to remain in the UK will be considered – it may be straightforward to pursue claims from abroad
- Longer grants may be appropriate having regard to the best interests of the child or other particularly exceptional compelling or compassionate reasons – there is no requirement to grant ILR which should be sought under other routes (eg LOTR, MIL 4.2.1)
- Applications will be considered in a timely and sensitive manner
- The SSHD sees trafficking obligations as generally arising from statutory obligations now rather than from international obligations (save for participating in investigations, s65(2)(c)) – this is a change of policy from the pre-31 January 2023 position
- Applications will be treated as withdrawn if the applicant leaves the UK
- There is no need to reconsider trafficking assessments before granting VTS

- VTS applications should not be stayed behind asylum claims
- Applications to stay to pursue compensation depend on capability and reasonableness of seeking it from abroad
- Extension applications are required; initial consideration will be automatic, though investigating authorities may also request VTS extensions to assist their enquiries
- If no application is made for a dependant child the HO should request one is made to regularise their position
- Applications are made on Form FLR (HRO) - fee waiver requests are possible through the online waiver request form, for those whose leave expires during consideration of a fee waiver, 10 working days are given within which time to make an application without treating leave as expired – relevant considerations are imminent destitution risk and promoting/safeguarding child welfare
- Cancellation of VTS may follow where the beneficiary no longer meets the criteria or on conducive to the public good/criminality grounds: there should normally be an opportunity to rebut the allegation and cancellation may be immediate or at a future date as appropriate to permit ongoing assistance to the investigations of public authorities
- One reconsideration (not AR) may be sought within 14 days of a decision, of the refusal or length of VTS – new evidence may also justify reconsideration

KTT [2021] EWHC 2722 (Admin) (upheld on appeal in EOG & KTT [2022] EWCA Civ 307) holds that pursuit of an asylum claim based on re-trafficking risk is capable of being a "stay" which is "necessary owing to their personal situation" in accordance with Article 14(1)(a) of the Convention. Accordingly discretionary leave should be granted pending resolution of such an asylum claim. Under the discretionary leave policy, those eligible for leave under KTT before 30 January 2023 receive special dispensation. Leave is granted if a positive conclusive grounds decision was made before that date and a trafficking-related asylum claim/further submissions was then outstanding, and still awaits final determination by way of decision and appeal.

SSA (Ethiopia) [2023] UKAITUR JR2021LON001894 holds that the protection claim must include a *material* fear of re-trafficking (ie it need not be the sole or substantial basis of the claim). It would be unlawfully discriminatory to defer a claim for ECAT leave because of a person's status as an asylum seeker.

PK (Ghana) [2018] EWCA Civ 98 (confirmed in EOG [2022] EWCA Civ 307) notes that Article 14(1)(a) of the Trafficking Convention requires a residence permit to be given to a person where this is necessary in the light of their personal situation, which does not give the HO an open-ended discretion as to when to grant leave. Rather any grant of leave had to be directed towards the purposes of the Convention itself. A central consideration was a person's recovery, possibly including medical and/or psychological care, and/or legal/social services. These were obligations which endured during the victim's residence in the UK. The Guidance cited did not have regard to these considerations.

Furthermore, the requirement for *compelling* or *so compelling* circumstances was excessive. This elevated the threshold too high, particularly given the context in which those terms were used elsewhere in the guidance for Discretionary Leave to Remain. It suggested that applications would rarely and exceptionally succeed.

Advisors making applications for those recognised as Trafficking Victims should accordingly make representations which identify the Convention objectives which the grant of leave would secure: a focus on recovery, having particular regard to medical and/or psychological care, and/or legal/social services, would be a firm starting point. Of course the NBA 2022 regime has now replaced the policy guidance which was the subject of PK (Ghana) and now the objectives of the trafficking convention are, it seems, relevant only so far as reflected in domestic legislation and Rules.

In FM [2015] EWHC 844 (Admin) the court noted that once a potential victim of trafficking is identified, Article 12(1) of the Convention required the state to assist in his or her 'physical, psychological and social recovery'. The HO Guidance made it clear that DLR should be granted to allow a victim to finish a course of treatment that would not be readily available abroad.

SV [2022] UKUT 39 (IAC) held that ECAT does not prohibit the SSHD's policy of granting leave "*normally*" for (at most) 30 months. The policy Guidance states that such longer grants were appropriate only where they "*can be distinguished to a high degree from other cases*". The UT explained that this must mean that decision makers should carefully examine all the circumstances to determine whether a longer period leave was in fact "*necessary*", and did not involve a particularly high threshold.

The Court in JP [2019] EWHC 3346 (Admin) held that the scheduling rule which required that decisions be taken on asylum claims before being taken vis-á-vis trafficking residence permits was a rational one in terms of how state resources were allocated. However, it unjustifiably interfered with the rights of asylum seekers to investigation of their trafficking status, to private life and the right to property (via access to benefits). This was because the psychological impact of prolonged uncertainty on potential trafficking victims was such that the effects of the rule on the rights of asylum seeking victims outweighed the administrative convenience it achieved.

In DA & Ors [2020] EWHC 3080 (Admin) the Court found that the failure to ask the questions "why have you come to the UK?" and "please outline your journey to the UK" posed a serious risk that individuals who would be picked up as potential victims of trafficking in the light of the answer to those questions would go unnoticed. The SSHD has undertaken to ask these "Journey Questions" before deciding to detain or remove anyone screened between 30 March and 16 November 2020.

4.3.10 Assessing the claim

The SCA Guidance warns that an account should not necessarily be doubted merely because of being incoherent, inconsistent or the victim has delayed in giving details of material facts. The guidance states that when these issues arise the SCA must take account of such factors as

- trauma (mental, psychological, or emotional)
- inability to express themselves clearly
- mistrust of authorities
- feelings of shame
- painful memories (including those of a sexual nature)

It goes on to recognise:

- that children may be unable to disclose or give a consistent credible account due to additional factors such as their age, the on-going nature of abuse throughout childhood and the fear of traffickers, violence, or witchcraft;
- that a key symptom of post-traumatic stress is avoidance of trauma triggers, or of those things that cause frightening memories, flashbacks or other unpleasant physical and psychological experiences. Because of these symptoms a person may be unable to fully explain their experience until they have achieved a minimum level of psychological stability. The SCA must not view a delay in disclosing of facts as necessarily manipulative or untrue. It may be the result of an effective recovery and reflection period and the establishment of trust with the person to whom they disclose the information; and
- that as a result of trauma, victims in some cases might not be able to recall concrete dates and facts and in some cases their initial account might contradict their later statement. This may be connected to their traumatic experience. However, the need to be sensitive does not remove the need to assess all information critically and objectively when the SCA considers the credibility of a case;
- lies may be told for many reasons including one's trafficking experiences and decision makers should concentrate on the central rather than peripheral aspects of a claim

There is no requirement for corroboration for a trafficking claim to be accepted, and a decision letter which suggests the contrary may well be struck down: see e.g. Mutesi [2015] EWHC 2467 (Admin) at [61]. The standard of proof is that of the *balance of probabilities*: MN [2020] EWCA Civ 1746. From January 2023 the *Modern Slavery Statutory Guidance* was amended to require 'reasonable grounds to believe, based on objective factors but falling short of conclusive proof'. However after much criticism from the sector, and reductions in the recognition rate, in July 2023 references to "objective factors" were removed. Now the Guidance states that '*Where available, specific, and general evidence should be considered for all referrals*'.

TVN [2021] EWHC 3019 (Admin) gives an interesting precis of the modern judicial thinking on witness assessment. It can be unrealistic to expect an honest person to give precisely the same account of past events from memory on different occasions months and years later. It was wrong to equate strength and vividness of memory, or to attribute weight to a witness's confidence in their own recollection. Memories were fluid and malleable rather than fixed at the time of the relevant experience. Memory was particularly vulnerability to interference and alteration when a person is presented with new information or suggestions re an event where the memory was already weak.

The significance of any dishonesty should be expressly considered, bearing in mind relevant evidence as to trauma, PTSD, and complex PTSD. Complex PTSD might well justify an assumption that multiple and repeated trauma has been suffered and high quality reasoning should be provided to rule out trafficking as its cause. That reasoning should explain why inconsistencies are found to be evidence of lies rather than being the product of a disordered mind responding to exposure to trauma.

AA (Sudan) [2021] EWHC 1869 (Admin) finds that it was arguably unlawful for the SSHD to have had in place a secret policy which went directly against the terms of her published policy and which directly impeded her in her duty to consider whether asylum seekers have been trafficked en route to this country, a matter recognised as arguable but not determined in DA [2020] EWHC 3080 (Admin).

Expert evidence is admissible as to a person's psychiatric or psychological stage or of the methods of criminal gangs abroad, though not (at least in litigation) as to their credibility, as that would trespass onto the ultimate issue to be determined by the court: AAD & Ors, R. v [2022] EWCA Crim 106.

4.3.11 Challenging NRM decisions

Individuals may request a reconsideration of a RGD or CGD. If the complaints relates to the application of guidance vis-á-vis the original material submitted, then this must be done within three months of the decision date. Reconsiderations based on fresh evidence can take place at any time. Anyone may make the request though it is recommended that a Support Provider or First Responder assists. The relevant competent authority will confirm whether a reconsideration is being made. See generally *Reconsideration of Reasonable Grounds or Conclusive Grounds decision* within the *Modern Slavery: Statutory Guidance*.

If that fails, JR in the Administrative Court will be required.

In H [2019] EWHC 3457 (Admin) the Court looked at trafficking reconsideration decisions, emphasising that they should not involve any lesser application of the Competent Authority Guidance or a less rigorous scrutiny of the case than did the original decision. The extent of the reconsideration required depended upon the facts and the nature of the new material.

In JS [2020] EWHC 500 (Admin) the Court emphasised that the HO Guidance stresses the importance of a "second pair of eyes" to review NRM decisions. Any such review had to be evidenced by a clear file note, otherwise the decision may be set aside if challenged on JR.

There is no ground of appeal by which decisions of the SCA on trafficking can be reviewed directly in immigration appeals. In ES [2018] UKUT 335 (IAC), the UT notes that decisions under the NRM are made on the balance of probabilities, whereas decisions in relation to international protection are determined on the 'real chance' standard, as shown by cases such as Karanakaran. Accordingly, decisions by the NRM could not be viewed as *binding* in appeals where trafficking was relevant to an international protection context.

The Supreme Court in MS (Pakistan) [2020] UKSC 9 confirms that the immigration tribunals are not bound by NRM decisions when determining human rights and asylum appeals. The tribunals determined appeals afresh, their primary obligation being to ensure that they respected the UK's international obligations under the Refugee Convention, ECHR and European Convention against Trafficking. They reviewed the merits of appeals and did not exercise a JR jurisdiction, and were free to look at the latest evidence. Any other approach would chill the willingness of trafficking victims to engage with the NRM process before pursuing an immigration appeal.

NRM decisions might retain some relevance to the Tribunal's reasoning, depending on the extent that new evidence and further consideration entered the equation.

Where the Tribunal identifies a trafficking victim in the course of its decision making, it is necessary to decide whether their removal from the UK would amount to a breach of any of the positive obligations in article 4 of the ECHR. Those obligations include the need for an effective investigation into a breach of Article 4 which goes beyond simply protecting a victim from future harm. An effective police investigation and any ensuing prosecution could not be conducted without the full assistance and co-operation of the victim, which would prevent the victim's removal from the UK. COL v DPP [2022] EWHC 601 (Admin) holds that there may be a duty to prosecute an employer, even where they can invoke diplomatic immunity.

Refusals of claims based on the SSHD's duties under Art 4 ECHR may give rise to a right of appeal on human rights grounds.

Further, in an Article 8 claim, one may readily imagine circumstances in which trafficking would have had an impact on a person's private life and the public interest in their removal, given the damage to a person's physical and moral integrity that might result from trafficking and the public interest in ensuring that victims are appropriately treated.

4.4 Statelessness

As the UNHCR Handbook on the Protection of Stateless Persons begins:

> In the last decade there has been a renewed impetus on the part of the international community, supported by the United Nations High Commissioner for Refugees (UNHCR), to address the plight of stateless persons. As the Universal Declaration of Human Rights makes clear, everyone has a right to a nationality. Without nationality, individuals face an existence characterised by insecurity and marginalisation. Stateless people are amongst the most vulnerable in the world, often denied enjoyment of rights such as equality before the law, the right to work, education or healthcare. Despite the actions of many States to prevent or reduce statelessness through measures such as reform of their nationality laws, new cases of statelessness continue to arise. Stateless persons can be found in almost every country. Indeed, some families have been stateless for generations.

Individuals who can establish they are stateless, as defined under Article 1(1) of the 1954 United Nations Convention relating to the Status of Stateless Persons can now benefit from specific provisions in Part 14 of the IRs.

The Convention itself at Article 31(1) states only that *'The Contracting States shall not expel a stateless person lawfully in their territory save on grounds of national security or public order'*. But beyond this, there is no non-refoulement (i.e. anti-expulsion) measure beyond this, making it much less useful than the Refugee Convention. So the stateless have to be present lawfully in order to benefit from that Convention. The IRs help by providing a gateway to lawful residence that triggers the Convention's benefits.

The central provisions in Part 14 are Rules 401 and 403:

> For the purposes of this Part a stateless person is a person who:

(a) satisfies the requirements of Article 1(1) of the 1954 United Nations Convention relating to the Status of Stateless Persons, as a person who is not considered as a national by any State under the operation of its law;
(b) is in the United Kingdom; and
(c) is not excluded from recognition as a Stateless person under paragraph 402.

The requirements for leave to remain in the United Kingdom as a stateless person are that the applicant:

(a) has made a valid application to the Secretary of State for limited leave to remain as a stateless person;
(b) is recognised as a stateless person by the Secretary of State in accordance with paragraph 401;
(c) is not admissible to their country of former habitual residence or any other country; and
(d) has obtained and submitted all reasonably available evidence to enable the Secretary of State to determine whether they are stateless.

It can be seen that simply being stateless is not enough. That is just the first requirement to be considered under Rule 403. Additionally, there is the need to establish that they are not admissible to any other country. So, the essential requirements are:

- that a person is not considered as a national by the law of any country and that they have provided 'all reasonably available evidence' on this
- that they are not admissible to any other country, including anywhere they have previously been habitually resident

JM (Zimbabwe) [2018] EWCA Civ 188 holds that r403(c) does not allow for a stateless grant of LTR where it is open to the applicant to register as a citizen of a country and they would therefore be 'admissible' to that country. The question was *whether it lay within a claimant's power to obtain admission to a particular country*, not simply whether they would be admitted if they presented themselves at its border as things now stood. So a person who had failed to take appropriate steps towards securing the necessary registration that would open the door to admission to a country whose nationality they potentially held could not meet the requirements of the Rules. Admissibility issues could always be clarified in the course of an appeal via an adjournment.

NB: registration as British citizens of stateless persons under the age of 22 and resident in the UK for five years (MIL 12.3.9).

AZ [2021] UKUT 284 (IAC) looks at the meaning of "*admissibility*" holding that it connotes the ability to enter and reside lawfully in the country in question. But not that any such lawful residence needed to be a gateway to permanent residence.

Questions of statelessness are to be considered on balance of probabilities, not via the lower standard of proof that operates in asylum claims, because generally speaking the evidence of nationality status (and attempts to acquire it) should be readily available. Where it is not, the Secretary of State must consider whether it is appropriate to assist in finding it: AS (Guinea) [2018] EWCA Civ 2234.

Johnson [2022] EWHC 3120 (KB) holds that a finding of de facto statelessness following a person's release from detention does not undermine their prior detention's lawfulness.

Leave to remain will not be granted where a person is excluded for one of the following reasons:

- Behaviour or status similar to the exclusion clauses of the Refugee Convention (i.e. receiving support from UNRWA (who work in the Gaza Strip, the West Bank, Syria, Lebanon and Jordan), being able to reside in a state which gives them rights akin to nationality, having committed international crimes or serious non-political ones or acted contrary to the purposes or principles of the UN (r402) (see MIL 8.8 for refugee exclusion)

- If there are reasonable grounds for thinking them to be a danger to the UK's security or public order (r404(b))
- If they fall foul of any of the general refusal reasons under Part 9 (these are of course very extensive and include almost any level of criminality) (r404(c))

The HO's Stateless guidance can be accessed directly from the Operational Guidance section of the GOV.UK website. For those representing stateless persons, the UNHCR has published a very useful Handbook on Protection of Stateless Persons, and further resources are available from Asylum Aid.

Applications under the Rules are made on form FLR(S)and are free of charge. A successful applicant will now be given 5 years leave with no conditions (that they are entitled to have recourse to public funds):

If they continue to meet the requirements for LTR in the route they may apply for ILR after spending a continuous period of five years in the United Kingdom with lawful leave, the last period of which must have been as a stateless person.

There are some cases that are especially likely to give rise to issues of statelessness: those of Kuwaiti Bidoons, Nepalese from Bhutan, persons caught up in the aftermath of border changes in the old Soviet Union or affected by the Ethiopia/Eritrea split or the Western Sahara situation. But the Rules potentially operate in any scenario, whatever the countries involved.

> **Example**
>
> Bishal is of Nepalese ethnicity and was raised in Bhutan. He lived there until 1990 when he was expelled to Nepal where he subsequently lived for many years until he left the country to look for work elsewhere. He arrived in the UK in 2007. He claims asylum based on his political activities in Bhutan. The claim fails because whilst he was accepted to be at risk in Bhutan he would not be in danger in Nepal where he was thought able to return to continue residing. However the HO have not managed to return him there and all attempts to document him have failed: he has provided them with a lot of information about his life in Nepal to no avail. Whilst the situation has improved in Bhutan, it is clear that the government does not accept back people of Nepalese origin.
>
> Bishal appears to have a good case for saying that he is stateless and that he cannot gain admission to any other country: he cannot return to Bhutan. He has a decent case to argue that he is not admissibile to his country of former habitual residence, Nepal, and can realistically content that all reasonably available evidence has been supplied.
>
> Bishal's twin brother Yash has the same background he does. However, when he arrived in the UK he was prosecuted for entering on false documents. He was sentenced to imprisonment for one year. He was subsequently the subject of deportation proceedings and a deportation order was made against him.
>
> Yash does not qualify under the Statelessness Rules: having a deportation order made against him = mandatory refusal under Part 9 r9.2.1.

The test for determining whether a person must be given leave to remain because they are irremovable is, in a non-statelessness case, a very high one (MIL 4.2.18).

CHAPTER 5: Long Residence and Private Life; Children; Proportionality in ECHR Art 8 cases

5.1 Introduction

Because this route is the one under which many claims with a human rights dimension will be argued and determined, it is the most appropriate chapter for us to deal with the approach to the assessment of Article 8 ECHR outside the IRs (thus Chapter 10, on human rights generally, focuses on rights beyond private and family life). So what follows is our central reference point for the consideration of Article 8 and should be referred to for a discussion of the relevant general principles.

The long residence and private life provisions are at r276A and Appendix Private Life. They should be read alongside:

1. Long residence Guidance; and
2. Private life Guidance
3. Family life (as a partner or parent) and exceptional circumstances Guidance: no longer intended to govern the issue with the introduction of Appendix Private Life but still relevant

Until 9 July 2012, there were two routes to settlement on the grounds of long residence for persons of good character whose residence would not offend the public interest:

- 10 years continuous and lawful residence, or
- 14 years of continuous residence (whether lawful, unlawful or a combination of the two).

The 14 year category is now closed (except for people granted an extension of stay on this basis following an application made prior to 9 July 2012, who will be able to apply for indefinite leave to remain once the requirements of the old rule are fully met: 276A2).

Since 9 July 2012, the 14 year rule has been replaced for post July 2012 applicants by the provisions of the 'private life' category: until 20 June 2022 in r276ADE(1) and now Appendix Private Life: i.e. it shifts from being a '14-year rule' to being a '20-year rule' (for those who are not the special cases heralded below). Or should that be '30-year rule': because that 2 decades of unlawful residence is just the gateway to a 10-year settlement route via 30 months grants of leave.

Thus now there is only one direct route to *settlement* on long residence grounds for persons of good character whose residence would not offend the public interest, under rule 276B, which requires:

- 10 years continuous and lawful residence

However there are some other avenues under Appendix Private Life. Despite its obscure title it is in fact one of the most cited rules, because it is the rule under which many people put their back-up case. The routes are for people who have been resident here for significant periods such that they can make a case built on private life grounds: these result in *30-month grants* of limited leave on a *10-year settlement* route. You will see that these are 'long residence' routes to a greater or lesser extent, though the length of residence is far less for the young and for those who cannot integrate abroad. These require:

- 20 years unlawful residence for those who are not children or young people who have lived half their lives here, or who are unable to show there are very significant obstacles to their integration in the country of return
- seven years' residence for a child who can show their departure would be unreasonable
- residence of half their life for a young person aged under 25

- any period of residence for a person who can show there are very significant obstacles to their integration in the country of return

5.2 Ten-year rule

5.2.1 Continuous lawful residence

Under the 10-year rule (276A to 276D), the leave must be continuous and lawful. The terms 'continuous residence' and 'lawful residence' are defined in rule 276A(a) and (b) respectively:

Continuous residence is residence for an unbroken period, and is not broken by absence of up to six months or less at any one time, so long as the applicant had leave to enter or remain on leaving and returning, but is broken if they:

- are removed, deported or depart following a refusal of leave
- leave evidencing a clear intention not to return or where there is no reasonable expectation of lawful return
- are convicted and sentenced to a custodial non-suspended sentence
- are abroad for more than 18 months during the relevant period

Lawful residence is that:

- with leave to enter or remain, or where one is exempt from immigration control: but not as an Appendix V visitor or under Appendix Short-term Student (English language), or Appendix Temporary work – Seasonal Worker (or any relevant predecessor routes) or
- with temporary admission (but not immigration bail) where leave is subsequently granted (e.g. where the application which led to a grant of temporary admission subsequently succeeds, as with an asylum claim made at the port of entry)

The disqualifications of periods as a visitor etc and immigration bail were introduced for applications made from 13 April 2023. Note that under 276A(a), absence from the UK for a period of six months or less does not break a person's continuous residence, provided that the applicant in question has existing limited leave to enter or remain upon their departure and return – there is no requirement that they must have the same form of leave on return as on departure – so they might return abroad with extant student leave and return as a Skilled Worker (subject to the other provisions in 276A(a)).

The guidance goes further than the customary condoning of 28 days overstaying (or 14 days on or after 24 November 2016 if r39E applies) which we often find in the rules. Generally the Rules condone a short spell of current overstaying. But this rule makes clear that historic gaps for applications made after up to 28 days of overstaying will not break continuity of lawful residence.

In Chang [2021] UKUT 65 (IAC) the UT examines the phrase "*has spent a total of more than 18 months absent from the United Kingdom during the period in question*" within r276A(v). The SSHD's Guidance states that 18 months should be construed as 540 days. The UT disagrees: under the Interpretation Act 1978 months are generally to be considered as varying with the calendar and there was no justification for deviating from that approach when construing this Rule. It was appropriate to adopt a common-sense approach which recognised that 18 months represented a year and a half, it was appropriate to treat it as comprising 548 days. The Guidance now reflects this, adding that 6 months = 184 days.

Creative but misconceived arguments (according to the courts!) have been pursued by many individuals wishing to establish a decade of lawful residence in order to meet the requirements of Rule 276B. Many have tried to argue that the fact that r39E gives the HO discretion to grant applications made late somehow magics the period of overstaying into lawful residence. However as discussed at 1.5.2.3, this argument has failed.

- How should periods of overstaying in the period of asserted long residence be treated?

- For a while the case of Ahmed [2019] EWCA Civ 1070 found that the fact that short periods of overstaying could be disregarded *once the decade had been clocked up* did not mean that such periods could form part of the qualifying decade in the first place
- Its thinking was overruled in Hoque [2020] EWCA Civ 1357 which lays to rest some arguments about the scope of the long residence rule
- Hoque goes on to explain that one does need a solid ten years ending with a period of lawful residence for a r276B application to prosper. There was a difference between open-ended overstaying (ie running up to the date of decision) and book-ended overstaying (ie periods condoned by a subsequent grant of leave). The latter could contribute towards acquiring a decade of lawful residence, but the former could not

How should the 10 years of lawful residence be calculated? Whilst some people will be lucky enough to have accrued a decade of consecutive periods of leave, others may have breaks in their leave. Do such breaks in leave condoned by the subsequent grant of leave under r276B(v) (for being made within 28 days pre-November 2016 or as per r39E thereafter) count towards the ten years of lawful residence? After a brief period where the UT and CoA thought they might, Afzal [2021] EWCA Civ 1909 holds that they do *not* count. So you need a decade of lawful residence via formal leave/permission *on top of* any periods where you were without leave. But watch this space: Afzal has been granted permission to appeal to the Supreme Court and the appeal has been heard.

In Waseem [2021] UKUT 146 (IAC) the UT looked at the history of policies which had run alongside the 10-year route. The route's introduction in 2003 reflected the ratification of the European Convention on Establishment and the primacy of the 10-year period of lawful residence, while still recognising the practice of permitting regularisation of status to those here illegally, necessarily for a longer period. The policy was perfectly consistent with Hoque and its approach to different kinds of overstaying. The exercise of discretion always remained relevant and will necessarily be fact specific: but it would undermine the policy of the route to disregard the core attribute of continuous lawful residence.

Can the decade of lawful residence include a period as a visitor? Mungur [2021] EWCA Civ 1076 finds that this is indeed acceptable. A visitor lawfully present was "resident" within the meaning of the relevant rules. A person present with the benefit of a visitor's visa might have a reasonable expectation that he would lawfully be able to return. Though the Rules changed from April 2023 (see above).

Marepally [2022] EWCA Civ 855 explains that a failure to adequately notify appeal rights may well justify extending time for giving notice of appeal, but did not otherwise render a decision ineffective. So one could not rely on such a failure to revive lawful residence retrospectively.

Iyieke [2022] EWCA Civ 1147 laments the ongoing failure of the SSHD to redraft the long residence rule. When r276B(v)(a) referred to disregarding overstaying where an application had been made within 28 days of leave expiring, that necessarily referred to an application which succeeded, not simply to any historic unsuccessful application. This is a litigious area: this case has also been granted permission to appeal to the Supreme Court.

Example

Walter is from Kenya. He entered the UK on 1 December 2004. He has entry clearance as a student valid until June 2007. On 24 July 2007, he leaves the country. He returns to the UK on 22 August 2007 with entry clearance granted on 25 July 2007.

His continuity of residence is broken – he did not have 'existing limited leave to enter or remain upon ... departure and return' under rule 276A(a), and given that he overstayed for more than 28 days before leaving the country, 276B(v) does not assist him.

Harvey is from the USA. He enters the UK on 1 December 2002 and is granted leave to remain until 1 May 2004 as a student. He left the UK on 27 April 2004 and returns on 26 September 2004, with a new entry clearance operating as leave to enter, again as a student.

> His continuity of residence is not broken – he has 'existing limited leave to enter or remain upon ... departure and return' and he was not absent for more than six months.

The *Long Residence* guidance is very useful. It shows:

- There is a discretion to ignore a break in residence *following the 10 years having accrued* exceeding 28 days (i.e. a discretion *outside* the rule that is more generous than the rule itself). It is available where
  - the applicant has acted lawfully throughout their stay and has always sought to obey the rules.
  - There are 'exceptional reasons why a single application was made more than 28 days out of time' (e.g. postal strike, HO error, hospitalization, unexpected or unforeseeable causes including unavoidable circumstances)
- Once an applicant has built up a period of 10 years continuous lawful residence, there is no limit on the length of time afterwards when they can apply. This means they could leave the UK, re-enter and apply for settlement based on a 10-year period of continuous lawful residence they built up in the past. This is subject to the provision that the applicant must not be in the UK in breach of immigration laws at the date of application, except for any period of overstaying 14 days or less allowed by r39E
- Time spent in the Republic of Ireland, Channel Islands or the Isle of Man does not count as residence in the UK for the purposes of long residence even though they form part of the common travel area
- Time spent in the UK with a right to reside under the EEA regulations will be treated as lawful residence (by way of an exercise of discretion outside the Rules). But this only applies where the residence was based on an outright entitlement, as was the case for EU nationals and their family members. Macastena [2018] EWCA Civ 1558 holds that the mere possibility that a residence card *might* have been issued to an extended family member based on a durable relationship (had an application been made) did not make such periods lawful. Whether residence with derivative rights can be included is not clear.
- Time spent awaiting an appeal hearing can count towards long residence. The Guidance says thatwhere the 10 years of residence has accrued during a period of continuing leave under s3C or 3D of the IA 1971, the matter can be raised on appeal. Not via an application to the HO (and any such application will be voided and the fee returned), but via the submission of "further grounds" to the Tribunal. This is probably a reference to a one-stop notice under s120 of NIA 2002
- Where a late appeal is granted an extension of time, s3C leave revives from that moment (in fact as per Akinola, see MIL 1.5.2.3, s3C leave revives from the date the late appeal is lodged). Which means it is not treated as extant for any period between time for appealing expiring and the late appeal being granted the extension. However, if the appeal is subsequently allowed, or dismissed but in circumstances where further leave is nevertheless granted following an "in-time" further application made, that gap will be treated as if it was lawful residence. The same goes for withdrawn decisions.

When writing representations in a long lawful residence case, bear in mind that the HO are not greatly concerned with the periods where leave has been granted: they are very unlikely to delve into those periods. Though you do need to check whether the immigration history held by the HO accords with your own understanding (where a refusal letter exists, the HO's understanding will usually be set out therein). However, they will be very interested in any breaks in leave, so you will need to explain carefully how it is that section 3C protection, or some other factor, extends leave or otherwise protects your client's position.

When arguing long residence cases outside the Rules by reference to private life, compliance with the Rules and guidance set out by the HO may still be important – so the fact that the Rules condone short breaks in leave or excess periods abroad for compassionate or humanitarian reasons may justify an appeal succeeding by reference to Article 8 ECHR.

> **Example**
>
> Vallerie is subject to immigration control. She has lived in the UK for just over 10 years, via various grants of leave to remain as a student. She wishes to apply for ILR under the long residence route: she still has leave as a Student. However, she has accumulated excess absence abroad as she was away for seven months in a single year.
>
> This excess absence disqualifies her from succeeding under the Rule, but the HO guidance states that 'it may be appropriate to exercise discretion over excess absences in compelling or compassionate circumstances, for example where the applicant was prevented from returning to the UK through unavoidable circumstances'.
>
> So it will be important to investigate the justification for the delay in her return. If she has a good explanation relating to circumstances beyond her control and can show she returned to the UK as soon as she was reasonably able, then discretion might be exercised outside the Rules.
>
> Alternatively, depending on how much leave to remain she has presently, she could postpone her application, and calculate whether the excess absence in question will drop out of the calculation if she can time her application such that it is split over two consecutive years.

5.2.2 Other considerations: character, conduct and the public interest

If satisfied that 10 years of continuous lawful residence has been established, the HO will then consider whether:

> (ii) having regard to the public interest there are no reasons why it would be undesirable for him to be given ILR on the ground of long residence, taking into account his:
>
> (a) age; and
> (b) strength of connections in the United Kingdom; and
> (c) personal history, including character, conduct, associations and employment record; and
> (d) domestic circumstances; and
> (e) compassionate circumstances; and
> (f) any representations received on the person's behalf;

These factors enable the HO to exercise discretion not to grant leave.

The applicant will also have to meet the knowledge of English language and life in the UK requirement in Appendix KoLL (MIL 2.2.6). If they have not yet done so, or settlement is delayed by the 'suitability' requirements of paragraphs S-ILR.1.5. or S-ILR.1.6. in Appendix FM, they will be granted a further 30 months.

Applications under the 10-year long residence category are made on forms FLR(LR) and SET(LR).

> **Top Tip**
>
> What can you suggest to a client who is nearly but not quite at the 10 year point of continuous lawful residence in the UK? An application under the 10-year rule cannot be made more than 28 days before the qualifying period is met. However, so long as they arguably satisfy the requirements of a different category, they can apply for an extension of stay under that category. If they then reach the 10-year point before that application is decided, and meet the KoLL requirements, they can then apply to vary that application: i.e. submit a new application under the 10-year rule which will replace the earlier undecided application. They will have reached the 10-year point whilst their leave is extended under s3C of the 1971 Act but that is no problem. Their leave has been lawful and continuous: they are entitled to vary their application so long as it has not yet been decided.

Their leave will be extended under section 3C of the IA 1971 whilst an appeal or administrative review can be brought or is pending. So this might fill the gap and take them up to the necessary 10 years, So their original application could be refused, but they could clock up the missing period whilst those remedies are pursued.

There may well be a right of appeal, as the HO often accepts that lengthy residence justifies treating a refusal as amounting to the refusal of a human rights claim. Then the applicant can seek to rely on the 'statement of additional grounds' procedure, so long as they received a one-stop notice under s120 of the 2002 Act when refused, to raise the 10-year rule as part of their appeal. The Long Residence Guidance specifically raises this possibility.

On the appeal it can then be argued that they have strong UK connections amounting to private life with which their removal would significantly interfere. And that their ten years of lawful residence and good character effectively shows that the public interest would not be threatened by the grant of leave: ie their application's refusal would be disproportionate (MIL 5.5.3).

But: the UT has held that the fact of attaining 10 years lawful residence *is* a 'new matter' which requires HO consent to be raised on the appeal: see OA Nigeria [2019] UKUT 65 (IAC). So reading the *Long Residence* guidance in the context of OA Nigeria one might think that consent could not reasonably be withheld, so long as the HO had time to conduct criminal record checks.

5.3 Private life under the rules

The concept of 'private life' comes from Article 8 of the ECHR, the 'right to respect for one's private and family life, his home and his correspondence'. It has become government policy from July 2012 to seek to define private life for Immigration Rule purposes, rather than leaving it to the case law.

Indeed the HO are generally disinterested in pre-July 2012 rulings.

Appendix Private Life (formerly r276ADE), allows an applicant to apply to regularise their stay in the UK on private life grounds: essentially long residence, lawful or not. Key features are:

- The usual validity regime, including a requirement to be in the UK on the application date (PL1.2)
- Fee & IHS, documents establishing identity and using the Private Life application form, are waived if the claim accompanies an asylum claim, or is detained, or if the HO gives consent for the issue to be raised on appeal (PL1.3) – and where a human rights claim that passes the fresh claim test is raised in response to removal directions (IR400)
- Limited Suitability criteria (PL2): cross-referencing some of the Appendix FM and Part 9 criteria
- Four routes, as set out below
- Residence periods exclude time spent in prison (PL7.2) but include unlawful residence (PL7.1)
- Continuous residence is broken by absence from the UK for more than 6 months at any one time, or spending more than 550 days absent over the relevant period, has been removed, deported or leaving left the UK after an application's refusal, or with no reasonable expectation of return (PL7.3)
- Applications that fail to meet one of the four routes' criteria still receive residual consideration under ECHR Art 8, subject to criminality & good character thresholds (PL8) (MIL 5.4)
- PTSP is granted for 30 months at a time – unless a child or young person (PL9) (MIL 5.7.1)
- Dependent children may join (PL19): applications are required unless being made alongside a protection claim or further submissions, or in an appeal with HO consent (PL19.4): the usual child dependency regime applies (MIL 2.2.8), with access to ILR (PL26 onwards) where the parent has or is being granted ILR or has become British whilst the child is on the PL route or was born before ILR was acquired, and satisfies English language at B1 and Appendix KOL UK

Appendix Private Life maintains four routes to leave to remain on private life grounds, respectively for a person who:

- has lived continuously in the UK for at least 20 years (discounting any period of imprisonment) (PL.5.1(a)); or
- is under the age of 18 years and has lived continuously in the UK for at least 7 years (discounting any period of imprisonment) and it would not be reasonable to expect the applicant to leave the UK (PL3.1); or
- is aged 18 years or above and under 25 years and has spent at least half of his life living continuously in the UK (discounting any period of imprisonment) (PL4.1(a)); or
- is aged 18 years or above, has lived continuously in the UK for less than 20 years (discounting any period of imprisonment) but there would be very significant obstacles to the applicant's integration into the country to which he would have to go if required to leave the UK (PL.5.1(b)).

These points arise:

- PL6.1 bars asylum seekers facing removal to a third country from this route
- the route is subject to 'suitability' requirements (PL2.1-2.2), cross-referencing to those in Appendix FM at Section S-LTR of the partner category: we deal with these below), but barely to the General Grounds for Refusal in Part 9.
- on appeal, the Rules specify a historic time-line (eg *'at the date of application ... is under the age of 18'*), and in these circumstances the appeal must focus on whether the evidence available at the hearing establishes that it would have been unreasonable for a child to relocate abroad at the date of the decision against which the appeal is brought (AQ (Pakistan) [2011] EWCA Civ 833 at [41]; Pankina [2010] EWCA Civ 719 at [39]).
- periods of imprisonment will be deducted from the total period of residence, (i.e. rather than restarting the clock from scratch following release)
- the clock stops re the acquisition of residence at 'the date of application' at each sub-rule. This may mean that a child who lacked the relevant residence at the date of application, but acquires it by the date of hearing, may need to argue their seven years' residence wholly outside the Rules (where it will be relevant because of s117B(6) NIAA 2002)
- Appendix Private Life PL5.1(b), the sub-rule under which all applicants are residual assessed if they lack the qualities of 20-year residence or youth for sub-rules (iii)-(v), requires 'very significant obstacles' to integration: this tends to raise particular obstacles for individuals of high calibre who lack ties abroad, as PL5 looks more to ability to integrate in the country generally than into resuming relationships
- there may be an explanation why assertions are unsubstantiated and private life must be assessed in the round, not compartmentalised: see Miah [2016] UKUT 131 (IAC)

The evidential requirements for proving length of residence are set high. It is expected that applicants will be able to provide independent evidence of each 12-month period they have lived in the UK, plus travel documents covering the whole period, unless a very good explanation has been provided as to why they cannot. A large envelope will be required.

Khan [2016] EWCA Civ 416 holds that it was wrong to attempt to restrict the forms of evidence that could satisfy a decision maker of the fact of long residence. It was likely that those lacking status would not have access to the 'official' documentation which the HO guidance seemed to demand.

Example

Hossain is a citizen of Pakistan aged 26. He has been present in the UK for five years as a student. His sponsor has lost their licence and although the HO has given him 60 days to find a new one, he has not managed to do so. Accordingly his application for further leave as a student has been rejected. He is not sure what to do next.

Hossain can make an application under Appendix Private Life, but given his age and length of residence in the UK the only route open to him will be PL5.1(b) & very significant obstacles to integration. As a person who has studied in the UK and who may well have been funded through those studies by family in Pakistan, it is very hard to see that he will be able to sustain a case based on facing very significant obstacles to integration in his country of origin.

> Mitsuda is a citizen of Japan aged 23. Her father was an international businessman who separated from her mother when Mitsuda was very young. She and her mother went to live in New Zealand and various other countries before she came to study in the UK aged 18 as a student whilst her mother remained abroad. Her studies have now come to an end and she is considering applying to remain in the UK on a longer term basis. She does not speak Japanese and has no friends in Japan: her mother now lives in Canada.
>
> Mitsuda's application under PL5.1(b) might succeed. Absent close family or language skills she may be able to establish very significant obstacles to integration. However the challenge she will face is that she has qualifications and the HO may take the view that she is essentially an independent young person who can make her way as well in Japan as in the UK. A judge on appeal might be more sympathetic.
>
> Fawaz is a citizen of Bangladesh aged 69. Her husband died some years ago. She came to visit her sons in the UK and remained here after her visit visa expired because she was taken ill. She did not return following her recovery and now several years have passed. The rest of her children have relocated to other parts of the world.
>
> Fawaz can argue that she lacks the social capital to integrate back in Bangladesh.
>
> Farid is a citizen of Afghanistan. He came to the UK as an unaccompanied minor aged eight. He is now aged 17½ having been repeatedly granted discretionary leave to remain once he came to the attention of the authorities having been looked after by his older brother for a few years after he arrived here. His leave to remain is just about to expire.
>
> At the present time Farid would need to show that his return to Afghanistan would be unreasonable given that he is still aged under 18. However if he made the application after attaining the age of 18 he would have lived in the UK for more than half his life and so would not have to show that departure was unreasonable.

5.3.1 Suitability

The general refusal reasons at 9.1.1(b) exempt a private life application from the general grounds for refusal in Part 9 of the IRs (sham marriage aside). Instead, the first consideration will be whether it falls to be refused under the 'suitability' requirements in paragraphs S-LTR 1.2 to S-LTR 4.5 in the 'Family life with a partner' category of Appendix FM (PL2.1-2.2) – for criminality, character and conduct, failing to provide information, false representations, and NHS/litigation debts (MIL 6.1.5.2).

5.3.2 PL3.1 – Children and when it is reasonable to expect them to leave the UK

This requirement appears both in the private life rules for children (PL3.1), and in the Exception (paragraph EX1) which applies to partners and parents under Appendix FM who have children who are British citizens or have lived in the UK for seven years or more (MIL 6).

One preliminary point to emphasise is that the test is one of **reasonableness**: obviously that is very different to a test based on 'insurmountable obstacles' or 'exceptional circumstances', thresholds cited elsewhere in the Rules. Indeed the Guidance Family life (as a partner or parent) and exceptional circumstances (on the analogous provision in Appendix FM at EX.1.(b)) itself recognises that insurmountable obstacles represents 'a different and more stringent assessment'.

Nevertheless, the test is one of seven years' residence *plus* reasonableness: so the mere fact of seven years' residence is not sufficient on its own, albeit that it does represent something of a presumption as to a certain level of ties having developed.

In the world of immigration law, there is a hierarchy of children:

(a) **British citizen children** are the best protected: because the rights flowing from nationality must be taken into account
(b) **7-year resident non British citizen children** are next best protected: because they have the benefit of the "reasonableness" test
(c) **All children** have some protection: because their best interests must be assessed

Principles relevant in all cases involving children

Before we say more about the proper approach to the cases of *qualifying* children, it is useful to set out the principles that apply *generally*.

There are three dominant considerations in these cases, which overlap:

- Section 55 of the Borders, Citizenship and Immigration Act 2009 and the general duty to ensure that immigration functions safeguard and promote child welfare (see Chapter 2 for an introduction to s55). Although much new immigration legislation has entered force since 2009, none of it should undermine s55: thus s71 of the IA 2014 stresses that nothing in the 2014 Act is intended to diminish the child safeguarding duty under s55 BCIA 2009 (see more on this in section 5.4.8 *Part 5A, 2002 Act considerations*, below). SM Algeria [2018] UKSC 9 §19 confirms this applies in entry clearance cases too, and so policy is broader than the statutory wording. Section 55 is the means by which UK law recognises the relevance of the UNCRC to immigration cases. Which leads us onto:
- The UK's obligations enshrined in the UN Convention on the Rights of the Child (UNCRC). Perhaps the most important part of the UNCRC is Article 3:

    In all actions concerning children, whether undertaken by public or private social welfare institutions, courts of law, administrative authorities or legislative bodies, the best interests of the child shall be a primary consideration

- The notion of a child having sufficient connections outside the family unit as show private life in their own right. Article 8(1) of the UNCRC expressly proclaims that 'States Parties undertake to respect the right of the child to preserve his or her identity'. As it was put in E-A Nigeria [2011] UKUT 00315 (IAC).

    Absent other factors, the reason why a period of substantial residence as a child may become a weighty consideration in the balance of competing considerations is that in the course of such time roots are put down, personal identities are developed, friendships are formed and links are made with the community outside the family unit. The degree to which these elements of private life are forged and therefore the weight to be given to the passage of time will depend upon the facts in each case.

Of course there are many children who have UK connections albeit they have not been resident here for seven years and are not British citizens. In their case, the test is that set out by the Strasbourg Court in Jeunesse: decision makers must assess

> the practicality, feasibility and proportionality of any removal of a non-national parent in order to give effective protection and sufficient weight to the best interests of the children directly affected by it.

The facts of the case must be examined with care. The ability of a relative to care for children should not be assumed without proper enquiry: see B [2010] EWHC 2471 (Admin) where the judge made the point that any serious investigation:

> would involve at least an inquiry as to the age, income, physical and mental health and housing circumstances of the grandmother, with a view to asking whether the availability of the children's grandmother represented a tenable alternative childcare option, not merely immediately following return but in the following years of the children's minority.

We can see a more detailed set of considerations identified in EV (Philippines) [2014] EWCA Civ 874:

> A decision as to what is in the best interests of children will depend on a number of factors such as:
>
> (a) their age;
> (b) the length of time that they have been here;
> (c) what stage their education has reached;
> (d) to what extent they have become distanced from the country to which it is proposed that they return;
> (e) how renewable their connection with it may be;
> (f) to what extent they will have linguistic, medical or other difficulties in adapting to life in that country; and
> (g) the extent to which the course proposed will interfere with their family life or their rights (if they have any) as British citizens.

Many principles in the case law are usefully summarised by Lord Hodge in Zoumbas [2013] UKSC 74:

- A 'best interests' assessment is integral to the proportionality assessment under ECHR Art 8
- A child's best interests are primary though not paramount and thus no other single consideration can be treated as inherently more significant than the child's best interests, albeit that a number of other factors might outweigh them on balance
- It is wise to take a structured approach to assessing proportionality and best interests
- It is important to clearly identify a child's circumstances and their best interests before balancing them against other considerations
- A child should not be blamed for matters for which they are not responsible such as a parent's conduct (we can quickly see that this could be very relevant where the parents have founded a family notwithstanding having overstayed their leave in the United Kingdom). But this must now be read with KO (Nigeria) [2018] UKSC 53 holding that the essentially common sense position must be that it is reasonable to expect the children of parents with no justification for overstaying to depart the UK (MIL 2.3 & 5.3.2)

The Supreme Court in HH [2012] UKSC 25 at [33] discusses the importance of family life to children:

> ... children need a family life in a way that adults do not. They have to be fed, clothed, washed, supervised, taught and above all loved if they are to grow up to be the properly functioning members of society which we all need them to be. Their physical and educational needs may be met outside the family, although usually not as well as they are met within it, but their emotional needs can only be fully met within a functioning family. Depriving a child of her family life is altogether more serious than depriving an adult of his.

The seminal case considering the role of the UNCRC in immigration cases is ZH (Tanzania) [2011] UKSC 4 where Lady Hale demonstrates how the UNCRC has influenced Strasbourg case law and prompted the passage of section 55. She stresses the importance of properly considering the impact of immigration decisions on children as individuals in their own right, the need to consult with them, the importance of recognising that the child's best interests are a primary consideration (no other consideration can be given more weight) and the right of British children to grow up in their country of nationality.

Qualifying Children

The factors so far identified apply in all cases involving children. However, a child who has been resident in the UK for seven years or more at the application date is in a much improved position than those resident for shorter periods. This is because, under the Rules:

- Rule 276(iv) addressing private life in the child's own right recognises a viable claim where the child

(iv) is under the age of 18 years and has lived continuously in the UK for at least 7 years (discounting any period of imprisonment) and it would not be reasonable to expect the applicant to leave the UK; or

- The Ex.1 Exception for parents and partners in Appendix FM opens up the possibility of an application succeeding where there is 'a genuine and subsisting parental relationship' for a pre-application seven-year resident child (or, indeed, a British citizen child)

There are further advantages enjoyed by British citizen children, because of the special status that their nationality gives them; we deal with this in the next section.

Ultimately these cases come down to the facts of the individual case. Key principles are:

- In KO (Nigeria) [2018] UKSC 53 the Supreme Court made it clear that parental conduct should not be held against children when assessing the child's best interests

- Runa [2020] EWCA Civ 514 emphasises that there is no automatic rule that it will be unreasonable to expect a child to leave the UK just because only one parent has the right to live here. It is a fact-specific question in each particular case. It would be wrong to pose the question whether it would be *reasonable*, were it accepted that one parent would be leaving the country contrary to the child's best interests, for the other to raise the child alone. Because the statutory test focusses only on whether it would be reasonable *for the child to leave the UK*

- NA (Bangladesh) [2021] EWCA Civ 953 reiterates that s117B(6) is a benevolent provision:
    - where it applies, it can only operate in an appellant's favour and not adversely to them
    - where it did not apply, a full proportionality assessment should nevertheless follow
    - the conduct of parents was indirectly relevant to the circumstances of the children given that if the hypothesis is that the parents must leave the country, it will normally be reasonable for their children to be with them. It was wrong to suggest that in these cases it would not be reasonable for a seven-year child to be expected to leave the United Kingdom unless there were "*powerful reasons to the contrary*"

- Children are often adaptable, but one should not jump to conclusions. The judge in B [2010] EWHC 2471 (Admin) thought it wrong to equate a change of education system (between the UK and abroad) to a mere change of school within the UK

- The basic idea behind the seven-year residence proviso builds on the notion we have already seen: the longer the residence, the greater the likelihood of the child forming independent links outside the family unit. Thus the <u>Family life (as a partner or parent), private life and exceptional circumstances recognises</u>:

    'that over time children start to put down roots and to integrate into life in the UK.'

- The Court of Appeal made the same point in MA (Pakistan) [2016] EWCA Civ 705:

    'After such a period of time the child will have put down roots and developed social, cultural and educational links in the UK such that it is likely to be highly disruptive if the child is required to leave the UK. That may be less so when the children are very young because the focus of their lives will be on their families, but the disruption becomes more serious as they get older. Moreover, in these cases there must be a very strong expectation that the child's best interests will be to remain in the UK with his parents as part of a family unit, and that must rank as a primary consideration in the proportionality assessment.'

- In MT and ET Nigeria [2018] UKUT 88 (IAC) the UT looked at the case of a somewhat run-of-the-mill immigration offender who came to the United Kingdom on a visit visa, overstayed, made a claim for asylum that was found to be false and who has pursued various legal means of remaining in the United Kingdom. They found that this did not provide sufficiently powerful reasons to counteract the child's best interests when assessing reasonableness

- In KO (Nigeria) [2018] UKSC 53 the Supreme Court found that the fact that both parents lacked immigration status such that the family unit should be expecting to return to their country of origin was very relevant to the assessment of reasonableness. So whilst the *severity* of a parent's immigration history is not relevant, their original lack of immigration status forms the context in which reasonableness is to be assessed

- Building on that thinking the UKVI Guidance presently states:

  'The starting point is that we would not normally expect a qualifying child to leave the UK. It is normally in a child's best interest for the whole family to remain together, which means if the child is not expected to leave, then the parent or parents or primary carer of the child will also not be expected to leave the UK …

  'The parents' situation is a relevant fact to consider in deciding whether they themselves and therefore, their child is expected to leave the UK. Where both parents are expected to leave the UK, the natural expectation is that the child would go with them and leave the UK, and that expectation would be reasonable unless there are factors or evidence that means it would not be reasonable.'

The Guidance Private life gives useful insight into how the HO works. Decision makers.

- Are likely to focus on a comparison between extended family and social connections in the UK as opposed to within the parents' country of origin, having regard to the extent that the child is dependent on, or supported by, relatives beyond their parents.
- The impact on the child of a transition from support from extended family members here in the UK to support from those abroad
- If there are much stronger connections in the UK, then it is more likely that a child's relocation will be considered unreasonable. If there are extensive family connections abroad, though, relocation may well be thought appropriate.
- Recent visits to the country of origin by the parents are likely to indicate some strength of ties there
- The extent to which the family lives amongst their country's diaspora, which is likely to contribute towards a child's familiarity with cultural norms there
- The parents' and child's ability to speak the language of that country, or to do so within a reasonable period

We can make some general points about the nature of the reasonableness assessment:

- It is clear that there is a two-stage enquiry: the best interests of the child need to be assessed, and the overall reasonableness of the child's removal must then be considered (though there is no absolute requirement to take the questions in this order). The immigration history of the parents should not be held against the child when assessing the first question; but it may be relevant to the second. MA (Pakistan) again:

There is nothing intrinsically illogical in the notion that whilst the child's best interests are for him or her to stay, it is not unreasonable to expect him or her to go.

- The enquiry is a hypothetical one:

  AB (Jamaica) [2019] EWCA Civ 661) explains provides that decision makers must consider whether it is reasonable to expect a child to leave the UK regardless of whether the child would in practice actually be leaving the UK.

- When cases are considered outside the Rules on appeal, then section 117B(6) NIAA 2002 also kicks in. That provision

  o Gives protection to both seven-year resident and British citizen children: and
  o Focuses on the date of *hearing*, not on the date of the underlying immigration *application*.

Children who have achieved seven years' UK residence during the appeals process will therefore benefit from the more generous assessment when their case is assessed outside the Rules, even though they may not succeed under the Rules.

Saleemi [2020] ScotCS CSIH_32 notes that the Rules focussed on the child's age *at the application date*. They thought it arguable that the question as to whether it *"would not be reasonable to expect"* a child's relocation should be looked at from the perspective of their age at the date of application throughout the subsequent appeal process. So attaining majority by the date of the appeal hearing should not prevent the 'best interests of the child' principle being considered.

Azimi-Moayed [2013] UKUT 197 (IAC) remains a good summary of the thinking of most Tribunal judges:

- The usual starting point will be that if parents are facing removal from this country then their children should accompany them unless there are reasons to the contrary.
- It is generally in the interests of children to have both stability and continuity of social and educational provision and the benefit of growing up in the cultural norms of the society to which they belong.
- Lengthy residence in the UK can lead to development of social cultural and educational ties that it would be inappropriate to disrupt, in the absence of compelling reason to the contrary – seven years has been consistently identified as a relevant period.
- It may be presumed that seven years' residence after the age of four are more likely to be significant to a child that the first seven years of life. Very young children are focussed on their parents rather than their peers and are adaptable.

If the Tribunal has not been provided with sufficient information to determine a child's best interests, it may be necessary for it to call for further material, see MIL 2.5.

5.3.2.1 British citizen children

As made clear in ZH (Tanzania), nationality is particularly important, because a national of a country is entitled to enjoy its protection and support, socially, culturally and medically, and to benefit from educational opportunities owed to citizens. Lady Hale sums it up thus, by reference to the Australian case of *Wan*:

> 'Although nationality is not a "trump card" it is of particular importance in assessing the best interests of any child. The UNCRC recognises the right of every child to be registered and acquire a nationality (Article 7) and to preserve her identity, including her nationality (Article 8). In *Wan*, the Federal Court of Australia [referred to these factors]:
>
> > "(a) the fact that the children, as citizens of Australia, would be deprived of the country of their own and their mother's citizenship, 'and of its protection and support, socially, culturally and medically, and in many other ways evoked by, but not confined to, the broad concept of lifestyle' ...;
> >
> > (b) the resultant social and linguistic disruption of their childhood as well as the loss of their homeland;
> >
> > (c) the loss of educational opportunities available to the children ...; and
> >
> > (d) their resultant isolation from the normal contacts of children with their mother and their mother's family."'

Examples

Maria and David are from the Philippines. They have lived here lawfully, with Maria having been a Student/Tier 4 migrant from their arrival here 7½ years ago, David being her dependent; she subsequently became a post study worker. They cannot find any obvious route under the Rules other than within the private life category. Their two children, Isabelle and Maria, were born in the Philippines and are aged eight and ten; in this country they have been in education since joining reception classes at primary school.

The children have a very strong case under Appendix Private Life taking into account the children and the reasonableness route at (iv): the children have been in education here for over seven years, and their residence includes more than seven years at an age greater than four, so is the kind of residence recognised as presumptively creating private life that it would be unreasonable to interfere with. The parents will have to rely on s117B(6) of the 2002 Act (MIL 5.4& PD Sri Lanka [2016] UKUT 108 (IAC)) as the Rules do not give them the same protection as their child.

Sohail and Afsana are citizens of Pakistan. They have lived in the UK for four years. Sohail has been a student and Afsana is his dependent. They have one child here, Mohammed, born three years ago. Following the loss of his college's sponsor licence, Sohail no longer has leave to remain, or any real prospect of finding a new sponsor. Their case is difficult having regard to Appendix Private Life. Mohammed is part of the family unit and it is doubtful he has much by way of links outside it. This is a case that decision makers will see as one where the child's interests are wholly subsumed in the family unit, and where he can reasonably be expected to return abroad with them.

Top Tip

When you are working on an application which involves children, make sure you carefully follow up every possible avenue of enquiry. Think about anything that shows that any relevant children have an independent life outside of the family unit with which they face removal.

Remember that:

- following Azimi-Moayed you have a real advantage if a child has been here for more than seven years at a time of their life when they are integrating socially beyond the family unit.
- the younger the child, the more work you need to do to show integration outside the family.
- at any age, interrupting a critical moment of life or study during formative years is likely to be very important.
- family life with extended family members will often be important for the children

Think carefully aboute the precise advantages of British citizenship where a child holds it. For example, do they have the citizenship of the country where they will otherwise be residing? For all cases involving children, relevant evidence will be:

- independent assessments from teachers
- reports from social workers or other child-centred professionals
- letters from family friends talking about relationships with other children
- letters from figures in the community speaking of the child's involvement with sports clubs, youth groups or the church

Print outs of health records from a doctor's surgery are perhaps the least impressive of the possible documents, but may be better than nothing. It is best practice to be sparing in the provision of reports which are largely repetitive, for example just selecting recent ones together with occasional past reports that give a flavour of the child's progress generally.

5.3.2.2 British Citizen Children living abroad with a parent applying as a partner

In SD Sri Lanka [2020] UKUT 43 (IAC) the UT gives very close attention to the relevance of British citizenship to an entry clearance application involving children. A spouse had applied to join her British citizen Sponsor in the UK; their two children, aged around 5 and 7 at the UT hearing date, were also British citizens. As the application could not meet the financial requirements, the best interests of the

British citizen children were of central importance. The UT emphasised the importance of social and economic rights protected by the welfare state including free education and the NHS, the right of abode and the opportunity to participate more fully in the life of their local community as they grow up (which should allow fuller integration here). But these had to be compared with the equivalents abroad, and the possibility of greater extended family support there. Even without clear evidence one could readily infer that the children's welfare would be significantly diminished by not having one parent living with them. But the reluctance of a parent to relocate abroad was not a significant factor absent strong reasons justifying that stance: effectively a UK resident Sponsor would need to show insurmountable obstacles or some other special factor to successfully argue that moving abroad was disproportionate.

5.3.2.3 Proving relationships via DNA and other evidence

It can be difficult to prove family relationships. The HO is often slow to accept documentary evidence which does not meet modern biometric standards. Birth certificates are often rejected when obtained long after the date of birth and other forms of identity document may be suspect where it is unclear what underlying documentation was provided to obtain them in the first place. So DNA evidence can be of critical importance.

UK birth certificates are presumed reliable. If the application asserts that the wrong father is named on the certificate then a correction must be made via the Births and Deaths Registration Act 1953 and the Registration of Births and Deaths Regulations 1987. The Registrar General will instruct registration officers to obtain evidence for the purpose of verifying the facts of the case.

The DNA Policy Guidance addressing inviting applicants to volunteer evidence (at their own cost) to demonstrate a biological relationship, including DNA evidence. It sets out

- The HO may not insist on DNA evidence and so general refusal reasons cannot be relied on where it is absent nor may an adverse inference be drawn from its absence
- If the decision maker considers that there is insufficient evidence of a biological relationship to decide a case, they should give a reasonable opportunity to provide such evidence (or a reliable alternative, eg where children are in the UK, a declaration of parentage, by the Family Court or High Court under section 55A of the Family Law Act 1986)
- A DNA testing laboratory must hold accreditation to a suitable International Organization for Standardization (ISO) standard - usually ISO/IEC17025 or ISO 15189
- The DNA collection standards must be followed: the sample-taking must be observed by an independent witness such as a testing laboratory representative, each person to be tested must provide facial photographs that ideally meet HMPO photograph standards, or another format that can be validated. The independent witness stating "I certify that this is a true likeness of [title and full name of adult or child who is providing a DNA sample]", a photographic document must be provided to the independent witness (unless held by UKVI), persons over 16 must provide a written consent to the process (and the parents of younger people must give written consent)
- Concerns about a report must be verified directly with the testing laboratory
- Test results must not be disclosed outside of the HO and care must be taken in notifying families of a decision which may be inconsistent with their understanding of biological relationships

5.3.3 PL5.1(b) – Very significant obstacles to integration

PL5.1(b) asks whether *'there would be very significant obstacles to the applicant's integration into the country to which he would have to go if required to leave the UK'*. PL6.1 excludes asylum seekers from consideration over any period their asylum claim is deemed inadmissible.

The significant obstacles test is future looking. Preparing a case on this basis will focus on the problems they will face in returning to their country of origin. Indeed, this is a significant difference between the approach to a private life case within the rules and outside them: the rules focus heavily on the prospects of integration abroad, whereas Article 8 looks first to the strength of connections here.

Relevant considerations in assessing the prospects of integration abroad are identified in the *Private Life* Guidance:

- The possibility of (re-)integrating in one's own country is to be assumed, the burden of proof being on the applicant to show otherwise
- Unsubstantiated assertions will not count for much
- A *very significant obstacle* is one would would seriously inhibit integration and/or cause very serious hardship
- Routine problems such as learning a new language or finding employment are not enough

The guidance then sets out the HO's specific approach to the following factors: cultural background; length of time spent in the country of return; family, friends and social network; faith, political or sexual orientation of sexual identity. Only really serious problems will qualify: this is an example from the Guidance: "*A very significant obstacle may arise where the applicant would be at a real risk of prosecution or significant harassment or discrimination as a result of their sexual or political orientation or faith or gender, or where their rights and freedoms would otherwise be so severely restricted as to affect their fundamental rights, and therefore their ability to establish a private life in that country.*" On the other hand, the Guidance suggests a more generous test for health cases than otherwise available under human rights law (MIL 5.6): '*independent medical evidence could establish that a physical or mental disability, or a serious illness which requires ongoing medical treatment, would lead to very serious hardship*'.

What follows on from this is a list of arguments as to why the following 'common claims' on their own do not necessarily constitute 'very significant obstacles': absence of family or friends in the destination country; applicant never having lived there (or only for a brief period); inability to speak the local language; absence of employment prospects.

Relevant factors appearing in the guidance as showing that there are no very significant obstacles are:

- living amongst their country of origin's diaspora here
- family connections abroad (including ones which could potentially be strengthened in the future) which may be shown by the family or friends visiting, perhaps sponsored by the applicant or their extended family
- The presence of family, friends or social networks organisations abroad that could assist them in integrating

Top Tip
Factors that might be relevant to establishing very significant obstacles will include (from casework experience and extrapolating from HO policy): ☐   The age they came to the UK. The more experience they have had of living in the country to which they would return or be removed, particularly as an adult, the weaker their case will be ☐   The extent to which they will be able to find work and accommodation in that country. In some countries, it is hard find work without the practical support of family or social connections, even to the extent of setting oneself up as a roadside trader. Expert or other evidence may be useful here in establishing the relevant cultural norms. Bear in mind the extent of any funds that might be expected for their support from family and friends in the UK, or available to them under the HO's voluntary return arrangements. ☐   Their sex or sexuality, or any other factor which might lead them to being exploited or oppressed, particularly where young or psychologically vulnerable ☐   The extent to which their country is in a state of upheaval (e.g. by reason of war or environmental disaster)

In Parveen [2018] EWCA Civ 932 looks at 'very significant obstacles to integration'. There was a heavy burden on an applicant under this route. One could not hope to get anywhere by simply baldly asserting one had lost touch with family members. Applicants needed to show that how it was that they had lost all connections abroad, via a close account of the life they originally had in their country of origin and precisely what family and friends they originally had there. It would then be necessary to explain how it was they had lost touch with all such links, having regard to the likelihood that modern means of communication would be available to stay in contact with one's past circle of acquaintance.

Kamara [2016] EWCA Civ 813, an appeal against deportation, upheld the Tribunal's view that the appellant, who arrived in the UK from Sierra Leone at the age of six, and had lost all contact with his country a long time ago, would face very significant obstacles to integration:

> The idea of 'integration' calls for a broad evaluative judgement to be made as to whether the individual will be enough of an insider in terms of understanding how life in the society in that other country is carried on and a capacity to participate in it, so as to have a reasonable opportunity to be accepted there, to be able to operate on a day-to-day basis in that society and to build up within a reasonable time a variety of human relationships to give substance to the individual's private or family life.

So Kamara shows that *integration* under the Rules infers the ability to actively participate and be accepted within society such that one can operate on a day-to-day basis.

In AS [2017] EWCA Civ 1284 the Court of Appeal found that 'generic' factors such as intelligence, employability and general robustness of character are relevant to the 'broad evaluative judgement' required in assessing whether there are very significant obstacles to integration abroad.

YD (Algeria) [2020] EWCA Civ 1683 finds that having to conceal one's sexual orientation because of social, cultural and religious pressures might severely limit one's life but does not provide a very significant obstacle to reintegration. Kamara did not assist someone who had lived in the country of proposed return until the age of 15, spoke the language, and was resourceful and able to adapt to circumstances there.

Some individuals raise matters within their human rights claim to the HO that could alternatively be advanced as an asylum claim (eg risks of serious harm from the authorities or third parties in their country of origin). JA Nigeria [2021] UKUT 97 (IAC) observes that "*serious harm*" claims of this nature must be determined by the decision maker.

- A serious threat to a person's life might well amount to very significant obstacles to integration; though one could imagine very significant obstacles to integration falling short of this.
- Where the HO noticed overlapping claims being made, they should advise applicants of the possibility of claiming asylum
- Failure to claim asylum might be taken into account on appeal given the implication of a "*refusal to subject oneself to the procedures that are inherent in the consideration of a claim to refugee or humanitarian protection status*"
- The international protection grounds of appeal would not be available in the ensuing appeals
- One might add to the UT's points the fact that any such claim would have to be proven on balance of probabilities both as to past facts and future risks

Decision makers should advise applicants if there is missing or inadequate information with a view to giving them an opportunity to make good their application (as per the Guidance).

5.3.4 PL 5(1)(b)(a)) – 20 years' residence

Making a successful application on the 20 year route will depend on:

1. The evidence in relation to continuous 20-year period of residence, which can be partly or wholly unlawful

2. Countervailing or mitigating any relevant factors which could otherwise lead to a suitability refusal
3. Should the 20 year period of residence not be fully corroborated (which can be difficult), evidence underpinning the alternative argument that the applicant would fit within PL5.1(b) (very significant obstacles to integration), and evidence supporting any relevant Article 8 private life arguments

Example

Maria is from Ecuador. She tells you that she has been in the UK for just over 20 years. She entered as a visitor and overstayed, working for various individuals over the years as a cleaner. She lost her original passport during one of her many moves between temporary addresses, but she has a photocopy. She is destitute and cannot afford the fee for an FLR(FP) application.

Her first problem is proving when she entered the UK. But even if she can do that, she also has to prove she remained for the relevant period. Even if she had one, a passport with an entry stamp and no other stamps since then would not prove her length of residence as, UKVI may argue, she may have travelled abroad and returned on a different passport.

Nevertheless, Maria must now apply for a new passport to enable her to make a valid application. Some embassies require proof of lawful residence in the UK and advocacy with the embassy may then be required. If this is unsuccessful, any evidence of attempts to obtain a passport can be used to argue r34(5)(c)(vii) – that Maria's application should be accepted as valid despite inability to provide a passport as this is due to circumstances outside her control.

Attempts must always be made to obtain official or semi-official records, as almost no one retains sufficient documentation to cover 20 years. In Maria's case, a UKVI subject access request should show her visit visa application if she made one, and any subsequent applications she may have attempted, and the free application process is accessible here. In addition to the photocopy of her expired passport, you will need to countersign a new passport photo of Maria confirming it is a true likeness of Maria, for ID purposes.

If Maria is concerned that this request may bring her to the attention of the HO and that they may then attempt to remove her, you can use your organisation as a "care of" address in making the request, instead of her own address.

As the evidence gathering process can take many weeks, it is also important to go on record with the HO, here. As a further informal strategy, a fee waiver request can be made early to give notice that Maria is in the process of applying to regularise her status. The fee waiver department, most recently available via FHR9DestitutionQueries@homeoffice.gov.uk or FHRUDecisionservice@homeoffice.gov.uk, has been amenable to extending the 10-day deadline to lodge the substantive application following a fee waiver grant. A simple email to the fee waiver team should suffice. It is not in the department's interest to process another, near identical application once Maria is ready to make the substantive application. You can offer instead to update her financial evidence at that point. As no s3C leave is in play, nothing is lost if no extension is given. You can simply resubmit the previous fee waiver request with updated evidence together with the approved previous request. In the meantime, Maria benefits from the knowledge that UKVI is aware she will be applying for leave.

For further evidence of her residence, in addition to the UKVI SAR, if she has a GP, Maria's GP surgery should be contacted and full medical records should be applied for (electronic records sometimes only reach back to around 2012 whereas full records can go back decades). These requests are sometimes free but if not are capped at £50. If Maria does not have a GP, an NHS subject access request can be made, and individual hospitals can be contacted directly for any records. .

Library, dentist or college records are further examples of evidence which may be obtained, and whatever is available in a given case should be pursued. Bank statements or utility bills, requested from the bank or provider from the beginning, obviously help. However, an undocumented migrant like Maria may well not have generated such records. Sometimes employers past or present are willing to give evidence, which would be very helpful.

Support from well-respected members of the community who are willing to vouch for the applicant's length of residence from their own experience may help too. Friends and family will usually be willing to give evidence, though this will not always be given a great deal of weight, and will certainly never lead to a grant of leave on its own.

In relation to the Suitabililty grounds (found in Appendix FM Partners at S.LTR), you must check:

1. Whether Maria has ever been billed for NHS hospital care, as one of the discretionary refusal grounds is on the basis that the HO has been notified of an outstanding NHS debt of £500 or more. If she has, contact the overseas charging department of the relevant hospital and negotiate a repayment plan that is affordable, which can then be used in mitigation.

2. Whether it is possible that she owes any unpaid litigation costs to the HO. The latest of her previous immigration lawyers' files needs to be requested, which should include all the previous. If not, and she mentions JR without legal aid, dig deeper.

3. Whether Maria has any criminal convictions – if so, apply for a subject access request from ACRO. This information will allow you to make the appropriate representations regarding offences and rehabilitation periods.

4. Whether, in any previous HO application, misleading information was provided or deception used. If so, explore the possibility whether previous representatives were aware or even advised Maria to be dishonest, as is sometimes the case. A complaint would need to be made and a firm reported to their regulator, for any mitigating arguments to hold any weight.

If Maria had been in the UK for less than 20 years, the case would be very different. In order to meet the rules, she would need to show very significant obstacles to re-integration into Ecuador, which may be difficult if she left the country as an adult.

Her case should be argued on three alternative bases:

(1) as a 20-year residence case under PL5.1(a)

and then, should it not be accepted that she can prove this length of residence:

(2) on the basis that there are 'very significant obstacles' in her case to relocation abroad under PL5.1(b), and

(3) outside the Rules and under any applicable Article 8 case law, based more on her connections here than on her difficulties abroad. Each strand of the case must be supported by as much objective evidence as can be found. Outside the rules, she would need to show very substantial and compelling ties to the UK above and beyond the normal friendships one would make over time, usually requiring, at least, cumulative factors which might include a large extended family here and very substantial activities in her community.

> **Top Tip**
>
> When presenting the evidence in a long residence application, make it easy for the decision maker and everyone else who ever reads the paperwork by providing a table of the evidence, showing the date that each piece of evidence covers, and using a witness statement to introduce the documents (e.g. 'from 2002–2003 I lived at this address and I worked nearby' (reference tenancy agreement and pay

slips), and explain why there may be periods that are not covered (e.g. 'unfortunately when I lost my job I also lost my accommodation soon afterwards, and I became homeless').

5.3.5 Young person living half their life in the UK

PL4.1 provides a route for young people who have arrived in the UK as a child and lived half their life here. An applicant aged 18 years or over and under 25 years must have arrived in the UK as a child and have lived continuously in the UK for at least half their life at the date of application. As the Guidance puts it: *'The rationale for the half of life test is that the greater the proportion of a child or young person's life has been spent in the UK, the more likely it is that the child or young person can be said to have established their own private life in the UK.'*

Whereas a child has to show *reasonableness plus seven years' residence*, a young person who has lived here for half their life *does not have to show reasonableness at all*. So an applicant who has lived here for 10 years would have a watertight case under the rule on their 18th birthday, whereas the day before they would have had to satisfy the more subjective test of reasonableness too, although they would have had a very strong case indeed on that limb. Some arithmetic is needed to work out whether a youngster has lived half their life here.

Once within the route, extensions are possible notwithstanding that the age limit is exceeded.

5.4 Private life outside the rules

From 20 June 2022 there is very little scope for considering private and family life applications outside the Rules, because all Appendix FM applications (GEN 3.2) and most Private life applications (PL 8) are to be considered within the Rules (MIL 5.7.1). The *Statement of Intent: Family Migration* which introduced the 9 July 2012 reforms explained that failing to meet the Rules would normally indicate that no ECHR Art 8 claim could succeed.

Essentially, the government has run with notions expressed in the Huang litigation (such as Lord Bingham's reference to 'the general administrative desirability of applying known rules if a system of immigration control is to be workable, predictable, consistent and fair as between one applicant and another'). The Rules proceed as if Parliament has now, via its partial stamp of approval of the IRs addressing family and private life (which received some rather modest debate before it), given a careful expression of the public interest in maintaining immigration control. Accordingly there is much less scope for cases to succeed outside the rules. As it was put in MM (Lebanon) [2017] UKSC 10:

> although the tribunal must make its own judgment, it should attach considerable weight to judgments made by the Secretary of State in the exercise of her constitutional responsibility for immigration policy.

The historic case law which we discuss in this Module was often decided before the modern era in which most ECHR Art 8 cases are addressed within the Rules. In general the cases emphasise the need to assess Article 8 with regard to the position struck in the core Rules, because these provide the starting point for assessing proportionality. The HO Guidance may also be useful – however the Guidance addressing Article 8 is not exhaustive (ultimately Article 8 assessments have to be evaluative): see MM (Lebanon) [2017] UKSC 10 §66.

> 'A … misconception is the implication that article 8 considerations could be fitted into a rigid template provided by the rules, so as in effect to exclude consideration by the tribunal of special cases outside the rules. As is now common ground, this would be a negation of the evaluative exercise required in assessing the proportionality of a measure under article 8 of the Convention which excludes any "hard-edged or bright-line rule to be applied to the generality of cases"'

The Immigration Staff Guidance on the 10-year route sets a high threshold for private life applications not meeting the IRs: whether there are exceptional circumstances which would render refusal a breach of ECHR Article 8 **(because it would result in unjustifiably harsh consequences for the applicant or their family)**

The guidance Family life (as a partner or parent), private life and exceptional circumstances suggests that the HO has finally got the message from years of litigation (eg Agyarko [2017] UKSC 11 §56) that

> Exceptional circumstances' means circumstances [where] refusal could or would result in unjustifiably harsh consequences for the applicant, their partner or a relevant child, or would result in unjustifiably harsh consequences for another family member whose Article 8 rights it is evident from the application would be affected by a refusal.
>
> 'Exceptional' does not mean 'unusual' or 'unique'. Whilst all cases are to some extent unique, those unique factors do not generally render them exceptional. For example, a case is not exceptional just because the criteria set out in the IRs have been missed by a small margin. Instead, 'exceptional' means circumstances in which refusal of the application could or would result in unjustifiably harsh consequences for the individual or their family such that refusal would not be proportionate under Article 8.

Cases are not, therefore, to be approached by searching for a unique or unusual feature, and in its absence rejecting the application without further examination. Rather, as per Agyarko, the test is one of proportionality. The reference to exceptional circumstances in the European case law means that, in cases involving precarious family life, 'something very compelling ... is required to outweigh the public interest', applying a proportionality test.

Exceptional factors identified in the Guidance include:

- the extent to which roots were put down whilst the applicant was in the UK legally
- exceptional legal or cultural factors which prevent or severely limit the applicant from enjoying private life in their country of origin
- specific barriers to communication (such as a disability that would prevent the applicant from learning the language of the country of origin)
- cumulative factors, such as family relationships where they cannot be counted as giving rise to family life

There seems to be a high rate of refusal once cases are considered outside the rules. Where there are particularly strong elements though, the UKVI may decide not to certify the application as clearly unfounded, allowing the applicant an in-country right of appeal.

The case law establishes that a judge who finds the rules are not met, must go on and make a full proportionality assessment on established Article 8 principles when deciding the appeal. The first case that established this was MF (Nigeria) [2013] EWCA Civ 1192. In MM & Ors [2014] EWCA Civ 985 it was made clear that at the second stage:

> in any event it would be necessary to apply a 'proportionality test' with regard to the 'exceptional circumstances' guidance in order to be compatible with the Convention and in compliance with *Huang* ...

However, for a case to succeed at the second stage, it has to have some force: the vogue term is that it needs to be 'compelling' (effectively a simile for the HO's *unjustifiably harsh*). Eg Agyarko [2017] UKSC 11:

> In general, in cases concerned with precarious family life, a very strong or compelling claim is required to outweigh the public interest in immigration control

See AT (Eritrea) [2016] UKUT 227 (IAC) (MIL 9.7.3.2) for the approach to refugee family reunion when it was not catered for under the IRs.

In Ganesabalan [2014] EWHC 2712 (Admin) the High Court laid down useful principles in approaching cases outside the Rules. The case is rather old now, but nevertheless it provides some inspiration when challenging a HO decision on private and family life cases outside the Rules by way of JR, where there is no right of appeal.

- The more complicated and individualised the case, the more the decision will have to engage with the supporting evidence, engaging with all relevant factors
- The discretion, described variously by reference to 'exceptional circumstances' or 'unjustifiable hardship', involves the Secretary of State applying a proportionality test and asking whether removal would be disproportionate by reference to Article 8 standards
- All relevant considerations have to be balanced up both inside and outside the Rules: so aspects of family and private life should not be discounted when it comes to assessing a case *outside* the Rules just because they did not reach the relevant standard required *inside* the Rules
- It is important to add up all relevant family and private life factors and balance them against the public interest, rather than simply taking aspects of Article 8 individually

The present state of black letter law, policy and case law is rather complex in this area. Encourage any judge who might allow an appeal on human rights grounds outside the Rules to remind themselves in their written decision that the Rules are themselves the starting point for consideration and that they represent the government's own evaluation of the public interest in human rights cases; and that a case that succeeds outside the Rules is to some extent exceptional or compelling, having regard to principles of proportionality. And that the section 117B factors are always relevant.

Example

Ismail is a citizen of Pakistan. He comes to the UK to study. After two years, his sponsor loses their licence because of documented dishonesty in their practice of recruiting and teaching students. Ismail tries to find an alternative sponsor but is unable to do so within the 60 days grace period given to him by the HO. He has made a few friends from his course.

Mira is a citizen of the Philippines. She comes to the UK under the work permit scheme working as a senior carer and has now been here for almost a decade. She subsequently extends her leave to remain as a Skilled Worker. She is refused a further extension of leave to remain because her employer has inadvertently failed to increase her earnings to the relevant level required under the Rules notwithstanding having promised her that they would do so. She is shown by letters from the old people's home where she works to play a very important role in their daily life.

Ismail's case will probably be treated as catered as very largely for by the Rules & Guidance, bearing in mind the HO policy to give a reasonable opportunity to find an alternative sponsor and his relatively short time in the country and limited connections (MIL 7.8.2). So if he cannot show very significant obstacles to integration back in Pakistan, Article 8 ECHR does not add much to his case (and the authorities such as Patel and Nasim at 5.4.2 below are against him).

However Mira may be on better ground: she has a more unusual case, has been let down through no fault of her own and has not failed to avail herself of a policy designed to help people in her situation, has resided here a long time lawfully, and seems to have strong connections where she works with a vulnerable community: all this is a long way from the situation on which PL5.1(b) focuses. So in her case it would easier to argue that the rules do not really envisage her situation and so there is a greater 'gap' between the rules and Article 8 ECHR, making it easier for an appeal to be allowed on pure Article 8 grounds. Hopefully, anyway: there are some quite tough decisions relating to migrants who are disadvantaged by sponsor errors under the PBS (MIL 7.10). But those are usually cases where any private life was rather exiguous.

5.4.1 Article 8 and the case law interpreting it

These established principles under ECHR Art 8 are relevant where the claim fails under the rules.

Article 8 provides as follows:

(1) Everyone has the right to respect for his private and family life, his home and his correspondence.

(2) There shall be no interference by a public authority with the exercise of this right except such as is in accordance with the law and is necessary in a democratic society in the interests of national security, public safety or the economic well-being of the country, for the prevention of disorder or crime, for the protection of health or morals, or for the protection of the rights and freedoms of others.

In paragraph 17 of the important case of Razgar [2004] 2 AC 368, Lord Bingham set out five questions that must be posed in assessing whether an act of removal from the UK would breach Article 8 in a given case:

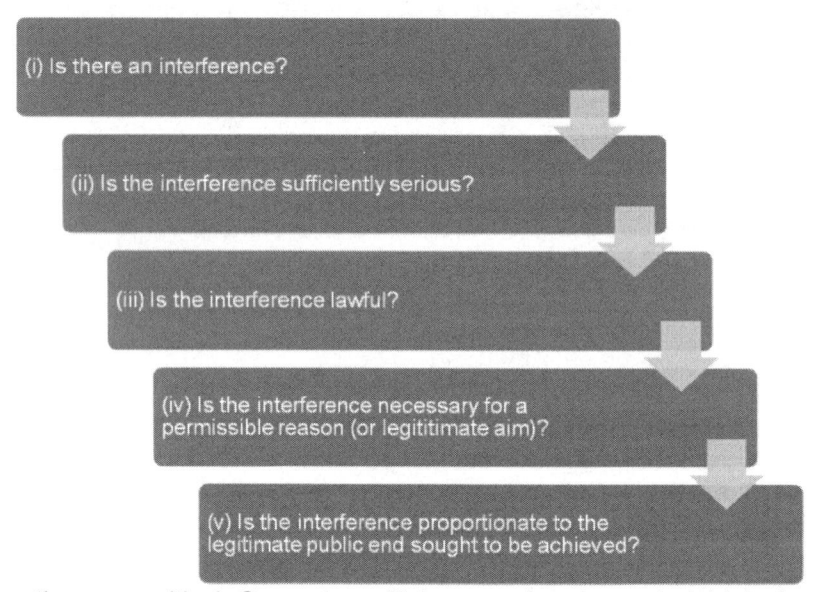

(i) Is there an interference?

(ii) Is the interference sufficiently serious?

(iii) Is the interference lawful?

(iv) Is the interference necessary for a permissible reason (or legititimate aim)?

(v) Is the interference proportionate to the legitimate public end sought to be achieved?

These five questions are critical. Once stage (ii) is passed and a material interference with Article 8 ECHR is identified, then the burden moves to the state to justify that, by showing it is lawful, for a legitimate aim, and proportionate. The section 117B statutory criteria do not replace this analysis: it simply gives some additional structure to stage (v) when the public interest is assessed.

Firstly, the five step approach provides an essential tool for analysing any Article 8 factual scenario. Secondly, it has been recognised that it may well amount to an error of law for an immigration judge to fail to follow the five step approach.

5.4.2 Interference with Article 8 rights

In order to establish that that there will be an interference with an Article 8 right, it is first necessary to show that private life is actually established in the United Kingdom.

Establishing private life

The concept of private life as protected by Article 8 has repeatedly been held to be a very broad one. There is a very thorough summary in Ni Chuinneagain [2022] NICA 56. The key protected dimensions are:

- Relationships with other human beings, see e.g. Niemietz v Germany (1992) 16 EHRR 97 where the ECtHR said:

    Respect for private life must also comprise to a certain degree the right to establish and develop relationships with other human beings ... [including] activities of a professional or business nature since it is, after all, in the course of their working lives that the majority of people have a significant, if not the greatest, opportunity of developing relationships with the outside world.

- Including 'the totality of social ties between settled migrants such as the applicant and the community in which they are living': see e.g. Khan v United Kingdom 6222/10 [2011] ECHR 2253 [32]
- Article 8 may also prevent a person's removal where their private life would face flagrant violations abroad, as where an 'alien homosexual' faced expulsion albeit that their treatment would fall short of Article 3 ill-treatment. However, such a breach would need to be flagrant – see Ullah at [47].
- Mental health: thus in Razgar, Lord Bingham recognised that private life extended to:

> the consequences for his mental health of removal to the receiving country ... 'private life' in article 8 ... [extends] to those features which are integral to a person's identity or ability to function socially as a person.

See also, regarding mental health, the Strasbourg court in Bensaid v UK (2001) 33 EHRR 10.

> "Mental health must also be regarded as a crucial part of private life associated with the aspect of moral integrity. Article 8 protects a right to identity and personal development, and the right to establish and develop relationships with other human beings and the outside world. The preservation of mental stability is in that context an indispensable precondition to effective enjoyment of the right to respect for private life..."

Below read more on human rights and health (MIL 5.6). In this chapter we deal with health only in so far as it may be a factor in an Article 8 case built on connections here generally.

The concept is clearly exceedingly broad; there is a convenient summary of the themes above in Suppiah & Ors [2011] EWHC 2 (Admin):

> the right to respect for private life protects the individual's identity, self-determination, physical and moral integrity, maintenance of relationships with others and a settled and secure place in the community. It also protects a right to identity and personal development and the right to develop relationships with other human beings and the outside world.

Applying these principles, in Janjanin [2004] EWCA Civ 448 the Court of Appeal recognized that valuable and responsible work in the National Health Service could constitute private life.

It can readily be seen that private life as recognised under the IRs is very much narrower than the forms of Article 8 rights that are protected by the judicial interpretation of the ECHR itself. The central difference in focus is that Article 8 looks first to connections here, whereas the Rule looks at the hardship of return abroad. The principal omissions from the Rule (read against the case law) are:

- The failure to cater for relationships with the community, church, and business — see the ECtHR in Niemietz quoted above
- The failure to take a sufficiently nuanced approach to studies (and indeed business and professional connections), see e.g. CDS Brazil [2010] UKUT 305 (IAC):

> people who have been admitted on a course of study at a recognised UK institution for higher education, are likely to build up a relevant connection with the course, the institution, an educational sequence for the ultimate professional qualification sought, as well as social ties during the period of study. Cumulatively this may amount to private life that deserves respect because the person has been admitted for this purpose, the purpose remains unfilled, and discretionary factors such as mis-representation or criminal conduct have not provided grounds for refusal of extension or curtailment of stay.

Students and private life

In general the more intertwined a person's study, work or business is with their personal identity and the 'inner circle' of their life, the greater will be the impact upon their 'private life' of a measure that interferes with that work or business. Most of the cases that have reached the higher courts have involved students, so the case law tends to focus on them. However, the same thinking appears in Onwuje [2018] EWCA Civ 331 the establishment of a business here. The Court accepts that in some circumstances an entrepreneur's ownership and involvement in their business may be seen as an aspect of their private life, and that a person's work could certainly be integral to their 'physical and social identity'. But finds it unlikely that refusals of their applications would be disproportionate.

CDS Brazil does not necessarily encourage students to expect long term residence here beyond their studies – that would be inconsistent with Lord Carnwath in Patel [2013] UKSC 72 – but it does show that an interruption of genuine studies that would seriously compromise a person's educational and professional development might well be disproportionate where based only on some technical failure to provide specified evidence (particularly given that that regime was reformed from 2020 see MIL).

Patel makes it clear that Article 8 should not be used as a general dispensing power to avoid the consequences of the IRs in cases to which the Tribunal is sympathetic. More recently, though, in Ahsan [2017] EWCA Civ 2009, the Court of Appeal reiterated that:

> a student's involvement with their course and their college can itself be an important aspect of their private life

Lawful residence for a limited period does not necessarily bring with it any real foundation for a human rights claim, even where the person is of good character: see Nasim [2014] UKUT 25 (IAC), where the Tribunal, having noted that there seemed little justification for extending CDS Brazil towards post study stay, found that:

> A person's human rights are not enhanced by not committing criminal offences or not relying on public funds. The only significance of such matters in cases concerning proposed or hypothetical removal from the United Kingdom is to preclude the Secretary of State from pointing to any public interest justifying removal, over and above the basic importance of maintaining a firm and coherent system of immigration control.

Top Tip

When representing a student, if you intend to raise private life human rights issues based on studies, make sure you provide a cogent, evidence-backed case that looks at issues such as

- their overall investment in studies
- the professional and educational relationships established here
- the friendships they have here and the relationships they have in the community
- the consequences to their professional development and personal identity of the loss/interruption of all this, in the light of their circumstances abroad

The same ideas can be carried over to cases where lawful residence is the foundation for setting up a business. The important thing is to ensure that there is rather more to the case than just an assertion of lawful stay plus good character: it is *connections* which are critical.

5.4.3 Third party rights

In Beoku-Betts [2008] UKHL 39 the House of Lords made it clear that, even if a narrow reading of the (then, IAA 1999) appeal provisions suggested that only the human rights of a migrant facing removal were to be considered by an immigration judge (and thus not those of other family members remaining here), they needed to be interpreted broadly so as to permit the whole family's interests to be considered:

... 'there is only one family life', and ... assuming the appellant's proposed removal would be disproportionate looking at the family unit as a whole, then each affected family member is to be regarded as a victim.

Evidence from family members may prove crucial re:

- Strength and depth of relationship and/or attachment, and what the applicant means to the family member concerned.
- Reasons why the family member(s) cannot or should not be expected to relocate to the country concerned.
- Information regarding the effect on any children affected, ideally from family court proceedings (a court order may well needed for disclosure MIL 6.2.6.2), child psychologist or from an Independent Social Worker.

Beoku-Betts was followed by another landmark House of Lords case, EM (Lebanon) [2008] UKHL 64. The Lords held that the rights of the child in this case had to be considered separately to the mother (both were facing removal) and also suggested that separate representation for a child might be appropriate in some cases.

5.4.4 Threshold for interference with private life: domestic cases

The threshold for establishing a private life that engages Article 8(1) is not "a specially high one": AG (Eritrea) [2007] EWCA Civ 801, a case concerning the private life of an unaccompanied minor.

5.4.5 Threshold for interference with private life: foreign cases

In 'foreign cases' (a term used in Ullah and Do), i.e. cases where an arguable human rights breach will take place *abroad* in the future, *post-removal* from the UK (e.g. the applicant faces a lack of fair trial abroad), rather than inside the UK itself by the action or inaction of the UK authorities (e.g. being separated from one's UK-based family), it has to be shown that there will be a 'flagrant denial' of the right in question where the right in question is not an absolute one.

The leading case is EM (Lebanon) [2008] UKHL 64. The facts there were extreme, involving a mother who came to the United Kingdom as a fugitive from Shari'a law, wishing to avoid the situation where her son's physical custody would pass by force of law to his father or another male member of his family. In proceedings from which she would be all but excluded. It was therefore accepted that she and her son faced destruction of the very essence of the family life that mother and child had hitherto shared together; the House of Lords allowed the appeal because of the compelling humanitarian considerations (see MIL 10.3).

5.4.6 In accordance with the law, legitimate aim and necessary in a democratic society (proportionality)

Decisions made in accordance with the HO's view of how immigration control should be secured will generally be seen as in accordance with the law for Article 8 purposes by the courts.

In the vast majority of cases, there will presumably be a legitimate aim present: because the courts have accepted that immigration control is aimed at securing the UK's public safety and economic well-being, preventing disorder and crime, and protecting the rights and freedoms of others.

5.4.7 Necessary in a democratic society

Having shown a legitimate aim for the interference, the HO must also show that it is necessary in a democratic society. This is the fifth question posed by Razgar. The legal profession's shorthand for this enquiry is to ask whether the decision is disproportionate.

The concept of proportionality is central to the application of Article 8, although it is very important to follow the five-step approach and not jump straight to proportionality.

The modern position on proportionality was summarised by Lord Sumption in Bank Mellat v Her Majesty's Treasury (No. 2) [2013] UKSC 39:

> the question depends on an exacting analysis of the factual case advanced in defence of the measure, in order to determine (i) whether its objective is sufficiently important to justify the limitation of a fundamental right; (ii) whether it is rationally connected to the objective; (iii) whether a less intrusive measure could have been used; and (iv) whether, having regard to these matters and to the severity of the consequences, a fair balance has been struck between the rights of the individual and the interests of the community.

Proportionality in the context of the exercise of immigration control usually boils down to a question of identifying those cases where the adverse effect on the individual is so disproportionate to the need to maintain an effective system of immigration control that it is unlawful. We can see some of the considerations as set out by Lord Bingham stated in Huang [2007] UKHL 11 at [24]:

> Human beings are social animals. They depend on others. Their family, or extended family, is the group on which many people most heavily depend, socially, emotionally and often financially. There comes a point at which, for some, prolonged and unavoidable separation from this group seriously inhibits their ability to live full and fulfilling lives. Matters such as the age, health and vulnerability of the applicant, the closeness and previous history of the family, the applicant's dependence on the financial and emotional support of the family, the prevailing cultural tradition and conditions in the country of origin and many other factors may all be relevant.

Assessing proportionality is sometimes compared to a balancing exercise. The scales and the weights on each side of the fulcrum can be represented thus:

State
- Maintain immigration control
- Public safety (deportation cases)

Individual
- Family life elements, e.g. spouse, children
- Private life elements, e.g. long residence, employment
- Other parties affected
- Home Office defaults, e.g. delay

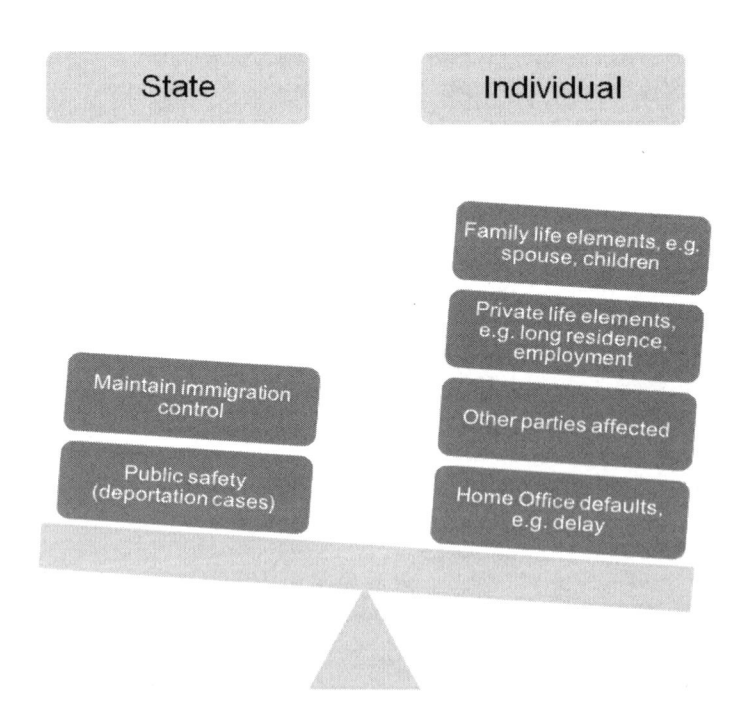

For example, here is the Court's reaction to the case of one young man, in AG (Eritrea) [2007] EWCA Civ 801:

> The private life established in this country by a lone 14-year old whose asylum claim is not processed for four years, who has no known family in Eritrea and cannot speak the language,

and who has acquired an education, psychological support and a social circle here, not only brings him very plainly within art. 8(1) but raises an obvious question about the necessity and proportionality of removing him notwithstanding the legality and proper objects of immigration control.

The Rules and Guidance give a strong indication of where the public interest lies in any particular case, see MM (Lebanon) [2017] UKSC 10:

> although the tribunal must make its own judgment, it should attach considerable weight to judgments made by the Secretary of State in the exercise of her constitutional responsibility for immigration policy ...

> The tribunal is entitled to see a difference in principle between the underlying public interest considerations, as set by the Secretary of State with the approval of Parliament, and the working out of that policy through the detailed machinery of the rules and its application to individual cases. ... By contrast rules as to the quality of evidence necessary to satisfy that test in a particular case are, as the committee acknowledged, matters of practicality rather than principle; and as such matters on which the tribunal may more readily draw on its own experience and expertise.

So it is easier for the Tribunal to depart from a HO decision based on the kinds of evidence that show that maintenance is available, than it is to differ from the level of income actually required (cf BF & Ors v Switzerland [2023] ECHR 542 - MIL 9.7.3). But when determining whether enough funds are available, the real question should be the likelihood of the applicant being a burden on the state, having regard to all forms of support that might be available including the prospect of the applicant finding employment following their arrival in the UK. Again in MM:

> They are entitled to take account of the Secretary of State's policy objectives, but in judging whether they are met, they are not precluded from taking account of other reliable sources of earnings or finance. It is open to the Secretary of State to indicate criteria by which reliability of such sources may be judged, but not to exclude them altogether.

5.4.8 Part 5A NIAA 2002

When considering proportionality, the starting point for the courts and tribunals is to 'have regard' to the considerations laid out under Part 5 of the 2002 Act, inserted as from 28 July 2014 by the Immigration Act 2014.

> **117A** ... (2) In considering the public interest question, the court or tribunal must (in particular) have regard—
> (a) in all cases, to the considerations listed in section 117B, and
> (b) in cases concerning the deportation of foreign criminals, to the considerations listed in section 117C.
> (3) In subsection (2), 'the public interest question' means the question of whether an interference with a person's right to respect for private and family life is justified under Article 8(2).

> **117B** Article 8: public interest considerations applicable in all cases
> (1) The maintenance of effective immigration controls is in the public interest.
> (2) It is in the public interest, and in particular in the interests of the economic well-being of the United Kingdom, that persons who seek to enter or remain in the United Kingdom are able to speak English, because persons who can speak English—
> (a) are less of a burden on taxpayers, and
> (b) are better able to integrate into society.
> (3) It is in the public interest, and in particular in the interests of the economic well-being of the United Kingdom, that persons who seek to enter or remain in the United Kingdom are financially independent, because such persons—
> (a) are not a burden on taxpayers, and

(b) are better able to integrate into society.
(4) Little weight should be given to—
(a) a private life, or
(b) a relationship formed with a qualifying partner, that is established by a person at a time when the person is in the United Kingdom unlawfully.
(5) Little weight should be given to a private life established by a person at a time when the person's immigration status is precarious.
(6) In the case of a person who is not liable to deportation, the public interest does not require the person's removal where—
(a) the person has a genuine and subsisting parental relationship with a qualifying child, and
(b) it would not be reasonable to expect the child to leave the United Kingdom.

A number of points can be made:

- These considerations are only part of the assessment, given the words of s117A(2): there is no suggestion in the statute that other factors should be excluded, even though the statutory ones should be evaluated 'in particular', so the existing case law on Article 8 ECHR remains relevant (see Dube) [2015] UKUT 90 (IAC))
- There is no obligation on the HO to have regard to these factors in its own decision making: s117 is aimed at 'a court or tribunal'
- The factors at 117B(2) and (3) may count in favour of many migrants, where they are economically self-sufficient and speak English: though to prevent the HO from relying on public interest considerations, they would need to be made good at the level of the requirements of the IRs: see AM Malawi [2015] UKUT 260 (IAC)
- At (4) little weight is to be given to 'a relationship with a qualifying partner' established on the basis of unlawful residence – but this does not bite on broader Article 8 relationships beyond partnership, including those with children
- At (6) the 'seven-year rule', based on a child's lengthy residence plus reasonableness, is now enshrined in statute; indeed s117(6) amounts to a straightforward statement of the public interest rendering other considerations largely irrelevant, so long as no issue of deportation arises, that in such cases, removal would disproportionate. This also seems to answer the question left open by Appendix Private Life 3.1, which addresses the child rather than the parent, by stating the consequence for the caring parent of a child whose own removal would be unreasonable under that sub-rule
- The section 117B considerations bite on the private life of a child or young person, though the context of their age and external influences on them must be taken into account, see Miah [2016] UKUT 131 (IAC):

    a moderate period of residence is likely to be of greater impact ... it is less likely that a child will be aware of, much less responsible for, his immigration status ... a series of considerations which could potentially outweigh the public interest ... might include matters such as parental dominance and influence; trafficking; other forms of compulsion; and the absence of any flagrant, repeated or persistent breaches of the United Kingdom's immigration regime by the child concerned

- As to s117B(5), in Rhuppiah [2018] UKSC 58, the Supreme Court ruled that anyone who lacks indefinite leave to remain is present on a precarious basis. However, where the private life has particularly strong features, the general guidance to give it little weight could be exceptionally overridden.
- GM (Sri Lanka) [2019] EWCA Civ 1630 shows that a decision which adversely impacts on family members who are on a route to settlement it will be easier to show a decision was disproportionate: there the family including children who the HO had expected to leave the country with the applicant had thereby lose a pathway to settlement to which their possession of DLR otherwise entitled them.
- Indeed, as found in AM Malawi [2015] UKUT 260 (IAC), immigration status may be 'precarious' even for a person with ILR, or for a person who has obtained citizenship, either because that status is revocable by the Secretary of State as a result of their deception or because of their criminal conduct. In such circumstances, the person will be well aware that they have imperilled their status and cannot viably claim thereafter that their status is other than precarious.

Nevertheless, in determining whether the public interest in enforcing immigration control trumps the private life in question, think carefully about the circumstances that made immigration status 'precarious': these may still be relevant where the private life has a *compelling* character:

- o a person may have had been in an immigration route that would have led to ILR subject to circumstances outside their control, directly (because the rule itself permitted a settlement application to be made), or because case law recognised that it should do so as in the HSMP litigation, see e.g. HSMP Forum Ltd [2008] EWHC 664 (Admin)
- o a person may have been exercising European Treaty rights in the past – see e.g. Heritage [2014]UKUT 441 (IAC)
- o they may have come here for reasons outside their control, ranging from historic trafficking to an asylum claim that was undermined by a post-departure change of circumstances by which time they had put roots down in this country – see e.g. Shala [2003] EWCA Civ 233, where it was accepted that the applicant's family unit originally had a strongly arguable claim to be entitled to enter this country because of the dangers they had faced at the time they came to this country
- o they may have come here as a minor at a time when decisions as to their future were made on their behalf (as is accepted, in a different context, in ZH Tanzania) and when they could not reasonably be expected to do anything else than make a life for themselves here as best they could, such that it might be thought unfair for the precariousness of their position to count strongly against them

- MS Belgium [2019] UKUT 356 (IAC) considers the relevance of unlawful residence in the context of EU nationals. Of course, in recent times they have had the benefit of the EEA Regulations and EU law to rely on. But where those issues are not available to them (as where they have brought an appeal on human rights grounds alone) EU law residence may still have some relevance. These ideas retain relevance not with standing the end of ongoing EU law residence rights.
    - o The UT accepts that where an EEA national brings an appeal on human rights grounds, s117B of the NIAA 2002 is relevant to their case. Thus considerations such as speaking English and financial independence are relevant. However, section 117B(4) refers to being in the UK "*unlawfully*", which raised a more difficult question, because a person's EEA residence rights are not simply established by formal grants of leave. Nevertheless, of course EEA residence rights are not necessarily automatic: they usually ensue from taking advantage of free movement to work and study etc.
    - o The UT holds that an EEA national will be present unlawfully at any time when they cannot demonstrate holding Treaty Rights. But this analysis left open the possibility that a child could lose out, as their residence would have been dependent on parents whose own residence rights based on their own EEA status may no longer be ascertainable. In such cases it might be appropriate to accept that they were present lawfully, particularly where their right of residence had never been questioned. This meant that when it came to consider the deportation provisions of the Rules they could be treated as individuals who had lived in the UK for more than half their lives.

Nevertheless, the Strasbourg case law has long drawn a distinction between the expulsion of 'settled' migrants with rights of residence in the host country and the refusal to admit, or the removal of, migrants with no such rights.

In Agyarko [2017] UKSC 11 the Supreme Court identifies these relevant considerations:

- what the ultimate outcome of immigration control measures was likely to be, regardless of the person's present status: so that there might be no public interest in enforcing departure where a person was certain to be granted leave to enter if they returned abroad to seek entry clearance
- one might envisage someone being under a reasonable misapprehension as to their ability to maintain a family life in the uk - a less stringent approach might then be appropriate

In Birch [2020] UKUT 86 (IAC) the UT considers the situation of a Jamaican national who had resided in the UK since 1999, having overstayed her student leave from 2001. However a few years later she was the victim of fraud, when a person claiming to be an immigration officer charged her £3,000 for a passport stamp appearing to confer ILR. In 2015 the false stamp came to light when she applied for a driving licence, and the SSHD served her with notice of removal. She lodged a human rights claim, which was refused, and then pursued an appeal.

The UT in Birch goes on to cite Agyarko §53 for the proposition that a person might be under a reasonable misapprehension as to the lawfulness of their UK residence. Agyarko concerned a person with limited leave who was being contrasted with someone with ILR. The UT rules that that thinking could extend beyond the cases of people with leave; it was also relevant to someone such as Ms Birch, now shown to be an overstayer. A period during which someone [reasonably] *thought* they held leave should be treated differently from periods when they knew otherwise.

5.5 Common considerations when assessing proportionality

5.5.1 Contribution to the community

A person who makes a significant contribution to the community outside work (see UE (Nigeria) [2010] EWCA Civ 975) or who has close relationships in the UK such as being someone's carer, might be able to build a case. In UE the Court noted that there might be a

> public interest in the retention in this country of someone who is of considerable value to the community [which] can properly be seen as relevant to the exercise of immigration control. It goes to the weight to be attached to that side of the scales in the proportionality exercise

In Thakrar [2018] UKUT 336 (IAC) the UT looks at how to approach this kind of activity. President Lane rules that a Judge should only attribute weight to community contributions where they are 'very significant' – in practice, this is likely to arise only where the matter is one over which there can be no real disagreement. Judges should exercise restraint in making judgments of this nature.

5.5.2 Policies and proportionality

We discussed HO policies above (MIL 2.4). For now, we should recall that not only may a policy be relevant given the public law requirement to take account of relevant considerations, but that policies also have human rights implications: because, as was stated in AG Kosovo,

> a judicial decision-maker has to take into account any applicable policy, because if the policy itself 'tells in favour of the person concerned being allowed to stay in this country' it is a factor that has to be incorporated into an assessment of the argument going to the importance of immigration control.

5.5.3 Meeting the Rules and 'near miss' cases

Additionally, the policy positions reflected by the IRs may themselves be relevant to assessing cases outside the Rules. Under the old-style appeals system, simply meeting the Rules meant that an appeal would be allowed. But these days the focus is on a breach of the Human Rights Convention, so where a person is refused leave to remain because they do not meet the Rules, the Judge has to look at the broader question of whether there is actually a disproportionate interference with private and family life. The fact that the FTT finds that the Rules are now met on appeal does not of itself guarantee it's success. But of course, meeting the Rules must take an Appellant a long way towards their goal.

The UT first looked at the relevance of meeting the requirements of the Rules in visitor appeals, which were the first class of appeal to have the grounds restricted to human rights only. In Kaur [2015] UKUT 487 (IAC) the UT found that where there was no significant gap between the visitor rules and what Article 8 requires, the claimant's ability to satisfy the IRs was

> capable of being a weighty, though not determinative factor when deciding whether such refusal is proportionate

Eventually the Court of Appeal rammed the point home in TZ (Pakistan) and PG (India) [2018] EWCA Civ 1109 §34:

> "where a person satisfies the Rules, whether or not by reference to an article 8 informed requirement, then this will be positively determinative of that person's article 8 appeal, provided their case engages article 8(1), for the very reason that it would then be disproportionate for that person to be removed."

Beyond the Rules, a judge on appeal has to take account of section 117B factors in assessing the proportionality of an interference with private and family life. However given that the Rules tend to deal with those factors (which are essentially English language proficiency, financial independence and lack of precarious immigration status subject to other features of the case), one might think that there would be little obstacle to an appeal being allowed on human rights grounds once the Rules are satisfied.

Whilst the courts have repeatedly stated that the fact that the application's refusal was in the context of a 'near miss' in satisfying the requirements of the rules is not sufficient to make a decision disproportionate, nevertheless a 'near miss' is still relevant. Lord Carnwath in the Supreme Court in Patel & Ors [2013] UKSC 72 stated that:

> the balance drawn by the rules may be relevant to the consideration of proportionality.

And see SS (Congo) [2015] EWCA Civ 387:

> If an applicant can show that there are individual interests at stake covered by Article 8 which give rise to a strong claim that compelling circumstances may exist to justify the grant of [leave to enter] outside the Rules, the fact that their case is also a 'near miss' case may be a relevant consideration which tips the balance under Article 8 in their favour.

And the Supreme Court in MM (Lebanon):

> The issue is not whether there has been a 'near miss' from the figure in the rules, but the weight to be given to any factors weighing against the policy reasons relied on by the Secretary of State to justify an extreme interference with family life. One such factor may be the extent to which the family, while not complying with the [minimum income requirement], would in practice be a burden on the state.

This is summarised very well by the UT in Caguitla [2023] UKUT 116 (IAC):

> *Because this is a human rights appeal, the immigration rules have an indirect, but important, role. First, an applicant may be able to show that, contrary to the position implied by the decision under appeal, he or she actually met the requirements of the Immigration Rules at the relevant date. In such circumstances, the balance of public interest against the individual circumstance of the appellant clearly falls in favour of the appellant, because the immigration rules demonstrate that there is no public interest in excluding a person who meets their requirements. Secondly, an appellant who does not meet the requirements of the rules may be able to show, by relying on the terms of the rules, that it would be disproportionate to exclude an appellant who falls in a very similar category to one who would meet the requirements of the rules. That will not be so if the problem is that the appellant misses (even narrowly misses) a quantitive or numerical requirement of the rules; but an appellant may be able to show that the public interest demonstrated by the rules ought to be read in exactly the same way in relation to the appellant's own circumstances, despite the latter not precisely meeting the terms of the rules.*

5.5.4 Third party failings

In OA (Nigeria) [2008] EWCA Civ 82 the Court of Appeal noted the Applicant had been seriously let down by her legal advisors who failed to proceed properly with an application before her leave to remain had expired; this was an important factor in the subsequent decision of the Court upholding the view of the Tribunal below that her removal would be disproportionate (MIL 4.2.6).

5.5.5 Historic wrongs and individual injustices

The historic immigration wrong suffered by a group when deciding whether an interference with family life is proportionate is something which can be attributed significant weight, given NH (India) [2007] EWCA Civ 1330 which discusses the past injustice suffered by British Overseas Citizen female heads of households who were unable to apply to settle in the United Kingdom and may be decisive in the appropriate case. Similar ideas appear in the decision in Gurung [2013] EWCA Civ 8 addressing the inability of dependent relatives of Gurkhas to come to this country sooner because former Gurkha soldiers had unfairly been denied the chance to settle in the UK until 2008.

Sometimes relatives, typically adult dependent children of UK sponsors, apply to rejoin their family in the UK arguing that some 'historic wrong' led to their separation. In these cases a decision maker must focus on whether the family unit was living together up to the time that the UK-based individuals migrated, rather than upon the separation being due to 'choice': eg Rai [2017] EWCA Civ 320.

In a wider context, HO decision making can, at times, be shown to have started off on the wrong footing. Litigants seeking to rely on relatively ancient mistakes in their case history often cite the doctrine of *historic injustice*. Usefully Hysaj [2020] UKUT 128 (IAC) reminds us that that doctrine was not wholly extinguished by the Supreme Court's rather negative decision on the topic in TN (Afghanistan). As shown by Mousasaoui [2016] EWCA Civ 50 it could still be relevant, though only where there was some demonstrable *illegality* rather than simply maladministration. Any such illegality had to be shown to have caused *practical detriment* to the migrant.

A good example is the English language test fraud cases. There the SSHD made allegations of serious dishonesty against students based on information from the test provider, ETS. This could lead to drastic consequences: curtailment of leave in-country, cancellation of leave at the port of attempted re-entry, or an unexpected refusal of an application based on events many years earlier. Any of this would be likely to leave the person as an overstayer, stuck in the hostile environment, and with serious problems.

Many of these individuals were subsequently vindicated by judges on appeal or by reconsideration of their cases by UKVI. In Ahsan [2017] EWCA Civ 2009 §120 gives important guidance for approaching the situation of migrants whose honesty has been vindicated some time down the line.

> "The starting-point is that it seems to me clear that if on a human rights appeal an appellant were found not to have cheated, which inevitably means that the section 10 decision had been wrong, the Secretary of State would be obliged to deal with him or her thereafter so far as possible as if that error had not been made, i.e. as if their leave to remain had not been invalidated. In a straightforward case, for example, she could and should make a fresh grant of leave to remain equivalent to that which had been invalidated. She could also, and other things being equal should, exercise any relevant future discretion, if necessary "outside the Rules", on the basis that the appellant had in fact had leave to remain in the relevant period notwithstanding that formally that leave remained invalidated."

So the HO must find a way to interpret the Rules, or make a decision outside the Rules, that restores the migrant to their former position. This may well require untypically creative thinking.

In Pathan [2020] UKSC 41 the Supreme Court, by a majority, finds that there was a duty on the SSHD to notify an applicant with an outstanding application promptly of the revocation of his sponsor's licence, it being procedurally unfair not to do so. Their reasoning apparently extends to a duty to notify of any other development which is within the SSHD's knowledge but not within that of the applicant. However there is no public law duty on the SSHD to confer any period of leave. Judges could not go that far, as that would impermissibly cross the boundary between procedural and substantive fairness. But this duty does not extend to overstayers: see eg Ullah [2022] EWCA Civ 550 (MIL 7.4.3.5).

Musico [2020] EWCA Civ 1389 further develops the requirements of fairness. An ambassador's domestic worker had been treated by the entry clearance officer as if she was exempt from immigration control. This proved problematic some years later and caused confusion. The Court opined that where a person was prejudiced by being wrongly treated by a decision maker, arguably they should not suffer any ongoing prejudice. So in this individual's case, fairness might have been required her be to put in the same position as if she had in fact been exempt in the first place. Such a person would have received 90 days leave under s8A of the IA 1971 in order to regularise their status at the end of their work for an Embassy. This did not help Ms Musico, however, as she had learned of the problem more than 90 days before she took action to protect her position.

In Patel [2020] UKUT 351 (IAC) the UT distinguishes **historic** from **historical injustices**.

- **Historic injustices** involve a belated recognition by the UK authorities that a particular class of persons was wrongly treated, in immigration terms, in the past; and that this injustice should be recognised in dealing with applications made now. The existence of this kind of injustice has a profound (or even determinative) effect in assessing a person's immigration position.
- **Historical injustices** involve individual failings by the SSHD such as unreasonable delay in determining an application, failing to apply a relevant policy, or making a mistake as to the applicant's conduct. In these cases the injustice would be uncontroversial and not dependent on any interaction between the applicant and the SSHD. Those who come to the United Kingdom for the purpose of study or employment may experience difficulties and disappointments, for not every teaching institution will be of the highest standard. Not every employer will be ideal. These latter disappointments and inadequacies were unlikely to reduce the public interest in enforcing immigration control

5.5.6 Severity of the interference with Article 8 rights

Always bear in mind whether the consequence of an application failing will represent a 'mere' interference with the underlying rights or will effectively extinguish them. A person who in future will be able to return to this country on a visit basis, or a family whose history and resources suggests could easily travel to meet the person now facing expulsion, will find it more difficult to show that the interference is disproportionate

A lack of physical proximity between members of the family unit is likely to be more serious where children are involved, as was accepted by the Tribunal in Omotunde [2011] UKUT 247 (IAC) making the point that 'modern means of communication' cannot equate to the on-going physical and emotional relationship available to people who reside together or nearby one another. Similar thinking is shown by Hussini [2017] ScotCS CSOH_80: if members of a family enjoy family life in an inter-dependent household of partners and minor and dependent children it is no comfort to say that they can continue to enjoy that family life by telephoning each other, emailing, or video conferencing.

5.5.7 Home Office delay and other maladministration

The definitive case on delay by the HO as a factor in assessing proportionality is that of the House of Lords in EB (Kosovo) [2008] UKHL 41. In summary, the three ways in which Lord Bingham says that delay may affect an Article 8 claim are as follows:

- The Article 8 family and/or private life rights will develop and grow during a period of delay.
- Delay reduced the weight given to a relationship being entered into in the knowledge of its precariousness owing to immigration control. To put it another way, a decision maker must recognise that delay has allowed Article 8 rights to become established and entrenched.
- Delay reduces the significance of the Article 8 (2) consideration of the need to maintain immigration control because delay gives rise to 'a dysfunctional system which yields unpredictable, inconsistent and unfair outcomes'.

The HO policy on delay was set out in Chapter 53 of the Enforcement Instructions archived 19 October 2017 but still accessible here). Delay was recognised as particularly relevant in some scenarios. The syntax of the policy is not very clear and we have done our best to make sense of it. This requires its decision makers to give weight to its own delay in making a decision on an asylum or human rights claim or in setting removal directions following refusal of such a claim of three years or more in the case of children or six years or more in the case of adults (MIL 2.4). See earlier section on HO policies for details. In Okonkwol [2013] UKUT 401 (IAC), the Tribunal made it clear that this does not equate to a principle that those who have been in the UK for six years or more should be given leave under the policy

In such cases it is desirable to show that the client has not 'acquiesced in the delay'. As the Tribunal put it in MM Serbia and Montenegro [2005] UKAIT 00163:

> Evidence of some formal pressure on the Home Office (either by way of solicitors' (or other representatives') letters ... intervention by an MP (as here), or personal appearance at the Home Office, resulting in an attendance note recorded on the file by an official) is likely to be required to show that an appellant has not acquiesced in delay.

In the summer of 2009 the HO amended Chapter 53 of the Enforcement Guidance and Instructions in order to attach more weight to length of residence in the UK and delay by the HO when considering whether to enforce removal of failed asylum seekers.

The relevant passages of that Guidance are at 53.1.1 in the section dealing with exceptional circumstances. This indicates that, subject to questions of character and conduct, caseworkers should, when determining human rights applications, place weight on significant delay (presumably this might be relevant either in assessing the strength of connections here, i.e. the establishment of private and family life with which there might be an interference, and in the proportionality balancing exercise: see the discussion above regarding EB Kosovo).

Saliu [2021] EWCA Civ 1847 holds that delays in entry clearance decision-making may *reduce* the quality of the family life rather than enhance the claim. Delay was relevant in the EB (Kosovo) sense, only once family life was shown to be firmly established. The notion of "*delay*" connoted unreasonable or unjustified behaviour – in contrast to a need to consider a complex case.

Family cases

Family cases are those where there is a family unit comprising a parent caring for a child/children and who are emotionally and financially dependent on the parent and under the age of 18 at the date of the decision

- where delay by the HO has contributed to a significant period of residence
- where factors preventing departure have contributed to a significant period of residence
- additionally where, following an individual assessment of the prospects of enforcing removal, and exceptionally, where the dependent child has lived in the UK for three years or more whilst under the age of 18.

Other delay cases

- where a person has been in the UK for more than six years in the context of exceptional delay by the HO following an individual assessment of the prospects of enforcing removal
- where a person has been in the UK for more than six years in the context of there being exceptional factors preventing departure, following an individual assessment of the prospects of enforcing removal. The UT looked at an older version of the policy that referenced 'residence of between four to eight years' in Okonkwo [2013] UKUT 401 stating that whilst such a period in non-family cases 'may be considered significant [...] that is residence following an initial assessment of the prospect of removal'.

So it can be seen that *irremovability* plus *HO delay* seems to have a special character which may help a case succeed when proportionality is assessed in the context of policy positions that can be taken as reflecting the public interest.

It will be seen that the question of *prospects of removal* will be important in many of these cases. The guidance goes to explain that a grant of discretionary leave may be appropriate provided there is credible evidence that:

- the migrant is undocumented
- has made genuine efforts to secure appropriate travel documentation to facilitate voluntary departure from the UK but has been unable to do so for reasons beyond their control, or
- it is accepted that the prospects of securing a document and/or return to the country of origin are unrealistic

The Appellant in Hysaj [2020] UKUT 128 (IAC) relied on the old HO position not to initiate deprivation proceedings for those *"resident in the United Kingdom for more than 14 years"*. The same notion was found in the IRs generally before the 14 year period was extended to 20 years(in July 2012). The UT concluded that the policy would not apply in situations where imprisonment for criminal offending effectively broke the continuity of residence (see MIL 4.2.18 re limbo).

Old country-specific exceptional leave to remain policies and deliberately delayed consideration of an asylum claim

In the case of S [2007] EWCA Civ 546 the Court of Appeal held that it was unlawful for the HO to have delayed consideration of a person's case in order to meet new targets they had been set for consideration of new cases, thereby depriving that person of a benefit to which he would otherwise have been entitled. The details of the case do not really matter anymore, as there will be few, if any, migrants who can still benefit from any failure to consider them under these policies as they will now have had many years during which to challenge the treatment of their case, it is now too late to argue that they should have benefited under the policy so giving them a water-tight case for leave to remain: see S & Ors [2009] EWCA Civ 142.

Top Tip

When preparing Article 8 cases generally, consider

☐ Friendships that exceed the average, e.g. those established at times of hardship or trauma involving an unusual level of emotional support
☐ Delay for which the migrant is not responsible (so awaiting a decision on an outstanding application, or being irremovable because of fears of generalised human rights abuses in a particular country, is a much better form of delay than simply going to ground following an unsuccessful asylum claim; staying at the same address waiting for an update for the HO carries rather less weight once there is no outstanding application)
☐ Whether the migrant's individual history includes a period when they would/should have benefited from a HO concession but on which they missed out for reasons outside their control
☐ Involvement and best interests of children, whether or not they are part of the family unit facing removal
☐ Being let down by a trusted figure, e.g. employer, government department, relative or lawyer
☐ Narrowly missing out on an application's success because of some technical requirement (though this must not be expressed purely in 'near miss' terms)
☐ Intention on arrival being consistent with the possibilities for extension of stay in the relevant immigration category
☐ Each of the relevant section 117B criteria and whether they are in the client's favour (e.g. English speaking and economic independence are often in their favour; precarious residence often counts against them)

And think very hard about what corroboration is available for every assertion that is made.

5.5.8 Present and historic entitlements to British citizenship

Any present entitlement to British Citizenship is central to a human rights appeal, as no refusal could be in accordance with the law if it resulted in a British citizen facing expulsion. If a person is in fact British then clearly a refusal by the HO would be unlawful. MS Belgium [2019] UKUT 356 (IAC) considers the relevance of arguments regarding *past* entitlement to British citizenship to a human rights appeal.

The UT held that no material weight should be given to the fact that there may have been a good (even indisputably good) case to be registered as a British citizen when assessing the proportionality of removal. The decision in Akinyemi had found that it was wrong to treat someone who could have registered for British citizenship during their childhood as having been present "unlawfully" over that period for the purpose of section 117B NIAA 2002. But this did not mean that anyone who had been eligible to apply for discretionary registration as a British citizen under s3 BNA 1981 during their childhood could cite that as a factor counting against their expulsion. Appeals would concentrate on current UK ties.

5.6 Unavailability of medical treatment abroad

It is argued in some cases that a difference in medical treatment between the UK and the country to which a person is to be removed will cause suffering or death and that removal would therefore breach the person's human rights and engage the UK's responsibilities. This raises issues both under Article 3 ECHR and Article 8 ECHR, but because they often overlap, it is convenient to deal with everything together.

- Under Article 3 ECHR it may be argued that the suffering will be so serious as to amount to a breach of Article 3, relying on a principle established in the case of D v UK (1997) 24 EHHR 423, subsequently developed in the case of N v UK and more recently in Paposhvili
- KH (Afghanistan) [2009] EWCA Civ 1354 shows that the same threshold should apply to mental illness re Article 3.
- The other is to argue that although the suffering would not be so serious as to engage Article 3, the suffering allied to other issues may engage Article 8, relying on the case of Bensaid v UK (2001) 33 EHRR 205. This is not a soft option

5.6.1 The Article 3 line of authority – From N to Paposhvili and AM Zimbabwe

The approach to human rights claims based on a lack of treatment for ill-health has significantly shifted over time. Essentially

- On 5 May 2005 the House of Lords in N [2005] UKHL 31 found that the test was (as summarised by Lady Hale)

    "whether the applicant's illness has reached such a critical stage (ie he is dying) that it would be inhuman treatment to deprive him of the care which he is currently receiving and send him home to an early death unless there is care available there to enable him to meet that fate with dignity."

    The difficulty for a claimant succeeding is shown by Lord Hope, who noted that the applying this test the claim would fail even though there was no doubt that N herself would "*face an early death after a period of acute physical and mental suffering.*"

- The Grand Chamber of the ECtHR essentially agreed with that approach in N v UK [2008] ECHR 453

- In Paposhvili (Application No 41738/10; 13 December 2016) the ECtHR's Grand Chamber revised its approach, concluding that inhuman and degrading treatment would result where an individual

    although not at imminent risk of dying, would face a real risk, on account of the absence of appropriate treatment in the receiving country or the lack of access to such treatment, of being exposed to a serious, rapid and irreversible decline in his or her state of health resulting in intense suffering or to a significant reduction in life expectancy.

- On 29 April 2020 the Supreme Court decided AM (Zimbabwe) [2020] UKSC 17. It held that

  o There was no good reason not to follow Paposhvili

  o The ECtHR had clearly referred to 2 distinct scenarios: a *serious, rapid and irreversible decline* in health resulting in

    - intense suffering or

    - a significant reduction in life expectancy: this meant *significant* given the individual's own circumstances, so a significant loss of life expectancy had to be recognised as even more important to a younger person – this is a very different approach to that prevailing in the N period where only a truly dramatic curtailment of life expectancy (eg with death just six months ahead) was recognised as a tenable claim

  o The burden of proof in human rights claims was generally on the applicant. But where necessary judges needed to consider where there was a *prima facie* case that the Paposhvili test was met

    - Effectively this meant that where the evidence so far supplied met the test if not challenged or countered, the SSHD would have to provide evidence about the *availability and accessibility of suitable treatment* in the receiving state

    - This would include the situation where the evidence was such that there were *serious doubts* as to whether the test was satisfied

- AM Zimbabwe [2022] UKUT 131 (IAC) proposes a way of analysing these claims.

  o First determining whether the evidence (usually from treating doctors) establishes the individual to be seriously ill

  o Second, assessing if the evidence was "*capable of demonstrating*" substantial grounds for believing that the serious, rapid and irreversible health decline resulting in intense suffering, or to a significant reduction in life expectancy, was due to the absence of appropriate treatment (or of access to it). Mere worsening of the condition on removal (even if there were serious and detrimental effects) was not enough

  o Evidence (being for the migrant to adduce) on the availability of and access to treatment in the receiving state was more likely to be found in reports by reputable organisations and/or clinicians (eg providing treatment & services there) and/or country experts with contemporary knowledge of or expertise in medical treatment & conditions

  o Only if these tests were satisfied would the procedural obligations on the SSHD to provide her own evidence arise

The procedural obligation applied in Paposhvili and AM Zimbabwe has been considered at Tribunal level too. In AXB Jamaica [2019] UKUT 397 (IAC) the UT holds that where the applicant's evidence is not challenged or countered by material from the SSHD and that evidence is sufficient for a decision maker to conclude that there is a real risk that Article 3 would be breached by removal, then the SSHD can only argue that removal is lawful if concrete evidence is produced pointing the other way. This might be:

> (a) general evidence;
> (b) specific enquiries made by the SSHD of the authorities or other organisations in the Receiving State; and
> (c) the obtaining by the SSHD of specific assurances from the Receiving State relating to the person facing expulsion (see assurances more generally: MIL 10.3.2.1)

There was no need for the applicant to show "clear proof" of their likely fate; some degree of speculation was inevitable given the nature of the issues.

Health law continues to develop. Savran v Denmark [2021] ECHR 1025 looked at the case of a person suffering from schizophrenia. A relapse leading to aggressive behaviour and a significantly higher risk of offences against the person of others were matters that might be very serious and detrimental generally but did not imply any intense suffering for the applicant (in contrast to a self-harm case).

Even before the important re-positioning in AM (Zimbabwe), a number of scenarios have been accepted as meeting the high threshold, or departing from it.

- In CA [2004] EWCA Civ 1165 the expulsion of a sick mother and child where the mother would have to watch her child suffer and die (post-Paposhvili that threshold needs to be revised downwards to suffering life expectancy deterioration or serious irreversible harm etc) was considered exceptional, as Laws LJ put it:

    It seems to me obvious simply as a matter of humanity that for a mother to witness the collapse of her new-born child's health and perhaps its death may be a kind of suffering far greater than might arise by the mother's confronting the self-same fate herself:

- Where there is **discrimination** in the healthcare available to the sick, see e.g. RS (Zimbabwe) [2008] EWCA Civ 839 discussing the possibility that there might be a deliberate withholding of medical care or food
- In GS and EO India [2012] UKUT 397 (IAC), the Tribunal noted a claim might succeed where health problems were exacerbated by an **absence of resources through civil war or similar human agency** (see further Ainte at MIL 8.9.2)
- Laws LJ in GS (India) & Ors [2015] EWCA Civ 40 recognised another possibility where treatment of critical value is imminently due and would be lost if removal proceeds:

    If there is a real possibility of this transplant in the near future ... there may be a question whether GM's removal from the United Kingdom before it is carried out would violate Article 3 on the specific footing that to deprive him of such an imminent and transformative medical recourse amounts to inhuman treatment.

- In MM (Zimbabwe) [2017] EWCA Civ 797 the Court of Appeal considered it arguable that to return someone to a country where they are likely to suffer a profound mental collapse, effectively leading to destruction of their personality, might infringe the right under Article 3 to protection against torture and inhuman treatment
- Medical problems may ensue other than from a want of resources, e.g. where the human rights interference is caused not by the difference in treatment between here and abroad and the repercussions of that difference, but where the act of removal actually causes a deterioration in physical or mental health. See J [2005] EWCA Civ 629 where it was the trauma of removal bringing with it an enhanced risk of suicide rather than any 'want of resources' that led to the human rights interference
- A lower threshold of suffering should apply to children than adults. There is considerable authority behind the proposition that treatment or punishment that would not breach the rights of an adult may nevertheless breach the rights of a child: see E v Chief Constable of the Royal Ulster Constabulary [2009] 1 AC 536
- Health may be considered alongside other factors within a private life claim as raising very significant obstacles to integration (MIL 5.3.3)
- If the UK is responsible for aggravating an individual's ill-health, eg via their treatment in detention or during a removal attempt, then once again this would not be a situation of '*naturally occurring illness*' and the relatively high threshold in Paposhvili would not be the only relevant consideration
- Suicide risks may engage ECHR Art 3
    - J [2005] EWCA Civ 629 explains that the risk must be serious and linked to removal, having regard to the objective reality of the person's foreseeable circumstances abroad (but also their subjective reaction to it) and to the availability of effective mechanisms to diminish the risk at all stages of (and after) the removal.
    - MY Occupied Palestinian Authority [2021] UKUT 232 (IAC) explains that the Paposhvili threshold applies when assessing suicide risk cases. The question in this context was whether

the applicant would face a real risk of Paposhvili consequences on account of the absence of appropriate treatment in the receiving state or the lack of access to such treatment. It would take its place within the J test. So the existence of mechanisms in the sending or receiving state that might reduce the suicide risk were relevant as was any subjective perception contributing to suicidal ideation.
- As it was put in Carlos [2021] EWHC 986 (Admin) a viable Article 3 claim must evidence risks arising not from a voluntary act but from impulses which cannot be controlled because of one's mental state.

5.6.2 The Article 8 line of authority

As per Bensaid (MIL 5.4.2) that mental health must also be regarded as a crucial part of private life associated with the aspect of moral integrity.

In JA (Ivory Coast) [2009] EWCA Civ 1353 the Court accepted that lawful residence where leave to remain was granted in the context of full knowledge of a person's health situation might differentiate the case from the norm:

> JA's is a markedly different case. Her position as a continuously lawful entrant places her in a different legal class from N, so that she is not called upon to demonstrate exceptional circumstances as compelling as those in D v United Kingdom. There is no finding by the AIT that she has much if any hope of securing treatment if returned to Ivory Coast, or therefore as to the severity and consequences of removal (see Razgar [2004] UKHL 27). Depending on these, the potential discontinuance of years of life-saving NHS treatment, albeit made available out of compassion and not out of obligation, is in our judgement capable of tipping the balance of proportionality in her favour.

This approach is exemplified in Akhalu [2013] UKUT 00400 (IAC). Here, the Appellant had arrived in the UK legally in 2004 to study, but was then diagnosed in the UK as suffering from end stage kidney failure. It was accepted that she was not aware of the illness prior to arriving in the UK. After successfully completing her studies, she received a kidney transplant and thereafter required carefully monitored medication to ensure that the transplanted organ is not rejected. It was accepted that she could not afford such treatment in Nigeria and would therefore die soon after returning there.

In upholding the allowed appeal, the UT concluded that the FTT had been right to allow the appeal, for the judge had made:

> 'a holistic assessment, drawing on the truly exceptional level of engagement with her local community that was disclosed by the evidence he alluded to and which he did not need to set out extensively in his determination and a comparison of her ability to enjoy any private life at all in Nigeria, as well as the foreseeable consequences for her health should she be removed to Nigeria.'

In SQ (Pakistan) & Anor [2013] EWCA Civ 1251 the Court of Appeal showed that health cases involving children brought via Article 8 should be assessed via a balancing exercise (and certainly could not be dismissed out of hand):

> On the one hand, MQ can pray in aid his lawful entry and his status as a child with the protection of the ZH approach. On the other hand, he arrived with his serious medical conditions at an advanced stage and, although not an unlawful entrant, it will be relevant to consider whether his arrival here was a manifestation of 'health tourism'. If it was, that would fall to be weighed in the balance.

However Akhalu also shows that a person whose health care must come from the state will have an uphill struggle to show their removal is disproportionate.

> The consequences of removal for the health of a claimant who would not be able to access equivalent health care in their country of nationality as was available in this country are plainly

relevant to the question of proportionality. But, when weighed against the public interest in ensuring that the limited resources of this country's health service are used to the best effect for the benefit of those for whom they are intended, those consequences do not weigh heavily in the claimant's favour but speak cogently in support of the public interests in removal.

A case might be rather stronger where the critical factor is the need for personal care from a close friend or family member resident in the United Kingdom.

From the above you can see that it is very difficult for a health case to prosper. But the situation may be different where questions of health and dependency arise in a context where other Article 8 rights are established: as was noted in MM (Zimbabwe) [2012] EWCA Civ 279 where

> the appellant ha[s] established firm family ties in this country, then the availability of continuing medical treatment here, coupled with his dependence on the family here for support, [may] together establish 'private life' under Article 8 ... Such a finding would not offend the principle ... that the United Kingdom is under no Convention obligation to provide medical treatment here when it is not available in the country to which the appellant is to be deported.

However the case is argued, clear medical evidence must be provided, and the UKVI guidance sets out requirements that it must satisfy: it must be dated within three months of receipt.

Savran v Denmark [2021] ECHR 1025 stressed the need for the national authorities to determine that the required level of criminal culpability was present where an offender's behaviour was affected by mental health concerns. The weight given to this factor was more limited where criminal culpability was impacted by mental illness.

Example

Jamil is a citizen of Pakistan aged seven. He entered this country with his mother as a visitor. He has always suffered from a serious bone disease. It has been treated with only moderate success abroad and his life expectancy is shorter by some years if he cannot find anything better. He and his mother visit your office and ask about the prospects of staying here because of his health. They do not have the money to qualify under the medical visitor route in the future.

It is very difficult to see an Article 3 case succeeding in these circumstances. There is not a complete absence of medical care abroad and he has his mother to look after him.

Nor is an Article 8 case likely to succeed: firstly because it suffers from the same problems as the Article 3 case, secondly because, unless there has been some significant recent change of circumstances, it would seem that his mother has deliberately entered the country in full knowledge that an application to remain longer than the permitted visit would be inconsistent with the intention to leave the country at the end of the stay which is a condition of the visa being granted.

The situation might be different had Jamil entered school and established a health care regime in this country. He could not be blamed for taking advantage of the opportunities: indeed Lord Hope in ZH (Tanzania) emphasised that the sins of parents should not be held against their children.

Top Tip

Health cases are not necessarily all doom and gloom. In an Article 3 case look for:

- Individual factors in a case which amount to compelling humanitarian grounds
- An absence of social and family support
- Whether or not medical treatment is in practice available

> - Imminence of death if adequate treatment is not received; the expelled person's degree of decline and the consequent indignity
> - A mother's natural distress at seeing her child's decline
> - The greater impact of suffering upon a child than on an adult
> - Whether there is any discrimination in government provision of healthcare services
> - Removal at a critical moment in transformative treatment
>
> In an Article 8 case look for, in addition to the factors above:
>
> - A combination of established family/private life in the United Kingdom, and health issues (see MM Zimbabwe – discussed further below)
> - A lack of treatment abroad compared to an established treatment regime here
> - Lawful residence in this country – of particular relevance are grants of leave in the knowledge of the applicant's health situation
> - Private health insurance which would reduce the public interest in restricting access to the limited resources of the NHS

5.6.3 Health claims and leave to remain

Applications on health grounds (e.g. due to suicide risks or to their inability to access suitable treatment) must be made on Forms FLR(HRO). They are free of charge if made solely, or predominantly, relying on Article 3. Leave is granted by way of

- 30 months rolling grants
- on a 10-year route to settlement
- though if leave was first granted under this route before 9 July 2012, the old DLR policy will be honoured so that ILR is granted after six years

See the HO guidance on *Human rights claims on medical grounds*.

5.7 Making a private life application

A valid application on under Appendix Private Life must be made on form Application to remain in the UK on the basis of family life or private life, and currently costs £1,048 (plus £1,000 for the IHS). The Guidance *Visa decision waiting times: applications inside the UK* sets out typical waiting times as 11 months for private life and 10-year route family cases.

An application for a fee waiver can be made where the person does not have accommodation or the means of obtaining it, or they cannot meet their essential living needs (MIL 1.5.7.4). As mentioned above, the procedures and fees are relaxed in some circumstances (MIL 1.5.3).

5.7.1 Decisions in private life cases: duration and conditions of leave, and ILR

Decision makers should request missing documents if anything material appears to be missing (MIL 2.2.2). There are two regimes for granting permission (the first of which replaces the young persons' early settlement concession that appeared from October 2021):

- A period of either 30 or 60 months is granted (as per the applicant's request, the longer IHS being paid for the route in question) for those, at the application date or when first entering the route, who are
    - Under 18 (PL10.1)
    - On the young adult aged 18-25 route (PL10.2)
- Everyone else gets 30 months (PL10.3)

The Guidance states the rationale: 'these applicants did not make a conscious choice themselves to move to the UK and are not responsible for any time spent in the UK without permission as any applications to regularise their stay would have had to be made by others on their behalf.' Should a child have a viable application under a family life as well as a private life route, they should receive a grant that 'gives the child the most favourable grant of leave and allows a shorter route to settlement' (even if this means the child receives a different length of stay).

Successful extension applications will have any remaining period of permission left at the application date (up to 28 days) added to their next grant of permission (PL10.4).

So, children and young people aside, new entrants to the route will need to make three further applications to extend their stay. Children and young persons can continue to extend their stay in the route notwithstanding that they become over age for the category.

The GEN.3 exceptions within Appendix FM (MIL 6.1.4) now require that residual consideration to be given to family life even when the various technicalities of the individual Rules within Appendix FM are not met. So it is quite hard to see any real scope for consideration of a family life case *outside of Appendix FM*. From 20 June 2022, Appendix Private Life moves closer to that position: if applications fail to meet the core routes under the Appendix (20 yeears' residence etc), ECHR Art 8 must still be considered (PL8.1). Unless there are significant adverse Suitability considerations PL8.2: ie the usual exclusions for custodial sentences exceeding a year or offences of persistence/serious harm, or good character issues, The Guidance advises that decision makers should '*consider whether refusal would result in a harsh outcome(s) for the applicant, which is not justified by the public interest, including in maintaining effective immigration controls, preventing burdens on the taxpayer, promoting integration, and protecting the public and the rights and freedoms of others.*'

Where appeals are allowed, the HO will look to the Implementing allowed appeals guidance. And as per the *Private Life Guidance*, where the FTT accepts that the rules are met, HO will grant the leave sought on the route. 30 months LOTR is granted where the appeal succeeds outside the Rules in pre-Appendix PL cases. Lifting the NRPF conditions should be considered where the appropriate evidence is available.

The HO Guidance *Private life* emphasises that cases failing on human rights grounds should still be considered for Leave outside the Rules where compelling compassionate factors exist.

Imposition and lifting of the NRPF condition

Grants are, by default under PL10.5(c) (and GEN1.10 for family life cases) subject to the condition to have "No Recourse to Public Funds"(subject to the usual "recourse to public funds" regime MIL 1.3.6.6).

5.7.2 ILR & early access to ILR

ILR is available subject to suitability criteria. Aspects of the Appendix FM Suitability regime are cross-referenced (PL12): refusal for breach of deportation order, past and present false representations and non-disclosure, and the bans for minor convictions. Additionally the *private and family life ILR conduct suitability regime* applies subject to dispensations for young people (MIL 6.2.10.1).

ILR is available

- For children born in the UK, after 7 years, where it would be unreasonable to expect them to leave the UK (PL13)
- For those granted PTS on the route as a child and young persons meeting the half-life test (MIL 5.3.5), after a continuous qualifying period of 5 years which may include
  - most private/family life routes: partner/parent under Appendix FM or via "family permission", under the private life route, the children of Appendix FM partners/parents or via ECHR Art 8 on private life grounds more generally (PL14)
  - any other settlement route so long as they did not enter the UK illegally and have held PTS under this route for at least a year
- For other adults, when they have completed at least 10 years months of continuous leave on private life grounds (PL14.2)

Other points

- English language proficiency is required (B1) and life in the UK knowledge is to be shown via Appendix KOL UK (PL16-17)
- Continuous residence must be shown via Appendix Continuous Residence (PL15 – see (MIL 7.7.15)
- The ILR to PTS regime applies (PL18 – see MIL 1.3.2.1)
- Children born to a person on the route may apply for ILR (PL26) where their parent is being granted ILR at the same time or is already settled or is a British citizen having last been on the PL route and where the applicant held permission as the parent's child on the route or was born before the parent was settled – the criteria are typical of those for dependency routes (MIL 2.8.1)

The more generous approach for children and young people now found in the Rules alleviates the need for bespoke arguments in individual cases. However, perhaps there will still be cases where the best interests of a child suggest settlement should be granted sooner rather than later. A clear evidence-backed case needs to be put as to why the general principle of 'staged settlement' via consecutive short grants of leave should not apply: Alladin [2014] EWCA Civ 1334. Before the Rule change, Guidance recognised that there could be cases where 'the precariousness of limited leave would create such serious distress as to have a disproportionately detrimental effect on the person's health or welfare that it would prevent recovery or development.'

Conversely, shorter grants than 30 months may be appropriate where leave is given due to some finite objective such as taking exams or completing medical treatment.

In Gornovskiy [2021] UKUT 321 (IAC) the UT looked at when ILR might be granted to a person who was not presenty removable for ECHR reasons. The applicant had put a strong case that there was no foreseeable change of circumstances in Russia permitting his return there. The SSHD had to confront that case on a clearly reasoned basis. However there was no duty to consider the precise seriousness of any conduct leading to exclusion from refugee status.

The LOTR policy emphasises that "*there may be an exceptionally unusual case where ILR is the only viable option, because a short period of leave is not appropriate because there are the most exceptional compeling compassionate grounds*".

Refusals of leave to remain on private life grounds will carry the right of appeal, being the refusal of a human rights claim, unless certified as clearly unfounded (under s94 NIA 2002, MIL 14.3.1-14.3.2) or raised unjustifiably late (under s96 NIA 2002, MIL 14.3.2; the same effect may result from a finding that they do not meet the fresh claim standard if they are made by way of further representations following an earlier claim's refusal: MIL 14.2.3).

CHAPTER 6: Family-Based Applications

6.1 Family Life under Appendix FM

Subject to the transitional provisions (see below), applications made to join or remain wiith settled family members in the UK are made under <u>Appendix FM to the Immigration Rules</u>. When brought into force on 9 July 2012, these rules represented a huge shake up to the system of family migration into the UK.

We will explain here the rules under Appendix FM. and, where necessary, the 'old' rules (in brief, which are in Part 8 of the Rules) for those applying und the transitional provisions.

Appendix FM deals with four categories of family migration, providing a route to enter and remain in the UK for those with family life as:

A partner
- including those whose relationships have ended due to domestic violence or bereavement

A parent
- of a child in the UK

A child
- of a partner or parent

An adult dependent relative

In all categories, applicants will always need to meet 'suitability' and some 'eligibility' requirements.

The suitability requirements largely mirror the grounds for refusal in Part 9 of the IRs, i.e. grounds for refusal relating to criminality, deception and owing money to the NHS, but there are some material differences.

The eligibility requirements relate to one or more of the following criteria;

1. **Relationship**
   - Always mandatory. Sponsor must be
   - a British citizen; or
   - settled or in the UK; or
   - in the UK with limited leave:
     a. under rEU3 of Appendix EU (i.e. pre-settled status as a person in the UK since before the transition period) or
     b. as a worker or business person under Appendix ECAA Extension of Stay
2. **Financial**
   - Minimum Income Requirements for partner and child categories
   - Adequate Maintenance for parents and others
   - Adequate accommodation
   - No financial requirements where EX1 applies
3. **English language**
   - Basic English UK partners and parents
   - No English requirement where EX1 applies
4. **Immigration status**
   - Switching in-country

- Except for fiancees and adult dependant relatives
- Few immigration status requirements where EX1 applies

As per GEN 1.1 of Appendix FM (below), Appendix FM aims to incorporate family life considerations into the rules. And to incorporate the government's duty to safeguard and promote the welfare of children in the UK (i.e. the 'best interests of the child' principle). And at the same time, to take account the public interest considerations implicit in Article 8(2) ECHR: respecting private and family life, protecting public safety, health and morals, the economy, and the rights and freedoms of others, and preventing disorder and crime.

As with the private life category, where the Appendix FM requirements are not met, the government's intention is that family life applications should be allowed only where removal from the UK would be unjustifiably harsh. However there is an important structural difference between the private life and family life rules. The private life routes do not claim to cater for all scenarios (MIL 5.7.1), thus leaving room for LOTR by the yardstick of justifiable harshness. Whereas for all cases considered under Appendix FM, GEN.3.2 provides that cases should receive a residual consideration within the Rules: even where some requirement of Appendix FM is not met. Thus, for family life cases generally there is a 3-stage consideration (the HO refer to a two-stage process in the _Exceptional Circumstances Guidance_ but this comes down to the same thing):

(1) Consider the case under the relevant sub-route within Appendix FM: partner, parent, adult dependent relative etc
(2) If it fails, conduct a residual consideration applying the test of "unjustifiably harsh" circumstances under rGEN.3.2 (MIL 6.1.4)
(3) The third stage (MIL 6.2.5) exists in the partner and parent 'in-country' routes, which insert an intermediate stage between (1) and (2): ie where the person is in breach of IRs, or fails to meet the financial or English language requirements, their application may still succeed if it would be unreasonable for a qualifying child to leave the UK or where there are insurmountable obstacles to a couple's relocation abroad, under rEX1.

6.1.1 Navigating Appendix FM

Navigating Appendix FM is never easy. The individual paragraphs of Appendix FM are referenced by a complex lettering scheme that takes some time to familiarise oneself with (provoking Underhill LJ in Singh [2015] EWCA Civ 74 to say that 'I do not doubt that some subtle intelligence is at work, but the system is quite 197ould197nto the uninitiated and adds to the difficulty of finding one's way around').

The sections are, however, helpfully grouped under the following drop-down index here:

- General
- Exceptional circumstances
- Family life with a partner
- Section EX: Exception to certain eligibility requirements for leave to remain as a partner or parent
- Bereaved partner
- Victim of domestic violence
- Family life as a child of a person with limited leave as a partner or parent
- Family life as a parent of a child in the UK
- Adult dependant relative
- Deportation and removal

To give a rough idea of how the lettering system in the main body of the Appendix works, the table below provides a brief glossary:

Letters at the start – type of rule	Letters in the middle – type of leave	Letters at the end – category
S = Suitability E = Eligibility D = Decision	EC = Entry Clearance LTR = Leave to Remain ILR = Indefinite Leave to Remain	P = Partner BP = Bereaved Partner, DV = Victim of Domestic Violence C = Child (of a person with ltd leave) PT = Parent (of a child in the UK) DR = Dependent Relative
NB: The Suitability provisions applicable to all categories are those in the Partner category		

6.1.2 Operational guidance

Broadly, guidance on Appendix FM can be found in the Immigration Staff Guidance 'Family of people settled or coming to settle'. This collection now contains

- Family migration: adequate maintenance and accommodation
- Adopted children and children coming to the UK for adoption caseworker guidance
- Chapter 08: appendix FM family members (immigration staff guidance)guidance on specific requirements under Appendix FM such as the English language and financial requirements
- English Language requirement: family members
- Family life (as a partner or parent) and exceptional circumstances (note private life dropped out of this as of 20 June 2022): though there may often be cross-over between the issues dealt with in Private life: caseworker guidance ('*Exceptional circumstances*' Guidance)
- Partners, divorce and dissolution
- Victims of domestic violence

Other guidance is found in the IDIs Chapter 08: family members. This contains

- the transitional provisions for persons granted leave under the pre-July 2012 family migration routes are at rules A277 to A280 of Part 8 of the IRs (these cases being rare now)
- other guidance pertaining to these

6.1.3 Section GEN

Appendix FM begins with Section GEN: General. This section defines terms used elsewhere in Appendix FM, and includes an important procedural provision at GEN.1.9. as to when a fee-paid application is unnecessary.

- GEN.1.2. defines the relationships considered under the 'family life as a partner' category (spouses, civil partners, fiancé(e)s/proposed CP, and those in a relationship akin to marriage who have been cohabiting for two years).

- GEN.1.3. allows applicants living outside the UK with their British citizen or settled partner or child to seek entry clearance to accompany them to the UK (b) – normally a sponsor must be physically 'present' in the UK.Those with LTR under Appendices EU or ECAA Extension of stay, however, must be in the UK. Both these sponsor categories are defined here, too.
- GEN.1.4. defines references to the word "specified" as referring to the critically important 'specified evidence' regime found in Appendix FM–SE.
- GEN.1.6. lists the majority-English speaking countries whose nationals will automatically meet the English language requirement in the partner and parent categories.
- GEN.1.8. incorporates into Appendix FM the provisions in Part 8 of the rules relating to polygamous marriages and the children thereof.
- GEN.1.9. outlines the circumstances in which there will be no need to make a valid application (ie. fee-paid and using the right form) in order to access consideration of one's case under the family life provisions in Appendix FM (MIL 6.1.6).
- GEN.1.10 confirms that where leave is granted under 'exceptional circumstances' in GEN.3.1.(2) or GEN.3.2.(3) (see below), the grants of leave will be subject to a condition of no recourse to public funds unless the decision maker considers, with reference to paragraph GEN.1.11A, that the applicant should not be subject to such a condition (MIL 1.3.6). The grant of leave will be as per these categories:
    - D-ECP.1.2. (grant of 33 months entry clearances a partner with 'exceptional circumstances' on the 10-year route)
    - D-LTRP.1.2. (grant of 30 months leave to remain as a partner with EX. 1&2 or 'exceptional circumstances' on the 10-year route)
    - D-ECC.1.1 (child entry clearance duration in line with parent)
    - D-LTRC.1.1 (child LTR in line with parent, settlement via para 298)
    - D-ECPT.1.2. (grant of 33 months entry clearance to a parent with EX.1 or 'exceptional circumstances' on the 10-year route)
    - D-LTRPT.1.2. (grant of 30 months leave to remain as a parent with EX.1 or 'exceptional circumstances' on the 10-year route)

NB: references to leave outside the Rules in these paragraphs were deleted on 10 August 2017. This is of course consistent with the objective of all family life cases being considered within the general framework of Appendix FM, either by meeting the full criteria for parents/partners etc, or where some requirement cannot be met, via the EX1 or GEN.3.2 dispensations.

- GEN.1.11. allows the HO to apply conditions as it considers appropriate in a particular case – that is even if the Rules applying to that particular type of leave do not specify that such a condition should be applied
- GEN.1.11A provides that leave listed in GEN.1.10. will normally be granted subject to a NRPF condition (MIL 1.3.6)
- GEN.1.15. provides that where a person applies for ILR, but the HO considers they qualify only for LTR, , they shoud be given the option to pay the IHS (which they would have had to pay if they had applied for limited leave): if they do so, LTR will follow if they don't, the application will be rejected
- GEN.1.16. Where an application or claim raising Article 8 is considered under Appendix FM and EX.1. applies, the requirements of paragraphs RLTRP.1.1(c) and R-LTRPT.1.1.(c) are not met. In other words, the conditions for the five-year route settlement for parents and partners will not be met in these circumstances and any grant will be on the 10-year route
- GEN.1.17: reminds us that 10-year ILR applications are dealt in Appendix Settlement Family Life
- GEN 2.1 emphasises the need for a passport to be granted leave to enter: the individual Appendix FM routes now make this clear too

6.1.4 Exceptional circumstances

GEN.3.1.(1) to GEN.3.3.(2) now form their own 'exceptional circumstances' regime. In short, these paragraphs operate as a two-stage consideration procedure. In a nutshell:

- 3.1. helps out those who cannot meet the financial requirements via the appropriate specific evidence
- 3.2. assists those who have any other flaw in their case which would otherwise bar access to consideration under Appendix FM (and who cannot fit within EX1)

See MIL 6.2.7 for more on GEN.3.1.

GEN.3.2. applies to:

- applications made or considered under the Appendix FM categories of partner, child or parent entry clearance or leave to remain, as well as (reading GEN.3.2.(3)&(4) together) adult dependant relative entry clearance
- in which any of the Appendix FM requirements are not met or where any relevant general grounds for refusal apply.

Under GEN.3.2.(1), the decision maker 'must' consider, on the basis of the information provided by the applicant, whether there are

> …exceptional circumstances which would render refusal of entry clearance, or leave to enter or remain, a breach of Article 8 of the European Convention on Human Rights, because such refusal **would** result in unjustifiably harsh consequences for the applicant, their partner, a relevant child ***or another family member whose Article 8 rights it is evident from that information would be affected by a decision to refuse the application.*** (GEN.3.2.(2). [own emphasis]

The difference in wording between GEN.3.1&2 ("*could*" vs "*would*") implies more evidence is needed to show the latter standard.

Lal [2019] EWCA Civ 1925 §68 explains that GEN3.2 amounts to a balancing exercise essentially the same as that found ECHR Art 8 itself. A decision will be unjustifiably harsh if it is disproportionate to the private and family life with which it interferes.

6.1.5 Suitability and the applicable grounds for refusal

Those applying under either Part 8 or Appendix FM categories (and Private Life, which is in Part 7) must not fall foul of the the 'suitability' provisions. They apply regardless of the date the application was made, and are located in sections S-EC, S-LTR and S-ILR under the Appendix FM partner category (though they are located within the partner category, they are cross-referenced from the Private Life rules and all the family categories, so they apply across the board).

Appendix FM applications are, since 11pm on 31 December 2020, subject to the following grounds for refusal (see also MIL 2.3.3):

- EC or PTSheld *must* be cancelled on SSHD's personal direction of exclusion (9.3.2) or where presence is not conducive (9.3.3)
- EC or PTS *may* be cancelled for a prison sentence of less than 12 months or non-custodial sentence or out of court disposal (9.4.5)
- EC or PTS *may* be cancelled for false representations etc or failure to disclose information (9.7.3) (for PTS applications only – see more detailed provision below and in the rules)
- EC or PTS held *may* be cancelled, where A fails without reasonable excuse to comply with a reasonable requirement to be interviewed, provide information or biometrics, undergo a medical test or provide a medical report (9.9.2)
- Mandatory and discretionary grounds re: failure to produce a recognised passport (see details for 9.15.1-3 in section 2.3 Part 9 grounds for refusal in Module 2)
- EC or PTS held *may* be cancelled if granting entry would be against the advice of a medical inspector (9.16.2)
- EC or PTS held *may* be cancelled, for a customs breach, irrespective of whether criminal prosecution is pursued (9.19.2)

- EC or PTS held *may* be cancelled if there has been a sufficiently significant change in circumstances since EC or permission was granted (9.20.1)
- EC or PTS held *may* be cancelled if they cease to meet the requirements of the rule under which it was granted. (9.23.1)
- EC or PTSheld by P as a dependent *may* be cancelled if the person on whom is a dependent has, or has had, their permission cancelled. (9.24.1)
- An application for EC/PTE *may* be refused for previous breaches of immigration laws where an application is made outside the re-entry ban period (9.8.2(a)&(c) – refer to the detail below and in the Rules)

Thus, most of the grounds for refusal which are applicable to Appendix FM applications are discretionary (as indicated by the word "may" rather than "must").

Whilst Appendix FM does not impose a mandatory ban on return to the UK for breach of immigration conditions, r9.8.2 (contriving to frustrate the Immigration Rules) does apply to family applications made under Appendix FM. It is often the basis upon which entry clearance applications, particularly those made under the partner category, are refused, where the applicant has what is considered by the HO to be a very poor immigration history.

When advising potential Appendix FM applicants, any potential issues under the applicable grounds for refusal must be explored, as well as any under the Suitability grounds.

As with the general grounds, the suitability provisions can be mandatory or discretionary. Whilst located in the partner route they are cross-referenced from all Appendix FM categories as well as Private Life.

6.1.5.1 'Suitability' at the entry clearance stage

The suitability requirements for entry clearance are mandatory for

- being subject of a deportation order (S-EC.1.3)
- where SSHD personally directs that exclusion is conducive to the public good (S-EC.1.2)
- exclusion is for the public good owing to:
    - convictionand imprisonment for either: at least four years (S-EC.1.4(a)); at least 12 months to less than four years (where sentence ended within 10 years before application)(b); up to 12 months (where sentence ended within five years before application) (S-EC.1.4)(c)
    - other convictions with non-custodial sentences, or for reasons of, including, character or associations making entry to the UK undesirable (S-EC.1.5)
- noncompliance, without reasonable excuse,with a requirement to attend an interview; provide information or physical data; or undergo a medical examintion orprovide a medical report (S-EC.1.6)
- where medical reasons make admission to the UK undesirable (S-EC1.7)
- having left or been removed from the UK within five years pre decision, as a condition of a caution under s22 of the Criminal Justice Act 2003 (S-EC.1.8)
- where SSHD considers the applicant's parent/partner poses a risk to the applicant for reasons of being a registered but non-compliant sex offender (S-EC.1.9): the Guidance discusses this ground at length

The suitability requirements for entry clearance are discretionary for

- provision of false information, statements or documents by anyone in connection with the application, including false information given to anyone else to obtain a supporting document, or failure to disclose important facts in relation to the application, even where the applicant was unaware (S-EC.2.2)
- failure to provide, where requested or required, a maintenance undertaking (S-EC.2.4)
- having received, within a year before application, a non-custodial sentence or other out of court settlement which appears on the criminal record, or SSHD views offending as having caused serious harm, or views the applicant as a persistent offender with a particular disregard for the law (S-EC.2.5)
- failure to pay litigation costs awarded to the HO (S-EC.3.1 – see Immigration Staff Guidance on Litigation Debt) or outstanding overseas NHS charges of at least £500 (S-EC.3.2)

Analysing the entry clearance Suitability Rules we see that:

- There is no mandatory ban for historic dishonesty unless it is thought to fall within S-EC.1.5, i.e. 'conduct ... character ... or other reasons'
- For some categories leave *may* be refused - ie there is no presumption of refusal.
- These rules are sometimes based on a simple factual finding (e.g. an extant deportation order under S-EC.1.3) and sometimes on a judgement which will have to be made following the evaluation of relevant evidence e.g. that there was no 'reasonable excuse' for non-compliance with information gathering efforts (S-EC.1.6)
- Given appeals are now on 'human rights' grounds only, the relevance of the general refusal- and suitability reasons is indirect. They are a factor counting in favour of the public interest against the rights of the individual. The FTT can depart from whatever evaluations were made by the HO if it finds that there are strong private and family life interests with which the interference is disproportionate.
- Where criminality is involved, the Appendix FM guidance refers to Criminality: Article 8 ECHR cases in 'criminality and detention (Immigration Staff Guidance). Art 8 representations in any case involving criminality should always address IR 398-399 in Part 13.

6.1.5.2 'Suitability' at the leave to remain stage

The suitability requirements for applications leave to remain are similar to those on entry clearance, but not identical.The mandatory grounds for refusal on the basis of criminality and past deception are certainly tougher for in-country applicants.

Additionally:

- A person *may* be refused on suitability grounds for the previous use of deception (S-LTR.4.2-4.3.). That provision does not apply in respect of entry clearance, though if a person who is likely to caught by that provision decides to make the application from outside the UK, they may well get caught by r9.8.7.
- A person *will* be refused if their presence is not conducive to the public good because the Secretary of State has excluded them from protection,or would have done so if they had applied for it (S-LTR.1.8.)
- Advisers will need to address any issues in the person's immigration history which might lead to the application being refused for the previous use of deception (allegations of which may not have been raised by the HO when that previous application was refused). A subject access request (see Chapter 2 at 2.1.1) might help anticipate problems which can then be addressed in the application, on the presumption that the HO will spot any inconsistencies in information provided in support of the application and previous applications, potentially going back many years.
- The exact wording of the Rule against any criminal offending is always important. For example section 38(2) of the UK Borders Act 2007 addressing Interpretation sets out that 'the reference to a person who is sentenced to a period of imprisonment of at least 12 months— (a) does not include a reference to a person who receives a suspended sentence (unless a court subsequently orders that the sentence or any part of it (of whatever length) is to take effect).' The r6 definitions of "custodial sentence" and "period of imprisonment" appliy this definition to the Rules generally.
- It is necessary to be realistic in assessing the public interest – ZH (Bangladesh) [2009] EWCA Civ 8 and Aissaoui [2008] EWCA Civ 37 held that illegal working does not necessarily exclude a person from the benefits of the then-extant 14-year 'unlawful residence' rule.

The suitability requirements for leave to remain are divided into 3 kinds: automatic refusals, cases where the misdemeanour brings a presumption of refusal, and pure discretionary cases. The mandatory ones (**'will be refused'** S-LTR.1.1) are

- being the subject of a deportation order (S-LTR.1.2)
- the applicant's presence not being conducive to the public good (disregarding any legal or practical reasons militating against removal – S-LTR.3.1), owing to:

- o having a conviction and prison sentence of between 12 months and under 4 years, unless 10 years have passed from the end of the sentence
- o having a conviction and prison sentence of 4 years or more
- o offending which has caused serious harm or its persistence shows particular disregard for the law (S-LTR.1.5); other convictions or conduct, character, associations or other reasons making their presence undesirable (S-LTR.1.6);
- having been excluded from refugee status or HP; or disentitled to protection from non-refoulement (for reasonable grounds to view them as a danger to security, or due to conviction for a particularly serious crime); or where SSHD would have thus decided had an asylum claim been made in which those issues were addressed (S-LTR.1.8) noncompliance, without reasonable excuse, with a requirement to attend an interview; provide information or physical data; or undergo a medical examination or provide a medical report (S-LTR.1.7)

One set of suitability requirements for leave to remain are discretionary, albeit with a presumption of refusal ('**will normally be refused**' – S-LTR.2.1) for

- providing false information, statements or documents, by anyone, regardless whether to the applicant's knowledge, including false information given to anyone else to obtain a supporting document, or failure to disclose material facts, in relation to the application (S-LTR.2.2)
- failure to provide, where requested or required, a maintenance undertaking (S-LTR.2.4) or comply with a marriage investigation as notified under s50(7)(b) of the 2014 Act (S-LTR.2.5)

Another set of suitability requirements for leave to remain are discretionary without any such presumption ('**may be refused**' – S-LTR.4.1) for

- have made false statements or failed to disclose material facts in any previous HO application for entry clearance, leave to enter or remain or a variation of leave, or in a human rights claim; or for a document to support applications, including for [EEA] residence documentation; regardless of whether the application succeeded (S-LTR.4.2/4.3)
- failure to pay litigation costs awarded to the HO (S-LTR.4.4) or outstanding overseas NHS charges of at least £500 (S-LTR.4.5)

NHS debts

Detainees and refugees are exempt from the NHS charging regime. NHS treatment for conditions caused by torture, female genital mutilation (FGM), domestic violence or sexual violence is also, under Reg 9 (f) of the The National Health Service (Charges to Overseas Visitors) Regulations 2015, exempt, so long as the patient did not come to the UK to seek this treatment. Patients who have been trafficked are also exempt (Reg 16). However, Maternity Action in its November 2019 report points out a real problem. Reg 9(f) requires that the condition for which treatment is sought is caused by the violence . Proving a direct link is very difficult given the complexity of most womens' situations: meaning this exemption is not par'icularly he'pful.

Where an NHS debt has already been notified to a client, they may wish to contact the overseas charging department to negotiate a repayment plan before making a human rights claim, to guard to some extent against a refusal on this ground.Where a migrant was not in fact liable to NHS charges representations should be made to the hospital .

6.1.5.3 'Suitability' at the indefinite leave to remain stage

The suitability requirements for ILR are mandatory ('will be refused' S-ILR.1.1) for:

- being subject of a deportation order (S-ILR.1.2)
- the applicant's presence not being conducive to the public good (disregarding any legal or practical reasons militating against removal – S-ILR.3.1), owing to:
- having a conviction and prison sentence of at least 4 years (S-ILR.1.3); of at least 12 months to less than 4 years (end of sentence less than 15 years ago) (S.1.4);

- a prison sentence of less than 12 months (end of sentence less than 7 years ago) (S-ILR.1.5); conviction for or admission of an offence, with a non-custodial sentence or out of court settlement entered on criminal record (within 2 years of date of decision) (S-ILR.1.6) *NB: where one of these two grounds is or would be the sole ground for refusal of ILR, further leave can be applied for or granted until the relevant barring period has passed. This is true for all Appendix FM categories (see generally the second 'Decision' paragraph under ILR for each category)*
- offending which has caused serious harm or its persistence shows particular disregard for the law (S-ILR.1.7); other convictions or conduct, character, associations or other reasons making their continued presence undesirable (S-ILR.1.8)
- having been excluded from refugee status or HP; or disentitled to protection from non-refoulement (for reasonable grounds to view them as a danger to security, or due to conviction for a particularly serious crime); or where SSDH would have thus decided had an asylum claim been made in which those issues were addressed (S-ILR.1.10)
- noncompliance, without reasonable excuse, with a requirement to attend an interview; provide information or physical data; or undergo a medical examination or provide a medical report (S-ILR.1.9)

The suitability requirements for ILR are discretionary ("will normally be refused" – S-ILR.2.1) for

- provision of false information, statements or documents, by anyone, regardless whether to the applicant's knowledge, including false information given to anyone else to obtain a supporting document, or failure to disclose material facts, in relation to the application (S-ILR.2.2)
- failure to provide, where requested or required, a maintenance undertaking (S-ILR.2.4)

The suitability requirements for indefinite leave to remain are discretionary ("may be refused" – S-ILR.4.1) for

- having made false statements or failed to disclose material facts in any previous application for EC/LTE/LTR; or for a supporting- (or EEA residence) document; whether or not the application succeeded (S-ILR.4.2 & 3)
- failure to pay litigation costs awarded to the HO (S-ILR.4.4) or outstanding overseas NHS charges of at least £500 (S-ILR.4.5)

6.1.6 Making a Family Life Application

Fiancé(e)s/proposed civil partners (unless they are also unmarried partners as defined in GEN.1.2.) and adult dependent relatives can only apply from overseas. Other applicions can be made from overseas or from within the UK. For basic information on entry clearance see this UKVI page.

A valid application will not be required (GEN.1.9) when the human rights claim is made if the claim accompanies an asylum claim, or is made from detention, or if the HO consents for the issue to be raised on appeal (MIL 14.2.7) – and where a human rights claim that passes the fresh claim test is raised in response to removal directions (IR400).

Some points arising from this Rule:

- A human rights claim can be made as further submissions under the fresh claims procedure (IR353) or via a Statement of Additional Grounds (a s120 Notice MIL 14.2.6). Of course supporting evidence is required.
- Whilst representations can be made in response to a s120 notice, the SSHD is under no obligation to decide them until a person's removal is imminent: see Shrestha [2018] EWCA Civ 2810. This allows the HO to essentially sit back and await a fee paid application until the moment of removal, and indeed the *Further representations Guidance* says as much (MIL 4.2.18).
- HO consent is required in appeals where the 'relevant provisions' of NIA 2002 are in force, i.e. after 6 April 2015.

- Where an Appendix FM partner case is brought via this route, it will result only in leave under the 10-year route: see GEN.1.9.(b).
- Refusals will generate a right of appeal, unless it involves a bereaved partner or domestic violence: see Appendix AR at AR3.2(c)((viii) (MIL 14.2.3).

Applications for leave to remain should be made on form FLR(M), for partners who meet all the requirements of the rules, or otherwise on form FLR(FP) for any (inclung 5-year route) parents, those relying on the Exception (i.e. para EX.1.), or those relying on GEN.3.2.

Appendix FM includes the usual condoning of 14 days of overstaying (MIL1.5.4). There is also a policy to permit late applications after this period which due to delays from unexpected or unforeseeable circumstances such as' serious illness, postal or travel delays and an inability to provide essential documents for exceptional and unavoidable circumstances beyond the applicant's control including HO fault or delay, or theft, fire and flood –these excuses must be evidence-backed.

6.1.7 Appendix FM-SE

Appendix FM-SE contains many substantive and complex requirements in addition to those in Appendix FM. These apply largely, but not wholly, in respect of financial requirements. These include:

- The decision-maker will only consider documents that have been submitted with the application unless they have contacted the applicant under the evidential flexibility rule at paragraph D(b) (MIL 2.2.2)

- Where a specified document is missing or in the wrong format or does not contain all the specified information, the decision maker should contact the applicant and give them a few days to provide the correct document unless the application also falls to be refused on other grounds.

- Those relying on income from salaried employment, will be able to use their gross annual salary at its current level from their current employment only where they have been employed with the same employer for a minimum of 6 months, and only where they have been paid at that level for that 6 month period (i.e. the level of gross annual salary will be taken as being the lowest income of that 6 month period). If this provision is not met, the sponsor will need to rely on their actual earnings over the previous 12 months.

- Where the British citizen is living outside the UK with their partner, they will both need to meet the financial requirement in respect of income earned abroad, and have a source of income available to them when they return to the UK (see e.g. paragraph 4).

- Under Appendix FM-SE, an application cannot rely on third party support, other than for maintenance payments, income from a dependent child of age 18 or over who remains part of the household, gifts of cash savings held for at least 6 months, and a maintenance grant for studies (paragraph 1(b)).

- Appendix FM-SE requires a great deal of specified evidence to be provided of the partners and applicants income, in its various forms, and savings. Eg those relying on income from salaried employment, must provide wage-slips, bank statements and a letter from the employer (answering 5 specified questions) for the 6 month or 12 month period. Additionally, the HO reserves the right to request P60s and a contract of employment. For those relying wholly or partly on self-employed or other forms of income (eg from employment/shares in a ltd company para 9, or for self-employed income abroad "a reasonable equivalent" to the equivalent UK-based specified evidence) completely different but even more onerous requirements apply.

- Detailed provisions as to the form that documents must take are laid out in paragraph 1. An application can be refused, for example, if the employer's letter is not on company-headed paper and signed by a senior manager.

CHAPTER 6: Family-Based Applications

- The specified documents evidencing income and savings are provided for in paragraphs 2 to 11. Where the sponsor is relying on certain benefits under E-ECP3.3, only paragraphs 12 and 12A apply.

- On the basis of the specified evidence provided under paragraphs 2 to 11, the income will then be calculated in accordance with paragraphs 13-20A. Paragraph 21 removes benefit and tax credit payments and any other source of income not specified elsewhere from the gross annual income calculation.

- Earnings must be "*lawfully derived*": Appendix FM-SE para 1(d), to be assessed on a case-by-case basis (Fatima [2022] UKUT 155 (IAC)): the mere fact that one's employer shirked appropriate tax arrangements did not undermine those earnings' lawfulness

Even where the applicant meets the financial requirements, many will find it very difficult to provide all the specified evidence. Unless paragraph D(e) applies, their application stands to be refused if they do not.

> (d) In addition to the financial requirements, Appendix FM-SE specifies the evidence required to prove the marriage or civil partnership, that the English Language requirement is met, and for all the key requirements of the adult dependent relative category.

Top Tip

If you are seeking to evidence the available income in a category such an Appendix FM where the requirements are rigorous, don't just leave it to the decision maker or judge to try and fathom out the meaning of a bundle for themselves. Remember they might not see things like you do.

Specify:

(a) what the requirement is and
(b) how it is met

- ☐ Explain the level of income you have to show under Appendix FM
- ☐ Explain the form of income which you are relying on to satisfy that requirement
- ☐ Reference and set out the relevant sub-rule which governs the acceptable evidence under Appendix FM-SE
- ☐ Cross reference the witness statement or Representations to the pages of the evidence bundle that demonstrate that the requirement is satisfied

For example, if relying partially on rent, explain that the evidential requirement is at para 10 of Appendix FM-SE and that you have satisfied it thus:

'Please find enclosed –

- ☐ proof of ownership by way of mortgage statement (page …)
- ☐ 12 months of bank statements with the rent receipts marked (pages … to …)
- ☐ A rental agreement between my client and his lodger ………. dated ……….nd covering the whole of this 12 month period (page …)'

6.1.8 Sponsors with LTR under Appendices EU and ECAA (EEA/Swiss or Turkish sponsors)

Sponsors with leave to remain under

- rEU3of Appendix EU (pre-settled status holders who were resident continuously before the end of transition – GEN.1.3(d)), and
- under Appendix ECAA Extension of stay were added, at the end of the transition period (MIL 11.1) to the potential sponsor list under Appendix FM.

You might think: why proceed under the cost and formalities of Appendix FM when the EUSSch is available? But don't forget that some people face a significant wait before clocking up ILR via moving from EUPSS to EUSS. So an Appendix FM application may a long separation between new partners in the meantime. Some partners might be able to find an alternative immigration route but that depends on the vagaries of immigration opportunities and sponsorship to remain with their UK based partner in the UK.

Be alive to any alternative potential EUSSch applications (MIL 11.7): eg EUPSS-holders may sponsor family members under the EUSSch as a 'Relevant EEA Citizen' So long as the family relationship existed before 11pm on 31 December 2020 – eg if partners were in a durable relationship by then (11.7.5.2), or on an ongoing basis for children of EUPSS-holders so long as they apply within three months of their birth/adoption.

Other points are:

- LTR holders under both appendices can sponsor **Partners**, including fiances, for EC (E-ECP.2.1(d)&(e)) or LTR (E-LTRP.1.2(d)&(e)) and consequently those applicant's children under the category "**Family life as a child of a person with limited leave as a partner or parent**" (i.e. as the child of the applicant partner of the sponsor).
- The bereaved partner (**BPILR**) and domestic abuse (**DVILR**) settlement categories are only open to pre-settled status holders under Appendix EU, not LTR holders under Appendix ECAA.
- EUPSS holders who are children can, additionally, technically "sponsor" their parent in the "**Parent of a Child in the UK**" category for EC (E-ECP|T.2.2(c)) and LTR (E-LTRPT.2.2.(c)).
- However, settlement for such a parent is excluded until the child becomes settled (E-ILRPT(1A)&(1B)). This should not be a problem as the child will have already begun their 5-year route to settlement under Appendix EU when their parent applies to commence their own (at least) 5-year route to settlement under Appendix FM.
- Further to the parent category, a pre-settled status holder can also be the "other" parent where the applicant is a single parent with access rights (E-ECPT.2.3(b)(i) & E-LTRPT.2.3(a)&(b)).
- It is hard to see the Exception at EX1(a)) (MIL 6.2.5 below) helping children cases, as a child with EUPSS would not normally have lived in the UK for 7 years (EUPSS last for not more than 5 years)
- However, under EX1(b), a partner with whom the applicant has a relationship, the continuation of which abroad would face insurmountable obstacles, *can* be a LTR holder under either Appendix EU or Appendix ECAA.
- **Adult dependent relatives** can be sponsored by EUPSS holders for entry clearance (E-ECDR.2.3(b)(iv)). ILR on the ADR route requires that a pre-settled status holding sponsor, for the applicant to be eligible for ILR, to have at least made a valid application for ILR by the time their adult dependent relative applies to settled (E-ILRDR.1.3.(b)), which reflects the position of ADRs of refugees or HP holders of LTR, who are covered by the same subparagraph.
- Given the remaining EUSSCH option for many family members, this sponsorship category is likely to become more useful as the post-Brexit period advances. Of course by 30 June 2026 most of the holders should have attained EUSS, subject to mishaps and late applications.

6.2 Family life as a partner under Appendix FM

This category provides for entry clearance, leave to remain and ILR for partners, defined at GEN.1.2. as:

(i) the applicant's spouse;
(ii) the applicant's civil partner;
(iii) the applicant's fiancé(e) or proposed civil partner; or
(iv) a person who has been living together with the applicant in a relationship akin to a marriage or civil partnership for at least two years prior to the date of application, unless a different meaning of partner applies elsewhere in this Appendix.

Unmarried partners must show two solid years of cohabitation.

In addition to the suitability criteria, there are relationship, financial, English language and immigration status requirements. Where 'Section EX: Exception' applies, the applicant will not need to meet the financial, English language or most of the immigration status requirements. This difference is what allows the immigration community to talk of the 'five year' and 'ten year' routes to settlement – because someone who qualifies only under the more limited requirements that operate when the EX exception is established will be granted leave, but under the longer settlement route. Since 10 August 2017, there have been grants on the 10-year route where even EX1 is not met but applications succeed after consideration under the 'exceptional circumstances' two-stage procedure in GEN.3.1. and GEN.3.2. (see above), which are also on the 10-year route to settlement. Cases succeeding under the GEN3 exceptions (MIL 6.1.4) are also on the 10-year route.

It is important to realise that many relationships between partners may fall outside Appendix FM altogether. These cases will be considered under GEN.3.2, and, on appeal, with the section 117B NIAA 2002 in mind. For example couples:

- where the migrant has been excluded for suitability reasons
- who have not cohabited for two years (in accordance with the GEN definition of partner)
- where the sponsor is not a British citizen, settled or holder of refugee/HP leave, or a holder of LTR under EU3 of Appendix EU, or under Appendix ECAA Extension of Stay (E-LTRP.1.2)
- where either is aged under 18 at the date of application
- where the applicant is present as a visitor or with other leave, save for that of fiancé or due to extant family proceedings, granted for six months or less (E-LTRP.2.1)

The possibility of cases falling through the gaps in Ex.1 is shown by Sabir [2014] UKUT 63 (IAC). EX.1 is not 'free standing', making it clear that one must pass Suitability under Appendix FM to benefit from the exception.

As we saw above, GEN.3.2 now provides for a residual consideration of cases under Appendix FM even though one of the key criteria under Appendix FM is not met, or the case falls foul of the General Refusal reasons. So the historic strictness of the eligibility hurdle has been removed for post-August 2017 cases. GEN.3.2 apparently authorises consideration of an application where those involved do not meet the "partner" requirements, for example for a couple who lack 2 years' cohabitation. Of course, in such a case, the relevant wider 'exceptional circumstances' necessary meet the GEN.3.2 threshold would have to be met. GEN.3.2 applies to all applications considered under Appendix FM (except bereaved partner and domestic violence provisions – see GEN.3.2(4)).

Family Policy Family life (as a partner or parent) and exceptional circumstances, sets out its definitions of "exceptional circumstances, "exceptional", "unjustifiably harsh consequences" and a "relevant child" and identifies matters relevant to the best interests of the child (see also MIL 5.3.2).

On appeal, however, a judge will be more concerned with Article 8 ECHR than the exact letter of the HO policy, albeit having regard to the fact that the Rules aim to be a comprehensive code and should be departed from only where there is a strong Article 8 case; and having regard to the statutory criteria in s117B of NIA 2002. The impossibility of applying bright-line rules to human rights cases was discussed in MM (Lebanon) [2017] UKSC 10 (MIL 5.4). Where family life is established on a precarious basis, compelling circumstances are required to justify departing from the Rules: Agyarko [2017] UKSC 11.

What exactly constitutes a 'precarious basis' for establishing one's UK ties? The answer is any residence short of ILR: Rhuppiah [2018] UKSC 58. However, the Supreme Court accepted that the 'generalised normative guidance to give private life *little weight* may be overridden in an exceptional case by particularly strong features of the private life in question. See GM (Sri Lanka) [2019] EWCA Civ 1630 where the applicant was a failed asylum seeker, whilst her husband (with whom she had two children) held DLR and was on a pathway (alongside the children) to settled status. Showing the potential loss of an entitlement of this nature would point to a decision being disproportionate - even though the situation of all the individuals involved might be said to be "precarious" (see generally MIL 5.4).

As you can see, there are a series of questions arising in an Appendix FM case. We summarised these at the start of this Module: but now we set them out in a bit more detail. Firstly, taking the example of the in-country partner:

(a) Does the case succeed under the Rules i.e. have the Suitability, Eligibility, Immigration and Financial Requirements been satisfied, in which case the appeal succeeds under the IRs without regard to the Exception at Ex.1?
(b) If not (a) for the sole reason a partner applicant fails to meet the Financial requirement, can 'Exceptional Circumstances' para GEN.3.1. be applied for the applicant to benefit from the wider list of financial sources and evidence in para 21A Appendix FM-SE?
(c) If para 21A of App FM-SE cannot be satisfied, or if the Immigration or English requirements are not met, is the Exception within the Rules at Ex.1&2 in play?
(d) If not (a), (b) or (c), can 'Exceptional Circumstances' para GEN3.2. be applied? Does ECHR Art 8 render the immigration decision disproportionate, having regard to compelling/exceptional circumstances causing unjustifiably harsh consequences?

Remember, Article 8 representations should be made with reference to the Appendix FM framework: LOTR is for non-ECHR issues (MIL 4.2.1).

The pandemic's impact may be relevant: the Guidance <u>Family life (as a partner or parent), private life and exceptional circumstances</u> states that "*A commitment has been made to ensure family and private life applicants are not unduly affected by reasons beyond their control due to COVID-19. The pandemic may have caused disruption to travel plans, causing breaks in continuous lawful immigration status/residence requirements.*"

The Guidance also explains some features of the route:

- Irish citizens are treated as settled
- Crown servants (ie UK government and Scottish, Welsh and Northern Irish equivalents, and permanent British Council members, can commence their probationary period (apparently a reference to the pre-ILR LTR period): the partner must return to the UK to apply for further LTR during their leave's currency
- It is preferable to grant leave under Appendix FM than LOTR or under private life where the application turns on family life

6.2.1 Relationship

The applicant's partner must be:

(a) a British citizen in the UK, subject to paragraph GEN.1.3.(c); or
(b) present and settled in the UK, subject to paragraph GEN.1.3.(b); or
(c) in the UK with refugee leave or with humanitarian protection; or
(d) in the UK with LTR under rEU3 Appendix EU; or
(e) in the UK with LTR under Appendix ECAA Extension of Stay.

The reference to GEN.1.3 (MIL 6.1.3) concerns British citizen and settled partners living outside the UK and returning to the UK with the applicant. The partners will be treated as being in the UK for the purposes of the application.

Additionally:

- The applicant and partner must be aged 18 or over at the date of application.
- The applicant and their partner must not be within the prohibited degree of relationship.
- The applicant and their partner must have met in person.
- The relationship between the applicant and their partner must be genuine and subsisting.
- If the applicant and partner are married or in a civil partnership it must be a valid marriage or civil partnership, as specified.

- If the applicant is a fiancé(e) or proposed civil partner they must be seeking entry to the UK to falicitate their marriage or civil partnership.
- Any previous relationship of the applicant or their partner must have broken down permanently (unless polygamous, via the reference to r278(i)).
- The applicant and partner must intend to live together permanently in the UK.

For ILR applications Appendix Relationship with a Partner governs the relationship criteria.

Categories of partner

'Pre-flight' partners of refugees and those with humanitarian protection continue to be dealt with under the family reunion provisions in Part 11 of the IRs (MIL 9.7.3). Sub-paragraph (c) above relates only to whose relationship (as defined in GEN.1.2.) was formed after the partner left their country of nationality.

Fiancé(e)s and proposed civil partners must apply for entry clearance (E-ECP.2.8., E-LTRP.1.12). They must be seeking entry to the UK to enable their marriage or civil partnership to take place within six months of arriving here. They cannot apply for leave in this Appendix FM category from within the UK.

Present and settled

The meaning of 'present and settled' and 'settled in the United Kingdom' is set out in Rule 6 of the IRs and in essence means possession of ILR or the right of abode combined with physical presence in the UK. An EEA national or non-EEA family member with a permanent right of residence in the UK was considered as present and settled until the grace period ended on 30 June 2021.

Validity of marriage

The parties to a marriage or civil partnership will need to show that they are legally married according to the laws of the country in which the marriage took place (although see below for polygamous marriages), or that they have contracted a legal civil partnership in a country in which such partnerships are recognised. These countries are listed at Schedule 20 of the Civil Partnership Act 2004. At the time of writing this numbered some 75 jurisdictions (see: the IDIs at Chapter 8, section 2, Annex H for the list as it was in January 2013).

The rule that marriages will be recognised if legally contracted in the country in which they take place is a long standing rule of international private law: (Berthiaume v. Dastous [1930] accept 79 and Rule 67 of *Dicey* 14th edition). This means that even quite unusual marriage arrangements, such as marriages by proxy where one or both participants are in the UK whilst the marriage is formalised in their country of origin, must be recognised (CB Brazil [2008] UKAIT 00080). For a while the UT thought that proxy marriages in EU law had to be recognised in the EEA Sponsor's (EEA) country of nationality: this misapprehension was corrected in Awuku [2017] EWCA Civ 178.

Where there are complications in evidencing the legality of the marriage, an option would be for the person to come to the UK as a fiancé(e), and then register the marriage once here.

The requirement that the marriage is legal may mean that relevant formal divorce papers or other evidence of a divorce that was effective in the country in which it took place will need to be produced. The complex issue of domicile may also arise: see The *Legitimacy and Domicile Guidance*.

Applicants must also demonstrate an intention to live permanently with the sponsor (defined as below, IR 6) and that the marriage or civil partnership is genuine and subsisting.

'Intention to live permanently with the other' or 'intend to live together permanently' means an intention to live together, evidenced by a clear commitment from both parties that they will live together permanently in the UK immediately following the outcome of the application in question or as soon as circumstances permit thereafter. However, where an application is made under Appendix Armed Forces the words 'in the UK' in this definition do not apply.

'Subsisting' and having met

The words 'subsisting marriage' have no precise definition. GA Ghana [2006] UKAIT 00046 held that this required a more than formal legal validity. An examination of the present state of the relationship rather than looking backwards or looking forwards in time, and that the past conduct of the parties can provide an indication of future intention.

If an ECO believes that the marriage is a sham marriage entered into for the sole purpose of gaining entry to the UK and that the spouses actually have no intention of living permanently with each other, then these two sub-rules will form the basis of refusal. However, they are not equivalent to the old 'primary purpose' rule, which used to require applicants to demonstrate that the application was not being made for the primary purpose of gaining entry to the UK, irrespective of whether the couple actually did intend to live together afterwards.

The guidance (Partners, divorce and dissolution) sets out potentially relevant factors when assessing the reality of a marriage, such as concrete evidence of the relationship's duration, any cohabitation, shared financial responsibilities, having visited each other's families, and practical arrangements for life together here.

Evidence of pre-marital co-habitation and joint living arrangements may corroborate a genuine relationship; so too their absence. In some cultures it is traditional for the household accounts, bills etc. to be in the name of the male head of the household (who could be the male partner or their father or grandfather) (the Guidance *Relationship with a Partner* is a good guide to HO thinking: MIL 6.2.10.1).

Detailed witness statements addressing all these factors are essential.

The couple must have met at the time of the application. This allows for arranged marriages, where the couple do not meet until the day of the wedding, but it may exclude some marriages that would be legal in the country in which they take place, such as marriages in absentia, by telephone or by proxy, unless the couple have met by the time of the application.

There are no specified evidence requirements in the partner rules for proving that the relationship requirements are met. So it is a matter of collecting the best available evidence that the relationship is legally valid, genuine and subsisting. Interviews and home visits by the UKVI are not unusual, and nor indeed are Immigration Officials turning up as unwanted guests at marriages in the UK and whisking one party into detention.

Goudey [2012] UKUT 00041 (IAC) and Naz [2012] UKUT 00040(IAC) help in proving a relationship is genuine and subsisting. As was said in Goudey:

> Evidence of telephone cards is capable of being corroborative of the contention of the parties that they communicate by telephone, even if such data cannot confirm the particular number the sponsor was calling and the country in question. It is not a requirement that the parties also write or text each other

Applicants and their partners should submit:

- evidence of registered relationships (e.g. birth, divorce and marriage certificates), with translations where necessary
- statements from both parties giving some history to the relationship and intentions for the future
- evidence of cohabitation
- photos and other evidence of any ceremony, and time spent together (but not DVDs or video cassettes)
- phone records – with itemised billing where possible, but phone cards if that is all there is (see *Goudey* above)
- other evidence of contact (e.g. emails, social media, cards, plane tickets)

Whilst there is no longer a requirement to seek HO to marry, registrars may notify the HO of suspicious marriages. The IA 2014 provides that notice of a marriage of 28 days must be given; registrars must notify the HO of all marriages involving a non-EEA party who is not settled in the UK. The immigration authorities may then delay marriages for up to 70 days whilst they investigate the immigration status of the parties, the genuineness of the marriage, and take enforcement action where appropriate. Read more on these provisions in Immigration Bill Factsheet 12.

Top Tip

In any case where the genuineness of the relationship is disputed, always check the documents provided to show cohabitation carefully:

☐ Has any permission that is required for co-occupancy been obtained?
☐ Are there any potential inconsistencies between the contents of the documents and the relationship history?

Issues such as these need to be explained carefully by detailed witness statements

---

Polygamy, prohibited relationships and age

Under the IRs the spouse in a polygamous marriage is not permitted to enter or remain in the UK on the basis of the marriage if there is another person living who is the spouse of the sponsor and who at any time since their marriage has been in the UK or has been granted a certificate of entitlement (IR278). So polygamous marriages may be recognised here, but only one spouse from such a marriage may enter the UK.

'Prohibited degree of relationship' is defined (IR6) as having the same meaning as in the Marriage Act 1949, the Marriage (Prohibited Degrees of Relationship) Act 1986 and the Civil Partnership Act 2004 and the list is set out in the Family Policy: Partners, divorce and dissolution Guidance.

The minimum age for both the person seeking a visa and the UK-based sponsor is now 18 (at the date of application). An earlier rule change raising the age to 21 was found to be unlawful by the Supreme Court in Quila [2011] UKSC 45.The justification put forward by the HO at the time of the change was that it would help to prevent forced marriages. The Supreme Court found that the rule change was not a lawful way of deterring or preventing forced marriages. The actual effect, at least in some cases, was to force the young British spouse to live abroad until aged 21, away from home, friends and family.

6.2.2 English language requirement

See MIL 2.2.6 for the general approach to proving English language proficiency. Appendix FM follows that general scheme though has its own precise criteria, E-ECP.4 and E-LTRP.4, with specified evidence being set out at Appendix FM-SE (paras 27 to 32).

There is Guidance: English language requirement: family members under Part 8, Appendix family member and Appendix Armed Forces.

The English language requirement (A1 for entry clearance, A2 for extensions) can be met in five ways:

- by being a national of a specified majority English speaking country listed in GEN.1.6 via the proof of nationality at FM-SE paras 28-30.
- by having passed an approved English language speaking and listening test at level A1 (or A2) If a test was passed in a previous application at the required level, this will satisfy the requirement. (see Appendix FM-SE 27(ii) – then test certificates can be accepted past their validity date, and where test providers or test centres are no longer approved (32D(d) of App FM-SE)

- have an academic qualification which is either a Bachelor's or Master's degree or PhD awarded by an educational establishment in the UK; or a qualification taught in English confirmed by Ecctis as degree-level plus: FM-SE para 31 gives the details to be provided
- on extension applications, by having previously met the criteria E-LTRP4.1
- by exemption (E-ECP.4.2)

Exempt from the requirement are:

- those aged 65 or over at the date of application
- those who have a physical or mental condition that would prevent them from meeting the requirement
- where there are exceptional compassionate circumstances that would prevent the applicant from meeting the requirement.

Where an applicant is unable to take the test, the Guidance states that they must demonstrate they are unable to learn English before coming to the UK or it is not practicable or reasonable for them to travel to another country to take an approved English language test and via independent and verifiable evidence. They must provide evidence of previous efforts to access learning materials or to travel overseas and the obstacles to doing so.

This might be accepted where the applicant:

- is a long-term resident of a country in international or internal armed conflict, or where there is or has been a humanitarian disaster, including in light of the infrastructure affected.
- has been hospitalised for several months immediately prior to the date of application.
- is the full-time carer of a disabled child also applying to come to the UK.
- is a long-term resident of a country with no approved A1 test provision and it is not practicable or reasonable for the applicant to travel to another country to take such a test.
- is a long-term resident of a country in which the applicant faces very severe practical or logistical difficulties, which cannot reasonably be overcome, in accessing the learning resources required to acquire English language speaking and listening skills at CEFR level A1.
- A test centre was closed or inaccessible due to Covid-19

Lack of or limited literacy or education will not in itself be accepted as exceptional circumstances.

Ali and Bibi [2015] UKSC 68 finds pre-entry English language testing for spouses lawful. However:

> [whilst] there is no basis for striking down rule E-ECP 4.1 in Appendix FM to the IRs, the guidance, because of the narrowness of the exceptional circumstances for which it allows, may result in a significant number of cases in which people's article 8 rights will be breached. To avoid that unfortunate outcome, the Government may need to take further steps toward providing opportunities for spouses and partners to meet the requirement or may need to amend its guidance.

Now GEN.3.2. provides an opportunity to circumvent any problem, including English language difficulties, posed by the Appendix FM requirements, but the threshold to be reached before a decision maker 'must' grant leave despite failure to meet elements of the rules is high.

Paragraphs 32A-32D of Appendix FM-SE deal with the aftermath of the English language fraud debacle (MIL 2.3.5.6). Applicants previously relying on suspect certificates can be required to provide new ones.

- Where the decision maker has reasonable cause to doubt that an English language certificate was genuinely obtained, or has received information that the test provider withdrew the test result, they *may* discount the test certificate and require a new one to be provided.
- Where the test result is invalid for other reasons yet was previously accepted as part of the evidence supporting a successful application for leave, then it *will* be accepted as valid.

The Guidance English language requirement family members explains that applicants should be exempted from the requirement where a test centre was closed or inaccessible due to COVID-19 at the application date. Where there are delays in being able to take the test by the application date, applications may be placed on hold and the test accepted once received.

6.2.3 Financial requirement under the Rules

Applicants under Appendix FM must meet the specified income threshold (in addition to having adequate accommodation) unless the partner is in receipt of specified disability-related benefits.

The Guidance Family Migration: Appendix FM Section 1.7A – Adequate maintenance and accommodation and Family Migration: Appendix FM Section 1.7 Appendix Armed Forces Financial requirement provides for COVID concessions:

- A temporary loss of employment income between 1 March 2020 and 31 October 2021 due to COVID-19 is disregarded so long as [the financial requirement] was met in the preceding 6 months
- Those who are furloughed are deemed to receive 100% of their income
- A temporary loss of annual self-employment income due to COVID-19 between 1 March 2020 and 31 October 2021 will generally be disregarded
- Evidential flexibility should be applied where evidence cannot be obtained for reasons related to COVID-19

This does not cater for every eventuality; Tfhe concession cutoff date of 31 October 2021 could have harsh consequences for many families (see generally MIL 4.2.19).

For applications for entry clearance under the Partner category:

E-ECP.3.1. The applicant must provide specified evidence, from the sources listed in paragraph E-ECP.3.2., of-

(a) a specified gross annual income of at least-
(i) £18,600;
(ii) an additional £3,800 for the first child; and
(iii) an additional £2,400 for each additional child; alone or in combination with

(b) specified savings of-

(i) £16,000; and
(ii) additional savings of an amount equivalent to 2.5 times the amount which is the difference between the gross annual income from the sources listed in paragraph E-ECP.3.2.(a)-(d) and the total amount required under paragraph E-ECP.3.1.(a); or

(c) the requirements in paragraph E-ECP.3.3.being met.

In this paragraph 'child' means a dependent child of the applicant or the applicant's partner who is-

(a) under the age of 18 years, or who was under the age of 18 years when they were first granted entry under this route;
(b) applying for entry clearance as a dependant of the applicant, or the applicant's partner, or is in the UK with leave as their dependant;
(c) not a British Citizen, settled in the UK or in the UK with valid limited leave to enter or remain granted under paragraph EU3 or EU3A of Appendix EU to these Rules; and
(d) not an EEA national with a right to be admitted under the Immigration (EEA) Regulations 2016.

CHAPTER 6: Family-Based Applications

E-ECP.3.2. When determining whether the financial requirement in paragraph EECP.3.1. is met only the following sources will be taken into account-

(a) income of the partner from specified employment or self-employment, which, in respect of a partner returning to the UK with the applicant, can include specified employment or self-employment overseas and in the UK;
(b) specified pension income of the applicant and partner;
(c) any specified maternity allowance or bereavement benefit received by the partner in the UK or any specified payment relating to service in HM Forces received by the applicant or partner;
(d) other specified income of the applicant and partner; and
(e) specified savings of the applicant and partner.

E-ECP.3.3. The requirements to be met under this paragraph are-

(a) the applicant's partner must be receiving one or more of the following –

(i) disability living allowance;
(ii) severe disablement allowance;
(iii) industrial injury disablement benefit;
(iv) attendance allowance;
(v) carer's allowance;
(vi) personal independence payment;
(vii) Armed Forces Independence Payment or Guaranteed Income Payment under the Armed Forces Compensation Scheme; or
(viii) Constant Attendance Allowance, Mobility Supplement or War Disablement Pension under the War Pensions Scheme; or
(ix) Police Injury Pension; and

(b) the applicant must provide evidence that their partner is able to maintain and accommodate themselves, the applicant and any dependants adequately in the UK without recourse to public funds.

E-ECP.3.4. The applicant must provide evidence that there will be adequate accommodation, without recourse to public funds, for the family, including other family members who are not included in the application but who live in the same household, which the family own or occupy exclusively: accommodation will not be regarded as adequate if-

(e) it is, or will be, overcrowded; or
(f) it contravenes public health regulations.

References to 'specified' refer to the mandatory provisions of Appendix FM-SE.

Detailed guidance Appendix FM 1.7: financial requirement. Where the partner is in receipt of one of the benefits listed in E-ECP.3.3/E-LTRP. 3.3, the guidance as to maintenance and accommodation is in Appendix FM 1.7a: maintenance.

The entry clearance guidance MAA summarises the approach taken to accommodation.

Points to note:

- a specified gross annual income of £18,600 is required (unless relying on E-ECP.3.3.)
- plus an additional amount for each child

- The definition of 'child' excludes children who are settled, British citizens, or who have a right to admission under the EEA Regulations, but includes those already in the UK with limited

leave. Note that where a British partner has children living abroad, these children will often be British citizens, and there will therefore be no increased income threshold in such cases.
- For entry clearance applications, it is only the sponsor's income from employment which is relevant (i.e. the applicant's current income or income from future employment is ignored). Where the application is made in-country, the applicant's income from lawful employment and self-employment can count towards meeting the income threshold
- Where the income of the partner, or where relevant the partner and applicant, is below the minimum threshold, savings may make up the shortfall. A complicated formula must be applied to savings. The first £16,000 of savings are disregarded. The balance must then be divided by 2.5, and the resulting figure can then be treated as incomeYou may find it easier to:

    - take the shortfall (i.e. the minimum income level that applies less the actual income)
    - multiply that figure by 2.5 and
    - add £16,000

    to give the level of savings that will make up the shortfall.

- Where the sponsor is on benefits as listed in E-ECP.3.3, the income threshold does not apply. The financial requirement will be met by 'adequate maintenance and accommodation' as defined in paragraph 6 of the rules (MIL 2.2.3).
- The minimum income threshold survived challenge in the relevant considerations summarised in MM (Lebanon) [2017] UKSC 10.
- GEN.3.1s allow alternative or additional sources of income to be taken into account. The decision maker 'must' take these into account, but only where *there are exceptional circumstances which could render refusal of entry clearance or leave to remain a breach of Article 8 of the European Convention on Human Rights, because such refusal could result in unjustifiably harsh consequences for the applicant, their partner or a relevant child* (GEN.3.1.(1)(b) (MIL 6.2.7)

As noted, the Rules concentrate on maintenance ability at the application date. In Begum [2021] UKUT 115 (IAC) the UT considers the wording of the maintenance requirements, drawing attention to the express focus to meeting the Rules at the application date and the period leading up to it. The only interpretation that this drafting permitted was that post-decision changes in a family's ability to meet the Appendix FM financial requirements pending an appeal hearing were not relevant. Accordingly an appeal on human rights grounds would normally succeed so long as the rules were met historically. This was subject only to there being public policy reasons nevertheless making the interference with ECHR Art 8 rights proportionate, as where the evidence showed that the relationship was in truth a forced marriage. HJT would suggest that when considering under the residual GEN3.2 *'unjustifiably harsh'* threshold, the date of hearing is relevant.

6.2.4 Immigration status

The immigration status requirements for applying for leave to remain (i.e. from within the UK) as a partner are:

E-LTRP.2.1. The applicant must not be in the UK-

- as a visitor;
- with valid leave granted for a period of 6 months or less, unless that leave is as a fiancé(e) or proposed civil partner, or was granted pending the outcome of family court or divorce proceedings

E-LTRP.2.2. The applicant must not be in the UK-

- on immigration bail, unless
    o SSHD is satisfied they arrived over 6 months prior to application and paragraph EX.1. applies; and
    o Paragraph EX.1 applies; or

CHAPTER 6: Family-Based Applications

- in breach of immigration laws (except that, where paragraph 39E of these Rules applies, any current period of overstaying will be disregarded), unless paragraph EX.1. applies

Under E-LTRP.2.2.(b), for those applying before 24 November 2016, there was the more generous disregard of 28 days. This has now been replaced by r39E, limiting overstaying to 14 days, only where it is beyond the control of the applicant or their adviser.

Oddly, an illegal entrant or overstayer can rely on EX.1. to apply under the rules, but a visitor or person granted leave for six months or less cannot. Applicants in this position must use their judgement when deciding whether to apply outside the Rules while they have that leave, or overstay before doing so. As always GEN.3.2 can come to one's aid: but that requires the refusal being 'unjustifiably harsh' so one would need a really good excuse for evading the implication that visitors should be returning abroad to seek entry clearance.

On 22 July 2020, the guidance Family life (as a partner or parent), private life and exceptional circumstances was first updated to incorporate COVID concessions applicable generally to family-and private life applications. These are collated on the last pages of the policy and currently include:

- Discretion to disregard failures to meet the immigration status- or continuous residence requirements, including where an applicant is in the UK as a visitor or with leave of only up to 6 months; or where an applicant is in or outside the UK with no leave, where they show that they were unable to travel or apply due to coronavirus between March 2020 and 31 August 2020.
- Visitors in the UK whose leave expired past 31 August 2020 could still apply until 30 June 2021 in-country for categories normally requiring entry clearance. They had to prove why their application was so urgent that they should be permitted to apply from within the UK rather than wait until they were able to apply from abroad.
- Fiancees and proposed civil partners whose wedding or civil ceremony was delayed due to the pandemic can apply for extra time under the "exceptional assurance" scheme (MIL 4.2.19)
- Those whose leave expired while abroad and who were unable to return or apply will have up to 6 months' break in continuous residence disregarded
- A second period of leave to enter will exceptionally count towards ILR.

Please refer to section 4.2.19 for our overview of Covid-related policies.

Example

Emanuel is from Malaysia; her partner David is a British citizen. They formed a relationship in recent years whilst he worked in Malaysia. He has now returned to the UK for a lengthy period of contract work. They are planning to make an application for her to join him on a spouse visa in the future. In the meantime he will visit her several times a year, whilst she will make one lengthy visit a year here. She enters the United Kingdom as a visitor together with their young daughter, Hannah. Hannah is taken ill whilst here and they wish to make a partner application under Appendix FM.

Emanuel's leave as a visitor rules out 'switching' for both the five- and 10-year settlement routes. This is an example of a case where 'an application for ... leave to ... remain ... does not otherwise meet the requirements of this Appendix or Part 9 of the Rules' and so we have to look at GEN.3.2. Emmanuel and David would have to argue that the GEN.3.2. is satisfied but, even if they succeed in doing so, they would still need to deal with the possible suspicion that the visit application had been a vehicle for making an otherwise impermissible in-country application all along. The health of a British citizen child will clearly be a very important factor. This would be treated as a 'primary consideration' (GEN.3.3.(1)) if they succeed in having the application considered under para GEN.3.2. Depending on all the circumstances it may still be preferable to return abroad and apply for entry clearance, to avoid the delay, cost and stress of possible refusal and subsequent lengthy appeal proceedings, so long as their lifestyle and patterns of earnings are such that their income/savings can meet the financial evidence requirements.

6.2.5 Section EX: Exceptions to certain eligibility requirements for leave to remain as a partner or parent:

This is the bespoke exception for limited applicants under Appendix FM: only partners and parents. It does not protect those who do not satisfy the core requirements as to relationship and some of the immigration status requirements.

> EX.1. This paragraph applies if:
>
> (a) - (i) the applicant has a genuine and subsisting parental relationship with a child who-
>
> - is under the age of 18 years, or was under the age of 18 years when the applicant was first granted leave on the basis that this paragraph applied;
> - is in the UK;
> - is a British Citizen or has lived in the UK continuously for at least the 7 years immediately preceding the date of application; and
>
> (ii) it would not be reasonable to expect the child to leave the UK; or
>
> (b) the applicant has a genuine and subsisting relationship with a partner who is in the UK and is a British Citizen, settled in the UK or in the UK with refugee leave or humanitarian protection, and there are insurmountable obstacles to family life with that partner continuing outside the UK.
>
> EX.2. For the purposes of paragraph EX.1.
>
> (b) 'insurmountable obstacles' means the very significant difficulties which would be faced by the applicant or their partner in continuing their family life together outside the UK and which could not be overcome or would entail very serious hardship for the applicant or their partner.

Note:

> Where paragraph EX1 applies, an application for leave to remain under the Appendix FM 'partner' or 'parent' categories will only have to meet the 'suitability', 'relationship' and part of the 'immigration status' requirements. (see for example paragraph R-LTRP.1.(d)). The financial and English language requirements will not apply.
> EX1 does not apply to entry clearance applications. An application for entry clearance that does not meet all the requirements of the Rules will be considered under 'Exceptional Circumstances' as per GEN.3.1. & GEN.3.2: oe without;; refusal result in unjustifiably harsh consequences.
> - Migrants can rely on EX1 where they are in the UK irregularly as illegal entrants or overstayers, or cannot meet the financial or English language requirements and, for failing to meet any other requirement, where the thresholds are met, they may rely on 'Exceptional Circumstances'.
>
> - Pre-Appendix FM, these cases would have been considered outside the rules and a successful applicant would have been granted three years discretionary leave on a six-year route to settlement. Now they are all granted 30 months within the rules but on a 10-year ILR route.

6.2.5.1 Reasonable to expect the child to leave the UK

See MIL 5.3.2 for the key principles. Albeit the subject matter of the application will be a partner's right to stay rather than the child's. The reasonableness question posed by Ex.1 is similar to that which judges are required to consider under s117B(6) of the 2002 Act which states re parents that:

> (6) In the case of a person who is not liable to deportation, the public interest does not require the person's removal where—

(a) the person has a genuine and subsisting parental relationship with a qualifying child, and
(b) it would not be reasonable to expect the child to leave the United Kingdom.

A qualifying child under the Act is defined in exactly the same way as under EX.1. If it can be established that the child cannot reasonably be expected to leave the UK, as per Appendix Private Life PL3.1 (MIL 5.3.2), a parent who falls into the partner definition, or who can satisfy the requirements of the parent route will succeed in their application.

6.2.5.2 Insurmountable obstacles

The 'insurmountable obstacles' test that appears in the rules at EX.1 originates in some very early domestic case law on Article 8 (see e.g. Mahmood [2000] EWCA Civ 315. It will be appreciated that it chiefly applies to partners without children: because cases where there are seven-year resident or British citizen children within the family unit refocus the enquiry on whether their departure is *reasonable* (and children with less solid UK connection must still have their best interests considered).

The test has had its ups and downs. Mahmood adopted it for domestic purposes because it was used as a benchmark by the ECtHR when interpreting the Convention. But by the late 2000s, the Court of Appeal viewed it as only one of a series of criteria: and Huang in the House of Lords heralded a significant period where there was essentially a bare balancing exercise. The public interest was not given greater weight than private and family life rights.

So the insertion of the 'insurmountable obstacles' into the rules some years after its judicial rejection was driven by the SSHDe's objective of narrowing the circumstances in which Article 8 could be used to thwart removal. It is now accepted, given the change in government policy, as generally relevant where family life has been established where there was no expectation of remaining in the UK. See eg Nagre [2013] EWHC 7200 (Admin):

> ... in a precarious family life case, where it is only in 'exceptional' or 'the most exceptional' circumstances that removal of the non-national family member will constitute a violation of Article 8, the absence of insurmountable obstacles to relocation of other family members to that member's own country of origin to continue their family life there is likely to indicate that the removal will be proportionate for the purposes of Article 8.

As stated by the Supreme Court in Agyarko [2017] UKSC 11:

> It appears that the European court intends the words 'insurmountable obstacles' to be understood in a practical and realistic sense, rather than as referring solely to obstacles which make it literally impossible for the family to live together in the country of origin of the non-national concerned.

Lal [2019] EWCA Civ 1925 shows that where the family life in question had been established during a period of precarious residence, it nevertheless should be afforded appropriate weight, depending on its strength. This required a nuanced consideration. In assessing precariousness it was important to have regard to the strength of residence rights: a person would be in a stronger position if they had been on a path to settlement than if they were here on a more short-term basis

EX.1 must be read with EX.2. '*Insurmountable obstacles*' are those causing:

> very significant difficulties which would be faced by the applicant or their partner in continuing their family life together outside the UK and which could not be overcome or would entail very serious hardship for the applicant or their partner.

Agyarko considered that this formulation was consistent with the Strasbourg approach. This is a high threshold. Where a case fails under Ex.1, it will still have to be assessed under the residual test of unjustifiably harsh consequences.

In Lal [2019] EWCA Civ 1925 the Court explained that when assessing whether insurmountable obstacles exist to a couple's relocation abroad, there are two questions:
  (a) Do the problems amount to a very significant difficulty
  (b) If so, can the difficulty be overcome by reasonable steps without very significant hardship

Very importantly, Lal notes a significant difference between assessing cases under the Rules by reference to benchmarks such as "*insurmountable obstacles*", and analysing them more broadly. Of course these days under Appendix FM the broader assessment takes place by reference to GEN3 (MIL 6.1.3). The Court explains that these balancing exercises could be approached via the HO test of whether the decision is *unjustifiably harsh*. The word "*unjustifiably*" emphasised the need for a balancing exercise between the public interest and the strength of family life, and did not require that there be any serious hardship if the couple moved abroad.

> **Example**
>
> Carlos is a failed asylum seeker from Colombia, but has been living in the UK with a Colombian man with refugee status for two years in a genuine and subsisting relationship akin to marriage. Duncan has a current well-founded fear of persecution in Colombia so there are insurmountable obstacles to the couple returning there to live, and Duncan can therefore rely on EX.1. He can apply for leave to remain as a partner - subject only to the suitability requirements. He will be granted 30 months leave as a partner on a 10-year route to settlement.
>
> Elena came to the UK as a visitor from Kazakhstan. Whilst here, she has a relationship with a British man and falls pregnant. The couple marry. She overstays and the child is born British. She can rely on EX1 to overcome the fact that she has overstayed. She can argue that it is unreasonable to expect her British citizen baby to leave the UK. And, depending on the problems abroad, that there are insurmountable obstacles to the family living in Kazakhstan. If she is no longer in a relationship with the baby's father, she can run the same arguments under the parent category.

> **Top Tip**
>
> Always look at the Guidance *Family life (as a partner or parent) and exceptional circumstances* to see what inspiration it provides. Bear in mind it should be construed sensibly and flexibly. Possible factors to take instructions on in an insurmountable obstacles case are:
>
> ☐ Pregnancy – the expectant mother's health and the conditions for birth abroad, including family and medical support
> ☐ Relationships with family and friends in the United Kingdom particularly where there are questions of dependency
> ☐ The best interests of any children, whether of the immediate family unit or others with children who might face relocation
> ☐ Ability of the partner lawfully resident in the UK to enter and reside in proposed country of relocation
> ☐ Cultural barriers leading to social isolation and discrimination
> ☐ Mental or physical disability
> ☐ The security situation including whether the Sponsor has was granted leave to remain based on protection needs, and whether those remain current
> ☐ Beware of those factors that may appear relevant, but which the HO guidance opines are not sufficient – language difficulties, uprooting from family and friends, and a material change in quality of life; nevertheless all these are clearly relevant albeit that they should be explored in detail rather than being blandly asserted

6.2.6 Partners outside Appendix FM and the exception

As noted above, where an application fails to meet the mainstream Appendix FM criteria, under GEN3.2 the question remains:

> whether there are exceptional circumstances which would render refusal ... unjustifiably harsh ... for the applicant, their partner, a relevant child or another family member

So it seems that the intention of the HO is that all aspects of Article 8 are to be considered inside the Rules. It will still be important to follow the five-stage test for approaching Article 8 rights as set out in Razgar [2004] 2 AC 368 (see further MIL 5.4.1, 5.6.2).

The essential questions in most cases will break down to the existence of family life, whether there will be a significant interference with it caused by the immigration decision and whether that will be disproportionate. See the relevant considerations summarised in MM (Lebanon) [2017] UKSC 10, in turn citing the Strasbourg case of Jeunesse:

> There is no general obligation to respect a married couple's choice of country in which to reside or to authorise family reunification. It will depend upon the particular circumstances of the persons concerned and the general interest. Factors to be taken into account are the extent to which family life would effectively be ruptured; the extent of the ties in the host country; whether there are 'insurmountable obstacles' ... in the way of the family living in the alien's home country; and whether there are factors of immigration control (such a history of breaches of immigration law) or public order weighing in favour of exclusion (para 107). If family life was created at a time when the people involved knew that the immigration status of one of them was such that persistence of family life in the host state would from the outset be precarious, 'it is likely only to be in exceptional circumstances that the removal of the non-national family member will constitute a violation of article 8' (para 108; note that this was expressed as a prediction rather than a requirement) ...

Jeunesse also emphasised that in the cases of children *"national decision-making bodies should, in principle, advert to and assess evidence in respect of the practicality, feasibility and proportionality of any removal of a non-national parent in order to give effective protection and sufficient weight to the best interests of the children directly affected by it."*

When assessing proportionality, MM (Lebanon) explains §61, 66:

> "the ultimate issue is whether a fair balance has been struck between individual and public interests, taking account the various factors identified ... the evaluative exercise required in assessing the proportionality of a measure under article 8 of the Convention ... excludes any 'hard-edged or bright-line rule to be applied to the generality of cases"

6.2.6.1 Family relationships beyond partners and children

Case law and common sense tell us that family life can include various relationships. It is useful to see how the Strasbourg Court has approached family life over time, beginning with the core family unit but going onwards, and how the UK courts have drawn on that approach.

Relationships between near relatives will constitute family life whether or not family links are 'legitimate', see e.g. Marckx v Belgium (1979) 2 EHRR 330:

> 'Article 8 ... makes no distinction between the 'legitimate' and the 'illegitimate' family. Such a distinction would not be consonant with the word 'everyone', and this is confirmed by Article 14 ...with its prohibition, in the enjoyment of the rights and freedoms enshrined in the Convention, of discrimination grounded on 'birth.'

> '[F]amily life', ... includes at least the ties between near relatives, for instance those between grandparents and grandchildren, since such relatives may play a considerable part in family life.'

AA [2021] UKAITUR JR016522020 is an example of a case where the SSHD's decision making was found unlawful because the presumption of family life between a parent and their natural child was not given proper weight.

The ECHR in Berrehab v Netherlands (1988) 11 EHRR 322 held that cohabitation, is not an essential feature of family life, although it is strong evidence of its existence:

> ... cohabitation [is not] a sine qua non of family life between parents and minor children ... the relationship created between the spouses by a lawful and genuine marriage [is such that] that a child born of such a union is ipso jure part of that relationship; hence, from the moment of the child's birth and by the very fact of it, there exists between him and his parents a bond amounting to 'family life', even if the parents are not then living together ... Subsequent events, of course, may break that tie ...

Where a child is involved the State must ensure a child's integration in their own family unit: Kroon v The Netherlands (1995) 19 EHRR 263:

> 'Where the existence of a family tie with a child has been established, the State must act in a manner calculated to enable that tie to be developed and legal safeguards must be established that render possible as from the moment of birth, or as soon as practicable thereafter, the child's integration in his family'

Singh v ECO New Delhi [2004] EWCA (Civ) 1075 examines Strasbourg case law which shows that family and private life is a question of fact and can cover a range of diverse situations, noting the Strasbourg Court's tolerant indulgence of cultural and religious diversity and stressing that the real question is one of 'close family ties':

> The existence or non-existence of 'family life' for the purposes of Article 8 is essentially a question of fact depending upon the real existence in practice of close personal ties

AA v United Kingdom (Apn no 8000/08; 20 September 2011) & HK (Turkey) [2010] EWCA Civ 583 accept that the family life of young adults does not terminate simply because they reach majority, when they continued to live at home.

The relevant close personal ties might though, in certain circumstances, be ones that have only recently been re-established. ECHR Art 8 obligations require a state not only to refrain from interference with existing life, but also from inhibiting the development of a real family life in the future: Ahmadi [2005] EWCA Civ 1721) (where two Afghan brothers were found to have family life where there was significant emotional dependency between them notwithstanding a lack of recent cohabitation).

But family life will not necessarily be accepted to be established between adults (e.g. adult children and their parents, adult siblings), see Advic v United Kingdom [1995] ECHR 57:

> Although this will depend on the circumstances of each particular case, the Commission has already considered that the protection of Article 8 ... did not cover links between adult brothers who had been living apart for a long period of time and who were not dependent on each other .... Moreover, the relationship between a parent and an adult child would not necessarily acquire the protection of Article 8 ... without evidence of further elements of dependency, involving more than the normal, emotional ties ...

As the Court said in MT (Zimbabwe) [2007] EWCA Civ 455, *Advic*, whilst stressing the need for an element of dependency over and above the normal between that of a parent or parent figure and adult child, also stresses that everything depends on the circumstances of each case.

In ZB (Pakistan) [2009] EWCA Civ 834 the question to be asked was put, thus:

> Where ..., the focus is on the parent, the issue must be: how dependent is the older relative on the younger ones in the UK and does that dependency create something more than the normal emotional ties?

Speaking of the situation where parents had migrated abroad in circumstances where their children could not follow them in the short-term, Rai [2017] EWCA Civ 320 summarised these authorities as meaning that family life was established where there was *sufficient* (but not any extraordinary or exceptional) *degree of financial or emotional dependence* between adults. The parental decision to migrate to and settle in the UK should be assessed in the light of the practical and financial realities leading to it. Decision makers should focus on whether as a matter of fact an adult child had family life with his parents which existed at the time of their departure and endured beyond it.

Uddin [2020] EWCA Civ 338 emphasises that there was no special test for the relationship between a child and their foster carers (here in the context of a UASC still living with his foster parents after reaching majority). The existence of family life was a question of fact depending on the real existence in practice of *close personal ties*. And:

> The irreducible minimum of what family life implies ... whether support is real or effective or committed.

Mobeen [2021] EWCA Civ 886 explains that co-habitation is generally a strong pointer towards the existence of family life: also relevant is the extent and nature of any support from other family members and the existence of any relevant cultural or social traditions. In the cases of parents, the issue will be the extent of the dependency of the older relative on the younger ones in the UK and whether or not that dependency creates something more than the normal emotional ties amounting to whether or not this is a case of "effective, real or committed support" or whether there is "the real existence in practice of close personal ties".

6.2.6.2 Family proceedings

Decisions such as MS (Ivory Coast) [2007] EWCA Civ 133 and Ciliz v Netherlands [2000] ECHR 365 relate to an applicant's potential expulsion in the course of family proceedings. Ciliz involved an applicant in the process of seeking a contact order. Decisions may violate Article 8 ECHR if they prejudice the removee's effective involvement in family proceedings. RS India [2012] UKUT 00218 (IAC) lays out the proper approach to immigration appeals which involve family proceedings. The case stresses the advantages that the family courts have in determining best interests over the Immigration Tribunals. The immigration judge will need to determine these questions:

1. Does the claimant have at least an Article 8 right to remain until the conclusion of the family proceedings?
2. If so should the appeal be allowed to a limited extent and a discretionary leave be directed?
3. Alternatively, is it more appropriate for a short period of an adjournment to be granted to enable the core decision to be made in the family proceedings?
4. Is it likely that the family court would be assisted by a view on the present state of knowledge of whether the appellant would be allowed to remain in the event that the outcome of the family proceedings is the maintenance of family contact between them and a child resident here?

CJ [2022] UKUT 336 (IAC) notes that in modern appeals on human rights grounds the FTT should simply allow the appeal where it finds that extant contact proceedings render expulsion disproportionate.

Further considerations identified in RS (India) arise in criminal deportation cases, such as whether there is reason to think the family proceedings amount to an attempt to stave off removal without there being any genuine underlying family life and whether realistically any such proceedings will make any difference to the appeal's outcome. CJ [2022] UKUT 336 (IAC) explains that this is likely to meet the "very compelling circumstances" threshold in deportation proceedings.

Communications between the Family Court and the Immigration Tribunals in such cases are governed by the Protocol on communications between judges of the Family Court and Immigration and Asylum Chambers of the First-tier Tribunal and Upper Tribunal.

As made clear by the High Court Family Division in F v M & Anor [2017] EWHC 949 (Fam), practitioners acting in family proceedings have an ongoing duty to remain on top of the immigration side of things, and vice versa. There appears to be no published guidance on granting leave where family proceedings are pending, but in practice it seems that leave outside the rules will be granted for three or six months at a time until the proceedings are concluded. A person who has been granted leave pending the outcome of family court proceedings may be able to apply to extend that leave under the parent category of Appendix FM at the conclusion of the proceedings (see rE-LTRPT.3.1(b) in Appendix FM).

Disclosure of Family Court documents to UKVI or the Tribunal (IAC)

These cases may well involve dealing with Family Court orders. Beware!

- The Family Procedure Rules at r12.37 essentially allow legal representatives to obtain these but not to disclose them to any other party (which includes the HO and IAC!) without committing contempt of court, unless consent for disclosure is first sought from the court.

- Normally a family court judge can give consent for disclosure for no charge and via an emailed request. You should ring the Family Court first and obtain a contact person to chase this up.

6.2.6.3 Applications for entry clearance that rely on Article 8 ECHR

It is possible to make an application to join family members in this country even though there is no route under the rules; alternatively Article 8 may be relied on as an alternative ground of admission. The principle is clearly recognised above in cases such as Singh v ECO (New Delhi).

In these cases the focus will often be on the existence of family life: given that, unlike in the more usual expulsion scenario, the family members are not presently residing together, it may be difficult to establish that they enjoy family life.

Once the question of proportionality is reached, one central question will be the circumstances in which family life arose. This was discussed in SS (Congo) & Ors [2015] EWCA Civ 387, where a former refugee, now a British citizen, who could not afford to accommodate his 'post-flight' spouse to the standard required by the minimum income requirements of the Rules, applied for entry clearance to bring her here:

- where family was life originally established in ordinary and legitimate circumstances at some time in the past, as in the case of a refugee who flees persecution or a British citizen who establishes a relationship abroad at a time when they hold no intention of returning to live here, then there is no requirement of exceptional circumstances: merely a requirement to show a compelling case, recognising that the rules are not a complete answer to the situation in hand
- if someone from the UK marries a foreign national or establishes a family life with them at a stage when they are contemplating trying to live together in the United Kingdom, but when they know that their partner does not have a right to come there, then their case is to be approached on the same basis as if the relationship had been established in this country on a precarious basis: i.e. essentially applying an exceptional circumstances test
- in either case, the fact that the interests of a child are in issue will be a countervailing factor which reduces the width of the margin of appreciation which the state authorities would otherwise enjoy

That reasoning does not appear to have been overturned by subsequent outcome of the appeal to the Supreme Court (when the case became part of the MM (Lebanon) cohort).The CoA had found the case was not an exceptional one. The UKSC overturned that thinking in one of the appeals before them, that of SS (Congo), finding that the extensive ties of the couple in the UK, and the fact the applicant had two children here, and their inability to live together in the Democratic Republic of Congo, were collectively sufficient to outweigh the public interest considerations enshrined in the Rule.

The reasons for separation may be very important: as was stated in H (Somalia) [2004] UKIAT 00027:

> It cannot be right to approach the disruption to family life which is caused by someone having to flee persecution as a refugee as if it were of the same nature as someone who voluntarily leaves, or leaves in the normal course of the changes to family life which naturally occur as children grow up.

Some people with poor immigration histories return abroad rather than stick things out here. If they do so and apply to return, they should be in a better position regarding their immigration history than had they made the application 'in-country': see LH [2006] UKAIT 00019 where the then Tribunal President noted that such a person:

> will not have the very significant burden which weighs in the scales against him presently, of currently being in the United Kingdom unlawfully in breach of the IRs. The Article 8 claim will not be tainted by that illegality. It can be considered in the round, with such fresh evidence as may be available.

However, these individuals must still run the gauntlet of IR9.8.2 - being thought to have contrived to frustrate the purposes of the IRs (MIL 2.3.5.8).

Top Tip

Relevant matters to take instructions on in an entry clearance case involving family life will be;

- ☐ the period over which the relevant family members cohabited in the past
- ☐ the reasons for their separation
- ☐ the means of ongoing contact and communication

6.2.7 The income threshold and Article 8 – MM and exceptional circumstances within the Rules

The minimum income requirement was accepted as lawful in MM (Lebanon) [2017] UKSC 10, though only on the basis that the Rule was capable of being operated compatibly with Article 8 ECHR by taking a sensible approach to those cases that did not meet it. Relevant considerations were:

- It would be essential for government decision makers to take a broad view of cases that did not meet the financial requirements, particularly where this was down to an inability to meet the specified evidence requirements by which the level of income is proved
- On appeal judges should take a realistic view and it would be more open to them to depart from the administrative decision maker's assessment where the flaw was down to a failure to meet the specified evidence requirements than where it related to a more fundamental aspect of the Rules: so evidence of third party support that was cogent and verifiable should be accepted
- Where the income threshold criteria could not be satisfied, the question would be whether the policy objectives served by that Rule were outweighed by the individual facts of the case

GEN.3.1 addresses the circumstances where the entry clearance financial requirements are not met, both for partners and for the parents with limited leave of a child who is seeking entry clearance or leave to join them. Where:

> it is evident from the information provided by the applicant that there are exceptional circumstances which could render refusal … [an ECHR Art 8 breach] result[ing] in unjustifiably

CHAPTER 6: Family-Based Applications

harsh consequences for the applicant, their partner or a relevant child ... the decision-maker must consider whether such financial requirement is met through taking into account [certain] ... sources of income, financial support or funds

GEN3.1 does not apply to the 'parent' category, where the financial requirement is to show 'adequate maintenance' which permits a more flexible assessment of the availability of funds than the super strict criteria of Appendix FM. (MIL 2.2.3). The phrase "could render refusal [a breach]" contrasts with that used in GEN3.2 "would render refusal [a breach]" and apparently indicates a lower threshold.

Those sources are identified in paragraph 21A of Appendix FM-SE as:

- Credible guarantees of third party financial support
- Credible prospective earnings from prospective employment of the applicant or sponsor, and
- Any other credible and reliable source of funds that will become available to them during the period of leave applied for – loans are generally excluded unless taking the form of a mortgage on property owned by one or both of the couple.

The applicant should be given 21 days to provide this alternative evidence (if not provided initially), as per the Guidance *Family life (as a partner or parent) private life and exceptional circumstances.* The Guidance explains that the para 21A criteria are relevant but not decisive, as "*Each case will be considered on its merits*": the more criteria that are met, the stronger the merits of the case will be.

Decision makers, in determining whether the 'exceptional circumstances' threshold is met, are reminded to take into account, as a primary consideration, the best interests of any relevant child. The guidance Family life (as a partner or parent), private life and exceptional circumstances sets out in great detail the 'Relevant Factors' as to exceptional circumstances and 'best interests'It is essential to consult and address these directly when writing representations.identified 'Best Interest' factors listed reflect existing case law such as EV Philippines and ZH Tanzania (MIL 5.3.2).

The 'exceptional circumstances' text includes this:

[…] the continued separation of family members does not of itself constitute exceptional circumstances or unjustifiably harsh consequences, particularly where the family have chosen to commence or continue their relationships in separate countries. […]

So the applicant's and sponsor's statements should explain why, despite historic migration choices, their plans to reunite in future, as a family, were not an unreasonable expectation to hold.

The absence of governance or security in another country […]

Examples given are a country-wide breakdown of public order due to civil war or natural disasters, but the guidance then steers the decision maker away from FCO information which 'should not normally be referred to', and towards the HO's own country information. Though presumably the FCO information will have more relevance where it is a British citizen who is expected to face circumstances abroad.

The immigration status of the applicant and their family members

This requires the decision maker to look at immigration history and the 'precariousness' counterpoint against weight accorded to family and private life. The paragraph, in particular, requires the questioning of visitor applicants' true intentions at time of visit visa application/entry.

In an appeal where the proportionality of an interference with private and family life is in issue, it being accepted or established that neither rule (nor the Ex.1 exceptions in an in-country case) are made out, the judge will need to consider whether the application of the financial requirement in the particular circumstances of the case is incompatible with Article 8. For in-country extension applications, applicants may be saved from the difficulties faced by entry clearance cases because, even if the financial requirements are not met, they can rely on EX.1 if they can establish insurmountable obstacles to living elsewhere or unreasonable relocation for a relevant child. And all applicants can point to 'exceptional circumstances' under GEN.3.1. or GEN.3.2 which can include UK connections.

6.2.8 Chikwamba – return abroad to seek entry clearance

Another argument re the proportionality of a partner refusal is whether the person who is in the UK irregularly can apply to return here by seeking entry clearance in the normal way. This consideration is not found in the IR themselves. It was considered in Chikwamba [2008] UKHL 40, which found that it was more sensible to assess the proportionality of enforcing the entry clearance route at the date of decision/appeal, particularly in family cases involving children. So to place this in the modern context, an applicant can

- First rely on the "core" Rules including Ex.1: eg by showing there are insurmountable obstacles to a couple's relocation abroad or that it would be unreasonable re their childrens' best interests: if they make their case on this basis, then Chikwamba does not enter the equation

- Secondly rely on "unjustifiably harsh" circumstances beyond Ex.1 (ie GEN 3.2): at which point the HO can rely on the 'entry clearance' argument as part of their case

Chikwamba [2008] UKHL 40 had taken a different approach re the previous IRs, . holding §40 that it was more sensible to assess human rights at the point of application, particularly in family cases involving children.

The role and relevance of the Chikwamba principle is an ongoing issue.

- Hayat [2012] EWCA Civ 1054 held that a sensible reason was required for enforcing entry clearance :

    Where Article 8 is engaged, it will be a disproportionate interference with family or private life to enforce such a policy unless, to use the language of Sullivan LJ, there is a sensible reason for doing so.

Essentially there would need to be a particularly bad immigration history before a return abroad was justified.

- Chen IJR [2015] UKUT 189 (IAC) holds that requiring an applicant to jump through administrative hoops might be disproportionate. But only if an evidence-backed case established that relocation would have harsh consequences.
- The Supreme Court in Agyarko [2017] UKSC 11 strongly vindicated the Chikwamba doctrine, stating that in a case where it was certain that entry clearance would be granted were a person to return abroad, then there might be no public interest in their removal.
- Younas [2020] UKUT 129 (IAC) holds that where the evidence indicated entry clearance would be granted on application, the degree of disruption should be assessed: a very young child might not materially be affected by temporary relocation.
- The fact that partner entry clearance rules were certain *not* to be satisfied was, conversely, one of the factors *militating against* requiring the appellant to re-apply from abroad in Tikka [2018] EWCA Civ 642. The reaction of the UK authorities to the application was made clear by the decision presently appealed against and there was no point in requiring an applicant to endure a presumably identical entry clearance and run round the whole appeal system again.
- Chikwamba thinking now looks set to decrease in importance following Alam [2023] EWCA Civ 30. Alam holds that the arguable unreasonableness of an entry clearance application being required from abroad should only be considered where the HO have squarely refused on that basis. It stresses that Chikwamba came from the era before the Rules dealt comprehensively with family life applications and before the s117B(4) proviso that little weight should be afforded family life established unlawfully.

6.2.9 Grants of leave and conditions for partner applications under Appendix FM

Spouses, civil partners and unmarried partners will be granted (see Section D-LTRP):

- 33 months leave to enter, or
- 30 months leave remain
    - on a 60-month route to settlement, or
    - on a 120-month route if relying on EX1, GEN.3.1 or GEN.3.2

Fiancé(e)s and proposed civil partners will be granted six months LTE.

In all cases, including those of a fiancé(e) or proposed civil partner granted six months LTE who has now registered their relationship, further leave to remain will usually be granted for 30 months at a time until the migrant becomes entitled to ILR.

Where the applicant has extant leave at the date of decision, the remaining period of that extant leave up to a maximum of 28 days will be added to the period of limited LTR granted under that paragraph (which may therefore exceed 30 months).

A person granted 30 months leave on the 120-month route will, if they meet all the requirements of the rules for their next extension application (i.e. they no longer have to rely on EX1), be able to switch into the 60-month route at any point without having to wait for their current grant to come to an end, but any time spent on the 120-month route will not count towards the 60 month requirement. This will reduce their route to settlement from 120 months to 90 months (see also MIL 6.2.10.1).

There is a prohibition on employment, and no recourse to public funds for fiancé(e)s and proposed civil partners. From 4 June 2020, the marriage must take place in the UK, presumably to prevent proxy marriages from being carried out in other countries .

There is generally no recourse to public funds in these routes: see MIL 1.3.6 for exceptions.

6.2.10 Indefinite leave to remain

When applying for ILR under the partner category in Appendix FM, substantially the same relationship and financial requirements apply as for LTE/R.

The couple will need to show their relationship is subsisting and that they continue to intend to live together permanently in the UK. The financial requirement under Appendix FM (MIL 6.2.3) is relaxed for those whose income is low such that they need to rely on savings: the whole of the savings above £16,000 can be added to income, not the excess savings divided by 2.5 (E-ILRP.1.3(1A))..

There are 'suitability' provisions (S-ILR). There is 15-year bar on ILR after prison sentences of one to four years, a 7-year bar for lesser prison sentences, a 2-year bar for non-custodial disposals, and an indefinite ban for longer ones (S-ILR.1.3 to 1.6); there can also be refusals for offending which is persistent or causes serious harm, good character, failing to comply with the information-gathering or interview process, having been excluded from (or being excludable) from international protection, breaching support undertakings, failing to pay litigation or NHS costs, and dishonesty.

Applicants for settlement under the age of 65 must meet the knowledge of English language and life in the UK (KoLL) requirements under Appendix KoLL unless exceptions apply (MIL 2.2.6).

Where the KoLL requirements are not yet met, or ILR is delayed due to the criminality time bars, the applicant will be able to apply for further limited leave. See MIL 5.7.1 for early ILR applications at.

6.2.10.1 Appendix Settlement Family Life (Appendix SFL) & Appendix Relationship with Partner

From 20 June 2022 Appendix SFL address ILR for partners & parents on the 10-year route. It makes it easier to mix different kinds of leave, under Appendix FM or otherwise. Different periods of leave with an ECHR Art 8 dimension (as a partner, parent, on a private life route, or with LOTR – as defined in SETF3.1), may be combined, without resetting the clock. Additionally any other residence on a settlement route can qualify so long as one year has been spent under Appendix FM (SETF3.2) and that permission has been based on the current for at least one year (SETF7.3). Under the previous regime, entering the partner/parent routes could put the applicant back to square one.

The core validity criteria apply (SETF1.1-1.2) (MIL 1.5.3) as does the standard immigration status proviso (SETF2.7) (MIL 1.5.4); one must have last had Appendix FM permission (SETF1.3). Appendix Continuous Residence must be satisfied (SETF4.1), as must Appendix English Language in speaking and listening to B1 standards (SETF5) and Appendix KOL UK (SETF6.1).

The ILR-to-LTR concession applies (SETF9) (MIL 1.3.2.1).

Alongside Appendix SFL the relationship criteria for partners applying for ILR departed Appendix FM and moved to Appendix Relationship with Partner (Appendix RWP). This addresses age (over 18: RWP1.1), prohibited degrees of relationship (RWP2.1), prior breakdown of any previous relationship (RWP3.1), validity in the country the marriage/civil partnership took place (RWP4.1), two years' extant relationship cohabitation for durable partners (RWP5.1), having met in person and being in a genuine and subsisting relationship (RWP6.1), only relying on a polygamous/polyandrous relationship where no other partner has sought or been granted leave/ILR or the right of abode (RWP7.1). This Appendix is cross-referenced from numerous immigration routes beyond Appendix FM.

There is supporting Guidance *Relationship with a Partner*. It provides detailed information on assessing the validity of marriages and degrees of relationship, the fact of prior relationship having ended which requires separation pursuant to a permanent end to the relationship even if divorce is not possible due to law or custom, and points out

- The requirement is for two years' extant *relationship* (not *cohabitation*) so long as there is good reason for them living apart
- '*Official and verifiable evidence carries the most weight. Statements without supporting evidence have less weight. Applicants are not encouraged to provide photographic evidence or evidence of interaction over email, WhatsApp or other social media as they can be falsified and are difficult to verify*'
- The end of a previous relationship can be assumed from the fact of a new marriage/CP unless the decision maker is satisfied that the assertion is false
- Generally the relationship need not be re-assessed where previously the subject of a grant absent new information – for first-time assessment, direct checks with third parties are possible as well as close analysis of the information on the form and supporting evidence, and numerous documents over an extended period are less important than those for the last 12 months (showing both names or at least covering the same time period)
- Evidence is to be assessed on balance of probabilities and via an interview if the documents do not suffice, and always bearing in mind that relationships don't always start, develop and subsist in the same way as is common in the UK, and that a Service and Support centre may not have retained all the documents though should have at least logged them. Evidence may be
    - **Strong**: documents issued on an official basis and verified by an organisation and/or service provider that carries out checks on the person involved (eg marriage certificates, tenancy agreements, bank/mortgage statements)
    - **Acceptable**: documents from an organisation and/or service provider though without verified checks, in which case more than one piece of evidence may be required (eg electoral register confirmation, student finance documents, domestic bills)

- **Weak**: evidence from individuals with no official capacity, or unverified, which may be considered sufficient only in conjunction with strong/acceptable evidence or with an explanation of the wider circumstances explaining the lack of other evidence (communications and social media records, written statements from friends/community)

Essentially the same Suitability criteria apply as under S-ILR: subject additionally to the private and family life ILR suitability regime

- An indefinite ban on ILR for any conviction with a sentence exceeding 12 months (SETF2.2)
- A 10-year ban for lesser sentences (and the applicant must then have held 10 years of permission in a private or family life route, of which 5+ years post-dates their sentence) (SETF2.3)
- A 10-year ban for involvement with sham relationships, dishonesty, litigation or NHS debts, or breaching one's conditions, unless completing 10 years in a private or family life route of which 5 years post-date the matter coming to HO attention (SETF2.4)
- A 10-year ban for entering the UK illegally unless they are a child or young adult with permission under private life (SETF2.5)

Children (including those over 18) may apply (SETF10-17) if they have a parent applying on the route or who already has ILR or British citizenship, so long as they were born in the UK or last had permission as a dependent child. They are subject to the same regime re suitability, English language, Appendix KOL UK, ILR to LTR concession as above. The usual rules apply regarding both parents being in the UK lawfully and for UK care arrangements (MIL 2.2.8).

6.2.11 Getting married in the UK

There is no requirement for migrants planning to marry in the UK to seek HO permission. The Certificate of Approval scheme requiring such permission was abolished on 9 May 2011. The scheme was held to be unlawful by the House of Lords in 2008 in the case of Baiai [2009] 1 AC 287. After several modifications it was finally abandoned.

One part of the original scheme does remain, which is the requirement to give notice to marry or register the civil partnership at a 'designated office'. All registration offices in Scotland and Northern Ireland are designated offices, as are 76 offices in England and Wales. Both parties will need proof of their name, age and nationality, but there is no prescribed way of evidencing these.

When this regime was introduced, the HO estimated that 35,000 marriages per year would need to be referred to themselves for potential investigation and that 6,000 marriages would then be actively investigated. Molina [2017] EWHC 1730 (Admin) explains the difference between a **sham marriage** and **a marriage of convenience**: the former involves a marriage where there is no genuine relationship between the parties (see s24(5) of IAA 1999), whereas the latter connotes one contracted to secure an immigration advantage, whether or not there is a genuine bond between the participants. The test for a marriage of convenience is whether the *predominant*, rather than *sole*, purpose of the marriage was to gain immigration rights: see Saeed [2022] UKUT 18 (IAC). A marriage of convenience *may* involve deception (as where a party knowingly enters into it knowing there to be no genuine relationship), in which case it will also be a sham.

A new referral scheme was introduced on 2 March 2015, contained in part 4 of the Immigration Act 2014. Under it, any proposed marriages or civil partnerships in the UK from which a person could benefit in immigration terms can be referred to the HO. and be investigated under an extended notice period of 70 days. Now, notice of all marriages in England and Wales must be given at least 28 days in advance of the marriage taking place. There are two key conditions, labelled A and B:

- Condition A:
    - Either only one, or neither, party is an exempt person: ie a British or Irish citizen, a person with EUSS/EUPSS or a pending application under the EUSSch

- They hold appropriate immigration status, EU permanent residence, exemption from immigration control, or ILR – or a marriage or civil partnership visa under the IRs or a, fiancée or proposed civil partner visa (inside or outside IRs)
- Condition B: "*reasonable grounds for suspecting that the proposed marriage or civil partnership is a sham*"

If the HO decides not to investigate then it HOHO should inform the registrar and the marriage can proceed after the conclusion of the normal 28-day notice period. If the HO does decide to investigate further, then the notice period is extended to 70 days to allow time for investigation and for enforcement action to be taken.

The HO may prevent the marriage taking place where the parties fail to co-operate with the investigation.

Examples of risk factors which may raise suspicions include (*Sham Marriages and Civil Partnerships Background Information And Proposed Referral And Investigation Scheme*, Home Office November 2013):

- Being of a nationality at high risk of involvement in a sham, on the basis of objective information and intelligence about sham cases.
- Holding a visa in a category linked by objective information and intelligence to sham cases.
- Having no immigration status or holds leave which is due to expire shortly.
- Having had an application to remain in the UK refused.
- Having previously sponsored another spouse or partner to enter or remain in the UK.
- Being or having been the subject of a credible section 24/24A report, which explains for example how the couple could not communicate in a common language and did not know basic information about each other.

The Marriage and civil partnership referral and investigation scheme: statutory guidance for HO staff sets out processes for considering sham marriages, stressing that EEA/Swiss nationals are now within its scope from 1 July 2021

6.3 Bereaved partners and domestic abuse

Normally, if a marriage or partnership has ended during the *probationary period* (the term traditionally given to the period of limited leave prior to settlement being granted), the foreign national is expected to leave the UK unless they can qualify under another category (e.g. as the parent of a child in the UK). However, in the following two circumstances partners will be able to apply for ILR notwithstanding the end of the relationship.

They initially applied only to partners of British citizens and those with ILR but from 10 January 2019 also to partners of refugees.

These categories do not include any exceptional route akin to Ex.1, unlike the parent and partner routes under Appendix FM. And GEN3.2(4) excludes them from its own exceptionality regime. So if the claim fails *under* the rules, consideration would have to move straight to a further assessment based on whether there are compelling circumstances *outside the IRs*, in the light of the five stage Razgar analysis (MIL 5.4.1, 5.4-5.5). It might, for example, be relevant that the individual in question has severed ties abroad and come to this country in the expectation of settling here. However, if their former partner is their only meaningful link with this country, then it is difficult to see such cases getting off the ground.

6.3.1 Bereaved spouses or partners

Bereaved partners will be entitled to apply for ILR if the partner they joined in the UK died during the 24, 60 or 120 month probationary period if the relationship was genuine, permanent and subsisting, at the time of the bereavement (BPILR.1.1-BPILR.1.4). Applications are to the Suitability provisions, but not the KoLL requirement.

6.3.2 Victims of domestic abuse

Partners under Appendix FM who are victims of domestic abuse (formerly termed as 'domestic violence' or DV) may be granted ILR where the marriage or relationship breaks down permanently during the probationary period as a result of domestic abuse (DVILR rules). The 'probationary period' is the term given to the period between the person first being granted leave as a partner, and the date on which they will be entitled to apply for ILR as a partner. That period will be of two, five or 10 years, depending on the route under which the leave was granted.

HO guidance on this route is in the Immigration Staff Guidance: Victims of domestic violence

COVID-19-specific guidance for victims of abuse is available here.

The gateway to entering the route initially was exclusively the possession of leave in the partner category where the sponsor was British or settled (or leave under the DDVC, discussed below). Accordingly the letter of the Rule excluded a person who entered the UK by being the partner of a person granted international protection. A [2016] ScotCS CSIH_38 found that this discriminated against the spouses of refugees, and that the differential treatment was not justified by the public interest: it was wrong to say that individuals granted international protection were in the same position as those present on a temporary basis such as students and workers. Indeed, it seemed the government had given no consideration to the difficulties of the partners of refugees. The rule was subsequently amended to reflect this so that and those who entered under refugee family reunion provisions are now also eligible.

There is no requirement to have current leave at the date of applying for ILR, so long as the relationship broke down due to domestic abuse whilst the person had leave, which reflects the fact that victims may have long overstayed by the time they are able to make the application.

Public funding is available for these applications for those who cannot afford to pay for advice and representation. Applications are made on form SET(DV). The normal fee for settlement applications is payable, but a fee waiver is available for those who can show they are destitute, either by having been granted three months' leave following a successful DDVC application (free application which can be emailed – see https://www.gov.uk/government/publications/application-for-benefits-for-visa-holder-domestic-violence)

The suitability provisions in S-ILR apply (see section on Suitability, above). Where a person is unable to meet the requirements for ILR because of the sanctions in S-ILR.1.5. or S-ILR.1.6, which delay settlement for those with convictions, the person will be granted 30 months leave rather than ILR. In that case, the DV Rules do not provide for any condition to be placed on the grant of limited leave, so the person should be allowed recourse to public funds (subject to the HO's discretion under paragraph GEN.1.11.). That person will then be able to apply for ILR when the sanction period is over.

There are no financial or English language or Life in the UK requirements to meet in this category.

6.3.2.1 Definition of domestic abuse

It will always be necessary to show that the relationship has broken down permanently *as a result of* the domestic abuse. It is not enough to show only that the relationship has permanently broken down and that there was domestic abuse before it did so. The applicant's statement will need to explain the relationship, the abuse and the breakdown in appropriate detail to present a compelling case to the HO - and the causative link between the violence and the end of the relationship.

Domestic abuse can be physical, emotional, sexual or financial. It can come from a person other than the partner (e.g. from the wider family). As stated in the Immigration Staff Guidance Victims of domestic violence referring to the cross-government definition of domestic violence and abuse:

The definition of domestic violence and abuse is any incident or pattern of incidents controlling, coercive or threatening behaviour, violence or abuse between those aged 16 or over who are or have been intimate partners or family members regardless of gender or sexuality. This can include, but is not limited to, the following types of abuse:

- psychological
- physical
- sexual
- financial

Controlling behaviour is a range of acts designed to make a person subordinate and/or dependent by:

- isolating them from sources of support
- exploiting their resources and capacities for personal gain
- depriving them of the means needed for independence
- resistance and escape, and
- regulating their everyday behaviour.

Coercive behaviour is

- an act or a pattern of acts of assault, threats, humiliation and intimidation, or
- other abuse that is used to harm, punish, or frighten their victim.

Domestic abuse is thus widely defined, including controlling and coercive behaviours as well as violence, and an adviser needs to be sensitive to certain behaviour even if the client does not recognise it to be domestic violence. Domestic violence and abuse can include forced marriages, threats as to honour, destructive criticism, verbal abuse, pressure tactics including disconnecting the telephone or taking children away, disrespect and humiliation, breaking trust, enforced isolation by monitoring communications, threats, harassment, sexual or physical violence, denial or encouraging suicidal thoughts. Each of these is usefully expanded at http://www. southallblacksisters.org.uk/domestic-violence/).

6.3.2.2 Proving the claim

The HO specifies in the Immigration Staff Guidance certain types of evidence that they expect to be submitted, and the types of evidence are classified in the following, paraphrased 'Table of Evidence', which is preceded by an explanation that the list is *indicative* and that all the evidence should be considered in the round.

Conclusive

- criminal conviction relating to domestic violence
- police caution, as accepting a caution is an admission of guilt
- final order in a civil court (e.g. non-molestation- or occupation order) where judge found DV occurred

Strong

- final order in a civil court (e.g. non-molestation- or occupation order) where no finding of fact is recorded
- MARAC (Multi Agency Risk Assessment Conference) referral confirmed by a person who is a member of MARAC
- charging decision
- domestic violence protection order
- forced marriage protection order

CHAPTER 6: Family-Based Applications

- prohibited steps order and contact orders (strong if evidence is that DV was a factor in granting the order)
- letter from social services, or welfare officer connected to HM Armed Forces
- letter from organisation supporting DV victims (including a refuge) confirming their assessment of the applicant as being a DV victim and detailing support provided
- letter or statement from an independent witness – strong if they confirm that they witnessed the incident first hand and have 'no vested interest', 'for example, they are not related to the applicant'

Moderate

- arrest (further information and evidence should be sought from the police in relation to the progress of their investigation and outstanding enquiries
- ex parte orders (such as molestation- or occupation order) – moderate value only because these orders 'are made on the evidence of one party only' (obtain further orders if there is a follow-up hearing)
- interim order (the weight will depend on how far the case has progressed and the terms of the order)
- undertaking to court – not conclusive unless there is a clear admission of guilt (ask for further details of the court proceedings and further evidence e.g. police reports, medical reports, professional assessments)
- police attendance at DV incident - attendance at an alleged incident is not itself proof of DV – evidence of police follow-up action or supporting evidence, e.g. medical evidence, will generally be required
- hospital reports confirming injuries or condition consistent with DV – 'report should include whether the hospital appointment was a referral from the doctor or any further treatment required. Many reports are lacking sufficient depth'
- other medical reports confirming injuries or condition consistent with DV – 'the medical report should be provided by the GP who provided the consultation and give details of any hospital treatment needed'

Weak

- power of arrest – weak because these are routinely included in non-molestation orders, not indicating the evidential weight of the order
- letter or statement from official sources, such as advice agencies or refuges, repeating applicant's account without confirming that applicant has been assessed as DV victim and is being treated and supported as such
- statement from applicant – 'decision makers would expect to see further evidence such as police reports, refuge assessment and medical evidence'
- letter, statement, email, text or photos repeating applicant's account of DV – 'limited value but must be considered in light of the rest of the evidence' (e.g. photos can be linked to medical reports)

The guidance does tell caseworkers that other evidence may be considered, and all evidence is to be considered in the round, but in practice anything that is not considered to be 'impartial and objective' or, according to the new guidance, 'conclusive' or 'strong' evidence risks rejection.

The applicant's own testimony, despite the guidance classifying this as 'weak' evidence, is essential and will need to be as compelling (i.e. as detailed) as possible, including an explanation as to the lack of other evidence.

It is clear from the above that as much corroboration as possible will need to be sought to back up potential gaps in evidence. The following evidence should be sought without delay:

- <u>Medical records</u> request (to the GP practice)

- Police records request (in the case of victims of crime, this is to the local police force which dealt with arrests and incidents – a request in writing, and a copy of proof of ID is required – and a photo, but only where CCTV footage is requested). A list of links to the local police forces is at the bottom of this page.
- Social services records request (to the local authority)
- UKVI Subject Access Request – often, controlling behaviour includes withholding information, misstating facts or contacting UKVI, so it may be vital to find out what information has been put to the HO
- Family Court documents (either from a family lawyer or the client and Family Court, if unrepresented) (MIL 6.2.6.2 addresses avoiding accidentally committing contempt of court)

Where the types of evidence on the HO's wish list is not available, the more relaxed approach to evidence laid down in Ishtiaq [2007] EWCA Civ 386 is very helpful, including at the application stage. Where evidence of domestic violence is clearly insufficient to meet any of the evidential requirements, but your client has a strong family/or private life case, an FLR(FP) application may be preferable – this has to be weighed against the onerousness of the lengthy settlement period and high application fees.

Suliman [2020] EWHC 326 (Admin) emphasises that the SSHD had to consider all relevant evidence when determining an application for leave to remain on domestic violence grounds outside the Rules. Where the evidence tended to evince the typical response of an abused partner in a relationship the SSHD should be slow to reject the application simply because the applicant had not originally attributed their injuries to domestic violence when receiving medical treatment.

Unscrupulous sponsors are known to entrap their migrant partners into travelling abroad to abandon them there, unable to access the DVILR route. This is known as transnational marriage abandonment (TMA), now a recognised form of domestic abuse. AM [2022] EWHC 2591 (Admin) recognises that there was no justification for the discrimination against this group when their plight was measured against that of victims of spousal abandonment in the UK who could rely on the DVILR immigration route.

Top Tip

DVILR does not require the applicant to possess leave at the time of application. However, the relationship must have been caused permanently to break down during the two-year probationary period, which can be a problem where there has not been a clean separation between the couple. LA (Pakistan) [2009] UKAIT 00019 reminds judges to 'be careful to assess the evidence in the round, looking at the totality of the evidence and remembering that a broken marriage may have ended before the parties separate and the marriage may have broken down as a result of domestic violence even if other grounds are given in matrimonial proceedings or raised before the Tribunal'.

6.3.2.3 Refusals of Bereaved Partner- or Domestic Abuse applications

The HO deems certain applications, including most of those made under Appendix FM, as involving human rights claims, so that the remedy on refusal is an appeal (see e.g. Appendix AR (AR3.2(c)(viii)). However, Appendix AR (AR3.2(c)) excludes domestic abuse or bereaved partner applications. So the normal remedy is (with JR to follow if needed).

These applications will not necessarily be deemed to be human rights claims such that their refusal generates a right of appeal (MY (Pakistan) [2021] EWCA Civ 1615, upholding MY [2020] UKUT 89 (IAC)). . The MY litigation holds that the HO may control access to how applications were considered. It was only where the HO actively engages with a human rights claim and made a reasoned decision to reject it, that the right of appeal would ensue. So a distinct case will have to be put, on ECHR Art 8 grounds (presuming there to be no asylum claim), to have a chance of accessing the appeal system (MIL 14.2.3) – and the application will need to be made under an alternative family or private life route to have the best prospect of a right of appeal. The stronger the evidence for DVILR purposes, the stronger the rationale for trying the bespoke Appendix FM route first.

Where a DV refusal proceeds to appeal, the question for the FTT would be not simply whether the DV Rules are satisfied. Its jurisdiction is to determine whether the refusal infringes the ECHR, so the primary question will be whether a person's ECHR Art 8 rights are infringed, i.e. applying the traditional five stage test in Razgar. So the Appellant needs to show a firm foundation of private and family life in the UK to get their appeal off the ground (MIL 5.4 to 5.5 - plus 5.6.2 if there is a mental health dimension).

6.3.2.4 Destitution domestic violence concession (DDVC)

This concession allows destitute prospective applicants for ILR via the DV rule to apply for three months of discretionary leave to allow them to claim benefits and secure temporary accommodation whilst they make and await a decision on the DV application.

Details of the concession and an application form are at: https://www.gov.uk/government/publications/application-for-benefits-for-visa-holder-domestic-violence – there is an interesting speech in Hansard (Vol 656, 20 March 2019). A person granted DDV leave will not have to pay a fee when applying for ILR under the rules.

The application is very straightforward, can be emailed to the HO, and will be decided in a few days. Having been granted DL in this capacity, the person will then be expected to make their ILR application within the three-month period following the grant (in which case they will remain entitled to recourse to public funds due to s3C of the 1971 Act, see Chapter 1).

FA (Sudan) [2018] EWHC 3475 (Admin) emphasises that an applicant had to have entered the UK via the appropriate immigration route under the Rules to qualify for such an application. As the concession tracks the DV rule, the spouses of sponsored workers cannot exercise the domestic violence concession, whilst EUPSS-holders can. SWP [2023] EWCA Civ 439 finds that this discrimination was justified, albeit that the former had a stronger claim to being on a settlement route than visitors and students: they were still not in the same position as refugees. It is not unfair to treat migrants on a settlement route differently to refugees, however, given the wide margin of judgment that the government had in social policy issues.

6.4 Parent of a child in the UK (Appendix FM section EC-PT onwards)

The Appendix FM category, 'family life as a parent of a child in the UK' is, according to the guidance *Family life (as a partner or parent)and exceptional circumstances*:

> ... not for couples who are in a genuine and subsisting partner relationship. An applicant cannot meet the parent route if they are or will be eligible to apply under the partner route, including where for example the definition of partner cannot be met, or other eligibility criteria for access to a 5-year route are not met. Applicants in this position must apply or will only be considered (where they are not required to make a valid application), under the partner route, or under the private life route.

Thus this route is not for parents of children when the parents remain in an enduring cohabiting relationship. If they do so, and neither have leave, they will need to make an application relying on the GEN.3.2 exception (MIL 6.1.4)).

For entry clearance applications, the applicant must be 18+ & have:

- sole parental responsibility for the child (E-ECPT.2.3)
- direct access (in person) to the child, as agreed with the parent or carer with whom the child normally lives or as ordered by a court in the UK- in addition in such cases E-ECPT.2.2):
    - the parent or carer with whom the child normally lives must be a British citizen in the UK or settled in the UK, or in the UK as a pre-settled status holder under rEU3 of Appendix EU, and not the partner of the applicant
    - the applicant must not be eligible to apply for entry clearance as a partner under Appendix FM

For LTR applications, the following requirements must be satisfied:

- the applicant has sole parental responsibility for the child or
- the child normally lives with the applicant and not their other parent (who must be a British citizen or UK-settled, or here with EUPSS under rEU3 of Appendix EU), and the applicant must not be eligible to apply for leave to remain as a partner under Appendix FM
- the parent/carer with whom the child normally lives is a British Citizen or UK-settled

In all cases, the applicant must provide evidence that they are taking, and intend to continue to take, an active role in the child's upbringing.

In Khattak [2021] UKUT 63 (IAC) (upheld by CoA in Khattak [2021] EWCA Civ 1873) the UT looks at the limitation on entering the parent route by reference to the partner proviso. As noted the E-LTRPT.2.3 limits applicants by reference to the requirement that "*the applicant is not "eligible to apply for leave to remain as a partner"*. One might readily think that this is intended to rule out those applicants who are in a *present* relationship with the relevant child's other parent. However that is not the only possible reading, as the UT's ruling recognises. In this case the SSHD had refused the application because the applicant was in a new relationship with a person with whom they had not yet lived for 2 years and had not married. So there was an issue as to whether or not they could be a "partner" under the Appendix FM definition.
The UT accepts that an applicant would not be eligible to apply under the partnership route where they had not cohabited with another person for 2 years at the application date: for then they would not meet the "partner" definition in GEN.1.2. Now the Guidance *Family life … exceptional circumstances* clarifies that applicants should not be treated as eligible to apply as partners unless they both meet the partner definition and have a qualifying sponsor enabling them to access a 5 or 10 year partner route, for example a partner who meets the immigration status requirement.

Additionally, the applicant must be either the primary carer of the child, or exercising access rights.

6.4.1 Relationship requirements

'A parent' is defined under IR 6:

a) the stepfather of a child whose father is dead and the reference to stepfather includes a relationship arising through civil partnership;
b) the stepmother of a child whose mother is dead and the reference to stepmother includes a relationship arising through civil partnership (the definition for the purposes of Appendix Ukraine covers stepparents whether or not a biological parent is dead); and
c) the father as well as the mother of an illegitimate child where he is proved to be the father;
d) an adoptive parent, where a child was adopted in accordance with a decision taken by the competent administrative authority or court in a country whose adoption orders are recognised by the United Kingdom or where a child is the subject of a de facto adoption in accordance with the requirements of paragraph 309A of these Rules (except that an adopted child or a child who is the subject of a de facto adoption may not make an application for leave to enter or remain in order to accompany, join or remain with an adoptive parent under paragraphs 297-303);
e) in the case of a child born in the United Kingdom who is not a British citizen, a person to whom there has been a genuine transfer of parental responsibility on the ground of the original parent(s)' inability to care for the child.

6.4.2 Entry clearance as a parent

For applications for entry clearance as a parent, the relevant child must be under 18 at the date of application, a British citizen or settled in the UK, and living in the UK (or if the child is a British citizen, it must be one who is coming to the UK to live or have contact with the applicant). Relevant criteria:

- The parent must have sole parental responsibility, or access rights to the child, and provide evidence that they are taking and intend to continue to take an active role in the child's upbringing (E-ECPT.2.3-2.4.)
- Financial requirements: are whether maintenance and accommodation can be provided 'adequately' (E-ECPT.3.1-3.2 – see Chapter 2 addressing maintenance for a discussion of how these kinds of requirement are to be established)
- English language requirements as discussed above for the partner route E-ECPT.4.1-4.2) (MIL 6.2.2)
- Section S-EC: Suitability–entry clearance applies

6.4.3 Leave to remain as a parent

6.4.3.1 Three-route structure – (a) all requirements met for 5 year ILR route, (b) EX1 exception or (c) GEN.3.2 met for 10 year ILR route

For applications for leave to remain, we see the same three-route structure as for partners:

1. If all the requirements of the route are satisfied (i.e. financial and English language requirements as above, plus sole parental responsibility, or access rights to the child, and taking and intending to continue to take an active role in the child's upbringing), then there is a five-year route to settlement under R-LTRPT.1.1.(c) and D-LTRPT.1.1, via two consecutive 30-month grants of limited leave
2. If some of the relevant requirements are not satisfied, then there is a 10-year route to settlement where paragraph EX1 applies, i.e. where there is a **seven-year resident or British citizen child whose relocation abroad would not be reasonable** (MIL 5.3.2). The requirements that are lifted are those for adequate maintenance and accommodation without recourse to public funds, relevant English language proficiency, and immigration status – see R-LTRPT.1.1.(d) and D-LTRPT.1.2.
3. If Ex.1 cannot be satisfied, then GEN.3.2 may assist if refusal would be *'unjustifiably harsh'* (MIL 6.1.3).

MM (Lebanon) [2017] UKSC 10 would apply at that third stage: decision makers would have to:

> … advert to and assess evidence in respect of the practicality, feasibility and proportionality [of any such removal of a non-national parent] in order to give effective protection and sufficient weight to the best interests of the children directly affected by it.

6.4.3.2 Ineligibility for this route

As with the partner route, one can be completely excluded from the parent one: eg it is not available to

- those here as visitors (any length of visitor leave) and others who hold less than six months leave unless it was granted specifically pending the outcome of family/divorce proceedings (E-LTRPT.3.1. being a requirement of R-LTRPT.1.1(d)(ii)). This part of the immigration status requirement, unlike that regarding overstayers and those on immigration bail, cannot be circumvented by application of EX1
- those who are eligible to apply for leave under the Appendix FM partner route (see paras E-ECPT 2.3 (b)(iii) and E-LTRPT 2.3 (b)(iii))
- as usual under Appendix FM, the generic suitability criteria at Section S-LTR: Suitability leave to remain are cross referenced in as a requirement
- As at the EC stage, one must not be eligible to apply as a partner: E-LTRPT.2.3(a)

Of course, once again this is subject to the GEN.3.2 dispensation. One can still be granted leave so long as one demonstrates unjustifiably harsh consequences to a refusal.

On appeal, a seven-year resident (or British) child may come to the rescue via s117B(6) NIAA 2002. It provides that the public interest does not require removal of a parent where it would not be reasonable to expect the child to leave the UK (MIL 5.3.2 and 6.2.5.1).

6.4.3.3 Parenting roles, relationships and sole parental responsibility

A parent applying to exercise access rights to a child must be 'taking [in the present tense] an active role in the child's upbringing'. This requirement is designed to prevent a parent who has not previously taken an active role from applying under the rule in order to begin doing so. A parent who has yet to take an active role for whatever reason, even if it is because they are outside the UK, but now genuinely wants to do so, will have to make an application outside the Rules.

The concept of 'sole parental responsibility' is not defined in the rules (though 'sole responsibility' has its own case law, MIL 6.7.3. In the Family Policy Family life (as a partner or parent), private life and exceptional circumstances it is used interchangeably with the term 'sole responsibility'. See the guidance:

> Sole responsibility means that one parent has abdicated or abandoned parental responsibility and the remaining parent is exercising sole control in setting and providing the day to day direction for the child's welfare.

'Parental responsibility' is a legal concept and a central part of the regime for parents as set out in the Children Act 1989. In normal circumstances both parents will have parental responsibility from the child's birth if both appear on the birth certificate. There is no suggestion though that that Act is a reference point for assessing the parental roles under the IRs.

To add to the confusion as to the various parental relationships referred to in the rules, we have the concept of 'a genuine and subsisting parental relationship with a child' which appears in EX1. It is not clear how this concept contrasts with 'sole responsibility', 'sole parental responsibility', 'parental responsibility' and 'taking an active role'. The five-year route guidance states that 'in all cases, the applicant must provide evidence that they are taking, and intend to continue to take, an active role in the child's upbringing'. In addition, clear evidence of the parental relationship is necessary. Suggested (but not prescribed) evidence is set out for each in the Guidance at 9.2.4. The guidance states:

> The burden of proof is on the applicant to provide satisfactory evidence. In some instances it may be appropriate to interview an applicant to establish whether they have sole responsibility for the child, or to contact the other parent (with the consent of the applicant) to confirm they have no parental responsibility.

In SR [2018] UKUT 334 (IAC) the UT noted that there are two very different tests specified inside and outside the Rules: at that time there was no GEN.3.2 route .

- Appendix FM addresses parents within their own sub-route; there the question is put as to whether the applicant has an ongoing *'active role in a child's upbringing'*.
- However, once a case is assessed outside the Rules, then section 117B(6) of the NIAA 2002 focuses on whether there is a *'genuine and subsisting parental relationship'*.

The test under the Rules does not necessarily require direct contact between the children and parent; as the UT noted in JA (India [2015] UKUT 225 (IAC)), to so interpret it would render the entry clearance route useless for most applicants. However, it will presumably involve some element of the applicant parent's involvement in the decision making. The intention to take on a role in the child's life alone were not enough. Pure 'access rights' without more did not necessarily establish sufficiently close involvement as to satisfy the Rule. Relevant considerations would include the age, wishes and feelings of the child, the nature and extent of direct and indirect contact, its duration, whether the parent has 'parental responsibility', and the nature and extent of the parent's role in decision making.

On the other hand, the test posed by section 117B(6) on appeal focusses on the existence of a *'genuine and subsisting parental relationship'*. It could readily be imagined that such a relationship might exist notwithstanding the absence of involvement in a child's upbringing, particularly where contact had only recently resumed on a limited basis. Its essence was having some genuine subsisting relationship of a parental nature. Accordingly, the UT accepted that contact limited to three hours a fortnight, during which time the father provided direct parental care to his child, was sufficient.

6.4.3.4 *Zambrano* parents

A parent who succeeds in establishing a right to reside under the CJEU judgement in Zambrano (Reg 16(5) EEA Regs 2016 & under Appendix EU - MIL 11.6.3.3 and 11.7.5.2 – bearing in mind that that route has become much more difficult even before its 8 August closure) will also usually be entitled to a grant of leave under the parent category (because satisfying the criteria of sole carer is likely to satisfy both the EEA and parent routes, as the relevant child/children would be at risk of having to leave the European Union if their sole carer's residence here was in jeopardy). See further 11.6.3.3.

Litigation now indicates that a Zambrano application can only be made where attempts to regularise one's status under the domestic rules have failed. HO Guidance used to state that parent applications facing refusal should be passed to the European Casework section.

6.4.4 Other requirements

The 'suitability' requirements always need to be met. Unless Section EX: Exception applies, the same immigration status and English language requirements apply as for the Partner category. That includes the additional English language requirement for those whose first grant of leave under this category expires from 1 May 2017 (E-LTRPT.5.1.A). The financial requirement is for the applicant to adequately maintain and accommodate themselves and any dependants in the UK without recourse to public funds and not the far higher minimum income requirement in the Partner and Child categories of Appendix FM.

6.4.5 Grants of leave

As with the Partner category, successful applicants will be granted 33 months on entry clearance or 30 months leave to remain, to begin a 60-month route to settlement, or 120 months where EX1 has been applied at any stage. There will be a condition prohibiting recourse to public funds unless they can show they are destitute.

For extensions beyond their youngest child's 18th birthday, parents will need to show the child remains dependent on them. This is defined in IR6 as not having a partner, living at home subject to being at boarding school, college or university as part of their full-time education, and being wholly or mainly dependent on the parent financially and emotionally.

ILR after five years is only available where both grants of leave were on the five-year route (i.e. in both applications the HO accepted that all requirements were satisfied). We address ILR for parents under the 10-year route at MIL 6.2.10.1.

6.5 Children of partners and parents

This Appendix FM category (Section EC-C and Section R-LTRC for entry clearance and leave to remain respectively) is for a child whose parent has or is being granted limited leave as a partner or parent under Appendix FM. Children applying together with their parent can be added to the parent's application.

Children whose parent or parents are settled or applying for settlement in the UK will apply under the IRs Part 8 (MIL 6.7).

As with other provisions for children in the IRs, the child must be under 18 at the date of their first application in this category, but not when making subsequent applications. This means that a child who reaches 18 before they are entitled to a further extension of leave or settlement will still be treated as if they are under 18 when the subsequent application is considered. For all children though, regardless of age, whether on initial application or at any stage before they are settled, they must not be married or in a civil partnership, must not have formed an independent family unit and must not be leading an independent life (as defined IR6).

For entry clearance, the child must be coming to the UK with or to join a parent, who has limited leave as a partner or parent. Where that parent is not the partner of the child's other parent, the parent must have sole responsibility for the child, or there must be serious and compelling family or other considerations which make exclusion of the child undesirable. We consider the definitions of 'sole responsibility' and 'exclusion undesirable' below in the section 6.7 *Children of settled parents*.

For applications for leave to remain, there is no immigration status requirement, so the child can be here irregularly. The financial requirement is the same as the Partner and Parent categories, depending on the parent's leave. If granted under the partner category, the minimum income requirement applies; if as a parent, the lower 'adequate maintenance'. It will be the parent's income and savings that is relevant, not the child's. There will be no financial requirement to meet where the parent is on the 120-month route to settlement. Leave will be granted in line with the non-settled parent.

The child's application for ILR at the end of the parent's 5- or 10-year route will be made under rule 298 at the same time as the parent's application (MIL 6.7).

6.6 Adult dependent relatives

The Appendix FM category, 'Adult dependent relative' (ADR), replaced the Part 8 (Rule 317) provisions for 'Other family members' for applications made on or after 9 July 2012. Applications from 1 June 2023 will be determined under Appendix Adult Dependent Relative. In very narrow circumstances, it provides the opportunity for sponsors (with limited leave, ILR or British citizenship: see E-ECDR.2.3 & MIL 6.6.1) to sponsor a parent, grandparent, sibling or child over 18 to settle in the UK.

JCWI's report on the ADR category, 'Harsh, Unjust, Unnecessary', published in July 2014, records that for the first year of its operation, only 34 settlement visas were issued (even then often only after appeal) and states that:

> It is almost impossible to succeed in this visa category. Fit and healthy parents and grandparents cannot even apply. The All-Party Parliamentary Group on Migration (APPG) has stated that this visa category has 'in effect been closed'.

Judges have become more confident in allowing appeals since the Britcits litigation (MIL 6.6.2). Applications under this category can only be made from outside the UK (as shown by the fact that there are simply no sub-routes headed 'leave to remain').

There is Guidance *Family Policy Adult dependent relative*.

Some features of the Rules:

- Applications for PTS are possible where a Sponsor holds PTS but only where the applicant entered the UK via entry clearance in this route (ADR2.2) and they must remain reliant on the original Sponsor (ADR4.3); PTS will be granted in line with the Sponsor's (ADR9.2) – if an applicant applies for PTS with a British citizen/ILR-holder they will be granted 30 months - when the time comes to apply for ILR (where the Sponsor has obtained British citizenship, ILR, protection status or EUPSS), the *private and family life ILR conduct suitability regime* applies (MIL 6.2.10.1)
- Grants are subject to conditions: no recourse to public funds, work and study permitted (ADR9.4)
- As usual with human rights related decisions, the remedy is a right of appeal rather than administrative review (AR3.2(c)(xii), AR5.2(a)(vi))

6.6.1 Relationship requirements

Applicants must be aged over 18 (ADR1.2(d)). Eligible relatives are (ADR4.1):

> (a) the parent; or
>
> (b) the grandparent; or
>
> (c) the son or daughter; or
>
> (d) the brother or sister,
>
> of a sponsor who is in the UK and is a British citizen, or UK-settled, or holds protection status or EUPSS (ADR4.2).

If the applicant is the sponsor's parent or grandparent they must not be in a subsisting relationship with a partner unless that partner is also the sponsor's parent or grandparent and is applying for entry clearance at the same time as the applicant (ADR 5.3A.1). Grandparent includes both biological relationships and those created by adoption (r6).

6.6.2 The 'threshold' requirement

The Rules provide:

> ADR 5.1. The applicant or, if the applicant and their partner are the sponsor's parents or grandparents, the applicant's partner, must as a result of age, illness or disability require long-term personal care to perform everyday tasks.
>
> ADR 5.2. Where the application is for entry clearance, the applicant, or if the applicant is applying as a parent or grandparent, the applicant's partner, must be unable to obtain the required level of care in the country where they are living, even with the financial help of the sponsor because either:
>
> (a) the care is not available and there is no person in that country who can reasonably provide it: or
>
> (b) the care is not affordable.

Where a parent/grandparent apply as partners, only one need meet the care criteria. Those criteria have two dimensions:

- a requirement for *long-term personal care* ('help performing everyday tasks, for example washing, dressing and cooking' suggests the Guidance) to perform *everyday* tasks due to *age, illness, or disability*
- which cannot be met via help from the sponsor because it is *wholly unavailable* (whether from family members or otherwise: the Guidance suggests 'friend or neighbour, or another person who can reasonably provide the care required, for example a home-help, housekeeper, nurse, carer or care or nursing home') or *unaffordable*

An indication of the difficulty of meeting this requirement is given in the examples provided in the HO Guidance:

Example

A person (aged 85) lives alone in Pakistan. With the onset of age he has developed very poor eyesight, which means that he has had a series of falls, one of which resulted in a hip replacement.

> His only son lives in the UK and sends money to enable his father to pay for a carer to visit each day to help him wash and dress, and to cook meals for him. This would not meet the criteria because the sponsor is able to arrange the required level of care in Afghanistan.

The Guidance also holds out the possibility of an ECO referring an applicant for a medical examination at a British Embassy/High Commission using the powers in the IRs 36-39.

Evidential expectations are set out in the Guidance (and thus are no longer via Appendix FM-SE §33-37):

- Birth/adoption certificates to prove family relationship
- Independent medical evidence from a doctor or other health professional re care needs
- Evidence re available care options abroad from a central or local healthy authority, a local authority, or a doctor or other health professional
- Proof of why any private care arrangements cannot continue including proof of financial support and its future non-availability

The ADR regime was challenged in the Britcits litigation: whilst those claims failed in the Administrative Court [2016] EWHC 956 (Admin) and then again in the CoA [2017] EWCA Civ 368, the decisions show that applications might succeed. The CoA made it clear that the provision of care in the home country must be objectively reasonable both from the perspective of the provider and the applicant, and the standard of care must be that required by that particular applicant, having regard to emotional and psychological requirements verified by expert medical evidence. And these extracts from the Administrative Court judgment show how extreme the interference with family life may be in some of these cases:

> "The new rule is certain to interfere with the family life of a significant number of frail and elderly parents [re] the ability to interact personally between applicants and their children and grandchildren and vice versa; the ability of their adult child and sponsor and his family to provide physical care and emotional support for them within a home shared by some or all; the ability to receive personal care from family members rather than strangers. ... valued aspects of family life are inevitably going to be interfered with for the elderly who are fit. By limiting eligibility to those whose personal care needs cannot be met in their country of origin, only those who would be bereft of assistance may be considered."

The Guidance reminds decision makers to '*bear in mind any relevant cultural factors, such as in countries where women are unlikely to be able to provide support in some circumstances.*' Much useful inspiration can be found in the JCWI report mentioned above.

6.6.3 Financial requirement

There is a generalised requirement for adequate maintenance and accommodation (though not via the thresholds and calculations that are necessary for the partner route) (ADR6.1); sponsors without international protection (British citizens and those settled here) must provide an undertaking of responsibility for maintenance, accommodation and care for five years (ADR6.4) where ILR is being granted; or otherwise the duration of PTS (the undertaking must be renewed on each PTS application). The sponsor's undertaking will be legally binding (r35) and steps to recover public funds subsequently received in breach of it may be taken ADR6.5; it is made via the *Sponsor Undertaking Form*. The forms of relevant evidence showing income or cash savings are at ADR6.2:

(a) Bank statements covering the last six months;
(b) Other evidence of income – such as pay slips, income from savings, shares, bonds – covering the 6 months prior to application, salaried employment may alternatively be for last 6 months before a period of maternity, paternity, adoption or sick leave; self-employment income must be for past 12 months; non-employment income must be for past 12 months

(c) Certain forms of income and savings must be evidenced via the criteria set out in Appendix FM-SE
(d) Relevant information on outgoings, e.g. Council Tax, utilities, etc, and on support for anyone else who is dependent on the sponsor;
(e) A copy of a mortgage or tenancy agreement showing ownership or occupancy of a property; and
(f) Planned care arrangements for the applicant in the UK (which can involve other family members in the UK) and the cost of these (which must be met by the sponsor, without undertakings of third party support).

6.6.4 Decision

Successful applicants sponsored by a British citizen or settled person will be given indefinite leave to enter (ADR9.1). They will have no recourse to public funds for the length of the sponsor's undertaking (i.e. five years from the date of entry). The Guidance refers to full access to NHS treatment being available to successful ILR applicants. The government could decide that the NHS is nevertheless entitled to be reimbursed for the cost of any such treatment by the person signing the undertaking.

Those sponsored by a relative with limited leave will be granted leave in line (D-ECDR.1.2), and can apply for ILR at the same time as the sponsor (E-ILRDR.1.1-1.5) (ADR9.2). The sponsor will not need to provide an undertaking on entry, but the applicant will have no recourse to public funds as a condition of entry. The five-year sponsorship undertaking will have to be signed by the sponsor at the ILR stage.

6.6.5 Adult dependent relatives beyond the core Rules

Before the 1 June 2023 creation of a bespoke Appendix, and as with other Appendix FM categories, GEN.3.2 authorised a proportionality balancing exercise for those failing to meet any of the core route criteria (MIL6.1.3). ADR7.1 is to similar effect, though applications may be refused for the more serious of the suitability grounds such as criminality and character (ADR7.2).

One strategy used to bypass the 'entry clearance only' aspect of this route has been to apply on private life grounds, either wholly outside the Rules or by reference to the relevant private life rules. The HO have been known to reject such applications as invalid and to require that the application is made on form FLR(O) (now FLR(HRO) rather than FLR(FP)) as they took the view that there was simply no route under the Rules for an adult dependent relative applying in-country. Time will tell if GEN.3.2 is to be interpreted as creating a route for adult dependent relatives to apply from within the immigration. Perhaps in future FLR(HRO) may be a safer option as FLR(FP) is likely to be amended in line with its intention that, with 'exceptional circumstances', Appendix FM now provides a complete code for consideration under Appendix FM.

Applying SS (Congo) & Ors [2015] EWCA Civ 387, these will presumably be cases where family was life originally established in ordinary and legitimate circumstances at some time in the past and so there is no requirement of exceptional circumstances: merely a requirement to show a compelling case.

It will be necessary to demonstrate that:

- Family life exists (having regard to the cases such as Advic and MT (Zimbabwe) mentioned above at section 6.2.6.1 *Family relationships*) – and it is the strength of that family life which is likely to represent the most significant difference between the case's prospect inside and outside the Rules
- That there has been an interference with that family life (ECOs routinely assert that there is no such interference where the status quo is maintained, though this may be thought inconsistent with Quila [2011] UKSC 45 in the Supreme Court as conveniently summarised by Aikens LJ in MM [2014] EWCA Civ 985 at [116], finding that refusal of entry clearance was likely to be an interference with family life)
- That the interference is disproportionate to the legitimate aim sought to be achieved: see the considerations in our 'Top Tip' below

- In Ribeli [2018] EWCA Civ 611 it was held that where the sponsor could feasibly join the applicant to provide care but decides not to do so, out of choice rather than necessity, then refusal of entry clearance will be proportionate.
- The requirements of the Rules are a useful reference point: where there is a 'near miss' under the Rules, it is more likely that the policy objectives of the Rules are not greatly threatened by the application's success
- Mobeen [2021] EWCA Civ 886 emphasises that the IRs in Appendix FM provide the conventional pathway for entry to UK as an ADR. Where, deliberately or otherwise, someone circumvents that route by coming as a visitor to the UK, overstaying and then applying for leave to remain outside the Rules, they are seekinig present the SSHD with a "fait accompli". This was just the kind of behaviour referred to in Agyarko as undermining a state's right to control its borders.

> **Top Tip**
>
> Relevant factors in a dependant relative case are likely to be:
>
> ☐ Medical evidence demonstrating that a high level of care required: reports from abroad are often sparse compared to UK equivalents. But should still show the diagnosis including severity, prognosis and treatment of conditions
> ☐ Evidence showing this cannot reasonably be provided outside of the family unit e.g. psychological issues, or issues of trust and/or dignity: family tree showing location and non-availability of care within the family
> ☐ Evidence showing there is no publicly funded system of care for the elderly
> ☐ Evidence showing there is no culture of privately funded care, and that experience or research shows that those individuals who might be employed as carers are not capable of addressing issues of emotional and psychological need (make speculative applications outlining care needs)
> Consider obtaining evidence from an independent expert on the care facilities in the country of origin
>
> Remember that these cases may be run in the alternative via ECHR Art 8 (including showing unjustifiably harsh consequences as per ADR7.1). Look for:
>
> ☐ Evidence that family life is established (visits, other forms of communication)
> ☐ That separation was for reasons other than pure choice, or that circumstances have changed since any real choice was exercised
> ☐ Support of the dependent relative without any danger of recourse to public funds
> ☐ Realistic care arrangements amongst a loving family in this country contrasted with isolation abroad, bearing in mind that the European Court said in Pretty v United Kingdom (2002) 35 EHRR 1 at [65] that 'The very essence of the Convention is respect for human dignity and human freedom.'

6.7 Children of settled parent(s)

This category remains under Part 8 of the IRs, IRs 296 to 300, and unaffected by Appendix FM.

We set out the IR 6 definition of 'parent' at MIL 6.4.1. But in summary:

Position of the parents
- All remaining parents in or coming to UK
- OR sole responsibility
- OR exclusion undesirable

Position of the child
- Under 18
- Not living independent life

Under IR296, where a parent is party to a polygamous marriage, and that parent would be refused under IRs 278 or 278A, their children may be refused too (even where they would otherwise meet the requirements of IR297). This was looked at in SG Nepal [2012] UKUT 00265 (IAC).

For entry clearance, the child must be seeking to join or accompany a parent or is present and settled in the UK in the following circumstances:

1. both parents are present and settled or being admitted for settlement or
2. one parent present and settled and the other being admitted for settlement or
3. one parent present and settled or being admitted for settlement who can show that they have had sole responsibility for the child's upbringing or
4. one parent is present and settled in the United Kingdom or being admitted on the same occasion for settlement and the other parent is dead or
5. a parent or another relative present and settled or being admitted for settlement where there are serious and compelling family or other considerations which made the exclusion of the child undesirable and where there are suitable arrangements made for the child's care

Under options 1, 2, and 4, the application will be relatively straightforward. In addition to proving that both parents are settled in the UK, or that one parent is dead, the applicant will need to show they are not leading an independent life (as defined IR6, MIL 2.2.8), and that they can be maintained and accommodated adequately without recourse to public funds.

It is in respect of options 3 and 5 that complications can arise. It can be seen that there are additional requirements that apply where one of the parents resides outside the UK with no intention of joining the child in the UK, or where the child is seeking to join a relative who is not a parent. In such cases, the UK-based parent or relative will have to show a very good reason why the child should be allowed to settle in the UK rather than continue their life in the country in which they are living. These reasons, (i.e. 'sole responsibility' and 'exclusion undesirable') are examined in more detail below.

Prior entry clearance is required where the child is applying from abroad. A child may also apply for ILR from within the UK, whether they have lawful residence or not (as there is no control on switching). The HO does not always accept the reality of claimed parent/child relationships (MIL 5.3.2.3).

6.7.1 In-country applications

Under IR298, a child who is under 18 at the date of application can apply for ILR if they have or have had limited leave in any category. A child who is here as avisitor, for example, can apply from within the UK to settle in the UK if both parents are settled, or one is settled and the other is dead, or the parent here has sole responsibility, or a parent or relative is settled and exclusion of the child is undesirable.

If the child is over 18 at the date of application, they must have previously been granted limited leave as a child in a category leading to settlement, and must still not be leading an independent life.

6.7.2 Not leading an independent life

See MIL 2.2.82).

6.7.3 Sole responsibility

In order to show that the sponsoring parent in the UK has sole responsibility for the child, notwithstanding that they live in different countries, they will need to show that they have been, so far as is possible at arm's length, exercising the normal role played by a caring parent. It is acceptable that the child's day to day care is delegated to another person in the child's own country but evidence that ultimate control rests with the sponsoring parent is required.

The IDIs (chapter 8, Section 5A Annex M) elaborate on the meaning of sole responsibility and state that the following factors are to be used as guidance on how to assess it:

- the period for which the parent in the United Kingdom has been separated from the child;
- what the arrangements were for the care of the child before that parent migrated to this country;
- who has been entrusted with day to day care and control of the child since the sponsoring parent migrated here;
- who provides, and in what proportion, the financial support for the child's care and upbringing;
- who takes the important decisions about the child's upbringing, such as where and with whom the child lives, the choice of school, religious practice etc;
- the degree of contact that has been maintained between the child and the parent claiming 'sole responsibility';
- what part in the child's care and upbringing is played by the non-UK resident parent and other relatives.

The IDIs also say that sole responsibility should have been exercised for a substantial period of time: however in Nmaju v ECO [2000] EWCA Civ 505, the court took a different view, saying that 'Time cannot on its own be a conclusive factor'.

TD (Yemen) [2006] UKAIT 00049 summarises the case law on this issue and holds that the test is whether the parent has continuing control and direction over the child's upbringing, including making all the important decisions in thchild's life. Where the child's non-UK resident parent took any role in the child's upbringing it would have to be clearly established that they had abdicated any responsibility for the child and helped out only under the Sponsor's direction. In Buydov [2012] EWCA Civ 1739 emphasises that TD (Yemen) addressed the situation where both parents remained involved in a child's life, rather than holding that exceptional circumstances were essential before sole responsibility could be found exist in such a case.

> **Example**
>
> Fatima, from Egypt, entered the UK as a work permitholder and has worked as a nurse for over five years. She now has ILR. She is sponsoring her husband and child to come to the UK. This will be a straightforward application on both counts.
>
> However, if Fatima was applying for only the child to come to the UK to join her, it would be a far more problematic application if the father remains involved in the child's life. She would have to demonstrate sole responsibility (i.e. that the father did not financially support or take any important decisions in the child's life) or that the exclusion of the child would be undesirable.
>
> If there is no father involved, and the child has been looked after by Fatima's family in Egypt whilst she has been in the UK, Fatima will still need to show that she meets the sole responsibility requirement, that is that she has directed the child's upbringing and has not fully delegated that direction to her family.
>
> In either scenario, if the child's well-being was threatened, however, then she might have a viable case under the 'serious and compelling circumstances' limb of the rule that we address next.

> **Top Tip**
>
> Factors to look out for in a sole responsibility case are:
>
> ☐ Letters from school(s) in the country where the child lives confirming that they have dealt with the sponsoring parent
> ☐ A formal legal agreement assists: though an explanation will be needed if it gives access rights to the other parent or is unclear: and it doesn't remove the need to document the whole picture
> ☐ Travel by the sponsoring parent to the country where the child lives
> ☐ Records of financial arrangements by which the sponsor pays for education and other needs
> ☐ A lack of contact with the other living parent and an explanation of the reasons for this, and the location of that parent if known
> ☐ Detailed evidence regarding what steps have been taken to provide educational, social, behavioural, and religious guidance

☐ Whether the child(ren) is/are old enough to usefully provide a witness statement

6.7.4 Serious and compelling family or other considerations making exclusion undesirable

There is no particular definition of what may constitute serious and compelling circumstances. Clearly it could cover the scenario where the child faces real problems abroad, as where recent care arrangements have broken down. The phrase 'family or other circumstances' suggests that real benefit to the child *or* to the sponsoring parent/s or other relative is relevant.

Hardward (00/TH/01522; 12 July 2000), suggeststhat the key factors are:

- willingness and ability of the overseas adult to care for the child
- poor living conditions – but not necessarily intolerable
- greater vulnerability of small children.

Article 8 and 'best interests' principles will usually now play an important role in showing the test is met. In Mundeba, the Upper Tribunal adopts a more inclusive approach to the 'exclusion undesirable' test than has traditionally been the case, reading into it at least some of the more child-centred modern considerations one would expect in this day and age. Still, though, the test seems to require something more than best interests. Even where it is difficult to show *serious and compelling* circumstances, ECHR Art 8 still applies of course. See MIL 6.2.6.1 for relevant ECthR decisions. Note though that Mundeba concerned an application for a boy to join his settled adult sister in the UK. A relationship between a parent and child will be seen as generally more compelling, including emotional factors relating to the sponsoring parent.

There is a useful summary of the Secretary of State's view of relevant considerations set out in SG Nepal [2012] UKUT 265 (IAC), The ECO should consider all the evidence as a whole, deciding each application on its merits:

- Are the circumstances surrounding the child exceptional in relation to those of other children living in that same country?
- Are there emotional/physical factors relating to the sponsoring parent in the United Kingdom?
- Are there mental/physical factors relating to the non-sponsoring parent? Where the physical/mental incapability of the non-sponsoring parent has been established, an entry clearance should normally be granted.

The mere fact that the UK offered a higher standard of living than in the child's own country was not relevant, however.

Top Tip
Look out for:
☐ Emotional ties going beyond the normal situation where a family has chosen to live apart ☐ Original separation due to reasons beyond the family's control ☐ Motivation for travel here other than the standard of living ☐ Explanation of why extant care arrangements are no longer available

6.7.5 Adopted children

The admission of adopted children and those being brought to the UK for adoption is provided for in IRs 309A to 316F, glossed by the Guidance *Adopted children and children coming to the UK for adoption*.

The Guidance notes

- Not every combination of foreign law can be catered for expressly and further enquiries may be necessary as to the substantive relationships involved: but '*A clearly demonstrated parenting role in a young child's life that is not provided by anyone else, which it is clear will continue, and where it is also clear that the legal status of adoption into that family will be the outcome in the United Kingdom, will always warrant serious consideration*'
- Though more circumspection is required when the adoption is of an older teenager where the opportunity to adopt has ostensibly long been present

6.7.5.1 Qualifying adoptions

There are several routes under the IRs:

- Hague Convention adoptions: IR316D-316F authorise leave to enter for a child accompanying persons wishing to adopt them who has been entrusted to those persons' care subject to a Hague Convention agreement
- Adoptions from countries whose adoptions are recognised under UK law (listed at *Intercountry adoption: information for adoption agencies*):
    - IR310-313 authorise ILR where both adoptive parents were previously resident abroad or settled in the UK at the time of the adoption
    - IR314 allows limited leave with a view to ILR
- Adoptions to take place in the UK (IR316A-316C)
- *De facto* adoptions, where the child has previously lived with the putative adopting parents but where there was no access to a legal system formally recognising adoption (qualifying under both the IR310-313 and IR 314 regimes)

The rules for adopted children apply to some *de facto* adopted children as well as those adopted through an appropriate and acceptableourt process. *De facto* adoption – not a formal one – or one that is formal but not recognised in the UK is defined IR309A. It must be shown that:

- immediately preceding the application the adoptive parent/parents have been living abroad (if two parents, living together) for at least 18 months of which the 12 months preceding the application must have been spent living with the child
- the adoptive parents must have assumed the role of the child's parents since the beginning of the 18-month period so that there has been a genuine transfer of parental responsibility

Otherwise, the child must have been adopted in accordance with a decision taken by the competent administrative authority or court in his country of origin or the country in which he is resident, being a country whose adoption orders are recognised by the United Kingdom.

Countries which are not appended to the Adoption (Recognition of Overseas Adoptions) Order 2013 are not so recognised. However, there is a oute to recognition of an adoption by a High Court order which succeeded in *W v SSHD* [2017] EWHC 1933 (Fam), and whose criteria are:
 (i)The adoptive parents must have been domiciled in the foreign country at the time of the foreign adoption
 (ii)The child must have been legally adopted in accordance with the requirements of the foreign law
 (iii)The foreign adoption must in substance have the same essential characteristics as an English adoption.
 (iv)There must be no public policy reason to refuse the adoption.

6.7.5.2 Other criteria

Once an eligible adoption is established, then the usual dependency criteria for children apply (MIL 2.2.8) (IR310(i)). Additionally there are a further set of requirements in addition to those for natural children (IR310(vii)-(xi)).

CHAPTER 6: Family-Based Applications

These require that the child:

- has the same rights and obligations as any other child of the adoptive parent's or parents' family; and
- was adopted due to the inability of the original parent(s) or current carer(s) to care for him and there has been a genuine transfer of parental responsibility to the adoptive parents; and
- has lost or broken his ties with his family of origin; and
- was adopted, but the adoption is not one of convenience arranged to facilitate his admission to or remaining in the United Kingdom.

Sometimes a Certificate of Eligibility is required from the relevant Central Authority in England, Wales, Scotland or Northern Ireland. The _Adoption Guidance_ explains the requirements in some detail.

If successful, the child will be granted indefinite leave to enter the UK.

Where a child is joining adoptive parents who have limited leave to remain with a view to settlement, they may apply under IR314 and begranted limited leave to enter. IR316B provides for limited leave to enter with a view to adoption. At the ILR stage for both these categories, under IR311, from 6 July 2018 the KoLL requirement applies to applicants who have turned 18 by the time of the settlement application. If the KoLL requirement is not met, the grant will be of 30 months with no recourse to public funds.

Giv that the provisions for adopted children are so narrowly drawn, adoption cases are often argued under Article 8 ECHR. See e.g. the case of Singh v ECO New Delhi [2004] EWCA Civ 1075. It is possible, if one of the adoptive parents is related to the child through blood or marriage, for an application to be made under IR297(i)(f) if there are 'serious and compelling family or other considerations' which make exclusion of the child undesirable, but this is a high hurdle to cross.

K & Ors [2021] EWCA Civ 1038 observes that the requirement in r309A for _de facto_ adoptions might be unlawful in some cases. Where a prospective adopting parent is a refugee it may be irrational to require them to have lived with the child for the 12 months "_immediately preceding the making of an application for entry clearance_". It was probable that in this scenario the proposed parent would have spent the immediately preceding period fleeing the country of origin and obtaining refugee status, not living in the country of originwith the child. Howeever the issue did not have to be finally determined in this particular case.

6.8 Children born in the UK

A child born in the UK who is not a British citizen nevertheless lacks the right of abode and thus is subject to immigration control. However they are not treated as present unlawfully, as discussed in the HO guidance Nov 09 IDI Chapter 8 Section 4A _Children who are not British Citizens_.

IRs304-309 allow for a child born in the UK to be given leave in line with their parents, which will be particularly important if the family want to travel and return to the UK. The requirements are essentially that (IR305(1)).

- they have at least one parent here with leave, or who is a British citizen or otherwise has the right of appeal or
- parental rights and duties are vested solely in a local authority
- the child is under 18
- was born here
- is not married and is not independent
- if applying for leave to enter, has not been away for more than two years.

Leave will be granted:

- where the parents have limited leave, in line with the parent with daily responsibility for the child's care who themselves has the longest leave (IR306)

- where there is a parent who is a British citizen or has the right of abode, or parental rights are held by a local authority case, by way of ILR (IR308)
- even where the parents are here without leave, a child *may* be granted leave for a period not exceeding three months if both of his parents are in the United Kingdom and it appears unlikely that they will be removed in the immediate future, and there is no other person outside the United Kingdom who could reasonably be expected to care for him (IR307).

The © Guidance is in the IDIS at Chapter 8 Section 4A. It understandably stresses the need to check that any such child has not in fact become a British citizen already. So decision makers should obtain the passports of any such child.

6.9 Refusals of leave to remain on family life grounds and appeals

Refusals of leave to remain on family life grounds will potentially carry the right of appeal, being the refusal of a human rights claim.

This will be either because they are deemed to constitute such a claim in most cases, see Appendix AR at AR3.2(c)((viii), though not domestic violence and bereaved partner cases. Or because the application expressly makes a human rights claim, unless certified as clearly unfounded (under s94 NIA 2002) or raised late (under s96 NIA 2002; the same effect may result from a finding that they do not meet the fresh claim standard if they are made by way of further representations following an earlier claim's refusal) (MIL 14.2, 14.2.3). However the courts have accepted the Home Office can control access to a right of appeal by requiring that applications are made via a particular route (see MIL 6.3.2.3 in domestic violence context & MIL 14.2.3 generally).

CHAPTER 7: Immigration for Business, Work and Study

7.1 Introduction to the Business immigration routes

In this paper edition of *Mastering Immigration Law* we are simply giving an overview of business immigration. The routes are dealt with in far more detail in the online version of MIL, where we provide practical hints and examples, explain the mechanics of each route in detail, and point out aspects of the Guidance that supplement the Rules – we also address Sponsor duties and obligations, and remedies against revocation and suspension of licences there.

As the Eligibility dimension of each route requires the acquisition of points, they are sometimes labelled the Points Based System (PBS). At one time all the PBS routes were found in Part 6A of the mainstream IRs but are now largely located in their own bespoke Appendices – eg Appendix Representative of an Overseas Business and Appendix Skilled Worker. Now only legacy routes (closed to new entrants but with ongoing potential for extension and ILR, subject to sunset clauses) such as Entrepreneurs and Investors remain in Part 6A.

Business immigration requires points to be accumulated for various qualities, depending on the route in question: skills and salary for workers, investment funds and innovative talents for innovators, qualifications and course criteria for students, etc.

It's worth remembering that one doesn't always need a business visa to conduct some business activities. For example visitors may conduct certain business activities under Appendix Visitor: Permitted Activities (MIL 3.3): such as attending meetings, conferences and seminars, giving non-commercial talks, negotiating and signing deals and contracts, attending trade fairs for non-selling promotional work, carrying out site visits and inspections, gathering information for their employment overseas, and being briefed on the requirements of UK based customers for work done outside of the UK.

7.1.1 The business and managed migration routes

These are the various business immigration routes as at Autumn 2023:

- Innovator Founders
- Global talent
- Skilled Work routes
    - Skilled Worker
    - T2 Minister of religion
    - International sportsperson
    - Scale-up workers
- Global Business Mobility routes
    - Senior or Specialist Worker
    - Graduate Trainee
    - UK Expansion Worker
    - Service Supplier
    - Secondment Worker

    - Study in the UK is also structured in line with the business managed migration routes:
        - Student
        - Child student
        - Short-term (English language) student
- Graduate
- High potential individual
- Domestic workers
- Youth mobility scheme
- Temporary work

- Seasonal workers
- Creative worker
- Religious worker
- Charity worker
- International agreement
- Government authorised exchange
- Service providers from Switzerland (MIL 11.13)
- UK ancestry (increasingly treated as an economic route by the HO; MIL 4.1.3)
- Legacy routes
  - Investors
  - Entrepreneurs
  - Representatives of overseas businesses

7.1.2 The scheme of the Rules

The Rules follow roughly the same scheme throughout the business immigration routes. Of course, it is essential to read the precise criteria of each route, but there is very significant overlap between the PBS routes, and in general the validity, suitability, and entry criteria requirements are very similar, as are the criteria for establishing English language proficiency and meeting the financial criteria.

These are the general features of the route. Of course, advisors should carefully read the precise criteria against these generalities.

- **Validity** addresses issues such as

  - Using the relevant form, paying fees and health charges, biometrics, providing satisfactory identity documents by way of passport/travel document
  - Having a Certificate of Sponsorship (CoS) or endorsement issued within 3 months of the application; for students, a Certificate of Acceptance for Studies (CAS) issued within 6 months; the Immigration Health Surcharge must be paid
  - Typically being aged 18 or over, and obtaining written consent to the application if previously funded by a Government or international scholarship agency
  - For in-country applicants the switching criteria are located within validity: one can apply so long as one is not a Visitor, Short-Term Student, Parent of a Child Student, Seasonal Worker, domestic worker in a private household, or hold leave outside the Immigration Rules
  - Applications deemed invalid will be *rejected* (rather than *refused* with the ensuing right to administrative review and s3C protection) - the applicant would then become an overstayer and enter the compliant environment whilst waiting for their application to be determined (MIL 1.3.6)

- **Entry requirements**: applicants outside the UK must obtain entry clearance prior to arrival, and provide a negative TB screening certificate if having spent more than 6 months in an Appendix T country immediately prior to their application
- **Suitability** is subject to the general refusal reasons as well as not being on immigration bail or not being in breach of immigration laws (eg being an overstayer) otherwise than where IR39E of the Rules is satisfied (MIL 1.5.4)
- **Eligibility** is typically satisfied by scoring points re one or more criteria relating to their sponsor, role, contents of their CoS/CAS (start date, details of remuneration/studies, whether Appendix ATAS (MIL 7.2.9) applies, and route specific criteria)
- The **CoS, CAS or endorsement** must be valid and uncancelled, bear the applicant's name, details of sponsorship including job and salary – no reuse of a CoS previously used in a prior application that was granted or refused (though reuse is possible if the application was rejected as invalid, made void or withdrawn); it will confirm if the ATAS requirements apply - CoSs, CASs and endorsement letters are generally valid for 3 months pre-application
- **Genuineness** provisions: an applicant has to satisfy the decision maker that their role is genuine This criteria manifests in various aspects of the work routes

- The job must truly "exist" without being a "sham" or be created for immigration rather than employment reasons: "*created mainly so the applicant can apply for entry clearance or permission to stay*"
- No temporary or permanent '*third party hire*' – ie acting as an agency or providing contract workers for a non-sponsoring third party by way of an ongoing routine service in a way that undermines the sponsorship system because the true employer is not the immigration Sponsor. Migrant workers may be supplied to another organisation so long as the Sponsor retains full responsibility for their duties, functions and outcomes, or outputs of the job
- No suspicion that the job description has been massaged to fit a SOC code which it does not truly merit: an assessment that will take account of whether the role is genuinely needed and the applicant's working history and whether they have appropriate skills, qualifications and experience, and the Sponsor's compliance history

• For work routes, **salary conditions**
- Usually expressed as the higher of a fixed sum or the "going rate" (found in Appendix Skilled Occupations), and by reference to a minimum hourly rate
- Only include guaranteed basic gross pay, pre-tax, including employee's national insurance/pension contributions
- Exclude other pay and benefits, eg non-guaranteed pay due to fluctuating hours, shift, overtime or bonus pay (guaranteed or not), employer's national insurance/pension contributions, allowances for accommodation or cost of living, in-kind benefits, one-off payments, payments re immigration costs or business expenses eg travel to and from the applicant's country of residence, equipment, clothing, travel or subsistence
- Only include salary for the first 48 hours a week (so salary based on additional hours worked above that limit will be pro-rated downwards)

• Routes requiring **job creation** such as legacy Entrepreneurs and modern Innovators need to show new employment roles existing for 12 months complying with all relevant UK legislation including working time and minimum wage requirements, for at least 30 hours a week, with some scope for aggregating hours worked in part-time roles

• Occasionally Tables, of varying complexity and sometimes with the criteria within them divided up into a series of Rows, set out the principal criteria to be satisfied, which are then explained in more detail in the following provisions: for example in Skilled Worker there is a Table at SW.4.2 explaining the various options for acquiring tradable points and then SW.8 to SW.14 explains in detail how each option works

• **Financial requirements**

- met automatically for a person previously lawfully UK resident for 12 months
- those resident for less time or seeking entry clearance must usually show £1,270 as per the evidence laid down by Appendix Finance, unless their endorsing body/sponsor confirms they have been awarded equivalent funding or will otherwise maintain and accommodate up to the end of their first month of employment or first month of the grant of permission
- Re maintenance/investment, funds held abroad must be freely transferable to UK and convertible to sterling – it can be presumed that funds in banks are transferable (so too for FCA-regulated foreign accounts) but other financial institutions should confirm this expressly

• **English language** must be established to the proficiency required by the individual route as per Appendix English language (MIL 2.2.6.1)
• **Dependants** are usually permitted, under the usual PBS regime (though from 1 January 2024 only if studying for a PhD, other doctoral/research-based higher degree. However those funded by Government awards, those already within the route and children born in the UK are not caught by this restriction

- Maintenance balances are £285 for a partner, £315 for the first child and £200 for other children, all additional to the applicant's own required finances, shown as held for 28 days before the application date

- Permission is granted in line with the principal migrant for partners, and in line for whichever parent's leave first expires for children – or in both cases for 3 years if the partner/both parents has/have ILR/British citizenship)
- Conditions will be no public funds access, work permitted with usual caveats, & study subject to ATAS
- Applications are made on *Form Dependant partner/child visa* if abroad, or *Form Dependant partner/child* in the UK
- The usual switching limitations apply as for in-country extensions
- English language at B1 standard
- Partners must be
    o 18+ years of age
    o the partners must be married or in a civil partnership, or be cohabiting in a similar relationship for 2 years pre-application
    o the relationship must be genuine and subsisting with an intention to cohabit during their UK residence
    o any previous relationship must have permanently broken down and they must not be so closely related that marriage or civil partnership would be prohibited in the UK
- Children (the criteria are now largely found in the cross-cutting Appendix Children)
    o must be the child of a parent with (or now being granted) permission in the sub-category or the partner of such a person
    o the parents must either be applying at the same time or be present in the UK with permission (except as a visitor) or
    o where one lacks permission in the route in question, is a British citizen or otherwise has the right to enter and remain in the UK without restriction, and is ordinarily resident
    o one parent is applying as the sole surviving parent, or has sole responsibility for the child's upbringing, or there are serious and compelling reasons for the child to reside with the parent in the sub-category
    o or they must have been born during the time when the principal or partner has permission in the sub-category and
    o a full birth certificate showing both parents' names is required to prove UK birth
    o there must be suitable arrangements for their care and accommodation in the UK complying with relevant UK legislation and regulations
    o they must be under 18 at the application date, unless last granted permission as a dependent of the parent who has (or is applying for) permission in the sub-category
    o must be under 18 unless previously granted as a dependent; if aged over 16, must not be living an independent life
- ILR applications from dependants:
    o The dependant must have already been present as such in the route in question
    o The principal upon whom the applicant is dependant must be applying for ILR at the same time, or already hold it or have become a British citizen on the basis of ILR via the route in question (so long as the applicant was already dependent at that time, or was a UK born child)
    o Partners must have met the relationship requirements throughout their residence
    o For children, the same care and age criteria apply as before, the sponsor must be the sole surviving parent, or solely responsible for them, or there must be serious and compelling circumstances for ILR

- Administrative review is available to challenge refusals – and JR as a last resort
- When new immigration routes are introduced, outstanding applications made before the date the rules entered force will be determined via the old rules: this transitional provision is found in the Statement of Changes introducing each route
- Typically, a permission grant will be subject to all the following conditions:

    - no access to public funds
    - usually, some ability to work additionally to the core business/study in addition to (b), often including self-employment and voluntary work, but not as a professional sportsperson (including as a sports coach)
    - study is permitted, subject to the ATAS condition in Appendix ATAS

- ILR applications, where available, are similarly structured, with the same criteria for validity and suitability. There are additional requirements
    - to be in the UK on the application date
    - to have (or have last been granted) permission in the route in question
    - meeting the criteria in Appendix Continuous Residence: the qualifying period varies, though is typically 5 years, and often time in different routes may be combined
    - meeting the knowledge of Life in the UK requirement as per Appendix KOL UK
    - there may be route-specific earnings requirements
    - to have maintained continuous residence, which is a whole subject in its own right (7.3.10 below)

Legacy routes such as Investors and Entrepreneurs are structured differently, remaining in the traditional PBS format before December 2020. The immigration requirements are in Part 6A of the mainstream IRs, the technical requirements of the investment funds are found in Appendix A, the English language requirements in Appendix B and the maintenance requirements in Appendix C. IR 39B sets out mandatory requirements for specified documents: an equivalent document or an explanation as to the possible availability of such documents in a covering letter would not suffice. There was no provision to correct defects in an application apart from the provisions of IR245AA permitting decision makers to request an extra document where information is missing from the document provided or it is in the wrong format. Another legacy route, that for 'sole representatives' of an overseas business, had adopted the modern structure before it closed for new applicants.

Supporting evidence for modern business routes should be assessed via a more benign attitude from decision makers. The IRs are less strict in the supporting evidence sought, and the guidance now encourages reversion to applicants where documents or information is missing. In general, a *'fair and proportionate'* approach should be taken to the available evidence. Evidence in the expected format is more likely to be helpful to a decision maker and alternative evidence can be sought if that provided is thought inadequate.

Each modern route is accompanied by Guidance. Legacy routes tend to have one set of Guidance for decision makers, one for applicants. Much of the Guidance simply explains the route, often in language barely different from the Rules themselves. However, there are also extra pieces of information found in Guidance: there may be hints on how the HO think about a particular kind of scenario, e.g. by providing practical examples. And explanations are given for other relevant IRs beyond those in the particular route. Sometimes related procedures are explained such as the Immigration Skills Surcharge. And there is discussion of general issues that are in fact applicable across a great many immigration routes, repeated within each individual piece of Guidance, eg validating and translating documents, TB certificates, the ATAS requirement, access for EEA, EU and Irish citizens, and the Immigration Skills Charge. But there are very few examples of meaningful discretion within the Guidance that adds to the Rules.

Migrants and Sponsors in these routes are more concerned to get on with their business than they are to litigate. But sometimes they are nevertheless entangled in unwelcome refusals, so some case law has sprung up:

- Alvi [2012] UKSC 33 held that all mandatory requirements relevant to a grant of leave/permission, including evidential requirements, must be listed in the IRs (MIL 2.4.1). The Guidance is a free-standing code for Sponsors – their duties and entitlements are not set out in the IRs
- Suny [2019] EWCA Civ 1019 notes the central importance of predictability and clarity within the PBS. Those objectives might be compromised if the HO raised concerns beyond the '*parameters set out in the rules*'. Borderline points could always be raised with an applicant within the application process
- Pathan [2020] UKSC 41 held that there is a duty on the SSHD to notify an applicant with an outstanding application promptly of the revocation of their sponsor's licence, it being procedurally unfair not to do so (see fairness more generally MIL 2.6 & 5.5.5). The Guidance now provides that all sponsored workers will be notified of revocation (though not the reasons) to give them a chance to take appropriate action

7.2 The business, work and study routes
7.2.1 Innovator Founders

This route is for establishing a business in the UK based on an innovative, viable and scalable business idea which the applicant has generated, or to which they have significantly contributed.

Previously there were two sub-routes, for Start-ups and Innovators. Start-ups must not have previously established a UK business which commenced trading, unless in their immediately previous period of permission within the Start-up, Graduate Entrepreneur; or as a student on the doctorate extension scheme. They only had to work on the business for the *majority* of their time. Their businesses were assessed more on their development potential than their actual achievements. The Innovator route required £50,000 of investments funds.

Innovator Founders must propose innovative, viable and scalable businesses.

Key features of the route:

- Investment funds are no longer required
-
- Whilst the view of the endorsing body is central, the HO still have the last word, and Innovators are likely to be interviewed
- There must be a genuine, original business plan that meets new or existing market needs and/or creates a competitive advantage, which is realistic and achievable based on the applicant's available resources, where the applicant has, or is actively developing, the necessary skills, knowledge, experience and market awareness to successfully run the business; and there is evidence of structured planning and of potential for job creation and growth into national markets
- Innovators must be sole/instrumental founders with a key role in the business's daily management and development, and have joined the business before it commenced trading, demonstrate that it is active, trading and sustainable, and show significant achievements against the business plan
- Innovators may only work for the business in question, in a capacity contributing to its daily management and development
- Following a cull in Spring 2023 there are only four endorsing bodies (see the list on the www.gov website)
    - Provide endorsement letters valid for three months
    - Should have frank discussions as to the business's present viability before issuing an endorsement – delay may be appropriate
    - Poor immigration compliance of endorsed migrants will not normally be held against an endorsing body, unless there is evidence of systemic non-compliance or deliberate immigration abuse
- Legacy endorsing bodies can continue to endorse their existing client base (endorsed before 13 April 2023)
- Multiple innovators (including co-directors of a company) can apply under the route, but each must receive an endorsement in their own right
- Contact point meetings at which an endorsing body must assess an applicant's progress with their business informing the HO if there is a lack of reasonable progress with the business: at least 2 within their PTS normally after 12 & 24 months
- Two scenarios amongst the general refusal reasons are particularly likely to impact in these categories: withdrawal of an endorsement (r9.25.1) and loss of endorsing body status (r9.32.1) (MIL 2.3.8.3)
- Innovators can attain ILR after 3 years– though only if the business truly prospers, meeting two out of seven objectives: one is easy enough (meeting the business plan & investing the £50k) but the others are tough: doubling customers over that 3 years, engaging in 'significant research and development activity' and applying for intellectual property protection, minimum annual

gross revenue of the business of £1 million, or £500,000 including £100,000 exports, generating 10 full time jobs for settled workers or 5 full time jobs which average salary of £25k
- There are pandemic concessions, eg a one-off extra 12 months' permission for Start-up applicants whose business was impacted by Covid so long as their endorsing body confirms reasonable progress

7.2.2 Global talent

Global Talent and its Exceptional Talent predecessor are routes for talented individuals wishing to work in the UK within in the field of science, engineering, humanities, medicine, digital technology or arts and culture who can show they have exceptional talent or exceptional promise. They will either already be recognised leaders in their field or have been identified as showing exceptional promise such as they are likely to become such.

Applications must be backed by an endorsing body, chosen because of their clear expertise in assessing excellence in their fields of operation: Tech Nation for the IT world, Arts Council England for the arts, and The Royal Society, The Royal Academy of Engineering and The British Academy for the sciences. There is a two-stage application process: firstly an application to the endorsing body, then the immigration application to the HO.

One useful sub-route is permitted work for research organisations as employers for people who have received a research grant or award from an endorsed funder (an approved UK Higher Education Institution or research institute with an established track record of awarding funding based on a rigorous peer review process). This means that individuals working within science, engineering, humanities and medicine applicants can benefit from a fast-track application process where they have the relevant UKRI backing via an appropriate employer and funder. Fast track also applies where they have been appointed to a sufficiently highly ranked research fellowship, received a highly ranked research award, or been appointed to an eligible senior academic or research position.

Applicants who hold one of the prizes listed in Appendix Global Talent: Prestigious Talent do not need to apply for endorsement by an EB. They can make a 'Part 2' application simply with evidence of their prize.

Those in the Arts and Culture, Architecture and Fashion sub-categories must show media recognition via detailed independent reviews, critiques, evaluations or profiles, from credible critics in recognised newspapers or magazines, TV, radio or websites.

Features of the route:

- The HO acts as intermediary between applicant and the endorsing body, forwarding the former's application to the latter, though applications can be made direct to Tech Nation. The HO effectively rubber-stamps the endorsing body's decision. Thus an unreported UT decision (Short [2023] UKAITUR JR2022LON000085) holds that endorsing bodies may be subject to judicial review applications
- The relevant criteria are tailored to the needs of each sector typically split into requirements for track record and for evidencing that record.
  - Arts, culture and architecture applicants must be professionally engaged in producing outstanding performed, presented, distributed or internationally exhibited work, and show regular professional engagement in their field in the last 5 years, evidenced via letters of recommendation from cultural organisations that are established nationally or internationally and eminent individuals with recognised relevant expertise. This is then backed up with supporting evidence of media recognition, prize winning, proof of appearances etc. There are equivalent requirements for fashion and film
  - In the Digital Technology field, technical applicants must demonstrate proven technical expertise in building, using, deploying or exploiting a technology stack and building technical infrastructure. Business applicants must demonstrate proven commercial, investment, or product expertise in building digital products or leading investments in significant digital product businesses

- Science, Engineering, Humanities and Medicine applicants (with the British Academy, the Royal Academy of Engineering, the Royal Society, and UKRI) must be active researchers in a relevant field and have a PhD or equivalent research experience. There are three fast-track routes, for those with an individual fellowship for current or recent holders of listed peer-reviewed research fellowships or named awards; academic and research appointments at a listed institution; and endorsed funders carrying out research at a UKRI-listed research organisation funded by a UKRI-listed endorsed funder
- Exceptional Talent is for those who can already make a case for being a leader in their field (including some degree of international recognition) and Exceptional Promise is for potential leaders
- No genuineness testing by the HO
- No English language requirement within Global Talent (or its predecessor Exceptional Talent) route until the settlement stage is reached
- No maintenance requirement
- No annual cap on applicant numbers
- Extensions are possible so long as the original endorsement remains valid and has not been withdrawn, and the applicant has earned money in their endorsement field or, if a prize-based applicant, the field of their prize
- When applying, applicants must request a period of leave from 1 to 5 years. If their application is successful they will be granted the period of leave they requested; there is no maximum limit on time spent in the route
- There is access to ILR after 5 years for Tech Nation endorsees, 3 years for others; they must be applying from the Global Talent route though their residence may mix periods as an Innovator or within the skilled work routes (though not Graduate Entrepreneur). They must have earned money in their field during their UK residence
- Dependants may join principal applicants and seek ILR (though only after 5 years)

7.2.3 Skilled Workers

These routes enable UK employers to recruit workers to fill a particular skilled vacancy. Whilst those travelling from abroad need prior entry clearance there are now much more significant opportunities to switch into the routes than was the case vis-á-vis their predecessors in the old Tier 2.

The general policy is that migration under this route should not displace settled workers suitable for the role in question. However, this is achieved by focussing on recruitment into genuinely skilled occupations rather than demanding formal proof of an advertising campaign. One can only apply for jobs at a certain skill level, as set out in the Tables in Appendix Skilled Occupation. The resident labour market test has been abandoned (although evidence of the vacancy's genuineness must still be provided). So too have other aspects of the red tape that long plagued the Tier 2 routes: there is no longer a cap on numbers, nor is there a cooling off period barring one's return to the UK, nor a ceiling on the time spent in the route.

Instead we have genuineness testing (above, 7.1.2), aimed at ensuring that the migrant is the right fit for the role. Decision makers will carefully consider whether the salary and job description have been massaged to inflate a role that does not truly warrant the grant of a visa.

Features of the route:

- Points are acquired via sponsorship, appropriate skill level job and English language
- Appendix Skilled Occupations lists the jobs which can be sponsored
  - Table 1 lists most of those which qualify, Table 5 lists those too unskilled to qualify, and Tables 2-4 list health and education roles
  - Table 1 gives the Occupation Code, then gives any related job titles, and provides the going rate by way of annual salary and hourly rate. It also conveniently provides the discounted rates for each Code within the tradeable points categories: these variously allocate points for discounted salaries depending on the qualifications or scarcity of the skills of the worker

CHAPTER 7: Immigration for Business, Work and Study

in question. Notably the jobs are all based on a 39-hour week so some arithmetic may be needed for working weeks of different lengths.
- Appendix Shortage Occupation list relevant jobs – this changes based on recommendations from the Migration Advisory Ctte: from 2022-2023 we saw new roles added in the agriculture and fishing trades, carpenters, joiners & bricklayers
- There is a sub-route, the Health and Care route for qualified doctors, nurses and allied health professionals (including within the social care sector) who have been trained to a recognised standard and who have good working English: found in the *Health and Care Guidance*
- A change of employment application is required where there is a change of employer, or of core duties sufficiently to change SOC code or depart the Shortage Occupations list
- There is no longer a 'cooling off' period before workers can return to the UK to resume a new job
- The usual work **Genuineness** criteria apply
- **Sponsorship** requires
  - A valid CoS (which cannot be reused if previously part of a refused or granted application) bearing salary and PAYE details
  - A start date within 3 months of the application
  - An A-rated Sponsor unless extending permission
  - The job must have been allocated to the Sponsor in entry clearance cases: this is a *Defined CoS* requested for the specific job and salary shown where for an entry clearance application, ie not from an employer's general allocation
- **Appropriate skill level** requires
  - An eligible occupation code listed in Appendix Skilled Occupations
  - The genuineness criteria for jobs
- Sponsors must pay the Immigration Skills Charge, subject to exemptions eg for students switching to Skilled Worker, where entry clearance is sought for less than 6 months or workers consistently in the route since before April 2017 workers. Small or charitable sponsors pay a lower ISC: ie those with charitable status, or subject to the small companies' regime as set out in the Companies Act 2006, or with no more than 50 employees. The scale ranges from £364 to £1,820 dependent on the length of the visa for these small firms; or £1,000 to £5,000 for medium and large sponsors
- There are various salary thresholds within the tradeable points option. Thus the earnings target may be £26,200, £23,580, or £20,960, depending on an applicant's qualifications, on whether it is a shortage occupation, and on whether they are a new entrant to the occupation. There are six options, Option A to Option F, by which salary points can be traded. Options A-E require an hourly rate of at least £10.75 (except for Option F). It must not be circumvented by claiming that some of the hours are "overtime". Then:
  - **Option A** (SW8): **Salary > £26,200** and the going rate for the occupation code
  - **Option B** (SW9): **PhD**: eligible job, UK or Ecctis-recognised qualification (evidenced on initial application), a credible explanation for PhD's relevance to the job (necessary on each application), points being awarded for a single qualification, and salary exceeding £23,580 or 90% of the SOC's going rate. Not all occupations are eligible for tradeable points for a relevant PhD qualification: one must check the "Eligible for PhD points (SW)?" column in Table 1 of Appendix Skilled Occupations.
  - **Option C** (SW10): **PhD** as per option B, but in a **STEM subject** (science, technology, engineering or maths), with salary exceeding £20,960 or 80% of the SOC's going rate
  - **Option D** (SW11): **skill shortage job** in the relevant UK nation where it is based as per Appendix Shortage Occupation List – unless job was removed from that List on or before date COS was assigned where applicant is extending as a shortage occupation Skilled Worker and is in same job with same sponsor, with salary exceeding £20,960 or 80% of the SOC's going rate. The Guidance notes that there are some SOC codes where not all the jobs within the code are on the shortage occupation list: in which further information should be sought
  - **Option E** (SW12): for New Entrants (ie the various alternatives at SW12.2(a)-(g)): of which the sixth is the much-vaunted return of a "post study work" option). The HO should revert if

the claim to meet an Option is unclear. In this sub-route the total period of leave/permission should not exceed 4 years in total as Skilled Worker/Tier 2 Migrant/Graduate. Salary exceeding £20,960 or 70% of the SOC's going rate, and then one of the following sub-categories:
- *aged under 26* on application date
- *postdoctoral position* in one of the SOC codes specified for chemical, biological, physical, social and humanities scientists, nature and science professionals or higher education teaching professionals,
- working towards a *recognised professional qualification* in a *UK regulated profession*: the website for The Centre for Professional Qualifications (CPQ: the organisation which covers all aspects of professional qualifications in an international context) has a list of the various kinds of regulated professions
- working towards full registration or chartered status with the *relevant professional body*
- *for an extension application, where most recent permission was as a Graduate Entrepreneur or Graduate*
- an extension application where most recent permission (other than as a visitor) was *as a student which expired less than 2 years before application date* (or where one still holds permission as a Student), at level of UK Bachelors/Masters/PhD/ Postgraduate Certificate in Education or Professional Graduate Diploma of Education, and the course is completed (or will be completed within 3 months – PhDs may just have completed 1st year)

- **Option F** (SW13): Table 2 job in Appendix Skilled Occupations (ie **health and education**) with salary exceeding £20,960 or the SOC's going rate, though for nurses and midwives there may be a temporary salary dip for up to 8 months where they are returning to work or working towards their NMC registration
- Re salary
  - going rates will be pro-rated to working pattern, based on a 39-hour week for roles in Table 1 of Appendix Skilled Occupations
  - there are some transitional arrangements for those who were previously on the Tier 2 general route, permitting guaranteed allowances to count towards salary threshold, salary of £20,800 or the '*going rate*' sufficing for those first entering route before 24 November 2016, and for scientists and higher education teaching professionals
- English language ability at B1 for all four language components (reading, writing, speaking and listening)
- Some further employment beyond the sponsored work is permitted
  - Supplementary employment is permitted. This refers to extra work other than for the job specified on the CoS if it is in either a job in Appendix Shortage Occupation List or a job in the same occupation code as the job for which the CoS was assigned, for no more than 20 hours a week outside the CoS's working hours
  - Secondary employment refers to work which does not fall under supplementary employment. Such employment must be sponsored so requires its own CoS and the HO must authorise the change of conditions of the original permission granted to cater for the change. This cannot be sought until the migrant has begun work for the first sponsor
- Dependants are allowed: generally in line with the Sponsor or three years where the Skilled Worker is being granted ILR
- Principals in the route receive entry clearance/permission for 14 days after expiry of their CoS (up to a maximum of 5 years from the CoS's start date) (specialty-training doctors get an extra 4 months to give them a chance to find a sponsor)
- ILR is available for both the principal and dependants after 5 years in the route: time in some other business routes can be aggregated. Skilled Workers must still retain their licensed Sponsor who should confirm they still require them and will pay the relevant salary (£26,200 or the '*going rate*' if higher) subject to being within certain shortage occupations or health/education/scientific/higher education roles in which case £20,960 suffices.

7.2.4 Ministers of Religion

This route is for a Minister of Religion undertaking preaching and pastoral work, or for a Missionary, or Member of a Religious Order, taking up employment or a post/role within their faith community. The route is to be contrasted with the Temporary Work - Religious Worker role, which is for more routine religious duties short of the full responsibilities of a Minister of Religion. Ministers are expected to lead the congregation in performing rites, rituals and preaching the essentials of the creed as its core duties.

- The specific eligibility criteria are

    - being qualified to do the job of a T2 Minister of Religion;
    - being a member of the sponsor's religious order (if the sponsor's organisation is such a thing); and
    - performing religious duties within the sponsor's organisation or directed by the sponsor's organisation in the UK (which may include preaching, pastoral and non-pastoral work); and
    - fulfilling a role excluding mainly non-pastoral duties, such as school teaching, media production, domestic work or administrative and clerical work, unless the role is a senior position within the sponsor's organisation; and
    - showing pay and conditions at least equal to those given to settled workers in the same role and compliant with the national minimum wage; and
    - being based in the UK

- English language ability at B1 for all four language components (reading, writing, speaking and listening)
- Permission is granted for
    - Entry clearance: the *shorter* of these two periods: 3 years and 1 month, or up to 14 days after the job on the CoS ends
    - Permission to stay: the *shorter* of these three periods: 3 years, or up to 14 days after the job on the CoS ends, or the difference between 6 years and the period they have already been granted in this route or as a Sportsperson/Skilled Worker (or any combination of these routes)
- Partners and children can join
- The route leads to settlement
    - After 5 years in the route, or in combination with periods as a Sportsperson, Skilled Worker, Tier 1 routes save for Graduate Entrepreneur, representative of an Overseas Business, or Innovator or Global Talent
    - The Sponsor must confirm they still require the migrant and retain their own sponsorship status

7.2.5 International Sportspersons

- Points are scored via the offer of a job by a governing body endorsement, a financial requirement and possessing a valid CoS – additionally English language at level A1 is required if permission is being sought beyond 12 months
- A letter from the Sports Governing Body and the CoS must establish that the applicant
    - is internationally established at the highest level
    - can show their employment will make a significant contribution to the development of their sport at the highest level in the UK
    - is qualified to undertake the job
    - has been issued a unique endorsement number from the appropriate governing body specified in Appendix Governing Bodies which identifies the various governing bodies); and
    - intends to be based in the UK
- The Guidance indicates that genuineness will seldom be an issue unless there is some overt evidence that calls the job into question

- Permission is subject to the usual conditions - with the additional employment option as a sportsperson for the applicant's national team while their national team is in the UK, playing in British University and College Sport (BUCS) competitions, and temporary engagements as a sports broadcaster providing guest expert commentary on a particular sporting event
- ILR is available after 5 years (as per same combinations as for Minister of Religion above):
  - Having been granted permission >12 months at some point in the route,
  - Sponsor must confirm they still require the migrant and retain their own sponsorship status and will pay the applicant at least £35,800 per year via basic pay (excluding overtime and other allowances/benefits, and shares as an employee-owner), though some guaranteed allowances are permitted

7.2.6 Scale-up Worker

The Scale-up Worker visa, introduced on 22 August 2022, allows individuals to come to the UK to do an eligible job for a fast-growing UK business. Applicants require a confirmed job offer to work for an approved scale-up business for at least 6 months, a valid CoS, a job offer on the list of eligible occupations and to be paid a minimum salary. After that probationary sponsorship period, they are free to take alternative work or self-employment options

- There is an initial two-year grant and then unlimited three-year extensions; ILR after five years
- Dependants are permitted
- A scale-up business is one specifically HO-approved to sponsor in this route having grown by 20% annually for 3 years from a base where it had at least 10 employees (& must be A-rated)
- Eligible jobs are those found in the Guidance *Scale-up: going rates for eligible occupations* (Appendix Skilled Occupations identifies these too)
- Earnings during the sponsored period must be the higher of £34,600 per year, £10.75 per hour or the 'going rate' for the type of work: the generic salary criteria apply
- For the unsponsored period after 6 months in the route:
  - monthly PAYE earnings equating to £34,600 (£33,000 if their last recent permission was off a CoS assigned pre-11 April 2023) for at least half the time in the route are needed, allowing for absences for parental/adoption/sick leave, based on guaranteed gross pay including employee contributions to tax/national insurance, though no other earnings (no self-employment, non-UK earnings, employer contributions, etc)
  - There should be no reasonable grounds to believe the PAYE earnings, or any part of them, is fabricated, inflated or unrelated to genuine employment, having regard to proof of the paying business's existence and its lawful genuine trading, payments from other parties and anything else
- English language at B1 and the usual financial requirements
- ILR is available after 5 years continuous residence (in this route alone or combining most other work categories). The usual criteria apply re validity and suitability, the salary must be £33k/34,600 pa at the application date, and at that same level for 2 of the 3 preceding years (subject the usual permitted absences, earnings restrictions and genuine earnings proviso).

7.2.7 Global Business Mobility

These are all sponsored routes. As always, the Rules should be read alongside the relevant guidance documents. For applicants, the guidance is *Global Business Mobility Routes* ('GBM caseworker guidance'). There is separate sponsor guidance, *Sponsor a Global Business Mobility worker* ('GBM sponsor guidance'), which should also be read to give a complete picture of the routes. Appendix Skilled Occupations addresses eligible occupations and going rates.

Some of the criteria are generic between the routes.

- Validity, including switching, Suitability and Entry criteria are the same as for the business immigration routes generally

- Sponsorship requirements - applicants in each route score twenty points by meeting the generic requirements, plus some route-specific sponsorship requirements set out under the relevant headings below
  - A valid CoS. The Sponsor must be authorised by the HO to sponsor workers under the relevant route. Sponsors must normally be A-rated, unless the worker one is applying to extend their leave in the same GBM route with their existing sponsor, or is applying as a UK Expansion Worker, is the sponsor's authorising officer and the sponsor has a provisional rating
  - The CoS must contain the necessary specified information: the applicant's name; details of the job and salary offered, for Senior or Specialist Workers, Graduate Trainees or UK Expansion Workers, details of any allowances, and PAYE details, if applying as a Service Supplier or Secondment Worker, confirmation that the job's pay complies with the National Minimum Wage, the job's start date, within three months of the application date, confirmation whether Appendix ATAS applies, and details of the working history abroad; and for Service Suppliers or Secondment Workers, confirmation of which of the Sponsor's HO-registered contracts they will work on
  - No reusing of a CoS in a prior application that was granted or refused (though reuse is possible if the application was rejected as invalid, made void or withdrawn)
  - Applicants must have worked outside the UK, as relevant, with the sponsor group, as an overseas service provider, or for the overseas sponsor business, for a specified period: see the relevant route-specific headings below. IR 6 defines '*sponsor group*' and '*overseas service provider*':
  - 'Sponsor group' means "*the sponsor and any business or organisation that is linked to the sponsor by common ownership or control, or by a joint venture on which the applicant is sponsored to work*"
  - 'Overseas service provider' means a business based outside the UK with no commercial presence in the UK, that is
    "*(a) a natural or legal person that has a contract to provide services to a UK business, where that UK business is on the register of licensed sponsors maintained by the HO; or*
    (b) a natural or legal person that is subcontracted to provide services to a UK business by a natural or legal person coming within paragraph (a)"
- **Genuineness requirements**. No points will be awarded if the decision-maker has reasonable grounds to believe that the job does not exist, is a sham, or has been created mainly for immigration purposes. Where there are concerns about genuineness, the application may be put on hold pending a compliance visit to the Sponsor (as explained in the GBM caseworker guidance). If the decision-maker believes the applicant may be complicit in any lack of genuineness, they may invite the applicant to interview and put this allegation to them. There may be no third party hire: see the provisions for Skilled Workers above
- **Sponsorship requirements**: each route requires applicants to score 20 points by meeting sponsorship requirements. The Senior or Specialist Worker, Graduate Trainee and UK Expansion Worker routes then require a further 40 points, made up of 20 each for the applicant's job being at the appropriate skill level and their salary at the required level. The Service Supplier and Secondment Worker routes require only a further 20 points, for the applicant's job being at the appropriate skill level.
- **Salary** – applicants under the Senior or Specialist Worker, Graduate Trainee and UK Expansion Worker routes receive points scored by meeting or exceeding both of the 'general salary requirement' and 'going rate requirement'.
  - When calculating these requirements, 'salary' includes only guaranteed basic gross pay, guaranteed allowances throughout the employment period or paid as a mobility premium or to cover the cost of UK living. If an allowance is solely for the purpose of accommodation, it will only be counted up to a maximum of 30% (for Senior or Specialist Workers and UK Expansion Workers) or 40% (for Graduate Trainees) of the total salary
  - Salary does not include any other pay or benefits. To minimise the scope for confusion, each route lists examples of pay and benefits which will not be counted, such as one-off 'golden hellos', in-kind benefits, or bonuses. The GBM caseworker guidance suggests,

however, that pay given up as part of a salary sacrifice schemes will not be deducted from the salary calculation
- The general salary requirement applies where the applicant's job is in an occupation code listed in Table 1 of Appendix Skilled Occupations. (ie all roles except health and occupation codes with going rates based on national pay scales.) The salary requirement is £45,800 yearly for Senior or Specialist Workers and UK Expansion Workers, and £24220 yearly for Graduate Trainees. Only the first 48 hours of work a week count towards this requirement.
- There are transitional provisions for Senior or Specialist Workers applying for permission to stay if previously granted leave as a Tier 2 (Inter-Company Transfer) Migrant under the rules in force before 6 April 2011
- The going rate requirement for Senior or Skilled Workers and UK Expansion Workers is 100% of the relevant occupation code's pro-rated going rate, identified in Appendix Skilled Occupations. For Graduate Trainees it is 100% of the pro-rated going rate for Table 2 occupations (health and occupation codes with going rates based on national pay scales), or 70% for Table 1 occupations (all other roles). Occupation codes in Table 1 set the going rate assuming 39 weekly working hours

- **Established connection with Sponsor** - applicants are required to have an established connection with their sponsor or any linked overseas business. In general, they must have (a) worked outside the UK for the sponsor or a linked business for at least twelve months, which do not need to be consecutive; (b) worked for the sponsor or a linked business (outside or inside the UK) for the twelve months preceding the application; and (c) be currently working for the sponsor or a linked business. Breaks in the period of continuous work are permissible for maternity, paternity or parental leave, statutory adoption leave, sick leave, assisting with a national or international humanitarian or environmental crisis, with the agreement of the sponsor group, and participation in organised industrial action
  - What is an eligible linked overseas business depends on the route being applied under, as explained in the GBM caseworker guidance.
  - For Senior or Specialist Workers and Graduate Trainees, businesses or organisations (a) linked to the Sponsor by common ownership or control or (b) having a joint venture with the Sponsor, on which the applicant is being sponsored to work.
  - For UK Expansion Workers, a business or organisation linked to the Sponsor by common ownership or control.
  - For Service Suppliers, (a) an overseas service provider with a contract to provide services to the sponsor, on which the applicant will be working, (b) the applicant's own self-employed business as a service provider that is contracted to supply services to the sponsor, and (c) a subcontracting business (including self-employed) that will provide services to the sponsor via a contractual chain
  - For Secondment Workers, an overseas business that has a contract with the sponsor that forms the basis for the secondment

- **Maximum length of assignments** - there is a limit on how long applicants can spend on GBM routes: the '*maximum cumulative period*'. The limit is 5 years in any 6-year period. For Senior or Specialist Workers applying as a high earner, the limit is 9 years in any 10-year period. (Senior or Specialist Workers not applying as a high earner are subject to the same '5 years in 6' limit as other GBM applicants.)
  - All periods of permission under the GBMs in the 6 or 10-year window count towards this maximum, including leave extended by section 3C of the Immigration Act 1971. Permission granted on the old Intra-Country Routes is also counted. The maximum cumulative period covers all GBMs. For example, time spent as a Graduate Trainee will count towards the maximum cumulative period if later applying as a Senior or Specialist Worker
  - In most cases, if an applicant's job end date would take them beyond the maximum length of assignments, permission will be granted for whatever shorter period is permissible. In the case of Graduate Trainees, however, permission will be refused. The GBM caseworker guidance explains that this is because Graduate Trainees are undertaking structured training programmes, which they would be unable to complete if not granted permission up to the requested end date.

- **Conditions of permission**: no access to public funds, work is restricted to the job for which the applicant is being sponsored, voluntary work, and working out a contractual notice period for a job held lawfully in the UK at the date of application.
  - Senior or Specialist Workers extending leave formerly held under the Intra-Company routes; they are permitted supplementary employment in a job on the shortage occupation list, for no more than 20 hours a week, and outside the CoS's working hours. Study is permitted, subject to Appendix ATAS
  - The period of permission varies between the routes.
    - For Senior or Specialist Workers, whichever is shortest of (a) 5 years from the job's start date; (b) 14 days after the job's end date, or (c) the maximum period to avoid exceeding the maximum length of assignments
    - For Graduate Trainees and UK Expansion Workers, the shortest of (a) 1 year from the job's start date; (b) 14 days after the job's end date; or (c) the maximum period compatible with the maximum length of assignments requirement
    - For Service Suppliers, the shortest of (a) 14 days after the job's end date; (b) the maximum period compatible with the maximum length of assignments requirement; or (c) the 'maximum single assignment period'. If the applicant is covered by the UK-EU Trade and Co-operation Agreement or Temporary Agreement between the Swiss Confederation and the United Kingdom of Great Britain and Northern Ireland on Services Mobility, the 'maximum single assignment period' is 12 months. Otherwise, the 'maximum single assignment period' is 6 months
    - For Secondment Workers, the shortest of (a) 1 year from the job's start date; (b) 14 years from the job's end date; (c) the date at which the applicant will have had continuous permission as a Secondment Worker for 2 years; or (d) the maximum period compatible with the maximum length of assignments requirement
- **Dependant partners and children** – as per PBS dependants generally
- **Administrative review** of refusals is available

7.2.7.1 Senior or Specialist Worker

This sub-route of the GBM enables senior managers or specialist workers to come to the UK to work for a UK business linked to their overseas employer. It replaces the Intra-Company Transfer route.

The key features of the route are:

- Points are acquired for Sponsorship, Job at an appropriate skill level and Salary at required level
- **Sponsorship** requires a valid CoS showing current employment for the firm in question
- **Appropriate skill level** requires an appropriate code that is considered genuine in the sense of the most appropriate code having been identified, and there being a genuine need for the job, for which the applicant has the appropriate skills, qualifications and experience, and the Sponsor's compliance history. The skill level criteria is relaxed for some applicants in creative roles such as artists, authors, actors, dancers, choreographers and product/clothing designers who were present under the GBM's predecessor routes
- **Salary:** certain requirements vary depending on the level of the applicant's salary. Applicants earning a salary of at least £73,900 (based on a maximum 48-hour working week) are classed as '*high earners*' (r6) and benefit from certain criteria being relaxed.
  - The maximum length of assignments for high earners is nine years in any ten, rather than five years in any six
  - Applicants for permission to stay who (a) were granted leave as a Tier 2 (Intra-Company Migrant) under the rules in force prior to 6 April 2011, or as a Work Permit Holder and (b) since then have continuously held permission as an Intra-Company Migrant or Senior or Specialist Worker:
    - Do not need to meet the general salary requirement, though they must still meet the going rate requirement

- o Are not subject to the maximum length of assignments requirement. They will therefore be granted leave for whichever is shortest of (a) 5 years after the job start date or (b) 14 days after the job end date, without reference to the maximum length of assignment
- **Immigration skills charge** must be paid

7.2.7.2 Graduate Trainees
Most of the criteria are as for generic GBM.

- Graduate Trainees are subject to the length of overseas work requirement as per other GBM routes, but only need to show 3 months of work for the sponsor group outside the UK, as opposed to the normal 12 months
- They are subject to an additional skill level requirement - their job must be part of a structured graduate training programme, with clearly defined progression towards a managerial or specialist role within the sponsor organisation

7.2.7.3 UK Expansion Workers
This route is the heir to the sole representative route (see 7.2.8), and is significantly more restrictive than its predecessor. It describes itself as for overseas workers who are undertaking temporary work assignments in the UK, where the worker is a senior manager or specialist employee and is being assigned to the UK to undertake work related to a business's expansion to the UK. The business must be linked to the sponsor by common ownership or control, and not have begun trading in the UK. Dependants by way of partners and children can qualify.

- Normally Authorising Officers for the purposes of sponsorship must be UK-based. The *Workers and Temporary Workers: guidance for sponsors (Part 1: Apply for a licence)* explains that the Authorising Officer may be based overseas for this route. That same Guidance goes on to explain that pending the migrant's arrival, they must sponsor themselves with a CoS allocation of 1
- UK Expansion Workers benefit from the same distinction between high earners and others as Senior or Specialist Workers. High earners are those with a gross annual salary of £73,900 or more, based on a maximum working week of 48 hours
- They do not need to meet the length of overseas work requirement, but only need to show that they are currently working for the sponsor group
- Unlike Senior or Specialist Workers, high earners in the UK Expansion Worker route are subject to the same maximum length of assignments requirement as other applicants, namely five years in any six
- There is also an exception to the overseas work requirement for Japanese nationals seeking to establish a UK branch or subsidiary of their sponsor group under the UK-Japan Comprehensive Economic Partnership Agreement. Like high earners, these applicants only need to show that they are currently working for the sponsor group.

7.2.7.4 Service Suppliers
- Service suppliers must be applying to work on a contract with an overseas service provider. The contract must be registered with the HO, and the service must be covered by one of the UK's international agreements (CARIFORUM-UK (the Organisation of African, Caribbean and Pacific States), Australia & New Zealand)
- The details of the contract must be stated on the Certificate of Sponsorship
- Service Suppliers have two ways to meet the skill level requirements, called option A and option B. Option A matches the skill level requirement in other routes, and is met if the applicant is sponsored for a job in an eligible occupation code, and the sponsor has chosen the most appropriate occupation code. Option B concerns educational and professional qualification and length of relevant work experience. Its requirements are:
    - The applicant must hold a university degree or equivalent level technical qualification, subject to exceptions for particular service industries: fashion and modelling or entertainment services do not need one, chef de cuisine services can rely on an advanced technical qualification, advertising or translation services just need to show 'relevant

qualifications', and applicants providing technical testing and analysis services may rely on a degree or 'a relevant technical qualification'
- The applicant must hold any professional qualifications or registrations needed to lawfully provide the relevant services in the UK
- Applicants must have three years' experience working in the relevant sector. For self-employed overseas services providers, and those supplying chef de cuisine services under the CARIFORUM-UK Economic Partnership Agreement, the requirement is for six years of experience
- There is also a nationality requirement not found in the other routes: applicants must be a national of the country or territory in which the overseas service provider is based, unless the service is covered by a commitment in a relevant international agreement such as the General Agreement on Trade in Services or the UK-EU Trade and Cooperation Agreement
- Re the overseas work requirement, the guidance explains that this should be interpreted as continuously working in the same sector as the service they are providing to the sponsor for the 12 months immediately before the date of application. This work can be both self-employed or employed and in or out of the UK

7.2.7.5 Secondment Workers

Secondment Workers must:

- To meet the sponsorship requirements, be working on a contract (detailed on the CoS) between their Sponsor and an overseas business which is registered with the HO
- If extending their stay in this sub-route to continue working for the same sponsor, they do not need to meet the length of overseas work requirement

7.2.8 Representatives of overseas businesses

Overseas businesses looking to establish a branch or subsidiary in the UK should now use the Global Business Mobility UK Expansion Worker route. But one long-standing business immigration route which predated the Points Based System was for representatives of businesses based overseas. It was commonly known as the *sole representative* route and was in place for many years, permitting individuals to move to the UK to represent their companies here. The route is now only open to media representatives.

Previously there were 2 routes:

(1) Sole representatives of overseas businesses
(2) Media representatives: ie employees of an overseas media agencies on long-term UK assignments

But from 11 April 2022 the "sole representative of overseas business" limb closed to new entrants, being replaced by UK Expansion Worker, one of the Global Mobility routes. Existing migrants may extend their permission.

The media representatives route is for employees of an overseas newspaper, news agency or broadcasting organisation being posted on a long-term assignment as a representative of their overseas employer. Its criteria have consistently been significantly more relaxed than those for sole reps.

- There is no limitation to being a sole employee
- There is no particular requirement for seniority: the guidance gives examples as producers, news cameramen & front-of-camera personnel (but not secretaries or administrative support staff)
- However, they must intend to work full-time as their employer's representative

Features of the sole representative of an overseas business route:

- Key criteria were being a senior employee of an active and trading overseas business, the business abroad having no active UK branch, subsidiary or other representative coming for the purpose of representing that business in the UK and establishing and supervising a registered

branch or wholly-owned subsidiary – the UK had to actively trade in the same type of business as that overseas business - applicants could not own more than 50% of the overseas business
- A1 English language was required and proof of maintenance and accommodation
- From June 2020 stricter rules were brought in - applications were increasingly scrutinised closely for "*genuineness*" of business expansion including the overseas company's track record and the applicant's skills and experience
- The overseas business may carry out a few very limited activities before sending a sole representative to the UK, for example creating an independent legal existence as a legal entity, setting up a bank account and identifying and setting up business premises. But this work cannot be carried out by direct employees of the overseas business. Any business conducted in the UK must be via distributors or intermediaries
- Dependants were permitted

Extensions of permission remain possible (for 2 years on a 5-year settlement route) where the applicant has established the registered branch or wholly-owned subsidiary and

- can maintain and accommodate themselves adequately
- is not in breach of the immigration laws other than via the permitted overstaying under IR39E
- can show
  - that the overseas business still has its headquarters and principal place of business outside the UK
  - evidence of salary paid by the employer in the 12 months immediately before the date of application and details of the renumeration package
  - that he is still required for the employment in question, as certified by his employer,
  - that he has generated business, principally with firms in the UK, on behalf of his employer since his last grant of leave, via accounts, copies of invoices or letters from firms who the applicant has done business with, including the value of transactions and a Companies House certificate of registration as a UK establishment (for a branch), and
  - a certificate of incorporation (for a subsidiary) with either a copy of the share register or a letter from the company's accountants confirming that all shares are held by the parent company

There are then similar criteria for ILR though English language is then required to B1 standard.

To extend permission in the route media representatives must show they are still engaged in the relevant employment, are still required for the employment in question and that they are in receipt of a salary from his employer, evidenced via the salary paid in the previous 12 months and the remuneration package's details.

7.2.9 Student routes

There are presently three student routes (though of course many immigration routes permit study, as will be found in the '*conditions of leave/permission*' heading of the relevant route).

- Appendix Student, for applicants aged 16 or older seeking to study an approved qualification with a licenced sponsor
- Appendix Child Student, for applicants aged between 4 and 17 seeking to study at an independent school
- Appendix Short-Term Student (English Language), for applicants intending to study an English language course for 6 to 11 months

Each Appendix details the requirements an applicant must satisfy to be granted entry clearance or permission to stay in the UK. Though the Appendices are largely self-contained, to completely understand their requirements it is also necessary to refer to Appendix Finance, Appendix English language and the Introduction to the IRs which defines a number of important terms.

There are significant similarities between the Student and Child Student routes. Key to both routes is the need for a Sponsor, who issues a Confirmation of Acceptance for Studies (CAS) which underpins the visa application. A CAS must comply with numerous formalities, such as the provision of information about every aspect of the proposed studies. The Short-term Student route is unsponsored.

- **CAS**: The Student route allows students to come to the UK to study with a sponsoring institution. The sponsor will issue a CAS which underpins the visa application – like a CoS, it is the electronic record and not any paper printout which matters. It must have been issued within the last 3 months before the application and may not be reused where previously part of an application which was granted/refused (though may be reused if the application was invalidated), and should show course fees/accommodation costs and payments already made towards them. The CAS should record how English language has been assessed. Entry clearance applications may not be made more than 6 months before a course starts (3 months for in-country extensions)
- **Sponsors and their duties:** Numerous aspects of immigration control are essentially devolved downwards to the Sponsor, who has significant record-keeping and reporting duties
    - They must report students who they suspect have breached any conditions of their leave or not sufficiently engaged with their course
    - If a student's Sponsor loses their licence during their studies for failure to maintain adequate standards of compliance, students' permission will normally be curtailed to end 60 days from the date of the HO's notification letter, presuming they are not deemed complicit
    - The status of the Sponsor institution impacts on the courses they may study, the conditions of the grant, and sometimes on the evidence supporting their application. Broadly, applicants whose Sponsor has a track record of compliance get a better deal so long as they are a '*higher education provider*, ie education institutions offering higher level courses such as degree courses, post-graduate courses, or courses for the Certificate in Education
    - Legacy Sponsors are not permitted to sponsor any new students but can continue to sponsor their extant students. Thus a CAS emanating from a Legacy Sponsor will only be acceptable where the relevant studies are for completion of a course already commenced, by way of re-sitting examinations or repeating a module of a course
- Applicants under the Student route, and applicants under the Child Student route who are aged 16 or 17, must satisfy the decision maker that they are *genuine students*. The decision-maker will first consider the material a prospective student provides with their application. If at this stage the decision-maker doubts that the applicant is a genuine student, in general they must then invite the applicant to a credibility interview. They will then decide whether, on the balance of probabilities, the applicant is a genuine student, having regard to study and career plans, immigration and education history, knowledge of the course and the broader personal and financial picture
- Study must be at an **appropriate level**, depending on the status of the sponsor's licence (more limited if only a probationary licence is held), and lead to an approved qualification. There are limitations on the ability to study "below degree level" courses for more than 2 years, or on studying courses "at degree level" for more than 5 years (always in the sense of the total leave granted, not merely the period spent studying or the length of courses). There is no specified maximum period of study for '*above degree level*' courses. Degree level is defined as Level 6 Regulated Qualifications Framework (RQF) or Level 9 or 10 Scottish Credit and Qualifications Framework (SCQF). Ecctis-recognised institutions abroad may have their students pursue short-term study abroad at degree level plus in the UK, and there is scope for Foundation Programmes for postgraduate dentists/doctors and pre-sessional courses in B2 English language
- **Place of study**: all study must generally take place on the premises (subject to pandemic concessions) except for course-related work placement, overseas study abroad programme or pre-sessional courses
- **Course requirements**:
    - There must be a single course of study leading to an approved qualification (including ones validated by Royal Charter, awarded by a UK recognised body, at or above RQF level 3 (SCQF level 6 in Scotland)). If the Sponsor has a track record of compliance this may be part-time or full-time; otherwise the course must be full-time
    - If below degree level it must involve a minimum of 15 hours classroom-based daytime study per week between 08:00 and 18:00 on weekdays
    - There is some scope for pre-sessional English language courses

- If the course involves a work placement, the placement must be assessed as an integral part of the course, and must not take up more than half/a third of the course length for studies respectively above/below degree level
- If the student will be studying towards an ACCA accountancy qualification or Foundation qualification, the Sponsor must be an ACCA-approved learning partner at Gold or Platinum level
- Alternatively, the Student may study a pre-sessional course, such as an English language primer in anticipation of degree-level study
- The applicant's **Qualifications** to enter the route must be evidenced by transcripts or certificates
    - The '*differential evidence*' rule benefits nationals of EU Member States, Australia and the USA, those with British National (Overseas) status, or with passports issued by Hong Kong SAR, Macau SAR, or Taiwan, in which case the evidence of finances and qualifications is relaxed, subject to HO discretion to request to see the full material
    - Foreign qualifications are assessed by Ecctis (formerly UK NARIC), the UK body which recognises and compares international qualifications and skills, confirming that the level of the academic, vocational or professional award is equivalent to a relevant UK qualification
- **Full-time studies:** Students will ordinarily study full-time, but there is provision to permit part-time study at sponsoring institutions with a track record of compliance with immigration law. Those studying at institutions with a track record of compliance get a better deal generally
- **Part-time studies** are permitted at higher education providers with a track record of compliance. Neither the Rules nor Guidance define any particular number of hours as comprehensively amounting to full-time or part-time study; the latter suggests that a course can be defined as part-time by the sponsoring institution
- **Maximum study period:** Students are not permitted to return to the UK repeatedly to study at the degree level or below. There is a maximum of two years' permission for studies below degree level, and five years above degree level. There is no restriction on studies above degree level
- **Academic progression**: applicants seeking further permission to stay must always show "*academic progression*"; i.e. that their new course of study will be at a higher level than their present or former study
- **Academic Technology Approval Scheme (ATAS)**: Appendix ATAS requires some students to obtain an ATAS certificate to ensure their studies do not empower weapons of mass destruction, generally research orientated, eg mathematical and computer sciences, biological sciences etc, though there are some exempt nationalities: all EEA states, Switzerland, Australia, Canada, Japan, New Zealand, Republic of Korea (South Korea), Singapore and the USA, issued by the FCO's Counter-Proliferation Department
- **Student Union Sabbatical Officer**: The Student route may be used by those seeking to work as a Student Union Sabbatical Officer during or immediately after their studies. The post must be full-time, salaried and elected, and based at the sponsoring institution unless elected to a National Union of Students. Applicants may either be in the course of their studies or be sponsored to fill the position for the academic year immediately following graduation and may then work in this position throughout the period of leave, for up to 2 years
- **Parental consent**: Applicants under 18 must have the written consent of their parents or guardians. If one parent has sole legal responsibility, their consent will be sufficient. Legal guardianship is determined according to the local law of the applicant's nationality. This consent must confirm support for the application itself, the applicant's living and care arrangements in the UK and, where relevant, the arrangements for the applicant's travel to and reception in the UK
- **General refusal/cancellation reasons** bespoke to students: for withdrawal of Sponsorship, breaching conditions, failing to engage with their course, or being required to withdraw for academic or disciplinary reasons, and for loss of the Sponsor's licence
- **Finances**: Applicants will be required to show they have sufficient funds to support their study in the UK for full course fees for the first year and living costs for nine months. The necessary funds will be made up of course fees and living costs, which will vary depending on the applicant's living arrangements and place of study, as per Appendix Finance criteria. Money must be held in the student's own account or that of a parent/guardian/UK carer, and may come from an official student sponsor (a government, educational institution or the British Council) or from the student and their family. Student loans must be dated within 6 months of the

application. The financial requirements vary according to whether the studies are located in the Greater London Area or outside it (£1,334 or £1,023 per month)
- **English language**: Applicants applying to study a course below degree level must demonstrate ability at level B2, or B1 at degree level or above
- **Conditions**:
    - No access to public funds
    - Only studying at the course for which the CAS was assigned, or at their Sponsor's partner institution, and there is more ability to switch courses if at a higher education provider
    - Supplementary studies in any subject are permitted so long as not on a scale that might itself require sponsorship
    - **Work** (including voluntary work) is permitted to certain degrees (though not in roles which would fill a permanent full-time vacancy unless awaiting a successful switch to Skilled Worker):
    - Full-time students at degree-level or above may work 20 hours per week during term-time if their sponsor is either a higher education provider with a track record of compliance or an overseas higher education institution. Outside of term-time these students may work full time
    - Full-time students at below degree-level may work 10 hours per week during term-time if they are sponsored by a higher education provider with a track record of compliance. These students may work full-time outside of term-time
    - All students may undertake work as part of a work placement
    - Students seeking to switch to working routes must have completed the course of studies for their extant CAS, or if on full-time degree-level+ courses with sponsors with track records of compliance may apply so long as their CoS has a start date no earlier than their course completion date, or by studying at PhD level+ with the CoS starting no earlier than 24 months from their CAS start date (these restrictions are found within the destination work routes)
    - Students on a recognised Foundation programme may work as a postgraduate doctor or dentist
    - Students may not be self-employed or engage in business activity
- **Covid concessions**: The pandemic's impact on studies is addressed in the Guidance. Absences need not be reported whether for sickness or self-isolation, there is no need to report changes in teaching regime, and sponsorship can continue for those on distance learning so long as blended or in-person teaching resumed by 30 June 2022, CAS allocations will not normally be reduced where Educational Oversight inspections are delayed, and course start-dates, and studies, may be deferred, the latter beyond 60 days. Digital copies of record-keeping documents are acceptable where in-person checks are not feasible (see also MIL 4.2.19)
- **Period of grant**:
    - All successful applicants will be granted permission for the duration of their course, plus a period before and after the course depending on how soon entry clearance is granted before the course start date, and the length and type of course. This is intended to permit a certain amount of time to get established in the UK, then a period to identify a way to extend one's permission or plan one's return abroad
    - All courses of 6 months or longer (and pre-sessional courses of any length) will lead to the applicant being granted 1 month before the course start date. However, this period will be cut down if entry clearance is granted within 1 month of the course start date, in which case the applicant will be given a period of leave starting 7 days before their intended date of travel. If entry clearance is granted less than 7 days before this intended date of travel, it will be granted with immediate effect
    - A course of 12 months or more will lead to a period of 4 months following the end date of the course being granted. If the course is longer than 6 months but shorter than 12, 2 months after the end date of the course will be granted. If less than 6 months the period post-course will be 1 month for a pre-sessional course and 7 days otherwise. Lastly, postgraduate doctor and dentistry courses are a special case, and will always see a period of 1 month post-course being granted.

The **Child Student** route is for children aged 4 to 17 years looking to be educated in the UK at an Independent School. Academies and schools maintained by a local authority cannot sponsor students under this route. If a foster carer or a relative (not a parent or guardian) of the applicant will be responsible for the applicant's care then there are detailed arrangements for their welfare. These arrangements must be evidenced via confirmation that the accommodation is a private address, and of the intended care arrangements and the availability of adequate funds for maintenance. Students who are still minors require the consent of their parents or legal guardian to their proposed study, reception and care arrangements. Specified documents are required to establish the parental relationship.

The **Short-term Student** route is for those coming to the UK to study an English language course for between 6 and 11 months. Applicants are not required to have a sponsor, and there is no Confirmation of Acceptance of Studies; though the prospective student must still provide written confirmation from their course provider that they have been accepted onto a suitable English language course. The route does not specify exact financial requirements. Instead it simply requires that applicants have sufficient funds to support themselves. Grants of permission are subject to strict requirements that Short-term students undertake no work or other study while in the UK.

However, the precise funds and level of English language proficiency required continue to be specified in the student routes themselves, and the 'general' Appendices contain rules specific to applications under the student routes.

Across all three routes, students will have no recourse to public funds. They may only work subject to strict conditions, if at all, and Students and Child Students must restrict themselves to the course of study stated on their CAS. Work placements which are part of the assessed element of their course and employment as a Student Union Sabbatical Officer are also permitted. For child students, there is a bar on working under the age of 16.

7.2.10 The Graduate Route

The return of a post-study work route was long awaited in the managed migration sector. Expectations were finally met with the introduction of Appendix Graduate on 1 July 2021. In one sense it replaced the Doctorate Extension Scheme which closed on that date. The basic idea is to provide an opportunity to work following the successful completion of an eligible course of study at UK bachelor's degree-level or above. There are no financial requirements for maintenance or accommodation; nor are there English language criteria: the SSHD is able to rely on successful negotiation of the Student route as an assurance in those respects.

Features of the route:

- The relevant qualification is being previously present as a Student at degree-level (plus certain professional courses where statutory requirements make the qualification a prerequisite of performing "*reserved activities*" within the profession)
- Aside from the typical validity and suitability criteria, there are three substantive criteria: successful completion of studies (at a higher education establishment with a track record of compliance) with respect to a qualification of a particular level (degree-level plus and certain professional courses), completing a minimum period of study physically in the UK (the whole course for studies under a year or 12 months of longer courses, with some dispensation for remote learning due to the pandemic)
- For shorter courses of up to 12 months the full duration of the course must have been in the UK; for longer ones, 12 months must have been completed here. There are saving provisions to help out students where pandemic measures replaced their in-person studies with distance learning
- This working route does not require a Sponsor, nor a CAS (though details of the last CAS will be needed to apply). It does not lead to settlement
- Permission to stay is non-renewable: 2 years is normally granted (or 3 years for PhD level-plus applicants, 2 years being apposite for a student on an integrated PhD course who has completed the lower postgraduate element)
- Dependants are allowed, but only where they were already a student dependant; they do not need to apply at the same time as the Graduate
- The Rules are found within Appendix Graduate; there is also Caseworker Guidance and a Fact Sheet. The Guidance explains that during the pandemic era, those who Student permission has expired, but who have a valid exceptional assurance, will be able to switch into the Graduate route. The application fee is £822

7.2.11 High Potential Individual route

This route was created from 30 May 2022 with a view to encouraging migration of graduates from the world's leading universities. Applicants must be aged over 18 at the application date. Entry clearance or permission to stay will be granted for 3 years for PhD+ qualifications, 2 years for other qualifications. This is a route that gives access to unsponsored work opportunities, though it is not a settlement route. Applicants must not have been previously granted permission under the Student Doctorate Extension Scheme, as a Graduate or as a High Potential Individual

Points are acquired via obtaining a degree from an appropriate institution, English language proficiency (level B1 at reading, writing, speaking and listening) and financial criteria (10 points – £1,270 for those without 12 months' lawful UK residence met by holding relevant funds as per Appendix Finance for 28 days.

The degree must be confirmed by Ecctis as meeting UK Bachelors/postgraduate standards from an institution on the Global Universities List at the date of the degree award.

7.2.12 Temporary Workers

These routes are for certain types of temporary workers helping cultural, charitable, religious or international objectives including volunteering and job shadowing. There are six sub-categories:

1. **Creative workers** – for people coming to the United Kingdom to work or perform as sports people, entertainers or creative artists for up to 12 months (subject to further extension of up to 24 months)
2. **Charity workers** – for people coming to the United Kingdom to do unpaid voluntary work for a charity
3. **Religious workers** – for people coming to the United Kingdom to work as religious workers in a supporting role including preaching, pastoral and non-pastoral work
4. **Government authorised exchange** – for people coming to the United Kingdom through approved schemes that aim to share knowledge, experience and best practice
5. **International agreement** – for people coming to the United Kingdom under contract to provide a service that is covered by international law: for example, the General Agreement on Trade in Services
6. **Seasonal workers** – generally for seasonal agricultural roles

The general rationale of CoSs granted under the temporary worker route is that the individual will not be basing themselves in business here or posing any threat to the resident labour force. As always applications are assessed for genuineness, where there is reasonable suspicion as to their ability to fulfil the role in question. For this reason, the role must be a *supernumerary* one in most of the sub-categories – ie one that is beyond the usual requirements of the employer and which they would not otherwise be recruiting to fill (eg where the worker offers pastoral support to others as part of their own personal development but would not be replaced if they were no longer available). This ensures that the Temporary Work migrant is not filling a genuine vacancy that should have be made available to a settled worker.

It is difficult to switch into a Temporary Work route. Generally speaking one must have permission in already, making them entry clearance only routes. However Students who previously studied at UK recognised bodies/higher education institutions may switch into the Government authorised exchange worker route. .

Conditions are typical of business immigration routes: no recourse to public funds, study subject to Appendix ATAS, and only employment as specified in the CoS, subject to certain caveats: supplementary employment for most sub-routes, other voluntary work for charity workers, Sponsor-authorised roles for Government Authorised Exchange, and work in other households for private servants in a diplomatic household.

Creative workers

These visas are for Creative Workers. Those who can make a unique contribution to the UK's rich cultural life eg as an artist, dancer, musician or entertainer, or as a model contributing to the UK's fashion industry. Dependents are allowed. There is no route to settlement. One can switch into the route only if present with permission as a standard visitor in the UK undertaking permitted activities in the creative sectors where the CoS was assigned before entering the UK; permission may be extended if already on the route. Creatives enjoy a dispensation as to the place from where they may apply for entry clearance: they may apply to an entry clearance post where they are residing at the time of the application, provided that the relevant post is one which has been designated as appropriate for this route, and the applicant is living there lawfully for a similar purpose to the activity proposed for their UK stay.

Charity workers

This route is for those wanting to undertake voluntary fieldwork with a Sponsor authorised for this route contributing directly to the Sponsor's charitable purpose in the UK. The work is classed as unpaid, though reasonable expenses as defined in the National Minimum Wage Act 1998 may be paid. The role must not be of a sort which might replace a permanent position, including on a temporary basis.

The Guidance explains these are activities which would not normally be offered at a waged/salaried rate and which does not include work ancillary to the charitable purpose. So roles in routine administrative work, retail/sales work, fund-raising and maintaining the office are excluded. They must not have held permission in the route in the 12 months before their application, unless they can prove they were not in the UK at any time over that period.

They receive entry clearance for the shorter of 12 months or the period of the role in the CoS plus 14 days extra before and after. In PTS cases, they are granted the shorter of the role's period as set out in the CoS plus an extra 14 days, or the difference between the period already spent in the UK as a charity worker and 12 months.

Religious workers

Religious workers will be performing religious duties, via work within or directed by the Sponsor's organisation, which may include preaching, pastoral work and non-pastoral duties: these duties must be outlined in the COS. This must not be of the same order as the work of a Minister of Religion, who leads the congregation in performing rites, rituals and preaching the essentials of the creed as its core duties (the higher level role being found in the Minister of Religion route).

The role requires the applicant be a member of a religious order (where the Sponsor *is* such an order), with pay and conditions equal to those of a settled worker in the same role and at the national minimum wage threshold. There remains a resident labour market test in this sub-route, which requires that national records of all putative candidates who are settled workers who could fill the role are supplied and confirmation that none is in fact available, and that a national recruitment search was undertaken, advertised via appropriate national media or on the sponsor's website if that is the means by which it normally reaches out to the relevant community, or via Jobcentre Plus/Job Centre Online or in the employment section of a national newspaper; advert reference numbers and the period of advertising (for at least 28 days before the CoS was issued) must be provided.

Government authorised exchange

This route is for those coming to the UK through approved schemes aiming to share knowledge, experience and best practice via work placements, whilst experiencing the wider social and cultural setting of the UK. It must not be used to fill job vacancies or import unskilled labour. The maximum period of grant depends on the relevant exchange scheme. Typically, applicants may come for 12 or 24 months depending on the scheme, but there are exceptions (e.g. the Jamaica Nursing Exchange has a maximum period of 10 months).

The central idea is that individual employers and organisations cannot act as Sponsors, with the exception of schemes for sponsored researchers approved by the Department for Innovation, Universities and Skills, and Government Departments and their Executive Agencies. So, applicants must identify and apply to the appointed overarching body, which in turn must have the support of a UK government department. These bodies oversee numerous schemes, and range from the Bar Council to the Scottish government. Both sponsors and the various approved schemes are listed in Appendix Government Approved Exchange Schemes.

There are four types of scheme within this route:

1. **Work Experience Programme** – volunteering, job-shadowing, internships and approved work experience programmes
2. **Research Programme** – only those working on specific scientific, academic, medical or government research projects at UK higher education institutions or other research institution operating under the authority and/or financial sponsorship of a relevant government department;
3. **Training Programme** – only those receiving formal, practical training in the fields of science and/or medicine, those receiving training by HM armed forces or UK emergency services, or those who obtained a UK degree at Bachelor's or Master's level during their last grant of leave who are sponsored for required postgraduate training/work experience in that degree's field who are not filling a permanent vacancy in the sense that the Sponsor would be aiming to employ them in that role at the training's end.
4. **Overseas Government Language Programme** – schemes that are fully or partially funded by overseas governments or government sponsored organisations, for those undertaking development placements to build and/or enhance foreign language skills and foster good cultural relations in the UK.

Permission may be extended in this category. A person may switch into these schemes from student leave if they were last sponsored by a higher education provider with a track record of compliance, or an overseas higher education institution (to do a short-term study abroad programme in the UK). However students may do so only where they have completed a UK recognised bachelors or postgraduate degree during that last period of permission, are currently sponsored for a period of postgraduate professional training or work experience which is required to gain a professional qualification or registration in the same field as their degree, or an internship for up to 12 months which is directly related to their degree. And students must not be filling a permanent vacancy and their sponsor must not intend to employ the applicant in the UK once the training or work experience is completed.

The CoS must confirm that they meet the relevant Appendix GAE Schemes requirements, that the role will not fill a vacancy in the domestic workforce, and is listed in Table 1 or Table 2 of Appendix Skilled Occupations.

Applicants may be under 18 so long as they have written consent from both parents or legal guardian. Permission from one parent is enough if they have sole legal responsibility for the applicant. This consent must confirm support for the application, the applicant's living arrangements in the UK and, if the application is for entry clearance, the applicant's travel arrangements.

The maximum time in the route is specified in a separate set of Rules, Appendix GAE Schemes. GAE workers are granted entry clearance for the shorter of: the relevant maximum period therein or the period of the role in the CoS plus 14 days extra before and after. Permission to stay is granted for the shorter of: the CoS plus 14 days extra, or the maximum period permitted by Appendix GAE Schemes and the time spent under the route already, or the difference between 25 months and their actual PTS within the GAE route including any period when IIR39E applied.

International agreement

There are various sub-routes here.

- Private servants in diplomatic households
- Employees of overseas governments and national organisations (the Sponsor must guarantee the migrant will not try to change to a different sub-category within the international agreements after entering the UK)

- Via an international agreement, i.e. the General Agreement on Trade in Services, or equivalents such as the EU-Andean multiparty trade agreement, the EU-Chile trade agreement and the EU–CARIFORUM (post Brexit, now the CARIFORUM-UK) agreement

This route formerly included contractual service providers and independent professionals. They are now dealt with under the Global Business Mobility routes.

Private servants in diplomatic households

There are the main criteria:

- They must be employed as a private servant by, and in the household of a named member of staff of a diplomatic or consular mission or a named official employed by an international organisation recognised by the UK government with diplomatic privileges or immunities under UK or international law
- Where they had permission under the rules in place from 6 April 2012 and are applying to extend their permission they must still be working for the same employer, and have done so throughout their time in the UK in this sub-category. Once they have built up 3 years in the route, they may be granted a further period of leave to take them up to 5 years in the route; they were then able to apply for ILR (until 9 November 2022 when HC719 deleted this route)
- They must not be undertaking any other role than private servant in the household, must intend to work full-time in that role, must not be their employer's relative (or their spouse's relative) by blood or marriage. They must intend to leave the UK at the end of their stay, be paid at least the national minimum wage, and must provide evidence that they are not carrying out the kind of work identified in reg 57 of the National Minimum Wage Regulations 2015 (which includes the requirement that they are not treated as a family member benefitting from the provision of living accommodation and meals and the sharing of tasks and leisure activities)
- There is a specimen employment contract for overseas domestic workers set out in Appendix Domestic Worker Statement. This must be provided as part of the eligibility requirements.

They are granted entry clearance for the shorter of: 24 months, or the period of the role in the CoS plus 14 days extra before and after. In permission to stay cases, they are granted the shorter of: the role's period in the CoS plus 14 days extra before and after, or 24 months, or the difference between five years and the period already spent in the UK since their last grant on the International Agreement route.

International Agreement Workers

These are for employees (under a contract of employment) of overseas governments or other international organisations. They must have a degree level qualification subject to certain exemptions and possess any professional qualifications/registrations required in the UK. They must be employed by a company based in a country with a relevant trade agreement under which they are supplying services, which has no commercial presence in the UK with a contract to supply appropriate services under that agreement (and the sponsor must be the final consumer of the services provided, the contract must not exceed 12 months and must have been awarded via an open tendering procedure or another procedure guaranteeing its bona fides).

These routes were amended to include EU nationals and Swiss nationals (and permanent residents in Switzerland) to take account of the United Kingdom-European Union Trade and Cooperation Agreement and the Temporary Agreement between the Swiss Confederation and the United Kingdom of Great Britain and Northern Ireland on Services Mobility. Thus EU nationals, Swiss nationals and permanent residents of Switzerland can benefit from the routes.

Applicants may extend their permission to stay if they continue to meet these requirements and the CoS is issued by the same sponsor and for the same contract. They receive permission for periods in line with domestic servants above.

Seasonal (Edible Horticultural Sector) Worker

The impact of Brexit on farm labour and related activities has received much publicity. The seasonal worker route was created from 10 January 2019 to address the needs of the edible horticultural sector. Occasionally other occupations with labour shortages such as pork butchers, poultry workers and lorry drivers enter the route. Applications must be made online on gov.uk on the "Temporary Worker visa" form. There is no provision to apply for permission to stay: this is an entry clearance-only route. The general refusal reasons apply with full force.

Under this route one must be sponsored by an A-rated sponsor who continues to be approved at the date the application is decided. Sponsors must also be endorsed by the Department for Environment, Food and Rural Affairs (re the Seasonal Worker route) and hold a license by the Gangmasters and Labour Abuse Authority). The Guidance states that only two overarching bodies (the "scheme operators") have been approved: Concordia (UK) Ltd and Pro-Force Limited. This pilot is subject to an annual quota of 10,000, set by the HO, and divided between the 2 scheme operators. The job offer must also remain current since the CoS was issued.

The CoS must make it clear that it is issued for a role in the edible horticulture sector, identified as those growing precisely defined produce, ranging from field and glasshouse vegetables to cut flowers and pot plants.

7.2.13 Youth mobility scheme

This route is for sponsored young people (aged 18-30) from participating countries and territories who wish to live and work temporarily in the UK – to experience life here, as the Guidance puts it. Applicants must either

- Be from a country listed in *Appendix Youth Mobility Scheme: eligible nationals*, namely, Australia, Canada, Hong Kong, Iceland, India (for whom this is packaged as the India Young Professionals Scheme visa), Japan, Monaco, New Zealand, the Republic of Korea, San Marino, Taiwan & Andorra (from 31 January 2024); or
- Be a British Overseas Citizen, British Overseas Territories Citizen or British National (Overseas) (there is no annual cap on numbers for these applicants)

British Overseas citizens, British Overseas Territories citizens, and British Nationals (Overseas) do not need to meet any sponsorship requirement.

- There are a certain number of places reserved for each of the countries in the Eligible Nationals Appendix, so it is always necessary to be alive to how many places remain available at the relevant time (eg Australia has 30,000 places, Japan has 1,500)
- Japan, Taiwan, Hong Kong, the Republic of Korea and India are subject to *Invitation to apply arrangements* whereby the SSHD selects applicants at random from those expressing an interest in the scheme; applicants must act within the stated period in the subsequent invitation to apply (further details are given in the Eligible Nationals Appendix and the Guidance on how to enter the ballot system)
- Nationals of Hong Kong, India, Japan, the Republic of Korea and Taiwan are subject to 'invitation to apply' arrangements. Prospective applicants must submit an expression of interest to the HO, who will select at random individuals to invite to apply for leave
- In addition to invitation to apply arrangements, there are some other country-specific criteria (not for nationals of Australia, Canada, Monaco or New Zealand, who only need to meet the financial criteria). Nationals of India must hold a qualification at Level 6 RQF or equivalent, proven by written confirmation from the issuing institution, or have three years' or more work experience in a professional role listed in Appendix Skilled Occupations; they, as well as nationals of San Marino and Iceland must provide letters from the police authorities or their equivalents as to their good character issued within the last six months
- Applicants must be below the age of 31 at the date of application (35 years for nationals of New Zealand; Australia & Canada too from 31 January 2024), and over the age of 18 by the time their entry clearance becomes valid. They may not have any dependent children, either living with them or financially dependent on them and must hold funds of £2,530

- Entry clearance is given for two years; PTS for 3 years is available to nationals of New Zealand (Australia & Canada too from 31 January 2024). This is not a settlement route

Conditions attaching to entry clearance/permission will be no access to public funds & study as per ATAS restrictions. Work is permitted, though not employment as a professional sportsperson/coach, and self-employment only where the individual owns no business premises beyond their home, has no employees and has equipment not exceeding a total value of £5,000.

7.2.14 Tier 1 Entrepreneur

For a person with sufficient means and the right frame of mind, the Entrepreneur route represented one of the more accessible ways of entering the UK for business immigration purposes. Although the Entrepreneur route is now closed to new applicants, existing Tier 1 Entrepreneurs can apply to extend their visa until 5 April 2023 (or 6 July 2025 if they ever had leave as a Graduate Entrepreneur). The requirements are found in Table 5 of Appendix A and r245DD.

However, the route was, and continues to be, fraught with challenges:

- the genuineness test (by which HO decision makers assess not only the *credibility* of the application but also its *feasibility* as a business venture),
- the fabulously detailed supporting document requirements which are likely to frustrate any but the most devoted reader of small print
- the difficulties in meeting the consistent employment requirements for an extension of leave. Therefore, it is crucial when entering the route to understand the requirements for future extensions: otherwise the path to further leave may be blocked

Points to note:

- A person could apply in their own right or as a member of a two-person entrepreneurial team
- The investment funds could come from the applicant, or from a third party, such as a family member, or from one of the external sources identified by the Rules which independently vet the quality of the business proposal, like seed funding competitions and UK government departments. Where funds came from a third party, there were numerous details that had to be provided in the supporting documents, including some that were known to unhorse some applicants, like the need for the bank to confirm that the funds promised to the applicant on this application had not also been affirmed as available to someone else. There is a specimen template letter at Annex D of the Guidance to applicants, Document 1
- The investment had to be made into the business via cash funds, a director's loan or shareholding. Those who had already made all or part of the investment before they applied had to do so only via investing in a way that showed up in the company accounts, bringing into play a broader variety of specified evidence. Investment funds had to remain available to the applicant until spent for business purposes
- Certain business activities were ruled out: particularly property development and management, and also activities that amounted to disguised employment such as simply working for another business. The general requirement was to hold funds of £200,000. However, this was modified in some circumstances, eg where the applicant had sourced funds from certain trusted sources which had independently verified the business, such as winners of seed funding competitions or those backed by UK government departments, and for Graduate Entrepreneurs. The investment funds had to go towards the expansion and establishment of the business: thus, any element of initial investment that was then paid back to the applicant by way of remuneration did not count. So, it paid to scrutinise the proposed investment in the context of the business model
- A business plan had to be provided in order for the decision maker to understand and assess the application. The business idea could be tested by the HO for genuineness: this was as much about assessing the viability of the business as it was about its credibility. The genuineness testing stage was the main contributor to the high refusal rate in this category: at least half of all applications were refused. An extension can be refused when evidence that had permitted entry to the route was re-assessed in a broader context (see also MIL 11.10.2.3)

There was a separate route for Graduate Entrepreneurs (now Start Up visa), who may apply if they have been endorsed by a UK higher education institution *or the Department of International Trade*. They could exit their sub-category into the general Tier 1 Entrepreneur route, and only required £50,000 of investment funds when so doing.

One could switch into the Entrepreneur route from Tier 1, Tier 2 and from Tier 4 where there was a trusted sponsor. Over time the *switching opportunities* to enter the route diminished: eg at one time Tier 1 General migrants could apply, but that route closed on 6 April 2015; similarly, Post-Study Workers could apply, until their own cut-off of 11 July 2014. Only businesses established before those dates qualified, and so applicants via those routes faced additional evidential requirements to satisfy a decision maker that their business had started trading sufficiently long ago. They also had to show they were making a contribution to the economy at a particular skill level, measured by the National Audit Office's Standard Occupation Codes.

Extensions of leave can be granted within the route. Applicants must show:

- They have registered as a director or as self-employed no more than six months after the date they entered the route.
- They have been self-employed, a member of a partnership or working as a director of a business three months before they apply for the extension.
- They have created at least **two full time jobs** that have existed for **at least 12 months** during **their last grant of leave**, and this has to be evidenced via very strict requirements, including that payments to workers have been made via HMRC's Pay As You Earn requirements (this requires that printouts of Real Time Full Payment Submissions are provided).
- A business plan and evidence that they only work for their entrepreneurial business: and their business cannot simply involve contracts of service for other businesses such as to amount to 'disguised' employment
- They can support themselves.
- They have invested into one or more UK businesses either £200,000 in cash or £50,000 in cash, the amount depends on the level of funds the initial application was based on. At the time the route closed, Graduate entrepreneurs were allowed to make applications based on the lower sum.
- They should include any dependants who are on the current visa in the application to extend - including children who have turned 18 during the stay in the UK.
- They must apply online.

See https://www.gov.uk/tier-1-entrepreneur/extend-your-visa

There is specific guidance (found within the general Coronavirus advice for visa applicants) on job creation impacted by the global Covid pandemic. There is a concession recognising the likely difficulties caused for small businesses which

- Relaxes the need to create 2 jobs lasting a year each in order to obtain ILR in favour of creating 24 months' worth of jobs during the (presumably still during the last period of leave)
- Includes furloughed staff
- If even this dispensation does not help, provides for at least a further grant of limited leave

The criteria for ILR are amended from 6 October 2021 to cater for the possibility of an extension having been granted under this concession. ILR may be granted to concession beneficiaries so long as 2 jobs have been created which have lasted for a year by the time of the ILR application (Appendix A Table 6 line 3, 4th para).

The prudent applicant will ensure that they explain their business in a covering letter, which will also give them the opportunity to address any issues that might be thought to arise from their business plan. The Guidance states this is appropriate for "unusual or particularly complex" cases where the case for scoring points may not otherwise be clear or where an extension application needs to clarify the establishment or joining of a business and the subsequent jobs creation. It then goes on to emphasise that the provision of a letter is no substitute for the provision of the necessary evidence and information within the application itself.

The covering letter may well provide the best opportunity to plug any gaps left by the business plan that might trouble a decision maker when assessing the genuineness of the application: a judge on a judicial review application would certainly expect it to be taken into account by a decision maker.

Where the business has been established and succeeded, there would seem little scope for a genuineness refusal at the extension stage. However sometimes the extension is sought on the back of a new business, at which point the test might kick in. The kinds of issue that come up in Entrepreneur refusals on genuineness grounds are sometimes what one might expect from an unstructured exercise in management consultancy conducted by a civil servant. Nevertheless, likely concerns may be dealt with up-front in a well-prepared application. Always look at the checklist in the Guidance: key issues are likely to include knowledge of the business plan and of every aspect of one's business, one's management experience and the commercial plausibility of any investment by third parties, and success in getting the business off the ground so far.

Settlement for Entrepreneurs

Tier 1 Entrepreneurs may obtain settlement, more quickly if they have created significant numbers of jobs or income (10 or more new jobs, or £5 million more income). Once the Entrepreneur has been in the route for 5 years (3 years under the accelerated proviso), they may apply for indefinite leave to remain.

They must make their applications by

- 5 April 2025 when the route will finally close for ILR purposes
- 6 July 2027 for applicants who spent time under the Graduate Entrepreneur route

The requirements are found in Table 6 of the Rules and r245F.

An applicant must have been living continuously in the UK

- For three years if they have created 10 new full- time jobs or generated £5 million in a three year period
- For five years if they do not meet the three year requirement

The three or five years can include time they have had a Business person or Innovator visa

The essential criteria are:

- Demonstrating that the required investment into a UK business was completed
- Registering with HMRC as self-employed or with Companies house as a Director within six months of entering the UK or within six months of their last grant of leave, and that that registration took place more than three months before the ILR application
- Creating two full time jobs which lasted for at least 12 months of the applicant's last period of leave (see above for the Covid concession).
- The application can still be tested for the genuineness of the underlying investment and the associated business, and applicants must demonstrate that they intend to continue with the business.

As usual they are subject to the continuous residence requirement. Thus they cannot have been outside the UK for more than 180 days in any 12 months during that time.

Applicants aged between 18 and 64 must also pass the Life in the UK Test and meet the English language requirements.

The general refusal reasons apply (MIL 2.3), so as always it is important to check for any relevant misconduct or criminal convictions before making the application.

7.2.15 Tier 1 Graduate Entrepreneurs

The Graduate Entrepreneur route was closed to new applicants on 6 July 2019. There are no further applications or extensions available in this category. In practice these individuals may be switching from the Graduate Entrepreneur into the Start Up for a further year or into the Innovator route.

As with other closed applications in this category it is necessary to understand the old route in order to see how one can extend one's leave.

The route was for

- UK graduates identified as having developed **genuine and credible business ideas and Entrepreneurial skills** to justify their stay in the UK after completing their studies
- Graduates identified by the Dept for International Trade as **elite global graduate Entrepreneurs** to establish businesses here

The businesses could have been set up as a sole trader, partnership or registered company. Those applying from abroad needed entry clearance before travelling. Applicants were not expected to provide documentary evidence of their immigration history as the HO would note their current status from their passport and HO records.

The route operated in a very similar way to its successor, the Start Up visa. The change-over has been quite smooth. Applicants needed to demonstrate the relevant entrepreneurial initiative to obtain leave and secure the backing of a higher education institute in the UK–registered as one of the <u>authorised endorsing bodies</u> listed on the finding website or of the Department for International Trade.

The applicant also had to establish their academic credentials by proving that they had a degree level qualification via tightly specified documents, together with the usual English language and ability to maintain themselves. There were a finite number of applications granted annually.

An in-country applicant could switch into the route only if they had leave as a student, or from Tier 2 General if they were a post-doctoral researcher whose place of study was endorsing their business. There was the possibility of a single extension under the route. There was no provision for ILR under the route, and whilst they could switch into the mainstream Entrepreneur route, they would not accumulate residence for ILR purposes whilst a Graduate Entrepreneur. They could have their leave curtailed if the institution endorsing them lost its status or stopped backing them.

The obvious extension opportunities for Graduate Entrepreneurs were into the Innovator or Start Up categories. It is possible to switch from the route to Skilled Worker under Tradeable points option E (see above 7.2.3). Time in the route does not generally count towards continuous residence for ILR purposes in other economic routes.

7.2.16 Tier 1 Investors

The investor route closed to new applicants with almost indecent haste, without notice by way of a Statement of Changes or consultation with stakeholders, at 4pm on 17 February 2022. UKVI say the need for this approach was to avoid a rush in the manner of a "closing down sale". Closure was brought about by the perception that the route added little to the economy and failed to prevent reliance on illicitly obtained funds.

Outstanding applications are to be decided as per the Rules then in force. Those still in the route may apply to extend their leave and for ILR (see generally the opening passages of the current Guidance Tier 1 (Investor).

The general purpose of this route was to allow generous immigration consequences for people with a high net worth who might make a substantial financial investment in the UK. They enjoyed certain benefits seldom available to other migrants: for example, there was no English language requirement in this route, the rationale being that they would not need to work in order to support themselves. The financial firepower they needed to evidence in order to be granted a visa was such that there were no separate maintenance requirements: it was simply presumed that they will be able to look after themselves given their overall wealth.

The route was tightened up over time: from 6 November 2014 the overall investment required was doubled. Previously, the requirement was for £1 million to be available for investment, of which at least £750,000 was invested in UK government bonds, or in share or loan capital in actively trading UK companies, and the remaining £250,000 had to be held in assets or money on deposit – this class of investor had to exit the route into ILR by 6 April 2020. Thereafter, the requirement changed to simply having appropriately invested £2 million. From 29 March 2019 more scrutiny was applied to the origin, control and transfer of investment funds, which henceforth had to be held for a significantly longer period, UK banks were mandated to carry out all due diligence on the origin of funds, intermediary vehicles in an investment chain all needed to be FCA-regulated, government bonds were ruled out as an eligible investment, and stronger evidence was required that the firms invested in were truly trading in the UK.

The investment had to be completed made before the application was made, though not more than a year previously. If the investment had not yet been made, then the money that underlaid it had to be shown to be available to the applicant for UK investment: either because it was held in an institution here, or freely transferable to the UK and convertible to sterling.

Money for these purposes could include funds held by the person's spouse, civil partner or unmarried partner, so long as they were under the applicant's control and they were free to invest them. Wang [2023] UKSC 21 held that the scheme should be construed purposively, realistically, and in the round. Applicants had to be in control of their assets, investments, their own and their borrowed money, such that they had a real choice on how investments were made. Certain documents had to be produced to demonstrate that the relationship was a genuine one, and that the funds were truly available to the applicant: so their partner had to demonstrate their intention by evidencing a gift of beneficial ownership, backed up by a legal advisor's letter confirming the gift was valid and enforceable in the country where it was made.

Those newly entering the route had to have held the investment monies for 90 days before applying (ending no more than a month before the application is made). The money had to be evidenced via portfolio reports from the institution holding it where an investment professional was in charge of the investment, or, for those managing their own investments, official company accounts or statements showing the value of holdings in shares/bonds/trust funds and so forth, or via bank statements or a letter from a regulated bank confirming the funds were found in the relevant bank balance. If the investment monies had not been held for 90 days, then there was a very long set of criteria for every imaginable source of funds, specifying the documents needed to back up their heritage: gifts, asset sales, business accounts, inheritances, divorce settlements, prize winnings, and any other source.

The investment in question had to be in share or loan capital in actively trading UK companies. There were specific limitations on the available investments which qualified: money held offshore was generally excluded, as was investment in open-ended investment companies, investment trust companies, investment syndicate companies or pooled investment vehicles, and leveraged investment funds; investment in property investment, management and development companies; bank, building society and other funds held on deposit, ISAs, premium bonds and national saving certificates.

Those seeking extensions of leave must demonstrate that they maintained their investment throughout their residence. There are different regimes for pre- and post-November 2014 investors. The former must, if investments within the portfolio are sold, replace them ('topping up') within six months or before the next reporting period (if sooner). Modern investors do not need to keep the investment at its original value; but they must reinvest the gross proceeds of any sales. Fees must be paid from surplus funds over and above the requisite investment: it is perfectly permissible to pay them from the investment funds, but only where those funds have contained a consistent surplus so that fee payments do not cause dips below the relevant threshold.

Leave may be curtailed (or an extension refused) if the appropriate investment has not been maintained throughout one's stay. Pre-November 2014 applicants had to keep their portfolios topped up to the same level as supported their points award when entering the route; modern applicants only have to reinvest gross proceeds of any sales.

As with other immigration routes, there is a sense that the HO reserve the greatest scrutiny for applicants who are seeking to settle in the UK. So investment arrangements which satisfied the original decision makers might get a closer audit at the ILR stage. And the specified documents requirements require particular kinds of financial reports, so it is important to look ahead.

Dependants were allowed.

7.3 Generic concepts within the work and study routes and family members of work and study migrants
7.3.1 Sponsors and Certificates of Sponsorship

The Sponsor is central to the PBS. Few routes are free from the requirement (Global Talent and Innovators/Start Ups require endorsing bodies who take a similar role – albeit that endorsing bodies do not have a "*policing*" role; Graduates, High Potential Individuals, and Scale-ups after the first few months, are unsponsored options). The sponsorship system is a creation of HO Guidance rather than being set up via the Immigration Rules.

There are three lengthy guidance documents which are central to the Sponsor role:

- Part 1: Apply for a licence
- Part 2: Guidance for sponsors on sponsoring a worker
- Part 3: Sponsor duties and compliance

Paying a supplemental fee to use the priority service guarantees a quicker sponsor licence decision.

A licensed Sponsor must satisfy onerous requirements as to their system of reporting and record keeping regarding the migrants for whom they are responsible. For example the Sponsors of Students and Workers must report a person who does not turn for the first day of work, if they are absent for more than 10 working days without permission, if the period of engagement ends including resignation or dismissal, if information as to the migrant breaching the conditions of leave comes to light or if there is reason to believe they are engaged in terrorism or other criminal activity; and must also record any significant changes of circumstances such as a job change or salary change, though not a change of job title or an annual pay rise.

The Certificate of Sponsorship, be it a Certificate of Acceptance for Studies (CAS) for Students or a Certificate of Sponsorship (CoS) for the Skilled Worker, ICT, T2 and Temporary Work worker routes, is a virtual document like a file on a database. Each has a unique reference number and contains information about the role for which it is issued.

Only one CoS can be issued for a period of leave and once this is done, no other Sponsor may issue a CoS reference number. It may well be advisable to give personal details such as passport number to a prospective Sponsor for whom the migrant will definitely be working. If a migrant does not want to take up the job for which a CoS has been issued, they should notify the Sponsor and request its withdrawal, giving them five days to action the request before sending a reminder. If it is not cancelled, they should contact the Sponsor Licensing Unit at sponsorlicensing@homeoffice.gsi. gov.uk providing relevant details: the Sponsor they no longer want, their own full name and nationality, the CoS to be cancelled and the reason, and the dates of contacting and chasing the Sponsor.

A CoS will expire three months after it is assigned if it is not activated by a person coming to the UK. A CoS may be withdrawn or cancelled at any time by the HO or sponsor and then becomes invalid.

The CAS is equally central to the student route. It is valid to support an entry clearance application for six months once issued (three months for PTS) and applications must not be made more than three months before the course's start date. A CAS is valid only for so long as the sponsoring educational establishment retains its licence, and it has to provide specified information regarding the course of studies.

7.3.2 Loss of a Sponsor's licence

A Sponsor may have their licence suspended or revoked for failing to meet the record keeping and reporting conditions. For their sponsored migrants, this means

- If the licence is suspended, the Sponsor may no longer issue new CoSs or CASs, but this does not immediately impact on the migrants working or studying there
- Individuals may apply for further leave during a period of suspension – however the application will be held pending the suspension being (hopefully) lifted
- If the Sponsor's licence is revoked, then presuming the migrant is not suspected of complicity in the issues leading to revocation, their leave should be curtailed to 60 days from notification of curtailment (or they will be allowed to retain their existing leave if they have less than 60 days outstanding): they may seek to find a new Sponsor over this grace period. Any CoS or CAS issued becomes invalid upon revocation of the licence.
- Those who have travelled to the UK will be allowed to enter the UK and start their work notwithstanding suspension of a licence: however, the recommendation in the Guidance is nevertheless not to travel once the applicant becomes aware of their Sponsor's difficulties. If possible, the HO will contact such applicants before they travel to advise them of the situation

If a Sponsor is taken over by another organisation, then the new employer must apply to become a licensed Sponsor within 28 days of the takeover. Otherwise leave will be curtailed in line with the regime above. CoSs will become invalid if no Sponsor application is made. If such a Sponsor does not renew their licence, leave will similarly be curtailed, and CoSs will become invalid.

Premature termination of employment will have similar consequences as to the treatment of outstanding leave.

Pathan [2020] UKSC 41 finds that there is a duty on the SSHD to notify an applicant with an outstanding application promptly of the revocation of their sponsor's licence, it being procedurally unfair not to do so (MIL 2.6 and 5.5.5). The Guidance now provides that all sponsored workers will be notified of revocation (though not the reasons) to give them a chance to take appropriate action.

7.3.3 Criminal record certificate (CRC) – Entry clearance routes only

The CRC is only required for some entry clearance routes – eg for Skilled Worker at SW.16.1, for roles in the health and education sector; but not in the GBM routes which are silent on the issue.

- A CRC must be obtained from the relevant authority in any country in which they have been resident for 12 months or more, whether continuously or in total, in the last decade, whilst aged 18 plus
- A person who cannot provide a CRC may seek exemption from the requirement which the HO may grant *if it is not reasonably practicable* to obtain one (SW16.2) (the Guidance refers to exceptions including the situation where there is no procedure for issuing certificates, fleeing the country for humanitarian reasons, or where humanitarian disaster or armed conflict prevents the issue of documents)

The Guidance *Criminal record certificate* explains that some countries have regional rather than national criminal record certificates in which case one must be produced for each area of the country where the applicant resided. Pending prosecutions may require an application to be put on hold, unless there is no reasonable prospect of resolution in which case the nature of the offences charged should be considered.

7.3.4 Regulated financial institutions

A regulated financial institution is one which is regulated by the appropriate regulatory body for the country in which the financial institution operates. There used to be strict rules on this including a list of unacceptable financial institutions in the old Appendix P.

Now Appendix Finance provides that the institution must be one which is appropriately regulated, uses electronic records, and is one where the decision maker can make satisfactory verification checks.

A person subject to any applicable financial sanctions regime must provide confirmation from HM Treasury that the funds are transferable and disposable in the UK (see by analogy the Investor Guidance on money being transferrable to the UK).

7.3.5 Calculating conversion rates

Many routes require a certain level of funds to be held to demonstrate an ability to maintain oneself. Sometimes funds held abroad qualify. Funds in a foreign currency will be converted to pounds sterling (£) using the spot exchange rate which appeared on www.oanda.com on the date on which the application was made.

7.3.6 Expedited visa applications

Applications may be expedited. It is important to be confident that the application is a straightforward one, however: any complications may lead to the decision maker being unable to complete consideration on the day, which may waste the premium fee.

In-country applications may be expedited via the Priority Service (5-day service) or Super Priority Service (the latter aims to make decisions within 24 hours of receiving the papers). Most of the PBS routes can benefit as per the *Faster Decision* Guidance. There are similar options available out-of-country.

7.3.7 Verification of documents

Documents supplied in support of the application will not necessarily be taken at face value, and are subject to verification. The Guidance explains the process (e.g. the *High Potential Individual caseworker guidance* at the heading *Verifying documents*). Essentially:

- Verification checks will be made where there are *reasonable doubts* backed by *clear reasons* about the document being genuine – 'based on the facts we have'
- They will be made with employers, an embassy or high commission, government departments in the UK or abroad, banks, universities or professional bodies
- There is a rather obscure further process known as 'other checks' where less cogent suspicions appear to justify checks being made
- Verification checks may inevitably delay the progress of the application
- Passports will always be verified.
- Sometimes verification checks will be omitted notwithstanding concerns about a document because there are other reasons for refusal

There are three possible outcomes:

1. **The document is confirmed as genuine** – in which case the application will be considered as normal
2. **The document is confirmed as false** – in which case the application will be refused under the general refusal reasons (MIL 2.3), though it will probably also be refused because no points can be awarded regarding the criteria which that document was aiming to support
3. **Verification check inconclusive** – if checks do not confirm or undermine a document's genuineness, then the application will proceed to decision. The suspect document will not be

awarded points, but if other non-suspect documents were put forward then the application may still succeed

Results of verification of falseness will be reported via a standard Document Verification Report form.

7.3.8 Extension and ILR requirements

Whatever stage an applicant is at, it always pays to look ahead. There are particular requirements for maintaining job creation and investments within the Entrepreneur and Investor routes, for example, and a client should be advised as to how to ensure they give themselves the best shot at being able to extend their stay or settle in the UK. Though they should also be warned that the Rules can always change, and the case law says that that a disadvantaged migrant cannot complain about a decision taken based on the Rules then in force (MIL 2.1.2).

7.3.9 Appendix Finance and Appendix C: Financial maintenance requirements

Applicants under the PBS and related routes have to prove they can maintain and accommodate themselves. The Guidance emphasises that this is to ensure that there is no burden on public funds during their time in the UK. Appendix C previously governed this issue until it was replaced by Appendix Finance.

7.3.9.1 Appendix Finance

Appendix Finance applies to applications under the work and study appendices from December 2020: new immigration routes are added to the list as they are introduced.

The content largely replicates the previous rules, with the following main changes:

- Appendix P, which contained the list of financial institutions whose documents were not verifiable, is replaced by para FIN 2.1 in this appendix. This requires that financial institution, in which funds are held, are regulated, use electronic record keeping, and are capable of conducting UKVI verification checks (FIN 2.1).
- Third parties who are not the applicant's partner are permissible account holders where the route in question allows this (FIN 5.1.(d)).
- Financial evidence must be held within 31 days of the date of application (FIN 7.1).
- A wider range of accounts than cash or cash savings can be relied upon, so long as funds are accessible immediately (FIN 8.1).
- The formatting requirements for bank statements are removed and applicants may rely on unstamped electronic bank statements

The appendix is structured as follows:

- FIN 1.1 Currency
- FIN 2.1 Financial institutions
- FIN 3.1 Overdrafts
- FIN 4.1 Requirement to have legally earned or acquired funds, savings, or income
- FIN 5.1-3 Account holders
- FIN 6.1 Third party support
- FIN 7.1 Dates of financial evidence
- FIN 8.1-3 Accounts
- FIN 9.1-2 Evidence of financial sponsorship for students

Some general points:

- Where amounts are held in one or more different currencies, the spot exchange rate on www.oanda.com is to be used to convert it to pounds sterling (**FIN 1.1**)

- Funds will not qualify if held in a financial institution in relation to which satisfactory verification cannot be undertaken (a); which is not regulated by its country's appropriate regulatory body (b); or which does not use electronic record keeping (c) **(FIN 2.1)**
- Overdraft facilities are not counted towards meeting financial requirements **(FIN 3.1)**
- Funds, savings or income earned or acquired while A was in the UK must have been earned or acquired lawfully, while A had permission and was not in breach of any of its conditions **(FIN 4.1)**
- Accounts relied on must be in the applicant's name (including with other persons jointly) **(FIN 5.1-3)** unless:
  - Their partner is the account holder who is applying alongside them or has previously been granted permission; or
  - For a Student, Child Student, Short-term student, or a dependent child, the account holder is their parent or legal guardian; or
  - For a Child Student, the account is held by a close relative or private foster carer who cares for them under an arrangement which complies with CS 9.3-5 in Appendix Child Student; or
  - The particular application category allows for accounts held in the relevant third party's name
- The account holder must have control of the funds (FIN 5.2)
- Students or Child Students relying on funds held by their parent or legal guardian must provide evidence of that relationship and written consent from the parent or legal guardian to use those funds (FIN 5.3)
- Promises of future third party support are only acceptable as evidence of funds where the individual route specifies that this form of financing is permitted **(FIN 6.1)** - for example Appendix Hong Kong British National (Overseas) (HK6.4) that "*The applicant may rely on credible promises of future third party support*"
- The most recently dated piece of financial evidence must be dated within 31 days before the application date (FIN 7.1) and the length of time for which funds are held is calculated by counting back from the date of the closing balance on the most recently dated piece of financial evidence (FIN 7.2). The evidence must cover the whole period for which funds must be held (FIN 7.3)
- Funds may be held in any form of personal bank or building society account so long as this allows the funds to be accessed immediately (FIN 8.1). Funds held in other accounts or financial instruments from which they cannot be withdrawn immediately are not acceptable (FIN 8.2)
- Students or Child Students meet the financial requirements if they can evidence any, or all, of (FIN 8.3):
  - Money held in an account that meets the requirements above by being held by a parent/guardian/close relative etc and is immediately available to them
  - Funds provided by an official sponsor – ie the UK government or the government of the country of A's nationality; the British Council of any international organisation, or a company, university or independent school
  - A student loan provided by a government, a government sponsored student loan company, or an academic or educational loans scheme by a financial institution regulated for the purpose of issuing student loans by the Financial Conduct Authority or the Prudential Regulation Authority, or the official regulatory body for purpose of issuing student loans in the country where the institution is and where the money is held
- For Students or Child Students relying on an official sponsor's funds, the CAS must refer to the funds provided and the sponsor must also provide a letter of confirmation (FIN 9.1)
- Student loans must be evidenced by a student loan letter from the lender which must be dated with within 6 months of the application; and confirm *all* of the following (FIN 9.2):
  - The amount of the loan and that the applicant is the recipient
  - The loan is a student loan by the relevant government or a government sponsored student loan company or an academic- or educational loans scheme
  - The funds will be available to the applicant before travel to the UK, or will be paid directly to the student sponsor before travel here (with the living cost portion being made available on UK arrival), or will be available before the course starts, if the loan provider is A's national government

7.3.9.2 Appendix C

Appendix C (which previously governed all the managed migration routes) is now renamed Appendix C: maintenance (funds) Tier 1 (Entrepreneur), reflecting the limited category of cases it now covers.

Appendix C had a series of Tables (of which only the one for Tier 1 (Entrepreneurs) remains), which set out the levels of money that must be held. There are then some general provisions at 1A regarding where funds must be held, and the content of bank or building society statements or passbooks and the period over which they must be produced, and the evidence required to show that funds are under their own control. There were then some specific requirements for each of the Points Based System routes, which were much more extensive for Tier 4 students (whose precise source of funding had to be evidenced) and Tier 4 child students (the requirements for whose care arrangements, as well as maintenance requirements, were found in Appendix C).

7.3.10 Continuous residence

Most routes are governed by Appendix Continuous Residence (similar criteria for investors and entrepreneurs are at r245AAA).

Applicants must have spent the qualifying unbroken continuous residence period required by their route lawfully in the UK.

No more than 180 days absence per year are normally allowed. This is calculated in particular ways depending on the period covered (reflecting a change in approach in January 2018):

- Before 11 January 2018, absences are calculated within each consecutive 12-month period ending with the ILR application date: this gives an opportunity to remove unhelpful periods of excess absence
- For leave granted after 11 January 2018, the applicant must not have been outside the UK for more than 180 days in *any* 12-month period

Some absences are excluded from counting towards the 180 days (CR 2.3):

- Assistance with a national or international humanitarian or environmental crisis, for sponsored routes (with the sponsor's consent)
- Travel disruption due to natural disaster, military conflict or pandemic
- Compelling and compassionate personal circumstances such as life threatening illness of the applicant or a family member, or death of a family member
- Certain research activities by Skilled Workers or Global Talent migrants
- Time spent in the Channel Islands or the Isle of Man is treated as time spent in the UK if the latest grant of permission was in the UK

There is a similar regime for dependants.

Continuous residence is broken by any of the following, being:

- sentenced to prison (unless suspended) or detained in another institution
- subject to a deportation or exclusion order or an exclusion direction
- subject to removal directions under s10 of the 1999 Act
- an overstayer unless
  - They have since been granted permission via IR39E
  - They held permission on leaving the UK and successfully applied to extend it while it was still valid or within 14 days of its expiry
  - The proviso in CR 4.2 applies
- absent from the UK for longer than the relevant 180-day period where no relevant exception applies

Overstaying before 24 November 2016 breaks continuous leave unless

- the subsequent successful application was made within 28 days of the previous leave's expiry or
- permission expired while the applicant was abroad but the subsequent successful application was made before it expired

Lawful presence is required: imprisonment or detention is not treated as lawful. Nor is overstaying unless condoned by IR39E (MIL 1.5.4).

Continuous residence is calculated by counting back from whichever is the most beneficial date for the applicant. This gives a limited opportunity to engineer one's best five year period in terms of excess absence though it only really helps vis-á-vis pre-January 2018 overstaying. The possibilities are:

- Date of ILR application
- Any date up to 28 days after date of ILR application
- Date of decision

The continuous residence regime for those routes which are still governed by r245AAA (investors and entrepreneurs) is similar to that described. The Guidance: *Indefinite leave to remain - calculating continuous leave* should be reviewed to determine any relevant differences.

7.3.11 Appendix KOL - Knowledge of life in the UK and the English language

The notorious "life in the UK" test is aimed to ensure those settling here have adequate knowledge of UK culture. There are two sets of provisions dealing with knowledge of life in the UK: Appendix KOLL (MIL 2.2.6.2) and Appendix KOL UK, which governs ILR for modern business, work and study routes.

The introduction to this appendix states that it sets out how the Knowledge of Life in the UK requirement is met in ILR applications. First it addresses relevant exemptions and then it details the knowledge of Life in the UK requirement. The Guidance *Knowledge of language and life in the UK* applies.

Applicants are exempt from the Life in the UK requirement if on the application date:

- They are aged 65 or over or
- They are aged under 18 or
- They have a physical or mental condition which prevents them from meeting the requirement or
- For dependants, they are aged >18, are exempt from the full English language requirements because they have lived in the UK for >15 years, have achieved A2 standard in English, and have studied for 75+ hours in the previous year and their teacher confirms they are unlikely to attain the higher standard

The knowledge requirement is met via a valid digital reference number from an educational institution or other person approved for this purpose showing they have passed the Life in the UK Test or its equivalent in one of the Islands.

CHAPTER 8: International Protection

8.1 The refugee definition

The fundamental provision of the UN Convention Relating to the Status of Refugees 1951 (read with the 1967 New York Protocol), usually referred to as the Refugee Convention, is Article 1(A)(2). A refugee is defined therein as a person who:

> owing to well-founded fear of being persecuted for reasons of race, religion, nationality, membership of a particular social group or political opinion is outside the country of his nationality and is unable or owing to such fear, is unwilling to avail himself of the protection of that country; or who, not having a nationality and being outside the country of his former habitual residence is unable or, owing to such fear, unwilling to return to it.

This provision deals with the situation of both persons with a nationality and those without (i.e. the 'stateless'). The courts have interpreted the requirements of the definition to be the same in both cases.

The definition can be broken down into its constituent parts:

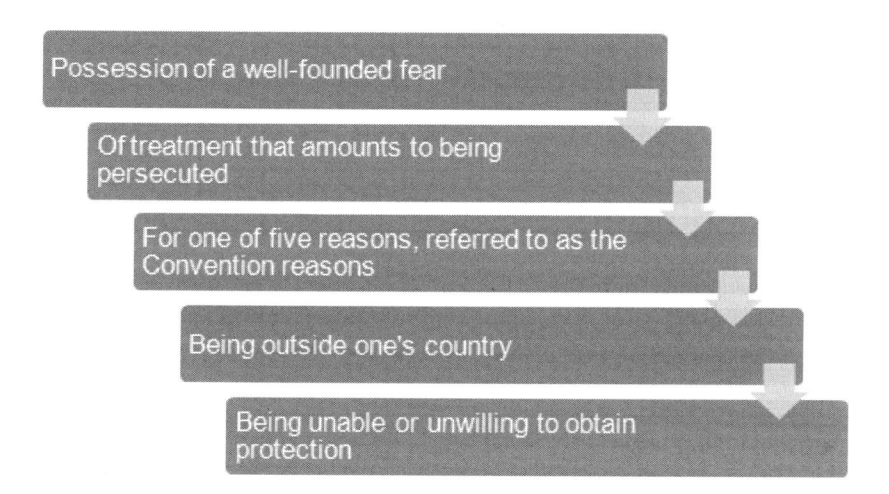

- Possession of a well-founded fear
- Of treatment that amounts to being persecuted
- For one of five reasons, referred to as the Convention reasons
- Being outside one's country
- Being unable or unwilling to obtain protection

We can paraphrase the most relevant questions thus:

- Will it happen (credibility plus country evidence)
- What will happen (persecution)
- Why will it happen (Convention reason)
- What might stop it happening (protection or internal relocation)

The location of the principles underlying these concepts have moved around.

- At one time they were found solely in domestic case law

    From October 2006 until 31 December 2020 they were governed by EC Council Directive 2004/83/EC – the 'Qualification Directive' (transposed into UK law through The Refugee or Person in Need of International Protection (Qualification) Regulations 2006 and modifications to the asylum section of the IRs at Part 11).
- From 31 December 2020 until 27 June 2022 they were retained EU law

- The NBA 2022 puts the EU legal regime (previously found in the Protection Regs) onto a domestic statutory footing found in Part 2 of the NBA 2022. It enters force for claims made from 28 June 2022 – and now there are two sets of Guidance for before and after the changes: *Assessing Credibility and Refugee Status* in asylum claims lodged before 28 June 2022 and

Assessing Credibility and Refugee Status in asylum claims lodged post 28 June 2022. It Introduces some radical measures , eg casting doubt on the veracity of asylum claims where supporting evidence is produced late and (probably) changing the standard of proof for establishing past events to the balance of probabilities; as well as creating a two-tier system of rights for refugees and persons granted HP.

- The HO *Assessing Credibility and Refugee Status* guidance states:

    the 2022 Act departs from previous caselaw in some aspects, so in practice it is important to follow this guidance, rather than caselaw that predates the passage of the Act

- UK judges will need to work out how CJEU case law is to be applied in the UK context in future given that CJEU decisions will have been interpreting exactly the same language as now found in domestic legislation.

8.1.1 Sources of refugee law

The Refugee Convention has existed for over 60 years and inevitably there are various authorities that provide guides to the meaning and construction of the Convention principles including, most importantly:

- The *Handbook on Procedures and Criteria for Determining Refugee Status*, published by UNHCR in 1978 in Geneva, is a fundamental text for any practitioner, particularly in the paragraphs (193-219) where it explains best practice in determining the underlying facts of an asylum claim.
- UNHCR also gives guidance beyond the UNHCR Handbook, in terms of occasional statements on best practice in status determination and on how to approach the refugee definition – you can see the full list in their extensive *Protection Manual*; in the UK they intervene in individual cases only occasionally, increasingly doing so via legal interventions in test cases; they also provide guidelines on risks in particular countries. Their online facility Refworld is a very impressive and useful database of national and international legal authority relevant to refugee law.
- The Preamble to the Refugee Convention is a useful reminder that the Convention is related to other international legal materials such as other human rights instruments (e.g. the Universal Declaration of Human Rights, the International Covenant on Civil and Political Rights, and the Charter of Fundamental Rights – so, for example, the definition of persecution, found in the domestic Protection Regulations at Reg 5(1), references those fundamental human rights which are absolute and from which there can be no derogation).
- Case law of the UK courts, the CJEU, the ECtHR, and of other jurisdictions representing signatories to the Convention.
- G (A Child: Child Abduction) [2020] EWCA Civ 1185 contains a useful discussion of the relationship between the Refugee Convention, UK law and the EU law, including the general direction of travel from January 2021 (for details, see further section 9.7.7).

> **Top Tip**
>
> HJT strongly recmmends reading the following ILPA best practice guides, which are essentially asylum skills guides. They are written by skilled, experienced practitioners who have distilled their learning into readable and accessible form. Aspiring practitioners should not pass by the opportunity to learn from them! They are available for free download at http://www.ilpa.org.uk/pages/ publications.html.
>
> ☐   The *Best practice guide to asylum and human rights appeals*, by Mark Henderson is an excellent practical guide to evidencing and running asylum claims. Updated versions can be found periodically, electronically via the Electronic Immigration Network and on paper published by the Legal Action Group
>
> ☐   Making an asylum application: a best practice guide, Jane Coker, Garry Kelly and Martin Soorjoo (2002) – whilst this is clearly out of date on substantive law and HO procedures, it is still very useful on issues such as taking instructions and ethical questions

CHAPTER 8: International Protection

> ☐ For current thinking on particular issues in asylum claims, country-based or otherwise, the Refugee Legal group (RLG) is an essential forum. For details of how to join, find its page on the Asylum Aid website
> ☐ And if you are interested in reading further into the subject, the leading domestic textbook is Symes and Jorro Asylum Law and Practice – the third edition is due early Summer 2023

8.1.2 Asylum seekers

An asylum seeker is a person who has left their country of nationality or habitual residence, and has made a claim in a signatory country (i.e. an asylum claim or application) to the effect that they are entitled to protection there under the provisions of the Convention. The asylum seeker will hold that status until the asylum application is finally decided by that country. A similar definition is given to 'asylum applicant' at r327 (in Part 11 of the IRs).

The HO will then be obliged to consider whether they are entitled to 'humanitarian protection' under the Qualification Directive (and r339C).

If the asylum seeker is refused under both protection regimes, they will no longer be an asylum seeker. In some circumstances, they may be able to make a further claim on asylum or human rights grounds under the 'fresh claim' procedure (r353). If they are not able to establish their claim for protection, or the right to stay in the UK on any other basis, they will be removable (subject to practicalities) to their own country.

8.1.3 Well-founded fear

There are two aspects to the possession of a well-founded fear: well foundedness and fear. The 'fear' test is in practice something of a red herring. It is very hard to imagine an asylum seeker losing their appeal because they are accepted as being at risk of serious harm but are not frightened at the prospect. So really the question of 'fear' collapses into the question of 'credibility': i.e. are they telling the truth?

8.1.3.1 Getting the story across and types of asylum claim

Procedurally, the asylum seeker will have an opportunity to establish that they do have a genuine fear of returning to their country in their asylum interview, with a detailed statement of their claim (if they are properly represented), and any corroborative evidence they may be able to submit to the HO. On the basis of this information, the HO will make an assessment of the truthfulness (or as the HO likes to call it 'credibility') of the asylum seeker. They will ask themselves if the asylum seeker is telling the truth about their profile or about what happened to them in the past?

The HO sometimes need reminding that an asylum seeker may lie about some or all of their claim, or exaggerate their fear, but may still have a well-founded fear of persecution.

- For example, if they are a member of a class or group of persons who are at risk (e.g. members of Somali minority clans or Eritrean military service evaders) an asylum seeker might succeed in showing an entitlement to refugee status, notwithstanding the rejection of their own account.
- A person may also be at risk if forced to return to a particular country, not because of anything they have said in their asylum claim, but because of the view taken by the authorities of that country of asylum seekers returning from abroad in general or from the UK in particular, as has been found from time to time regarding countries such as Sudan and Zimbabwe, and currently Syria.
- Merely claiming asylum or even merely having been in the UK can put a person at risk on return (see e.g. KB Syria CG [2012] UKUT 426 (IAC)).

Of course, it is easier to succeed if the asylum seeker is accepted as telling the truth about the entirety of their account, but many asylum seekers do not, often because they are poorly advised (not by inadequate lawyers so much as by agents, interpreters, members of their community or others they come across before or during the asylum process). But the examples above show that claims can succeed even if most of the individual facts put forward are might be rejected.

8.1.3.2 Well-foundedness

This is an objective test and concerns, in part, the claimant's account being looked at in the light of the conditions in the applicant's country of origin. It also requires a consideration of future risk. The claimant might fear return, but is that feawell founded in the sense of there being a sufficient likelihood of those fears being realised?

The standard is that of '*well-founded fear*', now found in the Qualification Directive at Article 2(c); the classic domestic expression of this was in the House of Lords decision of Sivakumuran [1987] UKHL 1, which put the question as whether there was '*a reasonable degree of likelihood*' of persecution.

Historic fact
- Standard of proof
- Credibility/Plausibility

Future risk
- Country information
- Past persecution
- Specific or general risk
- Activities in the United Kingdom
- Future behaviour

8.1.4 Standard of proof

The standard of proof for determining well-founded fear (in the sense of future risk) is that of 'a reasonable degree of likelihood', which is lower than the civil standard of the balance of probabilities andis sometimes expressed as 'substantial grounds for believing' or 'real risk'. The leading case is Ravichandran [1996] Imm AR 97.

In Karanakaran [2000] Imm AR 271 the Court of Appeal found that an asylum claim could succeed even though the person assessing it (HO decision maker or Immigration Judge) might doubt parts of the account (whereas if the evidence was assessed on the traditional standard of proof in civil proceedings, the balance of probabilities, they would have to reject evidence that they doubted). The Court held that the first three of the following four categories of evidence identified by a decision maker are relevant for this purpose:

- evidence they are certain about
- evidence they think is probably true
- evidence to which they are willing to attach some credence, even if they could not go so far as to say it is probably true
- evidence to which they are not willing to attach any credence at all.

MAH (Egypt) [2023] EWCA Civ 216 explains that the central issue in refugee status determination is the assessment of risk rather than establishing facts on balance of probabilities. An account might be true whether or not corroborative evidence was available; it was always important to consider giving the asylum seeker the benefit of the doubt. Ilogical reasoning was an error of law.

However for asylum claims lodged from 28 June 2022 NBA 2022 s32 provides for the balance of probabilities to apply when assessing past facts. Its impact will need to be interpreted via case law. Its novelty and importance demands that we set it out in full.

> '**Article 1(A)(2): well-founded fear**
> (1) In deciding for the purposes of Article 1(A)(2) of the Refugee Convention whether an asylum seeker's fear of persecution is well-founded, the following approach is to be taken.
> (2) The decision-maker must first determine, on the balance of probabilities—

(a) whether the asylum seeker has a characteristic which could cause them to fear persecution for reasons of race, religion, nationality, membership of a particular social group or political opinion (or has such a characteristic attributed to them by an actor of persecution), and

(b) whether the asylum seeker does in fact fear such persecution in their country of nationality (or in a case where they do not have a nationality, the country of their former habitual residence) as a result of that characteristic.(See also section 8 of the Asylum and Immigration (Treatment of Claimants, etc) Act 2004 (asylum claims etc: behaviour damaging to claimant's credibility).)

(3) Subsection (4) applies if the decision-maker finds that—

(a) the asylum seeker has a characteristic mentioned in subsection (2)(a) (or has such a characteristic attributed to them), and

(b) the asylum seeker fears persecution as mentioned in subsection (2)(b).

(4) The decision-maker must determine whether there is a reasonable likelihood that, if the asylum seeker were returned to their country of nationality (or in a case where they do not have a nationality, the country of their former habitual residence)—

(a) they would be persecuted as a result of the characteristic mentioned in subsection (2)(a), and

(b) they would not be protected as mentioned in section 34.

(5) The determination under subsection (4) must also include a consideration of the matter mentioned in section 35 (internal relocation).'

Some points arising:

- There is a two-stage process: the Guidance *Assessing credibility and refugee status post 28 June 2022* gives breaks this down into First and Second Stage assessments
- The existence of a Convention **characteristic** (ie Convention reason) (s32(2)(a)) and **fear** are to be assessed on balance of probabilities (s32(2)(b))
- If the two s32(2) questions are answered positively, then other matters are assessed on the reasonable degree of likelihood standard: persecution (s32(4)(a)), state protection (s32(4)(b)) and internal relocation (s32(5))
- The *intention* seems to be to have past facts assessed on **balance of probabilities** whereas future risks are assessed on **reasonable degree of likelihood** – thus the Guidance states
  'In order to make this assessment, when making findings about the material elements of the claim, decision-makers must only accept those elements that meet the standard of the balance of the probabilities'
- Query whether the language achieves this: the cross-reference to s8 AITCA 2004 and the targeting of **fear** (rather than **historical facts** expressly) might be interpreted as looking only at the subjective state of mind at the asylum seeker
- Whatever the approach to historical facts regarding the asylum seeker's account of past events generally, internal relocation itself may well involve factual assessment
- There appears to be no equivalent provision addressing Humanitarian Protection claims: suggesting that in future decision makers will need to assess the two different claims on two different standards of proof even though the relevant facts are the same (MIL 8.9.1)

8.1.5 Credibility

The assessment of past facts in asylum cases is a complex process. There are statutory provisions that have an impact on the assessment of credibility as well as the IRs and case law. When seeking inspiration in relation to what credibility issues might arise, the Rules and s8 AITCA 2004 are a very good place to start.

KB and AH Pakistan [2017] UKUT 491 (IAC) gives a useful overview about how judges should assess the credibility of an asylum seeker. Relevant indicators of a claim's truthfulness are sufficiency of detail, internal and external consistency, and plausibility. Nevertheless, the evidence must still be assessed globally 'in the round', having regard to the relevant factors in the domestic and EU framework. Some are identified in s8 AITCA 2004 (overt dishonesty, failing to claim asylum in an EU Member State, claiming asylum after arrest or receiving an immigration decision, and destroying documents). Others were at that time derived from Art 4 of the Qualification Directive though remain relevant (efforts to corroborate their account: r339L(i), the timing of the asylum claim (s8 AITCA 2004), and the need to give the benefit of the doubt where they have done their best to give a coherent account: *Assessing Credibility* Guidance).

That last point is consistent with other sources - the benefit of the doubt applies only where the account is generally credible (UNHCR Handbook paras 196 & 204). The HO clearly recognise the ongoing importance of the benefit of the doubt in assessing credibility in the Guidance *Assessing credibility*:

> '*decision-makers must only accept those elements that meet the standard of the balance of the probabilities, **after the benefit of the doubt is applied**, and no longer accept those material elements that are only reasonably likely to be true.*'

8.1.5.1 Immigration Rules relevant to assessing asylum claims

Rule 339L provides that when assessing credibility:

- the burden of proof is on the individual asylum seeker in general
- however where they have made every effort to substantiate their account, and provided a story which is coherent and plausible in the light of the country evidence, and explained any lack of corroboration, and are generally credible, they should be given the benefit of the doubt

The full text of Rule 339L reads:

> 339L. It is the duty of the person to substantiate the asylum claim or establish that he is a person eligible humanitarian protectionor substantiate his human rights claim. Where aspects of the person's statements are not supported by documentary or other evidence, those aspects will not need confirmation when all of the following conditions are met:
>
> (i) the person has made a genuine effort to substantiate his asylum claim or establish that he is a person eligible humanitarianprotection or substantiate his human rights claim;
> (ii) all material factors at the person's disposal have been submitted, and a satisfactory explanation regarding any lack of other relevant material has been given;
> (iii) the person's statements are found to be coherent and plausible and do not run counter to available specific and general information relevant to the person's case;
> (iv) the person has made an asylumclaim or sought to establish that he is a person eligible for humanitarian protection or made a human rights claim at the earliest possible time, unless the person can demonstrate good reason for not having done so; and
> (v) the general credibility of the person has been established.

This should be the starting point for the assessment of credibility. The rider that the applicant must be generally credible enables decision makers to attach appropriate weight to inconsistencies and other credibility issues, but this paragraph provides a useful reminder that corroborating evidence is not always required and that the benefit of the doubt should be given where it is not. But an asylum seeker must, where possible, corroborate a claim, and where attempts to do so have been made, but have failed, these should also be explained to the decision maker. It is not unreasonable for a decision maker to expect corroboration from sources that would appear to be available, particularly in this country, such as witnesses and relatives (and given modern ease of international communication via social media and email).

In FG v Sweden [2016] ECHR 299 the ECtHR stated that the special situation of asylum seekers meant that the benefit of the doubt should be given them when their credibility is assessed and any supporting documents evaluated, but where there are strong reasons to question the veracity of their claim they must provide a satisfactory explanation for any alleged discrepancies

One of the most important modern authorities on the appropriate approach to take when assessing credibility is UNHCR's *Beyond Proof – Credibility Assessment in EU Asylum Systems* which advises that the relevant factors that need to be taken into account include:

- the limits and variations of human memory, in particular the wide-ranging variability in people's ability to record, retain, and retrieve memories; in the accuracy of memories for dates, times, appearance of common objects, proper names, and verbatim verbal exchanges (the recall of all of which is nearly always reconstructed from inference, estimation and guesswork); directly relevant are also the impact of high levels of emotion on the encoding of any memory and the influence upon memory of the questioning and the way questions are asked;
- the impact of trauma and other mental ill health on memory, behaviour and testimony;
- the influence of factors such as disorientation, anxiety, fear, lack of trust in authorities or interpreters on the disclosure of material facts and submission of other evidence;
- the influences of stigma, shame, fear of rejection by family and community, which may also inhibit disclosure. Stigma may also account for the lack of documentary or other evidence, including under-reporting of incidents of violence, and limits on their inclusion in country of origin information;
- the influence on knowledge, memory, behaviour and testimony of aspects of the applicant's background, such as age, culture, education, gender, sexual orientation and/or gender identity, profession, socio-economic status, religion, values, and past experiences.

Example

Irene was a journalist in Zimbabwe writing under a pseudonym. She cannot easily prove that it was she who wrote the articles in question, nor is it easy for her to obtain copies of the articles from Zimbabwe.

To an extent, she can address this with a witness statement and explain everything she remembers about the articles she wrote and the process of getting them published. However, her case would be much stronger if she could obtain copies of the articles or something that links her to the pseudonym she used, such as a letter from the publisher.

Failing that, most immigration judges would view her case more sympathetically if she could at least demonstrate that she has tried very hard to obtain the relevant evidence and show copies of letters written, calls made and so on, and explain in her statement what steps she has taken to try to obtain the evidence. This would distinguish her case from someone who makes a claim but makes no attempt to substantiate it, at least as far as the judge can see. IRs 339L(i) and (ii) lend support to this approach.

8.1.5.2 Section 8 AITCA 2004

Section 8 of AITCA 2004 demands that specific types of 'behaviour' by an asylum seeker after they left their own country be treated by decision makers, including judges, as damaging credibility:

- reliance on false documents and destruction of documents,
- claiming asylum after receiving an immigration decision or after arrest,
- not claiming asylum despite having had a reasonable opportunity to do so in a 'safe' third country (safe third country is given a specific meaning later in the section),
- s8(3)(da) (from 28 September 2023) adds failing to provide on request anything required to access electronic devices found on the person, or which appears to have been in their possession

SM Iran [2005] UKAIT 00116 holds that even where s8 applies, the evidence should be assessed as a whole: a balanced assessment of the case as a whole is essential.

Nevertheless, s8 behaviour should as far as possible be addressed in witness statements. Both the HO and the Tribunal will be obliged to take them into account.

The statutory presumption re failing to claim asylum in a 'safe' third country applies only to those countries defined as 'safe' in section 8(7) itself: this is essentially whether they are European Union countries. And remember that the courts have accepted, in Adimi, &Ors [1999] Imm AR 560, that there is some element of choice open to a refugee as to where they actually claim asylum. The *HO Sovereign Borders International Asylum Comparisons Report* indicates that the main causes of claiming asylum in particular destinations are trusted social networks, diaspora communities, and a shared language and/or colonial history.

KA (Afghanistan) [2019] EWCA Civ 914 considered the relevance of a child asylum seeker's failure to claim asylum in a 'safe' third country, however the principle can be applicable to adult cases. It found that the public domain country evidence available regarding countries such as Hungary was such that careful reasoning would be required before a person's credibility was treated as damaged due to a failure to claim asylum there. Reasons would always be required in holding this factor against any asylum seeker, let alone a child: for example, there may well not have been an opportunity to claim asylum in a 'safe' country through which a claimant has passed while concealed in the back of a lorry.

However, an explanation should always be sought as to a failure to claim asylum abroad, particularly if there has been a lengthy stopover. A desire to join relatives in the UK, 'r a pre-arranged journey with only transit stops abroad, might be possible explanations; as might an ability to speak English, so might conditions in the third country (e.g. colonial or diplomatic relationships with the asylum seeker's country of origin might encourage or discourage an asylum claim).

Regarding delays in claiming asylum, much depends on the individual circumstances. Many asylum seekers who attempt to enter the country before making their claims will do so for the good reasons laid out by agencies such as the UNHCR, e.g. the effects of trauma, language problems, lack of information, previous experiences with authority and feelings of insecurity, rather than with a view to falsifying their claims with the assistance of contacts in this country. The UKVI *Assessing credibility* guidance mentions a lack of knowledge or misinformation about the asylum system, fear of detention, fears whether objectively warranted or not, being under another's control or having another form of leave as plausible reasonable explanations.

KG (Turkey) [2022] EWCA Civ 1578 emphasises that there is no need to cite s8 so long as the potentially adverse impact of any relevant period of delay (particularly where raised by the HO) on credibility is considered and the reasoning explained. NBA 2022 s19 will amend s8 to require the FTT to specifically engage with any s8 behaviour and its precise reasons for its conclusions on the issue.

8.1.5.3 Entering the country

The capacity in which a person enters the country ought not to carry decisive weight in the analysis of their claim to need international protection. Someone might claim asylum having entered as a visitor: the UNHCR has warned that this will often arise out of an understandable desire to secure some form of temporary stay in a country, to avoid simply being returned home from the border.

Again, look at Adimi:

> Most asylum seekers who attempt to enter the country before making their claims will do so for the reasons suggested by UNHCR rather than with a view to falsifying their claims with the assistance of friends and contacts here.

8.1.5.4 Inconsistencies

Although there are lots of possible explanations for discrepancies, inconsistencies are often thought to justify rejection of a person's story – because if a person gives different versions of an event, this may well be because he or she is making it up rather than drawing on genuine recollections. For this reason one of the practitioner's most important functions is taking full and accurate instructions, in order to:

- avoid unnecessary discrepancies; and

- ensure that any existing inconsistencies are adequately explained.

If you do have any inconsistencies in the case that cannot be otherwise explained, bear in mind that the client may be a victim of torture. The specialist international Tribunal regarding torture, the United Nations Committee against Torture (UNCAT), has warned that complete accuracy is seldom to be expected from victims of torture: Alan v Switzerland (UNCAT) [1997] INLR 29 (& see MIL 4.3.9 for the analogous approach to modern slavery victims with PTSD).

The Joint Presidential Guidance Note No 2 of 2010 addressing *Child, Vulnerable adult and sensitive appellants* requires judges to bear in mind a person's vulnerability as a possible explanation for discrepancies (see also: JL China [2013] UKUT 145).

Another potential source of vulnerability which may give rise to inconsistencies in a client's account is that they may be a victim of sexual violence, which they may find very difficult to disclose. For the particular issues to be aware of when dealing with male victims, the UNHCR Guidelines Working with Men and Boy Survivors of Sexual and Gender-based Violence in Forced Displacement (2012) are essential reading.

> **Top Tip**
>
> There is no such thing as perfect recall and no human being is capable of giving a completely consistent account of the same events on different occasions. The reasons for this lie in the way that memories are made.
>
> Firstly memories must be recorded. Bystanders to the same events always perceive the same events differently and attach significance to different aspects of those events. The human brain searches for patterns and where information is absent (or even where it is present sometimes) the brain completes the 'picture' by filling in blanks.
>
> Secondly, memories must be stored. Sometimes memories are simply lost or partially lost and blanks filled in. Minor aspects of events, such as sensations, may be recalled long after the event even though major events are forgotten. The passage of time generally degrades memories.
>
> Thirdly, memories must then be recalled and recounted. There is ample opportunity for memories to be recalled differently on different occasions. For example, the use of leading questions will often change the way that memories are recalled, particularly in children.
>
> Despite this, the fact is that in many asylum cases the only evidence is the witness's own testimony. If it is perceived as flawed, it will be rejected.
>
> Always consider possible explanations for discrepancies such a lack of formal education or a bad memory.

Due allowance must be made for the different stages of the asylum process, and the various ways in which information is elicited - the nature of the process is such that a single perfectly consistent telling of the story is unlikely. While the Tribunal has agreed that inconsistencies between accounts given at different times can properly be referred to for the purpose of assessing credibility, it will be necessary to consider all the circumstances of the interview process, including whether an explicit opportunity was given to add information in the context of the complexity for the questions and the scope for misunderstanding (DA Turkey [2004] UKIAT 104). In KS it was stated §99 that

> a child-sensitive application of the lower standard of proof may still need to be given to persons if they are recocunting relevant events that took place at a time when they were minors...

> **Top Tip**
>
> Not all additional information is necessarily inconsistent with an earlier account. It is the very nature of the process that further questions are asked later about an account that has already been given. Indeed, this is the whole purpose of a HO asylum interview. It would be truly absurd, then, to say that the provision of additional information is an elaboration of an account that is in some way not credible.
>
> However, providing additional information is not the same as making changes to an account or adding new events, which are likely to cause significant credibility issues.
>
> Contemporaneous complaints about unsatisfactory interviews will be more telling than late challenges at appeal.

Failure to read back the contents of the interview to its subject may make the interview a very unreliable basis for criticising an account, though see DA Turkey for the fact that an objection to an interview's conduct plus a mere failure to sign does not of itself mean an interview should be disregarded without analysing the surrounding circumstances. The screening interview is not intended to explore the substance of the asylum claim. AA (Sudan) [2021] EWHC 1869 (Admin) observes that the SSHD's practice of completing some screening interview boxes as if the answer had come from the asylum seeker was potentially misleading.

Another issue with interviews is the propriety of the questions actually asked: thus in A, B, and C (C-148/13 to C-150/13) the CJEU looked at the ways in which an asylum claim based on the individual's sexuality might be assessed, and stressed that the methods used to assess the case had to be consistent with the right to respect for human dignity and private and family life. This means

- questions about sexual practices are a "no go" area
- stereotyped notions about how people behave should be avoided
- "testing" for sexuality is an unreliable process, and the filming of intimate acts is unlikely to take things further reticence in revealing intimate aspects of one's life cannot be a factor counting against the acceptance of the claim's truthfulness

8.1.5.5 Plausibility

Asylum claims are often rejected because the story put forward is thought to be implausible. However, there are various caveats to be considered before a claim is so rejected.

Repressive regimes may act in a way that is unpredictable: see Suleyman (16242; 11 February 1998):

> It is clear to us that a repressive regime ... may well act in ways which defy logical analysis. A person who is genuinely a victim of such a regime may well find that the partial account he is able to give of its activities as they have affected him is not something which will stand up to a strictly logical analysis. The regime may seem to govern by confusion; it may engage in other activities, of which the Appellant knows nothing; it may simply behave in a way which a person sitting in safety in the United Kingdom might regard as almost beyond belief.

Other considerations regarding plausibility are:

- the need to assess the account in the light of the relevant country evidence, see e.g. Horvath [1999] INLR 7;
- Events in the kinds of countries that produce asylum seekers may well be rather more chaotic than the life experience of a decision maker in this country might expect: see HK [2006] EWCA Civ 1037:

  > Inherent probability, which may be helpful in many domestic cases, can be a dangerous, even a wholly inappropriate, factor to rely on in some asylum cases. Much of the evidence will be referable to societies with customs and circumstances which are very different from

those of which the members of the fact-finding tribunal have any (even second-hand) experience. Indeed, it is likely that the country which an asylum-seeker has left will be suffering from the sort of problems and dislocations with which the overwhelming majority of residents of this country will be wholly unfamiliar.

And again, See Bingham MR quoted in Y [2006] EWCA Civ 1223:

No judge worth his salt could possibly assume that men of different nationalities, educations, trades, experience, creeds and temperaments would act how he might think he would have done or even – which may be quite different – in accordance with his concept of what a reasonable man would have done.

Another element of plausibility is demeanour – it would be wrong to presume that a witness would necessarily give evidence in a particular emotional state: see the Tribunal in M (Yugoslavia) [2003] UKIAT 00004.

But none of this means that an account must be accepted at face value or that the decision maker must suspect their own judgement entirely. It will be for an adviser to anticipate and identify areas where an account may be found to be implausible and then take sufficient further instructions to show as far as possible how and why the events happened as claimed. Where necessary country information can be found to help corroborate the account or at least show it is consistent with what happens in that country.

Language proficiency may be relevant to determining a person's origin. At one time the HO used a language analysis agency, Sprakab, to try to determine this issue: MN and KY (Scotland) [2014] UKSC 30 raises various concerns including that the reports' authors had not adequately evidenced their asserted knowledge of country and culture. From around 2015 concerns increasingly arose about the reliability of these reports; by 2022 the HO only relied on Sprakab reports vis-á-vis disputed Somali Bajuni cases. ASA [2022] UKUT 222 (IAC) states that where expert evidence of language proficiency is provided, it should refer to the individual's speech, by reference to morphology, syntax, phonology and vocabulary, relevant features. It may also be relevant to opine on how speech compares with other young people, bearing in mind that in the modern era there is likely to be less variation in speech patterns.

8.1.5.6 Dishonesty

Proven, or admitted, dishonesty inevitably counts against any person who seeks to demonstrate their story's truthfulness, but a lack of veracity on one issue does not necessarily disprove the remainder of the account. Any acts of dishonesty must be specifically explained (for example entering the country on false documents).

A famous case says that the core of an account may be credible even though some elements are not made out: Chiver (10758; 24 March 1994). However this is rather an old authority now. The idea is more clearly expressed in MA (Somalia) [2010] UKSC 49:

People lie for many reasons.... so the significance of lies will vary from case to case.

8.1.5.7 Corroboration

Whilst for understandable reasons there can be no absolute requirement of corroboration in an asylum case, one should always carefully consider what support may be available. In general the potential sources will be

- witnesses by way of family members, friends or activists/office holders in groups sympathetic to the asylum seeker's situation (e.g. the UK branches of political parties or religious groups from their country of origin)

- documentary evidence particular to the asylum seeker and material to the case that they are putting – e.g. proof of nationality, proof of the asylum seeker's employment, political activities, indications of official interests in them by way of arrest warrants etc.
- media reports from the country of origin specific to the case mentioning the asylum seeker by name (though they are only of real use if they can be verified as genuine, as may be the case if they can be seen on the official online version of the source in question)
- medical expert evidence going to the consistency of their mental health presentation with PTSD and their physical presentation with torture or other ill treatment (see also Chapter 14 at section 14.5.4 *Expert evidence*)
- public domain country evidence
- expert country evidence both on credibility (i.e. whether their account of past events is consistent with known conditions in the country) and risk (i.e. the likely consequences of the return to the country of origin of a person with their characteristics) (see also Chapter 14 at section 14.5.5 *Country expert reports*)

8.1.5.8 Approach to documents; and enquiries in the country of origin

Merely producing a document from the country of origin does not necessarily advance an asylum claim: its relevance needs to be carefully explained, as does its provenance, including how it was that it was brought to the UK (as an account of how a document was obtained may easily undermine some aspect of the client's core account). In Tanveer Ahmed [2002] UKIAT 00439 (starred) (perhaps the most infamous of Tribunal decisions in relation to immigration procedure generally), we see the Tribunal setting down the relevant principles, which are essentially that:

- If an allegation of forgery of a document is made by the HO, then it bears the burden of proof in establishing that assertion. However, in most cases forgery is not the relevant issue, given that documents may be obtained through illicit means in many countries without being a forgery (i.e. a bribe might produce a 'valid' yet unreliable document).
- The general principle in asylum and human rights cases is that the applicant bears the burden of proof, which in turn requires that they establish the reliability of any document on which they seek to rely.
- The decision maker should consider whether a document is one on which reliance should properly be placed after looking at all the evidence in the round.
- In practice this means that the general findings on a person's credibility are likely to be a determination of the approach taken to any particular document, unless its genuineness is supported by other evidence such as some form of verification report.

A number of Strasbourg decisions (including Singh v Belgium (33210/11)) have indicated that sometimes a state will have to must investigate a document before rejecting it as genuine. Otherwise a real risk of inhuman and degrading treatment may be left unexplored.

- In MJ (Afghanistan) [2013] UKUT 00253 theUT found that where documents were of a nature where verification would be easy, and the documentation came from an unimpeachable source, a duty to investigate might arise
- PJ (Sri Lanka) [2014] EWCA Civ 1011 developed this thinking, ruling that where attempts to verify documents were not made when the duty to do so arose, the government might be precluded from challenging their authenticity subsequently
- MA (Bangladesh) [2016] EWCA Civ held that this duty may arise where a disputed documentis at the centre of the request for protection: if so, the decision maker should ask themselves whether a simple process of inquiry will conclusively resolve its authenticity and reliability
- HKK ([2018] UKUT 386 (IAC) notes that where a judge satisfied of a document's reliability, the SSHD may be unable resist the conclusion that the asylum seeker is at risk, absent conducting their own enquiries into that document.In QC [2021] UKUT 33 (IAC) the UT expressed its view as to what should follow where the SSHD had failed to verify a document in the limited and exceptional (in the sense of rare) circumstances that such an obligation arose
    - In such cases, the SSHD would not be able to challenge the document's *authenticity*. However, the SSHD could still challenge its *reliability*. Its provenance and contents remained relevant

- It was especially important to bear in mind that official documents from abroad which recorded complaints rather than officially-sanctioned investigations might be suspect. Thus where a First Information Report from countries such as Pakistan and Bangladesh was relied on, the fact the accusation has been made is in no sense probative of the fact that the relevant authority believes the accusation, let alone of its veracity
- PA [2018] UKUT 337 (IAC) looked at the duties on the SSHD when making enquiries in relation to an asylum claim in the asylum seeker's country of origin.
    - Here the appellant was a citizen of Bangladesh who claimed to have been active in the BNP; the supporting documents were First Information Reports and charge sheets from a police station, said to corroborate his fears of persecution.
- The UT drew attention to Article 22(b) of the Procedures Directive (the same provision remains in IR339IA(ii)) which provides that any information sought in the country of origin needed to ensure that the alleged persecutors were not directly informed of the making of any asylum claim such as to jeopardise the asylum seeker's family's safety. So long as this risk did not arise, there was no requirement to obtain the person's consent before making such enquiries. The SSHD explained that present practice when investigating such documents would be for a FCO official to request to see the relevant register without giving any reference number, so that there would be less chance of the asylum seeker being linked to the enquiry. Previously the reference number had been provided, which as noted by the UT would raise the possibility, if the charge was genuine, of alerting the authorities to the fact of the international protection claim. The UT confined itself to observing that confirmation of the document's authenticity would very significantly strengthen the asylum claim in question
- See also MIL 9.7.6 re family law proceedings.

8.2 Assessing risk: country evidence

As already mentioned, an asylum seeker needs to demonstrate that they face an objective risk of their fear that underlies the asylum claim: i.e. they must show that there is a *real chance* that they will face serious harm if they return home.

Such risk needs to be shown by a combination of evidence:

- their own account which will show what individual factors are present in their case
- reports about circumstances in their country of origin

SB (Sri Lanka) [2019] EWCA Civ 160 stresses the importance of adequate reasoning on credibility and objective risk . Here the reasons for rejecting the asylum seeker's claim did not stand up to scrutiny. The risk categories identified in the Country Guidelines were important but could never represent an exhaustive guide to whether someone was at risk.

8.2.1 Country information

Country information is an essential tool for demonstrating future risk, and often credibility too. It is often referred to as 'objective' evidence. Given that most reporters write from one standpoint or another, absolute objectivity is difficult to demonstrate. However some sources are more respected than others. The reliability of the evidence must be established by the party relying on it.

There are many different sources of country information, and each source has its advantages and disadvantages. A high quality source to which weight is likely to be attached would possess the following qualities:

- **Up to date**: the source would be a recent one, or failing that there would be information that suggested the situation or subject matter of the report was unlikely to have changed.
- **Objective**: there is no such thing as an entirely objective source, but clearly biased sources or sources more likely to have an agenda of some kind may be considered less reputable. However, even a biased source might include useful factual information: much depends on how the information is used and presented.

- **Identifiable origins**: the sources used by a report would be as well-informed as possible and their research methodology would be clear.

Common types of information source include:

- **Government reports:**
    - Eg: the UKVI's Country Policy and Information notes (CPINs) (used by the SSHD's decision makers to make decisions in asylum cases), US Department of State reports, which may reflect the agenda of the government or government department concerned but subject to public review. There is a difference between those reports that are a compilation of sources (which the UKVI has often done rather well) and those documents which represent guidance to caseworkers on how to determine appeals: the latter are not necessarily neutral. The Independent Chief Inspector of Immigration has been critical, see eg the 2017 Report re HO *production and use of country information*
    - UB (Sri Lanka) [2017] EWCA Civ 85 holds that the SSHD should always put their country policy material before a decision maker: this is an important and very useful principle that may permit poorly represented unrepresented claims to be reopened where relevant material was withheld
    - Some governments sponsor fact-finding missions to particular countries: these have been criticised by the ECtHR where they rely on anonymous sources, see Sufi and Elmi [2011] ECHR 1045; the UT in CM Zimbabwe CG [2013] UKUT 00059 (IAC) decided that country evidence from unnamed NGOs could be given weight in certain circumstances
- **Inter-governmental or supra-national reports**, e.g. UNHCR, African Union. May be compromised by the agendas of different constituent governments or by the organisation's own agenda or remit. Tend to be infrequently updated. The view of UNHCR carries special weight given its status and role in international law, expertise and experience, especially re matters within its particular remit or where it has special expertise: AAA (Syria) [2023] UKSC 42
- **Non-governmental reports**, e.g. Amnesty International, Human Rights Watch. May reflect campaigning agenda of the organisation concerned, but research methodology may be clear and the organisations have their reputations to protect. Annual reports are infrequent but updates are sometimes published
- **Press**, e.g. national or international newspapers and websites. Some articles may be the product of good quality journalism, others less so. May have the advantage of being very recent or precisely linked to a particular asylum claim.

Example

The suitability of a source depends on the context in which it is used. Normally, a blog post from an anonymous blogger in the country of origin would be given little weight. However, if the blog is long standing and appears unconnected personally to the asylum seeker, it might be useful corroboration of a claimed fact of some sort, particularly if backed up directly or indirectly by other sources.

An opposition newspaper might be expected by the reader to be highly critical of the government it opposes and to contain 'biased' information that suggests the opposition is badly treated. However, it may be corroborated by other sources and may contain specific facts or details that have a direct bearing on the account of a given asylum seeker.

Unusual sources should not lightly be disregarded merely because they can be said to be biased, but they should be used with care and further corroboration should always be sought.

8.2.2 Country Guidelines cases

Once it comes to assessing the country evidence, there are obvious advantages to achieving consistency of approach. For this reason the Tribunal has introduced a system of giving country guidelines, made in the context of particular asylum appeals which have reached what is now the Upper Tribunal. The higher courts have accepted the value of such a system and indeed the ECtHR itself often cites UT decisions.

A list of current Country Guidelines (CG) sometimes referred to as Country Guidance cases is kept on the MoJ's website page addressing Upper Tribunal – Immigration and Asylum Chamber Decisions here and is regularly updated; you can also find a list of pending cases and the issues they engage there. It is essential to be familiar with any relevant CG case relating to client's country of origin.

- Most CG cases include clear pointers as to future risk for various categories of asylum claimants
- They may also include other useful information: for example details of expert witnesses, opinion evidence by such experts which may be relevant to your particular case even though it did not find its way into the conclusions of the CG decision itself, or citations of country evidence which are, again, useful to you even though they may not have borne on the outcome of the CG case
- FTT judges must follow the findings in CG cases – a failure to do so is an error of law (see the Practice Directions of the Immigration Tribunals at paragraph 9.2-9.4)
- You may be able to distinguish your client's case from unhelpful CG findings because of individual factors that are present in your case: CG cases are supposed to be guides rather than straitjackets, see e.g. OD (Ivory Coast) [2008] EWCA Civ 1299:

    > The task of the immigration judge is not a simple tick box exercise. It should involve making an assessment of risk on the full evidence before the tribunal; that is why we have enxperienced immigration judges.

- Alternatively the country situation may have changed – the test to persuade departure from CG findings is to show that 'cogent evidence' has been provided justifying departure from the relevant guidance, see SG Iraq [2012] EWCA Civ 940
- KK and RS (Sri Lanka) [2022] EWCA Civ 119 emphasises that only cogent evidence will justify (hopefully infrequent) revisitations of Country Guidelines

The most efficient way in which to research and present country evidence is to take materials in this order:

- Relevant CG findings (because if your client fits iimmigration a risk category as so identified, your country evidence work is done)
- A policy position struck by the HO (because if their own guidance suggests a class of person is at risk, it is very hard for them to argue against that position)
- The HO's own published country evidence compilations (which are found within their CIG reports: why repeat their work if they have made your case for you?)
- Other human rights reports (and then media reports, which are only necessary if the respected reporters like Amnesty have not covered the necessary ground, or where they post-date other evidence and show a worsening situation)

Always bear in mind that CG cases can be a fabulous source of inspiration for issues that may be relevant in future asylum claims from other countries. For example, the cases on Zimbabwe and loyalty testing may give food for thought on relevant issues when other regimes freely attribute political opinions to opponents; and the approach to Ahmadi religious asylum claims from Pakistan may carry over to other stigmatised religions elsewhere.

Relevant considerations are (see further MIL 14.5.4, 17.4.2):

- impartiality of experts
- campaigning backgrounds
- their precise expertise
- the range of sources they have drawn upon
- the currency of their expertise in the light of the durability of the country situation
- their awareness and treatment of views contrary to their own (particularly well known views of government sources)

8.2.3 Relevance of past experiences to future risk

The past is always a useful guide to the future, and this common sense notion is adopted by IR339K:

> The fact that a person has already been subject to persecution or serious harm, or to direct threats of such persecution or such harm, will be regarded as a serious indication of the person's well-founded fear of persecution or real risk of suffering serious harm, unless there are good reasons to consider that such persecution or serious harm will not be repeated.

Past persecution is therefore useful as an indicator of future risk, so long as you have at least some evidence, by way of relevant CG findings or a recent country report, to demonstrate that the country situation remains the same. In JK v Sweden 59166/12 [2016] ECHR 704 the Court indicates that the burden shifts to the Government to 'dispel any doubts' about risk on return in circumstances where there was a 'strong indication' arising out of past persecution of risk from non-state actors.

8.2.4 Specific individual risk

It is always important in an asylum case to look at individual risk factors thrown up in the individual case. These may be positive, such as individual history and/or association with family members or political/religious figures who are themselves at risk, prominence locally and nationally, a record of detention by the security forces; or negative, for example:

- leaving the country of origin on their own passport (which might imply that the authorities were not interested in them – but think about issues such as corruption, resources, access to information technology, or indeed whether the authorities are perfectly happy to be rid of some individuals)
- delaying in leaving the country (which may suggest they are not really at risk)
- staying in the homes of relatives before departing (which might be thought an obvious place for the security forces to look)
- being of too low a profile to be at risk (either as shown by CG findings or based on the HO assessment of the country evidence generally)
- having been released from detention without suffering significant ill treatment which would not have happened if they were genuinely at risk (but think about whether, by their flight from their country, they have inevitably breached reporting conditions imposed on their release or shown their refusal to become informers or without cooperate with the authorities)
- any of the section 8 AITCA 2004 factors: whilst these are originally formulated as *credibility* points (i.e. '*you are not telling the truth because ...*'), they may also crop up as *risk* points (i.e. '*if you were really at risk, whether you are telling the truth or not, you would have claimed asylum sooner*')

All of these points are better answered by *evidence* than the citation of authority. It is very difficult to argue with recent objective relevant country evidence.

8.2.5 Generic risk cases

Where an individual is relying for their claim of persecution not on a desire by officials or non-state actors to target them as an individual, but rather from general problems (e.g. poor prison conditions: see Batayav [2003] EWCA Civ 1489 and again at [2005] EWCA Civ 366), then it will be necessary to show that the matters complained of are truly endemic.

- Thus the Tribunal may be right to look for a 'consistent pattern of gross and systematic violation of fundamental human rights': see Hariri [2003] EWCA Civ 807;
- the correct test is whether there is a consistent pattern of serious ill treatment see e.g. AA (Risk for involuntary returnees) Zimbabwe CG Rev 1 [2006] UKAIT 00061

8.2.6 Future activities

In the case of HJ (Iran) [2010] UKSC 31 the Supreme Court fundamentally changed the approach to the issue of how future behaviour will be considered relevant to the assessment of entitlement to refugee status. The previous legal analysis was a very pragmatic one. Essentially, whether future behaviour could make a person a refugee was a simple question of fact: would the person in question in fact, despite the dangers, behave in a way that would expose them to persecution?

HJ (Iran) establishes that where a person would in future refrain from behaving in a way that would expose them to danger because of the risk of persecution that behaviour brings, that person is a refugee.

The leading judgment in HJ (Iran) is that of the late Lord Rodgers, who explains the series of issues that arise thus §82:

- Will the person be liable to persecution if they lived openly?
- If so, would this individual live openly on a return?
- If they would live openly on return, then had they a well founded fear of persecution?
- If they would live discreetly on return, was this because of a risk of persecution?
- If so, then they also had a well founded fear of persecution; however if their discretion was merely due to social pressure or embarassment, then they would not.

The context in HJ (Iran) is sexuality – would a gay person have to conceal aspects of their sexuality in order to avoid persecution – and UKLGIG has published useful guidance on how the principles from the case should be applied in practice.

However, the legal principle is a wider one of profound significance. If a political or religious activist wants to continue their activities in future but would be prevented from so doing because of the risk of persecution, it is no answer to say that it would be reasonable for them to return to their country and just keep a low profile. Thus following HJ Iran the RT (Zimbabwe) [2012] UKSC 38 held in the case of that asylum seekers cannot be expected to lie or dissemble about their political beliefs in order to achieve safety in their own country (eg when actively tested for their loyalty). The test was neatly paraphrased in KK and RS (Sri Lanka) [2022] EWCA Civ 119:

> "if a person would be persecuted on return for the manifestation of their political opinions, it is no answer to say that they could avoid persecution by concealing those opinions; accordingly, if it is found that but for the threat of persecution they would manifest those opinions they are entitled to international protection."

So RT (Zimbabwe) applies equally to a committed political activist and to a person with no politician convictions: neither can be expected to lie. The latter of course would not suffer persecution in the HJ Iran sense if they were unable to express opinions they did not in truth hold.

The principle applies to religious claims too: WA (Pakistan) [2019] EWCA Civ 302. KK and RS Sri Lanka (CG) [2021] UKUT 130 (IAC) considers HJ (Iran) re returning Sri Lankan asylum seekers. The UT emphasises

- Factual findings must be made as to the genuineness of the beliefs held, the consequences of open expression of such beliefs and likelihood of detection and mistreatment (bearing in mind the likelihood that a particular interest is taken in returnees), and the reasons why they would act discreetly (if that is what the evidence suggests would happen): having regard to whether they would be monitored by the authorities
- That there is no need for any equivalence between activities in the UK and abroad.
- One would have to bear in mind whether organisations with relevant political activities were active in the country of origin – but the absence of such organisations would not prevent an individual wishing to act on an individual basis.

- The beliefs in question might not be genuine: but presumably the likelihood of wishing to manifest beliefs that an asylum seeker did not truly hold, particularly if serious adverse consequences would ensue, was remote.

8.2.7 Activities in the United Kingdom and claims made in bad faith

Activities in the United Kingdom

Refugees can base their claim for asylum on their own activities that post-date their departure from their country of origin, or in changes in the situation there (e.g. a coup that places all those holding their political affiliation at risk; or it may be that whereas they might not have been at risk hadthey never left the country, the increased attention they will attract on a return at the border will itself create a risk of persecution). These are known as 'sur place' claims.

Immediate risk on return at an airport has been explored in considerable detail for some countries, such as Zimbabwe and Turkey, and is also argued for other countries, such as Eritrea and Sri Lanka. Compelling evidence is usually needed to succeed with such arguments as they affect a large number of asylum applicants. There may be relevant Country Guideline decisions.

Returnees cannot be expected to lie about their beliefs or how they have spent their time in the UK – see IK Turkey CG [2004] UKIAT 00312 – re Turkey, butof interest in any 'questioning on return' case. And as we have just mentioned above, if they have to act discreetly in relation to expressing their political opinions on a return, that in itself should be recognised as persecution if their discretion is caused by a desire to avoid serious harm: RT (Zimbabwe).

If a claimant has engaged in activities directed against his or her own government while in the UK, it will be difficult to obtain evidence that the government in question (a) monitors UK-based opposition activities, (b) communicates that information to the domestic authorities and (c) that those authorities make use of that information to target the individuals concerned.

In YB (Eritrea) [2008] EWCA Civ 360 the Court of Appeal dealt with this question in the context of Eritrea and concluded that a common sense approach should be followed rather than an overly analytical approach which wrongly sought evidence of matters that could be readily inferred, such as the likelihood that repressive regimes probably monitor the internet for information about their political opposition or filmed nationals who demonstrated in front of their Embassies. The real question was what would be the consequences for the asylum seeker in question of the information-gathering in question. Similarly KS (Burma) [2013] EWCA Civ 67 found in a case concerning political 'hangers-on' that it would be wrong to presume that regimes with a record of persecution would make careful and rational assessments of which potential targets to pursue. Thus in HJ (F/E) [2022] ScotCS CSOH_69 holds that the FTT should consider carefully whether a regime is sufficiently repressive that it is likely to analyse photographs or online sources to pursue political opponents. The CoA returned to this theme in WAS (Pakistan) [2023] EWCA Civ 894 emphasising that direct evidence about 'the level of and the mechanics of monitoring' cuold not realistically be expected, particularly given the ease with which anyone could simply take pictures using their 'phone.

BA Iran CG [2011] UKUT 36 (IAC) identifies a number of factors and 'a spectrum of risk' likely to be relevant when assessing the evidence. The non-exhaustive list of factors in BA is grouped under a number of headings: nature of sur place activity; the chance of being identified as participating in such activities; factors triggering inquiry/action on return; the consequences if the asylum seeker is identified and thus associated with such activities, and the risk of that actually happening. Each heading is then illustrated and amplified.

Evidence from social media sources is an increasingly important aspect of international protection appeals.

- PA054792016 [2017] UKAITUR (24 May 2017) is a useful unreported public case on the assessment of Facebook evidence. The UT stresses the importance of reviewing the available

evidence with care to determine the likelihood that posts will have been seen by possible actors of persecution, bearing in mind privacy settings and the individual's following
- XX Iran CG [2022] UKUT 23 (IAC) records interesting evidence re
  - Facebook's responses to requests from information from foreign governments for disclosure of certain data (see biannual Transparency Reports re government authorities' user data requests)
  - Deletion of Facebook accounts: possible, though with a 90 day lag for full efficacy across the Facebook system and without removing records of messaging or posts etc shared on people's accounts
  - The possibility that search engines may retrieve and cache material for certain periods, and that foreign intelligence services are more likely to trawl and cache themselves than simply conduct enquiries at the border (and are especially interested in a person's social graph/network)
  - Stresses the importance of using the "Download your information" function to give a full picture of activity on the account
- *XX* concludes that the possibility of closing one's Facebook account and not volunteering the fact of its prior existence may be relevant to considering future actions which might mitigate risk. So long as this avoids the *HJ (Iran)* scenario where the reason for so doing is suppression of a characteristic that they have a right not to suppress. There was no fundamental right to have access to a particular social media platform as opposed to the right to political neutrality
- When relying on such evidence, it would be advisable for the lawyer to produce a witness statement tieing together the meaning of particular postings and explaining matters that might otherwise be unclear, such as the settings on the account and the number of followers

Activities conducted in bad faith

The issue of the wilful creation of an asylum claim through activities found to be conducted in 'bad faith' outside the country of origin (for example, cynical attendance at demonstrations outside an embassy) has occasionally arisen. In Danian [2000] Imm AR 96 the Court of Appeal held that the motive behind activities is irrelevant, the only question is whether there is a well-founded fear of being persecuted for a Convention reason.

Rule 339J(iv) states that the Secretary of State must take into account in making an asylum decision:

> whether the person's activities since leaving the country of origin or country of return were engaged in for the sole or main purpose of creating the necessary conditions for making an asylum claim or establishing that he is a person eligible for humanitarian protection or a human rights claim, so as to assess whether these activities will expose the person to persecution or serious harm if he returned to that country.

This rule has been interpreted as encouragling close scrutiny of claims made in bad faith. But no judge appears to have rejected an asylum claim where that close scrutiny leads to a finding of persecution for reasons of attributed political opinion. Thus KS (Burma)[2013] EWCA Civ 67 concluded that

> 'It is unpalatable that someone may become entitled to refugee status as a result of his cynical manipulation but if, objectively, he has a well-founded fear of persecution by reason of imputed political opinion, that may be the reality.'

8.2.8 Risk and route of return

There has been significant debate over the years over the extent to which risks arising from the manner of return and journeys back to the asylum seeker's home area are relevant to assessing an entitlement tinternational protection. The HO has often argued 'Your original claim based on political activities has been assessed as not showing a real risk of serious harm. You say you would be harmed at the point of return, or during the journey home, or would go hungry without identification documents, but as we do not propose returning you until things improve, you do not face any of those dangers.'

A series of decisions have now found the way to the present compromise:

- Where the route or method of return was uncertain, then risks arising from that aspect of the case could not be assessed until the practicalities were finalised and return was enforced. So a claim might fail for lack of certainty as to the mode and route of return, and once removal directions were set, further representations would have to be submitted, backed up by JR if refused without recognition as a fresh claim: HH (Iraq) and JI [2013] EWCA Civ 279 (a case where the human rights monitoring arrangements necessary for the safe return of a national security suspect were not yet in place).
- In AA (Iraq) [2017] EWCA Civ 994, the Court of Appeal found that it was illogical to exclude destitution risks from assessment on the basis that a person was not returnable. Confusion had arisen in the Country Guidelines case leading to the Court of Appeal decision, the UT finding that destitution risks from an inability to establish one's identity to the satisfaction of the authorities providing social support should be treated in the same way as risks arising at the border without travel documents. The Court of Appeal explained that the latter risks were hypothetical, arising only if return became possible, but the former were integral to an asylum claim (MIL 10.3.2.5).
- Thus an undertaking by the HO not to remove pending safely obtaining the documents required to access critical social entitlements cannot be accepted on appeal: see eg SA Iraq [2022] UKUT 37 (IAC)
- The HO must specify the point of return where this is possible: SA Iraq [2022] UKUT 37 (IAC)
- SA Iraq also rules that a Refugee Convention appeal ground will fail where voluntary departure would enable a safe journey: because a person refusing to take up that option would not be outside their country of origin due to a well founded fear of persecution. However an ECHR Art 3 ground of appeal would succeed where they refused voluntary departure: because the appeal focusses on whether removal would contravene the ECHR. Which thus includes enforced removal.

8.3 Being persecuted

There are two main elements to examine in the context of the requirement to show a risk of being persecuted:

Actors
- State
- Non-state

Acts
- Human rights analysis
- Subjective element
- Role of Convention reasons

8.3.1 Actors of persecution

NBA 2022 s31(1) specifies that the following actors can act as persecutors for the purposes of assessing cases under the Refugee Convention:

- the State;
- any party or organisation controlling the State or a substantial part of the territory of the State;
- any non-State actor if it can be demonstrated that the state & non-state actors just mentioned, including any international organisation, are unable or unwilling to provide protection against persecution or serious harm.

8.3.2 Acts of persecution

NBA 2022 s31(2) sets out a minimum definition of what might constitute acts of persecution:

> the persecution must be:

(a) sufficiently serious by its nature or repetition as to constitute a severe violation of a basic human right, in particular a right from which derogation cannot be made under Article 15 of the Convention for the Protection of Human Rights and Fundamental Freedoms(1); or
(b) an accumulation of various measures, including a violation of a human right which is sufficiently severe as to affect an individual in a similar manner as specified in paragraph (a).

Key to this definition is a requirement that the act must be sufficiently serious to amount to a non-derogable right under the ECHR. The non-derogable rights are Article 2 (right to life, except for deaths resulting from lawful acts of war), Article 3 (torture and inhuman or degrading treatment or punishment), Article 4(1) (slavery and servitude), and Article 7 (retrospective conviction).

NBA 2022 s31(3) then goes onto give specific examples of persecution:

- physical/mental/sexual violence
- discriminatory or disproportionate official measures, prosecution, punishment, and denial of judicial redress
- prosecution or punishment for avoiding military service which would have involved conduct leading to exclusion from refugee status (i.e. committing war crimes or crimes against humanity, or serious non-political crimes, or acts contrary to the purposes of the United Nations: all of which we address generally in section 8.7.2).

One particular class of serious harm is where someone is deprived of their nationality, as where a political activist or person of a persecuted ethnic origin is denied the opportunity to return home. MA (Ethiopia) [2009] EWCA Civ 289 held that denying a person return to their country would deprive them of virtually all the rights attaching to citizenship and would thus amount to persecution; however there has to be a link between the reasons why they left the country and their inability to return.

In general persecution must be assessed via its impact on the individual in question (see e.g. UNHCR Handbook para 55).

8.3.2.1 Prosecution and persecution

Straightforward fugitives from justice are not refugees. However to suggest that anyone who flees forms of harm that arise via prosecution is a criminal rather than a refugee is to over-simplify the question and it is clear from NBA 2022 s31(3) that there are circumstances where prosecution will amount to persecution: ie where it is disproportionate or discriminatory.

Thus the use of criminal justice powers such as prosecution may be persecutory where it is in itself discriminatory or implemented in a discriminatory way, be this in the original measures themselves, or via the prosecution or punishment that ensues, or because of a denial of judicial redress (Reg 5(2)(a)-(d)).

In X, Y and Z C-199/12, C-200/12 and C-201/12 the CJEU found that the fact that a country's criminal law targeted homosexuals supported a finding that they were members of a particular social group.

8.3.2.2 Military service

The HO view on these cases can be seen in the Guidance *Military service and conscientious objection*. Sepet [2003] UKHL 15 established that there is no international human right to conscientious objection. The necessary implication is that prosecution for refusal to perform military service will normally be a legitimate prosecution for breach of a state's criminal law.

The question of conscientious objection may require revisiting given subsequent developments in the Grand Chamber of the ECtHR. In Bayatyan v Armenia (Apn No. 23459/03; 1 June 2011 - & see more recently Avanesyan v Armenia (Application no. 12999/15)) the ECtHR ruled that states have a duty to take account of individuals' right to conscientious objection to military service in order to respect the right to freedom of thought, conscience and religion (ECHR Art 9). The case concerned a Jehovah's Witness who was sentenced to two and a half years in prison following his refusal of military service on the grounds of conscientious objection.

That aside, the general position in Sepet _does not apply_ where:

> such service would or might require him to commit atrocities or gross human rights abuses or participate in a conflict condemned by the international community, or where refusal to serve would earn grossly excessive or disproportionate punishment.

As explained in Krotov [2004] EWCA Civ 69, these internationally condemned actions equate to "acts contrary to the basic rules of human conduct." These are the core of humanitarian norms generally accepted between nations as necessary and applicable to protect individuals in war or armed conflict and, in particular civilians, the wounded and prisoners of war. Their breach constitutes to the commission of international condemned actions: there is no need for any formal statement to that effect.

As above, s31(3)(e) of NBA 2022 includes as persecution:

> prosecution or punishment for refusal to perform military service in a conflict, where performing military service would include crimes or acts falling under [the exclusion provisions].

Those exclusion clauses are found in Art 1F of the Refugee Convention (MIL 8.8) and essentially cover war crimes, serious non-political crimes and acts contrary to UN principles. If tthe service in question involves such activities, then punishment for avoiding it is likely to be persecution so long as it reaches a minimal level of severity: see generally the CJEU in Shepherd [2015] EUECJ C-472/13.

In PK and OS Ukraine CG [2020] UKUT 314 (IAC) the UT summarised key points from the earlier case law, adding some points of its own:

- The conduct in question must be committed on a systematic basis, as the result of deliberate policy or official indifference to the widespread actions of a brutal military.
- The asylum seeker must demonstrate that it is reasonably likely that their military service would involve the commission of acts contrary to the basic rules of human conduct, or that it is reasonably likely that, by the performance of their tasks, they would provide indispensable support to the preparation or execution of such acts
- The asylum seeker must also show that they hold a political opinion that is opposed to such actions. In practice this is unlikely to be difficult unless the evidence shows that they have previously been complicit in such conduct
- There must be no alternative to participating in the militaimmigrationservice (eg a procedure for conscientious objection)
- Any punishment will be persecution, including the imposition of a fine or non-custodial sentence, so long as it is more than negligible

8.3.2.3 Civil war

In order to secure refugee status, the House of Lords in Adan [1998] Imm AR 338 found that persons fleeing civil war must demonstrate that they face *a differential impact over* and above the general risks of a civil war in which law and order has broken down completely. The reasoning is essentially that of 'collateral damage': the ordinary victims of civil war are not being specifically targeted, rather they are simply in the way of the opposing factions and are accidentally caught in the crossfire.

Thus the Refugee Convention has not proven helpful to many victims of civil war: Article 15(c) of the Qualification Directive (MIL 8.9.3.2) was intended to fill some of the resulting protection gap. For now the IRs still maintain its protection.

Civilians who can show that they are specifically targeted for a Convention reason or who suffer a differential impact in related activities such as looting and robbery following the breakdown of law and order can potentially make out a claim for refugee status.

> **Example**
>
> In the case of Adan, it was found that there was a general state of civil war and lack of law and order in Somalia. All or many citizens of Somalia could be said to be victims of the civil war in a wide sense. In the leading judgment Lord Lloyd cited a number of authorities, including Hathaway: 'victims of war and conflict are not refugees unless they are subject to differential victimisation based on civil or political status. The same reasoning would not necessarily apply in a country such as 1994 Rwanda, where victims of genocide were being targeted for the very specific Convention reason of race. This went far beyond the normal threat from a general civil war.'

8.4 The Convention reasons

The Convention reasons are central to the Refugee Convention. A refugee is a person with a 'well-founded fear of being persecuted for reasons of…'. There must therefore be a causal link between the harm suffered and one of the five Convention reasons. A person who faces serious harm other than for a Convention reason may receive Humanitarian Protection. From October 2006 to 28 June 2022 the rights of refugees and beneficiaries of HP were the same – so arguments about the existence of a Convention reason were less relevant. There was then a period of differentiated family reunion rights and access to ILR (MIL 9.7, 9.8) which would make proving a Convention reason much more important in practical terms. But the pause of that policy in summer 2023 (MIL 9.7.1) leaves the statuses equal once again.

In addition, as described above, the Convention reasons can have a transformative effect on certain types of harm. For example, imprisonment as a result of criminal behaviour does not amount to persecution, whereas imprisonment for reasons of a Convention reason would amount to persecution. The Convention reasons are as follows:

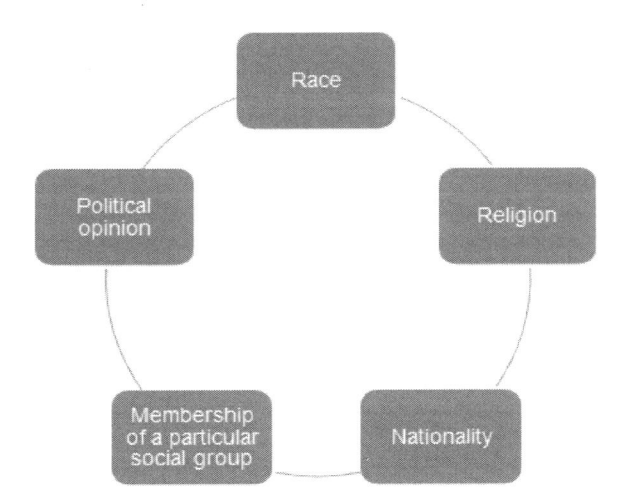

- Race
- Religion
- Nationality
- Membership of a particular social group
- Political opinion

8.4.1 Race

'Race' is interpreted to include '…all persons of identifiable ethnicity' (quote from Professor Hathaway's *The Law of Refugee Status*). The Qualification Directive states that 'the concept of race shall in particular include considerations of colour, descent or membership of a particular ethnic group'.

8.4.2 Religion

NBA 2022 s33(1)(b) offers a very inclusive definition of religion, covering the holding of theistic, non-theistic and atheistic beliefs, the participation in, or abstention from, formal worship in private or in public, either alone or in community with others, other religious acts or expressions of view, or forms of personal or communal conduct based on or mandated by any religious belief.

Cases of religious conversion can be controversial, and are best prepared by anticipating possible HO objections to the credibility of any conversion. Decision makers must "carefully consider the claimant's motivation behind withdrawing from a religious identity, and/or the conversion and their journey to their new faith" (*Assessing Credibility etc* Guidance). However, the depth of religious conviction of the apostate should not be permitted to obscure the fact that the agents of persecution may not be overly concerned about the theological commitment of the convert.

In its judgment in Y and Z the CJEU explained that this provision demonstrated that religious persecution encompassed both protection from serious acts interfering with the applicant's freedom to practice his faith in private circles but also to live that faith publicly. It will be appreciated that the principles in HJ Iran set out above carry over to religious cases as much as gender preference and political opinion ones.

In PS Iran CG [2020] UKUT 46 (IAC) the UT makes some observations of general relevance to religious asylum claims, noting that it is very difficult to peer into someone's soul to assess the reality of their beliefs.

Thus decision makers would have to rely largely on the observations of others to determine whether someone is, or is not, a 'genuine' Christian. 'he focus should be on whether the authorities of the country of origin would treat the asylum seeker as a convert rather than on where the UK decision makers themselves considered they fell on the path to Christianity.

In MH Iran [2020] UKUT 125 the UT observed that witnesses from an asylum seeker's church are able to provide factual evidence about ' claimed convert's attendance at church and their other activities as a Christian. They are also able to provide their opinion as to whether the individual has genuinely converted to Christianity. They should be treated as witnesses of fact; they were not expert witnesses.

When assessing the genuineness of a conversion, relevant considerations would include attendance at a place of worship, the timing of the conversion, the individual's knowledge of the faith, and the opinions of other members of the congregation as to the genuineness of the conversion.

8.4.3 Nationality

NBA 2022 s33(1)(c) defines this thus:

> the concept of nationality shall not be confined to citizenship or lack thereof but shall in particular include membership of a group determined by its cultural, ethnic, or linguistic identity, common geographical or political origins or its relationship with the population of another State.

8.4.4 Membership of a particular social group

Discrimination is the focal point of determining whether a person is a member of a particular social group. Other relevant criteria are whether the discrimination is on the basis of an immutable characteristic of the individual: i.e. one that is either beyond the power of an individual to change (i.e. is innate) or one that it would be contrary to their fundamental human rights for them to forgo (i.e. is non-innate).

Innate characteristic
- e.g. gender, sexuality

Common background that cannot be changed
- e.g. being a former teacher or policeman

Fundamental belief or characteristic
- e.g. home schooling

Shah and Islam [1999] UKHL 20 held that women in Pakistan constituted a particular social group. They shared the common immutable characteristic of gender, were discriminated against as a group in matters of fundamental human rights and the State gave them no adequate protection because they were perceived as not being entitled to the same human rights as men.

NBA 2022 s33(2)-(5) runs with the Shah and Islam approach but also elevates societal attitude to a strict requirement; it clearly states that both the conditions that it defines, shared characteristic and distinct identity, have to be shown to establish that there is a social group.

> (2) A group forms a particular social group for the purposes of Article 1(A)(2) of the Refugee Convention only if it meets both of the following conditions.
> (3) The first condition is that members of the group share—
> (a) an innate characteristic,
> (b) a common background that cannot be changed, or
> (c) a characteristic or belief that is so fundamental to identity or conscience that a person should not be forced to renounce it.
> (4) The second condition is that the group has a distinct identity in the relevant country because it is perceived as being different by the surrounding society.

This legal regime seems more restrictive than the previous understanding of the Refugee Convention. Pre-NBA 2022 the UK followed the EU asylum regime which made the Refugee Convention the cornerstone of international protection. So there was some scope for interpreting this provision's Qualification Directive predecessor, in similar terms, creatively. Thus in K and Fornah [2006] UKHL 46 the House of Lords indicated that the Qualification Directive seemed out of line with the internationally understood interpretation of the Refugee Convention. DH Afghanistan [2020] UKUT 223 (IAC) found §72 that it is necessary to read these as alternative rather than cumulative requirements. But on this very issue the *Assessing credibility and refugee status* Guidance says the new Act's definition should be followed.

A social group cannot be defined by the persecution which a potential member is experiencing. It has to exist independently of the persecution, although the persecution may play a role in the group becoming identifiable. This does not prevent future victims of Female Genital Mutilation constituting a particular social group: K and Fornah.

Particular social groups that have been recognised include:

- In SB Moldova CG [2008] UKAIT 00002, **'former victims of trafficking'** and **'former victims of trafficking for sexual exploitation'**: because of their shared common background or past experience of having been trafficked
- In K and Fornah the Law Lords accepted that **the family** was a particular social group. This may enables, for example, individuals whose fears arise from a family involvement in blood feuds to make good their claims for asylum
- **Gender preference and identity** cases: the CJEU accepted in X, Y and Z (C-199/12 etc.) that 'a person's sexual orientat'on is a ch'racteristic so fundamental to his identity that he should not be forced to renounce it [...] it is important to state that requiring members of a social group sharing the same sexual orientation to conceal that orientation is incompatible with the recognition of a characteristic so fundamental to a person's identity that the persons concerned cannot be required to renounce it'. This will include gender identity, such as identifying as 'non-binary' (falling outwith the fixed gender binary of female-male). It is important to respect an individual's gender identity, private life and personal dignity when determining these claims/appeals: Mx M (El Salvador) [2020] UKUT 313 (IAC)
- **Victims of Female Genital Mutilation** K and Fornah: '... FGM is an extreme expression of the discrimination to which all women in Sierra Leone are subject, as much those who have already undergone the process as those who have not. I find no difficulty in recognising women in Sierra Leone as a particular social group for purposes of article 1A(2)'
- **People with mental disabilities**, see DH Afghanistan [2020] UKUT 223 (IAC): they 'can be said to share a common uniting characteristic that sets them apart from those within society who have no such concerns.' The UT noted that this was a complex question of fact and law.

'Serious mental illness' includes diagnoses which typically involve psychosis (losing touch with reality or experiencing delusions) or high levels of care, and which may require hospital treatment, the most common of which are schizophrenia and bipolar disorder (or manic depression). The mere fact there might not yet be a firm diagnosis of the precise disorder did not prevent it being treated as an innate characteristic or part of a common background that could not be changed. Here the Appellant suffered from serious"mental health problems leading him to act in a disinhibited way, particularly towards women, putting himself at risk from onlookers due to his transgression of social norms

8.4.4.1 FGM and children

A (A Child) [2020] EWCA Civ 731 discusses the jurisdiction of the family courts to make protection orders for persons at risk of FGM (FGMPOs). Family judges must have regard to all the circumstances including "*the need to secure the health, safety and well-being of the girl to be protected.*" They should have regard to immigration decisions from the FTT and UT addressing FGM risks from family members, albeit that any such findings are not binding. Additionally the immigration proceedings may involve different evidence and have a different focus, one in which a child's interests were *primary* rather than *paramount*. X (FGMPO No.2), Re [2019] EWHC 1990 (Fam) lists the relevant considerations when the family court assesses the risks §91. GW (FGM and FGMPOs) Sierra Leone CG [2021] UKUT 108 (IAC) looks at the converse situation, emphasising that the relevance of findings in family proceedings will depend on their cogency, the different issues in play, and the extent to which the evidence overlaps. A FGMPO may be relevant to assessing the likelihood of persecution and the availability of protection.

8.4.5 Political opinion

Express political opinion is perhaps the most often cited Convention reason. Most obviously it will reflect a political opinion against the interests of the state itself, but NBA 2022 s33(1)(c) makes it clear that it may equally well arise on the basis of political opposition to powerful non-state actors:

> the concept of political opinion shall include the holding of an opinion, thought or belief on a matter related to a potential actor of persecution and to its policies or methods, whether or not that opinion, thought or belief has acted upon it

This may include opinions and beliefs contrary to the interests of powerful criminal gangs whose role in society is so pervasive as to be political: EMAP [2022] UKUT 335 (IAC).

We have already seen above (MIL 8.2.6) that a person who acts discreetly to avoid a serious risk of persecution should nevertheless be accepted as facing such a risk. RT (Zimbabwe) shows that this applies to political opinions as well as other Convention reasons.

Where a person claims asylum based partly on activities in the United Kingdom, Immigration Rule 339P warns that these cases may succeed:

> in particular where it is established that the activities relied upon constitute the expression and continuation of convictions or orientations held in the country of origin.

So it will always be important to take careful instructions on the extent to which the expression of political opinions in this country are consistent with the person's history abroad.

8.4.6 Attributed Convention reasons

The NBA 2022 has re-arranged the way this issue is dealt with but without changing anything: thus the possibility of imputation of opinions/characteristics is addressed under the well founded fear provision rather than under Convention reason directly. Thus s32(1)(a)) asks whether '*whether the asylum seeker has a characteristic which could cause them to fear persecution for reasons of race, religion, nationality, membership of a particular social group or political opinion (or has such a characteristic attributed to them by an actor of persecution)*'.

Attributed political opinion has traditionally been the best known possibility: but this provision shows that one could have a viable asylum claim based on an imputation of any other Convention characteristic too (a person wrongly thought to be gay might be attributed membership of a particular social group, or a person carrying out a particular trade might be presumed to be Christian). YMKA Iraq [2022] UKUT 16 (IAC) observes that the Refugee Convention does not offer protection from social conservatism per se and that there is no protected right to enjoy a socially liberal lifestyle. But refugee status may ensue where a "*westernised*" lifestyle reflects a protected characteristic such as political opinion or religious belief, or where there is a real risk that the individual concerned would be unable to mask his westernisation and where such protected characteristics would subsequently be imputed to him.

8.5 Protection and relocation

Note that these provisions of the NBA 2022 and the IRs apply to Humanitarian Protection claims as well as refugee ones.

8.5.1 Protection from non-state persecution

The issue of the availability of protection arises most acutely in non-state persecution cases. In Horvath, the House of Lords held that persecution by non-state actors is only persecution within the meaning of the Refugee Convention if the state is unable to provide a system of protection.

This approach is also followed in NBA 2022 s34:

- Persecution can be carried out by the State, or a party/organisation controlling it or a substantial part of it, or any non-State actor against whose actions the State or a controlling party/organisation do not offer protection (Rs34(1));
- Protection can be provided by the State, or a party/organisation controlling it or a substantial part of it (s34(2(a))) ;
- Protection is generally provided when the relevant actors *take reasonable steps to prevent the persecution by operating an effective legal system for the detection, prosecution and punishment* of the persecution in question which the asylum seeker can access (Rs34(2(a)-(b)).

Horvath is a difficult judgment to read as none of their Lordships offer a clear definition of what is meant by a system of protection. The consensus among asylum lawyers and judges is that the Horvath test is:

- whether or not there is a system in place to offer protection and
- whether there is a reasonable willingness in the country to operate such a system.

All of the judgments differ in emphasis but perhaps the most practical test is that provided by Stuart-Smith LJ in the Court of Appeal stage of the Horvath proceedings and adopted by Lord Lloyd. Key questions (always bearing in mind that no state can guarantee the safety of its citizens) are whether there is

- widespread and systemic indifference to the plight of a class of citizens by the law enforcement agencies
- a system of laws that provide punishments commensurate with the gravity of the crimes in question
- reasonable willingness by the law enforcement agencies to detect, prosecute and punish offenders, bearing in mind that inefficiency and incompetence is not the same as unwillingness unless extreme and widespread

As can be seen, the NBA 2022 s34(2) test is simpler, and it refers explicitly to the protection being both available to the person concerned and the system of protection including an '*effective legal system for the detection, prosecution and punishment of acts constituting persecution*'.

In both tests, the focus should be on the plight of the individual, and whether they can avail themselves of the protection of their country. Obviously past failures of protection, as well as the modern capacity of the actors of persecution as well as the relevant authorities who might offer protection, are relevant.

The greater the link between the authors of harm and the state itself, then the more attention must be paid to the made by the state to provide protection. The steps that can be taken to rein in 'uniformed persecutors' may be more extensive than those possible for individuals with no association with the state, see Svazas [2002] EWCA Civ 74.

OA v SSHD [2021] EUECJ C-255/19 holds that the Qualification Directive's protection and cessation provisions refer to the applicant's country of origin's ability to prevent persecutory acts. Mere social and financial support (eg from clans or family members) was inherently incapable of either preventing acts of persecution or of detecting, prosecuting and punishing such acts, and was thus irrelevant to the effectiveness or availability of state protection. That reasoning may well represent an early opportunity for the UK courts to consider the relationship between the NBA 2022 approach to the Refugee Convention and CJEU precedents.

> **Example**
>
> Leroy is from Jamaica. He witnessed a murder and has been targeted by the criminal gang responsible.
>
> Jamaica is a democracy and although there are serious problems with crime and organised crime, the criminal justice system does broadly function, albeit not very well. The case of AB Jamaica CG [2007] UKAIT 00018 deals with this subject and states that cases have to be decided on their own facts; some asylum claimants will be able to show inadequate protection is available given their particular circumstances. Depending on what has already happened to Leroy, he might well have a strong claim for protection.

8.5.2 Internal relocation

Situations arise where an individual may face persecution in a particular part of their country of origin but will be expected to relocate to a different part of their country where they can live in safety. This usually arises in non-state persecution cases, as it is difficult to imagine where a person might be able to relocate within the territory of a state while fearing persecution by that state. Januzi [2006] UKHL 5 held that there is no legal presumption that internal relocation is not viable in state persecution cases.

NBA 2022 s35 provides:

> (1) An asylum seeker is not to be taken to be a refugee for the purposes of Article 1(A)(2) of the Refugee Convention if—
> (a) they would not have a well-founded fear of being persecuted in a part of their country of nationality (or in a case where they do not have a nationality, the country of their former habitual residence), and
> (b) they can reasonably be expected to travel to and remain in that part of the country.
> (2) In considering whether an asylum seeker can reasonably be expected to travel to and remain in a part of a country, a decision-maker—
> (a) must have regard to—
> (i) the general circumstances prevailing in that part of the country, and
> (ii) the personal circumstances of the asylum seeker;
> (b) must disregard any technical obstacles relating to travel to that part of that country.

Logically, there should be three stages of reasoning:

(i) Is there persecution in the 'home area'?

- If there is no persecution in the home area then the question of internal relocation does not arise. However, in other cases it is still important to start with this question because you cannot properly assess whether an applicant will be safe after return in another area if you have not examined the nature and severity of the threat they face in their home area.

(ii) Is there a 'safe place' to which the person can relocate?

- In cases of state persecution the answer to this question will often be 'no' but cases might arise where a person has been targeted by local government and could relocate to another area. In cases of non-state persecution, the influence and reach of the non-state actors will need to be assessed, particularly though country information.

(iii) Is it reasonable to require the person to relocate there?

- If there is a safe place, the last and most difficult question is whether it is reasonable to expect a person to relocate there. There may be inhospitable jungle or desert in a given country where a person would be free from persecution, but it would be unduly harsh to expect the person to live there.

In AH Sudan [2007] UKHL 49 the House of Lords upheld an immigration Tribunal decision finding that relocation to refugee camps around Khartoum by Darfuri refugees was reasonable. The House of Lords did however stress that it would be an error of law to hold that relocation was only unreasonable if the proposed safe haven exposed the asylum seeker to Article 3 ECHR violations. both the conditions in the home area and in the proposed area of relocation were relevant to reasonableness . The approach was summarised thus by Lord Bingham:

> The decision-maker, taking account of all relevant circumstances pertaining to the claimant and his country of origin, must decide whether it is reasonable to expect the claimant to relocate whether it would be unduly harsh to expect him to do so... The decision-maker must do his best to decide, on such material as is available, where on the spectrum the particular case falls... All must depend on a fair assessment of the relevant facts ... [having regard to] the situation of the particular applicant, whose age, gender, experience, health, skills and family ties may all be very relevant.

Baroness Hale alongside him helpfully placed weight on UNHCR's intervention in the case:

> ...the correct approach ... is to assess all the circumstances of the individual's case holistically and with specific reference to the individual's personal circumstances (including past persecution or fear thereof, psychological and health condition, family and social situation, and survival capacities) ... in the context of the conditions in the place of relocation (including basic human rights, security conditions, socio-economic conditions, accommodation, access to health care facilities), in order to determine the impact on that individual of settling in the proposed place of relocation and whether the individual could live a relatively normal life without undue hardship.

Later the situation changed and the HO accepted that it was not reasonable to expect a Darfuri refugee to relocate to the refugee camps around Khartoum.

SC (Jamaica) [2022] UKSC 15 holds that the internal relocation test should not take account of what might be considered "*due*" to an asylum seeker on accountof their criminality. Another commonly recurring issue in asylum claims was the safety of the Afghan capital, Kabul; the country's law and order breakdown and the poor living conditions for those without family to support them has made Afghan cases an internal relocation battleground. AS (Afghanistan) [2019] EWCA Civ 873 summarised things thus:

- It may be reasonable, and not unduly harsh, to expect a refugee to relocate even if conditions in the safe haven are, by the standards of the country of refuge, very bad.
- However, this does not mean that it will be reasonable for a person to relocate to a safe haven, however bad the conditions they will face there - – conditions may be normal but nevertheless unduly harsh
- There was no need to try and identify whether there was a '*significant minority*' living at subsistence level (which might be 'relatively normal' in a particular country) in any particular country: that was simply one relevant consideration, but was certainly not a governing factor
- The UNHCR guidelines must be considered in any assessment of reasonableness

- Underhill LJ rejected 'objective baseline standards' by way of minimum human rights standards – it was open to decision makers to compare conditions in the safe haven with those that apply generally in the country in question

> **Example**
>
> AA (Uganda) [2008] EWCA Civ 579 held that it was not reasonable to expect a particularly vulnerable single young woman to relocate from her home area to the capital, where she had no connections and an expert had concluded she would be forced to make a living as a prostitute. Evidence rather than generalised assertions is necessary in these cases.

YD (Algeria) [2020] EWCA Civ 1683 looks at internal relocation for the LGBT community. There the UT had found that the fact that a gay man would not 'live openly in Algeria for social, cultural and religious reasons was not sufficient to amount to persecution. Answering the questions posed by HJ (Iran) the UT concluded that, given that finding, the asylum seeker would be living discreetly because of social pressure and not because of persecution. The Court of Appeal considered that approach lawful. But was such a lifestyle nevertheless unduly harsh? Not on the facts of that case. UNHCR's generic evidence that being compelled to conceal one's sexual orientation may result in significant psychological and other harm did not persuade the Court that relocation would necessarily be unduly harsh.

8.6 Non-refoulement

The previous sections have all dealt with Article 1A of the Refugee Convention, which sets out the definition of a refugee. Other clauses set out the rights that a refugee should enjoy. Article 33(1) sets out the most important right for refugees, the right not to be returned to the frontiers of territories where they fear persecution (note there is no absolute right to non-return to other territories).

> No Contracting State shall expel or return ('refouler') a refugee in any manner whatsoever to the frontiers of territories where his life or freedom would be threatened on account of his race, religion, nationality, membership of a particular social group or political opinion.

Even this fundamental right has limitations however, see below. The word 'refouler' is used because it implies return to the frontier of a territory where life or freedom would be threatened. This provision is at once the great strength and a significant weakness of the Refugee Convention. The strength is that sovereign states generally exercise complete control over their borders: but they have given up an element of that sovereignty for a common humanitarian objective. The weakness is that it is only return to the borders of countries where life or freedom would be threatened that is forbidden: returns to third countries where there would be no persecution are not prohibited. It will be readily be seen that this legal framework lies at the heart of much of the political discourse surrounding relative responsibility for refugee arrivals, including asylum seekers crossing the Channel.

Article 32 requires states not to expel a refugee lawfully in their territory save on grounds of national security or public order. This offers more generous protection than Article 33 which only protects against refoulement. In ST (Eritrea) [2012] UKSC 12, the Supreme Court found that there was nothing to prevent the HO from making a decision to remove a woman of Eritrean descent to Ethiopia, despite the fact that her asylum appeal against a decision to remove her to Eritrea had been allowed on Refugee Convention grounds.

As she remained on temporary admission (immigration bail is the modern equivalent) it was found that she was not yet 'lawfully present' in the UK and could not therefore benefit from Article 32: she only had the protection against expulsion to a place of real danger under Article 33, not the greater protection from any expulsion save on public policy grounds within Article 32. So 'lawfully present' requires lawful residence as a matter of domestic immigration law.

8.6.1 Article 33(2)

Article 33(2) of the Refugee Convention lifts the ban on return to the frontiers of territories where they fear persecution ('non-refoulement') for refugees thought on reasonable grounds to be a danger to the security of the country in which he is, or who have been convicted of a particularly serious crime. It is not limited to crimes committed outside the country of asylum, which is a difference between Art 33 and Art 1(F)(b). Thus someone
- Of whom there are reasonable grounds for regarding as a danger to the security OR
- Who has been convicted by a final judgement of a particularly serious crime

loses the benefits of non-return.

8.6.2 Section 72

NIAA 2002, section 72, reflects the considerations within Article 33(2). In effect it excludes from refugee status those deemed to fall within the terms of that Article. And a Judge has to consider s72 before embarking on any further consideration of their asylum claim.

Note:

- This provision only bites on refugee status: the applicant retains the right to establish that his removal would be in breach of the ECHR, so this provision prevents people becoming refugees rather than condemning them to a return abroad to face or inhuman treatment etc.). Thus there would be no inhibition on their arguing that their removal would infringe their Article 3 rights on appeal
- The individual whose refugee claim is so certified will presumably have no viable arguments on Humanitarian Protection grounds, because although there is no equivalent of section 72 for a HP claim, the exclusion grounds for HP are rather wider than under the Refugee Convention, including simply having committed a serious crime (r339D(i))
- Commissaire general aux refugies and aux apatrides (Refugie ayant commis un crime grave) [2023] EUECJ C-8/22 emphasises that conviction of a particularly serious crime is not enough: the ultimate question is whether the threat is to one of the fundamental interests of society and is genuine, present and sufficiently serious such that the revocation of refugee status is a proportionate measure. Bearing in mind the penalty imposed, the crime's nature, any aggravating or mitigating circumstances: Staatssecretaris van Justitie en Veiligheid v MA (Case C-402/22). These CJEU decisions may have some relevance to pre-28 June 2022 s72 decisions

Section 72 NIAA 2002 creates a presumption that a person convicted of certain criminal offences for which he was sentenced to a period of imprisonment of one year (s72(2)(b), from 28 June 2022: previously the bar was set at two years) either in or outside the UK
- has committed a particularly serious crime
- and represents a danger to the community
- Both those presumptions are rebuttable:
  - The first under the principle recognised by EN (Serbia) [2009] EWCA Civ 630 (the argument against the presumption will depend on the severity of the offence taking account of all relevant circumstances such as desperation, social exclusion and mental health difficulties of the refugee)
  - The second under the express words of section 72(6) (here the case against the presumption will concentrate on questions of re-offending risk)
- Certificates mean that, unless the appellant persuades the immigration judge that the presumption should not apply to him, or is rebutted, the Refugee Convention grounds of appeal must be dismissed. Given that Article 33(2) offending will normally have taken place after arrival in the United Kingdom, it is unlikely that there will be any connection between the claimed offending and the Refugee Convention case, and so it is more likely a judge will be able to rule on this at the outset of the appeal, though many will still prefer to consider the whole case after the hearing has finished

The SSHD passed an Order setting out certain offences, which, under section 72(4) and (5), gave rise to the presumption that the appellant is a danger to the community, regardless of the sentence. However, this order was declared unlawful in EN (Serbia). The ensuing years have not seen any attempt to replace the offending provisions.

8.7 Cessation Clauses

Refugee status is not necessarily permanent as the Refugee Convention includes several cessation clauses governing the circumstances in which a recognised refugee's status as a refugee ceases. Here we look at Article 1C, under which a person may cease to be recognised a refugee if they have:

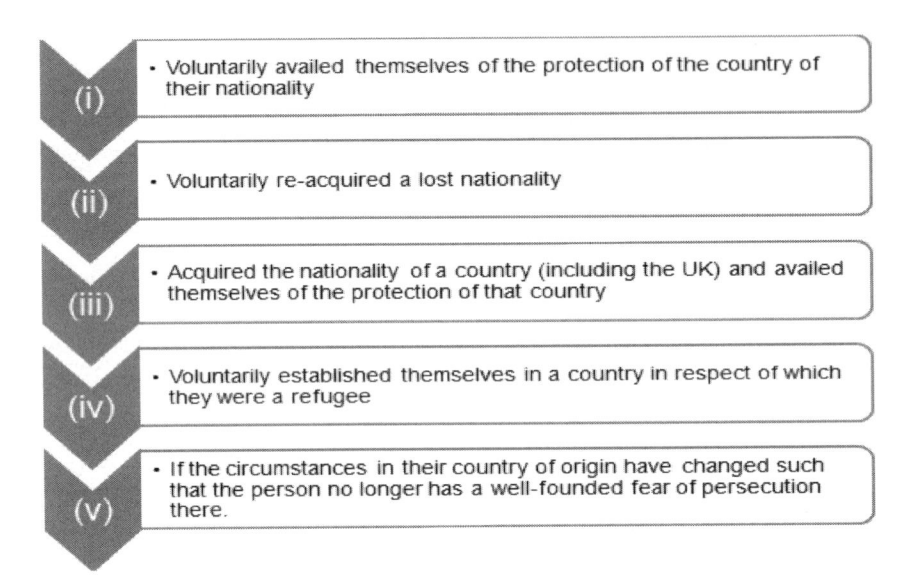

- (i) Voluntarily availed themselves of the protection of the country of their nationality
- (ii) Voluntarily re-acquired a lost nationality
- (iii) Acquired the nationality of a country (including the UK) and availed themselves of the protection of that country
- (iv) Voluntarily established themselves in a country in respect of which they were a refugee
- (v) If the circumstances in their country of origin have changed such that the person no longer has a well-founded fear of persecution there.

It can be seen that the Refugee Convention does not oblige States to offer settlement to refugees.

Successful asylum claimants are recognised as a refugee and granted LTR (IR339QA). At the end of that period they can apply for ILR under Appendix Settlement Protection (MIL 9.7.2). The HO will then consider whether to apply the cessation clause at Article 1C (IR339A). Though they may also take action during the period of LTR if relevant adverse behaviour comes to its attention.

As things stood until February 2016, ILR would normally be granted, subject to the absence of criminal convictions and the person not having re-established formal ties with their country as per Article 1C(i), (ii), or (iv) above. The HO previously never generally considered the person's protection needs when considering whether to grant ILR, under (v) above, unless for some other reason they have decided to apply the active review policy.

The only exception was where a Minister had issued a ministerial declaration that a particular country was now considered to be generally safe. However the February 2016 version of the Guidance on Settlement protection refers to a "*safe return review*" of protection needs before ILR is granted.

Some applicants for ILR, who have close family members in their countries of origin, have been asked by the HO to provide further information to support their settlement claims. Instances have been reported that this has started to happen to nationals of countries where the HO believes, with some support from the UT, that peace has broken out (ie Somalia and Zimbabwe).

There are some procedural protections for refugees facing potential cessation. There is a right of appeal against a revocation decision once made.

The IRs and Guidance *Revocation of refugee status* explain:

- Renunciation of refugee status is possible, as where the refugee wishes to return to their country of origin or switch to another immigration route
- Criminal offending should bring a speedy review of whether there remain extant protection needs – other triggers include obtaining a passport or returning to the country of origin, or going abroad for more than 2 years in which case the returning resident route should be used (MIL 4.1.3)
- Revocation can take place for misrepresentation or omission of facts, including the use of false documents, where decisive for the grant of refugee status (IR339AB)
- The procedure may take place when the refugee is abroad (IR339BC) and indeed their return may be prevented (Article 13(7) ILERO 2000)
- Acquiring British citizenship automatically revokes refugee status (IR339A(iii), 339BB(i))
- The refugee must be notified of the intention by the HO to do so and given a chance to submit representations in response (as per r339BA) and '*every reasonable effort*' should be made to locate them – but the Guidance treats interviews as optional and necessary only where information needs to be clarified
- Any refugee grounds, even if different from the original ones, must be considered, with the burden of proof on the HO and the standard of proof (for the refugee's evidence of ongoing protection needs) remaining at the same low level as is applicable to first instance decisions
- Any private and family life grounds should be considered as to whether a grant on an alternative basis might be appropriate, should revocation go ahead – '*compassionate reasons*' might justify non-revocation
- UNHCR must be consulted before revocation is effected (r358C) (usually before the refugee makes their own representations, so UNHCR can comment on these)

There are some important substantive law principles that have developed over the years.

There is a high threshold, see the requirement for "non-temporary" change – this may well amount to assessing whether the "*refugee's fear of persecution may be regarded as having been permanently eradicated*" (Abdulla C-175/08). The decision maker must have regard to all relevant international protection concerns (see Abdulla §76) which requires assessment of whether "that person has no other reason to bear being 'persecuted'"

- Under its policy on revocation of refugee status, the HO recognises it can terminate status for a change of circumstances under Article 1C(5) if the changes in the country situation are **significant** and **non-temporary** such that a fear of persecution can no longer be regarded as well-founded:

    The overthrow of one political party in favour of another might only be transitory or the change in regime may not mean that an individual is no longer at risk of persecution. The changes must be such that the reasons for becoming a refugee have ceased to exist and there are no other reasons for an individual to fear return there.

However there is no requirement for a complete change in country conditions including the development of a system for protecting human rights generally (ie beyond protecting against the persecution feared in the case in hand). Decision makers in a cessation case are simply auditing the original fear of persecution, and any new factors, as to whether there is a present well founded fear of persecution for a Convention reason against which the country in question does not offer effective protection: MA (Somalia) [2018] EWCA Civ 99.4

- Cessation may take place where the country situation indicates an internal relocation alternative to international protection is now available: MS (Somalia) [2019] EWCA Civ 1345 The fact that only one part of a country is now considered safe may be relevant to whether the changed conditions in question are sufficiently durable, but this will depend on the facts of the case

    o The protection of the cessation provisions only apply to people granted international protection via the status determination procedures in the UK. Thus they do not necessarily to the family members of those granted asylum

PS Zimbabwe [2021] UKUT 283 (IAC) gives a concise summary of the rest of the case law. Key principles are the search for risk being *permanently eradicated* and the conditions surrounding the refugee status grant having *ceased to exist* rather than simply a change of circumstances; this may flow from the refugee's circumstances or conditions in the country of origin. UNHCR's views are of considerable importance though not decisive. If cessation is established, it will still be necessary to assess removal against ECHR Art 3

- The UK practice at one time was to grant immigration status on a rather casual basis to the family members of people recognised as refugees here. They would be granted "leave in line" and their documents might well record this as refugee status. When such people get into trouble years down the line, as where criminal offending means the HO searchlight shines on them, they are liable to have their situation scrutinised carefully. Understandably they may consider themselves to be refugees. therefore they would want to rely on the protections contained in the cessation clauses. If they could do so, only a truly durable change of circumstances in conditions in their country of origin would justify ceasing their status

    o However, the Court of Appeal in JS (Uganda) [2019] EWCA Civ 1670 and KN (DRC) [2019] EWCA Civ 1665 has explained that family members will not normally be owed these benefits. Where they entered the UK under various historic family reunion policies, without any assessment of their own claim to refugee status, they were never in reality recognised as refugees and they do not have the benefit of those generous cessation protections. The only bar to their removal will be a modern claim on Refugee or Human Rights Convention grounds. Of course, they may be able to show they are at risk of serious harm because of their connections to the family member granted asylum, but that will be a question of fact to be assessed on the present country evidence, not based on any presumptions due to their existing status. Occasionally there may be special cases where refugee status was awarded to the whole family for reasons that are not obviously connected to the Refugee Convention, as had happened in the case of Mosira [2017] EWCA Civ 407. But that was a historic piece of good luck which represented a special exception which was different to the family reunion scenario

- Little-noticed provisions of the Refugee Convention state that a person should not be deprived of their refugee status, following an alleged change of circumstances in their country of origin, if they have suffered **atrocious past persecution**.

    In Hoxha [2005] UKHL 19 the House of Lords ruled that this provision was a legacy of the conditions prevailing at the time the Refugee Convention was drafted and did not apply to modern refugees. However, lawyers representing asylum seekers have relied on the provisions from time to time by analogy. Its relevance has again become topical given the increase in the use of cessation by the Secretary of State.

    o Although the House of Lords has ruled out the modern applicability of the provision, the HO Guidance, in a humanitarian vein, still has regard to the concept. Thus it states that where refugees or their family members have suffered truly atrocious forms of persecution and it is unreasonable to expect them to return to their country of origin, the cessation provisions will not be invoked against them. Examples given are ex-camp or prison tainees, survivors or witnesses of particularly traumatic violence against family members, including sexual violence, and those who are severely traumatised.

    o In AMA [2019] UKUT 11 (IAC) the UT looks at the relevance of this piece of guidance to appeals on Refugee Convention grounds. The UT notes that it goes beyond the requirements of the Refugee Convention, and so is not relevant to Tribunal appeals. Of course, it might still be relevant in JR challenges to HO decision making. In short, the HO has to take account of the principle as part of its administrative decision making, even though it is not part of international protection law.

In Bilali [2019] EUECJ C-720/17 the CJEU explained that a grant of international protection must be revoked where it transpires that it was granted without the requsiite refugee status condtions being met. This was the case even though the asylum seeker may have been innocent of any wrong doing. International protection granted due to some misunderstanding of the true facts (in Bilali, the availability of return to another country where there was no fear of persecution) should be corrected.

A grant of refugee status abroad does not bind the HO in first instance asylum decisions. But it is a very important factor, and a contrary decision should be underpinned by reasoning addressing the refugee status grant in terms sufficient for cessation see LW Ethiopia [2005] UKIAT 42. This effectively puts the burden onto the indefinite leave to remain to justify departing from the thinking found in the decision granting status abroad.

Safe return reviews now take place upoindefinite leave to remainLR applications for refugees which runs the risk of cessation at the settlement stage (MIL 9.7.2).

8.8 Exclusion clauses

The Convention contains several forms of exclusion clause:

- Article 1D for, essentially, Palestinians and others assisted by UNRWA
- Article 1E if there is a country beyond their country of nationality where they possess rights akin to nationality ('*a person who is recognised by the competent authorities of the country in which he has taken residence as having the rights and obligations which are attached to the possession of the nationality of that country*')
- the second limb of Article 1A(2) for dual nationals – i.e. a person with more than one nationality must show a fear of persecution in each country (or at least show they are not admissible to one country of nationality leaving them exposed to return only to the other one)
- the better known Article 1F exclusions for crimes against international law and serious criminal activity of a non-political nature.

But even those accepted to be refugees may face limitations as to the duties owed to them, because of Article 33(2) (MIL 8.6.1-8.6.2).

Multiple provisions empower exclusion from Convention protection, and set out the procedure for so doing, whether the case is being considered at the original application stage or whether the excludable activities are only identified later. These include:

- NBA 2022 s15 makes asylum applications from EU nationals inadmissible
- 334: provides for protection to be denied to a refugee under Article 33(2)
- 338A: provides for refugee status to be revoked or not renewed
  - under Article 1C (r339A)
  - under Articles 1D, 1E, or 1F (r339AA, referring to NBA 2022 s36)
  - under Article 33(2) (r339AC)

When a person's refugee status is revoked or not renewed any limited or indefinite leave which they have may be curtailed or cancelled (r339B). The procedure for revocation is at r339BA (the proposed decision should be notified with an opportunity for written representations/personal interview, though not where the situation is due to acquiring British citizenship or unequivocally renouncing their status r339BB; the procedure may take place whilst they are abroad r339BC). The Guidance *Suitability: Exclusion from Asylum or Humanitarian Protection* indicates HO procedures in practice.

8.8.1 Article 1(D)

This provision (replicated in the Qualification Directive at Article 12(1)(a)) is only applicable to Palestinian refugees receiving UNRWA assistance (because UNRWA's work in the Middle East represents the only current non-UNHCR protection work being carried out by the UN – they work in the Gaza Strip, the West Bank, Syria, Lebanon and Jordan, as their website explains). It states:

> This Convention shall not apply to persons who are at present receiving from organs or agencies of the United Nations other than the United Nations High Commission for Refugees protection or assistance.

When such protection or assistance has ceased for any reason, without the position of such persons being definitively settled in accordance with the relevant resolutions adopted by the General Assembly of the United Nations, these persons shall ipso facto be entitled to the benefits of this Convention.

Building on the approach of the CJEU in El Kott, C-364/11, Said [2012] UKUT 413 (IAC) holds that:

- a Palestinian forced out of the protection of the UNRWA region by virtue of circumstances beyond their control, such as armed conflict in their refugee camp, may well be entitled to the benefits of the Refugee Convention (because they are not presently receiving protection from a UN body, and given that the Palestinian question has not been finally resolved), regardless of whether or not they also possess a well-founded fear of persecution for a Convention reason under Article 1A(2) of the Refugee Convention
- the right to protection under 1D applied to all those Palestinians who had received the protection of UNWRA, and not just those who were receiving it at the date the Refugee Convention was concluded (i.e. in 1951)

- One can be excluded from refugee status both because of UNRWA operations in one's country of origin and where one subsequently establishes a further country of habitual residence where UNRWA operates: Alheto [2018] EUECJ C-585/16
- Protection does not cease where the applicant voluntarily travelled from an area where it was available and where their personal safety was not at serious risk to a dangerous location where it was not available. However when making any such assessment the possibility of unforeseeable developments such as border closures and the outbreak of conflicts should be considered: Bundes v XT (C-507-19) and Secretary of State for the Home Department [2022] EUECJ C-349/20 holds that the relevant date for assessing whether protection has ceased is that of assessing status. Whether protection had ceased due to UNRWA's intentions, acts or omissions was not the question - the focus should be whether protection was unavailable for reasons beyond the asylum seeker's control
- OFPRA v SW (Case C-294/22; 5 October 2023) holds that UNRWA assistance or protection ceases when UNRWA becomes unable to ensure stateless Palestinians have access to the healthcare and medical treatment necessary to avoid a real risk of imminent death or suffering a serious, rapid and irreversible decline in health or a significant reduction in life expectancy

Palestinians get a rough deal under the international protection regime. For example, when the SSHD set up the Vulnerable Persons Resettlement Scheme, she failed to appreciate that Palestinians stranded in Syria would not qualify: because UNHCR was chosen to administer eligibili"y under the scheme and UNHCR could not assist Palestinians. Palestinian refugees registered with"UNRWA are deemed by UNHCR to be receiving assistance from another UN agency, and are therefore excluded in practice from UNHCR's mandate (including its resettlement mandate). Turani [2021] EWCA Civ 348 notes that it has never been any part of UNRWA's mandate to provide durable solutions to Palestinian refugees, including resettlement elsewhere. Even though UNRWA reported that Palestinian Refugees from Syria registered in Lebanon live "*an extremely fragile and precarious existence and are forced to subsist on humanitarian handouts*", there was no unjustified discrimination in excluding them from the Scheme.

8.8.2 Article 1(F)

The following forms of behaviour lead to a person who would otherwise be a refugee being excluded from the Convention by virtue of Article 1F (and are included in the Qualification Directive at Art 12(2) and the Qualification Regulations at Reg 7):

- (a) Has committed a crime against peace, a war crime, or a crime against humanity, as defined in the international instruments drawn up to make provision in respect of such crimes
- (b) Has committed a serious non-political crime outside the country of refuge prior to his admission to that country as a refugee
- (c) Has been guilty of acts contrary to the purposes and principles of the United Nations.

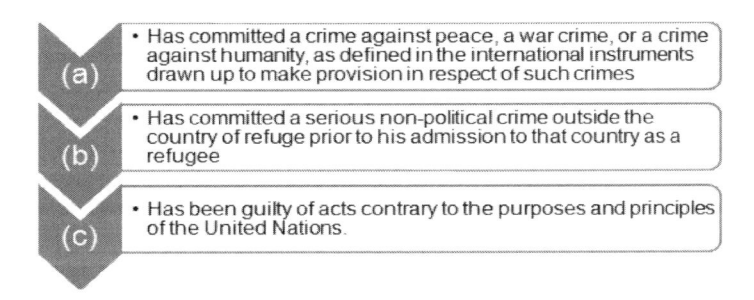

HO guidance on exclusion under Article 1F (and Article 33(2), see below) is here: Exclusion (Article 1F) and Article 33(2) of the Refugee Convention

8.8.2.1 War crimes and crimes against humanity, etc.

The modern definition of these crimes is best found in the Rome Statute (of the International Criminal Court), representing as it does the considered view as to which crimes shouldbe treated as the responsibility of the international community: crimes against humanity include murder, enslavement, forcible transfer of populations, torture, sexual violence and other inhumane acts; war crimes are more focussed on grave attacks against the civilian population.

8.8.2.2 Serious non political crimes

Consistent with its Qualification Directive predecessor, NBA 2022 s36(3) adds words to the Refugee Convention definition, so that regarding Art 1F(b) '*serious non-political crime*' cases, '*prior to his admission*''is to be interpreted as prior to '*the day on which they are issued with a relevant biometric immigration document by the Secretary of State*'. So one can be excluded for a crime committed *within* the United Kingdom *before* refugee status was awarded, whereas Art 1F(b) looks only at crimes committed *outside* the country of asylum.

Discussion of Art 1F(b) cases has often concentrated on whether a crime is *political* or *non-political* in nature. The House of Lords in 'T' [1996] Imm AR 443) rejected the idea that any crime that was incidental to a political cause could be insulated from categorisation as 'non-political'. Acts of terrorism, being incidents of depersonalised and abstract violence coldly indifferent to the human rights of the victims, are sufficiently divorced from the objectives they are thought to serve to sever them of true political ontent. A '*particularly cruel*' action may lead to exclusion: s36(2).

The Guidance Exclusion under Article 1F and 33(2) of the Refugee Convention states "More important than the sentence is the nature and context of the crime, the harm inflicted, the part played by the claimant and whether most jurisdictions would consider it a serious crime." It also gives examples of those who are thought to constitute a danger to the community or to the security of the country: those on the sex offenders register,those whose character, conduct and associations threaten national security, and those who engage in unacceptable behaviours such as fomenting, justifying or glorifying terrorist acts, or fomenting hatred that may lead to intercommunity violence.

8.8.2.3 Activities contrary to the purposes and principles of the United Nations

KJ (Sri Lanka) [2009] EWCA Civ 292 held that acts of a military nature committed by an independence movement (such as Sri Lanka's LTTE) against the military forces of the government are not themselves acts contrary to the purposes and principles of the United Nations. An armed campaign against a government would not necessarily constitute acts contrary to UN purposes and principles.

Al-Sirri [2012] UKSC 54 explained that such acts had to be of real severity (there, carrying out military activities against the UN-mandated forces in Afghanistan). Eg:

> human rights violations and acts which have been clearly identified and accepted by the international community as being contrary to the purposes and principles of the United Nations

> ... in extreme circumstances by activity which attacks the very basis of the international community's coexistence [with] ... the requisite serious effect upon international peace, security and peaceful relations between states.

They added that in general the clause:

> should be interpreted restrictively and applied with caution.

AE (Iraq) [2021] EWCA Civ 948 looked at the relevance of a sentence of imprisonment of 3½ years for posting online statements encouraging jihad. The Court observed that criminal sentencing was relevant to the Article 1F(c) enquiry, but was undertaken in separate proceedings on a different legal basis from assessing seriousness for exclusion purposes. Factual assessments were not always crystal clear; their precise basis may be debatable. Sentencing remarks may quite properly contain language which is evaluative rather than factual in nature and the boundary between fact and comment is not always obvious.

8.8.2.4 Guilt by association

Article 12(3) of the Qualification Directive states that exclusion:

> applies to persons who instigate or otherwise participate in the commission of the crimes or acts mentioned

A number of cases have looked at the extent to which an asylum seeker has to be *complicit* in the activities that bring exclusion:

- In KJ (Sri Lanka) [2009] EWCA Civ 292 it was accepted that mere membership of an organisation that, among other activities, commits acts of terrorism does not suffice to bring the exclusion into play. Whereas a foot soldier who has not participated in terrorist acts within an organisation that conducts both conventional military and terrorist activities would avoid exclusion, a person with a higher rank who might be expected to understand the overall picture might be excluded, as would any active member of an organisation which concentrates on terrorism
- In Youssef [2016] UKUT 137 (IAC), the UT upheld the exclusion of an Egyptian lawyer for explicit direct encouragement or incitement to acts of terrorism, as a result of his eulogies to various leaders of Al-Qaeda broadcast on YouTube. The Court of Appeal then held in Youssef [2018] EWCA Civ 933 that general incitement of terrorist offences can satisfy the threshold in Art 1F(c). There is no requirement for there to be a link between the incitement and a specific terrorist act.
- In JS (Sri Lanka) [2010] UKSC 15 the Supreme Court identifies the relevant factors:
    (i) the nature and (potentially of some importance) the size of the organisation and particularly that part of it with which the asylum-seeker was himself most directly concerned,
    (ii) whether and, if so, by whom the organisation was proscribed,
    (iii) how the asylum-seeker came to be recruited,
    (iv) the length of time he remained in the organisation and what, if any, opportunities he had to leave it,
    (v) his position, rank, standing and influence in the organisation,
    (vi) his knowledge of the organisation's war crimes activities, and
    (vii) his own personal involvement and role in the organisation including particularly whatever contribution he made towards the commission of war crimes.

- This was the summary of liability for complicity given in JS:

    > if there are serious reasons for considering him voluntarily to have contributed in a significant way to the organisation's ability to pursue its purpose of committing war crimes, aware that his assistance will in fact further that purpose.

8.8.3 Evidence and procedure

Obviously exclusion is a serious issue and requires the most serious consideration (via the policy, process and procedures set out in the Guidance *Revocation of Protection Status*):

- The decision maker needs to identify *serious reasons for considering* exclusion to be appropriate: this requires clear, credible and strong evidence, based on a considered judgment, albeit not requiring proof beyond reasonable doubt: Al-Sirri [2012] UKSC 54. (Post-script: Mr Sirri ultimately succeeded in his asylum appeal, see Al-Sirri Egypt [2016] UKUT 448 (IAC).)
- The exclusion clauses are part of the refugee definition, whether we take it from the Refugee Convention or from NBA 2022, and so can and indeed must be considered by the Tribunal even where the HO has not raised them, subject to giving an adequate opportunity to deal with such issues – the foreseeability of the issue arising will be relevant to the need for an adjournment
- In Gurung (AKA IG Nepal [2002] UKIAT 04870, the Tribunal held that issues of exclusion may arise on appeal even though the point was not taken in the refusal letter
- The SSHD cannot raise such issues, though, after an appeal has been allowed, if they previously have foregone the opportunity to raise exclusion during the appeal process itself (TB (Jamaica) [2008] EWCA Civ 977).
- As discussed in the Guidance *Exclusion: Article 1F of the Refugee Convention*, the HO may certify an appeal under Section 55 of the IANA 2006 on the grounds that the Appellant is not entitled to the protection of the Refugee Convention because (in its view) Article 1F applies. The Tribunal (or SIAC) is then required first to decide whether it agrees with the certificate. If it does, the appeal must be dismissed on asylum grounds (though the hearing will need to continue to consider whether removal will breach Article 3) – however, in many cases issues of inclusion and exclusion will be bound together, as discussed in Gurung.

8.9 Humanitarian Protection

Under the Refugee Convention, a person whose removal from the territory would threaten their life or freedom is entitled to remain in the country of asylum, and to various other rights to be enjoyed for the course of stay as a refugee (including non-discrimination). From 2 October 2000 the ECHR effectively supplemented the Refugee Convention as an alternative way of receiving protection. However the ECHR simply forbids exposing someone to a human rights violation abroad. It does not promise any form of immigration status. In essence the only right is to be free from torture, etc.; there are no other rights such as any particular grant of leave, family reunion or travel documents.

From 10 October 2006 the EU Qualification Directive entered force. It brought a new era of protection by covering both refugee status and subsidiary protection: the latter intended to plug (some) gaps in the protection afforded by the Refugee Convention. The UK implemented this Directive by applying the same term previously given to some beneficiaries of non-refugee protection to the new special EU legal status: which it thus called Humanitarian (rather than subsidiary) Protection.

- It is important to realise that HP prior to that date was no more than a form of leave to remain given by virtue of HO policy – i.e. an administrative discretion
- HP after then was a form of international protection given under directly effective EU law. Whilst the name may be the same, the legal basis was quite different
- HP, after the IRs changes coming into effect alongside the NBA 2022 on 28 June 2022, is seen by the HO as purely domestic law: hence the downgrading of the leave granted to 30 months. Indeed there are now two sets of Guidance on HP for claims breach and after that date: *Humanitarian protection in asylum claims lodged before 28 June 2022* and *Humanitarian protection in asylum claims lodged on or after 28 June 2022*
- HP claims are to be considered first as asylum applications (IR 327EC)

8.9.1 Serious harm

The fundamental requirement for eligibility for Humanitarian Protection is that a person faces a real risk of 'serious harm' in one of the following forms, see Article 15 of the Directive:

- (a) death penalty or execution; or
- (b) torture or inhuman or degrading treatment or punishment of an applicant in the country of origin; or
- (c) serious and individual threat to a civilian's life or person by reason of indiscriminate violence in situations of international or internal armed conflict.

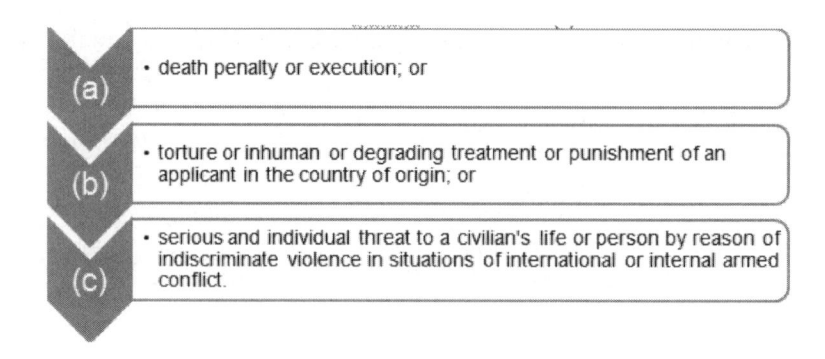

As per MIL 8.1.4, the standard of proof in Refugee Convention claims is now balance of probabilities when establishing the reality of the asylum seeker's fears, and real risk for assessing the likelihood of future events. But this split does not apply to HP claims, see the *post-28 June 2022 HP Guidance*:

> 'As a result of the lower, 'real risk', standard of proof which is applicable to all elements of considering whether a claimant qualifies for humanitarian protection, you must reconsider all material facts to the lower standard ... you must note that your credibility assessment when considering humanitarian protection must be undertaken to the lower standard of proof of a 'real risk'.'

8.9.2 Inhuman and degrading treatment or punishment, death penalty & execution

This class of HP emanated from Articles 15(a) and (b) of the Qualification Directive whilst the UK was part of the EU asylum regime. It represents a relatively uncontroversial addition to the protection given to asylum seekers, and covers much of the same ground as Article 3 ECHR. For convenience we can go straight to the terms by which Article 15 has been incorporated into the IRs (r339C). The location where the serious harm was feared changed on 11 May 2022 from "*country of return*" to "*country of origin*": to prevent HP claims being made vis-á-vis expulsion to locations such as Rwanda.

Grant of humanitarian protection

> 339C. A person will be granted humanitarian protection in the United Kingdom if the Secretary of State is satisfied that:
>
> > (iii) substantial grounds have been shown for believing that asylum applicant person concerned, if he returned to the country of origin, would face a real risk of suffering serious harm and is unable, or, owing to such risk to avail himself of the protection of that country [...]
>
> 339CA. For the purposes of para 339C, serious harm consists of:
>
> > (i) the death penalty or execution;
> > (ii) unlawful killing;
> > (iii) torture or inhuman or degrading treatment or punishment a person in the country of origin; or
> > (iv) serious and individual threat to a civilian's life or person by reason of indiscriminate violence in situations of international or internal armed conflict.

Basically, then, the question is whether the individual faces a real risk of 'serious harm' of one of the four defined species.

- The forms of harm are reminiscent of some of the more basic protections afforded by the ECHR (IR339C(ii) is based on the right to life protected by Article 2 ECHR; IR339C(iii) resembles Article 3 ECHR)
- Note that unless a person is excluded from HP for wrongdoing, it will be wrong to say that one is relying on Article 3 ECHR as a fall-back if Refugee Convention arguments fail – because in

fact one is relying on HP, which has a different legal originWhere the country evidence suggests a risk of imprisonment, decision makers should review the HO country evidence. And make a case-specific enquiry to HO CoI researchers if none is available.

Article 3 ECHR can in extreme circumstances cover health and destitution (MIL 5.3, 10.3.2.5). What of destitution rather than deliberate mistreatment?

- As explained in NM Iraq UKUT 259 (IAC) whilst HP often gives status to individuals facing Article 3 violations, it does not cover the same ground as Article 3 itself. It is also necessary to show that substantial grounds exist for believing there to be a real risk of serious harm by virtue of actors of harm intentionally depriving that individual of appropriate health care in that country. This will require proof of a sufficiently strong causal link between a relevant actor's conduct and health care deprivation. Simply relying on degraded healthcare infrastructure due to an armed conflict will not generally suffice. NM disapproves the contrary view in Ainte [2021] UKUT 203 (IAC). See also M'Bodj (Case C-542/13) [2015] 1 WLR 3059.

The UT noted in DH Afghanistan UKUT 223 (IAC) that even where the SSHD conceded the need for HP, an asylum seeker was entitled to pursue their claim for refugee status, which being a superior entitlement still needed to be determined.

8.9.3

8.9.3.1 Torture victims and Humanitarian Protection

One class of beneficiary has been recognised by the CJEU when interpreting Article 15 of the QD who might not haved succeeded under the ECHR or Refugee Convention. MP [2018] EUECJ C-353/16 holds that:

- a third country national who in the past has been tortured by the authorities of his country of origin and no longer faces a risk of being tortured if returned to that country,
- but whose physical and psychological health could, if so returned, seriously deteriorate, leading to a serious risk of him committing suicide on account of trauma resulting from the torture he was subjected to,
- is eligible for subsidiary protection if there is a real risk of him being intentionally deprived, in his country of origin, of appropriate care for the physical and mental after effects of that torture

This is an important decision. Generally speaking asylum seekers have to show a present need for international protection, whether their application is for refugee status or humanitarian protection. A person who is no longer in danger of persecution or serious harm against which their government will not protect them does not usually have a viable claim. However, where national authorities fail to meet the international standards relevant to their care on return may be able to sustain a humanitarian protection claim. This possibility exists even though there may be no threat of further torture.

8.9.3.2 Protection of civilians from indiscriminate violence from a civil war

Article 15(c) QD (post-Brexit, IR 339CA(iv)) finds no obvious reflection in pre-existing human rights law, and has sufficiently excited the courts to have inspired a whole string of cases ever since KH Iraq CG [2008] UKAIT 00023. The challenge for judges and lawyers has been to find some protection therein which was not already recognised by Article 3 ECHR – after all, nobody would seriously dispute the possibility that civilians fearing serious injury or death in wartime would have an Article 3 claim if the risk was sufficiently severe. Indeed, the Strasbourg court has recognised this in the context of Article 3 ECHR in cases such as NA v United Kingdom [2008] ECHR 616.

Mastering Immigration Law is not the place to explore the learning on these differences. What we can say is this:

- In QD Iraq [2009] EWCA Civ 620 it was said that Art 15(c) 'seeks to cover ... real risks and real threats presented by the kinds of endemic act of indiscriminate violence'.
- The conclusion of the Court of Appeal in QD was that 'the critical question' was:

    Is there in [the country in question] or a material part of it such a high level of indiscriminate violence that substantial grounds exist for believing that an applicant ... would, solely by being present there, face a real risk which threatens his life or person?

- The CJEU in Elgafaji [2009] EUECJ C-465/07 decided that 'indiscriminate violence' refers to a high intensity of violence: so high, in fact, that the side effects of armed conflict 'may extend to people irrespective of their personal circumstances'
- There may be classes of individual at enhanced risk due to personal factors (Elgafaji). In UK case law, examples given in GS Afghanistan were the disabled person who cannot flee shellfire as swiftly as the able-bodied civilians around them, and members of groups who might be sought out by parties to the conflict, or taking advantage of the conflict, for special attention; the HO HP policy suggests a child or someone of advanced age, disability, gender, ill-health, ethnicity or, for example, by virtue of being a perceived collaborator, medical professional, teacher or government official
- Past exposure to violence in a conflict might show a likelihood of a repetition of such experiences absent a change of circumstances
- In GS Afghanistan CG [2009] UKAIT 00010 the UT found that 'indiscriminate violence' would include that meted out by criminals taking advantage of the law and order vacuum created by the conflict
  The most useful overview is now found in HM Iraq CG [2010] UKUT 331 (IAC). The following key principles emerge:

    o a real risk of a relevant threat, threats being defined as the kinds of harm that flow from modern military conflict – it must extend to significant physical injuries, serious mental traumas and serious threats to bodily integrity
    o including indirect harm for which the conflict was an operative cause (as where the harm is caused by a breakdown in law and order)

- ZMM Libya CG [2017] UKUT 263 looks at the relevance of governance

    o Conditions were not necessarily stable or durable even in the occasional oases of peace in which some communities might currently live
    o The question of whether the government had the capacity to address the violence: relevant considerations were economic crisis, that governance was not high on the agenda of the competing national authorities, that there was a power vacuum leaving the authorities beholden to internal and external forces such as militia allegiances and objectives, and that the state apparatus had largely disappeared
    o It was important to take account of the uncounted victims of violent crime, human rights violations by militias, collateral damage, and PTSD

Various internal armed conflicts have been recognised by the Tribunal: eg in Iraq (as above), Somalia (AMM Somalia CG [2011] UKUT 445 (IAC)) and Afghanistan (GS Afghanistan). [2009] UKAIT 10. However, civilians in Afghanistan and Iraq were found not to be at sufficient risk to enliven Article 15(c); Somalia and Libya have been accepted as featuring violence such as to engage protection.

Top Tip
When putting a case based on risks to civilians due to armed conflict, investigate: ☐ The rate of civilian casualties of all kinds ☐ The extent to which there is under-reporting of casualties ☐ The geographical extent of the conflict and casualties ☐ The indirect impact of the conflict on the quality of life and the death rate because of interference with food and other vital supplies ☐ Availability of humanitarian assistance (including access of NGOs and health professionals)

And always remember that if you can establish a local risk from the internal armed conflict in your client's home area, then all they have to show in the rest of the country is that return there would be unreasonable.

8.9.4 Exclusion and revocation of Humanitarian Protection

The IRs at r339D largely tracks the UK's approach to the Refugee Convention exclusions: (taking the same approach to pre-biometric document criminality and 'particularly cruel' actions, r339DA, MIL 8.8.2.2), asking whether there are serious reasons:

- For considering a person has committed or instigated or otherwise participated in an international crime as per the Refugee Convention exclusion clauses, or a serious non-political crime (IR339D(i)-(ii))
- For considering a person has committed or been involved with acts contrary to UN purposes or principles (IR339D(iii))
- For considering a person constitutes a danger to the UK's community (as per the s72 NIAA 2002 regime MIL 8.6.2) or security (IR339D(iv)-(v))

Exclusion should not be automatic and must be preceded by a fact-sensitive consideration of the case. AH (Algeria) [2012] EWCA Civ 395:

> Sentence is, of course, a material factor but it is not a benchmark. In deciding whether the crime is serious enough to justify his loss of protection, the Tribunal must take all facts and matters into account, with regard to the nature of the crime, the part played by the accused in its commission, any mitigating or aggravating features and the eventual penalty imposed.

Decision makers are signposted to the Guidance *Exclusion under Article 1F and 33(2)* (MIL 8.8.2.2).

HP may be revoked because facts justifying exclusion have come to light post-grant (IR339GB), and where

- there is a change of circumstances so that protection is no longer required though as in refugee cases, in applying this test the question is whether the change is of a significant and non-temporary nature (IR339GA);
- there was misrepresentation or factual omission, including the use of false documents, which were decisive to the grant of HP (IR339GD).

Kakarash [2021] UKUT 236 (IAC) holds that neither the IRs nor the SSHD's Guidance on HP introduced a requirement that a person who *has committed* a serious crime must *also present a danger* to the UK in order to be excluded. The Guidance emphasises the need to give applicants an opportunity to rebut the presumption of being a danger to the community.

CHAPTER 9: Asylum Process and Practice

9.1 Claiming asylum

Reforms of the UK asylum procedure took place from 28 June 2022. But they only apply to claims lodged from that date. UKVI Guidance generally states that the new regime will not apply (see eg Guidance *Permission to stay on a protection route for asylum claims lodged on or after 28 June 2022* to

> 'individuals who sought to register an asylum claim before the commencement date of 28 June 2022 but were provided with an appointment to attend a designated place to register their asylum application on or after 28 June will be considered to have 'made an asylum claim' before the commencement date, but only if they attend their scheduled appointment (or, in the event that it is cancelled or rescheduled by the Home Office, the rescheduled appointment).'

However no such latitude will be granted to individuals who miss the appt without good reason of which they inform the HO (with evidence). Some aspects of the regime have in fact been paused for now (MIL 9.7.1), being deemed unnecessary because the IMA 2023 regime is so much more extreme.

An 'asylum claim' is defined at s113 of NIAA 2002:

> 'asylum claim' is a claim made by a person to the Secretary of State at a place designated ... that to remove the person from or require him to leave the United Kingdom would breach the United Kingdom's obligations under the Refugee Convention

Asylum claims must be made in person at the port of entry or by appointment at the Asylum Screening Unit in Croydon. From 28 June 2022 there are specific criteria for validity: being made in person at a designated place, in person by a non-British citizen, being particularised, and passing the '*fresh claim*' test (IR327AB).

The designated places within the UK (though not in our territorial waters)): a place designated by notice as an asylum intake unit, an immigration removal centre, a port, and a place where a person is HO-authorised to accept a claim or to where a person has been directed to make a claim (NBA 2022 s14(2)) (further glossed in Guidance *Screening and routing*).

Although MIL 9 addresses asylum, human rights claims are made alongside asylum ones so often that we should look at those too. Whereas a human rights claim is defined (s113 NIAA 2002 again):

> "human rights claim" means a claim made by a person to the Secretary of State at a place designated by the Secretary of State that to remove the person from or require him to leave the United Kingdom or to refuse him entry into the United Kingdom would be unlawful under section 6 of the Human Rights Act 1998 ... (public authority not to act contrary to Convention)

But IMA 2023 (s5(5)) defines a human rights claim more narrowly for inadmissibility purposes:

> A human rights claim is within this subsection if it is a claim that removal of a person from the United Kingdom to—
> (a) a country of which the person is a national, or
> (b) a country or territory in which the person has obtained a passport or other document of identity, would be unlawful under section 6 of the Human Rights Act 1998

See MIL 5.3-5.4 for private life claims, MIL 5.5 for proportionality, 5.6 for medical treatment, 5.7 for making applications; MIL 6 for family life claims; & MIL 10 for human rights law outside private and family life and health.

There are essentially two inadmissibility regimes which capture two kinds of asylum claim:

- Firstly claims from EU nationals (NIAA 2002 Part 4A, s80A) (MIL 9.6.2)

- Secondly claims from non-EU nationals returnable to a third country (NIAA 2002 Part 4A, s80B) (MIL 9.5)

See MIL 9.1.8 for delays in the asylum process.

Detailed guidance on asylum policies and processes is provided for Home Office staff, and is available on the GOV.UK website, in the Asylum decision making guidance. The key procedures are found in the IRs (Parts 11, 11A, 11B and 12). NBA 2022 sets out various procedural changes in terms of access to a two-stage appeal process and expedited detained appeals: but it now seems these may never see the light of day in practice: see the Tribunal Procedure Committee *Consultation reply*.

9.1.0 The Illegal Migration Act 2023

Truly dramatic changes to the procedure are now proposed by the Illegal Migration Act 2023 which was being rushed through Parliament with extreme haste and received Royal Assent on 20 July 2023. Key aspects are introducing an absolute duty on the HO to remove adults entering the country illegally (and a discretion to do so re children), suspending trafficking obligations except where victims are cooperating with law enforcement agencies re offences where they are the victim, disregarding asylum and human rights claims and banning them from ever being granted permission to stay, ILR or British citizenship. Its proposed effect on other legislation is found in this *Keeling Schedule*. Radical new powers permit detention without the usual protections of the common law: for example it will be for the HO to decide whether a particular length of detention is reasonable, not the court. There will be no challenge to detention for the first 28 days by way of conventional judicial review.

The IMA 2023 unusually states its purpose at its outset (s1(1)). Namely "to prevent and deter unlawful migration, and in particular migration by unsafe and illegal routes, by requiring the removal from the United Kingdom of certain persons who enter or arrive in the United Kingdom in breach of immigration control." Its provisions are generally to be construed by reference to this purpose (s1(3)), probably with a view to making it more difficult for judges to interpret the legislation consistently with international international human rights laws (in the event such laws clash with this purpose). The duty to read legislation compatibly with the HRA 1998 does not apply (s1(5)). The IMA's premise might be thought to be the availability of "safe and legal routes" by which to come to the UK (MIL 9.1.10).

It must be remembered that much of the regime is not yet in force: MIL specifies where provisions have been commenced. Once in force, the s2 regime will demand that the SSHD makes arrangements for the removal of persons who meet four conditions:

- Entering without LTE or EC or ETA where such is required or obtaining it by deception, or in breach of a deportation order, or being excluded under a sanctions regime (s2(1))
- Entering the UK from 20 July 2023 (s2(2))
- Not coming directly to the UK from a country in which the person's life and liberty were threatened for a Refugee Convention reason (s2(3)) (which includes the situation where "in coming from such a country, they passed through or stopped in another country outside the United Kingdom where their life and liberty were not so threatened" (s2(5))
- They require LTE/LTR but do not have it (s2(4)) (leave given to unaccompanied children under s4(1) is to be disregarded)

Whilst the person is an unaccompanied child (ie being <18 & having no carer at the relevant time (s4(5)) the absolute duty does not apply (s4(1)); there is a power but not a duty that the SSHD "may make arrangements" (s4(2)). For minors, removals are permitted only to destinations (s4(3))

- permitting reunion with a parent, or
- to safe states listed in s80AA NIAA 2002 (EU/Switzerland/Albania) on the basis that is their country of nationality/travel document issue, or
- where they have not made an asylum/protection claim, to their country of nationality/travel document issue/embarkation to UK
- in such other circumstances which may be specified in Regs

CHAPTER 9: Asylum Process and Practice

The removal duty continues regardless of protection, human rights, and slavery/trafficking claims; and regardless of a JR application (s5). Nor will the duty to consult the Independent Family Returns Panel apply (s14). A human rights claim is defined (s5(5)) as one contesting removal to the country of nationality or from where an identity document has been obtained (s5(5)). Removals must be as soon as *"reasonably practicable"* (s6(1)) and may be to destinations as follows:

- in general, to the country of **nationality** or country/territory from **where a passport/travel document has been obtained**, or to that of **embarkation** or where there is **reason to believe the individual will be admitted** (s6(3))
- if a **protection or human rights claim has been made**, to the country of nationality or from where a passport/travel document has been obtained – but only where the country is on the **NIAA 2002 s80AA list of safe countries** (essentially EU countries + Switzerland + Albania, the "*EU+ safe countries*") and where there are no exceptional circumstances present (s6(4)) (those circumstances are essentially those previously justifying inadmissibility for nationals of EU states (s6(5)) (MIL 9.6.4)
- if the **individual is *not* a national and lacks a passport/ID document from a s80AA country** (ie the EU+ safe countries), they **may only be sent to a country of embarkation/believed admissibility if it is on the IMA 2023 Sch 1 list**: these are essentially the same countries as presumptively safe for "clearly unfounded" certification purposes under s94 NIAA 2002 (EU states + those listed at MIL 9.6.1 *minus* Ukraine & Macedonia) – further countries may be added to this list if they are places where there is in general no serious risk of persecution and where removal would not generally contravene the ECHR (s7) and individuals may be sent there if they claimed asylum after 20 July 2023 and their claim is undecided when the addition happens (s6(14))

There are specific provisions re interim relief:

- Courts and Tribunals may not grant interim relief that prevents or delays the removal of the person from the United Kingdom (s54). Whether or not ECHR rights are in play
- If an application is made to the ECtHR which then indicates an interim measure in relation to such a removal (MIL 10.1.5) then a Minister *may* determine the s2 duty does not apply (s55) – bearing in mind the UK's opportunity to present observations and information before the measure was made, the form the decision containing the measure took, whether future government representations will be taken into account by the ECtHR, and the measure's likely duration in the light of the ECtHR's decision on the underlying application

If a person's age and thus liability to the mandatory s2 removal duty is disputed then no appeals may be brought under NBA 2022, should such appeals ever be introduced (s57(2)); and any JR will proceed only on the grounds that the decision was wrong in law, not in fact (ie the judge will conduct a review of lawfulness rather than determine the merits for themselves: in contrast to the general approach presently - MIL 9.3.4-5).

There are new detention provisions addressing both immigration detention generally but also detention for the s2 cohort (MIL 13.1.1.1, 13.1.6, 13.2.1).

One aspect of the IMA 2023 is the lifetime ban on grants of EC/ETA/LTE/LTR and nationality for those who are caught by s2. Whilst s2 has not yet entered effect for the purpose of inadmissiblity, the machinery for the lifetime bans has been commenced. From 20 July 2022 s8AA of IA 1971 provides that persons meeting the four s2 conditions must not be granted EC/ETA/LTE/LTR. However this is subject to provisos, where

- They have left or been removed from the UK and to do otherwise would breach the ECHR or where there are other exceptional circumstances (s8AA(3), (4))
- Though for LTR only on exceptional circumstances grounds where s8AA(3) had led to their entry here – but for LTR also on grounds of "any other international agreement" (s8AA(4))

The grant of s8AA LTE/LTR does not prevent liability from s2 treatment (s8AA(7)).

CHAPTER 9: Asylum Process and Practice

This regime appears to permit the HO to grant LTR to asylum seekers in limbo where for example their family or private life is subject to disproportionate interference by the lack of LTR. Perhaps where the best interests of children, or the mental health of the asylum seeker or their family, and the difficulties posed by the compliant environment (MIL 1.3.6), are such that the public interest does not justify the damage to ECHR Art 8 interests. These cases after all cannot simply be equated with the end-of-the-line deportation cases where LTR can be countenanced only as a last resort (MIL 4.2.18). Also

- Pending the commencement of the s2 regime itself, LTE/LTR may be granted on any grounds subject to the following provisos
- If a person to whom s2 applies leaves or is removed from the UK, they may not be given LTE/LTR under s8AA(3)-(4) (s8AA(5)-(6))

There is also a lifetime ban on obtaining full British citizenship for s2 victims ("ineligible persons") via registration or naturalisation (s32(1)) or obtaining other forms of British citizenship (s33-35). However the SSHD may determine applicants are not ineligible (s36).

This is the procedure for removability to a third country:

(1) The third country removal notice ("TCRN") must identify the suspensive claim period

(2) The claim period (8 days (s42(7), s43(7)) must have expired, or the person must have notified the HO orally or in writing that they do not intend to bring a suspensive claim (s8(2)-(3)) – disavowing a claim does not rule one out in the future until they have been removed from the UK (s8(4)-(5))

(3) A person may raise a serious harm suspensive claim ("SHSC"), or a removal conditions suspensive claim ("RCSC"), against the TCRN

- A **SHSC** is a claim supported by compelling evidence (s42(5)) that removal would cause them to "*face a real, imminent and foreseeable risk of serious and irreversible harm*" (death, persecution as defined in NBA 2022 s31 (MIL 8.3.2), torture, inhuman and degrading treatment or punishment) – and not lesser forms of persecution, harm resulting from lesser healthcare standards, and probably not pain or distress due to a medical treatment available in the UK not being available abroad (IMA s39) – bearing in mind any assurances from the government abroad, support or services provided by that government, and where it is reasonable to expect certain evidence which has not been forthcoming from the applicant (s42)

- A **RCSC** must be supported by compelling evidence (s43(5)(a)) that at least one of the 4 conditions under s2 IMA 2023 is not met (s38(7))

(4) The HO must determine the SHSC and/or RCSC by the end of the decision period (4 days from the claim being made or from (s42(7), s43(7)) – the decision period may be extended where the HO considers it appropriate to do so (s42(6), 43(6))

(5) The HO may decide that the claim is clearly unfounded

(6) If the claim is not certified as clearly unfounded, appeal lies to the UT automatically – compelling evidence that the relevant SRSC/RCSC is made out is required & the UT must take account of the factors at (3) above (s44)

(7) If the claim is certified as clearly unfounded, appeal lies to the UT only with permission s44(2)) (see also MIL 14.6.4)

- which may only be granted if the UT considers there to be compelling evidence of the SHSC/RCSC s44(3)-(4))
- these applications are determined via written submissions and evidence unless the UT thinks justice requires a hearing s44(5))

- notice of appeal must still be given once permission to appeal against clearly unfounded certification is given s49(1)(a)(ii)

(8) The UT may only consider new matters raised after the claim period with the SSHD's consent or where the UT considers it appropriate: in either case due to a compelling justification (s48)

(9) Appeals must be speedily brought and determined (s49):

- Notice of appeal must be given within 7 working days of receiving notice of the decision
- The UT must give its decision on substantive appeals within 23 working days of notice of appeal being given
- The UT must give its decision on clearly unfounded decisions and out-of-time declarations within 7 working days
- These periods may be extended by the UT if that is the only way to secure justice, and anyway by 3 working days where a new matter is raised

(10) Appeals may proceed in the SIAC if certified on national security grounds (IMA 2023 s53, SIAC Act 1997 s2AA)

(11) UT decisions are to be "*final and not liable to be questioned or set aside in any other court*" re new matters, out of time and clearly unfounded cases: save for questions as to validity of notice of appeal or the UT's constitution, or where it has acted in bad faith or in a way so procedurally defective as to be a fundamental breach of the principles of natural justice (s51)

(12) If a SHSC/RCSC is made outside the claim period, and has not previously made such a claim in relation to the same TCRN, the HO must decide whether there are compelling reasons for the failure; if the HO accepts there are, it must determine the claim, if it does not, the person may apply to the UT for a declaration that there were in fact such compelling reasons (which will be determined without a hearing) (s46)

(13) Removal may not take place pending decisions on these claims, or on admitting a late claim, or during the time for bringing an appeal and during its currency (s47(1))

(14) Successful appeals suspend removal, subject to a change of circumstances (including unsuccessful human rights claims and JRs) in which case a new removal notice may be issued and the procedures above begin again and removal may proceed absent a successful SHSC/RCSC or appeal (s47(3)-(5)). So success in an appeal simply puts one back into the inadmissibility limbo

9.1.1 The procedure

Simply put, the process for most asylum seekers, if their claim is refused, is broadly as follows:

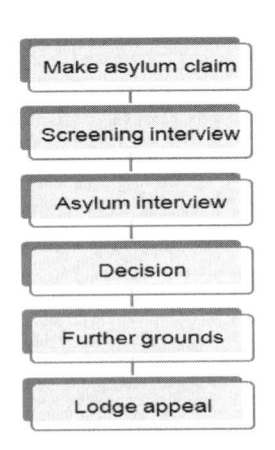

- Make asylum claim
- Screening interview
- Asylum interview
- Decision
- Further grounds
- Lodge appeal

In theory asylum seekers for whom other countries are deemed responsible will be excluded from this process following the screening interview. Though for now, post Brexit, returns to EU Member States do not seem feasible.

There is a lengthy policy *Asylum screening and routing* guidance on the screening and routing regime. There is also an *Information booklet about your asylum application*.

CHAPTER 9: Asylum Process and Practice

- As of 23 February 2023 the HO announced *Streamlined asylum processing*. Pre-28 June 2022 asylum applications are now styled "legacy" claims (a backlog which the Prime Minister expected to process by the end of 2023: *PM statement on illegal migration*: 13 December 2022). Modern claims are styled "flow cases". Streamlining can apply to both classes.
- Decision makers will have greater flexibility to make positive decisions without an interview for applicants from Afghanistan, Eritrea, Libya, Syria, Yemen and Sudan. Rumour has it that Iran and Iraq will be the next target countries: those nationals should use this *Questionnaire: continue your asylum claim*
- There is *Streamlined asylum processing for children's casework*, both UASCs and accompanied children
- The *Asylum decision-making prioritisation Guidance* explains the case-by-case system used: Hague Convention child abduction matters (MIL 9.7.7), extradition, foreign national offenders, complex or severe physical/mental health cases, and other cases of severe vulnerability – evidence-backed expedition requests may be sought via the email address Asylumcentralcommunicationshub@homeoffice.gov.uk
- Cases may also be paused under that Guidance: to wait for material evidence, a medico-legal report, due to a pending prosecution, or due to a country situation
- An asylum questionnaire will be despatched will be sent to candidates for the scheme to seek further details of their claims and identify changes of circumstances – they have 20 days to respond, with a prompt and a further 10 days given absent a response, subject to reasonable and proportionate extension of up to 20 days, and longer in exceptional circumstances. Claims may be treated as withdrawn if not addressed within that period.

Publicly funded legal advice is available for those seeking asylum.

There are specific provisions for dependants of an asylum seeker (r349).

- Spouses, civil/unmarried partners (latter only if 2 years' cohabitation is established), and minor children (ie those established or appearing to be under 18), accompanying the principal asylum seeker, may claim asylum as part of the latter's family unit
- Or they may claim asylum in their own right: in which case they may be interviewed
- Claims in one's own right should be made as soon as possible: or risk an adverse credibility inference
- As explained in G v G [2021] UKSC 9, a parent's international protection claim naming a child as a dependant is also an application by the child, if objectively it can be understood as such, because it is inherently likely that the parent's claim identifies risks applicable to the child too - a child's failure to raise a claim in their own right cannot reasonably be seen as a matter of choice. The Family Asylum Claims process has been introduced to implement the Supreme Court's judgment, aiming for a single process that assumes the child's protection needs reflect those of the relevant parent and avoiding any need to particularise a aim unless they have separate/additional protection needs. Any individualised claim needs to be identified by decision makers during the consideration of the parent(s) claims.

9.1.2 Screening interview and initial steps

Once a claim has been made, the next step is the screening process.

- This includes fingerprinting of the applicant with a view to 'locking' them to one identity – but the UK no longer participates in the Europe's EURODAC system so it is only possible to detect prior applications in other EU countries by other methods)
- Applicants are given a form of induction during which they receive an Application Registration Card (ARC) (explained in the *ARC Guidance*) which contains their personal details and acts as a form of identity. IR359 requires the HO to provide document certifying their status as such, within three days of their arrival
- The ARC guidance explains that an applicant with a current, valid BRP should retain it - & also receive an ARC (there is an ARC enquiry form if problems arise with the ARC)
- The HO must inform asylum seekers, 'within fifteen days after their claim for asylum has been recorded of the benefits and services that they may be eligible to receive and of the rules and

procedures with which they must comply relating to them' (IR358) in a language they understand, in writing and where appropriate orally (IR358A)
- A screening interview takes place
    - which concentrates on obtaining personal details and mode of entry and travel to the UK – its stated aim is to address identity and nationality
    - also addressing whether the applicant has potentially committed a criminal offence under s2 of the 2004 Act (MIL 15). If the answers given by the applicant suggest the offence may have been committed, a referral to the police and CPS will be considered
    - During which the interviewer should be alert to individual factors that may affect the ability of the asylum seeker to communicate:
    • "listening to the unspoken", including pauses, phrases or euphemisms that may indicate the person is trying to say something of a sensitive nature, such as sexual violence or torture, without directly saying so
    • when a claimant wants to show scarring
    • checking for indicators of trafficking
    • handling threats of self-harm and suicide
    • offering breaks where required

One initial procedural step found unlawful was the seizure of asylum seekers' mobile 'phones: HM [2022] EWHC 695 (Admin). As the policy was unlawful, the subsequent interferences with private life were not in accordance with the law, unlawful for Data Protection Act purposes, and undermined the Data Protection Impact Assessments. It might be permissible to retain 'phones in individual cases as part of an intelligence operation or to sift data, though even then officers would need to conscientiously consider the dangers of reading legally privileged messages. IMA 2023 s15 & Sch 2 plugs this gap by conferring powers to seize and retain such things, and to access, copy and use information stored on those things.

9.1.3 Routing

Having been screened, usually the asylum case will be referred, via the National Asylum Allocations Unit (NAAU) (or detention gatekeeper), to a regional asylum team where their case will be allocated to a case owner. The regional asylum teams are situated in Cardiff, Glasgow, Leeds, Liverpool, Central London, West London and Solihull.

Some classes of more specialist case are not immediately referred to the ART: previous absconders, children, those convicted of a serious offence, those with damaged fingerprints, cases suitable for the Detained Casework process, EEA nationals, medical cases, prosecution cases, repeat applications, Third Country Unit cases, and those who appear to be Victims of Trafficking. All of these will be dealt with in accordance with the relevant policies.

9.1.4 The role of the representative

Unless the asylum seeker is to be removed from the UK without a decision being made on their asylum application under the Safe Third Country procedure, the asylum seeker will need help in preparing their asylum claim. Public funding remains available for this purpose. Where the asylum seeker is detained, a representative from a legal aid firm may be available on site. Otherwise, they will need to find their own representative.

The adviser will need to take instructions to establish the basis for and the merits of the asylum claim, and to give appropriate advice. The adviser will then take more detailed instructions with a view to drafting a statement of the claim and preparing the asylum seeker for their interview.

The process of taking an statement from the asylum seeker should help prepare them for the asylum interview. An experienced adviser will build trust but then closely question their client, challenging them (in a friendly manner) where potential issues arise as to plausibility and consistency, and ensuring that the asylum seeker is aware of the level of detail they will need to provide as to their background and fears. The ILPA best practice guides on asylum applications and appeals remain essential reading for advisers on taking their clients instructions and drafting representations.

A good statement will set out the asylum-seeker's background, the events that led to her needing to flee her country of origin, the process of leaving, arriving in the UK, activities and private/family life since arrival and comments on the screening interview. Many legal representatives prefer to serve the statement before the interview and update it afterwards to take the asylum-seeker's comments on the interview into account. Alternatively the statement can be completed post-interview and given to the case owner with detailed representations and any corroborative evidence available, before the asylum decision is made.

Even where the statement is not served pre-interview, it is good practice to prepare a draft, to give the client a chance to recall all relevant aspects of their account, and to address inconsistencies.

In some cases, a Preliminary Information Questionnaire is sent to representatives. This was published online in May 2020, here. The answers should be kept brief and general, but should always be read back to clients with an interpreter before sending, to ensure its contents do not give rise to inconsistencies. The benefit of having already prepared a statement at this point is that you and your client can ensure the questions in the PIQ are addressed consistently with the draft statement.

9.1.5 Asylum interview

Once an asylum seeker has been screened and accepted into the asylum procedure, the next big step in the decision making process will be the substantive asylum interview. This differs from the screening interview in that it concentrates on the substance of the asylum claim. See the Guidance asylum interviews.

Representatives are not funded to attend interviews unless the asylum seeker is a minor or particularly vulnerable. Given this problem the HO should, on request, tape record the interview: Dirshe [2005] EWCA Civ 421. A failure to do so does not render the interview inadmissible: MB Iran [2012] UKUT 119 (IAC). This potential resource should be borne in mind where credibility is disputed.

Top Tip

If there is a dispute about whether or not questions were clearly put and understood at the interview, then the matter should be followed up in writing and if necessary a complaint should be made: this will encourage a judge on any subsequent appeal to take the matter seriously. Relevant steps when checking the fairness and adequacy of the interview process will be to:

☐ obtain the recording of the interview, if there is one, and check and the recording and the transcript for accuracy against the asylum seeker's instructions (see the *Asylum Interview* guidance for details on the interview recording policy).
☐ check not just for accuracy but for the interviewer's tone and whether they encouraged a full explanation to be given, and for corrections to be made.
☐ consider whether there was an interpreter present and their competence, did they appear to interpret everything or were things left out?

If there were any inadequacies, then a complaint should be made at once.

Interview by video conference

In an effort to clear backlogs and speed up decision making, the HO introduced asylum interviews by video conference. Such a setting can be highly problematic for obvious reasons. It is important to be aware that, where an interview is to take place via a video conference, a claimant should always be given the opportunity to explain why they wish to opt out. The API Asylum interviews states:

> ...any reasons given by the claimant for not wanting an interview to be conducted by VC must be carefully considered. This may include, but is not limited to, cases involving sexual orientation or gender identity, victims of torture or other trauma where recording was part of

the persecution, victims of sexual violence or other forms of gender-based persecution, victims of modern slavery or claimants with mental health conditions.

The policy further provides that, where it becomes clear during a video conference interview that the claimant cannot participate fully, the HO decision maker *must* suspend the interview and seek advice from a senior HO caseworker or technical specialist. If the interview cannot then continue via video link, it must be rearranged as a face to face interview.

9.1.6 Women

The Home Office have now incorporated elements of the best practices contained in the old IAA Gender Guidelines and elsewhere in their Asylum Policy Instructions such as Gender issues in the asylum claim. Bear in mind:

- various sorts of ill-treatment that may particularly affect women include persecution: marriage-related harm; violence within the family or community; domestic slavery; forced abortion; forced sterilisation; trafficking; female genital mutilation; sexual violence and abuse; and rape;
- women may be subjected to discriminatory treatment that is enforced through law or through the imposition of social or religious norms that restrict their opportunities and rights, e.g. family and personal laws; dress codes; employment or education restrictions; restrictions on women's freedom of movement and/or activities; and political disenfranchisement;
- there are cases where women are persecuted solely because of their family or kinship relationships, for example, a woman may be persecuted as a means of demoralising or punishing members of her family or community, or in order to pressurise her into revealing information. Whilst many women will be involved in such conventional political activities and raise similar claims this does not always correspond to the reality of the experiences of women in some societies. The gender roles in many countries mean that women will more often be involved in low level political activities for instance hiding people, passing messages or providing community services, food, clothing or medical care. 'Low level' political activity does not necessarily make it low-risk. The response of the state to such activity may be disproportionate because of the involvement of a section of society, namely women, who because of their gender it is considered inappropriate for them to be involved at all.
- Victims of sexual assault may suffer trauma (see MIL 4.3.9). The symptoms of this include persistent fear, a loss of self-confidence and self-esteem, difficulty in concentration, an attitude of self-blame, a pervasive loss of control and memory loss or distortion. Beware of inhibitors to taking instructions – the presence of family members, for example.
- FGM is recognised as a serious human rights violation. X (FGMPO No.2), Re [2019] EWHC 1990 (Fam) lists relevant considerations when assessing risks §91 (in the family law context but still of general relevance) (MIL 8.4.4.1).

9.1.7 Decision; Withdrawal of claims

Decisions can follow quite quickly from asylum interviews, although the time taken by individual case owners varies, depending on their working speed and whether they agree to wait for additional evidence or submissions. We noted the difficulties with determining asylum claims above (MIL 9.1).

Upon a refusal of the claim, a s120 one stop notice will be served, requiring notification of any grounds for remaining in the UK beyond asylum. Refusal of an asylum claim will normally carry the right of appeal (see s82 NIA 2002), subject to being certified as clearly unfounded. We deal with s120 procedures and appeal rights in Module 14.

An asylum claim may be expressly withdrawn by the asylum seeker (via signed disclaimer), or the HO may deem it withdrawn under the r333C regime: for failing to maintain contact with the HO or provide up-to-date contact details, attend reporting events, attend the personal interview or failing to complete the asylum questionnaire as requested, or leaving the UK without authorisation prior to the application being concluded. Unless the applicant can show within a reasonable time that this was due to circumstances beyond their control. Emails to AsylumOutcomeReview@homeoffice.gov.uk can contest a withdrawl decision: there may be rather a lot as the legacy backlog of pre-June 2022 claims is cleared.

The Statement of Changes introducing this (HC1496) states that it aims to ensure efficiency, preventing potential absconder scenarios, & enable decision-making resources to be concentrated on those who genuinely wish to continue with their asylum claims. It has been suggested that the addition of contact detail/reporting events failures in July 2023 is intended to permit many more claims to be deemed withdrawn.

The Guidance *Withdrawing asylum claims* provides detailed procedures.

9.1.8 Delays in determining asylum claims

In recent years the HO has struggled to manage its asylum caseload. Whilst numbers of claims have not greatly changed (35,737 applications in 2019 and 48,540 applications in 2021, and 84,132 in 2002). At June 2021 there were 125,000 cases in the backlog, of whom 57,1000 were awaiting an initial decision. In 2020 the average delay was 449 days (550 for UASCs

There is a significant volume of case law about delay, mostly in the asylum context. From which we learn:

- In general there is a duty on the HO to decide cases in a reasonable time: S [2007] EWCA Civ 546
- However the HO has a lot of leeway when it comes to allocating resources to asylum claim determination and delays will only be unlawful if (FH & Ors [2007] EWHC 1571 (Admin))
    - so excessive as to be manifestly unreasonable
    - there is some concrete detriment which the HO has failed to alleviate
- Delay is much more objectionable where there is effectively a vested right awaiting implementation (this & the position generally is well summarised in O [2019] EWHC 148 (Admin))
- Delay in determining childrens' cases may be unreasonable: whilst in general the system was found lawful in MK [2019] EWHC 3573 (Admin), as per General Comment 14 from the UN Ctte on the Rights of the Child which enjoins that: "*procedures or processes regarding or impacting children be prioritized and completed in the shortest time possible*"
- Arguably damages might be available for undue delay in issuing confirmation of status by way of a status letter once a refugee had been recognised as such: Aruchanga [2023] EWHC 282 (KB)

9.1.9 Right to work for asylum seekers

Asylum seekers can apply for permission to take up employment (not self-employment or setting up a business r360A), although only in shortage occupations (MIL 7.3.1.1), and excluding self-employment, if a decision at first instance has not been taken on their asylum application within one year of the date on which it was recorded – so long as the delay is not attributable to them (r360). Those with further representations pending determination as fresh claims also benefit during the claim's processing including subsequent appeals (r360C: required by ZO (Somalia) [2010] UKSC 36). Permission would last until the claim is finally determined (r360B). Outside of this regime there is no general right to work for asylum seekers as the state is entitled to set policy at a high level to protect the UK's economic interests: Rostami [2013] EWHC 1494 (Admin).

The policies supporting these Rules must recognise the possibility of exceptions, including the possibility of granting permission outside shortage occupations: C6 [2021] UKUT 94 (IAC). Additionally the best interests of the child must be considered having regard to the possibility that a refusal of the right to work might impact on a child: Cardona [2021] EWHC 2656 (Admin).

The *Permission to work and volunteer for asylum seekers Guidance* now has regard to those requirements. It explains that the purpose is to maintain a clear distinction between economic migration and asylum, to prevent illegal working, and to clarify that volunteering in the community is encouraged as it assists integration. The impact on a child's best interests must be balanced against the public interest generally. Children may access education including work experience placements or training.

Discretion may be exercised where rare and exceptional circumstances so demand, such cases being referred to a 'technical specialist' for decision.

9.1.10 Safe and legal routes

The SSHD will be making Regs capping the number of asylum seekers who can come to the UK via safe and legal routes, consulting local authorities as she does so (IMA 2023 s60). There will be a report in January 2024 explaining precisely what these routes may be at the publication date and in the future (s61).

There have been specific regimes for asylum seekers to enter the UK in the past: children transferred from the EU under the 'Dubs Amendment') or under the special Calais route (MIL 4.2.16, 4.2.17). Those are closed schemes. Those regimes which are currently operational are set out in the *Resettlement Guidance*: the *UK Resettlement Scheme* (UKRS: via which UNHCR assess refugees including torture survivors according to their protection and medical needs, depending on UK local authority capacity), *Community Sponsorship Scheme* (as per the UKRS but via local communities rather than local authorities), and the *Mandate Resettlement Scheme*. Other routes to come to the UK include the family reunion provisions of the IRs (MIL 9.7.3), as well as the special schemes for citizens of Afghanistan, Hong Kong and Ukraine (MIL 4.2.15, 4.2.20-21). There is a useful *House of Commons Briefing*.

The Fact Sheet on Safe and Legal Routes states that "It is our longstanding principle that those in need of protection should claim asylum in the first safe country they reach. For many people, it is in their best interests to stay close to the region or in a neighbouring country where there are often similarities in culture and language, and they can be supported by international organisations, including the UN."

9.2 Asylum support & benefits for refugees
9.2.1 Asylum support generally

Asylum support, often still referred to as NASS support, a reference to the now defunct National Asylum Support Service, is available to asylum seekers (and those who have made a claim under Article 3 ECHR) aged over 18 and their dependants who would otherwise be homeless and/or destitute. Unaccompanied children will be supported by their local authority under Section 20 of the Children Act 1989 and not by the HO. From March 2020 the numbers of asylum seekers being accommodated has soared: from 8,042 then to an estimated 99,000 at the end of September 2022 (MQ [2023] EWHC 205 (Admin) cites these figures). The government has stated that as at Spring 2023 the annual cost of hotal accommodation was £2.3 billion.

Applicants are deemed to appear destitute if:

- they and their dependants do not have adequate accommodation or any means of obtaining it (irrespective of whether other essential living needs are met); or
- they and their dependants have adequate accommodation or the means of obtaining it, but cannot meet essential living needs.

Support can be provided in three different ways under section 95 of the 1999 Act:

- Accommodation only, or
- subsistence only (regular cash payments), or
- both accommodation and subsistence

Asylum support can be claimed immediately on claiming asylum. Correspondence from the HO in June 2023 indicates that the application can be made and granted before a screening interview. The level is set by the Asylum Support Regulations 2000: it went up to £40.85 weekly on 21 February 2022. The High Court in CB [2022] EWHC 3329 (Admin) held this was inadequate and in breach of the SSHD's statutory duties; on 17 July 2023 the rate for support under s4(2) and s95 of the IAA 1999 was put up to £47.39.

Information on asylum support is in the Asylum support (asylum instructions). Very useful advice for advisers is provided by the Asylum Support Appeals Project (ASAP: http://www.asaproject.org/about-asap/).

Support is provided under s95 IAA 1999. It is subject to a means assessment and takes the form of allocated accommodation, if the asylum seeker requires it, and a weekly income equivalent to approximately 70% of income support. Emergency accommodation will be provided if necessary. The asylum seeker will then be dispersed somewhere outside of London.

Asylum support can be denied to an asylum seeker who has not made a claim as soon as reasonably practicable after arriving in the UK, generally three days, (a 'section 55 decision'). An asylum seeker cannot though be left destitute (see Limbuela [2005] UKHL 66). Beneficiaries must comply with the strict terms of asylum support - failure to do so can lead to its termination.

Additional support may be paid for pregnant women and children <3. These payments must be focussed on the person-specific essential living needs, including appropriate food for a young child on reasonable demand, and cannot be reduced because of the partial provision of needs via accommodation: HA [2023] EWHC 1876 (Admin).

If an asylum seeker is refused asylum support, or support is withdrawn, they can appeal to the First-tier Tribunal (Asylum Support). See further the *Ceasing Section 95 Support Instruction* which addresses various situations where ceasing support is appropriate, eg on the refusal or withdrawal of an asylum claim, and where leave is granted.

JM [2021] EWHC 2514 (Admin) makes the point that s95 support is typically 42% of the standard Universal Credit allowance for single people aged over 25. The deduction of or lack of, a modest amount of money might be significant where a person's entire needs must be met from asylum support. Travel and communication are to be regarded as essential living needs for the generality of asylum seekers as ways of maintaining essential interpersonal and social relationships as well as cultural and religious life. The restrictions on mobility imposed under the pandemic lockdown regime justified a reduction on travel payments. It was wrong to assume that all asylum seekers generally had access to a mobile phone given the self-evident possibility that genuine claimants might have had to flee their country of origin without regard to the possessions they took with them. AXG [2022] EWHC 56 (Admin) holds that the SSHD failed to provide asylum seekers with money for healthcare goods during the Covid pandemic. There was a hard-edged minimum standard to the essential living needs to be provided under ss.95 and 96(1)(b) IAA 1999, the power to provide support effectively being converted to a duty by the Reception Directive which remained in force for these purposes.

Asylum support obligations end once an asylum application is granted or leave is granted on other grounds, or an appeal is allowed. 28 days notice of support ending is then prescribed; additionally, 7 days notice to quit must be provided, on top of the full notice period if the latter has not been given.

Sch 3 NIAA 2002 addresses the Withholding and Withdrawal of Support, providing that a long list of benefits are not payable to ineligible persons, including failed asylum seekers. There are exceptions where British citizens or children would be affected, or where a HRA 1998 breach would ensue. Birmingham CC v Clue [2010] EWCA Civ 460 held that this provision could not allow people pursuing non-hopeless further representations to be denied benefits if to do so would effectively prejudge the merits of their claim; a local authority might have to conduct a human rights assessment for children leaving care (MIL 4.2.12.1).

9.2.2 Asylum Support via Accommodation

A family's accommodation needs must take account of issues such as a child's safety awareness, behaviour and needs, and any educational disruption that a move would involve: O [2019] EWHC 2734 (Admin). The HO's affordability criteria could not be treated as an absolute answer to the need to find appropriate accommodation.

Different accommodation may be provided for asylum seekers depending on the stage their case has reached and their compliance with bail and support under the HO's *Allocation of Accommodation* Guidance. We address immigration bail accommodation at MIL 13.2.2.

IAA 1999 s97 sets out a "no preference" regime; the HO must have regard to the accommodation being temporary and the desirability of providing accommodation where there is a ready supply. Relevant considerations include previous compliance with conditions of support and bail, and the stage a claim has reached including whether they have been notified of its inadmissibility (s97(3A) IAA 1999).

MQ [2023] EWHC 205 (Admin) emphasises that accommodation may become inadequate over time even if adequate at the outset of the procedure. It sets out the SSHD's evidence on expediting accommodation requests.

Accommodation provided on behalf of the Home Office for asylum-seekers will not require an HMO licence from a local authority during a specified period: The Houses in Multiple Occupation (Asylum-Seeker Accommodation) (England) Regulations 2023, due to enter effect later in 2023.

9.2.3 Section 4 support

Another vital mechanism is '*section 4 support*' (i.e. under s4(2) of the 1999 Act). This is available to those who are destitute and refused asylum where there are practical obstacles to them returning home: eg an outstanding fresh claim, or JR proceedings where permission has been granted, or no viable route of return. S4 support consists of accommodation, and a weekly sum via a payment card. It is available where claims are deemed inadmissible. It is typically provided on a 'no choice' basis usually outside London and the south east, subject to medical reasons. There is Guidance *Section 4(2) policy and process*. Inadmissiblity decisions under NBA 2022 count as an asylum claim's rejection (IAA 1999 s4(2)(b)).

9.2.4   Local authority support

Those asylum seekers who, because of age, mental or physical ill health, disability or any other circumstances, are in need of care and attention which they cannot access anywhere else (i.e. which cannot be met by the provision of s95 or s4 support) may be entitled to support from a local authority under Section 21(1) of the National Assistance Act 1948. This is a complex area of law and advice should be sought from a community care specialist adviser or lawyer.

There is specific provision for asylum seekers experiencing domestic abuse whilst receiving asylum support. The Guidance *Asylum support domestic abuse* explains that the presumption should initially be to believe the applicant, and that there should be an immediate offer of safe alternative accommodation.

9.2.5 Support JRs

SA [2023] EWHC 1787 (Admin) discusses how a support JR challenge works. The court may assess conflicts of evidence on uncontested photos and documents. The first question was whether, in fact, the accommodation provided met an objective minimum standard; and the second was a public law assessment of the reasonableness of the accommodation provided for the family's needs. Relevant considerations were vulnerability due to pregnancy, space for play, eating and homework, the length of residence bearing in mind that a short period in contingency accommodation might be acceptable, but that children needed better facilities than that to achieve developmental milestones.

9.2.6 Portland Barge & ex-MOD accommodation

The *Accommodation Allocation Guidance* states that currently ex-MoD accommodation sites are only to be used to accommodate single, adult males between the ages of 18 to 65.

In NB & Ors [2021] EWHC 1489 (Admin) the court looked at the decision to require asylum seekers to reside at Napier Barracks. The accommodation standards for reception arrangements had to ensure an asylum seeker's essential living needs achieving a dignified living standard adequate for health and subsistence. Whether this was met was an objective question, not a matter for the SSHD's judgment alone. The accommodation arrangements were not intended to be for those with mental or physical health vulnerabilities. The lack of ventilation and overcrowding, particularly when the accommodation was within a detention-like setting for an indefinite period, was a material consideration, given the experiences of many asylum seekers, particularly those travelling via land and in small boats where the likelihood was that they would be more vulnerable as to their mental health which might be undermined by conditions there. The process for selecting asylum seekers for detention in Napier Barracks did not meet the *Tameside* standard – ie there had been no adequate lawful enquiry into a person's suitability for the accommodation. The Inspection visit leading to a *March 2022 report on Napier Barracks* noted various improvements albeit regretting *'the lack of privacy, the noise levels, and disruption to sleep as issues that affected everyone in the shared dormitories'.*

The £6 million daily cost of housing 51,000 asylum seekers in hotels has led the government to announce the use of barges as an alternative: see the *Factsheet: asylum accommodation on a vessel in Portland Port*. 500 asylum seekers will be housed from June 2023 after screening (single adult males will be the focus) with a view to staying there for 3-6 months. This is not detention and arrangements will be made consistent with port security standards. Exercise and communal recreational facilities, and health and safety measures, to support well-being are promised.
Issues foreseeably arising will include
- Adequacy of screening measures
- Whether there is de facto deprivation of liberty
- Undue impact on physical and moral integrity
- Discrimination on disability or racial grounds
- Access to legal advice

The Bibby Stockholm is the first barge to be proposed: an outbreak of legionella caused an early evacuation. An early *legal challenge by the Mayor of Portland* argued the decision was unlawful for circumventing the proper planning process, though ran aground as the court believed the wrong Defendant had been targeted. It too is for single male adults only <65. The Guidance *Failure to travel to Bibby Stockholm vessel* explains 5 working days will be given to make representations, which will be considered within 5 working days; it necessary referral should be made to the HO Asylum Support Medical Adviser (who may advise on fitness to travel & accommodation needs) and/or the HO Psychiatrist. Late representations re suitability should generally be accepted only with verifiable expert or professional evidence of exceptional circumstances such as bereavement or serious medical emergency; further representations will be considered only exceptionally & where they fundamentally alter the case put. A refusal to relocate will lead to 5-days warning of eviction from their present accommodation & support will be discontinued.

9.2.7 Refugees and benefits

Where an asylum claim is finally determined, their asylum support will come to an end unless they have a dependent child. If the claim is successful, the asylum seeker (now a refugee) will be able to apply for mainstream benefits. At one time the HO recognised that in the meantime support should continue until their residence permit arrived. But now as per the *Ceasing section 95 support* Guidance asylum support continues for only 28 days meaning that the first welcome many recognised refugees receive is to be rendered street homeless.

Adnan [2022] CSIH 2 and DK [2022] EWCA Civ 120 confirm that provisions that enable refugees to make backdated child tax credit claims from the date they sought asylum continue to apply where that date was before the introduction of full service universal credit. Backdating claims must be made within 1 month of the status grant (Reg 3(5) of Tax Credit Immigration Regs).

9.3 Representing asylum seeking children

Representing asylum seeking children requires significant expertise, particularly where they are unaccompanied. There is a *distinct procedure* for family asylum claims (ie where children claim as dependents – accompanied asylum seeking children (ASSCs)). The rest of this section deals with unaccompanied asylum seeking children (UASCs). Useful sources of information:

- Coram Childrens' Legal Centre *Seeking Support' guide: asylum process* (bearing in mind that some of the support and other provisions might not be up to date, and further changes will be introduced as Part 5 of the Immigration Act 2016 comes into force)
- ILPA's *Resources Guide for Practitioners Working with Refugee Children*

When representing children:

- be aware of the *Streamlined asylum processing for children's casework Guidance* which provides for determining claims without interviews where possible for nationals of Afghanistan, Eritrea, Sudan, Syria and Vietnam via a Preliminary Information Meeting (PIM) with the child and a responsible adult to be held not before 2 weeks from lodging the asylum claim or enterilng local authority care, with a view to granting claims unless significant discrepancies emerge. Family tracing will take place via the Children and Secondary Case Progression Unit - from July 2023 asylum decision makers will concentrate on progressing cases rather than tracing family, leaving the latter to specialists. The objective is to resolve cases via the PIM with a substantive asylum interview only if required; SEFs are now discouraged
- make sure advisers working with children are accredited to IAAS Level 2, are suitably experienced, and have had enhanced criminal record checks (now termed Disclosure and Barring Service (DBS) checks) undertaken
- UASCs they should be referred to the Refugee Council's *Independent Unaccompanied Asylum-Seeking Children Support Service*
- bear in mind the possible need for counselling and a psychiatric report
- a decision on their claim should be made quickly, within a month if there is no good reason to delay it: there are repeated references to avoiding delay in the Home Office Guidance *Processing an asylum application from a child*
- remember in making appointments for children to ensure they attend with an appropriate adult who is responsible for the child's welfare (e.g. panel adviser, foster parent or social worker). Try to avoid appointments that will disrupt school.
- Bear in mind social work records as a means of corroborating a child client's credibility. This is an essential source of information, because it may record contemporaneous reactions to distressing news from abroad and extensively catalogue the child's behaviour in the light of their past experiences: indeed *Processing an Asylum Application from a Child* at page 38 expressly notes that 'child psychological and physical health and development reports or information from welfare and health support professionals to whom the child may have disclosed relevant evidence' are a relevant source of supporting material.
    - On appeal, bear in mind the Joint Presidential Guidance Note No 2 Judges must bear in mind whether any discrepancies are due to the age, vulnerability or sensitivity of the witness, in the decision as well as when conducting the hearing; objective indications of risk should receive particular attention (MIL 14.5.8))
    - Note the policy regarding children in the care of local authority: MIL 4.2.12
    - The Guidance *Screening and Routing* now provides that children should be seen as having made asylum applications in their own right even when dependents within a family unit

9.3.1 Relevance of age

Being assessed as a child has multiple impacts for an asylum seeker – most importantly:

- how they are to be supported in the UK (for example they will be supported by social services, and may benefit from their support even after becoming an adult)
- how their asylum claim will be assessed – there is a more generous approach to credibility for children, and thus, when assessing *credibility*, the Guidance *Processing an asylum application from a child* makes clear the care that must be taken before discrepancies are held against a child asylum seeker
- what will happen to them if their asylum claim is refused (if they are a UASC, i.e. one applying in their own right without a primary carer in this country (r352ZD) they will receive leave to remain until the age of 17.5 under r352ZC so long as there are no adequate reception arrangements in the country of return and no public interest reasons to the contrary)

9.3.2 Assessing credibility in children's claims

The credibility of a child needs to be assessed with care.

- There is also a more liberal attitude to risk assessment, see AA Afghanistan CG [2012] UKUT 16 (IAC) explaining the difficulties that children may face via sexual exploitation and vulnerability to forced recruitment into the armed forces or militias, and to trafficking
- The Child Processing Guidance just cited explains that an adverse credibility inference should not be drawn from omissions in a child's knowledge or account where their age or maturity may be responsible. Decision makers should consider what it is 'reasonable' to expect a child to know, given their circumstances, their age, maturity and education. Both generally when considering their account, and also when bearing in mind "section 8" considerations (MIL 8.1.5.2)
- The UNHCR Guidelines on *International Protection: Child Asylum Claims* warn that children cannot be expected to provide adult-like accounts of their experiences, due to reasons such as trauma, parental instructions, lack of education, fear of State authorities or persons in positions of power, use of ready-made testimony by smugglers, or fear of reprisals. Thus a liberal application of the benefit of the doubt may be essential. And

    "They may be too young or immature to be able to evaluate what information is important or to interpret what they have witnessed or experienced in a manner that is easily understandable to an adult. Some children may omit or distort vital information or be unable to differentiate the imagined from reality. They also may experience difficulty relating to abstract notions, such as time or distance. Thus, what might constitute a lie in the case of an adult might not necessarily be a lie in the case of a child. It is, therefore, essential that examiners have the necessary training and skills to be able to evaluate accurately the reliability and significance of the child's account. This may require involving experts in interviewing children outside a formal setting or observing children and communicating with them in an environment where they feel safe, for example, in a reception centre."

- This approach is reflected in IR351:

    "A person of any age may qualify for refugee status under the Convention and the criteria in paragraph 334 apply to all cases. However, account should be taken of the applicant's maturity and in assessing the claim of a child more weight should be given to objective indications of risk than to the child's state of mind and understanding of his situation. An asylum application madeon behalf of a child should not be refused solely because the child is too young to understand his situation or to have formed a well founded fear of persecution. Close attention should be given to the welfare of the child at all times."

In KA (Afghanistan) [2019] EWCA Civ 914 looks at the relevance of a child asylum seeker's failure to claim asylum in a 'safe' third country (MIL 8.5.2)

Very little attention should be paid to interviews early in the process with UASCs where no appropriate adult is present. Breaches of the HO guidance on interviewing children may well require that interviews, or aspects of them, are disregarded (e.g. AN and FA [2012] EWCA Civ 1636). Key requirements are that:

- a responsible adult should be present,
- there should be a short informal conversation on a non-asylum topic to break the ice,
- the interview should be conducted by a specially trained caseworker who makes clear their understanding that the child is giving information in an alien environment and may be distrustful, and
- Strict fairness is observed: an interviewer must 'put all inconsistencies in the child's subjective evidence or between the subjective and objective evidence to the child at the interview, to allow them an opportunity to explain further'.

The IRs r352 require that any child aged over 12 be offered an interview, unless unfit or unable to be interviewed, or where protection status can be granted without one. The interviewer must be specially trained, and a parent, guardian, representative or another adult independent of the SSHD who has responsibility for the child must be present. Children must be allowed to express themselves in their own way and at their own speed, with deferral of the interview if they appear tired or distressed. A representative of a specified kind (legal rep, social worker etc) must be appointed to advise the child of the importance of the interview.

Breaks should be offered during interviews as often as required: interviewers should ensure they use appropriate language and pace of delivery. Information should be sought from other sources where possible: from parents, adults, or objective material regarding the country. It should be recognised that children may be particularly liable to suggestability from an interviewer (see *Psychological Research Evidence in Refugee Status Determination* (Herlihy & Ors, Journal of Refugee Studies, 2023).

There is also a more liberal attitude to risk assessment which recognises that a broad array of harms may threaten the well-being of children (see AA (unattended children) Afghanistan CG [2012] UKUT 16 (IAC) for a good explanation of the difficulties that children may face by way of sexual exploitation and vulnerability to forced recruitment into the armed forces or militias, and to trafficking). In this regard there is no 'bright line' separating children aged under 18 from slightly older young adults (KA (Afghanistan) [2012] EWCA Civ 1014).

9.3.3 Family tracing

The Asylum Seekers (Reception Conditions) Regulations 2005, SI 2005/7 (Reg 6) impose obligations to trace an unaccompanied minor's parents. These Regs originally transposed EU law obligations and so are EU retained law:

- As part of the best interests duty the HO "*shall endeavour to trace the members of the minor's family as soon as possible after the minor makes his claim for asylum*"
- Where there may be a threat to the life or integrity of the minor or their close family, the HO must ensure that the collection, processing and circulation of any relevant information is undertaken on a confidential basis without jeopardising their safety.

These obligations have been found by the courts, in numerous cases culminating in MA and AA (Afghanistan) [2015] UKSC 40, to have a limited impact on Home Office decision making. A tracing failure may, however, be relevant to assessing an asylum seeker's claim where it had an 'effect on the nature and quality of the available evidence':

> If the appellant has identified people who might be able to confirm his account, but the respondent has not pursued that lead, the tribunal might fairly regard the appeint's willingness to identify possible sources of corroboration as a mark of credibility, but this would be an evidential assessment for the tribunal [73].

The HO's guidance on Family tracing is in the Children (asylum policy guidance) (see also MIL 9.3).

9.3.4 Age assessment

There has been considerable litigation around disputed age assessments of young asylum seekers. It is important to understand the basis of the system:

- Social services depts ('SSDs') have statutory responsibility for looking after children, so it is for them to assess a child's age
- Age is also relevant to assessing the route an asylum claim should take, which is HO territory: but given the time taken for a SSD assessment, the HO often needs to take a preliminary view
- The initial assessment process is often carried out by untrained and inexpert HO staff simply on the basis of a visual assessment

CHAPTER 9: Asylum Process and Practice

This is a volatile area. The NBA 2022 (Part 4) implements significant changes to the existing system, introducing "scientific methods" to assist "designated persons" to assess age (via decisions binding on the HO) – and it has been planned that age assessment appeals will replace the present JR regime though some sources indicate this initiative may fall by the wayside given the more Draconian response to asylum seekers found generally in IMA 2023. From 31 March 2023 local authorities must either conduct an age assessment themselves (on balance of probabilities), or inform the HO that they accept the claimed age without further assessment, or refer an age-disputed person to an official who the SSHD has designated for the age assessment role (NBA 2022 s50(3)), providing the HO with the underlying evidence on which they rely if so requested (s50(4)). Assessments by designated persons are provided for by s51 and are binding on local authorities and the HO (s50(7)) subject to (the presently non-existent) appeal. Pending introduction of appeals, designated persons must re-assess under a transitional provision (s50(7A), found in the Commencement No. 5 and Transitional Provisions Regulations 2023) if significant new information comes to light creating a realistic prospect of success. The local government lawyer newsletter on 20 Sept 2023 *reported concerns from various experts* that the use of X-rays was inaccurate and unethical.

BF (Eritrea) [2019] EWCA Civ 872 found that the previous HO policy (whereby the test was whether appearance and demeanour very strongly suggested they were aged over 18) was unlawful. It noted that if children are wrongly assumed to be adults, this will lead to their applications for asylum and other international protection being assessed by processes designed for adults rather than children.

- They might be detained, as with adults
- Their vulnerability as a child may go unnoticed, which as just mentioned can be relevant both to the assessment of their credibility and to the forms of serious harm they may face abroad)
- Age is also a central part of a child's identity and a failure to believe that they are children could lead to them losing all confidence in the decision making system and failing to disclose further and necessary details about their past persecution and future fears
- They will be refused accommodation under Section 20 of the Children Act 1989 and will be dispersed to NASS accommodation as adults

The Supreme Court disagreed, overturning that ruling in BF (Eritrea) [2021] UKSC 38. The policy at Criterion C (ie permitting treatment as an adult where their physical appearance/demeanour very strongly suggests that they are significantly over 18 years of age and no other credible evidence exists to the contrary) lawfully set out the relatively generous degree to which the benefit of the doubt should be applied to a person claiming to be a child.

The current policy Assessing Age (post-BF Eritrea in the Supreme Court) requires that claimants are only to be treated as adults prior to a formal age assessment if

- two HO members of staff, one at least of Chief Immigration Officer or Higher Executive Officer grade, have independently assessed that the claimant is an adult because their physical appearance and demeanour very strongly suggests that they are over 18 and there is little or no supporting evidence for their claimed age; or
- there is credible and clear documentary evidence that they are 18 years of age or over

If social workers with knowledge of the individual believe the person to be a child, it would be highly unlikely that HO staff could conclude adulthood to the "very strongly suggests" standard

In TN [2020] EWHC 481 (Admin) the Court emphasises the fact that children cannot be detained in any but the briefest and most extreme circumstances. A person should be treated as a child once the HO has accepted an age assessment from social services as Merton compliant. That will apply both to the future and the past. So a modern age assessment may demonstrate that historic detention was in fact unlawful, if it shows that the person detained was a minor at the time. BF (Eritrea) [2021] UKSC 38 confirms that a child's detention will be unlawful even though the immigration officers acted reasonably (at the time) in determining age.

Having been given the benefit of the doubt, an unaccompanied minor will be put under the care of a local authority which should then carry out a 'Merton complaint' age assessment (i.e. one that complies with the procedural safeguards identified by Stanley Burnton J in R (B) v Merton LBC [2003] EWHC 1689 (Admin)). The HO are likely to accept the view of social services though the SSHD will still consider the matter for themselves, giving significant weight to the assessment and having regard to all reliable evidence. The *Assessing Age* Guidance specifies numerous relevant considerations such as ethnic and genetic background, the range of physical development during adolescence, the impact of a long and traumatic journey, and the impact of poverty or manual labour during childhood. Particular care is required when assessing demeanour, with a firm understanding of the possible background to a false or mistaken statement by the child as to their age.

Given the numerous benefits of being correctly treated as a child, HO guidance and case law has developed in relation to age assessment challenges. There is no consensus on the right methodology: the report *Biological evaluation methods to assist in assessing the age of unaccompanied asylum-seeking children* sets out that there is no infallible method for either biological or social-worker-led age assessment that will provide a perfect match to chronological age, and goes on to identify relevant considerations. Care should be given for any X-ray process leading to radiation doses. There should be further research into the impact of socioeconomic factors and their effect on growth and maturational timing, particularly those factors likely to be experienced by UASC.

Critical features of a Merton compliant assessment are:

- an assessment of age in the light of a person's general background including their personal circumstances and history, education and recent activities (and certainly not on appearance alone)
- having regard to procedural fairness which would require a provisional assessment of age to be put to the person in question (M v London Borough of Waltham Forest [2021] EWHC 2241 (Admin) looks at this issue. A failure to do so would undermine a decision unless it was very clear that there was no answer to the assessment conclusions)
- the benefit of the doubt should be given where there is uncertainty
- trained social workers should make the evaluation

In T v London Borough of Enfield [2004] EWHC 2297 (Admin), the judge held in addition that it was necessary to ask the individual why they believed that they were a minor and take into account any evidence which indicates that they are suffering from trauma and/or have any special educational needs. HAM [2022] EWHC 1924 (Admin) emphasises that Merton did not lay down any set checklist: the central tenets were the absence of any burden of proof, and a duty of fair and reasonable (though not exhaustive) enquiry. There was no professional or legal consensus that accurate age assessment required two social workers nor that an independent adult's presence was essential to fairness.

The pressures of arrivals on the south coast have required special measures. At one time a team of suitably qualified social workers were embedded in the Kent Intake Unit (KIU) working alongside UKVI staff to provide social worker support and advice in relation re unaccompanied children, including those whose claimed age was doubted. MA & Anor [2022] EWHC 98 (Admin) looks at the Kent Intake Unit Social Worker Guidance which included a 'short' age assessment. It finds that absent safeguards such as the presence of an appropriate adult and "minded to refuse" process, the process was unlawful: so the KIU Guidance was withdrawn on 14 January 2022.

9.3.5 Challenging an age assessment

The sequence of challenges will normally be as follows (pending the introduction of appeals):

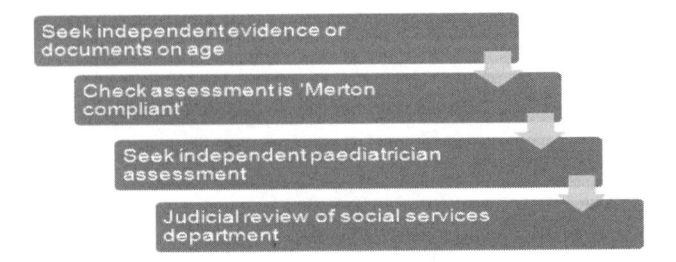

- Seek independent evidence or documents on age
- Check assessment is 'Merton compliant'
- Seek independent paediatrician assessment
- Judicial review of social services department

CHAPTER 9: Asylum Process and Practice

> **Top Tip**
>
> Before seeking to challenge a Home Office age assessment it is important to obtain any independent evidence available as to a person's age. Any such evidence will carry weight with whoever conducts an age assessment. Relevant materials include the Social Services *Practice Guidelines for age assessment*,
>
> - Verify any documentation the child may have with them in the form of passports, national or school identity cards, family records or similar
> - Chase schools, doctors, hospitals, local officials, NGOs in the field and other objective sources of data about age
> - Obtain statements and affidavits from family and community members
> - Ensure that a credible account has been provided of the child's background: their account of why they are present in this country, usually on asylum grounds, is an important part of this
> - Ensure there is relevant country evidence that supports the child's account for example as to the education system
> - Ensure the interview process complied with best practice requirements
> - Expert medical opinion, despite much criticism (see e.g. R v London Borough of Croydon [2011] EWHC 1473 (Admin)), may be useful, particularly where it is linked to the more reputable methods of age assessment such as a sustained dropping off in height and weight gain, and the full emergence of the third molar: AM v Solihull MBC (AAJR) [2012] UKUT 118. See more on the issues surrounding dental evidence in M v LB of Waltham Forest [2021] EWHC 2241 (Admin) noting that it was hard to imagine a case where dental records and/or a person's height could be determinative

If the social services age assessment is unfavorable, there are different courses of action that can be pursued, including:

1. Seeking alternative independent evidence of age as suggested above. Should new evidence become available social services will need to conduct a new age assessment.

2. Seeking a paediatrician age assessment. This is simply one form of independent evidence, but it is a controversial one – eg A v Croydon [2009] EWHC 939 (Admin) found that such assessments are inherently unreliable bearing in mind the difficulty of the exercise and the admitted margin of error of around two years either way – he was scathing about the particular expert report before him. Now though the Guidance *Assessing Age* recognises expert evidence must be considered albeit it does not necessarily merit greater weight than social worker opinions.

3. JR of social services. A v Croydon [2009] UKSC 8 held that an age assessment by social services for the purposes of section 20 of the 1989 Children Act is not to be approached via the limited scope of a normal JR application:

   > rather the question whether or not a person is a child is ... a question of fact which must ultimately be decided by the court

   This is very helpful when it comes to challenging a social services department. The judge on JR has to try the issues for themselves and make up their own mind as to age, giving a declaration as to their conclusion . The UKSC case came after the judgment of Mr Justice Collins (they are related but distinct cases) and undermines key parts of the reasoning of the earlier case, so it may prove to be the case that pediatrician assessments will be given more weight in the future – though the methods of some well known experts have received damning criticism.

Disputing age assessments has become a specialist area. Age assessment JRs are usually heard now by the Upper Tribunal (and are routinely transferred there by the Administrative Court following R (FZ) v Croydon LBC [2011] EWCA Civ 59 and R (JS and YK) v Birmingham City Council (AAJR) [2011]

UKUT 00505 (IAC)) because it is a more suitable forum for assessing evidence and are reported at https://tribunalsdecisions.service.gov.uk/utiac/decisions with an 'AAJR' prefix to the citation.

Possible flaws in age assessment decisions identified in the case law (see decisions such as AS v London Borough of Croydon [2011] EWHC 2091 (Admin) AZ v Hampshire County Council (AAJR) [2013] UKUT 87 (IAC), AM v Solihull Metropolitan Borough Council (AAJR) [2012] UKUT 118 and the Merton case itself):

- Failing to give a suitable margin for error
- Failing to disclose the age assessment reasons in good time
- Failing to give the subject an opportunity to comment on them
- Using obscure language which is difficult to understand
- Failing to follow best practice on building rapoort, Not paying attention to 'tiredness, trauma, bewilderment and anxiety', or ethnicity, culture, and customs of the person being assessed
- Automatically adopting a Home Office age assessment
- Making an unwarranted departure from a finding of age made on appeal by the tribunal
- Not having an interpreter present consistently
- Having regard to physical appearance without taking account of relevant life history
- Holding the absence of corroborative documents against the subject without considering the kinds of difficulties in obtaining and carrying documents abroad which are well known to the Immigration Tribunals
- Failing to give an opportunity to comment on the provisional decision if minded to find the interviewee to be an adult
- Conducting an unduly confrontational interview
- Failing to properly explain the nature and purpose of the process in advance
- Failing to ensure the presence of an appropriate adult: though this is not decisive, see eg SB [2023] EWCA Civ 924

Important considerations when assessing age might include (eg G v Royal Borough of Greenwich [2021] EWHC 3348 (Admin)):

- The benefit of the doubt must be afforded to the applicant given that age assessment is not a scientific process
- Evidence from teachers/family members who can point to supporting instances of consistent attitudes over time are likely to carry weight that observations made in the artificial surroundings of an interview cannot
- Evidence of the reactions of peers, likely to be of assistance particularly if allowance for any cultural differences can be made

AB v Kent County Council [2020] EWHC 109 (Admin) assesses the lawfulness of an age assessment conducted by social services on an abbreviated basis. Such assessments were *potentially* lawful – but it was essential that they clearly took account of the significant margin for error that age assessment always involved. The possible margin would depend on the facts of the case, but here an abbreviated age assessment which had given an age range of 20-21 years was too close to the age of 18 to be lawful. AB also provides a useful 21-point summary of the previous case law.

In the unreported JR decision of DK [2021] UKAITUR JR011052020, the UT holds that when making age assessment challenges, potential claimants should promptly make subject access requests of those nations through which they have passed and have given details including fingerprints. Such documentation may be relevant where it relates directly to the details given by the claimant to, for example, EU member states as to age and identity on detention or in an asylum claim outside the UK. Relevant documents which are reasonably available (bearing in mind EU authorities are obliged to respond to a subject data request under Article 15 of the GDPR) should be placed before the court to assist and enable it to make just and fair decisions in age assessments. There is actually Guidance on the processes for obtaining information relevant to age assessment from Eurodac & Dublin 3: *Eurodac and Article 34 information for age assessment purposes.*

Darboe and Camara v Italy [2022] ECHR 586 holds that the procedural obligations under ECHR Art 8 extend to the determination of an asylum seeker's age given the importance of personal relationships as well as a fair and appropriate asylum procedure to a young person.

BG [2022] UKUT 338 (IAC) explains that the duty of candour applicable to parties in JRs includes the need for those representing children to analyse and disclose relevant social media messages. They must ascertain what social media are used, analyse the content, and consider whether anything adverse to the client needs to be disclosed. A disclosure statement setting this out might be appropriate explaining the scope of the research and that the work undertaken was reasonable and proportionate. Disclosure of social media accounts may be an interference with a young person's private life and so excessively broad disclosure would not necessarily be appropriate (eg giving a local authority's legal team one's passwords would likely be disproportionate).

It may well be very important to preserve the disputed person's entitlement to be treated as a minor pending resolution of the legal challenge. An interim relief application (MIL 14.8.4) may be necessary if the local authority proposes placing the young person into an adult support regime. MA v Liverpool City Council [2023] EWHC 359 (Admin) explains relevant considerations: a well-conducted age assessment by qualified social workers may well be better than a brief assessment by the court, though the availability of witnesses supporting the asserted age is likely to show there is a serious issue to be tried. The protective precautionary approach recognised the importance of Parliament's wish that children receive necessary and desirable provision - though child protection issues could cut both ways as it might be as unsatisfactory to house an adult with children, as to house a children with adults (see also BAA [2023] EWHC 252 (Admin)). However in most cases the greater danger was in placing children with adults rather than temporarily supporting a young adult: AF [2023] EWHC 163 (Admin).

HP v Greenwich [2023] EWHC 744 (Admin) discusses the relevant considerations when subsequently awarding support where age has been wrongly assessed: the degree of unfairness/culpability by the local authority, delay in exercising the power and seeking a remedy, the continuity of services as between those received as a child and now sought, and the needs of the applicant (including those assessed by reasonable enquiries and the needs now known following judicial process). See this article *The discretion to provide support services to young adults: legal principles*.

9.4 Fast-track appeals

The detained 'fast track' (DFT) procedure was one whereby the asylum decision and appeal took place in a very short time frame. Although the DFT does not currently operate, we address it in the following section because it may be reinstated in one form or another. NBA 2022 s27 may one day introduce expedited appeals, as may IMA 2023 which proposes appeals against third country removal direct to the UTa right of appeal direct to the UT (MIL 9.1.0, 14.6.4). Procedure Rules may ensure that these appeals "*are determined more quickly than an appeal … in the normal course of events*".

Those subject to the DFT were detained throughout the process. In December 2014, Detention Action [2014] EWCA Civ 1634 found that the detention of asylum seekers in the DFT who were not at risk of absconding whilst their appeals are pending was unlawful. The detention policy did not meet the required standards of clarity and transparency, and was thus unjustified.

That was merely one of a series of blows struck against the fast track in litigation throughout 2014 and 2015. Ultimately The Lord Chancellor v Detention Action [2015] EWCA Civ 840 closed down the whole system. There the Court ruled that the DFT was systemically unfair. It noted the complex issues often raised in a context where instructions had to be obtained from individuals in detention whose lawyers had to perform varied tasks, and found that the limited power to adjourn proceedings was not sufficient to see fairness done.

The Court was particularly concerned that it would be difficult to persuade the Tribunal that the appeal could not be justly determined within the proscribed timetable as there may not have been time to complete the relevant enquiries into the available corroborative evidence, and there was an inevitable tension between having to argue that the available evidence was insufficient whilst being aware that such evidence would be all that could be used to support the case if an adjournment was refused.

Asylum seekers whose cases were heard in the DFT can apply for the decisions of the First-tier Tribunal to be put aside because of the lack of fairness. It would seem a good idea to highlight specific evidence which was not available because of the speed of the process or seek to show other forms of unfairness. The FTT President has clarified that rule 32 of the Tribunal Procedure (First-tier Tribunal) (Immigration and Asylum Chamber) Rules 2014 can be relied on by the FTT to set aside a decision which disposes of proceedings (32(1)) where it is in the interests of justice to do so (32(1)(a)) because there has been a procedural irregularity in the proceedings (32(2)(d)). But only so long as the decision in question was made pursuant to the 2014 Rules.

This litigation involved only the 2014 DFT Rules. Their 2005 predecessors were very similar, and so unsurprisingly the DFT appeals process under the 2005 Rules was also found to have been unlawful. TN (Vietnam) [2018]EWCA Civ 2838 (upheld by TN (Vietnam) [2021] UKSC 41) found that decisions made under the older Rules were unlawful for the same reasons of unfairness as the Court of Appeal had already identified. However, most of these decisions were relatively old, and many had not been challenged by way of JR or appeal. Accordingly, there was an issue as to whether the past proceedings should be revisited. The court concluded:

- The FTT does not have jurisdiction to set aside decisions made under the 2005 Rules
- Thus the only procedure for reopening asylum claims will be to make further representations to the SSHD pointing to actual unfairness within the appeal process (i.e. concrete corroboration such as documents, reports or witnesses would need to be identified that was not previously available within the strict time limits): once unfairness is established, it will be difficult for the SSHD to resist recognising a fresh asylum claim generating a new right of appeal, even if status is not granted

FTT decisions made in the DFT process will always need to be scrutinised with some care. MW [2019] UKUT 411 (IAC) finds that they remain the starting point when future appeals are heard. This is because of the Devaseelan principle (MIL 14.5) which requires judges hearing appeals involving previously determined issues to treat earlier FTT decisions as the starting point for any subsequent consideration of the case. Judicial fact-finders could depart from previous decisions on appeal on a principled and properly-reasoned basis. The burden would be on applicants to advance detailed evidence-backed forensic criticism of the decision.

The key features of fast track appeals were as follows:

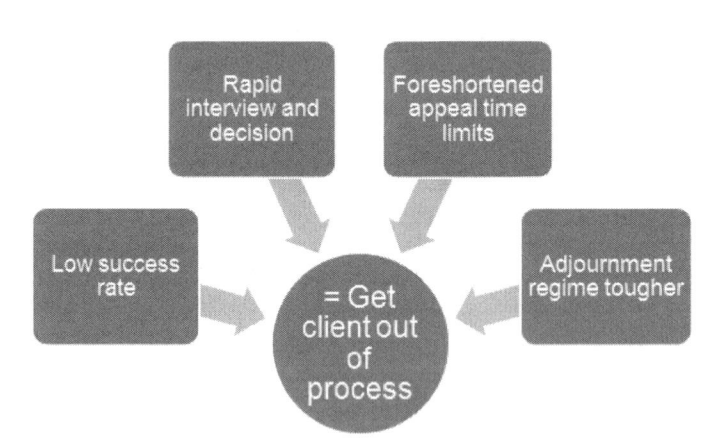

- Rapid interview and decision
- Foreshortened appeal time limits
- Low success rate
- Adjournment regime tougher

= Get client out of process

As can be seen, everything about the fast track process pointed to the need to extract one's client from it if at all possible. The DFT success rate was consistently very low. Was the HO spectacularly successful at selecting low merit cases for the process? Or did any case that went through the process thereby have a drastically reduced chance of success?

Those who were allocated to the fast track processes at Harmondsworth and Yarl's Wood received a decision on their claim within three days of arrival and were subjected to an expedited appeals procedure.

Examples of cases which were unsuitable for the DFT as shown by the case law were:

- Those turning on authenticity of documents, see Lord Phillips MR in the Court of Appeal in ZL and VL [2003] EWCA Civ 25
- Those where the HO had what amounted to expert evidence by way of a local authority age assessment which the appellant needs an opportunity to rebut: SH (Afghanistan) [2011] EWCA Civ 1284
- Those where the basis for the case cannot 'be reliably established without evidence from sources external to the claimant himself' where further time is legitimately required to obtain that evidence: JB (Jamaica) [2013] EWCA Civ 666 (as where gender preference can only realistically be established by finding various witnesses from the community)

On a removal from the process, any time periods for acts to be done which were then running were to be replaced by their equivalent in the principal rules (Rule 31).

We discuss the DFT process further in the context of detention (MIL 13.1.9.6).

9.4.1 Detained asylum casework

In July 2015, following the demise of the DFT, asylum policy guidance was published, addressing how the Home Office would henceforth deal with asylum claims from people in detention: Detained Asylum Casework (DAC) – asylum process.

Cases are deemed suitable for the DAC if the claimant is suitable for detention under detention policy; **and**

- Is already detained, and their detention is authorised according to the standard detention policy requirements; or
- The claim is likely to be certified as clearly unfounded under ss94(1) or (4) NIAA 2002 2002 (the officer authorising detention must be grade 7+) (MIL 9.6.1)
- There are other exceptional circumstances eg past criminality which justify their detention (the officer authorising detention must be at SCS or higher level of seniority)

In all cases, the Detention Gatekeeper Team must consider the suitability of the claimant for detention.

As to time frames and flexibility, the policy states:

> The DAC team operates to an indicative timetable for interviewing the claimant and deciding their asylum claim. This timetable exists to support case progression, to help minimise the time an individual is detained. However, this timetable is not rigid. Flexibility must be exercised in the asylum process wherever fairness demands it, with claimants being given additional time whenever it is appropriate. ...
>
> Requests for flexibility may be made orally or in writing by the claimant or their legal representative, at any time during the asylum decision process. Where requests are unclear, officers must take reasonable steps to obtain clarification. The issues raised must be properly considered, and flexibility given where appropriate.

Claimants must always have:

1. at least 5 full working days between the time their legal representative is confirmed and the asylum interview
2. at least 5 full working days after their asylum interview to submit further representations before any decision is made and further time can be requested
3.

The mainstream 2014 Proedure rules govern appeals.

Detention must be reviewed regularly having particular regard to the applicant's need to obtain further evidence and

- any vulnerabilities, having particular regard to those identified in the relevant policies in the Enforcement operational guidance under 'offender management').

The above policies include torture victims, whose cases will not normally be suitable for the DAC process if supported by independent evidence of torture via a (Detention Centre Rules 2001) rule 35 report (MIL 13.1.8), and those whose medical or mental health issues cannot be adequately managed in detention.

It is possible to bring a JR challenge against a person's continued detention and a judge may order suspension of the decision-making process to avoid the possibility of unfair prejudice resulting from unduly speedy consideration of a claim.

The challenges to the DAC have so far resoundingly failed – in TH (Bangladesh) [2016] EWCA Civ 815 the Court of Appeal refused permission to appeal against the decision of the Administrative Court below, noting that the safeguards including those designed to prevent inappropriate cases entering the system in the first place and that the DAC system involved lawyers at an early stage which significantly contributed towards achieving fairness.

ZA (Pakistan) [2020] EWCA Civ 146 looks at the detention of an asylum seeker during the period in which their asylum claim was under consideration. Decision makers should not simply presume that an asylum claim under this procedure would be refused. The SSHD was normally entitled to factor in the possibility that a detainee would be granted asylum and thus released from detention, and not simply to assume that the claim would be refused and that appeal proceedings would follow. Once the target period of 28 days for making a decision on such a claim had expired things might be different.

9.5 Third country cases

An asylum applicant cannot normally be removed from the UK without their claim being considered on its merits) (s77 NIAA 2002) (i.e. considered *substantively*, as it is sometimes expressed). An exception to this is where the HO intends to remove the asylum applicant to a safe third country. In recent years this has been the country which is responsible under EU law for allocating asylum seekers to particular countries depending on their place of arrival and their connections with individual Member States. Thus NIAA 2002 s77(2A)-(2B) provides that asylum seekers may be sent to places where their life and liberty would not be threatened for a Refugee Convention reason or suffer ECHR Art 3 mistreatment, and which will not send them onwards incompatibly with the Refugee Convention or their ECHR rights. These provisions, plus Sch 3 of AITCA 2004, provide that EU Member States are presumed to satisfy these criteria, as are other states which may be designated by a list. However whilst safety is deemed for Refugee Convention purposes, an asylum seeker may argue there are ECHR problems there, both in the territory itself or posed via the threat of being sent elsewhjere by the authorities there, due to their particular circumstances (eg Sch 3 para (1A)).

9.5.1 Third Country cases and Brexit
For a time IRs suggested that Dublin returns could continue regardless of Brexit. That proved optimistic.

9.5.2 Pre and Post Brexit arrangements for third country returns

9.5.2.1 Farewell to Dublin

EC Council Regulation Number No 604/2013 (Dublin 3) is the instrument governing the procedures by which one European Union Member State only will be identified as responsible for a particular asylum claim (see the relevant API here). The UK having departed the EU its provisions are no longer relevant to how new asylum claims are processed here. In practice Dublin 3 tended to allocate responsibility to the State where the individual was first detected as entering the EU territory (subject to having relatives or family members present in other countries, or other special circumstances such as having been granted a visa for another country). Damages may be available for serious harm to a person's private and family life caused by a failure to respect Dublin 3 rights (MIL 14.10 - or for detention, particularly before March 2017, MIL 9.5.2.3).

Dublin 3's demise was sudden. As per the House of Commons briefing paper cited below re the UK's ability to return anyone under Dublin 3:

> *The UK and EU haven't agreed a common set of transitional arrangements for outstanding Dublin transfer cases at the end of the transition period.*

For now the HO aspire to negotiate returns on a case by case basis. The *Home Office response to the Independent Family Returns Panel Report 2019 to 2020* (19 November 2021) states that *"We are pursuing bilateral negotiations on post-transition migration issues, including returns processes, with key countries with whom we have a mutual interest"*. This isn't going terribly well - as the Chief Inspector of Immigration puts it in the report *An inspection of asylum casework* August 2020 to May 2021 - *"none of the 3,379 claimants [receiving inadmissibility notices] had been returned"*. For now we will keep our discussion of Dublin 3 in the online version of MIL.

9.5.2.2 The third country regime from June 2022

The UK has now departed the Dublin 3 regime. There is an interesting discussion in the House of Commons briefing "*Brexit: the end of the Dublin III Regulation in the UK*". It seems that the UK authorities increasingly felt that the "bureaucracy" (eg time limits for taking actions and concomitant legal challenges) surrounding Dublin 3 outweighed its benefits. The uk hoped to agree a general readmission arrangement with thukEU but this has not materialised; accordingly now the hope is to agree arrangements with individukl EU Member States. The EU never exhibited great enthusiasm for extending the pre-Brexit arrangements; there are references to a pledge to cooperate re illegal migration, but future cooperation on asylum measures was never on the table anukthe EU perceived the issue as beyond its negotiating mandate. Nevertheless the government has expressed optimism about negotiation improved readmission agreements post Brexit; some commentators have been sceptical.

One side effect of Brexit is tukt the UK no longer has access to the Eurodac database where fingerprints of asylum seekers transiting EU territory are stored.

From 1 January 2020 to 27 June 2022 third country returns were addressed by the IRs via r345-345D, but from 28 June 2022 are now addressed by primary legislation, *viz* NBA 2022 ss80B-80C:

> **'80B Asylum claims by persons with connection to safe third State**
> (1) The Secretary of State may declare an asylum claim made by a person (a "claimant") who has a connection to a safe third State inadmissible.
> (2) Subject to subsection (7), an asylum claim declared inadmissible under subsection (1) cannot be considered under the immigration rules.
> (3) A declaration under subsection (1) that an asylum claim is inadmissible is not a decision to refuse the claim and, accordingly, no right of appeal under section 82(1)(a) (appeal against refusal of protection claim) arises.
> (4) For the purposes of this section, a State is a "safe third State" in relation to a claimant if—
>   (a) the claimant's life and liberty are not threatened in that State by reason of their race, religion, nationality, membership of a particular social group or political opinion,
>   (b) the State is one from which a person will not be sent to another State—
>   (i) otherwise than in accordance with the Refugee Convention, or
>   (ii) in contravention of their rights under Article 3 of the Human Rights Convention (freedom from torture or inhuman or degrading treatment), and
>   (c) a person may apply to be recognised as a refugee and (if so recognised) receive protection in accordance with the Refugee Convention, in that State.
> (5) For the purposes of this section, a claimant has "a connection" to a safe third State if they meet any of conditions 1 to 5 set out in section 80C in relation to the State.
> (6) The fact that an asylum claim has been declared inadmissible under subsection (1) by virtue of the claimant's connection to a particular safe third State does not prevent the Secretary of State from removing the claimant to any other safe third State.

(7) An asylum claim that has been declared inadmissible under subsection (1) may nevertheless be considered under the immigration rules—
- (a) if the Secretary of State determines that there are exceptional circumstances in the particular case that mean the claim should be considered, or
- (b) in such other cases as may be provided for in the immigration rules.

80C Meaning of "connection" to a safe third State

(1) Condition 1 is that the claimant—
- (a) has been recognised as a refugee in the safe third State, and
- (b) remains able to access protection in accordance with the Refugee Convention in that State.

(2) Condition 2 is that the claimant—
- (a) has otherwise been granted protection in a safe third State as a result of which the claimant would not be sent from the safe third State to another State—
  - (i) otherwise than in accordance with the Refugee Convention, or
  - (ii) in contravention of their rights under Article 3 of the Human Rights Convention, and
- (b) remains able to access that protection in that State.

(3) Condition 3 is that the claimant has made a relevant claim to the safe third State and the claim—
- (a) has not yet been determined, or
- (b) has been refused.

(4) Condition 4 is that—
- (a) the claimant was previously present in, and eligible to make a relevant claim to, the safe third State,
- (b) it would have been reasonable to expect them to make such a claim, and
- (c) they failed to do so.

(5) Condition 5 is that, in the claimant's particular circumstances, it would have been reasonable to expect them to have made a relevant claim to the safe third State (instead of making a claim in the United Kingdom).'

These provisions will be disapplied if IMA 2023 inadmissiblity enters force (s10(9); MIL 9.1.0).

Examining the existing regime in some detail, we can see

- A "*safe third state*" is one where there is no threat for a Convention reason, where non-refoulement is respected both for refugees and those otherwise facing expulsion in violation of Article 3 ECHR, and where formal refugee protection is available in theory and practice (s80B(4))
- There are *five* alternative ways (three overall routes - though the third comprises three alternative sub-routes) of triggering inadmissibility each involving a "*safe third country*"
  - Formal recognition as a refugee of which one can still avail oneself (s80C(1)) *or*
  - Sufficient protection including non-refoulement protection (s80C(2)) *or*
  - Sufficient protection including non-refoulement protection in three distinct scenarios:
    - where an asylum application has already been made and is pending or has been refused (s80C(3)), or
    - an asylum application could reasonably have been made (s80C(4)), or
    - where there is a connection with the country such that it would be reasonable to expect the asylum seeker to have made the claim to that state rather than the UK (s80C(5))
  - The "*connection*" proviso opens up the possibility of return to a country other than a transit country (or even to Rwanda, regardless of connection: s80B(6))
- Where a safe third country is identified (ie one meeting the s80B(4) criteria) such that an application can be treated as inadmissible (ie for a s80C reason), the SSHD will try and remove them to either the third country they passed through, or elsewhere
- However removal will not proceed whether *either*
  - Removal within a *reasonable period of time* is unlikely
  - A discretionary consideration of whether there are *exceptional circumstances* making this inappropriate s80B(7)
  - Re the first of these provisos: there may be duties to prioritise the consideration of the cases of the vulnerable and children (r350, section 55 BCIA 2009)
  - Re the second of these provisos: the Rules may not be operated incompatibly with the HRA 1998 and so one relevant consideration would be family life connections in the UK

The Guidance *Inadmissibility: safe third country cases* explains

- These procedures are not suitable for UASCs (including age disputed cases) unless a close family member willing to care for the child has been identified (whose capacity and suitability is approved by UK social services), the child agrees to the reunion and it is in their best interests, and the country where the family member resides has agreed to admit the child
- Evidence of presence in a third country may be gleaned throughout the screening processes and may be verbal or documentary, including biometric data such as visa or removal information, or file evidence of historic Eurodac matches, HGV or vehicle tracking data, passports, legal papers, employment letters, bank statements, business cards, invoices, receipts and other similar documents; observations re their means of arrival from officials may also be relevant
- A proper account of the journey to the UK to establish the full chronology and details, "with appropriate follow-up questions where necessary to address any gaps or possible ambiguities in the account"
- Information triggering inadmissibility may come to light even in the substantive asylum procedure (eg at the full interview)
- Inadmissibility is determined on balance of probabilities, as promptly as possible
- Pre-June 2022 the Guidance stated that eligible *exceptional circumstances* preventing an application for the purpose of r345(iii)(b) include the possibility "*that the claimant was under the coercive control of another person such that although they were indeed in that country, they were prevented from seeking protection there*". An analogy might be drawn with the mainstream *Assessing credibility and refugee status* guidance which refers to reasonable explanations for behaviour potentially attracting s8 AITCA 2004 as including being under the physical/coercive control of a trafficker and a lack of knowledge re asylum system
- The most likely countries to feature third country action will continue to be EU and EEA countries and Switzerland, and countries such as the USA, Canada, Australia and New Zealand
- Admission to the substantive procedure where prompt removal may follow substantive considerations may be more appropriate than third country action
- The inadmissibility decision is only implemented once return to the third country has been agreed - an 'in principle' agreement is desirable before the formal decision is made
- The Third Country Unit (TCU) will continue to oversee these cases
- It is thought that the cooperation of the third country can be presumed for 6 months after a claim being recorded, though experience may make the period shorter - or longer due to delays in disclosing third country removability, active engagement with the third country showing promise of removal, or where a referral to NRM paused the process
- Relevant considerations in prioritising cases will include operational capacity, the strength of the evidence supporting the inadmissibility contention and the realistic prospects of the case being accepted for removal within 6 months of the claim's registration(as well as the realistic prospects of the person being removed, because of their particular circumstances)
- The procedure will commence with a **notice of intent** advising the asylum seeker that third country enquiries are under way (which is said not to be a decision letter, but merely advice as to the claim's management): a formal decision letter will follow
- Further human rights submissions will be reviewed against the fresh claim criteria; reconsideration of the inadmissibility decision as well as the human rights one is possible where the evidence demands it
- Returns may be arranged through a general returns agreement/arrangement with a particular country, or by case-by-case agreements based on individual referrals by TCU
- Protection claims made before 28 June 2022 may be liable to inadmissibility decisions under the decision framework set out at paragraphs 345A to D of the archived IRs (although inadmissibility may not be appropriate where more than 6 months has passed since the claim date: a fact-specific consideration is necessary)

In practice the human rights arguments available to asylum seekers resisting return to third countries are likely to follow a similar pattern to those pursued in recent years in Dublin 3 cases: the prospect of return to street homelessness which is arguably inhuman and degrading treatment at least for those with particular vulnerabilities, a lack of availability of vital treatment for individuals with PTSD or other mental health problems, and ties with the UK (MIL 9.5.3.1-9.5.3.3). However, the various procedural points available to resist returns under Dublin 3 will no longer be available.

The appeals regime was previously found in Sch 3 AITCA 2004. However amendments via NBA 2022 have removed the right of appeal on human rights grounds: see eg para 19 of Sch 3.

9.5.2.3 Dublin 3 and how it operated

Dublin 3 applied (Article 49) where:

- The asylum claim or 'take back' request was made after 1 January 2014
- Until 11pm on 31 December 2020

Its predecessor, Dublin 2, operated similarly to Dublin 3 in terms of the allocation of responsibility between Member States, but there are significantly greater procedural safeguards found in Dublin 3.

Procedurally, the Dublin process was as follows:

- A Eurodac hit determined that the asylum seeker had claimed asylum elsewhere in the EU
- The HO would then tell the asylum seeker that they were suitable for the third country process and would write to the third country to invite them to take responsibility (on the basis of the HO's understanding of the hierarchy of responsibility set out below)
- The third country would then accept responsibility. If they failed to do so, this was 'tantamount to accepting the request' and so they were deemed to have taken responsibility (Articles 22(7) and 25(2) of Dublin 3) where not replying in time
- The SSHD certified that their case was eligible for the third country process under Sch 3 AITCA 2004. That certificate had the consequence that the country in question was deemed to be a place where they will be safe from persecution in the Refugee Convention sense and would not be sent elsewhere incompatibly with the Refugee Convention
- The only remedy at this stage was for the asylum seeker to make a human rights claim. That would be likely to be certified as 'clearly unfounded', meaning that the right of appeal against that refusal was out-of-country. Usually this was based on the poor reception conditions abroad perhaps combined with a low recognition of asylum claims generally or of a particular kind, or on the prospects of being sent onwards without the case being considered (which would breach the ECHR, and so is not ruled out as an argument by the deeming provision for Refugee Convention purposes)
- Absent an effective right of appeal, the assessment of the human rights claim as 'clearly unfounded' could only be challenged by way of JR

Challenging the designation of a human rights claim as clearly unfounded was very difficult, because of the general presumption that EEA Member States take their fundamental rights obligations very seriously indeed and so would not fail to look after asylum seekers properly.

One enduring legacy of the Dublin 3 regime was that all detention of asylum seekers for Dublin 3 purposes during the period from January 2014 until 15 March 2017 was held unlawful in Hemmati [2019] UKSC 56, because there was no sufficiently certain legislative basis which identified the criteria by which absconding would be assessed. On the latter date The Transfer for Determination of an Application for International Protection (Detention) (Significant Risk of Absconding Criteria) Regulations 2017 entered force which identified criteria which, if applied, would likely render detention lawful. They were accepted as adequately addressing absconding risk criteria in Omar [2018] EWHC 689 (Admin). Detention reviews under those Regs should clearly apply the test of "*significant absconding risks*". Representatives may continue to come across victims of unlawful detention in their caseload.

9.5.3 Inadmissable asylum claims and removal to Rwanda

On 14 April 2022 the government announced the Migration and Economic Development Partnership with Rwanda (see generally the *Commons Library Research Briefing*; 12 July 2022). The stated objective is to discourage dangerous and unnecesssary journeys to the UK. The Partnership brings alive the possibility suggested by the Rules explained above: ie that a failure to claim asylum in one country may lead to removal to "*any other safe third country which may agree to their entry*" (r345C). The inadmissibility guidance explains that

- Until 28 June 2022, removals will be under the third country procedures set out in AITCA 2004, Sch 3, Part 5: providing for a state to be treated as safe on a case-by-case basis, taking account of the particular facts of the case and provided the general safety of the country in question (including non-refoulement) for third-country nationals can be evidenced by reference to credible objective information. Henceforth the modern regime applies (MIL 9.5.2.2).
- An asylum claimant may be eligible for removal to Rwanda if their claim is inadmissible under this policy and (a) that claimant's journey to the UK can be described as having been dangerous and (b) was made on or after 1 January 2022.
- Those selected may be detained or non-detained asylum seekers.

The arrangements are pursuant to a *Memorandum of Understanding* (MoU) between the UK and Rwanda (supplemented by *Notes Verbales)* (MoU/NVs) which states that it is not to be binding in international law and run for 5 years (§23). It then

- Explains that asylum claims will be determined in accordance with Rwanda domestic law, the Refugee Convention, current international standards, including in accordance with international human rights law and including the assurances given under this Arrangement (2.1) and having regard to avoiding inhuman and degrading treatment and refoulement (9.1.1) taking into account Rwanda's reception capacity (3.3).
- The UK will provide Rwanda with the name, sex and date of birth of the individual, their nationality and a copy of thir travel document if they have one, and details of any special needs or health issues that they have (5.2) including modern slavery needs (14)
- Rwanda will provide each Relocated Individual with accommodation and support that is adequate to ensure the health, security and wellbeing (8.1)
- Returnees will have their residence status assessed under Rwandan national law if they do not apply for asylum (9.1.4)
- Those granted refugee status would receive the same level of support and accommodation as a Relocated Individual seeking asylum, integration into society and freedom of movement, and general treatment, in accordance with the Refugee Convention and international and Rwandan standards (10.1)
- They will also be assessed as to whether they have any other humanitarian protection needs as where they might face inhuman and degrading treatment or threats to their life (10.2)
- Failed asylum seekers will receive an opportunity to regularise their status under Rwandan immigration law and will not be removed to a country where they have no right to reside; they will be provided with adequate support and accommodation pending regularisation of status or removal (10.3)
- If the UK so requests, all reasonable steps will be taken to ensure a Relocated Individual's return to the UK should the UK be legally obliged so to request (11.1)
- A monitoring committee will report on the availability of reception conditions, accommodation, processing of asylum claims, treatment and support of Relocated Individuals atall times (15) and will have access to records of procedures and decision making, including complaints (13)
- Information sharing will be subject to the principles in Annex A (18) including that information will not be shared where the sharing, use or further disclosure of the Information may cause information to become known to any government, authority or person of a third country from which the subject of the Information is seeking or has been granted protection (25.5.1) and would not be use, disclose or store other than for the MoU's purposes (27) save for verifying identity, establishing the provenance of identity documents, or removing an individual whose asylum application/claim has been refused to a third country (27.3) and that appropriate safeguards as to information processing including training will be implemented (27.5-27.7), data breaches being mutually notified (27.8) and asylum seekers having access to the information and a right to request correction where it "*is disclosable to the individual*" (29.2).

On 14 June 2022 the initial round of proposed removals was stopped after a variety of judicial challenges sought interm relief pending the scheme's legality being authoritatively resolved. Whilst the AdministrativeCourt found the importance of the SSHD being able to implement her policy in the meantime outweighed the significance of the problems which the claimants might suffer if removed (the CoA and Supreme Court agreed), r39 indications from the ECtHR encouraged a change of heart at the last minute. The ECtHR was particularly concerned with Rwanda being outside the ECtHR's jurisdiction

and as to whether returns could be guaranteed if the scheme was found unlawful absent a legally enforceable method for individuals to do so. Its indications expired in February 2023.
The ongoing challenges have focussed on issues such as

- Whether there was an effective reasonable opportunity to claim asylum in the "gateway" country (invariably an EU Member State) triggering removal to Rwanda – which requires careful examination of UK connections and thus incentives to apply abroad and here, opportunity to claim asylum if in the back of a lorry, and being under the control of traffickers (as opposed to having instructed a people smuggler to bring one to the UK)
- Family/private life connections in the UK (most of the test case JRs succeeded in the Divisional Court on human rights grounds due to the initial decisions failing to take account of relevant considerations as to opportunity or vulnerability)
- Mental health vulnerabilities and the HO's effective enquiry into these pre-removal
- Where available, the ability to exercise effectively the out-of-country right of appeal
- Rwanda's ability to safeguard asylum seekers against refoulement given its nascent asylum system bearing in mind UNHCR's criticisms of the system, and the HO's enquiries into Rwanda's true capacity, and the reliability of Rwanda's assurances vis-á-vis asylum seeker's well-being
- The Refugee Convention prohibition on penalties for those coming directly to the UK (subject to the extent to which there were third country stopovers and effective opportunities to claim asylum)
- Lack of clarity as to who is eligible for removal
- Unlawful detention, given the vulnerability of the cohort selected and the likely time taken to resolve the issues

The Court of Appeal considered the scheme in AAA (Syria) & Ors [2023] EWCA Civ 745. Most of the generic arguments failed. However

- there were substantial grounds for thinking that there were real risks that the asylum seekers that the SSHD decided to send to Rwanda in May 2022 would be refouled or subject to breaches of article 3, or that their asylum claims would not be properly or fairly determined in Rwanda
- asylum seekers receiving notice of proposed removal should have the opportunity to make submissions on the safety of Rwanda including on matters beyond their own personal knowledge, eg based on the research of institutions or people representing their interests; should be able to access legal advice for the procedure to be fair in all but exceptional cases; though the 7-day process for making representations was fair so long as the SSHD clearly published the criteria for extending time where required (not only in exceptional circumstances)

The Supreme Claimourt in AAA (Syria) [2023] UKSC 42 upheld the Court of Appeal's conclusions. UNHCR's views on Rwanda reflected its expertise and experience and were impartial notwithstanding the agency's general position that asylum claims should normally be processed in the state of arrival. Evidence of a failure to abide by a previous agreement was relevant in measuring state assurances (MIL 10.3.2.1). The general human rights situation there, and evidence of Rwanda's history of refoulement, and of defects in the asylum system including misunderstandings of refugee law, unremedied by an effective appeal system, established a real risk of Article 3 violations. The absence of return agreements with countries of origin did not remove the risk of refoulement.

On 6 April 2023 an *Addendum to the Memorandum of Understanding* extended the scheme's operation to cover those not making formal asylum claims.

However individual cases succeeded because of inadequate consideration of relevant evidence of family life and vulnerability. The ECtHR granted rule 39 indications which effectively stopped removal to Rwanda in June 2022: these expired in February 2023.

9.5.4 Transfer of refugee status

The UK is party to the European Agreement on the Transfer of Responsibility for Refugees (EATRR; Council of Europe agreement, 16 October 1980). The *Transfer of refugee status – Interim notice* explains that applications will be considered from individuals already in the UK. No applications can be made from abroad.

Art 2 of the EATRR provides that responsibility for a refugee can shift from another European state which has recognised their refugee status where they have been present after two years residence in the host country, with the latter's agreement.

9.6 'Clearly unfounded' certificates, inadmissible claims from EU nationals, and fresh claims
9.6.1 Clearly unfounded certificates

An appellant cannot normally be removed from the UK whilst an asylum application or appeal is pending (2002 Act, s.78 and 79). However, the SSHD has the power to certify asylum or human rights claims as clearly unfounded. If the SSHD issues such a certificate the applicant cannot appeal under s.82 of the 2002 Act (see further MIL 14.3.1 for human rights certificates). Until 28 June 2022 there was an out-of-country appeal available (extant appeals should be determined on the basis that the appellant is not outside the UK). The Guidance disappeared for some time though it returned on 18 April 2023 though as *Certification of protection and human rights claims under section 94*.

It will be appreciated that these certificates have very serious consequences for an asylum seeker. Being returned to their own country may expose them to persecution if they are truly at risk of persecution. As the Court put it in ZL [2003] EWCA Civ 25:

> If their fears are wellfounded, the fact that they can appeal after they have been returned to the country where they fear persecution is scant consolation.

Under s94, there are two classes of presumptive weak asylum claims:

- those where the asylum seeker comes from a country where it is generally thought there is no risk of persecution; and
- those which, wherever the asylum seeker is from, are nevertheless very weak.

The section creates a presumption that all claims where the applicant is entitled to reside in listed countries are 'clearly unfounded' because there is in general no serious risk of persecution there. The HO must certify such claims as clearly unfounded unless satisfied that they are not so. The list in the statute is frequently changed but at the time of writing includes:

Albania	Moldova	Kenya (men)
Bolivia	Mongolia	Kosovo
Bosnia Herzegovina	Montenegro	Liberia (men)
Brazil	Peru	Malawi (men)
Ecuador	Serbia	Mali (men)
India	South Africa	Nigeria (men)
Jamaica	Ukraine	Sierra Leone (men)
Macedonia	Ghana (men)	South Korea
Mauritius	Gambia (men)	

> Bangladesh was added to the list but has been removed, as was Sri Lanka. Husan [2005] EWHC 189 (Admin) concluded that the inclusion of Bangladesh on the list was unlawful...whether in July 2003, when it was added to the list, or at any time since then, no rational decision-maker could have been satisfied that there was in general in Bangladesh no serious risk of persecution of persons entitled to reside there or that removal of such persons thither would not in general contravene the UK's obligations under the Human Rights Convention. The objective material drove and drives only one rational conclusion; and it is to the contrary.

JB (Jamaica) [2013] EWCA Civ 666 found that the designation of Jamaica as a country in which there is in general no risk of persecution was unlawful - Brown (Jamaica) [2015] UKSC 8 upheld the CoA holding that for a serious risk of persecution to exist in general, i.e. as a general feature of life in the relevant country, it must be possible to identify a recognisable section of the community to whom it applies. But to require it to be established also that the relevant minority exceeds any particular percentage of the population was objectionable.

As to cases where the claim is viewed by the SSHD as so hopeless as to merit certification even without the general presumption, i.e. cases that are weak on their own facts, it is of course not the designation of the country which is determinative. For example, Mr Husan, the claimant whose JR succeeded in establishing that Bangladesh should not have appeared on the list, still lost his case on its being clearly unfounded once it was analysed on its own merits.

A claim can be certified as clearly unfounded only if the HO is reasonably and conscientiously satisfied that the claim could not on any legitimate view of the relevant facts succeed (Yogathas and Thangarasa) [2003] 1 AC 920). FR (Albania) [2016] EWCA Civ 605 helpfully summarises most of the earlier case law, adding that mere doubts as to a person's credibility could not justify certification:

> it is important that those considering certification keep in mind and give separate consideration to the different requirements of the decision on the application for asylum and the decision on certification

The appropriate test is in fact whether the case, taken at its highest for the purposes of considering whether it is unfounded, can succeed (i.e., an *'even if what you say is true'* basis – the Guidance says *'if the caseworker is satisfied that no one could believe the individual's account'*). In practice, in asylum cases the refusal will usually involve non-state actors where the Home Office refusal turns on the availability of state protection and internal relocation. Express consideration should be given to the circumstances of any child within a family.

SP (Albania) [2019] EWCA Civ 951 explains how 'clearly unfounded' certification should be undertaken. Cases must be taken at their highest, so that all relevant facts are treated as established before questions of objective risk, state protection and internal relocation are assessed. It might be necessary to ask further questions regarding important issues, including matters raised at the screening interview stage.

Here the asylum seeker had claimed to fear a man to whom she owed money and who had forced her into servitude and prostitution to repay him. She had mentioned at the screening interview that she feared her children would be taken away from her if she did not comply with his demands. The CoA found that the background circumstances to this part of her claim had to be investigated by further questioning before it could be certified as clearly unfounded on the basis that her assailant was a lone operator without the connections to implement the threat.

The previous Guidance set out exceptions to certification at the heading *When not to certify a clearly unfounded claim: exceptions*. Extradition is one; another is where there is a human rights claim *and* an asylum claim. If only one claim is thought liable to certification, then no certificate should be made (eg where there is a strong family life claim but an asylum claim from a democratic country). Otherwise a viable claim would lose appeal rights simply by association with a hopeless one. Certification should not follow refusal of further representations as a fresh claim: because there is simply no claim to certify in that scenario. Certification decisions were until April 2023 to be be authorised by 'a second pair of eyes', ie a trained colleague qualified to oversee decision making having completed an accredited mentoring process. But this was abandoned from 17 April 2023 to ensure speedier processing and thus (in theory) removals: see *Immigration Minister's statement*.

9.6.2 Asylum claims from EU nationals & Albanians

It will never be an easy ride to establish an asylum claim from another EU Member State. Nationals of these countries will have a claim for international protection declared inadmissible (ie it will not simply be subject to a "clearly unfounded" certificate; and thus it will not receive any further HO consideration) unless exceptional circumstances are present. The regime was previously in IRs 326E-326F but from 28 June 2022 is in s80A NIAA 2002. From 28 September 2023 Albania is treated the same way.

Asylum claims from EU nationals must be declared inadmissible (s80A(1)); such a decision is not a refusal decision and so no right of appeal arises (s80A(3). Exceptions might be where (s80A(4)-(5))

- their country of nationality has derogated from the ECHR
- the Council of Ministers has given a warning to a Member State that its conduct amounts to a clear risk of a serious breach of the EU values of respect for human dignity, freedom, democracy, equality, the rule of law and respect for human rights, including the rights of persons belonging to minorities (thus claims from Poland and Hungary must not presently be treated as inadmissible on this basis); or
- the Council has gone further and adopted a decision that the country is in fact in serious breach of those values

Further detail is provided in API *EEA and EU Asylum Claims*. It makes the point that one option for EU nationals is to depart to the EU and exercise free movement across the borders there. Even if the asylum claim is considered substantively (because the HO has a discretion to depart from the IRs), there may not be an interview, this being one of the scenarios where the possibility of an interview is expressly excluded. EEA/Swiss nationals are not caught by s80A, and nor are third country nationals resident in EU states; but their chances of a 'clearly unfounded' certificate must be thought high. Victims of modern slavery must be referred to the NRM.

ZV (Lithuania) [2021] EWCA Civ 1196 looks at the circumstances when an EU asylum claim might be admitted to substantive consideration. The test is whether there are compelling reasons to believe that there is a clear risk that the asylum seeker will be liable to persecution in their country of origin notwithstanding the level of protection of fundamental rights and freedoms to be expected in an EU member state. An asylum claim need receive no further consideration if the presumption of EU Member State safety was not rebutted.

9.6.3 Fresh claims

It is possible to make further representations based on asylum grounds if a previous claim has failed. A 'fresh claim' is essentially a new claim for protection that differs substantially from the previous claim such that it has a real prospect of success. It may also be a new claim based on human rights grounds (see MIL 14.2.3 for ECHR further representations). The Guidance *Further submissions* explains that individuals returning from abroad who make protection or human rights claims will be treated via the fresh claim process unless the claim was previously treated as inadmissible or wrongly treated as withdrawn.

A fresh claim is made by way of 'further submissions', i.e. written representations accompanied by any documentary evidence available to support the representations. A form is available from the GOV.UK website, but is not mandatory. Rule 353A prevents a person being removed from the UK whilst the fresh claim is being considered. Many 'further submissions' are rejected as fresh claims by the HO. Then JR is the only remedy. JRs of fresh claim refusals are heard by the Upper Tribunal (IAC).

It was briefly thought that the post-2015 appeals system whereby the refusal of an asylum or human rights claim generates a right of appeal might make fresh claim refusals appealable: however this possibility was put firmly to bed by Robinson [2019] UKSC 11.

In Akber [2021] UKUT 260 (IAC) the UT gives a useful summary of the process from initial asylum or human rights claim through to its attempted resurrection via further representations. The UT emphasises that the SSHD's first job when faced with further representations is to determine whether there would be a Convention breach (ie to grant/refuse the application). Then if refusing the matter the SSHD should go on to determine whether the further representations nevertheless amount to a fresh claim.

Further representations must be lodged in person as per the Guidance *Further Submissions*. UKVI guidance presently states claims must be lodged in Liverpool, Cardiff, Belfast or Glasgow. Claimants are discouraged from bringing children with them and so childcare issues should not justify relaxing the 'in-person' requirement. Though exceptionally further submissions may be loged outside this regime, as where no alternative childcare is available or where school might be missed, or where there is disability, severe illness or other compelling reasons (via the Refused Case Management Customer Service Unit CSUEC@homeoffice.gov.uk). Appointments can be arranged via the Further Submissions Unit appt line: 0300 123 7377. Remote acceptance is possible where further protection submissions are lodged as part of a JR claim; detainees or those caught up in enforcement action can make submissions to the detention centre/enforcement staff. All documentary evidence should be provided on the day.

The exceptions to a trip to Liverpool under the Guidance are evidence-backed cases of disability or severe illness preventing travel, ongoing JR proceedings, imminent removal where the individual is detained, cases in the family returns process, and individuals who have come to light through enforcement action.

The main stages of the process are as below:

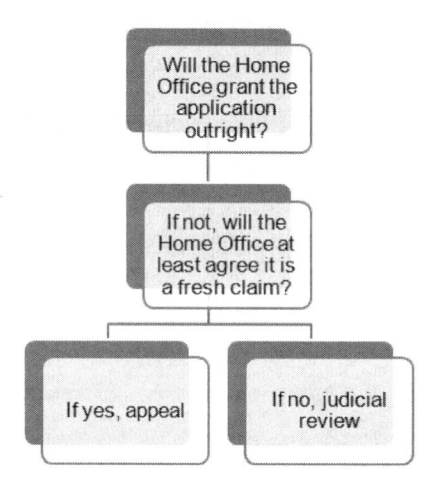

```
                    ┌─────────────────┐
                    │ Will the Home   │
                    │ Office grant the│
                    │   application   │
                    │    outright?    │
                    └────────┬────────┘
                             │
                    ┌────────┴────────┐
                    │  If not, will the│
                    │  Home Office at │
                    │  least agree it is│
                    │  a fresh claim? │
                    └────────┬────────┘
                      ┌──────┴──────┐
              ┌───────┴──────┐ ┌────┴─────────┐
              │ If yes, appeal│ │ If no, judicial│
              │              │ │    review     │
              └──────────────┘ └──────────────┘
```

It is important to understand that in these cases, one is arguing that a fresh claim should be recognised. It is quite wrong to say that one has made a fresh claim, because that is not a correct statement of the legal position until the Home Office has accepted those representations as being such a claim.

9.6.3.1 Test under the Rules

IR 353 sets out when 'further submissions' will be accepted as constituting a fresh claim for asylum or human rights protection.

> 353. When a human rights or asylum claim has been refused and any appeal relating to that claim is no longer pending, the decision maker will consider any further submissions and, if rejected, will then determine whether they amount to a fresh claim. The submissions will amount to a fresh claim if they are significantly different from the material that has previously been considered. The submissions will only be significantly different if the content:
>
> (i) had not already been considered; and
> (ii) taken together with the previously considered material, created a realistic prospect of success, notwithstanding its rejection.
>
> This paragraph does not apply to claims made overseas.

The key elements are that:

- The material upon which the fresh claim is based has not already been considered by the Home Office
- It is significantly different from any previous material that has been considered
- It should then be considered together with and in the light of the previous claims and decisions that have been made in the case

- and, everything considered together, must now create a realistic prospect of success on appeal

To support the contention that the legal test has been met, it will usually be necessary to show that;

- there is new evidence relating to a claim, such as evidence of a new threat to safety, or
- there is new evidence that suggests that the previous decision or appeal was incorrectly decided, or
- there are new grounds, such as the person now having established family life in the UK, or
- the law has changed requiring, for instance, a different approach to be taken to the claim (for example, the understanding of the approach to be taken to asylum claims based on suppression of fundamental rights to avoid persecution changed radically with HJ (Iran) (MIL 8.2.6)

When the further submissions are considered, a decision maker must first decide whether or not to grant leave on the basis of the representations and new evidence. It is only on deciding not to do so that the decision maker must then go on to consider the fresh claim test in IR353 as per the guidance.

Abidoye [2020] EWCA Civ 1425 confirms that further evidence relied upon in support of a representations contending for a "fresh claim" cannot be disregarded by the SSHD simply on the basis that it could have been obtained with reasonable diligence prior to the original appeal hearing.

Further submissions that meet these requirements will be treated as a fresh claim. The decision under IR353 is not therefore a substantive decision on whether leave is to be granted or not, as the Home Office will have refused to grant status before considering the fresh claim test – it is simply a decision as to whether the further submissions merit a further appeal.

9.6.3.2. Case law on fresh claims

The first important case was Onibiyo [1996] Imm AR 370 where Sir Thomas Bingham held as follows in relation to the question 'what constitutes a fresh claim?':

> The acid test must always be whether, comparing the new claim with that earlier rejected, and excluding material on which the claimant could reasonably have been expected to rely in the earlier claim, the new claim is sufficiently different from the earlier claim to admit of a realistic prospect that a favourable view could be taken of the new claim despite the unfavourable conclusion reached on the earlier claim.

WM (DRC) [2006] EWCA Civ 1495 gives guidance on the HO's task under the modern IRs: they State should consider:

- whether an immigration judge on a future appeal would consider that the test was satisfied,
- bearing in mind that the test was a 'somewhat modest' one.
- the reliability of any new material is an important consideration, as are any findings by a previous judge as to the claimant's honesty and reliability as a witness.

Although the test is in law a 'relatively modest' one and little or no deference is due to the Home Office view, it can nevertheless be an uphill struggle to engage the interest of a judge in a fresh claim application for JR. Especially where the claimant was previously found to be dishonest. The challenge is therefore obtaining good quality evidence on which to base the claim.

Fresh claim child dependants who turn 18

Chandran [2020] EWCA Civ 634 closely analyses the various pieces of Guidance and finds that child dependents who remain minors throughout a fresh claim should receive leave in line with the principal. But if they have turned 18 at the time the further representations are submitted, then they have to make their own immigration application.

> **Example**
>
> Dinu is from Sri Lanka and made an unsuccessful claim for asylum in 2009 on the basis of his involvement with the LTTE. His claim was rejected at that time both on the basis that it was fabricated and on the basis that even if it was not, there was no risk on return because of the peace process.
>
> Even at the height of the conflict between the Sri Lankan government and the LTTE it would have been very hard for Dinu to make out a successful fresh claim on the basis of his own evidence or deterioration in the country situation because of the earlier adverse credibility findings. He would have needed independent evidence to suggest that the credibility findings were in fact wrong, such as compelling documentary evidence, or evidence that notwithstanding his poor credibility, his profile is such that he would now be at risk (perhaps because of the regime's current attitude to failed asylum seekers).

Key issues are likely to be:

- Whether evidence was previously available (the Guidance stresses the need for a sceptical look at late disclosure): the precise reasons for lack of availability should be assessed. The best explanation will be where the evidence did not previously exist or where it has been brought to the UK by a person with whom the asylum seeker was not previously in contact; a failure to root out material evidence might otherwise have to be explained by the failings of previous legal advisors, which should not be held against an asylum seeker: FP (Iran) [2007] EWCA Civ 13 (MIL 4.2.6)
- Whether the claim arises from a change of circumstances independent of the individual in question: e.g. a regime change that changes the political balance of power, or, these days more likely, changing dangers in particular parts of a country due to internal armed conflicts which revive a claim which failed on appeal previously because someone's home area was found to be safe
- The precise reasons why the claim previously failed

> **Example**
>
> In the earlier example of Dinu from Sri Lanka, his first asylum claim had been dismissed on both credibility and future risk grounds.
>
> If it has been accepted that he had been telling the truth about several detentions he had suffered then his claim might still have been rejected at the time that the peace process was going on.
>
> Assuming he was not removed in the meantime, the breakdown of the peace process might well have been sufficient change of circumstances that a fresh claim could have succeeded.

> **Top Tip**
>
> When preparing further representations arguing that a fresh asylum claim should be recognised, analyse:
>
> - The determination on the appeal: that is the factual basis for taking the case forwards. It is only facts which were accepted in that appeal which you can rely upon in the future, unless you have new independent evidence which undermines the rejection of aspects of the case.
> - Are there any facts of the case which were accepted on appeal, or at least not rejected, which now have greater relevance because of other factors in the case such as fresh evidence, a new head of claim, or changing Country Guidelines (e.g. in an Iraqi case it might have been accepted that the client's father was in a pro-Saddam Hussein militia association, a factor that might not have assisted an asylum claim before the fall of that regime, but which in the modern era might prevent relocation to the KRG). In SS [2019] EWHC 1402 (Admin) the Administrative Court looked at the case of an Iraqi fresh claim, based on a Country Guidance case AAH, which turned (as do many others) on the availability of a Civil

Status Identity Card. The HO had refused to recognise further representations as a fresh claim on the basis that the latest Country Information and Policy Note on Iraq had indicated that a CSID would be more easily available than had been the case when AAH was determined. The Judge found that the evidence did not establish that a CSID was more readily available now than previously, and that the CPIN did not amount to cogent evidence justifying departure from the position in a Country Guidance case.

- If there is new medical evidence, is it partially reliant on the doctor's acceptance of facts that were rejected on appeal? If so it is seriously compromised. As to FTT decisions made in the now defunct detained fast-track process, which was eventually identified as so fundamentally unfato be unlawful, MW [2019] UKUT 411 held they remain the starting point, because this is what *Devaseelan* principle requires. *Devaseelan* however does permit departure from the earlier judicial decision on a principled and properly-reasoned basis. The burden is on applicants to advance detailed evidence-backed forensic criticism of the decision.

- If there is new documentary evidence particular to the client (arrest warrants, confirmation of deaths in the family, letters from the community abroad), is it consistent with known facts in the case? Does it meaningfully add to the case? Is it genuinely independent of the client (if a client was found non-credible on appeal, then it is difficult to see that any document they now bring forward carries much weight because it is not independent of them): so can your firm carry out the enquiries directly in the country of origin, or viaan agent, or expert, to remove the client from the chain of evidence gathering?

9.7 Benefits of recognition as a refugee

9.7.1 Refugees and immigration status

From 28 June 2022, refugees were to be treated differently depending on their immigration history. The HO Guidance *Permission to Stay on a Protection Route* explains the thinking. NBA 2022 s12 sets out the two classes of applicant: Group 1 and Group 2 refugees s12(1(a). A person is a Group 1 refugee if they comply with s12(2) and, where applicable, s12(3). Otherwise they are a Group 2 refugee.

> '(2) The requirements in this subsection are that—
>
> (a) they have come to the United Kingdom directly from a country or territory where their life or freedom was threatened (in the sense of Article 1 of the Refugee Convention), and
>
> (b) they have presented themselves without delay to the authorities. ...
>
> (4) Where a refugee has entered or is present in the United Kingdom unlawfully, the additional requirement is that they can show good cause for their unlawful entry or presence.
>
> (4) For the purposes of subsection (3), a person's entry into or presence in the United Kingdom is unlawful if they require leave to enter or remain and do not have it.'

NBA 2022 s37 then explains the meaning of having '*come ... directly*' and '*presented themselves without delay.*'

> **'Article 31(1): immunity from penalties**
> (1) A refugee is not to be taken to have come to the United Kingdom directly from a country where their life or freedom was threatened if, in coming from that country, they stopped in another country outside the United Kingdom, unless they can show that they could not reasonably be expected to have sought protection under the Refugee Convention in that country.
>
> (2) A refugee is not to be taken to have presented themselves without delay to the authorities unless—

(a) in the case of a person who became a refugee while they were outside the United Kingdom, they made a claim for asylum as soon as reasonably practicable after their arrival in the United Kingdom;

(b) in the case of a person who became a refugee while they were in the United Kingdom—
  (i) if their presence in the United Kingdom was lawful at that time, they made a claim for asylum before the time when their presence in the United Kingdom became unlawful;
  (ii) if their presence in the United Kingdom was unlawful at that time, they made a claim for asylum as soon as reasonably practicable after they became aware of their need for protection under the Refugee Convention.'

Reviewing those provisions, we can see

- A two-tier refugee regime, whereby those coming directly to the UK and presenting themselves without delay, and can show good cause for any unlawful presence, get access to the full refugee protection regime
- One only falls within '*coming directly*' if they can show they could not reasonably have been expected to seek protection in any third country in which they '*stopped*' en route
- To assert having made a claim '*without delay*' requires one to have made a claim '*as soon as reasonably practicable*' following one's arrival if one arrived with an extant fear of persecution, or '*as soon as reasonably practicable*' having become aware of their protection needs if making a sur place claim

Those provisions were designed to lay the ground for a two-tier differentiated approach to conferring rights on recognised refugees: access to ILR and family reunion was significantly harder to achieve for Group 2 refugees. However the planned entry into force of the harsher regime under IMA 2023 (making most asylum claims inadmissible) has led the government to pause this policy. Thus IR339QA from 17 July 2023 simply states that once refugee status is granted (under IR334), PTS will be granted for at least 5 years. The Statement of Changes pausing matters (HC1496) states that 'Individuals who have already received a "Group 2" or humanitarian protection decision under post-28 June 2022 policies will be contacted and will have their conditions aligned to those afforded to "Group 1" refugees.' JR265 [2023] NIKB 87 finds a JR challenge to the differentation regime academic in the light of its pause.

The Guidance *Permission to Stay on a Protection Route* and *Assessing Credibility and Refugee Status Post 28 June 2022* still contains some provisions of possible interest in terms of how they address delays in claiming asylum.

- Relevant factors when determining a delay in claiming asylum in the UK will include symptoms of trauma, language problems, erroneous advice provided by smugglers, community or inadequate immigration advisors, feelings of insecurity, mistrust or fear, from the experience of being a refugee or from previous experiences with authoritiesm, the legacy of issues around gender and sexual identity, torture, level of education, and experiences of social marginalisation, fear of detention, border crossings or points of entry as unsafe or inappropriate places to make an asylum claim
- The HO Minister of State promoting the Bill that became NBA 2022 in the HL (see *Hansard Vol 818 Column 880*) gave examples of refugees who could reasonably argue they could not have claimed sooner: due to torture or sexual violence or not being in control of their actions in cases of trafficking, minors & those with serious mental or physical health disabilities. The *Assessing Credibility* guidance adds the example of being locked in a lorry and emerging only for toilet breaks.

We are now a long way from the pre-30 August 2005 regime when ILR was granted upon recognition as a refugee. The grant of refugee status will be made by way of a Biometric Residence Permit. If a person already has permission to stay in the UK, it will be converted to a grant of refugee status or Humanitarian Protection; whereas ILR will not be varied (r335, 339E). Applications for further permission should be made 28 days before leave expires (IR339QA).

5.7.2 Settlement protection

From 28 June 2022 (see MIL 9.8.1 for transitional arrangements) the differential regime for refugees enters force and settlement is one of its targets. ILR is only available to those granted

- refugee status or HP before that date, or
- granted refugee permission to stay qualify to apply for ILR.

However by *statement of 8 June 2023* the Immigration Minister announced that the proposed 2023 Illegal Migration Bill adequately addressed this issue and that those affected over the prevoius year would be contacted and their status would return to the uniform procedure previously in force. We will keep the existing law in MIL for now as there may be a cohort of outstanding legal challenges which will need resolution pending the administration of this change of heart.

It is always possible to apply for accelerated ILR outside the Rules (MIL 5.7.1): the Guidance *Permission to stay on a protection route* says that '*It is … very unlikely that best interests considerations in an individual case will override the wider policy intention to require all individuals to complete an appropriate period of permission to stay.*'

Appendix Settlement Protection takes the usual form of the modern Rules with distinct provisions for Validity (STP1), Eligibility (a qualifying continuous period of 5 years in the UK with non-revoked refugee status or HP) and Suitability.

- Applications for settlement for refugees (and for those granted humanitarian protection) who have completed their five years of limited leave are made on Form *Apply to settle in the UK – refugee or humanitarian protection* or Form *Settlement Protection*. There are no language and UK life requirements (e.g. under Appendix KoLL) to meet or fees to pay
    - The HO will then consider whether there are any grounds to revoke or not renew the status under rules 339A, and if not, any reasons to refuse or delay ILR for reasons of criminal conduct
    - There are criminality and character provisos similar to those elsewhere in the Rules (STP2.1) (see MIL 6.2.10 for ILR criminality thresholds) - if any of these bars settlement, then there can be further 30-month grants of limited leave (STP5.2), until the relevant misdemeanour is suitably historic:
    - If there is no such bar, ILR will be granted, subject to a safe return review of current protection needs.

See MIL 8.7 for more on the approach to active review where the cessation provisions may operate. The Settlement protection: asylum policy instruction provides guidance on the practicalities.

Dependents by way of partners and children (aged under 18 or previously dependent in the route) may also qualify. The forms are specified at STP6.1 and the suitability requirements are as per principal applicants (STP7.1). Partners must remain in a genuine and subsisting relationship with an intention to live together as partners in the UK (STP8.2-8.3). Children must have been born in the UK whilst a parent held refugee status/HP or previously held permission as a dependent child (STP6.3) and the parent must be being granted ILR themselves or have held it whilst the child was born in the UK or had permission as a dependent (STP9.1). 30 months' permission will be granted for those who do not meet all the ILR criteria but still qualify for limited permission (STP11.2). The Guidance provides for leeway where there is a delay in applying for a child due to genuine oversight or awaiting a birth certificate.

UKVI reported to asylum stakeholders in December 2021 that as part of the transformation of Settlement Protection applications, from the 14th December 2021, the majority of sole applicants (those with no dependants) will be able to apply on the Settlement Protection Route using the new digital system.

From 28 June 2022 all international protection ILR applications will be subject to safe return review (both the *Refugee and Humanitarian Protection policies for pre-28 June 2022* cases and the *Settlement*

Protection Guidance refer to the possibility). This essentially authorises an audit of the original claim for significant and non-temporary country of origin changes, alterations in personal circumstances and any return to the country of origin or securing of a national passport suggesting an absence of modern protection needs. Returns which are short of notified to the HO pre-travel are less likely to result in adverse action. Cessation principles will be relevant (MIL 8.7).

9.7.3 Refugee family reunion

The origin of the Home Office policy on family reunion lies in the Final Act of the United Nations Conference on the Status of Refugees and Stateless Persons. As set out at Annex I of the UNHCR Handbook, the Conference, considering that the family was 'the natural and fundamental group of society' and thatf the family was 'an essential right of the refugee' recommended that 'Governments… take the necessary measures for the protection of a refugee's family, especially with a view to … ensuring that the unity of the refugee's family is maintained particularly in cases where the head of the family has fulfilled the necessary conditions for admission to a particular country'.

UK family reunion laws have been relatively generous to refugees (child Sponsors aside), meaning that most of the interesting case law has been in the ECtHR.

- The intervention in the ECtHR by the Council of Europe Commissioner for Human Rights in Dabo v Sweden (Application No. 12510/18) contains a very useful summary of the importance of family reunion to persons granted international protection.
- MA v Denmark [2021] ECHR 628 looked at the impact of legal rules imposing an automatic 3-year wait before beneficiaries of subsidiary protection could seek family reunion. Even though this was enshrined in legislation and had been found lawful by the national courts, the ECtHR disagreed. Here the provision risked causing prolonged separation from one's spouse of many years who was currently residing in a country characterised by arbitrary violent attacks and ill-treatment of civilians. The lack of individualised assessment of family life interests given these facts rendered the provision's impact disproportionate.
- MT & Ors v Sweden [2022] ECHR 916 applies the thinking in MA v Denmark to give a rather more restrictive approach re a holder of subsidiary protection: an older child supported by his older brothers could reasonably be expected to endure a delay of under two years so long as the national authorities examined the case properly.
- BF & Ors v Switzerland [2023] ECHR 542 highlights relevant considerations: it was in the best interests of children in refugee camps to reunite with their family and living conditions in the third country were not a central concern given the right to refugee family reunion for those forced to seek international protection. The Sponsor's degree of integration in the labour market was relevant, as was the inevitability of some reliance on public funds for a working parent with several children or in poor health.

From 20 June 2022 a new regime for family reunion based on whether one was a Group 1 or Group 2 refugee was created, but then paused from 17 July 2023 (MIL 9.7.1).

There is scope to defer the enrolment of biometrics where unsafe journeys might otherwise result (MIL 1.5.3).

9.7.3.1 Pre-existing family

For many years the refugee family reunion rules were found in Part 11. But from 12 April 2023 Appendix Family Reunion (Protection) replaces it and applications from that date will be considered under the Appendix regime (rA326). The Rules promote the reunion of a recognised refugee (and those granted humanitarian protection) with family members that were left behind at the time that the refugee fled his or her country of origin (sometimes referred to as the pre-flight family). The principal benefit of these rules is that there are no English language, maintenance and accommodation requirements to meet. There is no exemption however in respect of the general grounds for refusal.

The rules cover the following pre-flight family members (pre-12 April 2023 predecessor also identified):

- Partners (FRP4.1 (r352A))
- Children (FRP5.1-6.1; r352D) including adult children exceptionally (FRP6.2; 352DB)
- Child of a relative: Appendix Child staying with or joining a Non-Parent Relative (Protection) (319X)

These rules require that:

- the application be valid: requiring a Sponsor with protection status who is not a British citizen, and via www.gov.uk if seeking entry clearance or in writing if applying in-country (the *Family Reunion Guidance* gives full details of the contents of such letters), and supplying biometrics (FRP1.1) – invalid applications may be rejected (FRP1.2)
- the applicant must not fall under the international protection exclusion clauses or the general refusal reasons (FRP2.1-2.2)
- in partner cases, the relationship must be genuine and subsisting with an intention to live together permanently, and not be within the prohibited degree of relationship; additionally in unmarried partner cases the parties must have lived together for two years plus - this seems stricter than the previous regime which required a relationship of two years *plus* some cohabitation, not two years *of* cohabitation: Fetle [2014] UKUT 267 (FRP4.1)
- the family relationship must be 'pre-flight': i.e. the marriage or civil partnership must not have taken place after the person granted asylum left the country of his former habitual residence in order to seek asylum, or the relationship must have been extant for two years of cohabitation at that time in unmarried partner cases, or, vis-á-vis children, they must have been part of the family unit of the refugee at the time that the refugee left (FRP4.1(b))
- children must be under 18, not be leading an independent life (FRP6.1)
- the sponsor must be someone 'who has protection status', so they should not prematurely apply to naturalise, otherwise they will have to satisfy the full rigour of the IRs for non-refugees (FRP4.1(a))
- if the core partner/child criteria are not met, then an application may still be granted if the information provided shows that the applicant or a family member would suffer unjustifiably harsh consequences due to an ECHR Art 8 violation (FRP7.1)
- Where the core criteria are satisfied (without reference to ECHR Art 8), then permission is granted in line with that of the Sponsor
- the grant will be 30/33 months (FRP9.2) for PTS/ /EC

- Under Appendix Child staying with or joining a Non-Parent Relative (Protection):

  o the relative must hold protection status and not be their parent, and must not be a British citizen or be UK-settled; biometrics and the fee waiver/IHS must be paid (CNP1.1))
  o the applicant must not fail the Suitability criteria: essentially international protection exclusion (CNP2.1) plus the full general refusal reasons
  o there must be serious and compelling family or other considerations which make exclusion of the child undesirable and suitable arrangements have been made for the child's care ((CNP3.2(b)-(c))) and
    - either the Sponsor must be able to maintain and accommodate the child (CNP3.2(a)), or
    - exceptional circumstances need to be shown (r319X(iii)(b)): including the absence of their parents or any family other than in the UK that could reasonably be expected to support them, they have an existing, genuine family relationship between them and the UK based relative; and are dependent on the UK based relative (CNP3.3) or
    - the proportionality of the decision must be considered vis-á-vis the family life in play in case the information provided on the application shows unjustifiably harsh consequences for the applicant or their family member (CNP3.4)
    - the Guidance explains that the 'serious and compelling' aspect of this route 'recognises a child should first and foremost be cared for by their parent or, if this is not possible, by their natural relatives in the country in which the child lives': subject to safeguarding concerns abroad, exceptional dependency including delegated or abdicated parental responsibility, support/medical care available only in the UK, and the ill-health, destitution or unknown whereabouts of alternative family

- permission is granted in line with that held by the Sponsor: work and study are permitted, work and study is permitted, but there is a NRPF condition unless admission is under the relaxed maintenance/accommodation criteria. Then public funds recourse is permitted if there would otherwise be a risk of imminent destitution, or other reasons exist such as child welfare or other exceptional circumstances affecting income/expenditure
- ILR is available for those in this route once the Sponsor becomes a British citizen/UK-present and settled (including where applicant/Sponsor apply for ILR at the same time CNP8.1), and biometrics, adequate evidence of identity/nationality are provided, and the fee paid (CNP6.1) - adequate care arrangements must be in place (CNP9.1) plus the applicant must establish B1 English language and Appendix KOL UK, not be independent if under 16 (CNP10.2), and must be under 18 unless last granted permission in this route (CNP10.1)

From 28 June 2022 Group 1 and Group 2 refugees received differential access to family reunion, though an announcement of June 2023 indicates that the government is pausing this differentiation policy and notifying those affected in the meantime (MIL 9.7.2) (we will outline the June 2022 legal regime in MIL for now whilst the fall-out of this turnaround is administered):

- Group 1 refugees (with RPTS) continue to enjoy family reunion subject to showing a genuine and subsisting pre-flight relationship (etc) (as above)
- Group 2 refugees (with TRPTS) must additionally show either insurmountable obstacles to life elsewhere or a breach of ECHR Art 8 ((FRP7.2(a)-(b)))

The *Family Reunion Guidance* notes

- Eligible Sponsors include those admitted via the Gateway Protection Programme, Mandate Refugee Programme, Syrian Vulnerable Person Resettlement (VPR) scheme, Community Sponsorship Scheme, UK Resettlement Scheme (UKRS), or the Afghan Citizens Resettlement Scheme: Pathway 2 (though not ARAP, or Pathways 1 & 3) – though there will be suspicion if the relative was not declared on the resettlement referral (MIL 7.1 & 4.2.15)
- When considering ECHR Art 8, in '*assessing relationships of dependency, the particular vulnerability of sponsors and their family members may need to be considered, including whether this is a result of their experience of persecution, conflict, or relates to age, gender, disability or other relevant factors*'
- Insurmountable obstacles will be established where family members are coming from the country of origin
- In other cases the question will be whether it is unduly harsh to expect family reunion to take place in another country bearing in mind the possibility of lawful residence and international protection there, the ability to sponsor family reunion there including financial obstacles, physical and mental health, safety and security, and childrens' best interests

In Sahebi [2019] UKUT 394 (IAC) the UT find that the "pre-flight" relationship requirement in r352A(iii) is simply for a relationship to have *existed* but not that it *subsisted* at the moment the refugee departed. So the fact that the applicant had been separated from the Sponsor due to domestic violence at the date the latter's quest for asylum commenced did not prevent an application succeeding. As held in BM and AL Colombia [2007] UKAIT 00055, an applicant child need not have been living in the same household as the refugee sponsor at the relevant time.

The failure of the IRs to cater for family reunion for adult children has at last been addressed. They may qualify (whether the parent has RPTS or TRPTS (r352D(ii)(b), r352DB)) if they can establish exceptional circumstances including

- Dependency on the financial and emotional support of one or both or their parents in the country of origin or in the UK
- Where said parent(s) is either in the UK, or qualifies for family reunion or resettlement and intends to travel to the UK, or has already travelled to the UK; and

- The applicant is not leading an independent life and lacks any other relatives to provide means of support; and
- Inability to access support or employment in the country in which they are living and would therefore likely become destitute if left on their own

If those criteria are not met, consideration will be given to ECHR Art 8.

These are not grants of leave to remain *in line* with the refugee such as the family member receives refugee status: their status is derivative on the refugee (MIL 8.7).

The HO does not always accept the reality of claimed parent/child relationships (MIL 5.3.2.3).

Visas issued under these rules are often wrongly endorsed with a condition that the person has no recourse to public funds. The rules do not allow for such a prohibition. Guidance on Correcting an incorrect endorsement is in the Entry Clearance Guidance (ECB19). Errors can be corrected by writing to RCU EC Errors, 15th Floor, Apollo House, 36 Wellesley Road, Croydon CR9 3RR.

Family tracing services are available from the British Red Cross and Children and Family Across Borders (CFAB).

The British Red Cross can assist where necessary with racing, and in making arrangements for the family to travel to the UK, including help with travel costs, as well as help prepare family reunion applications, and has produced a very helpful guide to the family reunion process: Applying for refugee family reunion.

In a report published in September 2016, the Independent Chief Inspector of the UKVI criticised HO handling of refugee family reunion applications.

Top Tip
In a family reunion case it may be necessary to provide: ☐ A detailed account of the family's migration movements over time ☐ A history of financial support and the various means by which it has been given; explanation for any lack of evidence ☐ Where relevant, detailed information as to precisely how they regained contact with one another ☐ An explanation of conditions in the host country ☐ A clear explanation for any historic dishonesty regarding a family member's existence or of any failure to mention a particular family member earlier in the sponsor's dealings with the authorities in this country

9.7.3.2 Post flight and other family members

New and existing family members not entitled to family reunion under the Part 11 rules can be sponsored under provisions in Appendix FM. These will include new partners, and adult dependent relatives. Where a family member cannot meet the requirements of Appendix FM, it may be possible to make an application under GEN.3.2 arguing that refusing the human rights claim would be *unjustifiably harsh* (MIL 6.1.4).

The Family reunion casework guidance states that relatives beyond partners and children are ineligible for family reunion. However, applications must still be considered and granted where there are exceptional or compassionate circumstances, bearing in mind the best interests of other children in the family. Relevant considerations being

> that the applicant would be left in a conflict zone or dangerous situation and become destitute on their own; have no other relatives that they could live with or turn to for support in their country; are not leading an independent life and the rest of the family intend to travel to the UK.

In March 2016, in AT (Eritrea) [2016] UKUT 227 (IAC), the UT President allowed the appeal of the mother and brother of a refugee child from Eritrea. The mother and brother were the appellants and the child in the UK was the sponsor. The appellants had fled Eritrea after the sponsor and ended up in a refugee camp in Sudan. They had applied to come to the UK to join the child but were refused on the basis that there was no provision in the IRs for the entry of relatives of a child refugee: this lack of a considered government response to applications of this nature was found to make it more likely that the decision was disproportionate.

In KF Syria [2019] UKUT 413 (IAC) the UT looks at family reunion applications for the parents and younger (child) siblings of an 18-year old refugee Sponsor. The Tribunal noted that the critical Article 8 rights in play were those of the Sponsor: because only he was present in the UK.

> The section 55 "best interests" duty did not apply to the chiltn abroad, as they were not present in the UK. However the spirit of that duty had some relevance given that Article 3 of the UN Convention on the Rights of the Child, which was international law relevant to the scope of family life, emphasised the need to pay heed to a child's best interests. There was no absolute duty on entry clearance officers to facilitate the family reunion of cases involving child applicants. Nevertheless, Home Office policy in *Every Child Matters* recognised the importance of protection and safeguarding vulnerable children abroad. It was desirable that decision making was in harmony with Article 3 of the UNCRC, though it was not a provision which should necessarily be given substantial weight in the proportionality balance.
>
> Relevant public interest factors counting against family reunion in this case werethe fact that there were several family members who did not speak English and the fact that the family would foreseeably be a significant burden on public funds, and that they were not family catered for by the IRs. However, the serious mental health problems of the Sponsor outweighed those considerations, given the expert medical evidence that he would improve only with the support of close family members and that the more remote relatives, who were in the UK, could not take their place. There had been a significant delay in the SSHD processing the family reunion application (indeed complaint had been upheld)and this meant that the Sponsor had lost out on the advantage of section 55 duties applying to him as he was no longer a child when the application was refused. Any possibility of visiting the family in Jordan would be too short-term to help the Sponsor's mental health and anyway their immigration status there was precarious given the country was not a Refugee Convention signatory.

The *Family Reunion* Guidance now states these cases should be considered for exceptional circumstances and compassionate factors in the light of a child's best interests, on their 'individual merits'.

9.7.4 Travel documents

Recognised refugees are entitled to a Refugee Convention Travel Document (CTD), under Article 28 of the Convention (see general guidance for a *refugee travel document* and the fuller *Home Office travel documents* guidance).

- These CTDs are blue in colour and resemble a passport in appearance. They can be used for travel to any country that is a signatory to the Convention other than the country from which the holder is a refugee
- Applications, which now include an application for a biometric residence permit, are made on form TD112 or online. The cost is £82 (£53 for a child). The document will be valid for thel ength of the refugee's leave, or for 10 years if the refugee is settled (five years for a child)
- Dependants also qualify: defined as those treated as such on the asylum application or via family reunion (r344A(iv))
- Pre-existing family members of refugees are often issued a CTD on request but this does not constitute recognition as a refugee so will not entitle them to sponsor further family reunion (MIL 7.1): MS (Somalia) [2010] EWCA Civ 1236

CHAPTER 9: Asylum Process and Practice

9.7.5 Refugees and work, benefits and education

Any person with refugee status, indefinite leave to remain (ILR), exceptional leave to remain (ELR), humanitarian protection, or discretionary leave has the right to work in the UK and does not need to ask permission from, nor inform the Home Office, before taking up employment or setting up a business.

A refugee or person granted humanitarian protection may apply for a loan to assist with their integration into the community; for a rent deposit, household items, or for education and training for work: see https://www.gov.uk/refugeentegration-loan/overview for more details.

> Refugees will be treated as home students for the purpose of tuition fees and student support, as will their dependants who were pre-flight family members. Those granted discretionary leave will be treated as overseas students. They will have to pay higher fees and will not be entitled to student support.

9.7.6 Confidentiality of asylum claims

Generally speaking asylum claims, involving as they do the gravest risks to personal security, need to be treated as highly confidential (MIL 8.1.5.8).

However, there can be a tension between asylum confidentiality and fairness in family law proceedings. This might arise where an asylum claim has succeeded on the basis of threats from a family member (against which no national protection is forthcoming etc). Those allegations, and the reaction of decision makers in the asylum process to them, may be of interest in family law proceedings.

It is a fundamental principle of fairness and natural justice that a person is entitled to have sight of all materials which may be taken into account by the court when reaching a decision adverse to him. Sometimes the need for confidentiality in asylum proceedings will have to be measured against the public interest in ordering disclosure of important documents that may be relevant in answering allegations made in family law proceedings: RH [2020] EWCA Civ 1001.

9.8 Benefits of Humanitarian Protection
9.8.1 Immigration status

'Subsidiary protection' status (as it is called in the Qualification Directive) or Humanitarian Protection (HP) as it is called in the UK is generally equivalent to refugee status. HP holders receive leave for five years and can then apply for ILR (IR339QB). The policy intention under NBA 2022 that grants from 28 June 2022 would be ineligible for ILR was paused from 17 July 2023 (MIL 9.7.1).

9.8.2 Family reunion and travel documents

Those granted HP before based on asylum claims made before 28 June 2022 were entitled to family reunion on the same terms as per refugees. However claimants from that date are now in the same position as Group 2 refugees (MIL 9.7.3). They have to show insurmountable obstacles to family reunion abroad before pursuing it in the UK (r352FA(viii), r352FG(vii)).

Adult children dependent on UK-resident parents who lack support abroad may apply on grounds similar to adult children of refugees (r352DB, r352FG(ii)(b), r352FGA) (MIL 9.7.3.1).

A person with Humanitarian Protection can obtain a travel document named in this case a 'Certificate of Travel' from the HO, ' where that person is unable to obtain a national passport or other identity documents which enable him to travel, unless compelling reasons of national security or public order otherwise require': Rule 344A(ii). The *Guidance* refers to the need to show an application has been unreasonably refused.

If such a person can theoretically obtain such documents but has not done so, then a travel document may be issued if 'he can show that he has made reasonable attempts to obtain a national passport or identity document and there are serious humanitarian reasons for travel': Rule 344A(iii).

A Certificate of Travel (COT) does not carry the weight of a Convention Travel Document. The current cost is £280 for adults and £141 for children (also £280 if born before 1 Sep 1929 – this was previously lower) – check current fees here. The application is made on form TD112, or online.

Several countries, currently including Austria, Belgium, Denmark, France, Germany, Greece, Iceland, Italy, Luxembourg, the Netherlands, Portugal, South Africa, Spain and Switzerland, do not accept Certificates of Travel in lieu of a national passport. Wherethe HO issues a COT, but thinks that the person should use it to travel to a country where they can obtain a national passport, they must do so. In these circumstances the Certificate of Travel will be issued for one year, and may not be renewed.

CHAPTER 10: Human Rights Law

10.1 Human Rights Act 1998 & ECHR 1950

Although we deal generally with the European Convention on Human Rights in this chapter, we deem Chapters 5 and 6, addressing private and family life, as the most appropriate ones within which to deal with the approach to the assessment of Article 8 ECHR outside the IRs. We also address health and human rights in Chapter 5, because the tendency for health claims to raise issues both under Articles 3 and 8 makes it preferable to deal with them ccomrehensively in one place. Thus in this chapter we focus on rights beyond private and family life.

The Human Rights Act 1998 came into force in the United Kingdom on 2 October 2000. It brought the European Convention of Human Rights and Fundamental Freedoms (ECHR) into domestic law and made the rights protected by the ECHR directly enforceable in the British courts.

The Act has had a very important impact on immigration and asylum law.

Mechanisms for protection of human rights
- Interpretation of statute and rules
- Binding on public authorities
- Damages and compensation for breaches
- Ground on which immigration appeals can be allowed

For some time the HRA 1998 was under threat of significant reform via The Bill of Rights Bill introduced to parliament in June 2022. But on 27 June 2023 the Justice Secretary confirmed it would not proceed.

10.1.1 Interpretation of statute

Decisions and other material emanating from the European Court of Human Rights (ECtHR, often referred to by the shorthand 'Strasbourg' as this is where the court sits) must be taken into account by judges here (section 2(1) HRA). Over the first 15 years over which the HRA 1998 operated, the English judiciary indicated that itwould not deviate from the Strasbourg approach. Alconbury [2001] 2 WLR 1389 §26:

> In the absence of some special circumstances it seems to me that the court should follow any clear and constant jurisprudence of the European Court of Human Rights.

Section 3(1) of the HRA is the key to the interpretation of English statute that must be taken in future by the judiciary (though occasionally statute aims to exempt its application MIL 9.1.0):

> So far as it is possible to do so, primary legislationand subordinate legislation must be read and given effect in a way which is compatible with the Convention rights.

The system of immigration control as a whole is compatible with the HRA so long as cases can succeed inside or outside the rules (i.e. the rules do not themselves have to recognise every kind of application that could succeed, so long as discretion will be exercised to make good any gaps outside the rules): see e.g. Mahad [2009] UKSC 16, and more recently MM (Lebanon) [2017] UKSC 10 which found the minimum income threshold under Appendix FM to be lawful.

10.1.2 Effect on public authorities

Section 6(1) of the HRA demonstrates that the ambit of the Act is in no way limited to the review of statutory material – rather, any acts of a public authority may be challenged if they conflict with the fundamental rights and freedoms recognised in the ECHR:

It is unlawful for a public authority to act in a way which is incompatible with a Convention right.

This includes the HO and also the courts and tribunals, including the Immigration Tribunal. Do note that the proper ground of appeal is not compatibility with the European Convention on Human Rights but with the HRA 1998.

Uunder the HRA 1998 itself, s7(1), a person who claims that a public authority has acted (or proposes to act) incompatibly with the ECHR brings proceedings against the authority under the HRA 1998 in the appropriate court or tribunal, or may rely on the Convention right or rights concerned in any legal proceedings. Under the post-2015 appeals system, people will enjoy a right of appeal to the Tribunal, so long as they establish that the decision made against them amounts to the refusal of a protection or human rights claim (MIL 14.2.3); challenges to breaches of human rights in the UK (e.g. regarding conditions of detention in reception centres, NASS withdrawal leading to destitution sufficiently severe to raise Article 3 issues, etc.) will go via the JR route.

One must demonstrate being a victim of the act to have standing (s7(3) HRA 1998).

10.1.3 Damages and compensation

Under section 8(2) HRA 1998 damages may be awarded only by a court which has power to award damages, or to order the payment of compensation, in civil proceedings. Outside of JR claims, the UT lacks powers of this kind: only the higher courts can award damages.

Section 9(3) HRA indicates that the opportunity to obtain damages for judicial errors regarding human rights will be limited, except, perhaps, in bail cases:

> In proceedings under this Act in respect of a judicial act done in good faith, damages may not be awarded otherwise than to compensate a person to the extent required by Article 5(5) of the Convention.

Section 8 of the HRA authorises the payment of compensation where this is necessary to afford just satisfaction, taking into account the principles applied by the ECtHR in relation to the award of compensation under Article 41 of the Convention. There are three pre-conditions to an award of just satisfaction:

(1) a violation of a relevant human right;
(2) where there is no adequate remedy under domestic law (this can often be the case in public law proceedings, as discussed below); and
(3) 'just satisfaction' to the injured party requires an award.

The issues are discussed in Greenfield [2005] UKHL 14. Generally speaking awards will be moderate, and more in line with those made in Strasbourg than in analogous domestic proceedings: Anufrijeva v London Borough of Southwark [2003] EWCA Civ 1406.

The great value of HRA damages is that they may be available against a public authority which could not be realistically challenged for misconduct which is merely negligent. There is a potential action under the common law, for misfeasance in public office, but such an action has a very significant obstacle to surmount: the need to show targeted malice by a public officer, i.e. conduct specifically intended to injure a person or persons, or at least reckless conduct (Three Rivers DC v Governor and Company of the Bank of England (No 3) [2003] 2 AC 1; see also the uncertain possibility of a negligence action, Husson [2020] EWCA Civ 329). SW v UK 87/18 [2021] ECHR 541 observes that the UK may fail to offer an adequate effective remedy at domestic level where a judge acted disproportionately. There is a 1-year time limit to bring a claim: Rafiq [2022] EWHC 584 (QB) discusses the rather tough criteria for extending time when the issue is not raised in previous proceedings.

10.1.4 Human rights as a ground of appeal

When a migrant is refused permission to enter or remain in the United Kingdom, and where that decision involves the refusal of a human rights claim, there will be a right of appeal under NIAA 2002(MIL 14.2.1).

Challenges to breaches of human rights in the UK (eg regarding conditions of detention in reception centres, withdrawal of support or accommodation leadading to destitution sufficiently severe to raise Art 3 issues etc) will go via the JR route.

10.1.5 The ECtHR – interim relief by way of Rule 39 indications

The ECtHR's rules permit an application for interim measures as per r39 which permits the ECtHR to *"indicate to the parties any interim measure which they considers should be adopted in the interests of the parties or of the proper conduct of the proceedings"*. Applications may be made online via the Rule 39 site.

For now the Home Office will defer removal on receipt of a r39 application. The procedure attracted particular controversy during the Rwanda litigation. IMA 2023 empowers their being ignored unless a Minister has determined that the usual removal duties thereunder do not apply, having regard to the form of the decision, its duration, and whether the UK government had an opportunity to present its case before the indication was given (and whether in any event it can seek reconsideration of the issue) (MIL 9.1.0).

10.2 European Convention on Human Rights
10.2.1 Articles of the ECHR

The ECHR has a very useful website with the full texts of the Convention and Protocols and the Rules of Court along with all of the judgments and admissibility decisions of the Court and the old Commission. It is found at http://www.echr.coe.int. It includes a search engine, known as HUDOC. It also publishes a series of *Case Law Guides*.

Section 1 of the Human Rights Act explains which Convention rights are incorporated. The rights and fundamental freedoms protected are, in summary:

Article 2	Right to life
Article 3	Prohibition of torture or inhuman or degrading treatment of punishment
Article 4	Prohibition of slavery and forced labour
Article 5	Right to liberty and security of the person
Article 6	Right to a fair trial
Article 7	Freedom from retrospective criminal offences and punishment - "no punishment without law"
Article 8	Right to respect for private and family life
Article 9	Freedom of thought, conscience and religion
Article 10	Freedom of expression
Article 11	Freedom of assembly and association
Article 12	Right to marry and found a family
Article 14	Prohibition of discrimination in the enjoyment of Convention Rights
1st Protocol	Art 1: Protection of property; Art 2: Right to education; Art 3: Right to free elections
13th Protocol	Art 1: Prohibition on death penalty

CHAPTER 10: Human Rights Law

Article 1 ECHR requires the contracting states to secure to everyone 'within their jurisdiction' the Convention rights and freedoms. This was not actually incorporated into domestic law by the Human Rights Act 1998 – nor was Article 13, the requirement to provide an 'effective remedy'.

As you can see, the UK has not signed up to every ECHR Protocol. A full list of the obligations we have signed up to is found at *Human Rights: The UK's international human rights obligations*.

> **Top Tip**
>
> Although it is important to know about all the rights enshrined in the ECHR, the most useful and frequently relied on by immigration lawyers are Articles 3 and 8.
>
> The other rights are frequently relied on but very rarely successfully so.

10.2.2 Categories of rights

The rights and freedoms dealt with by the European Convention on Human Rights can be categorised in three ways:

Unqualified rights
- Those rights which apply absolutely without qualification and from which there can be no derogation by the state party even in time of war or public emergency threatening the life of the nation.
- e.g. the right to life, the right not to be condemned to the death penalty or executed except in time of war, the right not to be subjected to torture or to inhuman or degrading treatment or punishment, the right not to be held in slavery or servitude and the right not to be punished by retrospective laws.

Limited rights
- Those rights which display some limitation on their face (and which when read in context with the whole of the European Convention on Human Rights are subject to exceptions and which in time of war or public emergency threatening the life of the nation may be the subject of derogations).
- e.g. the right to liberty and security, the right to fair trial, the right to freedom of thought, conscience and religion, the right to education and the right to enjoy Convention rights and freedoms without discrimination.

Qualified rights
- Rights which are expressly qualified on their face and which must be balanced against, and may have to give way to, other competing public interests.
- e.g. the rights to respect for private and family life, home and correspondence, freedom to manifest one's religion and beliefs, freedom of expression and to hold opinions, freedom of peaceful assembly and association, and freedom of movement.

10.2.3 Standard of proof

The standard of proof for assessing whether the likelihood of a human rights breach is sufficient for the ECHR to be engaged is whether there is a 'real risk' of the claimed problem actually happening, or 'substantial grounds for believing' a breach will occur. The test is essentially the same as the 'reasonable degree of likelihood' test for assessing future risks in refugee cases: the government has no present plans to change this standard of proof (see MIL 8.1.4, 8.9.1 for refugee and HP regimes).

However, in some cases, the claimant may assert that they will be subject to a generalised risk of a breach of their rights, for example by being exposed to poor conditions in a country's prisons system or generalised problems in military service in a given country. In such cases it is necessary to show that anyone in the applicant's circumstances would face a certain minimum level of risk. Some judges have described the test as being whether there are gross, flagrant and systematic breaches of human rights extant: only then will it be established that all members of the relevant category are at risk. Hariri [2003]

EWCA Civ 807 posits the simpler question: whether the situation to which the appellant would be returning was one in which such violence was generally or consistently happening.

10.3 ECHR and immigration law – Articles 2, 3 and 8

The protected Convention rights are universal and intended to apply to everyone within the United Kingdom's jurisdiction, not just to British nationals. Furthermore, the preamble of the ECHR describes the rights as having a universal quality – they apply to all persons regardless of nationality, race, sex or other 'status'. In the SIAC field, generally beyond MIL's scope, we see the limitations on extra-territorial application of the HRA 1998. Eg it does not apply to those deprived of their citizenship having left the UK voluntarily: R3 [2023] EWCA Civ 169.

There are two broad categories of case where the ECHR has an impact in the field of immigration and asylum law, identified by the House of Lords in Ullah and Do:

Domestic cases
- Acts or omissions by the UK authorities
- e.g. breach of private and family life established in the UK
- e.g. catastrophic deterioration of medical condition owing to absence of treatment after removal

Foreign cases
- Acts or omissions by a foreign state after removal
- e.g. detention in breach of Article 5
- e.g. total deprivation of contact with child

Ullah and Do [2004] UKHL 26 established definitively in UK law that all of the articles of the ECHR can potentially be relied on in foreign cases. The Strasbourg cases of Soering v UK (1989) 11 EHRR 439 and Chahal v UK (1996) 23 EHRR 413 had already established that Article 3 could operate to prevent removal where there was a real risk of a future breach of human rights. However, for Articles other than Article 3, it is necessary to show that there would be a 'flagrant breach' of the right or rights in question, or that the right or rights would be completely nullified. This is sometimes referred to as the Devaseelan [2002] UKIAT 00702 test after the starred determination that first set out this test, later approved by the House of Lords in EM (Lebanon) [2008] UKHL 64.

There are some principles which are over arching and may be relevant in the interpretation of any of ECHR rights. As the European Court said in *Pretty v United Kingdom* (2002) 35 EHRR 1, para 65:

> The very essence of the Convention is respect for human dignity and human freedom.

This is worth bearing in mind whenever, for example, an old or vulnerable person faces living alone in circumstances that threaten their dignity.

10.3.1 Article 2

Article 2 of the ECHR is as follows:

1. Everyone's right to life shall be protected by law. No one shall be deprived of his life intentionally save in the execution of a sentence of a court following his conviction of a crime for which this penalty is provided by law.
2. Deprivation of life shall not be regarded as inflicted in contravention of this article when it results from the use of force which is no more than absolutely necessary:
    - in defence of any person from unlawful violence;
    - in order to effect a lawful arrest or to prevent the escape of a person lawfully detained;
    - in action lawfully taken for the purpose of quelling a riot or insurrection.

So far, in immigration cases, the article tends to be argued in addition to Article 3, for the simple reason that death or execution would be rather likely to be considered in the modern world to cross the threshold for Article 3 ill treatment in any event. There has not yet been a removal case in the UK or at Strasbourg that has succeeded on Article 2 but not on Article 3. It is worth remembering that in Soering the claimant feared execution and the experience of 'death row', and his case succeeded on the latter ground only.

The UK has duties to preserve the welfare of those under government control. Which includes preserving relevant evidence re deaths in detention (MIL 13.1.8).

Protocol 13, Article 1 contains an absolute prohibition on the death penalty. Following UK ratification of the 13th Protocol reference to Article 13 has now been inserted into the HRA 1998 (see SI 2004/1574, in force from 22 June 2004). Thus, where there are 'substantial grounds for believing' that following a removal from this country a person will be condemned to death or executed, even if for murder, such removal would be to breach their human rights. The Article reads:

> The death penalty shall be abolished. No-one shall be condemned to such penalty or executed.

10.3.2 Article 3

The right is expressed in these terms, and is notably unqualified:

No one shall be subjected to torture or to inhuman or degrading treatment or punishment.

There are therefore three forms of ill treatment, but each is afforded the same level of protection in immigration proceedings:

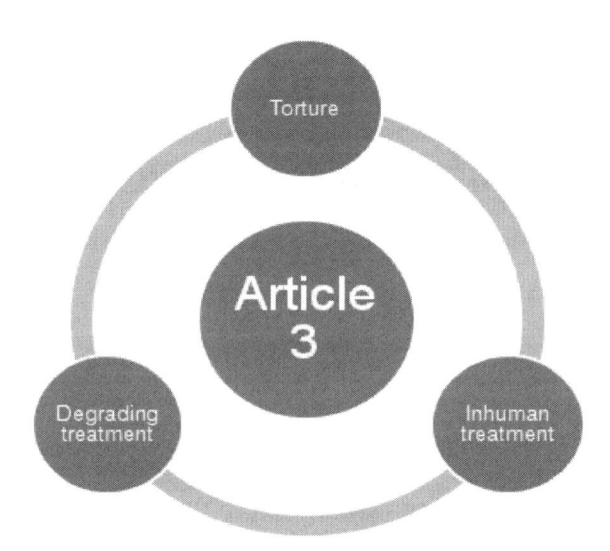

Outside an immigration context, these three forms of ill treatment can be seen as a spectrum, with torture at the most serious end, going through inhuman treatment and then degrading treatment. However, for ill treatment to amount to torture it would probably always have to be deliberately inflicted and intentional, whereas, as is discussed below, inhuman and degrading treatment canpotentially be passive in nature.

10.3.2.1 Absolute nature of Article 3

Article 3 is absolute in nature, meaning that there are no circumstances in which it can be derogated from, nor can there be any justification for failure to observe it. This means that even very unpleasant individuals who have committed very serious crimes can benefit from its protection.

In Soering, the claimant was mentally ill and had horribly murdered two people in the United States. His extradition to stand trial there was being sought. Strasbourg held that he could not be extradited because of the real risk of exposure to the death row experience, which would breach Article 3.

In Chahal, the claimant was accused of being a terrorist extremist and a danger to the UK's national security, but the ECtHR in Chahal v UK (1997) 23 EHRR 413 found that because right is absolute his removal to India was not permitted because 'the activities of the individual in question, however undesirable or dangerous, cannot be a material consideration' (para 80).

Whether Article 3 is breached or not in an individual case is a question of fact, based on measuring up all the relevant considerations – so it is always necessary to examine the impact of the feared future treatment on this individual. The courts say that (e.g. Ireland v UK (1978) 2 EHRR 25 at para 162):

> …ill-treatment must attain a minimum level of severity if it is to fall within the scope of Article 3. The assessment of this minimumis, in the nature of things, relative; it depends on all the circumstances of the case, such as the nature and context of the treatment or punishment, the manner and method of its execution, its duration and its physical or mental effects.

The right operates so as to prevent removal of a person within a country's territory to another territory in which there would be a breach of Article 3 ofthe ECHR. It is, therefore, irrelevant from an immigration perspective whether the breach of which the claimant complains will be one that amounts to torture, inhuman treatment or degrading treatment. For the purposes of understanding Article 3 is it is nevertheless important to explore the nature of each type of ill treatment.

The ECtHR has held open the possibility that diplomatic assurances may be sought of a receiving state in order to facilitate the removal of someone who might otherwise face a real risk of inhuman and degrading treatment. These tend to be encountered in the context of national security cases or serious criminals, though may also be relevant to "health" cases given the case law on Article 3 ECHR and health and the expelling state's possible duty of enquiry into healthcare arrangements abroad (MIL 5.6.1).

- The criteria for evaluating such assurances were set out by the ECtHR in Othman v United Kingdom (2012) 55 EHRR 1: the availability and terms of the assurances, their specificity, whether their author can bind the receiving state and how seriously they will be taken by local/central actors, whether the treatment in question is legal or not, the quality of bilateral relations between the sending and receiving state, previous ill treatment, and whether there are effective human rights monitoring systems and a system that protects against torture there
- Zabolotnyi [2021] UKSC 14 emphasises that assurances are likely to be taken especially seriously when from ECHR signatories & EU Member States, and that the compliance record of the issuing state is of central importance
- The court must assess assurances for itself: AAA (Syria) [2023] UKSC 42. Giving weight to the government's view: where that view reflects the advice of officials with relevant experience and expertise (recalling that such advice have been ignored). It may not be necessary to resolve conflicts of evidence if the overall picture suggests a real risk of mistreatment. Apparent failures to fulfil undertakings under previous similar agreements are relevant

---

Top Tip

Always focus on the individual facts of the case – what is the impact of a particular kind of treatment on a particular individual?

Are there circumstances of their case making them particularly vulnerable, such as age, physical or mental health or life experiences?

10.3.2.2 Torture

In Ireland v UK (1978) 2 EHRR 25 at para 167 torture was defined as 'deliberate inhuman treatment causing veryserious and cruel suffering'. This was said to be a very high threshold, and very few cases were found to reach this high level.

In Selmouni v France [1999] ECHR 66, the ECtHR revised this approach and derived assistance from the UN Convention against Torture. The new definition was essentially whether 'physical and mental violence, considered as a whole, committed against the applicant's person caused "severe" pain and suffering and was particularly serious and cruel'. So this seems to set the torture threshold rather lower.

In the case of Aydin v Turkey (1998) 25 EHRR 251 the ECtHR found that rape amounted to torture.

10.3.2.3 Inhuman treatment or punishment

Ireland v UK (1978) 2 EHRR 25 at 167 saw the European Court finding that a combination of forms of ill-treatment of detaineesdeprivation of food, drink and sleep, hooding, subjection to noise and being stood up against a wall) amounted to inhuman and degrading treatment.

> The five techniques were applied in combination, with premeditation and for hours at a stretch; they caused, if not actual bodily injury, at least intense physical and mental suffering to the persons subjected thereto and also led to acute psychiatric disturbances during interrogation. They accordingly fell into the category of inhuman treatment within the meaning of Article 3 (art. 3).

Pretty v UK (2002) 35 EHRR 1 at para 52 shows that natural illness, if made worse by certain conditions, may cross the threshold:

> As regards the types of 'treatment' which fall within the scope of Article 3 of the Convention, the Court's case law refers to 'ill-treatment' that attains a minimum level of severity and involves actual bodily injury or intense physical or mental suffering... Where treatment humiliates or debases an individual showing a lack or respect for, or diminishing, his or her human dignity or arouses feelings of fear, anguish or inferiority capable of breaking an individual's moral and physical resistance, it may be characterised as degrading and also fall within the prohibition of Article 3.... The suffering which flows from naturally occurring illness, physical or mental, may be covered by Article 3, where it is, or risks being, exacerbated by the treatment, whether flowing from conditions of detention, expulsion or other measures, for which the authorities can be held responsible...

The workings out of this principle are found at MIL 5.6.

The death row phenomenon can constitute inhuman punishment, see Soering v UK (1989) 11 EHRR 439.

10.3.2.4 Degrading treatment or punishment

In Ireland v UK held, re degrading treatment:

> The techniques were also degrading since they were such as to arouse in their victims feelings of fear, anguish and inferiority capable of humiliating and debasing them and possibly breaking their physical or moral resistance.

The ECHR has held that prison conditions can amount to degrading treatment, and even inhuman treatment. See for example Kalashnikov v Russia (2002) 36 EHRR 34:

> ...The suffering and humiliation involved must in any event go beyond that inevitable element of suffering or humiliation connected with a given form of legitimate treatment or punishment ... the State must ensure that a person is detained in conditions which are compatible with respect for his human dignity, that the manner and method of the execution of the measure do not subject him to distress or hardship of an intensity exceeding the unavoidable level of suffering inherent in detention and that, given the practical demands of imprisonment, his health and well-being are adequately secured ... account has to be taken of the cumulative effects of those conditions, as well as the specific allegations made by the applicant.

AD v Malta [2023] ECHR 794 summarises more recent thinking, having regard to personal space, physical conditions including natural light, ventilation & sanitation. A comprehensive record must be kept re the detainee's state of health & their treatment while in detention, diagnosis and care must be prompt and accurate and that, where necessary, supervision is regular and systematic, including a comprehensive therapeutic strategy aimed at adequately treating the detainee's health problems or preventing their aggravation, rather than addressing them on a symptomatic basis. Batayav [2003] EWCA Civ 1489 warns of the dangers of finding that Article 3 was not engaged by Russian prisons when the ECtHR had recently found the contrary. Complaints re general prison conditions in a country need to demonstrate a consistent pattern of gross and systematic human rights violations (MIL 10.2.3). But cases can succeed (eg PS Ukraine CG [2006] UKAT 00016). Interestingly the ECtHR considers that prisoners must have available space of at least $3m^2$ in multi-occupancy accommodation subject to occasional minor reductions VB (Ukraine) [2017] UKUT 79 (IAC).

Life sentences with no prospect of parole can also amount to an Article 3 breach, where the sentence is grossly disproportionate to the offence in question or where it is no longer justified in penal terms and incapable of reduction: Babar Ahmad v UK [2012] ECHR 609.

Top Tip

While the law says that a person cannot be removed if they are going to be detained in conditions that would be contrary to Article 3 ECHR, it is not at all easy to prove that the conditions will in fact be so bad as to meet this threshold. A line from a US Department of State report will not be sufficient.

Expert evidence will be needed, and/or specific reports on detention conditions in that country by a relevant international NGO or monitoring organisation of some sort, such as Penal Reform. ECHR signatories are monitored by the Committee for the Prevention of Torture, an official organ of the Council of Europe. The reports of the CPT were instrumental in VB (Ukraine). Unfortunately, such detailed and influential reports do not generally exist outside Council of Europe countries, so other forms of evidence must be sought.

Always check HUDOC, the ECtHR's case database for decisions involving the detention conditions sin the country in question

---

In Tyrer v UK (1980) 2 EHRR 1 the ECtHR held that corporal punishment of a minor amounted to degrading treatment or punishment, but said that the punishment must exceed the usual element of humiliation involved in the criminal justice system, and that 'a punishment does not lose its degrading character just because it is believed to be, or actually is, an effective deterrent or aid to crime control'.

Ocalan v Turkey (2003) 37 EHRR 10 §220 also emphasises whether the object of the ill-treatment is humiliation or debasement:

In East African Asians v UK (1981) 3 EHRR 76 the court concluded that discrimination based on race could, in certain circumstances, of itself amount to degrading treatment.

> [207] ... that discrimination based on race could, in certain circumstances, of itself amountto degrading treatment within the meaning of Article 3 ... The Commission recalls in this connection that, as generally recognised, a special importance should be attached to discrimination based on race; that publicity [sic] to single out a groupof persons for differential treatment on the basis of race might, in certain circumstances, constitute a special form of affront to human dignity; and that differential treatment of a group of persons on the basis of race might therefore be capable of constituting degrading treatment when differential treatment on some other ground would raise no such question.

The Tribunal in S&K [2002] UKIAT 05613 accepted that racial motivation could tip the balance in some cases.

10.3.2.5 Specific features of Article 3 cases

You might wonder, given the availability of international protection by way of refugee status and Humanitarian Protection, quite what role Article 3 ECHR plays in the 'asylum' context. It mainly operates where a person is excluded from international protection: given that the thresholds for exclusion are relatively moderate (particularly for Humanitarian Protection), and arise both in relation to international or other criminality abroad, and for offending in this country, an increasing number of people have to rely on the residual protection offered by Article 3.

Absence of exclusion clauses

Article 3 is subject to no limitation, and unlike the Refugee Convention, there are no exclusion clauses to deprive an individual of the rights which it recognises, see Chahal v UK (1996) 23 EHRR 413. Nevertheless whilst the SSHD cannot remove some individuals, they can be treated differently vis-à-vis the form of leave to remain conferred (MIL 10.5.3).

Absence of Convention reasons

Unlike Refugee Convention, there is no ECHR requirement that the harm feared be linked to the individual's race, religion, nationality, membership of a particular social group or political opinion. In cases where the individual faces serious ill treatment or harm on return but behind which there is no Convention reason, the individual may not be entitled to refugee status but may not nevertheless be removed. Subject to criminality, Humanitarian Protection may well be available.

Sufficiency of protection

Bagdanavicius [2005] UKHL 38 holds that although there was some difference in wording between the Horvath formulation of the standard of protection required by the Refugee Convention and the Strasbourg formulation in HLR v France (1998) 26 EHRR 29, the tests were to all intents and purposes the same.

It is therefore not possible to argue that the 'sufficiency of protection' test does not apply in human rights cases or that it is a different test to that which applies under the Refugee Convention. Basically everybody has to show that, firstly, they are at real risk of seriousharrm/persecution, and secondlythat there is no effective system (which they can access) capable of protecting them.

Destitution in the UK

A number of cases have explored the circumstances in which the problems that ensue from denying support might engage Article 3 of the ECHR, e.g. Limbuela [2005] UKHL 66. You can see the issues in Ganpot [2023] EWHC 197 (Admin) (MIL 13.2.2).

Destitution abroad

The rights found in the ECHR were originally conceived as offering protection against state harm; over time this has come to include protection from powerful non-state actors against whose actions the state does not offer protection. As we saw when we addressed health and human rights (MIL 5.6.1), the ambit of the Convention has been developed by the Strasbourg Court to cover, very exceptionally, health cases for which nobody could seriously suggest such actors are responsible. This has a knock-on effect for the consideration of destitution too.

In Paposhvili ([2014] ECHR 431 the ECtHR's Grand Chamber reviewed its approach to inhuman and degrading treatment, which could result where an individual

> although not at imminent risk of dying, would face a real risk, on account of the absence of appropriate treatment in the receiving country or the lack of access to such treatment, of being exposed to a serious, rapid and irreversible decline in his or her state of health resulting in intense suffering or to a significant reduction in life expectancy.

This thinking presumably carries over to destitution cases too, where ilfe is threatened due to "*naturally occurring*" phenomena. In MSS v Belgium and Greece [2011] ECHR 108 and Sufi & Elmi v United Kingdom (2012) 54 EHRR 9 the Strasbourg Court has held that the N test applies if "*dire humanitarian conditions ... were solely or even predominantly attributable to poverty or to the state's lack of resources to deal with a naturally occurring phenomenon.*"

The abandonment of the N threshold for health necessarily impacts on the analogous test of when destitution equates to inhuman and degrading treatment. We noted in MIL in 2020 that the precise analogy between a "*serious, rapid and irreversible decline ... resulting in intense suffering or to a significant reduction in life expectancy*" in health and destitution cases will need to be explored, and that life on the streets that involves intense suffering or a foreseeable threat to life expectancy now potentially falls within the ambit of Article 3.

We were prescient in so doing. Ainte [2021] UKUT 203 (IAC) accepts that if destitution caused intense suffering *or* a significant reduction in life expectancy such that the humanitarian case for granting leave is compelling, then it should be accepted as amounting as inhuman and degrading treatment.
- A resident of a poorly equipped and run camp, where food supplies are short and at the mercy of exploitative gatekeepers who take the meagre aid intended for the camp's inhabitants for themselves, could be accepted as facing inhuman and degrading treatment. Sustained and extreme deprivation was a material condition likely to lead to a "*significant reduction in life expectancy*"
- Even the strongest and most resilient individual can experience "intense suffering" where conditions are bad enough
- if poor living conditions were preponderantly due to a locust plague rather than the actions of parties to an armed conflict, the Sufi and Elmi approach would not apply
- The failure of a non-ECHR signatory to meet its own human rights obligations (such as regional treaties) could not be treated as analogous to a Sufi and Elmi situation

These thresholds are still pretty high of course.

- However sometimes destitution does not arise from natural events. As where an EU Member State has breached legal duties to protect the vulnerable (see MSS v Belgium and Greece, probably extending to the relatively unexplored issue of mental health deterioration attributable to detention in the UK) or where the destitution is the legacy of armed conflict (e.g. Sufi & Elmi). Then the conventional Article 3 test applies. Perhaps immigration tribunals will one day have to rule on whether climate change is manmade or a natural event: see for "*climate change refugees*" more generally, the Teitiota litigation including the action against New Zealand
- OA (Somalia) (CG) [2022] UKUT 33 (IAC) explains that destitution cases
  - Require a causal link between the real risk of the returnee being exposed to those conditions, and the SSHD's action in removing the individual to the country concerned. So the intense suffering had to be foreseeable at the time of return, bearing in mind the possibility of changes in living conditions due to improving economic circumstances. Simply pointing to some unknown future point where living conditions might cause intense suffering would not suffice
  - The breach of obligations under international treaties such as the ICESCR and the Kampala Convention (which require a state to make 'very effort to use all its resources to alleviate suffering) was not relevant. It was too difficult to determine the nature of those obligations in Somali's national law, and wrong in principle to impose obligations on the UK due to another country's compliance with its own obligations

These issues overlap with Humanitarian Protection applications: see MIL 8.9.2. Access to social assistance in the country of origin may be essential to avoid conditions inconsistent with Article 3 ECHR: see for example the Iraqi CG cases such as SMO and KSP Iraq [2022] UKUT 110 (IAC).

Unavailability of medical treatment abroad

It is argued in some cases that a difference in medical treatment between the UK and the country to which a person is to be removed will cause suffering or death and that removal would therefore breach

CHAPTER 10: Human Rights Law

the person's human rights and engage the UK's responsibilities. As in practice this overlaps with Article 8 private life cases, we address health cases and the human rights issues they raise elsewhere (MIL 5.6).

Successful Article 2, 3 and 8 claims and leave to remain

A person succeeding on the basis that their Article 2 or 3nights would be breached in the country of return because of the actions of non-state actors would be entitled to humanitarian protection under r339C.

10.4 ECHR Articles 4, 5, 6, 8 and 14

10.4.1 Article 4

Article 4 (1) is the absolute right amongst the parts of this Article, which could capture cases involving the future threat of trafficking, forced prostitution, or bonded labour:

> (14) No one shall be held in slavery or servitude.
>   1. No one shall be required to perform forced or compulsory labour.
>   2. For the purpose of this article the term 'forced or compulsory labour' shall not include:
>   (a) any work required to be done in the ordinary course of detention imposed according to the provisions of Article 5 of this Convention or during conditional release from such detention;
>   (b) any service of a military character or, in case of conscientious objectors in countries where they are recognised, service exacted instead of compulsory military service;
>   (c) any service exacted in case of an emergency or calamity threatening the life or well-being of the community;
>   (d) any work or service which forms part of normal civic obligations.

In Rantsev v Cyprus and Russia (Application no. 25965/04), the European Court of Human Rights held that trafficking falls within the scope of Article 4 of the Convention and that there is a procedural obligation under Article 4 to investigate alleged trafficking.

See further MIL 4.3.

10.4.2 Threshold for interference in foreign cases

The other articles that we now address are all qualified and/or limited ones.

The courts have styled scenarios where the rights violation eventuates abroad as 'foreign cases' (MIL 5.4.5).

10.4.3 Article 5

Article 5 ECHR provides, relevantly to immigration, as follows:

> 1. Everyone has the right to liberty and security of person. No one shall be deprived of his liberty save in the following cases and in accordance with a procedure prescribed by law:
>
>   (f) the lawful arrest or detention of a person to prevent his effecting an unauthorised entry into the country or of a person against whom action is being taken with a view to deportation or extradition.
>
> 2. Everyone who is arrested shall be informed promptly, in a language which he understands, of the reasons for his arrest and of any charge against him.
> 3. Everyone arrested or detained in accordance with the provisions of paragraph 1.c of this article shall be brought promptly before a judge or other officer authorised by law to exercise

judicial power and shall be entitled to trial within a reasonable time or to release pending trial. Release may be conditioned by guarantees to appear for trial.
5. Everyone who is deprived of his liberty by arrest or detention shall be entitled to take proceedings by which the lawfulness of his detention shall be decided speedily by a court and his release ordered if the detention is not lawful.
6. Everyone who has been the victim of arrest or detention in contravention of the provisions of this article shall have an enforceable right to compensation.

In Saadi & Ors [2001] EWCA Civ 1512 (a case which made its way from the House of Lords and then on to Strasbourg), the judge accepted that short-term detention of asylum seekers is permissible, even absent any risk of their absconding, for the purposes of processing their asylum claims.

ECHR Art 5 may become more significant from 28 September 2023 given that the Hardial Singh test has been replaced a statutory one (MIL 13.1.6). AD v Malta [2023] ECHR 794 summarises the ECtHR's approach. The State's categorisation of liberty restrictions is not conclusive as to whether it amounts to detention; close analysis is necessary as to whether the underlying evidence justifies a restriction of liberty for the stated public interest purpose, and whether the restriction is on balance necessary. To avoid being arbitrary under Article 5(1)(f) ECHR detention must be carried out in good faith; it must be closely connected to the ground of detention relied on by the Government; the place and conditions of detention should be appropriate, bearing in mind that the measure is applicable not to those who have committed criminal offences but to aliens who, often fearing for their lives, have fled from their own country; and the length of the detention should not exceed that reasonably required for the purpose pursued.

As mentioned above, damages are available under section 9(3) of the HRA, even for judicial acts carried out in good faith. There have been a number of successful claims for damages in immigration detention cases: excellent reviews of the relevant considerations are found in Dunlop and Denholm, *Detention under the Immigration Acts: Law and Practice* (Oxford University Press) and Dubinsky with Arnott and Mackenzie, *Foreign National Prisoners: Law and Practice* (Legal Action Group). HJT also offers a bespoke unlawful detention resource which can be provided in tandem with in-house training.

Liberty may be lost only pursuant to 'a procedure prescribed by law'. Thus the HO must reveal any policies which underlie detention decisions. Nadarajah [2003] EWCA Civ 1768 found that, given that the ECtHR had held that the phrase 'prescribed by law' in Article 10(2) required that the law must be adequately accessible. Those subject to the law must have an indication which is adequate in the legal circumstances of the legal rules which are applicable to the given case.

The Article may also have extra-territorial application. As discussed above, the risk of a flagrant breach of qualified/limited Articles can inhibit removal to a country, in relation to Article 5 where a person's liberty and security of person might face nullification or flagrant breach. Given that only the authorities of a country can lawfully deprive of an individual of their liberty pursuant to law, there must be an argument that loss of liberty at the hands of non-state actors constitutes a fundamental breach of the Article.

10.4.4 Article 6

Article 6 ECHR reads as follows:

1. In the determination of his civil rights and obligations or of any criminal charge against him, everyone is entitled to a fair and public hearing within a reasonable time by an independent and impartial tribunal established by law. Judgment shall be pronounced publicly but the press and public may be excluded from all or part of the trial in the interests of morals, public order or national security in a democratic society, where the interests of juveniles or the protection of the private life of the parties so require, or to the extent strictly necessary in the opinion of the court in special circumstances where publicity would prejudice the interests of justice.
2. Everyone charged with a criminal offence shall be presumed innocent until proved guilty according to law.
3. Everyone charged with a criminal offence has the following minimum rights:

(a) to be informed promptly, in a language which he understands and in detail, of the nature and cause of the accusation against him;
(b) to have adequate time and facilities for the preparation of his defence;
(c) to defend himself in person or through legal assistance of his own choosing or, if he has not sufficient means to pay for legal assistance, to be given it free when the interests of justice so require;
(d) to examine or have examined witnesses against him and to obtain the attendance and examination of witnesses on his behalf under the same conditions as witnesses against him;
(e) to have the free assistance of an interpreter if he cannot understand or speak the language used in court.

10.4.4.1 Article 6 & legal proceedings in the United Kingdom

MNM (00/TH/02423; 1 November 2000) (starred) confirmed that, as per the ECtHR in Maaroui v France, Article 6 does not apply in immigration appeals. Because immigration rights are not 'private' in nature and therefore do not amount to civil rights and obligations. However the Tribunal took the view that the common law would guarantee everything that Article 6 would provide, anyway, so this should not matter very much. The only real difference was the requirement that the hearing be held within a reasonable time. Which the Tribunal hoped that, absent procedural disasters, should not be a problem. The breadth of the non-applicability of ECHR fair trial rights was reiterated in ALO [2022] EWHC 2380 (Admin).

Article 6 rights may require a person's return to the UK to participate in legal proceedings ((online) MIL 3.5).

The Home Office does accept in that guidance (on the authority of the Quaquah case) that Article 6 may be engaged when the applicant is bringing legal proceedings against them, for example seeking damages for unlawful conduct, and was removed before the conclusion of those proceedings having made an allegation of bad faith as to the circumstances of that removal.

10.4.4.2 Article 6 and its extra-territorial application to resist removal

As discussed above, authorities such as Ullah show that a flagrant denial of justice abroad may prevent removal. Article 6 may also have some limited applicability in preventing removal if a lack of fair trial would be the gateway to Article 3 breaches.

RB (Algeria) [2009] UKHL 10 held that whilst the overriding test was whether there was a real risk of a total denial of the right to a fair trial, nevertheless§136-137:

> A trial that is fair in part may be no more acceptable than the curate's eggWhat isrequired is that the deficiency or deficiencies in the trial process should be such as fundamentally to destroy the fairness of the prospective trial.

The important question was the potential consequences of unfairness by way of further human rights violations.

10.4.5 Article 8

Article 8 provides as follows:

> (1) Everyone has the right to respect for his private and family life, his home and his correspondence.
>
> (2) There shall be no interference by a public authority with the exercise of this right except such as is in accordance with the law and is necessary in a democratic society in the interests of national security, public safety or the economic well-being of the country, for

the prevention of disorder or crime, for the protection of health or morals, or for the protection of the rights and freedoms of others.

Because of the overlap between private and family life inside and outside the rules, we address Article 8 in Chapters 5 and 6.

Normally Article 8 cases involve interference with private and family life relationships in the UK. So they are domestic cases and no especially high threshold is involved. It is possible, though very rare, to run a case relying on a violation of Article 8 rights abroad (MIL 5.4.5).

10.4.6 Article 14

Article 14 prohibits discrimination only when it can be linked with a lack of respect for one or more of the rights otherwise set out in the ECHR – it is the enjoyment of those rights which must be secured without discrimination

> "*on any ground such as sex, race, colour, language, religion, political or other opinion, national or social origin, association with a national minority, property, birth or other status.*"

The ambit of grounds of appeal for post-2015 appeals under the relevant provisions of the NIAA 2002 to HRA 1998 grounds (and thus the substantive Articles of the ECHR) (ie Human Rights Convention grounds) means that Article 14 continues to be available.

The courts have looked at the ambit of Article 14 in the immigration context in the context of who might be recognised as having an appropriate "*other status*":

- Being an immigration detainee may qualify: SM [2021] EWHC 418 (Admin)
- Secretary of State for the Home Department v First-tier Tribunal (Social Entitlement Chamber) [2021] EWHC 1690 (Admin) recognises that being a failed asylum seeker was arguably an "other status" for discrimination purposes
- So too are the "Windrush generation", in the sense of all those who had a right to remain in the United Kingdom by virtue of section 1(2) of the 1971 Act who, prior to 1 January 1988, could have obtained British nationality by registration: Howard [2021] EWHC 1023 (Admin), Vanriel [2021] EWHC 3415 (Admin)
- As is being an asylum seeker: JP [2019] EWHC 3346 (Admin)
- And presence abroad: AM [2022] EWHC 2591 (Admin)

The "other status" is something which must exist independently of the treatment complained of: SM [2021] EWHC 418 (Admin).

10.5 Discretionary leave

This is a residual form of leave given to some individuals who neither qualify for leave under the IRs nor for LOTR. It is governed by the *Discretionary Leave* guidance. It covers exceptional circumstances on non-private and family life grounds where removal would be unjustifiably harsh (elsexceptional compassionate circumstances or there are other compelling reasons).

Applications are free of charge if made solely, or predominantly, relying on Article 3. Leave is granted by way of:

- 30 months rolling grants
- on a 10-year route to settlement
- though if leave was first granted under this route before 9 July 2012, the old DL policy will be honoured so that ILR is granted after six years of DL (after active reviews at each stage)

There are three different types of leave granted in similar but slightly different circumstances.

- Discretionary leave
- Restricted leave – essentially, DL for domestic and international law criminals
- Leave outside the rules (MIL 4.2.1)

10.5.1 Pre-July 2012 DL

The most common situation where you would, pre-9 July 2012, have expected to see a grant of DL was in Article 8 cases where removal would breach the person's or their family's right to a private and family life in the United Kingdom, or where a person's medical condition would render their removal in breach of Articles 3 or 8.

In those circumstances, a person would normally have been granted three years DL, followed by an active review, a further three years DL if successful, and then ILR. Those on that route under the old policy will continue on that route under *Section 10: Transitional Arrangements* of the new policy.

The August 2015 API Discretionary Leave states the policy to be to "normally" grant ILR to those who have completed two 3-year periods of DLR. As explained in Ellis [2020] UKUT 82 (IAC) the word "normally" did not compel the grant of DLR but requires that caseworkers should consider whether there are circumstances that warrant a departure from the usual position. Even if the wrong form was used for an application outside the Rules (in this case, SET (LR) rather than SET O), this did not matter where the SSHD had considered the application under the DL Policy in any event. Reasons had to be given for departing from the "normal" position.

10.5.2 Modern DL

The *Discretionary Leave Guidance* explains that DL has a very restricted ambit: it essentially arises only where there are human rights grounds for leave other than under ECHR Art 8:

- medical cases which would not give rise to a grant of Humanitarian Protection (MIL 5.6)
- where there is a flagrant breach of a qualified or limited right
- pre-30 January 2023 and the introduction of temporary permission to stay under NBA 2022, in certain trafficking scenarios (MIL 4.3.9) (where a trafficking victim articulates a claim with sufficient clarity the HO should consider it) (DL will normally be granted where there is a pending asylum claim, unless the claim has been deemed inadmissible: DL may be appropriate where an inadmissibility decision is pending)
- exceptional circumstances: eg where a positive decision is made due to length of UK residence, character and conduct etc under IR 353B (MIL 4.2.2) – though decisions based on compassionate reasons should not undermine the policy objectives which generally animate the Immigration Rules
- From 2 September 2011, the Restricted leave policy replaced DLR for persons excluded from international protection: renewal applications from old-style cases should go to the Special Cases Unit or Criminal Casework to shift to the RL route

DL may also be granted where further submissions are considered under r353, where, having considered the factors set out and the guidance in Chapter 53.1 of the Enforcement Instructions and Guidance (EIG) (withdrawn 19/10/17 but archived version available here) removal is no longer considered appropriate. Some such cases will be entitled to an immediate grant of ILR under the pre-20 July 2011 policy.

Grants of DL will usually be for 30 months. An application for extension can be made where there is a continued need for such leave. Children born in the UK to parents with DL will receive leave in line. A person with DL under the new policy will not usually be able to apply for ILR until they have had DL for 10 years. There is sometimes scope for accelerated ILR (MIL 5.7.2) though the Guidance emphasises that ILR is a privilege and generally should not be allowed to shortcut other routes (such that the facts are "*not just unusual but can be distinguished to a high degree from other cases*"). Different periods of leave may be appropriate if a child's best interests are in play and if there are particularly compelling circumstances ILR may be appropriate, eg in serious and chronic health cases to give a greater degree of certainty for the purposes of their continued treatment or mental wellbeing. As each application for an extension will be subject to an active review, the course to settlement will be uncertain (see also MIL 5.7.2).

There are provisions for revocation of DL. However, given that DL does not normally result from any 'protection' need but rather is based on relationships or care in the UK, travel to the country of origin and use of one's own national passport does not bring with it the same negative connotations as in asylum and humanitarian protection cases.

There are no provisions which entitle a person with DL to sponsor family members to join them in the UK. They will need to assert ECHR Art 8 rights.

AZ [2020] ScotCS CSOH_15 notes the possible relevance of the different higher education tuition fees in Scotland as opposed to those in England & Wales. The Judge finds that the different fees (and the financial barrier to higher education that follows) might be a relevant consideration for considering the grant of ILR to a person with DLR. But an applicant would have to raise the issue expressly in their application.

The active review policy applies when applications are made for an extension of DL and for ILR. If there have been material changes in the person's circumstances such that the basis for the earlier grant of DL no longer exists, the HO may refuse the extension or ILR. Where, in those circumstances, the person has some other basis to stay, usually because of other Article 8 reasons, they may then be put on to the new 10-year route. Where they do not, their application will be refused. They may be a right of appeal if the application they made amounted to a human rights claim.

Where the person granted DL had previously made an asylum claim, the form to apply for an extension, and for ILR, is FLR(DL). Otherwise it will be FLR(HRO) or SET(O) (MIL 1.5.7). The fee will be £1,048 (plus £500 IHS) for an extension (subject to qualifying for a fee waiver), and £2,885 for ILR.

Unaccompanied minors refused asylum used to be granted DL until they were aged 17½ years. From 6 April 2013 they receive leave under IR352ZC.

10.5.3 Criminality and Restricted Leave

Criminals generally

Where a person has a criminal record, then they may be excluded from the usual 30-month slices of leave that may lead to settlement. Where they do not fall into the ambit of the restricted leave policy (which we deal with next), they may receive DL.

They can apply for ILR only after 10 years. AO [2011] EWHC 3088 (Admin) finds that the 10 year policy for exclusion cases was an unlawful fettering of HO discretion. In an exceptional case, it will therefore be possible to argue that a person should not have to wait 10 years before ILR will be considered (MIL 5.7.2).

Those successfully resisting deportation via an ECHR Art 8 claim receive leave under the IRs (MIL 13.4.4).

Restricted leave

Individuals who would have qualified for Refugee status or HP or leave as stateless persons but for committing international crimes that have caused their exclusion or otherwise behaving such as to be deemed a danger to the public will usually receive leave for periods of six months at a time. This includes individuals barred from the EUSSch as a "relevant excluded person" (MIL 11.7.7, 11.7.9.1) having regard to whether the individual's disposition is hostile to the fundamental values enshrined in the EU Treaties (human dignity, freedom, democracy, equality, the rule of law and respect for human rights including childrens' rights). The policy is subject to its own distinct regime as governed in the relevant guidance on *Restricted Leave*:

- The policy pursues the objective of public protection by monitoring working and living arrangements, upholding the rule of law internationally and
- cases will be reviewed regularly with a view to removal as soon as possible and only in exceptional circumstances will individuals on restricted leave ever become eligible for settlement or citizenship
- there will be restrictions on the right to work, which may be limited to voluntary work, or imposed so as to avoid exposure to vulnerable individuals having regard to previous behaviour, the roles identified by the Disclosure and Barring Service checks being a relevant benchmark – and a restriction on study, to emphasise the impermanence of stay and preserve public funds (having regard to previous conditions where the individual first received leave before RL was introduced on 2 September 2011)
- there will be no recourse to public funds unless there would otherwise be a risk of destitution or there are exceptional circumstances bearing in mind any childs' best interests, having regard to previous support arrangements, disposable assets and savings, and assistance from family members here and abroad
- there will be a condition as to residence: any change of address will have to be notified to the HO (possibly in advance), and they may be required to live in a specified area if their accommodation is publicly provided (though the more extreme requirements to notify the SSHD of short spells away was dropped in January 2022)
- there will be regular reporting restrictions (typically monthly)
- family members cannot be sponsored under the Rules: so any such family members must make applications in their own right, and where the principal of the family is granted restricted leave then the rest of the family should receive leave outside the rules
- regard should be had to any factors shown by cogent independent evidence such that the grant of RL will cause *real and unreasonable hardship* or have a detrimental effect on an existing health condition – regard must also be had to the best in interests of the child and the private and family life of the applicant and other family members
- if the individual travels abroad and leaves the Common Travel Area then their leave will normally lapse if granted for more than 6 months; consideration should be given to cancelling longer grants of leave if information as to a person's travel abroad comes to light
- one cannot duck RL by not claiming asylum, as the policy applies also to those who would be excluded from international protection if they applied
- the conditions and reasons behind the grant must be clearly explained in writing
- there will be active review for changes of circumstances (ranging from safer return possibilities to a child no longer being dependent on the principal) when extension applications are made (which are free and do not any particular form)
- permission is granted on a rigorous "no recourse to public funds" basis (see generally MIL 1.3.6.6 but limited to destitution risk and "exceptional circumstances"

Numerous challenges to the regimes for granting limited periods of leave to persons excluded from more generous residence regimes have been brought, and have largely failed: for example in Kardi [2014] EWCA Civ 934 the short grants of leave and reporting requirements (there, monthly ones), restriction on working (to general trader only) and residence (to notify changes of address) were all found proportionate on the facts of that case. However the Court was concerned as to the reasonableness of restricting his the Claimant's studies where this to prevented him from taking up a short English language course where removal was not imminent (MIL 5.7.2).

10.5.4 Travel documents

A person granted DL will be expected to travel on their national passport (on the basis that the grant is not normally based on any lack of protection by their national authorities). They can apply to the HO for a certificate of travel, but only if they have been unreasonably and formally (i.e. by letter) refused a national passport.

A refusal of a national passport will not be accepted as unreasonable where motivated by a failure to complete military service, a failure to provide evidence to confirm identity, or due to having a criminal record in their country.

Children need to apply for their own travel document. All applicants will now have to enrol their biometrics with the HO.

The GOV.UK website sets out the requirements for amendments to applications and travel documents. In virtually all cases a full further application form (and full fee) needs to be sent together with extrinsic evidence (e.g. on a change of name, the relevant legal documentation must be produced; if documents are lost or stolen, a police report must be provided). If details on the travel document that is issued are incorrect, and the HO are at fault, then there will be no further fee. The documents are not extendable, and if they expire whilst the holder is abroad, then it will be necessary to apply to the nearest British embassy or High Commission for advice.

There will be an investigation into the loss - the HO warns that applications to replace lost documents can take considerably longer than the usual period.

A person with DL should ensure they do not travel at a time when their leave is due to expire. They will not have any right of re-entry if they return after their leave has expired, as they will no longer benefit from Article 13 of the ILERO 2000 which permits travel and return whilst one holds current leave.

CHAPTER 11: European Union Law

11.1 Underlying legal principles, retained and saved free movement law and the EU Settlement Scheme

The UK left the EU on 31 January 2020. The Brexit transition period ended at 11pm on 31 December 2020, the Grace Period on 30 June 2021). Nevertheless EU legal principles that we adderss in 11.1-11.6 below remain relevant for ongoing cases. HJT has moved with the times and we now aim to describe the EU free movement and citizenship regime as a historic rather than present status. To summarise the continuing relevance of the following sections:

- 11.1 outlines the shift from EEA residence rights to the EU Settled Status Scheme (EUSSch).
- 11.2-11.6 summarises key EU law rights and concepts. For now aspects of the EEA Regs 2016 remain relevant because the EUSSch refers to them. And some knowledge of these areas will continue to be relevant: due to the need to establish 5 years lawful residence under EU law or some other gateway to permanent residence for those relying on historic residence for an outstanding/late EUSSch application, for outstanding appeals, and for determining when naturalisation is available
- 11.8 re *Excluding and removing EEA nationals from the UK*. These principles will continue to be applied to pre-2021 conduct for those successfully accessing the EUSSch
- 11.9 on EEA Rights of appeal, which remain relevant to refusals of applications made under the EEA Regs "pre-TP end" (before the end of the transition period)
- 11.10 Turkish Nationals – we give a brief summary of the Ankara Agreement regime for Turkish workers and businesspeople. MIL then concentrates on the modern Rules Appendix ECAA: Extension of Stay and Appendix ECAA Settlement which will remain relevant for years to come
- 11.11 The Charter of Fundamental Rights and General Principles of EU law –the Charter does not form part of retained EU law post-Brexit. However the General Principles developed in CJEU case law are retained EU law, in so far as extant pre-31 December 2020. So we will keep this section for now. The CFR may inform future CJEU decisions which will remain relevant to the decision making of the domestic courts
- Damages may be available for breaches of EU law (MIL 14.10)
- All of section 11.7 on the EU Settlement Scheme will remain significant well beyond 30 June 2021 as there is no deadline for certain family members to join their sponsors under it. Late applications under Appendix EU by those to whom the 30 June 2021 deadline applied will continue for the foreseeable future.
- Section 11.12 on S2 Healthcare Visitors. Any such applicants must have healthcare in place before 31 December 2020, so the pool of potential applicants will dwindle. But leave can be extended beyond the initial 6 months. So this section will remain relevant
- Section 11.13 on service providers from Switzerland will remain a fixture. 31 December 2025 is the end date for any periods of 90-day leave granted on this route

The changing basis of UK immigration law post-Brexit means Module 11 may undergo further restructuring in due course as the relative importance of its sections changes.

For the time being we are keeping the above structure for Module 11 whilst ensuring it is up-to-date. We use abbreviations throughout Module 7: **FM** = family member, **EFM** = extended family member, **EUSSch** = EU settled status scheme under domestic Rule generally, **EUSS** – EU settled status itself, **EUPSS** = EU pre-settled status, **WWA** = Withdrawal Agreement, **EEA Regs 2016** = The Immigration (European Economic Area) Regulations 2016. **Introduction and current context**

We are addressing European Union (EU) law (or European Economic Area (EEA) law, as it is to nationals of the EEA (and Switzerland) that the free movement regime applied). Free movement for EEA/Swiss nationals in the UK, and for UK nationals in the EEA/Switzerland ended with the transition period at 11pm on 31 December 2020, but some free movement rights and entitlements were preserved during the "grace period".

The founding purpose of the European Economic Community was to create a common market and guarantee the four freedoms: freedom of goods, capital, services and people. That purpose has been set out in various Treaty and subordinate provisions of EC and EU law since 1957 and is currently found in the Treaty on the Functioning of the European Union (TFEU) and Directive 2004/38/EC(the Citizens' Directive). These provisions allow EEA nationals and their family members to move freely among Member States to work and study – the self-sufficient benefitted too. These activities were the all important exercise of Treaty Rights. The rights are not wholly unrestricted, particularly regarding the ability to secure residence for family members, but they are powerful nonetheless.

In simple terms, EU law on free movement of persons was intended to, and usually did, make it as easy to move from Bilbao to London as it is from Birmingham to London. As such it was the antithesis of immigration control. EU law was designed to encourage movement; UK immigration law aims to restrict it.

Directive 2004/38/EC (29 April 2004) (the 'Citizens' Directive') contains the basis for the current rules of free movement within the EU.

Free movement rights also applied to the family members of EEA or Swiss nationals, whether those family members were EEA or Swiss nationals or not. Sometimes those rights would apply in the UK to the non-EEA national family members of UK nationals, where the UK national had exercised their free movement rights elsewhere in the EEA or Switzerland, and had returned to the UK.

At the end of transition, free movement ended. Following the end of the grace period at 11pm on 30 June 2021, we now find ourselves at the final stage of the four seminal periods created by Brexit.

1. **Pre 31 January 2020**: the EU Treaties and the Citizens Directive, largely transposed into UK law via the EEA Regs 2016, ruled supreme
2. **Transition period** following the UK's withdrawal from the EU at 11pm on 31 January 2020: the EU Treaties and the Citizens Directive (and EEA Regs) continued to apply, preserved in effect under the WWA (the Specialised Committee on Citizens' Rights oversees the effective implementation of the WA)
3. **Grace period** following the end of the transition period at 11pm on 31 December 2020 until 11pm on 30 June 2021: the EU Treaties and the Citizens Directive no longer applied. The UK transposition of the Directive – the Regs 2016 - was repealed at 11pm on 31 December 2020 but has been saved with modifications. Its modified provisions continued to apply to EEA/Swiss nationals who were resident lawfully in the UK before the end of transition, and to their family members until the end of the "grace period" (and beyond that if they applied under the EUSS before its end)
4. **Post-Grace period era**: no new applications for EEA residence documents can be made. Even some EUSSch routes begin to shut down (eg Surinder Singh, Zambrano: MIL 11.7.2.5). Appendix EU is the only basis for family members joining EU nationals here; whilst EU nationals themselves must have regularised their immigration status via their own distinct applications under Appendix EU
   - EU law is now effective only if it is retained EU law as defined in the European Union (Withdrawal) Act 2018 (see MIL. 8.1 for its interpretation)
   - The WWA will have the same feel as EU law traditionally had: a supreme legal document whose letter and spirit will need to be interpreted with EU principles in mind (appeals provide for a WWA ground)
   - This effectively requires it to either have been transposed into UK law as EU-derived domestic legislation or to have avoided repeal if it was originally directly effective: and in the migration regime, everything relevant to free movement has been repealed. Over time we will learn whether the courts think that Appendix EU contains any "EU-derived domestic legislation". A useful outline of what post-Brexit retained EU law is can be found in this article from Monckton Chambers.
   - Outside of immigration law, rights recognised in the case law may also survive: but for our purposes, para 6 of Sch 1 to the Immigration and Social Security Co-ordination (EU Withdrawal) Act 2020 is a pretty comprehensive wipe-out of that source:

CHAPTER 11: European Union Law

> 'Any other EU-derived rights, powers, liabilities, obligations, restrictions, remedies and procedures cease to be recognised and available in domestic law so far as—
> (a) they are inconsistent with, or are otherwise capable of affecting the interpretation, application or operation of, any provision made by or under the Immigration Acts (including, and as amended by, this Act), or
> (b) they are otherwise capable of affecting the exercise of functions in connection with immigration.'

5. The domestic law regime for EEA nationals, the EU settled status scheme (EUSSch), was fully available throughout periods (1)-(3). Following the general application deadline on 30 June 2021, applications under the EUSSch will only be accepted either by family members of existing EUSSch status holders and by those upgrading their status, from EUPSS to EUSS, or where the HO agrees that there were reasonable grounds to apply late (MIL 11.1A). The only alternative for EEA/Swiss citizens and their family members not fitting any of those cases is to apply for status under the domestic immigration routes.

Free movement rights

Under EU law, essentially the exercise of Treaty ('*free movement*') Rights generated residence rights; as did the possession of an EU Member States' citizenship. Brexit terminated this regime: any doubt being resolved by Shindler [2023] EUECJ C-501/21P holding that withdrawal from the EU was a sovereign choice and ended the possession of Member State nationality and its associated rights.

- This might either have been because the principal applicant was an EU national themselves (or a British citizen treated as such via exercising Treaty Rights in another EEA state). Or a family member might have relied on the EU national, who was in that sense a 'sponsor', to use a popular term from domestic immigration law.
- No application was generally needed to generate the rights, which existed by operation of law for EEA/Swiss nationals exercising treaty rights, and their direct family members, though it would of course normally be essential to physically reach the UK, to show one's status once here. EFMs, by contrast, did not have such automatic residence rights. They only benefited once the SSHD exercised discretion in their favour to issue a residence document. Both Appendix EU and the WWA run with this thinking, making the issue of a residence document pre-11pm on 31 December 2020 critical.
- Over time, many new classes of EU right were identified in the case law of the CJEU, ranging from citizenship-driven rights to different derivative rights.
- The free movement scheme ended with the transition period. However there are some transitional protections flowing from the WWA, which we address below.

The EUSSch (see MIL 11.7 below) is based on the same EU system. But there are some differences.

- It is a domestic Immigration Rule route and so to benefit, you have to make an application: there are no inherent rights.
- Applicants can be granted settled status (EUSS) or pre-settled status (EUPSS).
- And whilst the same idea of an EEA 'sponsor' for family members is required, the trigger is *not* that person's exercise of Treaty Rights, but simply the fact of residence in the UK. So to that degree it is much more generous than the free movement regime. Anyone residing on UK soil, however briefly, by 11pm on 31 December 2020, could join the EUSS system
- The scheme has had numerous amendments, aimed at capturing the development of free movement and citizenship rights. Sometimes these changes have been catching up with decisions from 2006 to the inception of the EUSSch; others have been necessitated by case law during the EUSSch's existence. By the end of 2020 it was difficult to find people who would have protection under the EEA Regs 2016 who lacked a route into the EUSS. At least if they were aware of the need to do so and properly advised (see 11.1A re late applications). The Migration Observatory has written reports on the likelihood of individuals not learning of their rights in time: see eg the report *Unsettled status*.
- The EUSSch has a sunset provision itself. To derive rights under it, one has to have arrived before the end of the transitional period ie before 11pm on 31 December 2020. Or to have been

within (or born from) a relevant relationship that was formed by that date. The general deadline for applications was 30 June 2021 although some people who can apply later.

One of the most significant aspects of EU law residence rights has always been its relatively strong protection against expulsion (MIL 11.8). Successive UK government measures have lowered the threshold for deportation for those who are not EU nationals or their relevant family members. Domestic law provides that only "unduly harsh" consequences for partners and children, or "very compelling" circumstances, will save someone convicted of more serious offences from deportation. But under EU law there are much stronger protections.

- One feature of the post-Brexit system is that conduct by EEA citizens and their family members, committed, after 31 December 2020 will attract the domestic *'conducive to the public good' regime*. The distinction had already been drawn under the Suitability provisions of Appendix EU for the EUSS which provide for the domestic regime to apply to post-transitional period conduct. Under The Citizens' Rights (Restrictions of Rights of Entry and Residence) (EU Exit) Regulations 2020, those protected by the Citizens Rights provisions of the WWA will continue to benefit from the protections set out in the EEA Regs 2016 (Reg 2(1))
- This protection applies to those granted leave under Appendix EU and entry clearance under Appendix EU (FP) or may in future have a right to such leave; and to those protected by the EEA Regs 2016 at the time a decision to remove them was made (Reg 2(2))
- The Schedule to the Restrictions of Rights of Entry and Residence Regs then retains various provisions of the EEA Regs 2016 (including Reg 27, which contains the essential protections on proportionality grounds) in order to continue to bestow such protection

The UK left the EU on 31 January 2020 under the WWA. Art 126 mandated a *"transition or implementation period"*, beginning when the UK left the EU and ending on 31 December 2020.

Until 11pm on 31 December 2020 the UK was within that transitional period (or implementation period: some of the new legislation refers to 'IP completion date' to signify that era's end)). Until its end, EU law continued to apply in the UK by way of savings provisions and retained EU law.

A trade deal between the UK and EU was reached in late December 2020 and the UK entered its new relationship with the EU on 1 January 2021. EEA and Swiss nationals and their families generally had until 30 June 2021 to apply for status under the EUSSch (so long as the relevant EEA/Swiss national was here before the end of 2020 and the relevant relationships existed before then) (MIL 11.7.2.5 sets out other deadlines for specific categories via the *"required date"* definitions). The legal foundation for the June 2021 longstop is Art 18(1)(b) of the WWA:

> *the deadline for submitting the application shall not be less than 6 months from the end of the transition period, for persons residing in the host State before the end of the transition period.*

Loyal to the WWA, the Citizens' Rights (Application Deadline and Temporary Protection) (EU Exit) Regulations 2020 (the "Grace Period Regulations") introduced a Temporary Protection regime for the first half of 2021. These provide that

- The Appendix EU regime generally ended for main applicants and their family members with no other leave on 30 June 2021 (Reg 2)
- The period from the end of the transitional period until then (ie 11pm on 31 December 2020 to 30 June 2021) was a **grace period** and some provisions of the EEA Regs 2016 remained in force to secure their position (those specified in Regs 5-10, including protections for accessing benefits and public services: Reg 11)
- So both EEA nationals and their family members living in the UK lawfully under the EEA Regs 2016 since before the end of the transition period were protected - including those who held permanent residence in the five years before 31 December 2020 (Reg 3) (and did not require leave to enter or remain: Reg 12)

CHAPTER 11: European Union Law

- Those who applied before the application deadline continue to enjoy the protection of aspects of the EEA Regs 2016 pending their application being determined or any appeal rights being exhausted (Reg 4)
- The burden of proof as to whether protection arose under the EEA Regs 2016 will be on the applicant (Reg 13)
- The legislative method for addressing outstanding applications under the EEA Regs 2016 is a little mind-bending. First off, those Regs were repealed from 1 January 2021. However, for those making applications during the Grace Period or with a reasonable excuse thereafter, that repeal is suspended. Instead, each individual provision is given effect either intact, or with various modifications:
  - So first one must find the relevant provision: imagine we were focussing on "*right of admission*" which inhabits Reg 11. We might remember that one used to be able to prove one's admission right at the border if lacking an EEA family permit
  - Then one checks The Citizens' Rights (Application Deadline and Temporary Protection) (EU Exit) Regulations 2020, Part 3, to see if any changes are made: you can just read through the list of individual regulations there
  - Admission is addressed under "*Provisions relating to residence rights*". When we get to Reg 6(a), we see that whilst Reg 11 of the EEA Regs 2016 is partly preserved, at 6(a)(iii) we discover it is to be read "*with the modifications that … paragraph (4) were omitted*".
  - As Reg 11(4) was the proviso for entry without a family permit, we can then deduce that that aspect of the old regime has been abolished

The WWA represents the agreement between the UK and the European Union for how the residence rights of EU nationals here (and our nationals in the EU) survive Brexit. Given the labyrinthine structure of Appendix EU, experienced practitioners often refer to the WWA first, and then, having identified a relevant right, only then look to see if they can locate it in the Appendix. It also contains procedural protections, of which the following are salient:

"(e) the host State shall ensure that any administrative procedures for applications are smooth, transparent and simple, and that any unnecessary administrative burdens are avoided'
(f) application forms shall be short, simple, user friendly and adapted to the context of this Agreement; applications made by families at the same time shall be considered together …
(o) the competent authorities of the host State shall help the applicants to prove their eligibility and to avoid any errors or omissions in their applications; they shall give the applicants the opportunity to furnish supplementary evidence and to correct any deficiencies, errors or omissions; ...
(r) the applicant shall have access to judicial and, where appropriate, administrative redress procedures in the host State against any decision refusing to grant the residence status. The redress procedures shall allow for an examination of the legality of the decision, as well as of the facts and circumstances on which the proposed decision is based. Such redress procedures shall ensure that the decision is not disproportionate."

From 1 October 2023 any claim governed by the *Civil Procedure Rules* (ie high court rather than Tribunal matters) relating to a breach of citizens' rights under the withdrawal agreements must be notified to the Independent Monitoring Authority.

Difference between EEA free movement and EUSSch

Non-permanent residence documentation issued under the 2016 EEA Regs in relation to rights to reside were a mere snapshot of confirmed rights at the time of application. They did not confer rights (merely confirming that the SSHD recognised their existence at the decision date). When conditions were no longer fulfilled, the right to reside ceased to exist despite the holder remaining in possession of the document.

By contrast, by applying for EUPSS, EU nationals (and their family members) obtain leave to remain.

- As with the Immigration Rules generally, leave continues until its stated end date unless the HO takes a positive decision to curtail or cancel that leave
- Leave is not automatically affected merely because one's circumstances change

- Para EU4 in Appendix EU requires EUPSS -holders to continue to meet the eligibility requirements they met at the date of application, or that, if they do not, they meet alternative eligibility requirements for EUPSS (cf the automatic extension of EUPSS, MIL 11.7.2).
- A3.4(c) in Annex 3 to Appendix EU provides for curtailment of EUPSS where the conditions of leave are no longer met. Although this set of provisions may be stricter than envisaged in the WWA, it remains a fact that EUPSS is not simply lost by its holder no longer meeting the eligibility requirements. Active steps would need to be taken by the HO to curtail it. We will have to see how this works out in practice.
- Always remember: under Article 13(4) of the WWA, the UK '*may not impose any limitations or conditions for obtaining, retaining or losing residence rights*'.

Rights to reside and benefit entitlements after Brexit

EU nationals arriving for the first time from 1 January 2021 need to obtain leave to enter and remain as per the European Union (Withdrawal Act) 2020.This is the case unless they have a EEA/Swiss family member who can be their "relevant sponsor" for an application under the EUSSch as their "joining family member". See further MIL 11.7.

Benefits and housing entitlements during the transition period and the grace period

EU law, which applied in the UK before the UK left the EU on 31 January 2020, continued to apply until the end of the transition period by operation of sections 1A and 1B of the European Union (Withdrawal Act) 2018. Because of this, holders of EUPSS who exercised treaty rights were still able to prove their entitlements to benefits and housing by showing their continued exercise of treaty rights.

The same applied during the grace period for EUPSS holders who exercised treaty rights in the UK before the end of the transition period, due to the preservation of rights and saving of most of the 2016 Regulations by the Grace Period Regulations.

An announcement of 6 August 2021 stated that the rights, not only of those who applied before the deadline, but also those with accepted late applications awaiting an outcome are to be protected (see MIL 11.7.9.2).

Vulnerable EUSS applicants

- Community organisations, funded by the HO to assist vulnerable persons with EUSS applications, have raised concerns about planning in this regard, particularly in relation to children in care, DV victims and those of no fixed abode, who face extra barriers in applying. A list of these organisations is found under EU Settlement Scheme: community support for vulnerable citizens.

11.1A Missing the deadline for EUSS applications

Generally speaking, any EU nationals and their family member who did not apply under the EUSSch by 30 June 2021, will need to apply for alternative leave to remain under the IRs based on family/private life ties (MIL 5 and 6) or the business/work/study routes (MIL 7). Those routes have been generally expanded to accommodate them. Otherwise they will become overstayers, unless they are eligible but can show '*reasonable grounds*' for their failure to apply in time. From 9 August 2023 applications that are deemed not to show reasonable grounds will be treated as invalid rather than receiving a substantive refusal (EU9(e)). So there will be no right of administrative review or appeal. The Statement of Changes HC1496 reassures applicants that validity will not be re-assessed if already confirmed as valid by the issuing of a Certificate of Application. There may be a legal challenge to these arrangements, as the WWA guarantees a right of judicial redress.

Note that different deadlines apply to certain categories of persons (MIL 11.7.1 gives a full table).

CHAPTER 11: European Union Law

Examples of "reasonable grounds" in the EUSS guidance include:

- **Children** whose parent, guardian or local authority fails to apply on their behalf (actual detail of the reasons for the oversight irrelevant)
- People in **abusive or controlling relationships** who were prevented from applying: no mandatory evidence - lack of access to documents, person's self-awareness of their situation, immigration history, HO records. Ongoing cohabitation with abuser is not conclusive as to the abusive nature of the relationship
- **Victims of modern slavery**: if recognised as such via NRM, that suffices; otherwise NRM referral will be considered. The consideration of reasonable grounds need not await NRM decision. Relevant factors will be immigration history, length of delay in applying and reasons for this, as well as barriers to document access, and self-awareness
- Those lacking **physical or mental capacity** to apply (evidence "*may include*" formal arrangements eg Power of Attorney, doctors/professionals' letters, applicant's letter "*explaining situation and authorising an appropriate third party to act on their behalf*", DWP evidence of care role: letter re medical condition from health professional, or carer/lawyer/appropriate 3rd party). This ground would cover the applicant's dependents too
- Serious **medical condition or significant medical treatment** (eg bed-bound or hospitalised, or "*unable to perform day-to-day tasks in the months before, or around the time of, the deadline applicable*")
- **Childbirth** ("*a difficult child birth or where a new-born child is in need of medical treatment*")
- **Other compelling practical or compassionate reasons**: eg no internet access, had limited computer literacy or limited English language skills or had been living overseas, lack of permanent accommodation, complex needs, Covid impact, failed to obtain paper form in time, "overlooked the need to apply or they overlooked the deadline" due to personal circumstances – evidence could include information from the person themselves, or from charity or DWP
- **Compelling practical or compassionate reasons** might include the pandemic and its impact on nationality and identity documents
- **Holders of EEA documentation** which expires after the deadline and who can convince UKVI that they were not aware of the need to apply

Note that:

- Under the guidance, those accepting support under the Voluntary Returns Scheme will be notified of the EUSSch. Failure to apply then will normally rule out acceptance of a subsequent application
- Those encountered via immigration enforcement measures from 1 July 2021 will receive a notice to which they must respond with an EUSS application with a reasonable excuse within 28 days. Enforcement will normally be suspended in meantime
- The guidance, somewhat counterintuitively, does not permit reasonable grounds to be found where an application is lodged post deadline when a previous in-time application was made (but it does permit consideration of reasonable grounds in relation to a *second* out of time application. ILPA is currently asking for clarification. UKVI stated in a response to *Here for Good's* letter of 18 January 2022 that the mere fact that an application was made following an in-time application's refusal *would not normally* constitute reasonable grounds for an extension of time.

Before 9 August 2023, if the HO did not accept "reasonable grounds" were established there should have been a reasoned eligibility refusal. With a right of administrative review and/or an appeal to follow.

11.1B Immigration options for EEA/Swiss nationals newly arriving from 2021

The loss of EU migrant labour able to easily service the UK labour market required new immigration routes. The new, simplified immigration system, which applies to new EU arrivals as well as non-EU nationals from 1 January 2021, was introduced, largely on 1 December 2020 (for work and study routes). Another Brexit impact was the need to recognise family migration routes for those now on a long-term route to ILR in the UK. Thus from 31 December 2020 EUPSS holders and some Turkish workers/businesspeople were classed as eligible Sponsors under Appendix FM.

The Skilled Worker route was adjusted to remove the cap on numbers, lower skilled work levels, and end the "cooling off" period which prevented a return within a year of last working here (see MIL7.3.1-7.3.3). Furthermore all the business, work and study routes are available to EEA nationals (MIL 7.1.1).

- All the pre-existing business immigration routes (eg representatives of an overseas business, innovators and start-ups) are of course also available now to EU nationals
- The Global Talent Scheme (MIL 7.2.3) is now open to EEA and Swiss nationals
- The only 'low-skilled' worker categories will consist of an expanded seasonal agricultural scheme (see Module 7, section 7.5.6) and some Tier 5 categories (see MIL 7.5)
- For visits of up to 6 months, EEA and Swiss nationals will be 'non-visa nationals', meaning visit visa applications need not be made before travelling.
    o The same advice as to other non-visa nationals applies. Visit visa conditions must be understood: when passing through immigration control you are effectively being granted a visit on specific conditions. Sometimes it's a good idea to apply for entry clearance in advance (MIL 3.2.4).
    o Prior to 6 October 2021, EEA/Swiss nationals aiming to qualify as joining family members could not switch into the EUSSch from being visitors under paras EU11A and EU14A – except for marriage visitors who had married their sponsor
    o On 21 July 2021 a temporary concession was added to the main EUSS guidance, relaxing the general bar on applications from visitors as JFMs. This covered those who entered the UK between 1 January 2021 and 30 June 2021 with 6 months' leave, or thereafter with less than 6 months' leave, so long as it expired before 30 December 2021. Plus those applying late with reasonable grounds who held visitor leave at the time of application
    o From 6 October 2021, the restriction on JFMs applying while they are visitors was deleted from Appendix EU paras EU11A and EU14A. So the "visitor" definition's exemption for marriage visitors was also deleted, now being redundant. But do bear in mind that anyone who enters the UK as a visitor with a view to then applying as a JFM could be seen as having engaged in deception. Because the "genuine visitor" requirements would rule out entry for that purpose. Presumably, the removal of the restriction is intended to benefit those visitors whose intentions changed post-arrival
- Biometrics will be requested from EEA and Swiss citizens in the form of a digital photo submitted via a smartphone app, while the current system will continue to apply to other applicants: the UK has moved to a '*digital by default*' paradigm by which one's eVisa is accessed via the ID Check app, see eg *Your immigration status: an introduction for EU, EEA and Swiss citizens*
- EEA and Swiss ID cards were accepted at the border until 1 October 2021. Thereafter ID cards won't be enough.
    o One will also need (rEU11A(b)-(g)) entry clearance as a Service Provider from Switzerland), a grant or pending application under the EUSSch (or any such equivalent status issued by an Island), an EUSS family permit, a frontier worker permit, and S2 Healthcare visitors
    o See the Guidance *Visiting the UK as an EU, EEA or Swiss citizen Entering the UK under the EU Settlement Scheme and EU Settlement Scheme family permit* and r11A and 11B (Part 1 of the Immigration Rules)
    o So whilst those with EUSSch applications pending are included, those applying as "joining family members" (i.e. people without continuous UK residence starting pre-end 2020) are not included (r11A(c))

11.1C Current status of EEA and Swiss nationals

The HO advice to employers was that until 30 June 2021, EEA and Swiss nationals could prove their right to work in the UK by producing their passport or national ID card. The page warns

> You have a duty not to discriminate against EU, EEA or Swiss citizens. You cannot require them to show you their status under the [EUSSch] until after 30 June 2021.

Employers anxiously awaited news of the new "*right to work*" regime for EEA nationals. This was left vague during the Grace Period (the first half of 2021). The *Employer's guide to right to work checks* states that from 1 July 2021 an EEA or Swiss national passport or national ID card is no longer proof of right to work.

Employers are now required to check the "share code" for EUSS online status unless the individual has a frontier worker permit, a service provider of Switzerland visa, or another visa. If the share code is not available, and there is a pending application made pre-end Grace Period, then a Certificate of Application (CoA) issued within the last 6 months, plus a positive verification from the Employer Checking Service, will suffice.

Note that the guidance for landlords, NHS and DWP also provides for CoAs for applications lodged before the deadline to be accepted as evidence of rights and entitlements.

The rights of those who applied before the end of the Grace Period, but who did not exercise Treaty Rights before the end of the transition period, are not protected under the Grace Period Regulations while their application is pending. Nor are those who have applied late and whose application is pending.

However, a government announcement of 6 August 2021 states that even the latter enjoy the protection of their rights. It is not clear at the time of writing whether the legal footing of this guarantee will be achieved via an amendment of the Regulations, or whether it will be purely policy-based.

The Guidance confirms that there is no requirement for retrospective checks on EEA citizens who entered into employment up to 30 June 2021 so long as adequate checks were made when they were taken on.

So, technically, an EEA/Swiss national who arrived after the end of the transition period (without any continuous residence pre-end transition period) and who had their passport or ID card checked by their employer before 1 July 2021 would be unlikely to be picked up by this system for as long as they remain in their employment and their employer chooses (as is their right) not to conduct a retrospective check, despite the fact they are not eligible for the EUSSch. The right advice here would be that it is not in their interests to let this situation continue. To do so is likely to impact their future UK immigration applications. They should ideally leave the UK voluntarily as soon as possible and seek advice regarding alternative application categories to lawfully return.

There may need to be litigation as to whether the Grace Period Regulations are more restrictive than the WWA. Article 18(3) of the latter appears to protect the rights of anyone with a pending EUSS application. UKVI policy has at times been more lenient than the letter of the Grace Period Regulations, particularly since the announcement of temporary protection on 6 August 2021 mentioned above.

11.1.1 EEA Member States

The EEA (European Economic Area) is made up of the EU member countries plus Iceland, Norway and Liechtenstein. Switzerland has a bilateral agreement with the EU adding it to the free movement regime. Nationals of all 31 countries enjoy free movement around the EEA and Switzerland.

The EU member states are:

Austria	France	Malta
Belgium	Germany	Netherlands
Bulgaria	Greece	Poland
Croatia	Hungary	Portugal
Cyprus	Ireland	Romania
Czechia	Italy	Slovakia
Denmark	Latvia	Slovenia
Estonia	Lithuania	Spain
Finland	Luxembourg	Sweden

It is important to remember that free movement rights are enjoyed by those moving or who have moved within the EEA or Switzerland, so will not normally be enjoyed by nationals of a country in whose territory they remain (even if they are dual nationals of another of the other countries, see 11.3.2 on 'dual nationals' below).

11.1.2 Interaction of UK and EU law

11.1.2.1 Rights not privileges

There was a very important difference of principle between UK immigration law and EU freedom of movement rights. In UK law, if a foreign national wishes to come to the UK, they must first make an application and await a positive decision. There is no pre-existing 'right' to enter the UK. Entry and stay in the UK is contingent on it being permitted by the HO: see section 1(2) of the Immigration Act 1971.

The position was very different under EU law. Certain individuals had a right to reside in the UK by virtue of their citizenship of another EEA country and their economic activities, or through their family relationship with such a person. The UK was bound by EU law to recognise and promote this right.

A great deal flowed from this distinction between inherent rights and discretionary privileges, and for those schooled in UK immigration law many aspects of EEA free movement law always seemed counterintuitive. The fact that family permit applications were free, that EEA documents (i.e. family permits and residence documents) were unnecessary for the exercise of free movement rights, and that Immigration Officers could not stamp the passports of EEA nationals were all natural consequences of the nature of pre-existing free movement rights in EU law.

Recent governments had decided to make free movement rights a major focus for its policy of reducing migration into the UK. Consequently, the EEA Regs 2006, the first domestic expression of the Citizens Directive regime, were repeatedly amended, sometimes controversially so, to tinker with the available rights. The EEA Regs 2016 wre effective from 1 February 2017) – they were also amended to take account of CJEU developments. Whilst the EU Commission were unhappy with some aspects of the amendments only some these issues were be resolved before the UK left the EU. Sometimes case law required the EEA Regs 2016 to be amended too, usually favourably to migrants.

The central purpose of the Citizens' Directive was to 'simplify and strengthen the right of free movement and residence of all Union citizens' (Recital 3). The HO, for example, were suspected of requiring far more evidence be provided than was strictly lawful or necessary (see Article 8 and 10 of the Citizens' Directive) when EEA nationals and their family members sought to document their status. That mindset was often shared by the Tribunal, who expect to see documentary evidence in support of every aspect of an EEA claim. Indeed, in AG Germany [2007] UKAIT 00075 the Tribunal stated:

applicants and appellants seeking to rely on EEA rights ... unless able to point to a specific provision of Community law limiting the need to produce evidence ... must expect that a failure to produce relevant evidence may well mean that the decision in their case will be a negative one, based on their failure to substantiate that they have any EEA right.

Those refused EEA entry and residence documents may still have a right of appeal to the FTT. In the past the advice was that it would make more sense in terms of time and cost to apply again with better evidence, than to appeal. Now, where, for example in the case of EFM applications for their first residence card or family permit, the opportunity to re-apply no longer exists, and the only access point to the EU Settlement Scheme (EUSSch) is to possess such a document, the advice in those cases must be to pursue the appeal.

11.1.2.2 Implementation of EU law

These were the general principles:

- EU law, in the form of the Treaties and relevant Directives, principally the Citizens' Directive which consolidated most pre-existing European legislation, was the foundation of residence rights – note that the relevant Treaty will be the Consolidated Version of the Treaty on the Functioning of the European Union (TFEU), sometimes known as the Lisbon Treaty (older cases may refer to previous numberings of particular Treaty rights)

- Such rights were found in the EU's legislation which put into effect the Treaty's objectives, for example the Citizens' Directive, regarding most free movement rights
- And in the Articles of the Treaty itself – for example the rights of EU nationals to retain the benefits of their citizenship, shown by the Zambrano principle
- In UK law, EEA free movement rights are laid out in the Immigration (European Economic Area) Regulations 2016 (which we refer to below as the 'EEA Regs 2016'). These were *repealed* at 11pm on 31 December 2020 but *saved* for certain individuals with modifications. Those are the Regs to which we refer throughout MIL 11. The EEA Regs were designed to implement the changes to EU free movement law that were introduced by the Citizens' Directive
- However, EU law, in the form of the Treaties, the Citizens' Directive and the decisions of the Court of Justice of the European Union (CJEU – previously the European Court of Justice), were directly effective in the UK, and would therefore trump any contrary provision or practice. This was often called the Marleasing principle
- Citizens rights post-Brexit were of course agreed upon between the UK and EU in the WWA, on which the EUSSch is based. Additional rights (not appearing in Appendix EU or UKVI policy) may be found there. In the EU law era people could derive rights from the Directive which might be more expansive than those found in the EEA Regs 2016
- UKVI Guidance on EEA residence rights and application procedures is in the EEA section of the Immigration Staff Guidance. This sets out the HO's way of thinking about EEA law
- However, where the EEA Regs (or UKVI guidance) were more restrictive than the principles they supposedly enshrine, then it would be the original EU version which would triumph
- The other side of the coin is that the UK's implementation of EEA law might occasionally be more generous than that of the EU. The EU does not prohibit a more generous approach than its own provisions. This is reflected in decisions like AP and FP [2007] UKAIT 00048 re dependent family members and Rose [2011] UKUT 276 (Rose found that the EEA Regs created a discretion to treat EFMs as full family members, and thereby benefitting from the protections against deportation afforded the latter, even though this was not a consequence of the Citizens' Directive)
- If a client fitted into the terms of the EEA Regs, their rights therein should be respected. But those residence rights were only European (as opposed to domestic) ones if found in the Directive itself or in the case law of the CJEU.

Top Tip

For most practical purposes, mainly to understand clients' immigration histories, it is important to understand the key principle by which EU law operated in the UK. The EEA Regs provided a reasonable exposition of the rights set out in the Citizens' Directive. But one would always need to check whether there were more extensive rights in the Directive itself. There could then be a long battle ahead through the appeals system to test the theory. Going forwards, the relationship between the EUSSch and the WWA may have a similar "feel".

11.1.2.3 EU law: General Principles and fundamental rights

Article 6 (2) TFEU provides:

The Union shall respect fundamental rights, as guaranteed by the European Convention for the Protection of Fundamental Freedoms signed in Rome …. And as they result from the constitutional traditions common to the Member States, as general principles of Community law.

Whilst the EU is not yet a signatory to the ECHR, its own EU Charter of Fundamental Rights (CFR) became part of the EU Treaties on 1 December 2009. The CFR contains rights that often equate to rights found in the European Convention on Human Rights, and some additional ones (MIL 11.11). Note that the CFR itself does not form part of retained EU law.

There also exist General Principles of European Union law: for example the right to good administration (YS [2014] EUECJ C-141/12) and the proportionality principle: EU rights may be circumscribed for reasons of public policy, but national measures adopted on that subject had to be be necessary and appropriate to attain the objective pursued.

Unlike the CFR, the General Principles are retained EU law where they have been clearly recognised in case law before 11pm on 31 December 2020. Watch this space for some interesting legal developments going forwards as the UK courts try and work out the relationship between the CFR and the General Principles.

11.1.2.4 Choice between using free movement or the Immigration Rules

Generally speaking family members had a 5-year route to PR or ILR meaning there was nothing to gain by relying on the IRs rather than EEA rights. However those with PR could bring children under 18 into the UK under IR297 thus gaining ILR. There were various other advantages: no English language or strict financial criteria, the domestic public policy did not regime, and children could join under the EEA regime at any age whilst still dependent.

From 1 December 2020 Appendix FM has permitted EUPSS holders to sponsor family members (MIL 6.1.8).

A person's presence here under UK law would not detract from rights they also had under the EU law. In some cases, it could be appropriate to pursue both simultaneously (e.g. an application as a parent under Appendix FM and an application for a Derivative Residence Card (DRC)). These provisions were not mutually exclusive. The DRC application was cheaper, but the parent application provided for a clear route to settlement (which the DRC did not).

Where necessary, a person relying on their EU right to reside could apply for leave to remain via the partner category of Appendix FM. Eg a dependent child of an EU national whose residence rights were based on ongoing dependency might marry someone person present and settled in the UK who now supports them. This might terminate their dependency, undermining their EU right to reside. So a domestic route would be more appropriate.

There was a time when the HO wrote of 'election' of the EEA route as opposed to the domestic law one: but it was difficult to see how anyone could contract out of fundamental EU rights. So a person whose immigration history does not overtly feature EU rights might nevertheless have been exercising them, which should always be borne in mind when assessing EUSSch eligibility.

11.1.2.5 Legal and procedural framework for EEA free movement – law, policy, forms, validity

The main sources of law and policy were.

- Immigration (European Economic Area) Regulations 2016 ("EEA Regs 2016") (NB: these applied for the duration of the Grace Period, and to applications made before that Period. The Regs are saved from the version immediately applicable before the end of transition (that consolidated version being available in HJT's OISC exam resource booklet) with modifications for EEA/Swiss nationals resident lawfully since before the end of transition. The savings and modifications are found in the Grace Period Regs. See 11.1.1 for how the system works
- EEA Immigration Staff Guidance
- EEA case law, summarised by UKVI: EEA Immigration Staff Guidance: EEA case law and appeals and available via other free case law sources, such as Bailii and UT decisions
- Citizens' Directive 2004/38
- Consolidated Version of the Treaty on the Functioning of the European Union (TFEU)

We list open access sources here - legal subscription databases have the great advantage of providing up-to-date consolidated versions which track amendments over time.

Application forms and validity of applications in EEA free movement applications

These were, but are no longer, available on the general UKVI forms page and set out whether there is also an online version and who was is eligible to apply online.

CHAPTER 11: European Union Law

- Form EEA(QP) was for an EEA or Swiss national applying for a registration certificate
- Form EEA(FM) for a Regulation 7 (direct family member), and Form EEA(FM) for a Regulation 8 (EFM) residence card
- Form EEA(PR) was used by an EEA or Swiss national to apply for a document certifying permanent residence, or by a non-EEA or non-Swiss national family member of an EEA or Swiss national to apply for a permanent residence card
- DRF1 for a Derivative Residence Card
- Various ECAA forms for the Turkish Association Agreement

Note that the various CR forms for Croatians and their family members were withdrawn upon restrictions on Croatian nationals becoming inapplicable from 1 July 2018. Croatians henceforth applied on the mainstream forms above.

Family permit applications remained free. The application would normally be made online, but a hard copy application would have been on form VAF5.

On 1 February 2017, the EEA Regs 2016 made the use of forms mandatory (Reg 21), by providing for invalidity where a specified form is not used (Reg 21(4)). Before that date, a simple covering letter with enclosed evidence could be used. Thereafter applications not on specified forms could proceed only if the decision maker circumstances outside the applicant's control prevailed.

On 24 July 2018, Reg 21 was amended in effect to require that all documentation is sent with the application rather than allowing that further evidence is later 'joined' (Reg 21(2)). Also on that date Reg 21(4A) was added which provides for invalidity where the applicant is subject to a removal decision under Reg 23(6)(b), a deportation order under Reg 32(3) or an exclusion order under Reg 23(5).

11.2 Who benefited from EU rights?

Below, we take the following approach to explaining the effect of the freedom of movement provisions:

- Who benefited from EU Treaty rights including free movement?
- What were those rights?
- When could those rights be removed?

Having dealt with EEA nationals who would have benefited fully from Treaty Rights, we go on to look at the rights of beneficiaries of lesser arrangements — Accession State workers and the Association Agreements

Top Tip

When working out if a client had an EEA solution to their needs, one would look at

Their position within the EEA Regs: were they are a qualified person or a family member

The type of residence under the EEA Regs that that status would have given them (e.g. extended, retained, permanent)

Had they already attained permanent residence because of the historic enjoyment of Treaty Rights

Whether there was any discretion involved before a residence card should have been issued

The exercise or engagement of Treaty rights underpinned EEA residence rights. Eg because

- the EEA national was themselves exercising Treaty rights giving a right to residence or permanent residence for themselves and their relevant family members under the Citizens' Directive

©HJT

- the EEA national enjoyed the right to European Union citizenship which they could not be compelled to forgo (because Article 20 of the Treaty proclaims that Citizens of the Union shall enjoy the rights and be subject to the duties provided for in the Treaties: demanding departure from the UK would undermine that benefit)
- the family member benefited from a relationship with an EEA national who was exercising rights recognised by the Treaty but not found within the Citizens' Directive or the EEA Regs, eg where an overriding Treaty objective, eg free movements of citizens, or freedom of movement for workers/service providers, would otherwise be hampered

We deal with each in more detail later on, but for now it is useful to have an overview of the main categories.

11.2.1 Residence rights in summary

11.2.1.1 Residence rights under the Citizens Directive and the Immigration (EEA) Regulations 2016

The rights of residence under the Directive and the Regs were as follows (we give references to the EEA Regs 2016 as a reference point):

Qualified persons and their family members – "extended" rights of residence – Reg 14

- as a person who was *economically active* as a jobseeker, worker or providing services, or who was *studying or self sufficient* (all 'qualified persons' as set out at Reg 6)
- those individuals had the right to enjoy the presence of various relatives such as *family members* their spouses and dependent children and relatives in the ascending line as of right (Reg 7), though students only had the right to have their spouses and dependent children here; and
- they had the right to have a discretionary consideration of whether their *EFMs* (unmarried partners, more remote dependent relatives who have been dependent or cohabiting with them in the past and present, and a person for whom the care of the EEA national is essential) should be allowed to reside with them here (Reg 8)

Permanent residents and their family members – Reg 15

- as a person who *was* present in one of those capacities but who gained *permanent residence* after five years' exercise of Treaty rights (Reg 15(1)(a)) or because they *ceased activity* in relevant circumstances (Reg 15(1)(c) read with Reg 5)
- as the family member of a person who had themselves *lived here for five years under the EEA Regs*, either consistently as the family member of a qualified person or down to a combination of entitlements, e.g. family membership followed by retaining a right of residence, who thus gained *permanent residence* (Reg 15(1)(b) and (f))

Retained rights of residence – Reg 10

- as the family member of a person of an EEA national *worker or self-employed person* residing with them when they died, the EEA national having previously resided here for two years or dying because of an accident at work or occupational disease, who thus gained *permanent residence* (Reg 15(1)(e))
- as a person who has *retained a right of residence* because he or she *was* the family member of an EEA national who *was* economically active as a jobseeker, worker or providing services, or who was studying or self sufficient, or who was permanently resident here, specifically as the child who was in education when their EEA parent died or left the UK and their primary carer (Reg 10(3), (4))
- as the family member who had resided here for the year prior to the death of an EEA national who was a qualified person or who had permanent residence (Reg 10(2))
- as the spouse/CP whose marriage/partnership was terminated subject to it having endured three years' including a year of residence here, or had custody or access rights to their child,

or whose relationship ended in particularly difficult circumstances including domestic violence (Reg 10(5))

Derivative rights of residence – Reg 16

- as a person who *enjoyed European citizenship*, the benefits of which they *could not be compelled to lose* – these people enjoyed the right to reside and to be accompanied by their primary carer, for example where they are self sufficient here (as in the Chen case, addressed domestically in Reg 16(2)) or when the departure of their primary carer would compel their own departure from the European Union and thus nullify their EU citizenship rights (those holding Zambrano rights would require residence for their primary carers too: Reg 16(5))
- as the *child of a person formerly exercising Treaty rights*, and as the primary carer of such a child (as in the Ibrahim and Teixeira cases, addressed domestically in Reg 16)

11.2.1.2 Residence rights found in the Treaty but not in the Citizens Directive – in summary

Surinder Singh

- as the family member of an EU national who is exercising the Article 45 Treaty right of freedom of movement for workers, who must be given a *derivative right of residence* if the worker would otherwise be discouraged from effective exercise of their rights (Surinder Singh (C-370/90; [1992] ECR I-4265); S v Minister voor Immigratie [2014] EUECJ C-457/12)
- as the family member of an EU national where the relevant family life was created or strengthened during genuine residence in the host Member State following the exercise of free movement rights, where the worker now wished that family member to accompany them on return to their EU state of origin (O v Minister voor Immigratie [2014] EUECJ C-456/12 discusses the importance of a spell of residence in the host Member State of sufficient quality to establish a real exercise of Treaty Rights there)

Family members of frontier workers

- as the family member of an EU national who is exercising the Article 56 Treaty right of freedom to provide cross-border services, which 'could not be fully effective if [he was] deterred from exercising it by obstacles raised in his country of origin to the entry and residence of his spouse' (Carpenter [2002] EUECJ C-60/00, S v Minister voor Immigratie [2014] EUECJ C-457/12) (as shown by O cited above, this applies to workers as well as service providers)
- The Citizens' Rights (Frontier Workers) (EU Exit) Regulations 2020 provide for EEA nationals who, by 31 December 2020, are working or self-employed in the UK but living elsewhere (ie not primarily resident here) to continue to work in the UK for as long as they remain a frontier worker. They also provide for the restriction of those rights and establish a scheme for frontier worker permits. This is an important exemption from the general effect of Brexit on EU free movement rights: generally speaking EU nationals enter the immigration control regime and have to regularise their status, but Frontier Workers can continue their pre-December 2020 cross-border working, albeit obtaining the relevant permit is a good idea to achieve certainty and avoid any suggestion they have misled immigration officers as to their true status when passing through the border
- those Regs essentially replicate the regime familiar from the EEA Regs 2016 for EEA citizens generally to cater for the particular situation of frontier workers: they contain provisions for admission and protections against expulsion, and for retaining frontier worker status
- Guidance Frontier workers in the UK: rights and status deals with the situation before and after the transition period.

Posted workers

- as the third country (i.e. non-EEA) national employee of a company (in EU legal language, as the *posted worker* of a relevant *undertaking*) established in another Member State exercising the Article 56 Treaty right of freedom to provide services, where they were lawfully and habitually employed in another Member State, would not take other employment in the UK and would leave the country at the end of their posting (Vander Elst v Office des Migrations Internationales [1994] EUECJ C-43/93), given grudging acceptance by the guidance *Non-EEA and Swiss nationals working in the EU (Van der Elst and Swiss posted workers* and entry clearance guidance Non-EEA and Swiss nationals working in the EU: EUN04. This category receives no ongoing protection from the WWA

11.2.2 Exercising Treaty rights

The term 'exercising Treaty rights' will often be inadequate to accurately define the rights and status of an EEA national or family member. A person exercising Treaty rights will have had a right of admission, an initial right to reside, and an extended right to reside; or a right to permanent residence. Each type of status had different requirements and may give rise to different rights at different times. We will address these in more detail later on, but to give a flavour of them now, the EEA Regs provided:

- There was an unconditional right of admission (Reg 11) and residence for an initial period of three months (Reg 13) for all EEA nationals and their family members. Note that the right of admission was one of the rights which were saved for EEA/Swiss nationals resident before TP end and their family members, though in a partial form, during the grace period (see MIL 11.6.1)
- There was then an extended right to reside (Reg 14) thereafter for students and those who have entered the UK to seek work, who are economically active as workers or self-employed, or the self-sufficient - this right endured for so long as the criteria which gave rise to it were satisfied
- Those who held a continuous right to reside for 5 years (and some others, e.g retired workers under Reg 5) became permanently resident (Reg 15). Permanent residence provided a right to reside in itself (i.e. the person no longer needed to be a qualified person – thus Reg 15 beneficiaries were dealt with separately to qualified persons throughout the EEA Regs). PR could only be lost by an absence from the UK for a continuous period of two years or exclusion. The right of PR remained effective for the rest of the Grace Period only. Though a mistaken belief that PR meant what is said might justify a late EUSSch application (MIL 11.7.2.5)

11.2.2.1 Benefits and Treaty rights

EU nationals could only get access to mainstream benefits where they had a "right to reside." This required them to be exercising Treaty Rights or have certain kinds of derivative rights (eg as a primary carer of a child in education but not as a person with *Zambrano* residence rights).

Now, as per the DWP's benefits guidance notes, those with EUPSS are not eligible to claim benefits automatically. They must therefore demonstrate that they have an existing qualifying 'right to reside' – such as worker status – to receive UK benefits (MIL 11.7.4). Those with EUSS will qualify for mainstream benefits so long as they are habitually resident here.

11.2.3 Qualified persons and family members

The main characters in the EU law story were:

Qualified persons, i.e. the EEA nationals themselves when engaged in the relevant forms of economic activity set out in Reg 6, i.e:

- A jobseeker (Reg 6(1)(a))
    - the Regs basically permitted up to 91 days of jobseeking from entering the UK before you were expected to leave the country and wait 12 months before returning
    - however one could retain jobseeker status for long via *compelling* evidence of seeking employment with a genuine chance of being engaged
    - those constraints in the Regs might not have been consistent with EU law: the matter was never finally determined pre-Brexit, but Antonissen [1991] ECR I-745 (Case C-344/95) & AG & Ors [2007] UKAIT 00075 indicate that the real test was whether a reasonable period

CHAPTER 11: European Union Law

had been exceeded, having regard to intentions on entry to the UK, job-seeking history in the context of the relevant labour market, and the chances of getting employment

- A worker (Reg 6(1)(b))

    o to establish worker status one needed to show a level of activities that were real and genuine rather than marginal and ancillary: Lawrie Blum (1986) ECR 2121 – a few hours a week might suffice. So a person might be present as a student and still meet the worker definition
    o The HO would look for a genuine relationship between employer and employee, the regularity of work, length of employment, hours worked and earnings: the guidance indicated the HO would make further enquiries of those earning below the HMRC's Primary Earnings Threshold (£166 per week in 2019/20, £183 in 2020/21) – rough sleeping did not rule out worker status but would be a relevant consideration
    o One would not lose worker status due to

- **Temporary inability to work owing to illness or accident** (Reg 6(2)(a)) – for these purposes 'temporary' meant any non-permanent absence from work, see FMB Uganda [2010] UKUT 447 (IAC)
    o So long as one was in '**duly recorded involuntary unemployment**' and registered as a jobseeker (Reg 6(2)(b)(i) & (c)(i)) without If employed here for more than a year, Reg 6(2)(b) applied and they could retain worker status, for six months provided the person provided *evidence of seeking employment and having a genuine chance of being engaged* (Reg 6(6)), & after six months only if they could provide *compelling evidence* of seeking employment with a genuine chance of being engaged (Reg 6(7)(a))
    o If employed here for less than a year, Reg 6(2)(c) applied and they could retain worker status only for a maximum of six months (Reg 6(3)), and only if the person provided *evidence of seeking employment and having a genuine chance of being engaged* (Reg 6(6))
    o Query whether the true arbiter in EU law was the Antonissen test rather than this domestic scheme (see jobseekers above)

- **Embarking on vocational training** – if unemployment was voluntary then such training had to be related to the previous employment (Reg 6(2)(e)); if involuntary, then it could be of any kind (Reg 6(2)(d)), see Yusuf [2015] UKUT 433 (IAC) holding found that courses mandated by the DWP to assist a person in finding employment would be vocational

- A mother leaving a job (or stopping actively seeking employment) because of the physical constraints of the late stages of pregnancy and the (reasonably assessed) aftermath of childbirth, provided she returned to work within a reasonable period of childbirth (Saint Prix [2014] EUECJ C-507/12). Weldemichael [2015] UKUT 540 (IAC)) suggested that the relevant period (of absence from the labour market) had to be for no more than 11 weeks before the expected date of confinement – though the physical constraints of pregnancy might have justified an earlier time of departure from work but cogent evidence would be needed to support such an inference — and should not exceed 52 weeks in total. SSWP v SSF [2015] UKUT 0502 (AAC) suggested the period could potentially exceed 52 weeks

- Other unidentified eventualities – Saint Prix indicates that Article 7(3) of Directive 2004/38 gives examples, rather than listing exhaustively, the circumstances in which a former migrant worker may nevertheless continue to benefit from worker status.
    o A worker or self-employed person became permanently resident under Reg 15(1)(c) if ceasing activity in one of the following circumstances (Reg 5):
    o Retirement having resided in UK for 3+ years, working for at least a year prior to retirement, & reaching state retirement age or taking early retirement if a worker: Reg 5(2)
    o Permanent incapacity to work due to an accident at work or an occupational disease bringing entitlement to a pension payable in full or in part by a UK institution, if resident in the UK for 2+ years immediately prior to this incapacity: Reg 5(3) (amended by EEA Regs 2019)

- o Resident in the UK as a worker or self-employed person for 3+ years and retaining a place of residence to which they returned as a rule at least weekly: Reg 5(4), no further prior UK residence necessary (Reg 5(5))
- o The criteria for periods of residence/activity did not apply where the person was married to or the civil partner of a UK national (Reg 5(6))

- **A self-employed person**

  - o Generally enjoying the same rights as the employed (with occasional exceptions: eg no early retirement proviso, unlike workers, and with a different set of rights for Turkish workers versus the self-employed under the Ankara Agreement, MIL 11.10) – from 24 July 2018 the EEA Regs 2016 were amended (Reg 6(4)) to prevent loss of self-employed status during temporary inactivity equivalent to involuntary unemployment or vocational training
  - o Self-employed status could be generated by a level of activity which was genuine and effective, whether or not it was full-time, by analogy to the approach taken to whether someone was working: Jany [2001] EUECJ C-268/99
  - o An activity is regarded as self-employed where it is carried out under an agreement with other commercial operators or consumers, but there is no subordination of one party or another into a relationship of salaried employment
  - o Characteristics of self-employment include whether a person is essentially in business for themselves and responsible for their enterprise's success or failure, profit and loss; whether they can set their own hours and hire a replacement for themselves if required, using their own tools, investing in business assets, and having multiple clients. See the government guidance on Employment Status. The HO focussed on self-employed registration & tax records with HMRC, invoices, business accounts, an accountant's letter, advertising and business bank statements

- **Self-sufficient persons**

  - o The self-sufficient were qualified persons (Reg 6(1)(d)) and thus enjoyed the extended right of residence, leading to permanent residence after five years, for as long as they could show that
  - o they had sufficient funds not to become dependent on benefits and
  - o they had comprehensive private health insurance (Reg 4(1)(c): MIL 11.5.4)
  - o Chen C-200/02 recognised the right of an EU national baby a few months old to reside in the host Member State and to be looked after by her mother, a third country national. Such primary carers would acquire a residence right to deliver the requisite care, so long as they had sufficient resources for the family unit not to become a burden on public finances, and provided that the minor was covered by appropriate sickness insurance. The fact that the family specifically went to the Member State where the child was born for the express purpose of the child's acquiring citizenship of the Union was irrelevant to the child's right to exercise her free movement and residence in the EU
  - o The Chen right of residence was incorporated into the EEA Regs at Reg 16(2), providing for a 'derivative' right of residence for the parents of a self-sufficient EU child: thus a Chen parent was entitled to a derivative residence card under Reg 20
  - o For some years the UK courts suggested that it would be necessary for Chen cases to be self-sufficient at the point of entry to the UK and that funds creating self-sufficiency could only come from parents whose earnings were lawful independently of the child's residence right: but the CJEU in Kuldip Singh [2015] EUECJ C-218/14 and Bajratari [2019] EUECJ C-93/18 explained that there was no particular requirement as to the funds' origin and so they might originate from a parent without any other form of immigration status. See also SSWP v WV (UC) [2023] UKUT 112 (AAC) explaining that it would be disproportionate to refuse residence rights where a third country national partner relied on welfare benefits flowing from his partner's disability to establish self-sufficiency.
  - o FE v HMRC (CHB) [2022] UKUT 4 (AAC) holds that when a minor has acquired a right of permanent residence under Art 16 of the Citizens Directive due to having previously lawfully resided for 5 years as a Chen child, her primary carer is entitled to a right of residence in order to give "*useful effect*" to the minor's rights - which suffices as a right to reside for child benefit purposes

- **Students**

EEA national students enjoyed a much more relaxed regime than third country nationals studying in the UK, as they could avoid the requirements for an educational sponsor and the set maintenance thresholds under Tier 4 of the PBS. Those seeking to enter another Member State solely for the purposes of study had to

- be enrolled at a relevant education establishment (not any college: it must have been either accredited or financed from public funds: the Guidance on *Qualified persons* interpreted 'accredited' as established by an endorsement from any recognised educational regulatory body)
- provide an assurance, in the form of a declaration or such like, that they were economically self-sufficient – following such an assurance admission was unrestricted and there was no need to back it up via documentary proof (Reg 4(1)(d)(iii))
- have comprehensive sickness insurance cover (Reg 4(1)(d)(ii)) (we address CSIC as a generic requirement of EEA cases, below). Note that the requirement for CSIC for students was not a straightforward one) (and, long after the event, was found to include NHS cover: MIL 11.5.4)

EU law students

- could only be joined by partners & dependent children
- Suffered no restriction on working so long as such work did not undermine the essential 'principal purpose of following a course of study' in Reg 4 (contrast the tight controls on students under the Student Appendices)
- would have access to UK loans to pay tuition fees and other forms of student support depending on whether the person was studying in England, Wales, Scotland or Northern Ireland
- if they were economically active alongside their studies sufficiently to meet the "*genuine and effective*" test to be a worker they would then benefit from the more generous rights afforded such persons (Reg 7(2)(a))

11.2.4 Qualified persons and other EEA national beneficiaries

Most forms of residence under the EEA Regs based on free movement rights were owed to those meeting the definition of being 'qualified persons'. The definitions were at Regs 4 and 6.

CHAPTER 11: European Union Law

11.3 British citizens who benefitted from free movement rights
11.3.1 British citizens exercising Treaty rights/Surinder Singh Route

The rights of EEA nationals to reside with their families were often stronger than those of British citizens (MIL 11.1.2.4). A British citizen residing in the UK could be treated as an EEA national by exercising their Treaty rights of free movement: for example, by going to work in another Member State and then returning to the UK. This route is found within Appendix EU which cross-refers to Reg 9 of the EEA Regs 2016: so we address Reg 9 in some detail.

The classic case, and indeed the one that to this day gives its name to this principle, is Surinder Singh (C-370/90). There, a British citizen married an Indian national living in the UK. They then travelled to Germany for some time where they lived together and worked. They later decided to relocate back to the UK. When the couple began divorce proceedings in the UK, the HO tried to remove Mr Singh on the basis that he no longer met the Immigration Rules' criteria as a spouse. He took the case to the ECJ, arguing that the right to go and work in other EEA countries must necessarily include a right to return to the UK afterwards on the same basis, and therefore that the European law of free movement applied to his return and re-entry, not UK immigration law. The court accepted this argument. This was one of those rights which were founded on the Treaty itself: it did not stem from the Citizens' Directive.

The principle is now reflected in the EUSSch via the notion of *Qualifying British Citizens* and their family members (MIL 11.7). The case law on Surinder Singh rights established that:

- Although the principle arose in relation to spouses, it could also apply to a British citizen who had been joined by a close relative abroad, as otherwise the former might have been deterred from free movement by the possibility that a way of life developed in the host Member State could not be continued on return to the home Member State: see Eind (C-291/05)
- Even a person whose free movement was unsuccessful in securing work might benefit: see (Eind)
- It applied even though the spouse or relative did not have a right to reside in the state of origin (the UK, for our purposes) before the EEA national (British citizen) travelled abroad (Eind)
- The work relied upon did not need to take place immediately before return: the test swa whether there was a sufficient link between the exercise of Treaty rights and the return, as was found to be the case notwithstanding a 13 month gap between work finishing and the time of return in OB Morocco [2010] UKUT 420 (IAC)
- The British citizen need not work or otherwise be economically active on their return to the UK; see eg HK v SSWP [2020] UKUT 73 (AAC)

Reg 9 of the EEA Regs 2016 incorporated the principle. Amendments, as a result of Banger ECJ C-89-17, came into force on 28 March 2019 expanding the applicability of Reg 9 to EFMs of British citizens. Reg 9 was maintained by the Grace Period Regs (Reg 5). Though EFMs could qualify only if their residence was lawful in the host country (Reg 9(2)).

To qualify under Appendix EU EFMs relying on Surinder Singh would have had to have returned to the UK with their British "sponsor" before the end of the transition period to take advantage fo the scheme (see definition of "family member of a qualifying British citizen" in Annex 1 to Appendix EU) (MIL 11.7.5.2).

The post-Brexit statutory regime retains the EEA Regs 2016 for the purpose of considering outstanding applications. Thus we see that The Immigration and Social Security Co-ordination (EU Withdrawal) Act 2020 (Consequential, Saving, Transitional and Transitory Provisions) (EU Exit) Regulations 2020 (at Reg 6) keep in place provisions including Reg 9. So below the text deleted by the Grace Period Regulations is still shown, crossed out, and the added text has been underlined and italicised, for ease of reference:

9.— Family members and extended family members of British citizens

"(1) If the conditions in paragraph (2) are satisfied, these Regulations apply to a person who is the family member ("F") of a British citizen ("BC") as though the BC were an

CHAPTER 11: European Union Law

>   EEA national *and BC is to be treated as satisfying any requirement to be a qualified person*
>   (1A) These Regulations apply to a person who is the extended family member ("EFM") of a BC as though the BC were an EEA national if—
>   (a) the conditions in paragraph (2) are satisfied; and
>   (b) the EFM was lawfully resident in the EEA State referred to in paragraph (2)(a)(i).
>   (2) The conditions are that—
>   (a) BC—
>   (i) is residing in an EEA State as a worker, self-employed person, self-sufficient person or a student, or so resided immediately before returning to the United Kingdom; or
>   (ii) has acquired the right of permanent residence in an EEA State;
>   (b) F or EFM and BC resided together in the EEA State;
>   (c) F or EFM and BC's residence in the EEA State was genuine;
>   (d) either—
>   (i) F was a family member of BC during all or part of their joint residence in the EEA State;
>   (ii) F was an EFM of BC during all or part of their joint residence in the EEA State, during which time F was lawfully resident in the EEA State; or
>   (iii) EFM was an EFM of BC during all or part of their joint residence in the EEA State, during which time EFM was lawfully resident in the EEA State;
>   (e) genuine family life was created or strengthened during F or EFM and BC's joint residence in the EEA State; and
>   (f) the conditions in sub-paragraphs (a), (b) and (c) have been met concurrently.
>   (3) Factors relevant to whether residence in the EEA State is or was genuine include—
>   ~~(a) whether the centre of BC's life transferred to the EEA State;~~
>   (b) the length of F or EFM and BC's joint residence in the EEA State;
>   (c) the nature and quality of the F or EFM and BC's accommodation in the EEA State, and whether it is or was BC's principal residence;
>   (d) the degree of F or EFM and BC's integration in the EEA State;
>   (e) whether F's or EFM's first lawful residence in the EU with BC was in the EEA State."

Reg 9(4)-(6) then provide:

- Reg 9 would not apply if the EEA State residence was as a means of circumventing any relevant immigration laws
- Where the requirements of Reg 9 were met, the British citizen ("BC") was deemed to be an '*EEA national who holds a valid EEA passport*' (Reg 9(5))
- Permanent residence acquired by the BC in the other EEA member state would only be recognised as such if it met the UK's domestic requirements in Reg 15 (Reg 9(6))

Then Reg 9(7) provided that

- In assessing whether BC would be a student/self-sufficient, the requirement to hold comprehensive sickness insurance needed only be met by their family member ("FM") and not the BC (Reg 9(7)(a))
- In assessing whether the BC retained worker status after stopping work, under Reg 6(2)(b) or (c) (in duly recorded involuntary unemployment after 1 year or more/less than one year, respectively), the requirement to be seeking work following exercising treaty rights as a worker, fell away (Reg 9(7)(b))
- In assessing whether the BC would be a jobseeker, the requirement to have entered the UK to seek work fell away, as did Condition C (the extra conditions where jobseeker status was previously enjoyed and lost, followed by an absence from the UK) (Reg9(7)(c))

NB: Reg 9(7) is omitted under the Grace Period regime.

Changes to Reg 9 since it was first introduced, over time, include additional requirements, as indicated above. These were that

- BC's 'centre of life' had, during their residence abroad, moved to the other EEA state
- residence there was 'genuine' according to specific criteria, e.g.: length of residence, level of integration and for an intention other than to circumvent the UK Immigration Rules
- the applicant must have been a family member during all or part of that residence and genuine family life was created or strengthened

ZA [2019] UKUT 281 (IAC) examined the Reg 9 regime. In so doing it held that the requirement to have moved the centre of one's life to the host Member State does not accurately reflect EU law. So that provision had to be omitted via the deletion of Reg 9(3)(a) in the saved version for Brexit purposes. The UT concludes:

(a) A genuine exercise of Treaty Rights did not require any attempt to settle in the host Member State, merely to establish oneself there. The CJEU case law did not support the EEA Regs 2016 in their reliance on a "centre of life" test. Nor was there any requirement to have severed ties with the UK or to solely reside in the host Member State.

(b) The individual's *intention* when making the move abroad is not of central importance. The fact that the move might produce some immigration benefit is not something to focus on, because motivation is not the test. Intention is relevant simply in so far as it assists in determining whether their residence was *genuine*. For example residence would be genuine where there was a real intention to exercise Treaty Rights: but not merely where a person only intended to take an extended holiday or work on a short fixed-term contract.

(c) Decision makers should not concern themselves with whether the work itself was genuine beyond asking whether it was paid work involving the payment of taxes, so long as the work reached the minimal level to constitute "work" for EU law purposes: ie that it is genuine and effective rather than marginal and ancillary.

(d) The factors relevant to "genuineness" are varied: those in the case law and in the EEA Regs 2016 are not exhaustive, and an applicant does not have to satisfy any particular criteria.

(e) The EU law doctrine of abuse of rights would not normally arise. It would do so only where the SSHD could show that there was no genuine exercise of Treaty Rights alongside a distinct intention to use an artificial constructed arrangement.

Christy [2018] EWCA Civ 2378 emphasised that the basis of residence in the host EU Member State is not critical. The issue of EEA residence documents there may be helpful but is not essential, and a refusal of such documents was relevant though not decisive.

When assessing permanent residence rights for family members of British citizens, decision makers might be looking back over a period prior to the EEA Regs 2016 entering force. In these cases, where residence cards were issued before 25 November 2016, the Guidance Direct family members of EEA nationals stated that a residence card should be accepted as proof of qualified person status. Thereafter concrete evidence of the British citizen having status equivalent to a qualified person, and proof of holding CSIC, was required for family members if the British citizen's sponsor's "EEA" status was as a student or self-sufficient person (Commissioners for HMRC was later to hold otherwise (MIL 11.5.4)).

So where a BC has not exercised Treaty rights in the UK after 25 November 2016, an EUSSch application will be the preferable option, as residence alone, rather than the positive exercise of treaty rights by the BC in the UK, suffices.

Appendix EU preserves Surinder Singh rights: via the provisions for *'family member of a qualifying British Citizen'*. But only for so long: until 29 March 2022 and until 31 December 2020 for some categories of family members (see 11.7).

11.3.2 Dual (British and EEA) nationals

It was at one time thought that British citizens living in the UK who also held the nationality of another Member State could benefit from the same free movement rights as EEA nationals who had moved here. That notion was dispelled by McCarthy Case C-434/09 ruling that dual nationals living in either country of nationality but who had never exercised free movement rights lacked residence rights based on either the Citizens' Directive or Article 21 TFEU.

Running with McCarthy thinking, at one time the EEA Regs ruled out dual EEA/British citizens from ever benefitting from free movement rights. But the CJEU in Lounes C-165/16 thought differently, explaining that taking the host country's citizenship after exercising free movement rights there represented a deepening of the migrant's integration. Accordingly from 24 July 2018 the EEA Regs 2016

- Defined EEA national as including dual British/EEA nationals who had previously exercised an enduring right to reside (Reg 2(1))
- Required that, to maintain EEA residence rights, the dual national satisfied the "*qualified person*" definition at the time of acquiring British citizenship and did not lose that status thereafter (Reg 9A(2))
- Offered access to permanent residence so long as the dual national satisfied the "*qualified person*" definition at the time of acquiring British citizenship or had acquired a right of permanent residence under the Regs (Reg 9A(3)-(4))

Transitional provisions existed for family members of dual EEA/British citizens who were residing in the UK on 16 July 2012, or had applied for residence documentation before that date, and who also held (or had applied for) a valid EEA residence document confirming this right on or before 16 October 2012. These are maintained in the saved provisions of the EEA Regs 2016 without modifications, and are found at Schedule 6, para 9. This is their text:

9.— Preservation of transitional provisions in relation to family members of dual nationals

(1) Where—
(a) the right of a family member ("F") to be admitted to, or reside in, the United Kingdom pursuant to these Regulations depends on a person ("P") being an EEA national;
(b) P would be an EEA national if P was not also a British citizen; and
(c) any of the criteria in sub-paragraphs (2), (3) and (4) is met;
P will, notwithstanding the effect of the definition of an EEA national in regulation 2, be regarded as an EEA national for the purpose of these Regulations.
(2) The criterion in this sub-paragraph is met where F was on 16th July 2012 a person with the right of permanent residence in the United Kingdom under the 2006 Regulations.
(3) Subject to sub-paragraph (5), the criterion in this sub-paragraph is met where F—
(a) was on 16th July 2012 a person with a right of residence in the United Kingdom under the 2006 Regulations; and
(b) on 16th October 2012—
(i) held a valid registration certificate or residence card issued under the 2006 Regulations;
(ii) had made an application under the 2006 Regulations for a registration certificate or residence card which had not been determined; or
(iii) had made an application under the 2006 Regulations for a registration certificate or residence card which had been refused and in respect of which an appeal under regulation 26 of the 2006 Regulations could be brought while the appellant was in the United Kingdom (excluding the possibility of an appeal out of time with permission) or was pending (within the meaning of section 104 of the Nationality, Immigration and Asylum Act 20022, as it applied on 16th July 2012).
(4) Subject to sub-paragraph (6), the criterion in this sub-paragraph is met where F—
(a) had, prior to 16th July 2012, applied for an EEA family permit pursuant to regulation 12 of the 2006 Regulations; or
(b) had applied for and been refused an EEA family permit and where, on 16th July 2012, an appeal under regulation 26 of the 2006 Regulations against that decision could be brought (excluding the possibility of an appeal out of time with permission) or was pending (within the meaning of section 104 of the Nationality, Immigration and Asylum Act 2002 Act, as it applied on 16th July 2012).

(5) The criterion in sub-paragraph (3) is not met in a case to which sub-paragraph (3)(b)(ii) or (iii) applies where no registration certificate or residence card was, in fact, issued pursuant to that application.
(6) The criterion in sub-paragraph (4) is not met where—
    (a) F was issued with an EEA family permit pursuant to an application made prior to 16th July 2012 but F had not been admitted to the United Kingdom within six months of the date on which it was issued; or
    (b) no EEA family permit was, in fact, issued pursuant to that application.
(7) Where met, the criteria in sub-paragraphs (2), (3) and (4) remain satisfied until the occurrence of the earliest of the following events—
    (a) the date on which F ceases to be the family member of P; or
    (b) the date on which F's right of permanent residence is lost.
(8) P will only continue to be regarded as an EEA national for the purpose of considering the position of F under these Regulations.

The upshot of these provisions is that

- Transitional protection is created for family members of individuals who had been recognised as owed EEA rights before legal changes jeopardised that status
- Firstly for those with permanent residence as at 16 July 2012 (Reg 9(2))
- Secondly for those with an extant residence document, or application for one pending decision, or had a refusal of one under appeal, as at 16 July 2012 (so long as a residence document was subsequently granted) (Reg 9(3) & (5))
- Thirdly for those with a pending application for a family permit (implying they were abroad at the time) pending or under appeal as at 16 July 2012 (so long as the application was granted and, if granted before 16 July 2012, the family member had been admitted within 6 months of its issue (Reg 9(4) & (6))
- The right under any of these routes endures until the date the individual in question ceases to be a family member or they lose their right of permanent residence (Reg 9(7))

For the procedures and issues surrounding naturalisation of EEA nationals and their family members, see MIL 12.5.2.

11.4 Family members of qualified persons

Family members of EEA nationals who enjoyed free movement rights under the EEA Regs included both EEA nationals that were not themselves exercising Treaty rights and non-EEA nationals. Both groups were entitled to accompany, or join and reside with an EEA national who had a right to reside in the UK.

There were two tiers of family member. They had to be related to either the EEA national (who had to have a right to reside in the UK) or to their spouse or civil partner.

The first tier (Reg 7 – saved, unmodified, until 30 June 2021 for family members of EEA/Swiss nationals lawfully resident before the end of transition) comprised immediate (sometimes called 'ordinary' or 'direct') family members. The benefits of being an immediate family member included:

- rights of entry and residence being innate and not depending on an exercise of discretion and
- which operated on proof of the underlying relationship: they did not rely on the possession of a particular EU entry or residence document

The second tier was the '*extended*' or '*other*' family member ("EFM") under Reg 8 (saved with a minor modification for the grace period, see below). This group:

- benefited from the same rights of freedom of movement as immediate family members, *but only if* discretion had been exercised in their favour

- if such discretion was exercised, then they would be granted the relevant entry or residence document: this proviso is proving very important as time moves on, with many EFMs seemingly being left high and dry for having failed to make a pre-31 December 2020 application
- enjoyed their rights as a matter of domestic legal provision alone, their European law rights being only procedural ones by which their applications had to be subject to an extensive examination.

11.4.1 Direct family members

Family members were defined at Reg 7 (consistently with Article 2.2 of the Citizens' Directive, and saved without modification for the grace period in respect of EEA/Swiss nationals resident lawfully before the end of transition, and their family members) thus:

(1) Subject to paragraph (2), for the purposes of these Regulations the following
persons shall be treated as the family members of another person—
(a) his spouse or his civil partner;
(b) direct descendants of his, his spouse or his civil partner who are—
(i) under 21; or
(ii) dependants of his, his spouse or his civil partner;
(c) dependent direct relatives in his ascending line or that of his spouse or his civil partner;

Note that there was no provision under Reg 7 for unmarried partners or fiancés. They were classified as EFMs and had to apply under Reg 8 as durable partners (MIL 11.4.2, 11.4.2.4).

Spouses and civil partners apart, other non-EEA family members did not have any EU right to be accompanied by their own family members (e.g. a non-EEA child of an EEA national did not have a right to be joined in the UK by their own non-EEA spouse unless the latter has a relevant family relationship as defined under the EEA Regs with the EEA national themselves or with their spouse or civil partner). They would need to rely on the UK's domestic Immigration Rules (Appendix FM) once they had acquired the right of permanent residence, usually after five years, or on Article 8 ECHR. Appendix FM was amended from 31 December 2020 to allow sponsorship by those holding EUPSS granted under rEU3, providing an earlier option to sponsor than was previously the case. This sponsor category however only includes EEA or Swiss nationals with EUPSS (the reference to EEA national in GEN 1.3(d) to "EEA national" is defined in r6 as including Swiss nationals). The reference to rEU3 grants means that they must have had pre-end of transition period UK residence (otherwise the grant would have been under rEU3A) (MIL 6.1.8).

For students (unless also qualified on another basis e.g. as a self-sufficient person or worker) the Regs on family members were more restrictive than for other qualified persons - only spouses/civil partners and dependent children qualified:

- children (regardless of their age) had to be dependent in order to be family members (Reg 7(2)(a)) and
- there was no provision for dependent direct relatives in the ascending line (Reg 7(2))

EFMs, once issued with relevant entry or residence documentation, were treated as if they were family members (Reg 7(3)).

See marriages of convenience under *Abuse of rights* (11.8.1) and "dependent" under *Dependency in EU Law* (11.5.1).

Top Tip

This tip remains relevant for EUSS applications as it was for applications under the EEA Regs.

If you want an application to be refused, provide minimal documents with no explanation of their contents by way of supporting representations – this leaves the decision maker entitled to refuse because of minor concerns as to a particular document's contents and their consistency with the case as put on the application form.

If you want an application to be granted, provide a detailed witness statement giving the history of the relationship, supporting evidence showing consistent cohabitation via utility bills and other "formal" correspondence addressed to both parties to the relationship over time. Explain the relevance of the documents – addressing your mind to this should in itself flag up any missing pieces in the chain of evidence.

If these are not available for one party because a lack of documented identity and/or immigration status means they are unable to obtain a bank account or produce relevant identity documents to officialdom and other third parties that allow them to receive correspondence in their own name, then some other corroborative evidence needs to be found: eg witness statements from friends and neighbours that are sufficiently detailed to have the ring of truth.

11.4.2 Extended family members

The Citizens' Directive at Article 3 addresses the situation of 'other family members', beyond those we have so far discussed and who do not fall within its own Article 2(2). It identifies three routes.

- the host Member State shall facilitate, according to its national legislation, the entry and residence of

    o the Union citizen's dependents or household members in the country from which they came, and
    o family members who, on serious health grounds, strictly require the personal care of the Union citizen, and
    o any partner with whom the Union citizen has a durable relationship.

- these cases shall receive 'an extensive examination of [their] personal circumstances'

The 2016 EEA Regs reflected these requirements at Reg 8, styling its beneficiaries as EFMs. Reg 9 was saved for the duration of the Grace Period. With one change - the extensive examination no longer needs to address whether an EEA national would be deterred from exercising their free ovement rights if the application were refused (by deletion of Reg 8(8)(c)). Originally the EFM category was divided up into four routes (the three routes within the Directive having been expanded by splitting family members into two):

(2) The condition in this paragraph is that the person is–
    (a)   a relative of an EEA national; and
    (b)   residing in a country other than the United Kingdom and is dependent upon the EEA national or is a member of the EEA national's household; and either–
        (i)   is accompanying the EEA national to the United Kingdom or wants to join the EEA national in the United Kingdom; or
        (ii)   has joined the EEA national in the United Kingdom and continues to be dependent upon the EEA national, or to be a member of the EEA national's household.
(3)   The condition in this paragraph is that the person is a relative of an EEA national and on serious health grounds, strictly requires the personal care of the EEA national or the spouse or civil partner of the EEA national.
(4)   The condition in this paragraph is that the person is a relative of an EEA national and would meet the requirements in the immigration rules (other than those relating to entry clearance) for indefinite leave to enter or remain in the United Kingdom as a dependent relative of the EEA national.
(5)   The condition in this paragraph is that the person is the partner (other than a civil partner) of, and in a durable relationship with, an EEA national or the child (under the age of 18) of that partner, and is able to prove this to the decision maker.

A 5th route was added via Reg 8(1A) to reflect the CJEU decision in SM [2019] EUECJ C-129/18. This addressed the Islamic system of Kafala adoptions used in countries including Algeria, which do not carry all the legal implications of other systems of adoption.

- This applied to those under 18 who had lived with an EEA national on the basis of a non-adoptive legal guardianship order that was recognised under the national law of the state in which it was contracted, so long as the child enjoyed family life with their EEA national guardian in the sense of a personal relationship of dependency and the assumption of parental responsibility, including legal and financial responsibilities
- Latayan [2020] EWCA Civ 191 noted that following SM the concept of a "*direct descendant*" required the existence of a direct parent-child relationship. The stepchildren of unmarried partners did not qualify: whilst a biological or a legal relationship would qualify, neither was present here

We shall look at each of these classes of EFM in turn, following our look at some general considerations.

11.4.2.1 Extended family members – general considerations

The EEA Regs required that an EFM be issued with a family permit or a residence card only if '*in all the circumstances, it appears ... appropriate*' (Reg 12(4), 18(4)). This indicated that the document needed to be issued only where a discretion was exercised in the applicant's favour, as was recognised domestically in AP and FP [2007] UKAIT 00048 and at CJEU level in Islam [2012] EUECJ C-83/11, which made it clear that there is no requirement for historic cohabitation in the country of origin prior to the EEA national's entry to the European Union. The objective is (as Islam put it):

> to 'maintain the unity of the family in a broader sense' by facilitating entry and residence for persons who are not included in the definition of family member of a Union citizen contained in Article 2(2) of Directive 2004/38 but who nevertheless maintain close and stable family ties with a Union citizen on account of specific factual circumstances, such as economic dependence, being a member of the household or serious health grounds.

Some relevant points re EFMs:

- As the grant of the application was discretionary notwithstanding the fact that the Reg 8 criteria were satisfied, the door was opened to consider criteria such as immigration history, and the ability to maintain and accommodate – Reg 8(8) identified express considerations such as a child's best interests, and the applicant's character and conduct
- A central question was the relevance of the relationship in question to the exercise of Treaty rights and whether refusal of the application would discourage free movement (Reg 8(8)(c)) (this however was removed from the saved provision during the Grace Period, there no longer being any free movement rights to encourage)
- Other factors were the degree of integration of both EEA sponsor and the applicant, and what degree of family and private life was in play
- The HO Guidance noted that where the parties were in a durable relationship, it would be difficult to refuse the application on discretionary grounds as 'it is likely that to refuse a residence card would prevent the relevant EEA national's free movement rights'
- Adverse immigration history would have to reach a certain level of severity to justify refusal: the Guidance suggested that a history of abuse and fraud will be more relevant than mere overstaying
- Because EFMs required the exercise of discretion before their residence was regularised, pending EEA applications and appeals were not treated as lawful residence. So if the application was granted, all well and good: the person had a residence card. But they would have a significant break in their lawful residence in any event: see generally Macastena [2018] EWCA Civ 1558 and AS (Ghana) [2016] EWCA Civ 133
- Lawful residence in another EU Member State is not required: MIL 11.5.2

Reg 7(3) provided that a person recognised as an EFM under Reg 8 via the issue of an EEA family permit, a registration certificate or a residence card was subsequently to be treated as if they were a (close) family member. So long as they continued to hold such documentation and satisfied the requirements which first brought them recognition as an EFM. The EUSSch also accords a different status to EFMs with EEA residence documents vs those without. Only those applicants already holding EFM residence documents, or who have a pending pre-TP end application, can access the EUSSch (MIL 11.7.5.2 Annex 1 definition of a "durable partner").

Top Tip

This tip retains its relevance for EUSSch applications:

When arguing these cases, always address the relationship giving rise to the factual claim including questions of dependency and cohabitation

-Provide a detailed witness statement giving the history of the relationship

-Look at the HO Guidance *Extended family members* for inspiration

-In a durable relationship case (as that Guidance suggests), provide, where relevant, evidence of cohabitation, joint finances, joint responsibility for any children, and any other evidence demonstrating their commitment and relationship, explaining the relevance of the documents

-If these are not available for one party because a lack of documented identity and/or immigration status means they are unable to obtain a bank account or produce relevant identity documents to officialdom and other third parties that allow them to receive correspondence in their own name, then some other corroborative evidence needs to be found: e.g. witness statements from friends and neighbours that are sufficiently detailed to have the ring of truth

-In a dependent relative case (again, see the Guidance) provide evidence of past dependency (remittances by way of bank statements (of the donor and recipient), money transfer records),

AND

-factors relevant to the exercise of discretion e.g.
-financial and emotional dependency
-discouragement of the Treaty right exercise
-periods of lawful residence
-reasoned explanations for any overstaying

Example

Francois is French. He is an eccentric artist, a 'character', who entertains and exasperates his family members in equal measure. Francois has lived in the UK on and off for 20 years. In the last 8 years, he has not been absent for more than 6 months in one year. He has never been in gainful employment for more than a few months at a time, and much of the work he did do was cash in hand with no records remaining.

In the last 10 years, he has regularly relied on his daughter, also French and UK-based Genevieve, who works in finance, for his upkeep and, at times, accommodation.

His long- term partner Grace is from Ivory Coast and an overstayer. Her previous application for a residence card, lodged in 2016, as a durable partner of Francois failed on the basis of Francois' lack of exercise of treaty rights.

Having requested evidence of Francois' dependence on his daughter you can see a consistent record of bank transfers and accommodation at Genevieve's address, starting 8 years ago, when he started living in the UK more consistently.

Having demonstrated that Francois has been his daughter's dependent relative in the ascending line for over 5 years he is therefore

- ☐ a "direct" family member under reg 7

- ☐ of a qualified person under reg 6

- ☐ who had an extended right to reside under reg 14 for 5 years and thus

- ☐ acquired permanent residence under reg 15(1)(b)

Francois acquired permanent residence not as a result of his own exercise of treaty rights. However, he has, at this point, been a permanent resident by operation of law for 3 years.

Presuming he had not applied for permanent residence before the end of the transition period, he retained that right in terms of his lawful status (and benefit entitlements etc) under the Grace Period Regs, but he had to apply for EUSS under rEU11 condition 1, before the Grace Period ended on 30 June 2021. Otherwise he will not enjoy Grace Period Regs protection unless and until the HO accept he has reasonable grounds for applying late and grants his application (MIL 11.7.2.5).

Unfortunately for Grace, it is now too late for her to enter the EUSSch as his durable partner as she would be relying on a period of residence before the end of the transition period during which she did not hold a residence card as a durable partner, and she cannot apply for such a card after the end of the transition period.

Francois would have to sponsor her under Appendix FM as a person settled in the UK once he is granted EUSS, but such an application would be highly unlikely to succeed as he lacks the income level required and Grace would have to meet paras EX1&2 as she has no leave.

Had she applied for a residence card before the end of the transition period, she might have succeeded by demonstrating all the above. Thus showing Francois was an EEA national with permanent residence.

Her prospects of success might have been better if he had been granted a document certifying permanent residence first.

Her prospects of succeeding in a durable partner residence card application would have been best if Francois started work, at least part-time, to be able to prove that he was a qualified person and thus able to "sponsor" her (in an evidentially much more straightforward manner) as a durable partner

If Grace had been granted a residence card as a durable partner following an application before the end of the transition period, even if the card was issued after 31 December 2020, she could then still have entered the EUSS.

11.4.2.2 Dependent relatives

Reg 8(2) was amended over time as decisions of the CJEU required its revision. The first route within it essentially provided for an EFM of the EEA national, who had previously been dependent on, or resided with, the EEA national themselves, abroad. Its essential features were:

- 'Relative', which was not defined under EU law, included, as acknowledged in HO Immigration Staff Guidance <u>Extended family members of EEA nationals</u>, a wide range of relations. The

CHAPTER 11: European Union Law

guidance stated that there was *'no limit on the distance of the relationship between the EEA national and the extended family member as long as they can provide valid proof of the relationship between them'*. Note that the guidance included those related by marriage to the EEA national
- Relatives could be either related to the EEA national or their spouse/CP (Reg 8(7)). For a while the EEA Regs suggested that only relatives of the EEA national could benefit: but this was corrected from 15 August 2019
- Household membership goes beyond mere cohabitation, whilst the CJEU and UKUT agree on the need for some dependency too, they otherwise differ a little as these two decisions show:

    o Sohrab [2022] UKUT 157 (IAC) holds that household membership requires a sufficient degree of physical and relational proximity to the EEA national through living in the household of which the EEA national is the head, living together as a unit, with a common sense of belonging, & a genuine assumption of responsibility by the EEA national for the EFM. Questions of the commencement of the assumption of responsibility and the duration of dependency or household membership are relevant. A case may be established even though the EFM arrived in the UK before the EEA national: usually where they were a household member abroad. Relevant factors are likely to include the duration of the separation, nature and the quality of the links during the time living apart, intention to continue life together as a household with the EEA national as the head, the extent to which the departing members of the household have established their own distinct household, any genuine assumption of responsibility (including financial responsibility) by the EEA sponsor for the putative EFMs during the period of physical separation, any corresponding dependence (including financial dependence) on the part of the EFM, and the immigration capacity in which the EFM has resided in the UK ahead of the EEA sponsor's arrival.

    o SRS and AA (Case C-22/21) defines household membership: a relationship of dependence with that citizen, based on close and stable personal ties, forged within the same household, in the context of a shared domestic life going beyond a mere temporary cohabitation entered into for reasons of pure convenience. However this did not require that the EEA Sponsor have been head of any particular household, and whilst some dependency was necessary, it need not be of such intensity that free movement rights would be deterred were the visa not be granted.

- The *dependency/household membership* must be between the dependent relative and the EEA national – i.e. dependency upon, or cohabitation with, the EEA national's spouse or civil partner will not suffice (Reg 8(2)(a)-(b))
- Reg 8(2) could be satisfied via a combination of prior and present dependency or household membership. As explained in Dauhoo [2012] UKUT 79, this could be done in any one of four different ways, each of which requires proving a relevant connection both prior to arrival in the UK and in the UK
- There was no requirement to show that the EEA national and their family member were in the same country during the period of dependency. The dependent could even arrive in the UK before the EEA national: see Aladeselu [2013] EWCA Civ 144
- However, continuous dependency was an essential requirement. In Chowdhury [2020] UKUT 188 (IAC) the UT examined a case where there was a break in dependency for a significant period following the third country dependant's arrival in the UK. It considered the phrase "has joined the EEA national in the United Kingdom and *continues to be dependent upon him or to be a member of his household*" in this context. The UT concludes that the italicised words require an applicant to establish that there has not been *any break* in their dependency on the EEA National sponsor. Chowdhury [2021] EWCA Civ 1220 finds the CoA agreeing: dependency is a matter for domestic law so long as the effectiveness of the Citizens Directive is not undermined. The relevant domestic law provision (Reg 8 of the EEA Regs 2016) required dependency to be a persisting state of affairs
- The UT has ruled that the EEA Sponsor should have been an EEA national throughout the relevant period of dependency: see Moneke [2011] UKUT 341 (IAC) Begum [2021] EWCA Civ 1878 confirms that the plain and natural meaning of Article 3(2) of the Citizens Directive is that the EU national must be a Union citizen at the time dependency is established

Reg 8(4) makes provision for a relative of the EEA national who would meet the requirements of the adult dependent relative category in Appendix FM of the Immigration Rules. That route requires a very high threshold to be met (see Module 6.6), basically that essential care is impossible to find or finance in the country of origin. Under Appendix FM the application must be made from abroad as the route is available only in relation to entry clearance, not leave to remain: Reg 8(4) with its reference to 'other than those [requirements] relating to entry clearance' relaxed this aspect of the Rule.

11.4.2.3 Serious health grounds requiring the EEA national's personal care

This provision clearly required s a high threshold to be established, as it was necessary to show:

- that a relative of the EEA national
- on serious health grounds
- strictly required the personal care of the EEA national or their spouse/CP.

TR [2008] UKAIT 00004 held:

- The use of the word 'serious' required the 'health grounds' to go well beyond ordinary ill health
- detailed medical evidence would be essential in support of any claim
- 'personal care' referred to a requirement for assistance with the daily physical tasks and needs of the person cared for

11.4.2.4 Partner of an EEA national in a durable relationship

This proviso was the EEA equivalent of the unmarried partner route under the Immigration Rules.

- There is no European Union law definition of 'durable' so each case had to be looked at on its own facts. In YB [2008] UKAIT 00062, the Tribunal held that national law must not seek to define EU law terms and it would be wrong to equate this concept with '*living together in a relationship akin to marriage which has subsisted for two years or more*'
- However the HO intermittently applied a rule of thumb of two years' cohabitation: the Guidance *Extended family members* did recognise '*If there is less than two years evidence, you can still accept this where there is evidence the relationship is durable*'
- A relationship could be durable whether or not it had entailed cohabitation (Dauhoo [2012] UKUT 79 at 19), though it would be very difficult indeed to make out durability where there has been no cohabitation
- The 2016 Regs provided in Reg 2 that the definition of durable partner did not include a durable partner of convenience. We discuss the definition below where we address marriages of convenience

The EEA Amendment Regs 2019 included the children of durable partners as EFMs – their best interests were identified as a relevant consideration at part of the "extensive examination".

Whilst not binding in UK law, the Supreme Court of Ireland's decision in Pervaiz [2020] IESC 27 is interesting its approach to durable relationships. These would typically be committed ones which have continued for some time and where each party would hope for it to continue for the foreseeable future. Such commitment might be shown in a short but serious relationship: relevant evidence might include the couple's social life and social network, finances and living arrangements, all of which would usually be recognised and acknowledged by their circle of family and friends.

Singh [2021] UKUT 319 (IAC) examines the ambit of duties to EFMs under the Citizens Directive noting that any obligations arise only in relation to a person who *has* such a relationship duly attested – ie the obligation arises only re current relationships. The Directive did not contain any protections for those formerly in such relationships, unlike for spouses. There was nothing in the Directive or elsewhere to prevent differential treatment of spouses and unmarried partners and so the discrimination was lawful – any rights as EFMs only accrued in the first place to those in an extant relationship.

11.5 Generic concepts: dependency, prior lawful residence, sham marriages and comprehensive sickness insurance

11.5.1 Dependency in EU law

Some EEA family members had to establish dependency before satisfying the requirements of the EEA Regs: this applied both to direct and EFMs:

- For close family members: dependent direct relatives in the ascending line (Reg 7(1)(c)) and adult children who were dependants (Reg 7(1)(b)(ii))
- For EFMs: to dependent relatives generally (Reg 8(2), 8(4))

The same principles essentially apply in EUSSch applications (see dependency definition at Annex 1 to Appendix EU, 11.7.5.2).

- SM (India) [2009] EWCA Civ 1426 held, following the ECJ decision in Jia [2007] EUECJ C-1/05 that whether dependency is established is a simple question of fact: it might be dependency *of choice* and need not be *of necessity*. This means that an enquiry is limited to whether a person is *in fact* dependent rather than *why* that person is dependent
- Voluntary dependency is not therefore excluded, eg giving up one's job to become dependent. In Lim [2013] UKUT 437 (IAC), the Tribunal found that a relationship of dependency could exist where a dependent has savings but chooses not to live on them
- Also, following Jia, 'dependency' must be in regard to the relative's material needs, generally taken to mean financial dependency. However, there may be other forms of dependency, recognised in Reyes [2013] UKUT 314:

    > questions of dependency must not be reduced to a bare calculation of financial dependency but should be construed broadly to involve a holistic examination of a number of factors, including financial, physical and social conditions, so as to establish whether there is dependence that is genuine ... bearing in mind the underlying objective of maintaining the unity of the family.

- For close family members (i.e. not extended ones who are subject to the express Reg 8(2) requirement of historic dependency/cohabitation), dependency need not have existed abroad: it can arise in the host state: Pedro [2009] EWCA Civ 1358.

The Guidance on Direct Family Members explained that a family member should be accepted as dependent where they could not meet their essential living needs without the financial support of that person. This could be established

- even if they also received financial support or income somewhere else (but which was at a level not adequate to meet their essentials needs): *"For example, an applicant can still be considered dependent if they receive a pension to cover half of their essential needs and money from the relevant EEA national to cover the other half"*
- For these purposes essential needs included accommodation, utilities and food.

Singh [2022] EWCA Civ 1054 notes that education could be an aspect of *'essential living needs'*.

11.5.2 No requirement for prior lawful residence and prior presence

Illegal entrants and overstayers could obtain EEA residence rights as family members, or EFMs. But EFMs would have to persuade the HO that discretion should be exercised in their favour notwithstanding their immigration history.

In the landmark case of Metock (Case C-127/08) the ECJ held that:

- the right of a national of a non-member country who was a family member of a Union citizen to accompany, join or remain with that citizen could not be made conditional on prior lawful residence in the EEA
- nor could the right be said to be conditional on physically accompanying a Union citizen from one country to another – it was the exercise of the rights of free movement in the wider sense (rather than physically moving between countries) by the Union citizen that triggers the right to be accompanied by the spouse
- a non-EEA national spouse of a Union citizen who accompanied or joined or sought to remain with that citizen could benefit from the Directive, irrespective of when and where the marriage took place and of how that spouse entered the host Member State
- it made no difference whether third country nationals who were family members of a Union citizen had entered the host Member State before or after becoming family members of that citizen

The Metock ruling meant that those who were in the UK irregularly – even those removable under UK law and facing imminent removal – would gain a right to reside immediately on becoming a genuine family member of a qualified person. Kutbuddin [2023] UKUT 76 (IAC) confirms that this approach applies to EFMs as well as to other EEA categories.

> **Example**
>
> Clare is French and permanently resident in the UK. She met and married Carl here in the UK. Carl is a failed asylum seeker who entered the UK unlawfully from a third country outside the EEA. Following Metock (and of course before the end of the transitional period), Carl would have obtained residence on the basis of his relationship with Clare. Only the public policy, public security or public health clauses might stand in his way: but of course they wouldn't have applied in most cases.
>
> The same is true under the EUSSch to some extent. Suppose the above scenario was set during the grace period (or thereafter with a reasonable excuse for lateness). Clare remains eligible to apply for EUSS, either under rEU11 condition 1 (as a holder of a documented right of permanent resident) or under condition 3 (on the basis of the 5-year residence she has accrued).
>
> Carl, as her spouse, was entitled to apply for EUSS under the same conditions (if he had also been granted permanent residence already under rEU11 condition 1, if not, under condition 3. If he has less than 5 years' residence as Clare's spouse, he would apply under condition 3 for EUPSS, as rEU14 allows for a grant of EUPSS where the only condition for EUSS which is not met is the residence requirement.
>
> Carl's lack of status should not prevent such an application from succeeding.

11.5.3 Sham marriage/ marriage of convenience

Free movement rights for a spouse or civil partner did not extend to a party to a marriage or civil partnership of convenience, nor to participants in sham marriages (see MIL 6.2.11 for the difference, & MIL 2.3.5.5 for procedures and guidance generally). The same is the case under the EUSSch. Agho [2015] EWCA Civ 1198 held that the burden of proof for proving whether a marriage is a sham for immigration law purposes rests with the HO:

What it comes down to is that as a matter of principle a spouse establishes a prima facie case that he or she is a family member of an EEA national by providing the marriage certificate and the spouse's passport; that the legal burden is on the Secretary of State to show that any marriage thus proved is a marriage of convenience; and that that burden is not discharged merely by showing 'reasonable suspicion'. Of course in the usual way the evidential burden may shift to the applicant by proof of facts which justify the inference that the marriage is not genuine, and the facts giving rise to the inference may include a failure to answer a request for documentary proof of the genuineness of the marriage where grounds for suspicion have been raised.

See further Rosa [2016] EWCA Civ 14, IS Serbia [2008] UKAIT 00031 and Papajorgji [2012] UKUT 38 (IAC) (and MIL 2.3.5.6 re the shifting burden of proof in immigration appeals generally).

Some other points on sham marriages:

- There is useful Commission guidance (COM (2009) 313 Final) on the approach to be taken to "marriage of convenience" allegations, specifying the kinds of consideration that might legitimately give rise to a concern. See further the Commission's Handbook on addressing the issue of alleged marriages of convenience
- Refusals on "sham marriage" grounds may be shortly followed by removal directions (MIL 11.9.3). In the EUSSch context, a removal decision may be issued and the application then refused on suitability grounds (see EUSS Suitability guidance under 'referral to immigration enforcement')
- An interview may be used to investigate the *bona fides* of a marriage. The Commission Handbook, as cited in Miah [2014] UKUT 515 (IAC), sets out that *'Contradictions, inconsistencies, lack of detail and implausible statements which are relevant for the decision making should be identified and explicitly put to the interviewed spouses.'* Miah goes on to emphasise that the interview record must be fully disclosed, including the interviewer's comments, subject to the need to protect anonymity in an exceptional case
- In Nimo [2020] UKUT 88 (IAC) the UT revisited Miah. That decision concluded that the SSHD was under a duty to disclose not only marriage interviews in immigration appeals, but also the interviewer's comments, usually found on form ICD.4605. The Nimo Tribunal disapproves Miah in so far as that case suggested interview comments (as opposed to interview records) should be disclosed But disclosure would be essential if the interviewer's notes included something that would actively assist an Appellant, eg a comment on their apparent state of health, which should then be provided: failure to do so would be contrary to the duty of litigants not to mislead the Tribunal
- Sadovska [2017] UKSC 54 reiterated and helpfully summarised the legal principles which should guide the handling of alleged sham marriage cases. If the EEA national faced enforcement action, they would enjoy the full protection of EU law. A person with permanent residence could not be removed under Art 28 of the Citizens Directive absent serious public policy grounds Decisions would have to be proportionate to the free movement rights with which they interfered, bearing in mind "he who asserts must prove". Sadovska then points out that (more limited) protections exist even for the non-EEA national partner who was an overstayer, removable as such and not yet a family member (as the couple had been prevented from marrying): as part of the "*extensive examination of the personal circumstances*" and reasoned justification for decisions owed to EFMs
- Elsakhawy [2018] 86 holds that PACE codes do not apply to marriage investigation visits or interviews, essentially because criminal prosecutions brought on the back of immigration enforcement questioning are very rare.The decision summarises the role of one of the individuals involved in researching the reality of a claimed relationship, who was both a criminal investigator and a digital media investigator. In the latter role he used open source material to investigate publicly available open source material, such as Facebook. Those advising clients whose immigration histories are such as to attract suspicion about the nature of their relationships may wish to consider taking instructions on social media records

Top tip

This tip also applies to appeals against refusals or curtailment under the EUSSch. These might arise as a straightforward suitability refusal on the false representations ground; or where the case was referred to immigration enforcement on an allegation of a sham marriage and a removal decision is made; or curtailment under the explicit sham marriage ground; or revocation of ILR on the basis it was obtained by deception.

Once an allegation is made that a marriage is one of convenience, it is important to put together a strong case on appeal that demonstrates the relationship is a genuine one. Think about:

- obtaining evidence independent of the couple: witnesses who know them well, be they friends, neighbours or work colleagues, particularly where they are figures of authority from a church, workplace or elsewhere
- obtaining social media records showing intimate expressions of affection
- explaining why discrepancies arose at the interview
- has a complaint been made about the interview? was it made before the decision on the application? should one have been made?

And always request a direction from the FTT that the underlying interview be disclosed

The Bilal Ahmed ruling means that the appellant may be removed before the appeal happens. As well as causing the person concerned to wait outside the UK for the duration of the appeal process (estimated at around two years at present) this would weaken any appellant's position considerably and made it even harder to address the routinely late and inadequate evidence from the HO. By providing better evidence of the relationship, if necessary by making a fresh application, the HO might at least be persuaded not to remove the person, pre-appeal.

It came to light in February 2021 that UKVI employs an algorithm in deciding upon which marriages raised suspicion, one factor being, simply, the nationalities of the parties to it. Awareness of this issue may be helpful in challenging the lawfulness of investigations, as the application of such an algorithm used in deciding visit visas was found to be unlawful and was abolished following JCWI's challenge in 2020.

11.5.4 Comprehensive sickness insurance cover

The possession of comprehensive sickness insurance cover (CSIC) was a prerequisite of meeting the definition of some forms of qualified person or family member:

- Students and the self-sufficient require CSIC (Reg 4(1)(d)(ii, 4(1)(c)(ii))
- So do their family members (Reg 4(2)(b))

This was a very important requirement in relation to EEA Regs 2016 applications. The EUSSch does not require CSIC. For a time it was said by HO Guidance to remain an issue in relation to the good character requirement in naturalisation applications (MIL 12.5.2).

Many people may have thought themselves safely exercising Treaty Rights over time because they were studying or financially independent. But they could be derailed by a lack of CSIC. However, years after many people had been (it was to transpire) wrongly refused, the CJEU ruled that NHS cover sufficed all along, such that anyone ordinarily resident in the UK did not require anything else. At the domestic level Ahmad [2014] EWCA Civ 988 had upheld the necessity of possessing a form of CSIC which is independent of the NHS. But Commissioners for HMRC [2022] EUECJ C-247/20 held that affiliation to the UK's public sickness insurance system (ie the) NHS sufficed as CSIC and did not represent a disproportionate burden on the state's public finances. The EEA Qualified Persons Guidance now confirms that under domestic law, people were entitled to access the NHS if they were "ordinarily resident" in the UK.

11.6 Rights of admission and residence (including Accession- and Association Agreements re the A8- and A2 states, Croatia, Turkey etc)

This section combines detailed information about the rights of admission and residence based on the 2004 Citizens' Directive, as transposed by the 2016 EEA Regs. As stated above, those Regs were repealed at 11pm on 31 December 2020 but saved with modifications by the Grace Period Regs 2020 in relation to EEA/Swiss nationals who resided lawfully (under the same Regulations) and their family members. These regulations confer rights of residence, entitlements to benefits and housing during the Grace Period. Keeping up one's continuous lawful residence is, of course, not just important in the immediate term for accessing services but also to future applications such as naturalisation. It remains important, therefore, to be able to determine who resided lawfully under the 2016 Regs before their repeal.

The rights under the 2016 Regs were as follows:

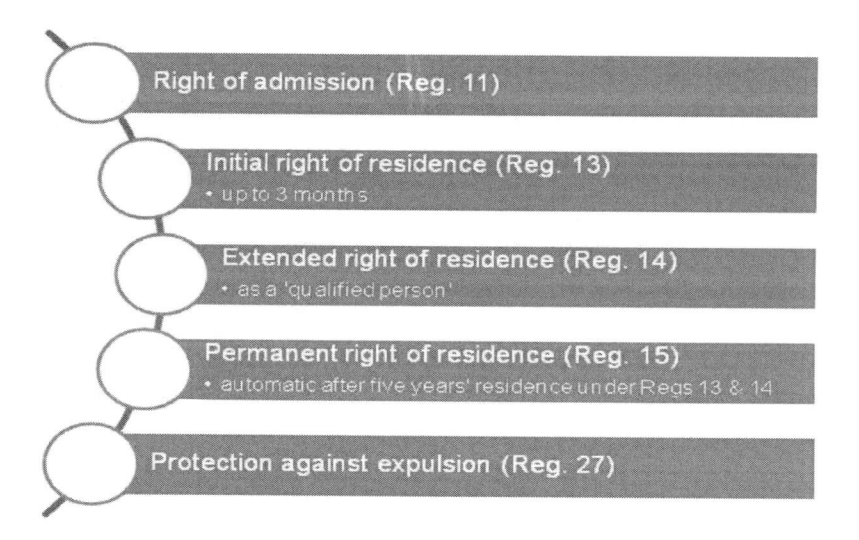

- Right of admission (Reg. 11)
- Initial right of residence (Reg. 13)
  - up to 3 months
- Extended right of residence (Reg. 14)
  - as a 'qualified person'
- Permanent right of residence (Reg. 15)
  - automatic after five years' residence under Regs 13 & 14
- Protection against expulsion (Reg. 27)

11.6.1 Right of admission

Before the end of the transition period, all EEA nationals and EEA family members had a right of admission (without requiring leave to enter or remain, under s7 IA 1988). That statutory protection was repealed on 31 December 2020 – then, typically of the technique of the legal drafting for Brexit, it was then preserved so that it applied over the Grace Period (by the "grace period" Regulations 2020/1209) to EEA/Swiss nationals who had resided lawfully in the UK before the end of the transition period, and to their family members (MIL 11.1.1). Thus all those individuals could *reside* in the UK without any other form of immigration leave until 30 June 2021.

Those EEA and Swiss nationals could also continue to *enter* the UK during the grace period with only their passport or national ID card under the preserved Reg 11.

But for other individuals, admission toughened up as of 1 January 2021:

- Family members who held neither an EEA Regs residence document and EUSS/EUPSS lost their right of admission
- The right of admission for those lacking a formal residence document was previously governed by Reg 11(4), which mandated immigration officers to "*provide every reasonable opportunity [...] to prove by other means that*" they were a family member with a right to accompany the EEA national or join them in the UK
- Reg 11(4) watered down the need for prior 'entry clearance' requirement by way of family permit (CO Nigeria [2007] UKAIT 00070) (presuming an airline would let someone board without a visa)
- However, Reg 11(4) was deleted by the Grace Period Regs as part of the savings modifications. In short, the right of admission for family members without a UK-issued residence document ceased to exist at the end of the transition period. Hitherto family members could also enter using an EEA residence document issued to them as a family member by another member state (Article 10 and 20 residence cards) (see updated guidance).

The UK has long operated and enforced the family permit scheme by which those asserting EEA rights should obtain a family permit before travelling. The EUSSch family permit, as its EEA Regs predecessor was, is free and the permit must be issued as soon as possible if the person qualifies.

From 1 January 2021 there are essentially two routes:

- Holding an EUSS family permit
- Or applying under Appendix EU for EUSS/EUPSS from abroad. However one needs "*required proof*" to do so. Summarising the definition of "*required proof of entitlement to apply from outside the UK*" in Annex 1 to Appendix EU this is:
    - For EEA/Swiss nationals, their valid passport or national biometric ID card
    - For third country nationals, an EEA residence card (biometric residence card, permanent residence card or derivative residence card) or a biometric EUPSS residence card, issued following an application made from 6 April 2015. The SSHD can agree to accept alternative evidence if they cannot produce the document for circumstances beyond their control or due to compelling practical or compassionate reasons

See the *Visiting the UK as an EU, EEA or Swiss citizen* Guidance for procedures and requirements for EEA/Swiss nationals crossing the UK border from 1 January 2021. Those with visas or pending applications for EUPSS/EUSS, or with Frontier Worker permits, or S2 healthcare or Service Provider from Switzerland visas, can continue to use their national ID card to enter the UK until at least 31 December 2025. Otherwise ID cards will lose their power to effect entry from 1 October 2021 and passports will be needed. You can read what sea and air carriers are told by the HO in the *General Partner Pack* which confirms that carriers are not yet obliged to check digital status.

The Guidance *UK residence cards* clarifies the importance of non-EEA citizens applying for an EUSS BRC to replace an expired, lost or stolen residence card to re-enter the UK before they travel abroad (should the card be lost abroad then a free EUSS travel permit may be obtained). Replacement of an expired BRC is free of charge.

11.6.2 Initial right of residence

All EEA citizens and their family members, before the end of the transition period, enjoyed what was referred to in the EEA Regs as an 'initial right of residence' (Reg 13). This enabled an EEA citizen to travel to the UK and reside here for three months (along with their family members) but without having to establish that he or she was a qualified person.

This provision enhanced the possibilities of free movement around Europe by allowing for an unchallenged right to reside in order to become established (for example, whilst one earns money to fund a course of studies or to set up a business). In the UK before the end of transition, it could be asserted simply on production of a valid identity card or passport by the EEA national (Reg 13(1)) or of a valid passport by the third country national (Reg 13(2)).

The only caveats to the initial right of residence were:

- not becoming 'an unreasonable burden on the social assistance system of the United Kingdom' (Reg 13(3))
- public policy: being subject to an extant decision such as removal on grounds of public policy/security/health; refusal to issue residence documentation, cancellation of a right to reside, misuse of a right to reside, revocation of admission; and an EEA exclusion or deportation order

Reg 13 was effective over the Grace Period with only one modification: admission could be refused for post-transition period conduct on the domestic "conducive" standard (Reg 27A).

Reg 13's effect is that

- any EEA/Swiss national and their family members who first arrived in the three months immediately before 31 December 2020 (and avoided recourse to public funds or public policy problems) automatically benefited from the Grace Period Regs 2020

- earlier arrivals will have to prove that they were exercising treaty rights immediately before the end of transition, or that they had by then attained a right of permanent residence

11.6.3 Extended-, retained-, and derivative right of residence

11.6.3.1 Extended rights of residence

Qualified persons had a right to reside in the UK as long as they remained qualified persons (Reg 14(1)). In addition, in some circumstances, they were permitted to retain a right of residence even though their qualifying activity had ceased, as is discussed above (MIL 11.2.4.2: i.e. temporary incapacity or temporary unemployment for workers and the self-employed: Reg 6).

This right was subject to the same public policy regime for refusals as the initial right of residence: ie there could be a refusal where was an extant public policy decision in force (Reg 14(4)).

During the 'extended right of residence', qualified persons could apply for a Registration Certificate on production of a valid identity card or passport plus proof of their status us such – applications had to be granted without delay (Reg 17). The application was made on form EEA(QP) and cost £65. This certificate was not essential: it merely evidenced the right, it did not create it. Nevertheless, such certificates could be useful, particularly for EEA citizens likely to be travelling in and out of the UK who might otherwise suffer the inconvenience of regular questioning by HM Immigration Officers.

Similarly, the right to extended residence for family members was set out at Reg 14(2). However, the document to evidence their status and right of residence was referred to as a residence card, the details of which were set out at Reg 18.

Qualified persons could carry out qualifying activities and could not be subjected to any form of discrimination compared to the national workforce. This means that rights to benefits and other advantages enjoyed by the national workforce had to be made accessible in equal measure.

A family member had a right to reside in the UK with the qualified person for so long as they remained as such. There were no additional limitations relating to maintenance and accommodation, intention to live permanently with the other or subsisting marriage. The family members of qualified persons enjoyed the same rights to take up activities in Member States.

The children of EEA nationals employed (both at the time and historically) in a host Member State were entitled to the latter state's general educational, apprenticeship and vocational training courses, under the same conditions as a national.

These rights had to be respected in an extremely proactive way. The rights were derived from the Treaty and were innate, meaning that it was for Member States to protect and promote these rights as far as possible. For example, when an EEA citizen or family member entered a Member State, the authorities could do no more than check that their documents were in order. They were not entitled to ask further questions about intention, availability of funds, sponsors or the like – although, so long as they had a reasonable belief that there could be grounds for it, they could investigate exclusion on the grounds of public policy, public security or public health. The new regime may be rather jarring for travellers used to the light touch of the EU law era.

> **Examples**
>
> It is May 2019. Anya is German and has been working in the UK for two years. She has never applied for a registration certificate. Nevertheless, by virtue of her work, she has automatically acquired a right to reside.
>
> It is May 2020. Herman is Canadian. He entered the UK as a visitor and overstayed his visa. He married Anya a year ago, and Anya has continued working. Despite the fact Herman has done nothing about his immigration status. he has automatically acquired a right to reside by virtue of his family relationship

> with Anya and Anya's position as a qualified person. Herman could have applied for a residence card before the end of the transition period if he wanted to but he did not have to. But for Brexit he would have been on a 5-year route to permanent residence after five years of marriage, presuming Anya retained her right to reside for that period, whether or not he applied for the relevant paperwork.
>
> Brexit however means that both Anya and Herman should have applied for status under the EUSSch before 1 July 2021; now they must show reasonable grounds for late applications if they failed to take timely action

11.6.3.2 Retained rights of residence under the EEA Regs 2016

Sometimes family members of EEA citizens acquired independent rights of admission or residence in the UK where they had lost their family connection to the EEA national on whom their own residence rights were based, by e.g. death, divorce, or the EEA national leaving the UK.

Eg in Baumbast C-413/99, an EEA citizen had been living and working in the UK but then returned to his own country. In the meantime, his wife and child had effectively settled in the UK and the child was attending an educational course. The mother did not want to leave the UK. The ECJ held that the child had acquired a right to reside in the UK to pursue their education and, in addition, that this right would be ineffective if the child's mother was not permitted to remain in the UK to care for the child.

There were essentially **four** routes to retaining rights of residence despite ceasing to be the family member of a qualified person, under Reg 10. These were largely replicated in Appendix EU for applications under the EUSSch (see MIL 11.7). Namely:

- Where the qualified person died but the family member had resided in the UK for at least one year and was either him or herself employed, self-employed or self-sufficient or was the family member of such a person (i.e. the child or dependent relative) (Reg 10(2))

- Where the family member was the child of a qualified person who had died or left the UK where the family member had been attending an educational course (or the child of the qualified person's spouse or civil partner in the same circumstances) (Reg 10(3))

- Where the family member was a parent with actual custody of a child as described immediately above (Reg 10(4))

- Where there was a termination of the marriage or civil partnership Reg 10(5). This, the most frequently encountered, had four sub-routes: either

- prior to the *initiation of the proceedings* for the termination of the marriage or the civil partnership the marriage or civil partnership had lasted for at least three years and the parties to the marriage or civil partnership had resided in the United Kingdom for at least one year during its duration (Reg 10(5)(d)(i)), or

- the former spouse or civil partner of the qualified person had custody of a child of the qualified person (Reg 10(5)(d)(ii)), or

- the former spouse or civil partner of the qualified person had the right of access to a child of the qualified person under the age of 18 and a court had ordered that such access must take place in the United Kingdom (Reg 10(5)(d)(iii)); or

- the continued right of residence in the United Kingdom of the person was warranted by *particularly difficult circumstances*, such as they or another family member having been a victim of domestic violence while the marriage or civil partnership was subsisting (Reg 10(5)(d)(iv)).

Of the four principal routes above (ie Reg 10(2)-10(5), **two** contained an additional essentially economic requirement. The family member had to, effectively, step into the shoes of the qualified person by themselves effectively working, studying or being self-sufficient. Any of those forms of activity analogous to Treaty Right exercise would do: (Gauswami [2018] UKUT 275 (IAC)).

By contrast, the EUSSch retained rights rule, contained in the definition of "*family member who has retained the right of residence*" in Annex 1 to Appendix UK

- Has no equivalent of the economic requirement (ie to step into the EEA family member's shoes in terms of exercising treaty rights from termination onward: Reg 10(6). This is because that system is residence-based only. From point of termination, the applicant need no longer prove their spouse/CP'UKUK residence *alongside* their own. They need only show their own *residence* from that point onward – as a person who has retained their right of residence.
- More significantly broadened the retained rights category to others: including extended family members (see further 11.7)

Separation does not terminate family membership

It is important to understand that the spouse/ civil partner of an EEA citizen continued to be a spouse/CP, and thus a family member, as long as the marriage legally persisted – not only until cohabitation ceased. Separation did not dissolve this relationship for the purposes of EU law, nor did a decree nisi. It was only when a decree absolute had been issued that the relationship was considered no longer to qualify (Diatta v Land Berlin 1986 2 CMLR 164). Thus, unless there was a divorce/dissolution, the case was not a retained rights case. It was simply a spouse/CP application.

The main problem in those cases was *proving* the EEA partner's continued UK residence and exercise of Treaty Rights. That had to be shown from the time the couple separated up to the moment that the non-EEA partner established permanent residence (ie the moment when 5 years of residence as a spouse/CP was achieved). Hard going where the separation was less than amicable. Similarly, under Appendix EU, continued proof of the EEA partner's UK *residence* must be provided (although the requirement for proof of *exercise of Treaty Rights* falls away).

When is the point of termination?

The case law shows:

- Kuldip Singh (Case C-218/14): the date at which the right of residence is retained is the date on which the *proceedings for divorce are initiated*. Therefore, it is not necessary to prove that the EEA national was a QP between that date and the date on which the marriage/civil partnership is finally terminated. Gracefully the SSHD accepted this in Baigazieva [2018] EWCA Civ 1088. This being a simple question of fact to be determined on a case by case basis
- The CJEU held in NA (C-115/15) that where there has been domestic violence, and the EEA national then leaves the UK, the divorce proceedings must have commenced before the EEA leaves the UK for the non-EEA spouse to have retained a right to reside. But this position was revisited in Belgian State [2021] EUECJ C-930/19. Contrary to NA it was now recognised that the objective of protecting spouses from blackmail on the basis of their immigration status could be served only if divorce proceedings may be initiated after the departure of the EU citizen from the host Member State, albeit within a reasonable period to achieve legal certainty (three years representing an unreasonable delay).

There is Guidance Free Movement Rights: retained rights of residence..

Evidencing that there was a right to be retained, up until termination

The retained rights regime often caused evidential problems for those family members who need to establish the whereabouts and activity of the relevant EEA national prior to termination. They needed to show that they **continued to have a right to reside** up until **the date of termination**. Or they would have nothing to retain. If they had lost contact with their ex-spouse, or the ex-spouse refused to assist them, it would often be difficult to provide evidence that their ex-spouse was in the UK with a right to reside on the relevant date.

They would need to do everything they could to find that evidence, up to and including the hiring of a private detective: but what if their efforts drew a blank?

- Case law held that the burden of proof on establishing that the applicant came within the EEA Regs lay upon the applicant, not the government: MJ [2008] UKAIT 00034. There the applicant sought to prove they retained rights after their EEA sponsor had left the UK, but they could not prove that fact. The same principle applied where the fact that needed to be proven was that the EEA family stayed in the UK and exercised Treaty Rights up until termination
- Balogun [2023] EWCA Civ 414 holds that residence rights as a family member of an EU national worker would have to continue seamlessly into the right to retain residence. So the third country national spouse must be working when the divorce decree becomes absolute, and imprisonment removing one from the labour market might prevent the seamless transition.
- Under s40(1)(j) of the UK Borders Act 2007 the HO has the power to obtain a person's National Insurance and other HMRC records if desired. In Amos [2011] EWCA Civ 552 the Court of Appeal agreed that the burden did nevertheless rest with the claimant but left open the possibility that the HO might assist a claimant if requested to do so or if directed to do so by the tribunal. Amos directions have since become very common
- HO practice was to generally refuse to assist the applicant in evidencing the position of the EEA national, unless there had been domestic violence, but they would do so in the event a direction was issued by the Tribunal (the FTT procedure Rules at 4(3)(d) empower a direction to 'a party or another person to provide documents, information, evidence or submissions to the Tribunal or a party')

So, in a retained rights case under the EEA Regs in the past, and in a retained rights case under the EUSSch, it might be necessary to make an application notwithstanding a lack of evidence. Then one must hope that the HO recognises a right of appeal. Where an appeal ensues, the Appellant may apply to the FTT for a direction that the HO provides any information that they have access to as to the whereabouts and activities of the EEA national.

Examples

Robert and Steve became civil partners in the Netherlands in 2014. Robert is South African and Steve is Dutch. They lived in the Netherlands for two years and came to the UK in 2018 when Steve was posted to the UK by his employer, an oil company.

In 2020, they separated and dissolved their civil partnership. As long as Steve remained employed, self-employed or self-sufficient, and continued to have a right to reside up to the initiation of dissolution of their civil partnership, and as long as Robert then started exercising Treaty rights, he could choose to apply for an EEA residence card under Reg 10(5)(d)(i), or apply for EUPSS under the retained rights category. EUSS applications require residence, not exercise of treaty rights by either partner.

From 1 January 2021, the residence card option fell away unless Robert had applied before that date and his residence card remained outstanding.

In any case an EUSS application by the 30th June 2021 would have been mandatory although a late application may be accepted if reasonable grounds for a late application are shown.

Proving that Robert has or had a retained right to reside required proof that Steve had a *right to reside* (EEA) or at least *residence* (EUSS) up to the date dissolution proceedings were initiated. Hopefully, Steve will assist him with that! If not, and Robert's application is delayed, he could argue that he has reasonable grounds to apply late. Eg due to "other compelling practical or compassionate reasons" (see main EUSS guidance).

Marie and Peter were married four years ago. Marie is French and Peter is from Cameroon. Marie was already living and working in the UK when they got married and Peter came to the UK directly. They have one child, Cecile, who is four years old and has just started attending school. Marie now wants to return to France but Peter does not want to leave his part-time job in the UK and he wants Cecile to grow up in the UK. They decide to separate and Marie returns to France, leaving Peter to care for Cecile in the UK.

If we were still within the transition period, Cecile would have retained a right of residence under Reg 10(3) and Peter under Reg 10(4). In addition both Cecile and Peter would soon have qualified for a permanent right of residence in the UK. They could also have applied under the EUSSch.

Now, following the end of the transition period, the EUSS is their only option.

If Peter and his daughter had already applied for EUPSS as family members of Marie, they would not be required to update the HO about the change in their eligibility category (but it would be a good idea to do so for peace of mind in view of their future EUSS application).

If they held no status under the EUSS before the general application deadline, they should have applied in time (and if they have not, will need to add reasonable grounds representations which will hopefully be accepted).

Either way, they qualify for EUPSS under the equivalent parts of the definition of "family member who has retained the right of residence" in Annex 1 of Appendix EU (paras (b) and (c)), and for EUSS once Peter has clocked up 5 years' residence (in a combination of being a family member and a family member with retained rights) under condition 3 of rEU11 in Appendix EU (enabling his daughter Cecile to settle slightly early under condition 7 in rEU11). Given the 30 June 2021 deadline has passed, reasonable grounds for delay must be shown (MIL 11.1A).

Top Tip

In a retained right of residence case where you require evidence of the ongoing activities (EEA) or at least residence (EUSS) of a former/separated spouse, consider:

- Witnesses with direct knowledge of their former/current employment
- Evidence obtained by an independent person (including the applicant's lawyer) making direct, possibly discreet enquiries
- Evidence from social media of ongoing economic activity
- Enquiries of Companies House for records of economic activity by any company which they set up
- Always bear in mind that even gaps in employment may not prevent their holding the relevant status, e.g. because they may have been a jobseeker in between periods of employment or have entered education.

Neither the Regs nor the Directive made provision for the breakdown of *durable partner* relationships, even where there has been domestic violence. Unlike the domestic Rules which provide protection in the domestic violence route under Appendix FM.

Things improved with the EUSSch. Anyone whose family relationship breaks down because of domestic abuse is covered, providing a more generous regime than the old.

Looking back at the system under the 2016 Regs, although EU law provided strong automatic residence rights for the family members of an EEA national who was, at the time, exercising Treaty Rights in the UK, the protection dropped off sharply when the EEA national lost that status. We have seen the various forms of retained residence rights above. These did not cater for all situations.

The most difficult situation arose where the EEA "sponsor" left the country. It was long thought that in this situation any family members with residence rights dependent on that Sponsor would simply lose EU law protection. And resort to whatever case they could make under the Immigration Rules, including a human rights claim on private life grounds. In Chenchooliah [2019] EUECJ C-94/18 the CJEU rather muddled the waters for individuals left high and dry in this situation. It points out in that case that the Citizens Directive provided a series of protections at Article 15 for the family members of EU workers facing expulsion on grounds other than public policy. Including where a former family member lost their temporary right of residence. These protections were equivalent to the procedural protections that a person excluded on public policy grounds would receive:

- To receive notice of the reasons for their expulsion and at least 30 days' notice of their departure date and an explanation of how to access an appeal
- There must also be the opportunity to apply for a suspensive appeal (essentially the same that applied under the EEA Regs 2016 under Reg 33)

There were also substantive protections:

- Their expulsion should only proceed after a full consideration of length of residence, "age, state of health, family and economic situation, social and cultural integration into the host Member State and the extent of his/her links with the country of origin" (Art 31(3), Art 28(1)).
- Plus at least one substantive right, via Art 15(4): there is be no ban on their return to the UK.

What impact might Chenchooliah have for the former family members of an EU national? Clearly the Citizens Directive does not treat them as immune to expulsion.

- However, their expulsion can proceed only after a full consideration of all relevant circumstances (and one that is clearly much wider than the criteria for the "private life" routes under Rule 276ADE)
- The mandatory bans on return that would normally apply to overstayers under r9.8.7 in Part 9 cannot apply
- We saw no further developments of the doctrine before Brexit. But the WWA (Art 21) requires Art 15 Citizens Directive protection to continue. So we may not have heard the last of Chenchooliah.

11.6.3.3 Derivative rights of residence

Reg 16 in the 2016 Regs addressed derivative residence rights. In so doing it incorporated case law developments in the understanding of Treaty rights. Such as the cases of Chen C-200/02, Ibrahim C-310/08 and Texeira C-480/08, and Zambrano C-34/09. Reg 16 was saved for the Grace Period. Reg was the original basis for the definitions of "*person with a derivative right to reside*" and "*person with a Zambrano right to reside*" in Annex 1 to Appendix EU as providing the basis for fitting those categories.

Entitlement to a derivative residence card ensued for those falling within one of the routes set out below. So long as the applicant was not 'exempt person'. Reg16(7) defined this as someone who has: any other right of residence under the 2016 Regs, an exemption from immigration control under s8 of the 1971 Act (seamen and aircrew exemptions); the right of abode (this includes British citizens) or ILR. The specific routes were:

- The **primary carer of a self-sufficient EEA national child** (i.e. the equivalent of the Chen case (MIL 11.2.4.4): Reg 16(2))
- The EEA Regs recognised the Teixeira and Ibrahim principle as including **a child of an EEA national** Reg 16(3) **who resided in the United Kingdom at a time when the EEA national parent was residing in the United Kingdom as a worker**; and
  - **was in education** in the United Kingdom (excluding nursery education but not excluding education before compulsory school age where this was at an equivalent level to school) (Reg 16(7)(a))
  - In Ahmed [2013] UKUT 00089 (IAC) the UT explained that the child need not have been in school whilst the EEA national parent was working in the UK. NA C-115/5 the CJEU confirmed that the former migrant worker parent did not need to have been resident in the Member State when the child began to attend school or university. Reg 16(3)(b) adopted

this position: thus when the EEA parent left the UK the family members could lose their right to reside in the UK, but then regain it, as a derivative right, on the child commencing school
- The **primary carer of the child, in education, of an EEA national** above: Reg 16(4) (this could be a non-EEA national or the EEA national parent themselves, where they had no other right to reside and are thus not an 'exempt' person under Reg 16(7)(c))
- The **primary carer of a British citizen who would be unable to reside in the UK if that primary carer were required to leave** (Zambrano: Reg 16(5)):
  - Reg 16(5) represented domestic recognition of the Zambrano principle, ie that not only positive exercise of free movement rights, but also threats to the effectiveness of the right to EU citizenship under Art 20 TFEU could require the grant of residence rights to avoid a child being compelled to leave the European Union due to their primary carer's lack of immigration status. The core notion (see further MIL 5.3.2.1) was that:

    'Article 20 TFEU … precludes a Member State from refusing a third country national upon whom his minor children, who are European Union citizens, are dependent, a right of residence in the Member State of residence and nationality of those children, and from refusing to grant a work permit to that third country national, in so far as such decisions deprive those children of the genuine enjoyment of the substance of the rights attaching to the status of European Union citizen.'

  - Following Zambrano the CJEU was slow to suggest any further extension of the principle. Subsequent cases emphasised that the protection focussed on avoiding a compulsion to leave rather than on respecting family unity.
  - Thus, where the EU citizen had a parent or carer entitled to live in the EU, the provision would not give rights to the other parent; e.g. where a parent was refused entry to the UK, or was facing deportation to a country outside the EU, that in itself would not deny the children a right to live in the EU if someone else was available to care for them: Sanade [2012] UKUT 48 (IAC); VM (Jamaica) [2017] EWCA Civ 255.
- The UK cases interpreted Zambrano such that the key issue was whether the EU national (usually child) would be driven out of the territory of the EU (not just the UK) by the consequences of the decision, either because their carer would physically take them abroad, or because their future quality of life would be so poor as to compel their departure. There was a very full discussion in Harrison [2012] EWCA Civ 1736
- However, family unity principles were identified as relevant in Chavez-Vilchez [2017] EUECJ C-133/15 where the CJEU explained that the mere availability of an alternative carer was not the whole question. A decision maker would have to assess the best interests of the child, having regard to everything relevant, including their age, physical and emotional development, and emotional ties to each parent, bearing in mind any threats to the child's equilibrium
- In Patel [2019] UKSC 59 the Supreme Court considered the circumstances in which a British citizen child could be said to be *compelled* to leave the EU. Before this case, Zambrano claims succeeded only where there had been absolutely no practical choice as to whether or not the child would have the UK: which tended to be the case only where the parents had been separated and the parent facing expulsion had been the primary carer. Building on the thinking in Chavez-Vilchez, the Supreme Court held that the fact that the other (Union citizen) parent was actually able and willing to assume sole responsibility for the child's daily care was *relevant* but not in itself *sufficient* to deem that there was no compulsion upon the child to nevertheless leave the country. It would be necessary to determine what would *in fact* happen having regard to the child's development and emotional ties. The fact that the Union parent was "*perfectly capable of looking after the child*" did not mean that there was no question of compulsion from the child's perspective: that would be sufficient for EU law purposes. This was a very significant step forward. If the evidence showed that the family felt driven to relocate abroad by their circumstances, this could be sufficient compulsion for Zambrano to bite
- Although Reg 16(4) was voiced by reference to a British citizen, Zambrano also applied where, for example, a child in the UK was a citizen of another EEA country: the test in all cases was whether the adverse decision would require the child to leave the territory of the Union: Ahmed [2013] UKUT 00089 (IAC)
- The Zambrano principle could be relied upon in entry clearance applications as well as to obtain rights whilst in the United Kingdom (Reg 11(5)(e)): the Entry Clearance Guidance *EEA nationals EUN01* expressly accepted this, as did the Tribunal in MA and SM Iran [2013] UKUT 380.

Staatssecretaris van Justitie en Veiligheid (Mere thailandaise d'un enfant mineur neerlandais) [2023] EUECJ C-459/20 explains that such applications could not be rejected simply because the child's EU residence was thought not in their real or plausible interests, and factors such as the third country national parent not always having had daily care of the child but now having sole care, or the fact that the Union citizen could assume the daily care role, were not decisive
- Velaj [2022] EWCA Civ 767 explains that decision makers should address the impact on the British Citizen if *in fact* the primary carer (or both primary carers) *would* leave the UK for an indefinite period: ie the reality of the situation, not hypotheticals. Now the *Chen and Ibrahim Teixeira cases* contains a distinct section on the Velaj assessment which sets out a two-stage consideration: (1) consider whether an applicant could obtain another lawful immigration status because of the possibility of obtaining an alternative domestic immigration status, which may require close analysis of whether they have previously held Appendix FM leave, or would have received it had they applied, having regard to an application's affordability (and fee waivers) and merits; (2) consider whether the person said to be dependent on the applicant would in fact be required to leave the UK for an indefinite period absent that person's residence here.

The focus above was on *children and their primary carers*. What of *adults* with care needs?

- Regs 16(4)-(5) did not refer to the British citizen being a child, but only to a primary care relationship: so a beneficiary might have been looking after an *adult with care needs* who, if compelled to leave the European Union to accompany their carer, would equally have lost the benefit of their EU citizenship
- The UT emphasised the difference between a child who lacked agency as to their own destiny versus an adult. There needed to be evidence of *compulsion* rather than merely the loss of a preferred carer (Ayinde and Thinjom [2015] UKUT 560 (IAC). Bearing in mind that it might be implausible to claim that one would seriously give up NHS & social welfare entitlements in this country to follow a relative abroad. Patel [2019] UKSC 59 makes the same point
- RM (Pakistan) [2021] EWCA Civ 1754 explains that the mere availability of state care could not act as a trump card in every appeal, although it would make it more difficult for many providing care to elderly relatives to bring themselves within the *Zambrano* principle. The actual dependency of the EU national on the applicant was always central. The fact of an adult's choice to leave (based on an understandable preference for their relative's care) will not be sufficient unless there is an absence of practical alternatives leaving them no choice in the matter.
- When considering derivative rights for a parent, particularly in a case where the person did not appear to meet the exacting requirements of Reg 16 or of the partner category in Appendix FM, it was useful to remember the provision in s117B(6) of the 2002 Act which states that the public interest does not require the parent's removal where they have a genuine and subsisting parental relationship with a qualifying child, and it would not be reasonable to expect the child to leave the United Kingdom. Where such an argument could succeed on Article 8 grounds, the parent would be entitled to leave under UK law. By contrast with a grant of a derivative rights card under the EEA Regs, that could preferable both in providing the parent with a possible route to settlement, and with the possibility of claiming public funds. The Zambrano category under the EUSSch does provide for settlement, but access to public funds remains disputed.
- As we can see, Zambrano protected an EU national's *primary carer* from expulsion.
    - This was defined in Reg 16(8) as a relative or legal guardian with primary responsibility for providing care, or a person who shares responsibility for that persons' care with one other person
    - There was once a requirement that, where care is shared equally with another person, the other person must not be an exempt person. It was removed on 24 July 2018
    - The EEA Regs 2016 at Reg 16(5) and (8) provided that a 'primary carer' had to be a *direct relative or a legal guardian* of an EEA national. The accompanying guidance set out that *direct relative* extended to relationships between siblings, children and parents, and grandchildren and grandparents, but no further
    - Saeed [2018] EWHC 1707 (Admin) decided that the relationship of nephew/niece did not fall within the class of direct relatives
    - L3 [2022] EWCA Civ 1357 holds that the Zambrano principle is not retained EU law (save for its express incorporation into the EUSSch)

CHAPTER 11: European Union Law

General points to note regarding derivative residence rights:

- The EEA Regs required the relevant children and their siblings to be under 18, which was contentious as generally under EU law a person was considered to be a child whilst they remain under the age of 21
- Persons with a derivative right to reside under Reg 16 would be entitled to apply for a derivative residence card under Reg 20
- Those with a derivative right to reside were excluded from becoming permanently resident (Reg 15(2)); though they could succeed under the long residence category of the Immigration Rules (at para 276B) (MIL 5.2.1 - the Guidance: Long residence holds that time spent in the UK under EU law was lawful residence). Note, under the EUSSch, EUSS is available to those with Zambrano- or other derivative rights
- At the point where the child reached the age of 18, or in the case of Reg 16(5) is able to live independently, the parents/carers would lose their right to reside. In regard to the EUSS adaptation of Reg 16, this has been remedied by allowing the child to be regarded as being under 18 where EUPSS was initially granted when they were still a minor
- Zambrano and Chen parents were denied recourse to public funds. R (HC) v SSWP [2017] UKSC 73 confirmed that Zambrano carers are not eligible to contribution-based benefits which have a 'right to reside' test (i.e. income support, child benefit, child tax credits, and housing and homelessness assistance). Zambrano parents would, however, have recourse, where necessary, to support under the Children Act 1989: Sanneh [2015] EWCA Civ 49)). Teixeira and Ibrahim parents, however, were entitled to recourse to public funds
- The Zambrano principle was recognised in cases where there was no public policy dimension. So for a while the scope of any public policy exception to the principle had been uncertain. Reg 16(12) provided that an enforcement decision could only be taken to those entitled to derivative residence cards on public policy grounds.. This was consistent with two linked cases, CS v UK C-304/14 and Marin v Spain C-165/14, where the CJEU had ruled that Zambrano-like derived rights of residence under EU law were not automatically lost if a crime was committed. Instead, each case had to be assessed on its merits and a judgement reached applying normal principles of EU law. Robinson (Jamaica) [2020] UKSC 53 confirms this. It holds that there is no requirement for the SSHD to show "exceptional circumstances": the only question is whether expulsion would be disproportionate to fundamental rights
- It seems that Zambrano applications are a last resort & thus required a person to have applied unsuccessfully (and failed) to obtain leave under the Rules first: (MIL 11.7.5.2 at "Annex 1 definition of a 'person with a Zambrano right to reside'")

11.6.4 Permanent residence

Reg 15 provided for permanent residence. This has been saved without modifications for EEA/Swiss nationals lawfully resident in the UK since before the end of transition, and their family members, by the Grace Period Regs 2020. The right to permanent residence can no longer continue to accrue under this provision but knowledge of this right, and the operation of Reg 15, is still relevant, eg:

- to determining what other rights (to entry, residence and public services) EEA migrants may hold under the Grace Period Regs 2020 if they have not yet been granted EUSSS
- to advise and assist clients with outstanding PR card applications, lodged before the end of transition (perhaps lodged to assist with proving past lawful status in support of a naturalisation application)
- a right of permanent residence, accrued in the past, may need to be proven to remedy subsequent gaps in exercise of Treaty rights as part of a naturalisation application (which looks for 10 years' lawful residence as part of the good character guidance)

Under the EEA Regs the following automatically acquired a permanent right of residence in the UK:

- EEA citizens who had lived here for five years in accordance with the EEA Regs (Reg 15(1)(a))
- Third country family members of qualified persons who had lived here for five years in accordance with the EEA Regs (Reg 15(1)(b))

- A worker or self-employed person who had ceased activity in the circumstances defined under Reg 5 (retirement, illness and incapacity in various circumstances), and their family members (Reg 15(1)(c), (d)) One relevant question was whether they had *"resided in the United Kingdom continuously for more than three years prior to the termination."* In Gubeladze [2019] UKSC 31 the Supreme Court held that this referred to *factual residence* rather than *"legal residence."* So the fact that an Accession country national might have failed to register their employment in line with the relevant Regulations applicable (during the period which that country's nationals were subject to restrictions on accessing the labour market) did not prevent them from later acquiring permanent residence as a worker who had ceased activities.
- Family members of a worker or self-employed person
  - who had died,
  - where the family member had resided with him immediately before his death, and
  - where he had been living in the UK for at least the two years immediately before his death or the death had been the result of an accident at work or an occupational disease (Reg 15(1)(e)

- Those who had resided in the UK under the EEA Regs for five years ending with a period during which they retained a right of residence (former family members whose qualified person had died or from whom they had divorced)

Other relevant considerations in relation to permanent residence:

- As was the case for initial and extended rights of residence, Reg 15(4) reiterated the public policy exclusions. Namely where one of these decisions was extant: removal on grounds of public policy/security/health; refusal to issue residence documentation, cancellation of a right to reside, misuse of a right to reside, revocation of admission; and, from 24 July 2018, an exclusion order under Reg 23(5) or deportation under Reg 32(3).
- Continuity of residence was not broken by periods of absence from the UK for six months or less per year, absence due to military service, or one absence not exceeding twelve months for an important reason (e.g. child birth, serious illness, study or an overseas posting) – though it would normally be broken by imprisonment or expulsion (Reg 3). Viscu [2019] EWCA Civ 1052 held that time in a young offenders' institution counted as imprisonment. But it might be recognised as less disruptive to integration than would be the case for an adult offender
- Permanent residence lapsed with two years continuous absence from the UK (Reg 15(2))
- As the language suggested, the *serious reasons* allowing excessive absence mentioned were not exhaustive: Babajanov [2013] UKUT 513 (IAC). The case held that it would be possible to continue to be resident in the UK notwithstanding absence abroad where a person is integrated here, as where a minor is stranded abroad after a parent returns here, because there is no adequate accommodation in this country
- Residence under previous Directives would count towards permanent residence (Schedule 4: Transitional Provisions of the EEA Regs, also saved during the grace period)
- The right of permanent residence, which in all respects was equivalent to ILR, brought with it enhanced protection from removal, as is discussed below
- A permanently resident person, whether an EEA national or a family member, had that status unconditionally: once permanent residence was established, there was no further requirement to be a qualified person or family member
- Rights of residence under European Union law prior to the Citizens Directive entering force could still be relied on in acquiring a right of permanent residence (MIL 11.6.4.1)
- Sometimes a person could have acquired a permanent right of residence some time ago, which could easily be overlooked, for example where the case has subsequently become more complicated and the focus has turned to questions such as a retained right of residence: Idezuna [2011] UKUT 00474 (IAC). So never forget to identify the historic rights of residence before going on examine more recent events
- Proof of permanent residence could be sought. Via a Document Certifying Permanent Residence for EEA nationals, and for non-EEA family members, a Permanent Residence Card on Form EEA(PR), both £65, issued under Reg 19. This was not essential but could help document one's identity
- Family members of workers who had obtained permanent residence under Article 17 of the Citizens' Directive on the grounds of retirement, permanent incapacity to work or three years of

cross-border working, themselves enjoyed permanent residence from the time they became family members (i.e. the fact they were not family members when permanent residence was acquired by the worker did not count against them): RM (Zimbabwe) [2013] EWCA Civ 775. However, Reg15(1)(d) of the 2016 Regs (unlike the 2006 Regs) stated that only those who were family members for EEA purposes at the time the worker themselves qualified for permanent residence would qualify.

11.6.4.1 Residence pre-2006

In Lassal (C-162/09), the ECJ stated that any continuous period of five years residence completed in line with EU law free movement rights could count towards qualifying for the right of permanent residence under the Citizens Directive. So this included residence under the legislation before the EEA Regs 2000 & 2016.

- For example, a person who entered the UK and remained here in a qualified capacity between 1999 and 2004 would have acquired a right of permanent residence under regulation 15 of the 2006 Regs so long as the period of residence was continuous
- The right of permanent residence could only ever be gained on or after 30 April 2006, when the right to permanent residence first began to exist
- Residence before an applicant's country of nationality acceded to the EU could also count where it was lawful and would have constituted them as a qualified person had they been an EEA national at the relevant time: Ziolkowski (C-424/10)

The earliest date at which permanent residence could be gained in line with Ziolkowski was either:

- 30 April 2006 (when the 2006 Regs entered force) if the applicant had completed 5 years residence under UK immigration law before that date and their country of nationality had since acceded to the EU;
- The date at which the applicant's home state acceded to the EU if later than 30 April 2006 and if the applicant had completed five years residence under UK law before that date

The CJEU in Ziolkowski at [62] said that this approach 'does not give retroactive effect to Article 16 [of the Citizens Directive] but simply gives present effect to situations which arose before the date of transposition of that directive'.

In Vassallo [2014] UKUT 313 (IAC) the UT accepted that a person could acquire qualifying residence for the purposes of exercising Treaty Rights arising before the UK became part of the European Community on 1 January 1973, relying on Ziolkowski. They also found, intriguingly, that the 2006 Regs were inconsistent with the Citizens Directive, because the stricture that pre-Regulation residence may qualify for EEA rights but would lapse with two years' non-exercise of Treaty Rights was not found in the Citizens Directive, which only provided for such lapse if a person spent more than two years abroad. Nonetheless, this provision was repeated in the 2016 Regs.

However, possession of a residence document where the underlying right did not exist did not contribute towards permanent residence: see Dias (C-325/09).

It was not only residence gained under the Citizens' Directive which provided benefits: residence rights under other EU provisions, e.g. Commission Regulation (EEC) No 1251/70, could also qualify. See for example the situation where an EEA national had resided continuously in the United Kingdom for more than two years and had stopped working as a result of permanent incapacity to work: RM (Zimbabwe) [2013] EWCA Civ 775.

11.6.4.2 Evidencing permanent residence

As explained above, this exercise will still remain a necessary competence for some time to come, for example when evidencing rights preserved during the grace period, or retrospectively in proving lawfulness of status under the good character requirement in a naturalisation application.

Evidencing permanent residence is not always easy. An EEA national may have had periods of economic inactivity in the relevant five year period, due to reasons that did not necessarily end their status as a qualified person, through illness, childbirth or unemployment, depending on the circumstances. Careful attention must be had to EEA Regs 4–15 to trace a five-year period of continuous residence entitlement, ensuring all relevant matters are fully evidenced. Reg 3 addresses absences from the UK during the five-year period.

EEA nationals from the A8 and A2 countries, and Croatia, may have had to meet certain documentary requirements to work lawfully in the UK during the accession periods (see next section). If they did not meet those requirements, they may only be able to rely on their right to reside in the UK from the date those accession periods ended when considering whether they have acquired permanent residence. For more on this, see the Immigration Staff Guidance, Qualified Persons.

The non-EEA family member's application will depend on themselves establishing five years of **continuous residence** under the EEA Regs, which will in turn depend on the evidence they can obtain of the EEA national's **continuous right to reside** in the UK during the same five year period.

Top Tip

Always remember that a person may have qualified for permanent residence if they have established five years residence in the UK as a qualified person or their family member

- this may include periods where a person is actually working, and
- periods where they retain worker status because of involuntary registered unemployment, vocational training and inactivity due to illness/accident (see above where we address *Workers*)
- the five-year period need not be the last five years – any continuous period of five years will qualify
- Evidence of a continuous five year period of residence in the UK can include (but is not limited to) tenancy agreements, utility bills, bank statements, school or nursery letters or immunisation records in support of applications for children
- Requests for HMRC records are free and can be made here (and the amount of earnings/NICs be reverse engineered by hourly rates to arrive at an average number of hours worked for each year), equally, a DWP subject access request, and client's GP and/or dentist appointment lists can help to prove residence.

11.6.5 Accession countries – the "A8", "A2" (Bulgaria and Romania), and Croatia

Further Member States acceded to the European Union throughout its history. Typically full rights of free movement were deferred at the moment of joining.

- Between 1 May 2004, when they joined the EU, and 1 May 2011, nationals of the Czech Republic, Estonia, Hungary, Latvia, Lithuania, Poland, Slovakia and Slovenia were required to register under the Workers Registration Scheme for the first 12 months of their employment. In all other respects they enjoyed free movement rights. TG [2015] UKUT 50 (AAC) holds that the extension of the WRS from 1 May 2009 to 30 April 2011 was unlawful. That means that workers who had failed to register under the scheme during that period were nevertheless lawfully employed in the UK. That decision was upheld on 7 November 2017 in Gubeladze [2017] EWCA Civ 1751
- Two further countries, Bulgaria and Romania, (the 'A2') then joined the EU on 1 January 2007 and, again, were not immediately granted full access to the UK labour market. They were treated even less generously than the A8 countries, restricting those entitled to be employed in the UK to those granted work permits
- The restrictions on A8 and A2 nationals ended as the maximum period the UK could apply them was for seven years from the date of their country's accession. Failure to comply with those restrictions however could still have implications for A8 and A2 nationals who seek to prove that they had accrued a right to permanent residence in the past
- Croatia joined the EU on 1 July 2013. Croatian nationals initially enjoyed limited free movement rights as, unless they were exempt (i.e. had been legally working here for a year before accession, or had no restrictions on their ability to work at that time), they required sponsorship

under the Tiers 2 or 5 of the PBS for the first 12 months of their employment in the UK. See generally the Accession of Croatia (Immigration and Worker Authorisation) Regulations 2013. The scheme ended on 1 July 2018 since when they have had full free movement rights. Nevertheless one comes across the scheme in immigration histories sometimes
- Sponsored Croatians did not need to apply for visas or extensions under the PBS, but required Certificates of Sponsorship reference number and a purple registration certificate
- There were three different types of registration certificate:
    - the blue registration certificate – to confirm unrestricted access to employment
    - the purple registration certificate – to confirm permission to work for a particular employer or specific employment category, and
    - the yellow registration certificate – to confirm the holder is exercising treaty rights other than as a worker (for example, as a student, self employed or self sufficient person).

11.6.6 Association Agreements with Turkey and other non-EU states

Association Agreements are signed between the EU and third countries, usually states interested in becoming members. All of the Accession States had entered into EC Association Agreements before joining. The only agreement with meaningful immigration consequences was, until the end of the transition period, with Turkey.

The EU-Turkey Association Agreement gave self-employed persons a right to establish themselves in business in the EEA, and allowed for some Turkish workers lawfully employed in the UK to extend their stay to continue their employment. The idea was to promote integration of the economy prior to full membership. Following the closure for new entrants using this Agreement, there is now only provision for those Turkish nationals extending their leave under the ECAA rules. Please refer, for details, to section 11.10.

In addition to the above Association Agreements, the EU has concluded a series of Association Agreements and Co-operation Agreements with countries such as Algeria, Tunisia and Morocco. The significance of these agreements in immigration terms is extremely limited in that they merely provide for non-discrimination clauses.

11.7 Settled and pre-settled status ('ILR/LTR under Appendix EU')

We outlined Appendix EU above (MIL 11.1). Now we provide an overview over the application categories within it, and how they relate to residence rights under the Directive and the EEA Regs. The sections above, on the underlying residence rights under the EEA Regs have all been updated to provide the more detailed context for their EUSS equivalents, and examples provided cover both EEA Regs application- as well as EUSS scenarios.

Appendix EU has been amended several times. These changes have aimed to capture the development of free movement and citizenship rights. Sometimes the result of a legal case has not stopped political realities requiring a particular approach to rights. Eg from 24 August 2020 Northern Irish nationals were recognised as eligible 'sponsors' for EUSS purposes even though the case law had not gone that far. For current applications, all that really matters is that one's circumstances are presently covered. The EUSS guidance can be consulted for a chronology of past changes. Unfortunately the drafting of Appendix EU is so convoluted that even experienced immigration lawyers and judges find it impossible to unravel: see eg the UT in EA138702021 [2023] UKAITUR. Nevertheless many applications have been determined: over 7 million at March 2023, with a grant rate of some 83% (see eg this HO letter to 3Million).

Law, guidance and policies

The rules pertaining to the EU Settlement Scheme are contained in:

- Appendix EU
- Appendix EU (Family Permit)

CHAPTER 11: European Union Law

- Appendix AR(EU)

The creation of this new body of law in conjunction with the time limited nature of the scheme and the high number of anticipated applicants, led to an exponential growth of the already voluminous amount of guidance. In the 'Immigration Staff Guidance' we find, contained in EU Settlement Scheme caseworker guidance:

- EU Settlement Scheme: EU, other EEA and Swiss citizens and their family members
- EU Settlement Scheme: suitability requirements
- EU Settlement Scheme: derivative right to reside (Chen amd Ibrahim/Teixeira cases)
- EU Settlement Scheme: family member of a qualifying British citizen
- EU Settlement Scheme: person with a Zambrano right to reside
- EU Settlement Scheme (interim guidance): Gender identity and sex markers on documents

From 6 October 2021, the pandemic concessions were inserted into Appendix EU (Annex 1 definition of "*continuous qualifying period*" (b)(i)) (MIL 11.7.5.1)). Previously they were found in the EU Settlement Scheme: coronavirus (COVID-19) guidance

There is also guidance EU Settlement Scheme: family permit and travel permit.

In Immigration Staff Guidance – other cross-cutting guidance – Administrative review, is Administrative review: EU Settlement Scheme etc.

The page 'EU Settlement Scheme: applicant information' currently contains the following:

- EU Settlement Scheme: evidence of UK residence
- EU Settlement Scheme: evidence of relationship
- EU Settlement Scheme: applying from outside the UK
- Using the 'EU Exit: ID Document Check' app
- EU Settlement Scheme: apply as the family member of a frontier worker
- EU Settlement Scheme: apply for an administrative review
- EU Settlement Scheme: Zambrano primary carers
- Support
- EU Settlement Scheme: ID document scanner locations
- EU Settlement Scheme: community support for vulnerable citizens
- **EU Settlement Scheme: looked-after children and care leavers guidance**
- Additional information
- EU Settlement Scheme: application processing times
- EU Settlement Scheme: how we use your personal information

A separate guide for applicants is entitled Stay in the UK ('settled status'): step by step", with the steps linking to some of the above information.

Relevant Enforcement Instructions are:

- EU, other EEA and Swiss citizens and their family members: consideration of administrative removal action
- Marriage Investigations (as to this topic also refer to the general guidance Suitability: Sham marriage or civil partnership and the European Commission's Handbook on dealing with the issue of marriages of convenience)
- Immigration Act 2014 Marriage and civil partnership referral and investigation scheme: statutory guidance for Home Office staff

As to practicalities, the following guidance pages are available:

- Entering the UK as the holder of an Article 10 or 20 residence card

- Visiting the UK: information for EU, EEA and Swiss citizens
- Check someone's immigration status
- View and prove your immigration status
- To update, replace or transfer BRCs, use this form

11.7.1 Key principles for understanding the EU Settlement Scheme following the end of the transition period and glossary of abbreviations used in this section

It's easy to get lost in the dense provisions of the EU Settlement Scheme (**"EUSSch"**), particularly following the extensive changes which have been in force since the end of the transition period (11pm 31 December 2020) referred to throughout this section as **"TP end"**. As the changes have resulted in very long-winded text, we use abbreviations to shorten the text.

11.7.1.1 Glossary of abbreviations used in this section

- EUSSch   = EU Settlement Scheme
- TP end   = end of transition period (11pm, 31 December 2020)
- Pre-TP end   = before that date and time
- Post-TP end = from that date and time
- REAACZ   = relevant EEA citizen
- JFM   = joining family member
- RS   = relevant sponsor
- QBC   = qualifying British citizen
- EUSS   = EU settled status
- EUPSS   = EU pre-settled status
- RPNI   = relevant person of Northern Ireland
- SRPNI   = specified relevant person of Northern Irelant

11.7.1.2 How does the EUSSch work?

The relevant provisions of Appendix EU are applied as follows:

Validity: an application must be valid under EU9 using the "required"...

- application process
- biometrics
- proof of identity and nationality
- proof of entitlement to apply from outside the UK if relevant (*EEA/Swiss ppt/ID or EEA/EUSS BRC*)
- and not making a late application without reasonable grounds:

Eligibility for settled/EUPSS is assessed under:

- EU11/EU14 condition 1 for REAACZ or their FM
- EU12/EU14 condition 2 for FM of QBC
- EU11A/EU14A for JFM of a RS

Suitability: the applicant must not fall for refusal under the suitability requirements in EU15 and EU16

Grants of settled/EUPSS are made under paragraphs:

- EU2/EU3 for REAACZ or their FM; or for FM of QBC
- EU2A/EU3A for JFM of a RS (these grants prevent sponsorship of others)

11.7.1.3 Structure of chapter

We want to ensure our readers can navigate the law and guidance and we aim to cover most of the common issues along a suggested structure in dealing with EUSSch cases. Surinder Singh applications (see MIL 11.3.1 for original concept) follow slightly different rules from the rest of the application categories. We therefore deal with these separately in a self-contained section (MIL 11.7.3.3).

11.7.1.4 Differences between the EEA Regs and the EUSSch and some general points

As already indicated, there is a great deal of symmetry between the EEA and EUSSch routes. The latter is modelled on the former. We address various technical differences throughout 11.7. However some particularly significant differences are:

For Sponsors:

- There is no requirement to be exercising treaty rights to be a relevant sponsor
- Relevant persons from Northern Ireland, even those who are dual British/Irish nationals by birth or solely British nationals, are treated as EEA citizens and can thus sponsor family members, whether or not they themselves have applied under the scheme

Extended family members – who's who?

This category can cause the most confusion as Appendix EU does not use the same language as the EEA Regs. Below we summarise how the EUSS treats different kinds of cases, so you know where your client fits.

- **Extended family members** do not comprise a single category in Appendix EU. Instead, they are addressed separately as "**durable partners**" and "**dependent relatives**".
- **Dependent relatives** do not include "**dependent parents**" (definition in Annex 1) or **dependent adult children** (included in definition of "child" in Annex 1).
- "**Dependent parents**" include grandparents, great grandparents etc; "**children**" include grandchildren, great-grandchildren etc, via their Annex 1 further definitions.
- **Children of durable partners**, and **children adopted by a sponsor under non-adoptive legal guardianship orders** are classed as dependent relatives.
- **Dependent relatives** must have held an EEA residence document to be eligible to apply, unless their sponsor is a relevant person of Northern Ireland (this is set out in the definition of "relevant document"). Dependent relatives who themselves lack pre-TP end continuous residence cannot apply under the EU Settlement Scheme.

Other general points on the EU Settlement Scheme

- Most routes to EUSS are barred should a **supervening event** occur. This is either an extant public policy expulsion, a removal or deportation order which remains in place against the applicant, or a consecutive 5-years absence following 5 years' residence. However supervening events do not bite on the children of spouses/CPs
- The scheme is open to applicants who have resided in the Bailiwick of Guernsey, the Bailiwick of Jersey or the Isle of Man: hence many provisions refer *the Islands* and their laws as well as that of the UK. Those whose residence must have been in the UK rather than the Islands are set out in the introductory para to the definition of "continuous qualifying period", abridged in 11.7.5.1 below
- There are some terms used to connote particular dates which permeate the system:
- "specified date": the transition period's end, 11pm on 31 December 2020. In relation to Surinder Singh applications, the specified date in some respect is 11pm, 29 March 2022
- "date and time of withdrawal": ie Brexit, the UK's withdrawal from the EU, on 11pm 31 January 2020 – this is the date by which Surinder Singh family relationships must generally have been formed, to benefit from the later return date and application deadline
- Dates of particular importance in the scheme (see for more MIL 11.7.2.5):

- o To enjoy rights as family members who are spouses/CPs, the marriage/CP must have been contracted by 31 December 2020, unless the couple were durable partners before that date and have married/contracted a civil partnership afterwards
- o To enjoy rights as a family member who is a durable partner, the relationship must be evidenced as durable before 31 December 2020
- Zambrano carers, with and without EUPSS, are excluded from most benefits as they are deemed to have no 'right to reside' for purposes of most benefits. There are exceptions: Personal Independence Payments and Carers' Allowance do not require a right to reside, hence are open to Zambrano carers. So aiming to secure settled status as soon as possible by applying for EUPSS should be a real advantage to them (so long as they are still Zambrano carers by the end of the 5 year residence period), EUSS will bring them mainstream benefits entitlement whereas residence under the 2016 Regs would not have led to the permanent residence that would so qualify them. All this being subject to the difficulties they face and the fact that the route has now closed (MIL 11.7.5.1, Annex 1 definition of a "person with a Zambrano right to reside")
- For the duration of the transitional period, both the rights under free movement law and under the settlement scheme existed side by side, and one could apply for, and hold, both simultaneously

Celik [2023] EWCA Civ 921 recognises the possibility that some applications under the EUSSch should be treated as having been made under the EEA Regs 2016. However the issue did not require determination in that appeal.

11.7.1.5 Can Appendix EU applications be made directly from abroad?

Yes ! Applicants must have the "required proof of entitlement to apply from outside the UK" which is:

- For EEA/Swiss nationals, their valid passport or national ID card (either must be biometric).
- For non-EEA/Swiss nationals: a valid biometric residence permit issued under the Regs or the EU Settlement scheme.

There is provision for the HO to accept alternative evidence of entitlement to apply from outside the UK "if the person is unable to produce" a document for reasons outside their control or compelling practical or compassionate reasons, as per the EUSS guidance. During the pandemic expired passports and ID cards might be accepted. National governments may extend the validity period of documents notwithstanding the date printed on their face, as with the secure French national ID card.

The benefit of applying under Appendix EU from abroad (instead of under Appendix EU (Family Permit) first) is to cut out an unnecessary additional application.

11.7.1.6 Multiple applications

On 6 April 2022, rEU10 clarified the EUSSch's own regime on multiple applications, entirely separate from that contained in r34BB (MIL 1.5.6). EU10 now provides that

- Where a further App EU application is submitted while a previous one is outstanding, the second will be considered as a variation of the first (EU10(2))
- Where one of two outstanding applications was made under App EU and the other under another part of the Rules (or outside the rules), irrespective of the order, both will be considered (EU10(3)); and where both fall to be granted, the applicant is to be given the choice which to withdraw. If neither is withdrawn within 14 days, the later of the two applications will be decided (EU10(4))

11.7.2 The mechanics of the scheme

It is useful to broadly summarise the mechanics of the "EU Settlement Scheme" ("**EUSSch**") before going into things in more detail, and to provide a roadmap as to how Appendix EU is applied to cases. Having done so we will itemise the conditions for "settled status" ("**EUSS**") at 11.7.3 and for "pre-settled status" ("**EUPSS**") at 11.7.4. As the "definitions" in Annex 1 to Appendix EU contain many of the

CHAPTER 11: European Union Law

substantive rules and requirements, and are difficult to read, we have provided abridged versions of the most important definitions at 11.7.5 to which it will be necessary to refer throughout. The Suitability requirements are addressed at MIL 11.7.7.

The workings of the scheme have been upended somewhat by the Administrative Court's decision in Independent Monitoring Authority for the Citizens' Rights Agreement [2022] EWHC 3274 (Admin). It finds that the EUSSch is unlawful for inconsistency with the WWA. A person with EUPSS automatically satisfied the Article 15 permanent residence right without making a further application. Accordingly once someone had entered the EUSSch successfully via a grant of EUPSS, it was unlawful to require a further application to confirm their acquisition of EUSS. The government have *confirmed they will not be appealing this decision.* Consequently from 9 August 2023 the HO has the power to 'extend that limited leave, regardless of whether the person has made a valid application under this Appendix for such an extension' (EU4). Thus the HO emailed the immigration sector generally on 12 September 2023 stating there would be an automatic two-year extension of EUPSS. Additionally EUPSS-holders will be switched to EUSS without an application wherever possible. Automated checks of EUPSS-holders against government-held information may assist in checking ongoing UK continuous residence.

11.7.2.1 Categorising applicants following the end of the transition period

Since the end of the transition period, applications are categorised, from the outset, by whether or not **the applicant** has resided in the UK continuously since before the end of the transition period (which ended at 11pm on 31 December 2020). We refer to this point in time, by way of shorthand, as "**TP end**".

- If the applicant has continuous pre-TP end residence, they will apply
  - either in their own right as a "relevant EEA citizen" ("**REAACZ**")
  - or as a "family member of a relevant EEA citizen" ("**FM of a REAACZ**")
- If the applicant has no continuous pre-TP end residence, they will apply as a "joining family member of a relevant sponsor" ("**JFM of a RS**").

The eligibility provisions for EUSS and EUPSS differ according to applicant category (see table below). Note that *Surinder Singh* eligibility is found under separate paragraphs and some different timelines apply, thus these are dealt with in self-contained section MIL 11.7.3.

Has **the applicant** resided continuously in the UK since pre-TP end?		
YES		**NO**
If the applicant is an EEA/Swiss national themselves, they will apply as a **REAACZ**	If the applicant is not themselves an EEA/Swiss national, they will apply as a **FM of REAACZ"**	The applicant will apply as a **JFM of RS"**
EUSS for REAACZ or their FM: • Eligibility conditions are in EU11 • grant is under EU2 EUPSS for REAACZ or their FM: • Eligibility condition is condition 1. in EU14 • grant is under EU3		EUSS for JFM of RS: • Eligibility conditions are in EU11A • Grant is under EU2A EUPSS for JFM of RS:: • Eligibility conditions are in EU14A • grant is under EU3A

11.7.2.2 EU Settlement Scheme step by step approach

We have now introduced the terminology, the relevant abbreviations, and the basic categorisation of applicants. We suggest the following sequence of steps to take in dealing with EUSSch cases, to ensure nothing is missed:

Top Tip

Always CHECK

1. whether the applicant has pre-TP end continuous residence and categorise the applicant (MIL 11.7.2.1)
2. whether the applicant fits the relevant definition of either a FM of a REAACZ or a JFM of a RS (MIL 11.7.2.3 and MIL 11.7.5.2 for individual applicant category requirements)
3. whether the sponsor meets the definition of either an REAACZ or an RS (MIL 11.7.2.4, and MIL 11.7.5.3 for individual sponsor category requirements)
4. the application deadlines in the Annex 1 definition of "required date" (MIL 11.7.2.5). For FM of QBC, the deadlines are below the table at MIL 11.7.3.3)
5. the eligibility conditions for EUSS. These are found:
   -For REAACZ and FM of REAACZ in EU11 (MIL 11.7.3.1)
   -For JFM of RS in EU11A (MIL 11.7.3.2))
   -For FM of a QBC in EU12 (MIL 11.7.3.3)
   If the applicant falls short of the settlement requirements, also:
6. the eligibility conditions for EUPSS (MIL 11.7.4):
   -For REAACZ and FM of REAACZ in EU14 condition 1
   -For JFM of RS in EU14A
   -For FM of a QBC in EU 14 condition 2.
7. the suitability provisions for possible refusal grounds (MIL 11.7.7)
8. the requirements of the Annex 1 definition of "required evidence of family relationship" (MIL 11.7.5.4)
9. whether an application under Appendix EU can be made from abroad (instead of a family permit) (this is possible where an EEA/Swiss passport/ID card is held, or a biometric residence document issued under the EEA Regs or the EUSS.
10. the validity requirements are met (follow the correct application process, biometrics process, proof of ID and nationality and proof of entitlement to apply from abroad if relevant - and lateness (MIL 11.1A)

11.7.2.3 Annex 1 definitions of "Joining Family Members" of "Relevant Sponsors", and "family member of a relevant EEA citizen" side by side

So: who can apply under Appendix EU? The answer to this question is found in the following two Annex 1 definitions. The first two of these definitions (JFM and RS) were introduced, and the third (FM of REEACSZ) changed at TP end. The overlap and areas of distinction between the definitions is best set out by presenting them side by side. The individual category definitions of those categories requiring further explanation are set out in abridged form below (MIL 11.7.5.2).

Comparative table of definitions	
Family member of a Relevant EEA Citizen ("FM of a REAACZ")	**Joining Family Member of a Relevant Sponsor ("JFM of a RS")**
A person who is (or was, at the relevant time) a spouse/CP since pre-TP end; or a spouse/CP who was the durable partner pre-TP end and remained so at TP end. *Check definition of "durable partner" as to whether in the circumstances an EEA Regs document must be held (MIL 11.7.5.2)*	
	Specified spouse or civil partner of a Swiss citizen (marriage/civil partnership contracted 1/1/21-1/1/26)
A person who is or was (for the relevant period) a durable partner, and the partnership was and remains durable since pre-TP end (see section below on durable partners)	
A child or dependent parent of the REEACZ/RS, or of their spouse/CP, and all the family relationships existed pre-TP end	
	A child born/adopted post-TP end of the RS, or of their spouse/CP
A dependent relative of REAACZ or their spouse/CP where dependency/ membership of household/strict need for personal care on serious health grounds existed pre-TP end and continues to exist (or did so for the period relied on). *A relevant document (under the EEA Regs) must be*	

CHAPTER 11: European Union Law

held or have been applied for pre-TP end except where their sponsor is a relevant person of Northern Ireland. Check the definition of "relevant document".	

As can be seen, spouses, durable partners, children and dependent parents can apply whether or not they have pre-TP end continuous UK residence.

11.7.2.4 Annex 1 definitions of "relevant EEA citizen" and "relevant sponsor" side by side

Who can sponsor under Appendix EU? The applicable definition in Annex 1 holds the answer– either a "relevant EEA citizen" (REEACZ) or a "relevant sponsor" (RS), both of which are presented abridged and side by side in the table below, for ease of reference.

Remember that a REEACZ sponsors those applicants who have their own period of residence which started pre-TP end, whereas a RS sponsors those who lack such residence.

Note that the definition of REAACZ comes in two parts according to whether the application is lodged before or after the end of the grace period (i.e. either before or from 1 July 2021); whereas, confusingly, the definition of RS incorporates both equivalent sets of rules within one single "definition", split into two parts ((a)& (b)) according to the date of application being before or from 1 July 2021.

NB: all categories of sponsors except frontier workers and naturalised British citizens (who can sponsor both, FMs of REAACZs and JFMs of RSs) must themselves have pre-TP end continuous UK residence. A frontier worker with had such continuous pre-TP end residence would be eligible for status under the EUSSch themselves rather than needing to rely on the frontier worker route! See MIL 11.7.5.3 for the individual sponsor category requirements.

Comparative table of definitions	
Relevant EEA Citizen ("REAACZ")	**Relevant Sponsor ("RS")**
For applications made during the grace period	
An EEA/Swiss national, resident continuously since pre-TP end	
NB: • *The above REAACZs can apply for EUSS/EUPSS in their own right.* • *All further REAACZ categories below are for REAACZs in the capacity as a sponsor for a FM of a REAACZ.* • *All RS categories are intended for sponsorship of JFMs.*	
An EEA/Swiss national • Resident continuously since pre-TP end; and • Held EUSS/EUPSS; or • Would have been granted EUSS/EUPSS if had applied before 1/7/21	
A relevant naturalised British citizen (no pre-TP end UK residence by this sponsor is required)	
A dual national BC (whose other nationality is EEA/Swiss) (where the post *McCarthy* transitional provisions in Sch 6 para 9 of the EEA Regs 2016 apply to the applicant as F): • Resident continuously since pre-TP end; or • Who, having been so resident, would have been (but for the fact they are a BC) granted EUSS if had applied before 1/7/21	
A relevant person of Northern Ireland (RPNI – this includes those with Irish, Irish/British or just British citizenship) • Resident continuously since pre-TP end (unless they are exempt from this as a SRPNI); or • Having been so resident, has been/would have been granted EUSS if had applied before 1/7/21 (if they were not BCs, should that be the case)	
A person exempt from immigration control	

	- Resident continuously since pre-TP end; or - Having been so resident would have been granted EUSS if had applied before 1/7/21
	A frontier worker (no pre-TP end UK residence by this sponsor is required)
For applications made from 1 July 2021	
REAACZ	**RS**
An EEA/Swiss national, resident continuously since pre-TP end	
NB: - *The above two REAACZ categories are those applying in their own right.* - *All further REAACZ categories below are for sponsorship of an FM of an REAACZ.* - *All RS categories are for sponsorship of JFMs only.*	
An EEA/Swiss national who has been resident continuously since pre-TP end, and who has been granted EUSS/EUPSS	
NB: if the family member applies under retained rights, PR, ILR or death of sponsor provisions the REAACZ need not have been granted EUSS/EUPSS	*NB: if the family member applies under retained rights or death of sponsor provisions, the RS need not have been granted EUSS/EUPSS*
A relevant naturalised British citizen who would (but for the fact they are a BC) have been granted EUSS/EUPSS had they applied before 1/7/21	
Dual national BCs (whose other nationality is EEA/Swiss) (where the post-*McCarthy* transitional provisions in Sch 6 para 9 of the EEA Regs 2016 apply to the applicant as F): - Resident continuously since pre-TP end; and - Would be (but for the fact they are BCs) granted EUSS/EUPSS had they applied before 1/7/21	
A relevant person of Northern Ireland - Resident continuously since pre-TP end (unless they are exempt from this as a SRPNI); and - Has been granted EUSS/EUPSS; or - Would have been granted EUSS/EUPSS (if applied before 1/7/21, and but for the fact they are a BC, if that is the case)	
A person exempt from immigration control, who has been resident continuously since pre-TP end and who would have been granted EUSS/EUPSS had they applied before 1/7/21.	
A frontier worker	
	In addition: unless the JFM applies under retained rights based on the death of their sponsor, the RS must be alive(!)

11.7.2.5 Annex 1 definition of "required date" (i.e. application deadlines)

The general deadline for applications under the scheme was at 11pm on 30 June 2021, the end of the grace period, but some categories of persons can apply later without having to prove "reasonable grounds" for doing so (MIL 11.1A). The deadlines are set out in the Annex 1 definition of "required date", which breaks down as follows:

If the applicant is/ arrives on (date):	...then the relevant application deadline is:
Not any of the below categories (i.e: this is the general deadline)	Before 1 July 2021
EUPSS (EUPSS) holder	Before expiry of EUPSS
Where a JFM arrives, or where a child is born or adopted on or after 1 April 2021	Within 3 months of arrival, birth or adoption
Where a JFM is a "specified spouse or civil partner of a Swiss national" (i.e. the marriage or civil partnership was contracted	Within 3 months of arrival and before 1 January 2026.

between 1 January 2021 and 1 January 2026) who arrives on or after 1 April 2021:	
Family member of a qualifying British national (*Surinder Singh*) **BUT not all categories – some must apply before 1 July 2021** (see MIL 11.7.3.3)	Before 11pm on 29 March 2022 – route closes altogether to new applications on 8 August 2023
Where an applicant holds leave under other parts of- or outside- the rules, which expires on or after 1 July 2021	Before leave expires. The HO will deem this to be a reasonable ground to apply after 30 June 2021. If made after expiry, evidence of reasonable grounds and consent by the HO are required as for all other categories (MIL 11.1A)
Where a person ceases to be exempt from immigration control on or after 1 July 2021:	Within 90 days of ceasing to be exempt. The HO will deem this to be a reasonable ground to apply late. If made outside the 90 days, evidence of reasonable grounds and consent by the HO are required as for all other categories.
Zambrano cases	Route closes altogether to new applications on 8 August 2023 – (a)(vi) & (vii) of "required date" definition

Note:

- The para in the definition headed "in addition" states that r39E (MIL 1.5.4) does not apply to applications under Appendix EU
- Re Zambrano aplicants, the Akinsanya litigation required a rethink of the HO's approach to Zambrano carers in Appendix EU. Applications for status lodged with 6 weeks of the Grace Period ending will be *deemed to have been lodged late on reasonable grounds*, and those with current leave to remain on human rights grounds can apply (MIL11.7.5)

The National Health Service (Charges to Overseas Visitors) Regulations 2015 were amended from 18 February 2023 so that those making late EUSSch applications must not be charged for relevant healthcare services provided to them whilst their application is under consideration - charges for services already made should be refunded.

Making the wrong application

Siddiqa [2023] UKUT 47 (IAC) looks at applications made on the wrong form. The UT accept that one HO online homepage was the route to access both EUSSch and EEA applications whilst the latter were still available: a dropdown box required a choice to be made between those routes. Thus a December 2020 application for a "European family permit visa" had expressly chosen the EUSSch route and there was nothing in the supporting correspondence to suggest otherwise. There was nothing in the WWA preventing the HO from operating a relatively simple process of this nature. This was to be contrasted with the situation in Ahmed (UI-2022-002804-002809) where the UT held that a covering letter which clearly set out legal submissions as per the EEA Regs 2016 effectively trumped the accidental choice of the wrong dropdown box.

11.7.3 Eligibility for 'EUSS'- all categories

Relevant EEA citizens (REAACZs) and their family members (FMs) vs joining family members (JFMs) of relevant sponsors (RSs)

The eligibility conditions for ILR/ILE under Appendix EU (collectively referred to as "EUSS" for "EU EUSS") are contained in in EU11 and EU11A, which compare, by way of an overview, as follows:

Comparative table of EUSS eligibility conditions **Relevant EEA citizens (REAACZ) or their family members (FM) vs** **Joining family members (JFM) of relevant sponsors (RS)**	
EU11 – EUSS for REAACZs or their FMs	**EU11A – EUSS for JFMs of RSs** *NB: essentially those lacking continuous pre-TP end UK residence*
1. PR holders (REAACZ or their FM)	*No equivalent*
2. ILR holders (REAACZ or their FM)	*No equivalent*
3. 5 years' residence (REAACZ or their FM)	1. Five years' residence as a JFM of a RS
4. REAACZ who has ceased activity	*No equivalent*
5. FM of an REAACZ who has ceased activity	2. JFM of a RS who has ceased activity
6. FM of an REAACZ who has died	3. JFM of a RS who has died
7. Child FM of an REAACZ or their spouse/CP *early settlement*	4. Child JFM of a RS or their spouse/CP *early settlement*

Para EU11A has four conditions instead of the 7 in EU11 because:

- JFMs, being by definition those lacking continuous pre-TP end residence, cannot be PR or ILR holders
- There is no equivalent of condition 4. of EU11 (REAACZ being the applicant who has ceased activity) in EU11A as the conditions for settlement in EU11A only apply to family members rather than the EEA national in their own right.

Other differences between FM of REAACZ and JFM of RS are:

- As the definition of JFM of a RS excludes those with Zambrano- or other derivative rights, those with no pre-TP end residence cannot qualify for settled or EUPSS in that category.
- Dual British citizens whose other nationality is EEA/Swiss (to whom the pre-McCarthy transitional provisions apply) are not included as relevant sponsors under condition 2 and 4 of EU 11A (FM of person who has ceased activity and early child settlement, respectively) but they do appear as eligible sponsors in conditions 5 and 7 in EU11 (the corresponding conditions).

EU 13 clarifies that, for the categories in which five years' residence must be accrued, applicants can combine periods of residence as:

- a relevant EEA citizen, their family member or a person with derivative or Zambrano rights to reside
- the family member of a qualifying British citizen (*Surinder Singh* cases)
- a family member with a retained right of residence based on a relationship with one of the above

Whether to apply under EU11 (MIL 11.7.3.1) or EU12 (MIL 11.7.3.3 for Surinder Singh) in those cases is determined by the relevant status at the time of the application.

11.7.3.1 Para EU11 - Eligibility for EUSS for Relevant EEA Citizens and their family members

The seven conditions (effectively individual gateways) under which "relevant EEA citizens" ("REAACZ") and their family members will be eligible for settled status ("EUSS") are outlined in this section. We address the components of the various definitions in 11.7.5.

CHAPTER 11: European Union Law

Where all requirements *except for the five years' residence* are met, an applicant will be eligible for a grant of 'EUPSS' under EU14 (see MIL 11.7.4).

Conditions 1, 3, 4, 5 and 6 also include the '*supervening event*' proviso: ie entitlement is forfeited by absence for more than 5 years or public policy refusal grounds. Doubtless the thinking behind *not* applying this to conditions 2 (ILR holders) and condition 7 (early EUSS for children) being that where one has domestic ILR, there is no reason to hold this against you, there being domestic immigration sanctions if required. And that issues of these nature should not be held against children. From 6 April 2022, conditions 1, 3 and 5 contain a clarification that the event is to be read as being in relation to the applicant.

The conditions are:

1. **Permanent residence holders:** A relevant EEA citizen, a current or former family member of one, or a family member who has retained the right of residence via a relationship with a relevant EEA citizen, and who holds a permanent residence document (issued under the Regs)
2. **ILR holders:** A relevant EEA citizen, a family member of one, or a family member who has retained the right of residence via a relationship with a relevant EEA citizen, and there is valid evidence they hold ILR or ILE
3. **EEA Citizens and their family members, and those with <u>Zambrano</u> or derived rights with 5 years' residence:** A relevant EEA citizen, a family member of one, or a family member who has retained the right of residence via a relationship with a relevant EEA citizen, or who is a person with a derivative or <u>Zambrano</u> right to reside; and who has accrued *five years' residence* in any (or any combination) of those categories
4. A **relevant EEA citizen who has ceased activity**
5. A current or former **family member of a relevant EEA citizen who has ceased activity**; they were a family member when activity ceased and were resident continuously immediately before their sponsor ceased activity. In all cases, the applicant's sponsor must have resided continuously in the UK since pre-TP end. The status requirements for the sponsoring REAACZ differ according to whether the application is made within or after the grace period:

Table re REEACZ condition 5 statuses Under condition 5. in EU11, if REAACZ is:	... then the REAACZ must have the following status for:	
	Applications during grace period	Applications from 1 July 2021
EEA/Swiss national	Holds EUSS/would have been granted EUSS	Holds EUSS
Relevant naturalised British citizen	Would have been granted EUSS if they were not British	Would have been granted EUSS if they were not British
Dual national (non-"relevant naturalised BC")	Has resided since pre-TP end OR would have been granted EUSS if they were not British	Would have been granted EUSS if they were not British
RPNI (Irish only)	Holds EUSS/ is being/ would have been granted EUSS	Holds EUSS/ would have been granted EUSS
RPNI (Irish/ British or BC only)	Would have been be granted EUSS if they were not British	Would have been granted EUSS if they were not British
Exempt from immigration control	Would have been granted EUSS	Would have been granted EUSS

NB: there is no reference here to EUPSS as those who cease activity are eligible for EUSS.

6. A **family member of a relevant EEA citizen who is deceased** and who was at time of death a worker or self-employed; the EEA citizen was resident in the UK and Islands for two years before death or the death was due to an accident at work or an occupational disease; the family member lived with them immediately before the death. *NB: Where the EEA citizen was neither a worker nor self-employed at time of death (nor held PR or ILR), the applicant may still come within*

condition 3, as a person who has retained a right of residence, so long as they resided in the UK as the family member of the deceased for one year before death – see definition of 'family member who has retained the right of residence' in Annex 1 to Appendix EU.

7. **A child (under 21) of a relevant EEA citizen, or of their spouse or civil partner (early EUSS)**. Where the parent is the partner of the REAACZ, the marriage/civil partnership must precede TP end or that parent must have been the REAACZ's durable partner pre-TP end and remained so at TP end. The status requirements for the sponsoring REAACZ or their spouse/CP differ according to whether the application is made within or after the grace period:

Under condition 7. in EU11, if REAACZ is:	... then the REAACZ must have the following status for:	
	Applications during grace period	Applications from 1 July 2021
EEA/Swiss national	Holds EUSS/would have been granted EUSS	Holds EUSS
Irish national (this is the only additional category compared with the table under condition 5.)	*Would have been granted EUSS*	*Would have been granted EUSS*
Relevant naturalised British citizen	Would have been granted EUSS if they were not British	Would have been granted EUSS if they were not British
Dual national (non-"relevant naturalised BC")	Has resided since pre-TP end OR would have been granted EUSS if they were not British	Would have been granted EUSS if they were not British
RPNI (Irish only)	Holds EUSS/ is being/ would have been granted	Holds EUSS/ would have been granted EUSS
RPNI (Irish/ British or BC only)	Would have been granted EUSS if they were not British	Would have been granted EUSS if they were not British
Exempt from immigration control	Would have been granted EUSS	Would have been granted EUSS if they were not exempt

NB: there is no reference in condition 7. to EUPSS as this category provides early EUSS for children whose relevant parent settles.

11.7.3.2 Para EU11A – Eligibility for EUSS by joining family members of relevant sponsors

The four conditions under which a "joining family member of relevant sponsor" (i.e. a person lacking pre-TP end continuous residence) will be eligible for settlement in the UK are outlined in this section. Please refer to the relevant definitions in 11.7.5.

Where all requirements *except for the five years' residence* are met, an applicant will be eligible for a grant of 'EUPSS' under EU14A.

Conditions 1, 2 and 3 below also include the '*supervening event*' proviso: ie entitlement is forfeited by absence for more than 5 years or public policy refusal grounds.

The conditions are:

1. **Five years' residence:** the person is (or was, for the relevant period) a JFM of a RS or a person with retained rights of residence via a relationship with a RS. They must have 5 years' continuous residence in any combination of these.
2. A current or former **family member of a relevant sponsor who has ceased activity**; they were a family member when activity ceased and were resident continuously immediately before their sponsor ceased activity. As this is the JFM category, their residence must have started *after* TP end. In all cases, the applicant's sponsor must have resided continuously in the UK since pre-TP end. The status requirements for the sponsoring RS differ according to whether the application is made within or after the grace period:

CHAPTER 11: European Union Law

Under condition 2 in EU11A, if RS is:	... then the RS must have the following status for:	
	Applications during grace period	Applications from 1 July 2021
EEA/Swiss national	Holds EUSS/would have been granted EUSS	Holds EUSS
Irish citizen	NB: Would come under the above category during the grace period	Would have been granted EUSS
Relevant naturalised British citizen	Would have been granted EUSS if they were not British	Would have been granted EUSS if they were not British
RPNI (Irish only)	Holds EUSS/ is being/ would have been granted	Holds EUSS/ would have been granted EUSS
RPNI (Irish/ British or BC only)	Would have been granted EUSS if they were not British	Would have been granted EUSS if they were not British
Exempt from immigration control	Would have been granted EUSS	Would have been granted EUSS

NB: there is no reference here to EUPSS as those who cease activity are eligible for EUSS.

3. A **family member of a relevant sponsor who is deceased** and who was at time of death a worker or self-employed; the EEA citizen was resident in the UK for two years before death or the death was due to an accident at work or an occupational disease; the family member lived with them immediately before the death. As this is the JFM category, this residence must have started *after* TP end. **NB:** *Where the EEA citizen was neither a worker nor self-employed at time of death, the applicant may still come within condition 1, as a person who has retained a right of residence, so long as they resided in the UK as the family member of the deceased for one year before death – see definition of 'family member who has retained the right of residence' in Annex 1 to Appendix EU.*

4. **A child (under 21) of a relevant sponsor, or of their spouse or civil partner (early EUSS).** Where the parent is the partner of the RS, the marriage/civil partnership must precede TP end or that parent must have been the RS's durable partner pre-TP end and remained so at TP end (see our summary of the "durable partner" definition)
   Where the applicant is the child *of the spouse or civil partner* of the RS, the spouse/CP must either hold or, be in the process of being granted, EUSS.
   - The marriage or civil partnership must either have been contracted pre-TP end or the now spouse/CP must have met the definition of a 'durable partner' pre-TP end; and
   - The parent can either
     - *have* been resident in the UK continuously since pre-TP end as a FM of an REAACZ who holds (or is being granted) EUSS under EU2; or
     - *not have* been resident pre-TP end as a FM of an REAACZ who holds (or is being granted) EUSS under EU2A; or
     - have been so resident but their continuous residence was broken by absence or imprisonment; or
     - have been so resident but a supervening event has occurred

The status requirements for the sponsoring RS or their spouse/ civil partner differ according to whether the application is made within or after the grace period:

Under condition 4. in EU11A, if RS is:	... then the RS must have the following status for:	
	Applications during grace period	Applications from 1 July 2021
EEA/Swiss national	Holds EUSS/is being granted EUSS	Holds EUSS
Irish citizen	Has not applied but would be granted EUSS	Would have been granted EUSS

CHAPTER 11: European Union Law

Relevant naturalised British citizen	Would have been granted EUSS if they were not British	Would have been granted EUSS if they were not British
RPNI (Irish only)	Holds EUSS/ would have been granted EUSS	Holds EUSS/ would have been granted EUSS
RPNI (Irish/ British or BC only)	Would have been granted EUSS if they were not British	Would have been granted EUSS if they were not British
Exempt from immigration control	Would have been granted EUSS	Would have been granted EUSS if they were not exempt

NB: there is no reference in condition 4. in EU11A to EUPSS as this category provides early EUSS for children whose relevant parent settles.

As with EU11, children under condition 4 are excluded from the application of supervening events. From 6 April 2022, conditions 1 and 2 contain a clarification that the supervening event is to be read as relating to the applicant.

11.7.3.3 Eligibility for EUSS for family members of Qualifying British Citizens

This is the EUSSch version of the Surinder Singh route (see MIL 11.3.1 for original EU regime). The four conditions, under which family members of 'qualifying British citizens' will be eligible for EUSS are in EU12 (see below).

Post-TP end deadlines for qualifying on this basis have now been put into the rules. They are best set out as part of the definitions in which they feature:

Annex 1 definitions of "qualifying British citizen" and "family member of a qualifying British citizen"

Qualifying British citizen

A QBC is a British citizen who:

(a) Has (or for the relevant period had) returned to the UK with the applicant:
  (i) Before 11pm on 29 March 2022): <u>or</u>
  (ii) <u>For the relationship categories in (a)(ii), (a)(iv), (a)(vii) or (a)(viii) of the definition of 'FM of a QBC': before TP end</u>. *NB: these are explained and set out in the left hand column of the table below, which sets out the definition of FM of a QBC.*

  or later if the HO is satisfied there were reasonable grounds for missing that deadline; and

(b) satisfied regulation 9(2), (3) and (4)(a) of the EEA Regs 2016 *NB: these are tthe Surinder Singh requirements for residence in another member state – see MIL 11.3.1 on Surinder Singh. The Annex 1 definition adds that service for HM forces may satisfy the condition of being a "worker".*
  (i) before TP end; and
  (ii) immediately before returning to the UK with the applicant
(c) was continuously resident in the UK under Reg 3 of the 2016 Regs

This route closes to new applications from 8 August 2023 (MIL 11.7.2.5)

Serving in HM forces counts for "worker status" and these rights can be acquired on the basis of service in the Sovereign Base Areas on Cyprus.

CHAPTER 11: European Union Law

Family member of a qualifying British citizen

Annex 1 definition of Family Members of a Qualifying British Citizen (FM of a QBC) – ("withdrawal date" = 11pm on 31 January 2020, when the UK left the EU)	
Deadlines for arrival in the UK to enter the EU Settlement Scheme in that category	
Before 11pm on 31 December 2020	**Before 11pm on 29 March 2022**
(a)(ii) Post-withdrawal date **spouse/CP** *with pre-TP marriage or civil partnership, where partnership was not durable pre-withdrawal*	(a)(i) Pre-withdrawal date **spouse/CP**, or current spouse/CP who was a durable partner before and on withdrawal date
(a)(iv) Post-withdrawal date **durable partners** *where partnership was durable pre-TP end and remains durable on date of application*	(a)(iii) Pre-withdrawal date **durable partner** who remains a durable partner at the date of application (or did so for the relevant period or immediately before British citizen's death)
(a)(vii) Pre-withdrawal date **dependent parent; or a child of a QBC's spouse/CP** *where marriage/civil partnership was formed between withdrawal and TP end and was not durable pre-withdrawal*	(a)(vi) Pre-withdrawal date **dependent parent; or a child of a QBC's spouse/CP** *where marriage/civil partnership existed pre- and on withdrawal date*
(a)(viii) **Other dependent relative of the QBC or of their spouse/CP** *The family relationship and person's dependency/membership of the household/strict need for personal care on serious health grounds existed before returning to the UK together and continues to exist at date of application or existed for the period relied on.*	(a)(v) Pre-withdrawal date **dependent parent of QBC; child of QBC**

In the Appendix EU (Family Permit) definition of a FM of a QBC, belatedly on 6 April 2022, the retained rights category of family member has been added ((a)(ix)), and the requirement to travel with the QBC to the UK or to join them there has been disapplied. The amendment in November 2022 to (b)(i) of the definition clarifies that it includes circumstances where the QBC might have returned to the UK ahead of the applying family member and a relevant child has been born or adopted to that QBC after the end of the transition period but before the family's return to the UK.

Application deadlines for family members of QBCs

These are found in the Annex 1 definition of "required date" (see 11.7.2.5 for full abridged definition). For *Surinder Singh* applicants to enter the EU Settlement Sceme, the deadlines are:

- Before 11pm on 29 March 2022 *but only* for the relationship categories in the right hand colum in the table immediately above this paragraph
- Before 1 July 2021 for the relationship categories in the left hand column.

Eligibility for EUSS for family members of QBCs – rEU12

1. **Permanent residence holders:** ie those who already hold a permanent residence document (issued under the Regs) or
2. **ILR Holders**: ie those with valid evidence of ILR or
3. **Family members with 5 years' residence:** those who have accrued five years' lawful residence (under Reg 9 of the EEA Regs 2016) in any (or any combination) of those categories (although the British citizen need not have been a qualified person) or
4. **Children**: the applicant is a child (under 21) of the spouse or civil partner of a QBC who would be in the UK lawfully under Regs 9(1)-(6) (disregarding exercise of Treaty rights by the British citizen), and that spouse/CP has been/is being granted EUSS. The marriage/CP must either have been contracted before 11pm on 31 January 2020 (withdrawal date) or the applicant's parent must have been the durable partner of the QBC before that date).

Conditions 1 and 3 also include the 'supervening event' proviso: ie entitlement is forfeited by absence for more than 5 years or public policy refusal grounds. From 6 April 2022, these conditions contain a clarification that the supervening event is to be read as relating to the applicant. As with the other EUSS categories, this proviso is not applied to ILR holders or children.

11.7.4 Pre-settled status – "leave to remain under Appendix EU" – all categories

EU14 allows for EUPSS to be granted to REAACZ or their family members under the following conditions

1. Condition 1: five years' residence have not yet accrued by the time of the application, where all other requirements of EU11 condition 3 are met (REAACZ or FM of REAACZ); or
2. Condition 2: five years' residence have not yet accrued by the time of the application, where all other requirements of EU12 condition 3 are met (*Surinder Singh* cases)

EU14A, which applies to JFM of RS, has only one condition, which is again that they would be granted EUSS if they did not fall short of the 5-year residence requirement.

From 6 April 2022, both EU14 and EU14A contain a new condition that no supervening event must have occurred *in relation to the sponsor*. From that date, the definition of "supervening event" changes its reference from "the applicant" to "the person".

Benefits entitlement for EUPSS holders

From 7 May April 2019 housing and benefit regulations were amended to make it clear that EUPSS is not a relevant 'immigration status' for claiming benefits or housing entitlements. This is in line with the general policy to permit access to mainstream benefits only to those with no restriction on their residence in the UK – and to EU nationals *exercising Treaty Rights*.

The relevant regulations are as follows:

1. The Allocation of Housing and Homelessness (Eligibility) (England) (Amendment) (EU Exit) Regulations 2019
2. The Social Security (Income-related Benefits) (Updating and Amendment) (EU Exit) Regulations 2019
3. The Child Benefit and Child Tax Credit (Amendment) (EU Exit) Regulations 2019

These changes were briefly found to be unlawful: Fratila [2020] EWCA Civ 1741 observed that EU law had long recognised the possibility that a right to social assistance may arise where a domestic right to reside was granted. Fratila [2021] UKSC 53 reversed that initial view. The CJEU by then had effectively determined the issue via their judgment in Case C-709/20 CG v The Department for Communities in Northern Ireland, which the Supreme Court accepted as the end of the matter. CG held that an EU citizen can claim equal treatment in respect of social assistance only if his or her residence in the territory of that member state complies with the conditions of the Citizens Directive.

EUSS (settled status) holders are fully entitled to benefits as they are in the same category as holders of any other type of ILR.

Zambrano carers (with and without EUPSS) are excluded from most benefits as they are deemed to have no '*right to reside*' for benefits purposes. There are exceptions: Personal Independence Payments and Carers' Allowance do not require a right to reside, hence are open to Zambrano carers. So aiming to enter the EUSSch as soon as possible is strongly advised. Remember that previous periods of residence under another category of family members can be combined with later residence as a Zambrano carer, to make up the 5 years' residence requirement for EUSS. Note that from 1 January 2021, only those Zambrano carers (and others with derivative rights) who have resided in the UK continuously since pre-TP end are eligible to enter the EUSSch.

Where a Zambrano carer is not close to achieving 5 years' residence and thus EUSS, they would need advice on the exact relative advantages and disadvantages of:

- Being locked in to a status excluding them from accessing most public funds for the remainder of their 5-year residence period (as opposed to leave to remain as a parent under Appendix FM, where the NRPF condition can be changed), but moving to ILR after a total of 5 years, with no fees or repeat applications
- Forfeiting the EUSS option by applying under the 10-year route under Appendix FM, with its high fees, fee waivers and change of conditions complications, as may be relevant. The high cost of this route compared with the free route above may put the time with no recourse to public funds somewhat in perspective

11.7.5 Substantive requirements contained in the Annex 1 "definitions"

From the first edition of Appendix EU, it has always appeared as if its structure, under which the Annex 1 "definitions" in fact contain many complex substantive requirements, may have been intended to make the rules on eligibility appear relatively short and straightforward. In practice, Appendix EU is now extremely difficult to navigate and the definitions are thick with cross references. To assist our readers we have abridged the most important definitions and, where appropriate, grouped them together, where they cross refer to one another substantively and are best read together.

As cross-referencing within Appendix EU is so ubiquitous, we have preserved section numbering within the definitions where possible, except where this results in the text becoming too expansive. In those instances, definitions have been presented as tables.

11.7.5.1 Key terms and requirements

In addition to the below, another key requirement is, of course the set of deadlines applicable to different categories of applicant. The deadlines are contained in the Annex 1 definition of "required date", which is set out as an abridged table above within the section "the mechanics of the scheme" (MIL 11.7.2).

Annex 1 definition of "EEA Regulations"

The 2016 Regs were repealed at TP end but saved with modifications (MIL 11.1). Within the sections on residence rights above, Appendix EU continues to refer to the Regs, and the Annex 1 definition of "EEA Regulations" sets out how this is to be done in that context:

(a) for something done pre-TP end: the 2016 Regs as they had effect immediately pre-TP end; or

(b) for something done during the grace period: the 2016 Regs as, following revocation, they remained in effect, with specified modifications, by virtue of the Citizens' Rights (Application Deadline and Temporary Protection) (EU Exit) Regulations 2020); or

(c) for something done from 1 July 2021, the 2016 Regs as they had effect immediately before they were revoked and, where the context requires it, on the basis that those Regulations had not been revoked

Annex 1 definition of "specified date"

This is the deadline for EUSSch applications:

(a) 2300 GMT on 31 December 2020; or

(b) 2300 GMT on 29 March 2022 for Surinder Singh family members (FMs of QBCs) **but only**

- spouses/CPs
- durable partners
- dependent parent of QBC/their spouse/CP
- child of QBC/their spouse/CP (unless born or adopted after 29 March 2022).

NB: This later date for some *Surinder Singh* family members is the specified date, before which the "continuous qualifying period" starts for FMs of QBCs who qualify for either EUSS or EUPSS on the basis of their own residence (i.e. under EU12 condition 3 for EUSS or EU14 condition 2 for EUPSS)

CHAPTER 11: European Union Law

Annex 1 definition of "continuous qualifying period", including the Covid-19 concessions

The introductory para to this definition states that this term refers to a period of residence in the UK and Islands, which for the following application categories, must have been in the UK, not the Islands:

- Surinder Singh – main provision based on 5 years' residence and EUPSS
- Those with retained rights on the basis of the sponsor's death or on the basis of termination of marriage/civil partnership whose marriage had subsisted for 3 years, one of which they spent living in the UK
- Cessation of activity by those who resided in the UK as a worker or self-employed person for 3 years before becoming a worker or self-employed person in the EEA/Switzerland while retaining a place of residence in the UK to which they return at least once a week
- Zambrano & other derivative rights

The text below follows the paragraph numbering of the definition, for ease of cross-referencing. The Covid-19 concessions, which between 11 June 2021 and 6 October 2021 resided in their own policy document entitled Coronavirus (COVID-19): EU Settlement Scheme, are found at (b)(i) and are emphasised in bold italics.

(a) The period must have started pre-TP end unless the person is a:
- Joining Family Member
- SRPNI or their dependent relative
- Person with an absence from the UK of 6-12 months for an important reason such as Crown Service, working in the UK marine area, or having had a removal, exclusion or deportation decision in place against them (which is revoked at the date of application)

(b) The period must have been unbroken by the following:
    (i) 6-12 month absence(s) from the UK and Islands, except for:
        (aa) a single absence for an important reason (such as pregnancy, childbirth, serious illness, study, vocational training or an overseas posting, *or Covid-19*); or
        (bb) a single absence not originally for an important reason but which is to be treated as such, because it exceeded 6 months *due to Covid-19*; or
        NB: the following types of second extended absences will not break continuity of residence but any period over 6 months is not counted towards the qualifying period, as stated identically in both (b)(i)(cc)&(dd).
        (cc) following a 6-12 month absence *because of Covid-19*, a second 6-12 month absence *for an important reason other than Covid-19*; or
        (dd) following a 6-12 month absence *for an important reason other than Covid-19* a second 6-12 month absence *because of Covid-19*; or
        (ee) a period of absence under any of paras (aa)-(dd) immediately above, which then exceeded 12 months because COVID-19 prevented the person from (or caused them to be advised against), returning earlier
        NB: Any period over 12 months under (b)(i)(ee) will not break continuity of residence but will not count towards the qualifying period.
        or
        (ff) an absence of any length on compulsory military service; or
        (gg) an absence of any length on Crown service, or as an accompanying spouse, civil partner, durable partner or child; or
        (hh) an absence of any length spent working in the UK marine area; or
        Get ready for some odd para numbers but this is what Appendix EU presently says!
    (ii) an absence of any length caused by having had a removal, exclusion or deportation decision in place against them, which is revoked at the time of application;
    (ii) the person served or is serving a sentence of imprisonment of any length in the UK and Islands, unless the conviction which led to it has been overturned; or
    (iii) an extant exclusion, deportation or removal order is in place against the person; and

(c) the period continues at the date of application, unless:
    (i) the period is of at least five years' duration; or
    (ii)

(aa) the person acquired the right of permanent residence, or they would have done so had the 2016 Regs not been revoked. This latter category is open only to those with reasonable grounds for applying after 30 June 2021 (MIL 11.1A); or
(bb) the period relates to:
> (aaa) a relevant EEA citizen (REEACZ) on whom the applicant relies:
>> (i) for all or part of their 5-year period on having been a family member; or
>> (ii) for being or having been a family member who has retained the right of residence.; or
>
> (bbb) a relevant sponsor (RS) on whom the applicant relies for all or part of their 5-year period or any shorter period for EUPSS on being a joining family member who has retained the right of residence; or
>
> *NB: for both the REEACZ or the RS as sponsors of those retaining rights, their period need not be continuous once they have resided in the UK for 5 years/have or would have acquired permanent residence/have acquired EUSS or hold other ILR. The residence of the sponsoring REEACZ/RS becomes irrelevant after the point at which the applicant retained their rights. Sub-paras (c)(ii)(bb)(aaa)(ii) and -(bbb) state this in identical terms for REEACZ/RS respectively;*

(iii) the person has valid ILE/ILR under Appendix EU; or
(iv) the person has other ILE/ILR; or
(v) a **relevant reference** is concerned

The term "relevant reference" is defined in the long para under "in addition", following on from the above. That merely sets out scenarios in which the sponsor's continuing residence need not be proven. The circumstances listed via extremely long-winded cross-references are simply where:

- The application is on the basis that the sponsor has died
- The applicant has already retained their rights
- The sponsor has already been granted EUSS
- The sponsor has the option to apply for EUSS but need not do so because they are Irish or exempt from immigration control, but would nevertheless have qualified for it before 1 July 2021
- The sponsor cannot apply for EUSS as they are British but would otherwise have qualified for it before 1 July 2021

11.7.5.2 Individual applicant category requirements

The specific requirements for each applicant category are found in the relevant Annex 1 definitions. In this section we address those which require further explanation.

Annex 1 definition of a "dependent relative"

"Dependent relatives" under the EUSSch are those dependent on a REEACZ or their spouse/CP <u>who are not</u>: spouses, civil partners, durable partners, children or dependent parents. They can only be sponsored as FM of REEACZ (meaning they must have started their own continuous UK residence pre-TP end). Exempt from this residence requirement for the sponsor are family members of a "specified relevant person of Northern Ireland" (see below),

The categories of "dependent relative" are:

- A member of the EEA Sponsor's household
- Those who strictly require the EEA Sponsor's care on health grounds ((a)(i))
- Those subject to a *non-adoptive legal guardianship order* (an example of how the EUSS aims to track CJEU case law, here SM Algeria [2019] EUECJ C-129/18) ((a)(ii))
- The children and adopted children of durable partners ((a)(iii)) (from 8 August 2023, to include within the EUSSch the child of a durable partner where the child has turned 18 since they were granted EUPSS)

Para (b) of the Annex 1 definition requires that they must also hold a document issued under the EEA Regs in that capacity. For dependent relatives of "specified relevant persons of Northern Ireland" (definition in MIL 11.7.5.3), this can be a family permit issued to them in that capacity.

Para (b) also permits those who applied for such a document pre-TP end, and which was issued only thereafter, to be deemed as having held it at TP end.

Following the end of the grace period, some EFM family permit applications and appeals under the Regs remained in the system. Post-grace period, successful applicants and appellants received a UKVI letter stating that they would have been entitled to such a document but that it could no longer be issued given the repeal of the EEA Regs; nor were they eligible for a family permit under the EUSSch as EFMs do not feature within the JFM category. Of course, had these cases received timely and correct decisions, this cohort would have been issued with EEA family permits. From 27 September 2021 a concession was introduced, which is now found in the "relevant document" definition permitting a letter from the HO confirming they would have qualified had the route not closed.

Annex 1 definition of "relevant EEA family permit case" (both Appendix EU and Appendix EU (Family Permit)

New definitions were added on 6 April 2022 to Annex 1 in both Appendices. These create new applicant categories for those who are neither JFMs nor required to have pre-TP end residence. The requirement for non-JFMs to have continuous residence which started pre-TP end is disapplied for this category by an amendment to the definition of "continuous qualifying period" (para (a)), see above.

The definition in Appendix EU (Family Permit) includes:

a) EFMs & derivative rights holders who applied pre-TP end;
b) those issued with EEA FP during the grace period but who had notified UKVI of inability to travel by 30/6/21 for compelling compassionate/practical or Covid reasons; or
c) those issued with an EEA family permit from 1 June 2021, who were unable to travel by 30 June 2021

All of these categories must show that there has been no significant change in circumstances, which would make a grant of EC in appropriate, since:

- the date of issue of the EEA family permit;
- the date on which the appeal against refusal of its issue succeeded; or
- the date on which they would have been issued with the EEA FP had the route not closed

The definition in Appendix EU is for EUPSS applications. It differs slightly from the App EU (FP) definition in that it refers to dependent family members and durable partners. At the EUPSS stage, these are now referred to as separate categories whereas under App EU (Family Permit) the reference is still to "EFMs", as at that stage the applications in question would have been lodged under the Reg 8 definition.

Annex 1 definitions of "child" and "dependent relative" by reference to dependency criteria

For children aged 21 and over and dependent parents, the applicant can be either dependent on the EEA citizen or on their spouse/CP. Where the marriage/civil partnership was contracted post-TP end, the partnership must have met the definition of "durable partner" pre-TP end.

Who is included?

- dependent "parent" means direct relative in the ascending line of EEA national/their spouse/CP (definition of "dependent parent" (a)).
- "child" includes all direct descendants of the EEA national/QBC or their spouse/CP (definition of "child" (a))

Dependency must be evidenced for:

- Children 21 or over, who do not hold EUPSS (see definition of "child"(b)(ii)(aa)-(cc))
- Dependent parents applying after 30 June 2021 as JFMs (see definition of "dependent parent" (b)(iii))

CHAPTER 11: European Union Law

Dependency need not be evidenced for:

- Dependent parents applying before 1 July 2021 but only if the EEA national was 18 or over pre-TP end (see definition of "dependent parent"(b)(i)-(iii)) Dependency must still be accurately stated.
- Children under 21 (definition of "child" (a))
- Dependent children 21 and over and dependent parents already granted EUPSS ("child" (b)(ii); "dependent parent" (b)(i)-(ii))
- Dependent parents where the applicant's spouse/cp with whom they reside has been granted

At which point in time must the dependency have existed?

- For children 21+ and dependent parents with pre-TP end residence: at TP end if application thereafter (or, if the application date was pre-TP end, on the date of application) ("child" definition (b)(ii)(aaa)/(bb); "dependent parent" definition (b)(i))
- For children 21+ and dependent parents without pre-TP end residence (i.e. joining family members): at the date of application ("child" definition (b)(ii)(cc); "dependent parent" definition (b)(iii)status as a dependent parent "dependent parent" (c))
- Dependency must continue throughout the child's UK residence: obtaining employment after entering the route would end residence rights unless the child was also still dependent on their parent: Ali [2023] EWHC 1615 (Admin)

Dependency (see MIL 11.5.1 for EU law approach) is defined in a subpara which is identical between the "child" and "dependent" definitions (emphasis added):

'dependent' means here that: having regard to their financial and social conditions, or health, the applicant cannot, or (as the case may be) for the relevant period could not, meet their essential living needs (in whole or in part) without the financial or other material support of the relevant EEA citizen (or, as the case may be, of the qualifying British citizen or of the relevant sponsor) or of their spouse or civil partner; **and** *such support is, or (as the case may be) was, being provided to the applicant by the relevant EEA citizen (or, as the case may be, by the qualifying British citizen or by the relevant sponsor) or by their spouse or civil partner;* **and** <u>there is no need to determine the reasons for that dependence or for the recourse to that support</u>"

Annex 1 definition of a "durable partner"

This category of persons can be sponsored as FM of a REAACZ or JFM of a RS. One major obstacle to applications succeeding has become apparent from 2021-2022: which is that often one needs a formal document issued under the EEA Regs 2016 pre-TP end: evidence of the relationship being genuine and subsisting does not suffice. Whether or not a residence document/family permit issued to them as a durable partner is required, or whether other durability evidence is permissible instead, depends on the nationality of the sponsor (i.e. whether the sponsor is a "relevant person of Northern Ireland"), or on whether the applicant resided in the UK continuously since pre-TP end, and if they did so reside in the UK without a durable partner document, whether they had leave in a different category. NB: where the marriage/civil partnership was contracted post-TP end, this durable partner definition must have been met pre-TP end.

(a) Person in a durable relationship (with an REAACZ, a QBC or a RS) at the relevant time, having lived with them in a relationship akin to marriage for at least 2 years unless there is other significant evidence of durability; **and**

(b)
  (i) The person holds a BRC/family permit as the durable partner of an REAACZ, QBC or RS for the period of residence relied on. Such a document is *deemed to have been granted* pre-TP end if it had been *applied* for pre-TP end; **or**
  (ii) The person does not hold such a document but can otherwise evidence the durability of the relationship at the relevant time. This is only permitted in the following circumstances:
    (aa) The date of application is after TP end [before that, the EUSS was not open to durable partners]; and
    (bb) the person

(aaa) if in the UK as a durable partner without a BRC/family permit in that capacity, had valid leave in a different category; or

(bbb) was in the UK pre-TP end but their continuous residence was broken through absence or imprisonment and after this, they were not resident in the UK again pre-TP end; or

(ccc) was in the UK pre-TP end but were then absent for 5 years and not resident again pre-TP end [i.e. they did not start a new period of continuous residence]. The relationship must have been durable pre-TP end (or for *Surinder Singh* cases before 31 January 2020).

People without an EEA residence card issued pre-TP end will thus often find themselves unable to qualify as a durable partner. The HO has defended this line successfully (its first arguments can be seen in the letter to *the3million* of February 2022), on the basis that the WWA only protected people whose residence had already been facilitated by EU law as at 31 December 2020 (by obtaining a residence card or at least making an application for one by that date). It would be wrong, says UKVI, to let them take advantage of unlawful presence particularly when many others had followed the Rules. UKVI's advice is for such applicants to leave the UK for 6 months, which means they will break their continuity of residence and thus qualify as a joining family member. Another letter from Kevin Foster MP states that a delay in being able to marry due to the pandemic should not have prevented a timely application for a residence card as a durable partner.

- The HO stance has been upheld by the UT in Batool [2022] UKUT 219 (IAC) which emphasises that an EFM who had not applied for facilitation of their UK residence by 31 December 2020 cannot claim any protection under either the EUSSch or the WWA. The UT noted that EEA family permit applications were no longer permitted after 1 January 2021, and that the HO website had clearly explained that the scheme for EFMs was closing on 31 December 2020.
- And in Celik [2022] UKUT 220 (IAC) the UT finds that those whose ability to escape EFM status by marrying pre-31 December 2020 was frustrated by the pandemic are similarly excluded from the EUSSch: no EFM residence card = no timely facilitation. In April 2023 the definition of 'durable partner' at (b)(ii)(bb) was clarified to make the HO interpretation clearer. The Court of Appeal upheld the UT in Celik [2023] EWCA Civ 921, holding that the WWA was clear and that neither human rights principles nor domestic public law could have any impact on this interpretation.

Elais [2022] UKUT 300 (IAC) holds that a post-IP period marriage is not admissible evidence on appeal of an improved status (ie spouse rather than durable partner) such as to materially alter the Appellant's prospects in an appeal. However, the fact of the marriage is admissible as further evidence as to existence and durability of the claimed relationship, though the bare fact of marriage did not necessarily establish that the relationship was indeed genuine and subsisting.

(c) The partnership is not one of convenience
(d) Neither partner has (or had, for the relevant period) another durable partner, spouse or civil partner with immigration status on the basis on that relationship.

The definition adds that where the application is on the basis of being a family member of a person who is deceased (i.e. an application under either condition 6. in EU11 or condition 3. In EU11A) the applicant must have met the durable partner definition at the time before death rather than the date of application. Both definitions require that the family member lived with the deceased person before the death.

Annex 1 definition of a "family member who has retained the right of residence"

Family members include those with retained rights. Those are essentially residence rights following the death or departure of the EEA citizen, or where the relationship has ended with divorce after a certain period (or where child access rights are at stake) (MIL 11.6.3.2).

- Retained rights are generally modelled on the EEA Regs 2016. Thus we can see that generally the Annex 1 definitions for *family member who has retained the right of residence* from (a)-(e) are the same for those benefiting from retained rights under the Regs, Reg 10(2)-(5)
- However one significant difference is that, by contrast to Reg 10, under the EUSSch not only *spouses/civil partners* can qualify following domestic violence. Thus a person can benefit where the applicant '*or another family member has been a victim of domestic violence or abuse before the relevant family relationship broke down permanently*'
- There is no requirement for the family member to be working, studying or self-sufficient after the relationship has ended (because there is no equivalent provision to Reg 10(6) of the EEA Regs 2016)
- The Appendix EU equivalent of Reg10(5) explicitly states that, where termination proceedings (divorce or dissolution of a civil partnership) are initiated but the EEA citizen leaves the UK before termination, they are *deemed* to have remained until termination.
- And of course, consistent with the general scheme of EUSSch which looks to a sponsor's residence rather than any Treaty Right exercise, the EEA citizen need not have worked or studied etc

Annex 1 definition of a "person with a Zambrano right to reside"

The EUSS includes Zambrano rights holders amongst its beneficiaries. It now contains similar text to the UK's previous Zambrano category defined in the EEA Regs 2016 (MIL 11.6.3.3 for detail on Zambrano rights). Thus those who can benefit are
- Non exempt persons who are not subject to extant EEA Regs expulsion decisions who are
    - Primary carers of British citizens where the latter could not live in the UK/EEA/Switzerland if the former left indefinitely (Reg 16(5))
    - Other children of such primary carers so long as they are under 18 and otherwise lack leave (aside from Appendix EU or via s3C IA 1971 or granted under Appendix EU (Family Permit) as a "specified EEA family permit" case) under the Rules (Reg 16(6)): and once granted leave under Appendix EU such children can be granted further leave (presumably EUSS itself) notwithstanding that they have reached majority and that they have now held leave under Appendix EU)

Also
- Applicants must be able to show they met the criteria throughout the continuous qualifying period on which they rely, including at 11pm on 23 December 2020
- Primary carers are defined in Annex 1 as direct relatives/legal guardians with, or sharing equally, care (beyond bare financial) responsibilities. However one cannot be a primary carer where sharing care responsibility with another person who had achieved derivative residence rights (under the EEA Regs 2016 or Appendix EU) before the applicant assumed equal care responsibility
- Applicants must not be exempt persons (ie those with a right to reside under the EEA Regs 2016, or with the right of abode, or exempt from immigration control, or holding ILR other than under Appendix EU) nor subject to public policy decisions under the EEA Regs 2016
- This route **closes to new applicants from 8 August 2023** (MIL 11.7.2.5)

Note that the derivative rights guidance, as well as the EUSS guidance on Zambrano, mandates refusals of all applications on Zambrano grounds:

1. where the applicant has never made an application under Appendix FM or any other Art 8 claim, or
2. where such a claim was refused but circumstances have changed so as to, now, allow for success.

Akinsanya [2022] EWCA Civ 37 holds that Zambrano rights do not apply where domestic law accorded the right to reside on other grounds: the right is one of last resort. However it was unclear whether the SSHD intended to grant leave to all carers whose removal would result in their EU citizen dependant having to leave the UK when framing Appendix EU and the Zambrano definitions. It was not for the court to presume any particular intention. However once the HO reconsidered things, the stricter approach (ie requiring exhaustion of other options) was maintained: see *Guidance EU Settlement Scheme: Zambrano primary carers*. HCLC have promised a further legal challenge.

Annex 1 definition of a "person with a derivative right to reside"

Essentially the same classes of beneficiary exist as under the EEA Regs 2016 (save for Zambrano cases who of course have their own route). Essentially they are primary carers of self sufficient children (route (a)), the children now in education of EEA nationals formerly exercising Treaty Rights here, including the self-employed (route (b)), and the primary carers of such children in education (route (c)).

Under the EUSSch primary carers of self sufficient children need not establish that the child holds comprehensive sickness insurance. The same provisos apply as to not being an exempt person and as to the primary carer definition as for Zambrano cases directly above. UK education *excludes* nursery education – though *includes* education received before compulsory school age if equivalent to that received after that age. Self-sufficient persons are those with sufficient resources not to become a burden on the UK's social assistance system: CSIC is not required.

Consistent with the HO and judicial interpretation of Zambrano rights (see Zambrano definition directly above), this category is a last resort where no other residence basis is available, save for limited exceptions.

Annex 1 definition of "specified spouse or civil partner of a Swiss citizen"

This class of persons is a special category of JFM of a RS, which has no equivalent for applicants with prior continuous UK residence. A specified spouse or civil partner of a Swiss citizen is defined as:

(a) the spouse/CP of a RS; and
(b) the RS is a national of Switzerland who is not also a British citizen; and
(c) the marriage or civil partnership was formed between 1 January 2021 and 1 January 2026; and
(d)
(i) the marriage or civil partnership continues to exist, unless the application is for EUSS on the basis of 5 years' residence in general or under retained rights, or death of the sponsor; or
(ii) if applying on the basis of 5 years' residence, it must have existed for the relevant period; or
(iii) where applying for EUSS on the basis of the death of the sponsor, the marriage or civil partnership existed immediately before death

Note that the use of the word "exists" is in contrast to "subsists". A subsisting relationship would normally require cohabitation, indicating that, to meet the definition, no cohabitation is required. However, for applications as a partner of a deceased person, of course, cohabitation immediately before the death *is* required.

11.7.5.3 Individual sponsor category requirements

The specific requirements for each applicant category are found in the relevant Annex 1 definitions. In this section we address those which require further explanation.

Annex 1 definition of "frontier worker"

Frontier workers do not require their own continuous UK residence starting pre-TP end. Because, if they had this, they would generally fall within the other category of an EEA/Swiss national with such residence (and thus have a viable EUSSch case). Annex 1 defines a frontier worker as:
a person who:
(a) is an EEA or Swiss national; and
(b) is not a British citizen; and
(c) satisfies SSHD by relevant evidence of this that they fulfil the relevant conditions of being a frontier worker set out in regulations made under section 8 of the European Union (Withdrawal Agreement) Act 2020, and that they have done so continuously since TP end; and
(d) has not been (and is not to be) refused admission to, or removed from, the UK by virtue of regulations of the type to which (c) above refers

The cross reference in (c) is to the Citizens' Rights (Frontier Workers) (EU Exit) Regulations 2020, which defines a frontier worker at Reg 3, as someone who:
- Was, pre-TP end, and has been continuously since then, an EEA national worker or self-employed person (or someone who has retained that status under Reg 4)
- Is not primarily resident in the UK i.e. they have been in the UK for less than 180 days in the preceding year; or have returned to their country of residence at least once in the preceding 6 months; or twice in the preceding 12 months (unless there were exceptional circumstances why they did not)

- In relation to Frontier workers, the following guidance is available (the applicant guidance links to the different respective application forms from inside and outside the UK):
- Frontier worker permit scheme caseworker guidance
- Frontier Worker permit
- Frontier worker permit for EU citizens
- Administrative review: Frontier Workers caseworker guidance (warning that unprecedented delays as at Spring 2022 mean that decisions could take 6 months)
- Frontier Workers: apply for a review of your Frontier Worker permit decision

Annex 1 definition of "relevant naturalised British citizen"

(a) an EEA or Swiss national in the UK continuously since pre TP end; or
(b) an EEA or Swiss national who, having been in the UK under (a) above, would, if they were not a British citizen, be granted ILE/ILR under EU2 of this Appendix, if they applied under it before 1 July 2021; *[b in short: who would be granted ILE/ILR were they not British]*

and in either case the person also:

(c) comes within (b) of the definition of "EEA national" in regulation 2(1) of the EEA Regs 2016 *[by either having become a permanent resident under Reg 15 or having held an extended right of residence under Reg 14. Excluded are those whose country joined the EU after they naturalised]*; and

(d) meets the criteria contained in Reg 9A(2) or (3) (to have been a qualified person or permanent resident, disapplying, from 6 April 2022, the CSI requirement) as the dual national ("DN") to whom those provisions refer (regardless of whether, save in conditions 5 and 6 in the table in EU11, they remained a qualified person under regulation 6 of the EEA Regs 2016 after they acquired British citizenship).

This is the text of Reg 9A of the 2016 Regs (see MIL 11.3.2):

9A. Dual national: national of an EEA State who acquires British citizenship
(1) In this regulation "DN" means a person within paragraph (b) of the definition of "EEA national" in regulation 2(1).
(2) DN who comes within the definition of "qualified person" in regulation 6(1) is only a qualified person for the purpose of these Regulations if DN—
    (a) came within the definition of "qualified person" at the time of acquisition of British citizenship; and
    (b) has not at any time subsequent to the acquisition of British citizenship lost the status of qualified person.
(3) Regulation 15 only applies to DN, or to the family member of DN who is not an EEA national, if DN satisfies the condition in paragraph (4).
(4) The condition in this paragraph is that at the time of acquisition of British citizenship DN either—
    (a) was a qualified person; or
    (b) had acquired a right of permanent residence in accordance with these Regulations.

Annex 1 definition of "specified relevant person of Northern Ireland"

This special category is defined as follows:

(a) the person is a relevant person of Northern Ireland who is British or Irish/British (i.e. not solely Irish); and
(b) the applicant is a non-EEA citizen; and
(c)
> (i)
> (aa) the applicant is a joining family member and the person is their relevant sponsor; and
> (bb) due to compelling practical or compassionate reasons, it was not possible for the person to return to the UK before the specified date while the applicant remained outside the UK; or
> (ii)
> (aa) the applicant is a dependent relative and the person is their sponsoring person as defined under "dependent relative" i.e. *a REEACZ/QBC or their spouse/CP. QBCs and their spouses/civil partners where their relationship post-dated the UK's EU withdrawal on 31 January 2020, they must have returned to the UK pre-TP end whereas those where it pre-dated withdrawal may return before 29 March 2022* ; and
> (bb) the applicant relies, as their relevant document on an EUSS Family Permit as a 'dependent relative of a specified relevant person of Northern Ireland', as defined in Annex 1 to that Appendix

Annex 1 definition of "dependent relative of a specified relevant person of Northern Ireland" (SRPNI) – Appendix Europe (Family Permit)

For the context, see MIL 11.7.1.4.

> the person:
> (a)
> > (i) is a relative of a SRPNI or of their spouse/CP, but not a spouse, civil partner, durable partner, child or dependent parent; and
> > (ii) is a dependant of a SRPNI or of their spouse/CP, a member of their household or in strict need of their personal care on serious health grounds; or
>
> (b) is a person who is subject to a non-adoptive legal guardianship order in favour (solely or jointly with another party) of a SRPNI (substituting 'SRPNI' for 'QBC' in the entry for 'person who is subject to a non-adoptive legal guardianship order' in this table); or
> (c) is a person under the age of 18 years who:
> > (i) is the direct descendant of the durable partner of a SRPNI; or
> > (ii) has been adopted by the durable partner of a SRPNI, in accordance with a relevant adoption decision

For ease of reference, the underlined cross reference to the next Appendix EU (Family Permit) definition modifies that definition, as follows:

> Annex 1 definition of a "person who is subject to a nonadoptive legal guardianship order" – Appendix EU (Family Permit) (as modified by Appendix EU definition of "dependent relative of a SRPNI")
>
> a person who has satisfied the entry clearance officer that, immediately before the specified date, they:
> (a) are under the age of 18 years; and
> (b) are subject to a non-adoptive legal guardianship order in favour (solely or jointly with another party) of a SRPNI that:
> > (i) is recognised under the national law of the state in which it was contracted; and
> > (ii) places parental responsibility on a permanent basis on the SRPNI (solely or jointly with another party); and
>
> (c) have lived with the SRPNI since their placement under the guardianship order; and
> (d) have created family life with the SRPNI; and
> (e) have a personal relationship with the SRPNI that involves dependency on the SRPNI and the assumption of parental responsibility, including legal and financial responsibilities, for that person by the SRPNI

Annex 1 definition of "person exempt from immigration control"

> a person who:

(a) is an EEA/Swiss national; and

(b) is not a British citizen; and

(c) is exempt from immigration control in accordance with section 8(2), (3) or (4) of the Immigration Act 1971

Sections 8(2)-(4) IA 1971 broadly speaking provides for such an exemption to, as the main EUSS guidance summarises: "foreign diplomats, consular staff, posted members of foreign armed forces, members of staff of certain international organisations and certain family members of theirs".

From 6 October 2021, this cohort is free to apply under the EUSSch without first having to wait for their immigration exemption to come to an end.

Annex 1 definition of "relevant person of Northern Ireland"

This is a person who:
(a) is:
(i) a British citizen; or
(ii) an Irish citizen; or
(iii) a British citizen and an Irish citizen; and
(b) was born in Northern Ireland and, at the time of the person's birth, at least one of their parents was:
(i) a British citizen; or
(ii) an Irish citizen; or
(iii) a British citizen and an Irish citizen; or
(iv) otherwise entitled to reside in Northern Ireland without any restriction on their period of residence

11.7.5.4 Evidential requirements

Annex 1 definition of "required evidence of being a relevant person of Northern Ireland"

(a) Birth certificate or passport showing the person was born in NI; and
(b) Evidence that when they were born one parent was
   (i) A British citizen; or
   (ii) An Irish citizen; or
   (iii) Both; or
   (iv) Entitled to reside in NI without restriction on their period of residence

Annex 1 definition of "required proof of entitlement to apply from outside the UK"

Not all applicants from 1 January 2021 have to apply for family permits. Some can apply for EUSSEurope for settled- or EUPSS from abroad, so long as they have the "required proof" for their entitlement to do so. The abridged definition is as follows (and immediately below are the further definitions referred to therein):
(a) For EEA/Swiss nationals:
   (i) their valid passport; or
   (ii) their valid national biometric identity card
(b) For non-EEA citizen, their valid "specified relevant document"

unless the HO agrees to accept alternative evidence of entitlement to apply from outside the UK, if the person is unable to produce the required document due to circumstances beyond their control or to compelling practical or compassionate reasons.

'valid' means that the document is genuine and has not expired, been cancelled or invalidated.

Annex 1 definition of "specified relevant document"

This term occurs only 3 times in Annex 1, namely within the definition of "required biometrics" (to exempt non-EEA applicants from having to attend an appointment to provide fingerprints); in the definition of "required proof of entitlement to apply from outside the UK" (to facilitate the bypassing of a family permit application); and in the definition of "required proof of identity and nationality".

It is defined as:
(a) A biometric residence card, permanent residence card or derivative residence card issued by the UK under the EEA Regs on the basis of an application made on or after 6 April 2015; or
(b) A biometric EUPSS residence card.

Note the difference to the broader definition of "relevant document" (immediately below), which is referred to more widely throughout Appendix EU. The latter category includes non-biometric documents issued to EEA/Swiss nationals, whereas "specified relevant document" only includes biometric documents issued to non-EEA/Swiss nationals.

Annex 1 definition of "relevant document"

This term is cross referred to from other definitions. Sometimes holding a document determines one's eligibility to apply (for durable partners and dependent relatives), sometimes the document represents an alternative way of proving the claimed relationship.

This definition also effectively modifies the evidential requirements for dependent relatives and durable partners of "relevant person of Northern Ireland" by allowing any cogent evidence of the claimed relationship to be *deemed equivalent to* a "relevant document" ((a)(i)(bb)).

(a) Any document issued under the EEA Regs applied for pre-TP end or, for family permits (including outside Appendix EU(Family Permit) before 1 July 2021 (only family permits for dependent relatives must have been applied for pre-TP end). A HO letter confirming entitlement to a family permit is, from 6 October 2021 also included here.
  (bb) For dependent relatives or durable partners of an RPNI: other evidence of the relationship is deemed to be equivalent of a document in (aa)
    (i) [mirrors (i) for the Islands]
    (ii) A EUPSS biometric residence card
(b) Which has not been revoked or fell to be revoked, because the relationship/dependency never existed or had ceased
(c) Unless (d) or (e) applies, it has not expired or otherwise ceased to be effective and had remained valid for the period relied on
(d) for dependent relatives and durable partners, the relevant document may have expired, where:
  (i) the new document was applied for before the old one expired. It must be on the basis of the same family relationship.
  (ii) this new document must be issued by the date of decision on the Appendix EU application I.e. this is likely to mean that a decision will be put on hold until that document is issued
(e) The document may have expired if
  (i) It is a family permit issued by the UK or the Islands; and
  (ii) It expired post-TP end and before the deadline date which applies to the applicant; and
  (iii) The applicant arrived during the grace period. Durable partners or dependent relatives can have arrived during *or before* the grace period.

Annex 1 definition of "required evidence of family relationship"

The explanation below is abridged from an extremely long-winded original version. To facilitate cross-referencing from other sections when dealing with the actual provisions in Appendix EU, we have retained the structure and numbering of this definition. However, the below is an abridged version where cross references contained in its subparas have been explained rather than retained, for readability.

(a) Spouses (without a documented right of PR which can be used for EUSS applications on its own under condition 1 in rEU11):
  (i) A relevant document issued on that basis, or a valid document of record of marriage (the latter being defined neither in rule nor guidance) recognised in the UK; and
  (aa) for marriages contracted after TP end, a relevant document issued as a durable partner of the sponsor. Specified spouses/CPs of Swiss citizens are excluded from this requirement. Post-TP spouses of RNPIs and JFMs of RSs (i.e. those without pre-TP residence) can evidence their durable relationship pre-TP end via the relevant evidence. They do not need to have a relevant document.

CHAPTER 11: European Union Law

      (bb) for spouses of QBCs who married post-31 January 2020, evidence of the durable relationship before and on 31 January 2020
- (b) Civil partners (without a documented right of PR, which can be used for EUSS applications on its own under condition 1 in rEU11):
  - (i) A relevant document issued on that basis or a valid civil partnership certificate recognised by the UK; or an overseas registration document which can be treated as a civil partnership under the Civil Partnership Act 2004
  - (ii) (aa) for civil partnerships contracted after TP end, a relevant document issued as a durable partner of the sponsor. Specified spouses/CPs of Swiss citizens are excluded from this requirement. Post-TP civil partners of RNPIs and JFMs of RSs (i.e. those without pre-TP residence) can evidence their durable relationship pre-TP end via the relevant evidence. They do not need to have a relevant document.
  - (bb) for civil partners of QBCs who married post-31 January 2020, evidence of the durable relationship before and on 31 January 2020
- (c) A child without a documented right of PR: a relevant document issued to them on the basis of being a child family member, or their birth certificate, and
  - (i) Children aged 21 and over, not previously granted EUPSS as a child: evidence of dependence
  - (ii) A JFM of a RS, born or adopted (or otherwise became a 'child') after TP end: , evidence that either their parent is Swiss or a spouse/CP of a Swiss national; or that both parents are an RS; or one is an RS and the other a BC; or one parent is an RS with joint or sole custody under UK, EEA or Swiss law, or recognised by those states (particularly as regards best interests of the child)
- *(d)* A dependent parent without a right of PR: a relevant document issued on that basis; or evidence of birth. Evidence of dependence is only required in applications from 1 July 2021 where no previous leave as a dependent parent is held.
- (e) A durable partner:
  (i) a relevant document as the durable partner of the REEAC (or of the QBC or of the RS). If this does not confirm the right of permanent residence, also: evidence which satisfies SSHD that the partnership remains durable at the date of application (or did so for the period of residence relied upon); or
  (ii) for applications after TP end and where no relevant document is held: evidence of durability if the applicant was not in the UK with continuous leave since pre-TP end.
  The evidence must show that the partnership was durable pre-TP end (or before 31 January 2020 for *Surinder Singh* cases)
- (f) Dependent relative:
  - (i) A relevant document as the dependant relative of their sponsor. If this does not confirm a right to PR, also: evidence that the relationship and dependency/membership of the household/strict need for personal care exist at the date of application (or did for the relevant period); or
  - (ii) In the case of a FM of a QBC: evidence that the relationship and dependency/membership of the household/strict need for personal care existed at TP end and at the date of application (or that it existed for the period relied on)

      In addition, the definition provides:
- (a) A death certificate or other evidence of death is required where the application is in a category relating to the death of a person
- (b) Any family member applicants of any nationality without a documented right of PR, the evidence of family relationship must include:
  (i) Proof of ID and nationality of the sponsoring person (REEACZ. QBC or RS)
  (aa) valid passport; or
  (bb) valid national ID card or confirmation they have been/are being granted EUSS/EUPSS
  (cc) for naturalised British citizens or those to whom the pre-*McCarthy* transitional provisions apply, their valid EEA/Swiss passport or national ID and "information or evidence which is provided by the applicant, or is otherwise available to the [SSHD] that the person is a British citizen"
  (dd) for relevant persons of Northern Ireland (RPNI): the required evidence of being a RPNI (see below), and:
  (aaa) If British: information or evidence which is provided by the applicant, or is otherwise available to the HO that the person is a BC
  (bbb) If Irish: valid passport or national ID card or confirmation that they have been/are being granted EUSS/EUPSS
  (ccc) If British *and* Irish: either of the above (not both)

unless (in any case) the Secretary of State agrees to accept alternative evidence of identity and nationality where the applicant is unable to obtain or produce the required document due to circumstances beyond their control or to compelling practical or compassionate reasons; and

(i) Evidence that a sponsoring family member does (or did for the relevant time) fit the relevant family member definition. This applies to:
(aa) REAACZ
(bb) QBC
(cc) RS (i.e. someone sponsoring a JFM)

(c) 'Valid' means a document is genuine and has not expired or been cancelled or invalidated
(d) Where a copy is provided the HO can request the original where there is doubt as to authenticity
The HO can require a certified translation of (or a Multilingual Standard Form to accompany) any document which is not in English, where this is necessary to decide the application

Annex 1 (of Appendix EU (Family Permit)) definition of "required evidence of qualification"

This contains the evidential requirements for family permit sponsors. The sponsor categories covered by this definition appear under the following definition subparagraphs:

a) REEACZ and, additionally Irish citizens where the person they are sponsoring applies from 1 July 2021
b) Relevant naturalised British citizens
c) SRPNI who may be British, Irish or both.
d) Person exempt from immigration control under s 8(2), (3) or (4) of the Immigration Act 1971. They must, of course, also be an EEA/Swiss citizen.

In order to sponsor the applicant, they must provide:

1. an original, valid EEA/Swiss passport or national ID card ("valid" meaning a document is genuine and has not expired/been cancelled/invalidated); and
2. (if they do not already hold status under the EU Settlement Scheme): *"information or evidence which satisfies the entry clearance officer"* that they would have been granted EUSS/EUPSS under EU2 or EU3 of Appendix EU (i.e. not as JFMs) had they applied before 1 July 2021; and
3. that this status would not have lapsed, been cancelled, curtailed revoked or invalidated before the date of application by the family member whom they are sponsoring.

Evidence can include *"information or evidence which is provided by the applicant, or is otherwise available to the entry clearance officer"* that the sponsoring person is British or exempt from immigration control. British citizenship must be evidenced for relevant naturalised British citizens and relevant persons of Northern Ireland who are British or British and Irish.

Where evidence (other than a passport or a national ID card) is submitted:

- as a copy, the Entry Clearance Officer can request the original *"if they have reasonable doubt as to the authenticity of the copy"*
- in a language other than English, the ECO can request a certified English translation of, or a Multilingual Standard Form to accompany, the document, *"where this is necessary to determine the applicant's eligibility for a family permit"*.

11.7.6 Losing continuity of residence; 'supervening events' which terminate permanent residence and EUSS; and cancellation, curtailment and revocation of EUSS/EUPSS

Both the EUSS and the EEA Regs 2016 have specific measures for

- Breaking continuity of residence for the purpose of acquiring permanent residence
- Losing permanent residence/EUSS once it is granted

Breaking continuity of residence

For exclusion from the benefits of the schemes

Continuity of residence is required to establish a right to permanent residence under the EEA Regs 2016 or ILR under the EUSSch.

- Under the EEA Regs 2016, a person would lose continuity of residence for the purpose of acquiring permanent residence if they are imprisoned (Reg 3(3)(a))
- Though if they have lived in the UK for more than 10 years and had forged integrating links here, continuity may be retained (Reg 3(4)) (reflecting the EEA regime MIL 11.8.4)
- Under the EUSS those whose eligibility requirements include having 5 years of residence need to show residence for a *continuous qualifying period* (eg Condition 3 of EU11) : continuity is broken if '*the person served or is serving a sentence of imprisonment of any length*'. However, this will not be the case if the conviction is subsequently overturned (Annex 1 definition of "continuous qualifying period" (b)(ii)).

Losing permanent residence/EUSS

Under the EEA Regs 2016, permanent residence may be lost through '*absence from the United Kingdom for a period exceeding two years*'.

Under the EUSS, only a '*supervening event*' suffices. Defined in Annex 1 as follows:

- An absence from the UK and Islands for five consecutive years since the applicant last acquired permanent residence or completed a continuous qualifying period of five years; or
- The making of one of the following decisions, which remains effective: removal or exclusion under Regs 23 or 32, other exclusion decisions, cancellation of a right of residence, revocation of admission under Reg 11; deportation outside the EEA Regs

Under the EEA Regs 2016 permanent residence lapsed after two years continuous residence outside the UK (Reg 15(2)). Gurskis [2022] EWHC 1305 (Admin) notes that it does not appear that an extradition request would cause an Appendix EU application to lapse. Under Appendix EU EUSS will remain in place unless five years is spent continuously outside the UK (Annex 1- definitions). Thus, Appendix EU is more accommodating than the Regs. Note that EUPSS is lost only after 2 consecutive years outside the UK, but eligibility for EUSS will be lost if continuous residence is broken during the 5-year period on which the applicant will be relying. It is important to advise clients of this carefully to avoid misunderstandings.

Cancellation, curtailment and revocation of leave granted under Appendices EU and EU (Family Permit)

Cancellation, curtailment and revocation under Annex 3 of Appendix EU

Until 6 April 2021 this regime was found by applying Part 9 of the Immigration Rules. However now Annex 3 represents a complete code (IR9.1.1(d)-(e) fully excluding Appendix EU/EU(FP)). EUSS/EUPSS *must* be cancelled for conduct post-transition on or before UK arrival, applying the "*conducive to the public good*" threshold to post TP end conduct (A.3.1) and where they are under a UK or UN Security Council travel ban (A.3.1A).

EUSS/EUPSS *may* be cancelled on or before UK arrival, *where proportionate*:

- On EEA public policy, public security or public health grounds (A.3.2(a))
- For material dishonesty re application/supporting documents (A.3.2(b))

EUPSS *may* be cancelled on or before UK arrival *if proportionate* where they cease to meet the Appendix's requirements (A.3.3)

EUPSS *may* be curtailed *if proportionate* to do so for

- material dishonesty re application/supporting documents (A.3.4(a))
- probable involvement in marriage of convenience (A3.4(b))

- ceasing to meet Appendix's requirements (A.3.4(c))

EUSS *may* be revoked *where proportionate* and where:

- deportation is not possible for legal reasons (eg ECHR rights) (A.3.5(a))
- EUSS obtained by deception (A.3.5(b))

Guidance document Revocation of indefinite leave- s76 emphasises that any deception must have been material to the grant. The list of examples of deception provided is non-exhaustive. It includes provision of fraudulent eligibility evidence, presentation by a non-EEA national as an EEA national, sham marriage and deception by a third party. It also states that discovery of a sham marriage may lead to deportation. Where the decision's subject is in the UK at the revocation date, their leave will be extended to permit an "in-time appeal" to be brought, though not if the removal is certified, in which case they should be detained or placed on immigration bail.

Cancellation and revocation under Annex 3 of Appendix EU (Family Permit) – current position

Entry clearance granted under App EU (FP) *must* be revoked for conduct post-transition:

- Applying the "*conducive to the public good*" threshold (A.3.1)

Entry clearance granted under App EU (FP) *may* be revoked, *where proportionate* and where:

- An exclusion order or decision relating to pre-transition period end conduct, exists (A.3.2(a))
- There has been material dishonesty re application/supporting documents (A.3.2(b))
- Since its grant there has been a change in circumstances as to eligibility (A.3.2(c))

Leave to enter following entry clearance granted under App EU (FP) *must* be cancelled where:

- Presence is not conducive to the public good on the basis of post TP end conduct (A.3.3)

Leave to enter following entry clearance under App EU (FP) *may* be cancelled *if proportionate* to do so for

- Public policy, public security or public health grounds (A.3.4.(a))
- Material dishonesty re application/supporting documents (A.3.4(b))
- Since EC was granted there has been a change in circumstances as to eligibility (A.3.4(c))

Leave to enter following entry clearance under App EU (FP) *may* be curtailed *where proportionate* for:

- Material dishonesty re application/supporting documents (A.3.5(a))
- Probable involvement in a sham marriage (A.3.5(b))

MIL 11.7.10 addresses appeal rights and extension of permission in some of these cases.

11.7.7 Suitability under Appendix EU and Appendix EU (Family Permit)

As in other parts of the Rules, applications can be refused for not meeting substantive requirements of the Rules. That notion (Eligibility) is what we have dealt with so far. But refusal (as well as cancellation and revocation, addressed above) may also be due to various misdemeanours. This is the concept of Suitability. Some refusal grounds are mandatory, others are discretionary.

Suitability grounds for refusal under Appendix EU

Mandatory refusals

- Being subject to an extant deportation order or exclusion decision (EU15(1) read with EU17)
- Being subject to a Islands deportation order (EU15(3) read with EU17)

- Presence deemed not conducive to public good (for post TP end conduct) (EU15(2))
- Discretionary refusals
- Being subject to an *Islands* extant exclusion decision (EU15(4) read with EU17)
- Where material "*false or misleading information, representations or documents*" (re application and its supporting documents) submitted, whether or not to applicant's knowledge if it is **proportionate** to refuse (EU16(a))
- Where a removal decision exists in relation to "*non-exercise or misuse of rights*" for pre-July 2021 applications if it is **proportionate** to refuse (EU16(b))
- For persons previously refused entry on public policy grounds under EEA Regs 2016 or Frontier Workers Regs or had Appendix EU- or App EU (FP) leave cancelled (EU16(c)(i))
- Where the EEA Regs 2016 "*public policy, public security or public health*" provisos apply for **pre-transition conduct** and it is proportionate to refuse, and re the "*conducive to the public good*" **thereafter** (EU16(c)(ii))
- For a "*relevant excluded person*" (ie a person who has been excluded from refugee status or HP for international or domestic criminality, or would be excluded were they to apply): if the EEA public policy proviso applies for pre-transition conduct, otherwise automatically (EU16(d)-(e))

Suitability grounds for refusal under Appendix EU (Family Permit)

- Mandatory refusals
- Being subject to an extant deportation order or exclusion decision (FP7(1) read with FP7(5))
- Presence deemed not conducive to public good (for post TP end conduct) (FP7(2))
- Discretionary refusals
- Being subject to an *Islands* extant deportation order or exclusion decision (FP7(3) read with FP7(5))
- Where material "*false or misleading information, representations or documents*" (re application and its supporting documents) submitted, whether or not to applicant's knowledge if it is **proportionate** to refuse (FP4 (a))
- For persons previously refused entry on public policy grounds under EEA Regs 2016 or Frontier Workers Regs or had Appendix EU- or App EU (FP) leave cancelled (FP4(b)(i))
- Where the EEA Regs 2016 "*public policy, public security or public health*" provisos apply for **pre-transition conduct** (and refusal is proportionate), and re the "*conducive to the public good*" **thereafter** (FP4(b)(ii))

11.7.7.1 EUSS applicants with criminal records

The EUSS Suitability guidance from page 14 sets out cases of applicants with criminal records which *must* be referred for immigration enforcement, and cases which *must not* be referred. If a removal or deportation decision is then made, this would additionally give rise to a suitability refusal. Therefore, as a representative, it is vital to know when UKVI could make such a referral within the policy. Where the guidance states that a client's case should *not* be referred to IE, this should perhaps be pointed out in the covering letter.

Under the guidance, cases ***must*** be referred for deportation or exclusion, which is to be considered on a case by case basis, where the applicant has had:

- Any prison sentence in the last 5 years
- Any 12 month prison sentence for one offence at any time
- Three or more convictions in the last 3 years, where the person has been resident for under 5 years. At least one of these must have occurred in the last 12 months.
- Involvement in serious deception such as assisting unlawful immigration or sham marriages/partnerships
- Being 'of interest', meaning the CCD were already considering issuing a deportation or exclusion order, for example where a prison sentence is currently being served

Cases ***not to be referred*** are where:

- A recorded decision has been made not to pursue deportation or to revoke a deportation order
- A tribunal has overturned a deportation decision, the HO has not appealed and there are no further offences meeting the referral criteria
- While in prison a conviction did not meet the referral criteria and there are no further offences meeting the referral criteria
- A past conviction or convictions were not referred for deportation under the policy in place at the time and there are no further offences meeting the referral criteria

Clearly there are many cases falling into neither category, particularly where there are additional, more recent, if minor offences, and thus it is not certain at this point how best to advise clients. This area of uncertainty was criticised by the ex-offenders charity Unlock in their report EU nationals, settled status and criminal records. A response from the HO providing no real clarity. ILPA has also made a number of recommendations in that regard in their updated report on EU residence rights after Brexit of 22 January 2020.

Overseas offences may also attract enforcement action. The guidance states that overseas criminal records checks may be requested where:

- Overseas criminality is declared; or
- Police checks reveal that the applicant was previously extradited, is subject to a European Arrest Warrant or interpol alert or has an overseas conviction

Applicants will be contacted and informed if such a check is to be undertaken. Currently they seem regularly to be informed that the checks will take 6 months. It may be advisable to request such records independently as this may result in a faster response. This also gives a client the chance to put any revelations in context before making their application to the HO. Information on how to request records from abroad can be found here.

Overseas criminal records requests will *not* be required, says the guidance, where the applicant has:

- Declared an overseas conviction; but
- Has 5 years' continuous UK residence; and
- Their UK PNC check is clear

Overseas offending revealed by such checks may lead to cases being referred for immigration enforcement.

Sometimes a putative applicant will have a prosecution pending against them (MIL 11.8.6)

The protections from expulsion for EEA nationals, in relation to conduct committed pre-TP end, remain the same criteria under the Citizens Directive, the effect of which is preserved by being directly referred to in the WWA (see below, section 11.8).

Top Tip

For the time being, the best strategy when dealing with EUSS clients with criminal records may be to
1. Make criminal records requests via ACRO in any cases where convictions disclosed by clients may meet the referral criteria for deportation.
2. Consider requesting records from abroad where overseas criminality is disclosed, https://www.gov.uk/government/publications/criminal-records-checks-for-overseas-applicants. If the HO is likely to request these anyway, your request may well be faster, so you may save waiting time for your client (and you will have the opportunity to take instructions and make representations in relation to their contents before the HO sees them).
3. Consider requesting probation reports and/or any evidence of rehabilitation where relevant.
4. Advise clients on the risk of deportation, and on the importance to be able to show rehabilitation, in challenging deportation, should this become necessary.
5. If risk is high, take instructions as if on an EEA deport case: take a full chronology to determine whether client has 10 years' lawful residence as well as permanent residence – HO would then need to show imperative grounds of public security

> 6. Signpost clients to services which may aid them in their rehabilitation such as, eg: homeless charities, counselling services, substance abuse support groups, language classes, volunteering or employment support wherever appropriate and beneficial to the client in any case, while their application is being prepared and then processed.
> 7. Submit the application, where time allows, only once records are received so as to advise more specifically on the likelihood of deportation and take further instructions, before submission.
> 8. Whether or not to submit legal representations in an attempt to pre-empt a referral for enforcement action will be a judgment call. Applicants with offending histories have nevertheless, anecdotal evidence shows, been granted EUSS, thus it may be better not to draw attention to a record which does not clearly fit the referral criteria.
> 9. Of course, the questions on criminality in the application form must at all times be answered truthfully, and the client must be advised on potential future cancellation or revocation on grounds of deception.
> 10. Even in cases of more serious, and/or recent criminality, it may be best to submit the application without representations at first, and wait for contact from the HO for further information, to then respond by making representations at that stage. In some cases, by then, there will be more evidence of rehabilitation available to be put forward, than there would have been at the time of the application

11.7.8 Application procedure and guidance

Aside from the Immigration Staff Guidance EU Settlement Scheme caseworker guidance, a body of online guidance is available under EU Settlement Scheme: applicant information. The latter appears to be aimed at applicants without representatives but contains a wealth of useful information which may be of use to advisers, too. A full list of all EEA and EUSS guidance is provided at 11.7. Concerns have been raised as to delays and other difficulties in the application process by the European Affairs Committee.

The HO takes the view across immigration law generally, including EEA applications, that the burden of proof is on the applicant. So it is rather rare for the HO to actively help an applicant to obtain evidence in these cases (cf Amos directions MIL 11.6.3.2),

However under the EUSS (including the EU(FP) Appendix) there is a more proactive approach. Under Annex 2 decision makers will have regard both to

> '(a) the information and evidence provided by the applicant, including in response to any request for further information or evidence made by the Secretary of State; and
> (b) any other information or evidence made available to the Secretary of State (including from other government departments) at the date of decision.'

There is some scope under the PBS and Appendix FM for decision makers to request further documents and information. The range of enquiry is fuller under the EUSS: Annex 2 provides

> 'they may (a) request that the applicant provide further information or evidence that they meet those requirements; or
> (b) invite the applicant to be interviewed by the Secretary of State in person, by telephone, by video-telecommunications link or over the internet.'

In relation to the eligibility requirements:

- the applicant may be invited to provide further information or evidence or to be interviewed
- the sponsor may be invited to provide further information or evidence about the relationship or be interviewed
- interviews may be conducted in person, by telephone, by video communication or over the internet

Where applicant or sponsor fail to respond or at least twice fail to comply with an interview invitation, the ECO may draw factual inferences about eligibility and refuse the application. But not relying on this failure as the sole refusal basis (A 2.2(3)-(5)).

Note that no such procedural safeguards apply to the meeting of the suitability requirements, and that, where fraudulent documents have been submitted, the process is either disapplied or truncated under the main EUSS guidance (see "validity considerations" and "consideration of applications: eligibility").

Once an application is made a Certificate of Application (EUCoA) is issued, without regard to whether the Eligibility/Suitability criteria are met. However this will not alone suffice for right to work/rent checks: a Positive Verification Notice is required from the Employer Checking Service. A Provisional Replacement Certificate (PRC) giving access to the NHS is issued to to individuals with a valid pending application to the EUSS, rather than an EHIC card. Many issues arising in the application process are addressed by this *March 2023 HO letter to the 3Million*.

Online application, using the EU Exit ID app

This procedure is used by EEA and Swiss nationals with current biometric passports or national ID cards and non-European family members with current valid Biometric Residence Cards. The same process can be used from abroad by those applicants who meet the Annex 1 definition of "required proof of entitlement to apply from outside the UK" (see MIL 11.7.5 – in short, they must have an EEA/Swiss passport or ID card and if non-EEA/Swiss, a biometric residence card).

The submission procedure is via the EU Exit ID app, which can only be downloaded to phones with Near Field Communication. This function scans the biometric information from the chip in passports and BRCs, and will take and submit directly to the HO a facial image. The rest of the application can then be completed online, here: https://www.gov.uk/settled-status-eu-citizens-families/applying-for-settled-status.

Online and postal application

This procedure is open to European applicants holding current, but non-biometric and non-machine readable documents. The application form is filled online, a digital photo uploaded, and once the online form is submitted the document must be sent to the address as notified by the online system.

Online form & biometrics appointment

Non-European applicants who do not hold a current valid Biometric Residence Card complete the online form as above, with a digital facial photograph, but once submitted the online application will direct the applicant to book an appointment with Sopra Steria. If it is impossible, due to a client's specific vulnerabilities (eg if they are currently residing at a mental health facility having been 'sectioned' under the Mental Health Acts) you can ring the resolution centre for alternative solutions. The HO has committed to facilitating applications from the vulnerable. Where warranted, it is even possible for the mobile biometrics unit to be deployed without charge.

Application by paper form

The system for beneficiaries of derivative- and Zambrano rights, Surinder Singh and Lounes applicants (FM of QBC and family members of relevant naturalised British citizens respectively) and for those unable to obtain ID documentation, is paper-based.

For applications from 4 June 2020, these forms could, temporarily, be emailed where an email address was stated on the form. The date of service was the date the email is registered on UKVI's system. This temporary procedural concession, introduced to assist with urgent applications before the 30 June 2021 deadline, was withdrawn on 5 July 2021

A paper application form must be requested from the UKVI EUSS Resolution Centre.

Grant of status

Once the application is granted this will be confirmed by email. For EU citizens they will then have an online profile confirming their status which they can access and which can be shown to employers or others via loggin in and requesting a "share code". This is all they will have.

Status must be updated when renewing passport/ID document linked to their online status, or if their email or phone number which they used to access their status changes, via this link: https://www.gov.uk/update-uk-visas-immigration-account-details

Non-EU applicants will receive a biometric card confirming their leave. If they already hold a residence card issued under the EEA Regs, EUSS will be 'linked' to this. Such a card can be exchanged for an EUSS card by using the process here: https://www.visas-immigration.service.gov.uk/product/biometric-residence-permit-replacement-service

11.7.9 Family Permits and Travel Permits - applications from abroad under Appendix EU(FP)

Appendix EU (Family Permit) was added to the Immigration Rules on 30 March 2019; there is accompanying Immigration Staff Guidance EU Settlement Scheme Family Permit. The objective is to provide a route for non-EEA family members of EEA citizens (or EEA nationals lacking pre-TP end residence) (and then for non-British citizens from 9 November 2022) to apply for entry clearance to come to the UK in order to make an application under the EUSS.

FP3. The applicant will be granted an entry clearance under this Appendix, valid for the **relevant period**, by an entry clearance officer where:

> (a) A valid application has been made in accordance with paragraph FP4 (in accordance with the "required application process", "required proof of identity and nationality" and "required biometrics"
>
> (b) The applicant meets the eligibility requirements in paragraph FP6(1), (2) or (3); and
>
> (c) The application is not to be refused on grounds of suitability in accordance with paragraph FP7.

The "relevant period" is 6 months from date of decision.

The eligibility requirements for EUSSch family permits in FP6(1)&(2) are that:

- The applicant is a person of any nationality except British.
- Under FP6(1): the applicant is a "family member of a relevant EEA citizen" or a "joining family member" *NB: different from under Appendix EU, these categories are not mutually exclusive, and there is no distinct category to sponsor JFMs either, i.e. there is no definition of a "relevant sponsor" – everyone is being sponsored by a REEACZ or QBC.*

- Under FP6(2): the applicant is a "family member of a Qualifying British Citizen"
    - The REEACZ/QBC resides in the UK or will travel to the UK within six months of the application
    - The applicant will accompany or join them in the UK
    - The applicant is not the spouse, civil partner or durable partner where such a partner (of the applicant or the EEA citizen) has already been granted entry clearance under Appendix EU(FP) or under Reg 12 of the EEA Regs
    - This route closes, in line with that in the mainstream EUSSch, from 8 August 2023 (applications after that date are deemed invalid: FP4): those with pending applications before that date which are granted, or succeed on appeal, will be able to come to the UK and join the EUSSch

For Travel Permits, the eligibility requirements in FP6(3) are that:

- The applicant is a non-EEA citizen holder of EUSS/EUPSS which remains extant
- They were issued with a "relevant document" under the EEA Regs or the EUSSch, which they have reported to the HO as being lost, stolen or having expired while abroad
- The applicant will be travelling to the UK within 6 months of application

The guidance page with a link to the online form, is here.

The suitability requirements in FP7 are almost identical to those at EU15 & EU17 of Appendix EU (MIL 11.7.7) except that under Appendix EU (Family Permit)

- the existence of a removal decision on the ground of non-exercise or misuse of rights is not one of the suitability grounds for refusal
- the ground under Appendix EU for relevant excluded persons (those who are or would be excluded from international protection) does not appear

Annex 1 contains the definitions which apply to Appendix EU (Family Permit). A 'relevant EEA citizen' here is defined as:

- an EEA citizen (including relevant persons from Northern Ireland, *McCarthy-* and *Lounes* naturalised British citizens, persons exempt from immigration control and frontier workers)
- who has been granted settled or EUPSS under paras EU2/EU3, or would have been granted this had they applied before 1 July 2021 (and if they were not barred from so applying by being British) – and the grant was not made in error
- which has not/would not have lapsed, been cancelled, curtailed or revoked
- which is evidenced by a HO reference number or other information and evidence

A 'family member of a relevant EEA citizen' is defined similarly to Appendix EU in so far as it caters for close family members of EEA citizens:

- Spouses/CPs and durable partners where the relationship was contracted, or durability achieved, by the end of December 2020
- Children or dependent parents of the EEA citizen or of their spouse/CP
- Specified spouses of Swiss citizens (the marriage must be contracted between 1 January 2021 and 1 January 2026)
- The amendment in November 2022 to (b) of the definition clarifies that it includes circumstances where the QBC might have returned to the UK ahead of the applying family member and a relevant child has been born or adopted to that QBC after the end of the transition period but before the family's return to the UK (& military service in the Sovereign Bases in Cyprus counts as work for these purposes)

Dependent relatives are not otherwise included (aside from dependent parents or dependent relatives of a SRPNI): so there is no route for EFMs. Nor for derivative rights holders.

Annex 1 of Appendix EU(FP) defines "required evidence of qualification" (MIL 11.7.5.4) specifying the evidence for family permit sponsors, and the proof of family relationship is defined at "required evidence of family relationship".

11.7.9.2 After the Grace Period - EEA nationals at the border

The Guidance *EEA nationals at the border post grace period*:

> "…sets out the operational processes for dealing with EU, European Economic Area (EEA) and Swiss passengers and their family members who arrive at the UK border after the end of the grace period, which ended at midnight on 30 June 2021. The guidance therefore came into effect at 00:01 on 1 July 2021."

The Guidance recognises the need to protect those who arrived during the Grace Period. Until 30 June 2021 the saved version of the EEA Regs 2016 performed this task. But with the repeal of those Regs, something was required to fill the gap for this cohort of arrivals, to ensure they can live, work, study, access public funds, and travel. This **Temporary Protection status** is not a form of leave, but it may be necessary to grant a period of Leave outside the Rules (LOTR) at the border to facilitate the entry of an individual who has Temporary Protection status. Where a grant of leave is required, it should be for 3 months on a Code 1A.'

A right of admission under saved Reg 11 of the 2016 Regs is, according to the guidance, enjoyed by:

- non-EEA nationals who have applied for status under the EUSSch *only if* they also hold a valid EEA Regs BRC. Where these documents are not held, and where there is no reason to disbelieve their family relationship, they *must* nevertheless be granted 3 months' LOTR (p43).
- holders of EUSS expired family permits who applied to the EUSSch before expiry. They hold leave in the UK under s3C but this is lost if they leave the UK. However, these individuals also *must* be granted LOTR.

The general position is that everyone except Irish citizens should have prior entry clearance. However a reasonably relaxed approach is taken to the assessment of evidence and the account of arriving passengers is not to be doubted without good cause. The table Saved rights or Temporary Protection lists circumstances in which persons are deemed to have Temporary Protection vs saved rights, and whether immigration bail or LOTR should be granted. Various kinds of EEA and non-EEA arrivals are then listed, divided up according to whether they have pending in-time EUSSch applications, or have made late applications, or no application. .

The guidance then goes into more detail on how certain cases are treated:

- Those encountered in the UK who appear to be eligible but have not applied are to be given a 28 Day Notice for EUSS" to enable them to do so, whereas those encountered at the border who claim to have been resident pre-TP end are asked to evidence this on the spot and border staff are encouraged to be pro-active in assisting them. If they succeed on the balance of probabilities, either LOTR should be granted or permission to enter refused and immigration bail granted (p59-60).
- Most grants of immigration bail will be of 28 days to allow enough time to lodge an application. Unsurprisingly, those in any category who cannot evidence their pre-TP end residence (where this is a requirement) or their family relationship are not protected. In certain circumstances, where neither saved rights nor Temporary Protection apply, caseworkers are cross-referred to "compelling circumstances" preventing removal.
- At juxtaposed ports (where UK border controls are undertaken abroad) LOTR must be granted where the person has an unexpired EEA Regs BRC or family permit (p 61).
- Children whose parents have EUSSch status or a pending application should be granted LOTR rather than refused entry and granted bail (p60).
- Long term residence in itself can be a compelling enough circumstance to warrant 28 days' LOTR when long-term residents are considered as part of the cohort who have failed to apply, but they should also be considered as being eligible for assistance under the Windrush scheme depending on whether their residence began before 1 January 1973 or whether they had obtained ILE/R prior to 31 December 1988 (p 44-5).
- Late EUSSch applications following refusal of leave to enter (but where 28 days' immigration bail has been granted to make an application) will not normally be a barrier to removal where no further evidence has been brought; where it was established at refusal of LTE that the person lacked pre-TP end residence and is not a JFM and they have brought no further evidence; they are subject to a deportation or exclusion decision; or the exceptions for criminality apply (p 58).

NB: the guidance applies a stricter rule in relation to continuous residence than Appendix EU, in requiring permanent residence under the Regs to have accrued rather than also, alternatively, 5 years' residence, before permitting longer absences from the UK (p 62).

Among the other issues dealt with in this guidance are:

- the requirements for Irish nationals, their family members and the Common Travel Area in general
- the use of "eGates" which remains open to EEA nationals aged at least 12 and accompanied by an adult. Entry through eGates will automatically grant 6 months permission to enter subject to the standard visit conditions, but S2 Healthcare Visitor leave can also be granted automatically.

Criminality will be considered before granting LOTR, but pre-TP end conduct by for principals and family members is assessed on the EEA public policy standard. The guidance states that deportation orders automatically invalidate any previous leave, and thus such an individual may be ineligible for Temporary Protection if they lacked lawful residence pre-TP end (but see the more nuanced assessment process set out at Pending EUSS applications and Temporary Protection). Exclusion orders are differentiated in that they do not necessarily have that effect unless accompanied by cancellation of leave (34).

11.7.10 Challenging EUSS refusals – appeals and administrative review

The Immigration (Citizens' Rights Appeals) (EU Exit) Regulations 2020 ("ICREx Regs 2020") introduce appeal rights for individuals receiving negative decisions in relation to the EU Settlement Scheme or frontier workers.

For the first few years of these Regs' operation, appeal rights were only available where a decision was made in relation to an application submitted after Exit Day: ie from 1 February 2020 (Reg 3(2)). From 8 May 2023 however, decisions made after that date will bear the right of appeal whatever the application date (Reg 3(2)). The rationale given in the Explanatory Note is that the closure of the scheme (subject to reasonable explanation for delay) meant that the option of applying again was no longer available.

Rights of appeal

Essentially the Regulations provide a right of appeal for persons re most imaginable EUSSch decisions:

In relation to leave under Appendix EU:

- Varying one's leave such that one does not have any leave (Reg 3(1)(a))
- Cancelling leave (Reg 3(1)(b))
- Refusing leave to enter or remain (Reg 3(1)(c))
- Refusing to grant EUSS (Reg 3(1)(d))
- Revocation of EUSS (revocation under s76(1) or (2) of the 2002 Act) (Reg 4)

From 8 May 2023 an equivalent to s3C leave is conferred on those receiving hostile variation and revocation decisions (ie under Regs 3(1)(a), 4): Reg 13A. With one drawback: no applications for alternative permission to stay can be made during this period.

For family permit entry clearance under Appendix EU-FP (Reg 5):

- Refusal of entry clearance (Reg 5(a))
- Cancellation/revocation of entry clearance (Reg 5(b)
- Refusal of leave to enter to a person with entry clearance (Reg 5(d)) & refusal of leave to enter on arrival (Reg 5(c))
- Cancellation variation of leave to enter (Reg 5(d)

In relation to deportation:

- A decision to make a deportation order (Reg 6) (though not where the decision was made under the EEA Regs 2016)

The ICREx Regs 2020 also provide a right of appeal against decisions under the Citizens' Rights (Frontier Workers) (EU Exit) Regulations 2020 (the "Frontier Workers Regs 2020") to:

- Refuse to issue or renew a frontier worker permit (Reg 6A(a)&(b))
- Revoke a frontier worker permit (Reg 6A(c))
- Refuse admission (Reg 6B(1)) but the right of appeal is conditional on a valid identity document (Reg 6B(2)(a)). Alternative evidence of being a frontier worker maybe brought where admission is refused before 1 July 2021 (reg 6B(3)(a) or where the person is Irish (b)
- Revoke admission (Reg 6C) or a removal decision under the Frontier Workers Regs 2020 (Reg 6D), the right in both cases being conditional on producing a valid ID document

CHAPTER 11: European Union Law

- Deport a frontier worker under s5(1) IA 1971 (not under the EEA Regs 2016), this right being conditional on a valid ID document and evidence of being a frontier worker (a permit in that capacity or other evidence) (Reg 6E)

Note that

- The appeal rights against deportation under the ICREx Regs 2020 do not apply to decisions under Reg 23(6)(b) of the EEA Regs 2016. EEA decisions including deportation are appealable under those Regs
- Wherever the ICREx Regs require valid ID to be produced but the person is unable to do so due to circumstances beyond their control, they can use alternative evidence of identity and nationality (Reg 6F)

Grounds of appeal

The grounds of appeal cover both EU law (under the Brexit Agreements) and domestic law. More precisely:

- **Rights under the WWA** (or for nationals of the EEA countries, Liechtenstein, Iceland, Norway or Switzerland, rights under the EEA EFTA separation agreement, and for the Swiss, the Swiss Citizens' rights agreement): Reg (8(2)
    - Migration rights generally: entry/exit, residence, permanent residence, rights to residence documents and equal treatment (Chapter 1, ie Articles 13-23 of the WWA)
    - Primary carers of the minor children of workers in education and dependent older children (Reg 24(2), Chapter 2 of the WWA) and similarly for descendants of the self-employed (Reg 25(2), Chapter 2 of the WWA)
- **Domestic immigration law** (Reg (8(3)), which means
    - The general refusal reasons so far as they are applied to EUSS (Reg 8(3)(a) read with Reg 3(1)(a)-(b))
    - The EUSS rules for refusals and variations of EUSS (Reg 8(3)(b) read with Reg 3(1)(c)-(d))
    - The statutory provisions on revoking ILR on grounds of non-removability and deception (Reg 8(3)(c) read with Reg 4)
    - The statutory provisions on deportation on conducive to the public good grounds (Reg 8(3)(b) read with Reg 3(1)(c)-(d))
    - The Frontier Worker Regs 2020 provisions set out in Reg 8(3)(e)&(f)

So it seems that EUSS appeals will have a similar scope to EEA appeals (MIL 11.9). Arguments can be put under the domestic Rules (and probably should be, for simplicity) where there is no difference between those Rules and the WWA. But if the latter ever seems to give more protection, then it can be relied on directly.

Arguments available under domestic legislation

For ease of reference, an overview of where the relevant domestic provisions are found:

Decision to be appealed	Immigration rule or legislation with which the decision was not in accordance
Refusal to grant leave	Appendix EU or Appendix EU (Family Permit) or the Frontier Worker Regs
Cancellation of status	the relevant grounds for refusal, in Part 9 of the Immigration Rules, on curtailment or cancellation at port or while outside the uk
Revocation of status	s76(1) or (2) of the 2002 Act under which ILR can be revoked where a person is liable to deportation but cannot be deported for legal reasons, or where leave was obtained by deception
Deportation under s5(1) of the 1971 Act	s3(5) or (6) of the 1971 Act.

©HJT

Deportation or removal decision of (frontier workers)	Reg 15(b) of the Frontier Workers Regs 2020
Decisison re: a frontier worker, under Frontier Workers Regs 2020	Regs 9, 11, 12, 14, 15(1)(a) or 15(1)(c) of the Frontier Workers Regs 2020

New matters in EUSS appeals

New matters may be raised in the form of a s120 statement, before or after the appeal is lodged (reg 9(1)-(3)). The HO's consent is required for these to be considered (Reg 9(5) and see MIL 14.2.7). New matters may include the usual grounds under s84 of the 2002 Act, namely that removal would breach the UK's obligations:

- under the Refugee Convention
- in relation to those eligible for Humanitarian Protection
- under the Human Rights Act 1998

In Celik [2022] UKUT 220 (IAC) the UT clarifies that a right of appeal is available on human rights grounds against an EUSSch refusal (because the Schedule to the ICREx Regs cross-references to the grounds of appeal in s84 NIAA 2002). However only where the HO consents to a new matter arising.

Forum and appeal deadline

Appeals will be to the FTT with onward appeals to the UT on points of law. Where the appeal is certified on grounds of national security, the appeal is to SIAC.

Reg 19 of the FTT Procedure Rules 2014 provides that notice of such appeals must be received 14 days after *being sent* the decision, unless the appellant is abroad, in which case the deadline is 28 days after *receipt* of the decision.

Option to apply for administrative review first *and* appeal later

Administrative review was available as an alternative to an appeal until 5 October 2023 (AR(EU)1.4). The same deadlines applied again from the date a negative decision on an Administrative Review was either sent or received (depending on whether the appellant was inside or outside the UK). AR was available as an additional option here, but not once an appeal had been lodged (MIL 14.7.9). This regime was achieved by r3C-r3D of the IAPRs 2014.

The decision to be appealed was not the AR decision but the original refusal.

Abandonment of Citizens Rights appeals

An appeal will be abandoned where EUSS or EUPSS is granted, unless the applicant gives notice to continue the appeal where they were granted EUPSS but think they are entitled to EUSS. Where the appeal is against revocation of EUSS, and EUPSS is granted instead, the appeal may be continued where the appellant wishes for EUSS to be restored.

Grant of a frontier workers' permit will deem the appeal abandoned (Reg 14(4A)); where the appeal is against refusal of admission, it is abandoned following admission to the UK ((4B).

Departure from the UK does not result in the abandonment of the appeal, reflecting the position under the 2016 Regs. This applies for both EUSS migrants and frontier workers.

In-country rights of appeal and certification of decisions

Appeals will be suspensive unless the decision is certified because the appellant is liable to deportation. Those appealing from abroad may, however, return to the UK to attend the hearing, unless this would cause 'serious troubles' to public policy or public security. While in the UK for that purpose they will be granted immigration bail. This is essentially the same regime as for expulsion under the EEA Regs 2016 (MIL 11.9.5).

Decisions can be certified under Reg 16(3) & 16A of the ICREx Regs 2020 where:

- it is decided to make a deportation order under s5(1) of the 1971 Act (ie on the basis that removal is conducive to the public good or has been recommended by a sentencing judge) or to deport under the 2016 Regs; and
- the tests at Reg 16(3)&(4) are met
- or (Reg 16A, from 8 May 2023) it is thought that the decision was taken in whole or in part due to abuse of rights or fraud (typically relationships of convenience and fraudulent attempts to gain leave under the EUSSch)

These tests are that removal would not:

- be unlawful under s6 Human Rights Act 1998 despite the appeals process not yet having been begun, or having been exhausted (Reg 16(3))
- expose the person to a real risk of serious, irreversible harm (Reg 16(4))

Any appealable decision can be certified if a deportation decision is made at the same time, or where there is an extant deportation order in place. The Guidance *EU Settlement Scheme – certification in National Security and deportation cases* explains that certification will not be appropriate for sentences of indeterminate length, prisoner transfer and extradition cases, for minors, and where the individual's whereabouts are unknown.

Section 3C leave where a EUPSS holder applies to vary leave

Section 3C(2)(ca) of IA 1971 now covers appeals against refusals of applications to vary EUPSS. i.e. to EUSS applications. Thus a person's EU leave will continue pending the appeal being finally determined. Section 2C of the SIAC Act 1997 is amended to enable certification of an exclusion decision in relation to EEA citizens protected by the Agreements or the domestic implementation of the Agreements where the grounds are met, enabling review by SIAC.

Appendix AR(EU) - administrative review of EUSS decisions, S2 Healthcare visitors and Service Providers from Switzerland

Administrative review was generally available under Appendix AR(EU). From 5 October 2023 AR is no longer available in category (3) cases below. The process is via an online form and the fee of £80 will be refunded if the review is successful. Further information, including contact details for assistance with using the form or complaints, is available on this page.

Para AR(EU)1.1 listed decisions eligible for Administrative Review as follows:

1) decisions under the EU Settlement Scheme, including Appendix EU eligibility refusals (AR(EU)1.1(a)), grants of EUPSS - (instead of EUSS) ((b)&(c)), cancellation of Appendix EU leave for ceasing to meet the requirements (d), cancellation of LTE under Appendix EU (Family Permit) for relevant eligibility changes (e)
2) eligibility refusals of applications, or refusal/cancellation of permission to enter on eligibility grounds, as an S2 Healthcare Visitor (f)(g)&(h) respectively
3) eligibility refusals of applications, or eligibility cancellations of permission to enter, as a Service Provider from Switzerland (i)&(j) respectively (applications may not be lodged however if the decision was made in the Channel Tunnel Control Zone and the applicant remains there)

Para AR(EU)1.2 excludes the following decisions from eligibility for administrative review:

4) refusals under Appendix EU EU6 on suitability grounds under paras EU15&16 (AR(EU)1.2(a))

5) refusals under Appendix S2 Healthcare Visitor para HV9.1 on suitability grounds (b)
6) refusals of permission to enter in relation to an entry clearance holder as an S2 Healthcare Visitor for a change of circumstances resulting in failure to mee the suitability requirements (c)
7) refusals of applications for entry clearance under Appendix Service Provider from Switzerland para SPS 7.1 on suitability grounds (d)
8) refusal of permission to enter in relation to an entry clearance holder as a Service Provider from Switzerland for a change of circumstances resulting in failure to meet the suitability requirements (e) (however AR is available for dishonesty/false representations)

Para AR(EU)1.3 excludes all rejections on validity grounds under Appendices EU, S2 Healthcare visitors, and Service Providers from Switzerland.

Appendix AR(EU) is more generous than Appendix AR in that

1. any information and evidence submitted with the application for the review, including information and evidence that was *not* before the original decision-maker can be considered
2. there is no automatic withdrawal if AR was applied for in-country and the applicant leaves the UK
3. the time limit to apply is in new 34R(1A) in Part one, and is 28 days from receipt of the refusal ((a)&(d) for those who are in the UK and not detained, and for those abroad, respectively). By contrast, under Appendix AR, which applies to refusals under other parts of the immigration rules, the shorter limit of 14 days applies for in-country applications for AR

those in detention have 7 days to apply (r34R(1A)(b)).

11.8 Excluding and removing EEA nationals from UK

Expulsion could, before the general repeal of the EEA Regs 2016, be justified due to any of the three scenarios found at Reg 23(6):

- lapse (where the individual no longer satisfies the requirements for the residence in question) or
- a person's entry or continued residence being considered not conducive to the public good on public policy grounds or
- misuse of rights

Public policy expulsion is a field where Brexit is of particular importance. Article 20 of the WWA states, referencing the Citizens Directive's expulsion protections:

> ARTICLE 20
> Restrictions of the rights of residence and entry
> 1. The conduct of Union citizens or United Kingdom nationals, their family members, and other persons, who exercise rights under this Title, where that conduct occurred before the end of the transition period, shall be considered in accordance with Chapter VI of Directive 2004/38/EC.

This is the reason the EEA Regs 2016 and the sections below dealing with its application to expulsions, will remain relevant for some time. Although they were repealed on 31 December 2020, they were saved with modifications. Those modifications relevant to restrictions of rights are found in the Schedule to the Citizens' Rights (Restrictions of Rights of Entry and Residence) (EU Exit) Regulations 2020 and The Citizens' Rights (Application Deadline and Temporary Protection) (EU Exit) Regulations 2020. Post-grace period, the EEA Regs 2016 are only saved for those lawfully resident in the UK immediately pre-TP end and who applied under the EUSSch before the end of the grace period, and who are awaiting a final decision, including appeals.

The effect of Art 20 WA is reflectedin the savings modifications below (the underlined text has been added):

CHAPTER 11: European Union Law

Reg 23 – Exclusion and removal from the United Kingdom

(1)-(5) are omitted by way of modification
(6) Subject to paragraphs (7) and (8), <u>a person protected by the citizens' rights provisions</u> who has entered the United Kingdom may be removed if—
(b) the Secretary of State has decided that the person's removal is justified on grounds of public policy, public security or public health in accordance with regulation 27; or on conducive grounds in accordance with regulation 27A or if the person is subject to a deportation order by virtue of section 32 of the UK Borders Act 2007
(7) A person must not be removed under paragraph (6)—
(a) as the automatic consequence of having recourse to the social assistance system of the United Kingdom;

Thus the new para 27A provides for the domestic "conducive" regime to apply for post-TP end conduct:

Reg 27A.— Decisions taken on conducive grounds
(1) An EEA decision may be taken on the ground that the decision is conducive to the public good.
(2) But a decision may only be taken under this regulation in relation to a person as a result of conduct of that person that took place after IP completion day.

We addressed the different expulsion regimes under <u>The Citizens' Rights (Restrictions of Rights of Entry and Residence) (EU Exit) Regulations 2020 above (11.1)</u>. Essentially, those protected by the Citizens Rights provisions of the WWA will continue to benefit from the protections set out in the EEA Regs 2016 (Reg 2(1)). In <u>Silva</u> (11 November 2021), the High Court signed off on a Consent Order declaring that a decision to deport under the EEA Regs 2016 does not terminate residence rights protected by the WWA. In this scenario Reg 23(9) of those Regs is of no effect where the deportee is protected under Article 18 of the WWA.

As to the EUSS scheme, this generally ensures that EU citizens who arrived in the UK pre-TP end, and who took adequate steps in reasonable time, enjoy similar rights as before. However a clear line is drawn in the sand regarding public policy exclusions. Conduct arising before 31 December 2020 is treated as a falling under the EU law protections; that arising afterwards is addressed via the UK's own view of what is conducive to the public good (Appendix EU 16(c)(ii)).

There are several cohorts whose cases, post-1 July 2021, need to be addressed via the EU protection standards for pre-31 December 2000 conduct. They are conveniently referenced in the *EEA public policy and public security decisions* Guidance.

- Those granted leave under Appendix EU/Appendix EU (Family Permit)
- Those with a pending application (with reasonable grounds for making a late application if post-deadline (MIL 11.1A)) or appeal
- Joining family members within the deadline to apply to join the scheme (eg 3 months from entering UK)
- Those under the other EU legacy arrangements: Frontier Workers, Swiss Service Providers and S2 Healthcare Visitors

EEA nationals may be detained pending their expulsion (see MIL 13.1.6 for restrictions on detention generally).

MIL 11.8 now goes on to address post-Brexit EU/EEA expulsions.

11.8.1 Removal on grounds of a person ceasing to be qualified and abuse of rights

As seen above, the provision for expulsion on this ground was deleted from Reg 23(6) as part of its savings modification. You may still encounter cases in which this element featured, and thus this section remains part of Module 11 for now.

A person who no longer satisfied the requirements of the EEA Regs ceased to have a right to reside and faced possible administrative removal (Reg 23(6)(a))). However, their removal was not permitted as the automatic consequence of having recourse to the social assistance system of the United Kingdom (Reg 23(7)(a))).

EEA nationals were in the past rarely removed and were able to simply return to the UK. That said, the HO, police and local authorities did sometimes remove rough sleepers; and lack of evidence of Treaty Right exercise was a convenient means of targeting people with criminal convictions. Non-EEA family members who lost their right to reside would need to find a route under UK law or ECHR Art 8 if they wanted to stay in the UK.

The Guidance *EU, other EEA, Swiss citizens, and their family members: consideration of administrative removal action* entered force from 30 June 2021. It explains that

- Decision makers should consider whether it is reasonable and proportionate to pursue enforcement action rather than voluntary return
- A 28-day notice of losing access to services and being required to leave the UK is essential: it will give an opportunity to make a late application for EUSS/EUPSS and if this is not taken up, enforcement action is more likely to become appropriate
- "*it is imperative that complete records searches are conducted… it is vital that you explore every practical means of gathering information to help justify your decision to proceed or not to proceed*" bearing in mind, before concluding they lack a residence right and are attempting to conceal this, that an individual has a legitimate right not to disclose personal data, and that a visa refusal does not necessarily mean there is no prior right to reside
- "*if there are any reasonable grounds to suspect that there is a credible but unsubstantiated claim to lawful residence, no notice of liability to removal should be served at that time but evidence regarding any potential civil penalty should be recorded and referred to CPCT. You should serve a 28-day notice for EUSS if one has not already been served*"- reasonable grounds should take account of evidence of vulnerability (in which cases referral to social services, or one of the funded organisations providing charitable assistance, may be appropriate), the circumstances of the individual being encountered, whether their statements are consistent with previously extant EEA Regs, the strength and consistency of information within available documentary evidence and the potential for corroboration, keeping an open mind as to re-evaluating the evidence in the light of further information
- in "no right to reside" cases, the decision maker must audit the case carefully for any entitlement to remain and must still act proportionately

Abuse of rights

The genuine exercise of Treaty rights could bring rights into play that permitted domestic immigration rules to be sidestepped. So it is no surprise that the HO sometimes refused applications relying on EEA rights because of a belief, right or wrong, that there had been an attempt to abuse the rights bestowed by European law.

In practice this kind of thinking typically arose in the context of

- Surinder Singh cases (i.e. those where British citizens seek to rely on their own exercise of free movement to gain residence rights for non-EEA family members) (see MIL 11.3 above)
- Turkish nationals seeking to rely on the Ankara Agreement to establish businesses in the United Kingdom (see MIL 11.10 below).

In O v Minister voor Immigratie [2014] EUECJ C-456/12) the CJEU summarised the relevant test as having two elements:

- a combination of objective circumstances in which, despite formal observance of the conditions laid down by the EU rules, the purpose of those rules has not been achieved and
- a subjective element consisting of the intention to artificially create an advantage from the EU rules

It would be for the HO to raise the issue of abuse of rights. So it is on them that the burden of proof lies to establish the proposition: see for example Sadovska [2017] UKSC 54.

> Reg 26 is headed *Misuse of a right to reside* and incorporates the O test. It provides an example of misuse as attempting to enter the UK within 12 months of a public policy removal absent evidence of exercising Treaty Rights in the future. During that period an application could be made to set aside the restriction. Decisions would have to be proportionate.

The Guidance (Abuse of rights, fraud and verification of European Economic Area (EEA) rights of residence) gives examples of perceived abuse. Eg repeated returns to the UK to pursue a "rough sleeping" lifestyle under the initial right of residence, without establishing some other exercise of Treaty Rights.

Gureckis [2017] EWHC 3298 (Admin) found that the large-scale operations against EU nationals who were rough sleeping and for that reason alone said to be abusing their Treaty rights was unlawful. There was not enough of a connection between the mere fact of rough sleeping and the rights set out in the EEA Regs 2016, such as the initial right of residence, or working, to justify a conclusion that rights were being abused.

11.8.2 Public policy removals and exclusions

Under the Citizens' Directive regime the HO could refuse to issue, revoke or refuse to renew a residence document for EEA citizens and their family members only if the refusal or revocation was justified on grounds of public policy, public security or public health.Immigration Officer powers to revoke a family permit on a person's arrival in the UK were similary constrained.

The HO could remove, refuse to admit or exclude a person claiming a right of entry or residence on the same grounds. Individuals could apply to return but still had to confront the public policy grounds for their previous exclusion.

Costea [2021] EWHC 1685 (Admin) notes that EU law protection under Art 27 of the Citizens Directive is required at every stage in the deportation decision making process - including all steps relevant to the adoption of a decision. The policy document *EEA decisions taken on grounds of public policy and public security* requires the SSHD to issue a notice of liability to deportation giving an opportunity to raise grounds as to why any such decision is disproportionate. Art 30 of the Citizens Directive gave important procedural rights to have such a decision notified to one in a language that one understood. However a notice merely of *liability* to deportation was not a *decision* requiring notification under Art 30 as it was only part of the expulsion process.

11.8.3 Different levels of protection against expulsion
Under Reg 27, different periods of residence are rewarded with different levels of protection against expulsion:

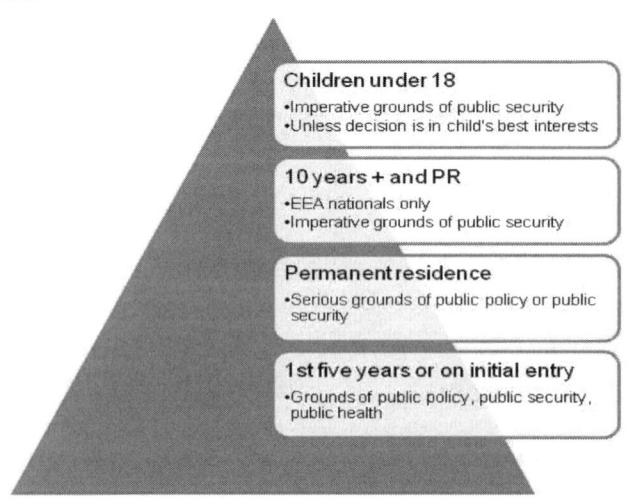

Children under 18
- Imperative grounds of public security
- Unless decision is in child's best interests

10 years + and PR
- EEA nationals only
- Imperative grounds of public security

Permanent residence
- Serious grounds of public policy or public security

1st five years or on initial entry
- Grounds of public policy, public security, public health

The saved Reg 27 for future cases replaces the reference to "*permanent residence*" with a reference to "*settled status*".

There are two ways in which the protection given by EU law is enhanced with the length of stay in the UK:

- there is firstly a narrowing of the grounds, from 'public policy, public security or public health', to 'public policy and public security', to 'public security' alone;
- secondly there is a raising of the threshold, from bare 'grounds', to 'serious grounds', to 'imperative grounds'.

Key issues likely to arise in EEA public policy cases.

- It is very difficult for the host state to justify expulsion based only on historic offending: unless it is very severe indeed
- Accordingly current offending risks are a central focus
- All the circumstances of the case are relevant when assessing the strength of the case against expulsion, assessed via proportionality - including the impact on rehabilitation
- The need for a proportionality assessment derives from a general principle of EU law that "*the content and form of Union action shall not exceed what is necessary to achieve the objectives of the Treaties*" - see article 5(4) TFEU
- Where the level of protection is to require serious grounds of public policy or security warrant a person's exclusion, the burden of proof is on the SSHD: Straszewski [2015] EWCA Civ 1245
- The UK's domestic public policy considerations: Sch 1 of the EEA Regs 2016 (MIL 11.8.6)

Surprisingly even at the end of the UK's EU membership there are two areas where the waters remain very muddy:

- The impact of imprisonment on residence rights
- The threshold the SSHD must show to establish imperative grounds

11.8.4 Identifying the level of protection – The impact of imprisonment

Length of UK residence and the impact of imprisonment on integration are crucial in identifying the appropriate level of protection.

A person who has misbehaved seriously enough to warrant exclusion from the UK will often be someone who has spent a significant period in prison. Such periods of imprisonment may well occur over a period which is potentially relevant to the acquisition of the higher levels of protection. The thorny question as to what extent residence in prison counts as residence for determining which level of protection still awaits an authoritative conclusion.

- Most of those facing expulsion having resided in the UK for a long time will do so because of serious criminal offending. And of course, that is likely to have involved a hefty prison sentence. So the question arises as to whether that period of imprisonment has broken their continuity of residence in the UK. The CJEU in B and Franco Vomero [2018] EUECJ C-316/16 & C-424/16) shows this will depend on the strength of their pre-imprisonment family and other ties here, the circumstances surrounding the offence, and the person's conduct during their sentence
- FV (Italy) [2012] EWCA Civ 1199 held that in determining whether accrued residence rights are lost by virtue of a period of absence or imprisonment, the test to be applied is an integration test. A period of imprisonment does not of itself prevent a person accruing 10 years residence and therefore engaging the imperative grounds of public security test. That was upheld by the CJEU, following a reference by the Supreme Court, in SSHD v Franco Vomero (C-424/16): see now the EEA Regs 2016 at Reg 3, and MG [2014] EUECJ C-400/12 referring to the relevant test being '*whether the integrating links previously forged with the host Member State have been broken*'
- Similarly, once 10 years of residence has been acquired, a period of imprisonment does not necessarily cause the person to lose the safeguard against deportation

- Imprisonment disrupts the acquisition of permanent residence: but once permanent residence is acquired it will not be lost through a period of imprisonment: see Franco Vomero [2019] UKSC 35
- In MG [2014] EUECJ C-400/12 it was held that the 10-year period of residence must be continuous and was to be calculated by counting back from the date of the decision ordering expulsion
- Thus imprisonment may break continuity of residence - but the overall impact of a period of custody must be considered. Relevant factors are the strength of any integrative links forged prior to detention and conduct while detained. The HO accepted that Hussein [2020] EWCA Civ 156 to the contrary was wrong, as recorded in the Order (short-circuiting a substantive hearing in the Supreme Court) in Hussein [2022] Lexis Citation 145.
- Hafeez [2020] EWCA Civ 406 holds that periods of imprisonment (or detention in a young offenders' institution) *do not count positively towards* establishing ten years' residence. An individual relying on imperative grounds protection who has served time in custody must prove *both* that
    - he has ten years' continuous (or non-continuous) residence ending with the date of the decision on a mathematical basis *and*
    - he was sufficiently integrated within the host State during that ten year period

Imprisonment will prevent a person *maintaining* their status as a qualified person:

- A person who is serving a prison sentence cannot claim to be exercising his Treaty rights during the period of incarceration (see Carvalho [2010] EWCA Civ 1406 and SO Nigeria) [2011] UKUT 164 (IAC)); so residence during imprisonment does not count towards the qualifying period for permanent residence
- Incarceration in a hospital pursuant to an order of the court under the Mental Health Act 1983 is not to be equated to imprisonment, as the individual has not been convicted of any criminal offence: a 'Hospital Order results from a finding that the individual suffers from a mental disorder and is not therefore criminally responsible for their otherwise culpable behaviour', see JO (Slovakia) [2012] UKUT 237 (IAC) (see MIL 13.4.1.2 for non-EEA authorities on this issue).

11.8.5 Imperative grounds of public security

The meaning of the phrase '*imperative grounds of public security*' (Reg 27(4)) awaits resolution.

- In MG and VC (Ireland) [2006] UKAIT 00053 it was said that HO's considered view was that the phrase '*public security*' was directed to the risk of '*terrorist offences*',
- By the time of LG (Italy) [2008] EWCA Civ 190 it was noted that '*public security*' was not to be equated with '*national security*' - the words might equate to a '*risk to the safety of the public or a section of the public*'.
- However in any event there was a need to show an actual risk to public security so compelling that it justifies the exceptional course of removing someone who has become 'integrated' by 'many years' residence in the host state. The Supreme Court suggested the test was not met vis-á-vis an appellant sentenced to eight years imprisonment for manslaughter in FV (Italy),
- Tsakouridis [2010] EUECJ C-145/09 holds that "*the fight against crime in connection with dealing in narcotics as part of an organised group is capable of being covered*"
- The concept includes imposing a direct threat to the calm and physical security of the population, remembering the particular values of the legal order of the Member State in question: P.I. v Oberbürgermeisterin der Stadt Remscheid (Case C-348/09)

B and Franco Vomero rules that the enhanced *imperative grounds* level of protection would only be enjoyed by those EEA nationals who have obtained permanent residence. This means those who have actively exercised Treaty rights for five years, for example by working, not merely those who have resided in the UK for a decade. Reg 24(4)(a) now includes this requirement.

In summary the important questions in these cases will be:

(a) Has the individual in question acquired permanent residence prior to imprisonment?
(b) Have they acquired 10 years' continuous residence prior to the date of the expulsion decision, the 10 year period to be calculated omitting time spent in imprisonment?
(c) If so, did those periods of imprisonment break the integrative links previously forged with the host member state with the result that he is no longer entitled to the enhanced protection?

11.8.6 Relevant factors in considering public interest expulsion

A wide range of factors must be balanced. These emanate from

- Principles derived from the case law (many helpfully summarised in Reg 27(5))
- Sch 1 to the EEA Regs 2016 containing a set of general public interest considerations to which judges '*must (in particular) have regard*'.

Regardless of which threshold of protection applies, the following factors must be considered when reaching any decision based on public policy and public security grounds. Reg 27(5):

- the decision must comply with the principle of proportionality
- the decision must be based exclusively on the personal conduct of the person concerned
- the personal conduct of the person concerned must represent a genuine, present and sufficiently serious threat affecting one of the fundamental interests of society
- matters isolated from the particulars of the case or which relate to considerations of general prevention do not justify the decision
- a person's previous criminal convictions do not in themselves justify the decision

There is a useful summary of the various aspects of proportionality in the unreported decision of DA003062019 [2020] UKAITUR. The overarching test for EU proportionality is in Lumsdon [2015] UKSC 41.

> '... first, whether the measure in question is suitable or appropriate to achieve the objective pursued; and secondly, whether the measure is necessary to achieve that objective, or whether it could be attained by a less onerous method.'

We have learned about Zambrano rights already. These, like other EU law rights, are subject to the public policy restrictions (MIL 11.6.3).

Robinson [2018] EWCA Civ 85 examines relevant considerations as to whether a public policy interest trumps Zambrano residence rights. However the thinking should inform any expulsion decision.

- Relevant considerations beyond those just set out would be the individual's length and legality of residence in the Member State concerned, the age and health of any child, and their economic and family situation
- The test for justifying expulsion in the face of fundamental rights did not require 'exceptional circumstances': the CJEU used that phrase to summarise the need for a proportionality exercise
- Although a current risk to public policy was normally required, there were still cases where past conduct and '*deep public revulsion*' might still be relevant. Eg

> "one whose facts are very extreme. It is neither necessary nor helpful to attempt an exhaustive definition but the sort of case that the court was thinking of was where, for example, a person has committed grave offences of sexual abuse or violence against young children.'

Thus Reg 27(5)(f) adds an extra principle, namely that

> 'the decision may be taken on preventative grounds, even in the absence of a previous criminal conviction, provided the grounds are specific to the person'.

Nevertheless, a 30-month sentence of imprisonment for supplying Class A drugs was not of the order to attract such revulsion – the 1974 Act concept of rehabilitation did not take things further as it did not apply under the relevant statutory scheme

In SA [2018] ScotCS CSIH_28 a property damage conviction did not justify deportation. Such an offence did not show '*a genuine, present and sufficiently serious threat*' to '*one of the fundamental interests of society*' as it did not indicate any propensity to violence against a person.

In public policy and public security (not public health) cases, account must also be taken of considerations such as the age, state of health, family and economic situation of the person, the person's length of residence in the United Kingdom, the person's social and cultural integration into the United Kingdom and the extent of the person's links with his country of origin.

GW Netherlands [2009] UKAIT 00050 holds that the '*fundamental interests*' of a society are to be determined re the legal rules governing the society in question. It is unlikely that conduct that is not criminalised or otherwise prohibited can be regarded as threatening those interests. The case concerned the attempt by the Secretary of State to exclude Geert Wilders from visiting the UK on the grounds of his unpleasant views about Islam. Mr Wilder's appeal was upheld.

The Guidance *EEA public policy and public security decisions* sets out a specific approach to pending prosecutions (ie being subject to a live police investigation or an extant arrest/summons), pointing out that these generally represent a barrier to removal, though sometimes the prosecuting authorities will conclude that deportation is preferable to completing the prosecution. Decision makers should decide whether decisions should be postponed pending the prosecution being completed: if there is only one pending matter and the maximum sentence predicted via the Sentencing Council guidelines is less than 12 months, and there are no previous convictions then there should be no delay. There is also bespoke *Pending Prosecutions* Guidance (cf MIL 2.3.5.3).

11.8.7 Prospects of rehabilitation

The prospect of the rehabilitation of an EEA national offender may be relevant to a decision based on public policy. Though it is likely to be more important where it is an EU national facing expulsion. As noted in Batista [2010] EWCA Civ 896: '*common sense would suggest a degree of shared interest between the EEA countries in helping progress towards a better form of life.*'

The UT looked at the role to be played by actual or potential rehabilitation in MC [2015] UKUT 520 (IAC).

1. The prospects of rehabilitation are a *potentially* relevant consideration
2. Those prospects will only be weighty where the offender has *permanent residence* and is integrated here
3. However rehabilitation only enters the equation where the offending in question reaches a level that it poses a genuine, present and sufficiently serious threat affecting a fundamental interest of society. At that point, the question of proportionality enters the equation, and it is here that rehabilitation prospects kick in
4. If the rehabilitation process has been completed, then it drops out of the equation
5. In determining whether the prospects of rehabilitation bear on the public interest in expulsion, the relevant question is whether there are *reasonable prospects of a person ceasing to commit crime* (not a mere possibility of the same)
6. The rehabilitation question must be considered whether or not the offender raises it
7. Affirmative evidence is required to show a difference in rehabilitation prospects in another Member State
8. Relevant factors are family ties and responsibilities, accommodation, education, training, employment, active membership of a community; the lack of access to a Probation Officer or equivalent in the other Member State should not, in general, preclude deportation

Around the same time the CoA in Dumliauskas [2015] EWCA Civ 145 observed:

- Rehabilitation was relevant in all EEA cases, particularly in the context of mental health and reoffending risks: if a person *'remains mentally healthy, he is unlikely to reoffend; if his mental health deteriorates, he is liable to reoffend.'*
- Rehabilitation must always be considered whether or not it is raised by the prospective deportee
- Substance misuse was relevant to rehabilitation: *'It is notorious that a great deal of offending is linked to illicit drugs and/or to alcohol. Addiction to drugs leads to crimes of acquisition, including theft, burglary and robbery, aimed at financing the purchase of drugs to feed the addiction. Alcohol affects self-restraint and is particularly associated with crimes of violence'*
- The SSHD was best placed to provide evidence as to rehabilitation services in another Member State: however the absence of evidence did not justify an automatic assumption that they were inadequate

11.8.8 Public policy, public security and the fundamental interests of society

The 2016 Regs enshrine the government's view of the public interest requirements, in line with the approach taken in domestic immigration law. With that in mind, Schedule 1 of the 2016 Regs contains a statement of policy. Brexit provided the opportunity to emphasise the weight to be given to the HO perspective (Sch 1 para 1).

Considerations of public policy and public security

1. The United Kingdom enjoys considerable discretion, acting within the parameters set by the law, to define its own standards of public policy and public security, for purposes tailored to its individual context from time to time

Schedule 1 continues as follows:

2. An EEA national or the family member of an EEA national having extensive familial and societal links with persons of the same nationality or language does not amount to integration in the United Kingdom; a significant degree of wider cultural and societal integration must be present before a person may be regarded as integrated in the United Kingdom.
3. Where an EEA national or the family member of an EEA national has received a custodial sentence, or is a persistent offender, the longer the sentence, or the more numerous the convictions, the greater the likelihood that the individual's continued presence in the United Kingdom represents a genuine, present and sufficiently serious threat affecting of the fundamental interests of society.
4. Little weight is to be attached to the integration of an EEA national or the family member of an EEA national within the United Kingdom if the alleged integrating links were formed at or around the same time as—

    (a) the commission of a criminal offence;
    (b) an act otherwise affecting the fundamental interests of society;
    (c) the EEA national or family member of an EEA national was in custody.

5. The removal from the United Kingdom of an EEA national or the family member of an EEA national who is able to provide substantive evidence of not demonstrating a threat (for example, through demonstrating that the EEA national or the family member of an EEA national has successfully reformed or rehabilitated) is less likely to be proportionate.
6. It is consistent with public policy and public security requirements in the United Kingdom that EEA decisions may be taken in order to refuse, terminate or withdraw any right otherwise conferred by the WWA, the EEA EFTA separation agreement or the Swiss citizens' rights agreement in the case of abuse of rights or fraud, including—

    (a) entering, attempting to enter or assisting another person to enter or to attempt to enter, a marriage, civil partnership or durable partnership of convenience; or

(b) fraudulently obtaining or attempting to obtain, or assisting another to obtain or to attempt to obtain, a right to reside under these Regulations.

6A. For the purpose of paragraph 6, a marriage, civil partnership or durable partnership of convenience means a marriage, civil partnership or durable partnership entered into as a means to circumvent any criteria that the party to the marriage, civil partnership or durable partnership would otherwise have to meet in order to enjoy a right to reside in the United Kingdom or a right to leave to enter or remain in the United Kingdom.

The rest of Sch 1 remains saved, unmodified:

The fundamental interests of society

7. For the purposes of these Regulations, the fundamental interests of society in the United Kingdom include—

   (a) preventing unlawful immigration and abuse of the immigration laws, and maintaining the integrity and effectiveness of the immigration control system (including under these Regulations) and of the Common Travel Area;
   (b) maintaining public order;
   (c) preventing social harm;
   (d) preventing the evasion of taxes and duties;
   (e) protecting public services;
   (f) excluding or removing an EEA national or family member of an EEA national with a conviction (including where the conduct of that person is likely to cause, or has in fact caused, public offence) and maintaining public confidence in the ability of the relevant authorities to take such action;
   (g) tackling offences likely to cause harm to society where an immediate or direct victim may be difficult to identify but where there is wider societal harm (such as offences related to the misuse of drugs or crime with a cross-border dimension as mentioned in Article 83(1) of the Treaty on the Functioning of the European Union);
   (h) combating the effects of persistent offending (particularly in relation to offences, which if taken in isolation, may otherwise be unlikely to meet the requirements of regulation 27);
   (i) protecting the rights and freedoms of others, particularly from exploitation and trafficking;
   (j) protecting the public;
   (k) acting in the best interests of a child (including where doing so entails refusing a child admission to the United Kingdom, or otherwise taking an EEA decision against a child);
   (l) countering terrorism and extremism and protecting shared values.

Several of the paragraphs are self-explanatory. Some observations :

- Para 2 requires integration in the UK beyond simply remaining in one's own community
- Para 4 discounts the weight given integration that took place around the same times as the criminality or when the individual was in custody
- Para 6 provides that fraudulent activity in relation to EEA rights (including participation in sham marriages/relationships) will be treated as contrary to public policy
- Judges *must* address these in each case: it is likely to be an error of law to fail to do so

11.8.9 Working when subject to expulsion – and returning to the UK

Lauzikas [2016] EWHC 3215 held that the HO could prevent such a person from working; the very grounds that militated against them remaining in the UK would justify a ban on working. However, on appeal to the CoA (C9/2017/0125), the case was settled by consent, the SSHD accepting:

"(a) the imposition of a work restriction limiting an EEA national's ability to work in another Member State is a limitation on a fundamental freedom protected by EU law,

(b) Such a work restriction may only be imposed following an assessment of whether the work restriction is proportionate (and thus also justified and necessary) in the individual circumstances of each case. Whilst the consideration giving rise to the decision to deport an EEA national will be relevant to that assessment, the decision to impose work restriction requires separate consideration and separate justification on the facts of each case."

However it was important to check that the individual *could* work. Often the probation licence might require consent for any, or specified, occupations. And the SSHD could well retain their passport or identity document with a view to securing their departure. So practical steps had to be taken to ensure that the theoretical ability to work is effective in practice.

If someone returns to the UK shortly after receiving an expulsion decision, the SSHD may want to rely on the previous decision as a basis for their removal. This is possible where there has been "*a genuine and effective termination of residence*". A brief departure abroad may not suffice: Staatssecretaris van Justitie en Veiligheid [2021] EUECJ C-719/19.

11.9 EEA rights of appeal

As per MIL 14, rights of appeal in immigration law generally arise under the NIAA 2002. However, one consequence of the modern appeal system's focus only on asylum and human rights is that EEA appeals then fell outside the mainstream statutory framework. At the same time, the new EUSS system has its own right of appeal created a specific set of Regulations. So to summarise there are various appeals available:

- NIAA 2002 appeals: but only on asylum or human rights grounds
- Appeals against EEA decisions under the EEA Regs 2016 (now largely legacy appeals)
- Appeals against EUSS decisions under the Immigration (Citizens' Rights Appeals) EU Exit) Regulations 2020: see above at 11.7.10

Why would one pursue an EEA appeal now EEA rights are historic? There are some reasons so to do:

- Some EUSSch applications (eg durable partners) require a document issued under the EEA Regs 2016. Applications for such documents cannot be made after 11pm on 31 December 2020. So the only way to get one, for a person who made an application before the transition period ended and whose application was refused, will be to pursue and win an appeal. That will then lay the ground for an EUSS/EUPSS application.
- Some applicants for EUSS/EUPSS may have previously been refused documents under the EEA Regs 2016 because it was thought their claimed relationship was not genuine or there was some other credibility issue. Sometimes better evidence can be produced on a subsequent application for EUSS/EUPSS but if the best case has already been put and been rejected, an independent FTT decision that resolves the factual issue in the appellant's favour is worthwhile: it lays the ground for an EUSS/EUPSS application that would otherwise be doomed to fail.

Presumably vindicating one's case via a statutory appeal would be a good reason for a late EUSSch application post-30 June 2021. One relevant document qualifying an applicant as the family member of a relevant EEA citizen is a letter from HO issued after 30 June 2021 confirming they would qualified for a relevant EEA residence card had the route not closed (MIL 11.7.5.2).

Features of the EEA appeal regime re:

- EEA grounds can be raised only in appeals arising under the EEA Regs, not in appeals arising only under the NIAA 2002
- But where a one-stop notice is served on a migrant, Hydar [2021] UKUT 176 (IAC) accepts that they might respond by raising an asylum or an EU ground of appeal. Then the matter would potentially fall within the Tribunal's jurisdiction. Grounds of this nature would require

"*consent*" where amounting to a "*new matter*" not previously considered by the SSHD (MIL 14.2.7)
- EEA appeals are expressly subject to the one-stop regime, so that human rights grounds of appeal can be raised following the refusal of an EEA document but only where a one-stop notice was served and returned

Geci [2021] UKUT 285 (IAC) provides a neat summary of the way in which the EEA Regs 2016 are preserved for appeal purposes post-Brexit and the end of the transition period. The UT explains that the complex array of provisions basically mean that the sole ground of appeal in EEA Regs appeals will be whether the decision appealed breaches the Appellant's rights under the EU Treaties as in force before 31 December 2020. Geci also notes that the HO has no power to refuse an EEA application where the documentary evidentiary requirements are met. If the SSHD failed to put a public policy case based on criminal convictions the Tribunal might be compelled to allow an appeal. A refusal to issue a residence card could impact on the practical exercise of free movement rights.

The critical questions in determining whether an EEA right of appeal arose, and its nature, were:

- Had an EEA decision been made (as defined in Reg 2)?
- Even if an EEA decision had been made, had the Secretary of State barred a right of appeal on grounds of insufficient evidence?
- Was the right of appeal in-country or out-of-country?
- Even if the appeal could be brought in-country, did it guarantee removal is suspended?

A few other general points re EEA appeals:

- EEA appeals are not deemed abandoned simply because an appellant leaves the country whilst they were pending (Reg 25(4))
- Nor when a residence document is issued. Ammari [2020] UKUT 124 (IAC) noted appeals brought under the EEA Regs 2016 were not deemed abandoned when a residence document is issued
- The procedures on appeal are those applying to the FTT generally under the FTTRs
- The Tribunal in Zubair [2013] UKUT 196 (IAC) thought that it might be unlawful to leave a family with arguable EEA rights without an opportunity to resolve their status on appeal

11.9.1 The existence of a right of appeal

Reg 2 of the EEA Regs 2016 defines an EEA decision as one which concerns a person's removal from the United Kingdom. Refusals of residence cards carried the right of appeal before the EEA Regs were amended to shutt down EEA routes in favour of the EUSSch.

Rights of appeal for EFMs were the subject of a significant saga for some years.

- Until Sala [2016] UKUT 411 appeals for EFMs preceded uncontroversially. That decision decided that there was no right of appeal for EFMs under the EEA Regs 2006
- Running with that thinking, the EEA Regs 2016 did not originally provide for a right of appeal. This meant that from their introduction in February 2017 until their amendment on 7 March 2019 there was no appeal for individuals refused a residence card as EFMs
- This gap in protection was recognised as unlawful following the CJEU proceedings in the case of Banger [2018] EUECJ C-89/17 (12 July 2018). The CJEU returned the case to the UK court ruling there must be a redress procedure to check that refusals are founded on a sufficiently solid factual basis
- Sensing the way the wind was blowing, on 28 March 2019, prior to Banger being heard in the UT, Parliament re-introduced appeal rights for EFMs were, by deleting the exemption in Reg 2 of the 2016 Regs. There was then no reference to EFMs in Reg 2 of EEA decisions and so no basis for awarding them less by way of appeal than close family members

- By now judges were lining up to disagree with Sala (which was a decision relating to the 2006 Regs). Khan [2017] EWCA Civ 1755 considered it wrongly decided; so too did the Supreme Court in SM (Algeria) [2018] UKSC 9
- The UT then resumed consideration of Banger [2019] UKUT 194 (IAC) finding that the CJEU ruling effectively required a remedy by way of a statutory appeal, which of course by the time of the 2019 hearing had already been recognised by the introduction of the appeal right in March 2019
- What of cases refused a residence card in between the introduction of the EEA Regs 2016 and this amendment? The answer given in Banger was that there should have been a right of appeal all along. Accordingly applicants left without an appeal over that period could either make a new application to the SSHD, which if refused would bear the right of appeal, or they could lodge a late appeal against the original refusal, or challenge any FTT or UT decision made in the interim period which had denied them an appeal right. In most cases the former route was simplest

11.9.2 Restrictions on accessing EEA appeal rights

There were some barriers to the right of appeal notwithstanding the making of what would otherwise be an appealable EEA decision.

- Where the SSHD certified that the decision under challenge was taken 'wholly or partly' in the interests of national security or relations with a foreign State there was no appeal to the FTT – but the saving grace was an appeal to the Special Immigration Appeals Commission (Reg 38).
- Additionally, the SSHD could prevent an appeal on a particular ground by certifying that the matter had been previously considered in an earlier appeal (Reg 36(7)).
- Much more commonly seen, however, were a number of restrictions, based on the quality of the evidence submitted with the application. These meant that even though an EEA decision had ostensibly been made, there will no ensuing appeal

These latter restrictions operated rather like certification of an asylum or human rights claim, in that they barred access to the Tribunal based on the HO's assessment of a person's case. They denied any appeal whatsoever, and they did not focus on the strength of the case taken at its highest, but rather on the nature of supporting evidence.

De Souza [2019] UKUT 355 (IAC) noted that Reg 26(3) of the EEA Regs 2016 barred an appeal where the evidence submitted did not, on its face, amount to proof of the claim being made. Thus, where an individual asserted that he or she was the *family member* of a person who plainly falls within the definition of "EEA national," the individual needed to put forward evidence to show that this is, as a matter of fact, the position. However, once the appeal had got off the ground, that Reg could not be invoked by the HO to restrict the arguments available to an Appellant.

In general it is for the FTT to determine its own jurisdiction (MIL 14.2.4). Where the question under Reg 26 was whether 'proof' of a relationship was required, and where the HO declined to recognise a right of appeal, the remedy should be to lodge an appeal with the FTT and ask them to recognise jurisdiction (rather than bringing JR proceedings).

Importantly, the HO recognised the fact that the evidence may be improved on appeal. So a person should not be permanently shut out from the appeal system just because they provided insufficient evidence with their application. Thus the Guidance *Rights of appeal* states:

> Where there is no right of appeal at the point of decision because specified evidence has not been provided, the person will be notified that there is no right of appeal against the decision. However, the applicant can lodge an appeal with the specified evidence and, if they do so, the appeal will be valid.

For example an EEA national who did not provide either valid evidence of nationality or an identity card issued by an EEA State to the HO would not have demonstrated that they had a right of appeal under Reg 26. However, if the person enclosed an EEA passport when appealing to the Tribunal they would have a right of appeal as they would have met the Reg 26 requirement by so doing at the point they appealed.

11.9.3 In-country and out-of-country appeals

Whether an appeal could only be brought out-of-country depended on the nature of the EEA decision made and the documentation held by the applicant.

Some appeals under the EEA Regs could only be brought from abroad (Reg 37). Where the decision was:

- to refuse to admit to the UK;
- to revoke admission;
- to make an exclusion order;
- to refuse to revoke a deportation order made;
- to refuse to issue an EEA family permit;
- to revoke, or to refuse to issue or renew any document under the EEA Regs where that decision was taken at a time when the relevant person was outside the UK; or
- to remove him from the UK after he has entered or sought to enter the UK in breach of a deportation order (unless asylum or human rights grounds are raised, and not certified: Reg 27(3)).

Sometimes individuals seemingly holding only an out-of-country right of appeal could still bring their case from within the UK. Essentially this was where they already possessed an EEA residence document or some other form of lawful residence – though not immigration bail. See generally Reg 37(2).

Other kinds of appeal could and still can be brought in-country. These include appeals against decisions refusing residence documentation from within the UK, and regarding expulsion.

Appeals can be *brought* in-country; but not necessarily *pursued* whilst remaining here. There is a very significant inroad on the extent to which EEA appeals are in truth suspensive. A series of authorities have held that whilst refusals or residence cards are *potentially* in-country, this does not prevent the SSHD removing a person. Section 78 NIAA 2002, which generally protects people against removal does not apply to EEA appeals, so there would have to be an express provision. And there isn't one.

Thus in Bilal Ahmed IJR [2015] UKUT 436 (IAC), the UT found that an appeal against refusal of a residence card did not prevent a third country national's removal under s10 of the IAA 1999 where the Secretary of State considered the marriage to be a marriage of convenience. That conclusion was then upheld by the Court of Appeal in Ahmed [2016] EWCA Civ 303. Those decisions related to the 2006 Regs; Shote [2018] EWHC 87 (Admin) carries this over to the EEA Regs 2016. The HO only seemed to use this power to remove pre-appeal in cases where the refusal extends beyond standard refusal grounds. Percieved sham marriages seem the main target. The only barrier to removal in these cases will be to argue that the right of appeal from abroad would not adequately protect EU rights: see Gheorghiu (MIL 11.9.5).

Public policy refusals may also involve an out-of-country appeal: see further 11.9.5.

If an appellant has an in country right of appeal under the Immigration Rules but only an appeal on an out-of-country basis under the EEA the UT will refuse to consider those EEA arguments in the context of the human rights appeal (MS Belgium [2019] UKUT 356 (IAC)).

11.9.4 Grounds of appeal

Although EEA appeals were governed by the EEA Regs, there was some cross-referencing to the appeals provisions of the NIAA 2002, in Sch 1 and Sch 4 to the EEA Regs.

- Schedule 1 of the EEA Regs states that *the only ground of appeal* is to be 'that *the decision breaches the appellant's rights under the EU Treaties* in respect of entry to or residence in the United Kingdom' which it styles 'an EU ground of appeal'
- Schedule 1 also incorporates the one stop notice procedure by reference to s120 NIAA 2002, stating that section 85 NIAA 2002 is to read as if the Tribunal has jurisdiction to consider a matter raised in a section 120 'one stop' notice, though only where the SSHD has already considered the application or consents to the matter entering the arena of the appeal
- Thus human rights (or, presumably much less often, asylum) grounds can be considered, where the one stop notice has been returned, and the HO has considered the matters raised in it (Amirteymour) [2017] EWCA Civ 353 – however HO practice has long been to decline to serve a s120 notice when applications for EEA documents are refused, so access to an appeal may remain elusive for those in this situation
- Oksuzoglu [2018] UKUT 385 (IAC) looked at this situation in practice in the EEA context. The UT notes that the 2016 Regs apply for all decisions made from 1 February 2017.
  - Here the original residence card application had been wholly based on a Surinder Singh argument, i.e. that the EEA sponsor (who was a dual British/Cypriot citizen) had worked on an enduring and genuine basis in another EU Member State before returning to the UK. However, on appeal the appellant sought to raise the argument that the sponsor was exercising Treaty rights in the UK and that this was another route by which residence could be recognised.
  - The UT found that this different case represented a 'new matter', given it had not been raised in the original application nor considered in the refusal letter. Accordingly it could be raised only with the consent of the HO. Such consent had to be given expressly, and could not be deemed simply from the fact that no objection had been made to the alternative case when it was raised in oral submissions.

- MS Belgium [2019] UKUT 356 (IAC) explains the relevance of EEA residence rights in a human rights appeal (MIL 5.4.8)

11.9.5 EEA deportation appeals

It has been government policy since summer 2014 to expel deportees following the refusal of their human rights claims notwithstanding that their appeals are still pending (see for non-EEA cases MIL 13.5.2.1: in practice difficulties with guaranteeing effective appeals from abroad have frustrated this policy). These principles carry over to the EEA regime: both regarding the general test mandating out-of-country appeals unless serious irreversible harm will then result, and as to requirement for a truly effective remedy. The EEA context is slightly different to the domestic deportation regime, though – because EEA nationals, even if expelled, can apply to return to the UK.

Reg 33 provides that:

- It applies to public policy/security/health removals (i.e. these being decisions made under Reg 26(3)(b) which is cross-referenced from Reg 32(3)) where an appeal could be lodged or is actually pending (Reg 33(1))
- Such an appeal no longer suspends removal where the Secretary of State has certified that return abroad will not contravene their human rights pending the appeal hearing and that the person would not face a real risk of serious irreversible harm if removed (Reg 33(2)-(3))
- However, the removee may apply to the court for an interim order to suspend removal proceedings and no removal may take place pending a decision on whether that application should be granted (Reg 33(2))
- Except where the removal decision is based on a previous judicial decision (e.g. an unsuccessful appeal), or where the removee has had 'previous access to judicial review', or where the expulsion is on grounds of imperative grounds of public security
- Garrec [2020] EWCA Civ 621 clarifies a procedural issue in appeals certified under Reg 33 of the EEA Regs 2016. The FTT lacks power to grant interim relief to prevent an Appellant's removal before their appeal hearing. So anyone wanting to prevent their own removal before the hearing will need to bring JR proceedings seeking interim relief

There is specific guidance on certification for non-suspensive appeals in EEA deportation cases. The particular considerations that must come into play when a judge considers an application to suspend certification were outlined in Gheorghiu [2016] UKUT 24 (IAC):

When considering whether or not to suspend certification of EEA appeals ... the decision-maker should take into account inter alia: (i) the status of the EEA national; (ii) the impact of removal on family members; (iii) evidence of continuing risk to the public; and (iv) the role oral evidence may play.

In addition, Hafeez [2020] EWHC 437 (Admin) addresses the protections available to EEA nationals against expulsion (under Reg 33 of the EEA Regs 2016) prior to their appeal being heard. It was necessary to read Reg 33 such that the *proportionality* of the interim removal had to be measured having full regard to the EU free movement rights with which they interfered.

The HO guidance was unlawful in stating that there was a strong public interest in interim removal and in so far as it suggested that the ability to return to the UK, to present one's appeal in person necessarily meant that the process would not threaten the efficacy of an appeal.

The relevant guidance on Regulations 33 and 41 has been updated to take account of Hafeez. All pre-Hafeez decisions have to be reconsidered in line with the proportionality test. Where intereim relief has been granted against pre-hearing expulsion, tthe SSHD would have to apply to the court which granted it to set the order aside, or seek an expedited JR or appeal, if she sought to reinstate the out-of-country dimension.

Under Reg 41:

- A person who has been removed pre-appeal hearing may apply to return once a date for their hearing has been set if they wish to make submissions in person
- They will be granted temporary admission (i.e. immigration bail) to do so if their application succeeds
- Their application may be refused only if their appearance 'may cause serious troubles to public policy or public security': this appears to be a higher test for the HO to satisfy than for deportation itself, as the threshold is one of 'serious troubles', e.g. it is very difficult to see that past convictions alone could represent such a threat
- The period granted will take account of the date(s) on which they will be required to make submissions in person
- They may be removed having made the requisite submissions pending the appeal being finally determined, though may return again if required
- They are liable to detention – Reg 41(7)

How far does the right to submit a defence in person extend? It might be thought that it would involve a significant period of residence in this country in order to effectively instruct one's legal team, for example. After all, EU law requires that rights are made practical and effective. The argument that this should allow sufficient time to instruct lawyers and prepare the case was rejected in Masalskas (IJR) [2015] UKUT 677 (IAC).

Gabor [2017] UKUT 00287 states the right will be achieved if '*the admission takes place within a reasonable time to enable the applicant properly to instruct his solicitors*'. A period of 2-3 days before the hearing is suggested as sufficient.

Careful consideration will have to be given to the case management of Reg 41 returns.

- The starting point is that individuals should return at their own expense, The Guidance countenances applications for financial assistance where there is evidence of an inability to fund one's return, no family or friends can help out, and where this poses a genuine barrier to matters proceeding.
- The SSHD may well insist on detaining the individual from their return. This may in turn cause problems in accessing legal advice or in obtaining last minute evidence from a social worker who could otherwise observe the family interacting together.

- The Guidance explains that one should not apply to return until one can provide evidence of the appeal having been listed. At that point all reasonable efforts will have to be made effort to persuade an entry clearance post to engage with the need to facilitate return. The FTT might have to be make a direction to move things forwards.

MIL 13.5.2.1 addresses the issues generally. But one cannot simply carry over the principles set out there to EEA cases, because the HO position in an EEA appeal may very well be that the individual in question can apply to return for their appeal hearing. Accordingly the disadvantages regarding inability to give oral evidence will not necessarily be present. Or, to be more precise, a challenge on those grounds may not be appropriate at the time of certification under Reg 33: it may only be realistic if permission to return is refused under Reg 41 (otherwise, of course, the Reg 41 application is an alternative remedy which would probably put a JR claim at risk of dismissal simply for being 'premature').

11.10 Turkish cases: from the Ankara Agreement to the ECAA rules

Under the European Community Association Agreement (ECAA) with Turkey, the 'Ankara Agreement', a Turkish national was able to apply to enter or stay in the UK to establish and run a business, and in some circumstances for an extension of stay to continue employment in the UK. Following Brexit the entry route closed at 11pm on 31 December 2020. The Immigration and Social Security Co-ordination (EU Withdrawal) Act 2020 disapplied certain directly effective immigration rights under EU law including provisions within the ECAA between the EU and Turkey. Nevertheless provision had to be made for the many Turkish nationals still in the route. So the HO decided to create a new extension route for these individuals. A route to settlement under the domestic rules had already been created.

In section 11.10 we will very briefly address how it was that the ECAA helped Turkish workers and businesspeople establish themselves in the UK. Then we discuss the Rules introduced from 11pm on 31 December 2020 for extending leave and seeking ILR. The Rules refer to the previous system as the ECAA Agreement whereas the new system is styled the ECAA rules: and collectively they are called the "ECAA route". Leave under the Agreement and under the ECAA Extension is also treated the same for the purpose of sponsoring dependents under Appendix FM (GEN.1.3(e)).

There is published guidance on the post-Brexit system: a *brief overview* on extending permission within the route and detailed *Appendix ECAA Extension of Stay* guidance.

11.10.1 The Ankara Agreement

The Ankara Agreement is the oldest Association Agreement, dating back to 1963, with an Additional Protocol of 1970. The rights granted to Turkish nationals were for many years not reflected either in the modern Immigration Rules or in the EEA Regs and anybody seeking to benefit from them had to refer directly to EU law and the provisions of the ECAA. Most of the relevant provisions though were found in old Immigration Rules which the HO eventually decided should feature in published UKVI Guidance. The ECJ & CJEU issued important decisions on Ankara rights.

Workers were allowed to reside in the UK to continue in legal employment (including au pairs and working students), so long as they were duly registered as belonging to the labour force. The longer they worked here, the greater were their rights to switch role/employer; and after 4 years they could take any employment.

There was also a 'standstill clause' for Turkish nationals wishing to provide services. Member States could not adopt new measures tending to make establishment (and thus residence) of a Turkish national in its territory subject to stricter conditions than those which applied at the time when the Additional Protocol entered into force re the Member State concerned. So Turkish businesspersons needed to be assessed via the IRs in force when the UK became party to the European Community on 1st January 1973, ie IRs HC 510 and 509 These were considerably more favourable than the current immigration rules pertaining to business people (HC395). Essentially applications from persons present as visitors were to be considered on their merits having regard to whether they were inputting their own assets and ability to bear the business's liabilities and to support oneself. If they were buying into an existing business they needed to show an active and controlling interest. None of the hurdles created by the later Innovator or Entrepreneur routes applied to them.

EK Turkey [2010] UKUT 425 (IAC) found that HC510 did not limit those switching into business status to those who had entered as visitors. Veli Tum [2004] EWCA Civ 788 and Tum and Dari [2007] EUECJ C-16/05 involved Turkish asylum seekers who had sought to exercise rights under the Ankara Agreement. The Court held that the Agreements applied whatever the basis on which the applicant had entered the UK - it was only those who had obtained entry via fraud who were excluded.

11.10.2 Appendix ECAA: extending leave for Turkish workers and businesspeople

So, to reiterate: the discussion above is of historic interest. It may well retain relevance in assessing immigration history which may bear on access to an extension of leave or settlement. But from now on, there is no way to **enter** these immigration routes.

11.10.2.1 Introduction to Appendix ECAA

These routes now take the usual form found in modern regular immigration routes: validity, suitability, eligibility, with specific provisions governing the length and conditions of permission, and for dependent partners and children.

The specified form is on www.gov.uk: "Turkish Businessperson or Worker". There is no fee for these applications.

To be valid applications must use that form and be from Turkish nationals providing the required biometrics, a passport/travel document satisfactorily establishing identity and nationality, and applicants must be in the UK (ECAA 1.2). Otherwise applications will be rejected (ECAA 1.3).

11.10.2.2 Suitability and conduct before and after 11pm on 31 December 2020

The suitability requirements reflect the general arrangements for persons previously benefitting from EU rights. There is a distinction between conduct before and after 11pm on 31 December 2020 when the transition period ended.

For conduct before transition ended (ECAA 2.1):

For workers: public policy, health or security grounds

For businesspeople: character, conduct or associations as set out in HC 510

For conduct after transition ended (ECAA 2.2):

Applicants must not be in breach of immigration laws; r39E applies to condone limited overstaying (MIL 1.5.4).

Applicants must not be on immigration bail.

Aspects of the general refusal reasons found in Part 9 of the Rules apply (ECAA 8.1 read with r9.1.1(h) (MIL module 4.3), which authorises:

> *refusal* of applications *to stay* under the ECAA rules where there are extant exclusion orders or grounds based on character and conduct, serious or minor criminality, involvement in a sham marriage, making false representations, and rough sleeping)

> *cancellation* of permission to stay and *refusal* of applications for entry clearance for those same reasons

So Turkish nationals under the ECAA route will enjoy the protection of EU law against expulsion on public policy grounds for pre-December 2020 conduct: see generally MIL 11.8.

> **Examples**
>
> Imagine advising these individuals of the impact of their conviction on their immigration status.
>
> Yismet is a Turkish builder with his own firm. He was granted entry clearance under the Agreement in October 2018. He committed a serious assault on 30 November 2020 and was sentenced to one years' imprisonment.
>
> This is pre-end transition conduct. Yismet is a businessperson. So his conduct is measured against the standard of the 1973 Immigration Rules: ie by reference to his "character, conduct or associations": ECAA 2.1(b).
>
> Erdogan is a Turkish chef working for a restaurant. He was granted leave to remain under the Agreement in October 2018. He committed a serious assault on 30 November 2020 and was sentenced to one years' imprisonment.
>
> This is pre-end transition conduct. Erdogan is a worker. He is protected by the EU public policy threshold (which essentially requires a future offending risk): ECAA 2.1(b) (MIL 11.8.3).
>
> Ilkay is a Turkish IT engineer. She was granted entry clearance under the Agreement in October 2020. She committed fraud on 5 January 2021 and was sentenced to one years' imprisonment.
>
> This is conduct after the transition period ended on 31 December 2020. It does not matter whether she is a worker or businessperson as the Suitability proviso in Appendix ECAA Extension makes no distinction. Part 9 of the Rules applies to her: ECAA 2.1(c). As she entered under the ECAA Agreement (rather than the post-2020 Rules in the Appendix) her circumstances are addressed by r9.1.1(h) rather than r9.1.1(i). We then see that r9.1.1(h) specifies that some of the criminality provisions apply: eg r9.4.2, which provides for cancellation of permission "convicted of a criminal offence in the UK or overseas for which they have received a custodial sentence of 12 months or more."

11.10.2.3 Specific requirements for Turkish workers and businesspeople

Given the two forms of economic activity recognised, there are two sets of criteria: workers at ECAA 3 and businesspeople at ECAA 4. The workers' requirements are more straightforward so long as there is documented work for the qualifying period. Businesspeople have to show a venture that the SSHD accepts is genuine, which gives more scope for different opinions.

For workers (ECAA 3.1):

- To be already present with permission in the route
- To have been lawfully employed in the UK for 3 years+ with the same employer or
- To have been lawfully employed in the UK for 4 years+ including 3 years+ with the same employer

The latter two differing criteria are important because they lead to different periods of stay.

And then:

That they will continue to be employed in the UK throughout the requested period (ECAA 3.2)

These criteria being established via a valid employment contract with the employer under which they continue to receive payment for services (ECAA 3.3)

Lawful employment will not be treated as broken for annual holidays, statutory maternity leave/paternity leave/shared parental leave, statutory adoption leave, sick leave (up to 6 weeks in any 12 months, or longer if there are compelling circumstances), absence due to an accident at work & periods of involuntary unemployment (so long as registered with relevant employment authorities and make reasonable efforts to rejoin workforce), jury service or appearing as a witness in a trial (ECAA 3.4),

The Guidance explains how these considerations will be assessed. There is specific Covid provision: furloughed workers in genuine and effective employment and remaining under contract will continue to be treated as workers where adequate evidence from the employer or DWP/HMRC is forthcoming. Three months grace will be given for finding a new job before needing to register with Jobcentre plus. There is specific information about how au pairs and agency workers should evidence their work.

Workers will be granted permission subject to these conditions (ECAA 6.1-6.2, 6.4):

- 12 months' permission where they have previously been lawfully employed in the UK for less than 3 years (ECAA 6.1 read with ECAA 3.1(b)): the Guidance says "after completing one year of self-employment applicants will normally be granted 3 years' further permission to stay if the provisions are met - where the ongoing success of the business is still to be proven a further 12 months' permission may be granted rather than the full 3 years" and "this is unless the circumstances of the employment are such that granting further short period of leave after 3 years would be unreasonable, for example the applicant is employed on a single contract basis"
- 36 months' permission where they have previously been lawfully employed in the UK for 4 years+
- Work only for the current employer or another employer in the same occupation, until they have been here for 4 years ECAA 6.4(a))
- No access to public funds & study subject to ATAS conditions

For businesspeople (ECAA 4.1):

- To be already present with permission in the route
- To have established a business (or intend so to do) as a sole proprietor, partner or director
- Which is viable and has operated (or will operate) genuinely
- Note that these provisions for extending leave ECAA 4.1(a), (d)) recognise the possibility that the business has not yet started trading.

The required evidence appears at ECAA 4.2:

- Of past/future investment of sufficient funds or assets in the business/businesses in the context of their interest therein, via funds/assets that are, and continue to be, their own
- Being able to meet their share of the possible business liabilities;
- Not being involved such as to amount to disguised employment
- Entitlement to sufficient profits to support themselves and any dependants (the Guidance notes that other sources of revenue such as sub-letting and rent should be excluded from maintenance calculations, though encourages the exercise of discretion where profits have been up and down, and where an applicant has managed to survive without recourse to public funds in the first two years of the business even if profits have not been enough to fully support the applicant)
- Where joining an existing business:

    (i) a written statement of the terms and conditions on which they are joining the business; and

    (ii) accounts for the existing business for the 12 months before the date of application; and

    (iii) evidence that there is a genuine need for their services and investment.

These factors will be taken into account when assessing the evidence (ECAA 4.3):

- Viability and credibility of the investment money's source
- A credible time frame (within 11 months) for any non-invested sums to be brought into the business
- The credibility of the financial accounts and of the applicant's proposed business activity in the UK
- Whether any mandatory accreditation, registration or insurance has been obtained (examples are given in the Guidance: eg a driving licence, environmental and utility registrations, licences for selling alcohol; it also notes that registering for tax and national insurance are not mandatory

under the Appendix, though this will be relevant depending on the business's longevity: relevant documents will be tax returns (P35), Unique Tax Reference number (UTR), self-assessment tax calculations (SATCs) and national insurance receipts (class 2 and 4))

The Guidance discusses these issues at length. It explains the differences between sole traders, partnerships and limited companies, and gives some examples of applications that might fail for want of individual control over one's own activities, or lack of experience. See also the government *guidance on Employment Status* and Dasdemir [2013] UKUT 121 (IAC).

The ECAA Guidance lists individual pieces of evidence that might be scrutinised: a business plan, business accounts for the previous 2 years (if appropriate), funding evidence, bank statements, overseas money transfers, bank loans, certificate of registration with Companies House (if appropriate), tax and/or national insurance (NI) registration and tax documents, a partnership agreement, copies of contracts and invoices, educational and vocational qualifications, testimonials, proof of advertising, premises agreements, any licences required/obtained, staff details, and insurance details. Up-to-date management accounts may be sought where the last filed accounts do not address the present situation.

Distinct matters that might give cause for concern and call for an interview include authenticity of the documents provided, any inconsistencies or omissions in the evidence (ie whether the invoices and contracts provided match up to the picture shown by the accounts), applications which are identical to others previously submitted, and the involvement of a third party (so beware of recycled business plans where the applicant's own input is limited). Decision makers are encouraged to look at the balance sheet (so beware any significant liabilities therein) and profit and loss account. Doubtless a large investment compared to the business's financial indicators will attract suspicion.

Viability is assessed by reference to the business's ongoing activities (eg recent invoices & advertising campaigns), its level of debt, whether any requisite accreditations or qualifications are held, and whether profits are inflated artificially by public funds. The business need not have UK clients so long as it is genuinely UK-based, as with online services.

The source of the investment funds will be assessed, as will any possibility that the funds are not fully under the applicant's control or might be withdrawn at short notice. Business revenue needs to cover loan costs. The source of any unusual or irregular deposits into the applicant's account needs to be explained (as where funds come from overseas, or are gifts). Bank statements should be provided even though the Rules do not expressly require them, as they may be relevant to the overall business picture. Decision makers are encouraged to use discretion where the level of financial investment is small in relation to the anticipated profits or comes via gifts from family (so long as they appear affordable).

There is similarly precise guidance as to assessing applications from partners and company directors: in short the information provided must be sufficient to ensure that the terms on which one is joining a business are clear.

There is particular guidance re the Covid pandemic: the business's length of operation and previous profits, its viability Covid aside, and use of Covid schemes eg loans and grants.

There continues to be a strong focus on whether the business activities are self-employed rather than amounting to disguised employment. The Guidance holds out the possibility of conducting an employment status check with HMRC, and highlights relevant considerations tending towards self-employed status as whether the individual runs their own business and takes responsibility for its success or failure, has multiple customers at the same time, can decide how, when and where they do their work, is free to hire other people to do the work or help at their own expense, and provides their own equipment. Whereas Applicants are probably employed if they work for one person at a time who takes on business risks, can be told how, when and where they do their work, can be moved from task to task and have to do the work themselves via a set amount of hours or set pattern of work for which they are paid a regular amount as per their hours including overtime pay, sick pay, holiday pay or bonus payments, and otherwise appear to be 'part and parcel' of an organisation receiving employee type benefits such as a pension & access to grievance procedures.

Previous experience is one area where the Guidance enjoins decision makers to seek further information (eg via references and certificates) if insufficient material is provided to grant the application. English language proficiency is recognised as an advantage in some enterprises; but sometimes *common sense will tell you that it may be possible for the applicant to establish in business with little or no English*. Agca [2023] EWCA Civ 56 holds that it was reasonable for the HO to require business experience for someone seeking to enter the route, even for a relatively small proposed business given that that would be relevant to managing the finances, sales and stock and to managing staff, and thus to the enterprise's future viability.

Businesspeople will be granted permission on these terms (ECAA 6.4):

- For 36 months (however the Guidance allows for 12 month grants where there is a suspicion as to whether the business is viable)
- Such that they may only work for the business they have established, joined or taken over (and not in the capacity of apprentice) (ECAA 6.4(b))
- No access to public funds & study subject to ATAS conditions

11.10.2.4 Dependents of Turkish workers and businesspeople

Dependents can accompany or join workers and businesspeople who are on the ECAA route (ECAA 10.1).

The Guidance states that those partners who have not already been granted leave need to apply under Appendix FM rather than under ECAA Extension. Thus we see that the partner route under Appendix FM now features an expanded class of eligible sponsor at both the entry clearance and leave to remain stage: E-ECP.2.1(e) and E-LTRP.1.2(e). The Guidance explains that children under 21 can enter the route via entry clearance or permission to stay; those over 21 can join the route only where they already held leave under the former ECAA route as at 31 December 2020.

Children seeking entry clearance must use the "Join or accompany a family" proviso within the "Find and apply for other visas from outside the UK" form; for extensions, partners and children can apply alongside the principal where applying at the same time, or use form ECAA 3 (ECAA 7.1).

Dependents face the usual generic requirements re validity (ECAA 7.2) and suitability (ie a ban on being on immigration bail or on overstaying other than that condoned by r39E) (ECAA8.3),

Unmarried partners are specifically defined in Part 1 r6 and ECAA 10.3-10.4. There is no 2-year cohabitation requirement; rather the applicant must be living with the sponsor presently, unless applying for entry clearance, and in a genuine and subsisting relationship where they intend to live together or continue to do so. They must be aged over 18 at the application date, any previous relationship must have permanently broken down and they must not be too closely related such as UK law would forbid the relationship (ECAA 10.2).

Children of the principal or their partner may apply where both parents are present in the UK or applying alongside the child unless one parent is dead, or one has sole responsibility or there are other serious and compelling reasons to grant the application (ECAA 11.2). Children are eligible to become dependents up to the age of 21,and may stay as dependents in the route for so long as they are not independent (ECAA 12.1-12.2). Whilst they are under 18 there must be suitable arrangements for their care and accommodation in the UK compliant with relevant legislation and regulations (ECAA 13.1).

Adequate accommodation must be available; for businesspeople maintenance must demonstrably come from the business profits (ECAA 14.2). The Rules do not specify a distinct maintenance requirement for workers.

There are nuanced requirements for refusal for misconduct given the need to respect EU law standards for those present before transition ended. The requirements are the same as for principals under the relevant route (see above) (ECAA8.1). Thus even children are liable to aspects of the general refusal reasons for post-transition conduct.

Permission will be granted in line with the ECAA worker to end on the same day as does theirs (ECAA 16.1); there is no access to public funds, but any work is permitted as are studies so long as they are ATAS-compatible (ECAA 16.2).

Administrative review is available for refusals (ECAA 16.3 – MIL 14.7.9).

11.10.3 Indefinite leave to remain for Turkish workers and businesspeople

In Aydogdu [2017] UKUT 167 (IAC) the UT decided that settlement rights fell outside the scope of the standstill provisions of EEA law, because the grant of settlement was not essential to the right of establishment; therefore any entitlement to indefinite leave to remain was a product of domestic UK rather than EEA law. So from 16 March 2018 the HO stopped accepting ILR applications in this category.

The statement of changes HC1154, on 6 July 2018, then added the new appendix ECAA to the Immigration Rules. This created a new settlement route under the Immigration Rules for Turkish ECAA business persons, workers and their family members. This is a 5-year settlement route. Previously ILR had been available after 4 years. A legal challenge to the longer period was rejected in Alliance of Turkish Business People Ltd [2020] EWCA Civ 553. This finds that no clear promise was ever made as to the scheme's future operation. So Turkish nationals could not claim a legitimate expectation that things would not change. There is guidance *Appendix ECAA indefinite leave to remain (ILR) and further leave to remain (FLR)*. The latest development is the creation of *Appendix ECAA Settlement* to govern these applications from 11pm on 31 December 2020.

Appendix ECAA Settlement provides

- The form is digital form ECAA4 and the fee £2,885.
- Dependents can also apply (see rules in ECAA Parts 5 & 6): partner (spouse/CP/unmarried partners) and children under 21 (over 21 in specific circumstances).
- Switching into the ECAA route is not possible
- If granted ILR, applicants will have full recourse to public funds, and can work, study or establish a business without restriction

There are distinct requirements for continuity of lawful residence (which includes time spent in the Islands with leave granted for an equivalent purpose ECAA 2.4). Unbroken valid leave is necessary (ECAA 2.1-2.3), ie:

- No absences over 180 days in any 6-month period except for absences proven to be to assist with a national crisis or international humanitarian or environmental crisis overseas, or due to travel restrictions or serious illness
- Holding limited leave on departure and return, though
  - a break of up to 28 days pending a successful entry clearance application incurred before 6 July 2018 is disregarded, and
  - absence on or after 6 July 2018 is disregarded where a successful application is made whilst the applicant still holds continuing leave and remains abroad
- Any absences must be consistent with the basis of the applicant's UK stay, or for serious and compelling reasons
- Absences are assessed on the basis most beneficial to the applicant, from a choice of application date, any date within 28 days thereafter, and the decision date
- The usual overstaying proviso under r39E applies

The applicant must

- be a Turkish national who has valid leave to remain under the ECAA either
- for the purpose of working here and have completed five years of continuous leave with the most recent period being under the ECAA worker route (though the overall period may combine time as a work permit holder or in a Tier 2 route except ICT (ECAA 3.1) or

- for the purpose of establishing themselves in business in the UK, and have completed five years of continuous leave (including time as a Tier 1 Entrepreneur), with the most recent period being under the ECAA business person route (ECAA 4.1) – and the business must meet the requirements for genuineness that we set out above at 11.10.5.3 (though now with a procedural safeguard in that additional information and evidence can be sought within 28 days to support that assessment, ECAA 4.4)
- have met the knowledge of language and life in the UK requirement (KoLL)
- not fall for refusal under the Part 9 General Grounds for Refusal
- have the ability to financially support any family members with them without recourse to public funds to which they are not entitled

A dependent child must (ECAA 5.1) satisfy the usual criteria (MIL 2.2.8) :

- be a child of a parent who has ILR, or is about to be granted it, as an ECAA worker or business person, or the child of their spouse, civil partner or unmarried partner (providing full birth certificate)
- have been granted leave as the child of an ECAA worker or business person, or their partner, or have been born in the UK
- not be married or in a civil partnership, or leading an independent life (where aged 21 they must provide additional documents as set out in Part 8 r319H-SD: ie two separate forms of proof of residential address such as bank/credit card/driving licence/NHS registration/place of education, plus any payments for rent/board, and if living away from the family home, the reasons for so doing including proof of educational commitments and financial dependency on the parents)
- have both parents lawfully settled in the UK, or currently being granted ILR at the same time unless the usual exceptions (sole surviving parent, sole responsibility, or serious and compelling reasons) apply
- meet the KoLL requirements if aged 18 or over
- have care and accommodation in the UK that is in line with current UK legislation and regulation
- not fall for refusal under the General Grounds for Refusal (as per the restrictions set out above at 11.10.5.2)

Partners must (ECAA 6.1-ECAA 6.4):

- be a spouse, civil partner or unmarried partner of an ECAA business person or worker who has been granted ILR via that route (or been granted British citizenship following ILR on that route)
- have leave as the spouse, civil partner or unmarried partner of the sponsor
- be in a genuine relationship, and intend to live permanently, with the ECAA worker or business person whom entry clearance or leave to remain was granted
- have lived with the sponsor for 5 years in a continuous relationship whilst the sponsor held leave in ECAA routes or any other lawful route
- not have any excess absence
- not fall for refusal under the General Grounds for Refusal (see above 11.10.5.2)
- have adequate accommodation and be maintained by the sponsor, who must do so without accessing public funds other than those to which they are entitled
- not be the UK in breach of immigration laws subject to the the usual exceptions

There is a route for further limited leave for partners who are still living with their ECAA sponsor in a subsisting relationship, including those who previously missed out on ILR for not meeting the 2-year residency requirement (ECAA 7.1):

- where their ECAA sponsor has ILR under the ECAA guidance operative before 16 March 2018, or has ILR (or British citizenship following ILR) under the current Rules, and
- the applicant was last granted leave as an ECAA dependent OR
- the applicant is in the UK without leave because their ECAA leave expired and they did not qualify for ILR due to not meeting the two years residency requirement and could not qualify

as a dependant of an ECAA business person to gain further leave to remain, due to the fact that the ECAA business person had already acquired ILR.

For business persons, these additional requirements apply. In relation to the business(es):

- the applicant must have established, taken over or become a director and genuinely operate that business whilst she or he had leave as a ECAA business person
- the business related to the applicant's visa must be viable during any qualifying periods
- the applicant must intend to continue to operate one or more businesses in the UK

Karagul [2019] EWHC 3208 (Admin) addresses the genuineness test (MIL 14.7.5).

11.10.4 Remedies under Turkish Association Agreement routes

The Immigration Rules provide that the remedy for a refusal of these applications is administrative review: Appendix AR3.2(d), ECAA 6.5 (entry clearance refusals also attract admin review for so long as decisions are made under the old Rules for applications before 11pm on 31 December 2020 AR 5.2(b)).

Pre-2015, refusals under either the ECAA businessperson or worker route would have received the right of appeal. The legality of this approach has to be assessed by reference to the standstill provision. Akturk [2017] EWHC 297 (Admin) found that the standstill provision applied to procedural rights and guarantees as well as to substantive ones, being 'inseparable from the rights to which they relate', and that administrative review (possibly with judicial review as a back-up) were no substitute for an appeal. However this generous decision was reversed by CA (Turkey) [2018] EWCA Civ 287. So admin review remains the relevant remedy.

Karagul (discussed above) shows decisions on genuineness grounds should not be made without the applicant being given an opportunity to respond via letter or formal interview.

It is important to bear in mind that conduct pre-dating the end of the Brexit transition period will attract the full protection of EU law. Indeed many of the decisions cited in EU expulsion cases from the CJEU have involved Turkish nationals. See generally MIL 11.8.

11.11 The Charter of Fundamental Rights

The EU Charter became binding across the European Union in December 2009. It operates only (but always) when a Member State is applying EU law, as was discussed in NS (European Union law) [2011] EUECJ C-411/10 (including cases when a discretion is exercised within the context of EU law) – in the immigration context, this applies most obviously in the field of free movement and international protection law (i.e., in the UK, in all EEA, asylum and Humanitarian Protection cases).

The Charter has long been a bugbear of the UK government. So it was one of the first legal casualties of Brexit.

The UK position post-EU exit on 31 January 2020

The position in the UK following our exit from the EU on 31 January 2020 in relation to EU law is set out in s5 of the EU Withdrawal Act 2018. The general scheme of the legislation is to retain much of EU law as domestic law for the time being. But s5(4) provides:

> (4) The Charter of Fundamental Rights is not part of domestic law on or after exit day.

So have we seen the last of the Charter? Maybe not. Because s5(5) then goes on to say that s5(4):

> does not affect the retention in domestic law on or after IP completion day in accordance with this Act of any fundamental rights or principles which exist irrespective of the Charter (and

references to the Charter in any case law are, so far as necessary for this purpose, to be read as if they were references to any corresponding retained fundamental rights or principles).

So there will be question going forwards as to which of the Charter rights represented pre-existing general principles of EU law rather than being novel creations. You can get inspiration from the Explanations written at the time the Charter entered force: they explain the background to the various rights.

It may well be relevant to the way that the CJEU continues to interpret EU law in the future, and CJEU decisions will continue to have some effect on our domestic court's interpretation of retained EU law generally.

The general position pre-exit date, for background

The Charter contains many rights similar or identical to those in the European Convention on Human Rights, and also some additional ones. The latter are understood to be derived from general principles of EU law. A useful guide to its rather controversial history in this country is found in the House of Commons European Scrutiny Committee report *The application of the EU Charter of Fundamental Rights in the UK: a state of confusion*.

Notable features were:

- Possessing the greatest legal force, akin to the Treaties themselves. Article 6 of the Treaty on European Union:

    The Union recognises the rights, freedoms and principles set out in the Charter of Fundamental Rights of the European Union of 7 December 2000, as adapted at Strasbourg, on 12 December 2007, which shall have the same legal value as the Treaties.

- A general principle of proportionality found in Article 52(1)

    Any limitation on the exercise of the rights and freedoms recognised by this Charter must be provided for by law and respect the essence of those rights and freedoms. Subject to the principle of proportionality, limitations may be made only if they are necessary and genuinely meet objectives of general interest recognised by the Union or the need to protect the rights and freedoms of others.

- EU law will reflect the meaning and scope of fundamental rights found in the ECHR where they correspond to Charter rights (Article 52(3)): though this provision shall not prevent Union law providing more extensive protection.
- Interpretation via the published series of Explanations

Some rights familiar to immigration lawyers are found in similar terms in the Charter as they are in the ECHR. For example, the rights to family life, and to be free from inhuman and degrading treatment, are found at Articles 4 and 7. The best interests of the child are protected by Article 24. In an EU free movement case, one should be referring to Article 7 of the Charter rather than ECHR Art 8, at least until it is clear that the case has moved beyond the scope of EU law altogether.

In Abdul [2016] UKUT 106 (IAC), involving the deportation of the Nigerian father of two British citizen children, who had acquired a permanent right of residence in the UK under EU law, the UT found that Article 24(3) '*Every child shall have the right to maintain on a regular basis a personal relationship and direct contact with both his or her parents, unless this is contrary to his or her interests*', creates free-standing rights. It is not though an absolute right. Nevertheless it is of interest in that it emphasises that in EU law there is a distinct right to ongoing personal and direct contact with a child's parents.

The other rights likely to be of the greatest interest in the immigration context are these:

CHAPTER 11: European Union Law

Article 1 Human dignity

Human dignity is inviolable. It must be respected and protected.

Article 18 Right to asylum

The right to asylum shall be guaranteed with due respect for the rules of the Geneva Convention of 28 July 1951 and the Protocol of 31 January 1967 relating to the status of refugees and in accordance with the Treaty establishing the European Community.

Article 47 Right to an effective remedy and to a fair trial

Everyone whose rights and freedoms guaranteed by the law of the Union are violated has the right to an effective remedy before a tribunal in compliance with the conditions laid down in this Article.

Everyone is entitled to a fair and public hearing within a reasonable time by an independent and impartial tribunal previously established by law. Everyone shall have the possibility of being advised, defended and represented.

Legal aid shall be made available to those who lack sufficient resources in so far as such aid is necessary to ensure effective access to justice.

Summarising points arising from these rights:

- Article 1 may offer support to arguments that seekers and beneficiaries of asylum (and Humanitarian Protection) status should be treated at a minimum level of decency; so too removees in cases with an EU dimension.
- Article 18 bestows a 'right' to refugee status – notoriously the Refugee Convention gives no more than a right *not to be removed* to territories where one's life or freedom would be threatened, not a right to *status*.
- The right to good administration at Article 41 seemed originally to be of interest (particularly in cases involving delay or other maladministration). However it has been interpreted as only binding the EU institutions themselves. Though it seems that Article 41 in fact stems from a general principle of EU law. So Member State authorities may nevertheless be bound by the same right as, albeit not in the form of a Charter right – see HN v Minister for Justice, Equality and Law Reform (Ireland) (Case C-604/12).

Article 47 has both a procedural and a substantive dimension. Procedurally it requires:

- An effective remedy before a tribunal
- Within a reasonable time
- With the possibility of legal representation
- Legal aid where effective access to justice would otherwise be threatened – see Gudanaviciene [2014] EWCA Civ 1622, holding that:

    if the Director concludes that a denial of [funding] would be a breach of an individual's Convention or EU rights, he must make an exceptional funding determination. But as we shall see, the application of the ECtHR and CJEU case-law is not hard-edged. It requires an assessment of the likely shape of the proposed litigation and the individual's ability to have effective access to justice in relation to it.

Substantively it requires effective review of government decisions ensuring that they are taken on a sufficiently solid factual basis with adequate reasons, see Bank Tejarat v Council (Judgment) [2015] EUECJ T-176/12.

11.12 Appendix S2 Healthcare visitors

The introduction to this Appendix outlines its purpose as relating to persons who before 11pm on 31 December 2020 had requested authorisation to receive planned healthcare under the S2 route, pursuant to Regulation (EC) No 883/2004. The S2 route entitles UK nationals to NHS-funded state healthcare treatment in another European Economic Area (EEA) country or Switzerland, and entitles EEA nationals to reciprocal rights here. The treatment in question must be provided under the national health scheme and must not be experimental or emergency; its need must be backed by a consultant's report. As the introduction adds, such persons may be accompanied by a person to provide care or support during the treatment. Caseworker guidance is published here.

As the Rules goes on, they use the abbreviations "P" for patient and "AP" for accompanying person.

The appendix is structured under the following headings and with the following paragraph numbers:

- HV 1.1-7 Validity requirements for entry clearance or permission to stay as an S2 Healthcare Visitor
- HV 2.1-4 Suitability requirements for an S2 Healthcare Visitor
- HV 3.1-8.3 Eligibility requirements for an S2 Healthcare Visitor
    - HV 3.1-4 Entry requirements for an S2 Healthcare Visitor
    - HV 4.1-3 Financial requirement for an S2 Healthcare Visitor
    - HV 5.1 Treatment requirement for an S2 Healthcare Visitor
    - HV 6.1-2 Patient (P) requirement
    - HV 7.1-5 Accompanying person (AP) requirement
    - HV 8.1-3 Consent requirement for child S2 Healthcare Visitor
- HV 9.1 Decision on application as an S2 Healthcare Visitor
- HV 10.1-2 Period and condition of grant for an S2 Healthcare Visitor
- HV 11.1 Cancellation and curtailment

There are no fees for applications under this route. The available guidance is as follows. The applicant guidance links to the application form, which for initial applications is intended for use outside the UK. Extensions can be applied for from within the UK but a form must be requested by email.

- S2 Healthcare Visitor caseworker guidance
- Enter the UK as an S2 Healthcare Visitor
- S2 Healthcare Visitors: apply for a review of a decision

HV 1.1-7 Validity requirements for entry clearance or permission to stay as an S2 Healthcare Visitor

EC applications must be made on online form "Apply for an exempt, diplomatic or official visit vignetter or S2 Healthcare Visitor visa" (HV 1.1) while outside the UK and to a post designated to accept such applications (HV 1.2).

PTS applications must apply on form FLR(IR) and must have or have last held, permission in this category (HV 1.3).

Applicants must provide biometrics (HV 1.4(a)); and a passport or satisfactory national ID card (b); or, if a non-EEA national, a passport or satisfactory travel document (c).

Where someone enters the UK from Ireland having travelled from outside the common travel area holding a certificate of entitlement to S2 treatment or proof of S2 leave, they are permitted to remain for 6 months by virtue of a statutory instrument. .. So they need only apply for PTS at the end of that period (and indeed, under Appendix S2, may only apply at that point) (art 5 of the Immigration (Control of Entry Through Republic of Ireland) 1972 Order read with HV 1.5).

One can only extend leave by obtaining further PTS (HV 1.6(a)) where one holds or last held, permission in this category (b).

An application not meeting all validity requirements is invalid and *may* be rejected and not considered (HV 1.7).

HV 2.1-4 Suitability requirements for an S2 Healthcare Visitor

Applicants *must* be refused where subject to a deportation/exclusion order or decision (HV 2.1 (a)&(b)). However, where such an order or decision relates to conduct before transition ends (ie before 11pm on 31 December 2020), it must be justified on the grounds of public policy/security/health under Reg 27 of the 2016 Regs. This is regardless of whether the EEA Regs otherwise apply (HV 2.2).

Under HV 2.3, an application *may* be refused, if proportionate, in the following scenarios:

(a) In relation to the application and whether or not to the applicant's knowledge, false/misleading information, representations or documents have been submitted including to obtain a supporting document, and this is material to a decision on the application; or

(b) For pre-11pm 31 December 2020 conduct, on grounds of public policy/security/health in accordance with Reg 27 of the 2016 Regs whether or not they apply ("EEA decision" to be read as "a decision under HV 2.3")

(c) For conduct thereafter on domestic law grounds (ie "conducive to the public good")

The same exclusion regime as for the UK applies where the deportation/exclusion decision relates to one of the Islands. Grounds HV 2.3 (d) and (e) are being subject to an Islands deportation order (d) or an Islands exclusion decision on direction by the relevant minister or other authority on conducive grounds (e), subject to the proviso in HV 2.4 which repeats the reference in (b) to the EEA standard to be applied.

HV 3.1-8.3 Eligibility requirements for an S2 Healthcare Visitor

HV 3.1-4 Entry requirements for an S2 Healthcare Visitor

HV 3.1. A person seeking to come to or stay in the UK as an S2 Healthcare Visitor must be a person to whom one of the following applies (ie that they had requested authorisation to receive a course of planned health care treatment pre-11 pmyigc on 31 December 2020):

(a) Article 32(1)(b) of the WWA [EU nationals]; or

(b) Article 31(1)(b) of the EEA EFTA separation agreement [citizens of Norway, Iceland and Liechtenstein]; or

(c) Article 26a(1)(b) of the Swiss citizens' rights agreement.

HV 3.2 provides for mandatory refusal of non-visa nationals lacking entry clearance. Non-visa nationals, however, may apply for PTE on arrival in the UK (HV 3.4)

HV 4.1-3 Financial requirement for an S2 Healthcare Visitor

Applicants must have sufficient funds to cover all reasonable costs in relation to their visit (inc cost of return journey) without working or access to public funds (HV 4.1). These must be shown in accordance with Appendix Finance (HV 4.2). A third party can cover the cost of travel, maintenance and accommodation if the decision maker is satisfied that they can and will do so for the intended duration of the stay (HV 4.3).

HV 5.1 Treatment requirement for an S2 Healthcare Visitor

The course of planned treatment must have been arranged prior to travel to the UK.

HV 6.1-2 Patient (P) requirement

The patient must provide their valid S2 certificate (HV 6.1).

Under HV 6.2, for PTS to complete a course of treatment, the patient must provide this valid S2 certificate demonstrating that the length of treatment extends beyond the period of EC granted (a); or a renewed or extended S2 certificate covering the extension period (b); or the original S2 certificate and a letter from the treating healthcare professional detailing the further treatment required (c).

HV 7.1-5 Accompanying person (AP) requirement

The accompanying person must evidence a right to reside in the EEA or Switzerland (HV 7.4) and be accompanying the patient (the S2 Healthcare visitor) on entry to the UK (HV 7.1(a); or joining P in the UK (b).

The relationship must be evidenced via proof of the patient's PTE as an S2 Healthcare Visitor (HV 7.2(a)); or their S2 certificate (b); and their passport of EEA national ID card (or other satisfactory travel document if P is not an EEA national).

For PTS applications, the accompanying person must also provide the person's S2 documentation (HV 7.4, 6.2).

The accompanying person can provide copies of documents but must provide originals where the decision maker has reasonable doubts as to their genuineness (HV 7.5).

HV 8.1-3 Consent requirement for child S2 Healthcare Visitor

If the patient is a child their parent or legal guardian must give consent who is not travelling with them (HV 8.1). The consent must cover the application (HV 8.2(a)); living and care arrangements (b); and, if for an EC/PTE application, the travel and reception arrangements in the UK (c). This consent must be available in writing on request (HV 8.3).

HV 9.1 Decision on application as an S2 Healthcare Visitor

If all suitability and eligibility requirements are met, the application *will* be granted, otherwise it *will* be refused.

HV 10.1-2 Period and condition of grant for an S2 Healthcare Visitor

PTE/PTS will be granted for up to 6 months (HV 10.1&2). The conditions on grants are no access to public funds (HV 10.3(a)); no work (b) or study (c).

HV 11.1 Cancellation and curtailment

EC/PTE/PTS in this category *may* be cancelled, where it is proportionate to do so:

(a) In relation to the conduct of the patient or accompanying person preceding the end of the transition period on grounds of public policy/security/health grounds under Reg 17 of the 2016 Regs. Decisions on Appendix S2 cases are treated as EEA decisions for this purpose; or
(b) In relation to conduct thereafter on conducive grounds
(c) On grounds of misleading or false information having been provided, whether or not to the applicant's knowledge and including for a supporting document, where this is material to the decision on the application
(d) On the ground the applicant ceases to meet the requirements of this category
(e) On the ground they have breached a condition in HV 10.3 unless EC or further permission was granted in knowledge of the breach.

11.13 Appendix Service Providers from Switzerland

This Appendix is in force from 1 December 2020. The introduction to this appendix summarises the route as allowing eligible employers, companies or self-employed individuals to carry out contracts with a UK based party for 90 days per calendar year in total (regardless of how many contracts are held). The contract must have been signed and commenced before 11pm on 31 December 2020. There is no provision for dependants to accompany migrants on this route.

This Appendix is structured under the following headings and with the following paragraph numbers:

- SPS 1.1-4 Validity requirements for Service Providers from Switzerland
- SPS 2.1-4 Suitability requirements for Service Providers from Switzerland
- SPS 3.1 Eligibility requirements for Service Providers from Switzerland
- SPS 4.1-10 Services requirement for Service Providers from Switzerland
- SPS 5.1 90 day limitation requirement for Service Providers from Switzerland
- SPS 6.1-2 Genuineness requirement for Service Providers from Switzerland
- SPS 7.1-2 Decision on an application as a Service Provider from Switzerland
- SPS 8.1-4 Period and conditions of grant for Service Providers from Switzerland
- SPS 9.1 Cancellation of entry clearance or permission of a Service Provider from Switzerland

The available is as follows (the applicant guidance links to the application form):

- Service Providers from Switzerland caseworker guidance
- Apply for a Service providers from Switzerland visa
- Service Providers from Switzerland: apply for a review of a decision about your right to enter the UK

There are no fees for applications in this category. Applicant guidance, linking to the form, is available here and caseworker guidance Service Providers from Switzerland here. Further applicant guidance on requesting an Administrative review is here.

SPS 1.1-4 Validity requirements for Service Providers from Switzerland

Applications are to be made on online form "other work visas for the UK (non points-based working visas)" on the "Find and apply for other visas from outside the UK" form (SPS 1.1).

The applicant must pay the fee and provide biometrics and a passport, Swiss national identity card or, if non-Swiss a satisfactory travel document (SPS 1.2). They must be aged 18 or over at application date (SPS 1.3).

An application not meeting all these requirements is invalid and *may* be rejected and not considered (SPS 1.4).

SPS 2.1-4 Suitability requirements for Service Providers from Switzerland

An application *must* be refused if at the date of decision the applicant is subject to a deportation or exclusion order or decision (SPS 2.1), but where such a decision related to conduct before 11pm on 31 December 2020 the order or decision must be justified on the grounds of public policy, public security or public health in accordance with Reg 17 of the EEA Regs 2016, whether or not those Regs apply to that person. In applying this provision, "an EEA decision" read "a decision under SPS 2.1" (SPS 2.2).

Under SPS 2.3, application *may* be refused, if proportionate, in the following scenarios:

(a) In relation to the application and whether or not to A's knowledge, false/misleading information, representations or documents have been submitted including to obtain a supporting document, and this is material to a decision on the application; or
(b) For pre-11pm 31 December 2020 conduct, on grounds of public policy/security/health in accordance with Reg 27 of the 2016 Regs whether or not they apply to A ("EEA decision" to be read as "a decision under SPS 2.3")
(c) For conduct thereafter on conducive grounds
(d) The same exclusion regime as for the UK applies where the deportation/exclusion decision relates to one of the Islands Grounds SPS 2.3 (d) and (e) are that A is subject to an Islands deportation order (d) or an Islands exclusion decision on direction by the relevant minister or other authority subject to the usual proviso (SPS 2.4) distinguishing between when EEA and domestic legal standards are applied.

SPS 3.1 Eligibility requirements for Service Providers from Switzerland

The applicant must apply for EC before their arrival in the UK.

SPS 4.1-10 Services requirement for Service Providers from Switzerland

If the applicant is a Swiss national they must be either established in self-employment or habitually employed in Switzerland (SPS 4.1) and if self-employed must be registered as such with the appropriate Swiss tax authority (SPS 4.2).

Non-Swiss nationals must be legally integrated into the regular Swiss labour market, be habitually employed there and if required must provide a copy of their Swiss residence or work permit (SPS 4.3).

SPS 4.4 provides that the applicant is legally integrated where they are an EEA national with the relevant residence status enabling them to work in Switzerland (a) or if a non-EEA, non-Swiss national they have permission to reside and have been working for an extended period within the regular labour market of Switzerland (b).

EEA or Swiss nationals need not evidence permission to reside in Switzerland if their country of nationality remains within the free movement system (subject to transitional provisions) (SPS 4.5).

An employer or company is eligible if legally formed in Switzerland (SPS 4.6 (a)); has their registered office, central administration or principal place of business in Switzerland (b); and remains active and trading (c).

Under SPS 4.8, a contract will be eligible if it is written (including electronically) and between a Swiss employer or company and a UK employer or company (formed legally in the UK) or an individual established in the UK (a); it is signed and dated before 11pm on 31 December 2020 (b); and performance has started before then (c). Conditions need not accord with the National Minimum Wage & Working Time Regs (SPS 4.11).

SPS 4.7 cross refers to the evidence required by SPS 4.9&10 for A to show they are required to travel to the UK.

The evidence required for employees to show they are required to travel to the UK, is set out at SPS 4.9: a letter (a), signed by a senior member of the organisation (b); including the author's credentials (c); a copy of the contract (d); including reasons why A is required to travel to the UK to execute it (e), confirming A has the professional qualifications to do so (f); and confirming the employer or company has not already used the 90 days per year to execute this or other contracts (g).

Self-employed Swiss nationals must provide a letter of self-certification meeting the same requirements as in SPS 4.9 except (a)&(b), and confirmation that the 90-day limit has not already been exceeded.

SPS 5.1 90-day limitation requirement for Service Providers from Switzerland

The employer, company or self-employed person must not have used up their 90-day annual limit.

SPS 6.1-2 Genuineness requirement for Service Providers from Switzerland

There is scope for "genuineness" testing. To be satisfied the route is not being abused, the decision maker must ensure that the applicant does not remain in the UK after the end of their permission (SPS 6.1 (a)), will not live in the UK for extended periods through frequent and successive visits or make the UK their main home (b); and is genuinely seeking entry as a Service Provider from Switzerland (c).

A must not, while in the UK, intend to access public funds or NHS treatment (apart from emergencies) (SPS 6.2(a)&(b)); study (c), marry/enter a civil partnership (d) or give notice thereof (e).

SPS 7.1-2 Decision on an application as a Service Provider from Switzerland

If all the requirements are met, the application *will* be granted, otherwise it *will* be refused (SPS 7.1). On refusal, administrative review is available under Appendix AR(EU: Admin Review (SPS 7.2)

SPS 8.1-4 Period and conditions of grant for Service Providers from Switzerland

Under SPS 8.1, grants will end on whichever is soonest: the end date of the eligible contract (a); the end date of the employee's fixed term work contract (b); the day before the expiry date of the applicant's permission to reside in Switzerland (c); or 31 December 2025 (d).

Multiple entry during the permission period is allowed, subject to the 90 day proviso (SPS 8.2). The company or employer (or self-employed person) must ensure the total number of days in the UK in this category does not exceed 90, regardless of the number of staff granted permission (SPS 8.3).

Grants are subject to the conditions in SPS 8.4: no more than 90 days' work in each calendar year (a); no work other than on the eligible contract (including self-employment and voluntary work (b); no study (c) and no access to public funds (d).

SPS 9.1 Cancellation of entry clearance or permission of a Service Provider from Switzerland

EC in this category *may* be cancelled, where proportionate, if

(a) Justified in relation to pre-TP end conduct on grounds of public policy/security/health grounds under Reg 17 of the 2016 Regs, regardless whether these apply to A. For an "EEA decision", read "a decision under SPS 9.1"; or
(b) Justified in relation to conduct thereafter on conducive grounds
(c) Justified on grounds of misleading or false information having been provided, whether or not to A's knowledge and including for a supporting document, where this is material to the decision on the application
(d) Justified on the ground the applicant has breached one of the conditions in SPS 8.4 unless further permission was granted in knowledge of the breach
(e) Justified on grounds that the applicant, the company or the employer cease to satisfy the Service Requirement at SPS 4.1-6 or the 90 day limit; or
(f) An agreement is concluded between the UK and Switzerland dealing with movement of natural persons for supply of services under WTO terms.

CHAPTER 12: British Nationality Law

12.1 A brief history of nationality law

Broadly, the subject of nationality law for our purposes covers two central questions; firstly, am I a British citizen and, secondly, if I am not, how do I become one?

British citizenship can be very important, as noted in O (a minor) [2022] UKSC 3:

> "It gives a right of abode in the UK which is not subject to the qualifications that apply to a non-citizen, including even someone who has indefinite leave to remain. It gives a right to acquire a British passport and thereby a right to come and go without let or hindrance. It can contribute to one's sense of identity and belonging, assisting people, and not least young people in their sensitive teenage years, to feel part of the wider community. It allows a person to participate in the political life of the local community and the country at large e."

It is useful briefly to review the historical development of different forms of British nationality to ensure fa familiarity with the key terminology of nationality law. Also an old passport, or the passport of someone who has died, may be for a category of British nationality that is no longer current but may be useful to establish a person's current entitlements.

The key stages of development are broadly as follows:

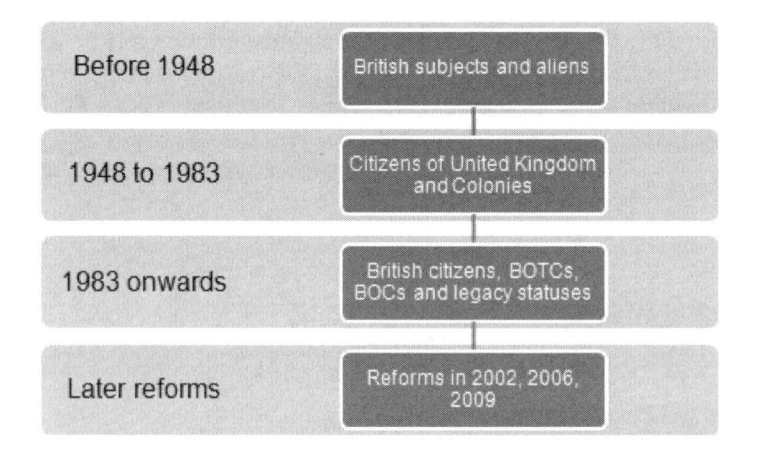

Before 1948	British subjects and aliens
1948 to 1983	Citizens of United Kingdom and Colonies
1983 onwards	British citizens, BOTCs, BOCs and legacy statuses
Later reforms	Reforms in 2002, 2006, 2009

12.1.1 Pre 1948

Until 1948 the terminology used in law was 'British Subject'. The world was divided into British Subjects, who were in the UK and overseas, and aliens, with the exception of British protected persons who were connected not to colonies but to British protectorates. They were not subject to immigration control.

12.1.2 1948 to 1983

The British Nationality Act 1948 created the status of a '**Citizen of the UK and Colonies**', often abbreviated to CUKC. All CUKCs had a right of abode in the UK. They were also, at the same time, British Subjects.

Citizens of colonies which had become independent were not CUKCs but they retained the status of British Subject and with it the right of abode. The term Commonwealth Citizen was also used for this group.

No change was made to British Protected Persons and the status of British Subject Without Citizenship was created for those for those who had not acquired the citizenship of the independent country, but were not CUKCs either.

As more colonies became independent after 1948 their citizens lost their CUKC status if they gained citizenship of the new country, and became British Subjects/Commonwealth citizens.

From the 1960s onwards, some CUKCs and some British subjects began to lose their right of abode. The IA 1971 introduced the term 'patriality'.

Patrial citizens were those who had a right of abode and thus were not subject to immigration control:

- **Patrial CUKCs** – who had acquired their CUKC citizenship in the UK (by birth, registration or naturalisation) had a parent or grandparent who had similarly acquired CUKC status in the UK, or had lived in the UK for five years or more; or CUKCs.
- **Non-patrial CUKCs** – all CUKCs not in the category above.

The right of abode was also withdrawn from certain British Subjects and Commonwealth citizens during this period.

In summary, the following people born before 1 January 1983 are British citizens:

- Those born in the UK pre-1 January 1983 (save the children of diplomats)
- Those born abroad pre-1 January 1983 whose father was born in the UK
- Those born abroad pre-1 January 1983 whose father was registered or naturalised as British before their birth
- Those adopted in the UK by a British fa father.

Murugason [2022] EWHC 3160 (Admin) holds that the IA 1971 s2(1)(b)(i) requires that a parent have obtained CUKC citizenship either by registration in the UK or by birth, adoption or naturalisation, also in the UK.

12.1.3 1983 onwards

With the coming into force of the British Nationality Act 1981 on 1 January 1983, what mattered primarily was parentage, rather than place of birth. The Act created three new categories of British nationals:

- **British citizens** – these were people who, on 31 December 1982, were patrial CUKCs. As British citizens they retained their rights of abode and are recognisable as the British Citizens of today.
- **British Dependent Territories Citizens** (renamed **Overseas** in the British Overseas Territories Citizens Act 2002) for people who, on 31 December 1982, were CUKCs because of their connection with a British Dependent Territory (e.g. Bermuda). Those who had the right of abode retained it.
- **British Overseas Citizens** for non-patrial CUKCs who did not fit into the category of British Dependent (Overseas Territories) Citizens.

Meanwhile,

- **British Protected Persons** retained their status.
- **Commonwealth Citizens'** status did not change (see MIL 4.1.2 for definition). Those who had the right of abode retained it.
- **British Subject** changed its meaning. It became the new name for British Subjects without Citizenship as defined in the BNA 1948.

As you can see, there are therefore several types of British national currently in existence. This guide is intended as an introductory text and therefore focuses on British citizens.

Section 11 of the BNA 1981 made provision for certain CUKCs to become British citizens on passage of the Act. The principal requirements were that a person, on 31 December 1982:

- Was a citizen of the UK and colonies
- Had a right of abode in the UK

12.1.4 2002 legislation

In 2002, the British Overseas Territories Act 2002 was passed. This Act renamed British Dependent Territories, British Overseas Territories. People became British Overseas Territories Citizens automatically on 26 February 2002 and on the 21 May 2002 they all became British Citizens with a right of abode in the UK, with the exception of those connected with the Sovereign bases.

NIAA 2002 amends BNA 1981 to address some injustices faced by holders of lesser forms of British citizenship.

12.1.5 Children of unmarried fathers

NIAA 2002 also finally abolished the patrial-centric approach of previous nationality laws; it also added s50(9A) to BNA 1981 to give unmarried fathers the same ability to transmit British nationality (subject to proving paternity) as unmarried mothers.

From 6 April 2015, s65 of the Immigration Act 2014 amended the BNA 1981 (by adding ss 4F to 4I) to provide for the registration as a British citizen, by right, subject to the good character requirement, for all those who missed out on being a British citizen at birth because their mother was not married to their father.

In Johnson [2016] UKSC 56, the Supreme Court decided, in an appeal against deportation, that it would be a breach of a person's human rights to impose the good character requirement into adult British citizenship registration applications for those affected by this historic discrimination, 'the denial of citizenship, having such an important effect upon a person's social identity, is sufficiently within the ambit of article 8 to trigger the application of the prohibition of discrimination in article 14'.

In the light of Johnson, on 25 July 2019, the British Nationality Act 1981 (Remedial) Order 2019 came into force. This removes the good character requirement for citizenship applications under BNA 1981 s4F (entitling registration under ss 1(3), 3(2) or 3(5); & ss 3C, 4G, 4H and 4I).

12.1.6 2006 legislation

The Immigration, Asylum and Nationality Act 2006 made further changes to nationality law, widening the power to deprive a person of citizenship (s56) or the right of abode (s57) to include 'conducive to the public good' and also removes registration as a British citizen as of right by inserting a good character test for all applicants. An Order passed in January 2010 also includes children aged 10 and over in the 'good character requirement'.

12.1.7 2009 legislation

The BCIA 2009:

- Enables registration as British of the children born outside the UK of members of the armed forces and confirms automatic British citizenship of children born in the UK of members of the armed forces.
- Allows registration of children born outside the UK under s3(2) of the BNA 1981 up to their 18th birthday (extended from 12 months after their birth or six years in exceptional circumstances).
- Permits registration of otherwise stateless BN(O)s.
- Enables registration of those born before 7 February 1961 with British mothers, if they would have become a British citizen at birth had women been able to pass on citizenship in the same way as men.

12.1.8 2014 legislation

The Immigration Act 2014

- Enables registration of those born before 1 July 2006 and previously excluded from acquisition of British nationality on the ground their parents were unmarried at the time of their birth by insertion, via s65 IA 2014 of sections 4E to 4J into the BNA 1981
- Extends powers to deprive a person of their British nationality by insertion, via s66 IA 2014, of s40(4A) into the BNA 1981

12.1.9 Windrush scheme – uncharged nationality applications and waiver of certain requirements

In April 2018 media exposure of the impact of the hostile environment on members of the Windrush generation and their descendants, some with entitlements to citizenship, led to a public outcry, a change of Home Secretary and the launch of the Windrush scheme on 30 May 2018. Where this applies, nationality fees and certain requirements are waived (MIL 4.2.14).

12.2 Nationality Guidance

The Nationality Instructions were archived here
http://web.archive.org/web/20170425005852/https:/www.gov.uk/topic/immigration-operational-guidance/nationality-instructions.

They were replaced by a set of documents, all posted 27 July 2017, as a set entitled 'Nationality guidance', accessible here https://www.gov.uk/government/collections/nationality-policy-guidance

Those archived NIs may be of assistance in cases of doubt.

Other guidance, fees and forms

Additional guidance is often available either in separate booklets appearing on the same page as the relevant nationality application form, or on the form itself. All citizenship application forms–are accessible here.

Nationality forms have no payment section and the payment slip is page 4 of this separate nationality fees list which must be printed and added to the form
https://assets.publishing.service.gov.uk/government/uploads/system/uploads/attachment_data/file/691774/Nationality-MasterFeesLeaflet_2018_Final_06-04-18.pdf

This list helpfully groups the categories of application and the relevant fees together.

The SSHD must bear in mind the best interests of children when setting fees: PRCBC [2021] EWCA Civ 193.Those seeking advice on behalf of child clients who are separated from their parents, such as children in care, should of course also be advised of the fact that all immigration and nationality immigration cases have been brought back within legal aid scope, meaning they can now seek free legal advice and assistance from legal aid providers (without the need for these to apply for Exceptional Case Funding). This reopening of funding for immigration cases explicitly includes nationality cases.

Organisations considering taking on such cases now should refer to new LAA guidance Separated migrant children - transitional guidance for organisations making civil legal aid applications for immigration matters concerning separated migrant children.

Passports will only be issued in the male or female gender: Elan-Cane [2021] UKSC 56 holds that the recognition of a third gender raises complex moral and ethical issues with wide implications and there was no consensus amongst EU Member States that passport should be available with an *x* marker. Passport fees for online applications are £82.50 for adults, £53.50 for children and varying fees for different priority and postal services; there are different rates for applications made by post or from abroad. There is Guidance *Passport Fees*.

12.3 Birth or adoption in the UK on or after 1 January 1983

The routes by which a child born in the UK is a British citizen by birth or can become so by registration under s1 of the BNA 1981 are as follows:

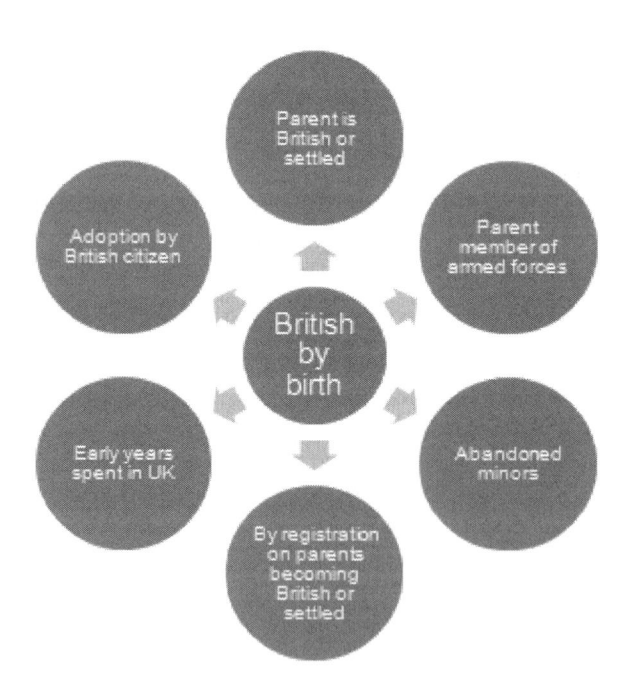

- Parent is British or settled
- Parent member of armed forces
- Abandoned minors
- By registration on parents becoming British or settled
- Early years spent in UK
- Adoption by British citizen

(British by birth)

12.3.1 Automatic acquisition – parent is British or settled at time of birth s1(1) BNA 1981

The plain fact of birth in the UK since 1 January 1983 does not usually create any entitlement to citizenship unless it is combined with a parental link to a person settled here:

> s.1(1) A person born in the United Kingdom after commencement, or in a qualifying territory on or after the appointed day, shall be a British citizen if at the time of the birth his father or mother is–
>
>> (a) a British citizen; or
>> (b) settled in the United Kingdom or that territory.

This form of acquisition of citizenship operates by law, so no registration or other forms need be completed. However, proof that a person meets the above criteria will be required to prove citizenship and apply for a passport.

Settlement is defined in the Immigration Act 1971 as 'being ordinarily resident in the United Kingdom ... without being subject under the immigration laws to any restriction on the period for which he may remain'. Effectively this means that the parent in question must have ILR.

At one time a child could establish his right to nationality via either parent so long as he was born within marriage. Whereas 'Illegitimate' children (for this was the effect of this provision) could trace entitlement only via their mother. BNA 1981 s47 improved things somewhat: a person born out of wedlock was to be treated as if they had been born legitimate (i.e. retrospectively) for the purposes of nationality law if their parents subsequently married.

This old fashioned and discriminatory approach came to a partial end as of 1 July 2006, though only for children born after that date, with the coming into force of amended s50(9A) of the BNA 1981, which redefined father as either:

> (a) the husband of the mother (regardless of who is the biological father – but see below at 12.3.3), or
>
> (b) & (ba) the person treated as the father under s28 of The Human Fertilisation and Embryology Act 1990, or under s35, 36, 42 or 43 of The Human Fertilisation and Embryology Act 2008, or
>
> (c) – *only* where (a) to (ba) do not apply: the person who satisfies the requirements of The British Nationality (Proof of Paternity) Regulations 2006 – either the person named as the father of the child in a birth certificate issued within one year of the date of the child's birth, or the person who otherwise satisfies the HO that he is the father (e.g. by way of a DNA test report – a list of HO approved DNA testing companies is available here: https://www.gov.uk/get-dna-test). In Alake [2020] EWHC 1956 (Admin) the Judge held that there would be some cases where HMPO should consider whether it was appropriate to assist an applicant with requesting their father to provide DNA evidence voluntarily.

Note that for birth certificates issued after 10 September 2015, being named as the father will no longer be sufficient to prove paternity. Under the British Nationality (Proof of Paternity) (Amendment) Regulations 2015, it will be left to the HO to determine who is the 'natural father' of the child.

A further step was taken to right this historic wrong by s65 of the IA 2014, which from 6 April 2015 provides the right to register for all those who missed out on British citizenship, by operation of law or registration, because their natural father was not recognised as their father for the purposes of nationality law because of the pre-July 2006 discrimination against children born illegitimately. Johnson [2016] UKSC 56 took this right yet another step forward by declaring that a refusal to register in these circumstances merely on 'good character' grounds would be a breach of human rights (see above under 12.1.5).

The *Legitimacy and Domicile Guidance* points out that not all countries have concepts of legitimacy so the national laws in the father's place of domicile needs to be checked. Absent a prohibition on not recognising illegitimate fatherhood, fathers should be recognised as legitimate. Relevant evidence where a father is unnamed on a birth certificate could include statutory declarations by parents or, if they are dead, others who may know the birth's circumstances, court orders, DNA tests or other evidence. Caseworkers should send the father a domicile questionnaire if information is missing, and consult the *HO Knowledge Base* and the *Laws on legitimacy outside the UK*, or make a case-specific guidance referral, to the HO's *Guidance & Quality, Operating Standards* unit. A change in the identified father in a new passport application may require nationality entitlement to be revisited.

As the Guidance explains, one acquires a domicile of origin at birth (usually one's father's at the date of birth) and may subsequently acquire a domicile of choice, because their father's domicile changes before they are 16 or they lose their links with their domicile of origin over time.

Example

Beatrice was born in the UK in 2005 to a French national mother and British father. The mother had only been present in the UK for 18 months and was not therefore settled. The parents were not married. Beatrice was not automatically born British, although she could almost certainly later have been registered as British (by discretion; from 6 April 2015, s50(9A) gives a right to register in these circumstances).

Bertie was born in the UK in 2007 to the same French mother and British father. The mother was still not settled here and the parents were not married. Bertie, however, was automatically born British because of the July 2006 change in the law.

12.3.1.1 Nationality and EU law rights: the Good Friday Agreement

The Good Friday Agreement recognises "*the birthright of all the people of Northern Ireland to identify themselves and be accepted as Irish or British.*" In De Souza [2019] UKUT 355 (IAC) the UT considered whether this provision had any material effect on British nationality law, such that persons born in Northern Ireland might be able to access Treaty Rights on the basis of self-identifying as Irish.

The UT concluded that, whether or not an individual so identifies, they are still excluded from benefitting from the EEA Regs 2016 if they are also a British citizen. It was not reasonably possible to read section 1(1) of the British Nationality Act 1981, conferring British citizenship on individuals born in the UK to a British citizen parent, such that the words "*if they consent to identify as such*" appeared there. The UT rules out this possibility. To do so would represent a radical departure from the existing law of British nationality, and an international Treaty such as the Good Friday Agreement could not have such effects. The Court of Appeal in Ni Chuinneagain [2022] NICA 56 looked at the issue from a different angle – whether a dual Irish/British citizen suffered disproportionate interference with their right to self-identification by the automatic acquisition of British nationality at birth (which required certain administrative steps to divest oneself of). The Court found not: the consequences were minor and the right to renounce citizenship was sufficient protection.

The EUSS scheme was subsequently amended in order to ensure the Good Friday agreement was properly reflected in UK law: see generally 11.7.1 above.

12.3.2 EEA nationals treated as 'settled' in the past –*Capparelli*

For a very long time (pre-Brexit) it was understood that EEA nationals exercising Treaty rights in the UK should be treated as 'settled' here if born here from 1 January 1983 to 2 October 2000. The old Nationality Instructions, Chapter 3, Part 1, para 3.5.1.4 provided that UK-born children before 2 October 2000 would need only to evidence that one of the parents was an EEA national who, at the time of the birth, was exercising EU Treaty rights in the United Kingdom. Roehrig [2023] EWHC 31 (Admin) notes that this remained HO practice until 11 October 2022 'as a matter of policy and fairness'. This factor can be relevant to the acquisition of British nationality by birth, as under section 1 of the British Nationality Act 1981, a person born in the UK after the Act's commencement is a British citizen if at that time a parent is a British citizen or settled here. Settlement is defined under section 50(2) of the BNA 1981 as being ordinarily resident in the United Kingdom or … without being subject under the immigration laws to any restriction on the period for which he may remain.

So potential candidates for British citizenship must show that:

1. They were ordinarily resident in the UK; and
2. They were not subject to a restriction under such immigration laws

Capparrelli [2017] UKUT 162 (IAC) and Roehrig destabled this understanding. The thinking therein no longer really matters. For a while the HO stance was that they would not revisit nationality decisions made before 11 October 2022 and that anyone recognised as a British citizen will continue to be treated as such: *British citizenship automatic acquisition Guidance*. From 28 June 2023 the British Nationality (Regularisation of Past Practice) Act 2023 places in statute the longstanding policy on British nationality that was disrupted by these cases. It amends BNA 1981 for EEA and Swiss nationals living in the UK, confirming that they should be treated retrospectively as not subject to any immigration restrictions on their length of UK residence.

12.3.3 Who is the father?

As you can see from the above, this is a vexed question in nationality law, where proving paternity may render a person British by birth or give them an opportunity to register. Unsurprisingly, the HO set a high bar for proving who the father is.

Section 1(1) of the British Nationality Act 1981 (BNA) sets out that a person born in the United Kingdom is automatically a British citizen at birth if at that time their mother or father was a British citizen or settled in the United Kingdom.

Section 50(9A) provides various routes by which the fact of fatherhood may confer nationality (MIL 12.3.1 above).

The BNA 1981 s50(9A)(a), read with (c), had the consequence that, where the child's mother was married to someone other than the biological father at its date of birth, the latter father cannot be the basis for any entitlement to British citizenship for their child. K (A Child) [2018] EWHC 1834 (Admin) found this to be unjustifiable discrimination against the affected children. Being born to a mother married to a person other than one's biological father represented an 'other status', given the need to treat people in a fundamentally equal manner as to their dignity and rights. HO discretion was not enough as a legal guarantee was essential. BNA 1981 s4E now addresses this difficulty.

Whenever there is a gap in registration entitlements the HO may well allow the child to register as of discretion, under s3(1) BNA 1981.

For children born on or after 1 July 2006 to a British father where the mother was married to someone else, there is now a fee waiver available. The fee waiver is not automatic and must be applied for. The application is made on form UKF(M). There two relevant sets of guidance which need to be consulted as to the practicalities of the fee waiver application:

- the form guidance
- general child registration guidance (updated in April 2020)

12.3.4 Qualifying territories

It is not only birth in the UK that can give rise to British citizenship. So too birth in the qualifying territories. This possibility arises for those born on or after 21 May 2002 in a a British overseas territory other than the Sovereign Base Areas of Akrotiri and Dhekelia in Cyprus, if a parent is a British citizen and settled in the UK or that qualifying territory.

The qualifying territories are: Anguilla; Bermuda; British Antarctic Territory; British Indian Ocean Territory (BIOT); British Virgin Islands; Cayman Islands; Falkland Islands; Gibraltar; Montserrat; Pitcairn Islands; Saint Helena, Ascension and Tristan da Cunha; South Georgia and the South Sandwich Islands; Turks and Caicos Islands (see list here: https://www.gov.uk/types-of-british-nationality/british-overseas-territories-citizen)

A new route for BIOT residents is available from 23 November 2022 (s17H BNA 1981. This recognises the impact that the combination of the removal of the Chagossians from the British Indian Ocean Territory in the 1960s and 1970s, and the limited recognition of their removal in nationality legislation, has had on their ability to access British nationality. The direct descendants of those born in the BIOT as CUKCs (or before 8 November 1965 in the BIOT) who have never been British overseas territories or British Dependent Territories citizens. Applications must be made within 5 years of the November 2022 commencement for those over 18; those under 18 at that date, or born within 5 years thereafter, must do so before attaining the age of 23. British citizenship otherwise than by descent ensues. There is a *fact sheet* available, a *pre-travel information pack*, and Guidance on *Support for Chagossians* (listing various community funds and scholarships), the possibility of contacting *We Are Digital* (where help with IT literacy us needed(and Guidance *Chagossian descendant* which explains that

- most applicants will be able to apply for BOTC and full British citizenship at the same time
- there is no fee
- direct descendents may be of any generation, onwards through great-grandparents, but do not extend outwards to uncles and aunts etc
- whilst a full birth certificate and a full set of consecutive birth records showing an unbroken line of descent are desirable, they may not be available, in which case medical or dental records suffice, marriage/CP certificates, change of name deed polls, and factual records including court proceedings
- there is no requirement for legitimate birth
- fathers will be those named as a birth certificate issued within 12 months of the birth before 10 September 2015 or a person who can establish themselves as such via court orders, birth certificates, DNA reports etc

12.3.5 Automatic acquisition – children born inside UK to members of the armed forces – s1(1A) BNA 1981

BCIA s2009 s42 provides a statutory basis for the acquisition of British citizenship for children born in the UK to members of the armed forces. This removes the need to treat parents of such children as if they were settled here, as the previous legal regime had done.

In 2010 s1(1A) was inserted into the BNA 1981, which provides that a person born in the United Kingdom or a qualifying territory on or after the relevant day (13 January 2010) shall be a British citizen if at the time of the birth his father or mother is a member of the armed forces.

12.3.6 Automatic acquisition – newborn infants found abandoned in the UK – s1(2) BNA 1981

Under s1(2), a newborn infant found abandoned in the United Kingdom on or after 1 January 1983 is regarded as born in the UK to a British or settled parent. Thus they acquire British citizenship applying s1(1):

This presumption applies unless the contrary can be proven by the HO.

12.3.7 Acquisition by registration of children born in the UK upon parents becoming British or settled – s1(3) BNA 1981

Minors are entitled to registration under s1(3) of the British Nationality Act 1981 if:

- they were born in the United Kingdom on or after 1 January 1983; and

- they were not British citizens at birth because at the time neither parent was a British citizen or settled here; and
- while they are minors, either parent becomes a British citizen or becomes settled in the United Kingdom (NB: unlike for naturalisation of adult EEA nationals, no prior issue of permanent residence documentation is required, only evidence of acquisition of PR by the parent); and
- they are minors on the date of application

> **Example**
>
> To continue with the example of Beatrice, above, if her mother becomes settled in the UK after five years of residence under EU law, Beatrice could be registered as British. Unlike with Bertie, this is a positive step that must be taken and it must be taken before Beatrice turns 18.
>
> Alternatively, Beatrice could probably have been registered under s1(3) after 1 July 2006, once her father was recognised in law as her father for nationality purposes, i.e. when one of her 'parents' became British.

12.3.8 Acquisition by registration of children or adults born in the UK due to early years spent in UK – s1(4) BNA 1981

Adults or minors are entitled to registration under s1(4) of the BNA 1981 if they:

- were born in the United Kingdom on or after 1 January 1983; and
- were not a British citizen at birth because at the time neither parent was a British citizen or settled here; and
- were aged 10 years or more on the date of application; and
- have lived in the United Kingdom for the first 10 years of their life; and
- during that "10 years have not been out of the United Kingdom for more than 90 days in any one of those years

The lawfulness of residence is irrelevant for this provision. BNA 1981 s1(7) gives a discretion to condone longer absences than 90 days. This statutory discretion receives a gloss from the Nationality *Guidance Registration as British citizens: children*: non-intentional longer absences should normally be permitted if:

- the number of days absent from the UK in any one of the years does not exceed 180 days and the total number of days over the 10 year period does not exceed 990 days
- the number of days absent exceeds 180 or 990 respectively but was due to circumstances beyond the family's control, such as a serious illness

12.3.8.1 Fees for childrens' citizenship applications

Note the form is the same for adults and children (Form T) but the fee differs – £1,214 for children, £1,431 for adults (see Nationality Fees list).

For some years it has been thought that requiring a fee before an application from the child of an impecunious family is accepted represents a real barrier to a child making good their rights. However, Williams [2017] EWCA Civ 98 and O (a minor) [2022] UKSC 3 upheld the fees requirements. PRCBC [2019] EWHC 3536 (Admin) noted a

> '*mass of evidence supporting the proposition that children born in the UK and identifying as British ... feel alienated, excluded, isolated, "second-best", insecure and not fully assimilated into the culture and social efabric of the UK.*'

In some circumstances this may be contrary to the best interests of the child, as indeed found in PRCBC. Not before time, the HO has introduced a fee waiver scheme (as per Immigration and

Nationality (Fees) Regulations 2018 Sch 8 paras 5, 8): *Affordability fee waiver: Citizenship registration for individuals under the age of 18.*

- Citizenship applications will be treated as made on the fee waiver date application if the applicant attains majority before the application is otherwise made
- Waiver is granted if applicants credibly demonstrate they cannot afford the fee and that their income is not sufficient to meet the child's needs, having regard to the need to promote and safeguard child welfare, bearig in mind the impact of lacking citizenship on the child and the broader public interest in funding the immigration system
- "*Clear and compelling*" evidence re lack of affordability is required via 6 months of all bank statements with a breakdown of monthly income/expenses, from themselves and from "*those who are supporting them*"; and a compelling reason must be given where relevant evidence is said not to be available
- Refusal may follow where reliable information is not provided, there is intentional disposal of funds, non-essential purchases have been made, excess savings are available, or there is a failure to show reasonable steps to ensure funds are available (though without reference to complicated financial options such as remortgaging) – having regard to who has responsibility for the family's support and accommodation (including absent parents) and their ability to pay the fee, income sources, all bank accounts, and surplus income (bearing in mind the costs of travel and communication to enable the supported persons to maintain interpersonal relationships and access a reasonable level of social, cultural and religious life) and luxury purchases
- There is no fee waiver for adults: but where an adult is applying for citizenship alongside a child, the cost of the adult's application should be factored into the family's overall finances
- Part payment fee waivers are possible where multiple children share a parent: generally issued to the eldest child first to reduce the risk of such a child turning 18 before an application
- Fees are not payable for children looked after by a local authority: see Fees Regs 2018 Sch 8 para 20A.3.1 & Guidance *Children looked-after by local authorities in England*

12.3.9 Acquisition by registration of stateless persons – Sch 2 BNA 1981

Schedule 2 of the 1981 Act provides for reducing statelessness, permitting registration where:

- there is a link with the UK via parental possession of one of the lesser forms of British nationality such as being a British overseas territories citizen, a British Overseas citizen and a British subject where the child would be otherwise stateless, and the child is born in the UK or in a British Overseas Territory (paras 1-2)
- a person born in the UK 1 January 1983 who is and has always been stateless if between the ages of 18 and 22 and resident in the UK for a period of five years (as long as absent for no more than 450 days during that period) (para 3)
- A person born in the UK or in a BOT applies whilst a minor, no UK absence > 450 days and is unable to acquire another nationality (para 3A). In this context, ability to acquire a nationality is limited to nationalities held by the applicant's parents, to which they have been entitled (by legal right not discretion) since birth, and where these are steps which it would be reasonable to expect of them. The Guidance *Registration as British citizen - stateless persons* suggests that '*simple steps*' such as completing forms would be reasonable; international travel might not be, and evidence of enquiries with the relevant national authorities will be expected. Registration is as a British citizen if they have spent more of the last 5 years in the UK than in a BOT, otherwise as a BOTC

This latter proviso is a reaction to MK [2017] EWHC 1365 (Admin) where a child born in the UK to Indian parents had been refused registration. The court accepted that a child born outside India to Indian parents is entitled to Indian citizenship by registration at an Indian consulate unlike children born overseas to British parents, who are British automatically (unless their parents are only British by descent themselves). MK adopts the definition of statelessness in the Convention relating to the Status of Stateless Persons 1954, namely of a 'stateless person' being a person who is not considered a national by any state under the operation of its law. This was the definition of statelessness adopted in Al-Jeddah [2013] UKSC 62 and Pham [2015] UKSC 19, both of which appeals against deprivation of British citizenship under s40 BNA 1981. MK concluded that the fact that the person *could* acquire a different nationality if he applied for it did not affect his entitlement to British nationality while he remains stateless. BNA 1981 Sch 2 para 3A changes things.

Perhaps in response to this, new evidential requirements over and above what this case requires have been added in new Nationality Guidance Stateless Persons on 26 Sep 2017.

Note the IRs addressing statelessness (MIL 4.4).

12.3.10 Automatic acquisition – minors adopted by British citizens – s1(5) BNA 1981

Section 1(5) o' the British Nationality Act 1981, as amended, explains which children adopted on or after 1 January 1983 acquired British citizenship automatically because of their adoption. Under s1(5), a child who is not already a British citizen becomes a British citizen from the date of an adoption order if

EITHER:

- the adoption is authorised by order of a court in the United Kingdom on or after 1 January 1983 or, on or after 21 May 2002, by an order of a court in a qualifying territory; and
- the adopter or, in the case of a joint adoption, one of the adopters is a British ci citizen on the date of the adoption order

OR

- it is a Convention adoption under the 1993 Hague Convention on Intercountry Adoptions; and
- the adoption is effected on or after 1 June 2003; and
- the adopter or, in the case of a joint adoption, oneof the adopters is a British citizen on the date of the Convention adoption; and
- the adopter or, in the case of a joint adoption, both of the adopters is habitually resident in the United Kingdom on the date of the Convention adoption.

    The current guidance is set out in Nationality policy Registration as a British citizen: children

- For adoptions non-compliant with the requirements set out in the policy, the old policy recommended registration if demonstrably in the child's best interests, whereas the new policy allows registration only if there are exceptionally compassionate or compelling circumstances.

12.3.11 Applications to change nationality by Local Authorities for children in their care

Local authorities have significant powers to take steps for the welfare of the children in their care. In Y (Children In Care: Change of Nationality) [2020] EWCA Civ 1038 the Court of Appeal held that whilst a local authority's powers which might include taking steps to change the nationality of a child in its care against the wishes of the child's parents, it must first seek the approval of the court.

12.3.12 Acquisition in connection with IRs Appendix EU

Under section 10A BNA 1981, a child will acquire British citizensip on the date one of their parents is granted settled status on or after 1 July 2021 if the child is:

- neither entitled to citizenship under other sections of the BNA
- nor exempt from immigration control

The parent must:

- Either have applied for settled status before 1 July 2021

CHAPTER 12: British Nationality Law

- Or have been eligible for settled status under any of the settled status eligibility categories in EU11 (relevant EEA citizens & family members) or EU12 (family members of qualifying British citizens – *Surinder Singh*); and
- Be ordinarily resident in the UK on the grant date.

12.4 Birth outside the UK

The routes by which a child born outside the UK can become British are as follows:

At birth
- To a parent who is a British citizen otherwise than by descent

On registration
- Any time up to age of 18
- On residence in UK with British citizen parents for 3 years
- If parent is or becomes a member of the armed forces

12.4.1 Automatic acquisition by descent – s2(1) BNA 1981

Section 2(1) of the BNA 1981 reads as follows:

> A person born outside the United Kingdom after commencement shall be a British citizen if at the time of the birth his father or mother:
>
> (a) is a British citizen otherwise than by descent; ...

This form of transmission of nationality operates by law, so no registration form need be completed, but evidence may be required that the person does meet the above requirements.

Example

Chris is a British citizen who emigrates to Australia with his Australian girlfriend, Clarissa. They do not get married. They have a baby boy, Clarence, in 2005, who was born in Australia. Clarence had no entitlement to British nationality when he was born, because his birth preceded the change in the law of 1 July 2006. However, following the further change of 6 April 2015, he can now register under s4G BNA1981. The application is free but in his case will confer citizenship by descent only (because this is the status he would have had, if his parents had been married, because of his birth outside the UK – s4G(2)).

Chris and Clarissa have another child, a baby girl called Carrie, who is born in 2007. Carrie is automatically born British and does not need to take any further steps to become British.

12.4.2 Acquisition by registration of children under the discretion in s3(1) BNA 1981

Section 3(1) can be used to register a variety of problem cases as it is a very wide discretion:

> 3(1) If while a person is a minor an application is made for his registration as a British citizen, the Secretary of State may, if he thinks fit, cause him to be registered as such a citizen.

Applications may be made either outright (on Form MN1) or argued as an alternative, for example where some of the evidence for registration by entitlement cannot be obtained.

The exercise of discretion under s3(1) should be conducted under the policy set out in Nationality Guidance <u>Registration as British citizen: children</u>. The Guidance is structured as a series of "*expectations*" to be taken into account when considering D's residual discretion. A central question is whether a child has a "*strong connection with the UK*". The identified factors are the child's future residence intentions, their parents' circumstances, the child's UK residence and the child's own immigration status. Where those expectations for registration are not met, any compelling compassionate circumstances should be assessed.

The child should be living in the UK with their future clearly shown as to lie here. Generally, the HO will exercise its discretion in favour of registering the child as British if the child has settled status and either both parents are British citizens or one is while the other is settled. However, if the child has lived in the UK for many years, it may be argued that, whatever the parents' circumstances, the child's future clearly lies in the UK and that it would be in the child's best interests to be registered as British. Children whose parents lack British citizenship will normally be registered after both child and parents have 5 years' lawful residence and then receive ILR – and normally 10 years' residence ending with a period of lawful residence (or exceptionally with unlawful residence throughout if they have lived here much of their life) also suffices. The Project for the Registration of Children as British Citizens (PRCBC) may be available for advice.

A suggested checklist of documents for this type of application:

- Original old and new passports or any biometrics card/immigration status documents
- Original full birth certificate may be necessary to prove identity and/or relationship with parents
- Proof of continuous residence in the UK since first arrival (baby book, confirmation letters from nursery, schools, GP, etc. original signed and dated)
- If child is aged 10 or over, a Police National Computer check should be requested https://www.acro.police.uk/Subject_Access_Apply_By_Post.aspx
- Medical/educational/social services details/reports of any serious medical condition(s)/special needs
- As many letters of support as possible from tutors, British friends, peers, support workers any other professionals and non-professionals involved in the child's life in the UK.
- Awards, Certificates of achievements, diplomas, photos of medals etc
- Photos covering as much as possible of the child's life since arrival in the UK, eg with school and British/settled friends/tutors/extra- curricular activities etc.
- Certified copy of any current immigration status document/biometrics or British passport(s)/registration/naturalisation certification of parent/s or legal guardian and siblings etc.

In the asylum context, Singh v Belgium finds the ECtHR holding that there might be exceptional cases when national authorities should verify documents (MIL 8.1.5.8). This may sometimes apply to nationality decision making: Kadir [2019] EWHC 1332 (Admin).

12.4.3 Acquisition by registration of children born outside the UK due to a connection with the UK – ss3(2), (4) &(5), and s4D BNA 1981

12.4.3.1 Section 3(2) BNA 1981

This section permits registration where there is a sufficiently strong link with the UK, looking back across the generations, as to make it unfair to decline to permit access to full British citizenship. The requirements, in the normal case, are as follows:

- As of 13 January 2010, the child to be registered must be under the age of 18. The previous rule until the relevant section of the BCIA 2009 came into effect was that registration had to take place within 12 months of birth or six years in exceptional circumstances.
- The child's parent has the weak form of nationality ('by descent') but their grandparent has the strong form of nationality ('otherwise than by descent').
- The child's parent has a residential link with the UK, in that they have lived here for a three year period some time prior to the birth of the child, and did not leave the UK for more than 270 days within that period (however, for a child born stateless, this requirement is waived).

12.4.3.2 Section 3(5) BNA 1981

This section permits another form of registration. This does not require the *grandparent connection* that we saw in s3(2), nor does it require the *historic* three-year stay in the UK that that section demands – however, it does require that the family including the child were in the UK *for the three years leading up to the application for registration*, and did not leave the UK for more than 270 days within that period. The application can only be made whilst the child is a minor.

> **Example**
>
> To continue with the story of the family of Chris and Clarissa, we saw earlier that Carrie was born British by descent by virtue of section 2(1) of the Act. Section 14 of the Act sets out a definition of a British citizen 'by descent' and Carrie falls within that definition.
>
> When Carrie grows up she has a child of her own, Colin, who is born in Australia. Colin is not automatically born a British citizen under the same section as Carrie, because section 2(1) states that the parent must be a British citizen 'otherwise than by descent'.
>
> However, Colin could be registered as a British citizen under section 3(2) if the proper procedures are followed, or could be registered under section 3(5) if he was later to qualify (see below).
>
> When Colin grows up, he has two children, Claude and Cedric. They have no entitlement at all to British citizenship by descent
>
> | | |
> |---|---|
> | British citizen otherwise than by descent s.1(1) | Chris |
> | British citizen by descent: s.2(1)(a) and s.14 | Carrie |
> | Eligible for registration: s.3(2) or s.3(5) | Colin |
> | Not eligible for British citizenship unless Colin registered under s.3(5) | Claude / Cedric |

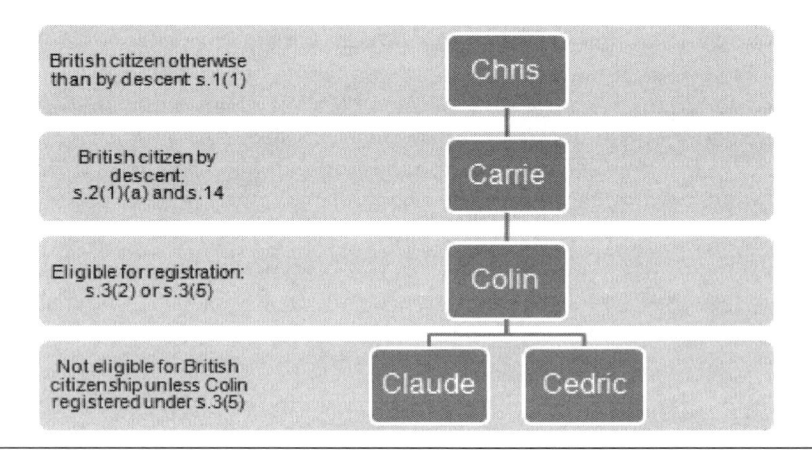

12.4.4 Acquisition by registration as an Adult – ss4(2), s4(4), ss4A-C & ss4E-I BNA 1981

Certain adults are also able or entitled to register as British citizens (useful Guidance includes *Registration as British citizen - children of British parents* and *Registration as a British overseas territories citizen and British citizen - children of BOTC parents*):

- Under s4(2), a person who is a British Overseas Territories Citizen, British National (Overseas), a British Overseas Citizen, a British Subject or a British Protected Person may register as a full British citizen if they have lived in the UK for 5 years lawfully and attained ILR (essentially as per naturalisation for British citizenship and show good character (excess absence can be condoned s4(4)(za) as can unlawful presence s4(4B))
- Under s4(4) & (5) there is a discretion to register those persons as a British citizen, even if the residence requirements are not met
- Under s4A, there is a discretion to register (as British citizens otherwise than by descent) a British Overseas Territories Citizen (refer to list of qualifying territories above) who does not have the citizenship only by a virtue of a connection with the sovereign base areas of Akrotiri and Dhekelia, who has not previously renounced citizenship

CHAPTER 12: British Nationality Law

- Under s4B, there is an entitlement to register (as British citizens by descent) BOTC, BN(O) BOC, British Subjects or BPPs who have no other nationality. The applicant must not have renounced, voluntarily relinquished or lost through action or inaction any citizenship or nationality after the relevant day (for BN(O)s 19 March 2009 and for the rest 4 July 2002)
- Under s4C, there is an entitlement to register (as British citizens by descent) those born outside the UK to British mothers before 1983. This is on Form UKM
- With effect from 13 January 2010, s4D of the BNA 1981 permits registration of certain children born outside the UK to a parent serving overseas in the UK armed forces if born from 13 January 2010 outside the UK and relevant territories, with parental consent.
- Under ss4E-I there is now the option to register for those disadvantaged by the law's pre-2006 discrimination against those born outside wedlock. This is on form UKF

The NBA 2022 amends the BNA 1981 to correct for historical inequalities in the abilities of mothers and fathers, and unmarried fathers, to transmit British nationality.

- A person who would have become a CUKC if mothers had been treated the same as fathers before 1983, and would subsequently have automatically become a British Overseas Territories Citizen, can now be registered as a British Overseas Territories Citizen: BNA 1981 s17A
- Before 1 July 2006, an unmarried father could not pass on British nationality to his children. This has previously been corrected for children of British citizens (MIL 12.3.1) but not for other British nationals. Ss. 17B-17G BNA 1981, inserted by NBA 2022 s2 now fill this lacuna for BOTCs. A person whose natural parents were unmarried when they were born, and who would have become a BOTC had their parents been married, can register for BOTC status if:
    - they have never previously been a BOTC or its predecessor status a British Dependent Territories citizen; and,
    - in cases of assisted reproduction, no other person was treated as the person's father
- BNA 1981 s4K allows those benefiting from the new anti-discrimination provisions in ss. 17A-17G to register as British citizens by descent, unless: the BOTC status derives from a connection with the Sovereign Base Areas of Akrotiri and Dhekelia; or the person has already been a British citizen. Applicants who would have been BOTCs automatically, but for the historic discrimination, do not need to pass a good character test; other applicants (who would have had to register for BOTC status) are subject to the good character test
- BNA 1981 s17 is amended by s. 5 NBA 2022 to remove the requirement for registration of a child as a BOTC by descent to be done within 12 months of birth. The application must now be made before the child turns 18, bringing s17 in line with s. 3(2) on British citizenship by descent (MIL 13.4.3.1 above
- It was held in Romein [2018] UKSC 6 that, to give effect to s4C(3A) BNA 1981, the consular registration condition in s5(1)(b) 1948 Act is to be treated as being inapplicable in cases where citizenship is claimed by descent from a mother. Now s6 NBA 2022 amends ss. 4C and 4I BNA 1981 to remove the historical registration requirement

There is also a residual discretion to register victims of historic injustice as British citizen. But unlike the other provisions, which tend to be very tightly defined to particular circumstances, this one is more general. BNA 1981 s4L, inserted by s. 8 NBA 2022, permits registration to correct for "*historical legislative unfairness*", an act/omission of a public authority, or any other "exceptional circumstances", without which the applicant would have been a British citizen (an equivalent power for BOTC status is in a new s17I BNA 1981). Previously, people in this situation would have had to rely on s. 3 BNA 1981, which was only open to applicants under 18. Registration under s. 4L is subject to the *good character* test.

BNA 1981 s4L(2) points to probable scenarios: essentially where men and women, or the children of unmarried parents or those whose mother was married to a person other than the natural father. The *Guidance* explains that there may be other cases encountered, probably involving discrimination against protected characteristics (as per the Equality Act 2010): caseworkers should refer these to the policy team.

Registration applications involve the completion of a form and payment of a fee (except UKM and UKF applications which are free). Applications for the registration of people living abroad will normally be made through a British Diplomatic Post as per the FCOwebsite. Applications for people living in the UK are made to the HO. Registration is evidenced by a certificate and the person can subsequently apply for a British passport.

If on receipt of an application the HO detect that a person does not need to register because they are already a British citizen, they will inform the applicant of this and refund the application fee. The public Citizenship Ceremony requirements apply to applicants for registration as for naturalisation but there are exemptions (see next section).

12.5 Acquisition by naturalisation as an adult – ss6(1) & 6(2)

Section 6 of the BNA 1981 deals with naturalisation, the process by which most adults will become British citizens. There are two routes for naturalisation, under s6(1) BNA 1981) or, where the applicant is the spouse of a British citizen, s6(2). The requirements for each route are then set out in Schedule 1 to the BNA 1981.

In addition to requirements as to length and continuity of residence and immigration status,

- an individual must be of good character,
- have sufficient knowledge of the English, Welsh or Scottish Gaelic language, and of life in the UK; and
- intend to make their principal home in the United Kingdom (if they are not married to a British citizen), or, if they intend to live abroad, that they work in Crown service or for a UK enterprise.

Provisions in the 2009 Act were set to change the route to naturalisation in a major way. They were enacted but never commenced, and the subsequent government scrapped them. Beware reference sources that print these provisions without clearly setting out that they are not in force.

The criteria are explained in Naturalisation as a British citizen by discretion: nationality policy guidance as well as the HO's Booklet AN and Guide AN available on the same page as application form AN.

The criteria for naturalisation are as follows:

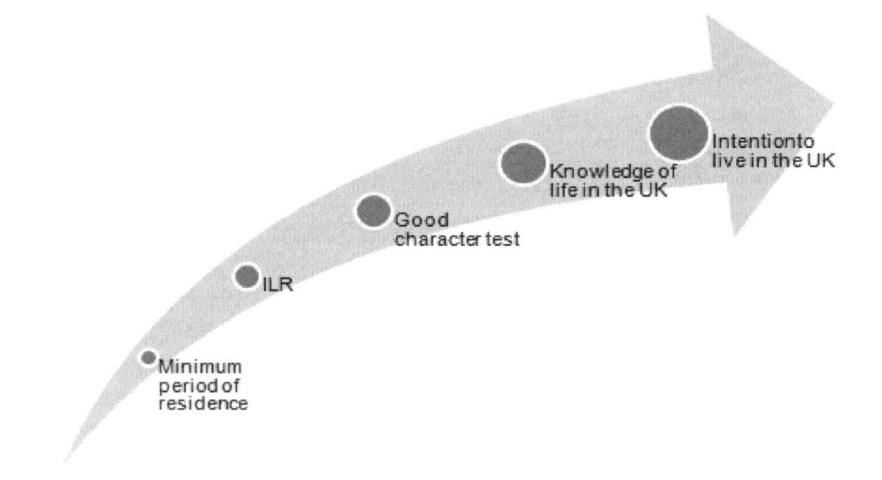

12.5.1 Period of residence

12.5.1.1 Non-spouse cases

The requirements of residence for those not applying as spouses are set out at Schedule 1 paragraph 2.

- subject to subsection (3), that he was in the United Kingdom at the beginning of the period of five years ending with the date of the application and that the number of days on which he absent from the United Kingdom in that period does not exceed 450; and
- that the number of days onwhich he was absent from the United Kingdom in the period of twelve months so ending does not exceed 90; and
- that he was not at any time in the period of twelve months so ending subject under the immigration laws to any restriction on the period for which he might remain in the United Kingdom.
- that he was not any time in the period of five years so ending in the United Kingdom in breach of the immigration laws.

The Naturalisation guidance explains that EEA permanent residence documents can only still be used post-30 June 2021 if the holder by then held a PRC card and has a pending EUSSch application.

So effectively these break down into these requirements:

- residence for the last five years without having been outside the country for more than 450 days;
- including residence for the last year without having been away for more than 90 days;
- possessing ILR or permanent residence for the year leading up to the application;
- not having been present unlawfully in the five years leading up to the application.

The residence conditions can be relaxed under HO discretion including where applicants are Crown servants; NBA 2022 amended BNA 1981 Sch 1 para 2(1) by adding (zb) and para 2(1B) potentially condoning excess absence and unlawful residence.

There is also reference in the guidance to a policy to allow applicants to "e-declare" their application where they failed to meet the requirement of presence in the UK at the start of their qualifying period. Discretion may condone excessive absences: for health problems, pandemic travel difficulties, removal pursuant to a decision that was later overtured, and wrongful refusal to permit permanent residence to be resumed. Discretion should be exercised for less than 30 days excess absence, and for absences under s6(1) of up to 900 days (540 days for s6(2) spouse cases), where the applicant has established their home, employment, family and finances in the UK, there has been 2 years residence without substantial absence before the 5-year period, and the absences are due to reasons including appointments abroad of a British citizen partner, Crown service postings, or an unavoidable consequence of the nature of the applicant's career, or exceptionally compelling reasons of an occupational or compassionate nature.

Vanriel [2021] EWHC 3415 (Admin) holds that it is discriminatory for Windrush victims to have to meet the 5 years lawfully in the UK proviso where the obstacle to so doing was wrongful denial of entry to the UK.

12.5.1.2 Spouse cases

Section 6(2) deals with applications of persons 'married to a British citizen'. The required residence period is 270 days, with the references to five years replaced by three years, in sub-paragraphs (a) and (d).

The restriction at 3(c) is lifted, so that there is no requirement to be free from immigration control (i.e. to have ILR) for 12 months prior to the date of application, with the practical consequence that a spouse can apply from the grant of ILR without waiting for a further year.

There is no requirement to make the UK their permanent home, though spouses must still meet the requirements of good character, English language proficiency, and have the requisite knowledge of life in the UK.

12.5.2 EEA nationals

There are three important considerations for EEA nationals and their family members who wish to naturalise.

Firstly, those whose country of nationality prevents straightforward acess to dual nationality (eg Austria & the Netherlands, Bulgaria, Germany and Lithuania) should carefully weigh up the pros and cons of naturalisation, given Brexit and the loss of their free movement rights which this would entail.

Secondly, as just noted, those not married to British citizens must hold a year's worth of freedom from immigration restrictions before seeking naturalisation. From 12 November 2016 require applicants relying upon an EU right of permanent residence ("PR") in the UK to apply for and be granted a PR document. That would establish that they were present without any restriction on their entitlement to be here. However, the date they acquired PR will be before, sometimes many years before, that document is issued. So a person relying on their EU right to PR needed not necessarily wait for one year from the date they are issued with that document in order to apply for citizenship. While the PR documentation would show a 'valid from' date of issue, usually after the date PR legally accrued, it is accompanied by a letter stating the date on which PR is deemed to have been acquired. EEA PR could be used as evidence of freedom from immigration restrictions only until 30 June 2021, as confirmed in the Naturalisation guidance.

Thirdly, from May 2020, the UKVI Guidance on naturalisation changed. It now raises the possibility of refusal of naturalisation to EEA nationals present with EUSS but who had not consistently exercised Treaty Rights over the previous five years. Gaps in 'qualified person' status may be treated as residence "*in breach of the immigration laws*". An example given was where those needing CSIC for lawful residence as students or self-sufficient individuals failed to obtain it; however that thinking was undermined when NHS cover was belatedly found to qualify as CSIC (MIL 11.5.4). Hence the Guidance now states that those ordinarily resident in the UK would have qualified for NHS cover and thus should not be treated as lacking CSIC; historic refusals of confirmation of lawful EEA residence should be reviewed with this in mind. This could trip the unwary: one might be granted EUSS (and thus hold ILR – the EUSSch does not require Treaty Right exercise, of course) but still be found to have been unlawfully present for failing to meet the criteria of the EEA Regs 2016 over an earlier period. Discretion to condone such failings should be exercised only for "*reasons … clearly outside the applicant's control, or if the breach was genuinely inadvertent and short*" Though there should be a full assessment of the relevant facts of the case.

12.5.3 In breach of the immigration laws

Where there are qualifying periods to be met, periods spent in the relevant territory 'in breach of the immigration laws' do not count. The meaning of 'in breach of the immigration laws' for the specific purpose of calculating residence is set out in s50A(4) of the BNA 1981.

The Nationality policy: Naturalisation as a British citizen by discretion sets out the circumstances in which one is considered to be in breach of immigration law in the qualifying period, and this, notably, includes those who have claimed asylum whilst in the UK illegally. Even if granted temporary admission or immigration bail during the consideration of their claim, the policy considers them in breach until leave to remain was granted. There is some discretion to disregard such 'unlawful residence', however, where the claim was made within one month of clandestine arrival or longer if there were 'extenuating circumstances'. Other circumstances in which unlawful residence may be disregarded include where the applicant

- was a minor at the time, or a victim of domestic violence whose abusive partner prevented a renewal of leave
- had an application invalidated but a fresh application was submitted within 28 days if before 24 November 2016
- made a late application, subsequently granted, no more than 28 days after overstaying began (14 if overstaying ended on or after 24 November 2016)

Unlawful residence during the qualifying period, unless exempt by discretion, do not count towards the qualifying period; but these, as well as other breaches of immigration law, are also taken into account in assessing 'good character'. See MIL 12.5.1 for discretion to condone unlawful presence.

12.5.4 The good character requirement

Good character will be in issue in applications to naturalise and register for those aged 10 years or over (by reason of s41A of the BNA 1981). 'Good character' is not defined in legislation and the policy is now contained in the Guidance Good character requirement. This leaves the HO with enormous discretion. It is always important to take careful instructions against the Guidance.

The good character test engages a person's behaviour before and after they arrived in the UK. It is not unusual, for instance, for a person recognised as a refugee to be refused citizenship due to events they disclosed as part of their asylum claim. This could arise from matters that would also justify exclusion from the Refugee Convention.

- SK [2012] EWCA Civ 16 holds that there is a difference between the approach to international crimes (like crimes against humanity) under refugee law and nationality law: in the former cases the SSHD bears the burden of proof, and it is an objective test, whereas under the latter the applicant bears the burden, and the test is relatively subjective, in so far as the SSHD simply has to point to good reasons for being dissatisfied re good character
- Al-Atabi [2021] EWHC 3075 (Admin) emphasises that the published guidance gives fair warning to most applicants of the possibility of refusal without an interview so long as an opportunity is given to answer the SSHD's concerns in writing
- AHN [2022] EWHC 582 (Admin) shows that consistency of decision making is important: had other members of the group said to raise a potential good character objection been granted naturalisation, the SSHD should address this in any subsequent refusals
-
- Alaian [2022] EWHC 3012 (Admin) holds that the HO is entitled to refuse citizenship on bad character grounds evincing lack of commitment to British values as where there has been support for an organisation falling short of close association with crimes against humanity

Ameen [2023] ScotCS CSOH 38 notes the HO has a discretion to disregard overstaying as relevant to good character whether or not an applicant was at fault.

All criminal convictions, however minor, including spent convictions, must be declared (immigration and nationality decisions being exempted from section 4 of the Rehabilitation of Offenders Act 1974).

For applications from 31 July 2023 the criminality thresholds found in Part 9 of the IRs will apply (MIL 2.3.5.3).

Broadly, convictions for applications made before 31 July 2023 will be dealt with as below:

Sentence	Impact on Nationality applications
4 years or more imprisonment	Application will normally be refused, regardless of when the conviction occurred.
Between 12 months and 4 years imprisonment	Application will normally be refused unless 15 years have passed since the end of the sentence.
Up to 12 months imprisonment	Applications will normally be refused unless 10 years have passed since the end of the sentence.
A non-custodial offence or other out of court disposal that is recorded on a person's criminal record	Applications will normally be refused if the conviction occurred in the last 3 years.

The guidance explains that some minor convictions may be disregarded, and useful advice is given as to the effect of receiving a fixed penalty and similar notices (including under the coronavirus Regs) which 'do not form part of a person's criminal record as there is no admission of guilt'. It also clarifies that the 'end of the sentence' is not the release date but the end of the sentence imposed, and that a suspended prison sentence is treated to fall within row 4 of the table above. There is a regime for Exceptional grants (eg where foreign convictions are not for matters deemed criminal in the UK, for offences committed over 40 years ago for the over-60s, or NHS debts incurred due to medical treatment for life-threatening conditions, or for offences a while back since when having actively engaged with youth and mental health charities and promoting the reduction of youth crime).

Checks are made on financial impropriety. A bankrupt will, where there has been fraud or they were discharged less than 10 years ago, be of insufficiently good character.

The person's immigration history will also be considered. In a major amendment to the good character guidance introduced in December 2014 and enforced until 28 June 2022, citizenship was normally refused *'if within the 10 years preceding the application the person has not been compliant with immigration requirements'*. All breaches will be taken into account, including illegal entry, failure to report, breach of conditions, overstaying, and failure to report. Al-Enein [2019] EWCA Civ 2024 upheld the lawfulness of this requirement. From 28 June 2022 possessing ILR was sufficient to satisfy the lawful residence criteria without further enquiry, presuming no further good character issues have arisen including other breaches of immigration law.

When applications for naturalisation are being made in the knowledge that there is some immigration history issue to be confronted, well reasoned representations backed by cogent evidence will still need to be carefully considered by decision makers. That is a general principle of public law. Decision makers have to be *responsive* to a reasoned case put to them. And the Guidance itself indicates that where non-compliance is the only reason for refusal, it can be disregarded where it was not the applicant's fault.

The good character requirement has been extended to include children aged 10 and over (who will be applying to register rather than naturalise). Between 13 July 2017 and 30 August 2018 the HO received 20,068 applications from 10-17 year olds, 28 of these were refused on good character grounds. A report by the ICI into the good character requirement for under 18s may assist in preparing a case with criminal conditions or cautions.

For further reading on this controversial issue, PRCBC on 20 September 2018 published a SLF-funded legal opinion by Ronan Toal, on the application of this requirement to children.

We addressed unlawful residence for EEA nationals above (MIL 12.5.2). Rose [2022] EWCA Civ 1068 examines the application of the "good character" requirement in relation to Windrush victims. There was no direct connection between good character and long residence and integration. Accordingly it was wrong to suggest that the Windrush policy of making allowances for the latter could be relevant to the former. Dispensing with good character requirements was a pure policy matter with which the court should be very slow to interfere.

12.5.5 Sufficient knowledge of language and life in the UK

BNA 1981 Sch requires all applicants for naturalisation to show sufficient knowledge of English, Welsh or Scottish Gaelic, and 'sufficient knowledge about life in the UK'.

The British Nationality (General) (Amendment) Regulations 2013 provide that the language and life in the UK tests are met in pretty much the same way as under Appendix KoLL for a person applying for settlement. Where the Appendix KoLL provisions have been met, an applicant for naturalisation will not have to meet them again. If they have not, guidance about English for citizenship is available on this page.

To pass the English language requirement, applicants will need to, either, come from an English speaking country listed in Schedule 2A to the Regulations, or have a degree taught in English, or pass a test specified in Schedule 2A (excluding those provided by the Educational Testing Service). For the life in the UK element, the applicant must have passed the Life in the UK test.

The HO possesses a discretion to waive the language requirement where it would be unreasonable to expect the applicant to fulfil it because of age or physical or mental condition. The language requirement will normally be waived where the applicant is aged 65 or over.

The grounds for exemption of younger people need to be compelling, such as where the applicant:

- is suffering from a long-term illness or disability which severely restricts mobility and ability to attend language classes; or
- suffers from a speech impediment which limits ability to converse in the relevant language; or
- has a mental impairment which means that they are unable to learn another language.

12.5.6 Intention to live in the UK

If a person is abroad or about to go abroad it may be important to explain this. For example, caring for a person overseas who is ill or dying is likely to be a temporary absence and should not be treated as evidence that a person has no intention to live in the UK. See generally the Naturalisation nationality policy guidance.

12.5.7 Citizenship ceremonies

BNA 1981 s42 to 42B and Schedule 5 provides that anyone over the age of 18 who acquires British citizenship, whether by registration or naturalisation, must do so at a public ceremony and is required to take the Oath of Allegiance (there is an affirmation to be used by people of different religions and of none) and now a new pledge as set out in these provisions. Section 6 of the *Become a British citizen* guidance has further details. Ceremonies are normally held in groups, although arrangements can be made (at a price) to have individual ceremonies. People can invite guests. A fee is payable.

Some people are exempted from the requirement by Section 42(2) of the 1981 Act. These are:

- those not of full age; or
- those who are already:
    - British citizens; or
    - British Overseas Territories Citizens; or
    - British Nationals (Overseas); or
    - British Overseas citizens; or
    - British Subjects under the 1981 Act; or
    - citizens of any country of which Her Majesty is Queen (Antigua and Barbuda, Australia, the Bahamas, Barbados, Belize, Canada, Grenada, Jamaica, New Zealand, Papua New Guinea, St Christopher and Nevis, St Lucia, St Vincent and the Grenadines, Solomon Islands and Tuvalu).

Where an applicant is required to take an oath of allegiance they must normally do so within the time limit of three months prescribed by the British Nationality (General) Regulations 1982 (or the British Nationality (General) Regulations 2003, as appropriate). Otherwise the applicant cannot be registered or naturalised unless the SSHD decides to extend the period.

Notification letters will advise the applicant to contact the local authority to arrange a ceremony, and online contact details for this purpose are made available via this gov.uk page. The HO will also notify the local authority.

If a person does not attend a citizenship ceremony within the time limit permitted, the HO should notify them that it will not be possible to become a British citizen because the Home Secretary is not able to register or naturalise a person who has not attended a ceremony and taken an oath/pledge. If the applicant still wishes to become a British citizen, and had an entitlement at the date of application, a certificate may be issued at any time on the basis of the original application on payment of the balance of fee and attending a citizenship ceremony and making an oath/pledge. In all other cases, the applicant will need to re-apply under an appropriate provision of the legislation.

In exceptional circumstances an exemption may be made in respect of any or all of the following:

- the requirement to attend a citizenship ceremony
- the requirement to make an oath of allegiance and pledge
- the time limit for attending a ceremony

12.6 Challenging nationality decisions

There are no appeals against refusal to grant nationality (contrast deprivation of nationality, where there is ' right of appeal, discussed below). A review of a decision can be requested on Form NR.

Page 5 of that form states:

> We may reopen applications where:-
>
> - we have not used the correct requirements or criteria to decide the application
> - we refused your application for lack of a response to enquiries when a response had been received but not linked with the application
> - we decided your application without allowing sufficient time for a response or completion of enquiries
> - we refused your application on character grounds due to a criminal conviction which was either later quashed on appeal or involved a case of mistaken identity (i.e. you were not the person convicted of the offence)
> - we have failed to take account of relevant documents or information in our possession
>
> This is not an exhaustive list.

Note the exceptional cases when the HO may have a duty to verify an applicants documents (Kadir [2019] EWHC 1332 (Admin)).
The fee at the time of writing is £372 - check here.

If a nationality review is unsuccessful, the only remedy is JR (MIL 14.8). Nationality JRs are brought in the High Court.

- Where nationality is refused in circumstances where a person's entitlement to British citizenship *is a question of right as opposed to discretion* (i.e. in the cases set out above where nationality is acquired by operation of law or non-discretionary registration), it is for the court to determine the question for itself: i.e. even though proceedings are by way of JR, they will effectively have the character of an independent appeal on the merits of the case with the court looking at up-to-date evidence for itself, and then making a declaration that the individual should be granted nationality if appropriate. See generally Harrison [2003] EWCA Civ 432.
- When determining nationality, Tariq [2021] EWCA Civ 378 emphasises that the question of a person's nationality is a *de jure* matter, *i.e.* to be determined by reference to the actual law of the state on the basis of expert evidence, not what agencies of the state may assert about that person's nationality. So simply obtaining a letter from the authorities abroad cannot necessarily be relied on – particularly if any assertions therein do not fit with an objective and evidenced legal analysis of the relevant provisions.
- GA & Ors [2021] EWHC 868 (Admin) notes that the weight to be given the HO Country Profile addressing matters of nationality law will depend on a number of factors, including: (i) whether the author(s) have expertise in the country or region concerned; (ii) the degree of specificity of the information reported; (iii) whether references are given for the sources of the information reported; and (iv) how regularly the document is updated or checked for accuracy.

Huson [2021] EWHC 885 (Admin) acknowledges that paternity can be established by other means than DNA evidence, and compelling circumstantial evidence, whilst not as conclusive as DNA evidence, would achieve this end. It was important for a decision maker to engage with any such alternative evidence.

JR of discretionary refusals such as naturalisation, however, is rather more limited. The BNA 1981 at s44 of the BNA 1981 has been amended to remove the original power to refuse naturalisation without providing reasons. In practice, however, the High Court will generally defer to the very wide discretion that the HO has to refuse applications on good character grounds and there is no requirement that she fully discloses the basis of the reasons in public policy cases.

12.7 Stopping being British

The different ways in which a person can stop being a British national or citizen fall into three categories:

- Loss
- Renunciation
- Deprivation

12.7.1 Loss of British nationality

British citizens cannot simply lose their nationality. However, as described above, when looking at the history of British nationality law, other categories of British national have lost their status at different points in the history of nationality law. To this must be added those who have lost rights and entitlements previously attendant on their status (as for example with the abolition of special voucher quota schemes). As noted above, British citizens by descent do not pass on their nationality to their children born outside the UK. These topics are beyond the scope of MIL presently.

Other forms of British national can still lose their British nationality. A British Subject who gains any other citizenship or nationality after 1 January 1983 will no longer be a British Subject unless they used to be a citizen of Eire and have made a claim to remain a British Subject under section 2 of the British Nationality Act 1948 or under the 1981 Act. Similarly, a British Protected Person will no longer be a British Protected Person on acquiring any other nationality or citizenship.

12.7.2 Renunciation of British nationality

A person can renounce their form of British nationality. People are likely to want to renounce British nationality if they wish to become or remain the national of a country that does not allow them to hold another nationality.

The requirements are that a British citizen, British Overseas Territories Citizen (see note below), British Overseas Citizen, British Subject, British National (Overseas) or British Protected Person may renounce that nationality if:

- they have a nationality other than the one it is sought to renounce; or
- can show that they will get another citizenship or nationality; and
- is over 18 (or under 18 but have been married); and
- is of full capacity (i.e. not of unsound mind).

A declaration of renunciation must be completed. The renunciation date is when it is registered. But if no other citizenship is obtained within six months, the declaration does not take effect and the person is considered to have kept their British nationality. Renunciation does not necessarily mean the individual reverts to any prior immigration status. So if possible an ILR application on long residence grounds may be advisable, if available (MIL 5.2).

If a person renounced their British citizenship or British overseas territories citizenship to keep or get another citizenship, they have a right to register and resume the citizenship they renounced: but only once. Any subsequent attempt to resume following a second registration will be at the SSHD's discretion (for British citizenship) or the Governor of a British overseas territory (for British overseas territories citizenship).

NIA 2002 s5 amended the BNA 1981 to give men the (superior) rights previously enjoyed only by women, who had renounced their UK and colonies citizenship before 1983 to qualify for registration on the basis of a connection with the UK or a British Overseas Territory by marriage. It is still necessary to meet all the qualifying requirements.

Other forms of British nationality cannot be resumed following renunciation.

12.7.3 Deprivation of nationality and declarations of nullity

12.7.3.1 Deprivation of nationality

Powers to deprive people of their citizenship are set out under the Section 40 and 40A of the BNA 1981 as amended. The Free Movement website calculated there to have been some 1,007 deprivation decisions from 2006-2021.

There are powers to deprive people of the different forms of British nationality on the following grounds:

- If the SSHD is satisfied that deprivation is conducive to the public good: s40(2).
  - This power may not be exercised if to do so would leave the individual stateless (s40(4))
  - Though there is a proviso to statelessness protection: it does not apply where citizenship resulted from naturalisation, the individual 'has conducted him or herself in a manner which is seriously prejudicial to the vital interests of the United Kingdom' and there are 'reasonable grounds for believing that the person is able, under the law of a country or territory outside the United Kingdom, to become a national of such a country or territory' (s40(4A))
- If the SSHD is satisfied that nationality obtained by registration or naturalisation was in fact obtained by fraud, false representation or concealment of a material fact (there is no protection here in respect of statelessness) (s40(3))

BNA s40A gives a right of appeal against deprivation of nationality.

- This is to the FTTIAC or to the Special Immigration Appeals Commission (SIAC).
- The HO must notify a person of the intention to deprive them of their nationality and the deprivationwill not take effect until any appeal has been finally determined (s40A(6)) or the time for appealing has expired.

The British Nationality (General) Regulations 2003 permit service to file.

- D4 [2021] EWHC 2179 (Admin) finds that Parliament intended an unqualified requirement to give written notice before making an order. So, if for whatever reason notice cannot be given, the order cannot be made; this was confirmed on appeal in D4 [2022] EWCA Civ 33
- Parliament has since decided deprivation may proceed without notice in some circumstances where it is impractical or contrary to public policy (s10 NBA 2022 commenced 10 May 2023)
- From 28 April 2022, a failure to notify a person of deprivation before that date does not invalidate deprivation orders made before that date (s10(6)-(7) NBA 2022) – the Guidance *Deprivation of British citizenship* summarises the position
- Where appeal lies to SIAC in national security cases, there is now a special procedure allowing for judicial oversight (NBA 2022 Sch 2): where the SSHD proposes to make a conducive grounds deprivation order without notice, she should apply to the SIAC within 7 days which will consider whether the SSHD's view that a condition in s40(5A) BNA 1981 said to justify not giving notice (national security, investigation/prosecution of organised/serious crime, risks to the safety of any person, & the relationship between the UK and another country) are met is '*obviously flawed*'

- C12 (SIAC; 16 September 2022) suggests that the pre-existing regime was rather fragile anyway, given it permitted service on one's last known address: beyond that there was no duty on the SSHD to attempt to locate someone in order to effect service of the deprivation notice

In Deliallisi [2013] UKUT 439 and Hysaj [2020] UKUT 128 the UT decided that a person deprived of citizenship does not automatically revert to having ILR (even if that was their status before becoming a British citizen). E3 [2022] EWHC 1133 (Admin) (upheld in E3 [2023] EWCA Civ 26) holds that the legal effect of withdrawing a deprivation of citizenship decision is *prospective* only: it does not alter the legal approach to past events. If it *did* have retrospective effect, there would be an argument that a child born between the deprivation decision's making and its subsequent withdrawal would retrospectively acquire British citizenship, based on their parent's British citizenship at the time of their birth. However the ruling in E3 rules this out: the statutory scheme is that one holds citizenship once one fulfils the relevant criteria but not during any period of extant deprivation order.

The precise scope of deprivation appeals has been debated for some time. The wording of section 40 of the BNA 1981 refers to the Secretary of State being 'satisfied' that dishonesty was used.

In Begum [2021] UKSC 7 the Supreme Court held that an appeal must satisfy the procedural requirements of the ECHR. Appellants must be able to challenge the human rights compliance of a revocation. However, when other grounds of appeal are considered, the statutory framework leaves some matters to the SSHD. This was certainly the case where the question was whether citizenship deprivation may be conducive to the public good.

This is the current state of the law on nationality deprivation:

- Re arguments as to '*conducive to the public good*', whilst Begum was a national security case, it is difficult to see that different considerations would arise in the FTT given that both tribunals are looking at the same provision, s40(2), where the words "*the Secretary of State is satisfied*" are found. The Supreme Court's reasoning would also seem to apply to s40(3) appeals, given the language used there is the same. All this suggests that nationality deprivation appeals will have more of a feel of public law JR proceedings than merits appeals going forwards. The focus will thus be on arguments such as whether there was evidence to support the SSHD's conclusions and whether relevant factors were taken into account, rather than upon the actual merits of the case.
- How should ECHR considerations apply? The core question that judges will examine will be the role that dishonesty originally played: this in itself raises no questions of family and private life whatsoever. If an Appellant establishes they did not act dishonestly, the appeal will presumably succeed. But where there has been dishonesty, it will be necessary to determine where the *reasonably foreseeable consequence of deprivation* would violate the Human Rights Act 1998. This is described in decisions such as Aziz [2018] EWCA Civ 1884 as a *proleptic* assessment: ie an exercise which anticipates future events. The stronger the person's UK connections (and thus their ECHR claim against removal), the less likely it is that they will face expulsion. If expulsion is unlikely then there is no real need for the FTT to have to consider its possibility.
- In Ciceri [2021] UKUT 238 (IAC) the UT looks at the proper approach in the light of Begum.

    - Presumably if a public law error is identified the appeal would need to be allowed. That would leave the matter outstanding before the SSHD to reconsider
    - If no public law error is identified, then it would be necessary to evaluate whether the decision breached the Appellant's Convention rights – usually private and family life. That decision would be made just as in any other immigration appeal, the judge making up their own mind on the issue having regard to all the available evidence including material that might not have been before the decision maker
    - If the FTT found that the SSHD's conclusion that fraud had been committed was lawful then that factor would necessarily weigh heavily on the public interest side of the scales

- Berdica [2022] UKUT 276 (IAC) finds that a judge should review the SSHD's decision as to dishonesty in acquiring nationality on a public law basis, in so far as the evidence before the FTT is the same as that before the original decision maker. Where there is further evidence post-dating the SSHD's decision, the question would be whether the HO could now take the same view of the case, given that material. Any assessment on ECHR grounds should however be a full merits review. It seems that post-decision evidence is admissible, notwithstanding the "JR" feel to the jurisdiction, both for public law and human rights arguments

- So far we have concentrated on *jurisdiction* on appeal. But what of the relevant factors to be balanced? Hysaj [2020] UKUT 128 reviews a number of recurring issues in these appeals:
    - Even 11 years of delay whilst the SSHD pursued clarification of the right legal approach was not unreasonable. Pursuing a legal challenge was not the same as running a dysfunctional system (Ciceri agrees). Only real prejudice would lead to that result.
    - The policy position (in place until 20 August 2014) not to initiate deprivation proceedings for those "resident in the United Kingdom for more than 14 years" could be helpful only to those whose decision making ended before its withdrawal, and even then it was subject to a "normally" proviso and to public interest considerations. Limbo between deprivation of citizenship and a decision on issuing expulsion proceedings was not significant, given that an opportunity would be given to make representations in response to a notice of an intention to deport, which would be considered within 6 weeks of receipt. If deportation did not proceed, then a short period of leave to remain would be granted. Whilst the individual would enter the hostile environment with its attendant disadvantages (MIL 1.3.6), one would need to assess whether their partner would be able to work and whether the family could rely on welfare safety net payments such as s17 of the Childrens Act 1989 or a lifting of No Recourse to Public Funds restrictions.
- Laci [2021] EWCA Civ 769 identifies relevant factors. Normally one would not expect an appeal to succeed where nationality had been acquired by fraud, unless the individual was somehow put into a *worse* position than they would otherwise have been in without the fraud: for example because they would now be stateless. Relevant considerations included the SSHD's delay in taking firm action having initiated the process in the first place, exposure to the hostile environment during a "limbo" period between losing an appeal and a final decision on granting further leave including the potentially serious effect of job loss, and mitigating circumstances, such as having originally been under the influence of an agent and then finding it difficult to extricate oneself from the consequences. The fact that the information leading to the SSHD becoming aware of the original fraud came from the Appellant themselves in the course of other dealings with the SSHD might deserve some very limited weight.
- Matusha [2021] UKUT 175 (IAC) involved a British citizen who had made an asylum claim based on false details – but that claim had failed and ILR had been granted under the Legacy programme; naturalisation followed. The UT concluded that a repeated and longstanding deception re nationality and age would have been material to a Legacy assessment had the SSHD been aware of it at the time given the need for caseworkers to take account of all relevant considerations. Thus the deception was directly linked to the grant of Legacy leave and in turn on the ILR which had laid the ground for the naturalisation application.
- P3 [2021] EWCA Civ 1642 explains that whilst the courts would need to defer to the SSHD on matters of high policy, at a granular level (including determining an individual's particular activities) it would be necessary to carefully scrutinise the evidence. The appropriate course for a person outside the UK at the time a nationality deprivation decision was made against them was to seek entry clearance to return here to fight the nationality appeal, and appeal against any resulting refusal. The SIAC would have to consider the extent to which ECHR Art 8 rights could be relied on in both appeals.
- Muslija [2022] UKUT 337 (IAC) finds it very hard to imagine circumstances where a "*proleptic*" analysis (into the hypothetical possibility of removal) could be appropriate. An example might be where the SSHD's only argument for deprivation was that removal was appropriate and "*places no broader reliance on ensuring that the individual concerned ought not to be allowed to enjoy the benefits of British citizenship generally*". Even lengthy periods of limbo were unlikely to involve hardship such as to tip the balance in the appellant's favour: as a factor alone, unless it would result in destitution rather than stressfulness, "it could not possibly tip the balance in the appellant's favour" and its precise length was unlikely to matter.
- Chimi [2023] UKUT 115 (IAC) looks at these appeals again:
    - Firstly it confirms, notwithstanding some debate due to decisionsof SIAC and the higher courts, that whether or not a fraud has been committed must be assessed by public law standards rather than being a merits appeal. So the appeal will turn on whether the HO

CHAPTER 12: British Nationality Law

took into account relevant evidence and considerations and made appropriate enquiries into the background facts. The FTT cannot make up its own mind
- Secondly, this was also the approach to take when assessing whether the HO had, if the fraud allegation was upheld, lawfully considered its discretion to proceed with deprivation notwithstanding the fraud
- Thirdly post-decision evidence was only admissible to show that an error of law had been committed. For example that had adequate enquiries been made or a fair procedure adopted, more evidence would have been forthcoming. It could not be admitted in the same way as in statutory appeals generally
- Allowing an appeal in these circumstances meant that the decision would return to the HO to be retaken
- Absent any public law error re dishonesty or discretion, the FTT could consider post-decision evidence when considering the human rights ground of appeal
- Shyti [2023] EWCA Civ 770 §91 acknowledges that the arguments against the Chimi position (ie that questions of fraud must be assessed by public law standards rather than on their merits) are rather strong. However the CoA decides not to address the issue given it was not essential to the matters before it.
- Dishonesty will not always mandate deprivation of citizenship. The Guidance in *Chapter 55: Deprivation and Nullity of British citizenship* explains that it must be material. The more promising arguments, both before and since Begum, would seem to be those based on failing to follow the Chapter 55 policy criteria:
  - Where the fraud does not bear on the reasons for naturalisation 55.7.4: "*where a person acquires ILR under a concession (e.g. the family ILR concession) the fact that we could show the person had previously lied about their asylum claim may be irrelevant*" (cf Matusha above) – or
    innocent use of a different name (55.7.4)
  - Fraud post-dating the naturalisation application (55.7.5): Walile [2022] UKUT 17 (IAC) notes that the opening words "*In general*" before the phrase "*Where fraud postdates the application for British citizenship it will not be appropriate to pursue deprivation actio* could justify deprivation in the light of very serious cases, observing that the application form did stress a continuing obligation to disclose relevant matters and that it was dishonest not to do so
  - Being a minor at the time of the citizenship application or the date of acquiring ILR subject to overriding public interest considerations (55.7.5) or at the date of the fraud leading to the DLR which founded subsequent ILR (55.7.8.2)
  - An absence of intention to deceive (55.7.7.1)
  - Applying the residual test of whether deprivation was "a balanced and reasonable step to take" (55.7.10.1) and usually not taking account of available evidence disregarded at the application date (55.7.10.2).
  - Also mitigating factors must be considered: relevant professionally-evidenced physical or mental impairment, or coercion bearing on ability to make independent decisions (55.7.11.3).

There is also Guidance *Deprivation of British citizenship*. This notes that
- Disadvantages such as losing one's job and access to benefits do not suffice to prevent deprivation proceeding
- If a person is abroad then any risks of inhuman and degrading treatment or threats to the right to life must be considered due to leaving them stranded abroad
- Involvement in serious organised crime re high harm offences, particularly those involving violent or sexual crime, human trafficking or facilitation of illegal immigration, money laundering or serious financial crime, organised drug importation and child sexual exploitation, may attract deprivation action
- False representations are those which are deliberately dishonestly made, and concealment of material facts requires deliberate operative steps, not simply innocent mistake; in either case having a direct bearing on the application. Innocent use of an alternative name, other than to mask issues relevant to criminality or character is an example of conduct that should not be treated as dishonest. Dishonest conduct would include giving false details in asylum or immigration applications which led to a grant of status, or failing to disclose a marriage being

invalid or void, or failing to reveal relevant information re dishonesty in immigration applications in the last decade
- An investigation letter should give 21 days for the recipient to make representations, with extension requests for up to 3 months
- Notice of the decision with full reasons, and appeal rights, should be appropriately served – including where notice could not originally be given because the individual was not in contact with the HO

The HO has recognised the problems to which revoking the nationality of a British citizen who is presently abroad might contribute. A self-made limitation on the exercise of deprivation powers aims to cater for this situation. In Begum [2021] UKSC 7 the SSHD's human rights stance in nationality deprivation cases was usefully summarised. The practice was not to deprive individuals of British citizenship when they are not within the UK's jurisdiction for ECHR purposes if the SSHD is satisfied that doing so would expose those individuals to a real risk of treatment which would constitute a breach of article 2 or 3 if they were within the UK's jurisdiction and those articles were engaged.

Passport issue/withdrawal versus nationality deprivation

As noted in Gjini [2021] EWHC 1677 (Admin), possession of a passport helps in establishing immigration status, which in turn facilitates the exercise of basic rights within the UK (under the so-called "Compliant Environment") including, the right to work, the right to rent, the ability to travel, the right to hold a bank account and the right to hold a driving licence, and absent a passport one might have no alternative means of evidencing his entitlement to rights in the UK, bearing in mind that UKVI Guidance indicated circumstances where one must rely upon certain key documentation to establish lawful residence.

Passports are issued under the Royal Prerogative (XH and AI [2017] EWCA Civ 41) and so the SSHD has significant discretion when making decisions (see eg TS [2022] NIQB 1 re the likely need for an interview). The Written statement to Parliament on *The issuing, withdrawal or refusal of passports* explains that decisions must be necessary and proportionate, the reasons should be conveyed subject to the case's individual circumstances, operational responsibility for passport issue/refusal is a matter for the Identity and Passport Service, and the key criteria are establishing British nationality, identity, and the absence of any other reasons for refusal: particular attention is given to any question of fraud.

An increasingly important issue in deprivation cases is the obligation to issue a passport. Passport issue is dealt with by HM Passport Office whereas nationality decisions are taken by UKVI. Both bodies are parts of the HO. The Passport Office is especially concerned with accurate identification of British passport holders. In what circumstances can passport facilities be withheld where nationality is disputed?

In Xhelilaj [2021] EWHC 408 (Admin) the Court finds that there are different approaches to be taken to decisions on nationality and passport issue. The decision of William [2020] EWHC 3499 (Admin) is on similar lines.

- In a nationality deprivation case, the burden of proof is on the SSHD; whereas the burden of proof is on the applicant in a passport issue case.
- The Chapter 55 policy on Deprivation and Nullity of British Citizenship showed that even where fraud, false representation or concealment of material facts is established, the SSHD will not necessarily take citizenship away, for example where mitigating circumstances or evidential difficulties in establishing a case were in play. This was relevant here, as nationality deprivation had not proceeded.
- Nevertheless, decisions to remove citizenship and withhold a passport were distinct and different in nature. The SSHD could still challenge a person's identity whether or not nationality deprivation was proceeding.
- The court would need to determine these issues for itself. Relevant considerations would be the failure of the applicant to provide a birth certificate, enlist the assistance of their national authorities or provide direct evidence for himself.

Gjini [2021] EWHC 1677 (Admin) looked at the situation where identity was *not* disputed. Enquiries showed that HMPO was able to issue a British passport to individuals whose details did not match those on their naturalisation certificate, eg following name changes. A mismatch between the details on the naturalisation certificate and a person's true details did not call into question a person's identity where identity was not otherwise in dispute – as where the fact of past dishonesty as to identity had now been admitted and the true identity verified had been verified by the SSHD. The "Changes to dates of birth" policy required the SSHD to update her records once she was satisfied of the Claimant's correct identity. Passport refusal because of historic deception would not necessarily be justified on public interest grounds given that was not one of the well-defined circumstances in the policy. An FTT appeal was not an adequate alternative remedy. Nor was the potential availability of their other national passport for dual nationals given that a British citizen's non-British passport could not be endorsed as belonging to a person subject to immigration control which would make travel impractical absent an undertaking from the SSHD to grant an emergency travel document.

The Guidance *Nationality policy – identity* addresses the SSHD's approach to identity and deprivation. HMPO will refer cases to the Status Review Unit where false information re identity comes to light, to consider whether deprivation or nullity action is appropriate. Whilst the person in question remains a British citizen, passport applications will be refused in the meantime if the individual has not provided reliable information as to their true identity. They should do so via a fee-paid application for a corrected naturalisation/registration certificate.

12.7.3.2 Declarations of nullity

The HO sometimes comes across information indicating that a person's route to British citizenship included deception. For example refugee status may have been granted based on a claim that was deceitful as to a person's nationality or some other key feature of their case. For a time the SSHD took the view that deceit as to one's nationality or other key bio-data was so fundamental that it voided the grant of citizenship. So there was no need to *deprive* them of citizenship: they simply didn't hold it in the first place. This thinking was very important, as the SSHD refused to acknowledge a right of appeal, leaving the only remedy as JR.

Hysaj [2017] UKSC 82 noted the SSHD's acceptance that it would be relatively rare for there to be circumstances where citizenship should be treated as a nullity rather than taking the deprivation route. Save for cases of outright impersonation of another individual, it will normally be appropriate to make a decision *depriving* them of their nationality rather than declaring that their nationality was *null and void from the outset*. Accordingly they can appeal to the FTT under section 40A of the BNA 1981.

The Guidance *Nullity of British citizenship* explains that nullity ensues where a person adopts the identity of a real person whose characteristics would permit a successful citizenship application. It does not result where an application is pursued in a false identity. Nor does it apply where '*X adopts the identity of Y, where Y is a real person, and in adopting the identity of Y, X acquires the characteristics required for citizenship.*' In short the test is whether there has been '*wholesale impersonation of another real person or if there are merely fictitious elements of the identity*'. A purported citizenship grant to someone who was already a British citizen would also be void. Children of individuals whose British citizen is a nullity may find their own citizenship at risk, though if born abroad only if they too became British in the identity of another real person, not where they registered in their own identity. The best interests of the child will have to be considered before making nullity decisions. The *No Time Limit* (NTL) Guidance applications for a biometric residence document for those with ILR, was updated in August 2018 with the following paragraph, which suggests that an NTL application may assist in cases of nullity:

> Where British citizenship has been declared a nullity, the applicant will revert back to their status at the time of the purported grant of citizenship. In the majority of cases, this will be indefinite leave to enter or remain. When considering an application for an NTL BRP, you must check the case information database (CID) to confirm whether:
>
> - the applicant has acquired British citizenship which has since been declared a nullity
> - the reasons for the nullity

Where a person has had their citizenship declared a nullity because they had either assumed the identity of another person or created a new identity, this may mean that they never had indefinite leave in the first place.

Where a client or their family member upon whose status the nullified British citizenship depended, may fall within the Windrush-type of cases, it may make sense to first contact the Windrush taskforce, Freephone: 0800 678 1925 Monday to Friday 9am to 5pm, Saturday and Sunday 10am to 3pm, Email: commonwealthtaskforce@homeoffice.gsi.gov.uk, as this may result in resolution of the situation for no fee.

CHAPTER 13: Enforcement; Detention, Removal and Deportation

In this chapter we deal with the hard edge of immigration control: detention, the circumstances in which people are removed from the United Kingdom, via administrative removal (for those who require leave but do not have it) and deportation (for those whose removal is conducive to the public good), including appeals against deportation.

The HO has over time used myriad forms to notify migrants of their liability to detention and expulsion: there is a useful list in the Guidance *Reporting and Offender Management Guidance* at the heading Decision notices.

13.1 Detention

Note that many of the issues dealt with in this chapter are addressed in some very useful Factsheets from the charity Bail for Immigration Detainees (BiD), particularly designed for those without legal representation. Despite the criticisms of the detention regime mentioned below, there are *media reports* of a very significant increase in the detention estate including 1,000 more beds at Campsfield and Haslar by the end of 2023.

13.1.1 Power to detain

There are four circumstances in which a person may be detained for immigration purposes, found in Schedules 2 and 3 of the IA 1971 (as amended):

- when they are being examined as to their suitability for entry;
- pending their removal;
- pending deportation; and
- as members of the crew of ships or aircraft.

The power to detain originated with the powers to remove a person under the 1971 Act. The 1971 Act essentially allows the HO either to let people enjoy their liberty into the UK, subject to conditions, or to detain them. For many years the former power was exercised by granting *Temporary Admission*. Temporary admission has now been replaced by the harsher sounding regime of Immigration Bail. Traditionally, bail was a term reserved for the grant of liberty subject to conditions, and was usually granted by the Tribunal, though a Chief Immigration Officer could also grant bail.

The NIAA 2002 extended the power to detain to include the situation where the HO is deciding whether to remove a person (s62).

A person will remain *liable to detention* even if they cannot currently be detained because they cannot be removed i.e. due to legal impediments arising out of international agreement, or practical difficulties or demands on administrative resources which impede or delay a decision to remove (s67). This is to enable the HO to keep a person on TA (now immigration bail) indefinitely, despite their irremovability. The *UKVI country returns guide* sets out documentation procedures by country, a relevant factor in relation to removability.

Legal aid remains available for detainees seeking advice and representation in regard to their detention (e.g. for applications for immigration bail), and for JRs of the legality of detention. It may not be available for the underlying immigration case of the detainee (unless they are seeking asylum, or are a victim of trafficking, or have been granted 'Exceptional Case Funding' for an Article 8 case).

Detainees in IRCs who volunteer for work are paid. However, this is at a rather low rate (£1 an hour), though not as low as in prisons. This was challenged in *Badmus* [2020] EWCA Civ 657 as potentially exploitative as it might lead the IRCs to try and meet some of their contractual obligations using cheap labour However the Court of Appeal found no evidence of exploitation, noting that in any event the decision to work was voluntary.

13.1.1.1 Detention under the IMA 2023

When the s2 regime commences, immigration officers will have the power to detain individuals potentially subject to the s2 regime at all times in the decision making process (as to whether the conditions are met, whether the duty applies, pending removal or when considering whether to grant LTE/LTR) (IA 1971 para 16(2C). There will be protection for pregnant women: no more than 72 hours' detention absent personal Ministerial authorisation for up to a week (para 16(2D)); and unaccompanied children will be detainable only pursuant to Regs (2F-2G). The same regime applies re the SSHD's detention powers pending removal from the UK (NIAA 2002 s62(2A)-(2M)).

There are duties on carriers such as ships' captains to prevent disembarkation before the removal directions have been fulfilled and to detain individuals on board, which is deemed to be legal custody (s8(11-13)).

13.1.2 Detention processes

Much of HO detention policy long resided in Chapter 55 of the Enforcement Instructions and Guidance. However from 9 June 2021 it was replaced by the *Detention: General instructions*.

Although the immigration legislation gives broad general powers to detain, it provides very little substantive control over how those detention powers will be exercised. So the General Instructions represent most of the 'law' that immigration lawyers will come across in their dealings with the HO.

Key features of the detention processes are:

- Initial reasons for detention must be given
- Subsequently there must be periodic reviews (recorded internally as a *detention review* and provided to the detainee as a *monthly progress report*)

Policies regarding detention should be published and reliance on unpublished guidance to justify detention may result in a migrant being held unlawfully (Lumba [2011] UKSC 12). MXK [2023] EWHC 1272 (Admin) emphasises the importance of publishing policies relevant to detention, subject to national security issues, because of the dangers of largescale unlawful detention.

The guidance requires that the SSHD promptly provide reasons for detention at its outset, using Form IS91R. A failure to do so renders the detention unlawful as a breach of ECHR Art 5 (Saadi v. UK [2008] ECHR 80). However this will not necessarily oblige the detainee's release from detention, if there are nevertheless good reasons for them to be detained.

Following the initial detention, regular reviews must be carried out by increasingly senior officers. This is the programme for reviews in a routine case (see Table 1 in *Detention General Instructions*):

Review Period	Review Authorised by:
24 hours	Inspector/SEO
7 days	CIO/HEO
14 days	Inspector/SEO
1st monthly	Inspector/SEO
2nd monthly	Inspector/SEO
3rd monthly	Inspector/SEO
4th monthly	Inspector/SEO
5th monthly	Inspector/SEO
6th monthly	Grade 7

7th monthly	Grade 7
8th monthly	Grade 7
9th monthly	Grade 6
10th monthly	Grade 6
11th monthly	Grade 6
12th and subsequent monthlies	Grade 5

Table 2 lays out the review programme for the Criminal Casework Directorate.

The Detention Centre Rules 2001 (updated) and the Short-term Holding Facility Rules 2018 (original version) set out the basic legal regime within detention centres and related locations. There is Guidance Detention on Reporting which sets out the modalities of detaining those subject to immigration control when signing on with the HO. It explains that exercising detention powers in a controlled environment can assist with securing removals and avoids the complications and cost of home visits. It may be necessary to alert the detention gatekeeper where the mitigating circumstances interview turns up new relevant information. The Detention Services Order 06/2013 Reception, Induction and Discharge Checklist and Supplementary Guidance also explains numerous procedures; Detention Services Order 06/2015 addresses *Marriage/Civil Partnership in Immigration Detention* and Detention Services Order 15/2012 deals with the *Fingerprinting of Detained Individuals*

There are limitations on how long someone can be held in short-term holding facilities: 7 days (and 96 hours in a holding room).

13.1.3 Exercising the power to detain

The power of detention is always available. However, that does not mean it should always be exercised.

The basic justifications for detention are these:

- To effect removal, or
- Initially, to establish identity or basis of claim, or
- Where there is reason to believe the person will fail to comply with conditions of temporary admission.

These justifications are set out in the *Detention: General Instructions* Guidance. There are implied limitations to these justifications, which are explored below. For example, a person cannot be detained to effect removal if there is no real prospect of their removal in a reasonable timescale. The burden is on the SSHD to justify detention as necessary. The SSHD must do so to the ordinary civil standard.

There are limitations on the use of the power which the SSHD must contemplate when determining whether to detain:

- The presumption in favour of liberty: the *Detention: General Instructions* state '*there is a presumption in favour of immigration bail*', also part of common law and Article 5 of the ECHR. There must be strong grounds for believing that a person will not comply with conditions of immigration bail to justify detention. The Guidance goes on to state that '*wherever possible, alternatives to detention must be used*'
- All reasonable alternatives to detention must be considered before detention is authorised
- Each case must be considered on its individual merits

However from 28 September 2023 detention law changes. IMA 2023 s12 provides that, vis-á-vis all forms of detention, the question as to whether the time period of detention is reasonable is for the SSHD – not the court.

> **Top Tip**
>
> In a bail application, if the HO cannot prove to the civil standard that detention is necessary for one of the above reasons, the person ought to be released on bail. This is certainly how a bail application should work.
>
> But the nature of the system tends to focus on the reliability of the individual bail applicant. So always challenge the premise of the detention. Emphasise that the burden of proof is on the SSHD.

13.1.4 The factors justifying detention

The *Detention: General Instructions* identifies these factors as influencing a decision to detain (so they should be addressed in representations/bail applications):

> All relevant factors must be taken into account when considering the need for initial or continued detention, including:
>
> - What is the likelihood of the person being removed and, if so, after what timescale?
> - Is there any evidence of previous absconding?
> - Is there any evidence of a previous failure to comply with conditions of immigration bail (or, formerly, temporary admission or release)?
> - Has the subject taken part in a determined attempt to breach the immigration laws? (For example, entry in breach of a deportation order, attempted or actual clandestine entry).
> - Is there a previous history of complying with the requirements of immigration control? (For example, by applying for a visa or further leave).
> - What are the person's ties with the UK? Are there close relatives (including dependants) here? Does anyone rely on the person for support? If the dependant is a child or vulnerable adult, do they depend heavily on public welfare services for their daily care needs in lieu of support from the detainee? Does the person have a settled address/employment?
> - What are the individual's expectations about the outcome of the case? Are there factors such as an outstanding appeal, an application for JR or representations which might afford more incentive to keep in touch than if such factors were not present? (See also 55.14).
> - Is there a risk of offending or harm to the public (this requires consideration of the likelihood of harm and the seriousness of the harm if the person does offend)?
> - Is the subject under 18?
> - Is the subject an adult at risk? See the separate guidance in Adults at risk in immigration detention

13.1.5 Deportation cases

A tougher line is generally struck for foreign national offenders, where the presumption is more likely to be displaced. Thus the Guidance states that special attention must be paid to individual circumstances and that the clear imperative of public protection, and/or the likely greater absconding risks that criminality may bring, will make detention more likely.

13.1.6 Removability as the basis of the power to detain

It can be seen that the power to detain is very extensive, in the sense that any person subject to immigration control can potentially be detained. We have just seen the main factors that are relevant when detention is considered. There is also an overriding consideration, which is that the power to detain will lapse in cases of lengthy detention if there is no realistic prospect of removal. Detention must be reasonable in all the circumstances, particularly having regard to the prospects of removal (the 'Hardial Singh principle') from the landmark detention decision in: <u>R (Singh) v. Governor of Durham</u>

Prison [1983] EWHC 1 (QB). Many judges have cited and sometimes rephrased the Hardial Singh requirements. An authoritative version is this from the Supreme Court in Lumba [2011] UKSC 12:

1. The SSHD must intend to deport the person and can only use the power to detain for that purpose
2. Detention must be no more than for a period that is reasonable in all the circumstances
3. If, before the expiry of the reasonable period, it becomes apparent that deportation cannot be effected within a reasonable period, the power to detain should not be exercised
4. SSHD should act with all diligence and expedition to effect removal

Judges sometimes refer to these as Hardial Singh (1)-(4). But they really come down to one thing: the length of detention must be *reasonable*. And a lack of reasonableness may be apparent if one sensibly assesses future likelihoods on the basis of present realities.

The detention regime from 28 September 2023 (via s12 IMA 2023) aims to alter the 2nd and 3rd principles. Albeit that the Guidance *Detention: General instructions* accepts that "*It remains the case that a person liable to detention may only be detained for such period as is reasonably necessary to enable the examination, decision, removal or directions to be carried out, made or given*". Now detention is permissible:

- "*for such period as, in the opinion of the Secretary of State, is reasonably necessary*" for whatever purpose the precise detention power is being used for and
- once the SSHD no longer considers the purpose will be achieved in a reasonable time, further detention is permitted "*for such further period as, in the opinion of the [SSHD], is reasonably necessary to enable such arrangements to be made for the person's release as the [SSHD] considers to be appropriate*"

The detention purposes are completing an examination of a passenger and their subsequent removal under IA 1971 Sch 2 para 17A, or effecting their removal under s62 NIAA 2002 2N-2R or considering/making a deportation order s36 (Sch 3 para 2A-2E IA 1971, s36 1A-1E UKBA 2007), or making decisions under the preserved EEA Regs 2016 (Reg 32). The Guidance *Detention: General instructions* emphasises that short-term barriers (short-term medical treatment or flight availability issues, or an upcoming appeal) should not affect the detention power; longer term barriers may well do so.

We will return to Hardial Singh when we come to address unlawful detention, removal and case progression. There are around 500 references on www.bailii.org to 'Hardial'. So we can see how often the principle comes up.

The cases show:

- The actions of the detainee, both past and present, can have an impact on whether it is reasonable to exercise the power to detain. R (A) [2007] EWCA Civ 804 found that a risk of absconding was relevant to the period before which detention becomes unreasonable, as was a refusal of voluntary departure from the UK and risk of re-offending. More recent case law has found detention for several years not to be unlawful whilst the HO persuaded the court that there remained some real prospect of removal, despite several years of trying
- Where the argument is based on non-removability, any **uncertainty as to removability** must be balanced against other factors: overall "*there must be a sufficient prospect of removal to warrant continued detention when account is taken of all other relevant factors*" (MH [2010] EWCA Civ 1112 §65)
- Lord Dyson in Lumba: "*It is necessary to distinguish between cases where return to the country of origin is possible and those where it is not. Where return is not possible for reasons which are extraneous to the person detained, the fact that he is not willing to return voluntarily cannot be held against him since his refusal has no causal effect.*"
- Samson Bello [2020] EWHC 950 (Admin) holds that the reference in §55.3.2.4 of the Enforcement Instructions and Guidance to removal being "*imminent*" if likely to take place in the next four weeks was no more than a guide. It was not a strict rule. The degree of uncertainty

in any upcoming removal had to be factored into the overall reasonableness of continued detention. This was a challenge made in the context of the ongoing uncertainty as to removability during the global pandemic

In SB (Ghana) [2020] EWHC 668 (Admin) the Judge accepts that further loss of liberty (following a significant period of detention) once an in-country appeal was lodged to the FTT would be unlawful, given that it could be assumed that such an appeal would take at least six months to progress to hearing in the FTT with the chance of applying for permission to appeal to the UT before appeal rights were exhausted

- Samson Bello [2020] EWHC 950 (Admin) holds that a detainee's use of lawful routes to challenge his deportation (even repeatedly and unsuccessfully) does not, on its own, suggest that he will seek to use unlawful ones. Only active evidence of absconding including the actions of one's family could justify inferring absconding risks

---

Example

Rahul is from Algeria. He is to be deported and his appeal rights were exhausted 18 months ago. However, he has been detained now for 21 months, allegedly pending removal.

The HO insist that they are doing everything in their power to remove Rahul, but the Algerian authorities are not co-operating. A face to face interview between Rahul and the Algerians took place 20 months ago in detention in order to obtain an Emergency Travel Document. The Algerians stated that they did not accept Rahul was Algerian. The HO asked Rahul to provide some written proof of his Algerian nationality. Being in detention in a foreign country, Rahul was unable to do so.

A second interview was arranged and took place 15 months ago. The Algerians maintained their position. It is not clear whether any new information was submitted by the HO.

A third telephone interview took place three months ago with the same result.

Rahul has applied for bail five times in the last 21 months and has been refused each time because he is a high absconding risk. There is strong support for this view, as Rahul has a very poor criminal and immigration record.

Rahul's detention may well be unlawful and probably has been for some time; arguably since the first interview, almost indisputably since the second. Tribunal bail applications have failed him so he must apply for habeas corpus and/or JR. On the claim form he should also specify that he seeks a declaration of unlawful detention and damages. Quantum could easily be tens of thousands of pounds in a case such as this.

Top Tip

One sometimes comes across a detainee who is, in immigration terms, 'at the end of the line' in terms of regularising their status, with no further options open to them. So the onus will be on the HO to enforce removal. Over time the SSHD has seen the virtue in publishing the procedures that have been established for challenging returns: you can see them in the Country returns guide. It sets out the kind of documentation required to secure (or enforce) a removal. You can assess the progress the HO has made by reference to the disclosed detention reviews against the criteria found in that guidance.

Many challenges have been brought over the years in these cases. So you can start your casework by standing on the shoulders of your predecessors' efforts. Use the www.bailii.org website and from the homepage search for, for example, 'Hardial Algeria'. This will bring up cases where detention has been challenged on Hardial Singh principles involving Algeria, and you should find a treasure trove of inspiration regarding the necessary stages in agreeing a person's return with the Algerian authorities. Then you can see how well the SSHD is doing by reference to those processes.

13.1.7 Detention of children, pregnant women, families, and adults at risk

On 12 July 2016, sections 59 and 60 of the Immigration Act 2016 were brought into force; requiring the HO to issue statutory guidance on those who would be particularly vulnerable to harm in detention, and limiting the detention of pregnant women.

The relevant guidance is in UKVI operational guidance, in 'Enforcement', both under 'offender management':

- Adults at risk in immigration detention : addressed in detail below
- Detention of pregnant women : essentially providing that
  - detention is permissible only for those who will shortly be removed (ie normally within 3 days, exceptionally up to 7 days where personally authorised by a government Minister), or
  - where there are **exceptional circumstances** which justify detention (posing a threat on criminal or national security grounds) or **very exceptional circumstances** (arising from breach of bail conditions or pending a decision to proceed with deportation: but not simply to secure removal)
  - The woman's welfare is central: when assessing it, all features of the pregnancy must be considered
  - Pregnancy must be proven from the outcome of medical examination or a pregnancy test, or records of appointments associated with pregnancy

The *Adults at risk* and *Detention of pregnant women* policy documents above largely replaced the provisions in the former Chapter 55 EIG, regarding those who are ordinarily regarded as unsuitable for detention, though the *Detention: General Instructions* retains two important general principles:

- Unaccompanied children must not be detained other than in very exceptional circumstances (55.9.4): though there is a more fundamental statutory safeguard now, at para 18B of Sch 2 of the IA 1971, providing that a child can only be detained in a short-term holding facility or if en route to one, and only if removal directions are in force or due to be set such that there is a reasonable belief that removal will be effected within 24 hours. This is consistent with the view in Strasbourg: MH v Croatia [2021] ECHR 949 finds the ECtHR reiterating its view that extreme vulnerability of children (whether or not they were accompanied by their parents) was a decisive factor that took precedence over considerations relating to the child's status as an illegal immigrant (see also Nikoghosyan v Poland [2022] ECHR 211). Detention can have an extreme negative impact on children's physical and mental health and development. The HO is alive to the possibility of litigation based on detention of a person who may be a child: see the Detention Services Order 02/2019 *Care and management of Post Detention Age claims* (January 2022) which stresses the importance of not detaining someone pending a *Merton* compliant age assessment subject to the usual exceptions (MIL 9.3.4).
- Families should only rarely be detained outside of the Family returns process (in the 'Returns preparation' section of 'Enforcement' operational guidance). See also the archived policies EIG ch's 45 a) b) and c)

Notwithstanding these safeguards, children are still sometimes detained. If you come across such a case:
- Bear in mind the statutory safeguarding duty under section 55 BCIA 2009
- The place of detention **must** have in place and implement a safeguarding children policy. When advising children or their parents it is crucial to have sight of the policy for the relevant centre and check the HO have acted in accordance with that policy and their duty under Section 55. Guidance on the HO approach is found in the Detention services order 19/2012: safeguarding children policy here

13.1.8 Detention of vulnerable categories of person: The Adults at Risk guidance

The Adults at Risk guidance was introduced in response to the Shaw report: the *Review of the Welfare in Detention of Vulnerable Persons* (Cm 9186). It essentially aims to identify vulnerable persons according to the cogency of the evidence supporting their case, and then balances their vulnerability against any immigration control factors in favour of detention. It replaced the previous regime, which focussed on whether there were exceptional circumstances justifying the detention of vulnerable groups, such as torture victims or those whose mental health could not be satisfactorily managed in detention.

When a person enters detention the *Detention General Instructions* explain that any risk factors must be identified in form IS91RA at the very first opportunity, and there is an ongoing obligation to identify any new risks. Those identified as at risk of suicide or self-harm must be managed using the Assessment Care in Detention and Treatment (ACDT) procedures which warns of the importance of alertness to triggers such as receiving immigration/removal decisions, illness, segregation, first days in detention, and a history of trafficking.

The intention of the Guidance on adults at risk in immigration detention (then in its original August 2016 version) was that 'fewer people with a confirmed vulnerability will be detained in fewer instances and that, where detention becomes necessary, it will be for the shortest period necessary':

> The clear presumption is that detention will not be appropriate if a person is considered to be 'at risk'. However, it will not mean that no one at risk will ever be detained. Instead, detention will only become appropriate at the point at which immigration control considerations outweigh this presumption. Within this context it will remain appropriate to detain individuals at risk if it is necessary in order to remove them. This builds on the existing guidance and sits alongside the general presumption of liberty.

The *Adults at risk* guidance defines an adult at risk as a person likely be particularly vulnerable to harm if detained in two circumstances:

- Where they have self-identified themselves as at risk, or have experienced a traumatic event (e.g. trafficking, torture or sexual violence)
- There is medical or other professional evidence, or observational evidence, of them having experienced such a traumatic event, whether or not they have highlighted it themselves

There is then presumption that 'at risk' persons should not be detained. The available evidence should be classified as follows:

- a *self-declaration* of being an adult at risk – should be afforded *limited weight*, even if the issues raised cannot be readily confirmed. Individuals in these circumstances will be regarded as being at **evidence level 1**
- *professional evidence* (e.g. from a social worker, medical practitioner or NGO), or official documentary evidence, which indicates that the individual is an adult at risk – should be afforded *greater weight*. Individuals in these circumstances will be regarded as being at **evidence level 2**
- *professional evidence* (e.g. from a social worker, medical practitioner or NGO) stating that the individual is at risk and *that a period of detention would be likely to cause harm* – for example, increase the severity of the symptoms or condition that have led to the individual being regarded as an adult at risk – should be afforded *significant weight*. Individuals in these circumstances will be regarded as being at **evidence level 3.**

The AAR Guidance now takes aim at some kinds of "*External medical report*" which will be the subject of particular scrutiny. In particular

- These standards apply in cases where the report arrives without any history of the condition's treatment in the community – they are not aimed at reports from physicians treating pre-existing conditions who may have insight re the detainee's condition in the community
- Relevant considerations will be the author's understanding of their independent role, access to a full set of health records, taking place in a suitably equipped consulting room, the need for a face-to-face examination unless that is unrealistic for reasons beyond the author's control, use of a professional interpreter, express consideration of the standard of primary care available in detention, and a statement of assurance re these standards being met by both the author and

CHAPTER 13: Enforcement; Detention, Removal and Deportation

- the instructing lawyer - and any health concerns should be speedily relayed to the health authorities at the detention centre
- Generic statements about detention will be disregarded
- Some individuals with a serious medical condition (ie where a medication interruption might be serious, or where their mobility is affected, they have difficulty in caring for themselves, or there are related complications, or fluctuating episodes or recent hospitalisation) may be on specialised medication or a treatment plan not available via GPs in the detention estate. All reasonable efforts must be made to support these arrangements' continuity; detention is unlikely to be suitable where this is not practical.
- Medical reports should explain the interpretation arrangements: they risk receiving limited weight absent professional interpretation.
- The *Guidance Interim Guidance: Requesting a second opinion for an external medical report/Medico-Legal Report* explains that in general medical reports external to the detention process will be referred to the Detained Medical Reports Team (DMRT) who will instigate a second opinion process via remote conference sending an Invitation to Assessment to the detainee, and to the resident healthcare team at the IRC or prison immediately upon receipt, and also internally for a second opinion as to maintaining detention. A HO-contracted doctor should conduct the second opinion. If the opinion cannot be obtained within 7 days then a decision on AAR status will need to be made without one (and vulnerability should be considered in any event); the Dr should write up their report within 5 days. Detention decision makers should give appropriate weight to both reports.

The *Equality Impact Assessment - Standards for consideration of external medical reports* laid the ground for that tightening of standards: it records that the HO considers the numbers of reports have gone up whilst their quality has gone down. Issues raised include not recognising the limitations of telephone assessments, failing to rely on objective health records and using non-diagnostic self-reporting tools, failing to explore the major symptoms underpinning the diagnosis, and not conducting formal tests for malingering.

The AAR Guidance sets out a *non-exhaustive* list of risk factors to 'inform' detention decisions:

- suffering from a mental health condition or impairment (including depression and serious learning difficulties)
- having been a victim of torture (individuals with a completed Medico Legal Report from reputable providers will be regarded as meeting level 3 evidence, provided the report meets the required standards)
- having been a victim of sexual or gender-based violence, including female genital mutilation
- having been a victim of human trafficking or modern slavery
- suffering from post-traumatic stress disorder (which may or may not be related to one of the above experiences)

- being pregnant (pregnant women will automatically be regarded as being level 3 risks)
- suffering from a serious physical disability
- suffering from other serious physical health conditions or illnesses
- being aged 70 or over
- being a transsexual or intersex person

The Guidance *Adults at risk Detention of victims of modern slavery* explains that identification of being a victim, either to the initial reasonable grounds, or conclusive grounds, thresholds, will place the person at level 2 AAR. A Modern Slavery Needs Assessment will be undertaken in order to identify the person's recovery needs arising from their experience of modern slavery and assess any support they may require. This will include an interview, referral to a Healthcare provider for an assessment of physical & mental health recovery needs, & consideration of the ensuing material by a caseworker.

The policy acknowledges that there may be other conditions that render a person particularly vulnerable to harm and that the nature and severity of a condition and the availability of evidence may change over time. Court or Tribunal judgements about the credibility of a person's account or about professional evidence may be taken into account.

The Detention Centre Rules 2001, at Rules 34 & 35, provide very important protections for vulnerable people:

- Rule 34 provides that every detained person shall be given a physical and mental medical examination within 24 hours of admission to the detention centre. Such an examination might reveal information of health problems or torture that would in turn lead to the examining doctor issuing a Rule 35 report.

- Rule 35 requires medical practitioners to report to the detention manager on any case
    - where a detainee's health is likely to be injuriously affected by continued detention, or the conditions of detention; or
    - where they believe a detainee may be a victim of torture.

DCRs r15(1) mandate the SSHD to ensure sufficient accommodation is provided for all detained persons' and that size, lighting, heating, ventilation and fittings are adequate. 5-yearly audits aim to secure compliance. There is Guidance *Accommodation: lighting, heating and ventilation*.

The 'adults at risk' guidance on vulnerable detainees identifies torture victims as one of the categories who should not normally be detained. When *Adults at risk* was first introduced, the definition of torture concentrated on governmental responsibility for the mistreatment, excluding non-state actors. Legal challenges caused a rethink. Medical Justice [2017] EWHC 2461 (Admin) held that the definition of torture should include that inflicted by non-state actors: the political question of whether or not the harm was inflicted by a state or non-state actor was not relevant to the question of vulnerability to harm via detention. So from 2 July 2018 the government brought forward legislation to correct this failure.

Now Rule 35 states:

> 'torture' means any act by which a perpetrator intentionally inflicts severe pain or suffering on a victim in a situation in which—
>
>> (a) the perpetrator has control (whether mental or physical) over the victim, and
>> (b) as a result of that control, the victim is powerless to resist.

Once an adult at risk has been identified, the case for detaining them has to be considered, in the context of the presumption against detention for such a person. Their vulnerability has to be assessed in the light of an *Assessment of Immigration Factors*.

The immigration factors are

- **Length of time in detention** – every effort must be made to ensure detention is for as short a time as possible
- **Public policy issues** – criminality, presenting a security risk, or being subject to deportation on conducive to the public good grounds
- **Compliance issues** – i.e. absconding risks, based on the individual's record

Detention has increasingly been under scrutiny in recent years. We can see:

- An unacceptably high death rate: 35 immigration detainees have died in detention and 35 in prisons since 2000. The 2016 deaths included the particularly poignant case of a Polish man detained in Morton Hall who killed himself after being refused bail just before Christmas 2016, dying on the same day as his partner gave birth to the couple's son. Medical Justice are on record as observing in January 2017 that '*Year after year, investigations into these deaths reveal ongoing systemic healthcare failings.*' Statistics obtained by the organisation *no-deportations.org.uk* also show the continued prevalence of incidents of suicide attempts and continuing elevated level of self-harm interventions: from 159 suicide attempts in 2007 to 393 in 2015, and 227 in 2017; there were 2,597 people on suicide watch in in 2015 and 1,055 in 2017.

- BID's analysis *Adults at Risk: the ongoing struggle for vulnerable adults in detention* has also shown that 80 per cent have been defined as being "at risk" by a medical practitioner on a 'Rule 35 report'. The diagnosed conditions and vulnerabilities were most commonly PTSD, depression and suicidal tendencies, with two thirds recorded as being torture victims.
- Research by charity Women for Refugee Women (Detained: women asylum seekers locked up in the UK) also revealed that 85 per cent of women who have sought asylum and been detained after the new policy came into force are survivors of rape or other gender-based violence, including forced marriage, female genital mutilation and forced prostitution.
- The HO's own sampling of cases revealed 226 cases between September and December 2016 who as survivors of torture should not have been detained.

It is worth keeping in touch with the latest published reports about detention. These can inspire general challenges to detention conditions as well as assisting in showing that a problem in your client's case may be part of a broader problem. Eg the Chief Inspector of Immigration's *Annual inspection of Adults at Risk in Immigration Detention* (for 2018–19; published 29 April 2020) identified ongoing problems in the detention system:

- Significant weaknesses included that:
  (1) Detention Gatekeeper staff do not have direct contact with the person referred for detention and have to rely on forms completed by various referring units, and;
  (2) neither party had any professional medical knowledge and therefore both are resorting to internet searches to try to understand the significance of medication found with the person being referred: 3.7-3.8
- There was force in the case for enhanced screening and assessment prior to detention: 3.9
- The scale and pace of progress on alternatives to detention needed to increase significantly for it to be more than a token: 3.12
- The inspection found issues with each stage of the admission process, including:
  - differences and gaps in the training different staff had received
  - different methods of recording and reporting the process, and what it discovered about the detainee
  - a lack of time to explore vulnerabilities, exacerbated by a detainee's state of mind on arrival, particularly if new to detention; and reluctance to talk about personal issues, especially traumatic experiences, such as having been trafficked or the victim of modern slavery or sexual abuse: 3.16
- There was clearly a lot more that the HO can and should 'o to make each component of the Adults at Risk process more efficient and more effective, and it is reasonable therefore to continue to describe it as a work in progress: 3.27

The *Third annual inspection* published in January 2023 (from a 3rd quarter 2022 review) recorded the Inspector's view that "*the pace of change was too slow and the enthusiasm to protect vulnerable people in immigration detention was held back by a narrative that placed abuse of the system ahead of protecting the vulnerable*". There was a common perception that the r35 process, which was under-resourced, was being abused with limited evidence to support that view; quality assurance was needed in the treatment of requests and responses to reports.

The *Brook House Inquiry Report* (19 September 2023) reveals 19 incidents with 'credible evidence of acts or omissions that were capable of amounting to mistreatment' contrary to ECHR Art 3 (including derogatory and humiliating remarks and aggressive and threatening language aimed at vulnerable detainees, and the use of an inherently dangerous restraint technique and physical violence, and makes 33 recommendations necessary to 'prevent a recurrence of any identified mistreatment'.

Overall it is difficult to be confident that the Adults at Risk policy regime has really improved things. NGOs and lawyers report that few detainees were released as a result of the attribution of that designation. Pierre Makhlouf, assistant director at BID has warned that AAR:

> '*has introduced a categorisation of types of evidence, absolving the Home Office of any requirement to follow up evidence where it doesn't meet a higher category. Instead, the lower*

categories are used as reason to refuse release, when in fact at the very least they should result in further enquiry.'

The Medical Justice report *Harmed Not Heard* (April 2022) sets out ongoing flaws in the identification of the vulnerable based on analysis of 45 clinical assessments in the 2nd half of 2021. None had had a safeguarding report from IRC healthcare to the HO, 67% had had no communication re possible health damage from detention from the IRC to the HO and 87% had suicidal and/or self-harm thoughts. The average wait for a safeguarding report was 29 days.

CSM [2021] EWHC 2175 (Admin) holds that the possible consequences of an interruption in HIV anti-retroviral treatment are sufficiently serious to engage ECHR Art 3. Detention staff needed to know that medication must not be missed and how to obtain it.

The credibility of a detainee will often be challenged where a false imprisonment claim involves disputed facts. Louis [2021] EWHC 288 (QB) emphasises that there are a number of reasons why errors can creep into a person's account of of their own history. These range from the obvious loss of recollection due to the passage of time, which may have had greater impact if relevant events took place in childhood, the impact of traumatic experiences, or a process of conscious or subconscious reconstruction or exposure to the recollection of another which has corrupted or created the recollection of an event or part of an event. Allowance should be given for a person's limited education and English language facility. Care must also be taken to recognise the impact the very different customs and practices of other countries may have on what has happened in a person's past and their ability to furnish information, bearing in mind that in many countries there is no national registry office where copies of birth, marriage, and death certificates are kept: local authorities issue these documents but do not keep copies for their records.

13.1.8.1 Capacity, disability and Equality Assessments

The detention system is becoming increasingly aware of the need to address the question of disability and capacity. One driving force has been the **Equality Act 2010** which requires equal access to remedies against grievances for the able and the disabled.

The Equality Act 2010 requires –

- Persons exercising public functions make reasonable adjustments (s29(7)(b)): the Code of Practice says that the duty is anticipatory and continuous and requires such steps as are reasonable
- Including the situation where a provision, criteria or practice puts the disabled person at a substantial disadvantage in comparison with those not disabled (s20(3)) (substantial disadvantage = unreasonably adverse experience: sch 2 para 2(5))
- For these purposes, a disabled person includes those with mental impairment having a substantial and long-term adverse effect on their ability to conduct daily activities (s6(1)) (substantial = more than minor or trivial: s212(1))
- A failure to make reasonable adjustments represents discrimination against the individual in question (s21(1), (2))

VC [2018] EWCA Civ 57 sees the Equality Act in action.

- a breach of the duty to make reasonable adjustments was found because detainees were not involved in the decisions to detain or to remove them from association and segregate them and there was no formal process for them to make representations to the SSHD though they could make informal representations in respect of the decisions after they have been made: VC 151; 188-190.
- In cases of alleged breach claimants must give *some indication as to the adjustments it is alleged should have been made*: VC 159.
- The burden of proof is on the SSHD to show that the duty has been complied with, once the possibility of a breach has been put in issue by the case's facts: VC 160-161.

On 23 July 2020, UKVI published guidance entitled Mental vulnerability and immigration detention. This document introduces its purpose as follows:

> The purpose of this Detention Services Order (DSO) is to provide non-clinical staff in immigration removal centres (IRCs), pre-departure accommodation (PDA) and residential short-term holding facilities (RSTHFs) with instructions on how to identify individuals who may:
> - lack capacity (see paragraph 14 below);
> - have a disability arising from mental impairment;
> - have a mental health condition.
>
> This is with a view to referring them, where appropriate, for assessment and setting up a process to ensure that appropriate support and, for those with a disability, reasonable adjustments are in place. This guidance is not intended to replace a clinical or professional mental health assessment.

13.1.8.2 Detention issues and Covid-19

Various information sources raised concerns about Covid-19 and the extra risks it poses to immigration detainees at an early stage in the pandemic. Detention is a stressful experience at the best of times and many detainees are already vulnerable with mental health issues. Early in the pandemic various steps were taken such as suspending bail reporting conditions and new detentions for those facing removal, closing IRCs to visitors, releasing very large numbers (from January to March to May 2020 there were 1,225 to 736 to 368 detained), reviewing all cases in order of approximate vulnerability.

13.1.9 Unlawful detention

So far we have set out the main principles regarding detention. MIL 13.2 addresses immigration bail, i.e. the regime for a person's admission to the UK via a supervision regime granted and administered by the SSHD and/or FTT. However, it is important to be aware of the possibility that an individual is, or has been, unlawfully detained.

Detention may become unlawful for many reasons. The most common reasons are that

- **Detention is too long**: i.e. contrary to the Hardial Singh principles, in that the period of detention has become unreasonable in the light of the progress in advancing removal and/or
- **Detention is contrary to HO policies**, most often with respect to vulnerable persons. For example, a person with mental health problems may wish to argue that their health is deteriorating in detention.
- **Detention is contrary to some other governing legal norm**: eg

    - the Equality Act 2010 (MIL 13.1.8.1)
    - the general prohibition on detaining children), or
    - where its impact on a vulnerable individual amounts to inhuman and degrading treatment contrary to Article 3 ECHR
    - it is contrary to ECHR Art 5

It is unusual directly to challenge the lawfulness of detention before applying for immigration bail, as an application to the SSHD (and thence to the FTT if that fails) is a shorter and simpler remedy for many people, especially those with strong community ties. However, the principles surrounding unlawful detention may still be relevant in immigration bail applications. There is also the possibility of securing compensation for a detainee for their unlawful detention after they have been released from detention. The possibility of **damages claims** was first recognised in ID and Ors [2005] EWCA Civ 38.

Challenges are usually brought via JR proceedings in the Administrative Court. A JR application may include a claim for damages. Once a person is released from detention, the Administrative Court often prefers that their case proceeds outside of the public law jurisdiction (i.e. the world of JR), so cases may be transferred to the Queen's Bench Division or a county court (i.e. the world of civil proceedings).

Even if the Administrative Court makes a finding on *liability* for damages, it is very unenthusiastic about assessing the *quantum* of damages for itself, so at that point, the claim is likely to be transferred to one of those courts for the quantum to be assessed. ZA (Pakistan) [2020] EWCA Civ 146 emphasises the importance of pursuing false imprisonment claims via civil actions rather than clogging up the Administrative Court. It was very important that all parties gave timely consideration to the issue of transfer to the County Court/QBD once a person had been released from detention.

Damages may be compensatory or nominal.

- The former is available where the detention is unequivocally unlawful, as where the only reasonable conclusion is that removal is not on the cards because the case has stagnated administratively.
- Nominal damages are likely to be awarded where there is a technical legal breach (eg of the review schedule) which means the detention power was unlawfully exercised – but the power to detain might remain intact, were it to be lawfully exercised.
    - In those cases the Court will have to consider the likelihood of detention having taken place had a lawful decision been made.
    - For example, in SK (Zimbabwe) [2011] UKSC 23, the Supreme Court held that a failure to conduct detention reviews at the required frequency and level of seniority rendered the detention unlawful. However, that left the question of whether, on the balance of probabilities, detention would have been authorised anyway.
- So there are two questions to ask in analysing a detention case which relates to in relation to mistakes regarding interpreting Home Office policy:
    (1) Was there a technical legal error, such as getting policy wrong?
    (2) If so, would detention have been authorised anyway? Put another way, are the risks of absconding, offending and danger to the public sufficiently great for a judge to be confident that detention would have proceeded even if the guidance had been followed? In that case, a judge would only award nominal damages.

FTT judges will concentrate on whether the exercise of the detention power is correct. Whereas judges in unlawful detention cases focus on whether the power to detain exists. Thus:

- **Bail is granted** where a person is liable to be detained, but they are thought to be a good candidate for release into the community because of their immigration history and social/family ties.
- **Detention is unlawful** where the power to detain is absent.

As it was put in B (Algeria) [2018] UKSC 5 approving and citing the earlier decision of Konan:

> 'An [immigration judge] in considering a bail application is not determining (indeed, he has no power to determine) the lawfulness of the detention. The grant of bail presupposes the power to detain since a breach of a bail condition can lead to a reintroduction of the detention.'

Of course, many arguments may be relevant under both the lawfulness of detention and its correctness – e.g. a lengthening period of detention might eventually become unlawful.

Length of detention is clearly relevant both to the reasonableness of detention (and thus its lawfulness) and also to whether bail should be granted. The less progress the HO is making in securing a person's removal, the greater the chance that the FTT will begin to question the need for detention. And the fact that the detainee is vulnerable and their health is suffering in detention is bound to weigh on a FTT Judge's mind. Nevertheless, beware: many immigration judges have been sold on the notion that they should steer clear of the territory of unlawful detention. Whilst this is technically true, it does not mean they should ignore issues of case progression and vulnerability.

Actions of this nature have become one of the most common brought in the High Court. Where lawfulness arises as an issue, it may be in the client's best interests to make an application for an Order to the High Court. This can be done simultaneously with an immigration tribunal bail application. The bail application is the fastest way to try to secure release for a client, but it is not a challenge to lawfulness and is not a basis for securing compensation.

Applications in such cases may be run by way of a *habeas corpus* application, which is an ancient and fundamental remedy, where the underlying power to detain is challenged. However, such applications are very rare these days. Habeas applications have a higher priority over JR with respect to listing of the hearing. However in general unlawful detention applications can be made as part of a JR claim made to the Administrative Court: typically seeking an Order for release, a Declaration that detention was unlawful, and a remedy by way of damages. IMA 2023 preserves habeas applications as a potential remedy during the initial detention period so the remedy may well come alive again (MIL 13.2.1).

The courts increasingly recognise the problems caused by a lack of proper legal advice in detention. A lack of access to the internet and to a mobile phone may pose major difficulties, as noted in Singh [2021] EWHC 158 (Admin). Detention Action [2022] EWHC 18 (Admin) notes the disconcerting statistics regarding some firms' conduct at legal surgeries: 5 firms had opened no legal help files for any of 292 clients during over 41 surgeries. But this was essentially a regulatory rather than a legal issue that was beyond the court's role to assess.

AO v The Home Office [2021] EWHC 1043 (QB) emphasises that if the SSHD fails to call evidence from witnesses with direct knowledge of the decision making (as opposed to witnesses who are simply reviewing the file) then the court may draw adverse inferences. This might be relevant to the SSHD's ability to demonstrate that detention would have continued absent the public law errors found by the court in order to discharge the burden of proof in showing that the errors did not bear on the detention. Here the Claimant's detention had not been robustly and formally documented and the decision maker had repeatedly failed to notice an adult at risk identification and appeared to have simply cut and pasted earlier detention reviews.

13.1.9.1 Mental illness

There is growing light being shone on the treatment for detainees with mental health issues. The IMB 2018 report into Immigration Detention found that "One of the most important and frequently-encountered aspects of detainee vulnerability is mental illness". The courts also highlight the states's duty to safeguard mentally ill detainees.

- The SSHD has statutory and public law responsibilities for safeguarding detainees, and cannot just leave this to the relevant health authorities or clinicians (HA (Nigeria) [2012] EWHC 979 (Admin) at [155] and [181]).
- The Tameside duty of enquiry is relevant (ie the public law duty to make enquiries essential to gathering the facts for a lawful decision to be made): R (O) [2016] UKSC 19 and Das [2013] EWHC 683 (Admin). In the detention context this requires conscientious reasonable inquiries as to the physical and mental health of the person who is being considered for detention, obtaining relevant reports from treating clinicians: where this is done, then the SSHD may rely on the responsible clinician's opinion (Das [2014] EWCA Civ 45 70), presuming there has been no negligence (HA (Nigeria)):

    o In Adegun [2019] EWHC 22 (Admin) the HO had no formal medical evidence when admitting the individual to the DAC but should have been §110 "*on notice that [he] claimed to be suffering from a serious mental health condition; the claim was backed by credible evidence that he had been "sectioned" under the Mental Health Act earlier that year and had been on medication*" meaning that the IRC healthcare staff should have been consulted at once

    o In VC [2018] EWCA Civ 57 the Court of Appeal finds §52-55 that in order to avoid circularity, it is important that enquiries are made where there is some reason for concern re mental health even though the individual may presently be well

    o Non-health matters may also require exploration: in BS [2018] EWHC 454 (Admin) the Court held that

- The availability of treatment in the community that can improve (as opposed to prevent the deterioration of) a detainee's health is also relevant to an assessment of whether to detain or maintain detention (R (O) [2016] UKSC 19)
- The SSHD need not search out every pos'ible treatment; but it was wrong to argue that the SSHD did not need to consider a treatment just because a detainee has not suggested it.
- A relevant consideration might be the possibility that a claimant refusing treatment could be compulsorily treated under the Mental Health Act, but not in a detention centre: VC
- A health condition may not be satisfactorily managed in detention if a person's health is deteriorating (VC: at [82] that "under the policy, satisfactory management of a condition at least requires the prevention of deterioration".
- But variations in the condition do not automatically mean it is not being managed: ASK [2019] EWCA Civ 1239 (below)
- See also MIL 10.3.2 for the ECtHR's position on detaining authority duties re health

13.1.9.2 Removability and other case progression

We have dealt with this at 13.1.6 above. For context, here are a couple of examples of successful cases.

In OA [2017] EWHC 486 detention pending deportation was held to have been unlawful as relevant considerations had not been taken into account when considering whether removal was imminent or possible within a reasonable time. In this case, these were that the applicant's Nigerian passport had expired, and the Nigerian Memorandum of Understanding requires that a returnee's citizenship was established beyond reasonable doubt, they were medically fit, had exhausted all legal remedies, and for those present in the UK for more than 15 years, proof of the existence of friends and relations as well as the capacity to integrate.

Delay in progressing an application, a VOT referral or a protection claim which unnecessarily prolongs detention are the other side of this particular coin– those caught up in such delays will usually be (or have been) FNPs (these are also Hardial Singh cases albeit that the *reasonableness* question turns on getting on with determining an application rather than enforcing removal). There is a useful summary in AC (Algeria) [2019] EWHC 188 (Admin):

- An application for asylum must be determined within a reasonable period of time
- It may be appropriate for the SSHD to take active steps to progress an asylum claim during a FNP's prison sentence (rather than awaiting the shift to detention under immigration powers) (Saleh [2013] EWCA Civ 1378)
- The assessment of what is a reasonable length of time will depend on all the circumstances including:
  - any applicable policy
  - other calls on the HO's resources
  - the extent to which the Claimant is compliant with the decision making process
  - the complexity of the claim and the information needed to determine the claim and how readily it can be secured
  - the extent to which the Claimant is prejudiced by delay in the determination of his claim ie whether the delay has the effect of prolonging detention

AO v The Home Office [2021] EWHC 1043 (QB) notes that there is a public law obligation upon those deciding whether to maintain detention to *consider* a Case Progression Panel (CPP) recommendation for release and to justify any departure from that recommendation. CPPs aim to provide consistency and oversight to the removals process, ensuring continued detention is properly justified, at 3-month intervals from the initial detention: see the Guidance *Detention Case Progression Panels*. The personnel should include Independent Panel Members with knowledge of public protection issues, management of potentially vulnerable people & multi-disciplinary environments.

13.1.9.3 Non-disclosure and cooperation

This area is another manifestation of the Hardial Singh doctrine, now applied in cases where a balance has to be struck between further action by the HO and compliance with necessary steps by the detainee. Where there were doubts as to, and between, two possible, nationalities, it was held in Qarani [2017] EWHC 507 that detention for 11 months was unlawful where only one of the two possible nationalities had been explored. Expedition following change of tactics would have been appropriate.

However, where complex investigations were necessitated by the detainee's non-cooperation, the HO was entitled to undertake these in a realistic timeframe given administrative caseloads Simukonda [2017] EWHC 1012.

It has been the settled policy of the Zimbabwean government since 2002 not to issue emergency travel documents (ETDs) to its nationals who do not wish to return. JM (Zimbabwe) [2017] EWCA Civ 1669 clarified that, under s35 of the 2004 Act, the HO is not entitled to require a possible re'urnee to tell officials at their embassy that they agree to return. The burden of proof in showing that foreign national authorities would issue an ETD to a person who did not wish to return (but would if they had to) was on the HO.

13.1.9.4 Bail and curfew

Sometimes the world of bail and unlawful detention can overlap. At one time the HO frequently imposed curfew conditions on detainees. However, the courts have policed the availability of this power with vigour.

> Jollah [2020] UKSC 4 shows that a curfew may well constitute imprisonment for the purpose of the tort of false imprisonment. There was a lack of any sufficiently clear legislative power to impose a curfew on migrants on bail
>
> The imposition of a curfew on an individual subject to a deportation order was unlawful because the HO had applied an unpublished policy in reaching that decision and there was no opportunity to make representations against it (Lupepe [2017] EWHC 2690).
> Para 2(1)(f) of Sch 10 to the IA 2016 might be interpreted as granting unlimited power to impose any suitable conditions on bail. One of them might be curfew. This remains untested.

13.1.9.5 Availability of accommodation

Increasingly in recent years the availability of accommodation has clogged up the possibility of release from detention. Where family or friends can provide satisfactory accommodation there are few problems. However where this is not available, or the individual's profile makes it unsuitable, then there can be a problem in sourcing the accommodation essential to release. BID's influential report *No place to go: delays in provision of s4(1)(c) bail accommodation* (September 2014) showed systemic problems and delays in the provision of bail accommodation to high risk immigration detainees. Subsequent litigation has used that report to challenge the way in which accommodation is obtained.

The problem can arise
- When seeking to provide an address for a bail application
- When conditional bail is granted subject to finding accommodation

The policy documents explain that there are 3 different levels of accommodation: level 1 (initial accommodation), level 2 (stand"rd dis"ersal accommodation), and level 3 (complex bail dispersal accommodation).

There have been a flurry of cases on these issues.

- Noorkoiv [2002] EWCA Civ 770 holds that the obligation to avoid delay in determining a person's right to be released is a more intense obligation than the duty to try a person accused of a crime within a reasonable time. Lack of resources and administrative necessity do not justify such delays.

    Sathanantham [2016] EWHC 1781 (Admin) holds that the system itself was being operated in a manner that was unlawful, and that in each case the time taken to resolve the application amounted to a breach of the SSHD's duty to deal with applications fairly and rationally. The judge commented that, *'when arrangements come to be made under the Immigration Act 2016 the failures of the existing system must be addressed'*.

- Baraka [2018] EWHC 1549 (Admin) involved a 10-month delay for a sex offender; essentially the SSHD will be given significant leeway when seeking out appropriate accommodation: the policy documentation noted that there was a very limited supply of Complex Bail Accommodation.

- Only an application made on the appropriate form can set off the SSHD's duty: Messaoud [2019] EWHC 2948 (Admin)

- Diop [2018] EWHC 1934 finds that steps needed to be taken re a perpetrator of domestic violence once "bail in principle" was granted, *"knowing the difficulties that a valid offender requiring level 3 accommodation would pose"*: summarised in DM (Tanzania) §74

    DM Tanzania [2019] EWHC 2576 (QB) summarising *Kedienhon*: "*where the period was in excess of a few days it would be reasonable to have evidence from the SSHD to explain the steps that had been taken and why it was not reasonably possible for the accommodation to have been found earlier, and why the balance of the relevant factors continued to justify the claimant's detention for the period.*"

    In DM (Tanzania) §148 the improved prospects of compliance brought by engagement with the asylum process combined with a failure to progress matters with the police and probation service meant that the failure to provide 'ccommodation became unlawful after 5 weeks: this case evinced §143 "*a sorry tale of a deeply unsatisfactory "system" operating between the SSHD, his suppliers, the Probation Service and sometimes the Police*"

- Gasztony [2019] EWHC 2879 (Admin) looks at the duties of the SSHD to help find accommodation for a migrant presently detained but who it is recognised should be released due to their mental health. Clearly it would not be in a detainee's interests to be released in circumstances where they had no support, even if detention would otherwise be unlawful. The SSHD might need to liaise with other agencies, but should nevertheless aim to make arrangements speedily where the support needs were clear cut. Where the needs were less clear, then they would need a reasonable time to be assessed. The SSHD needed to do everything within her power to influence the priority and urgency to ensure that arrangements were co-ordinated with appropriate urgency rather than leaving the timetable to be set by other agencies.

    However if at any point in the process the SSHD stops being able to show some meaningful progression of the search (or if the records show confusion between the responsibilities of the Probation Service and UKVI), detention may become unlawful. Thus in MS [2017] EWHC 2797 that homelessness is no legitimate reason, on its own, to prolong detention. At first the prospect of removal was reasonable. However, upon challenging his deportation in May, and the realisation in June that there would be no imminently available hearing date, the HO agreed to provide bail accommodation. At that point, the HO was entitled to take into account the claimant's personal circumstances (such as homelessness) in assessing his continued detention, but these factors would only render a short period lawful. It was held that, from July, the claimant's detention became unlawful.

- Humnyntskyi [2020] EWHC 1912 (Admin) finds that the present accommodation arrangements for offenders are unlawful, because only the cases of high risk foreign national offenders seemed to be advanced for consideration. The Judge also held that applicants should have a clear opportunity to make representations about their need for accommodation. Louis [2021] EWHC 288 (QB) finds that it is illogical and inconsistent to release a detainee, effectively onto the streets, having previously argued in the bail context that a person's previous conviction for robbery & a lack of access to means of support would be likely to lead a detainee to financial crime.

- Mohammad [2021] EWHC 240 (Admin) emphasises that an order to accommodate made as interim relief (ie on an emergency basis before the case was substantively heard) was not simply a direction to the parties about the procedure that should follow. It was an interim mandatory injunction: an order from the court. The obligation to comply remained even if the stipulated time had passed. The obligation was to achieve the result ordered, not to simply make reasonable efforts to comply. If that was not done, then a formal explanation and assurance that the breach was not intentional and that measures had been put in place to avoid a recurrence might mean further proceedings, including for contempt of court, would be unnecessary. Babbage [2021] EWHC 2995 (Admin) gives a succinct summary of the relevant test: where the decision-making records showed that release would have proceeded had accommodation been available, it would be clear that any breach of section 4 accommodation duties materially bore on the detention decision.

13.1.9.6 Detention following unlawful immigration decisions

For many years judges held that a decision maker was entitled to rely on immigration decision making that was thought lawful at the time to justify subsequent detention. Even if legal proceedings subsequently overturned such decisions. In DN (Rwanda) [2020] UKSC 7 the Supreme Court reversed this thinking. It held that detention that was founded on an unlawful immigration decision was inevitably unlawful §19:

> *the lawfulness of the detention is always referable back to the legality of the decision to deport. If that is successfully challenged, the edifice on which the detention is founded crumbles.*

DN (Rwanda) was an extreme case, in that the deportation was pursuant to a decision made under a statutory instrument which was subsequently identified as ultra vires: its makers had gone beyond the statutory powers which enabled such Orders. But Lord Kerr clearly saw the unlawfulness in question as extending to other cases. He cited *Lumba* for the proposition that:

> "*there is in principle no difference between (i) a detention which is unlawful because there was statutory power to detain and (ii) a detention which is unlawful because the decision to detain, although authorised by statute, was made in breach of a rule of public law.*"

PN (Uganda) [2020] EWCA Civ 1213 shows that reliance on the unlawful detained fast track procedures (MIL 9.4) and the unfair appeal proceedings that might have ensued was directly relevant to, and bore upon, the decision to detain. So it satisfied the test for mak"ng detention unlawful. Lawfully determining a claim's aptitude for the DFT required correctly identifying the basis for the persecution feared, the scope of documents sought to be relied on, and the availability of further evidence; the actual eventuation of material subsequently was relevant to this third question: Ali [2022] EWHC 866 (QB).

13.1.9.7 Detention in prisons

The *Detention: General Instructions* identify three classes of person as to whom the normal presumption is for detention in prison accommodation, *viz* cases involving:
- **National security**
- **Serious criminality**: involvement in serious offences involving the importation and/or supply of class A drugs, very serious violent offences with sentences of 5 years or more and/or those convicted of sexual offending involving a minor
- **Specific identification of harm** – those individuals who have been identified in custody as posing a risk of serious harm to minors, and those identified in custody as being subject to

harassment procedures who have previous breach history or refuse to sign the non-contact disclaimer

13.1.9.8 "Reception" in inadequate conditions with restrictions on liberty

Detention of asylum seekers in 2021 in the unsatisfactory conditions at Napier Barracks attracted significant media publicity. A court challenge held that there was no curfew strictly enforced at Napier Barracks meaning that there was no violation of ECHR Art 5 on that ground. However, the order that the camp was to put into strict isolation wrongly suggested a lawful underpinning: NB & Ors [2021] EWHC 1489 (Admin). Accordingly detention there was unlawful. Sadly the February 2022 report by the *APPG on Immigration Detention* recorded run-down, isolated andbeak conditions, a near total lack of privacy and private spaces at the site and inadequate access for residents to healthcare and legal advice.

13.1.9.9 EU law and detention re Dublin 3 returns

See MIL 9.5.2.3 for the likelihood of unlawful detention prior to March 2017.

13.2 Immigration bail

Temporary admission was abolished and replaced by immigration bail on 15 January 2018. All existing arrangements for those already on some form of bail were transferred over into the new system. We have already mentioned the general presumption in favour of liberty; this consideration necessarily infuses the bail process too. As the FTT Guidance puts it:

> Liberty is a fundamental right of all people and can only be restricted if there is no reasonable alternative.

There are several useful pieces of published guidance available:

- The guidance on Immigration bail
- For a brief overview, there is a basic UKVI information page and letters to ILPA outlining the operation, in practice, of the new system from UKVI, of 18 December 2017 and from the FTT, of 26 January 2018 (ILPA login required).
- The UKVI First-tier Tribunal bail guidance sets out FTT bail procedures specifically for Presenting Officers, see also *First-tier Tribunal bail - completing the bail summary*
- The release from detention procedures Guidance is aimed at staff at IRCs and in pre-departure accommodation.
- The organisations Bail for Immigration Detainees and the Asylum Support Appeals Project offer much useful information regarding the more specialist practical issues which inevitably arise.

The 2020 Covid-19 crisis shows the difficulties that a pandemic can create for detainees. The FTT became significantly more generous in its bail decisions: BID indicated of 45 applications made to mid April 43 had been successful. That was a 95.5% success rate, as against a 53.5% success rate pre-lockdown. The FTT *Help for Users* explained that during the pandemic *minded to grant* decisions are being issued to the SSHD in order to determine whether a hearing is sought to avoid unnecessary hearings.

Kaitey [2021] EWCA Civ 1875 records the SSHD's estimate that there were 90,000 people on immigration bail in December 2021. And that there is no requirement that a person be removable to be held on immigration bail. Powers of detention and to grant liberty involved different considerations.

13.2.1. Bail grants and imposition of conditions

Anyone who can be detained may be granted bail by the HO or by the Tribunal (under para 1 of Sch 10 to the IA 2016 – all references that follow are to Sch 10 unless otherwise stated)

- The HO can grant immigration bail and impose conditions
- So too can the FTT – however there are two notable limits on the grant of bail from the FTT:

- the Tribunal can grant immigration bail to those in detention who have been in the UK for eight days (para 3(3))
- where a person is facing imminent removal, the Tribunal's bail power is restricted: if the removal is set for within 14 days of the proposed bail grant, the FTT needs SSHD consent (para 3(4))
- The requirement for HO consent for release on bail where removal directions are imminent (under para 3(4)) is legally controversial, because it endangers the separation of powers between the executive and the judiciary. However, the provision survived challenge in Roszkowski [2017] EWCA Civ 1893, and so for now at least remains valid. The FTT Guidance stresses the importance of putting the SSHD to proof to show that removal directions have genuinely been set (para 119).Bail conditions can be imposed even on a person liable to detention (under Immigration Act powers generally, or because they are being considered for deportation) who can no longer be detained. Presumably this recognises the scenario where their detention would otherwise be unlawful. Thus the Immigration bail guidance gives as an example where 'there is no realistic prospect of the person's removal taking place within a reasonable time')
- Bail conditions may be varied via transfer to the SSHD (para 6(3)) if the FTT so directs (6(1)) – this is described as 'Transfer of bail to the Secretary of State' in the FTT Guidance (para 102ff). But BVN [2022] EWHC 1159 (Admin) holds that the SSHD cannot impose bail conditions inconsistent with those imposed by the High Court without applying to the court so to do.
- Bail ends where a person is granted leave, re-detained, leaves or is expelled from the country, or where their liability to detention otherwise ends (para 1(8))
- Bail decisions must be notified to the subject, giving start date and conditions, and where the FTT grants bail, to the SSHD (para 3(6), (8))
- A person may be arrested where an immigration or police officer considers there are reasonable grounds for thinking they are likely to breach, or have breached, a bail condition (para 10) (breaching these conditions is also a criminal offence under s24(1)(h) of the IA 1971)
- When the IMA 2023 inadmissibility regime enters force, there may be
  - no bail grant until the earlier of two periods in relation of detention for those purposes (ie under para 16(2C) of IA 1971 Sch 2, or s62(2A) NIAA 2002) began – either the end of 28 days from detention beginning, or the end of 8 days from a minor's detention: Sch 10 to IA 2016 para 10(3A)
  - no other legal challenge, where detention is under those provisions: "the decision is final and is not liable to be questioned or set aside in any court", unless the decision has been made in bad faith or is so procedurally defective as to fundamentally breach natural justice principles Sch 10, para 10(3A). However applications may be made for the writ of habeas corpus over this period para 10(3A)(5). This is an ancient remedy not much used in the era of modern judicial review.

The application form to apply to the HO is Bail 401. An applicant must provide

- full biographical and contact details
- their UK arrival date
- information regarding access to a travel document
- provision of an address at which to reside where available, and
- confirmation that they understand that a further two days in detention may be necessary to implement any electronic monitoring conditions considered appropriate.

Any available funds for a Financial Condition should be provided, including funds available from a third party (formerly known as a surety) whose own personal details including immigration status, occupation and relationship to detainee should be given. Grants are made via form BAIL 201.

There is no legal requirement to put up funds (see e.g. FTT bail guidance para 78), nor that the funds are necessarily available in cash. The UNHCR in their 1999 *Guidelines on Criteria and Standards Relating to the Detention of Asylum Seekers* make the point that asylum seekers should not be expected to produce sureties willing to offer prohibitively high sums of money.

Form B1 is used to apply to the FTT for bail. It includes a box to tick to confirm one's consent for future bail management to be transferred from the FTT to the SSHD. The Form requires information such as

- whether one has a legal representative
- whether an appeal is pending
- whether a prior bail application has been refused within the last 28 days
- the planned place of residence
- the amount of any Financial Condition proposed and any person supporting it
- whether an interpreter is needed for the hearing, and
- whether are any exceptional circumstances that might prevent a bail hearing by video link (which is the default option).

13.2.2 Bail conditions

Bail when granted must be subject to at least one of these conditions (see MIL 13.2.1 & BVN for limitations on SSHD's power to disagree with court-ordered bail conditions).

- **Residential and reporting conditions** (Sch 10 para 2(1)(c) & (d)): There should be no residence condition imposed on a person who proposes staying in private rented property where they are disqualified from renting (unless they have permission to rent) (see the *Immigration Bail* guidance, which itself links to the *Short Guide on Right to Rent* Guidance which outlines the circumstances where permission to rent is likely, as where there is a pending asylum or trafficking claim or there are outstanding further representations, an outstanding appeal which cannot be pursued from abroad, pending JR proceedings which have received permission). In person reporting is now supplemented by telephone reporting (from 12 April 2022) and digital reporting for those with smartphone/email access: HO *Immigration Bail Guidance* and *Reporting and Offender Management Guidance*.
- **Appearance before the SSHD or FTT** at a specified time and place (para 2(1)(a)): the *Immigration Bail* Guidance explains that this refers to one-off events rather than regular reporting, such as attending for return flights, self check-in returns, or attending travel documentation interviews (though the Guidance adds that attendance at the latter must not be *compelled* via a condition)
- **Occupational, work and study restrictions** (para 2(1)(b)): Study conditions are not essential (and in cases of doubt, there should be no such condition); children can lawfully access education until the age of 18 in the UK and so should be permitted to do so, and thereafter if they are at a point in their education that they are undertaking '*significant exams*'; asylum seekers should only face a restriction once their appeal rights are exhausted, and former unaccompanied minor asylum seekers should be allowed to continue their studies during 'leaving care' arrangements overseen by social services (see generally the *Immigration bail* guidance)
- **Financial conditions** can be added to other conditions from 2(1) (*or 2(3) once in force*) (para 2(4))
- **Electronic monitoring** (para 2(1)(e)):
  - From 31 August 2021 in England and Wales, the provisions of The Immigration Act 2016 Schedule 10 Part 1 paragraphs 2(2) and 2(3) enter force (via The (Commencement and Transitional Provisions No. 1) 2021) (applicable in Scotland/Northern Ireland from 31 August 2022).
  - These place a duty on the SSHD to electronically monitor those on immigration bail who could be detained if they are subject to deportation proceedings and reside in England & Wales, unless this would be contrary to their Convention rights or is impractical .
  - The *Immigration Bail* Guidance sets out that the EM devices may be issued at the current reporting centre or at one's home; one reason for impracticality in fitting a device is that there are not enough to go round, and past compliance is a good reason not to prioritise fitting one. The conditions will involve one's presence and absence from designated locations at a particular time. Curfews are not mandatory. 3 days will be given to make representations on EM conditions. Those subject to EM must be informed of their responsibilities and an invitation issued to raise concerns and questions. Where the duty is not applicable, EM should be considered where a person poses a high risk of harm and is less likely to be appropriate where immigration bail is granted from a position of liberty.

There is also further guidance for those on the pilot scheme *Immigration bail conditions: Electronic monitoring (EM) expansion pilot*. There are two kinds of device, fitted (ankle tags) and unfitted (which are palm size and require regular provision of fingerprints throughout the day); both use GPS to monitor movements.
- **Any other conditions** as the person granting bail thinks fit, 2(1)(f)
- Any HO view that bail conditions have been breached should be notified by form BAIL 204 giving an opportunity to make representations (*Bail Guidance*)

If there is no restriction placed on a particular activity (eg on working), we must presume it is permitted. These conditions may be varied, on notice to the individual and SSHD (para 6).

A person granted bail needs somewhere to live. Thus permission to rent will need to be granted following the grant of bail by a Tribunal or court. Where the bail grant includes a residence condition to live at a specified address, the SSHD may provide accommodation (para 9), where they could not otherwise support themselves and where there are exceptional circumstances. An application must be made in form BAIL409. Such circumstances are explained in the *Immigration bail* Guidance: essentially where the individual poses a *high risk generally* (as where they are involved in SIAC proceedings), where they pose a *high risk of causing serious harm to the public* or a *high risk of harmfully offending against individuals*. Ganpot [2023] EWHC 197 (Admin) holds that it would be contrary to the HRA 1998 to fail to provide immigration bail accommodation where someone would otherwise have to abandon a viable immigration application to return abroad where they lacked connections.

These arrangements may require probation service and local authority involvement in ensuring any risks to the community are appropriately managed. If sensible practical steps cannot be agreed to implement a decision to grant bail 'in principle', unlawful detention may arise. However this only applies where appropriately supervised accommodation is required by the grant of bail: if not, there will be no "specified address" requirement. The mere fact that a bail grant required "suitable" accommodation did not mandate a specified address: Bounar [2023] NIKB 94.

13.2.3 Mandatory considerations when assessing immigration bail

The SSHD / FTT must have regard to certain specified considerations under Sch 10 para 3(2):

- The likelihood of breaches of bail conditions or commission of offences while on bail – 3(2)(a)&(c)
- Previous convictions – anywhere, any time – 3(2)(b)
- Whether release could endanger public health/maintenance of public order – 3(2)(d)
- Whether detention is necessary for the person's own interest or the protection of others – 3(2)(e)
- Anything else considered relevant – 3(2)(f)
- Failures of cooperation with the process for administering leave or enforcing removal - 3(2)(ea)
- When the IMA 2023 inadmissibility regime enters force, whether there is a duty under s2 IMA 2023 to make removal arrangements, or where the applicant is a member of the family of such a person – Sch 10 to IA 2016, sub-paras 3(2)(eza)-(ezb)

13.2.4 Automatic bail hearings

One feature of the modern system is that the FTT must have the opportunity to consider whether a detainee should be granted bail – so the application is not wholly applicant driven. Thus the FTT Guidance styles it as 'auto-referral'.

- This applies to detainees not subject to deportation proceedings or the person is within the SIAC process and has been certified as unsuitable for bail (para 11(1)(a), 11(6)(a))
- The SSHD must *arrange a reference* (para 11(1)) within the *relevant date* (para 11(2)) – though an individual can opt-out by giving a notice that they do not seek such a reference (para 11(6)(b))
- Time for making the referral runs from either

CHAPTER 13: Enforcement; Detention, Removal and Deportation

- o the date detention began or
- o an intermediate *relevant event*: a bail decision by the FTT, withdrawal of a bail application, or withdrawal of an opt-out notice (para 11(3))
- The FTT then deals with these references as if they were a bail application (para 11(7))

13.2.5 Bail hearings before the FTT

The FTT Procedure Rules make specific provision for bail applications before the FTT at r38 onwards. The term *bail party* is used to describe both kinds of detainees likely to be involved: those applying for bail themselves, and those referred for a bail hearing. The Rules require, from a bail party making an application themselves (r38):

- Detailed grounds in support of the application
- Advanced service of a bail address
- Details of any Financial Condition and its Supporter

If the bail party is subject to a reference by the SSHD, the SSHD must provide details of the provisions under which they are detained and a copy of any decision by the SSHD on bail, and any documents relevant to these matters (r38(4A)). The bail party must be provided with notice of the reference as soon as reasonably practicable (r38(6)).

The HO must serve their bail summary, where opposing bail, by 2pm the day before the hearing, or as *soon as reasonably practicable* where the SSHD received less than 24 hours' notice of the hearing. This must identify any concerns regarding the para 3(2) factors, specify any removal directioin force, and the conditions sought if bail is granted (FTT Guidance para 17). The Guidance *First-tier Tribunal bail - completing the bail summary* explains the procedure including the importance of giving '*a fair and balanced reflection of the applicant's presence while in the UK*' and providing 'a realistic and factually-sourced timescale for resolving' any removal barrier due to litigation, casework decision making or travel documentation, bearing in mind the need to adhere to promised deadlines and to identify any potential accommodation entitlements.

> **Top Tip**
>
> It is an unfortunate fact that bail summaries are often woefully inaccurate and/or highly misleading. For example, the underlying facts are sometimes wrong, or important facts are omitted – such as difficulties the HO has had in obtaining an Emergency Travel Document. Sometimes a person will be accused of failing to report when in fact they did report, or were in immigration or criminal detention at the relevant time.
>
> It is crucial not to assume bail summaries are accurate and to take full instructions on them.

The FTT must serve its written decision on the parties to the hearing and the detaining body (r41). Where bail is granted, the decision must contain

- Its commencement date
- Any relevant information about Financial Conditions (r41(2), r42): the sum of money, when and how it is to be paid, and confirmation (by signature(s)) that all involved understand that the payment may be forfeited
- Confirmation of whether the SSHD has given consent where removal directions are due within 14 days, and confirmation that if no such consent has been forthcoming, that the bail should not be released on bail (r41(6)).

The FTTIAC has its own Guidance *Presidential Guidance Note No 1 of 2023* (from 1 March 2023).

It sets out some fine sounding *General principles*:

- It stresses that immigration detention is not to be used as punishment, or for coercive purposes, or to restrict the development of family life or the ability to put a case against removal
- Detention for three months would be considered a substantial period and six months a long period. Imperative considerations of public safety may be necessary to justify detention in excess of six months.
- An inquisitorial approach may be appropriate given the need for a Judge to efficiently collect relevant information

The FTT Guidance also gives more detail of bail procedures:

- Listing as soon as possible normally within three working days (para 17)
- Online hearings are increasingly available via MyHMCTs & should be available universally from the end of 2023 (para 20)
- A judge will decide if a request for a personal appearance at a bail hearing should be granted (para 22)
- The objective is for all involved to be present in the hearing room throughout the bail hearing, subject to judicial discretion (para 23)
- Financial Condition Supporters must be present to hear the decision and reasons (para 23): their *Privacy information notice* explains how their personal information is addressed and when it might be passed on, including to debt collection agencies
- A list of the key elements of the hearing, bearing in mind submissions should concentrate on the statutory factors under para 3(2) of Sch 10 to the IA 2016 the probable bail conditions and any removal directions (para 18) (the taking of evidence is not generally anticipated as necessary (para 26))
- Relevant considerations include the fact that absconding risks are likely to be low where the applicant is under a criminal licence or where they propose living at a stable address with supportive friends/relatives and an incentive to comply with immigration control (ie a pending application/appeal/JR) or no imminent removal prospect (para 38); licence arrangements should be presumed to adequately address risks of reoffending and HO risk assessments are unlikely to be afforded any weight being non-professional (para 51), threats to public order/health must be evidenced by the HO or will be given little weight. Immigration detention should not be used for collateral purposes such as mental health control.
- The minimum conditions of bail are likely to an appearance date condition, a residence condition and (where the appearance date is more than seven days ahead) a reporting condition (para 37, 59 onwards) (there may be additional safeguarding issues where the evidence expressly requires this para 49)
- Where a person cannot offer a bail address, the FTT must consider whether they may be eligible for support under Schedule 11 to the IA 2016: it is then common to grant bail subject to (and upon) such an address being provided (para 58)
- Decisions to refuse or record a bail application as withdrawn should be supported by typed written reasons (para 96)
- If someone on bail supported by a Financial Condition breaches their bail conditions, then the FTT will have to consider Payment Liability, by which all or part of the sum is forfeited (paras 89-90): the HO administers this pursuant to the FTT's consideration of representations
- The FTT has a discretion to permit the SSHD to vary bail conditions: the bail party must be given a chance to make representations on this, though their wishes are not decisive. One relevant consideration is whether the bail conditions being imposed are equivalent to those sought by the SSHD: in such a case it is difficult to see any chance of stricter conditions being imposed in the future, which is a reason for transfer (para 111)

Notice of hearing under the pandemic arrangements of 2020 and thereafter

The informality of the pandemic era has continued and hearing notices typically provide for remote hearings and give case management indications such as these:

- Date and time of telephone bail hearing will follow between Judge and the representatives
- 24 hours before reps are to email bailshattoncross@justice.gov.uk with a telephone number & any objection why *cannot* participate in this kind of hearing

- Applicant may be absent (unless unrepresented)
- Financial Condition Supporters may be absent but sometimes arrangements are suggested by which they might provide relevant information
- Hearing may proceed if you miss the call

13.2.6 Preparing bail applications

Bail summaries provided by the HO are known to be less than fully accurate. For example, the HO may allege that a person was an absconder when in fact they were not or may fail to record that a person has complied with previous conditions for bail or temporary admission. The FTT Bail Guidance requires express confirmation of the chronology provided therein (para 23(e)). It is therefore crucial to take instructions on the accuracy of a bail summary. Where possible, the original reasons for detention should be obtained (e.g. via a Subject Access Request): this should make it harder for an inventive bail summary to supplement them with reasons added after the event.

It can be very helpful to prepare a witness statement by a bail applicant. Such statements need not be long, but it should be borne in mind that live evidence at a bail hearing, particularly one by video link, is often unhelpful to the applicant. Any applicant for bail can be expected to state that they will comply with conditions, for example, and such assurances therefore carry little weight. Oral evidence is not routinely expected in bail examinations. In any event, cross examination of an unprepared bail applicant is best avoided.

When taking instructions from a bail applicant, ensure you cover:

- Their case in the light of each relevant detention criteria/factor
- Their proposed lifestyle following release from detention
- The underlying facts said to give rise to a power to detain – e.g. was the person working in breach of conditions, and/or are the HO right to say they have overstayed their leave?
- Presuming they are not at the end of the line in immigration terms, the strength of their case for leave on human rights or other grounds?

> **Top Tip**
>
> *Some thoughts on Financial Condition Supporters*
>
> It is important to adequately prepare the Financial Condition Supporters for a bail hearing: for example, they may be subjected to criminal records and address checks; their past record in backing the release of detainees may be investigated. Therefore, it is important that they are aware this will happen; otherwise they may get an unpleasant surprise at the hearing. Also ask them about the following:
>
> - ☐ Any criminal convictions (especially offences of dishonesty or related to immigration)
> - ☐ Their financial situation, including expenses and income – any recent large transactions into their account should be explained
> - ☐ Liquidity of assets – they may have to deposit the money in question, have they thought through how they might deal with the chance of having to forfeit it? Is the sum they are offering credible given their circumstances?
> - ☐ Evidence of support and accommodation – do the proposed funds come from sources that raise questions of ethics or immigration offences?
> - ☐ Plans regarding any trips abroad or other engagements which might impact on the effectiveness of their control over the bail party, or their ability to support subsequent extensions of bail.
> - ☐ How they know the applicant and how they intend to maintain contact with, or control over, them
> - ☐ What they would do in the event that the bailee did threaten to breach their bail conditions?
>
> Parents and partners are often not the best choice. This is because of their close relationship with the applicant for bail: an immigration judge may have had the unpleasant task of conducting forfeiture hearings with such family members and will consider them not best able to judge a bail applicant's character because of their closeness, or alternatively too much under the influence of the bail applicant

or willing to do anything to get the bail applicant out of detention, including forfeit large amounts of money.

Close friends or colleagues willing to put up substantial sums and who can explain that they understand the risk may be better choices.

Generally, Bail Circle volunteers or detention visitors are not considered good sureties by mosimmigration judges, because they are perceived as having limited knowledge of the detainee and only limited control over their future intentions.

Some thoughts on taking instructions from the client

Make sure you take instructions on:

- The key detention criteria:
- i.e. the client's perspective on their immigration history
- impact of immigration history on likelihood of breaching bail conditions, any immigration or other kinds of offending, its severity, and the likelihood of its repetition
- Do they have any pending application or appeal? In a nutshell, how strong is it?
- Whether the facts that are said to give rise to a power to detain are truly established e.g. was the person working in breach of conditions, and/or are the HO right to say they have overstayed their leave?
- Do they have an entitlement to remain in the UK under a HO policy?
- Ensure that any referrals are made that are shown to be necessary by the instructions – e.g. for mental or physical health care.
- Ensure that instructions are taken in a way that recognises any vulnerability of the client.

Preparation for remote bail hearings

Issues to address will include:

- The importance of concisely stating the case for release from detention
- Ensuring that all information reasonably available is obtained before applying for bail
- Seeking contact with the HO representative to ensure that all relevant issues are raised and understood
- Ensuring the hearing is limited to those issues previously notified
- Remember that rule 40 of the FTT Procedure Rules requires that
    … if the Secretary of State opposes a bail application, the Secretary of State must provide the Tribunal and the bail party with a written statement of the reasons for doing so — (a) not later than 2.00 pm on the working day before the hearing.

- Ensuring that the bail bundle includes the best possible evidence from Financial Condition Supporters including witness statement evidence of a person's good character.

13.2.7 National security cases

Under the NIAA 2002, the SSHD may certify that it is believed that the person's presence in the United Kingdom is a 'risk to national security' and that it is suspected that the person is connected to international terrorism. On certifying an individual is such a person the HO may take removal action.

Applications for bail are brought before the SIAC rather than the SSHD or FTT (see information here). Section 32 of the AITCA 2004 gives a right of appeal regarding the grant of bail, on a point of law, to the Court of Appeal, to which the normal SIAC processes then apply, i.e. an appeal may be brought only with the leave of the Commission or, if such leave is refused, with the leave of the appropriate appeal court.

13.3 Administrative removal

Most non-voluntary removals of foreign nationals from the UK take place by way of 'administrative removal'. Which isn't 'deportation': that takes place only where the HO has decided that the person's presence in the UK is not conducive to the public good, or where automatic deportation provisions apply due to certain criminal convictions. Both 'administrative removal' and 'deportation' involve the person being forced to leave the UK.

There is a safety-valve provision which must be considered before a person is removed if a case is reviewed: r353B (MIL 4.2.2). Any further submissions from a person should be considered quickly, explains the *Further submissions* Guidance, with a view to granting leave if necessary.

Once outside the UK, the removed person will be prevented from applying for re-entry for a 10 year period (Part 9 r9.8.1, 9.8.7, because this would be an involuntary return at public expense): unless the applicant is seeking to return under an Appendix FM category (subject to the "contriving to frustrate" the rules proviso r9.8.2). This distinguishes administrative removal from deportation, as a deportation order excludes the person forever unless the deportation order is revoked.

13.3.1 Administrative removal

Before April 2015, removing an illegal entrant or a person who had breached the conditions of their stay was a two-part process. Removal decisions were made under the old version of s10 of the IAA 1999, usually triggered by overstaying, leave breaching or use of deception. But first a decision on any application to extend their leave was necessary. This two-part process was cumbersome.

Now we have a streamlined removal process, requiring just one decision to refuse or curtail leave before the person can be removed: a process summarised as '*administrative removal*'.

The removal power applies to any person who '*requires leave to enter or remain in the United Kingdom but does not have it*', s10(1). Those who do have it, but are caught in breach (e.g. working in breach of a restriction or prohibition), will have their leave cancelled first. There is no further step required before removal can proceed.

The power also applies to a member of the family of the person facing removal, s10(2).

- A member of the family is widely defined to include partner, parent, adult dependent relative or child or child living in the same household where the person facing removal has care of the child, s10(3)
- The member of the family must either have leave to enter or remain on the basis of family life with the person facing removal or, in the opinion of the Secretary of State or immigration officer, if making an application for leave would not be granted leave in their own right but would be granted leave on the basis of family life with the person facing removal if the person facing removal themselves had leave, s10(4). The removal power does not apply if the family member is a British or Irish citizen or has permission under the EUSSch, s10(5)

If a notice of removal is served, the notice invalidates any leave previously possessed, s10(6).

Only limited notice will be given in these cases (essentially the policy is that the last refusal of an application will include notification that removal may subsequently take place at 72 hours notice, within a three month window running from shortly after the decision is served: MIL 14.2.6). Any notice of removal will be by way of courtesy, says the policy: but this must be read with the the fundamental constitutional right of access to the court, see e.g. Medical Justice [2011] EWCA Civ 1710. And, of course, a decision that is not communicated has no legal effect: see Anufrijeva [2004] 1 AC 604 at 621 at [26].Decisions to remove under s10 are not appealable immigration decision. One needs to put an . So it is only the subsequent making of an asylum or human rights claim, and its refusal, that can generate a right of appeal (MIL 14.2.3).

The *Administrative Removal: notification and implementation – interim guidance* (MIL 14.2.6 addresses removal windows) sets out that:

- RED notices are used to inform people of removal liability (and transit and final destinations): they may contain s120 notices stressing the last chance to raise grounds to stay (see MIL 14.2.6 for removal windows) – different reference numbers indicate different kinds of return, enforced/voluntary/family, whether an opportunity has been given to make a fee-paid application, RED.0001 MS is modern slavery/trafficking tag
- Indeed a s120 notice must be served at some point in every case
- Ministerial clearance is required if a MP has made representations; there are minimum levels of authority to authorise removal and authority may need to be obtained afresh after 10 days or where there have been significant changes of circumstances
- RED Cancellation notices do not invalidate pending applications
- There is specific wording for the liability to being classed as an illegal entrant where applicable, eg via an agent, with no credible explanation of entry, clandestinely

Immigration raids often catch people suspected of working in breach of their conditions.

- The Guidance on *Illegal working operations* explains the procedures
- Kanwal [2022] EWHC 110 (Admin) looks at the procedure for an illegal working interview and finds that on-the-spot questioning at the place where a migrant was encountered and suspected of illegal working was fair so long as the purpose of the enquiry was made clear to them at the time
- Shah [2022] EWHC 3033 (Admin) looks at the procedures adopted in dawn raids leading to cancellation of permission, noting that the "administrative caution" issued to suspects was not a criminal caution that required PACE safeguards. Allowance should be made for the stress of a dawn raid on an interviewee
- Campos [2022] EWHC 3299 (Admin) emphasises that JR is a poor remedy for resolving disputes about what was said during on-the-spot interviews: the court is likely to accept the immigration officers' version

13.3.2 Protections for children and families

There are some protections for children and families.

- **S78A of the NIAA 2002** provides protection from removal where a child is to be removed and a parent or person with care of the child or a person in the child's household is also to be removed.
- The provision provides for a 28-day grace period from exhaustion of appeal rights in which actual removal is forbidden for the child and for the adult where 'if, as a result, no relevant parent or carer would remain in the United Kingdom'. Preparatory steps towards removal such as the setting of removal directions or making of a deportation order are not prohibited.
- S54A BCIA 2009 requires that the Independent Family Returns Panel be consulted by the Secretary of State 'on how best to safeguard and promote the welfare of the children of the family':
- A 'family returns case' is a case where removal of a child is going to take place along with removal of a person who:
    - is a parent of the child or has care of the child, and
    - is living in a household in the United Kingdom with the child
- HO guidance on the Family returns process is in the Returns preparation section.
- There is no duty on the Secretary of State to abide by any recommendations, only to consult. Recommendations or comments could therefore be disregarded by the Secretary of State, although that would obviously call into question whether the Secretary of State was abiding by the duty imposed by s55 of the 2009 Act and reiterated by s71 of this Act, which provides:

> For the avoidance of doubt, this Act does not limit any duty imposed on the Secretary of State or any other person by section 55 of the Borders, Citizenship and Immigration Act 2009 (duty regarding the welfare of children).

> **Example**
>
> **Student caught working in breach of conditions**
>
> Meet Leonardo. He has made an application for further leave to remain as a Student (the following analysis would apply to any dependents he might have, too). The application is granted.
>
> Leonardo meets some Immigration Officers who think he may be working in breach of his conditions. As such a person, s10 permits his removal if he requires leave to enter or remain in the United Kingdom but does not have it. Now of course he presently has permission to be here: but that can be changed in an instant, as it is open to the HO, upon discovering that a person has breached their conditions, to ccancel said leave, under the IRs (r9.8.8). So, as long as a curtailment decision has been made, Leonardo has now become someone who requires leave to be lawfully present here, and lacks it. There is guidance in the 'Enforcement guidance' under 'Considering Immigration status and deciding enforcement action' entitled Liability to Administrative Removal (non-EEA): consideration and notification (formerly in Chapter 50: EIG) on the need for '*firm and recent evidence*' of a breach of '*sufficient gravity*' to warrant action being taken against him.
>
> Can he appeal against this decision? No. He can appeal only if he receives the refusal of a human rights or asylum claim.
>
> Can he bring an administrative review of the decision? No, the remedy is not available for a removal case like this (see Appendix AR of the IRs as to the type of decisions which are 'eligible' for AR).
>
> How about JR? Possible: because there simply is no alternative remedy by way of an administrative review or appeal. However, presuming cancellation was via the General refusal reasons , this may be unpromising: the UT on JR will just be determining the question on the evidence available to the decision maker, which is likely to be rather one-sided. Essentially the UT will be asking whether the SSHD acted reasonably in adjudging Leonardo's sporting of a chef's hat in the wrong part of a restaurant at the wrong time was irrational or overlooked relevant evidence: see Giri [2015] EWCA Civ 784.
>
> Whatever the theory, will there be an *effective opportunity* for JR? Tricky. He'll need to get a move on. The HO need give him no further notice of removal (see removal procedures in the Enforcement guidance' under 'Considering Immigration status and deciding enforcement action' entitled Liability to Administrative Removal (non-EEA): consideration and notification (formerly in Chapter 50: EIG).
>
> If Leonardo has powerful UK ties, his best bet will probably be to make a human rights application speedily (if he is detained, he need not follow the formalities of the right form and fee). This might include arguments about whether or not the HO was right to think he breached his leave. Then the HO will have to consider that application, and whether or not to certify it as 'clearly unfounded' if refusing it: see generally the discussion in Ahsan [2017] EWCA Civ 2009 §115ff.

13.4 Deportation
13.4.1 Power to deport

Deportation allows for the expulsion of a person whose presence is thought inconsistent with the public good; deportation orders also prohibit their return for significant periods.

By s5(1) of the 1971 Act the Secretary of State may make a deportation order against a person liable to deportation under s3(5). A deportation order requires the person to depart, invalidates any leave that they hold, and prohibits their return whilst such order is extant (s5). Before attempting to apply to return to the UK, the deportee must first apply for the deportation order to be revoked.

Section 3 of the IAA 1971 sets out that:

- A non-British citizen is liable to deportation if this is thought conducive to the public good, or they are a family member of such a person (s3(5))

- This includes where they are convicted of an imprisonable offence and recommended by a criminal court for deportation (s3(6))

This power is the launchpad for deportation generally. So the automatic deportation provisions of the UKBA 2007 are premised on decisions made under the 1971 Act.

Section 7 of the 1971 Act provides for exemption from deportation for long term residents who:

- are Commonwealth or Irish citizens and were such on 1 January 1971 when the 1971 Act came into force
- were ordinarily resident in the UK on 1 January 1973 ('ordinarily resident' has no statutory meaning but has been held to exclude unlawful residence)
- have been resident in the UK for five years at the time of either a court or the Secretary of State considering whether to make a deportation order.

There are three regimes for mainstream deportation cases: discretionary, automatic, and national security. The latter is largely beyond MIL's scope. And there is a different regime for those EU nationals and their family members who are protected by the Brexit Withdrawal Agreement (MIL 11.8).

It will be appreciated that there is fairly limited scope for discretionary deportation (which arises simply on the basis of s3(5) or (6) of the IA 1971), given the relatively low threshold that operates to attract automatic deportation (which is authorised by s3(5) or (6) read with s32 of UKBA 2007).

However, it can be utilised in instances where one of the exceptions to automatic deportation applies.

It is also the mechanism used to effect deportation in instances where an individual presents as a persistent offender, but where sentencing does not reach the automatic deportation threshold.

The processes are largely the same: those identified for deportation are provided with a s120 notice and are expected to raise any grounds they have for challenging the decision. If the HO declines to modify its view, and those grounds involved the making of an asylum or human rights claim, the person will have a right of appeal (subject to the certification regime – MIL 9.6.1 & 14.3.1 & 13.5.2.1). Perhaps the most notable procedural difference between automatic and discretionary deportations is that in the former, the deportation order itself is made very early in the process without the formal need for a notice of intention to deport or a notice of a decision to make a deportation order.

The Rules explain there is a general presumption in favour of deportation if the Refugee Convention or ECHR would not prevent it (r13.1.3), and summarise liability to deportation thus:

- Conviction of a criminal offence & receiving a sentence >12 months (r13.1.1(a))
- The SSHD considering deportation is conducive to the public good (r13.1.1(b))
- Being the spouse/partner/child of a deportee (r13.1.1(c))
- Though for Irish nationals, only where the court recommends deportation or the SSHD exceptionally considers the public interest requires it (r13.1.2)

The Independent Chief Inspector issued a damning report on the efficiency and effectiveness of the removals process in June 2023: *An inspection of the Home Office's operations to effect the removal of Foreign National Offenders*. There was a lack of reliable consistent data and management information available. This raised broader concerns for the Home Office in anticipation of a likely increase in immigration detention, removals and caseworking under the IMA 2023. The Early Removal Scheme (MIL 13.5.3) was not working well leading to unnecessary UK prison costs.

13.4.1.1 National security cases

Where the SSHD certifies that the decision to make a deportation order was taken on the grounds that the person's removal from the UK would be in the interests of national security (NIAA 2002 s. 97A), such a person will be able to appeal against the decision to deport only to SIAC and only from outside the country.

If the person then makes a human rights claim, they can appeal in-country unless the SSHD certifies that removal would not breach the person's human rights. In such a case, the person can appeal, in country, to SIAC against that certificate.

13.4.1.2 Automatic deportation

'Automatic' deportations were introduced in the wake of the foreign prisoner scandal in 2006 (wherein the press made much of the government's failure to deport foreign criminals). In fact, the process is not completely automatic as there are various exceptions to expulsion.

In outline:

- Section 32 of the UKBA 2007 places a duty on the Secretary of State to make a deportation order in respect of a person who is not a British citizen and who has been convicted in the UK of an offence and sentenced to a period of imprisonment of at least 12 months (i.e. 'Condition 1).
- Condition 2, for serious criminals not imprisoned for 12 month or more, is not operative.
- Imprisonment for 12 months or more does not include suspended sentences, or shorter consecutive sentences which only meet the test when aggregated (see s38).
- Section 32(4) introduced a statutory presumption that a deportation to which section 32 applies is conducive to the public good for the purpose of s3(5)(a) 1971 Act.
- The convictions must have taken place in the UK: SC Albania [2020] UKUT 187 (IAC).

This s32 duty applies to all foreign criminals except where they fall within one of the exceptions in section 33. Even where an exception does apply, deportation may still be considered appropriate under the existing discretionary deportation provisions of the IA 1971.

The exceptions in s33 UBKA 2007 are as follows:

1. breach of the ECHR or Refugee Conventions
2. age (under 18 at date of conviction)
3. breach of EU Treaty rights
4. extradition – where the person is the subject of extradition proceedings
5. mental health grounds – but only where specific sections of the Mental Health Act 1983 apply to the person
6. recognised victim of trafficking – it is acceptance by the Competent Authority, rather than the making of a claim, that is critical
7. possession of leave under the EUSSch system or under the Withdrawal Agreement or its EEA/Swiss equivalents

The burden is on the applicant to raise the operation of an exception and to evidence its application. Where one of these exceptions is held to be operative, either by the SSHD on receipt of representations or by a judge on appeal, the deportation order against an applicant wil be revoked. Foreign criminal status is to be determined at the date of the SSHD's decision to make a deportation order: Zulfiqar [2022] EWCA Civ 492.

Yussuf [2018] UKUT 117 (IAC) holds that a person can be deported under UKBA 2007 without any decision formally being made under IA 1971 addressing whether deportation is conducive to the public good.

The mental health protections have been examined in the case law.

- KE (Nigeria) [2017] EWCA Civ 1382 holds that offenders sentenced to a hospital order are caught by s117D(4)(d) and so fall under the automatic deportation provisions

- MZ [2020] UKUT 225 (IAC) looks at a person sentenced to a hospital order following a finding under section 5(1)(b) of the Criminal Procedure (Insanity) Act 1964 that he 'is under a disability and that he did the act or made the omission charged against him'. This was merely a finding and did not amount to a conviction. So he was not subject to automatic deportation nor to the 'unduly harsh' provisos re private and family life within A399-399 of the Rules, as he was not a foreign criminal

The Procedure for deportation

Turning then to the procedures for discretionary and automatic deportation decisions, the processes are slightly different, though the differences have few practical implications.

Discretionary Deport
- Secretary of State identifies a person subject to deportation
- Notice of liability to deportatin is issued and an opportunity is afforded to make representations
- Secretary of State determines whether to proceed with enforcement action, and if so notice of intention to deport is issued
- No deportation order is made unless and until any application/appeal is finally determined

Automatic Deport
- Secretary of State identifies a person subject to deportation
- An order is made upon identification of offending falling within the statutory scheme of the 2007 Act
- An opportunity to afforded to make representations for inclusion within the statutory exceptions contained in section 33 of the 2007 Act
- If inclusion within the exceptions is demonstrated, on application or appeal, the deport order is revoked

13.4.2 Criteria for deportation

13.4.2.1 Deportation criteria inside the rules

The IRs in respect of deportation have changed substantially over the years to reflect the ever-growing level of political attention given to foreign national prisoners. The courts and Tribunal struggle to keep up: you will often see that lead cases are interpreting the last set of rules, not the present ones.

The IRs governing deportation decisions were amended as part of the general human rights reforms on 9 July 2012 to incorporate the government's view of how Article 8 considerations should be applied, and again on 28 July 2014 to tighten things up rather more. Those latter changes took effect, according to their commencement provisions in HC532, on 28 July 2014 and apply to all ECHR Article 8 claims from foreign criminals *which are decided on or after that date*. The Rules were rewritten on 12 April 2023 – they are no longer numbered in the 390s (398-399 were especially famous) but take the format 13.1.1-13.4.5. The rules are glossed by Chapter 13 of the IDIs at: *Criminality guidance in Article 8 ECHR cases*.

CHAPTER 13: Enforcement; Detention,
Removal and Deportation

The r398-399 regime was usefully summarised by Pitchford LJ in AQ & Ors (Nigeria)[2015] EWCA Civ 250 from [66] onwards – and they are rather more concisely expressed in s117C of NIAA 2002 in the context of the general considerations to be taken into account by courts and tribunals when considering the public interest in deportation cases. In fact his summary remains useful for the latest Part 13 Rules.

Whatever the precise numbering of the Rules, the courts have made increasingly clear that the considerations under the IRs and outside them, under s117C, are effectively the same. They effectively set up a regime of three categories:

(1) **Minor offenders**: those sentenced to less than 12 months with no element of serious harm or persistent offending: they need to show that expulsion would be ***disproportionate to their private and family life***
(2) **Medium offenders**: those sentenced to imprisonment of 12 months plus or whose offending is significant because of a conviction causing serious harm or persistent offending:
   - they must establish that their expulsion would be ***unduly harsh*** where they can meet one of the exceptions under the Rules relating to a relationship with their partner or British citizen/7-year resident child, or where they can meet the private life proviso
   - and if they can't squeeze into one of those 3 exceptions, they must establish a ***very compelling*** case against deportation
(3) **Serious offenders**: those sentenced to imprisonment of 4 years of more: they must establish a ***very compelling*** case against deportation

SM (Zimbabwe) [2021] EWCA Civ 1566 stresses that the best measure of the seriousness of an offence is the length of the sentence. Gordon [2021] UKUT 287 (IAC) reminds judges that the public interest must be assessed by reference to the *actual sentence* imposed – not the sentence that might have been imposed before some discount was applied (eg for an early guilty plea). Normally that will be the sole relevant question. But where there are salient aggravating or mitigating circumstances surrounding the offence they may be taken into account. Though if doing so it is important to avoid double counting any particular factor: as those same circumstances may have featured in the sentencing remarks. Savran v Denmark [2021] ECHR 1025 stresses the relevance of mental health to culpability though questions whether reoffending due to mental health problems would constitute an Article 3 violation (MIL 5.6.2).

It would be wrong to say the Rules are a 'complete code'. However we can say they are a complete code once read with s117, see eg HA Iraq [2020] EWCA Civ 1176 (§13, 27-28):

> *'the statutory structure is a "complete code" in the sense that the entirety of the proportionality assessment required by article 8 can and must be conducted within it*
> …
> *the Strasbourg case-law about the application of article 8 in cases of this kind must and can be accommodated within the statutory structure.'*

In Binaku [2021] UKUT 34 (IAC) the UT emphasises that the appeal should be determined by reference to the factors identified in s117C NIAA 2002 *rather* than those in the IRs. If the Rules ever suggest a higher test should apply than s117C authorises, then it is the statute that should prevail.

The Rules apply in the case of a 'foreign criminal': i.e. a non-British citizen convicted of an offence and who (s117D(c) NIAA 2002) who:

(i) has been sentenced to a period of imprisonment of at least 12 months,
(ii) has been convicted of an offence that has caused serious harm, or
(iii) is a persistent offender.

S117C is laid out full below, in the sections under 13.6 '*The substantive law on deportation relevant to appeals*'. The Rules essentially provide (r13.2.1-13.2.6) that:

In the cases of medium offenders, where rr398(b) or (c) applies (i.e. where criminality was punished by imprisonment of between one and four years, or where the Secretary of State thinks the offending

©HJT

caused serious harm or considers that they were a persistent offender showing particular disregard for the law), the public interest in deportation will be outweighed only where

- **family life** is established via a genuine and subsisting parental relationship with a British citizen or seven-year resident child where it would be
  - unduly harsh for the child to live with the deportee abroad and -
  - unduly harsh for the child to live without them in the UK (r13.2.5: formerly r399(a));
  - The fact that the parents might claim to plan to take an action that would have unreasonable consequences for a child does not render the consequences unduly harsh: decision makers should presume that parents would ultimately act reasonably and their childrens' best interests. HA (Iraq) [2020] EWCA Civ 1176

- **family life** is established via a genuine and subsisting relationship with a British citizen or settled partner (r13.2.6: formerly r399(b)):
  - where the relationship was formed at a time when the deportee was in the UK lawfully and their immigration status was not precarious,- where it would be unduly harsh for the partner to live with the deportee abroad or without them in the UK: at one time the Rules expressly required compelling circumstances over and above the Appendix FM level as expressed in EX.2, i.e. exceeding 'very significant difficulties/very serious hardship'

- **private life** is established via (r13.2.3: formerly r399A):
  - lawful residence in the UK for most of the deportee's life
  - they are socially and culturally integrated here
  - there would be very significant obstacles to his integration into the country of return. For more on this test, see the section on Private life in Chapter 5.

Mahmood [2020] EWCA Civ 717 explains how to assess whether an offence has caused "serious harm" for the purposes of section s117D(2)(c) of the NIAA 2002.
- The SSHD bore the burden of proof and needed to prove each element of the definition on balance of probabilities. In so doing the SSHD could refer to sources such as the sentencing remarks
- The thinking in the refusal letter should be addressed by the FTT but carries no particular weight
- "Serious harm" included acts of emotional and economic harm.
- Whilst minor offending may cause serious harm to society, one could not say that any individual offence considered in isolation had done so. Acts of shoplifting might be a serious social problem but one could not reasonably say that individual acts of that kind caused serious harm either to the shopowner or the public. Specific evidence would be needed to link an immigration control offence to some serious harm to the public.
- Relevant considerations included the nature of the offence itself, the sentencing remarks and victim statements (though the SSHD need not adduce the latter as they were part of the background to the sentencing remarks)
- For attempted crimes, it could be expected that the sentence would exceed 12 months before one could say it was a serious one; offences of actual bodily harm for which imprisonment had been imposed could reasonably be thought to have caused serious harm
- The Sentencing Council Definitive Guidelines were likely to be of assistance though were not determinative

In Wilson [2020] UKUT 350 (IAC) the UT summarised its view of the assessment of serious harm on appeal, having particular regard to Mahmood. It noted that the potential deportee's evidence on knife crime should be treated with caution; the mere potential for a crime causing serious harm was irrelevant, and the fact that it contributed to a widespread problem was not sufficient absent distinct evidence of the actual offence's impact. In Wilson itself the sentencing remarks had emphasised that carrying a knife in a public place was a serious matter, However the UT found that the FTT had been entitled to have regard to the explanation that this was for self-defence, the fact that the knife had not been brandished, and had been voluntarily offered to the police.

Wilson also emphasises that judges must always carry out a proportionality balancing exercise in a deportation appeal. Simply finding that an offence had not caused serious harm was not enough to justify allowing an appeal.

LT (Kosovo) [2016] EWCA Civ 1246 questions whether *all* drugs offences are necessarily serious. But the SSHD's view that dealing in Class A drugs was always serious was reasonable.

The recent case of OH (Algeria) [2019] EWCA Civ 1763 confirms that references to past periods of imprisonment exceeding 12 months in the deportation provisions of NIAA 2002 could refer to any historic incarceration, however long ago it had taken place.

CI (Nigeria) [2019] EWCA Civ 2027 examines s117C(4) NIAA 2002 which provides an exception to deportation where a person is integrated in the UK, would face very significant obstacles to integration abroad, and has been "*lawfully resident*" in the UK for most of their life.
- When assessing UK integration, it was necessary to have regard to social ties: relationships with friends and relatives, and ties via employment or other paid or unpaid work or through participation in communal activities.
- A person's social identity was formed, at a deep level, by shared customs, traditions, practices, beliefs, values, linguistic idioms and other local knowledge which gave them a place in society or a social group and generated a sense of belonging.
- Pursuing a criminal lifestyle was likely to minimise ties of this nature, because of a disassociation from normal society and given that any spells of imprisonment would diminish one's social connections during the sentence and make one less employable thereafter.
- Even so, it was hard to see that criminality could destroy the integration of someone whose whole identity had formed during UK residence. When assessing the existence of "*very significant obstacles to integration*" abroad, positive evidence would be needed to justify an inference that a migrant raised in the UK had somehow gained knowledge of their country of origin's culture and traditions. The severity of offending would need to be assessed in the context of a person's childhood experiences: abuse and deficient parenting might reduce the public interest in deportation.

Definition of 'partner'

Partners are defined under Appendix FM as those in contracted relationships or engaged to one another, or cohabitees for more than two years. However that definition is not expressly carried over to the deportation regime, either for the deportation Rules or for s117C. Nevertheless, the UT in Buci [2020] UKUT 87 (IAC) observed that the scheme of both Rules and statute must be presumed to focus on relationships where there was genuine emotional commitment: not for example on transient boyfriend/girlfriend relationships which had not yet become sufficiently serious and committed. Ultimately, however, the impact of the deportee's departure on anyone with whom they had a relationship of any significance whatsoever would have to enter the equation where a Judge reached the point of considering whether there were "*very compelling circumstances*" in cases of sentences exceeding four years or where the partner, child or private life exceptions were not established.

In the cases of serious offenders, where r13.2.2 applies (i.e. where criminality was punished by imprisonment **exceeding four years or more**) or, for medium offenders who cannot show private and family life to the degree set out in the relevant exceptions (r13.2.1(b)), the public interest in deportation will only be outweighed by other factors where there are **very compelling circumstances over and above** the three private and family life routes just described (see e.g. AQ & Ors at [70]).

'Persistent offender', 'unduly harsh' and 'precarious'

The meaning of the term **'persistent offender'** (now r13.2.1) , and in the definition of 'foreign criminal' in s117D, NIAA 2002) was considered in Chege [2016] UKUT 187 (IAC):

> A 'persistent offender' is someone who keeps on breaking the law. That does not mean, however, that he has to keep on offending until the date of the relevant decision or that the continuity of the offending cannot be broken. A 'persistent offender' is not a permanent status that can never be lost once it is acquired, but an individual can be regarded as a 'persistent offender' for the purpose of the Rules and the 2002 Act even though he may not have offended for some time. The question whether he fits that description will depend on the overall picture

and pattern of his offending over his entire offending history up to that date. Each case will turn on its own facts.`

In SC (Zimbabwe) [2018] EWCA Civ 929 the CA approved Chege. In short, for the 'persistent offender' test to be satisfied, something more is required than mere repeat offending; furthermore, the status can be lost via a significant period of non-offending.

The UT in MAB [2015] UKUT 435 (IAC) (endorsed by KO (Nigeria) UKSC [2018] 53 looked at the meaning of **unduly harsh** in terms of the *threshold* for the severity of the problems that it implies, with a dictionary close to hand, and concluded in the headnote:

> Whether the consequences of deportation will be 'unduly harsh' for an individual involves more than 'uncomfortable, inconvenient, undesirable, unwelcome or merely difficult and challenging' consequences and imposes a considerably more elevated or higher threshold.
>
> The consequences for an individual will be 'harsh' if they are 'severe' or 'bleak' and they will be 'unduly' so if they are 'inordinately' or 'excessively' harsh taking into account of all the circumstances of the individual.

For some time the appropriate approach to the question of what was **'unduly harsh'** was uncertain There'were two possible interpretations. The phrase might refer to circumstances that are unduly harsh:

> (1) because a child's best interests or the impact on a partner were adversely affected to a degree that was unduly harsh
>
> (2) in all the circumstances, having regard to a child's best interests as a primary consideration, but not treating them as a trump card: so the severity of offending and issues of immigration history could overcome a child's best interests

The matter was resolved by KO (Nigeria) where the Supreme Court upheld (1) and rejected (2), holding that it would be wrong to hold the severity of offending against a child. Judges *should* assess the question of whether consequences are 'unduly harsh' by reference to the statutory criteria which distinguish between low level, medium and serious offenders; but beyond that, they should not hold the severity of offending against a child.

In Patel [2020] UKUT 45 (IAC) the UT carries out a detailed review of the relevance of British citizenship to a child affected by a parent's deportation. There was nothing in the statutory scheme or HO policy to show that having a British citizen child furnishes powerful reasons for finding that the effect of the deportation of a parent on the child would be unduly harsh. There would have to be some *substantial* interference with the rights and expectations that come with being British before the position could be seas one where the consequences for the child were *unduly harsh*.

SM (Zimbabwe) [2021] EWCA Civ 1566 emphasises that the "unduly harsh" threshold connoted circumstances logically falling somewhere between the low level faced by those subject to ordinary immigration removal and the very compelling threshold for serious offenders. The threshold was also subject to the almost infinitely variable range of circumstances in the cases of children where there is no baseline of ordinariness. An over-ready reliance on Sedley LJ's *dictum* in *Lee* that the breaking up of families is "what deportation does" was to be deprecated.

Precariousness is relevant to the question of whether someone is eligible for the partner route for medium offenders. Rhuppiah [2018] UKSC 58 holds that any immigration status short of ILR counts as 'precarious'. It also holds that when considering the statutory factors generally, it is necessary to apply some degree of flexibility. Some of the earlier case law probably survives this development (MIL 5.4.8).

What approach should be taken to periods where an application for leave was outstanding?
In SC (Jamaica) it was held that an asylum seeker was lawfully resident pending the outcome of their successful application for asylum. CI confirmed that this principle only protected refugees pending their formal recognition:

the interpretation which is most consistent with the aims of the legislation, including the aim of legal certainty, looks simply at the person's legal status at the relevant time (subject to the special case of successful asylum-seekers). If a "foreign criminal" has no legal right to be in the UK and is in breach of UK immigration law by being here, then that person is not "lawfully resident" in the UK. The fact that the Secretary of State has adopted a concessionary policy which means that no enforcement action would in practice be taken does not alter this position. Nor does the fact that an application has been made for leave to remain. It is only if and when the application is granted that the individual's legal status can be said to have changed.

This does not mean that it is always irrelevant to ask whether, if CI's application for leave to remain had been made or determined sooner than it was, the application would or should have succeeded.

There was no general principle that a period of temporary admission (now immigration bail) pending the outcome of an application which subsequently succeeds meant one was lawfully resident.

- Some individuals will have had the opportunity to register as British citizens during their childhood, but for whatever reason the chance was not taken up. In Akinyemi [2017] EWCA Civ 236 the Court of Appeal found that a person who had been in that situation for a significant period during their childhood could not be said to be present **precariously**.
- In Terrelonge [2015] UKUT 653 (IAC), the UT concludes that even a person with ILR has **'precarious'** immigration status from the time they fulfil the definition of 'foreign criminal', in either of its statutory senses: i.e. from
    o The taking effect of the UKBA 2007 on 30 October 2007 for persons sentenced to more than a years' imprisonment;
    o The taking effect of the NIAA 2002 s117D from 28 July 2014 for persons sentenced to a lesser period but who have been convicted of an offence causing serious harm or who is a persistent offender

Accordingly any relationship entered into from the point of attracting a relevant sentence would be treated as established at a time when their position was precarious.

See of GM (Sri Lanka) [2019] EWCA Civ 1630 for the relevance of being on a pathway to settlement to precariousness (MIL 5.4.8). It emphasises that may be relevant to assessing. .

Less serious foreign criminals

Those outside the 'foreign criminal' threshold are addressed at r13.1.3 which essentially applies a classical ECHR Art 8 test without any especially high thresholds being introduced.

This strongly indicates that the normal five-stage Razgar test is to be applied, without any requirement that a *particularly compelling* case be established, albeit having express regard to the public interest in deporting a person whose removal is considered by the Secretary of State to be conducive to the public good. The s117B criteria still apply too.

13.4.2.2 Deportation criteria outside the rules

Tthere is potential for consideration of private and family life both inside and outside the rules, in order that all the factors identified by the Strasbourg Court's case law are considered at some point. MF [2013] EWCA Civ 1192 held that the July 2012 deportation rules:

> are a complete code and that the exceptional circumstances to be considered in the balancing exercise involve the application of a proportionality test as required by the Strasbourg jurisprudence

That, however, was not the last word on the subject, and the debate as to whether the assessment is a one-stage or two-stage process was only finally laid to rest in Hesham Ali [2016] UKSC 60, where the Supreme Court explained that in order to be compatible with the UK's obligations under the Human Rights Convention, it would *always* be necessary to conduct an assessment having regard to any ECHR principles that were not captured by the terms of the Rules. Whilst the statutory scheme was comprehensive, the Rules alone were not.

Examples where there might be a case to be considered outside the rules will be where

- a non-British citizen child has lived here for less than seven years but nevertheless has very significant connections here (MIL 5.3.2)
- the deportee's connections are built on private rather than family life but they have lived here for a period less than 'most of their life', but are nevertheless socially and culturally integrated here and would face very significant obstacles to integration abroad: this is essentially the situation in Üner and Maslov discussed below
- an individual would have been born British if their parents were married at the time of their birth Johnson [2016] UKSC 56)
- There has been a significant delay in initiating deportation action subsequent to the index offence
- Anything else which is '***very compelling***'

NA (Pakistan) [2016] EWCA Civ 662 emphasises the need to consider the Strasbourg case law when considering cases outside the Rules. The case also explains that the same private and family life interests found within the Rules are relevant to whether there are '*very compelling*' circumstances outside them. So factors that did not individually reach the '*unduly harsh*' threshold should still be weighed in the overall balance.

LE (St Vincent And the Grenadines) [2020] EWCA Civ 505 involved a former serviceman who had served in Afghanistan with the Royal Marines, and had subsequently been convicted of defrauding an elderly woman of her savings. It was argued on his behalf that his active military service for the UK was a special feature of his case. The Armed Forces Covenant recognises that

> the whole nation has a moral obligation to the members of the Naval Service, the Army and the Royal Air Force, together with their families. They deserve our respect and support, and fair treatment

Those notions are developed in the guidance, the sections addressing Family Life and Support After Service emphasising the stresses that service may put on family life. However, the obligations go in both directions: for example: "*serving members should not bring the Armed Forces into disrepute in any of their actions*". The Court noted that the deportation regime made no express provision regarding the weight to be attached to military service. Thus, whether there were "very compelling" circumstances arising from a particular individual's military service would be an evaluative question that depended on the facts of each case: it was not a trump card.

One of the more detailed considerations of Article 8 in the context of a long resident migrant is found in Üner v. The Netherlands (Application No. 46410/99), where the applicant, who had a history of involvement in violent assaults, had triggered deportation proceedings by injuring one man and killing another: he was sentenced to seven years in jail. The ECtHR concluded that the correct balance habeen struck in favour of expulsion, setting out the following factors at [57]-[58] as relevant having regard to:

the special situation of aliens who have spent most, if not all, their childhood in the host country, were brought up there and received their education there:

- the nature and seriousness of the offence committed by the applicant;
- the length of the applicant's stay in the country from which he or she is to be expelled;
- the time elapsed since the offence was committed and the applicant's conduct during that period;
- the nationalities of the various persons concerned;

- the applicant's family situation, such as the length of the marriage, and other factors expressing the effectiveness of a couple's family life;
- whether the spouse knew about the offence at the time when he or she entered into a family relationship;
- whether there are children of the marriage, and if so, their age; and
- the seriousness of the difficulties which the spouse is likely to encounter in the country to which the applicant is to be expelled.
- the best interests and well-being of the children, in particular the seriousness of the difficulties which any children of the applicant are likely to encounter in the country to which the applicant is to be expelled; and
- the solidity of social, cultural and family ties with the host country and with the country of destination.

The subsequent decision of Maslov v Austria 1638/03 [2008] ECHR 546 was for some time understood as laying down the following principle:

> for a settled migrant who has lawfully spent all or the major part of his or her childhood and youth in the host country very serious reasons are required to justify expulsion … all the more so where the person concerned committed the offences underlying the expulsion measure as a juvenile.

Akpinar [2014] EWCA Civ 937 finds this was not a general rule. As that would not differentiate between the migrant returning to a developed country with similar prospects of integration as here, and a person being expelled to a country where they were unfamiliar within the language and culture. Rather such cases involved '*a conventional balancing exercise*'. D [2012] EWCA Civ 39 held that the Maslov approach did not apply to a case where the deportee has spent his time here unlawfully.

In Akinyemi [2019] EWCA Civ 2098 the Court of Appeal then revisited the approach to be taken to people facing deportation who had long been resident in the UK. Not knowing any environment other than the UK was of central importance and long residence of this kind should not be given little weight simply because one's presence had been consistently unlawful. There was a real a distinction between a foreign criminal who enters this country and offends and one who does so having been born here.

Nevertheless, Maslov is an important reminder to focus on the strength of ties in the UK rather than abroad, recognising that for a youngster who has grown up here, the UK may represent the totality of their life experience. Sanambar [2021] UKSC 30 emphasises that the four critical criteria identified in Üner are the nature and seriousness of the offence, length of stay in country of residence, time elapsed since the offence was committed and conduct during that period; and the solidity of social, cultural and family ties here and abroad. There was no separate requirement of "very serious reasons" justifying deportation beyond these criteria themselves. Nevertheless length of UK residence is a highly material factor in all cases and living here all one's life was due great weight in the proportionality assessment: Zulfiqar [2022] EWCA Civ 492.

TD (Albania) [2021] EWCA Civ 619 holds that factors such as the complete loss of family life (because modern means of communication would not foreseeably permit such family life to continue) and the absence of a breadwinner did not represent "*very compelling*" circumstances.

13.4.3 From Hesham Ali to HA (Iraq): the legislative scheme for deportation

The immigration community keenly awaited an authoritative judgement on the operation of the rather dense and confusing Rules which entered force from July 2012, and on cases falling outside them, and eventually this came with the decision of the Supreme Court in Hesham Ali. Key points made therein are:

- The overall question is whether a ***fair balance*** has been struck between the private and family life in existence, and the public interest
- However, a national government is permitted to weight the balance in favour of the public interest if it considers that is necessary – the United Kingdom has done this very thing

- That weighting of the balance was achieved by the requirement for *exceptional circumstances* in the various government policy statements: given the expertise that government had in assessing the public interest, courts and tribunals should *attach considerable weight to the Secretary of State's assessment*
- The requirement for exceptional circumstances implied, when deportation of a serious criminal fell to be considered, that a case could only succeed outside the Rules if *very compelling reasons* were established: they cited with approval the words of Laws LJ in SS Nigeria – the same test applied inside the Rules for those who had been sentenced to more than four years imprisonment, and both sets of applicants had to show '*a very strong case indeed*'
- Nevertheless, whatever the public interest to which considerable weight had to be given, it was *necessary to feed into the analysis the facts of the particular case*
- *Delay* by the government authorities in pursuing deportation reduces the public interest in expulsion
- It is relevant to consider whether the migrant's residence is *precarious* or whether they have *settled status*: in the former scenario, a whole further series of questions need to be considered, focusing on whether there are insurmountable obstacles or exceptional circumstances militating against'relocation abroad having regard to the strength of UK ties
- The ECtHR decision in Jeunesse is cited as offering a useful summary of the considerations in a case involving children. The general focus should be on:

    the practicality, feasibility and proportionality of any removal of a non-national parent in order to give effective protection and sufficient weight to the best interests of the children directly affected by it

- Judges may find it useful to assess proportionality via a 'balance sheet' of the pros and cons in the particular case: but not mechanistically so and it would be wrong to assess a case via a proscribed number of points as this would unnecessarily impose a limit on the weight afforded each discrete factor: KB [2022] UKUT 161 (IAC)
- When assessing the proportionality of interference with private and family life based on public interest considerations, Lord Kerr stated:

    The strength of the public interest in favour of deportation depends onsuch matters as the nature and seriousness of the crime, the risk of re-offending, and the success of rehabilitation

The relevance of rehabilitation has had its ups and downs over the years. Jallow [2021] EWCA Civ 788 confirms that rehabilitation can be relevant to the public interest assessment in deportation appeals. One example would be making a positive contribution to society via an offender's community activities to encourage others not to engage in crime. SM (Zimbabwe) [2021] EWCA Civ 1566 emphasises that the special features of rehabilitation (such as reconciliation with the victim) required specific attention notwithstanding that plain rehabilitation might not carry great weight. ZA v Ireland [2023] ECHR 236 finds the ECtHR observing that it might be unreasonable to expect rehabilitative steps beyond those specified in the criminal sentence. The best measure of the seriousness of an offence is the length of the sentence.

Lord Thomas in Hesham Ali considered that general deterrence was also important, albeit that decision makers should never forget 'the *degree* of strength of the public interest in the deportation of this particular foreign criminal, strong though "hat will"always be' (his emphasis). The same point is made in RF (Jamaica) [2017] EWCA Civ 124:

    It is relevant to the decision of a Tribunal whether an appellant received a sentence of, say 4 years or one of 10 years.

The actual severity of the offence matters more when assessing a *very compelling* case. The fact that one falls at the low or high end of medium offending (ie the 1-4 years range set by the Rules and s117C) does not really matter: because the statutory scheme treats those individuals the same. But outside of that range, sentence is important: as noted in KO (Nigeria) [2018] UKSC 53, it would be extraordinary if, for the purposes of the ultimate proportionality exercise which has to be performed where the Exceptions do not apply no distinction fell to be made, between, say, an offender who had committed offences attracting a term of four years' imprisonment and a multiple murderer.

Lord Kerr also noted, regarding the factors on the deportee's side of the balance:

> there is a public interest in families being kept together, in the welfare of children being given primacy, in valuing a person who makes a special contribution to their community, and in encouraging and respecting the rehabilitation of offenders. These factors all play a role in the construction of a strong and cohesive society.

However, it must be understood that the courts accept the basic premise of deportation proceedings. That premise is that deportation may well split up families and create some degree of hardship: thus in KO (Nigeria) the fact that children might be distressed or that their parent who remains in the UK may have to give up work in order to become their primary carer provider was not considered disproportionate.

In Imran [2020] UKUT 83 (IAC) the UT accordingly notes that the "*unduly harsh*" test will not be satisfied in a case where a child has two parents "*without more*" evidence than the general upset that will inevitably result from the physical absence of one of them. This was so even where it was accepted that the deportee played an important part of their lives.

There would have to be distinct evidence of the particular importance of one parent in the lives of the children and of the emotional dependence of the children on that parent and (therefore) of the emotional harm that would be likely to flow from separation. The form that such "*without more*" evidence would take was fact-sensitive, though firm evidence of psychiatric damage would suffice.

However, just because the consequences of deportation will routinely be severe does not mean that the individual facts of the case should be downplayed: HA Iraq [2020] EWCA Civ 1176 §56, warning of the dangers of minimising the *ordinary* consequences:

> '[ordinary] may be misleading if used incautiously. There seem to me to be two (related) risks. First, "ordinary" is capable of being understood as meaning anything which is not exceptional, or in any event rare. That is not the correct approach … There is no reason in principle why cases of "undue" harshness may not occur quite commonly. Secondly, if tribunals treat the essential question as being "is this level of harshness out of the ordinary?" they may be tempted to find that Exception 2 does not apply simply on the basis that the situation fits into some commonly-encountered pattern. That would be dangerous. How a child will be affected by a parent's deportation will depend on an almost infinitely variable range of circumstances and it is not possible to identify a baseline of "ordinariness". Simply by way of example, the degree of harshness of the impact may be affected by the child's age; by whether the parent lives with them (NB that a divorced or separated father may still have a genuine and subsisting relationship with a child who lives with the mother); by the degree of the child's emotional dependence on the parent; by the financial consequences of his deportation; by the availability of emotional and financial support from a remaining parent and other family members; by the practicability of maintaining a relationship with the deported parent; and of course by all the individual characteristics of the child.

HA (Iraq) represents a landmark re-statement of the relevant principles and its reasoning was upheld on appeal in HA (Iraq) [2022] UKSC 22, where the Supreme Court stressed that it would be wrong to hypothesise a child with baseline characteristics against which a potential deportation might be measured. Judges may have to recalibrate their thinking somewhat to ensure that their decision making is consistent with the proper approach. MI (Pakistan) [2021] EWCA Civ 1711 emphasises that emotional harm is as significant as physical harm, bearing in mind s31(9) of the Children Act 1989 defining "*harm*" as ill treatment or the impairment of health or physical, intellectual, emotional, social or behavioural development. A self-direction to look for evidence of the particular importance of one parent to a child or the emotional harm that would be likely to flow from separation of the child from that parent failed to perform the evaluative approach required by HA (Iraq). Sicwebu [2023] EWCA Civ 550 emphasises the relevance of an expert's citation of academic study that "*separation anxiety in children may be associated with increased risk of suicide*"; and that, when predicting the impact of deportation, taking care in equating a family's ability to negotiate short-term imprisonment with family visits as opposed to the long-term rupture in relationships caused by deportation. Real-world facts such as advanced pregnancy needed to be properly considered too.

Unuane [2020] ECHR 832 finds the Strasbourg Court looking at decision making in a UK case where a father facing deportation had received a 5½ year sentence for serious and large scale offending by way of numerous acts of falsifying immigration documents. Here the best interests of the children of the family were clearly for their father to remain in the UK (one had forthcoming surgery and their father's presence would clearly be beneficial to their recovery). In such a case, the fact that the offence committed by an applicant was at the more serious end of the criminal spectrum is not in and of itself determinative of the case. Rather, it is just one factor which has to be weighed in the balance.

Extant family proceedings where a childs' best interests await determination are likely to render deportation disproportionate for the time being (MIL 6.2.6.2).

13.4.4 Leave to remain granted where deportation is resisted

This is addressed by r13.3.1-13.3.2B, Part 13 of the IRs, whereby a person who sustains an Article 8 claim

- will be granted 30 months temporary permission, regardless of the leave they had (or lack of it) prior to the deportation proceedings
- will have any longer leave they previously possessed curtailed to 30 months (this was previously explicit but now seems implicit within r13.3)

13.5 Revocation of deportation order and appeal rights
13.5.1 Revocation of deportation order

The Rules set out a scheme whereby an application can be made for a deportation order to be revoked on the basis of certain identified circumstances, albeit that applications should be granted only after a certain period of time has expired, itself linked to the severity of the offending that led to the original deportation order. Some points to note generally regarding revocation:

- The classic application will be made from abroad, some time after the subject of the decision has complied with its requirements. However, an application may be made from within the UK prior to departure: this may be based on further representations arguing that a fresh asylum or human rights claim should be recognised with the appeal rights that would ensue
- Revocation of an order does not itself entitle a person to return: it simply opens the gateway to applying under an appropriate category of the rules (r13.4.1) – and only express revocation applications will be considered as such, the *Guidance* states; there is no particular form, a written application suffices
- Deportation orders remain in force until revoked or quashed by a court/tribunal (r13.4.2)
- When revocation cases are assessed on appeal, the public interest provisions set out in section 117A-D NIAA 2002 apply: IT (Jamaica) [2016] EWCA Civ 932

Rule 13.4 in Part 13 provides that a deportation order may be revoked (thus replacing its predecessor's rather vague terms):

- For sentences of less than 4 years, where the private/family life exceptions are met (r13.4.4(a))
- For sentences over 4 years, where there are very compelling circumstances (r13.4.4(b))
- Where a decision not to revoke would be contrary to the ECHR or the Refugee Convention (r13.4.4(c))
- For non-custodial sentences, where there is a material change of circumstances (r13.4.5)

Previously the Rules provided two routes under which revocation might be considered (an interpretation confirmed as correct in ZP (India) [2015] EWCA Civ 1197):

- R390A for individuals who have not yet been deported (i.e. 'in-country' applicants for revocation) and
- R391 for someone *who has been deported following conviction for a criminal offence.*

But there is no such distinction under the modern Rules.

Some reprobates are known to return to the United Kingdom in breach of a deportation order and then subsequently seek to assert a right to remain here based on the private and family life they have subsequently established or enhanced. Old r399D stated that in this scenario enforcement of the deportation order was in the public interest and will be implemented unless there are very exceptional circumstances. SU [2017] EWCA Civ 1069 emphasised that *'there is a particularly strong public interest in maintaining the integrity of the deportation system as it applies to foreign criminals'*. Clearly that public interest was especially threatened by return to the UK in defiance of a deportation order. However, in Binaku [2021] UKUT 34 (IAC) the UT finds that an Appellant who had returned to the UK in breach of a deportation order should not have to establish a higher threshold in order to show their expulsion was disproportionate than as set out in s117C itself: if the IRs suggested otherwise, then that was an unnecessary distraction. SU seemed to have overlooked this aspect of the legislative scheme.

13.5.2 Appeal rights

Those defined under s117D(2) of 2002 Act as a foreign criminal (see above) no longer have an automatic right of appeal. They will be served with a s120 notice giving them an opportunity to raise a human rights or asylum claim. The refusal of the asylum or human rights claim will then give rise to a right of appeal. The same should apply where a human rights claim is made as part of an application to revoke a deportation order, subject to meeting the fresh claim test if applicable. Some 15% of appeals of foreign national offenders (FNOs) succeeded in 2008/2009, some 2% on ECHR grounds; whereas 30% of appeals of FNOs succeeded in 2019/2020, some 14% on human rights grounds (Migration Transparency data in March 2022). Presumably the other successful appeals are protection-related.

13.5.2.1 Non-suspensive appeals absent serious irreversible harm

The appeals regime for deportees enables the HO to require any appeal against deportation to be brought from abroad, both in domestic and EU law cases (MIL 118). Thus s94B NIAA 2002 provides that:

- in any case where deportation is considered conducive to the public good by the SSHD or where a court has ordered deportation (s94B(1): this effectively catches all deportation cases)
- where the provisional HO view (i.e. that reached before the result of the appeal) is that removal would not breach the HRA 1998 (and therefore the ECHR) (s94B(2))
- in particular, an appeal will be certified where the HO considers that the deportee would not, before the appeals process is exhausted, face a real risk of serious irreversible harm if removed to the proposed destination (s94B(3)).
- The effect of the certificate is in amended s92 NIAA 2002: where the appeal has been brought from within the UK, the appeal must be continued from outside the UK

From 1 December 2016, the 94B certification procedure was in theory brought in for all human rights appeals, not just those involving deportees. For some time it seemed that the provision was only used in deportation cases. However, litigation for some time cooled the HO's ardour for using s94B certificates. Whilst *Clearly Unfounded Guidance* of 28 June 2022 stated the process was presently suspended, the procedure resumed from 5 June 2023 with the Guidance *Certification under section 94B*. See Ms Braverman's *letter to the Home Affairs Ctte* – for now foreign national offenders are again the target.

The ECtHR does not object to non-suspensive appeals in principle: eg De Souza Ribeiro v France [2012] ECHR 2066 expressly states that a remedy with suspensive effect, whilst essential in Article 3 cases, is not necessarily required in Article 8 proceedings. Thus the HO guidance says:

It is not appropriate to certify protection claims made on the basis of the Refugee Convention and/or ECHR Article 2 and Article 3 because there will arguably be a real risk of serious irreversible harm where a person's life or freedom from inhuman and degrading treatment is at issue.

Past HO guidance for both non EEA and EEA cases gave some clues to how certification would operate:

- the Guidance *Certification-under-section-94B* (following Kiarie there was a lengthy pause in certification) and
- the Regulation 24AA certification guidance for European Economic Area deportation cases) (no longer available whatsoever)

The guidance took the stance that:

- the test relates to the period between deportation and the conclusion of any appeal, after which the person will return to the UK if successful
- the test requires that the harm be serious AND irreversible
- whilst the legal burden of proof is on the HO to justify certification, once certification has happened, the evidential burden is firmly on the deportee, and only independent objective evidence will suffice. More weight will be given to recognised expertise, direct rather than hearsay knowledge, and to detailed rather than unsubstantiated assertions
- when exercising discretion to certify or not, the case should be assessed in the round focussing on the practicalities, including possession of a travel document and whether there is a credible case for being unable to leave the UK within a reasonable timeframe; any application for discretionary non-certification should be answered on a reasoned basis in the decision letter
- certification should proceed only where a videolink facility is available and where the country of return has agreed to the giving of evidence by that means: the Overseas Video Team should be consulted
- certification should not proceed when the deportee's whereabouts are unknown

MIL 11.7.10 addresses certification of Citizens Rights Appeals which is available on similar grounds. The Guidance *Conducive Deportation* now addresses the SSHD's view of how certification will operate, though it is vaguer than the former Guidance summarised above.

13.5.2.2 Circumstances which fall short of serious irreversible harm

Next, the guidance goes on to suggest situations that in the opinion of the HO would not meet the test, i.e. where:

- A person will be separated from their child/partner for several months while the individual appeals against a human rights decision
- A family court case is in progress
- A child/partner is undergoing treatment for a temporary or chronic medical condition that is under control and can be satisfactorily managed through medication or other treatment and does not require the person liable to deportation to act as a full time carer
- The FNO has a medical issue where removal would not breach Article 3 ECHR
- A person has strong private life ties to a community that will be disrupted by deportation (e.g. they have a job, a mortgage, a prominent role in a community organisation etc.)

It is debatable whether it would be compatible with the right to family life to restrict a person's ability to participate in family proceedings. A person usually needs to be physically present in the UK in contested family court proceedings as various assessments are often needed which require their physical presence. The considerations are dealt with in more detail in Chapter 6, section 6.2.6.2 *Family proceedings*.

13.5.2.3 Examples of serious irreversible harm

The guidance then goes on to give examples of situations that in the view of the HO would meet the test, coming up with these rather high hurdles:

- The person has a genuine and subsisting parental relationship with a child or partner who is seriously ill, requires full-time care, and there is no one else who can provide that care
- A court order for a trial period of contact likely to determine the extent of future contact is in place
- The person has a serious medical condition for which treatment is not available or would be inaccessible such that removal risks a significant/irreversible health deterioration
- There is *credible evidence* that the right of appeal would be rendered ineffective because their mental health or physical disability would impinge on their ability to put a case
- A close relationship of dependency with a close family member which could not be maintained remotely where the dying individual's life expectancy is shorter than the likely spell abroad were the appeal to succeed

The situation of children is recognised as being especially fact sensitive and necessarily to be assessed in relation to their best interests. The mere fact they are in education, would face some generalised disruption, and would lose close contact with their peer group, is not considered as being contrary to this: so an evidence-backed case would always need to be put.

13.5.2.4 Kiarie and Byndloss: The effectiveness of non-suspensive appeals

Kiarie and Byndloss [2017] UKSC 42 was a landmark decision on non-suspensive family life appeals. That decision and subsequent cases that follow it have found:

- The overriding public interest in cases where a right of appeal is afforded is that the right be effective – decision makers should focus on whether a removal pre-appeal risks serious harm *to the prospects of his appeal,* having regard to the fact that it is wrong for one party to an appeal to be entitled to weaken the other party's case (Kiarie)
- JRs of s94B certificates may need to conduct fact-finding (Kiarie) – however it is more appropriate in most cases for the FTT to consider the effectiveness of the right of appeal, within the statutory appeal process, rather than seeking JR (Nixon [2018] EWCA Civ 3, Watson [2018] UKUT 165), the FTT being under a duty to review the developing situation (Watson, even during the hearing Juba [2021] UKUT 95 (IAC) albeit that only JR proceedings could force the HO to bring someone back to the UK (AJ (Nigeria) [2018] UKUT 115 (IAC), FB (Afghanistan) [2020] EWCA Civ 1338)
- Back in 2017, remote hearings were thought unsatisfactory because of technological barriers and the perceived difficulty in judicial supervision of the evidence (Kiarie) – but things have greatly moved on due to the steps taken in the pandemic (FB (Afghanistan) albeit that the HO might need to fund an Appellant's expenses such as data charges and a laptop (Arman [2021] EWHC 1217 (Admin)). The ECtHR agrees that remote hearings may comply with fair trial rights: Jallow v Norway [2021] ECHR 1004 (having regard to the importance of an immediate impression of a witness, any objections made during the trial process, and whether a party had a broad opportunity to present their case (including consulting with counsel during the examination of witnesses, and having adequate access to documents). Agbabiaka [2021] UKUT 286 (IAC) mentions that the SSHD sees herself as under a duty to provide appellants subject to s94B certificates with video facilities to participate in their appeal hearing.
- Psychiatrists and independent social workers would struggle to assess risks and relationships remotely (Kiarie, AJ (Nigeria)): key issues in assessing an appeal's efficacy would be their ability to instruct professional witnesses, and their own lawyer, the practicalities of video evidence, and their ongoing relationship with the probation service: at all times the central question was impediment rather than inconvenience Juba particularly vis-á-vis legal advice – but the FTT should refuse to hear an appeal absent a fair process
- The criticisms of ineffectual appeal rights arose specifically in the context of viable appeals, not ones certified as clearly unfounded (Kiarie)
- Whether the right of appeal is effective or not is question of fact depending on the facts of the case (Nixon)
- Certification under section 94B establishes a potential interference with Article 8 rights and the HO will have to show that an out-of-country appeal is effective (Nixon [2018] EWCA Civ 3)
- If an appellant has been unlawfully removed, their return to the UK may be ordered as part of JR proceedings, subject to evidence of the efficacy of the appeal from abroad having regard to

concrete steps already taken, their ability to instruct legal representatives, and whether a judge had considered this issue pre-removal (Nixon [2018] EWCA Civ 3)

The public interest balance may play out differently in a national security case. In Begum [2021] UKSC 7 the Supreme Court held that when assessing the consequences of a right of appeal not being able to be effectively exercised, the court must have regard to the administration of justice, the nature and consequences of the decision in question, and any relevant provisions of the legislation. If the difficulty is of such an extreme nature that not merely is one party placed at a forensic disadvantage, but it is impossible for the case to be fairly tried, the interests of justice may require a stay of proceedings. If a vital public interest such as the safety of the public makes it impossible for a case to be fairly heard, then the courts cannot ordinarily hear it. The ECtHR decision in Jallow is consistent with this thinking.

Example

Mehmet was convicted of a crime and sentenced to 14 months' imprisonment. Irrespective of whether a recommendation for deportation is made by the sentencing judge, the sentence should trigger the automatic deportation process.

If the HO take the view that none of the 2007 Act s33 exceptions apply, Mehmet will be served with a Deportation Order when the HO sees fit, probably whilst he is serving his criminal sentence, or shortly afterwards when that ends and he enters immigration detention.

The right of appeal under s82 NIAA 2002 arises from the refusal of an asylum or human rights claim, or revocation of protection status; so Mehmet would be reliant on the HO following their usual process of requesting representations on those grounds and then refusing them.

It can be expected that the decision will contain a s94B certificate and the right of appeal will be out of country (i.e. Mehmet must depart the UK before the appeal hearing can go ahead). A human rights claim will not help to bring the appeal back in-country unless Mehmet is able to show that he faces a real risk of serious irreversible harm if removed to the country or territory to which P is proposed to be removed.

The only arguments available to Mehmet on appeal are whether any of the exceptions in s33 UKBA 2007 are available (and a private and family life case must be considered with the tough rules on deportation and s117C of NIAA 2002 in mind: we discuss the substantive considerations in significantly more detail below). If the appeal is successful, the deportation order will be revoked and he will be able to return to the UK if he has the leave to do so. If the appeal is dismissed, the order will remain in force and he will not be able to return to the UK, subject to a successful future application for its revocation

---

Top Tip

In a section 94B case, think carefully about the impact that removal will have both on the client's private and family life and on their prospects of winning their appeal, and about the kinds of evidence you might obtain to support each contention.

- Damage to businesses that employ British citizens
- Disruption of the family at a critical stage of a child's education
- Disruption of family law proceedings leading to a result that may be contrary to a child's best interests
- Inability to prepare the appeal from abroad: as non-asylum appeals are not publicly funded absent an exceptional case funding application succeeding, if present in this country the Appellant might be able to do a significant amount of the case preparation themselves, in terms of locating witnesses, but once abroad they may have use a lawyer more than would otherwise be the case
- Inability to access/afford video link facilities from abroad

CHAPTER 13: Enforcement; Detention, Removal and Deportation

☐ Whether video evidence can be given in conditions that ensure the remedy is effective: see e.g. Nare [2011] UKUT 00443 on the possible formality and witness supervision for giving video evidence, relaxed somewhat in Agbabiaka [2021] UKUT 286 (IAC)

13.5.3 Speeding up deportation: The Early Removal Scheme and the Tariff Expired Removal Scheme; the Facilitated Returns Scheme (FRS)

We inhabit a richly varied world, and not everyone wants to avoid deportation. Some seek to speed things along.

There is an Early Removal Scheme (ERS) for foreign national offenders serving a determinate sentence (ie a statute-specified fixed or minimum period) in England and Wales. The Tariff Expired Removal Scheme (TERS) is for those serving an indeterminate sentence (ie a sentence of confinement without a fixed length of time, but with a minimum "tariff" to be served before release is considered). TERS gives the Secretary of State the power to order removal from prison once a prisoner's minimum tariff date has expired without the need for authorisation from the Parole Board. Lopes [2021] EWCA Civ 805 explains that a person cannot be deported under the TERS absent a deportation order. Potentially eligible prisoners must be considered for removal, but relevant considerations included whether extradition rather than deportation should be prioritised.

From 28 June 2022 the Criminal Justice Act 2003 s260 provides for removal from prison (and thence the UK) following the minimum pre-removal custodial period: ie the longer of one half of the requisite custodial period, or the requisite custodial period less one year.

The FRS, as the *FRS Guidance* explains, encourages FNOs to leave the UK at the first opportunity and provides financial support for reintegration (£1,500 for those still serving a custodial sentence and each qualifying family member, £750 otherwise, paid by uploading a cash card; a discretionary further £500 is available for the vulnerable). All FNOs liable to deportation or administrative review are eligible, even those previously removed, so long as they are subject to enforcement action, are able to leave the UK voluntarily, have no outstanding applications and have not previously failed to comply with removal arrangements. It is not an alternative to deportation.

13.6 The substantive law on deportation relevant to appeals

If one manages to obtain an effective right of appeal against deportation, whether or 'in-country' or 'out-of-country', the battle is by no means over. This is because of the very high thresholds now set out in the IRs (MIL 13.4.2.1)..

NIAA 2002section 117C sets out statutory public interest considerations of the: these largely replicate the public policy position struck by the IRs themselves (it will be recalled that s117C is for the consideration of 'courts and tribunals'). These state:

117C Article 8: additional considerations in cases involving foreign criminals

(1) The deportation of foreign criminals is in the public interest.

(2) The more serious the offence committed by a foreign criminal, the greater is the public interest in deportation of the criminal.

(3) In the case of a foreign criminal (C) who has not been sentenced to a period of imprisonment of four years or more, the public interest requires C's deportation unless Exception 1 or Exception 2 applies.

(4) Exception 1 applies where—

(a) C has been lawfully resident in the United Kingdom for most of C's life,
(b) C is socially and culturally integrated in the United Kingdom, and

(c) there would be very significant obstacles to C's integration into the country to which C is proposed to be deported.

(5) Exception 2 applies where C has a genuine and subsisting relationship with a qualifying partner, or a genuine and subsisting parental relationship with a qualifying child, and the effect of C's deportation on the partner or child would be unduly harsh.

(6) In the case of a foreign criminal who has been sentenced to a period of imprisonment of at least four years, the public interest requires deportation unless there are very compelling circumstances, over and above those described in Exceptions 1 and 2.

(7) The considerations in subsections (1) to (6) are to be taken into account where a court or tribunal is considering a decision to deport a foreign criminal only to the extent that the reason for the decision was the offence or offences for which the criminal has been convicted.

13.6.1 The public interest in deportation

A judge determining an appeal must consider the case having regard to those statutory considerations, but additionally to the public policy considerations identified in the rules and thus (AJ (Angola) [2014] EWCA Civ 1636):

> through the lens of the new rules themselves, rather than looking to apply Convention rights for themselves in a free-standing way outside the new rules

The extent of the public interest must be expressly recognised (MA (Somalia) [2015] EWCA Civ 48) of

> the great weight to be attached to [the] public interest [and] that something very compelling is required to outweigh that public interest,

Whether or not a case is being considered inside or outside the rules, the public interest in deportation has multiple facets. As explained in SE Zimbabwe [2014] EWCA Civ 256:

> the decision-maker must consider three separate aspects of the criminal offence. These are (i) the risk of re-offending, (ii) the need to deter others and (iii) the need to express society's revulsion at the criminality.

Hesham Ali appeared to have disapproved the third of those public interest considerations, the judges finding that 'revulsion' had no place in the process – the relevant focus was upon the severity of sentencing.

However, in DW (Jamaica) [2018] EWCA Civ 797 the CA held that each dimension of 'public interest' must be distinctly evaluated; re-offending and deterrence *as well as* 'revulsion' – as the criticisms were not part of the majority judgement in Hesham Ali. One approach may be to address 'revulsion' in terms of the public's loss of confidence in the immigration system if the criminal avoids deportation. This was clarified in Zulfiqar [2022] EWCA Civ 492: there is indeed a third component, namely public concern, ie the public's view that whose who have committed serious offences should not normally be permitted to live in the UK subsequently, albeit that this should not carry the emotive term "*revulsion*".

The more serious the offence, the less the risk of re-offending may matter, at least 'for very serious crimes': N Kenya [2014] EWCA Civ 1094.

Barry [2018] EWCA Civ 790 looked at a deportation appeal which had been brought under the pre-2014 amendments to the deportation process. So this was a case where the section 117C presumptions were not in force. The Court noted that under this earlier regime, when the public interest was balanced against the private rights in play, neither side of the balancing exercise was to receive 'primacy'. When the public interest was considered, the strong public interest in deporting foreign criminals was of course relevant: but it was not a paramount consideration.

HA (Iraq) [2022] UKSC 22 holds that the nature of the sentence was often the surest guide to an offence's seriousness – subject to other issues not relevant to seriousness that might have reduced it, including an early guilty plea. Gosturani [2022] EWCA Civ 779 holds that convictions abroad are relevant to the public interest, so long as the possibility of conduct not being criminal in the UK is borne in mind. BWM, R. v [2022] EWCA Crim 924 notes that sentencing judges should not encourage guilty pleas by reference to time already served given that might lead to detention and deportation.

Top Tip

It is important to consider what arguments and evidence might be available in a deportation case. It is not easy to acquire good evidence in deportation cases but this will be decisive on appeal. Of course getting detailed testimony from your client, and expert evidence, will be far more difficult if they are to be outside the UK when preparing their appeal.

Evidence to seek might include:

- Sentencing judge remarks. Ensure a complete copy is obtained and do not leave it to the HO to do so. The HO often quote very selectively and a full copy may be helpful to the client.
- Up to date probation report. Some probation officers are helpful, some are not. Whether an up to date report on risk of re-offending can be obtained might be critical.
- Copies of all pre-sentence reports. There may have been a psychological or psychiatric assessment as well as a pre-sentence probation report.
- Solid and incontrovertible evidence of family life. The HO will question everything in a deportation case, including even the existence of children or a partner. Whether the client can get out on bail and therefore re-establish a current and strong family life before the appeal hearing can be a critical factor.

13.6.2 Conducive to the public good appeals

Some of the general refusal reasons (MIL 2.3) provide expressly for diverse public interest refusals.

There are mandatory grounds of refusal both at the entry clearance and leave to remain stages (IRs Part 9 r.9.3.1-9.3.2) where:

> The immigration officer deems the exclusion of the person from the United Kingdom to be conducive to the public good. For example, because the person's conduct (including convictions which do not otherwise reach the refusal threshold), character, associations, or other reasons, make it undesirable to grant them leave to enter.

13.6.3 Operation Nexus cases

In some of these cases the HO seeks to rely on evidence from police intelligence which has not been subjected to a court process leading to the appellant's conviction. This happens particularly in cases where Operation Nexus (a joint initiative between immigration enforcement officers and the police force) is involved. The forms of evidence relied upon are diverse, varying from reports from police officers to evidence from informants. One judge said in V [2009] EWHC 1902:

> whilst I see that this evidence inevitably loses considerable weight by being anonymous and (in part) hearsay, thereby preventing any direct challenge to the relevant witnesses, I cannot say that this evidence must inevitably be given no weight by the tribunal – or that to admit the evidence at all will inevitably deny the claimant a fair hearing

The two lead cases are Bah [2012] UKUT 196 (IAC) and Farquharson [2013] UKUT 146 (IAC), establishing that:

- Acts that lead to a charge, but not a conviction, may be established by the HO as 'conduct' capable of justifying a public interest in deportation

- The standard of proof remains the balance of probabilities
- Evidence is more likely to be impressive when allegations from informants are corroborated
- Suspicion should not replace proof
- The gist of how such evidence was obtained must be disclosed and if its gist is too sensitive to disclose, then the information should not be relied upon
- If the HO seeks to establish the conduct by relying on the contents of police Crime Reporting Information System (CRIS) reports, the relevant documents should be produced rather than bare witness statements referring to CRIS reports
- In summary (Farquharson at [65]):

> the weight to be attached to such material will depend on its nature, the circumstances in which it was collected or recorded, the susceptibility of the informant or original informant to error, and the extent to which the appellant is able to comment or rebut it.

In The Centre for Advice on Individual Rights In Europe [2018] EWCA Civ 2837, the Court of Appeal considered a challenge which maintained that the Operation Nexus approach amounted to 'systematic verification' of whether EU Treaty rights were truly being exercised, which was thus inconsistent with the general prohibition of such measures in EU law generally. The Court found that essentially the police were involved in legitimate 'information gathering' rather than verification, and that working with the immigration service was a legitimate police purpose.

13.7 Extradition

MIL does not aim to cover extradition in any great detail. However sometimes cases crop up that cross the jurisdictions of immigration and extradition.

- Unsurprising the Article 3 ECHR prohibition on torture and inhuman and degrading treatment/punishment applies to extradition (MIL 10.3.2.1)
- Being subject to extradition exempts one from the automatic deportation regime (MIL 13.4.1.2)
- Extradition is taken very seriously by the courts and so should proceed in preference to deportation early release schemes (MIL 13.5.3)

In Gornovskiy [2021] UKUT 321 (IAC) the UT looked at the relationship between extradition and immigration control. The Extradition Act 2003 intended that particular immigration decisions would have certain consequences for extradition proceedings, such that the SSHD would refuse extradition to category 2 territories pending an asylum claim's determination, and a discretion to refuse to issue a certificate vis-á-vis a person recorded by the SSHD as a refugee and where removal would infringe ECHR Art 2/3. Mere discharge from extradition did not prevent a person's removal. A recent and reasoned extradition decision might well prevent a decision to remove based on the same evidence; but circumstances might change, or a scantly reasoned decision might be revisited.

13.8 Voluntary Returns

Some migrants wish to return home and the HO may facilitate this via the Voluntary Returns Service (VRS). The *Practical information for applicants* and *Get help to return home if you're a migrant in the UK* explains that

- The VRS can assist those in the UK illegally and overstayers, asylum seekers, modern slavery victims, and those withdrawing applications for leave to remain – and those from the EU, Switzerland, Norway, Iceland or Liechtenstein living in the UK before 1 January 2021
- It is not available to those with a conviction & sentence >1 year (including pending investigations) and with leave to remain, nor to people in modern post-Brexit routes (EUSSch, Frontier Workers etc)
- Up to £3,000 may be available in financial assistance where applicants are returning to developing countries, failed asylum seekers, modern slavery victims, family groups, lone children, under 21 care leavers, those sleeping rough, and with medical conditions

- VRS may be able to assist with obtaining a temporary travel document for those without valid passports
- Medical support may be available, as may physical assistance from those with severe vulnerabilities and mobility issues

CHAPTER 14: Appeals, Administrative Review and Judicial Review

The online MIL details with practice, procedure and evidence in the FTT in detail. In the paper version we provide brief information, as below.

The orders of courts and Tribunals play a central role in the UK's unwritten constitution. Majera [2021] UKSC 46 holds it to be a well-established principle of the UK's constitutional law that a court order must be obeyed unless and until set aside or varied by the court (or, conceivably, overruled by legislation).

14.1 Appeals in the First-tier Tribunal

Under the 2002 Act, certain decisions of the HO give rise to a right of appeal before an independent judge of the First-tier Tribunal (Immigration and Asylum Chamber) (FTT). The FTT judge has the power to allow or dismiss an appeal, subject only to a further challenge on points of law to the Upper Tribunal (Immigration and Asylum Chamber) (UT).

The appeals system created by the extensive amendment of the NIAA 2002 by the IA 2014 entered full effect on 6 April 2015, although there was a lengthy overlap period whilst old appeals wended their way to conclusion.

We generally now deal with the modern appeal system, unless the text specifically states otherwise. The old appeal system is now mainly relevant to understanding someone's immigration history: as it may explain why a right of appeal was available or denied. Key features of the system are:

- Removal powers under the 'single decision' process, empowering removal via a single step for anyone who needs leave to enter/remain but does not have it, under which the Home Office says it will give only limited notice of removal beyond the provision of a 'one-stop' notice when the last application is refused (MIL 13.3)
- A clear ongoing duty to update the HO of any changes to one's circumstances (s120 NIAA 2002)
- No right of appeal unless the present immigration decision relates to a claim on human rights or asylum grounds
- No grounds of appeal other than human rights or asylum
- For those cases that lack a right of appeal, a potential remedy by way of administrative review for those decisions casts as 'eligible decisions', and a potential further remedy by way of judicial review (JR) (see more on these remedies at the end of this chapter) – and a few decisions, such as curtailment, have no administrative review option available, meaning that it is JR or nothing
- Appeals against EEA decisions arise not from the NIAA 2002 but from the EEA Regs 2016, but themselves become subject to the one stop regime, so that human rights can be raised in regard to an EEA decision only if a one stop notice is served on the applicant and returned to the HO: this class of appeal is dying out post-Brexit (MIL 11.9)

Note that:

- Encounters with the immigration authorities no longer generate a right of appeal absent an asylum/human rights claim (so decisions to issue removal directions or cancel leave to enter or remain will no longer carry the right of appeal until the relevant claim has been made and refused: section 120 notices should be issued when such encounters occur, so nobody should face removal before they have had the opportunity to respond to those notices by making a claim)
- Appeals against refusal of refugee status or Humanitarian Protection are available, notwithstanding the person has been granted leave to remain on a different basis (e.g. as a victim of trafficking, unaccompanied child, or on human rights grounds): because the grant of any form of leave to remain is irrelevant to the existence of a right of appeal, and the refusal of international protection itself generates a right of appeal

- The HO may control the raising of new arguments on appeal, via granting/withholding consent regarding matters sought to be raised late (i.e. raised for the first time after receipt of the appealable decision)

Post-decision evidence

The NIA 2002 addresses post-decision evidence at s85:

- In all appeals, whether in-country or involving entry clearance, the FTT may consider any matter which it thinks relevant to the substance of the decision, including a matter arising after the date of the decision (so there will no longer be any barrier to post decision evidence in an entry clearance appeal)
- However, do bear in mind the possibility that new evidence involves a new matter. Then it is admissible only if the SSHD has consented (see 14.2.7 below).

The FTT and UT operate in Scotland and Northern Ireland as well as England & Wales: UK immigration control, from the IA 1971 to the IRs, generally applies in each country. But there may be differences in how the local courts approach particular issues. Arturas [2021] UKUT 237 (IAC) notes that decisions of the appellate courts in different parts of the United Kingdom will be binding in the region where they were decided (eg MIL 2.5).

Where migrants have a choice as to their next step, the timetable for an appeal is of interest. These are provided by the _Tribunal Statistics Quarterly_. For example in the third quarter of 2022, the meantime taken to clear appeals across in the FTTIAC was 54 weeks for asylum/protection, 51 weeks for human rights and 37 weeks for EEA.

HJT runs occasional courses on appeals and advocacy where we give many more practical examples and more detailed discussion than is realistic here.

14.2 Rights and grounds of appeal
14.2.1 Rights of appeal

Appeals now arise under the system which fully came into effect on 6 April 2015 (following a staged implementation for different kinds of refusal). This was a very major change, and reduction, in appeal rights.

The practical operation of the appeals system, from the Home Office perspective, is explained in a series of Immigration Staff Guidance documents. Rights of appeal are at s82 of the 2002 Act, the full text of which reads:

> 82 Right of appeal to the Tribunal:
>
> (1) A person (P) may appeal to the Tribunal where—
>
> (a) the Secretary of State has decided to refuse a protection claim made by P,
> (b) the Secretary of State has decided to refuse a human rights claim made by P, or
> (c) the Secretary of State has decided to revoke P's protection status.

Under the pre-2014 Act system, with which immigration practitioners had long been familiar, a right of appeal arose with respect to an immigration decision (e.g. to refuse entry clearance, leave to enter or leave to remain, in the latter case only where current leave was held at the date of decision; to make removal directions against illegal entrants and overstayers; to cancel leave to enter; and so forth); then various grounds of appeal were available. The immigration decisions which gave rise to a right of appeal were set out in the 'old' s82 and s83 of the NIA 2002; the grounds of appeal in the 'old' s84. Now s82 and s84 still exist, but they have been amended to implement the current human rights/ protection-only appeals regime.

Appeal rights arise in EEA cases under the EEA Regs 2016 (MIL 11.8, 11.7.10).

14.2.2 Protection claims

A protection claim is one where a person alleges their removal would contravene the Refugee Convention or the UK's obligations in relation to Humanitarian Protection (s113 NIA 2002). Such a claim is refused where the Home Office makes a decision that removal would not breach the relevant Convention (in the form of a Notice of Decision accompanied by a Reasons for Refusal letter).

The protection claim will usually have been made in person at the port on entry to the UK, at the Asylum Screening Unit, or by delivering further submissions to the Further Submissions Unit of the HO in Liverpool. It can also be made on encountering an Immigration Officer having already entered the UK, or whilst the person is detained by the HO.

14.2.3 Human rights claims

Those lacking a viable asylum claim will only be able to access the appeals system via a human rights claim. A 'human rights claim' means a claim made by a person that to remove them from or require them to leave the United Kingdom or to refuse them entry into the United Kingdom would be unlawful under s6 of the HRA1998) as being incompatible with their Convention rights (s113 NIA 2002).

Note that although these claims will usually arise under Article 8 ECHR and involve family or private life, they may involve other rights. Article 3 (non-health) claims will usually be argued under the international protection ground. There are some other less commonly argued rights, e.g. Article 1 of Protocol 1 right to property.

A human rights claim under the 2002 Act can be made by way of

- A 'valid application' (on the appropriate form and paying the right fee) relying the family and/or private life provisions in the IRs or outside the Rules, or
- As 'further submissions' (though these have to pass the 'fresh claim' test within Rule 353 or
- By completion of a section 20 response to a 'one stop notice', or
- During the appeal process, though only where the SSHD consents, or
- Simply by representations.

We address the ways in which a claim can be made, aside from a fee-paid application (MIL 6.1.6). The short point is that unless the person has made an asylum claim or is in detention, the HO effectively controls how a human rights claim can be effectively raised. The only way to guarantee consideration (at least before the very moment of removal) is usually to make a fee-paid application.

Identifying a human rights claim

When will an application involve a *human rights claim*? Remember, appeal rights arise by operation of law. Of course, usually the HO identifies when they believe a claim has been made, by providing appeal forms. But the HO does not necessarily have the last word.

The SSHD treats some applications as deemed human rights claims. These are basically most of those involving conventional private and family life applications, i.e. those involving children and under the Appendices Private life, Settlement Family Life, Settlement Protection, Adult Dependent Relative, Family Reunion (Protection), Appendix Child staying with or joining a Non-Parent Relative (Protection). We can see this in Appendix AR at AR.3.2.(c), where the applications that do not give rise to administrative review are listed. The flip side of them *not* enjoying the right of administrative review is that they potentially enjoy a right of appeal, being human rights claims. Usefully the Home Office *Rights of appeal* guidance summarises the appealable routes (we have paraphrased somewhat):

Immigration Rule (Category of application)

- Paragraph 276B (long residence)
- Appendix Private Life
- Paragraphs 276U and 276AA (partner or child of a member of HM Forces)
- Paragraphs 276AD and 276AG (partner or child of a member of HM Forces) where the sponsor is a foreign or Commonwealth member of HM Forces and has at least 4 years' reckonable service in HM Forces at the date of application
- Part 8 of these Rules (family members) where the sponsor is present and settled in the UK or has refugee or humanitarian protection in the UK
    But not (under Part 8): paragraphs 319AA to 319J (PBS dependents), paragraphs 284, 287, 295D or 295G (sponsor granted settlement as a PBS Migrant)

- Part 11(asylum)
- Part 4 or Part 7 of Appendix Armed Forces (partner or child of a member of HM Forces) where the sponsor is a British Citizen or has at least 4 years' reckonable service in HM Forces at the date of application
- Appendix FM (family members)

   But not: section BPILR (bereavement) or section DVILR (domestic violence)

The guidance goes on to state that where human rights claims are made outside the Rules, they must be made on forms FLR(O) or SET(O). This does not grapple with the former's withdrawal on 1 December 2016. Family and private life claims made outside the Rules should be made on Form FLR(FP), and on other human rights grounds on form FLR(HRO) or FLR(DL).

Leaving aside the problem of which form to use for the human rights claim (which is discussed further in Chapter 1), it appears that applications made under the above listed categories will be accepted by the HO (and consequently the FTT) as being human rights claims.

Where human rights claims are made outside the rules, the guidance explains that:

> It is only where the applicant ticks the box 'Other purposes or reasons not covered by other application forms' that it should be treated as a human rights claim. Even if this box is ticked, the application may not be a human rights claim.
>
> You should consider the following three questions:
>
> 1. Does the application say that it is a human rights claim?
> 2. Does the application raise issues that may amount to a human rights claim even though it does not expressly refer to human rights or a human rights claim?
> 3. Are the matters raised capable of engaging human rights?

So where question 1 or 2, and 3 can be answered in the affirmative, the HO will accept the application is a human rights claim and acknowledge that a right of appeal is available if the application is refused.

The *Rights of Appeal* Guidance also provides that, in general, cases raising medical issues should be considered as claims under Article 3 or Article 8, and cases seeking leave to remain to participate in legal proceedings as a witness should be considered as Article 6 claims.

Outside the UK, applications based on a human rights claim outside the IRs must form part of a valid application for entry clearance.

Generally speaking, applicants with a potential human rights dimension to their case (eg a student with strong ties here, or a domestic violence survivor) will need to make a choice as the basis on which they put their application. It is open to the HO to be generous in their approach to the procedure, and treat an application as a human rights claim. But the case law would justify them refusing to do so.

In Baihinga [2018] UKUT 90 the UT considered the case of a person who applied to enter the UK as a returning resident. Her application referenced her family and community ties here. The UT held that an application may constitute a human rights claim, even if not in express terms or the application is not one which is deemed to be an human rights claim, if

> ...on the totality of the information supplied, the applicant is advancing a case which requires the caseworker to consider whether a discretionary decision under the rules needs to be taken by reference to ECHR issues ...The issue of whether a human rights claim has been *refused* must be judged by reference to the decision said to constitute the refusal. An entry clearance manager's decision, in response to a notice of appeal, cannot, for this purpose, be part of the decision of the entry clearance officer. A person who has not made an application which constitutes a human rights claim cannot re-characterise that application by raising human rights issues in her grounds of appeal to the First-tier Tribunal.

The ECO had effectively considered family life issues, given that the refusal questioned the strength of the asserted ties.

However, more common is the scenario where the HO effectively ignores the human rights dimension of an application made under Rules other than those deemed to count as human rights claims. In MY [2020] UKUT 89 (IAC) the UT considered a domestic violence application which was made under the domestic abuse route in Appendix FM. The supporting representations argued that a return abroad would exacerbate the applicant's vulnerability. The application was refused, and the only remedy suggested to be available was administrative review; the refusal letter stated that an application should be made using the appropriate form to pursue human rights issues. Nevertheless, the Appellant sought to appeal, arguing that the net effect of the refusal of the application under the Rules was to refuse his human rights claim. As such it carried the right of appeal.

The UT disagreed, stating that the SSHD was entitled to control access to how applications were considered. It was only where the SSHD actively engaged with a human rights claim and made a reasoned decision to reject it, that the right of appeal would ensue.

On appeal MY (Pakistan) [2021] EWCA Civ 1615 upheld this thinking. Whilst every domestic violence victim may have suffered an impairment of their physical and moral integrity such as to engage ECHR Art 8, this was due to the violence they suffered, not the SSHD's proposed act of removing them from the UK. The HO had a strict one-application-at-a-time policy which could lawfully separate the domestic violence application from any subsequent human rights claim.

The UT in MY also noted that in similar cases the FTT appeared to have begun a practice of inviting would-be Appellants to provide copies of their applications, in order to determine whether a human rights claim had been made and refused. That should no longer continue, as the question was not the content of the claim but the form which had been used.

Nevertheless, the UKVI Right of Appeal guidance still states:

> In order for an application to raise human rights, it is not necessary for the application form to say so. If the application does not state that it is a human rights claim you will need to consider what the applicant's reasons are for wanting to remain in the UK and decide whether those reasons amount to a human rights claim. ... You should ask yourself whether, having regard to the human rights protected by the European Convention on Human Rights (ECHR), is it obvious that the application relates to one of those rights. If it is obvious that the application relates to one of these rights, a human rights claim may have been made.

If the application was refused because documents provided with the application were overlooked, then administrative review, which is well-suited to that kind of complaint and is speedy, may well be more appropriate, at least where the Home Office would be unlikely to recognise a right of appeal.

Where does this leave us? It seems that

- If the HO refuses to consider a human rights claim implicit in (eg) a DV application, there is no refusal of said claim - and thus no right of appeal (MY)

- If the HO uses a form of words which shows that a human rights claim within (eg) a DV application has been considered and refused, there will be right of appeal (as was the case in AT [2017] EWHC 2589: see above at 6.3.2.3)

- The HO guidance actually encourages some active analysis of whether a decision contains an implicit human rights claim: so when challenging an adverse decision on a DV application, perhaps lawyers should consider whether the appropriate target is the reasonableness of declining to treat the contents of the application as a human rights claim. That approach could be challenged by JR. Though one might think that simply making an application overtly on human rights grounds would be more effective in terms of time and costs.

Sometimes the HO refuses an ILR application but grants limited leave instead. For example where an application is made for ILR based on a decade of lawful residence in the UK, where the representations also emphasise family connections here. Mr Mujahid was such a person: the SSHD refused ILR because of discrepancies in his reporting of earnings for tax as opposed to immigration purposes. But leave was nevertheless granted because of the family connections.

Mujahid [2021] EWCA Civ 449 concludes that, reading the NIAA 2002 appeal rights compositely, a person may appeal to the FTT where the SSHD has decided to refuse their claim that to remove them or require them to leave the UK or to refuse entry here would be unlawful under s6 HRA 1998. The natural meaning was thus that a right of appeal to the FTT arises where the SSHD's decision is that there is no lawful immediate or imminent impediment to removal/departure/refusal of entry. But if permission to stay was granted there could be no right of appeal.

Rights of appeal in the context of repeat and late claims

It was briefly thought possible that the new appeals system might have made refusals to recognise further representations as fresh claims appealable. However a series of decisions decided the contrary, culminating in Robinson [2019] UKSC 11.

Human rights claims may also be considered for certification under s96 NIAA 2002: the *Rights of appeal* Guidance under *Late claims* sets out that:

> if a person wishes to raise again a ground that has previously been refused supported by further evidence because his or her circumstances relating to that ground have changed, that information should be included in a section 120 response. For example, if a person has previously made an application on the basis of family life which was refused because he was a single man and he now claims to have established family life (such as marriage, children from the relationship), that information should be provided to the Secretary of State together with details of the claim for family life. In this type of case, you will want to consider any application under paragraph 353 (fresh claims) in the first instance.

See further MIL 9.6.4. When the further submissions are considered by the Home Office, a decision maker must first decide whether or not to grant leave on the basis of the representations and new evidence. It is only on deciding not to do so that the decision maker must then go on to consider the fresh claim test in r353.

There will be no right of appeal against decisions to curtail or refuse to extend leave, unless human rights or asylum grounds have been raised by way of pre-decision representations; or a s120 NIA 2002 one-stop notice has been provided in reply to the decision which generates, for example, a refusal of a human rights claim. Where a person raises an asylum or human rights claim in these ways, they will probably be told, unless they are in detention, that the application must be made in the normal way, e.g. by way of a valid application (which is provided for paragraph 400 of the IRs) or an asylum claim made in person at the Asylum Screening Unit.

14.2.4 Arguing for a right of appeal

As we have touched on above, a right of appeal arises by operation of law. The phrase sometimes uttered by those who should know better is that the HO '*grants a right of appeal*'. However, as we have seen, in reality a particular decision described by statute carries the right of appeal: i.e. a refusal of an asylum or human rights claim.

The Immigration (Notices) Regulations 2003 require that the decision maker issues a Notice of Decision, where the decision is appealable, with an accompanying statement explaining the right of appeal. Where there is an in-country right of appeal, the notice must be accompanied by a Notice of Appeal. A Notice of Decision which does not conform to the Notices Regulations may be invalid. Regardless of the validity of the notice though, if the HO has *in fact* made an appealable immigration decision under the terms of section 82, an immigration judge will have jurisdiction to deal with the appeal (subject to the exceptions and limitations in the Act).

If the HO have failed to acknowledge a right of appeal, then they have issued a decision that is incompatible with the Notice Regulations 2003. Though this does not necessarily mean the decision is invalid for all purposes, if left unchallenged (see Marepally [2022] EWCA Civ 855: MIL 5.2.1). If the HO wants it to take effect, they must re-issue it, carrying appropriate notice of appeal rights. However, someone who wants to get on with things may waive this failure: see e.g. LO [2009] UKAIT 00034.

The other side of the coin is that the HO may wrongly assert that there is a right of appeal, when in law there is not. For example they might serve an appeal form when refusing a straightforward PBS application, or alongside a decision on further representations which refuses to recognise them as a fresh claim. A person who tries to pursue an appeal in this scenario will be skating on thin ice: because the FTT must decline to hear the case if the SSHD spots the problem or if the FTT notes the mistake of their own motion (FTT Practice Statement para 3). There could be no legitimate expectation to the contrary: because any 'expectation' would be contrary to law.

There are nevertheless cases where the HO *does* have some discretion as to whether a right of appeal should be recognised (see also MIL 14.2.3). In particular:

- When deciding to reissue an earlier refusal of a human rights claim, in order to deliberately give a right of appeal – e.g. because the individual lost out on a right of appeal under the pre-2014 appeals system which did not award appeal rights to overstayers. See the Guidance *Requests for reconsideration of old human rights claims that were refused before 6 April 2015 with no right of appeal*
- When recognising that representations made in support of an application that is not *deemed* to be a human rights claim under Home Office policy nevertheless *in fact* amount to a human rights claim
- When deliberately denying the right of appeal, e.g. because the SSHD concludes that further representations do not amount to a fresh asylum or human rights claim (addressed above, & in Chapter 6)
- Where the SSHD does not consider that sufficient evidence has been put forward to establish a genuine relationship that is recognised as meriting an appeal for EEA purposes (MIL 11.8)
- Where there has been an allegation of dishonesty made against a migrant and the only sensible way of resolving the allegation is to give access to a right of appeal sooner rather than later. Eg pragmatically recognising the last application made as a human rights claim, even if that is stretching things: see Khan [2018] EWCA Civ 1684
- As noted above, where the migrant has applied under an immigration route that is not deemed to carry the right of appeal, the HO may well be entitled to refuse to recognise a right of appeal (MIL 14.2.1)

Where there is a debate as to whether there is a right of appeal to the FTT, normally an attempt should be made to bring such an appeal, whereby the FTT may determine its own jurisdiction – see e.g. Khan [2017] EWCA Civ 424. This might be determined as a preliminary issue (2014 Procedure Rules, r4(3)(e)). Time will not have begun to run where the Home Office failed to notify the (putative) appellant of the right of appeal.

14.2.5 Grounds of appeal

Section 84 of the 2002 Act, provides the grounds (or legal reasons or basis) for an appeal:

84 Grounds of appeal

> (1) An appeal under section 82(1)(a) (refusal of protection claim) must be brought on one or more of the following grounds—
> (b) that removal of the appellant from the United Kingdom would breach the United Kingdom's obligations under the Refugee Convention;
> (c) that removal of the appellant from the United Kingdom would breach the United Kingdom's obligations in relation to persons eligible for a grant of humanitarian protection;
> (d) that removal of the appellant from the United Kingdom would be unlawful under section 6 of the Human Rights Act 1998 (public authority not to act contrary to Human Rights Convention).
> (2) An appeal under section 82(1)(b) (refusal of human rights claim) must be brought on the ground that the decision is unlawful under section 6 of the Human Rights Act 1998.
> (3) An appeal under section 82(1)(c) (revocation of protection status) must be brought on one or more of the following grounds—
> (a) that the decision to revoke the appellant's protection status breaches the United Kingdom's obligations under the Refugee Convention;
> (b) that the decision to revoke the appellant's protection status breaches the United Kingdom's obligations in relation to persons eligible for a grant of humanitarian protection.

To summarise:

- Refusals of international protection claims (i.e. refugee status and Humanitarian Protection) decisions can only be appealed on refugee status and Humanitarian Protection grounds
- Human rights refusals can only be appealed on human rights grounds
- One implication of this is that an application may have been refused because of a relatively minor technical failure to meet the IRs: e.g. a partner application under Appendix FM may fail because the right bank statements are not submitted. The FTT Judge on appeal will not simply be looking at that particular Rule: they will be looking at whether there is a disproportionate interference with private and family life
- As the only available grounds for appeal are ones raising protection or human rights issues, appeals can no longer be allowed because the decision is 'not in accordance with the law': for many years this had previously provided a convenient solution for cases where an unfair decision had been made or a relevant policy had been overlooked or misunderstood. Now Judges must finally determine matters for themselves

14.2.5.1 Human rights appeals and the relevance of the Immigration Rules

An appeal against the refusal of a human rights claim can only be allowed (or refused) on human right grounds. Will a finding from the FTT judge that the application met the requirements of the Rules necessarily mean that the decision to refuse the application in breach of the Rules also breached the Appellant's human rights? It ought to, where there are sufficient Article 8 rights in this country with which removal would disproportionately interfere.

This approach was confirmed in TZ (Pakistan) [2018] EWCA Civ 1109 §34:

> ... where a person satisfies the Rules, whether or not by reference to an article 8 informed requirement, then this will be positively determinative of that person's article 8 appeal, provided their case engages article 8(1), for the very reason that it would then be disproportionate for that person to be removed.

So the major question then becomes whether the Appellant has shown by evidence that they have established private and family life ties with the UK. We can identify two species of human rights appeal:

1. Those relating to categories of the Rules which the HO deems to be human rights claims (i.e. those cross-referenced in Appendix AR and the Guidance *Rights of appeal* as listed above) and
2. Those under other categories which the HO does not necessarily see as a human rights claim, but where the facts nevertheless might engage human rights – the most obvious are domestic violence and visitor applications

In the first class of case, applying the thinking in TZ Pakistan, if the judge finds that the Rules are met, it is highly likely that they will also accept Article 8 is engaged (absent findings of a lack of private or family life). So a refusal which breaches the Rules in these circumstances is, under the Razgar framework, likely to be unlawful, have no legitimate aim, and be disproportionate (there being no public interest in refusing the application) – so would clearly breach Article 8.

What of the second species, for example an application to visit a close family member in the UK? There is no presumption under the visit rules that any particular family relationship engages Article 8. When considering the appeal on human rights grounds, the Judge must

- First, decide whether the nature of the family relationship does engage family life
- Second, determine whether the resulting interference with family life is disproportionate. This will require consideration of the extent to which the Rules, plus the statutory factors to be considered on appeal under NIAA 2002 section 117B (though not 117B(6), which applies only in expulsion cases) are satisfied

Where the visit concerns a very strong family relationship the Judge will presumably find that Article 8 is engaged. There will then be no difficulty in allowing the appeal on human rights grounds, presuming the application is now accepted as having met all relevant Appendix V Rules, including the intention to leave the UK at the end of the visit in circumstances where adequate maintenance and accommodation are available (eg Kopoi [2017] EWCA Civ 1511 - MIL 3.5).

It is probably a good idea to always remind Judges in human rights appeals that the Rules are the starting point, but that they also step back and consider the case in the round, having regard to the statutory criteria under section 117B too. In most cases, the fact that the Rules are satisfied will also demonstrate that section 117B factors point in the client's favour. For the relevance of the policy objectives found in the Rules when measuring proportionality see MIL 5.5.3.

14.2.6 Statements of additional grounds: section 120 notices, removal windows emergency

The 'one stop procedure' is a key element of the immigration control system. However its relevance to appeals is rather less than it used to be. Under the old appeal system, judges could consider all available grounds and facts that might allow a person to stay in the UK in one hearing. However the 'new matter' provisions of NIAA 2002 effectively give control of when new issues can enter appeals to the Home Office (see 14.2.7 immediately below).

The NIAA 2002 at s120 requires someone who is given a *Statement of Additional Grounds* (also called a 'section 120 notice') by the Home Office to declare any additional grounds for being allowed to stay in the UK other than those raised in their application. Under s120 the Home Office *may* serve a notice (NIAA 2002 s120(1)) where a person (P):

(a) P has made a protection claim or a human rights claim,
(b) P has made an application to enter or remain in the United Kingdom, or
(c) a decision to deport or remove P has been or may be taken.

A s120 notice is printed on the front of many of the specified application forms. Additionally, most refusal letters and decisions to deport now include a s120 notice. Applicants are also given a s120 notice soon after their first encounter with the Secretary of State where they are found to be in the UK in breach of immigration control, and asylum seekers are often given one shortly after claiming asylum. The HO Guidance on *Rights of Appeal* notes that Immigration Act 2014 *requires* the HO to serve a s120 on all those facing removal, but under the EEA Regs 2016 only that they *may* do so. However standard practice in EEA and EUSSch decision making was, and is, *not* to include a s120 notice.

Once a s120 notice has been served on an individual they may make a s120 statement in reply at any time in the future. There is no time limit. As explained in the *Rights of appeal* Guidance, although a time limit may be indicated, this is just to encourage speedy action: because s120 creates an ongoing duty which continues until the individual has either left the UK or has been granted leave.

If the time limit has expired, the SSHD must still consider the matter or grounds raised – but it is more likely that any subsequent claim will be certified as having been made late, so denying a right of appeal altogether (s96 NIAA 2002).

Having been given a s120 notice, the person can then raise, for example, Article 8 issues, other Convention rights, or their right to stay in the UK under other provisions of the rules or outside the rules. Where a s120 notice is completed before a decision is made on the original application, the Home Office will then have to make a decision on all the issues now before it.

Furthermore, under s120(5) there is a very clear ongoing duty to alert the Home Office of any changes of circumstances 'where P's circumstances have changed since the Secretary of State or an immigration officer was last made aware of them'.

The s120 regime underpins the UKVI policy of removing individuals without further notice, by reference to the concept of the **removal window**. The original HO policy envisaged giving no further notice of imminent removal once a person was given notice of being within a 3-month removal window. This was found unlawful in FB (Afghanistan) [2020] EWCA Civ 1338. The court accepted that there was nothing wrong in principle with the removal window idea in principle. However in practice the policy violated the right to important common law right of access to the court. Because, following an adverse decision material to their removal which is notified in the removal window, those involved are at risk of removal without any opportunity to challenge the relevant decision in a court or tribunal (MIL 13.3.1 addresses administrative removal procedures, 14.8 deals with JR generally).

Imminent removal can only realistically be challenged by judicial review – there is a distinct procedure in Part 54A of the Civil Procedure Rules requiring the HO to be served at once with a copy of the claim form. Exceptionally the court may accept there is good reason for failing to comply with that procedure, usually because full detailed grounds are not yet feasible. The application for JR will be accompanied by an application for a court-ordered injunction, ie interim relief, to suspend removal pending a decision on permission for JR.

The famous Guidance *Judicial reviews and injunctions* (filed under 'returns preparation') was replaced from 26 January 2023 (see also MIL 14.8 on JR). Now the removal window notice periods appear in *Administrative Removal: notification and implementation – interim guidance*.These set out that:

- There must always be at least 72 hours notice of removal
- Including at least 2 working days, and
- The last 24 hours must be a working day unless the period already includes 3 working days
- The removal window lasts for 3 months from notice of liability to removal being given
- Issue of notice RED.0006 may be apt– '*Whether or not they are detained, individuals must be allowed a reasonable opportunity to access legal advice and have recourse to the courts. The purpose of the notice period is to enable individuals to seek legal advice*'
- Issue of notice RED.0005 is appropriate where the applicant has made a protection claim or is an adult at risk, as evidence that the window no longer applies to them
- Where signed, Disclaimer form IS.101 must be explained to the individual and an opportunity for legal advice given: the notice period is then waived and the HO pays for the ticket home at public expense (see *Administrative Removal: notification and implementation – interim guidance*)

Other relevant issues arising from the Guidance:

- Claim forms lodged with detailed JR grounds will normally lead to deferral
- Urgent JRs are dealt with by Operational Support and Certification Unit (OSCU) who will decide whether to defer removal (whether or not a JR is lodged in time) – it is presumed there are 14 days maximum to respond to a JR threat
- An immigration factual summary must be provided: containing details of the applicant's arrival, any departures/removals, claims/applications made to the HO, appeals, further submissions, deportation proceedings, past JRs/injunctions, periods of detention, any non-compliance, removal directions, assisted voluntary returns or facilitated returns scheme offers, medical conditions & suicide/self-harm risks
- OSCU should aim to resolve meritorious representations without requiring JR to proceed
- A **Barrier Test** is applied to JR issues: as where new matters arise that should go via the further representations/fresh claim procedure, and a **Merits Test** too: where the JR grounds are very weak because they do not make sense or are generic, are obviously unarguable, or contrary to clear legal authority
- Removal will not be deferred (without a court injunction) if there has been less than 6 months since an appeal or previous JR concluded on the same/similar issues, or the same evidence, or the issues could reasonably have been raised in such proceedings or an injunction has already been refused or the court has indicated renewal of the JR is no bar to removal – nor if the removal is proceeding by Charter Flight (hence 5 working days notice should be given so there is a chance to obtain an injunction)
- Removal will always be deferred if an injunction is granted by the court, this is the first JR challenge to a certification decision such that there is no right of appeal or no in-country right and no injunction has been refused by the court, where JR permission is granted, or where this is the first challenge to a modern slavery claim rejection
- If the HO considers the claim has no merit then the court will be requested to expedite the claim
- All enforcement action should be suspended if permission for JR is granted; if permission is refused, the Merits and Barrier Tests should be applied, unless the permission refusal states that renewal is no bar to removal
- A reasonable opportunity to seek legal advice must always be given bearing in mind it is reasonable to expect someone to do so once an immigration application has been refused – via the detention advice surgeries where appropriate

Where someone faces a removal window but nevertheless has a case for remaining in the UK, they need to get their house in order *fast*.

- If they do not have an outstanding application with the SSHD they must make one as soon as possible. It is better to make a stronger application than a weaker one, but without an application pending, they are highly removable
- If they have an outstanding application with the SSHD, then they still need to consider making an urgent application to the UT for JR + interim relief against removal: otherwise they risk receiving an adverse decision and being detained and spirited away before they have a chance to challenge it. However this does not justify leaping to conclusions regarding the viability of a detainee's case. Advisors should always take full instructions and obtain the best available evidence. They must not commence JRs on a wing and a prayer: see SB (Afghanistan) [2018] EWCA Civ 215 (MIL 14.8.3).
- Making an application without full supporting evidence risks its refusal, of course. And once refused, any further application is likely to be assessed for whether it meets the *fresh claim* threshold. Furthermore, a poor quality application made in-country may prejudice future applications for entry clearance from abroad: for example, an application that is considered 'frivolous' could be refused under r9.8.2 of the General Refusal reasons, that being one of the relevant '*aggravating circumstances*'.

14.2.7 Considering new matters on appeal

There is a major difference between the old-style and new-style appeals systems, in that new sub-sections 85(5)-(6) of the 2002 Act prevent an Immigration Judge from considering new grounds of appeal after an application has been refused unless the Secretary of State has given the Tribunal consent to do so.

> (4) On an appeal under section 82(1) against a decision the Tribunal may consider any matter which it thinks relevant to the substance of the decision, including a matter arising after the date of the decision.
>
> (5) But the Tribunal must not consider a new matter unless the Secretary of State has given the Tribunal consent to do so.
>
> (6) A matter is a 'new matter' if—
>
>   (a) it constitutes a ground of appeal of a kind listed in section 84, and
>   (b) the Secretary of State has not previously considered the matter in the context of—
>   (i) the decision mentioned in section 82(1), or
>   (ii) a statement made by the appellant under section 120.

This means that compliance with the s120 procedure does not guarantee the availability of a new ground of appeal.

The Rights of Appeal guidance states that switching from Article 3 to Article 8, or from Article 8 private life to family grounds such as marriage to a British citizen, is caught by the provision so that their consent to raising the point is required: however a 'new matter' does not include additional facts or evidence of the original claim: e.g. a developing private life claim, the introduction of additional children to a parent application, or further risk factors in an asylum claim.

Where their consent is required, the Guidance goes on to explain that the HO will aim to consider the issue and decide the new matter before (or even at) the hearing, even if the new matter is not identified until very late in the day, but they are likely to withhold consent where there is insufficient time to do so, for example because the HO Presenting Officer needs to check whether a document is genuine, but helpfully concludes that in such cases:

> In order to make best use of tribunal resources, an adjournment should be sought for the SSHD to consider the new matter. Where possible, a single appeal should consider all matters that have been raised by the appellant.

The Guidance also states that where consent was refused and an appeal allowed, no action will be taken on a "new matter" until a new application or claim is made based on the matter in question.

Mahmud [2017] UKUT 488 (IAC) holds that a 'new matter' is a factual matrix not previously considered by the Secretary of State in the course of determining the application whose refusal led to the right of appeal.

This effectively upholds the interpretation given by the Home Office Guidance, which gives examples of new matters as a private life claim when previously only family life had been raised, or vice versa, or a family life claim that had previously been based on relationship between partners where there has now been a child born to the family.

The Tribunal noted that the Home Office Guidance encouraged active steps to be taken to ensure that an appeal proceeded considering new matters with consent where reasonably possible, but was of the view that any failure to follow that Guidance could be challenged only by JR.

NB: If the HO does refuse to consider the matter, and an adjournment is not granted, the judge will not consider the matter either.

In AK and IK (Turkey) [2019] UKUT 67 (IAC) the UT looks again at the 'new matter' provisions of the NIAA 2002. These are increasingly biting on some of the more creative attempts to make the most of

CHAPTER 14: Appeals, Administrative Review and Judicial Review

the appeal system. Here the migrants had applied for leave based on their private and family life, applications that had been considered under the family life route under Appendix FM to the IRs.

However by the time of their appeal hearings, the new Appendix ECAA for Turkish nationals was in force. This permits leave to remain to be granted to the partners of Turkish citizens on a more relaxed basis than Appendix FM would require. Accordingly they sought to rely on this as a matter relevant to the proportionality of their application's refusal, arguing that if they in reality now met the requirements of Appendix ECAA, the requirements of immigration control were significantly reduced.

The UT refused to permit this to be argued without HO consent. The UT concluded that where an attempt was made in an appeal to rely upon criteria from a different category of the IRs to make good an Article 8 claim than that relied upon in the application made to the Home Office, this would be a '*new matter*' within the meaning of section 85(6) NIAA 2002 even if the underlying facts (e.g. as to accommodation, maintenance etc) remain the same.

In Hydar [2021] UKUT 176 (IAC) the UT accepts that where a one-stop notice is served on a migrant, they might respond by raising an asylum or an EU ground of appeal. Then the matter would fall within the UT's jurisdiction. Grounds of this nature would require consent where it was a new matter not previously considered by the SSHD.

Some individuals clock up a decade of lawful residence in the course of their Tribunal appeal. Having done so, they may well wish to argue that the fact that they have a viable application for ILR under the long residence route (IR276B) means their appeal should succeed for that reason alone.

In OA and Others [2019] UKUT 65 (IAC), the UT notes the relationship between human rights grounds of appeal and the IRs setting out the SSHD's view of private and family life. It notes the longstanding position that matters of leave are for the SSHD. A finding on appeal that the criteria for a particular Rule was met (and thus that the human rights appeal should be allowed) did not necessarily mean that the appellant was entitled to leave of the precise nature and duration envisaged by that Rule: leave was generally a matter for the SSHD. The Tribunal's jurisdiction is limited to that set out in the relevant ground of appeal: i.e. (international protection cases aside), whether a decision is consistent with the Human Rights Convention.

The UT notes that even though the '10 years' lawful residence criteria of the long residence Rule may clearly be met, there will remain questions such as the *Suitability* of the applicant for the grant of leave having regard to the general refusal reasons: this may require checks to be made as to their character and conduct. The UT treated the fact that an appellant might now satisfy Rule 276B as a 'new matter' which required consent from the SSHD to be raised on the appeal. It is only where the SSHD accepts that *all* the requirements of the rule are currently met that the SSHD would subsequently have to grant ILR. Otherwise, the success of the appeal will simply mean that a grant of limited leave should be made, and a fee-paid application will still need to be made for ILR. It would clearly not be appropriate for someone to removed pending the making of such an application.

> **Top Tip**
>
> Always ensure that a one stop notice is provided at the same time as lodging grounds of appeal to the Tribunal: and ensure that the one stop notice actually goes to the Home Office (though it should be copied to the FTT as a matter of courtesy).
>
> It is absolutely essential to keep up to date with a client's circumstances and take full and detailed instructions when matters arise. The client, if refused, will have one chance to put arguments before an immigration judge. If this chance is lost, there is absolutely no guarantee that the arguments will ever be independently considered.
>
> If a s120 notice has not been served on the client at any time before the decision is received, or with the decision, and there are issues to raise before the tribunal in respect of which a s120 notice will have to be submitted, an adviser might sensibly consider whether to request the immediate service of a s120

notice: the policy statements indicating universal service should provide powerful support for such a submission.

Examples

A person refused leave to remain on private life grounds with an impending appeal hearing tells their solicitor they have a viable asylum claim which they wish to make. A s120 notice is submitted to the HO, copied to the Tribunal. The HO Presenting Officer declines to consent to this being considered by the Tribunal because the information is provided too close to the appeal hearing. The judge has no jurisdiction to hear the asylum element of the appeal. Nevertheless the asylum claim will have to be determined by the HO and an adverse decision will be a refusal of an international protection claim (which will give rise to a further right of appeal).

A person awaits an appeal hearing against the refusal of a parent application made under Appendix FM. Whilst awaiting the appeal, with continuing leave under s3C of the 1971 Act, they clock up 10 years of lawful continuous residence (and pass the KoLL requirements). They submit a s120 notice to the HO, asking for consent to raise the long residence application as a new matter (now seeking to rely on their Article 8 private life). The HOPO should consent, if possible, or agree an adjournment, but if they do not, or the judge refuses to adjourn the hearing, the appellant will be in a very difficult position. They can wait until the present appeal is over, but if the appeal is ultimately refused, their 3C leave must end before they can submit the long residence application to the HO. They will then be making the application at risk of all the privations that might be piled on them under the hostile environment, including the loss of their job. In such circumstances, they may wish to challenge the FTT's refusal of an adjournment if that is all that is standing between them and the opportunity to have their circumstances considered whilst they remain lawfully in the UK.

14.2.8 From where may appeals be brought?

Sections 92 and 94B of the 2002 Act address whether an appeal can be brought from inside or outside the UK. Section 94B means that most deportation appeals (i.e. where a human rights claim has been refused following notification of a deport decision) must be pursued from outside the UK, unless the appellant's removal pending their appeal will cause *serious irreversible harm* (MIL 13.5.2.1)). An appeal which can be brought in-country and prevents removal is often referred to as *suspensive*: because it suspends expulsion whilst still pending. The Guidance *Current Rights of appeal* addresses how the HO monitors this via its GCID or Atlas systems.

Under the amendments to the non-suspensive appeal provisions of NIAA 2002 which entered force on 1 December 2016, the HO have the power to certify *any* human rights appeal under 94B (and not just those relating to deportation), so that the person must leave the UK to appeal the decision. However at the time of writing s94B decisions are suspended (MIL 13.5.2.1).

NIAA 2002 s92(4) explicitly provides for out-of-country human rights appeals where a human rights claim is made from outside the UK, and subsection (5) provides that protection revocation appeals must be brought from inside/outside the UK depending on the Appellant's location at the time. Subsection (8) provides for appeals brought from within the UK to be treated as abandoned in most cases if the person leaves the UK (but not where the appeal is brought under the EEA Regs or certified under ss 94 or 94B). The definition of a pending appeal (i.e. one that is not finally determined) is in section 104 of the 2002 Act.

14.2.9 Who entered the new system and when?

It might be relevant when looking at your client's immigration history, to understand the way in which the commencement of the new appeals regime took place. Tranches of migrants entered the new system based on the refusal date, from 20 October 2014 onwards, as set out in a rather complex set of Commencement Orders. And all applications made after 6 April 2015 entered the modern regime. At the same time the IRs increased access to administrative review (Appendix AR).

CHAPTER 14: Appeals, Administrative Review
and Judicial Review

4.2.10 Applications and appeals processes

Now we have seen the statutory framework under the 2014 Act, we can take a look at how particular classes of case move through the system. Here are some examples, ignoring complications such as certification as 'clearly unfounded' (s94 NIAA 2002) or raised unduly late (s96 NIAA 2002).

How immigration decision making progresses

Overstayers

1. Migrant arrives in UK with leave to remain
2. They remain beyond the leave granted: hence they are now an overstayer
3. They are removable upon detection as a person who requires leave to enter or remain but does not have it (s10 IAA 1999)
4. They apply for leave to remain to regularise their status
5. Their application is refused
6. They have a right of appeal so long as they raised an asylum or human rights claim in that application and used the appropriate application form for private and family life routes (s82(1) NIA 2002) (presuming the claim is not certified)
7. This is an in-country right of appeal (s92 NIA 2002)
8. Once the appeal fails they are removable as a person who requires leave to enter or remain but does not have it (IAA 1999 s10)
9. There is no right of appeal against those removal directions
10. They should be notified of entering a removal window, within which they will have 72 hours of removal directions: MIL 14.2.6)
11. Any further application (with an asylum or human rights dimension) will attract a further right of appeal if it meets the fresh claim test (IR 353)

Regular Migrants

1. Migrant arrives in UK with leave to remain
2. They apply for an extension
3. The application is refused
4. See paras 6-11 above for overstayers

Illegal entrants

1. Migrant arrives in the UK without permission, or by making false representations
2. Migrant detected: illegal entry notice given
3. Any application, asylum or otherwise, is made
4. The claim is refused: see paras 6-11 above for overstayers

---

14.2.11 Right of appeal – The 'saved provisions' regime

There are a few old-style appeals still in the system, but they are rarely encountered. Anyone wishing for information about them should feel free to email the HJT office and we can provide an e-copy of some old text from earlier editions of this publication.

14.3 Certificates and out-of-country appeals

An appellant cannot normally be removed from the UK whilst an asylum application or appeal is pending (2002 Act, s78 and 79). However, the SSHD has the power to certify asylum or human rights claims as clearly unfounded. From 28 June 2022 these bar the right of appeal altogether (NIAA 2002 s94(3A)) – they no longer simply render an appeal out-of-country.

There are a series of different powers of certification: five in number in total, though of three types. They are:

CHAPTER 14: Appeals, Administrative Review and Judicial Review

- **Clearly unfounded certificates** [MIL 14.3.1] (usually made under s94 NIAA 2002, though there are also specific powers in third country cases under Schedule 3 to the AITCA 2004 and section 94(7) of NIAA 2002: there is quite a good discussion in the Rights of appeal Guidance under *Place from which an appeal may be brought or continued*): where the Secretary of State considers a case to be weak
- **Late claim certificates** [MIL 14.3.2] where the Secretary of State considers the claim should have been raised earlier, in an appeal or in response to a one-stop notice (s96 NIAA 2002) – this prevents the right of appeal altogether, rather than just making it out-of-country.
- **Section 94B certificates** [MIL 13.5.2.4] in deport and human rights cases where the Secretary of State considers that, having decided to proceed with deportation proceedings because there is no real chance of a human rights breach, additionally there is no threat of 'serious irreversible harm' such as to warrant an 'in-country' right of appeal

14.3.1 'Clearly unfounded' certificates

Within s94, there are essentially two kinds of 'clearly unfounded' cases:

- clearly unfounded asylum claims (MIL 9.6.1)
- clearly unfounded human rights claims

The guidance Certification of protection and human rights claims under section 94 of the Nationality, Immigration and Asylum Act 2002 (clearly unfounded claims) is of interest as it sets out suitable cases for certification:

- In parent cases, where there is no evidence of the child's existence, or of the parent's asserted involvement in their life, or no evidence of arguably unusual level of dependency where it is an adult child involved, or where a non-British child has been in the UK for less than seven years and there is no evidence of any arguably exceptional circumstances
- In partner cases, where there is no evidence that the relationship is genuine, or it is fairly new and more akin to 'girlfriend/boyfriend' than a permanent and enduring relationship, or where there are no circumstances put forward suggesting that family life could not continue overseas, absent exceptional circumstances
- In private life cases, claims based on limited job prospects abroad, medical claims absent evidence of the condition's existence, claims from students/workers absent proof of private life exceeding the normal level of social interaction, and, vis-á-vis adults over 25 who have not lived here for 20 years, evidence of circumstances suggestive of very significant obstacles to relocation by way of integration, or exceptional circumstances

The same principles apply on JR of clearly unfounded human rights claim certificates as regarding asylum ones. Such JRs will normally be in the UT.

As the test was put in Thangarasa [2002] UKHL 36:

> The question to which the Secretary of State had to address his mind….is whether the allegation is so clearly without substance that the appeal would be bound to fail.

In ZT (Kosovo) [2009] UKHL 6 the House of Lords held that the court reviewing a clearly unfounded certificate must (i) ask the questions which an immigration judge would ask about the claim and (ii) ask itself whether on any legitimate view of the law and the facts any of those questions might be answered in the claimant's favour.

Where there remains a right of appeal (due to a pre-28 June 2022 decision), a certificate may be made after the appeal has been brought and then the appeal must be continued from outside the United Kingdom (s92(6) NIAA 2002).

The UKVI Guidance sets out exceptions to certification at the heading *When not to certify a clearly unfounded claim: exceptions*. One of which deals with the situation where there is a human rights claim *and* an asylum claim. If only one is thought liable to certification, then in practice no certificate should be made. Otherwise a viable claim would lose appeal rights simply by association with a hopeless one.

From 28 June 2022 there is no longer any out-of-country appeal in these cases. This may well change the approach on JR – the courts may well review HO decisions more intensely.

14.3.2 'Late Grounds' certificates – prohibition on further appeals or raising grounds late

As well as clearly unfounded certificates, a certificate can be issued under NIA 2002 section 96. In these cases *an asylum may not be brought* at all (i.e. they do not merely lead to an out-of-country appeal). Certification is likely to follow

- where the claim or application to which the new decision relates relies on a matter that could have been raised in an appeal against an old immigration decision (s96(1)), or
- the appeal seeks to rely on a ground that should have been, but was not, raised in a s120 notice (s96(2)) and
- (in either case) there is no satisfactory reason for failing to do so

Before April 2015 the provision was very rarely used. Practitioners are now seeing it rather more.

Example

Ahmed is facing deportation. He was given a notice of decision to deport him under the non-automatic deportation provisions, and a s120 notice. He fails to mention that he has two children and an arguable family life in the UK. He does not lodge an appeal against the decision. A deportation order is made against him. Ahmed is in a difficult situation. If he puts forward his family life arguments now in an application to revoke the deportation order, he risks certification. He would need to show instead that he meets the test for a fresh claim (i.e. that he has a significantly different family life than he did when he had his right of appeal). It might also be worth investigating whether to make a late appeal to the Tribunal, if Ahmed had difficulty obtaining legal representation in detention, was not given appeal forms at the time of the immigration decision or something similar that led him to not appeal the earlier decision.

The only remedy against decisions to certify under s96 will be JR, i.e. an application to the UTIAC showing that there has been a misunderstanding of the situation or because of a failure to take account of all relevant evidence.

For example, in ROO (Nigeria) [2018] EWHC 1295 (Admin), the Court struck down a refusal of an asylum claim which had certified the claim as raised unjustifiably late under section 96 of the NIA 2002. The SSHD had acted unfairly in making a decision on the asylum claim prematurely. Had a Rule 35 report been obtained before the asylum interview, it should have become apparent that this asylum seeker was vulnerable and could not reasonably be expected to raise all relevant factors in her case during a rather confrontational interview process.

The provisions are designed to catch all circumstances, whether or not an appeal was brought, or if one was brought, whether or not it has been determined. Once an appeal has been instituted, however, there can be no certification (see NIAA 2002 section 96(7) – so if there is no certification in the fresh refusal letter, an appeal cannot be cut off by a subsequent certificate: this is in contrast to 'clearly unfounded' and s94B serious irreversible harm certificates which can stifle extant appeals).

These provisions apply whether or not the appellant has been outside the UK since the requirement to state additional grounds arose or since the right of appeal arose (2002 Act, s96(5)).

The operation of the old version of s96 NIAA 2002 was considered in J [2009] EWHC 705 (Admin), a decision which remains relevant as the statutory scheme remains generally the same, and which identified the relevant questions as whether:

- the individual was notified of an earlier right of appeal

- the matters now relied upon could have been raised earlier
- if they could have been raised earlier, there is a satisfactory reason for not doing so
- in all the circumstances, if there is no good reason for the late raising of the claim, certification is appropriate as a matter of discretion (for example, having regard to considerations such as the section 55 duty to secure the best interests of children, even if a parent has failed to act in a timely fashion)

14.4 Appeals in the FTT

The online MIL details with practice, procedure and evidence in the FTT in detail. In the paper version we provide brief information.

Practice in the FTT – the reformed appeal procedures & issue-based decisions

Lodging appeals and coming on/off the record

The Consolidated Practice Statements annexed to the User Guide now explain how appeals are to be lodged and processed. There is also a guide *Make an Immigration and Asylum Appeal using HMCTs*.

- Generally appeals should proceed online via MyHMCTs (3.5) (note that law firms need to register with MyHMCTs and obtain an account/password): unless in detention or relating to EUSSch. Some appeals may proceed online though not via HMCTs if the FTT accepts this is appropriate
- An appeal may not proceed if the FTT determines there is no appealable decision (3.2)
- Appeals will be stayed for 3 months if they have been wrongly commenced offline – online and offline appeals can be consolidated where two start running in relation to essentially the same refusal (3.5) though an offline appeal that does not makes its way online within the period of stay will be determined without a hearing
- There are sets of model directions for

  - Appeals commenced via MyHMCTs (Annex A)
  - Appeals proceeding online though not via MyHMCTs (Annex B)
  - Appeals without representatives proceeding online though not via MyHMCTs (Annex C)
  - For offline appeals where the FTT considers it in the interests of justice, appeals may proceed via case specific directions

- Grounds of appeal are no longer required
- Documents may only be provided to the FTT via uploading
- The standard directions provide (in an Annex A (ie represented) case)

  - For Respondent's bundle from HO within 28 days from providing Notice of Appeal, which must include refusal letter and any material supporting the application that has been refused
  - The Appellant must provide the appeal skeleton argument (ASA) on the later date of: 28 days from Respondent's bundle being provided, or 42 days after the Notice of Appeal, summarising their case, stating the issues, and making brief submissions as to why they disagree with the refusal: extensive quotations are not required
  - The Respondent must provide a meaningful review of their decision within 14 days of the ASA, particularising the maintained refusal reasons and giving a counter-schedule of issues if not agreed: proforma responses will be rejected
  - Material provided outside these time limits requires express leave to be relied on, and the admission of evidence provided within 5 working days of the hearing must be dealt with as a preliminary issue – no evidence may be admitted unless uploaded
  - Post-hearing evidence may be provided exceptionally if the judge so directs

- In an Annex B case, the parties must additionally provide contact details within 5 days of the standard directions and there will be active case management, though the directions are otherwise similar to Annex A

- In an Annex C case, contact details must be given as per Annex B, the HO must provide a Respondent's bundle within 14 days of directions, and the Appellant must provide an Explanation of Case (a less formal document than a skeleton) on the later date of: 28 days from Respondent's bundle being provided, or 42 days after the Notice of Appeal; to which the HO must provide a meaningful review. The FTT will then decide whether a Case Management Appointment is needed to advance things (and the parties may apply for one)

In Lata [2023] UKUT 163 (IAC) the UT emphasises that having received a focussed skeleton argument and a meaningful review the FTT can expect the parties to be focussed on their position at the hearing. There should not be a rolling reconsideration of either party's position. The parties should identify any matters arising from previous judicial decisions and the Devaseelan principle (MIL 14.5) relevant to their cases now. It was unlikely that a party would be entitled to seek permission to appeal on a matter not raised at the FTT hearing.

TC [2023] UKUT 164 (IAC) stresses that HO reviews should be **meaningful** and not proforma or standardised. The FTT should condense the parties' positions in a clear, coherent and concise issue-based manner to identify the principal important controversial issues. Permission to appeal grants should focus laser-like on grounds which are arguable. Issue-based decision making is now a major objective of the First-tier Tribunal.

Procedure in the FTT – the Rules

Immigration appeals in the FTT are governed by the Tribunal Procedure (First-tier Tribunal) (Immigration and Asylum Chamber) Rules 2014 ('the FTTRs'). Of interest:

Appeal time limits

- Time limits for bringing appeal (FTT Procedure Rules r19): 14 days from being sent decision for in-country cases, 28 days post-departure if in the UK when decision received but where the appeal is out-of-country, otherwise 28 days from receipt (ie entry clearance)
- Late appeals are possible – the test is the FTT's overriding objective of fairness/justice
- There are radical proposals in NBA 2022 & IMA 2023 for speedier appeals, including ones direct to the UT, but the provisions have not commenced at the time of writing (MIL 9.1.0)

Other important Rules

- The possibility of an award of 'wasted' costs, where a party has acted improperly, unreasonably or negligently (r9)
- There is some measure of judicial control over attempts by the HO to vary refusal letters because of the need for consent to vary a document and to alert the FTT of the basis for defending a case 28 days before the hearing via the response procedure (r23, r24) and within 14 days of so doing confirm via a written statement what aspects of the Appellant's case are opposed/accepted (r24A(3)): now Appellant's representatives must react to any such responses by providing a skeleton argument and any relevant supporting evidence on the later of the two dates (i) 42 days from giving notice of appeal or (ii) 28 days from the HO response (r24A(1-2))). The refusal letter can be amended but this requires permission (r4(3)(c)) and they must request permission to do so (r23(2)(b), r24(2))
- Supervision of withdrawal of HO decisions, because an appeal can be heard notwithstanding the withdrawal of the underlying decision where there is '*good reason*' (r17)
- Some decisions can be delegated to non-judicial legal staff, now titled Legal Officers, though there is a right to apply for a reconsideration of any such decision to a judge (r3)
- The overriding objective is to deal with cases fairly and justly and in a way which is proportionate, avoids unnecessary formality, ensures ease of full participation, uses the FTT's expertise and avoids delay subject to properly considering relevant issues (r2(1))
- Requiring a new representative notifying the Tribunal they are acting, ie "*coming on the record*": r10(3)
- A representative can take any step for the Appellant except for signing a witness statement, anything given to the Appellant *must* also be provided to their representative r10(4)-(6). There

CHAPTER 14: Appeals, Administrative Review
and Judicial Review

- are some contact obligations under r12A for Appellants themselves to ensure the FTT has their present address, and for the Respondent to alert the FTT if she removes someone from the UK
- Directions as to issues, evidence, expert evidence, and witnesses can be given under rule 14. Witnesses can be summoned to attend, or answer questions or produce documents on application of either party or on the FTT's own volition under rule 15
- Rule 6 allows the FTT to take what action as it considers just where there has been non-compliance with a rule or direction, including referring the matter to the UT to exercise its powers under section 25 of the 2007 Act (which are the same as those exercised by the High Court – i.e. scary ones which include powers to punish breach of an order to attend court by witness summons, or to produce documents, via contempt proceedings)
- Evidence has to be disclosed to all parties in general, though there are some powers under r13 to withhold disclosure if otherwise a person might be caused serious harm and where it is proportionate to the interests of justice to do so
- Grounds of appeal can be varied with the FTT's permission (r19(7))
- Adjournments must be applied for not later than 5pm a full working day before the hearing, otherwise there must be representation at the hearing to pursue the question of adjournment; see more on adjournments below
- Hearings generally take place in public (r27) subject to powers to exclude a disruptive person or one who might inhibit the giving of evidence or making of submissions, and to exclude a person where material that might cause serious harm is involved, or where the purpose of the hearing would be defeated by their attendance (anonymity might be ordered in the last scenario)
- The *Guidance Note on Anonymity Directions in the FTT* highlights cases involving children or vulnerable persons where the appeal may involve their personal information and their welfare may be injured by undue disclosure, and any cases where there is highly personal evidence that should remain confidential or might risk harm to individuals if disclosed
- An appeal may be heard in the absence of a party where due notice of the hearing has been given and it is in the interests of justice to do so (r28); and may be considered without a hearing (i.e. on the papers in the absence of both parties) by consent, or where the interests of justice or serious non-compliance with the Procedure Rules or directions make this a proportionate response to the situation, having given the opportunity to make representations from both sides (r25)
- An appeal may be deemed abandoned where an appellant has left the United Kingdom or been granted leave to remain in the course of the appeal (r16 read with s104(4A) of the NIAA 2002) – however if the appeal is re international protection, i.e. where leave short of HP or refugee status was granted, then an appellant may provide notice within 28 days of being sent notice of the grant of leave to remain that they wish to continue with their appeal (r16(3))
- If the HO wishes to withdraw a decision, then they must obtain the permission of the FTT, and the FTT may continue with the appeal if there is *good reason* to do so (r17(2))
- A wasted costs order may be made against a party if a person has acted unreasonably in bringing, defending or conducting proceedings (rule 9), the FTT doing so on an application or on its own initiative. The rule also contains the procedure for making such an application, and for a detailed assessment of the costs. There is a detailed discussion of the issues in Okondu [2014] UKUT 377 (IAC) and Cancino [2015] UKFTT 59 (IAC). Such orders may follow conduct which is unreasonable, improper or negligent. An application for costs is made to the Tribunal that heard the appeal, and served on the HO, within 28 days of conclusion of an appeal, i.e. within 28 days of either withdrawal by the HO or of notification of the appeal's success being sent. There is no specific form or fee for this application
- Costs orders may be made by reference to s194A of the Legal Services Act 2007, which applies where one of the successful party's legal representatives is acting partly/wholly free of charge: orders can be made that the HO pays a sum equivalent to what might have been incurred absent pro bono services to the *Access to Justice Foundation*

Other points of FTT practice

These points arise:

- The systems of starring (rare in recent times) and reporting aim to achieve consistency across the FTTIAC and UTIAC – as does the Country Guidelines regime (MIL 8.2.2)
- FTT appeals are generally lodged via the Reform Online Procedure

©HJT

- A fee is payable: £140 for an oral hearing and £80 for consideration on the papers. FTTJs may order the fee be repaid to a successful Appellant by the HO if their appeal is allowed. Typically if the appeal succeeds on the same evidence supplied on the refused application. Fee waiver is possible for those whose immigration application was subject to fee waiver, if on legal aid/asylum support or where there are children receiving local authority support, and some kinds of appeals: citizenship deprivation and protection status revocation
- A hearing date can be expedited for compelling/compassionate grounds
- In practice, standard directions issued with the notice of hearing sent to the parties will include a date by which directions must be complied with, and require the Appellant to produce:
    - witness statements of the evidence to be called at the hearing, such statements to stand as evidence in chief at the hearing – from May 2022 the directions state that witness statements should represent the *totality of the evidence in chief* and only *in exceptional circumstances and with the leave of the Tribunal* will further oral evidence be permitted;
    - a paginated and indexed bundle of all the documents to be relied on at the hearing with a schedule identifying the essential passages
- There is specific guidance as to liaison between the immigration and family courts where there are extant family law proceedings (see below). Where there are parallel family and immigration law proceedings extant, it is necessary to consider whether one set would benefit from findings made in the other. You can see the issues described in the case law, particularly the two stages of the proceedings in RS India [2012] UKUT 218 (IAC) and RS India [2013] UKUT 82
- Family court documents are confidential and care should be taken to avoid disclosing them without a court order so authorising (MIL 6.2.6.2)
- The FTTRs require the HO to send a bundle including decision notices, reasons for decisions, application forms, interview records, any other unpublished information referred to in the decision, and notice of any other appealable decision made re the Appellant (r23-24)
- Appellants may be represented by anyone permitted to provide legal services under s84 of the IAA 1999, whilst the HO may be represented by one of her employees
- Whilst in general a party may well have to accept the consequences of errors by their representative, this is not necessarily the case in asylum and fundamental rights cases, see FP [2007] EWCA Civ 13, though evidence that the failing is truly that of the (presumably former) representative and not the migrant themselves will be required: BT [2004] UKIAT 00311 – including pursuing a formal complaint
- Where the issues in an appeal have been determined in previous proceedings to which the Appellant was a party (or where their family member was a party & where they gave evidence relating to the same issues), the findings made in that decision are the starting point for future consideration of the case, subject to the availability of further evidence, and the provision of new evidence that might have been produced sooner should be treated with suspicion: Devaseelan [2004] UKIAT 000282.

Evidence

- The HO is under a duty to draw attention to relevant documents within its possession which the other party cannot access, and must draw attention to any policy, published or not, that might throw doubt on the HO case: BH Iraq [2020] UKUT 189 (IAC) – and any comment made by an interviewer or similar that might be relevant, eg as to the Appellant's state of health (though not as to the thinking of HO staff regarding the decision making, beyond the refusal letter itself)
- Immigration appeals are intended to be an informal procedure, in which the forms of material which may constitute evidence of facts (especially in asylum and human rights cases regarding the well-foundedness of the appellant's fears): so there is no strict need for corroboration, though the more obtainable evidence appears to be, the greater the chance of adverse inferences being drawn from its absence
- Oral evidence given from abroad requires the express permission of the relevant national authorities: the procedure is set out in Presidential Guidance Note No 4 of 2022 on *Evidence from Overseas*

Instructing experts

The instruction of experts (usually country experts and medical experts, both psychiatric and physicians) is regulated by Practice Direction: No 6 of the consolidated set.

- A party who instructs an expert must provide clear and precise instructions, together with all relevant information concerning the nature of the appellant's case, including their immigration history, the refusal reasons leading to the appeal, and copies of any relevant previous reports.
- It is the duty of an expert to help the Tribunal on matters within their own expertise; this duty is paramount and overrides any obligation to the person from whom they have received instructions or by whom they are paid.
- Expert evidence should be the independent product of the expert uninfluenced by the pressures of litigation, assisting the Tribunal by providing objective, unbiased opinion on matters within the author's expertise, and should not assume the role of an advocate.

Experts should:

- consider all material facts, including those which might detract from their opinion;
- make it clear when a question or issue falls outside their expertise; and
- state when they are unable to reach a definite opinion, for example because of insufficient information

Medical evidence can be of use in a number of scenarios.

- In establishing the facts of the case independently of the client's oral evidence, e.g. by showing that there is scarring present, and perhaps also that it does not have any obvious explanation than that offered by the appellant (e.g. bullet wounds, blade wounds to the back);
- In showing physical evidence of past problems that might exacerbate risk on return to the country of origin, or in showing that present health questions may attract discrimination (e.g. HIV in some countries);
- In establishing why the client cannot themselves give a coherent account, e.g. because they have mental health problems following serious ill treatment, or because it would be unusual for a victim of trauma to be able to give details of certain episodes in their life;
- In establishing that the client has health problems counting against their return to their country of origin, where this would amount to a breach of ECHR Article 3 or Article 8 – this will be particularly relevant where they cannot access health care there (see MIL 5.6).

Reports of scarring should be written by reference to the Istanbul Protocol addressing the examination and evaluation of evidence of torture. For each lesion and for the overall pattern of lesions, the physician should indicate the degree of consistency between it and the attribution.

14.5 Onwards appeals to the Upper Tribunal

Appeal via the FTT

An application form is provided on the FTT (IAC) section of the www.gov.uk website: IAFT–4: Application to the FTT for permission to appeal to the Upper Tribunal

The deadline for receipt of the application by the FTT is 14 days after the date on which the party making the application was provided with written reasons for the decision and 28 days where the appellant is outside the UK.

The application must:

- identify the decision of the Tribunal to which it relates,
- identify the alleged error or errors of law in the decision, and
- state the result that the party seeks.

An application for an extension of time can be made if necessary (r33(5)(c) – the touchstone for decisions generally in the UT & FTT is dealing with cases fairly and justly).

FTTRs 34-35 empower the FTT to review its own decisions rather than having to grant permission to appeal. The idea behind the power is that lengthy proceedings to the UT may be avoided by a timely review. This would be useful where a material error of law that undermines the entire decision is self-evident. Rule 34 requires that the FTT when considering an application for permission to appeal should always bear in mind the possibility of reviewing a decision for itself rather than granting permission to appeal onwards. Under Rule 35, the FTT may set aside the decision if it considers it contains a material error of law, notifying the parties of its view. Rule 35(3) states that a party may object to the 'set aside' decision if not given an opportunity to make representations.

Appeal to the UT direct

If the FTT refuses permission, or refuses to extend time for the application for permission, a further application can be made directly to the UT. Applications to the Upper Tribunal are governed by the Tribunal Procedure (Upper Tribunal) Rules 2008 (UTRs):

> The application to the UT must be received no later than 14 days after the date on which notice of the FTT's refusal of permission was sent to the appellant. The time limit is one month where the appellant is outside the UK (see UT r21). R5(3)(a) imparts the UT with discretion to vary any time limits, so if an application is made late reasons should be included.

The form provided (although not specified as compulsory in the Rules) for applications to the UT for permission to appeal to the UT is IAUT–1.

If permission to appeal to the UT is granted by the UT, written notice must be given to both parties.

UT appeals generally

Applications for permission to appeal to the UT are made only on the basis of an error of law. These are the most common errors likely to be pleaded as identified in R (Iran) [2005] EWCA Civ 982.

> 'i) Making perverse or irrational findings on a matter or matters that were material to the outcome ("material matters");
>
> ii) Failing to give reasons or any adequate reasons for findings on material matters;
>
> iii) Failing to take into account and/or resolve conflicts of fact or opinion on material matters;
>
> iv) Giving weight to immaterial matters;
>
> v) Making a material misdirection of law on any material matter;
>
> vi) Committing or permitting a procedural or other irregularity capable of making a material difference to the outcome or the fairness of the proceedings;
>
> vii) Making a mistake as to a material fact which could be established by objective and uncontentious evidence, where the appellant and/or his advisers were not responsible for the mistake, and where unfairness resulted from the fact that a mistake was made.'

AS (Afghanistan) [2019] EWCA Civ 873 reminds us that it is an error of law for a tribunal to reach a factual conclusion for which there is no evidential support.

Joseph [2022] UKUT 218 (IAC) reiterates the importance of identifying real points of law rather than simply disagreeing with factual findings.

CHAPTER 14: Appeals, Administrative Review and Judicial Review

The UT refuses permission: 'Cart' judicial reviews

Where the UT refuses permission to appeal to itself against a decision of the FTT, until 14 July 2022 (when s11A TCEA 2007 entered force) it was possible to judicially review the refusal in the Administrative Court: from that date UT permission refusals are unchallengeable unless the UT acted in bad faith or "i*n such a procedurally defective way as amounts to a fundamental breach of the principles of natural justice.*"

Initial and continuation hearings in the UT

The first issue to be decided in the UT will be whether there was in fact an error of law in the decision of the First-tier Tribunal. This test is a prerequisite to an appeal to the UT and must be satisfied in all cases, whether permission was granted by the FTT or the UT. The possible grounds for asserting that there is an error of law are addressed briefly above.

It will be unusual for new evidence to be relied on at this stage in the proceedings (unless it goes to procedural unfairness which actually took place at the hearing) because the focus must be the material that was before the decision maker who it is contended committed an error of law.

The procedure to be followed on appeal is set out in Practice Direction 3:

> '**3.2** The parties should be aware that, in the circumstances described in paragraph 3.1(c), the Upper Tribunal will generally expect to proceed, without any further hearing, to re-make the decision, where this can be undertaken without having to hear oral evidence…
>
> **3.3** In a case where no oral evidence is likely to be required in order for the Upper Tribunal to re-make the decision, the Upper Tribunal will therefore expect any documentary evidence relevant to the re-making of the decision to be adduced in accordance with Practice Direction 4 so that it may be considered at the relevant hearing; and, accordingly, the party seeking to rely on such documentary evidence will be expected to show good reason why it is not reasonably practicable to adduce the same in order for it to be considered at that hearing.'

In theory there is a clear steer towards the UT retaining cases for final decision rather than remitting them to the FTT. Over time the culture varies. In recent years the preference has seemed to be usually for remittal where significant further oral evidence is required.

Although there is much encouragement in the Upper Tribunal as well as in the Practice Directions and Statements for appeals to be finally determined at a single hearing, there are nevertheless many appeals which feature a two-stage process. First there will be hearing to establish where there is a material error of law, then (if the appeal requires a further hearing and is not remitted to the First-tier Tribunal) there is a continuation hearing.

A choice has to made as to whether the appeal should be prepared for full re-hearing in advance of an initial error of law hearing: if the preparation is done it may be wasted as no error of law may be established; if it is not done, then a UT judge may wish to proceed to the second stage of re-determining the appeal in any event.

It therefore seems safe to assume that where the error of law asserted is such that oral evidence would be necessary for a re-decision, witnesses need not attend the initial UT hearing and full up-to-date evidence need not be prepared. In all other cases, representatives have to assess whether it is 'reasonably practicable' to prepare and adduce any necessary further evidence.

Once an error of law is established, the UT has to decide whether any findings in the FTT decision still survive ('preserved findings'). The decision needs to be read carefully. UTJs will not want to disturb findings that are lawful simply because some other findings cannot stand. If not remitting the matter for re-hearing in the FTT, the UT will ultimately determine the appeal for itself. A party wishing to provide updating evidence needs to identify it and justify why it was not previously supplied, via a notice under r15A of the UTRs.

14.5.1 Suspensive appeals direct to the Upper Tribunal under IMA 2023

These appeals will be introduced if IMA 2023's inadmissibility regime is commenced, something likely to be affected by the outcome of the Rwanda litigation in late 2023 (MIL 9.5.4). We address the inadmissibility procedure generally at MIL 9.1.0 and pending publication of new appeals Procedure Rules address appeals there too for now.

In readiness for this regime all FTT judges have been potentially upgraded to UTR status (IMA 2023 s52).

14.6 Onwards appeal to the Court of Appeal

An Upper Tribunal decision can, exceptionally, be challenged in the Court of Appeal. An application must be made to the UT for permission to appeal to the Court of Appeal which, if refused, can be renewed directly to the Court of Appeal.

The deadline is set out at UT rule 44(3B) and is 12 days from the sending of the determination, or seven working days if the person is detained or 38 days if the person is outside the UK. Different time limits apply where the person was served personally or by electronic means.

An appeal to the Court of Appeal must be on a point of law (s13 TCEA 2007) and must also show:

(a) that the proposed appeal would have a real prospect of success, and raise some important point of principle or practice, or
(b) that there is some other compelling reason for the relevant appellate court to hear the appeal.

These criteria are sometimes referred to as the 'second appeals test'.

14.7 Administrative review
14.7.1 Overview of the process

Human rights aside, for most people whose immigration applications are refused, or whose leave is cancelled at the port of entry or return, an 'administrative review' (AR) will be available to challenge the decision. These are particularly aimed at those who had lost their right of appeal under the reforms introduced by the IA 2014. An AR involves the HO reconsidering its own decision to refuse leave (or to cancel leave at the border).

Appendix AR(EU) provides for administrative review of certain decisions under Appendix EU in relation to settled status for EU nationals (MIL 14.7.9).

The Explanatory Memorandum introducing Admin Review outlined an objective of determining matters within 28 days.

The AR process is wholly found in the IRs:

- Rules 34L-34X in Part 1 discuss the procedures such as time limit, form and fee
- Appendix AR explains the decisions that can be challenged and on what grounds , and
- Appendix SN provides for the service of AR decisions, and for notifying the person that an application is invalid

There is also Guidance *Administrative review*.

The Rules define an administrative review (AR) as (Appendix AR, paragraph AR2.1):

> the review of an *eligible decision* to decide whether the decision is wrong due to a *case working error*.

An AR is available where the HO makes an 'eligible decision'. An eligible decision cannot be appealed to the FTT (IAC) (contrast AR for Appendix EU cases where there is in fact a choice of remedy). The only remedy will be to seek AR (and/or, sometimes, to make a fresh application for leave). Eligible decisions are listed in AR3.2, AR4.2, and AR5.2, dependent on where the eligible decision is made (i.e. outside, at the border, or inside the UK). The list of potential 'case working errors' is at AR2.11-2.12.

Paragraph AR2.8 of Appendix AR confirms the Home Office will not seek to remove the applicant from the United Kingdom where AR is pending (as defined in AR2.9: ie until it gets a decision, so long as the AR is not invalid or withdrawn).

An application cannot be varied by way of an AR application (AR2.6). Subject to some specific exceptions for dishonesty allegations, an AR will be looking only at the decision to refuse an application, and not at post-decision facts.

The Independent Chief Inspector of Borders and Immigration published a report on the AR process in May 2016, one year after the process was introduced. The review was ordered in response to concerns of MPs and peers during the passage of the Immigration Bill about the effectiveness and independence of the proposed new process as a replacement of the right of appeal. The Chief Inspector was highly critical. It is notable, for instance, that ARs succeeded in a far lower proportion of cases than similar cases under the old appeals regime. However, where only an AR is available, that will be the individual's only option (with the possibility of JR to follow). The process has been criticised in other official reports over time: see those cited by Saini J in Karagul [2019] EWHC 3208 (Admin) §54-59.

In line with the introduction of the post-2015 appeals regime, the process of AR for in-country applications was brought in progressively, in four stages, for various types of application, becoming fully operative for all eligible decisions made on or after 6 April 2015. AR3.2 lists the relevant dates. For decisions at the border, and out of country applications, AR was introduced on the same date.

We discuss common arguments available in administrative review applications in the PBS module (MIL 7.15).

14.7.2 Extension of leave to remain

One important feature of the remedy is that it brings with it a statutory extension of leave to remain for in-country applicants. So long as it is made "in time". Section 3C of the IA 1971 extends leave when AR might be brought and over the period it is pending, in the same way that leave is extended for 'in-time' applications and appeals. Thus leave to remain is statutorily extended where:

> (d) an administrative review of the decision on the application for variation—
>   (i) could be sought, or
>   (ii) is pending.

Because this automatic extension of leave bars the making of another application once an application has been refused, it will be necessary for a person who wants to make a speedy further application rather than pursue the administrative review route to complete an 'Administrative review waiver form' (AR2.10). In any event the making of a further application of any kind is deemed as withdrawing any pending administrative review (r34X(4)) and thus bringing 3C leave to an end of the day before the application is made (AR2.10(b)).

14.7.3 Administrative review – the principles

There are two key concepts found in the administrative review process: *eligible decision* and *case working error*. Essentially the practitioner will be looking to see if their client's problem arises from an eligible decision (i.e. something which can be the subject to the administrative review process) in circumstances where the complaint involves a 'case working error' (effectively, a ground for appeal).

Both refusals of leave and grants may be challenged, the latter where the period or conditions granted are subject to challenge (AR2.12).

14.7.4 Eligible decisions

The decisions amenable to AR are divided into three sets: decisions re entry clearance (ie "overseas" as the rule is headed: AR 5.1), leave to remain ("in the UK: AR.3.1), and for arrival at the border (AR.4.1). Appendix AR is not the only clue as to whether AR is available though: these days individual modern immigration routes also say as much (see eg for short-term students, who previously did not have such a right, at STS 8.2).

Eligible decisions in relation to leave to remain (AR3.1):

An eligible decision is either a decision to refuse an application for leave to remain or a decision to grant leave to remain where a review is requested of the period or conditions of leave granted. The classes of decision are listed in order of the date that AR was made to relevant to the route in question, so runs from the old Tier 4 students decisions at AR.3.1(a), through various other older PBS routes (AR.3.1(b)) and non-human rights applications generally (AR.3.1(c)), up to the routes introduced by the major reform of immigration in December 2020 for principal applicants (AR.3.1(e)) and their dependents (AR.3.1(f)) and the introduction of the Hong Kong BNO route (AR.3.1(g)), the Appendices for Domestic Workers in Private Households and who are Victims of Modern Slavery and Appendix Graduate, International Sportspersons and the revised short term work routes (AR.3.2(h)-(j)) and on to High Potential Individuals and Scale-up visas, Appendix Ukraine, the Afghan ARAP route and Gurkha or Hong Kong military unit veterans & their family members. Eg decisions re:

- applications under the IRs generally (e.g. PBS, UK ancestors etc.), except;
  - Visitor cases (where the only remedy will be to apply again or seek JR or lodge an appeal where there was very strong evidence of family life such that the visit visa's rejection amounted to the refusal of a human rights claim), or
  - Asylum, including family reunion;
  - Applications and human rights claims under Appendix FM, r276B (long residence), Appendix Private Life, Appendix Settlement Family Life and Appendix Settlement Protection, Part 11 (ie asylum: presumably catching refugee family reunion), Part 8 of the Rules (except for PBS dependants), and various similar 'family routes' for members of the Armed Forces
  - However AR is available for bereaved partners and domestic violence cases, as well as PBS dependants (so that refusal of such applications cases *are* eligible decisions for AR, but not appealable)
- Turkish Association Agreement applications. The government decision to replace appeals with administrative review was challenged, but an initial success was reversed by the CoA: see MIL 11.10.7.

Eligible decisions in relation to leave held on arrival in the United Kingdom

- decisions to cancel leave to enter or remain due to change of circumstances, false representations or non-disclosure of material facts (AR4.1-AR4.2). Tthese applications cannot be made until leaving the Control Zone where one is seeking to enter through the Channel Tunnel: AR.4.3.

Eligible decisions in relation to entry clearance

- there is a very long list of eligible entry clearance decisions except for the exceptions which apply as for leave to remain, above (AR5.2)

AR2.11 and 2.12 address relevant *'Case working errors'*. AR2.11 identifies the challenges to refusals, ie where the original decision maker:

(a) Erred in:

(i) Refusing an application on the basis of an allegation of dishonesty or previous breach of the Rules (r9.7.1-9.7.2, 9.8.1-9.8.2); or
(ii) Cancelling leave to enter or remain which is in force, for false representations/documents under r9.7.3 ; or
(i) Cancelling leave to enter or remain under Appendix ECAA (Turkish businesspeople and workers) for deception;
(ii) Cancelling leave for false information/representations under Appendix EU or S2 health visitors or for Appendix Service Providers from Switzerland (before 5 October 2023)
(b) Erred in thinking that the date of application was beyond any time limit in the Rules;
(c) Failed to request specified documents under the PBS provision for seeking missing documents (r245AA) ;
(d) Otherwise applied the IRs incorrectly; or
(e) Failed to apply the HO's relevant published policy and guidance in relation to the application.

AR2.12 addresses challenges to grants. Where extension applications under the Rules are refused, an error as to the leave or conditions granted may be challenged.

Many kinds of challenge can doubtless be brought under these provisions, including:

- Arguments over the meaning of the rules, including the possibility that the interpretation of the rules does not conform to principles established by case law ('*applied the Immigration Rules incorrectly*').
- Disputes as to the correct exercise of discretion so long as the discretion was present under the Rule itself (e.g. Rule 39E addressing *Overstaying* expressly allows for some element of discretion ('*applied the Immigration Rules incorrectly*')
- Overlooking documents or failing to request documents ('*decision not to request specified documents... was incorrect*') or failing to carry out an interview (the Guidance for some routes permits an interview to explore issues further)
- Debate as to whether an Applicant's *credibility* was assessed lawfully: the Guidance states that when reconsidering credibility, 'the correct test to apply is whether it is more likely than not, based on the evidence and facts available, that the original decision maker made the right decision that the applicant is not credible' ('*failed to apply the Secretary of State's relevant published policy and guidance*')
- Challenges to the length of stay granted, which might be relevant to students where the HO has misunderstood the course's start and finish dates, and conditions placed on the grant of leave.

However, one has to be realistic as to how these Rules are likely to be interpreted by the HO. Applications are much more likely to succeed where they involve unequivocal overlooking of evidence that was previously supplied on an application, or where the wrong Immigration Rule has been applied; it is doubtful that the HO wants to enter debate as to the interpretation of the IRs or to be told that its policy on the application of a Rule is wrong. The HO has long been very slow to change their mind on credibility without corroborative evidence from some reliable source.

14.7.5 New evidence in administrative reviews

In some cases, fresh evidence can be admitted (though only at the request of the HO under AR2.5 in response to the AR application). This is where the relevant ground of review is under AR2.11(a), (b) or (c) above, i.e. where it is argued the decision maker was incorrect to:

- refuse or cancel on the basis of deception in the present (or a previous) application (or the application has been refused for other mandatory grounds relating to a previous breach of immigration control by overstaying, breaching the conditions of leave, or illegal entry); including cancellations for deception under the various EU legacy routes (Appendix EU, S2 Healthcare Visitors and Swiss Service Providers). But only if the allegation had not previously been made in another refusal (AR2.4(b))
- determine the application as having been made outside a relevant time limit in the Rules (eg beyond the r39E tolerance for overstaying)

- the original decision maker's decision not to request specified documents under paragraph 245AA of the Rules was incorrect

For example: one cannot rely on new evidence where the *genuineness* of a student (r245ZX(o)) application is challenged. But one can do so where the challenge is made expressly by reference to the mandatory general refusal reasons relating to deception.

Whether or not a genuineness refusal involves a dishonesty allegation is a question of fact. In a refusal because the SSHD is "*not satisfied that you genuinely wish to establish in business as proposed*", Karagul [2019] EWHC 3208 (Admin) held that this language effectively amounted to alleging misconduct or bad faith. In that particular context – not where a decision maker used genuineness to refuse an application on grounds that the business plan was unduly optimistic. It was then essential to give the chance to make representations in response to the allegation made, either via written representations following a letter, or via a formal interview. The administrative review procedure would only be lawful in such cases if a fair opportunity was given to provide further evidence.

A procedure at AR2.5 provides that 'the Reviewer' can contact the applicant to request relevant evidence is provided within seven days of the date of request where such a case working error has been identified. No fresh evidence will be considered other than that requested by the HO, so that any such evidence submitted with the AR application will be ignored.

14.7.6 Administrative review – procedure

Features of the process are that

- Written notice of an eligible decision must be given (i.e. conforming to the requirements of the ILERO 2000 (r34L). As with an appealable decision under the Immigration (Notices) Regulations 2003, a refusal must be accompanied by a statement of reasons, and information about how to apply for administrative review, including the time limit. A refusal that does not do this will be invalid and an applicant could argue that they should receive a fresh notice of an eligible decision
- Only one valid application for administrative review may be made in respect of an eligible decision, unless the administrative review does not succeed, but for different or additional reasons to those specified in the decision under review (34N(2)): in such a case, there may be a further application (AR2.2(d))
- The application must be made in the relevant location – whilst the applicant remains in the United Kingdom in relation to 'in-country' refusals, whilst they remain abroad vis-á-vis entry clearance applications, and whilst they remain here if it is a decision made on their arrival, though no application may be brought whilst they remain in the control zone (of the Channel Tunnel)
- Dependants can be included in the AR application where they were dependants on the application which resulted in the eligible decision (34S)
- It must be made in accordance with 34U if made online, or 34V if made by post. The paper form will only be available in exceptional circumstances (so says the Guidance) and where the initial application was on a paper form (r34O)
- An application will be treated as withdrawn on the applicant's notification to such effect, or if they request the return of their passport for the purposes of travel outside the United Kingdom, or if they actually travel abroad, or if they make a fresh application for leave (34X)
- Where an application is made online any specified fee must be paid, any section of the online application which is designated as mandatory must be completed as specified; and documents specified as mandatory on the online application or in the related guidance must be submitted in the specified manner (34U)
- A notice of the outcome of an administrative review application, or a notice of invalidity informing an applicant that their application is invalid, must be given in writing (Appendix SN)
- A application must be made online unless the original application was a valid paper application (34O)

14.7.7 Fees

The current fee for an AR is £80 (see Schedule 6 of The Immigration and Nationality (Cost Recovery Fees) (Amendment) Regulations 2014. According to the Guidance:

- Fee exemptions will be available for those who were fee-exempt on the original application, or where the application to a decision that has been re-issued following administrative removal with different or additional reasons to the original decision; or otherwise in exceptional circumstances
- The fee will be refunded if the original decision is withdrawn and leave is granted, or varied as to duration or conditions

14.7.8 Time limits for the application

Where notice of the eligible decision is sent by post to an address in the UK, it is deemed to have been received, unless the contrary is shown, on the second working day after the day on which it was posted.

The AR application is treated as being made on the marked date of posting, or on the date it is delivered by a courier or submitted online. The application must be made (34R):

- where the applicant is not detained, no more than 14 calendar days after receipt by the applicant of the notice of the eligible decision (seven days if they are detained); or
- where the applicant is abroad, no more than 28 calendar days after receipt by the applicant of the notice of the eligible decision;
- where the challenge is to the conditions of a grant, no more than 14 days after the biometric residence document is received

Note that whan an application for AR is made under Appendix AR (EU) the application must be made in 28 days if overseas or in the UK and not detained and 7 days if detained. The AR application may be accepted late if the Secretary of State is satisfied that it would be *unjust not to waive the time limit* and the application was made as *soon as reasonably practicable*.

In Hasan [2019] EWCA Civ 389 it was confirmed *receipt* of a decision by the applicant (r34(1)) includes deemed receipt under r34(3), actual physical receipt is not required. So the fact that the SSHD sent a decision letter to the applicant student's university address (as per his request) which then did not reach the student for some time afterwards did not stop time expiring – though, in this case, there seems to have been no real explanation of the reasons for the delay provided.

The Home Office policy guidance *Administrative Review* sets out that

- It is recognised that some applicants may accept that documents were missing and therefore that the refusal was correct overall, but they may still wish to request AR if they can show that the documents were genuine, even though this would not change the overall outcome of the original application
- AR is not available for EEA applications (though it is available for Appendix EU and EU-FP), human rights applications or protection claims, or to try and apply for leave on another basis from the refused application (as is evident from the Rules themselves and their limited list of eligible decisions)
- As the online AR application does not allow for the submission of further documents, where an online application is accepted as valid, an opportunity should be given at that point to provide any further documents which Appendix AR permits, before the case is reviewed
- Applications should be made online if possible; a postal application must, to be valid, use the appropriate application form, pay the specified fee, fill out all mandatory sections of the form (either identified as such in the form or in associated guidance), be appropriately signed, any mandatory documents must be supplied, and the form must be sent to the specified address
- Extensions of time will not be given for minor oversights, internet connection problems, minor illnesses or needing to discuss the matter with an advisor who was not available

CHAPTER 14: Appeals, Administrative Review
and Judicial Review

- Further evidence, where requested by the HO, must be supplied within 7 working days, plus 2 extra days for it to pass through internal mail, unless there are exceptional reasons justifying an extension of time
- If the Applicant's leave has expired and they remain in the UK, a section 120 notice must be provided when the original decision is upheld
- The AR process should proceed notwithstanding any challenge by way of JR
- If a challenge is brought by way of appeal to a decision which is liable to AR, the HO will defend the appeal on the basis that there is no jurisdiction for the appeal
- Where a person launches a JR following the refusal of an AR, time for the JR (i.e. the 3-month limit) will start running from the date the person receives the AR decision (and not the date of the original decision).

The Guidance also gives a useful set of 'example scenarios' as to whether a particular complaint amounts to a case working error and whether new evidence can be requested.

> **Examples**
>
> These are possible administrative review avenues given the possible case working errors that might lead to a reviewable refusal.
>
> An application is refused because enquiries of a bank lead to a response that the bank statements are not genuine. The applicant produces further evidence by way of a letter from the bank central office confirming an error in the original letter. This may be reviewed under Appendix AR2.11(a) and fresh evidence is admissible.
>
> An application is refused because it is believed that the applicant previously overstayed for 31 days. However they produce the original grant of further leave to remain which shows they were granted leave to a later date than Home Office records showed. This may be reviewed under Appendix AR2.11(b) and fresh evidence is admissible.
>
> In the next 3 examples, fresh evidence is not admissible. However this does not matter given the nature of the challenges brought, which involve failures to follow the Rules or policy based on the extant evidence submitted with the original immigration application.
>
> An application is refused because it is thought that there are insufficient tradeable points scored under Appendix Skilled Worker; however the decision maker has misread the salary in question. This may be reviewed under Appendix AR2.11(d).
>
> An application is refused because of an insufficient number of points but the decision maker overlooked the highest qualification submitted by the applicant. This may be reviewed under Appendix AR2.11(c).
>
> A student's extension application is refused because the decision maker checks the sponsor register and finds that their college is not on it. They therefore refuse the application because this invalidates the CAS. However they have overlooked the Student Guidance which says that a student in this situation should be given an opportunity to find an alternative place within 60 days. This may be reviewed under Appendix AR2.11(e) as relevant Home Office guidance has been overlooked.

> **Top Tip**
>
> When planning your strategy vis-á-vis administrative and JR, it is important to be clear on time limits. Where an application for administrative review is made and refused, it will be the date of that refusal (not the original refusal of the application) from when time for JR runs: Topadar [2020] EWCA Civ 1525.

14.7.9 Appendix AR (EU)

We deal with this in (see MIL 11.7.10). 14.8 Judicial review

The HO Judicial review guidance (Part 1), at chapter 27 of the IDIs, is a useful general introduction (from the government's perspective) to judicial review (JR) in the immigration context. For a wealth of specialist information, see the Immigration Appeals and Remedies Handbook (Symes and Jorro, Bloomsbury, 2021); and the HJT ebook on immigration JR in the Upper Tribunal. The online MIL contains more information about the processes. See MIL 14.2.6 for urgent removal JR procedures.

14.8 A fully worked example of different remedies – Appeal, AR and JR

> **Example**
>
> Leonardo makes an application for further leave to remain as a Student. The representations supporting his application argue that if his extension application is refused, he maintains that the amount of money he had invested in the UK and his very strong professional and educational links here amount to a private life claim, and that he should be granted leave on that basis instead to allow him to complete his studies.
>
> If Leonardo's student extension application is refused, what happens next? Let us imagine this is because he failed to provide adequate bank statements showing maintenance.
>
> Leonardo can only bring an appeal if he has made a human rights claim which the HO has refused. Whilst at one time various creative arguments were available about pursuing an appeal in circumstances where private life might have been established in the UK, the case law (MIL 14.2.3) is unreceptive to levering a human rights appeal out of a managed migration immigration refusal. So human rights applications generally have to be made via the appropriate forms.
>
> Things might be different if the decision maker had addressed the human rights arguments. That would have been the decision maker's choice. On that scenario Leonardo would have been able to run arguments involving his private life as a student who had invested in his studies and developed professional ties in the UK (MIL 5.4.2).
>
> Can Leonardo launch an administrative review? Perhaps based on a failure to take a sufficiently flexible approach to the evidence (MIL 7.1.2). AR will be the appropriate remedy in the mind of the SSHD – the HO thinking will be that he has not made a human rights claim which has been refused. He has been refused'leave to remain as a Student. So this is an eligible decision for administrative review under Immigration Rule AR3.2 found in Appendix AR. Note that he cannot pursue any human rights arguments under this route: because these would not flow from the refusal of the application as a Student (AR2.6, 3.2), but only from refusal of a private life application. And the argument he wants to make (i.e. that the Rules provided for the Home Office to give an opportunity to rectify an innocent error, see Rule 245AA) is perfect for the administrative review route.
>
> Such an application must be made within 14 days of receiving the decision (as he is not detained), online or by post, under the procedure set out from Rule 34L onwards.
>
> Oh no! A decision on administrative review is promptly made. But it is a refusal, made just days later. The reviewer writes 'The administrative review application shows no relevant casework error. A failure to provide bank statements is a serious omission and I do not consider that the Rules require every case that lacks relevant documents to receive another chance'. No further refusal reasons are given, so there is no further right of administrative review (as would be the if reasons were added, see AR2.2(d)) read with Rule 34M(2)).
>
> Can he bring JR proceedings? These is available where an administrative body makes an error of law. He should target the original refusal and the decision on the administrative review (time runs from the latter). Failing to follow the IRs must amount to an arguable error – either the decision maker and the

reviewer have overlooked the power to condone minor slips of this nature, or they have acted unfairly in failing to permit access to a procedure designed for just this scenario.

However, when Leonardo brings JR proceedings (in the UTIAC), he will be exposed to the government's legal costs (admittedly, usually only for a modest amount, just for drafting the Acknowledgment of Service, up to the stage of a renewed oral permission hearing). So he must hope for a realistic decision from a judge on the papers that makes the other side see sense early on.

Alternatively, upon having his AR application refused (and within the relevant deadline), Leonardo may be able to make a fresh Student application (presuming the refused application was made in-time such that s3C leave continues). That might be a viable option if his sponsor is willing to issue him another CAS, and he does not risk too much from becoming an overstayer for a few months. Note that he must factor this option into his decision to JR the refusal, as if he awaits a decision on the JR, he will almost certainly be too late to make the fresh application from within the UK.

14.9 Home Office maladministration, damages and ex gratia payments

The HO is not unknown to make mistakes, sometimes serious ones. This might be the subject of complaint via litigation and a damages claim: or by the ex gratia complaints scheme.

The Guidance *Complaints Procedure* explains matters should be raised within 3 months of the incident absent exceptional circumstances; a complaint will not change the decision making timetable, should be resolved in a satisfactory and timely manner with a reply in 20 working days normally, or within 12 weeks after an impartial investigation if involving serious professional misconduct. The online complaints form may used or a letter sent to the Complaints allocation hub, Central point of receipt, 7th Floor, Lunar House, 40 Wellesley Road, Croydon. Those dissatisfied with the response can request an administrative review and there should be a response within 20 days.

From late October 2022 the *Independent Examiner of Complaints* can investigate cases of unhappiness with the HO's final response to a complaint; the deadline is 3 months from that response. This can relate to a delay or error, poor service, advice, or information, and a failure to follow the correct procedures, though not where right of appeal/review are available, or where JR has been used.

CHAPTER 15: Criminal Offences

15.1 Overview, Article 31 and Trafficking
15.1.1 Introduction

Immigration legislation contains a plethora of offences. In addition the practitioner will find a range of other penalties, for examples the fines and civil penalties that can be imposed upon carriers under Part II of the Immigration and Asylum Act 1999. The _Charging Guide Procedures - A Guide for Carriers explains the system in practice._ AITCA 2004 is an early example of the ever-expanding range of offences, for example creating a new offence of failure to cooperate, without reasonable excuse, in one's documentation for removal or or deportation; or failing to possess a valid passport or similar document without reasonable excuse on arrival. There is Guidance _Criminal Investigations: Court proceedings_ explaining to HO staff how to commence prosecutions and allocate cases to courts.

It is also important to be aware that there are general offences of aiding and abetting the commission of a criminal offence, which can broaden the scope of who can be caught by an offence. See the Guidance _Dealing with potential criminality - ICE teams_ for an overview of offences and procedures, and of the constraints on the exercise of powers. The Guidance _Interviewing suspects_ sets out the HO's roles and responsibility for officers in criminal and financial investigation (CFI) teams and suitably trained and HO-accredited criminal investigators.

If sitting the accreditation examinations, it is important to bear in mind that criminal offences will be examined, but questions raising such issues may not be immediately obvious. As with the ethical dimension to the exams, practitioners are expected to identify when problems might arise without a specific 'pointer' to this effect. Practitioners should also beware that offences which have not been prosecuted remain criminal offences, and therefore statements such as 'the client has never committed a criminal offence' in relation to an overstayer, will be false.

15.1.2 Immigration officers and police powers

Immigration Officers have been granted increasing powers of arrest and search, previously the sole province of the police force. These powers have been extended by subsequent legislation. Section 145 of the 1999 Act provides for Immigration Officers to have regard to Codes of Practice in exercising these powers. Code of Practice Directions have been issued. These take as their starting point the PACE codes, and take the form of a series of instructions modifying those Codes. However it is also notable that some safeguards that apply to police officers do not apply to them, for example the requirement to give one's name when conducting certain searches.

Section 14 of AITCA 2004 considerably broadens the powers of arrest, and ancillary powers of entry, search and seizure, of Immigration Officers. They now possess powers of arrest when in the course of exercising a function under the immigration acts they form a reasonable suspicion that one of a wide range of offences under the general criminal law have been committed, including conspiracy to defraud under the common law, bigamy under the Offences Against the Person Act 1861, offences under s3 or s4 of the Perjury Act 1911, as well as aiding and abetting offences; a range of offences pertaining to obtaining by deception, false accounting and handling stolen goods under the Theft Acts and a range of offences under the Forgery and Counterfeiting Act. Perhaps this represents the development of a separate policing of persons under immigration control.

15.1.3 Article 31 defence against prosecution

Adimi [1999] EWHC Admin 765 examines the United Kingdom's obligations under Article 31 of the Refugee Convention. Article 31(1) states:

> The contracting States shall not impose penalties, on account of their illegal entry or presence, on refugees who, coming directly from a territory where their life or freedom was threatened in the sense of Article 1, enter or are present in their territory without authorisation, provided they

present themselves without delay to the authorities and show good cause for their illegal entry or presence.

As a result, section 31 was introduced into the 1999 Act. Section 31, by contrast, requires the refugee to have, under s31(1)(a)-(c):

- presented him/herself to the authorities in the UK without delay
- made a claim for asylum as soon as was reasonably practicable after his arrival in the UK (interesting cases have arisen where refugees have been deemed to have presented early enough to not be caught by the denial of support for late claims under s55 of the NIA 2002 but have nonetheless been prosecuted with the view being taken that they delayed in presenting themselves to the authorities)
- shown good cause for the illegal entry or presence

The Adimi case has led to successful applications for compensation for those imprisoned in violation of the UK's obligations under Article 31. Such cases are brought by first quashing the conviction and then making a claim for compensation, which has been paid for the Home Office's ex gratia scheme.

In R v Asfaw [2008] UKHL 31 the House of Lords considered the extent to which Article 31 and section 31 IAA 1999 afford protection against prosecution. The majority held that it was an abuse of process to prosecute offences not explicitly covered by the section 31(3) exclusions from prosecution, but which nonetheless fell within the scope of Article 31.

Lessons were not learnt though - Defendant's representatives, prosecutors, and judges continued to let prosecutions slip through. R v Mateta & Ors [2013] EWCA Crim 1372 revisited the issue: perhaps unfairly, it was only the defence representatives admonished for their failures. Abdulahi [2021] EWCA Crim 1629 again finds a criminal appeal being allowed due to a lack of reference to the s31 defence in the case history: a lack of knowledge or understanding of the statutory defence would justify extending time for such appeals. Setting aside a conviction required that substantial injustice would otherwise result, as where ILR would be denied thus having a continuing direct impact on one's life.

In SXH v CPS [2014] EWCA Civ 90, the Court held that section 31 was to be interpreted consistently with the Convention, absent any express indication of an intention to depart from it, and therefore, consistently with Adimi. Re-litigation of Adimi may follow in the light of s37 NBA 2022 (MIL 9.7.1). Elmi, R. v [2022] EWCA Crim 1428 points out that the s31 protection regime does not apply to Humanitarian Protection beneficiaries given they are not owed Refugee Convention obligations.

15.1.4 Trafficking

The Modern Slavery Act 2015 consolidated previous legislation:

- Holding someone in slavery/servitude, or conditions of forced/compulsory labour, bearing in mind the victim's vulnerability: s1 MSA 2015 (life, or up to 12 months imprisonment or a fine or both, on indictment/summary conviction: s5)
- Trafficking someone between countries, ie facilitating/arranging travel for the purposes of, or knowing the likelihood of, exploitation: s2 MSA 2015; s3 defines exploitation as slavery, servitude and forced or compulsory labour, sexual exploitation, organ removal, or where the person is subjected to force, threats or deception designed to induce him or her to provide services/benefits of any kind – including aiding, abetting, counselling or procuring such an offence s4 (10 years/up to 12 months imprisonment or a fine, or both, on indictment/summary conviction: s5, and for life on indictment for a s4 offence involving kidnapping/false imprisonment)

MSA 2015 s45 provides that a person who is compelled to commit an offence for reasons attributable to slavery or exploitation has an absolute defence. They must be aged 18+ at the time of the relevant act, have been compelled to do it, as direct consequence of slavery or relevant exploitation, or of being a victim of slavery/exploitation, where a reasonable person in the same situation as the person and having the person's relevant characteristics would have no realistic alternative to doing that act.

The CPS guidance gives the CPS a broad discretion to consider whether to prosecute offences in other circumstances. See MIL 4.3 for modern slavery more generally.

Extensive guidance was given on the prosecution of VOTs in AAD & Ors, R. v [2022] EWCA Crim 106. Abuse of process arguments (eg whether it was unfair and oppressive for a defendant should to be tried) are available in principle under MSA 2015. Indeed as shown by R v M(L) [2011] EWCA Crim 2327 & AAJ, R. v [2021] EWCA Crim 1278 they had been available previously too. The central issue was whether the alleged criminal acts were compelled by reasons of slavery or explitation. Sufficient protection was given to VOTs by the legal burden to the criminal standard resting on the prosecution once the defence had passed the evidential burden of raising the trafficking issue. Conclusive grounds decisions (favourable or not) were in principle admissible on a criminal appeal. Expert evidence was admissible as to a person's psychiatric or psychological stage or of the methods of criminal gangs abroad, though not as to their credibility. Failing to detect the accused being a minor victim of trafficking would most likely be fatal to a conviction's safety: AJW, R. v [2023] EWCA Crim 803, as would a guilty plea due to incorrect legal advice depriving someone of a defence which would probably have succeeded (albeit that the general principle that there should only be one chance to advance a defence absence very exceptional circumstances applied as elsewhere in criminal law): BSG v R [2023] EWCA Crim 1041.

15.2 Offences under the Immigration Act 1971

This is one of the main sources of offences under immigration law. The key offences are as follows:

15.2.1 Illegal entry and stay: s24 to 24A

Section 24 IA 1971 (heavily revised from 28 June 2022 by NBA 2022) criminalises entry into the UK in breach of a deportation order or knowingly without leave/entry clearance, overstaying and failing to comply with the conditions on which leave if granted without reasonable excuse – once commenced, knowingly arriving without an Electronic Travel Authorisation (ETA) will also be criminalised. By s24(1A) an overstayer is committing an offence throughout the period of overstaying but can only be prosecuted once in respect of overstaying the same leave. It is for the defence to prove that the person did in fact have leave, or that a stamp in a passport or travel document is wrong.

The s24 offence as a whole is subject to an extended time limit for prosecution as set out in s28. The offence can be tried if information is laid within three years of the commission of the offence provided that a senior police officer certify that this is within two months of the date on which there is sufficient evidence to justify proceedings. Otherwise, the more usual six-month time limit for trial in the magistrates' court applies.

From June 2022, both those entering the UK when requiring leave but lacking it (s24(B1)) and those requiring entry clearance and arriving without it (s24(D1), commit offences. This applies to asylum seekers just as much as to anyone else: Mohamed [2023] EWCA Crim 211. Ginar, R. v [2023] EWCA Crim 1121 notes the sentence increase from 6 months to 4 years for s24(D1) offending. Relevant considerations were that any deterrence objective should receive little weight given the desperate circumstances of many arrivals. There was nevertheless an important public interest in tackling knowingly illegal actions, undermining border controls and generating rescue costs, risking death and injury to travellers and the safety of rescuers, and disrupting a busy shipping lane. The starting point should be a 12-month sentence: aggraving factors would include operating the means of arrival and involvement in planning, and a history of unsuccessful immigration applications; mitigating ones would include good character, youth & lack of maturity, mental disorder, coercion/pressure, and the strength of an asylum claim.

Section 24A again applies to a person who is not a British citizen. It criminalises obtaining or seeking to obtain leave to enter or remain or securing or seeking to secure avoidance postponement or revocation of the giving of removal directions, making a deportation order, or actual removal, by deception. It can be tried either way and before the Crown Court the maximum penalty is four years imprisonment (five years for deportation order breach) and a fine. See further MIL 1.3.6.

15.2.2 Assisting: s25 to 25D

Section 25 provides for an offence to do anything

- to facilitate
- the actual or attempted entry, transit or stay in the UK
- of a person who is not a UK national
- in breach of the immigration law of any member State of the EU (& Norway/Iceland)
- if they know, or have reasonable cause to believe that the person is not a UK national

AND

- if they know or have reasonable cause to believe that the act facilitates a breach of immigration law.

Anyone can be prosecuted for an act done in the UK. All forms of British nationals can be prosecuted for acts done outside the UK and so can bodies incorporated under UK law. The maximum penalty is life imprisonment and a fine.

It is not an offence to make an application to regularise a person's status where that person is an overstayer or has entered illegally. Such an application would assist the person to attempt to stop being in the UK in breach of immigration law. Nor does the section override normal duties of confidentiality. If a person comes to you and you advise them that they are, or may be, in the UK in breach of immigration law, you have not facilitated their stay by giving them that advice. Nor would you do so if you took action on behalf to regularise their stay. Nor would you do so if you gave your advice and they said, 'thank you very much' and disappeared. Where you would be in trouble would be if you took steps to facilitate their remaining in the UK in breach of immigration law.

Small boat arrivals have shone light on the scope of s25 offences regarding "*entry*" to the UK (MIL 1.3.6.1). Bani [2021] EWCA Crim 1958 explains that where a boat is intercepted by the UK authorities and brought to a safe landing, those on board would not have "*entered*" the UK: rather they would remain in an "*approved area*" under s11 IA 1971 pending a decision granting them leave, immigration bail or authorising their detention. The helmsman of a boat would be liable to conviction if their act of facilitation was done in order to assist a migrant whose plans included the possibility of entering the UK without leave if there was no other alternative. If their sole objective was to be intercepted by the UK authorities then no offence would have been committed as it would be "*arrival*" not "*entry*". See also R v Khodamoradi [2022] EWCA Crim 37 re possible facilitation offences under ss 24-25 IA 1971 (before the NBA 2022 amendment) where they intended to deliver the migrants to a landfall outside the approved area of a port, or recognised that this was a possible outcome.

Section 25A makes it an offence to

- facilitate the actual or attempted arrival/entry in/to the UK of a person knowingly and for gain
- having reasonable cause to believe that the person is an asylum seeker (the definition of an asylum seeker also covers those who say that their removal would be contrary to the Human Rights Act 1998).

There is an exception to 25A in subs (3). To benefit from the exception, you must be acting on behalf on an organisation which aims to assist asylum seekers and which does not charge for its services.

Gain is not limited to financial gain. The exception is narrowly drafted. It will not help a person who is working for a 'not for profit' organisation if they are not acting in the course of their employment, and it will not help a person who works for an organisation existing to help people seeking asylum if the organisation charges for its services.

Section 25B (repealed for the future, but still in effect via the statutory Brexit arrangements: s25BA(5)(c)) creates an offence to do anything

- to facilitate an actual or attempted breach of a deportation order by an EU national in the knowledge or with reasonable cause to believe that the act facilitates a breach of a deportation, or to assist a person excluded from the UK (on EU law public law policy grounds)

All three offences carry a maximum sentence of 14 years in prison. All three offences carry a maximum sentence of 14 years in prison. IA 1971 ss25C-25D address deals with related powers to forfeit and detain ships aircrafts and vehicles.

Collectively these are labelled 'facilitation offences' by s25BA. The situation in the English Channel has necessitated special provisions:

- acts of facilitation are not offences if carried out by Her Majesty's Coastguard, or an overseas maritime search and rescue authority exercising similar functions (s25BA(1)), and
- there is a defence if acts of facilitation are in relation to an assisted individual in danger or distress at sea, and took place between that situation first arising and their delivery to a place of safety (s25BA(2)) – though not if the UK was not the nearest place of safety and there was no good excuse for landing here, nor if the act was steering the same ship as the assisted individual (s25BA(3))
- there is a defence in relation to stowaways if the ship's master reported the presence to the SSHD as soon as reasonably practicable when calling at a UK port, or for an individual who reported the matter to the ship's master as soon as reasonably practicable and were acting to ensure the person's security, general health, welfare or safety (s25BB)

15.2.3 General offences: s26

Section 26 lists a whole series of offences, all of which carry a maximum sentence of six months imprisonment and a fine, and to all of which the extended time limit for prosecution (s28) applies (see note above to s24). The offences are all linked to the administration of the immigration acts, and are concerned with:

Those under examination under Schedule 2 to the 1999 Act (i.e. clients) are criminalised if:

- they fail to submit to such examination without reasonable excuse
- they fail without reasonable excuse, or refuse, to produce documents in their possession or control which they are under examination to produce
- they fail to complete and produce a landing or embarkation card in accordance with an order made under Schedule 2 of the 1971 Act
- without reasonable excuse they fail to comply with reporting restrictions (or certificates of registration or payment of fees for same – i.e. requirements of regulations made under s4(3) of the IA 1971).

The last two offences in the section could catch anybody:

- Altering without lawful authority a certificate of entitlement, entry clearance, work permit or other document issued or made under or for the purposes of any of the Acts named; or (this later part for clients and third parties, probably under immigration control) using or having in one's possession for a document for such use which one knows or has reasonable cause to believe to be false.
- Obstructing an Immigration Officer or other person acting lawfully in the execution of one of the named Acts, without reasonable excuse.

15.2.4 Registration cards and immigration stamps – ss26A & 26B

Section 26A provides for a whole range of criminal offences in connection with ARC (Asylum Registration Card) issued to people seeking asylum including forgery, etc. Penalties vary with the offence to a maximum of two years in prison or a fine.

Section 26B criminalises having in one's possession an 'immigration stamp' – not the impression it leaves in a passport or on a document, but the device used to make that impression – or a replica of the same, without reasonable excuse. The maximum penalty is two years in prison and a fine.

15.2.5 Offences connected with ships or ports

IA 1971 s27 provides for criminalising captains, owners and agents of ships or aircraft for offences in connection with embarkation and disembarkation, including making arrangements in connection with a removal: highly specialist work.

15.2.6 Powers of entry and search

As detailed above, the IA 1971 gives broad powers for both the police and Immigration Officers, of arrest and to enter and search premises, with or without a warrant, in connection with immigration offences. These are broad powers but there is a protection for items subject to legal privilege. However, there is no protection for a solicitor's firm, voluntary organisation or other body, from searches for people taking place, and arrests being made, on the premises.

IA 1971 at ss28C, 28E, 28F and 28I gives search and arrest powers to immigration officers.

IA 1971 s28G allows searches, excluding strip searches but including searches of a person's mouth (5), at places other than a police station (1).

Failure to comply with a written notice to attend for fingerprinting makes a person liable to arrest without warrant under s142(3) of the Immigration Act 1999, and although no provision is made for a corresponding offence the person could no doubt be caught by the provisions of Part III of the IAA 1971, for example s26.

The *Criminal investigation guidance to the PACE (1984) Order 2013* addresses the role of criminal investigators generally. The Guidance *Obstruction* addresses the powers of Immigration Enforcement Officers during enforcement operations, including when arrest is necessary because the exercise of Immigration Act powers is being obstructed.

15.3 Offences under other legislation

The Law Society Practice Note *Statutory defences available to asylum seekers charged with document offences* is useful.

15.3.1 Offences under the 2004 Act

15.3.1.1 Immigration document offence: s2

Those who (or whose dependants) are unable to produce an 'immigration document' (passport or document of similar function) at an interview on arrival; for those already within the UK, they have three days grace to produce such a document.

There are defences: viz being an Irish national; or having a reasonable excuse for so doing or proving that a false document was used as an immigration document for all purposes en route to the UK, or proving that no immigration document was used on the journey at all.

Reasonable excuses will not include the fact that a document has been deliberately destroyed or disposed of, unless the disposal or destruction was for a reasonable cause or beyond the control of the person charged with the offence. Reasonable excuses do not include following an agent's instructions, unless in the circumstances of the case it is unreasonable to expect non-compliance with the instructions or advice. The burden of proof is on the applicant in these cases.

CHAPTER 15: Criminal Offences

In Thet v Director of Public Prosecutions [2006] EWHC 2701 (Admin) the Lord Chief Justice held that the section applies to genuine immigration documents, and if a genuine document is not held then the person has a reasonable excuse for not possessing it and can make out the defence at s2(6)(b). This decision drastically curtailed the number of s2 prosecutions.

15.3.1.2 Duty to co-operate: s35

The government says that currently more than 60 per cent of asylum seekers have no documents and this is the single biggest barrier to dealing with their claim and, if their claim is rejected, to returning them to their country of origin.

There is provision for certain steps to be taken to facilitate removal, by an enforced duty of co-operation with endeavours to obtain travel documents: see AITCA 2004, s35. A person commits an offence if he fails without reasonable excuse to comply with a HO requirement relating to arrangements for removal, including making arrangements with third parties, the provision of information, and complying with identification procedures.

R v Tabnak [2007] EWCA Crim 380 held that the 'reasonable excuse' had to render a person unable to comply with requests, rather than simply unwilling, and that fear of the consequences of removal was not sufficient to render the person unable to comply.

15.3.2 Offences under Identity Documents Act 2010

This act repealed the Identity Cards Act 2006. Section 4 criminalises 'possession of a false identity document with improper intent', including false passports and other immigration documents, and can lead to lengthy prison sentences. Those using false documents to gain employment and driving licenses, to rent accommodation and to open bank accounts may be prosecuted.

15.3.3 Offences in the British Nationality Act 1981

Section 46(1) makes it an offence for a person, for the purpose of procuring anything to be done or not done under the Act, to:

- make a statement which they know to be false in a material particular
- recklessly make a statement is false in a material particular

The offence carries a maximum penalty of three months imprisonment and a fine. It is subject to extended time limits for prosecution on the same terms as those contained in the IA 1971 s28 (see above).

Section 46(2) criminalises failure without reasonable excuse to comply with requirements the Act imposes on delivering up certificates of naturalisation. The maximum penalty is a level 4 fine, and there is no extended time limit for prosecution.

15.3.4 Employer and financial institution offences

Sections 15 to 25 of the IAN 2006 introduced a scheme of civil penalties for employers, with a criminal offence of knowingly employing someone who does not possess permission to work. The maximum fine per employee is presently £20,000 though these are set to soar in 2024. There is a system of appeals first within the HO then to the county court, against the level or imposition of a fine.

The Home Office had issued fines totalling almost £80m (collecting £25m) as of summer 2013. There are criminal penalties too: up to 5 years' imprisonment.

The PBS has radically increased the risk to persons involved with immigrants, namely education providers and employers. There is a concerted drive to transfer responsibility for policing migrants to these categories of person. It is now possible to be sentenced to up to two years for failure to make proper checks and keep records on non-EEA employees/ students. Employers and education providers also risk breaching discrimination legislation if they target foreign workers only, for record keeping purposes.

15.3.4.2 Sections 135 to 139 of the Nationality, Immigration and Asylum Act 2002

Employers or financial institutions can be required to provide information relevant to determining whether a person has committed an immigration offence, or an offence of fraud in relation to asylum support. Section 136 provides that employers or banks must reply to a notice issued by the HO requiring the information. Failure to do so, without reasonable excuse, is an offence (s137) for which a range of responsible people in the company (see s138) can be held responsible.

Information provided in a response to a s136 notice could be used in a criminal prosecution for a s137 offence. But notin other criminal proceedings against the person providing the information

15.3.5 Giving immigration advice: The OISC

15.3.5.1 Section 91 of the Immigration and Asylum Act 1999

Section 91 states as follows:

> 91(1) A person who provides immigration advice or immigration services in contravention of s84 or of a restraining order is guilty of an offence...

Section 82 defines the relevant terms as follows:

> *'immigration advice'* means advice which—
>
> (a) relates to a particular individual;
> (b) is given in connection with one or more relevant matters;
> (c) is given by a person who knows that he is giving it in relation to a particular individual and in connection with one or more relevant matters; and
> (d) is not given in connection with representing an individual before a court in criminal proceedings or matters ancillary to criminal proceedings;
>
> *'immigration services'* means the making of representations on behalf of a particular individual—
>
> (a) in civil proceedings before a court, tribunal or adjudicator in the United Kingdom, or
> (b) in correspondence with a Minister of the Crown or government department,
>
> in connection with one or more relevant matters.

15.3.5.2 Section 84 of the Immigration and Asylum Act 1999

Section 84 provides that no person may provide immigration advice or immigration services unless they are a qualified person. Qualified people are defined in s84 to include those registered with the Immigration Services Commissioner or employed by them or working under their supervision. They also include those authorised by a 'designated professional body' to and those working under their supervision. The bodies designated in the Act are the Solicitors Regulation Authority, ILEX and the Bar Council.

Section 92A gives the OISC a power to enter and search premises with a warrant, where there are reasonable grounds for suspecting that immigration advice or services are being provided by someone thereby committing a criminal offence under s91 of the 1999 Act and that material likely to be 'of substantial value (whether by itself or together with other material) to the investigation of the offence' is on the premises. Material subject to legal privilege is expressly included.

Advertising or offering to provide immigration or services when unqualified may receive a fine.

Akhtar [2022] UKUT 38 (IAC) holds that lawyers providing immigration advice and services from within the UK are regulated - but those doing so from abroad are not regulated. So there was no need for OISC regulation for businesses established abroad. A side effect of this ruling is that barristers qualified and regulated in England and Wales could provide advocacy in Scotland in remote hearings, though not "*in-person*" ones.

15.3.6 Offences connected with support

Provisions connected with asylum support can fall within the general scope of offences relating to all immigration acts, as detailed in the discussion of Part III of the IA 1971 above. However, there are also specific offences related to asylum support.

15.3.6.1 False and dishonest representations, delay or obstruction

Section 105 provides that a person is guilty of an offence if with a view to obtaining support under Part VI of the 1999 Act for themselves and any other person they:

- Make a statement which they know to be false in a material particular
- Give or cause to be given to a person exercising functions under Part VI a document they know to be false in a material particular
- Fail, without reasonable excuse to notify a change of circumstances when required to do so in accordance with support provisions or knowingly causes another person so to fail.

Section 106 relates to the more serious offence of dishonest representations. It contains all the same provisions as s105, but with the aggravating circumstance that the person does what they do dishonestly. In this case the maximum sentence is seven years imprisonment, or a fine. The provision is modelled on the Social Security Administration Act 1992. Although they are not part of the statute or an official statement of the law, Explanatory Notes to the Act said:

> This section is directed at cases of serious and calculated fraud, such as where a person makes a plan to extract as much from the Home Office as possible by deception.

15.3.6.2 Delay or obstruction

Section 107 of the 1999 Act provides that a person is guilty of an offence if without reasonable excuse they intentionally delay or obstruct a person exercising functions conferred by or under Part VI refuse or neglect to answer a question, give any information or produce a document when required to do so in accordance with support provisions. The maximum penalty is a level three fine.

15.3.6.3 Failure of a sponsor to maintain

Section 108 of the 1999 Act criminalises a sponsor who, having given a written undertaking to support and maintain under the IRs 'persistently refuses or neglects' without reasonable excuse, to maintain the person in accordance with that undertaking, resulting in the need for support. Sentence may be imprisonment for up to 3 months or a fine.

15.3.7 Offences under Schedule 3 of the NIA 2002

Schedule 3 of the NIA 2002 makes provision for withdrawal of support for different categories of person under immigration control. Its overriding philosophy is 'if you cannot afford to support yourself here and you can leave – please leave'. There are provisions to assist people to leave the UK, and to accommodate them pending their departure. Paragraph 13 of the Schedule makes it an offence to leave the UK in accordance with arrangements made under the Schedule and then return to ask for assistance in leaving again, or for support during the period pending departure. It is also an offence to request such support without disclosing that one has made a previous request. The penalty is six months in prison.

15.3.8 Offences under IA 2016

See also reference to these under 'hostile environment' in Chapter 1. The offences are listed against the section in the 2016 Act which inserted the relevant section:

- s34 IA 2016 – under s24B 1971 Act it is illegal to work while disqualified from working by reason of immigration status while knowing or at least having reasonable cause to believe that this is the case. The maximum sentence is 51 weeks imprisonment and a fine.
- S35 IA 2016 – s21 of IANA 2006 makes it illegal to employ a person without permission to work. There is no longer any need for *actual knowledge* of the employee lacking permission to work: *reasonable cause to believe* they don't have work permission suffices (maximum prison sentence is now five rather than two years – and closure and compliance orders can be imposed on the business).
- Sch 6 IA 2016, para 11 makes contravention of said closure and compliance orders illegal at a maximum penalty of 51 weeks imprisonment and a fine. Under s27 IA 2016, noncompliance with a Labour Market Enforcement Order is an offence with a maximum penalty of two years' imprisonment and a fine
- s39 IA 2016 – under ss33A-C IA 2014 it is illegal to lease premises to those 'without the right to rent'. The maximum sentence is 5 years' imprisonment.

The Guidance Right to rent: landlords' penalties may be helpful, as may Shelter's guide on Right to rent immigration checks

CHAPTER 16: Professional Ethics

16.1 Ethical issues and professional practice

Ethical issues are pervasive in immigration practice, and questions on ethics will always be asked in OISC and IAAS assessments. An understanding of ethics is such a central and critical part of an adviser's knowledge that a failure to answer correctly the questions on ethical issues may lead to the paper being failed for gross professional error, regardless of the overall test result.

In this section we consider various documents where mention is made of ethical issues, and where the duties of advisers are laid out.

Solicitors are now bound by the SRA Code of Conduct 2011 and OISC advisers by the OISC Code of Standards 2016 supplemented by the Commissioner's Guidance Notes 2016. It is the general principles that matter for the purposes of the accreditation exams and for everyday practice, and so for convenience we cite more often the SRA code because it is the one that Immigration Judges, for example, are more likely to be familiar with. Also relevant are

- The *Law Society Practice Notes* on Immigration appeals and judicial review; ILPA also has a set of Guidelines for members
- The opening section of the ILPA guide Representation at immigration appeals: a best practice guide, whilst a few years old, is very good on all of this
- The SRA Code of Conduct guidance on particular risk factors in immigration work is also essential reading
- In November 2022 the Law Society published their *Immigration Work Guidance* and *Effective Supervision Guidance*
- The OISC Criminal Enforcement Policy explains the OISC's practice on prosecutions, selecting charges, discontinuing criminal proceedings, and other sanctions such as cautions, warnings and restitution

The HO Guidance and practice notes for authorised immigration advisers links to a collection of relevant documents.

16.2 General duties

Salient requirements are to:

- Be aware of vulnerability of clients;
- Use appropriate interpreters;
- Avoid deceit or active misleading of the immigration authorities;
- Limit work in terms of competence and capacity;
- Maintain records.

16.3 Basic principles

The 10 mandatory principles of the Solicitor Regulation Authority Code of Conduct are that you must:

1. uphold the rule of law and the proper administration of justice;
2. act with integrity;
3. not allow your independence to be compromised;
4. act in the best interests of each client;
5. provide a proper standard of service to your clients;
6. behave in a way that maintains the trust the public places in you and in the provision of legal services;
7. comply with your legal and regulatory obligations and deal with your regulators and ombudsmen in an open, timely and co-operative manner;

8. run your business or carry out your role in the business effectively and in accordance with proper governance and sound financial and risk management principles;
9. run your business or carry out your role in the business in a way that encourages equality of opportunity and respect for diversity; and
10. protect client money and assets.

The guidance to the SRA Code of Conduct states that:

> Where two or more Principles come into conflict the one which takes precedence is the one which best serves the public interest in the particular circumstances, especially the public interest in the proper administration of justice. Compliance with the Principles is also subject to any overriding legal obligations.

The professional advisor may be forced to withdraw in a case where the client's conduct threatens compromise or impairment of any of the foregoing. On the other hand, so long as the client accepts advice that will prevent the problem arising, there will be no difficulty in continuing to act.

Spurred on by media reports, the SRA has seen fit to publish the *Warning notice: Immigration work* (27 September 2023). They note their experience of solicitors advising the pursuit of poorly drafted applications and meritless appeals. Worse, and as the press reported, there had been complicity in supporting false accounts and information to the HO. They add:

> All solicitors should act with honesty and integrity, upholding the high professional standards that we and the public expect of them. This is especially important in areas such as immigration and asylum where those involved may be among the most vulnerable in society. Consequences for this group can be particularly severe, long-lasting, and difficult to rectify. A client found to have submitted false or misleading information to the Home Office or relating to an appeal could face significant financial and personal consequences, including being made to leave the country ... Immigration and asylum law can be a complex, fast-paced and politically sensitive area of law. Solicitors must be able to demonstrate steps they take to maintain their own competence, and solicitors managing individuals in the provision of immigration work must also make sure those people are competent to carry out their role, and keep their professional knowledge and skills up to date ... Similarly, firms are also required to make sure that their managers and employees are competent and have the right knowledge and skills to carry out their role.
> If you become aware of an issue with an immigration client's previous legal adviser you should consider your obligations ... to report promptly to us (or other regulators, as appropriate) any facts or matters that could amount to a serious breach of regulatory arrangements.

16.4 False representations

Where a client indicates that they wish to represent a state of affairs to the Home Office which is not correct, including reliance on false documents, the advisor will find their duty not to mislead to be in conflict with the usual duty to act in accordance with the client's instructions. It is the duty of honesty which prevails. This may also be relevant where it is apparent to the advisor from the client's general conduct or from other information which comes to light that the facts of the case are not in truth consistent with the client's express instructions.

The OISC Code of Standards at 13. requires that 'advisers and organisation must, as far as reasonably practicable, satisfy themselves that documents supplied to them in support of an application are genuine'; and at 14. that they must '...not mislead the Commissioner, government departments or any other statutory or judicial body [and] not knowingly or negligently permit themselves to be used in any deception'.

Apart from potential breaches of ethical and professional standards by continuing to act where such dishonesty by the client becomes apparent, do not forget the potential breach of the criminal law by an adviser who assists a client to apply for leave by deception.

Where this is, or is strongly indicated to be, the case, you should advise the client that you are unable to act unless you can be satisfied that their instructions accord with the reality of the situation.

The usual requirement to give three days' notice for withdrawal from a case, as stipulated in OISC Code of Standards, does not apply in this circumstance (see OISC guidance on Code 43).

An adviser cannot, however, inform the immigration authorities, as mere dishonesty by the client is not one of the scenarios which attracts the waiver of confidentiality (see generally below): the solution for the professional advisor is to cease acting.

16.5 Appeals and duties to the court

Tthe Law Society Practice Notes stress the need to:

- Take all reasonable steps to comply with Rules and Directions of the tribunal;
- Prepare the case ensuring witnesses are properly advised and prepared (with properly approved witness statements that do not make legal submissions), and that the FTT is advised of any relevant vulnerability (MIL 14.5.8), and that a professional bundle is supplied in good time
- Previous guidance emphasises the importance of determining the retainer only for good reason and with reasonable notice, and addressing merits tests, funding and arrangements for the advocate, in good time before the hearing

There is also a *Practice Note re immigration JRs*.

The SRA Code of Conduct deals with these issues in greater detail, in Chapter 5: *Your client and the court*, including the following, other mandatory outcomes:

- Not attempt to deceive or knowingly or recklessly mislead the court, or being complicit in another person doing so (O(5.1&2))
- Not place oneself in contempt of court (O(5.4))
- Inform clients where duties to the court override your duties to the clients (O(5.5))
- Ensuring evidence relating to sensitive issues is not misused (O(5.7))
- Not offering payment to witnesses dependent on their evidence or the outcome of the case (O(5.8))

While the Code of Conduct Indicative Behaviours in each chapter are not mandatory, they are instructive as to the relevant expectations on how the outcomes tend to be achieved, and are essential reading. In Chapter 5 these include:

- Advising clients to comply with court orders, and advising of failure to comply (IB (5.1))
- Drawing the court's attention to relevant cases and statutory provisions, and any material procedure irregularity (IB (5.2))
- Ensuring child witness evidence is kept securely and not released to clients or third parties (IB (5.3))
- Immediately informing the court with client's consent where you have inadvertently misled the court; or where client has committed perjury or deliberately misled the court; *and* ceasing to act where consent is not given (IB (5.4, -5)
- Not acting as an advocate where any member of your firm will appear as a witness (IB (5.6))
- Not constructing facts or tampering with evidence; not drafting documents containing contentions which you do not consider to be properly arguable (IB (5.7, -11))
- Not making allegations of crime, fraud or misconduct unless instructed to do so, material to the case and supported by reasonable grounds (IB (5.7, -8))
- Not calling a witness whose evidence you know to be untrue; or attempting to influence a witness as to the contents of their statement, or persuade them to change it; and not calling into question the character of a witness unless they have the opportunity to answer the allegations during cross-examination (IB (5.9,-10,-11,-13))

- Not naming a third party in open court whose character would thereby be called into question unless necessary for proper conduct of the case (IB (5.12))

16.6 Costs and client care

The 2016 OISC Code of standards requires at 26 that:

26. A client care letter must contain:
    a. a statement identifying the client for whom the organisation is acting;
    b. a statement of the client's immigration status, if known;
    c. full details of the client's instructions, advice given and the work agreed to be done with estimated time frames;
    d. confirmation of the costs estimated or agreed;
    e. confirmation that if client money is held by the organisation on behalf of the client, such money remains the client's until the client is invoiced and payment is due;
    f. information explaining what, if any, additional costs may be incurred for which the client may become liable;
    g. contact details of the adviser dealing with the matter including their name, address, telephone number and email address;
    h. confirmation that if the client is required to hand over any original documents to the organisation, the client will, if necessary, be given copies of those documents as soon as reasonably practicable;
    i. the organisation's complaint-handling procedures;
    j. all other terms and conditions of the agreement, and, if online selling regulations are relevant, the client's protections under relevant legislation;
    k. confirmation that the organisation is regulated in the UK by the Commissioner and that the Commissioner has the power to examine the client's file; and
    l. confirmation that the organisation retains full responsibility for all work done on behalf of the client.

The SRA Code of Conduct deals with these issues in detail in Chapter 1: *Client care*, which suggest the elements above in similar terms as those above but also contains the suggestion at IB(1.3) to inform the client in writing of the status of the fee earner who would be carrying out their work as well as the name and status of the person responsible for overall supervision.

As to fees and costs, the Indicative Behaviours in the SRA Code of Conduct at IB(1.13-21) helpfully sets out in detail what is expected, whereas the OISC Code of Standards 2016 section fees and accounts (paras 58-69) sets out expectations with greater emphasis on handling client money.

16.7 Supervision

All staff must be supervised, whether they are employees or independent contractors, such as locums or consultants, and irrespective of where the work is actually carried out. The SRA Code of Conduct deals with the issue of supervision in Chapter 7: Management of your business, in particular at Outcomes 7.6 -11, including:

- Compliance with the statutory requirements for direction and supervision of reserved legal activities and immigration work
- Having a system for supervising clients' matters including regular quality checks which must be undertaken by suitably competent and experienced people
- Refraining from outsourcing legal activities to those not authorised to conduct them

The Law Society has historically warned against providing nominal supervision to non-solicitor businesses. Managers will remain responsible for this overall supervision and management within the practice, however day-to-day supervision may be delegated.

The OISC Code of standards, by specific reference to the OISC accreditation scheme levels, provides at 9., that a person may operate above their authorised level or in categories for which they are not authorised, so long as the organisation where they work, is so authorised if permission has been requested by the organisation and granted by OISC specifically to do so. If that is not the case, the work must be handed over to a member of staff qualified at the appropriate level and in the appropriate category. If no one in the organisation is appropriately accredited and authorised, an external referral, or signposting to an appropriately accredited organisation should be made.

The Law Society November 2022 *Effective Supervision Guidance* sets out detailed considerations vis-á-vis supervision. In fact the *Immigration Work Guidance* summarises the relevant criteria:

- Having an effective system for delivering competent work by competent staff
- Supervisors should robustly ensure they have clear oversight of work whilst it is live and that they are readily available to provide support
- Effective supervision requires having some knowledge of each matter being progressed bearing in mind the limited redress available to vulnerable clients – for complex cases this may require having sight of the whole course of a matter
- Bearing in mind vicarious trauma
- Checking the regulatory history of supervisees including taking up references and Disclosure and Barring checks and mitigating risks where appropriate

16.8 Liens – retention of documents

A client is entitled to the papers on his file which belong to him unless the solicitor can exercise a lien (i.e. a right to retain the client's papers) for unpaid costs. However, best practice is that the solicitor should transfer papers even though financial issues remain unresolved, obtaining undertakings from the new representatives as appropriate. The client should, if now acting for themselves, be given copies of material on file at their own expense, and be given access to the file.

Under the OISC Code of Standards 2016, the position is even clearer. Code 48 states:

> Where a client requires that their case be transferred to another organisation, irrespective of whether any payment is outstanding, all documents relating to the client's case and the client's file must be transferred as soon as possible and, in any event, no later than three working days of the request being made.

As stated in OISC News, July 2013: Codes 47 and 88 explained an adviser's obligations when a client requests their file. They made it clear that advisers should not place any unreasonable obstacles in the way of clients being given their files such as refusing to hand a file over until photocopy fees are paid. Further, where a client needs to take quick action such as lodging an appeal, no delay in handling over the file is acceptable.

Advisers were also reminded that they do not have a lien over a client's file. The client's file must be given to the client or sent to their new representative on request, and advisers should seek to recover any outstanding fees using civil remedies, as necessary.

16.9 Standard of work

The SRA Code of Conduct provides at Outcome (1.4) that it is essential that 'you have the resources, skills and procedures to carry out your clients' instructions'.

The Rules previously stipulated that this encompasses considerations of sufficient time, experience or skill to deal with the instructions.

In an urgent case, it is permissible to take on a client simply for the purpose of seeking an adjournment. However, if that is refused, and if continuing to act will do more harm than good, then representation at the hearing should be curtailed (which is not to say that the firm should not continue to act).

This is therefore a limited caveat to the general rule 12.03 of the previous Professional Conduct rules which states:

> A solicitor must not act, or continue to act, where the client cannot be represented with competence or diligence.

The OISC have recently released an online Professional Conduct Course to enable advisers to learn about the OISC Code of Standards.

The Law Society November 2022 *Immigration Work Guidance* details where solicitors can work when giving immigration advice, the supervision rules, providing a proper work standard in immigration practice and supporting the administration of justice. It notes

- Solicitors may work in SRA-authorised and BSB/Cilex-authorised firms, as employees for their employer/colleagues, and through non-commercial services eg law centres that are OISC-regulated
- Solicitors may only supervise other IAA-accredited staff – freelancers may not supervise within the IAA
- Solicitors must ensure they do not abuse their position by taking unfair advantage of others, do not overwhelm clients with information, assess vulnerability, be clear on pricing and disbursements, ensure documents use plain English, mitigate risks regarding cash payments and ensure proper record-keeping, ensure clients understand their complaints procedures and do not fear for their immigration application's success if they bring a complaint
- Solicitors must maintain competence reflecting on their practice, legal developments, feedback from clients and peers, and file reviews
- Solicitors must ensure they do not draft submissions that are not properly arguable, waste the court's time, and provide realistic merits assessments

16.10 Conflict of interest

Chapter 3 of the SRA Code of Conduct outlines this complicated set of rules, with helpfully hyperlinked glossaries of the relevant terms, as follows:

Conflicts of interests can arise between:

- you and current clients ('own interest conflict'); and
- two or more current clients ('client conflict').

You can never act where there is a conflict, or a significant risk of conflict, between you and your client.

If there is a conflict, or a significant risk of a conflict, between two or more current clients, you must not act for all or both of them unless the matter falls within the scope of the limited exceptions set out at Outcomes 3.6 or 3.7. In deciding whether to act in these limited circumstances, the overriding consideration will be the best interests of each of the clients concerned and, in particular, whether the benefits to the clients of you acting for all or both of the clients outweigh the risks.

You should also bear in mind that conflicts of interests may affect your duties of confidentiality and disclosure which are dealt with in Chapter 4.

In short: a firm may not act if there is a conflict of interests. A conflict of interests arises where the fee earner or firm owes separate duties to act in the best interests of two or more clients in relation to same or related matters and there is a significant risk of those interests conflicting. However, the firm may act where the clients give informed consent so long as it is reasonable to do so; unless

- the clients cannot be represented even-handedly or will be prejudiced by lack of separate representation (IB (3.5))

- the clients' interests in the end result are not the same (IB (3.11)) or are mutually exclusive (IB (3.13))
- or where it would be unreasonable to act because there is unequal bargaining power (IB (3.12))

Other points to bear in mind:

- You cannot use case-specific information gained in the course of acting for one client for the benefit of another client without the former's consent
- Once a conflict is identified, it may well be best to stop acting on each client's case
- You should instantly alert the clients involved, firstly of the possibility of conflict, and later of your considered decision on what your obligations entail as to their future representation
- In the case of Kaur (01/TH/02438) the Tribunal noted that in the case of a solicitor whose firm practises in the same centre as where they sit judicially, actual interest, not merely appearance of interest, arises if a member of the firm appears before them, so they should at once disqualify themselves from sitting.

16.11 Confidentiality

The duty of confidentiality is fundamental to the relationship of solicitor and client. It prevents the revelation of *any information* about your client to third parties – so, for example, it stops you informing the Tribunal or Home Office of the reasons you may no longer be able to act for a client or of disclosing documents, including non-reported decisions on their case, to third parties, without their consent. It exists as an obligation both in law, having regard to the nature of the contract of retainer, and as a matter of conduct. The OISC Code of Standard is very brief on confidentiality (para 27-28), whereas Chapter 4 of the SRA Code of Conduct better explains it.

- Confidentiality must be maintained save where disclosure is required by law or permitted by the client
- This overrides the otherwise general duty to disclose to the client any matter which the solicitor is aware is material to the client's case; this does not apply where there is a reasonable belief that to disclose would lead to serious physical or mental injury to any person due to the disclosure, or where disclosure is prohibited under money laundering or anti-terrorism legislation
- Even aside from legal professional privilege (which applies to communications between solicitor and client), there is a duty to maintain confidentiality
- It applies regarding any source of information
- It applies after the client's death or the end of the retainer
- A duty may arise even regarding a prospective client
- There is a duty to reveal confidential information to the extent necessary to prevent the client or a third party committing a criminal act that you reasonably believe is likely to result in serious bodily harm; and exceptionally where a child client reveals information which indicates continuing sexual or other physical or mental abuse but refuses to allow disclosure

Guidance specifically states that a client's address should not be disclosed without their consent.

16.12 Money laundering

The Solicitor Regulation Authority warns that if solicitors do not take steps to learn about the provisions of the Criminal Justice Act 1993, they may commit criminal offences, by assisting someone known or suspected to be laundering money generated by any serious crime, by telling clients or anyone else that they are under investigation for an offence of money laundering, or by failing to report a suspicion of money laundering in the case of drug trafficking or terrorism.

Accordingly, attention should be paid to: Unusual settlement requests, unusual instructions, large sums of cash, secretive clients (particularly where you do not meet them in person) and dealings with suspect territories where production of drugs or drug trafficking may be prevalent.

As at late 2004, the Law Society indicated that the problems that might ensue from the HO demanding that the lodging of the surety money is a condition of bail, given that the Proceeds of Crime Act 2003 can disadvantage a bail applicant who is unrepresented and can pose problems for solicitors with regard to the Law Society's conduct rules.

16.13 Terrorism, money laundering; confidentiality and GDPR

The SRA Code of Conduct requires compliance with legislation applicable to your business including any-money laundering and data protection legislation at O (7.5). For example, under Chapter 4: Confidentiality and disclosure, Indicative Behaviour (4.4) (c) contains a reminder that while normally, any individual who has responsibility for acting for a client or supervising a client's matter, is obliged to disclose all information material to that matter to the client, there are legal restrictions which effectively prohibit such disclosure under money laundering and anti-terrorism legislation.

It is therefore vital to be aware of relevant legislation.

Money laundering

The specific duties on legal professionals, firms and other businesses are helpfully set out in the SRA's ethics guidance notes on Anti-money laundering of 19 September 2017 (updated 9 March 2018), as well as guidance on the Money Laundering, Terrorist Financing and Transfer of Funds (Information on the Payer) Regulations 2017. In brief, the most important of these are that:

- It is an offence to provide assistance to a money launderer to retain the benefit of funds if that person should have known or suspected that those funds were the proceeds of terrorism.
- It is also an offence for any person who acquired knowledge or a suspicion of money laundering of terrorist funds in the course of their profession, not to report it.

Anti-terrorism legislation

Section 19 of the Terrorism Act 2000 creates a duty to disclose to the police any information where a person suspects that another person has committed a terrorist offence outlined in sections 15 to 18 (involving funding terrorist purposes and money laundering). This section is triggered where the belief or suspicion is based on information gathered 'in the course of a trade, profession, business or employment'. The duty comprises disclosing (a) the belief or suspicion in question and (b) the information on which it is based. The maximum penalty for the failure to disclose such information is five years imprisonment. There is a defence if the person charged establishes he had a 'reasonable excuse' for not disclosing the information. The Anti-Terrorism Crime and Security Act 2001 has introduced a further level of liability by developing this offence so as to require disclosure of 'information about acts of terrorism' in general. It is now an offence if the individual does not disclose 'as soon as reasonably practicable' information which can be of 'material assistance' in preventing an act of terrorism, or lead to the apprehension, prosecution, or conviction of a person involved in acts of terrorism. Once again there is a defence of 'reasonable excuse'.

GDPR

The UK General Data Protection Regulation (GDPR) sets out key principles, rights and obligations when processing personal data. The Law Society guide *GDPR for Solicitors* is useful.

- Lawyers inevitably hold personal data – their employees', their clients' and other people relating to their clients and their work
- This is classed as personal data if someone can be identified from the information held
- As data controllers they must: process personal data lawfully and fairly in line with data protection principles, process the data in a way that protects the subject (person), use the right systems, be accountable, operate with the ICO, and make sure they follow the rules when sending data abroad (cross-border data flows)

- Someone in the legal practice must be responsible for making sure data protection rules are followed
- Data subjects (ie clients) must be advised of their right to see any information held, correct it if wrong, request its deletion and that it not be used for certain purposes
- Firms should register with the Information Commissioner
- The principle of accountability means information must be processed fairly, lawfully and transparently, only processed for specified explicit purposes, in a way that is adequate, relevant and limited to what is necessary, kept accurate and for no longer than necessary, and handled securely
- A data breach must be reported within 72 hours

16.14 Complaints procedures

A complaint should be defined as any expression of client dissatisfaction – however it is expressed. This might be in writing, over the telephone or in person.

The firm's approach to complaints should be positive, as they alert you to problems that your clients have about the service and thereby provide an opportunity to maintain a good service.

The SRA Code of Conduct 2011 sets out the expectations as to complaints handling at IB(1.22-24), namely that

- the organisation must have a complaints procedure which is brought to the client's attention and is provided on request;
- which is easy to understand and allows complaints to be made by reasonable means, also taking account of the needs of vulnerable clients;
- under which complaints are handled promptly and fairly, with decisions based on sufficient investigation of the circumstances;
- which provides for appropriate remedies; and which does not involve any charges to clients for handling their complaint.

Clients must also be provided with all necessary information regarding the handling of their complaint.

The Solicitor Regulation Authority has recommended that firms consider having face to face meetings earlier in the process to discuss concerns given the potential needs of immigration clients.

Responsibility for complaints

Ensure that the client is aware of the names of individuals who are authorised to handle complaints (e.g. those to whom specific training has been given), or the level at which all complaints should first be handled (e.g. by the caseworker initially, with guidance from the supervisor or a manager). This will include the name of the individual who has ultimate responsibility in the organisation for tracking and monitoring complaints (this is often, but not always, the same person to whom complaints escalate if they cannot be resolved initially).

It is imperative that the firm has a system to report and record centrally every complaint made: so ensure complaints are passed onto this system, for analysis and review of all complaints at least annually by an appropriate person.

Ensure that you respond appropriately to any complaint. This will include identifying the cause of any problem of which a client has complained, offering any appropriate redress and correcting any unsatisfactory procedure.

Practical solutions

Make sure that you explain the circumstances behind any problem clearly to a client and explain what practical steps are available to remedy whatever problems have arisen (obtaining statements from inadequate interpreters or colleagues or third parties, writing representations, admitting one's error to the immigration authorities).

16.15 Third party instructions

The client is the individual for whom you are providing legal services. Third party instructions may be taken only where the client themselves has given written consent to this process.

16.16 Ethics questions in Accreditation exams

> **Top Tip**
>
> If there is a question with an ethics dimension to which you are unsure of the answer in the exam, you may wish to indicate that you would consult a supervisor and/or the Solicitor Regulation Authority Professional Conduct telephone line. A note on examination technique previously posted on the CLT website suggested this was a possible way of trying to extract a mark and it would seem particularly apposite for ethics questions.
>
> Also bear in mind the possibility of a criminal offence dimension to a particular exercise as well as a conduct/ethics dimension, as where conduct which is unethical, such as representing a false situation to the Home Office, might also bring liability in terms of seeking to obtain leave to remain via deception.
>
> And there may be an immigration dimension too – i.e. if the the present application is refused under the mandatory ban provisions of the general refusal reasons then future applications are likely to be refused. For example, if an application for leave to remain features dishonesty, it may be refused on a discretionary basis (r9.7.1); whereas future applications must be refused because of the historic dishonesty (r9.8.1, 9.8.7).

CHAPTER 17: Practical Skills

17.1 Introduction & best practice guides

In this chapter we look at a series of the most important skills for representing clients in the main immigration contexts. We deal with immigration applications first and then move on to asylum. Chapter 9 also deals with particular classes of asylum seeker, such as children and women; these also expert witness instruction (MIL 14.5.4). HJT runs a regular session *The Perfect Caseworker* that covers the most important skills for immigration practitioners.

> **Top Tip**
>
> HJT strongly recommends reading the following ILPA best practice guides, which are essentially skills guides. They are written by skilled, experienced practitioners who have distilled their learning into readable and accessible form. Aspiring practitioners would be mugs to pass by the opportunity to learn from them! They are available to download from the ILPA website.
>
> - *Best practice guide to asylum and human rights appeals*, Mark Henderson and Alison Pickup (2014)
>
> - *Making an asylum application: a best practice guide*, Jane Coker, Garry Kelly, Martin Soorjoo (2002)
>
> - *Working with children and young people subject to immigration control: guidelines for best practice*, ILPA/Heaven Crawley (2nd edition, March 2012)
>
> - *Representation at immigration appeals: a best practice guide*, Jane Coker, Jim Gillespie, Sue Shutter, Alison Stanley (2005)
>
> - *The detained fast track process: a best practice guide*, Matthew Davies (2008)
>
> - *Working With Refugee Children: Current Issues in Best Practice* (second edition, February 2012), Syd Bolton, Kalvir Kaur, Shu Shin Luh, Jackie Peirce and Colin Yeo for ILPA May 2011 (first edition)
>
> - *Resources Guide for Practitioners Working with Refugee Children*

17.2 Immigration applications
17.2.1 Taking instructions and advising

As solicitors and OISC firms do not operate under the cab rank principle (unlike barristers, who have to take on cases on which they are instructed), you are free to take on clients as you wish so long as you are not discriminatory in how you operate your business.

Ensure you deal with issues such as:

- Identifying who is the client, particularly where there is a sponsor as well as an applicant – remember you have full duties of disclosure and to act in the best interests of all clients
- Identify the client's objectives (obtaining limited leave, settlement, setting up a business) and the difficulty they presently have
- Identify their options in achieving their objectives, bearing in mind both options within the rules and based on policies and guidance
- Assess the merits, advantages and disadvantages of each option – e.g. think carefully about whether the client's best option is to actually make an application from within the UK rather than going abroad and applying from there

- Bear in mind particular aspects of the Rules that need to be satisfied, e.g. specified documents which in turn may require a certain level of earnings over a certain period of time to be established
- Ensure you take instructions on whether there are any issues under the general refusal reasons that might arise
- Ensure you obtain the full immigration history and copies of any correspondence from the Home Office and any judicial decisions on the case
- Identify any family members who may be relevant, because they generate access to a right of abode, a UK ancestry right, rights to regularise former EU residence rights via the EUSSch, or might provide a foundation for private and family life arguments
- Bear in mind future possibilities as to extension of leave to remain, access to settlement or citizenship
- If there is no merit in pursuing appeals or further applications, then might it be appropriate to contact the client's Member of Parliament to see whether they will support the case having been given a succinct summary of the matter

The client's file needs to be kept in good order

- to ensure speedy access to documents,
- copies of all correspondence, including the most mundane, need to be retained; envelopes should be kept where they show dates of posting of Home Office or Tribunal decisions that are later than the date borne by the decision itself
- all advice given, and instructions received, should be recorded

17.2.2 Dealing with interpreters

Ensure that:

- the interpreter is competent to interpret both in the client's language to English and back again
- interpreters do not interpolate information into questions or answers, nor summarise them, nor render 'comprehensible' answers that if not so decoded would indicate mental health issues.
- interpretation is in the first person ('I was tortured' not 'he was tortured')
- the interpreter is conversant with the client's dialect as well as language, and does not intimidate them
- you watch out for errors resulting from the use of an under-qualified interpreter, or one who speaks a different dialect or whose culture or background or gender inhibit communication
- interpretation is through a known person, friend or family member for example is often inappropriate where sensitive issues arise.
- interpretation through a known person is still interpretation; be sure that your instructions come from your client and not their family member who is acting as an interpreter.
- you make alternative arrangements rather than proceeding with an inadequate interpreter, explaining the issues to the client particularly where they prefer to use a trusted friend – otherwise you run the risk of breaching with the fundamental rules on acting in the best interests of the client and working on the case with due diligence
- if there is a difficulty with an official interpreter used by the Home Office or Tribunal where your own interpreter is present, they inform you first, raise the issue, request a short break to seek instructions as appropriate, determine whether the issue involves language difficulties or another form of misunderstanding of the client's evidence, and then make any appropriate application, e.g. for a change of interpreter

17.3 Asylum applications
17.3.1 Taking instructions

It is recommended that you are familiar with the ILPA *Making an Asylum Application* BPG, although we summarise most of the important issues as follows:

- Make sure you take instructions on other basis than asylum on which an application for leave to remain could be made, such as immigration history, the status of other family members,
- Ensure you are aware of all relevant documents held by the client (e.g. documents going to the basis of stay of relatives and witnesses in the United Kingdom be it ILR on the basis of refugee status, or lesser forms of leave to remain, and accompanying statements)
- Ensure you investigate whether there have been any other encounters with the authorities such as visa applications or other applications to remain in the United Kingdom
- Applications for asylum must be made in person, by appointment, and are often followed directly by the screening interview
- It is useful to send clients along with written materials confirming that the firm is on the record
- Give your client's name, firm's reference number for client, date of birth, and nationality, confirm the date you are instructed ('go on record', as it is sometimes said), together with a known contact at the firm.
- After a claim has been lodged, confirm that the Home Office have recorded these details, confirm the temporary admission/immigration bail address (and that it is the correct and permitted address)
- Obtain a copy of the screening interview record and discuss it with your client. Make representations immediately where there are errors.
- Advise on the need for prompt disclosure – if they cannot disclose details of their case for reasons of mental health, medical evidence should be sought to explain this on an objective basis
- Ensure that all relevant asylum claims are brought forwards – women or other dependants may have independent claims which are prejudiced by a failure to explore them sufficiently early on

17.3.2 Substance of asylum claim

Ensure you deal with issues such as:

- Internal relocation and State protection issues
- Delay in leaving country of origin
- Time in third countries
- Family members left behind
- Delay in claiming asylum
- Possession of a national passport

17.3.3 Initial advice

Ensure you deal with issues such as

- Possessing a nationality (or kind of case) liable to fast tracking, be that non-suspensive appeals with detention at Campsfield or elsewhere or accelerated appeals with detention at Harmondsworth or Yarl's Wood, or third countrying
- Liability to treatment as illegal entrant
- Being ready for the substantive interview, understanding the need to give a full account and not to leave out anything important, that interviews will not be read back, and that legal representation at the interview is not available under public funding – a recording of the interview can be requested, however
- Relevance of early disclosure of all material evidence, including where relevant, statements from supporting witnesses.
- Entitlement to Asylum Residence Cards and asylum support

Regarding witnesses, ensure that you know:

- Their immigration status (and have advised them of any possible adverse consequences of giving evidence, for example, whilst it is no doubt very unlikely indeed, there is a power to revoke leave available to the SSHD)

- If they are refugees or otherwise made applications to the SSHD, that you have details of those applications and any appeals (it can be a disaster if a statement or SEF turns up on the SSHD's file at court showing claims inconsistent with those already available).

17.3.4 Vulnerable clients

When dealing with vulnerable clients including those with a history of torture:

- bear in mind the difficulties occasioned by recent arrival: disorientation, and fatigue
- create a suitable atmosphere for the interview, seek rapport, using body language, eye contact and tone of voice (though it will be appreciated that these devices may not survive cultural divides)
- make sure the client understands they can have another interpreter or even representative so long as that choice is made on grounds that are not themselves discriminatory
- be aware of body language as a clue to distress; advise on the possibility of support and counselling from specialists
- the interview may be the first opportunity the individual has to relate the events to another person: this may lead to a release of pent-up emotion
- refer onwards to a health care professional where there are pressing health issue, including mental health concerns and any threat of self-harm: consider whether it is realistic to take instructions until this is addressed – the account may be provided via a statement or summary produced by such a professional absent any other alternative
- be alert to suggestions of sexual ill treatment (e.g. 'I found myself naked in the street'). Late disclosure of this is to be expected; but it still needs to be dealt with (watch out for relying on explanations such as gender of interviewer or interpreter only to discover that the sought-for combination was available earlier in the process). Do not probe unnecessarily for details, but nor should you fail to obtain clear instructions unless the client's well-being is threatened by this
- consider whether there are signs that your client has been trafficked, such as particular types of criminal offences, indications that the client has not had control over their situation, or reluctance to disclose types of work. Again late disclosure is to be expected, and your client is likely to find discussing this very difficult, or may not themselves known that they have been trafficked. See Chapter 4 for more information
- be alive to behaviour that suggests PTSD, such as extreme symptoms of, or a combination of: recurrent recollections (including nightmares) of past trauma; fear of figures of authority or other cues to past trauma; irritability; memory failure and poor concentration; fatigue
- do not underestimate the impact on yourself of a traumatic interview
- ensure the client understands that your own professional obligations will ensure you keep their claim confidential – an application may be made to the Tribunal to have their case held in private (r27(2) appeal procedure rules); the Home Office have confidentiality obligations too, e.g. Immigration Rule 339IA not to disclose details of the case to the actors of persecution)

Top Tip

These are likely to be important issues when dealing with the vulnerable.

(i) Where the client is an adult with a history of torture consider:

- ☐ Counselling
- ☐ Psychiatric Report
- ☐ Physical injuries report

(ii) Where the client is disabled consider:

- ☐ Their current health (e.g. are they well enough to attend an interview with us)
- ☐ Whether they will require assistance to attend your offices or any appeal
- ☐ Whether they will expect third parties to attend the interview

> ☐ Whether they will have special access requirements (e.g. parking close to the building, use of lifts, wheelchair access)

17.4 Skills guides – interviewing and drafting

We have produced a series of skills guides as below which give an indication of the issues that are relevant to interviewing and drafting both in practice and in the accreditation exam assessments for the Law Society and OISC.

17.4.1 Interview skills

Specific Criteria

Opening

- Explain purpose and structure of conference
- Acknowledge concerns held by client and timetable the way in which you will deal with them, without letting them override your objective of keeping control of the interview
- Explain purpose of questioning
- Identify any vulnerability and tailor your questions accordingly

Questioning

- Ask relevant questions to clarify and expand upon instructions
- Explore conflicts of fact
- Tackle omissions
- Keep your questions open, avoid suggesting answers to the question until your client has given you a clear picture

Advising

- Use the bullet points as to relevant considerations in asylum and immigration cases set out earlier in this chapter for inspiration
- Outline the relevant law simply and comprehensibly
- Outline relevant procedure
- Explain options with risks and benefits
- Give advice on issues raised
- Ensure the client understands your advice so as to make an informed decision

Concluding

- Invite outstanding queries
- Explain next stage in the proceedings (without going too far into future)

General Criteria

- Be clear and concise
- Maintain control
- Build and maintain rapport
- Maintain professional standards

17.4.2 Briefing expert witnesses

We cover all relevant considerations in Chapter 14.

17.4.3 Writing advice letters

Opening

- Explain purpose of letter
- Adopt rational structure (introduction, advice, summarised reiteration of advice)
- Use the bullet points as to relevant considerations in asylum and immigration cases set out earlier in this chapter for inspiration

Advising

- Summarise your understanding of your instructions so far
- Advise on strengths and weaknesses in case
- Identify and advise on options
- Advise on gaps in the evidence which need attention

Concluding

- Invite outstanding queries
- Explain next stage in the proceedings (without going too far into future)

17.4.4 Witness statements

Specific Criteria

Complete formalities:

- Deal with present address, adopt other statements
- Properly and appropriately set out introductory issues

Material content:

- Chronological (or, exceptionally, partly in another, logical) order.
- Include all relevant admissible facts and evidence
- Ensure it stresses the merits of the case and deflects away from the weaknesses
- Deal with other evidence in the case (e.g. explain relationship of persons whose ILR documents are in evidence; explain meaning and provenance of documents from country of origin)
- Deal with all human rights articles that might be relevant in the case
- Do not limit your points to answering the Home Office refusal letter – bear in mind that the case may have defects which the Home Office have not spotted
- Do not include caselaw or legislation unless your client is a lawyer

General Criteria

- Logical structure
- Be concise: do not repeat facts
- Be precise
- Use correct, plain and professional English
- Maintain ethical standards

17.4.5 Representations

Specific Criteria

Complete formalities correctly:

- Write in form of letter with salutation
- Provide client's full name, date of birth, nationality
- Explain stage case has reached (pre decision/post decision)
- Refer to documents that are being enclosed (a schedule is the clearest way for the reader to ensure that they have been sent everything)

Briefly set out all relevant introductory matters:

- Make clear what the factual basis of the case is
- Make it clear for whom you are applying for leave to enter (including dependants) and what form of leave you are seeking (e.g. discretionary outside the rules, or a form of leave to remain within the rules).
- Note any further evidence which is not yet available but which is imminent, unless there is a question over whether such evidence will actually support the claim.

Make substantive representations:

- Set out any relevant legal propositions, both Convention rights and case law interpreting those rights
- Apply to the facts of the case: ensure that for each proposition you identify (a) the fact(s) relevant from the client's case; (b) the country/medical evidence that supports the proposition; (c) the application of the law in the light of this combination of client-specific and independent facts.
- Show why any error in the case's processing so far has led to unfairness
- Cross refer between sources, such as to objective country evidence, medical evidence, to statements; show your drafting expertise by always succinctly summarising your source rather than including lengthy quotes; only quote verbatim where a passage is vital or particularly persuasive
- Address other material that has been provided (e.g. Home Office policy guidance).
- Offer explanations for any conduct which might antagonise the Home Office (failure to comply with immigration formalities, a change in a visit's purpose away from the original basis for entry clearance being granted).

General Criteria

- Logical structure
- Be concise: do not repeat facts
- Be precise
- Use correct, plain and professional English
- Maintain ethical standards
- Be persuasive